Think Sociology

Paul Stephens

Andy Leach

Laura Taggart

Hilary Jones

Stanley Thornes (Publishers) Ltd

First published in 1998 by:
Stanley Thornes (Publishers) Ltd
Ellenborough House
Wellington Street
CHELTENHAM
GL50 1YW
UK

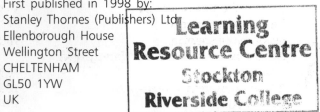

98 99 00 01 02 / 10 9 8 7 6 5 4 3 2 1

A catalogue record for this book is available from the British Library.

ISBN 0 7487 2563 6

Typeset by Florencetype Ltd, Stoodleigh, Devon

Printed and bound in Great Britain by Scotprint Ltd., Musselburgh, Scotland

Contents

Acknowledgements

The authors and publishers are grateful to the following for permissions to reproduce previously published material:

• **Ashgate Publishing Limited and Social & Community Planning Research** for extracts from Jowell et al (1992) (eds) *British Social Attitudes Survey 1991* (pp. 443, 444); (1994) *British Social Attitudes the 11th Report* (pp. 253–4) and Jowell, R., Witherspoon, S. and Brook, L. (1988) (eds) *British Social Attitudes Survey* (p. 193) • **Associated Examination Board** for extracts from (1995) *1998 Syllabuses GCE Advanced Level Sociology* (p. 7); (1995) *Chief Examiner's Report, Summer 1995 Examination: Sociology* (p. 16); (1996) *GCE Advanced Level Syllabus Support Material: Sociology* (p. 24); and examination questions contained in the Exam practice sections at the end of each chapter, with the exception of chapters 6, 9 and 10. (Any answers or hints on answers are the sole responsibility of the authors and have not been provided or approved by the Board) • **Cambridge University Press** for material from Crewe, I., Day, N. and Fox, A. (1991) *The British Electorate 1963–1987* (p. 395) and Bradshaw, J. Mitchell, D. and Morgan, J. (1987) 'Evaluating adequacy: The Potential of Budget Standards' in *Journal of Social Policy, vol.16, no.2* (p. 270, 271) • **Causeway Press** for the extract from Haralambos, M. (1995) (ed) *Developments in Sociology, vol.2*, (p. 430) • **Chatham House Publishers** for material from King, A. et al (1993) (eds) *Britain at the Polls 1992* (pp. 393, 394) • **Christian Aid** for extracts from *Trade for Change: Youth Campaign Action Pack* (p. 595, 596) • **CPAG Ltd** for extracts from *Poverty 91, Summer 1995* (pp. 305–7), the *National Welfare Benefits Handbook 1992/93 and 1995/96* (p. 273), Oppenheim, C. and Harker, L. (1996) *Poverty: the facts* (pp. 268, 274, 278 ,279, 281) and Amin, K. and Oppenheim, C. (1992) *Poverty in Black and White: Deprivation and Ethnic Minorities* (p. 283) • **Friends of the Earth** for use of statistics and *'Attractive Detached Residence'* postcard (p. 553, 568) • **Gerald Duckworth & Co. Ltd** for extracts from Humphreys, L. (1970) *Tea-room Trade* (p. 98) • **Guardian and Observer News Syndication** for extracts from *The Guardian* (pp. 154, 185, 187, 188, 189, 192, 341, 341, 342, 343, 346, 376, 387, 389); *Guardian Education* (p. 605); *Guardian Higher* (p. 242); *New Internationalist* (pp. 582, 586, 591, 603); and *The Observer* (pp. 382, 384, 385, 392) *The Observer Magazine* (p. 187) *The Observer Review* • **HarperCollins Publishers Ltd** for material from Reid, I. (1989) *Social Class Differences in Britain* (p. 144) • **Her Majesty's Stationery Office** for extracts from *Social Trends 22* (p. 513), *Home Office Research and Statistics Department Research Bulletin, Special Edition: Prisons and Prisoners, No.36 ,1994*, the OPCS *General Household Survey 1992* (p. 215) and *Summaries of the Health of the Nation: a strategy for health in England* (DoH, 1992) (p. 316) (Crown copyright is reproduced with the permission of the controller of Her Majesty's Stationery Office) • **Macmillan Press Ltd** for extracts from Alcock, P. (1996) *Social Policy in Britain: Themes and Issues* (p. 303) and Coxall, B. and Robins, L. (1994) *Contemporary British Politics, 2/ed.* (pp. 383, 389) and Jones L., (1994) *The Social Context of Health and Health Work* (pp. 353, 338) • **Office of National Statistics** for material from *Labour Force Survey* (1995, 1996) (pp. 228, 253, 278) *Social Trends 20, 22, 23, 25, 26, 27* (1990, 1992, 1993, 1995, 1996, 1997) (pp. 253, 286, 287,344, 429, 430, 432, 442) and *Population Trends 77* (1994) (p. 344), all are Crown copyright • **Olympus Books** for extracts from *Sociology Update 1995* and *1996* (p. 185) • **Open University Press** for material from Acker, L. and Abbott, P. (1996) *Social Policy for Nurses and the Caring Professions* (p. 351) and from Bell, J. (1987) *Doing Your Research Project, 1/ed* (pp. 36, 40–1) • **Oxfam Publishing** (274 Banbury Road, Oxford, OX2 7DZ) for graph from *The Oxfam Poverty Report* (p. 553) • **Oxford University Press** for extracts from Bruce, S. (1995) *Religion in Modern Britain* (p. 432), and (with UNICEF, 1994) a flow chart from *The State of the World's Children* (p. 609) • **Oxford University Press Inc. (New York)** for graphs from *Human Development Report 1994* by United Nations Development Programme (used by permission of Oxford University Press, Inc.) (p. 581) • **Penguin UK** for material from Townsend, P. (1979) *Poverty in the United Kingdon* (pp. 261, 262, 263) • **Philip Allan Publishers Ltd** for material from *Politics Review, April 1996, vol.5, no.4* (p. 393) • **Routledge** for extract from Mack, J. and Lansley, S. (1985) *Poor Britain* (p. 264) • **Sage Publications Ltd** for extracts from McQuail, D. (1987) *Mass Communication Theory 2/ed* (pp. 476, 483) and Van Zoonen (1994) *Feminist Media Studies* (p. 471) • **Scientific American Inc.** for material from *Scientific American, December 1949, international edition* (p. 588) (all rights reserved) • **The European** for use of extract from *The European, 7–13 July, 1995* (p. 482) • **The Green Party** for extract from the *Green Party Manifesto 1997* (p. 375) • **The Independent Newspaper Publishing PLC** for extracts from the *Independent* (pp.125, 381)and the *Independent on Sunday* (pp. 287, 392) • **The Institute of Education** (University of London) for material from Sammons, P. et al (1995) *Key Characteristics of Effective Schools: a review of school effectiveness research* (p. 223) • **The Politics Association** for figure from *Talking Politics, 5:2, Winter* (p. 395) • **The University of Chicago Press** for map from Shaw and McKay (1942) *Juvenile and Urban Areas* (p. 495) • **Times Newspaper Limited** (1996) for extracts from *The Times* (p. 477) and • **Walter de Gruyer & Co.** for material from *Organisation Studies 16, Issue 6* (pp. 232, 237).

We are also grateful to the following for permission to reproduce illustrations and for providing prints:

• **AFP Photos** (p. 403) • **BBC** (pp. 118, 132) • **BFI Stills, Posters and Designs** (p. 479) • **Channel 4** (pp. 84, 229) • **Colorific Photo Library Ltd** (pp. 498, 514) • **Da Costa & Co.** (p. 212) • **David Hoffman** (p. 84) • **Deborah Owen** (p. 125) • **Deutsche Telecom AG** (p. 449) • **EMI** (p. 68) • **Gerry Lewis and Co.** (p. 493) • **Getty Images Ltd** (pp. 86, 125, 548) • **Greenpeace** (p. 356) • **Guzelian Photography** (p. 197) • **Jackie Fleming** (p. 191, 192) • **John Hudson © The Conde Nast PL/GQ** (p. 508) • **Katz Pictures** (pp. 4, 80) • **Leeds Museums and Galleries Support Services** and **Leeds City Council** (p. 195) • **Los Angeles Times Syndication** (p. 561) • **Magnum Photos** (pp. 255, 256) • **Miam Davidson** (pp. 378, 544) • **Microsoft Limited** (p. 481) • **PA News** (pp. 174, 315, 355, 360, 408, 426, 547) • **Paula Solloway** (p. 175) • **Pictor International Ltd** (p. 158) • **Popperfoto** (pp. 491, 503, 560) • **Redferns** (p. 68) • **Rex Features Ltd** (p. 518) • **Richard and Sally Greenhill** (pp. 159 and 280) • **Ronald Grant Archive** (p. 112) • **Ros Parry Syndication** (p. 167) • **Sygma** (p. 492) • **Texas Instruments Ltd** (p. 67) • **The Advertising Archives** (pp. 462, 458, 459, 462) • **The Associated Press Ltd** (p. 80) • **The Guardian** (pp. 216, 358, 557) • **The Times Supplements Ltd** (p. 201) (**UNICEF** (p. 77) • **UPI/Corbis-Bettman** (p. 387) • **Wayland Publishers Ltd** (p. 54) • **Weimar Archive** (p. 59) • **World Bank** (p. 594).

Every attempt has been made to contact copyright holders, but we apologise if any have been overlooked.

About the book and the authors

The book

Background

During the summer of 1995, three sociology teachers – Hilary Jones, Andy Leach and Paul Stephens – met in York to discuss an idea proposed by Andy to write an A-level Sociology book. We eventually decided on a 'one-stop-shop' textbook, and this is it. Hilary suggested the appropriate title, *Think Sociology*, and she introduced the idea of Crit Think exercises to encourage students to do just that – to think sociology!

We asked another sociologist, Laura Taggart, to make a video to support the book. She agreed. Laura became the video editor, Andy the co-ordinator and Leeds University Television the producer. Andy, Paul and Hilary acted as programme advisers. In the summer of 1996, the video was completed. So impressed were we with Laura's work, that we asked her to join the writing team. Paul set the blueprint for the writing style and layout, Andy did the liaison work with the publisher, and Sarah Wilman – our publishing manager – expertly brought the project to completion.

We have written an A-level Sociology textbook that is comprehensive, easy to understand, up-to-date and fun to read. It accomplishes all of these things without trivialising the subject matter. On the contrary, its main strength is that it encourages students to engage sociology with critical thinking skills. *Think Sociology* covers all the main A/AS-level topics, and it also offers expert advice and guidance on exam skills and coursework.

Think Sociology will prepare you very well indeed for A/AS-level Sociology. Just as important, we think you will enjoy reading it.

Who wrote what?

Paul Stephens wrote the *introduction*, and the chapters on *sociological theories*, *sociological methods*, *social stratification*, *work, organisations and leisure*, *power and politics*, *mass media*, *deviance*, *sociology of locality* and *world sociology*. He co-wrote the chapters on *study skills*, *culture and identity*, *education* and *religion*.

Andy Leach wrote the chapters on *coursework* and *wealth, poverty and welfare*. He co-wrote the chapters on *study skills*, *education* and *religion*.

Laura Taggart wrote the chapters on *family* and *health*. She also wrote the booklet to accompany the *Think Sociology* video.

Hilary Jones co-wrote the chapters on *study skills* and *culture and identity*.

The authors

Paul Stephens

Paul Stephens obtained a B.Sc. and a Ph.D. in Sociology from the University of London. He was formerly Head of Social Sciences at a Leeds comprehensive school. From 1996 to 1997, he was a senior research social scientist at the National Foundation for Educational Research. He is now an associate professor at the Stavanger School of Education, Norway, where he teaches and researches the sociology of education.

I am indebted to the late Steve Schenk, my doctoral supervisor, who helped me to understand that sociology is an objective and an emancipatory discipline. I also want to thank my former A-level Sociology students for making me aware that scholarship should be good fun.

For Philip, a great brother and a fine writer.

Paul Stephens

Andy Leach

Andy Leach obtained a B.Ed. in Sociology from Liverpool University and an MA in Education from the Open University. He was formerly Head of Social Sciences at Lawnswood School in Leeds, where he is now Director of Sixth Form Studies and Co-ordinator of Vocational Education. He is also senior examiner, coursework adviser and INSET presenter for A-level Sociology (AEB).

I would like to thank my wife, Jacqui, for the many months of love and support received when the going got tough, and Nicholas and Sam for putting up with a part-time dad. I am also very grateful to my students for their honest and helpful feedback on early drafts of *Think Sociology*.

For my parents, Sylvia and the late Sid, who have encouraged and believed in me over the years.

Andy Leach

Laura Taggart

Laura Taggart obtained a B.Sc. in Sociology from the London School of Economics and an MA in Education from the Open University. She has taught Sociology in schools and at Leeds University, where she was also a researcher and a teacher educator. She is now a freelance researcher and consultant in education and media, and lectures Sociology and Social Policy to midwives at Leeds University.

I would like to salute the spurs to my educational achievement given to me by my physics and games teachers, neither of whom thought I would amount to anything.

For my parents, Gwen and William John Taggart, who believed otherwise, and to my two children, Isabel and Edward. I also dedicate this book to many friends in the Association for the Teaching of the Social Sciences.

Laura Taggart

Hilary Jones

Hilary Jones obtained a B.Sc. in Behavioural Sciences from Huddersfield University. Her interest in critical thinking led her to the USA, where she has trained in critical thinking skills. She is an experienced teacher and an examiner of A-level Sociology, and is currently Head of Social Sciences at Heckmondwike Grammar School in West Yorkshire. She also teaches on a teacher education programme at a college in Leeds.

My thanks go to my husband for his infinite patience and wisdom. I would also like to thank friends, Pam Bye and Ruth Alborough, for their helpful comments and good advice on drafts of the writing I did for this project. Last, but by no means least, thanks go to my students, past and present, for believing in me.

For my husband, Michael

Hilary Jones

1 Introduction

Topics covered in this chapter
- *A mixture of 'ologies'*
- *Sociology as science?*
- *Sociological theories*
- *About this book*

If you tell people you study a subject like biology, maths, history or English literature, they're unlikely to say, 'What's that?' Tell someone you're studying sociology, and you might have to explain what it is.

Sociology is the science of human social behaviour, would be a good reply.

A mixture of 'ologies'

When we're born, much of our behaviour is biologically driven, but biology immediately begins to interact with psychological and social environments. Once they enter the world beyond their mothers' wombs, humans don't just rely on their genes – they also acquire experience. Infants actually begin remembering language from the moment they're born, and these memories can influence later learning. Subsequent human behaviour is the result of biological, psychological and sociological influences, biology being the *nature* part of the equation, psychology being a *nurture* and *nature* part, and sociology being the *nurture* part.

Don't, however, think of nature and nurture as distinct and independent – they constantly bounce off and affect each other. Humans aren't just collections of brain cells; they're also members of society, and the brain cells and society both impose their imprints on the other. Illustrative of this interaction between the brain and society, traumatic life experiences (for example, being a victim of a violent crime) can create changes in the brain that then affect how an individual behaves. As the American psychologist, Drew Westen, writes:

'Research suggests that environmentally triggered episodes seem to lay down neural "tracks" that subsequent episodes employ, much as repeated use gradually blazes a trail in the woods.'

(Westen 1996: 616)

What Westen is saying is that experiences cause changes in the brain's wiring, and this wiring becomes strengthened if the same or similar experiences are encountered again.

You might be asking whether this is psychology rather than sociology – or is it biology? In fact, as mentioned above, human behaviour is the result of an intricate weave of all three 'ologies'. While we still don't know for sure how much of each is in the mixture, we can study the resultant behaviour on different levels:

- Biologists study the influence of anatomical structures and physiological processes on behaviour (for example, how being thirsty prompts the desire to drink).
- Psychologists study the influence of personal experiences on behaviour (for example, how an early bad experience with alcohol prompts a desire to avoid drinking beer).
- Sociologists study the influence of social factors on behaviour (for example, how the presence of friends at a social gathering prompts beer drinking – come what may!).

The final outcome here isn't, of course, pre-determined. Much will depend on particular circumstances and the relative strengths of the three influences. Separating out these influences is a tricky affair, but social scientists and natural scientists are giving that irksome problem their best shot, and they're making important progress.

Suppose, for example, you wanted to find out the extent to which social factors influence educational achievement. Here's how you might go about tackling that task:

1 Find two identical twins who have been adopted at birth by two different families.

2 Note the differences in the social circumstances of the two families (such as, social class, neighbourhood, etc.).

3 Test the mathematical and reading skills of the twins on their seventh birthday.

4 Compare the results, and, if they're significantly different, attribute the differences to the identified social factors.

If you were able to conduct the same 'experiment' on lots of pairs of identical twins, your findings would be even more accurate.

OVER TO YOU

What might you conclude if each pair of identical twins obtained the same test scores despite being separated at birth and raised in different social circumstances?

The extraction of the sociological portions from the range of factors that influence human behaviour can't ever be 100 per cent accurate, but all sciences – sociology included – look for regular, predictable patterns. If, for example, we find time and time again, that significantly more smokers than non-smokers get lung cancer, then it's entirely reasonable and eminently scientific to infer that smoking increases the risk of that disease. Similarly, if we repeatedly discover that children from low-income households are much more likely than children from middle-income homes to have poor reading scores, we can sensibly and scientifically conclude that low-income households increase the likelihood of that outcome. Of course, it's true that some non-smokers will develop lung cancer and some smokers won't, and some middle-class children won't read well and some working-class children will. What's important, however, from a scientific perspective, is *probability* – and that's what sociologists take account of. For example, they know from research that in the UK:

- men are much more likely than women – about 33 times more likely – to go to prison
- people from minority ethnic groups (especially black people, Bangladeshi people and Pakistani people) are about two and a half to three times more likely to be unemployed than white Britons
- life expectancy at birth is about seven times higher in the professional middle class than in the unskilled working class.

Sociology as science?

While the writer of this chapter adopts the view that human social behaviour can be studied scientifically, some sociologists argue that their discipline isn't and shouldn't attempt to be a science. They claim that how people behave is simply too unpredictable to pin down in the language of precise science. While I know that every time I toss a coin, it's going to fall to earth, I can't say, with the same degree of certainty, that every time I proffer my hand in friendship to a stranger, that this gesture will be reciprocated. The coin falls because that's the law of gravity – it's not negotiable. Different cultural conventions, a broken hand, a fear of contamination, a dislike of me or any number of other reasons might lead to my handshake not being met in kind. There are no social laws here, just the anticipation of convention.

And it's precisely here that scientific sociologists (known as *positivists*) and non-scientific sociologists (known as *interpretivists*) are at loggerheads. The scientists contend that convention is a reliable predictor of human social behaviour. The anti-scientists counter with the argument that each situation potentially creates its own rules of engagement. There is, to be sure, a middle ground: given specified social contexts, social outcomes are often but not exclusively predictable. This middle ground tends to be occupied by most sociologists, who either lean towards the positivistic or the interpretivistic side of the continuum. The 'middle-grounder' (not to be confused with the 'fence-sitter') often adopts a scientific approach towards some kinds of social phenomena (for example, the relationship between gender and occupational destiny), and a non-scientific outlook towards other issues (for example, the interpretation of what it means to be a woman or a man).

But isn't there a credibility gap here? Positivistic assertions are backed by science, which provides knowledge that can be trusted. Interpretivistic statements are, by definition, *interpretations* rather than hard evidence. We think it's important to recognise that some interpretations are better than others. If, for example, I want to find out what it feels like to fear an impending battle, I need to get into the shoes of front-line soldiers who have experienced that fear. By letting them tell their story, I'm able to privilege their interpretations of events above others (for example, a war movie representation of fear). This means that the sociology which emerges is *valid*.

Sociological theories

Now that you have an idea about the kinds of sociological approach to social phenomena, it's helpful to say something about how sociologists make sense of the world they investigate. This is where we enter the realm of sociological theories.

To theorise is to figure out how and why things happen, and the first step here is to come up with an intelligent hunch – to put forward an *hypothesis*. The verb 'to hypothesise' comes from Greek, and it means 'to think'. The origins of hypotheses are many: dreams, mishaps, successes, observations, the reflections that come from experience, or just plain sitting down and thinking things through.

Let's suppose that, based on my travels to the USA, I develop a hunch that the very high homicide rate there is linked to a 'no holds barred' culture which tolerates open displays of emotion and aggression when dealing with deviants. This hypothesis needs testing, so I look at some preliminary evidence, taking care to consider instances of disconfirming as well as supporting data. From what I already know about American culture, I theorise that quite a lot of Americans agree that homicide is a valid response to a wide range of provocations. In sociological language, I assume there's a relatively high degree of *consensus* about this. It's enshrined, for example, in the constitutional right to bear arms, and legitimated in the frontier mentality of the 'old west'. If, through very extensive social scientific research, I find these factors exercise a powerful and an enduring influence on the modern American psyche, such that the 'shoot first, ask questions later' maxim is widely accepted in defence of the person or of property, then my hypothesis is 'proven', and it becomes part of general theory – in this case, *functionalist theory*. Functionalists, as will be seen in Chapter 4, claim that when people share the same general outlook, certain types of behaviour – especially those that have the *function* of upholding the *status quo* – are very predictable.

Thereafter, my functionalist theory of human social behaviour in America becomes my starting point for further research. I might, for example, develop hypotheses which assume that Americans have commonly-held views about acceptable conduct that are perceived to keep deviant, *dysfunctional* behaviours strongly in check: great attachment to the star-spangled banner; the use of 'boot camps' to punish and correct young criminals; a sense of the parent in the person of the American President, and so forth. Functionalism is a 'big picture' theory. It begins with general assumptions about society-wide norms (accepted behaviours) and values, and then applies these assumptions to particular issues. For example, my assumption that most Americans agree on what constitutes acceptable behaviour might help me to explain why students in a San Francisco high school believe it's right to swear allegiance to the American flag before classes begin.

Functionalism shares with another important perspective – *conflict theory* – a broad canvas view of society, but parts company with that approach in other respects. For unlike functionalists, who say that society works because most people agree to abide by shared norms, conflict theorists believe that society is more accurately described in relation to confrontations between different groups. They concede that, on the surface, there often appears to be harmony, but claim that if you dig deeper you'll find discord. Thus, for example, social relations in a company might seem to be as nice as pie to the casual observer, until she or he starts probing and finds female secretarial staff who are sexually harassed by male managers, and bosses who intimidate trade union representatives. What we have here, say conflict theorists, is an 'enforced consensus', not a genuine sense of common purpose.

There's also a theory that operates on a small-scale level, as well as explaining small-scale phenomena. It's called *social constructionist theory*. Unlike the macro (large-scale) functionalist and conflict theories, social constructionist theory doesn't make prior assumptions about the 'nature of things'. It begins theorising at the point of entry: where the action is. In that sense, it tries to find out what 'theories' people have in their heads when they make decisions rather than imposing a 'we know better' sociological theory on things. For example, if I'm investigating the reason why a young man committed suicide, instead of explaining that event with a set theory of suicide, I piece together a theory based on the evidence to hand – a suicide note, a conversation with the young man's best friend, an interview with the coroner.

These three theories – functionalist, conflict and social constructionist – provide sociologists with ways of looking at the human social behaviours that are shaped by, and which also shape, society. You're born into an existing society that places its imprint on you, but you, in turn, with other people, bounce back and make your mark on society. If, for example, you grow up in a neighbourhood where crime is common, you might commit crimes yourself. But that doesn't mean you'll be a criminal for life. You might wake up one morning in a prison cell and say, 'That's it – no more breaking the law!', and act on that resolve. It happens. Your decision might have an effect on young people in the neighbourhood who have started stealing cars. Seeing you as a role model, they follow your example, becoming conformists rather than deviants.

Distilling the essential ingredients of the three main sociological theories, we can say that:

*human social behaviour is initially shaped by learning to follow commonly approved conduct (**functionalism**), becomes refined to a greater or lesser degree as individuals test – and contest – the boundaries of this conduct (**conflict theory**), and re-defined, in part, when individuals are able to construct new forms of conduct (**social constructionist theory**).*

Putting this into a real-life setting:

- As a child, I learn from my parents to obey their (and society's) rules.
- As I grow older, I begin to test and contest some of these rules.
- If my contesting is 'successful', I create some new rules.

None of the above denies the importance of biological and psychological influences. The pre-social child (the one who hasn't yet learnt society's ways) is a bundle of biological instincts and psychological predispositions. It's with this initial material that society works and upon which it impresses its culture. But as the pre-social child

Sociologists offer politicians the knowledge to make society a better place. Whether politicians decide to act on that knowledge is, of course, another matter. William Julius Wilson (pictured here) is a sociologist whose research into the causes of poverty in America and how to tackle the problem is influencing President Bill Clinton. His books, says Clinton, 'made me see race and poverty and the problems of the inner city in a different light'.

CRIT THINK CRIT THINK CRIT THINK CRIT THINK CRIT THINK

THINKING SOCIOLOGICALLY

The following extract is adapted from *Thinking Sociologically* by Sygmunt Bauman.

'Sociology is a way of thinking about the human world. One can also think about this world in other ways. One of these other ways is commonsense, that rich yet disorganised indescribable knowledge we use to make sense of daily life. Commonsense has next to nothing to say about natural sciences, like chemistry and physics, because such subjects rarely come within the sight of ordinary people. So those of use who are non-experts can't rely on commonsense to make sense of natural science. We have to rely on the experts – the scientists. Their vast and expensive experiments constitute property that only belongs to them.

With sociology, things are quite different. In sociology, there aren't any equivalents of giant accelerators or radiotelescopes. The raw material of sociology is the experience of ordinary people in ordinary, daily life. This experience, before it comes under the 'magnifying glass' of sociologists, has been lived by ordinary people, by non-sociologists who don't think sociologically, but who do think commonsensically. Before sociologists started looking at this experience, it was just commonsense. However, unlike commonsense thinking about commonsense experience, sociological thinking about commonsense experience is characterised by:

1 assertions supported by evidence rather than by provisional, untested guesses
2 horizons that go beyond just our own personal experience of life
3 social rather than individual explanations of human social behaviour
4 questioning what might appear as obvious rather than taking it on trust.'

(Adapted from Bauman 1992)

Discuss what it means to think sociologically, and how this differs from thinking in common-sense terms. Are there times when common sense might be more helpful than sociology? Consider the relationship between natural science and common sense, and social science – of which sociology is an example – and common sense.

CRIT THINK CRIT THINK CRIT THINK CRIT THINK CRIT THINK CRIT

becomes a social individual, she or he turns back on society – sometimes to be constrained, sometimes to win a partial (but rarely a total) victory. This – the making of the social individual and her or his making of society – is the stuff of sociology.

It's a 'making' whose explanation mustn't be left to common sense. Your background and the social forces within it that have played a part in shaping your attitudes and behaviour are far too important for that. You deserve a better understanding, and sociology offers that.

We hope that the Crit Think exercise has got you thinking about sociology, as well as thinking sociologically. We believe sociology is an exciting and an important discipline that offers people, through evidence-based decisions, the chance to make and live in a better society.

About this book

We want to share our enthusiasm for sociology – and, of course, our expertise – with you, the reader. Doing that and helping you to pass A-level Sociology are the principal aims of this book. It's a book written with A- and AS-level syllabuses in mind, especially the 0638 A-level and 0999 AS-level syllabuses of the Associated Examining Board (AEB). The book will also be helpful and informative to undergraduate students of sociology. No previous knowledge of sociology is required or assumed. The book is written in a direct, easy-to-read style, and the content is up-to-date, drawing on very recent research and examining current issues. The emphasis is on making sociological concepts simple without trivialising them. While we strongly recommend that all students of sociology extend their reading beyond any textbook, for the A-level student this is a one-stop-shop resource. It contains all of the AEB topics, and it addresses them comprehensively.

The layout of the book is as follows:

- *Chapter 2* offers expert guidance on study skills: how to achieve maximum proficiency in the AEB's skill domains (Knowledge and understanding, Interpretation and application, and Evaluation); how to write good sociology; and how to get the best out of revision.
- *Chapter 3* gets to grips with how to conduct a sociological study for the coursework option syllabus, offering practical advice on how to collect data, and how to present, analyse and evaluate the evidence.
- *Chapter 4* builds on this introductory chapter to reacquaint the reader with the main sociological theories, and to take the discussion further.
- *Chapter 5* examines sociological methods, considers the extent to which sociology may be regarded as a science, and investigates the relationship between sociology, values, and social policy. Taken together, Chapters 4 and 5 cover the Theory and Methods topic of the AEB A-level Sociology syllabuses.
- *Chapters 6 to 18* explore the remaining topics of the same syllabuses. Given that the Paper 1 topics of the syllabuses require somewhat less content knowledge than the Paper 2 topics, the chapters that examine Paper 1 topics are rather shorter than the chapters dealing with Paper 2 topics. One topic, Theory and Methods, features in both papers, and in terms of length is treated as a Paper 2 topic.

Here's how the topics and the chapters correspond:

- *Paper 1 topics:*
  Theory and methods (occurs in Paper 2 also): Chapters 4 and 5, respectively
  Culture and identity: Chapter 6
  Stratification and differentiation: Chapter 7
  Family: Chapter 8
  Education: Chapter 9
  Work, organisations and leisure: Chapter 10
- *Paper 2 topics:*
  Wealth, poverty and welfare: Chapter 11
  Health: Chapter 12
  Power and politics: Chapter 13
  Religion: Chapter 14
  Mass media: Chapter 15
  Crime and deviance: Chapter 16
  Sociology of locality: Chapter 17
  World sociology: Chapter 18.

You will find the following features in the chapters (some you have met already):

- *Questions* (to elicit content recall)
- *Over to you* (to take matters further)
- *Exam tips* (advice on how to keep the examiner happy)
- *Crit thinks* (to get you to *think* sociology)
- *Exam practice* (specimen exam questions for practice)
- *For and against* (a summary of arguments for and against a theory, view or method)
- 60.26 (to show links with the *Think Sociology* video in chapters 8, 12 and 16.)
- When a video icon and time clock appear in the text this signals that there is a section in the *Think Sociology: Voices* video which addresses the same issues as those covered in that section of the book. For example, in Chapter 16, next to the heading Defining Deviance, you'll find: 01.59 . At this point in the video, a political activist begins to address the issue of unjust laws. The same issue, in different contexts, is raised in the 'Defining Deviance' section of the textbook.

- a *Glossary of key terms* used in the chapter
- a list of *References* cited in the chapter.

You can do the questions and exercises alone, in groups or as whole-class activities – your teacher will advise you.

References

Bauman, Zygmunt (1992) *Thinking Sociologically*. Oxford: Blackwell
Westen, Drew (1996) *Psychology: Mind, Brain, and Culture*. New York: John Wiley & Sons, Inc.

2 Study skills

Topics covered in this chapter
- *The AEB A-level Sociology exam*
- *The AEB skill domains*
- *Answering the question*
- *Writing style in social science*
- *Classroom note-taking*
- *Effective revision*
- *The examiners' perspective*

Sociology describes, explains and interprets social phenomena, and evaluates its own propositions. Good sociology does this in clear, accurate language. It also avoids ageism, racism, sexism and other negative -isms.

The AEB and other examining boards set out what they expect from good candidates in A-level Sociology exams and coursework. This chapter focuses on exams, while Chapter 3 deals with coursework.

Although there are some differences of emphasis between examining boards over how exams are assessed, the AEB's so-called *skill domains* helpfully identify skills that all A-level Sociology students will need to acquire before they take their A-level. These are:

- Knowledge and understanding
- Interpretation and application
- Evaluation.

Added to these requirements, is the important AEB statement – again relevant for candidates of any examining board – that:

'In all components of these examinations [i.e. the various AEB A- and AS-level syllabuses] candidates will be assessed on their ability to organise and present information, ideas, descriptions and arguments clearly and logically, taking into account their use of grammar, punctuation and spelling.'

(AEB 1995a: 7)

This chapter will show you how to develop and apply the study skills that will help you get the highest possible score in A-level Sociology. Read it carefully, and actively learn from it.

The AEB A-level Sociology exam

For detailed information of the four syllabuses contained in this examination, consult the booklet: *AEB Syllabuses for 1988 Examinations, GCE Advanced Level Sociology*, published by the AEB (for the address, see page 21).

At the very minimum, ensure you obtain from your teacher a copy of the syllabus you're taking. In all cases, you'll be studying a core of Theory and Methods, plus a selection of topics. Throughout, these themes are integral features:

- sociological theories
- social order, social control and social change
- culture, identity and socialisation
- social differentiation, power and social stratification.

This book covers all of the above in comprehensive detail, but you're advised to read widely and, especially, to read some 'real sociology' (i.e. original studies in books and articles).

The four syllabuses all contain a common *data response* written paper. Data will be presented in different forms, including tables, graphs, and extracts from studies, newspapers and fiction. Candidates are required to *respond* to questions about the data. For example, a table which contains simple statistics on crime rates might contain a question like, *Referring to the table and elsewhere, what are uses and limitations of official statistics in sociological inquiry?*

The data response paper contains:

- one compulsory question on Theory and Methods
- two questions to be chosen from five questions. There's one question on each of these topics: Family; Education; Work, Organisations and Leisure; Stratification and Differentiation; Culture and Identity.

The second paper (in one of the modular syllabuses, this paper is divided into two papers) is essay-based. There are nine topics, each topic containing two essay questions. Candidates choose *four topics* and answer *one* question from *each topic* chosen. The essay paper contains these topics: Crime and Deviance; Health; World Sociology; Wealth, Poverty and Welfare; Mass Media; Sociology of Locality; Power and Politics; Religion; Theory and Methods (this last topic is compulsory in coursework syllabuses, and, in those syllabuses, it addresses coursework issues – more about that in Chapter 3).

In all syllabuses, the three data response questions count for 50 per cent of total marks.

In non-coursework syllabuses, the four essay questions count for 50 per cent of total marks.

In all coursework syllabuses, two essay questions, plus a compulsory section on Theory and Methods in Context, count for 30 per cent of the total marks. A coursework study of 5,000 words counts for 20 per cent of the total marks.

The AEB skill domains

These domains define the skills that are assessed in A-level Sociology. They're described under the three headings of:

- Knowledge and understanding
- Interpretation and application
- Evaluation.

This adds up to a total of five skills, all of which must be clearly demonstrated in the A-level exam.

It can be confusing and unhelpful to get over-technical here. Writing has to flow. We don't want you, for example, to stop mid-way through a Paper 2 essay, and agonise over whether you've demonstrated the exact amount of 'knowledge and understanding of the theoretical and practical considerations influencing the design and execution of sociological enquiry'. What counts is the spirit rather than the letter of the law.

So we're going to distil that spirit from the details of the AEB's assessment objectives contained in their skill domains. We'll also illustrate our points with some examples of good practice.

- *Skill 1: Knowledge* This means demonstrating to the examiner that you know the content of the syllabus or those parts of it for which you're prepared.
- *Skill 2: Understanding* This means demonstrating to the examiner that you understand the content of the syllabus or those parts of it for which you're prepared.
- *Skill 3: Interpretation* This means demonstrating to the examiner that you *do what the question requires you to do*, and, in the case of data response questions, that you *intelligently make sense of the data*.
- *Skill 4: Application* This means demonstrating to the examiner that you *select and use information and arguments relevantly*.
- *Skill 5: Evaluation* This means demonstrating to the examiner that you *weigh up information and arguments critically*. Being 'critical' doesn't mean being negative. It's about exercising good judgement, both for and against something.

We'll now demonstrate these skills in action in relation to the two types of exam paper in AEB A-level Sociology: the data response paper and the essay paper.

The data response paper

Opposite is some quantitative data (Item A), adapted and simplified, about suicide among white males in the USA. Read Item A and then look at our answers to three data response questions which relate to it. We've also indicated how our answers exemplify the different skill domains.

Question (a):
Under the marital status factor in Item A, which group of people are most at risk of committing suicide? (1 mark)

Answer:
The divorced/separated group

Skill domain:
Interpretation: addressing the question, and correctly interpreting the data

Question (b):
Referring to Item A, how much more likely, approximately, are people who live alone to commit suicide than people who live with others? (2 marks)

Answer:
About two and one-third times more likely

Skill domain:
Interpretation: addressing the question, and correctly interpreting the data

Item A

(NB In a complete data response question, there are normally two or three items.)

Hazards estimates of the effects of social factors on white male suicide in the US, 1979–85

Social factor	Risk factor*
Marital status:	
Married	1.00
Single	1.61
Divorced/separated	2.65
Widowed	1.97
Social isolation:	
Lives with others	1.00
Lives alone	2.36
Education:	
Less than 12 years	1.00
12 years	0.78
13+ years	0.84

*Where 1.0 represents the risk against which other risks are compared (for example, a widowed person is nearly twice as likely to commit suicide as a married person, the ratio being 1.97:1.00. A person who has received 12 years of education is about two-thirds as likely to commit suicide as a person who has received less than 12 years of education, the ratio being 0.78:1.00).

Question (c):
Referring to Item A and other sociological studies, to what extent is it helpful to produce statistics about suicide risks? (10 marks)

Answer:

The risk factors associated with suicide referred to in Item A help to define the scope for preventive intervention.

Skill domain:
Interpretation: addressing the question by referring to Item A, as required

Housing development plans that incorporate communal gardens might, for example, reduce the risk of suicides which are linked to social isolation. It would be helpful though to extend suicide research beyond the circumstances of white males. Women and black people, for example, would surely benefit from research-led policy initiatives in this area.

Skill domains:
Interpretation; Evaluation: addressing the question by tackling the issue of *helpful*. Starting to evaluate the extent of *helpful*

One of the world's leading authorities on suicide, the Norwegian psychiatrist Professor Nils Retterstol (1993), is, like Emile Durkheim, who pioneered the statistical study of suicide, a quantifier of suicide rates. Retterstol's statistical research supports Durkheim's contention (and the one implied in Item A) that social integration or lack of it is a key factor in the problem of suicide.

Skill domains:
Knowledge; Interpretation and application: knowing about sociological studies, addressing the question by bringing in *other sociological studies*, and weighing up Durkheim's contribution *vis-à-vis* Retterstol's support for it

However, while official suicide statistics help sociologists to identify the causes of suicide (for example, depression and unemployment are statistically linked to suicide), the same statistics are the products of complex social processes. This is where the social constructionists have much to offer. Their work into how some deaths come to be categorised as suicides cautions us against taking official suicide statistics too literally. In that context, social constructionists (for example, Jack D. Douglas 1967; J. Maxwell Atkinson 1973) argue that the decisions of coroners and other officials affect what deaths become part of the suicide statistics. Such factors must be taken into account when we consider the accuracy of suicide statistics. Commenting on the presence or absence of suicide notes, J. Maxwell Atkinson (1973) remarks: '. . . according to a police officer who had encountered many suicides, many notes end up on fires long before the law arrives on the scene.' The implication is that the notes are destroyed by friends or relatives of the deceased, so that the act of suicide is concealed and no social stigma arises. Unless these interventions are detected, coroners might not include some actual suicides in their statistics.

Skill domains:
Knowledge and understanding; Interpretation and application; Evaluation: Knowing about social constructionist studies and applying these *other sociological studies*. Understanding that suicide statistics can't necessarily be taken at face value, and evaluating this point in relation to post-suicide interventions (for example, by relatives)

Social constructionists alert us to the fact that the accuracy of official suicide statistics is crucially linked to the work that coroners do. If their diagnosis that suicide has occurred is correct – probably most of the time – the cause of death is accurately recorded. But when they get it wrong, what appears as an official suicide statistic is a socially constructed mistake. It would be folly though to imagine that there are no valid sources on suicide. All the above forms of evidence, in professionally trained and honed hands, give social scientists a reasonable approximation of the extent of suicide. To adopt an extreme ethnomethodological view that it's impossible to adjudicate between different claims to truth – the considered judgement of a coroner versus the hearsay opinion of a tabloid journalist – is unhelpful. Ultimately, some opinions are more trustworthy than others.

Skill domains:
Understanding; Evaluation: understanding that official suicide statistics are linked to coroners' work, and evaluating this point in relation to qualitative and quantitative arguments

> ### EXAM TIP
> You wouldn't be expected to give, as we have, the dates of studies, but you mustn't assume that the findings of a study from, say, the 1960s, necessarily hold true today. Some findings endure; others don't.

The essay paper

The following passage demonstrates the preceding skills as part of an essay answer to a question. Once again, the appearance of the skills is explicitly indicated.

Question:
Assess the argument that males are more likely than females to commit crimes.

Answer:
Albert K. Cohen and James F. Short Jr (1971) claim that the best predictor of becoming a criminal is being a male, and the best predictor for not becoming one is being a female.

Skill domains:
Knowledge; Interpretation and application: addressing the question, knowing about and applying relevant information and an argument

Their assertion is supported today by Pamela Abbott and Claire Wallace (1993), who maintain that: 'One of the reasons that "women and crime" has been a neglected area in sociology is that women appear to be remarkably non-criminal.' As for male crime, note Abbott and Wallace, much of it is associated with what it means to be 'a man': an exaggerated masculinity that prizes violence.

Skill domains:
Knowledge; Application; Evaluation: knowing and applying relevant information and an argument, and using them to evaluate an assertion

Although official statistics (Social Trends 1995) indicate that in 1990s England and Wales, males are more likely than females to be convicted of – or cautioned for – crime, it's important to ask whether these figures reflect real differences or harsher treatment by the police and criminal justice system towards males.

Skill domains:
Knowledge; Application; Evaluation: knowing and applying relevant information, and raising a critical question

Thus, for example, D. Steffensmeir (1980) asserts that women tend to be treated more leniently than men by courts, and therefore appear less often in the statistics.

Skill domains:
Knowledge and understanding; Application; Evaluation: knowing relevant information, understanding the critical question previously raised by applying relevant information and an argument, and using it to evaluate an assertion

However, such alleged leniency is rarely given to adolescent girls, who, notes Madeleine Leonard (1995), are more likely than boys to be put into care or receive custodial sentences. Thus girls are often referred to courts for being in need of care and of protection from their own promiscuity.

Skill domains:
Knowledge and understanding; Application; Evaluation: knowing relevant information, understanding the complexity of the issue by applying relevant information, and using it to evaluate an assertion

Even if allowances are conceded for some discriminatory behaviour on the part of law enforcers towards males, there are still likely to be quite big differences between rates of male and female crime. In other words, the differences recorded in official statistics are too big to be explained largely on the basis of gendered discrimination. We must therefore conclude that males really do commit more crimes than females.

Skill domains:
Understanding; Evaluation: understanding the complexity of the issue by evaluating an assertion

Answering the question

Having considered the use of the AEB skill domains in data response and essay questions, it's now helpful to look at the practicalities of answering the questions. Once again, we'll begin with the data response paper and follow with the essay paper.

The data response paper

Each complete question in this paper typically comprises up to four or five 'mini-questions' (hereafter referred to as questions). The marks allocated to each question vary, but add up to a total of 25. The questions address data that are usually presented in two or three extracts, called *items*. The time allocation for each complete question is one hour.

These are the steps that should be taken for each complete question:

1 Spend about five minutes reading through the items and about two minutes looking at the questions. Don't write anything. Just get a feel for things.

2 Read the first question again, and look at the part(s) of the item(s) to which it relates. Where required, think about other relevant information. Then, with a pencil, write down your answer in the answer book in note form. Pause very briefly, check the question again (and also the item(s) if necessary), resume thinking, and write up the finished answer in pen. Follow this procedure with the remaining questions.

3 Spend about five to ten minutes in total checking through each complete question, making alterations and corrections if necessary.

The amount of time you spend and the amount you write per question should vary according to the marks awarded. As a rough guide:

- 1–2 mark questions require two minutes of reading time, thinking and note-taking, and up to one minute of further thinking plus writing final script. *Total time: about 3 minutes*. Amount of writing ranges from one or two words to a couple of lines.
- 3–4 mark questions require up to three minutes of reading time, thinking and note-taking, and up to three minutes of further thinking plus writing final script. *Total time: about 6 minutes*. Amount of writing ranges from several words (if a list is required) to about a quarter of a side or slightly more.
- 5–7 mark questions require five minutes of reading time, thinking and note-taking, and up to seven minutes of further thinking plus writing final script. *Total time: about 12 minutes*. Amount of writing should be about half a side or slightly more.
- 8–9 mark questions require ten minutes of reading time, thinking and note-taking, and up to ten minutes of further thinking plus writing final script. *Total time: about 20 minutes*. Amount of writing should be between about three quarters of a side to a full side.
- 10–12 mark questions require 12 minutes of reading time, thinking and note-taking, and up to 13 minutes of further thinking plus writing final script. *Total time: about 25 minutes*. Amount of writing should be between about one side to one and a quarter sides.

NB It's unlikely that any single question will be awarded more than 12 marks.

Summarising the above points, the timing for each complete question should be as follows (allowing for some minor adjustments):

- all reading time plus pencil notes: 25 minutes
- final version pen writing: 30 minutes
- checking through: 5 minutes.

Here are some other helpful pointers:

- Given that data are provided in the items, somewhat more emphasis is placed in this paper on *Interpretation and application*, and on *Evaluation*, though *Knowledge and understanding* are still important.
- The information in the items is there to help you. Refer to it, unless specifically required by the question not to do so. You must, of course, refer to the item(s) when the question requires this. If the question says to refer to information *elsewhere*, do exactly that. Failing to follow these important instructions, means not earning valuable marks
- Questions that require very brief answers (for example, *Referring to Item A, what percentage of females are enrolled on undergraduate courses in medicine? 1 mark*), don't require answers in sentences. A few words will suffice (for example, *50 per cent*).

  The same applies to questions where an answer in the form of a list is appropriate (for example, *Item B refers to gender as a factor that influences educational achievement. Name three other factors that affect educational achievement. 3 marks*). Here your answer might read: *social class; being disabled; ethnic group*.
- Questions that require more substantial answers (for example, *Referring to the items and elsewhere, evaluate the argument that subject choice in schools is influenced by factors that often disadvantage girls. 10 marks*), should be answered in sentences. Treat them like 'mini-essays'.
- A good writing style will help you to obtain a high score. Consult the style sheet on page 13 for guidance here.

The essay paper

The time allocation for each essay question in this paper is 45 minutes.

We recommend that you spend about ten minutes thinking and making pencil notes, 30 minutes writing the final piece in pen, and five minutes checking through.

As with data response questions, so in essay questions, a good writing style impresses examiners. The style sheet on page 13 offers guidance. Meanwhile, here are some tips on essay structure.

An essay should be structured in three parts:

- *introduction* (up to half a side)
- *main body* (about two sides)
- *conclusion* (up to half a side).

Three sides is a good length for an essay. Two sides are an absolute minimum; less than that, and you probably won't write enough to be marked out of the full 25 marks

Introduction

There are two kinds of introduction:

- the 'in with a bang' kind
- the more considered kind.

Both can be equally effective, but the safer of the two is the second one. Here are examples of each, as openings to the same question:

'Television often presents "working-class" people in negative ways.' Critically assess this claim.

'In with a bang' introduction

In an interesting contrast to the claim made in the question, a very popular – and equally controversial – American television cartoon series, Beavis and Butt-Head, 'presents the revenge of youth and those who are terminally downwardly mobile against more privileged classes and individuals' (Douglas Kellner 1995). Beavis and Butt-Head sit in a shabby house most of the day, watching television – especially music videos. They hate school and also middle-class adults, especially white conservative males and liberal yuppies. Says Kellner, the series thereby enacts class and youth revenge against older, middle-class authority figures.

Even though the middle class suffer a bit of bashing at the hands of MTV's Beavis and Butt-Head, the young people who are the programme's main viewers aren't part of the mainstream media audience. It's in that section of the majority television viewing public that images of working-class people, as this essay will show, are often negative.

The considered introduction

In this essay, the extent to which working-class people are negatively presented on television will be critically evaluated. In order to determine the extent to which this does or doesn't happen, it's necessary to quantify negative presentations of working-, middle- and upper-class people. For to claim that working-class individuals often receive 'rough' treatment at the hands of television media – or not, as the case might be – only makes sense if these comparisons are made.

Before looking at working-class images on television, the essay first examines television presentations of middle- and upper-class people. Throughout, references are made to important sociological studies, and a critical stance is maintained. Thereafter, the final section of the essay arrives at a conclusion based on the sociological evidence.

Main body

This is where you develop the points made in the introduction and move them towards a conclusion. It's a good idea to consider three or four main issues, and to strike a balance between description and evaluation – both, of course, supported with reference to sociological concepts and cited studies. Be sure to keep the question in mind, referring back to key words contained in it (for example, *The Glasgow Group (1995) found that television news coverage of* working-class people *quite often focused on their negative involvement in industrial disputes*). Don't be afraid to take a stand. Examiners like a brave candidate, provided the argument is robust, and the opposing view is intelligently countered. Even if the examiner doesn't agree with your position, full credit will be given for good arguments.

A balanced appraisal which gives equal weight to different positions is acceptable, but avoid being a 'fence-sitter'. Better to write, for example, *Marxist and pluralistic theories both provide important but different contributions to the proposal contained in the question*, than, *Marxists and pluralists are equally right in their responses to the proposal contained in the question*.

Conclusion

Good conclusions are evaluative. They address the original question, weigh up the evidence and arguments that have been presented in the main body, and they deliberate. While the main body continually hints at what this outcome might be, the conclusion states it explicitly and succinctly. Here's an example of what we mean:

The evidence and arguments presented in this essay support the claim that, 'Television often presents "working class" people in negative ways'. Extensive research in this area by the Glasgow Media Group (1995) shows that television news programmes consistently link the coverage of working-class people's lives to 'social problems'. While programmes like Beavis and Butt-Head, as Kellner (1995) finds, take satirical swipes at middle- and upper-class people, the working-class image of these two characters is hardly flattering: 'low-life delinquent failures' who live in shabby surroundings, skip school and rarely work. Television adverts sometimes romanticise blue-collar masculinity, but images of garage mechanics and truckers reinforce the notion that working-class people do the 'dirty work' in society.

Answering the question set

We've already pointed out that answering the question set is an interpretation skill. Clearly, it's also the *most important single requirement in the exam*. For however good your answers might be, if they don't answer the question, you'll get few marks at best and none at worst. Teachers sometimes give the impression that candidates only have themselves to blame if they don't do what the question requires. We take a more sympathetic view. It's very easy for someone to get side-tracked when answering a question. Politicians have turned this into an art form! And we're sure you know teachers who indulge in lengthy digressions, thereby losing sight of the main issue.

Answering the question requires *focus*, especially in the pencil note stage. If you start right here, the chances are you'll keep on track. Study, intently, the exact words of the question, note down the key words in pencil in the answer booklet, produce a concise plan, and, in questions other than the very briefest data response ones, flag up the key words at intervals in the final script. Here's what we have in mind.

Question:
Assess the argument that western colonialism has left a legacy of racist stereotypes about the people who are citizens of the former colonies.

Pencil note plan:

KEY WORDS:
- *assess*
- *western colonialism*
- *legacy of racist stereotypes in former colonies.*

INTRODUCTION: define colonialism and racist stereotypes, and indicate how legacy will be examined.

MAIN BODY:
a) colonial representations of 'savage natives' (e.g. Frank)
b) legacy in relation to, e.g. media stereotypes, school books, etc. (e.g. Manuel)
c) counter-arguments, e.g. positive images of black people (e.g. Met Police anti-racist recruitment poster)
d) assessing the evidence.

CONCLUSION: Racist legacy endures, but has been challenged by new arguments and representations

Use the pencil notes as a guideline when writing up the final version. Make it clear to the examiner that you're answering the question by referring back to the key words contained in it. Be sure to heed rubric instructions like *assess, compare and contrast* – more about that later.

If new, relevant ideas enter your mind as you write, incorporate them into your answer, but continue to refer to your pencil notes, especially to the key words.

Terms used in exam questions

It's all very well to tell you to answer the question, but if you're not familiar with the terms examiners use (the so-called rubric), that advice isn't helpful. Here are the more common terms used in A-level Sociology questions, and explanations of what they mean:

- *Outline* and *evaluate* mean *describe* and *weigh up*. Other words that mean the same as evaluate are *assess*, and *critically examine*. For example, *Outline and evaluate the usefulness of modernisation theory to the sociological understanding of the relationship between poor and rich countries*.
- *Explain* means to *spell out* the meaning of something or why something happens. For example, *Referring to the term 'self-fulfilling prophecy' on line 6 of Item B, explain this concept.*
- *Compare* and *contrast* mean to identify *similarities* and *differences*. For example, *Compare and contrast the contributions of functionalism and marxism to sociological explanations of social change*.

Writing style in social science

We hope you've noticed that the writing style in the data response and essay 'model answers' that appeared earlier is direct and to the point. There's some use of technical language (for example, social constructionist) because sociology, like any academic discipline, has its own specialist terms. Other than that, the language is simple and factual. There's no need for lavish embellishments. Sociology isn't poetry or literary prose; it's a social science.

To help you write well in sociology, we've prepared the social science style sheet below. It contains advice which will improve your writing style and enhance your score potential in the exam.

A CONCISE SOCIAL SCIENCE STYLE SHEET

1. Use short, direct sentences and short paragraphs.
2. Pay careful attention to punctuation, grammar and spelling.
3. Generally avoid 'I', 'me', 'you' and 'we'. These words are acceptable in some contexts (for example, when reflecting, sociologically, on a personal experience), but are otherwise too subjective in tone. For example, write: *Sociological research helps policymakers to make informed decisions*, in preference to, *I think that sociological research helps policymakers to make informed decisions*.
4. Generally avoid 'believe', 'think' and 'feel' when presenting arguments. Instead, use the more robust 'argue', 'assert', 'claim', 'contend', 'maintain' and 'note'. For more tentative statements, 'propose' and 'suggest' are acceptable. For example, write, *Sociologists contend that gender is a powerful predictor of occupational life chances*, in preference to, *I feel that gender is a powerful predictor of occupational life chances*.
5. When challenging arguments, use words like 'counter', 'rebut', 'contest', and – by all means – 'challenge' too. For example, write, *Social constructionists contest the claim that suicide statistics should be taken at face-value*.
6. Social science has no place for ageist, racist, sexist or any 'negative -ism' language. Use, for example, 'black', 'African–Caribbean' and 'Asian', instead of 'coloured'; and she or he, or 's/he' instead of 'he' when the sex of the person is not known. It's politically correct in the US to refer to 'people of color'.

CRIT THINK CRIT THINK CRIT THINK CRIT THINK CRIT THINK CRIT THINK

TROUBLESHOOTING TECHNIQUES

This exercise focuses on troubleshooting techniques which will help you to write better answers to data response and essay questions.

Many study guides only offer advice on what makes for a good answer. This can be vague and unhelpful to the student who isn't used to writing in an academic, social scientific style. We set out to be different. We advocate thoughtful, interactional troubleshooting when preparing answers.

Here is our guide to troubleshooting.

Troubleshooting an answer

Sections *Yes/No*
(Write comments on a separate sheet)

Structure:
Doesn't address the question
Lacks clear development of points
No conclusion

Theories/Evidence:
Shallow conceptualisation
'Common-sense' claims and personal opinions
Lack of cited evidence
Over-stating anecdotal evidence
Use of inappropriate theories/evidence
An absence of sociological reasoning
One-sided arguments
Too much description and too little analysis

Language:
Incorrect sentence structure
Incorrect punctuation
Incorrect spelling
Disjointed sentences that lack flow and coherence
Inappropriate use of sexist and other offensive terms

Read the guide to troubleshooting. Then, working with a question you have already answered (a homework or a test piece will do nicely), write Yes or No against each point, accompanied by a thoughtful comment (for example, Structure: No conclusion – Yes. The argument is left dangling. Add a conclusion).

If possible, work with another student who has answered the same question. Discuss your respective assessments.

It's important to emphasise that 'troubleshooting' means precisely that – identifying trouble in the work you've produced. Don't think us unduly negative here. The goal is, once the problems have been identified, to do better next time around.

Don't forget to reflect upon the outcome of this exercise. Good sociologists are reflective thinkers!

CRIT THINK CRIT THINK CRIT THINK CRIT THINK CRIT THINK CRIT THINK CRIT

Classroom note-taking

The advice dispensed so far has concentrated on what to do in the exam room. We'll now consider what to do before the real event arrives, focusing on classroom note-taking and exam revision.

While we, as teachers, prefer our students to get actively involved in thinking aloud about sociological issues, note-taking is probably going to feature, to some extent, in the course you take. Admittedly, this can be dull, especially if lengthy dictations are involved. If you don't like taking notes, you might ask your teacher to provide you with a word-processed handout of the main content of the lesson. Then you'll only need to take the briefest of notes when the teacher introduces new ideas or embellishes the ones already contained in the handout.

If, however, as is likely, some note-taking is going to be necessary, here are a few helpful guidelines:

1 Don't write down too much; concentrate on the bold outlines. This takes practice, so be patient.

2 Consider taping important lessons; ask permission first. If permission is given, use a small reporter's audio cassette recorder.

3 Ask your teacher to be considerate: to slow down to dictation speed when key points are made; to allow you to cut in and ask questions as the lesson proceeds; to keep teacher-talk short; not to talk continuously (the use of video clips and other support material is helpful here); to write difficult words on the chalkboard.

4 Use suitable abbreviations when you take notes. Here are some examples: e.g. = for example; i.e. = that is; // = between.

5 Do a second, neat orderly set of notes after the lesson, as a final version. This should be based, of course, on the speedily taken jottings from the lesson.

Effective revision

Everyone has their own revision style, and, provided it works, who are we to say we know better? It's for you to take ownership of *your* revision programme, and, in that context, to be largely responsible for your own learning. This isn't to say that teachers don't have a role to play in offering advice and guidance. Do ask them for help here, and ask them to make revision an integral part of some classroom time, once the syllabus has been completed. This will mean re-visiting issues that have already been encountered, but on a more sophisticated and, hopefully, a more readily understandable level.

Other than advising you to take note of our counsel, and recommending that serious revision begins in the Easter holidays prior to the summer exam, what we have to offer is guidance on self-prepared revision notes.

The task is to prepare a three-page set of notes for each section within the topic headings that you're studying. Thus, for example, section C of the topic Family is *the diversity of contemporary family structure*. Sometimes it's helpful to combine two or more sections into one. This works well, for example with sections E and F of Education: *the sociological significance of teacher-pupil relationships and pupil sub-cultures*, and *the social construction of the concepts 'educational success' and 'educational failure'*, respectively. These sections contain interrelated themes, and, for revision purposes, can be treated as one section.

Now that the task is defined, these are the steps for accomplishing it:

1 Find the biggest table you can, and place on it all your notes, collections of articles, and books opened at the right page(s) which relate to one section.

2 Using the format of *introduction, main body* and *conclusion*, distil the essential contents of your various sources (with one or two nice, short verbatim quotes) onto three pages of A4 paper. Even though data response and essay topics require different answer techniques, this format works well for both in a revision context, because it's tightly structured. Some students like writing throughout in prose; others prefer prose for the introduction and conclusion, and notes for the main body. Adopt the system that works for you. Each section (and, in some cases, combined sections) should take about two to three hours to complete. But don't think of this as wasted time. As you read and distil, you're actively revising.

3 Use the completed three-page set for revision, remembering that this is second-phase revision, because it re-visits what you've already revised during the compilation of the set.

4 You might also want to make a one side summary of the three-page set, for last minute revision

5 Now it's time for the real event: the A-level Sociology exam.

We aren't suggesting that the above pointers are the only or even the best way for you to do your revision. Each person has their own preferences and style. In order to become better acquainted with each other's revision techniques, it's important that you exchange ideas in groups and in whole-class situations. The sharing of 'best practice' is always helpful. For example, do you and other students use any of these techniques:

- Read and re-read?
- Cue cards?
- Colour coding/highlighting?
- Short note summaries of topics?
- Flow charts?
- Other (please specify)?

OVER TO YOU

Tick Yes or No for each of the revision techniques listed above. When are certain techniques appropriate? Evaluate these techniques. You might want to write down your deliberations under these headings:

Technique	Yes/No	When appropriate	Evaluation

The examiners' perspective

Finally, it's time to say something about what happens when you hand in your coursework or leave the exam hall.

One of the most harrowing things about being an A-level student is having to wait for the results – the countdown to that Thursday morning, the fear of disappointment or the anticipation of exhilaration.

So who are these examiners who decide your fate? Which people are so committed to the subject that they would wish to mark hundreds of scripts or coursework assignments after a full teaching day? Actually, they're human beings and, just like you, they've taken exams and have been through the same uncertainties and anxieties.

They're sympathetic teachers and lecturers of sociology whose task is to mark positively. What this means is that all candidates start with a score of zero, and – rather like a taxi meter – points get added as and when sociological skills are appropriately displayed in the scripts or coursework. Nobody is out to take marks from you. That's not how the system works. You will get marks whenever you do what is required effectively.

Don't worry about arguing a particular case and fearing that the examiner will take a different view. Provided you use sociological arguments and evidence to support your assertions, the examiner will give you credit – even if she or he's a functionalist and you're a conflict theorist!

The marking process is a very thorough exercise, and – just so you know what goes on – this is what generally happens:

- *Stage 1: Posting the scripts* The exam scripts (including coursework, if you take a coursework option) are posted to the examiners who are responsible for your school immediately after each paper has been sat.
- *Stage 2: Pre-co-ordination meeting* The chief examiner (who has overall charge of everything), or the principal examiner (who has responsibility for one paper), meet with a team of senior examiners (called team leaders). They then sample-mark a number of scripts and coursework assignments, keeping closely to a common mark scheme. Deliberations and discussions eventually lead to marks that are agreed upon by all present. Using sociological language, a consensus is arrived at. The agreed standard obtains the formal approval of the chief examiner, and it subsequently becomes the benchmark for all examiners to follow across the country – a process called *standardisation*.

  Tony Lawson, the former chief examiner for AEB A-level Sociology, describes the procedure in these terms:

  'In examining, the establishment of fairness for every individual candidate is achieved by the rule that every candidate's work should be marked as if it was marked by the Chief Examiner him or herself, according to agreed mark schemes.'

  (Lawson 1996: 31)

- *Stage 3: Co-ordination meeting* The assistant examiners meet the next day with their team leaders to go over a sample of scripts and coursework which have already been marked by the team leaders and the chief or principal examiner. The role of the team leaders is to ensure that the judgements of the assistant examiners are 'standardised' (i.e. consistently correspond with the standards set by the chief examiner). The scripts and coursework are then second-marked by the assistant examiners, who will have been briefed on the marks already awarded and why. Unconventional answers are also discussed, and, if deserving, receive due credit. Through this co-ordination meeting, each examiner, notes Tony Lawson, 'has access to the Chief Examiner's views of particular scripts, which then act as bench marks for all other similar scripts' (Lawson 1996: 31).
- *Stage 4: Further samples* To ensure the team leaders and assistant examiners are continuing to mark to the required standard, further samples of their marking are requested by the exam board. These are checked by more senior examiners and, as appropriate, feedback and adjustments are made. If it's decided that an assistant examiner isn't marking to the correct standard, she or he will be removed from the team of markers.
- *Stage 5: Borderline marking* After the marking is completed, the chief examiner, the principal examiner, and team leaders meet to carry out further checks, and to set the grade boundaries (i.e. how the letter grades correspond to the marks gained) for papers and coursework assignments. These decisions are regulated and scrutinised by the Qualifications and Curriculum Authority (QCA), a national body which monitors all public exams in England and Wales.
- *Stage 6: The chief examiner's report* All assistant examiners and team leaders send their comments on the exam performances – taking account of strengths and weaknesses – to the chief examiner. These comments are collated and summarised by the chief examiner, published in the autumn term by the AEB, and sent to all schools and colleges where students sit A-level Sociology. A breakdown of candidates' marks for each paper is sent to each centre.

Make sure your teacher shows you a copy of the latest Chief Examiner's Report. It contains lots of helpful tips and pointers. Here's part of page 1 of the report for 1995, which focuses on key learning points and skills:

'on the whole, candidates were able to demonstrate the required skills across the whole ability range . . . The majority of pupils seem to be familiar with appropriate sociological material . . . Candidates continue to show improvement in interpretation and application skills . . . Evaluation continued to pose most problems for candidates. The better answers offer sophisticated and evaluative accounts of debates, and most candidates seemed to be aware of the need for evaluation and a conclusion.'

(AEB 1995b)

Two sociology teachers, Michael Moores and Tony Breslin, asked the chief examiners of all the exam boards what constituted a good sociological exam performance. Their question elicited very useful information. Three areas were commonly highlighted:

'CONTEXT: Studies should be understood in their context. That is, there should be an understanding of the background of such studies . . . in historical and sociological terms

INTEGRATION: The need to connect different areas of social experience, . . . theory, methodological understanding and substantive study . . . to illuminate social reality

AWARENESS: Cross cultural understanding and tolerance of a range of value systems and to be able to challenge commonly held assumptions.'

(Moores and Breslin 1991: 14–15)

When all is said and done, you can be assured that the examiners have the interests of each candidate at heart, and that they aim to ensure complete fairness.

OVER TO YOU

We'd now like you to participate in a similar marking exercise to the one your examiner will be involved in. You're going to mark a Paper 2 answer from the topic called Crime and Deviance. Obviously, at this stage, we don't expect you to be expert criminologists. So take a dip into this book by fast-forwarding to pages 497–9, 512–14 and 516–17. These sections address the major issues contained in the question below.

When you've read the sections, talk about them with your teacher and the other students. Then carry out the preparatory tasks listed below.

You should be ready to have a go, either now – or if you prefer, later in the course – at marking the question.

Question:

Critically assess the usefulness of the concept of 'youth subculture' as a sociological explanation for deviance.

Before you begin the marking, here are some important tasks to perform:

1. Define what you consider is meant by the following key terms contained within the question:
   - Critically assess
   - concept of 'youth subculture'
   - explanation for deviance (first, say what deviance is).
2. Make a list of sociologists who use youth sub-cultural explanations of deviant behaviour. Alongside this, as illustrated below, summarise their key explanations:

   Name of sociologist   Explanation given
3. Make a list of sociologists who challenge the preceding explanations:

   Name of sociologist   Nature of challenge
4. Read the mark scheme on pages 19–21, just to get a feel of things.

Now it's time to do some marking. Read the student's answer, making notes, as you proceed, of the following:

- sociologists referred to and explanations given
- evaluations offered
- demonstration, paragraph by paragraph, of these skills, as and when they occur:
  - Knowledge and understanding
  - Interpretation and application
  - Evaluation.

Then, using the mark scheme, give the candidate a mark out of 9 for all skills that demonstrate *Knowledge and understanding*, a mark out of 9 for all skills that demonstrate *Interpretation and application*, and a mark out of 9 for all skills that demonstrate *Evaluation*. This is exactly the same procedure that examiners go through.

This is the answer we'd like you to mark, presented exactly as it was written. So don your examiner's hat, and have fun!

Deviance is described as behaviour that is contrary to the norms of a particular society. Therefore deviance is relative to the society in which it takes place, for example, having two wives in Britain is not acceptable but in some Muslim countries it is regarded as normal. It is possible for deviance to be viewed as positive or negative, but the sociological study of deviance is confined to behaviour which is viewed as negative and contrary to the established norms of society.

Deviance is often associated with sub-cultures. These are groups who hold certain values which are contrary to those held by society as a whole, for example Orthodox Jews or Travellers. The members of these groups are likely to be ostracised by society because they refuse to conform to the established norms. When members of these groups are predominantly teenagers they are known as youth sub-cultures.

The youth sub-culture is an American concept. It was first described by Robert Merton in the 1930s. He argued that deviance results from the way in which society is constructed. He suggests that the 'American Dream' appears to offer everybody the same chance to achieve success through education, drive, determination and hard work otherwise known as the legitimate means. However, because the legitimate means of achieving success are not available to everybody because of unemployment, poor education, low pay, etc., some resort to illegitimate or deviant means. He suggests five ways in which the individual can respond to society's goals: 'conformity' – acceptance of the goal and the means of achieving it; 'innovation' – creating alternative means to achieve society's goals; 'ritualism' – abandonment of the goals; 'retreatism' – dropping out of society; 'rebellion' – creating alternative goals and means of achieving them.

Several other sociologists have developed Merton's work further. Albert Cohen concluded that deviance is more likely to involve a group of people rather than one individual. He also argues that, unlike society as a whole, success is not necessarily measured by monetary gain.

His studies have focused on lower working-class boys. He suggests that they have two sets of values, those of the middle class, which he sees as society's norms, and the values of the deviant youth, or delinquent sub-culture. The latter is marked by the reversal of society's values whereby violence and theft are regarded as positive behaviour. He argues that sub-culture are formed because everybody needs to achieve status but, as a result of poor educational achievement, some are unable to do so in mainstream society. In order to deal with the resulting frustration they join with other frustrated individuals and create their own goals and means of achieving them. Within the structure of the sub-culture an individual is able to achieve status but they are subject to pressure from the other members to continue to display deviant behaviour.

Cohen's theory is illustrated by an article about 'Gang Sisters' (Independent 1/12/93). It shows how a group of teenage girls have replaced society's goals with goals of their own. One girl joined the gang looking for family love and relationships that had been denied to her by society. In order to gain respect and status within the gang she was expected to commit acts of violence, even murder, deal in drugs, and commit other crimes. The penalty for disobedience or attempting to leave the gang was violent assault or even death.

As Cohen suggests the gang members display behaviour which reflects society's values. Like many women in mainstream society, these girls are trying to gain equal status with men. Wherever women compete against men they feel that, in order to be regarded as equal, they have to be higher achievers. This is reflected in the fact that the girls were prepared to commit acts more violent than many boys would contemplate. The attitudes of some male gangs are illustrated in an article in 'Time' magazine (2/8/93) about the use of guns by gangs in Omaha. Despite having constant access to a lethal weapon, the boys insist that their intention is to damage property and not take human life. In comparison, the 'Gang Sisters' insist upon the taking of life as part of the initiation process.

Cloward and Ohlin question why some gangs concentrate on theft and others on vandalism. They suggest that, as in mainstream society, the means to success vary. They describe three distinct groups, based on Merton's theory: the 'criminal sub-culture' – in lower working class areas where adults provide training for younger criminals; 'conflict sub-cultures' – arising where there is no controlling adult influence and resulting in gang violence; 'retreatist sub-cultures' – where the young fail to succeed in the other groups and resort to drugs.

Walter Miller contradicts Cohen's theory that deviance results from frustration due to lack of success. He puts forward the theory of 'focal concerns' which are held by the whole of the working class. He suggests that, because generations of low skilled workers have been employed in jobs which are repetitive and boring, they have developed a way of dealing with the tedium. 'Focal concerns' such as 'toughness', 'smartness' and 'excitement' have replaced the goals held by the rest of society.

Steven Box argues that, by their very nature, the young do not hold the same values as the rest of society. He disagrees with Cohen's theory that the young are reacting to their own shame at not being able to achieve society's goals. He suggests that they resent being labelled as failures by those in authority and their more affluent peers. Their deviant behaviour is a protest against the way they are judged by others. Taylor, Walton and Young point to Hippies and similar groups who have rejected society's goals but do not consider themselves to be failures.

Matza supports Box's view in his description of what he terms as 'subterranean values'. He lists these values as: enjoying oneself, acting on the spur of the moment, self expression, being aggressive and seeking excitement. He believes that these values exist in all individuals but that they are suppressed by those who conform to society's norms. These norms are only allowed freedom of expression when irresponsible behaviour is acceptable, for instance, at parties or on holiday. However, the delinquent, because he is not bound by society's conventions, is able to express these values in 'inappropriate' settings.

An overall conclusion can be drawn from the work of the American sub-cultural theorists. It seems that deviant behaviour in youth sub-cultures, whose members are drawn from the lower middle class, is a reaction against the goals set by middle-class society which they are unable to achieve. They are unable to achieve goals because of poor education which does not provide them with the legitimate means for achieving success. In order to achieve status, which every individual requires, they substitute their own means and goals but the form that these take are, in part, dependent on adult sub-cultures.

When examining deviant behaviour in Britain, youth sub-culture is useful but not comprehensive enough to offer an adequate explanation. This is partly due to the way in which society is structured and the social policy in existence in the two countries.

Britain has a welfare state which prevents the extremes of poverty present in American cities. The British police and public do not, as a rule, carry guns which, in America, are regarded by the young as status symbols. American policy in the 1960s to segregate Black and Hispanic people resulted in the formation of ghettos where unemployment and poverty have become serious problems. In these conditions, where the chances to succeed are small, the youth sub-culture thrives. Although Britain has areas where ethnic populations tend to congregate, failure to succeed in terms of a 'British dream' is not an issue.

The study of deviant behaviour in Britain is heavily influenced by Marxist and Interactionist theory. Marxists see society as a conglomeration of groups, each with conflicting interests, who compete against each other. This view is complimented by Interactionist theory which suggests that delinquent behaviour is created by the misinterpretation of the actions of individuals or groups of individuals by other individuals or groups.

Corrigan suggests that highly structured gangs are rare in Britain. He argues that deviant behaviour associated with gangs is simply a way of having fun. This is reflected in Matza's theory of 'subterranean values' as discussed above.

Downes in his study of Stepney and Poplar supports Corrigan's view. He suggests that youths have a desire to indulge in sport and leisure activities. However because of the lack of facilities provided by local government, they are forced to create other outlets for their energy.

These theories are supported by a recent newspaper article 'Bronx Violence, Sheffield Accent' (Independent 28/11/94). The article describes how a teenage boy had been murdered during what had all the appearances of an American style gang fight. However the evidence suggests that the 'rival gangs' were teenagers from two of the town's schools who had come together specifically for the purpose of settling an minor dispute. The article does not suggest that any of those involved were regular members of a gang. For the majority, the motivation for meeting in the park was the excitement derived from 'imagined danger'. The boy who committed the murder had a background of family violence. He was accompanied by a group of boys who dressed and behaved in a manner reminiscent of American films depicting gang violence. This suggests that, where British youths display behaviour associated with American youth sub-cultures, it may be due to media influence and not social issues.

A study of 'Girl Gangs' in Britain presented by Private Eye (18/11/94) showed similarities to the American 'Gang Sister'. One of the gangs called themselves the 'Ghetto Girls', a phrase which is reminiscent of American society and, again, suggests some media influence. The British girls were very violent and indulged in initiation rituals. The main difference between the British and American gangs was the individual's motivation for joining. The British girls said that they joined because they had nothing more interesting to do with their time while the American girls appeared to be looking for an alternative way of life.

Matza suggests that deviants share society's values but are able to 'neutralise' them when the situation demands. They deny that their behaviour is wrong and claim that activities such as joy riding are harmless fun. Also they may consider that they are doing society a favour by persecuting 'undesirable' members of society such as homosexuals. Matza argues that the individuals need to 'neutralise' society's values suggesting that no sub-cultural values exist. Otherwise they would be behaving in accordance with their groups' accepted values and would not find it necessary to justify their actions.

Howard Becker suggests that 'deviant behaviour is behaviour that people so label', therefore deviants are created by society. Society decides where and when a certain type of behaviour is permitted to occur. Anybody who breaks the rules is 'labelled' as deviant and all of their future actions are judged accordingly. Owen Gill's study of a Liverpool housing estate showed that the City Council had decided that it was fit only for the 'worst types of families'. He concluded that, as a result, the area had serious social problems including high levels of crime and deviance. Because of these problems an individual giving the estate as their address was immediately labelled as deviant. This had repercussions in their dealings with the police, other authoritative figures, and their peers.

Cloward and Ohlin's 'opportunity structure' would suggest that a criminal sub-culture existed which was responsible for the deviant behaviour on the estate. However this would assume that the labelling taking place was justified. Gill suggests that, on the whole, the labelling was unjustified ant that the situation was created by local government housing policy.

Youth sub-culture theories can be useful in explaining some aspects of deviance in both American and British society. The young are dissatisfied with society and the values that it imposes upon them and they use deviant behaviour to demonstrate their displeasure. There are run-down inner city areas which are marked by violence and poverty and contain a criminal element where deviant youths are bred. However both British and American societies are so complex that to rely on one set of theories to provide a comprehensive explanation for deviance could only, at best, give an incomplete, even distorted picture. In Britain, many of the problems which cause the young to turn to deviance are as a result of either a lack of adequate leisure facilities or the labels placed on individuals by society. It is unlikely that deviance in Britain is caused exclusively by the individual's failure to reach a goal set by society.

AEB mark scheme

NB. NO CANDIDATE CAN SCORE MORE THAN 25 MARKS FOR EACH ANSWER.

Knowledge and Understanding

0 No Knowledge and Understanding appropriate to the set question.

1–3 Candidates' answers will present a limited amount of knowledge relevant to the set question. Candidates' understanding of this knowledge may be implicit rather than explicit.

In this band candidates' answers are likely to be characterised by the poor logical expression of ideas and the use of a limited range of conceptual terms, perhaps often used imprecisely and/or inaccurately.

Spelling, punctuation and grammar may show serious deficiencies and frequent errors, perhaps impairing the intelligibility of significant parts of the answer.

4–6 Towards the bottom of this mark band candidates' answers will present an adequate amount of knowledge, including historical and comparative material if appropriate, and will begin to demonstrate their understanding of it.

Towards the top of the mark band candidates' answers will present an increased amount of empirical and/or theoretical detail, drawn from historical and comparative sources if appropriate, and will be more accurate and complete in the presentation of this detail.

In this bank, candidates' answers are likely to be characterised by the fair to good logical expression of ideas and the competent use of a reasonable range of conceptual terms.

Spelling, punctuation and grammar will be of a reasonable standard. Commonly used words and sociological terms will generally be spelt correctly. There may be minor errors of punctuation and grammar, but these will not seriously impair the intelligibility of the answer.

7–9 To achieve this mark bank candidates' answers will have to present a detailed, accurate, and coherent account of knowledge including historical and comparative material if appropriate, within the remit of the set question. The theoretical context of the answer will be clear, and there will be explicit links between the theoretical and empirical aspects of the answer; in so doing, candidates will demonstrate a sound understanding of the question asked.

In this band, candidates' answers are likely to be characterised by the very good to excellent expression of ideas and the precise use of a broad range of conceptual terms.

Spelling, punctuation and grammar will be of a very good to excellent standard. Commonly and less commonly used words and sociological terms will almost always be spelt correctly. Punctuation and grammar will be used correctly throughout to facilitate the intelligibility of the answer.

Interpretation and Application

0 No relevant Interpretation or Application appropriate to the set question.

1–3 Answers in this mark band are likely to attempt either Interpretation or Application, will possibly be confused and meet with limited success in answering the set question.

Attempts at the Interpretation of relevant material will be general, and may be embedded in a 'Catch-all' presentation of a study, theory or idea. Attempts to apply knowledge will be in the form of, for example, an undeveloped example, a reference to a contemporary event, a reference to a related area of Sociology, or a reference to a personal experience; one or more of these will feature but without sociological insight or context.

In this band candidates' answers are likely to be characterised by the poor logical interpretation of ideas and the application of a limited range of conceptual terms, perhaps often applied imprecisely and/or inaccurately.

Spelling, punctuation and grammar may show serious deficiencies and frequent errors, perhaps impairing the intelligibility of significant parts of the answer.

4–6 Some appropriate material will be interpreted and applied in a limited way. In essence, to reach this mark band candidates will present a more sophisticated, complete and clearly sociological answer to the set question.

In this band, candidates' answers are likely to be characterised by the fair to good logical interpretation of ideas and the competent application of a reasonable range of conceptual terms.

Attention will be paid to specific issues raised by the set question, and answers should demonstrate that candidates have made an explicit attempt to both Interpret and Apply some relevant sociological material, although this attempt may still be partial towards the lower end of the mark band, and more complete at the top end. Towards the top of the mark band there will be greater evidence of sensitivity in interpretation and sociological awareness in application.

Spelling, punctuation and grammar will be of a reasonable standard. Commonly used words and sociological terms will generally be spelt correctly. There may be minor errors of punctuation and grammar, but these will not seriously impair the intelligibility of the answer.

7–9 Both the Interpretation and Application requirements of the set question will be addressed in a complete and successful way.

Candidates' answers will demonstrate that, with reference to the set question, they are able to interpret relevant sociological material in an explicit way (for example, ideas, concepts, theories and studies), and that they are able to apply this material to, for example, an example, event, a related area of Sociology, or personal experience, although not all of these need be attempted. Towards the top of the mark band, there may be evidence of, for example, interpretation and application following a clear rationale, as well as demonstrating clear sensitivity in interpretation and sociological application.

In this band, candidates' answers are likely to be characterised by the very good to excellent interpretation of ideas and the precise application of a broad range of conceptual terms.

Spelling, punctuation and grammar will be of a very good to excellent standard. Commonly and less commonly used words and sociological terms will almost always be spelt correctly. Punctuation and grammar will be used correctly throughout to facilitate the intelligibility of the answer.

Evaluation

0 No attempt at evaluation or an irrelevant attempt at evaluation.

1–3 Candidates' answers may offer one or two critical comments/justifications on some aspect of their answer, but these remain undeveloped and/or partial and/or confused.

In this band candidates' answers are likely to be characterised by the poor logical evaluation of ideas and the use of a limited range of conceptual terms, perhaps often applied imprecisely and/or inaccurately.

Spelling, punctuation and grammar may show serious deficiencies and frequent errors, perhaps impairing the intelligibility of significant parts of the answer.

4–6 Towards the bottom end of the mark band candidates' answers may attempt either to offer a number of relevant criticisms of a particular study/idea/concept, etc., or will use one theoretical perspective to criticise another in a one-sided manner (i.e. a juxtaposition).

In this band, candidates' answers are likely to be characterised by the fair to good logical evaluation of ideas and the competent use of a reasonable range of conceptual terms.

Towards the top of the mark band candidates' answers should present a more balanced form of evaluative awareness in criticising/justifying both specific and general issues in their answer. Even at this level, however, there may still be a tendency to present a one-sided form of criticism, though this needs to be reasonably complete and accurate.

Spelling, punctuation and grammar will be of a reasonable standard. Commonly used words and sociological terms will generally be spelt correctly. There may be minor errors of punctuation and grammar, but these will not seriously impair the intelligibility of the answer.

7–9 To attain this mark band candidates' answers will have to present a successful appraisal of relevant issued as raised in their answer, with reference to the set question.

Answers should demonstrate balance in the critical comments offered as, for example, appreciating that all studies/theories have both strengths and weaknesses. Answers which present some of these evaluative qualities, but in a simplistic juxtaposed framework, cannot reach this mark band. Towards the top of the mark band, candidates' answers will present a full evaluation of the material used as well as any conclusions which are relevant within the remit of the set question.

In this band, candidates' answers are likely to be characterised by the very good to excellent evaluation of ideas and the precise use of a broad range of conceptual terms.

Spelling, punctuation and grammar will be of a very good to excellent standard. Commonly and less commonly used words and sociological terms will almost always be spelt correctly. Punctuation and grammar will be used correctly throughout to facilitate the intelligibility of the answer.

(AEB 1997: © AEB 1997)

We hope you were positive in your marking, giving credit when deserved, but not for things that didn't demonstrate the required skills in line with the set question. Now you know the criteria examiners use to judge different levels of performance, and, importantly, what they're looking for in a good answer. Ultimately, as the saying goes, we can only do our best. It's a good maxim, but best efforts, however well-intentioned, must address the task to hand. We hope this chapter has helped you to do just that.

Good luck in your A-level Sociology exam!

References

AEB (1995a) *1998 Syllabuses GCE Advanced Level Sociology*. Surrey: Associated Examining Board

AEB (1995b) *Chief Examiner's Reports, Summer 1995 Examination, Sociology*. Surrey: Associated Examining Board

AEB (1997) *Guidance notes in the use of general and question specific marking schemes for A/SOCGY/3, A/SOCGY/5 and A/SOCGY/6*. Surrey: Associated Examining Board

Lawson, Tony (1996) A response to 'Mixing it with an exam board', pp 30–1, *Social Science Teacher*, Vol. 25, No. 2, Spring

Moores, Michael and Breslin, Tony (1991) What is good sociology?, pp 14–16, *Sociology Review*, Vol. 1, No. 1, September

Address

The Associated Examining Board, Publications Department, Stag Hill House, Guildford, Surrey GU2 5XJ
Tel: 01483 506506, Fax: 01483 300152

3 Coursework

Topics covered in this chapter
- *Background considerations*
- *The rationale for coursework*
- *Research action plan*
- *The context section*
- *The methodology section*
- *The content section*
- *The evaluation section*
- *The bibliography, research diary and appendix*
- *The mark scheme*

There are few studies of sociologists at work. J. S. Coleman's book, *The Adolescent Society* (1961), took him seven years to complete. During that period, he changed the focus, hypothesis and methods of analysis, had financial difficulties, and the data didn't live up to expectations. Consider the research of C. McCaghy and J. Skipper, which led to two publications: 'Lesbian behaviour as an adaptation to the occupation of stripping' (1969) and 'Stripteasers: the anatomy and career contingencies of a deviant occupation' (1970). You can imagine the difficulties and sensitivities involved when two male sociologists conduct fieldwork into women's sexual behaviour. For starters, do you think that it's appropriate for males to be involved in this kind of study? And what do you think of a title that includes the word 'strippers'?

Whether you call it research, investigation, inquiry or a personal study, carrying out coursework is *sociology at work*. Even though your research won't be so controversial or time-consuming as that mentioned above, it'll be full of what Marten Shipman describes as 'frustrations and joy, inspiration and depression, false starts and premature finishes' (Shipman 1981: 9). Don't be put off by the suggestion that research is the province of 'Activities which are substantially removed from day-to-day life and which are pursued by outstandingly gifted persons with an unusual level of commitment' (Howard and Sharp 1983: 6). This is an imperious view of things, and isn't something that either Howard and Sharp, or we, subscribe to.

Background considerations

There are some issues that are commonly encountered in sociological research, including:

- What topic of study to choose?
- Which hypothesis and set of objectives to research?
- Which methods of research to use?
- How to use these methods?
- Is a pilot study needed?
- Is there access to respondents and institutions?
- How to collect, present and analyse the results?
- How to evaluate the results in relation to initial objectives?

Don't be intimidated by the statistical whizz kid or computational star who may appear in your A-level sociology group. Whatever the size of your undertaking, you'll need to devise a clear action plan, but this doesn't mean accessing every sophisticated research technique available. 'It is quite possible to produce a worthwhile study without using computers and with a minimum of statistical knowledge' (Bell 1992: Introduction).

Assessment format

With the introduction of new government regulations, your coursework will have a weighting of 20 per cent of the total marks for your A-level examination. The maximum mark for the coursework is 40 marks, and these are divided between the three skill domains:

- Knowledge and understanding – 12 marks
- Interpretation and application – 14 marks
- Evaluation – 14 marks.

For more about the skill domains, see Chapter 2, pages 8–10, and for the mark scheme, see pages 47–8 in this chapter.

What do I need to know before undertaking coursework?

The timescale for completing a piece of research is challenging. Your study must be about 5,000 words in length. There's a lot to do and little time to complete it. You cannot start the research until April of the first year of your course, and it must be ready to send to an examiner (called a coursework moderator) by April of the following year, so it will require dedication and organisation. However, you shouldn't spend a disproportionate amount of time on the research to the detriment of the written papers. The coursework timeline opposite might help you to keep to a manageable schedule.

> **EXAM TIP**
>
> If your coursework is well over the 5,000 word limit, it implies that you may have a very broad hypothesis and too many wide-ranging objectives, and/or you aren't focused tightly enough on the objectives you've set yourself.
>
> *You must have a focused study with manageable objectives.*

Group work

Group work is allowed up to and including the data collection stage of the study. The writing-up of all the stages should be your own work. However, avoid selecting a similar title to that of another student from your centre. It will be difficult not to communicate with them, and to use similar sources of information.

Presentation

Follow these guidelines:

- The coursework that is submitted must be the original, not a photocopy. You may, copyright permitting, attach photocopied inserts (such as tables) to the original.
- It should be word processed, typed or hand-written neatly on one side of A4 paper.
- Ensure each page is numbered in the correct order, including appendices.
- Include a clear lightweight title page which states the *study title, your name, candidate number,* and *centre number*.
- Include a *contents page* which lists all the section headings and page numbers, for example:

Rationale	1–3
Context	4–9
Methodology	10–15
Content	16–23
Evaluation and Conclusion	24–30
Bibliography	31
Research diary	32–34
Appendix A	35–36

- The whole study should be secured with treasury tags. Avoid ring binders or tight binding which will hide your text.
- You should have a *candidate assessment sheet* attached to the front of your study, which should be signed by you and your supervising teacher to authenticate it as your own work.

Ethical guidelines

As a student undertaking your own research, you must abide by what is grandly called the 'Statement of Ethical Practice' (British Sociological Association). This means that you must safeguard the interests of those involved in your research and ensure that your results are presented truthfully and accurately. The following factors should be carefully considered before embarking on any research:

- Do not override the rights of others – ensure that their interests, sensitivities and anonymity are respected and protected.
- Obtain the consent and trust of those who are participating in your research. Ask their permission to tape-record an interview and assure them that the recording will be deleted once the data have been analysed.
- If access to a participant is through an 'intermediary', do not 'inadvertently disturb that relationship unduly' (AEB 1996: 71). Remember, if someone has arranged an interview for you with a work colleague, their relationship will not end after your interview has been completed. Everyone participating in your research should be treated with respect at all times.
- Consider the dangers (to you and to others) of using covert research. Participant or non-participant observation may be an exciting prospect but, when the

Coursework timeline

Month	Action
Year 1:	
April	Your teacher will introduce coursework to you. Decide on a possible focus.
May	Hand in *coursework action plan* to teacher for feedback on suitability of area. Clear *hypothesis*, as appropriate, *and objectives* should be agreed. Coursework diary (*research diary*) launched.
June	First draft of the *rationale* is completed and handed in for comments. Draw up a list of possible *secondary source* contacts and write letters (remember to enclose a stamped addressed envelope). *Literature search* in libraries for *context section* commences. Be prepared to take information directly from reference books, photocopy specific articles or pages (follow copyright regulations) or, where it's unavailable, put in a book request or inter-library loan requisition. The latter can take ages so don't delay!
July	Continue literature search and make rough notes addressing *objectives*. Hand in second draft of the *rationale* for comment and clearance. Discuss with teacher possible *primary research methods* in the light of earlier action plan. Make contact with research respondents to arrange access for future social surveys, informal interviews and observations.
July/August holidays	Draw together notes from literature search and combine with other secondary material from organisations and contacts and produce *draft context chapter*. Design your *research schedule* and *formulate questionnaire, interview questions* and *observation techniques*, as appropriate. Pilot them, where possible, and make changes if appropriate. Ensure access has been agreed and all ethical codes followed.
Year 2:	
September	Hand in completed *draft context section* ensuring that information presented corresponds closely to objectives set, is coherent and evaluative. After teacher appraisal, amend and obtain clearance. Carry out *primary research* and collate information. *Draft methodology section* should be completed and handed in.
October	Respond to teacher comments on methodology section and complete. Draw together all results from primary research in preparation for *drafting content section*. Ensure that material covers each of the objectives, or you will need to arrange and collect further evidence. Discuss with teacher your plans for presentation of primary data and other secondary sources (where applicable). The use of appendices for complete transcripts of interviews, and questionnaire exemplars, may be useful, but clear reference will need to be made to them in the main text.
November	Under each objective, set out, in rough, evidence from your *primary research*. Scan secondary evidence within your context section, and look for any similarities or disparities between your own primary findings and secondary documentation. Draft the *content section* incorporating the above suggestions. Remember, it's not enough just to present results accurately. *Interpret* them too in relation to the objectives.
December	Hand in your *draft content section* for comment and complete your final and very significant *evaluation section*. It's important within this section that you're intellectually honest about the limitations of your methodology, and suggest possible alternatives. With your findings, it's essential that you signpost each of your objectives and show how the evidence within your study either supports or contradicts them. A final *conclusion* should then be composed relating specifically to your hypothesis.
January	Hand in *revised content section and draft evaluation section*. Revise as necessary based on teacher comments.
February	You should be in a position to draw together all the sections and make any minor amendments to spelling, punctuation and presentation. Ensure you have completed your *appendix, bibliography* and *research diary*. Count and number all your pages. Your teacher will now set you a date for completing your *final version* and handing it in. This is likely to be the end of February/beginning of March to allow time for it to be marked before the external sample is sent to the moderator.
Presentation	Your final version should be either typed or word processed. If you have very neat writing, that's also alright. You may find it easier to complete each section as it's checked and 'approved' by your teacher rather than leaving it all to the end. However, previous experience suggests that students usually find changes to be made towards the end of the process. You'll be able to collect your research from your teacher in October.

(Adapted from Walker 1993: 22)

activities are law-breaking, the consequences may be more than you were prepared for. Try explaining to the police at 3 a.m. that you were carrying out sociological research for your A-level!

- Special care should be offered to those who may feel threatened due to age, status or powerlessness.
- Under the Data Protection Act, you are required to ensure that no participant is identifiable. Use pseudonyms. National organisations may not be as concerned with anonymity, but do not assume this.
- Avoid sensitive topic areas such as child abuse, rape and domestic violence. You won't be able to carry out primary research with the offenders/victims without breaking ethical guidelines. If you want to study sensitive issues, use secondary sources. Any primary research should only be conducted with appropriate official organisations (for example, the NSPCC).
- Ensure the research – both primary and secondary sources – is collected independently of other students. The sources you use should be acknowledged in your study. At no time should you copy from other candidates' data or their secondary sources. If you do, your coursework may be cancelled.

QUESTIONS

1 Why do you think the British Sociological Association decided to produce a Statement of Ethical Practice?
2 What is meant by the 'integrity of sociological enquiry'? What will you as a researcher do to maintain this?
3 Why should you aim to complete the research within the suggested 5,000 word limit?
4 Draw up a list of coursework titles that would not be suitable for A-level, with appropriate explanations.

The rationale for coursework

The rationale is the *justification* for doing something. This is an important section of your coursework as it sets out and justifies what's to follow.

How do you decide on the focus of your study?

- From the topics covered this year in your course, which particular aspects have interested you enough to follow up in more detail?
- Browse through the range of sociology textbooks or books covering sociological issues available in your school or college. These may trigger ideas.
- From television programmes watched, or magazines and newspapers read, are there any specific issues that interest you? Is there any particular story in the news at the moment, or from the past, that could looked at from a sociological viewpoint?
- What are your main interests, hobbies, out of school activities, work experiences, etc? There may be an element of these that interests you sufficiently to conduct research. It's likely that you'll also have accessible respondents available.
- Are there any aspects of your own experience or home background that could be studied? Perhaps you're interested in the way you were brought up, or the role that each family member plays. What about that family down the road? And so on.

Research action plan

You've decided upon a possible area of focus, but before you go any further it's essential to set out and complete a research action plan or, as Barrat and Cole (1991: 26) define it, the 'Sociology Enquiry Proposal Form'. This should be an outline of *intention* which will help you to focus on significant aspects of your coursework (for example, objectives, methods of research, etc.). This should then be handed to your teacher who will advise you how to proceed.

The action plan should be completed under the following headings:

- *Overall area of focus* This is the area of the syllabus that you're going to research.
- *Specific hypothesis* This is an informed hunch directly related to your area of study that you 'test' against the evidence (or investigative title). NB 'Open-ended' research might not involve an hypothesis.
- *Objectives of the study* These are the questions you hope to answer as part of your research which will directly link to your hypothesis. Langley and Corrigan (1993: 10) express them as 'key areas to be investigated . . . a pathway through the project . . . you need to solve before you can reach final conclusions regarding your overall hypothesis.'
- *Operationalising your concepts* These are the key terms/words that will be derived from your hypothesis and objectives. They will need to be defined in your context section and measured through specific indicators in your methodology. For example, if you are examining social class differences, have you established what you mean by social class and which indicator you are going to use to measure it?
- *Proposed methods of research* Which methods are you going to use to address your hypothesis and objectives? Will you be able to combine the collection of 'first hand' primary data from questionnaires and interviews, with 'second hand' secondary sources of data such as official statistics and media reports?
- *Preliminary background sociological observations* Within your rationale you should include background material that relates to your area of study. It may be a 'stepping stone' to your hypothesis. It may be

information that you've read and is directly linked to your research which you hope to elaborate upon or analyse later.

- *Possible sources and contacts* It's essential that you access sociological (and non-sociological) sources of evidence which can be used in your study. These may be from books, newspaper articles, specific sociological studies, etc. You need to consider whether there are official organisations that you can write to, local representatives to interview, questionnaire and interview respondents available, etc.
- *Research diary* This is a record of everything occurring throughout the research study (see page 44).

OVER TO YOU

Find a newspaper or journal article that could be used in a rationale. Think of an hypothesis and a list of objectives that could evolve from it.

Summary

Your rationale should normally include:

- reasons for selection (for example, personal interest, contacts, experience or concerns)
- a clear hypothesis to be tested from the outset (or investigative title)
- a set of related objectives to be covered and directly related to the hypothesis
- brief reference to sociological arguments and themes, placing your research in the context of existing research and literature
- a plan of action outlining what you'll include in each section, with a potential set of sources of information.

Before you go any further with your coursework focus, consider these questions:

- Can you access sociological material and adapt non-sociological literature on the topic?
- Are there further contacts – both within national and local organisations, and other individuals?
- Is it possible to collect primary and secondary sources of data?
- Does the study abide by the statement of ethical practice?
- As appropriate, have you set out with a clear hypothesis to test and a limited number of manageable objectives?
- Will the research keep you interested?

EXAM TIP

Generally, the examples of students' written work in this chapter are presented as we found them, even when this includes errors. Where the original contains, for example, faulty punctuation, which makes it difficult for the reader to follow the text, minor 'corrections' have been made.

It is important that your use of English is as good as you can make it, otherwise you won't earn the marks that are awarded for good English. Furthermore, inaccurate language can confuse the moderator and adversely affect your overall score.

CRIT THINK CRIT THINK CRIT THINK CRIT THINK CRIT THINK CRIT THINK

A RATIONALE FOR COURSEWORK

The rationale on page 28 was produced by an A-level candidate.

1 *Read the rationale and highlight the following (if present):*
  - a *reasons for selection*
  - b *hypothesis*
  - c *objectives*
  - d *preliminary sociological background information – both argument and theory*
  - e *plan of action.*

2 *Do you think this choice of research is acceptable for A-level?*

3 *How far does this section demonstrate that the candidate has thought through the implications of her choice?*

CRIT THINK CRIT THINK CRIT THINK CRIT THINK CRIT THINK CRIT THINK CRIT

AN INSIGHT INTO THE CRIMINAL BEHAVIOUR OF TWINS WITH SPECIFIC REFERENCE TO THE KRAY TWINS

Rationale

This project focuses specifically upon twinship and its link with criminal behaviour, an area first researched by Dr Johannes Lange in 1929. I have chosen to study twins chiefly because they are a natural phenomena that have featured predominantly in history and have remained subject to close examination and suspicion.

The Bible features the power struggle of Romulus and Remus, and the deception of Jacob and Esau, whilst the Greek myths stage the battle of the twin heroes, Castor and Polydeuces. During the Second World War, the Nazi scientist, Joseph Mengele isolated twins within the Auschwitz death camp for experimentation. In contemporary society, media coverage of identical twins such as Freda and Greta Chaplin, whose bizarre relationship was the subject of a 'Short Stories' documentary in 1991, and June and Jennifer Gibbons, the 'silent twins', who are now detained at Broadmoor Special Hospital for arson, had added to the myth, mystery and gross misinterpretation which stigmatises the twinship role.

I have developed a strong interest in identical twins and the relationship with criminality through media coverage of the Kray twins, who controlled London's gangland in a ten-year reign during the 1960s, and who have since achieved legendary status in British criminal history. Identical twins tend to be relatively rare and occur all over the world at a rate of between three and four births in every thousand. The relationship between monozygotic or identical twins is a special and intimate bond, and this may be a predisposing factor in the link with criminality. The immediate questions posed when examining twins tend to focus upon the hereditary and environment debate because identical twins have the same hereditary endowment and should therefore provide the ideal material for research into crime causation.

I have not established a specific hypothesis in my project because the twinship area provides an abundant source of information which would be inhibited by a strict hypothesis. Instead I have employed an exploratory research technique through which I can hopefully achieve an unlimited insight in to the criminality of twins. The title of the research I wish to examine is:

'An insight in to the criminal behaviour of twins with specific reference to the Kray twins'

My project is going to be based on the following foundation questions which I hope will enable me to assess the concordance rate, or similarity of monozygotic twins and establish the motivation behind their criminality:

1 Identify whether there are a large number of criminal twins.

2 Sociological explanations for criminal behaviour.

3 a Collect secondary source material on explanations for criminal behaviour of twins.

b Compare the sociological explanations for crime with the secondary source material on twins.

4 Case study on the Kray twins as an example of criminal twins. How far do the Krays fit the sociological theories and secondary source material or reasons why they commit crimes?

In the context chapter, I will examine the sociological explanations for criminal behaviour of all offenders using theoretical perspectives on crime by both positivist and phenomenologist sociologists. By assessing, for example, the theory of subcultures and effects of urban environment, I will be capable of establishing the stimulus behind criminality in monozygotic twins and subsequently expand on the nature–nurture debate, which remains a contentious issue.

The methodology chapter in my project will be concerned with the research methods I have adopted to answer the foundation questions set in my rationale. However, through preliminary reading I have already established that my coursework is going to be limited to secondary source data, such as suggestions from written contacts like professors of criminology for example, and hopefully prisoners themselves. I will be employing a positivistic approach in the methodology chapter when I document the number of criminal twins from the official statistics. I aim to justify my use of secondary source data and predict the advantages and disadvantages of the research methods by highlighting the validity and reliability of those adopted.

In the content chapter, I will present the main body of my research, in which I will identify the reasons for criminal behaviour in monozygotic twins and establish whether their concordant offences are determined by environmental influences, genetic programming, or alternatively the psychological influence of the co-twin. In this chapter I will make specific reference to the Kray twins and examine how far they fit the sociological theories on criminal twins and any other secondary material based on criminological twin research.

In the concluding chapter, I will evaluate the foundation questions set in the rationale and offer satisfactory results and answers to my initial proposals, by establishing the 'insight'of criminal behaviour in twins. I will consider the success of my project and address the issues I have neglected by highlighting any methodological problems, and by providing a personal falsification or qualification of the sociological research I have assessed on the criminality of twins.

In embarking upon my research, my plan of action will primarily comprise of letters to Mr Reginald Kray and Mr Ronald Kray at their places of detention. I will request permission to enquire about their status as criminal twins and the motivation behind their criminality. Throughout my coursework, I will maintain a research diary documenting my correspondence, the conferences I have with my coursework tutor and the general procedure of my project as it develops and progresses.

The context section

This section is a *selected review* of relevant sociological and adapted non-sociological literature which focuses directly upon the objectives of your rationale. A common mistake in this section is not keeping the literature review specific enough and completing a broad review on the whole area of, for example, Sociology of Education.

This section will only contain *secondary source material*. Your own research findings will appear later in the content section.

> **EXAM TIP**
>
> To ensure that you cover each of the objectives in the rationale, it may be helpful to address them under sub-headings in this section.

If you are completing a study that relies totally on secondary source material, it may be advisable to separate the sources which are *specifically sociological* from those which are to be adapted from 'non-sociological' work, such as media cuttings and other organisations' data. You may find it easier to review the sociological evidence in the context section, and those sources initially non-sociological which are to be adapted to the study in the content section. Don't forget that you'll need to compare and contrast the two sources in the content section.

Examples from a student's context section on 'Female Stereotyping in Advertising' are used to illustrate this part of the chapter.

What needs to be in your context section?

You should provide clear coverage of each of the objectives you set yourself with secondary source evidence.

You need to define key terms contained within your hypothesis and objectives of study. If you remember, we called this *operationalising the concepts*. The example which follows shows how a student has operationalised the concept of stereotyping.

> Stereotype
> *In his book In the Eye of the Beholder Arthur Miller defines stereotyping as 'a generic process applicable to any socially defined group'[1]. This concept was first developed by Walter Lippman (cited in Miller) in the 1920s. Whilst Lippman emphasised the deficiencies of stereotyping in terms of its consequences he noted that it is a necessary process in society and that to abandon stereotypes would be to 'impoverish human life'. This, he argued, is because stereotypes help to define an individual's position in society and provide a justification and explanation for behaviour towards other members of society, by placing a control over social stimuli. He asserted that stereotyping is a reflection of our culture, language and manner of thinking, and it is therefore in all of us.*

You should include a selective review of related *sociological and non-sociological literature*. Don't worry if you can't find very up-to-date material. Just ensure that what you do use is relevant. Reference to recent *Sociology Review* articles and similar journals and textbooks will help you achieve this.

The next example shows how a student has reviewed a piece of the literature.

> POSITIVIST STUDIES
>
> Categorising Women – Content Analysis
> *Content analysis is a technique whereby hypotheses are tested by measuring certain aspects of the content of the media and it has been used to study gender stereotyping in magazines and TV advertisements. Two studies, by Butcher and Coward[7], and by Millum[8], noted that a number of common images exist, into which all women in advertisements can be categorised. Millum observed that the most common images of women portrayed in British magazines were mannequin, narcissist, hostess and wife/mother. Coward and Butcher reached similar conclusions, highlighting nine main categories into which women fall: official or professional women; sports women; criminal women; women with elite status; women with borrowed status; sexually attractive women; women as the object of humour; and women as a social problem . . .*
>
> ANTI-POSITIVIST STUDIES
>
> *It is important to note however that the positivist method of content analysis is just one approach to assessing the significance of advertisements in reinforcing social gender stereotypes. Gill notes that during the 1970s disillusionment with content analysis grew and researchers began to address a more interpretive method of investigation popular in France and evident in the works of Roland Barthes and Louis Althusser[15]. Such research used mostly qualitative methods concentrating on imagery, relationships and behaviour, and also the social effects of advertisements of society.*

It's essential that your review of selected literature has a *theoretical stance* (for example 'The functionalist and marxist approaches to the study of advertising'). This is illustrated in the following example.

> SOCIOLOGICAL PERSPECTIVES ON FEMALE STEREOTYPING IN ADVERTISING
>
> *There has been very little theoretical study on this topic to my knowledge. However, it is possible to outline the general arguments functionalists, Marxists and interactionists would put forward based on their views of women and their functions in society.*
>
> Functionalists
> *Functionalist anthropologists such as G. P. Murdock see women as fulfilling a primarily housewife/mother type role in society. He sees biological differences between men*

and women as the basis of the sexual division of labour in society . . .

Marxists

Marxists on the other hand would disagree strongly with the functionalist perspective. Supporters of Marxist arguments would point out that the family in particular plays a significant part in retaining stereotypes created for women in society. As many advertisements depict women in a domestic family role they arguably also contribute to the maintenance of stereotypes. Sue Sharpe notes that advertisers use stereotypes because it is in their interest to do so. Because women are worried about achieving their roles due to the pressures on them to be sexually attractive and successful as a wife and mother, advertisements are good for capitalism because they encourage women in particular to consume in order to achieve these roles . . .

Interactionists

An interactionist-based argument would note that individuals in society derive meanings from stereotypes and act in the light of them. Labelling theorists such as Becker and Lemert may argue that once a stereotyped role is applied to a woman her actions will be interpreted in the light of the label.

Use a variety of sources to cover your objectives (for example, newspaper articles, transcripts from television programmes and sections from publications). Ensure that they're relevant to your objectives, and interpreted and evaluated as you progress.

EXAM TIP

It may be useful to include a summary at the end of each objective completed or significant study examined.

Remember that the sources you're using may lack reliability or validity. So, it's essential that you highlight the merits and problems of using secondary sources within the methodology section.

OVER TO YOU

Here's an hypothesis that is being tested by a student in her/his research:
'There is a link between the closure of mental institutions and an increase in suicides by the mentally ill living within the community.'
Which key concepts would you need to operationalise from this hypothesis? Think of appropriate secondary sources that could be accessed.

The literature search

Don't succumb to data overload. Set out a literature search plan of action similar to this:

1. *Identify possible sources* You need material that will answer the set objectives. This must be collected within a limited time span. Access to copies of the books and articles you want may not be possible immediately so you must have other options.
2. *Identify collection points* For example:
   - sociology department library
   - school or college library
   - main local library
   - local university library (access will be for reference only, and permission should be sought from the university)
   - local/national organisations (that can be visited, contacted for an interview, or written to for information)
   - local/national media organisations who may be able to provide articles, references to follow up, interviews, etc.
   - computer facilities, including CD-ROM, the Internet, and other databases. Also microfiche or cuttings files that are held in libraries
   - local individuals whom you know or can safely contact, who have a particular knowledge or expertise of your area of study. Remember their time is limited and valuable so don't bank on an early or favourable reply.
3. *Access the literature* It's essential to have a focus before you start. Do you know exactly what you are looking for? Bell (1993: 24–6) suggests the following points should be considered when planning a search for literature:
   - selection of topic area
   - key terms to be defined and covered in the study
   - parameters set. Do you only want UK sources and material found in the area of sociology?
   - time period of search (for example, 1980 onwards)
   - type of material to be collected. Will it be from journals, books, official statistics, etc?
   - possible search terms. Be aware of synonyms under which your terms may be classified in the library
   - selection of sources. The library catalogue houses selected terms under its class number. Bibliographies with brief references of published works are found in *British National Bibliographies*. Reference sections which hold sociological journals, specialist magazines, official international surveys, statistics and specific books can't be removed from the library. Indices for articles are to be found, for example, in the *British Humanities Index* and *Social Science Index and Abstract*.

4 *Review the literature* Peruse the whole text first, and then use the contents and index to focus more specifically on particular aspects. I suggest that you employ a card index system for each text examined. On one side, record the authors, year of publication and name of publisher. If the material comes from a journal, record author and date, title of the article and volume and number of the journal. On the other side, record information, summaries and direct quotes that can later be incorporated into the chapter under specific objectives. Note page references throughout. By organising yourself in this way, the *bibliography* (see page 44) will be easier to complete at the end of the research process.

EXAM TIP

If you do include direct quotations, cuttings from newspapers and larger articles or passages and place them in an appendix, always clearly interpret and evaluate them in the main body of your text. Simply referring to them isn't sufficient.

5 *Analyse the literature* You may have a wide range of different sources, including historical, comparative, cross-cultural and statistical, as well as material from novels and pressure group pamphlets. You must decide *how* you're going to use the sources. The best way is to arrange the material under each of your objectives. Langley and Corrigan (1993: 42) also suggest that 'explicit connections between secondary data and your project need to be made using phrases such as "I will be retesting this conclusion"'. In other words, never take secondary data at face value. To show your understanding, it's essential to make an *assessment* (evaluation) of the stance in the literature and then perhaps make further remarks on it in the light of your own findings.

Here's an example of how a student has assessed some literature.

> CONCLUSIONS
>
> *After examining the various approaches previously applied to the study of gender stereotyping in advertisements, a number of observations can be made and some conclusions can be drawn. By using positivist methods such as content analysis, researchers have found that women in advertisements can often be categorised into a number of common images, supporting the notion that stereotypes do exist. It seems that women most frequently appear in advertisements as housewives within the home (as Courtney and Lockeretz, and Wagner and Banos concluded) or as sexually attractive objects.*

OVER TO YOU

For the following research areas:
1 The sociology of eating disorders
2 Sect and cult movements in the UK
3 Misuse of funds by charities

indicate appropriate examples of:
a sociological ideas/debates
b sociological theories
c specific sociological studies
d non-sociological studies/sources
e organisations/places to be contacted and/or visited.

Summary

Your context section should normally include:

- a collection of secondary source material that locates the study in a theoretical and sociological setting
- original work throughout. Don't copy extensively from any textbook or other source without acknowledging it. It's always better to express the information in your own words, but write like a sociologist
- application of all your source material to the objectives set in the rationale. Don't accept them at face value. Interpret and evaluate everything
- a varied and up-to-date (as far as practical) literature search. Always start your search early. You can't expect to find every source immediately or that organisations will reply quickly. Stamped addressed envelopes are essential with any communication, but don't always count on a reply.

The methodology section

In this section, you select research methods to enable you to address your hypothesis and objectives. Judith Bell indicates how difficult this selection is:

> 'The sad fact is that in spite of all the tried-and-tested methods that have been employed by experienced researchers over the years, there never seems to be an example that is quite right for the particular task. Inevitably, you will find you have to adapt or to devise a completely new approach, and all new systems need careful piloting and refining in the light of experience.'
>
> (Bell 1992: 97)

As you're probably now discovering, carrying out primary research is not something you can enter into lightly and without thought. The range of research methods available is extensive and the task of deciding which are the most appropriate for your study is critical.

Methods of research

We'll indicate here the four main methods that should be considered. Some examples from students' work are included.

For a detailed examination of methods, read Chapter 5.

Surveys

The aim of a survey is generally to gain representative statistical information based on *samples* from target populations.

Most surveys aim to collect *reliable* evidence. That is to say, 'anybody else using this method, or the same person using it at another time, would come up with the same results' (Patrick McNeill 1992: 14). Reliability can be checked if the same question is repeated in a different way during the questionnaire. However, you can't be sure that the answers the respondents give you are *valid* (i.e. truthful).

If the sample is representative of the population, you'll be able to infer that what is true of the sample is broadly true of the population. This is called *generalising*.

Surveys usually obtain data from two important research tools:

- *questionnaires*, which can be fixed-response, open-ended or a combination of both
- *interviews*, which can be structured, semi-structured or unstructured. A structured interview is, in fact, a questionnaire which is completed by an interviewer in response to replies from an interviewee.

In the case of questionnaires that people complete themselves, the data are returned to the researcher in – hopefully – complete, or near complete, form. However, when interviews are used, the interviewer is responsible for 'collecting' the data. This can be accomplished, for example, by:

- recording the interview on audio cassette for later transcription
- entering responses onto a schedule during the course of the interview. Big research organisations often use lap-top computers for this. You might have to settle for a notepad and pen!
- entering the responses onto a schedule straight after the interview.

Sampling is normally associated with survey methods of research, although you will naturally sample with all methods. Burgess distinguishes between *probability sampling* and *non-probability sampling:*

Probability sampling	Non-probability sampling
Random	Quota
Stratified random	Snowball
Cluster	
Multi-stage cluster	
Stratified cluster	

(Burgess 1993: 25)

- *Probability sample* – specifying for each element of the population the probabilty of it being included in the sample.
- *Non-probability sample* – no way of estimating the probability of being included in the sample.

According to Murray Morison, there are three levels to the sample:

'The first we call the *survey population* or *target population*. This is the overall population that we are hoping to draw conclusions about . . . It should be noted that this survey population is always a sub-group of some larger population. The second level is commonly called the *sampling frame*. It is from this group that the sample will actually be selected . . . The third level is the *sample* itself. This has been defined as a small scale representation – a kind of miniature model – of the population from which it is selected.'

(Morison 1989: 312)

Observation

Although used by some positivists, this method is commonly associated with interpretivist research.

There are four main types of observation in social science:

- overt participant observation
- covert participant observation
- overt non-participant observation
- covert non-participant observation.

These are important considerations:

- Gaining access to the people being observed.
- Ethics. Is it acceptable to 'go undercover' (covert) to observe the actions of others? Are you placing yourself at risk? Is there any likelihood of you witnessing or participating in criminal activities?
- If you are carrying out participant observation, how far will you become involved or remain aloof?
- The data are more likely to be valid as you're able to observe the person in her or his own natural setting.
- The data will only be relevant to a particular social context, but the research is more likely to interpret validly the meanings people attach to their actions.

Analysis of existing data

This method is commonly used across the positivist–interpretivist spectrum:

- Positivists, for example, identify 'causal' relationships by interrogating official statistics. Durkheim used existing statistical data to develop a better understanding of risk factors in relation to suicide.
- Interpretivists, for example, disclose stereotypes by conducting content analysis of the media. The Glasgow University Media Group have shown how journalists 'problematise' working-class strike action.

Students considering mass media research will find the content analysis of existing data useful in obtaining qualitative and quantitative information. In the context of the latter, content analysis can 'produce an objective record of the frequency of pre-selected items which the researcher is interested in' (Barrat and Cole 1991: 58).

On a practical level, content analysis is repeatable. You will need to select a media sample and then arrange a set of categories to be piloted. The categories can then be modified. Don't expect all the evidence to fall clearly into set categories. You'll discover data that doesn't always fit preconceptions. Generalisations can be made by comparing the statistical findings of different documents. This may be by measuring space, time allocation, frequency, stereotyping, different groups, issues, etc.

You might want to analyse a sample of media coverage to generate qualitative data, to disclose underlying messages. This is called *semiology*. Within a media coverage, photographs and words are open to a variety of interpretations. For example, the size of the text may have direct relevance to the image presented. You may focus on 'the headlines, layout, choice of words, length of sentence and story, the details provided and use of quotes' (Dutton 1989: 16).

Experiments

A controlled laboratory experiment is the one most closely associated with the natural sciences. The knowledge collected is regarded as objective and factual. You need to decide whether you could study aspects of human behaviour within these confines.

Few students and few professional sociologists use experiments, However, a key advantage of using the experimental method is the opportunity to make comparisons between different groups and situations. Some positivists argue that, through experiments, they're able to control and manipulate different variables to some extent in order to provide causal explanations for the behaviour of different groups.

Your study will probably involve *primary research* (i.e. your own, first-hand use of interviews, questionnaires, etc.) and *secondary research* (i.e. your scholarly reference to existing data and/or further analysis of such data).

Although it's entirely acceptable to use only secondary data in your study, there's a danger that this might turn into too much replication of textbook information. For this reason, we strongly recommend that you engage in both primary and secondary research. Suppose, for example, you use a small random survey to obtain information on what A-level students think about politics. You might supplement this primary research with secondary source commentaries on:

- the advantages of random sampling
- the effective use of random sampling in a published sociological study.

OVER TO YOU

The following coursework titles have been selected by students:

1 A focus on the attitudes of people towards cannabis, its use and its legislation
2 The working class and its presumed link to crime and deviance
3 Why should you be concerned about AIDS?

For each one, select:

a appropriate methods of research
b an appropriate sampling technique (if desirable)
c a sample size (what does your teacher think?).

What to include in the methodology section

Justification of the choice of the methodology

In the rationale, you will have indicated your proposed methods.

Your choice of methods will depend on the aims of your study. If you wish to make generalisations, you should select *quantitative* methods. Surveys will certainly 'fit the bill' here. On the other hand, if you require detailed information on how people make sense of social reality, a *qualitative* tool would be advisable (for example, informal interviewing or overt participant observation).

Practical constraints will influence your selection. You've a short time span and limited resources with which to work. You would be ill-advised to select a large sample or to select a study which only lends itself to participant observation.

Consider your theoretical position. Are you adopting a structural or a social constructionist approach (or both)? *Methodological pluralism (triangulation)* will help you to compare and contrast findings.

You will have identified and defined the key concepts in your study within the context section. Now is the time to consider how best to operationalise them.

Will the data be collected in an honest, accurate and ethical way? Discussion with and advice from your teacher are crucial here.

Is your aim to collect reliable, valid data, or both? The survey is more likely to be reliable because the respondents will have generally answered the questions in the same way and their responses will have been collected in an identical manner. Comparisons and generalisations can then be made from the data. An informal interview is more likely to be valid, that is to say, a truthful representation of what it claims to show. However, interview bias may occur during the interview.

Whether you use a self-administered questionnaire, an interview schedule or an observation schedule, you must *justify* its design and how it links to the objectives and hypothesis. This should include why you chose particular methods with reference to strengths and weaknesses. This shouldn't be a regurgitation of theory and method textbooks, but a logical, coherent process where you explain how that method relates closely to your own study. Drawing upon the methodological experiences of other sociologists and their work will help you to highlight the strengths and limitations of using particular methods.

It's also appropriate to justify why you haven't used other methods. However, you don't have to go through *all* the methods that you didn't use!

The following example demonstrates how a student justifies a particular methodological stance.

> 4.1 METHODOLOGY:
>
> *The main purpose of this study is to analyse the debate on the family within the context of one area – and how it adheres to the functionalist's account of the family; providing a valuable contribution to an evaluation of the hypothesis.*
>
> *The study, due to the limited amount of time, shall only examine the borough of Batley, in West Yorkshire. Within Batley approximately 65% belong to the working class in that they are predominately employed in manual work. Furthermore aproximatley 11% of the residents are of New Commonwelath and Pakistan origin (NGWP); mainly Indian and Pakistan – those of West Indian achieve a represent[ative] sample a proportion of New Commonwelth and Pakistan citizens shall need to be included.*
>
> *Furthermore, [questions in] questionaires can either be closed or open-ended. Closed questions enable ease of quantification but however, limit freedom of response, while on the other hand open-ended questions allow greater freedom of response which provides greater depth and complexity.*
>
> *Obviously one will not be able to quest'on all of Batley's population. Thus [I will] follow the usua practice of sociologist[s] and select a sample of peop e for interviewing. The method that shall be employed is questionaires. This method appeares to be the only feasible technique when considering the ntyre [nature] of the reseach. Other possible methods, such as unstructured interviews, may provide a more in-depth understanding, yet not with the necessary statistical information that is required. To this end, questionaires are a comparrtively cheap, fast and efficient process of obtaining large amounts of quantifiable data and [from] relatively large numbers of people.*

The pilot study

In primary research, piloting should be carried out with all methods, and a detailed rationale of any proposed changes made (copies of these should be included within this section or referred to and placed in an appendix).

Here's an example from a student's work.

> 4.2 PILOT STUDY
>
> *After administering the pilot study, it became apparent that the original questionaire required a great deal of alterations. The questionaire lacked orgnisation and were carelessly worded. There were some questions which appeared to be irrelevant. (refer to appendix 1).*
>
> *The survey is concerned in [about] obtainig information in the following areas:*
>
> - *The trends in remarriage, divorce, one - parent families, homosexuality and single persons.*
> - *The vareiety of family structures that exist.*
> - *Households consisting of more then the ideal number of chidren.*
> - *To what extent the ideology of male breadwinner and female housewife exist.*
> - *The extent of relationships between 'nuclear family' and kinship.*
> - *Should sex education should only be taught in the form of hetrosexuall family values?*
> - *Should homosexuals be allowed to form families legally?*
> - *What do the respondents understand by the term 'family'?*
>
> *Thereafter an appropriate questionaire was re-designed (refer to appendix 2 & 3).*

The questionaire was carried out on Friday 16th December '94 at midday. The advantage to this was that there were late Christmas shoppers and it was market day, both together aided me in collecting a representative sample, as it was busy.

Justification of the choice of questions in questionnaires and interviews

Justify the selection of questions you use in your questionnaire or interview. Ensure that they relate specifically to your objectives. The following example shows how a student justified the inclusion of a particular question.

Methodology

When it came to obtaining the information needed, I was aware of the fact that I will also be faced with a few problems. I knew from the beginning that it would be impossible for me to meet the offenders who were to become the sample for my study. I had to take into consideration the fact that not only were they under-aged but also that my presence could produce racism and sexism, and I felt that I would not be taken seriously enough because of my age. Therefore, I knew that I had to choose a different route to get in touch with them.

Where the issue of ethical problems arose, I made sure that my respondants knew what I was doing, why I was doing it and which college I was attending. I felt that I had a responsibility towards them and therefore stressed the fact that their responses would be treated with anonymity and confidentiality. I was aware of the fact that my approach had to be sensitive enough to avoid upsetting, annoying or offending anyone.

The Questionaires I was hoping to give to the offenders (see appendix) were formulated in accordance with my hypothesis 'Crime is a working class phenomena which is found mainly in young males'.

The first question was formulated to find out whether the offenders put on probation were mainly youngsters or whether other age groups were present, thus supporting or disproving my hypothesis of the main offenders being young.

Remember to give yourself time to prepare, pilot, amend and collect your data.

Summary

Your methodology section should normally include:

- a justification for the chosen methodology
- close links between the objectives of the study and methodology
- a consideration of theoretical issues that are linked to your research
- use of methodological techniques such as sampling and piloting
- reference to key terms (for example, representativeness, generalisation, validity and reliability)
- a discounting of alternative methods not employed, with reasons.

The content section

This section is a presentation of the main body of findings from your primary research. With this being only a small-scale study, your findings are more likely to be suggestive than generalisable. However, you may have collected a great variety of data, both quantitative and qualitative. These will need to be clearly organised, well-presented and interpreted in relation to your hypothesis and objectives. It's also essential that you make links between your own primary research and your context section. Also remember to place your findings in a theoretical context.

If you've completed a secondary source research study, the same thorough analysis of evidence will need to take place. It's likely that the secondary material you have collected from relevant organisations and media will be placed in this section.

It may be advisable to organise your material under specific sub-headings (or at least chronologically). This could be done in one of two ways, either by:

- arranging all your findings under specific types of data such as quantitative and qualitative, or by
- selecting the evidence and presenting it under headings for each of your objectives.

The key is to choose the way which gives you maximum clarity, focus and relevance. To assist you in this, what follows is offered as guidance. Student examples are included.

Presentation of quantitative data

'There are two broad categories into which statistical methods fall: Descriptive and Inferential.'

(Sandy Goulding 1992: 103)

Descriptive statistical methods are likely to be the ones most A-level students will use. They provide 'pictures' of the group under investigation through the use of bar charts, pie charts, percentages, averages and tables. The questionnaire and structured interview often generate these data.

The *inferential method* aims to draw inferences from the data.

Bell (1992) emphasises the need to plan the analysis of any quantitative data. She highlights the use of summary sheets onto which questionnaire responses can be transferred. Each question will be given a code number to allow for easier classifications (see the examples below).

Questionnaire

For each question, please circle the number which corresponds with your answer.

Q1 Male 1   Female 2

Q2 Age last birthday

16–20	21–25	26–30	31–35
1	2	3	4
36–40	41–45	46–50	51–55
5	6	7	8

Q3 I consider my promotion prospects to be good:

strongly disagree	disagree	neutral	agree	strongly agree
1	2	3	4	5

Summary sheet

(responses indicated by *)

RESPONDENT	Q1	Q2	Q3 etc.
You may have a code on each questionnaire for identification purposes	1 2	12345678	12345
01/C 02/C	* *	* *	* *

(Both examples adapted from Bell 1992: 106–7)

Examples of a coded questionnaire and a summary sheet

With open-ended questions, it's not possible to code the answers, so the responses would need to be collected together on separate pieces of paper and sifted for relevance. This should be a selection that represents the views of the respondents. With the closed, coded responses, it will be possible to represent these in a *diagrammatic form*. Information presented like this is easy to analyse and make comparisons with.

How well does the student in the example below interpret figures 6 and 7? For example, do the student's percentages make statistical sense?

> *Inherent in the functionalists analysis of the family is that it is '. . . based upon legal marriage' (Murdock, 1949). However, in the survey it was found that overall 39% (29) were single (refer to Figure 6). Of these 13% (10) were cohabiting couples. It could be argued that cohabitation may only be a temporary arrangement and shall eventuate in marriage. However, in light of the evidence it could be argued for a great number of couples cohabitation illustrates that marriage is becoming less popular and, further, couples are seeking more conventional alternatives to married life.*
>
> *The great numbr of marital brekdowns (refer to figure 7) further reflects a decline in the popularity of marriage. Furthermore, Parsons (1955) and Fletchers (1966) concept of divorce is reinstated by the survey. It was found that only 40% of divorces were childless and the remaining had more than one child. Moreover, 80% of the divorces (regardless of sex) took place within the age of 25 – 45. Although there is no evidence of the number of years the couples were married, it can be concluded from the data that it is not necessarily an occurrance that when couples 'settle down' and have children, divorce shall be hindered, as stated by Parsons et al.*

Percentage rep. of marital status in sample

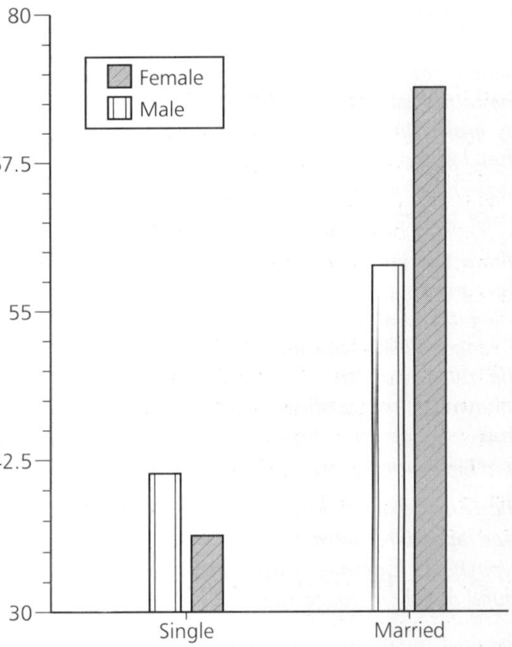

Fig 6

Rep. of family type in sample
(percentage of all females)

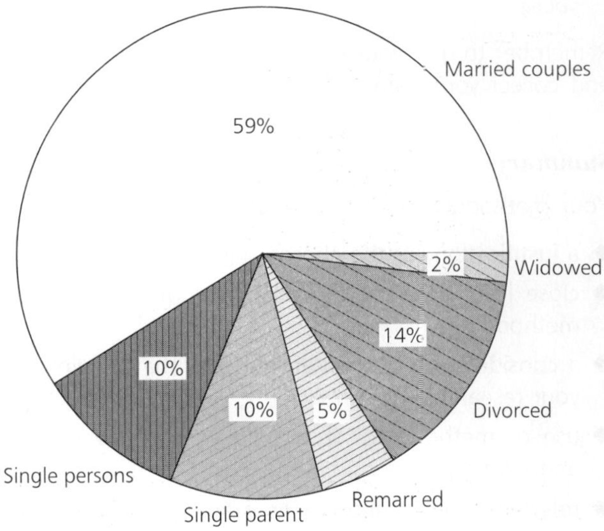

Fig 7

EXAM TIPS

- Ensure that in each diagram the headings are clear, categories are labelled, shading/colour is used to differentiate categories, and keys are included.
- 'One crucial decision you will have to make is how much of the statistics to use and display. This will be determined by the hypothesis you are testing or questions which you are exploring. You should only use the statistics which are necessary to support directly points which are being made.' (Tony Lawson, Former Chief Examiner, AEB Sociology [Lawson 1993:15])

Spreadsheet/graphics packages

Many students are now enhancing the presentation of their coursework by using spreadsheet/graphic packages and word-processing. You won't be penalised for not using these, but you should talk to your coursework teacher or information technology staff for advice and guidance.

If you use spreadsheet/graphics packages, it's essential that the information contained in your graphs is related directly to your hypothesis and objectives. Fancy, coloured diagrams have little relevance unless they're analysed. You're *interpreting* the information and *applying* it to your study. These are two of the coursework skill domains being assessed.

In the example below, how well do you think the student has interpreted the information from her or his diagrams and applied them to the study of crime levels? Note, for example, that Fig 8 contains an illegible label and omits important background information, while in Fig 9 the horizontal axis is not labelled with the years.

Crime levels

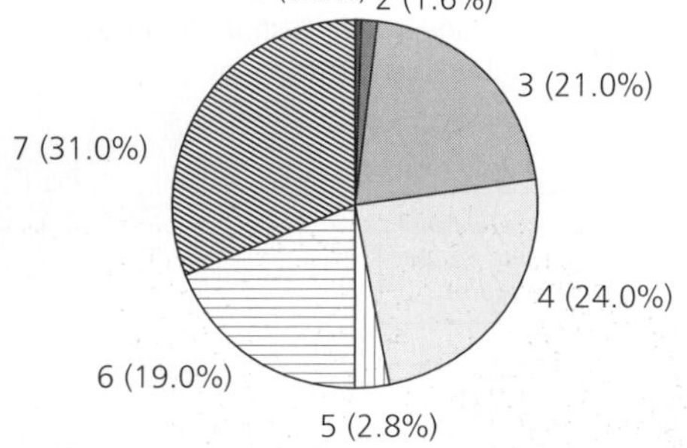

Fig 8

As far as my sample is concerned of the four main reasons by far the greatest factor which they believe is responsible for rising crime levels is unemployment.

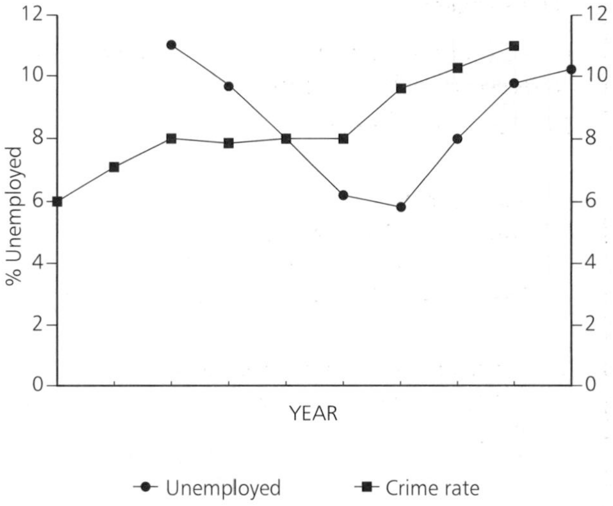

Fig 9

SOURCE: Unemployment: Regional Trends 1994
Crime rate: Home office statistical office

As can be seen from the above graph, unemployment & crime levels are directly related, when unemployment is high, crime levels increase and when unemployment is low, change in crime levels drop.

In a Guardian article 25 February 1993 p.4, Lord Whitlow, the former Home Secretary publicly acknowledged a link between youth unemployment and crime. This is in contradiction with the Prime Minister John Major who maintains that unemployment is not a key cause of crime and that it should not be used as an excuse for criminality (see Guardian article one).

The theory of unemployment and crime are again linked in a further article dated 29 April 1993 'Minister for the first time publicly acknowledged a link between economic deprivation and crime rates' (see article two).

This evidence shows that a link does exist between crime and social and economic conditions and is perceived to do so by others in society.

There is further support in Stuart Halls study 'Policing the crisis' (page 636–640 Haralambos)

The examples on page 38 show how data presented through Microsoft Excel and Logistix can look. (There are other packages available.)

EXAM TIP

Ensure all dates are recorded accurately when you use statistics, charts and tables. When referring to official statistics (for example, *Social Trends*) be mindful of words like UK, Great Britain, England and Wales, Scotland, etc. The use of these words tells the reader *who* is being referred to (for example, the UK population).

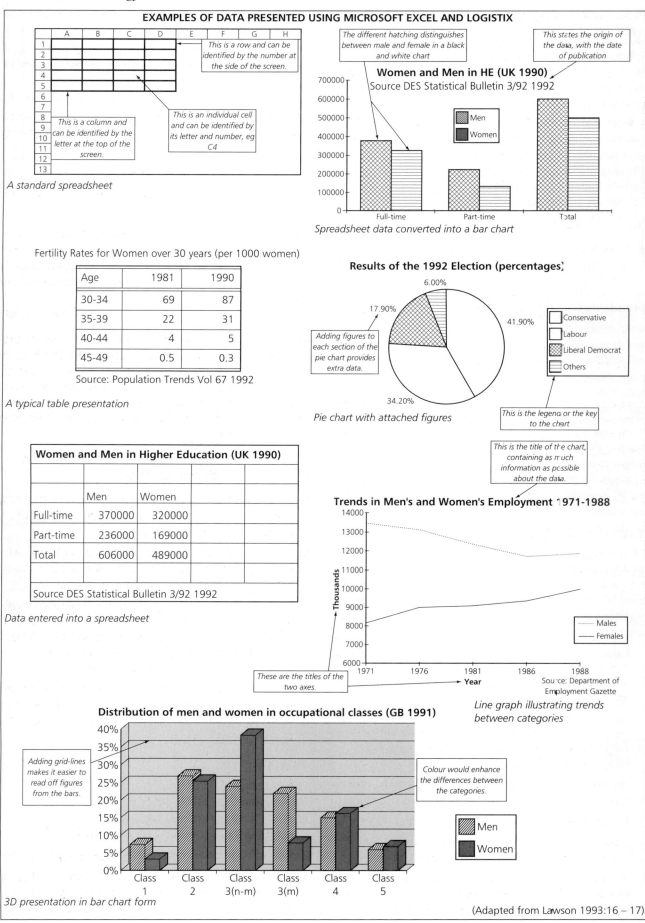

EXAMPLES OF DATA PRESENTED USING MICROSOFT EXCEL AND LOGISTIX

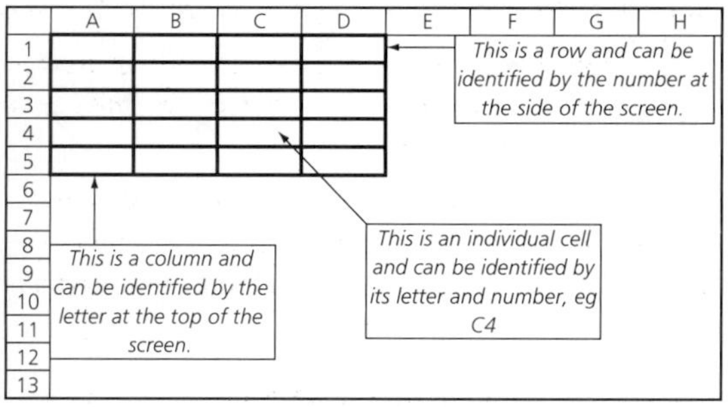
A B C D E F G H
1 2 3 4 5 6 7 8 9 10 11 12 13
This is a row and can be identified by the number at the side of the screen.
This is an individual cell and can be identified by its letter and number, eg C4
This is a column and can be identified by the letter at the top of the screen.

A standard spreadsheet

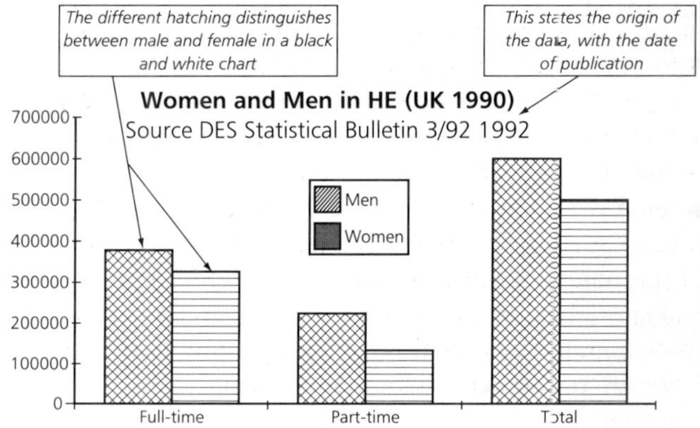
The different hatching distinguishes between male and female in a black and white chart
This states the origin of the data, with the date of publication
Women and Men in HE (UK 1990)
Source DES Statistical Bulletin 3/92 1992
Men
Women
700000 600000 500000 400000 300000 200000 100000 0
Full-time
Part-time
Total

Spreadsheet data converted into a bar chart

Fertility Rates for Women over 30 years (per 1000 women)

Age	1981	1990
30-34	69	87
35-39	22	31
40-44	4	5
45-49	0.5	0.3

Source: Population Trends Vol 67 1992

A typical table presentation

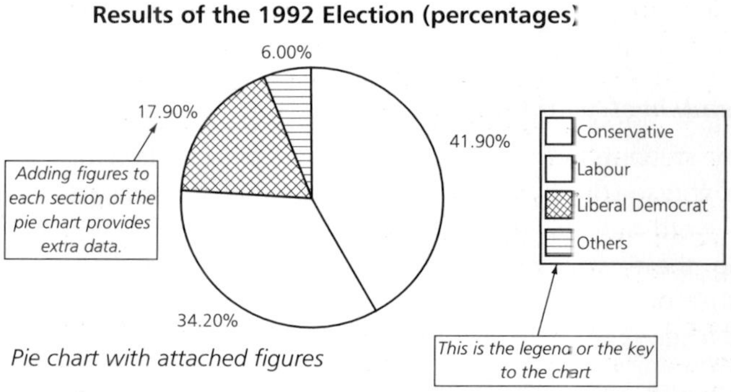
Results of the 1992 Election (percentages)
6.00%
17.90%
41.90%
34.20%
Adding figures to each section of the pie chart provides extra data.
Conservative
Labour
Liberal Democrat
Others
This is the legend or the key to the chart

Pie chart with attached figures

Women and Men in Higher Education (UK 1990)				
	Men	Women		
Full-time	370000	320000		
Part-time	236000	169000		
Total	606000	489000		
Source DES Statistical Bulletin 3/92 1992				

Data entered into a spreadsheet

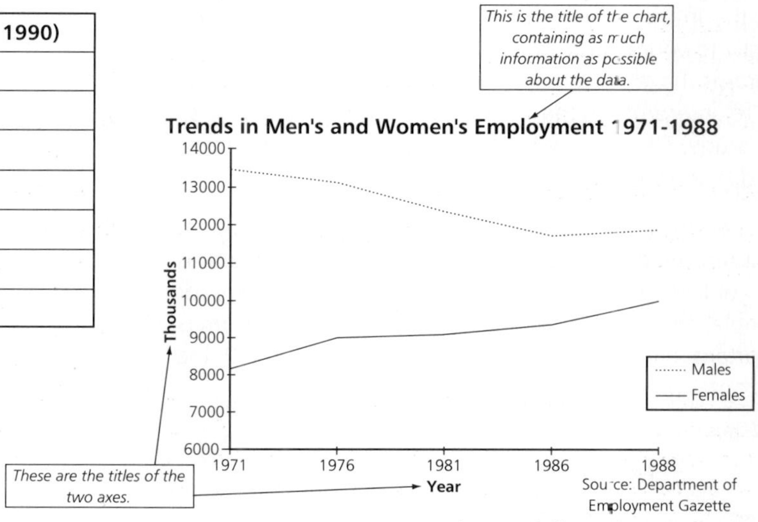
This is the title of the chart, containing as much information as possible about the data.
Trends in Men's and Women's Employment 1971-1988
14000 13000 12000 11000 10000 9000 8000 7000 6000
Thousands
Males
Females
1971 1976 1981 1986 1988
Year
These are the titles of the two axes.
Source: Department of Employment Gazette

Line graph illustrating trends between categories

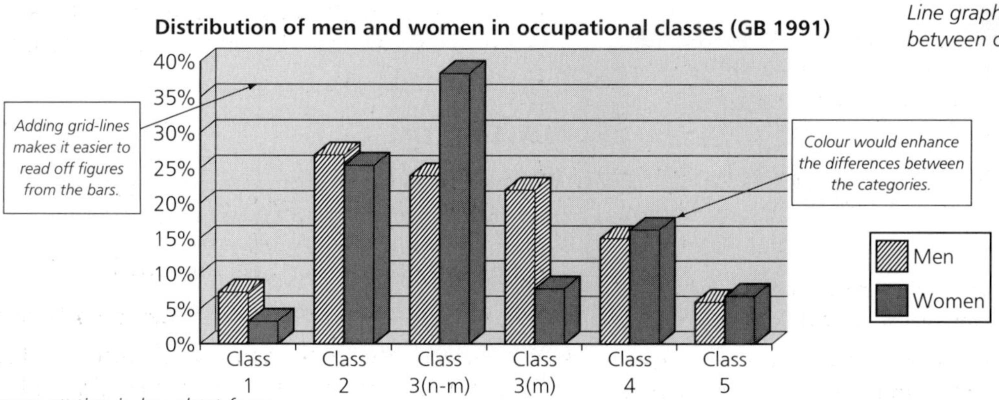
Distribution of men and women in occupational classes (GB 1991)
40% 35% 30% 25% 20% 15% 10% 5% 0%
Adding grid-lines makes it easier to read off figures from the bars.
Colour would enhance the differences between the categories.
Men
Women
Class 1
Class 2
Class 3(n-m)
Class 3(m)
Class 4
Class 5

3D presentation in bar chart form

(Adapted from Lawson 1993:16 – 17)

Presentation of qualitative data

Students often use *unstructured interviews* and *observation* to obtain qualitative data. If you have permission of the respondent to tape-record your interview, it will probably take you at least ten times the length of the actual interview to transcribe it verbatim. Another option is a summary transcription which includes key verbatim quotes. You could also devise a system to transcribe accurate notes as the interview proceeds. An interview schedule will help to structure the information under sub-headings, but it's likely that some of the conversation will be misrepresented or forgotten.

There are different ways of presenting the dialogue:

- ◆ You could include a complete transcript of the interview and place this in an appendix. You could then refer to particular aspects of the interview which relate specifically to your objectives. The organisation and presentation may be clearer if you use sub-headings for each objective.
- ◆ You could include 'snap shots' of the interview within the content section. This may include direct quotations from the interview.

It won't be enough just to present the transcripts. It's essential that you *analyse* all the material as you present it. This analysis will be related directly to your objectives. It's imperative that each respondent is given a number to protect their anonymity, whilst also assisting the reader to follow the information. A biography of each respondent may also be useful as background information.

Analysis of unstructured interviews

In the following example, the student integrates the analysis and quotation.

> *Unstructured Interview with Ten Women*
>
> *Method*
>
> *The interviews were conducted in an informal atmosphere because to the young women I was accepted as a friend. The women were interviewed in a group because I felt it would give them confidence to speak. This experiment was proved to be successful.*
>
> *As I came from within the community I could receive information which the interviewees would never tell an outsider. They felt that they should be united and strong in a white [male] dominated society.*
>
> *The ten women interviewed ranged from sixteen to twenty four. They were all interviewed in English.*
>
> *Unstructured interview*
>
> *I wanted to find out the difference between the religion, which is Islam in this case and the cultural traditions.*
>
> *All the women interviewed felt that women had been oppressed. They felt some people believed that women were inferior to men and could not enjoy the right to express their views, the right to an education or live as they wanted. The following quote supports this point.*
>
> > *'Woman has a high status in Islam, but our men want to keep us oppressed. Each person (man or woman) has a different role.'*
>
> *Most of the interviewees said that many educated Muslim women act out the role of being a good Muslim wife by acting docile in the presence of their husband and his family.*

Presenting observation findings

If you are using observation techniques, take heed of this advice:

'Observation . . . is not a "natural" gift, but a highly skilled activity for which an extensive background knowledge and understanding is required, and also a capacity for original thinking and the ability to spot significant events.'

(Nisbet 1977, in Bell 1992: 88)

As a researcher, you will be interpreting the events that you see and that may affect your objectivity. This is more likely if you become a participant observer. However, there are observation schedules available to assist researchers when observing individuals and groups in different social contexts. These schedules can be adapted for your purposes.

These are some of the techniques you could use for presenting your observation findings:

- ◆ *Interaction chart*, to indicate who interacts with whom, student pairings and further areas for investigation. It provides clues about relationships.
- ◆ *Content and interventions chart*, to highlight who speaks the most and on which topics. A line is drawn between each topic area to allow easier analysis.
- ◆ *Chart recording speaking contributions by individuals*, to keep a tally of who spoke and for how long. A vertical line shows half a minute speaking (or less); a following horizontal line shows the same person continuing to speak for the same set period.
- ◆ *A plan recording individual behaviour*, based on the Huthwaite Research Group and their study on management skills and behaviour. Observations are recorded as follows:
  - 1 = proposing
  - 2 = supporting
  - 3 = disagreeing
  - 4 = giving information
  - 5 = seeking information
  - 6 = extension of another's proposal.

  These observations are then recorded on a table plan.
- ◆ *A behaviour category chart*, which records observations in the same way as the plan recording individual behaviour, but this time they are noted on a chart.

- *A chart recording the content of a meeting*, which is likely to be used when analysing the content of a lesson or meeting.

Examples of these techniques are shown on the right.

The techniques described above have mainly been used in educational research, but could be adapted to other areas of observation such as the workplace, an old people's home or a youth club. Whichever method you use, you should record what is happening in a structured way. For example, enter the appropriate category number on your chart every five seconds. Clearly, some value-judgements are made when you assign a category to an aspect of behaviour. Own up to this. The reporting stage of your findings could be a written analysis accompanied by diagrams and charts.

If you're carrying out *participant observation*, you're likely to have a wide variety of field notes that you've collected over a period of time. However, your observations will probably have been hampered by the short time available; you, the observer, may have influenced the behaviour of the people being observed; there may have been legal or ethical constraints on the research process. Don't present the findings as a story. You should link closely with the objectives through sub-headings, and arrange the material to allow thorough analysis of the quotations and observations.

Many sociologists have also used the diary interview method in conjunction with participant observation. This involves the subjects recording, over a period of time, their activities. This is useful where direct observation by yourself isn't an option. You ask people to record information under suggested headings. This allows the people you are studying to convey their first-hand impressions about particular issues.

According to Simon Dyson:

'research diaries can help to give accounts of power relations experienced in the research process; they can act as a form of triangulation – confirming or refuting data from other methods; they help researchers to be self-critical of their role; they can document the social context of the research process; they can help document struggles between researchers and researched in defining the research role, and they can be a springboard to an alternative project.'

(Dyson 1995: 13)

Much of this is relevant in the evaluation section which follows.

Summary

Your content section should normally include:

- a clear and accurate presentation of the main body of the findings

MEETING: Governors of Bramhope High School
DATE: 1.12.86
TIME: 6.30–8.30 p.m.

Chairperson (Industrialist)	APPROX. TIME SPENT (in minutes) OR NUMBER OF TIMES TOPICS WERE MENTIONED	PERCENTAGE OF TOTAL RECORDED
ADMINISTRATION (Minutes, letters etc.)		
RESOURCES		
STAFFING (Appointment of new Scale I teacher of English)		
DISCIPLINE		
PTA		
CURRICULUM		
OTHER (Sports Day, Caretaker's illness, etc.)		

A chart recording the content of a meeting

Participants	
Mick	/// =
Fred	
Judith	/ ≡ //
Brendan	//
Ian	//// = / ≡
Stephen	//
Sandy	/ = //
Multiple speaking	///

A chart recording speaking contributions by individuals

Examples of techniques used for presenting observation findings

School: Bramhope High
Meeting: Governors
Date: 1.12.86

	Admin. (Minutes, etc.)	Curriculum (general)	Curriculum (resources)	Exams	New appointment	PTA	Discipline	Other	No.	%
Chairperson (Industrialist)	卌 卌			卌 //		/	卌 //	///	28	22.6
Secretary (ILEA official)	卌 卌							//	12	9.7
Mrs A (Parent governor)						//	///		5	4.0
Mrs B (Parent governor)									0	0
Mr C (Councillor)					/		卌	//	8	6.5
Mr D (Councillor)					///		//		5	4.0
Mr E (Bank manager)					/		/		2	1.6
Dr F (LEA adviser)	卌			//	////		/		12	97
Mrs G (Staff representative)					////	/	////		9	7.2
Miss H (Sixth-form representative)									0	0
Head	///	卌 /		卌	///		卌 卌	//	29	23.4
Deputy head	//	///				//	卌 //		14	11.3
Total time (in minutes)	30	9	0	14	16	6	40	9	124	100

A content and interventions chart

Participants	Categories 1	2	3	4	5	6	Totals
Chairperson (Mick)	✓✓✓						3
Secretary (Fred)	✓	✓	✓				3
Judith	✓	✓	✓✓				4
Brendan				✓	✓		2
Ian				✓✓		✓	3
Stephen	✓					✓	2
Sandy	✓		✓	✓			3
Totals	7	2	4	4	1	2	

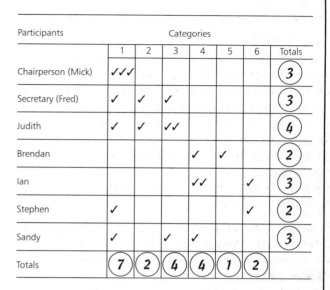

A behaviour category chart

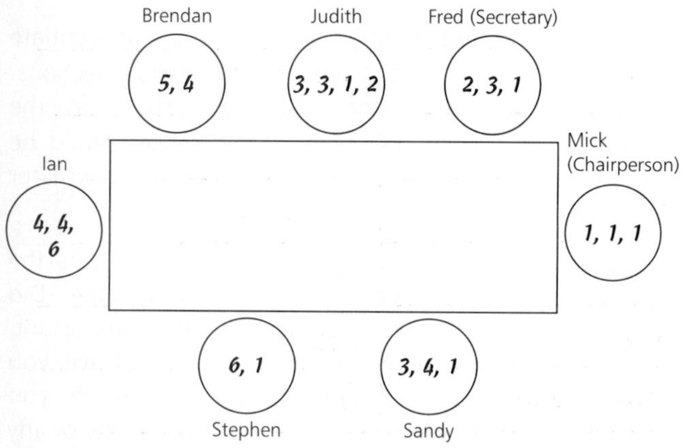

A plan recording individual behaviour

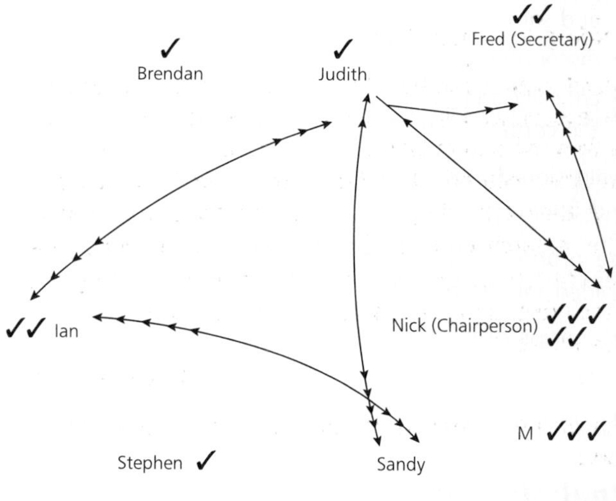

✓ = Communication in the whole group
M = Multiple speaking

An interaction chart

(Adapted from Bell 1992:91–6

- quantitative and qualitative data, and secondary source material (wherever possible)
- the use of sub-headings to assist in organising and presenting material
- a presentation of findings interpreted with sociological insight in relation to the hypothesis and objectives which were set in the rationale
- similarities and disparities between the context (secondary sources) and content (mainly primary sources) sections
- data and graphs/tables that are relevant, and not 'data for data's sake'
- the placing of findings in a theoretical context (wherever possible)
- secondary source material placed in the appendix, which is analysed in the main text.

The evaluation section

For some reason, many students don't consider the evaluation section to warrant the same rigour as previous sections. Experience suggests that it tends to be rushed, superficial and of minimal length. Students often consider it as merely a summary of the findings, failing to grasp its true importance.

Evaluation is a *skill* which must be evident *throughout* the coursework and the research process. It's not a 'bolt-on' extra. It takes place when:

- considering your selection of hypothesis and objectives
- interpreting and analysing the secondary source material
- justifying which methods are to be employed, piloted and sampled
- discounting alternative methods
- critically analysing your findings and linking them to the context section.

Evaluation draws together many of the issues, problems and findings in a coherent, reflective and critical way.

We propose that this section of your study should be divided into three sub-sections:

- analysis of methodology
- evaluation of material
- conclusion.

Analysis of methodology

You need to:

- re-examine the methods you used
- highlight clearly which strengths and weaknesses appeared in using them
- review your justification for selecting a method or methods
- make close reference to the methodology section
- discuss methodological problems which arose during the research process. Ask such questions as:
  - How effective was my choice of methodology?
  - Did I select the most effective combination of sources of data?
  - What other methods of data collection might have been possible?
  - Would my data have been different with the use of other methods?
  - Did theory play a significant role in my selection of methods?
  - Would I change my theoretical position now?
  - How well did I plan and carry out each method?
  - Did I pilot and sample adequately?
  - How effective was my operationalising of the concepts?
  - To what extent did I allow personal values and biases affect the collection of data?
  - Did I consider the ethical and access implications of my research design?
  - How far did I consider the methods I used in relation to representativeness, reliability and validity? (Adapted from Langley and Corrigan 1993: 89)
- explore a reasonable, viable, alternative methodology. If you were to complete the research process all over again, where and why might you change particular aspects? Avoid making common-sense remarks on possible improvements, such as increasing the number of persons interviewed or sample size to get better results from a questionnaire.
- refer to your research timeline. This gives you an overview of all the incidents that have occurred during the research process. Use them to show the problems which you have encountered and how well you did or did not deal with them.

Evaluation of material

Many students find it difficult to sort and differentiate material between the content and evaluation sections. They either presume that analysing material in the content section is sufficient or that evidence should be presented in the content section and then analysed later in the evaluation section.

You should review each section of the study. Were the hypotheses and objectives plausible and attainable? Did you explore all the available, or indeed vitally important, secondary sources in your context section? Have you analysed their shortcomings? Were the methods you selected appropriate? Did you present your results clearly in the content section? Was the evidence analysed with reference to your objectives?

The following example is an attempt by one student to draw together issues within sections and to review their appropriateness and success in meeting the objectives.

> *Critical analysis*
>
> *Context chapter conclusions*
> *After carrying out an examination of background studies on gender stereotyping two main approaches to the topic can be identified: Positivist and Phenomenological. As both have various strengths and weaknesses, the two approaches are complementary. Whilst the Positivist approach concentrates on quantitative research – measuring 'matter' and drawing conclusions from it, the phenomenological approach assesses the 'manner' of advertising. Looked at simultaneously then, a number of conclusions can be drawn . . . .*
>
> *Methodology chapter conclusions*
> *The first conclusion to be drawn concerning the methodology of this project is that two different methods of research were needed to analyse the two levels of stereotyping. Whilst content analysis measured the denotative aspect of the stereotypes present in my sample and the quantities of them, the more interpretative analysis I adopted examined the connotative aspect, looking at factors such as language, appearance and behaviour.*
>
> *Clearly, with more time, I could have extended my close analysis of advertisements to include a wider sample. However, as close interpretation in this way is very time consuming it was necessary to limit the number used to a very small sample. This raises problems however. As the samples for the administration of the questionnaire and analysis of advertisements were both small, they were not very representative . . . .*
>
> *Content – Conclusions*
> *After conducting my own examination of the hypothesis 'Do images in advertising reinforce the stereotyped roles of women in society?', it is clear that there are indeed two levels of stereotyping – denotative and connotative. Identification of the denotative stereotypes is concerned primarily with the roles women are portrayed in and the products they are associated with. At this stage it seems reasonable to conclude that there are four main stereotyped roles for women: sex object, housewife, professional woman and leisure woman. Advertising apparently has a specific range of stereotypes which cannot necessarily be applied to other areas of social life. Coward and Butcher identified a total of nine roles for women, however many of these categories were not represented in my sample, which suggests advertising stereotypes are not mediawide.*

When presenting the evidence, you should write an interpretation of the following under each objective:

- an assessment of the data's strengths and weaknesses
- how far the data confirm/refute the objectives
- a comparison between the evidence of empirical studies in the context section and your own research in the content section. Point out any comparisons or contradictions that appear
- your findings placed within a theoretical context. Which perspective appears to be of closest allegiance to your own findings?
- how far other variables may be relevant to your study and affect your findings
- an attempt to make general statements about the detailed issues which you have studied
- whether the primary and secondary data collected are representative, reliable and valid. This will link in closely with your analysis of the methodology. Did the choice of methodology ensure your data collection was accurate?
- how far you think you, as a researcher, affected the research process and collection of data. Did you spend enough time on the study? Was it a sensible choice? Were you able to use sufficient secondary sources? Did you research into the background to your topic adequately? If you were to begin again, would you do things differently?

The conclusion

This is only a 5,000 word study. No one expects any earth-shattering revelations. Nevertheless, try to make modest claims which are supported by the data. Guard against sweeping statements. The concluding statements will be made on each of the objectives, with a final discussion on your success in testing your hypothesis. Give examples to show how far your results, and those from the other empirical studies reported upon, support the conclusion.

Summary

Your evaluation section should normally include:

- a clear analysis of the methodology used with an appropriate justification, examination of problems and alternatives considered
- a full evaluation of the material throughout the study with appropriate judgements made on each section in a coherent, reflective and critical manner
- conclusions reached which relate to the hypothesis and objectives of the study
- reference to your research diary when examining the problems/solutions and links with the rationale
- an examination of the range of issues that affect the reliability, validity and representativeness of the research findings.

The bibliography, research diary and appendix

You'll need to complete and attach at the end of the study any sections which cannot be placed within the main text:

- the bibliography
- your research diary
- any appendices.

The bibliography

This is an alphabetical list of all the sources you have used in your study. It *must* include every text that has been used. As stated earlier, you may have your coursework cancelled for plagiarism if you don't follow this guideline from the exam board.

For an example of how to prepare a bibliography, look at the reference sections at the end of each chapter of this book.

In-situ references (i.e. those that occur within the main text) don't have to be so detailed as bibliographical references. Look at the way they are presented throughout this book.

The research diary

This should be a standardised system for recording each stage of your 'research timeline'. It might look like this:

Date started/ completed	Activity to be completed	How successful?	Changes to be made
21.6.98/ 12.7.98	Drawing up objectives of study	Discussion with tutor: second draft to take place	Too broad; require greater focus
22.7.98/ not complete	Sent letter to British Censorship Board	No response to letter	Decided not to follow up by telephone; alternatives considered

It's of little value if you don't refer to the diary when completing the analysis of your research study in the evaluation section. It helps you to recall events, some of which may have occurred nearly a year before.

The appendices

The number of appendices (singular: appendix) vary. They provide an effective means of placing bulky material (for example, copies of letters and replies sent to organisations, articles from newspapers, examples of questionnaires and interview transcripts) at the end of the study. They should be clearly labelled Appendix 1, Appendix 2, etc. Make sure you refer to and interpret appendix data in the main text.

The mark scheme

The structure of this chapter will help you to present your material in a way that attracts high marks. We will now look at each of the skill domains in turn and list the qualities required to obtain the top scores.

Knowledge and understanding

Context

You need to demonstrate:

- a clear and accurate theoretical context
- a selection of relevant, up-to-date sources – both empirical (data-based) and non-empirical which are appropriately structured to the objectives of your study
- research ideas and arguments that are presented in a clear, coherent and critical fashion
- explicit references to the context material throughout the study.

Methodology

You must:

- have a clear justification for the methods selected, and analyse the strengths and weaknesses of these methods (and alternatives discounted) in relation to the objectives of your study
- make reference to previous sociologists' studies where these methods have been used
- make connections between your choice of methods and sociological theories
- show clear understanding and application of sampling and piloting techniques.

Content

You must:

- refer throughout your study to a wide range of appropriate material
- show that you have an understanding of the key concepts used in your study
- demonstrate that a range of relevant sociological data have been accessed
- present a clear theoretical framework for the whole study
- show that evidence is structured clearly
- demonstrate that your SPAG (spelling, punctuation and grammar) are excellent.

Interpretation and application

Rationale

There must be:

- a clear statement of reason for selecting your topic of study
- interesting and relevant background material (sociological and non-sociological)
- 'stepping' from the reasons for selection to the hypothesis to be tested and objectives to be realised
- a conclusion drawn that signposts the rationale.

Application of methodology

You must:

- demonstrate that the chosen research methods were applied as successfully as possible to the context of the study
- show that sampling and piloting techniques were carried out and evaluated competently
- demonstrate that sensitivity was shown towards respondents
- show that you applied both positivist and interpretivist approaches, as appropriate, when collecting your range of data
- demonstrate that the methods applied were relevant to the study.

Presentation of evidence/argument/results

You must:

- present findings clearly in a range of formats (for example, graphs, tables, written form)
- demonstrate that these were interpreted with sociological understanding and were related to the hypothesis and objectives
- show that links were made between the evidence and other sections of the study
- draw conclusions from the findings
- demonstrate a clear analysis of data throughout.

Evaluation

Methodological justification and problems

You must:

- show an analysis of your own methodology and indicate strategies for improvement
- discuss alternative methods
- critically assess problems arising
- make reference to your research diary to address all the problems encountered in the study
- closely examine the validity, reliability and representativeness of the techniques employed.

Evaluation of material and conclusion

You must:

- bring together all your evidence with similarities and differences drawn out
- present coherent discussion of the issues explored and their sociological implications
- make direct reference to the objectives of the study and how far the material collected addresses them
- demonstrate that a *conclusion* is drawn that not only summarises your findings but 'tests' the original hypothesis.

Do ask for advice from your sociology teacher throughout the coursework process. It's vital that you are informed if any of the requirements for the top band of the mark scheme aren't being met. Ask for advice on how this can be rectified. It's possible to meet some of the criteria in two mark bands. In this case, your tutor will find an appropriate mark between the two bands.

Happy researching!

References

The Associated Examining Board (1995) *Chief Examiners' Reports Summer 1995 Examinations: Sociology*. Surrey: Associated Examining Board

The Associated Examining Board (1996) *GCE Advanced Level Syllabus Support Material: Sociology*. Surrey: Associated Examining Board

Barrat, David and Cole, Tony (1991) *Sociology Projects: A Students' Guide*. London: Routledge

Bell, Judith (1992) *Doing Your Research Project*. Milton Keynes: Open University Press

Burgess, Robert G. (1993) Issues *In Sociology: Research Methods*. London: Nelson

Clarke, Jane (1994) Writing up your coursework, pp 10–11, *Sociology Review*, Vol. 3, No. 3, February

Clynch, Ann (1991) Sociology A-level coursework 1991 AEB Syllabus 664, pp 15–17, *Sociology Review*, Vol. 1, No. 2, November

Clynch, Ann (1996) Coursework five years on! 1991–1995, pp 30–2, *Sociology Review*, Vol. 5, No. 3, February

Dunsmuir, Audrey and Williams, Lynn (1990) *Sociology In Action: How To Do Social Research*. London: Unwin Hyman

Dutton, Brian (1989) *Media Studies: An Introduction*. New York: Longman

Dyson, Simon (1995) Research diaries and the research process, pp 11–13, *Sociology Review*, Vol. 4, No. 3, February

Goulding, Sandy (1987) Analysis and presentation of information, pp 103–23, in Bell, Judith (1992) op. cit.

Hammersley, Martyn (1992) Introducing ethnography, pp 18–23, *Sociology Review*, Vol. 2, No. 2, November

Hitchcock, Graham (1995) Writing lives, pp 18–23, *Sociology Review*, Vol. 5, No. 1, September

Howard, K. and Sharp, J. A. (1983) *The Management of a Student Research Project*. Aldershot: Gower.

Langley, Peter and Corrigan, Peter (1993) *Managing Sociology Coursework*. Cooksbridge: Connect Publications

Lawson, Tony (1986) In the shadow of science, pp 36–41, *Social Studies Review*, Vol. 2, No. 2, November

Lawson, Tony (1993) IT graphics packages and coursework, pp 15–17, *Sociology Review*, Vol. 3, No. 2, November

Mann, Peter H. (1985) *Methods Of Social Investigation*. Oxford: Blackwell

McNeil, Patrick (1992) *Society Now: Research Methods*. London: Routledge

Morison, Murray (1989) *Sociology in Focus: Methods in Sociology*. London: Longman

Platt, Jennifer (1993) Case studies: Their uses and limits, pp 8–12, *Sociology Review*, Vol. 2, No. 3, February

Shipman, Marten (1981) *The Limitations Of Social Research*. London: Longman

Walker, Steve (1993) Starting coursework, pp 21–3, *Sociology Review*, Vol. 3, No. 1, September

Core and topics

The first three chapters of this book looked at the skills you need to develop. The following 15 chapters focus on the core of theory and methods and specific topic areas required by the A-level syllabuses.

Core

Substantive topics

4 *Sociological theories*

Topics covered in this chapter
- *Consensus theory*
- *Conflict theory*
- *Social constructionist theory*

Imagine arriving on a desert island and meeting the inhabitants there for the first time. Your initial overture had better be friendly because they're probably frightened of you and you're certainly scared of them. But how do you know how to be friendly in a way that they'll recognise as friendliness? A smile wouldn't be a bad start, and if you get a smile back, things are looking up. What you're doing and what they're doing is trying to figure each other out. Each of you is testing the water: the smile worked; try offering a gift; that didn't go down too well – maybe they think it's a weapon, so try something else. This testing of the water is called an *hypothesis*. It's an intelligent guess that what you expect to happen will happen.

One week on . . .

You've begun to get better acquainted. The hypotheses – theirs and yours – are turning into theories. Put another way, when you and they hypothesise correctly (for example, that you both like smiling at each other), the hypothesis becomes a reliable organising principle – *a theory* – for cueing into each other's customs and ways. Perhaps you've found that theirs is a touch culture where people greet each other by shaking hands and patting shoulders. You might also have discovered that behaviours which are considered undesirable elicit disapproving frowns. Maybe you've noticed too how some children test the boundaries of acceptable conduct by seeing how far certain forms of behaviour are tolerated by parents.

The theories of human social behaviour that emerge from the above encounter are based on the testing of hunches against the evidence. Sociologists are experts at this, so much so, that over the past 200 years they've come up with some very reliable ones. The three most common sociological theories – the ones we'll look at in this chapter – have rather complex sounding names. They are:

- consensus theory
- conflict theory
- social constructionist theory.

But don't let that worry you. By the time you've read the chapter, you'll be a bit of an expert yourself!

Having identified the three main sociological theories of society, it's important to add that consensus and conflict theories are conventionally called structural theories. These theories present a model of society that has a structure of *institutions* (family, school, etc.) which have a considerable influence on the ways people think and behave. Social constructionist theory goes by different names, more notably, as *interpretivist theory* and *social action theory*. The idea here is that people choose to *interpret* human social *action* (a term allegedly more akin than 'behaviour' to human choice) in lots of different ways, thereby making it difficult – but not impossible – for common behaviours to become incorporated into institutions. Incidentally, in this book, unless otherwise specified, we use the terms 'action' and 'human social behaviour' interchangeably.

Structural sociologists generally use scientific research methods when they study human social behaviour because their conception of society as a force that moulds and shapes people emphasises the importance of reliable measurement. Some social constructionist sociologists use scientific methods, recognising that people are, to some extent, influenced by 'measurable forces'. Others of their number regard empathy as a more appropriate research tool than science because they argue that people behave unpredictably.

The important issue of the relationship between theory and methods is considered in detail in the next chapter. Meanwhile, it's time to examine consensus, conflict and social constructionist theories more fully.

> **EXAM TIP**
>
> The AEB A-level Sociology syllabuses refer to 'consensus, conflict, structural and social action theories'. Remember:
>
> - consensus and conflict theories are *structural theories*
> - social constructionist theory is *social action theory.*

Consensus (functionalist) theory

'Consensus' means 'agreement'. Society exists because people decide to live together, to accept common values and to abide by common norms (codes of conduct). Put simply, society is possible because of consensus – agreed values and norms. Consensus theorists from August Comte to Talcott Parsons have documented this simple but important fact for the last 250 years. What they've observed and theorised about, is *interaction* – people behaving socially rather than privately. Put a human being in solitary confinement, and before long, she or he will become mentally ill. We need to be in the company of others because we're social beings.

Being together and interacting means following rules of engagement. When we act, we take account of other people. Shall I call my new GP by her first name or will she think that's too familiar? Will politely declining this invitation to attend a wedding cause offence? Do I need to greet Japanese guests by bowing or will they expect me to shake hands? These kinds of question enter our minds when there's uncertainty about how we should act. However, most of the time we follow convention without having to think about it too much. By doing what's expected, things *function* smoothly. That's why consensus theory is also – indeed, most often – called *functionalism.* In the nineteenth century, the British sociologist, Herbert Spencer, likened the functions of society to the functions of a biological organism. Just as individual organs work together for the good of the whole body, so, in this analogy, do individual institutions function in harmony for the benefit of society. These days, however, few sociologists invoke biological metaphors. We will use the terms 'functionalism' and 'functionalist' throughout this section when discussing consensus theory.

One ingenious way to test social convention is to break the rules, which is precisely what an American professor, Harold Garfinkel (1967), told his students to do. Garfinkel, though not a consensus theorist, recognised that many conventions in society are taken for granted. Break a convention and the startled response of onlookers confirms that the convention really exists. One of the things Garfinkel's students were instructed to do was to talk with people while, without indicating anything special was afoot, bringing their noses almost to touching point. The bewilderment on the part of the unwitting 'subjects' is dramatic confirmation that they abide by the convention of not intruding other people's body space, unless permitted.

Convention, note functionalist sociologists, is the defining feature of most societies. For convention spells social order. Think about it. Without social order, motorists in the UK would drive on the left, the right or the middle of the road according to personal whim. Chaos would prevail – and that's just on the roads! Imagine what confusion there would be if shoppers didn't queue at supermarket checkouts, if, when you went to the dentist, she asked *you* to check *her* teeth, or when you went to shake hands with your new bank manager, he punched you on the nose instead of proffering his hand. Without social order, society wouldn't be possible. That's why functionalists conceptualise the order they see as an enormous stage where all the parts of the play have their own important functions. In this setting, society (through institutions like family, school, place of worship, etc.) writes the different players' scripts – their *roles* – and it's important that every player agrees to play them. Attempts to step outside of one's allotted role – *deviance* – result in punishment or treatment, and the rule-breaker is either coerced or persuaded into accepting the script (*hard* or *soft social control*). In extreme cases, the deviant is removed from the stage altogether, as in life imprisonment or execution.

In 1964, some 80 per cent of American sociologists were, according to a national survey, favourably disposed towards functionalist theory. In an important sense, for them, sociology and functionalism were one. Yet today, it's considered by some sociologists – especially marxists and social constructionists – to be part of a deviant, highly conservative intellectual subculture. We think that's an unfair charge. Functionalists come in different shapes and sizes: conservatives and radicals; right-wingers and left-wingers. Indeed, far from being a conservative, the most famous functionalist of them all, the French sociologist, Emile Durkheim (1858–1917), was a self-proclaimed socialist. Given the magnitude of Durkheim's impact on functionalist theory, we'll now consider some of his more important insights.

Durkheim's theory

Durkheim's writings were profound and prolific. Here are some of his key theoretical propositions:

- The integration of individuals into society is what holds society together. The 'holding together' is guaranteed because, other than new-born infants, there's no such thing as a non-social individual.
- Social integration is achieved by the socialisation of individuals from birth into societal values that teach and enforce society's prescribed codes of conduct. Societal values refer, using Talcott Parson's definition, to 'conceptions of the desirable society that are held in common by its members' (Parsons 1967: 8). In this sense, they amount to – and here we use Durkheim's original French term – a *conscience collective*, namely, commonly held moral beliefs. When people base their actions on these beliefs, as most do, they conform.
- Socialisation – that is, the learning and acceptance of the *conscience collective* and the accompanying readiness to conform – is imparted through institutions like the family, the school, the place of worship, etc.
- Most people are socialised into conforming most of the time. If persuasion doesn't do the trick, there's always back-up in the form of tougher forms of social control, namely, punishment.
- Punishment restores and sustains social order by removing non-conforming individuals from circulation (notably, imprisonment and execution), and by reinforcing the sense of allegiance to the *conscience collective* among the citizen majority when they collectively condemn the criminal in their midst.
- The degree to which conformity is required and, if needs be, enforced, varies from society to society. In traditional societies, people are expected to be members of society first and individuals second. The reverse is the case in modern societies. This means that a high level of conforming behaviour characterises traditional societies, whereas much more levity towards divergent, individualised lifestyles – so long as they aren't disruptive – is found in modern societies.
- Traditional societies are held together through what Durkheim called *mechanical solidarity*, that is, a 'machine-like' adherence by people to a non-negotiable *conscience collective*. Mechanical solidarity emphasises social duty above personal identity or uniqueness – a kind of Three Musketeers 'all for one, and one for all' spirit. Some tight-knit communities (for example, public schools and monasteries) are still characterised by mechanical solidarity. But mechanical solidarity only thrives in small communities. As society, through population growth and urbanisation, gets bigger and concentrated in towns and cities, people escape the close surveillance of village life. They dare to be different. Moreover, their work becomes increasingly separated from home, and gets divided between specialised institutions: schools, hospitals, factories, etc. The parent who was once teacher, doctor and producer all rolled into one, now does one job, and the other functions are carried out by a range of specialists. Durkheim called this process the *division of labour*. Together, population growth and the division of labour are forces for *social change*. They lead to a different type of social bonding which Durkheim termed *organic solidarity*. The term is a metaphor of the human body, a biological organism whose overall health is maintained by ensuring that different organs work for the good of the whole. Similarly, in a society characterised by organic solidarity, different people perform different functions for the good of the 'social organism' that is society.

Durkheim's work was ground-breaking. It laid the foundation of sociology's basic contention that society is possible because social forces weld individual minds into common purpose. Critics claim that Durkheim underestimated the wilfulness of individuals who seek to go their own way. But Durkheim didn't ignore individuality. Indeed, he wrote about individuals, 'who resist this general current [large-scale industrialisation] and obstinately pursue their modest enterprises', adding that, 'The moral conscience of nations . . . prefers a little justice to all the industrial perfection in the world' (Durkheim 1964: 51, first published 1893). He did, of course, highlight the other side of the coin, namely, that when individuals interact with each other, the behaviour that issues is social in character.

OVER TO YOU

Describe some of the things that happen in two imaginary societies, one based on 'mechanical solidarity', the other on 'organic solidarity'. Justify your descriptions.

The main propositions of consensus (functionalist) theory

- Society is an interdependent structure of individuals and institutions. For example, most individuals are born into an institution called the family. In turn, the family has links (hence the idea of an interdependent structure) with other institutions. It hands over some of the functions of bringing up its children – *socialisation* – to an institution called the school, which depends on the family to have already instilled basic skills (for example, the ability to speak). The family, of course, depends on the school to take the socialisation of its children – especially in relation to learning and behavioural outcomes – further, as do other institutions (notably, universities and places of work). Some institutions (for example, police forces) have the function of enforcing consensus when socialisation doesn't ensure conformity within 'reasonable bounds'. In extreme circumstances, non-conforming individuals whose behaviour is considered dysfunctional (i.e. threatening to social order) are punished or treated.

◆ The 'social cement' that holds together the 'social structure' of society is *consensus* – what Durkheim called the *conscience collective*. It's through common beliefs that society lasts and that stability is maintained. Moreover, it's through the process of socialisation that an individual's mind becomes attuned to these common beliefs, for they, in large part, are what a maturing mind draws upon. Thus, for example, a British individual learns, through socialisation, that democracy is good. By accepting this belief and acting upon it, she or he also helps ensure that democracy endures. In a brilliant analysis of a different belief system – anti-Jewish nazism – the American historian, Daniel Goldhagen, showed how an upbringing in 1940s nazi Germany meant that many 'Germans massively complied with and enthusiastically lent support in a variety of ways to the antisemitic institutions, legislation, and policies of their country' (Goldhagen 1996: 32). That system lasted until a world war ended it. Durkheim astutely points out that even certain types of deviance can reinforce consensus in other quarters. When, for example, the international community publicly rebuked nazi murderers after the war, the principles of democracy and justice were given added momentum. In that respect, the condemnation of nazi crimes defined the boundaries of acceptable human behaviour.

Because most people act in conventional ways, human social behaviour is generally predictable. This means it can be studied scientifically because science explains predictable phenomena.

◆ The acceptance by individuals of common values is a matter of degree, for, as the mid-twentieth century functionalist, Talcott Parsons, notes, 'members of a going society will, to some extent, differ in their values . . . and they will, to a certain degree, fail to act in accordance with the values they hold' (Parsons 1967: 8). Herein lies one potential source for what sociologists call the process of *social change*. Individuals who aren't fully integrated into society (perhaps because they grew up in untypical circumstances) are more likely to resist social convention than the rest of us. Such people, especially if they rise to positions of prominence (for example, newspaper editors) sometimes persuade other people to break from tradition. There are also individuals whom, as Parsons (1964) correctly points out, are expected to bring about change. These are primarily scientists whose job it is to help society move towards a better future. Individuals aside, Parsons (1964) also observes that nature itself can be the cause of social change. Thus, for example, the depletion of a natural resource like oil might lead some societies to develop new technologies (such as solar energy), which, in turn, changes people's lives. Durkheim cited population growth and concentration as other important causes of change. These and the various circumstances that people face ensure that adaptation and change are necessary features of the human condition.

Change, argue functionalists, is more commonly *evolutionary* (gradual) than *revolutionary* (rapid) because convention is deeply embedded in the structure of society and takes time to pry free. From this perspective, change can be pictured as a 'shifting' from one stable state to another stable state. Imagine, for example, that a government raises income tax. Indignant citizens vigorously protest, thereby de-stabilising the existing 'equilibrium'. In response to public outcry, the government promises to delay the introduction of the tax rise for one year, and to then invest the increased revenue in more hospitals and schools. This strategy eventually quells most of the unrest and ushers in a new 'equilibrium': a delayed-reaction change linked to the promise of better public services.

EXAM TIP

It's commonly asserted that functionalism doesn't pay sufficient attention to social change. Avoid that error by informing the examiner that the notable functionalist, Shmuel N. Eisenstadt, wrote that 'tendencies to change are inherent in all human societies, because they face basic problems to which no overall continuous solutions exist (1964:712).'

To summarise, *functionalism envisages society as a social structure of interdependent institutions into which individuals are born and raised, but which changes gradually, mainly in response to problems that require new solutions.*

EXAM TIP

Don't assume that functionalism is a spent force in sociology. It still correctly reminds us that *most* forms of human social behaviour are predictable because *most* people conform to conventions *most* of the time.

QUESTIONS

1 How have Durkheim's ideas influenced the development of consensus (functionalist) theory?

2 How does society promote conforming human social behaviour?
3 What useful function(s) might deviant behaviour serve?
4 How does consensus (functionalist) theory explain social change?
5 What are some of the main arguments for and against consensus (functionalist) theory?

CONSENSUS (FUNCTIONALIST) THEORY

FOR

+ Functionalists correctly note that individuals are born into an existing society which exerts very powerful social forces on them to conform. All do, to varying degrees. In fact, a minimum degree of conformity to group demands is an absolute necessity for a satisfactory personal life. How, for example, could even a burglar get by in life without paying for some things? In its rejection of the possibility of a 'non-social' human being, functionalism convincingly demonstrates that human behaviour can't just be explained on the basis of individual psychologies. Being in a crowd, for instance, has social dynamics that 'push' some people into behaviours that they wouldn't contemplate doing on their own (for example, showing very public exuberance at a music concert).

+ Functionalists are adept at identifying what it takes, in relation to specific kinds of social arrangement, for different types of society to either endure or change. The key to endurance is, of course, the process of socialisation, whereby family, schools and other key institutions teach members of society the rules of the game. Change, while initiated by a range of possible factors, is typically brought about, argue functionalists, by: 'rebels' whose individuality sometimes overpowers social convention; innovators whom society encourages to be creative and scientific; natural events such as climatic change and the depletion of the earth's resources; and population growth and concentration.

+ Functionalism has had a powerful impact on the discipline of sociology. It would be fair to say that, from its inception in the first half of the nineteenth century up to the 1960s, functionalism has been the dominant theory in sociology. Indeed, sociology and functionalism were almost one and the same thing. The great contribution of this long intellectual history – which still endures, though not so prominently – is the important insight that human social behaviour is largely structured and generally predictable. Functionalism makes that claim on the basis of scientific evidence.

AGAINST

– Functionalism views society as a 'machine out there' which thinks and functions for itself. In that respect, functionalism allegedly invents 'scientific laws' of human social behaviour that don't derive from people's individual psychologies. That said, Parsons, for example, recognises that some individuals actively pit their own psychological dispositions against the 'social system'. He cites the example of artists in relation to 'the well-known association of art with "Bohemianism", with the repudiation of many of the main institutionalized patterns of ordinary life' (Parsons 1964: 410). It's not often though that one finds many concessions to the notion of wilful individualism in functionalist theory.

– Some functionalists (for example, Kingsley Davis and Wilbert Moore 1945) go beyond describing what they see to claiming that certain social arrangements (for example, people who do 'important' work deserve more pay than people who do 'less important work') are desirable. This leads to the intrusion of value judgements – sometimes of a conservative, right-wing nature – into sociological theorising. It must be emphasised, however, that the identification by functionalists of what it takes to maintain an 'unjust' society isn't automatically the same thing as saying this is morally acceptable.

– Functionalists tend to over-emphasise consensus and under-emphasise conflict, treating first appearances of stability as accurate readings. In that context, claim marxists, scratch the surface of what appears to be consensus, and you'll often find conflict underneath. For example, if you only spend a day in a primary school as an observer, staff relations there might appear very convivial. However, if you spend more time in the school, you might find that the strict disciplinarians on the staff don't get on at all well with the teachers who are indulgent persuaders.

– Functionalism is often charged with not adequately explaining change because it allegedly places too much emphasis on order and stability. We think, however, this accusation is largely unfounded. Functionalists do consider and account for change. Parsons devotes a whole chapter to the issue in his ground-breaking work, *The Social System* (1964). In Chapter 11 of that book, he concludes that it's not possible yet (the book was first published in 1951) to come forward with an all-embracing general theory of change, instead noting that there are various causes and process of change (for example, processes initiated by scientific advances).

Conflict theory

Given that conflict is the opposite of consensus, it seems at first sight as though conflict theory and consensus (functionalist) theory must be polar opposites. Such is not the case. They have their differences, but both theories accept that no society can be exclusively described in conflict or consensus terms. Indeed, this century's most eminent functionalist, Talcott Parsons, has noted how individuals sometimes have to ponder conflicting 'obligations'. In that context, he uses the interesting example of a white American who lives in the Deep South, and who caught in the conflicting expectations of conforming to 'the universalistic values of the wider society, the "American creed", but also as a Southerner in the pattern of "white supremacy"' (Parsons 1964: 281). This drama was played on a much wider stage in the nineteenth century during the American Civil War, and, more recently, in the American civil rights movement of the 1950s and 1960s.

Most of us carry around some sets of conflicting role expectations, but when these expectations become vividly crystallised and polarised in opposing social movements, it's time to make a 'choice' as to where we really stand. Am I going to march on the streets of London with black Britons and white Britons in support of equal rights for all citizens, or am I going to join a neo-nazi group and persecute people from minority ethnic groups?

While functionalist theorists accept that conflict is an integral feature of any society, they don't pay as much attention to it as conflict theorists. Both, however, concur that society is best theorised as a place where consensus and conflict co-exist (i.e. some people 'get on'; others 'fight'). In that context, functionalists do a good job at explaining the consensus side of the equation, and conflict theorists are equally proficient at figuring out why confrontations arise and where they lead to.

The most famous (some would say the most notorious!) proponent of conflict theory is the nineteenth-century social scientist, Karl Marx, whose profound and prolific writings have led two sociologists, David Lee and Howard Newby to propose that, as a thinker, he 'is probably the single most influential figure in the history of ideas since Jesus Christ' (Lee and Newby 1986: 113). Thus today, hundreds of millions of people live in societies that claim to be run on marxist lines. As with Christianity, so with marxism, claiming an allegiance to a set of beliefs that carries the name of Jesus or Marx is, of course, an assertion that needs to be tested. For it's not what people call themselves that counts, it's what they do.

Marx's theory

Marx's central argument is that society never stands still because conflict between the different groups who comprise it make for constant change. Marx recognises that consensus tends to exist within groups whose members have similar economic positions and common purpose, namely, within social classes. He pointedly adds, however, that the ruling class is adept at propagandising its view of things to society at large. Yet, beyond surface appearances, Marx notes that classes don't get on with each other because their economic interests are at odds. At crucial 'no turning back' moments in history, this conflict erupts into revolution, and the old society yields to a new age. Marx emphasised that revolutions only occur when obsolete social arrangements get in the way of new needs. As he put it, 'wherever there is a revolutionary convulsion, there must be some social want in the background, which is prevented, by outworn institutions, from satisfying itself' (Marx 1971: 1, first published 1891). When the time is ripe for radical and swift change, individuals are able to seize the moment and ride the wave of social change. To quote Marx again (1859, in Bottomore and Rubel 1975: 68), 'mankind therefore sets itself only such problems as it can solve.' By this, he meant that judging the moment for change, has to be 'precision-accurate' if the wave is to be successfully ridden.

Karl Marx (1818–83)

Marx spent many years in nineteenth-century England, and was able to learn from and apply his theories to the English Industrial Revolution. Early nineteenth-century English landlords invested more in agriculture than in industry. This brought them into conflict with a new social class, factory owners, who staked their economic futures on machines rather than farms. There thus developed a confrontation between the lords of land and the barons of iron. This, referring largely to Marx's interpretation, is what happened:

1 In eighteenth-century England, landlords and farmers owned the soil which, in turn, was worked by agricultural labourers who mainly used horse-drawn ploughs and other simple power sources. Contained in this description, we have two of Marx's key concepts: the *means of production* (in this case, land, horses and ploughs); and the *relations of production* (how people are related to the means of production: in this case, landowners own them; labourers work them).

2 New power sources – notably, steam and coal-driven machines – were invented in the second half of the eighteenth century, and were increasingly developed by a new kind of owner: the factory capitalist. Agricultural labourers gradually left the rural villages, and headed for the urban towns to become machine workers in mechanised factories. Cotton manufacture, in particular, flourished.

3 The relations of production began to shift in the following way: landowners and agricultural labourers yielded ground to factory owners and industrial workers.

4 The *new* means of production (factory machines) were *in conflict* with the landowner/agricultural labourer relations of production. Put another way, the factory system couldn't function in an agricultural society. This stand-off simmered on (*evolved*, to use a sociological term) for about a hundred years, but something had to give, and it did. Under enormous pressure from a powerful capitalist lobby which had economic muscle but limited political representation, the landlord parliament repealed legislation that had protected agricultural over industrial interests – the repeal of the Corn Laws in 1846. Marx referred to this event as a nail in the coffin of the landed aristocracy. It signalled a *revolution* that heralded the end of an era and the dawning of a new age. The landowners and agricultural labourers were replaced (outnumbered, would perhaps be a better description) by factory owners and industrial workers. Economic transformation ushered in a new political elite. By 1880, Parliament was represented with a majority comprised of businessmen and industrialists.

5 Once the economic system (the *base or infrastructure*, to use Marx's terminology) had been transformed, the other institutions in society (which Marx collectively called the *superstructure*) had to follow suit. Parliament, the linchpin of the *superstructure*, therefore had to drag – sometimes 'kicking and screaming' – other institutions into the new economic order. Schools, for example, were a priority on the new agenda because they imparted basic skills and instilled the discipline required of future factory workers.

And there you have it: Marx's theory that conflict in the economic system is the engine of *social change*. It's important to emphasise that Marx wouldn't have it any other way. According to him, all change has its origins in the material (i.e. economic) world.

To be sure, this is a 'bold outlines' description of a much more complex process, but the gist of it is there. While conflict existed on lots of different levels (between landowners and agricultural workers, for example, as well as between landowners and factory owners), the confrontation that ignited the English Industrial Revolution was between a landed aristocracy who wanted workers to remain in fields and an industrial capitalist class who wanted them to enter factories. The initial fuse was a long one – an *evolutionary* process towards a point of no-turning back – capped by a short-fuse (relatively non-violent) *revolution* leading to an industrial society.

The next stage, said Marx, would be a confrontation between the owners of the means of production (industrial capitalists, or as he called them the *bourgeoisie*) and the workers (the *proletariat*, to use Marx's term). Marx lived long enough to describe empirically the beginnings of this confrontation. He argued that the upper class employed workers on low wages, but made vast amounts of money on the worker-produced goods and services they sold. This meant that workers were exploited by a capitalist upper class because only an exceedingly small part of the value of the goods and services they produced was retained by them. The rest – the so-called *surplus value* – went to the upper class, who, even allowing for their expenditure on factories, machines and such like, reaped huge profits.

Marx didn't like what he saw, and he urged the working class to forge a more just world, reminding them that it wasn't enough to understand society, but also to change it for the better. His famous rallying call, now inscribed on his tombstone in Highgate Cemetery, London, was:

'The philosophers have only interpreted the world in different ways; the point is to change it.'

(Marx 1845, cited by Bottomore and Rubel 1975: 84)

Marx was aware of the difficulty of this mission because people live in a society that isn't entirely of their own making. Nevertheless it was a cautionary piece of advice that contained a good deal of optimism. People are shaped by society, but they're also the potential shapers of society. This important point has been developed by Anthony Giddens (1984) in his so-called *theory of structuration*. In this theory, Giddens envisages social structure as a wall – tough but replaceable – whose bricks are constantly being re-arranged by often wilful human social behaviour. Rarely is the wall, in this metaphor, entirely demolished, but rarely is it left entirely intact either. If, for example, I travel by train from York to Manchester Airport, I make a wilful decision to use this mode of travel. Once in the railway system, however, I abide by its structural rules – buying a ticket, not occupying a seat booked in someone else's name, etc.

In his futuristic – critics would say fanciful – exposition on the downfall of capitalism, Marx set out a series of stages that contained both shaping forces and a shaping role for a revolutionary working class. Here are the main outlines of his blueprint:

1. The means of production in industrial society eventually become so efficient that machines start taking over human labour, leading to mass unemployment.
2. Unemployed people are usually poor and can't afford to buy many goods and services.
3. Capitalists suffer the consequences of this because there's a reduced demand for their products.
4. Profits consequently fall.
5. Capitalists therefore lay off more workers and pay the remainder either lower wages or wages that don't keep pace with inflation.
6. The relations of production – owner capitalists and non-owning workers (some of whom are unemployed) – are out of alignment with the means of production. Put another way, who needs workers when machines can do their jobs?
7. The laying-off of workers and the pauperisation of those whose labour is retained, as well as the fall in capitalists' profits caused by diminished consumer demand, creates an economic crisis.
8. Workers seize the initiative and, in unity and common purpose, launch a revolution (violent or peaceful, depending on circumstances) in order to take over the means of production. *This is their point of entry as a force for change*.
9. The revolution is successful, and workers become the owners of the means of production, as well as members of a temporary socialist government (a *'dictatorship' of the proletariat*).
10. The temporary government steps down once it has ushered in a permanent socialist society (a *communist* one).
11. Under communism, people are attended to on the basis of need rather than on how much money they have. Classes disappear because machines and other forms of technology transfer to the collective ownership of the people. When machines take over from people, the drudgery of labour is replaced by unlimited leisure. People still get 'paid' though because the machines create enough wealth for everyone to have a relatively equal share of the cake.
12. Some societies become communist at the same time. Others follow suit until eventually the whole world is communist. This is the end of 'history' because thenceforth no significant changes occur in the social structure of society.

And that, in abridged form, is Marx's conflict theory of the future transformation of capitalist society into communist society.

While Marx, as Parsons claims, 'was probably the greatest social theorist whose work fell entirely within the nineteenth century' (Parsons 1967: 135), when he started predicting future trends, he entered the realm of prophecy. Some of his hunches (for example, the entry of the very richest industrial managers into the ranks of the industrial owner ruling class) have proven correct. Other anticipations, like the predicted shrinking of the middle class, haven't been borne out. Although it would be unfair to depict him as a crystal ball gazer, some of Marx's ideas undoubtedly had more to do with what he wanted to happen than with what the evidence would actually support.

This quite lengthy consideration of Marx is justifiable because his influence on conflict theory is so profound that the terms 'marxism' and 'conflict theory' are sometimes treated as one and the same. Certainly it would be true to say that most conflict theorists are marxist in orientation.

OVER TO YOU

Describe what life would be like in Marx's communist version of society, and discuss whether such a society (or something approximating it) would be possible and desirable.

The main propositions of conflict theory

- Individuals are born and raised in a society that socialises them into social human beings. The experience of socialisation, however, varies between different groups in society. Most notably, children from working-class backgrounds are socialised into conforming roles, whereas upper-class children are socialised into leadership roles. Middle-class children are socialised to manage the affairs of the upper class and to supervise the working class. The upshot of these different socialisation patterns is that the conflicting economic interests of the upper class and the rest of society are kept in check through a propaganda-manufactured consensus, backed up by force. Conflict theorists support their claims on the basis of evidence rather than opinion, placing great emphasis on the social *scientific* nature of sociology.
- While it's hard to step out of their socialised roles, individuals do have the capacity to break free. In order to realise this capacity, they need to stop acting on autopilot and start thinking about what they do and why they do it. In short, they need to become politically conscious. Political consciousness means understanding that society is 'shot through' with conflict. Once conflict is recognised, people can address it, especially

those who are being exploited. Thus, for example, coal miners who work in dangerous conditions for low pay in a privately-owned mine need to know that their interests are in conflict with those of the owner. When they realise this, they become politically conscious, and can then collectively fight for social and economic justice. A victory means overcoming social arrangements that normally constrain them. A successful intervention in the social structure like this is called *human agency*, the idea here being of 'free human agents' who change rather than succumb to the social structure.

- Linked to the preceding point, conflict theorists explain change on the basis of successful interventions by individuals, usually through collective action, in the social structure. However, to be successful, these interventions need to be precisely timed. If individuals take on a social structure that's showing signs of cracks and strains (for example, pre-apartheid South Africa just prior to Nelson Mandela's release from Robin Island Prison), then change is likely to happen. On the other hand, when individuals seek to overthrow a social structure that isn't 'ripe for change' (for example, present-day China), the social structure remains firm and

CONFLICT THEORY

FOR

+ It digs deep to get beyond surface appearances. On the surface, we see conformity in all kinds of social relationship: people standing in queues, secretaries politely complying with their bosses' instructions, students getting their homework assignments in on time. But sometimes this conformity is a very 'fragile peace'. Ask people if they think queuing for a movie is acceptable, and they might tell you that extra pay booths would mean not having to wait in line. Speak to secretaries about whether they willingly do what their bosses say, and some will tell you of the tyranny of office hierarchies. Talk with students about their assignment deadlines, and some will say they're forced to prioritise things that aren't at the top of their agendas. Conflict theory gets to the root of these underlying discontents, and cautions us not to take consensus at face value.

+ It combines a scientific awareness of the influence of social forces on human action with the recognition that individuals place their imprint on society too. Society is very powerful and it exists before you or I enter it. But we make 'choices' in our lives. The 'choices' are influenced by our upbringing and by the amount of power we have. Instead of pitting the important concepts of 'human agency' and 'social structure' against each other, conflict theory sensibly points out that we *can* have the one with the other.

+ It seeks to find ways of reducing inequality and promoting social justice. Conflict theorists identify conflict in society, but they would prefer to live in a society based on consensus. The consensus they long for, however, isn't the kind that exists in a society where powerful people exploit the weak. Rather, they look forward to a society where consensus is based on the collective belief that equality is good for everyone, liberating both the oppressor and the oppressed. For many conflict theorists, the task of sociology is to root out the conflict in society that causes so much damage and hurt, and to give people the initiative and the wherewithal to build something different and something better.

AGAINST

− It plays down the extent to which consensus in society is mutually arrived at, instead seeing conformity as a contrived outcome. The 'bad guys' – the contrivers – are the rich and powerful and their servants in the propaganda and law enforcement 'industries'. This paints a very manipulative picture which is at odds with the many instances of conforming behaviour that help us all. Thus, for example, everyone – not just the rich – benefits if people agree to abide by traffic regulations.

− It's sometimes difficult to disentangle the 'social scientific' (the *what is* part) from the 'ideological' (the *what should be* part) in conflict theory. This is very much a legacy from the writings of Marx, who at times was very scientifically composed about the circumstances he documented and analysed, and at other times brimming with 'righteous' anger about the conditions of the poor and under-privileged. One really has to ask conflict theorists if they shouldn't pay more attention to understanding human social behaviour than with telling people how to behave. They, of course, would reply that they do both! What do you think?

− Its tendency to predict future trends makes it a very speculative theory. While this was perhaps attributable to Marx, there's still a yearning among many conflict theorists to map out the society of tomorrow. Few conflict theorists these days would adopt Marx's nineteenth-century predictions wholesale. That would be a bit like trusting a Victorian 'science fiction' writer's vision of the world beyond the year 2000. Nevertheless, the left-wing political leanings of many conflict theorists makes one wonder whether their predictions have more to do with wish fulfilment than with what's actually going to happen.

things stay as they are – at least for the time being. It's this quality of being able to seize the moment, to strike while the iron's hot, that makes for change. In that respect, human agency is akin to a catalyst in science – it rapidly speeds up a process that's going to happen anyway. The difference is, without the catalyst, we get evolution; with it, we get revolution. Here we see how conflict theory incorporates both evolutionary and revolutionary concepts of social change. Revolutions don't just happen by 'spontaneous combustion'. There's a definite march of history behind them. When the march is steady but not swift, society is in what Marx called 'the course of historical evolution' (1965: 95, first published 1846). When it goes into a sprint, there's your revolution.

> ***EXAM TIP***
>
> Many candidates describe conflict theory as a revolutionary theory. It's actually a theory which contains both evolutionary and revolutionary concepts.

To summarise, *conflict theory envisages society as a social structure of conflicting social groups into which individuals are born and raised. Social change is the result of a continuous struggle between groups who support existing social arrangements and groups who fight for something different.*

> ***EXAM TIP***
>
> Don't make the mistake in a 'compare and contrast' question of claiming that conflict theory is ideological (makes claims about what kind of society is desirable), whereas consensus (functionalist) theory is not. Both are ideological!

QUESTIONS

1. How have Marx's ideas influenced the development of conflict theory?
2. How does conflict manifest itself in society?
3. How does conflict theory explain 'consensus'?
4. How does conflict theory explain social change?
5. What are some of the main arguments for and against conflict theory?

Social constructionist theory

Social constructionists have theories about the theories people construct in their heads and act upon. Perhaps you have a theory that if you assertively resist manipulative people, they'll eventually leave you alone. If your theory works in practice, it's added to the stock of 'recipe knowledge' that's stored in your long-term memory, to be called upon and used, as and when required. Social constructionists claim that there's no universal sociological theory of human social behaviour because each of us have our own theories. The task of sociology is to make those private theories public in order to find out how unique or common they are.

Socially-isolated individuals don't have much chance to learn and practise social skills. This sometimes leads to unpredictable and 'deviant' behaviour, for example, laughing when someone asks for street directions. Most individuals, however, derive their ideas about how to behave from interacting with other people. Allowing for some individual differences, we can be pretty sure that in fairly common social situations they'll follow a predictable social script. Ask them how to get to the bus station and, if they know, they'll more than likely give you the required information in a courteous manner.

Instead of explaining human social behaviour according to sociological 'laws', social constructionists claim that the best way to theorise is to align sociological ideas with people's ideas. People choose appropriate behaviour in relation to how they *interpret* different situations. If, for example, my *interpretation* – my theory – of a student's excessive anxiety over forgetting his exercise book is that he's scared of teachers, I would say something like, 'Don't worry about it. I forget things all the time.' Here I'm *constructing* my behaviour in a manner designed to change his *interpretation* of teachers, to get him to attach a different *meaning* to the people they are. If my efforts are successful, he'll *construct* and act upon a 'theory' that forgetfulness is 'human' the next time he forgets his book. Hopefully, his behaviour will then exhibit much less anxiety.

This and other kinds of 'theory' arise out of *social interaction*. They don't exist in sociological textbooks. The italicised words in the preceding paragraph draw attention to the essential vocabulary of social constructionist theory, namely:

Human social behaviour is <u>interpreted</u> during the process of <u>social interaction</u>. The <u>meanings</u> that are attached to the initial behaviour (for example, this student is scared of teachers) influences how subsequent behaviour is <u>constructed</u> (for example, I, as a teacher, behave in a way designed to defuse the fear).

One of the confusing things about social constructionist theory is that it goes by lots of different names. Among the most common you'll encounter are these: social action theory; symbolic interactionism; interactionist theory; labelling theory; ethnomethodology, and phenomenology. Making things a bit more simple, we can say that:

- Social action theory, symbolic interactionism and interactionist theory are *moderately social constructionist*. They propose that people socially construct social structure, and that social structure also influences the way people think and act. Although some purists would disagree, interactionist theory is a good all-purpose term for these 'theories'.
- Ethnomethodology and phenomenology are *very social constructionist*. They propose that social structure is very fragile indeed. It exists because people socially construct it, but it doesn't necessarily mould attitudes and behaviour. Ethnomethodologists and phenomenologists argue that 'social reality' is what people say it is rather than what sociology claims it to be. In that sense, the opinions of individuals are privileged above the 'scientific' conclusions of the sociologists who study them. While there are some differences between ethnomethodology and phenomenology, the two 'theories' are largely interchangeable. Probably, ethnomethodology is the more commonly used term in sociology. Phenomenology has its origin in philosophy.
- Labelling theory generally has a closer affinity with 'moderate' than with 'very social constructionist' perspectives. Nevertheless, it's used by all kinds of social constructionist sociologist. It's central proposition is that human social behaviour is judged in relation to how it's labelled. For example, in some communities a man who works as an 'au pair' might be labelled a 'cissy', whereas the same behaviour elsewhere might be judged as entirely 'normal'.

EXAM TIP

An important reminder: the AEB A-level Sociology syllabuses use 'social action theory' as the umbrella term for all the above 'theories'. The umbrella term in this book is 'social constructionist theory'.

Lots of sociologists have contributed to the development of social constructionist theory. Its main legacy though resides in the writings of the early twentieth-century German sociologist, Max Weber. Unlike the functionalist, Emile Durkheim, and the conflict theorist, Karl Marx, Weber wasn't a 'grand theorist'. That's not an insult. What it means is that Weber didn't come up with a general theory of society. He chose not to do so because he had a profound distrust of any theory which paid neither sufficient attention to the uniqueness of each social encounter, nor to the meanings attached to the encounters by the individuals who were party to them. He did, however, theorise about whole societies, but not in a manner that detracted from their unique characteristics. Moreover, he made it clear that all theories could only provide sociologists with a modest approximation of the real social world.

Weber's theory

Students new to sociology will be able to understand quite a lot about the theories of Durkheim and Marx by reading their original works. Weber, however, sometimes wrote in a style that even experienced sociologists find hard to comprehend. Intellectually, he, Durkheim and Marx were equals in the field of social science. But Weber preferred painstaking analysis to the grand heroic sweep of Durkheim and Marx, and this makes his writing difficult at times. We'll do our best though to make his profound contribution to sociology as simple to understand as possible.

Here, in abridged form, are Weber's main theoretical propositions:

- Each society is historically and culturally unique. Ancient Greek society, for example, for all its greatness, has been and gone. So too have the belief systems that underpinned its culture. Ancient Greeks thought lighting was a bolt from the hand of the god, Zeus; modern scientists know it's a powerful form of static electricity. Each society must therefore be theorised about in relation to its distinctive characteristics rather

Max Weber (1864–1920)

than on the basis of general sociological 'laws'. Weber wasn't against general theory and sociological 'laws'. But he believed that to obtain them would be a quest – not something achievable now. The best way to theorise is through empathy – to step into the shoes of the society one is studying, and understand it from the perspectives of its people. Understanding the intended motivations of individuals is the key to good sociology.

- Understanding a society can only be partial because what we see is the product of an infinite chain of cause and effect that stretches back into history. Take tea-drinking, for instance. It's a deeply ingrained part of British culture. If, as a sociologist, you wanted to understand why the British love their cup of tea, you couldn't possibly come up with all the answers. It would require digging up and assembling all the historical and present-day reasons for the popularity of tea-drinking – the influence of empire (tea plantations in India, etc.), brewing tea as a pick-me-up for troops returning from the field of fire, and so on. Sociology therefore has to be intellectually honest and unpretentious about its theoretical claims.
- A good way to build 'working theories' is to extract from the empirical social world aspects of its essential characteristics and deliberately exaggerate them, rather like a cartoonist caricatures the features of a well-known celebrity. This yields a concept which Weber called the *ideal type*. The connotation isn't of 'ideal' in a moral or perfect sense, but 'ideal' or 'good' for the purpose of understanding complex social phenomena. For example, one might study the essential ingredients of the causes of the American, French, Russian and Chinese revolutions, and, from this, develop an ideal type theory of revolutions. Not forgetting Weber's insistence on the unique feature of individual events, we might, nevertheless, be able to come up with the typical causes of revolutions in general. Weber wouldn't baulk at this, provided the typical causes were refined on the basis of the singular empirical characteristics of each revolution. Thus, for example, a general cause of revolution might be the marxist one of 'breaking point' class conflict. A singular case would be, for instance, the specific nature of the conflict between Tory landed aristocrats in England and self-made merchants in America prior to the American Revolution.
- In his famous study, *The Protestant Ethic and the Spirit of Capitalism* (1974, first published 1904), Weber developed a model of change based on individual human endeavour. The main pioneers of *modern* 'western' capitalism were, he argued, strict Protestants who belonged to a puritan sect called Calvinism, which was a product of the sixteenth-century Reformation. Calvinists believed God helps those who help themselves, and that success in business could be taken as a sign that they were among those who would go to Heaven. They therefore conducted their business as though it were a *calling*. This disciplined approach to enterprise had an affinity with the *spirit* of capitalism, whose prime characteristic was the rational pursuit of profit.

  Using the *comparative method* (in this case *comparing* different societies with each other), Weber estimated that material economic factors (for example, the discovery of precious metals) were as conducive to the development of modern capitalism in China and India as they were in Europe. He noted, however, that of the three, Europe was the main seedbed of modern capitalism. Weber therefore concluded that something other than economic factors 'caused' the development of this very distinctive economic system. He found what he was looking for in Europe: Calvinism. By encouraging its followers to pursue profit not out of greed but as a duty, Calvinism was the main driving force behind the rise of modern capitalism. On the last page of his book, Weber made it clear that a religious explanation for change – in this case, the development of modern capitalism – isn't the only explanation:

  > 'But it is, of course, not my aim to substitute for a one-sided materialistic an equally one-sided spiritualistic causal interpretation of culture and of history. Each is equally possible, but each, if it does not serve as the preparation, but as the conclusion of an investigation, accomplishes equally little in the interest of historical truth.'
  >
  > (Weber 1974: 183, first published 1904)

  In other words, *social change* can be caused by ideas, as well as by material (economic) factors. So don't come to conclusions about what's the best model of change until you've completed your investigation. One suspects that Weber is taking a gentle swipe here at the marxist theory of change, which starts with the assumption that the cause of any significant change in society must be found in the economic system.

Weber is properly regarded as a sociologist whose works had a profound influence on social constructionist theory. He, more than Durkheim and, arguably, more than Marx, emphasised that social structures are sufficiently flexible for concerted individual action to take hold and change the structures. This crucial insight, as will be seen, is the key to social constructionist theory.

OVER TO YOU

Explain the reasoning behind Weber's comparative study of economic factors in Europe, China and India, in relation to the development of modern capitalism.

The main propositions of social constructionist theory

- People make social structures through purposeful, goal-directed actions, but the structures then influence how people think and behave. Imagine, for example, that you and your associates start a wind surfing club. Before you arrived on the scene, the club didn't exist. You made it happen. You created its social structure – its admission procedures, its policy for recruiting qualified instructors, its tuition fees, and so forth. While it's true that you have to take account of other structures (for example, British health and safety regulations), you have *socially constructed* an institution. But institutions bite back! Now that it's up and running, its rules (including the ones you made) are binding on you and all the members and users of the wind surfing club. Social constructionist theory won't let us forget that individuals aren't detachable from society. They make society! Ethnomethodologists and phenomenologists suggest that the making and re-making of structures – their construction – by people is a continuous process because the social world is empty unless we impose meanings upon it. Moreover, these structures can be very personal, having no hold on people for whom they have no meaning. For example, you and your friends might construct a dress protocol for an end of school leaving party that means a lot to you, but nothing to those students who choose to wear something different.
- Adding to the preceding point, existing institutions only *exist* on the sufferance of people. We, as human beings, allow them to endure because we attach *meanings* to them that endorse their authority. For example, the majority of British parents agree to let teachers teach their children because the institutions where teachers work – schools – *mean*, among other things, a decent education and the chance of a good future. We also have meanings for lots of other things in life, many that are held in common (for example, a puppy means cute and cuddly for most people), but others which are personal (for example, the word 'police officer' has different meanings for a bank robber and a bank clerk). Some of the meanings we attach to daily events are part of our 'socialised' way of looking at them. But other meanings emerge because of new experiences, especially when we interact with people who look at things differently. If you've never heard of the band, REM, that term might only be meaningful to you as an acronym for 'rapid eyeball movement' – a phenomenon observed by psychologists when people dream. If you're introduced to someone for whom REM means 'great music by a great band', and you subsequently attend a live REM concert, perhaps you'll discover another meaning for the term too.
- It points out that people have a better understanding of what makes them tick than the sociologists who study them. This isn't to negate the importance of sociology as a discipline. Far from it. The task of sociology is to discover the theories people have in their heads rather than to invent theories that 'know better'. People aren't rocks or pieces of metal. They have opinions and they attach meanings to things. They have subjective (i.e. personal) outlooks that are worthy of study. Social scientists who insist it isn't the task of science to consider subjective matters are wrong at worse and imperious at best! Getting in touch with the subjective states of other people, requires empathy, the skill of stepping into other people's shoes and understanding things as they understand them. As will be seen in the next chapter, this often leads social constructionists to use intuitive research methods: analysing personal documents like autobiographies, diaries and letters; 'interviewing' people in an informal, conversational style; and observing people up close.

EXAM TIPS

- Whenever possible, make it clear to the examiner that you're aware of the distinction between being 'moderately' and 'very' social constructionist.
- In exam questions on sociology and science, point out that ethnomethodologists and phenomenologists are usually far less sympathetic to the term 'social science' than are interactionists.

QUESTIONS

1. How have Weber's ideas influenced the development of social constructionist theory?
2. What is the difference between interactionist theory and ethnomethodology?
3. What is meant by the claim that people attach meanings to social life?
4. How does social constructionist theory address the issue of social change?
5. What are some of the main arguments for and against social constructionist theory?

Before concluding this chapter, it's important to emphasise that, in keeping with the AEB A-level Sociology syllabuses, we've examined the three 'main' sociological theories. This doesn't mean that some sociologists wouldn't add to the AEB's three theories. Pamela Abbott and Claire Wallace (1997) have written a whole sociology textbook that adopts a *feminist* perspective. They

SOCIAL CONSTRUCTIONIST THEORY

FOR

+ While structural sociologists properly point to the endurance of 'structure', social constructionist sociologists show us that there are fragments of the social world which people are able to purposively construct. Some parts of our life (for example, encounters with powerful institutions) are to a large extent governed by structure. Other parts (for example, choice of entertainment) involve a considerable amount of personal goal-directed behaviour. These 'other parts' are the ones where social constructionist theory comes into its own. Without its emphasis on the challenges and the possibilities of human agency, sociology would surely exaggerate the extent to which 'society is destiny'.
+ As will be seen in ensuing chapters, 'labelling theory' is one of the most influential insights in modern sociology. Among the sociologists who use it are: the interactionist David Hargreaves (1976), who highlighted the self-fulfilling effects of positive and negative labelling on student behaviour in a secondary school; Stanley Cohen (1973), who showed how negative labelling can give some young people a 'bad reputation'; and Greg Philo of the Glasgow University Media Group (1995), who found how the mass media fuelled popular support for the Falklands/Malvinos War (1982) by describing Argentinean casualties in matter-of-fact language and British casualties in heroic and tragic terms.
+ It cautions against treating human social behaviour as though it were the same as natural scientific behaviour. While most structural sociologists are, these days, inclined to agree with this, social constructionists place more emphasis on the distinction between social and natural phenomena. Their main point is that humans are live, sentient, wilful beings, which isn't the case with chemicals in test tubes. Therefore, to understand people, empathy offers more valid insights than 'hard science'. Indeed, empathy is the best way to comprehend the human condition because it enables the sociologist to step into the shoes of the people she or he studies. Science might be high-powered and glamorous, but what counts is fitness for purpose, not image. If scientific methods are appropriate (for example, measuring the extent of poverty), most social constructionists – especially interactionists – aren't against their use in sociology. Where, however, intuitive human skills enable sociologists to 'tell it like it is' (for example, capturing the experience of being poor), they must be the methods of first choice. It's only among ethnomethodologists and phenomenologists that one is likely to encounter a blanket hostility towards the notion of 'social *science*'.

AGAINST

– Some versions of social constructionist theory, notably, ethnomethodology and phenomenology, push the capacity of humans to shape social life too far. They underestimate the impact of social structure on people's lives. Take poverty, for example. Old people on low fixed-income pensions have little option but to accept what institutions like government and social security decide they're legally entitled to. The extent to which people can make decisions having major consequences often has more to do with structure than with individual freedom. Thus, for example, members of the upper class can 'work the system' because they occupy or have privileged access to the major command posts – politics, the law, business, etc. – in the social structure.
– Its emphasis on the self-fulfilling nature of labelling (for example, 'Call me a thief, and I'll act as one') makes some of its proposals over-deterministic. By that, we mean that it portrays human social behaviour as over-determined by the opinions of others. This objection causes a great deal of embarrassment to social constructionist theorists because they're more used to accusing structural sociologists of being over-deterministic than of being charged with the same 'offence'. Being fair though, some sociologists who employ social constructionist insights (for example, the marxist-cum-social constructionist, Paul Willis 1978) claim that certain individuals fiercely resist and repudiate the negative labelling of their character and actions.
– Its antipathy towards 'hard science' as the norm for sociological inquiry leaves it open to the charge that its own assertions are merely informed opinions. If, as structural sociologists argue, science is the best kind of knowledge we have, opting for an unscientific approach is heading in the wrong direction. In science, conflicting claims to truth are settled on the basis of evidence. In extreme versions of social constructionism, it becomes impossible to adjudicate in these disputes because opinion counts for more than evidence. Moreover, one opinion is just about as good as any other if evidence isn't summoned. One is therefore inclined to ask of some ethnomethodologists and phenomenologists why we should take their opinions more seriously than anyone else's.

rightly point out that much contemporary sociology is 'malestream' in orientation – by which they mean that issues are often looked at from a male viewpoint. Feminist theory draws quite heavily on conflict and social constructionist theories, especially in relation to confrontations between female aspirations and male power structures, and to the negative labelling of 'feminine' gender roles. Abbott and Wallace's important work is considered in Chapter 7.

Then there are sociologists whose orientation is described as *postmodern*. They question the *modern world* privileging of the scientific outlook, arguing that all kinds of viewpoint are important and valuable. There are clear parallels here with ethnomethodology and phenomenology. There are 'out-and-out' postmodernists, like the French sociologist, Jean Baudrillard, whose critique of America (1993) was described by the *New York Times Book Review* as, 'A mixture of crazy notions and dead-on insights'. There are also 'selective postmodernists', like the British sociologist, Paul Willis, who doesn't knock 'modern' ways of looking at things, but urges us to take other viewpoints equally seriously. Willis (1990) intimates, for example, that twentieth-century conceptions of 'art' don't just have to be informed by nineteenth-century picture gallery art forms. Postmodernism is examined in Chapter 6.

Concluding remarks

Sociological theories help sociologists to understand and explain human social behaviour. Not content with basing arguments on hearsay and half-truth, sociologists test their hunches against the evidence, and build theories that honestly and faithfully describe what *is* rather than what *might be*. Some sociologists – notably, those of a structural orientation – claim that the best theories are based on scientific investigations. Others – mainly, ones who favour a social constructionist perspective – argue that empathy is as good as, and sometimes better than, science as a means of generating valid theories.

Occasionally, structural sociologists and social constructionist sociologists argue over how best to grasp the essential 'reality' of the social world. Structural theorists see, well, 'structure', where social constructionist theorists see 'human agency'. But are these differences reconcilable? We think, as do most sociologists these days, that they are. For any theory of society that focuses either on 'structure' (society as a shaping force) or 'human agency' (individuals as the shapers) is incomplete. Although much of his sociology is structural, Karl Marx acknowledged this important fact when he pointed out that people make history in circumstances not of their own choosing.

CRIT THINK CRIT THINK CRIT THINK CRIT THINK CRIT THINK CRIT THINK

USING THEORY TO UNDERSTAND THE MACABRE

The following extract is adapted from Daniel Goldhagen's account of the 'holocaust'.

'Captain Wolfgang Hoffman, a Police Battalion Commander, was a zealous executioner of Jews. He and his fellow officers led their men in the slaughter of tens of thousands of Jewish children, women and men in Poland. Yet this same man, whose conception of Jews as persons (humans would not likely be his word of choice) not deserving life, once stridently disobeyed an order from a superior officer that conflicted with his own sense of morality. The order commanded that members of his company should sign a declaration that they would not steal from Polish people. Hoffman was enraged by this effrontery. He wrote back pointing out that since his men were decent German soldiers, instilled with proper values and abiding by German norms of conduct, there was no need for them to sign this declaration. He added, in defiant tone, that, "As an officer I regret . . . that I must set my view against that of the battalion commander and am not able to carry out the order, since I feel injured in my sense of honor. I must decline to sign a general declaration."

The letter is astonishing and instructive. The genocidal murderer's honour was wounded. Clearly his conception of a German's obligations to the so-called 'sub-human' Poles was measurably much greater than that for 'inhuman' Jews. His judgement of his men was that they acted as killers of Jews with willing assent, from a conviction borne of commonly held inner beliefs.'

(Adapted from Goldhagen 1996:3)

How do functionalist theory, conflict theory and social constructionist theory all help to explain the macabre behaviours described in the passage?

CRIT THINK CRIT THINK CRIT THINK CRIT THINK CRIT THINK CRIT THINK CRIT

The three main sociological theories – functionalist theory, conflict theory, and social constructionist theory – all contribute to our better understanding of how human social behaviour is formed. Sometimes this behaviour is compassionate and decent, as, for example, when rescue workers risk their lives to save victims of earthquakes and other disasters. Other times, the behaviour is brutal and callous, as, for example, when German soldiers murdered Jews in the Second World War.

We hope you found that each of the three main sociological theories helped you to understand the events described in the Crit Think exercise. It's unlikely and, perhaps undesirable, that sociology will one day develop a unified theory of society. A more realistic and, arguably, a better goal is to develop good *theories* that don't contradict or confront each other, but which work together to find reliable and valid answers to lots of different questions.

Glossary of key terms

Conflict theory A sociological theory, substantially influenced by the writings of Karl Marx, and based on the perspective that human social behaviour is largely characterised by conflict between people who oppress and people who are oppressed

Consensus theory A sociological theory based on the perspective that human social behaviour is largely what most people agree it to be. This consensus promotes – but doesn't always guarantee – behaviours that are deemed to serve useful functions; also commonly called functionalist theory

Empirical evidence Data that are known and confirmed by the senses (for example, observation, smell, touch)

Ethnomethodology/Phenomenology Largely interchangeable theories that are profoundly social constructionist in orientation. Ethnomethodologists and phenomenologists claim that society isn't some real, 'out there' thing. People construct their own versions of society in their heads, and their actions are based on those constructions

Functionalist theory *see* Consensus theory

Human social behaviour Behaviour that occurs when human beings interact with each other (for example, collective worship, night clubbing); also called social action

Hypothesis An educated guess that needs to be tested against empirical evidence

Institution A grouping – large or small (such as family or school) – where established values and prescribed norms are clearly defined and endure

Interactionist theory A moderate version of social constructionist theory based on the perspective that people shape and are shaped by society

Norms Human social behaviours based on values (for example, showing tolerance)

Science Knowledge that's based on the reliable and valid analysis of empirical evidence

Social constuctionist theories Sociological theories that envisage society as more constructed by people than as something that shapes them

Socialisation The process, from birth onwards, whereby individuals learn and – in most cases – comply with the norms and values of society

Society A very large grouping of institutions, typically existing within a geographical boundary called a country

Structural theories Sociological theories that envisage society as a structure of institutions which exercise powerful influences on the ways people think and behave

Structuration theory Developed by Anthony Giddens, this theory develops Karl Marx's claim that people are both shaped by and shapers of social structure

Theory A systematic body of knowledge that has been repeatedly supported by empirical evidence; a collection of hypotheses that have 'graduated'

Values Things that people consider important or good (for example, liberty)

References

Abbott, Pamela and Wallace, Claire (1997) *An Introduction to Sociology: Feminist Perspectives,* Second Edition. London: Routledge

Baudrillard, Jean (1993) *America*. London: Verso

Bottomore, Tom and Rubel, Maximilien (eds) (1975) *Karl Marx: Selected Writings*, Second Edition. Harmondsworth: Penguin

Cohen, Stanley (1973) *Folk Devils and Moral Panics*. St Albans: Paladin

Eisenstadt, Shmuel N. (1964) Social change, differentiation and evolution, pp 711–29, in Coser, Lewis A. and Rosenberg, Bernard (eds) (1969) *Sociological Theory*, Third Edition. London: Macmillan

Davis, Kingsley and Moore, Wilbert (1945) Some principles of stratification, pp 24–9, *American Sociological Review*, Vol. X, No. 2, April

Durkheim, Emile (1964) *The Division of Labor in Society*. New York: The Free Press

Garfinkel, Harold (1967) *Studies in Ethnomethodology*. Englewood Cliffs, New Jersey: Prentice-Hall

Hargreaves, David H. (1976) *Social Relations in a Secondary School*. London: Routledge & Kegan Paul

Lee, David and Newby, Howard (1986) *The Problem of Sociology*. London: Hutchinson

Giddens, Anthony (1984) *The Constitution of Society*. Cambridge: Polity Press

Goldhagen, Daniel Jonah (1996) *Hitler's Willing Executioners*. London: Little, Brown and Company

Marx, Karl (1965) *The German Ideology*. London: Lawrence & Wishart

Marx, Karl (1971) *Revolution and Counter Revolution*. London: Unwin Books

Parsons, Talcott (1964) *The Social System*. New York: Free Press

Parsons, Talcott (1967) *Sociological Theory and Modern Society*. New York: The Free Press

Philo, Greg (ed.) (1995) *Glasgow Media Group Reader*, Volume 2. London: Routledge

Weber, Max (1974) *The Protestant Ethic and the Spirit of Capitalism*. London: Unwin University Books

Willis, Paul (1978) *Learning to Labour: How Working-Class Kids Get Working-Class Jobs*. Farnborough, Hants: Saxon House
Willis, Paul (1990) *Moving Culture*. London: Calouste Gulbenkian Foundation

Exam practice

Specimen exam questions for Theory and Methods appear at the end of Chapter 5, Sociological Methods, page 109.

5 Sociological methods

Topics covered in this chapter

- *Choosing the right tool for the right job*
- *Sociology: Science or something different?*
- *Theories and methods*
- *Can and should sociology be value-free?*
- *Choice of topic*
- *Choice of method(s)*
- *Conduct of research*
- *Social policy: Social science in applied form*
- *Methods in social science*

How would you respond if we told you that the reason it rains is that a giant in the sky has a bath now and then, and that the water overflows from her tub? You might say that only children would believe such stories. But if we asked you to disprove our assertion, you'd need to come up with a *method* that could do this. You might suggest that we take a plane ride when it's raining, and check if we can see a giant in a tub. If we don't see a giant, then you've used a method – observation – that shows our claim to be false. It's also possible to use methods to prove an argument is true. If, for example, you say that rain is caused by certain types of cloud formation, you might prove your point by getting us to observe rain clouds during that plane ride. You'd convince us even more that our *subjective* opinion was rebutted by *objective* evidence if you took us on several plane rides above rain clouds with no giant in a tub in sight. When methods are repeated and an assertion is continually confirmed by the same result, the assertion becomes *reliable* and *scientific*.

This chapter examines and evaluates the main methods that are used by sociologists when they investigate society. There aren't any giants in the sky for them to observe, but there are plenty of interesting things to study. Yet to study society isn't enough. Most sociologists believe that the findings of sociological inquiry should be used to make society a better and a more just place in which to live. The application of sociological and other social scientific knowledge for the benefit of society is called *social policy.* And since effective social policy relies on rigorous social scientific methods, it too is a subject for consideration in this chapter.

Choosing the right tool for the right job

You don't need a sledge hammer to crack a walnut, as the saying goes. A simple nutcracker will do the job. There are parallels in sociology. We don't take a fixed-response questionnaire to a case study of battered women living in 'safe houses'. Informal interviews

Saying that one of these bands is better than the other is a subjective statement, in this case, a matter of personal taste.

conducted by compassionate female interviewers would be more appropriate. The methods sociologists use to understand and explain human social behaviour, as well as to make some informed suggestions about social policy, distinguish it from common sense and hearsay. For its methods appeal to *empirical* evidence (things that can be observed rather than simply conjectured), and, in that respect, come back with tried and tested findings. That's why many, probably most, sociologists describe their discipline as a social *science*. By this, they mean that it takes an objective look at social life, keeping, as far as is possible, subjective thoughts out of the research process. Those two terms, 'objective' and 'subjective', are so important to the discussion that follows that it's helpful to define them as clearly as possible:

- To be *objective* means to produce findings that are knowable through empirical evidence.
- To be *subjective* means to make assertions that might or might not become knowable through empirical evidence.

It's very important to recognise that a subjective assertion isn't necessarily wrong. It just hasn't been tested. In that sense, it can be a hypothetical ('I think') belief that may or not be amenable to scientific testing. Among the 'may nots' are statements like 'The band Oasis are better than the band Blur' (that's purely subjective and can't, nor should it attempt, to 'graduate' to objective knowledge). The 'might bes' include assertions like 'Most Britons have a strong sense of their social class position.' It's an interesting proposition, but it must be corroborated or disconfirmed by empirical evidence.

Sociology: Science or something different?

Now there's a tough question. Before we try to answer it, we must first define what we mean by 'science'. Most scientists would probably say that *science is the description and explanation of objective reality*. Perhaps, more modestly, they'd claim that science is the best kind of knowledge we can know. These definitions assume a *realist stance* – that there is an objective reality that exists independently of what our own personal opinions might be. The two key themes here are 'objectivity' and 'autonomy': science explores a discoverable external reality that exists on its own terms. It can't be understood on the basis of *subjective interpretation* because reality exists solely on the basis of how the world is, not by dint of what you or I might think it to be. This all sounds very complex stuff. So what are those who call themselves scientists really saying? Essentially, they're claiming that science is based on the testing of hypotheses (intelligent hunches) against empirical evidence (what we find, through our senses, in the real world). Anything less than this, for a scientist, is inadmissible.

What we study in this real world – chemistry, economics, psychology, sociology, and so on – becomes scientific only when scientific methods are used. In other words, it's not what you study but *how* you study it that defines science. That said, it's helpful and important to make a distinction between natural science and social science.

Natural science

Natural science is the empirical study of the natural or physical world. Its main sub-disciplines are biology, chemistry and physics. Natural scientists study living and non-living matter, so don't imagine that rocks and test-tube chemicals are their only interests. Nevertheless, natural scientists tend to focus on those aspects of life behaviour that aren't usually conscious (for example, how the kidneys function, rather than how the self interacts with others). This division shouldn't, of course, be overstated. Both natural and social scientists are interested, for example, in the ways in which the brain physically processes social experiences.

Natural science provides explanations of how real-world events happen. Ask a natural scientist why the sky is blue on a clear day, and she or he will give an explanation that begins with 'because' (i.e. the cause of that is . . .):

because *the air molecules absorb all frequencies of visible light, apart from frequencies in the blue spectrum.*

Here we have a *cause and effect* explanation of the observed behaviour of air molecules in the sky. The cause is the why (because . . .); the effect is the outcome (i.e. us seeing the sky as blue). In science, the cause is commonly referred to as the *independent variable* (the thing that does the causing, for example, sitting in the sun), and the effect (the thing that is the outcome, for example, getting sunburnt) is known as the *dependent variable*. Try to remember those two terms.

You might, of course, ask the scientist to justify cause and effect explanations. In that case, she or he will refer you to a large amount of empirical evidence containing little or no disconfirming data. And if that doesn't convince you, our scientist will set up an experiment to prove her or his point. Of course, the scientist will expect you to accept that there is an objective reality 'out there' which is discoverable by the application of scientific methods. If you don't accept that premise, then, say scientists, you'll remain in the realm of the vaguely felt: a universe where anything goes, and all explanations are equally convincing. In such a universe, I could tell you that I'm the man in the moon, and you wouldn't be able to prove otherwise. Truth would be what anyone claims it to be, and no one would have to prove their case. That's why science comes to the rescue, for it alone offers acceptable evidence that can be observed, checked and verified.

Consider these two competing explanations of a real-world event:

- Water boils at 100°C at sea level because at that temperature the thermal motion (heat-generated movement) of the water molecules overcomes the external atmospheric pressure.
- Water boils at 100°C at sea level because at that temperature the water molecules decide that it's time to have a cup of tea.

The first explanation is scientific – it can be proven experimentally. The second explanation isn't scientific – it can't be proven experimentally.

OVER TO YOU

Give a scientific and a non-scientific explanation of why water freezes at 0°C at sea level.

The experiment is the favoured method of the natural scientist because it helps to show that one thing causes something else. For example, if a scientist *hypothesises* (thinks it likely; from the Greek verb meaning to think) that a certain type of solution causes iron to remain rust-free, in contrast to iron not so treated, she could carry out this experiment:

1. Get 20 pieces of rust-free iron in 10 cm by 5 cm rectangles, each 2 cm thick.
2. Place ten of the pieces of iron in a solution that is hypothesised to prevent rusting, removing them after 15 minutes. These ten pieces are called the *experimental group*.
3. Leave the other ten pieces of iron untreated. These ten pieces are called the *control group*.
4. Apart from the fact that one group is treated and the other untreated, ensure that all other conditions for the two groups stay exactly the same for two weeks: same level of humidity, same temperature, etc.
5. Check the experimental and control groups for rust. If the pieces of iron that were treated are rust-free and the untreated pieces have rusted, it can be inferred that the hypothesis is supported and that the solution has caused the pieces in the experimental group to remain rust-free. If there aren't any significant differences between the experimental and the control groups, then the hypothesis is unsupported.
6. If the hypothesis is supported, conduct the same experiment several times again, and if the results are always the same, this means that the hypothesis graduates to become a reliable proof (i.e. something that is confirmed through replication). If the hypothesis is unsupported the first time round, and subsequent experiments don't yield conclusive differences in rusting, then it can't be inferred that the solution prevents rusting.

The steps identified above represent, in simplified form, the most common form of natural scientific method. The next thing to consider is whether those steps, in different contexts (for example, the study of suicide rates rather than rusting), can be carried out by social scientists. If we consider the hypothesis that suicide-prone young males are less likely to commit suicide when they receive treatment than when they don't, this might be tested experimentally as follows:

1 Get 20 young males, all of whom are the same age and all of whom are prone, based on similar psychological profiles, to commit suicide.
2 Provide the first ten individuals with therapeutic intervention in the form of counselling and medication for one year. This is the experimental group.
3 Do nothing for the other ten individuals over the next year. This is the control group.
4 Apart from the provision of therapy for the experimental group and no intervention for the control group, try to keep all other factors in their lives as far as possible the same.
5 After one year, measure the suicide rate for both groups. If the suicide rate is significantly lower for the experimental group than for the control group, then it can be inferred that the hypothesis is supported and that therapeutic intervention has caused fewer males to commit suicide in the experimental group than in the control group. If there aren't any significant differences between the experimental and the control groups, then the hypothesis is unsupported.
6 If the hypothesis is supported, conduct the same experiment several times again, and if the results are always the same, this means that a reliable proof is established. If the hypothesis is unsupported in the initial instance, and subsequent experiments don't yield conclusive differences in suicide rates rate, then it can't be inferred that therapeutic intervention reduces the risk of suicide.

We hope, as you've been reading the 'suicide experiment' that thoughts like 'They can't be serious', 'Surely this is unethical', and 'You can't play with people's lives in this way', have been running through you mind. And, of course, we would entirely agree with such sentiments. Not only would the experiment be unethical, it wouldn't be appropriate to the reality of the human social world that we inhabit. How, for example, would it be possible to find 20 individuals with identical psychological profiles, or to ensure that, apart from the inclusion or exclusion of therapy, all other lived experiences would be the same during the coming year? Our reply is that these things wouldn't be possible. Is it conceivable to fit the complexities of authentic social experience into the limiting boundaries of a contrived experiment? We don't think so. These are issues that will be considered in more detail later under 'Experiments' (page 104).

Another important difference between natural and social scientific phenomena, is the extent to which their manifestation is influenced by particular contexts. While, for example, the temperature at which water boils is determined by its height relative to sea level (a contextual factor), when water boils it exhibits physical characteristics (emission of steam, scalding to the touch, etc.) that are recognisable in all cases (a non-contextual, or universal factor). Such isn't often the case with human social behaviour. How people behave is, to a large extent, contingent on social contexts. True, there are 'universals', like reflex blinking when a bee heads straight at your eyeball, but, in other respects, we are what our socialisation makes us. For example, a clinician who is unfamiliar with an individual's cultural background might incorrectly define as mental illness those normal variations in behaviour that are acceptable in this individual's society. For someone to say that they've seen a dead relative would be usually diagnosed as a form of psychotic mental disorder. But in some cultures, such an assertion might be regarded as acceptable and normal. There's the difference between the science of sociology and the science of the natural world: in the first, contexts must nearly always be taken into account; in the second, some phenomena are the same wherever they occur.

But don't think we're saying that sociology isn't a real science. What we're suggesting is that sociology is a social science, not a natural science. The methods of the sociologist are, because of what she or he studies, different in many important respects to those of the biologist, the chemist and the physicist. On a broader canvas, however, most scientists – social and natural – are committed to the objective pursuit of knowledge and to the discovery of 'cause and effect' relationships. In seeking to achieve these goals, they both know that methods must match the issues under investigation.

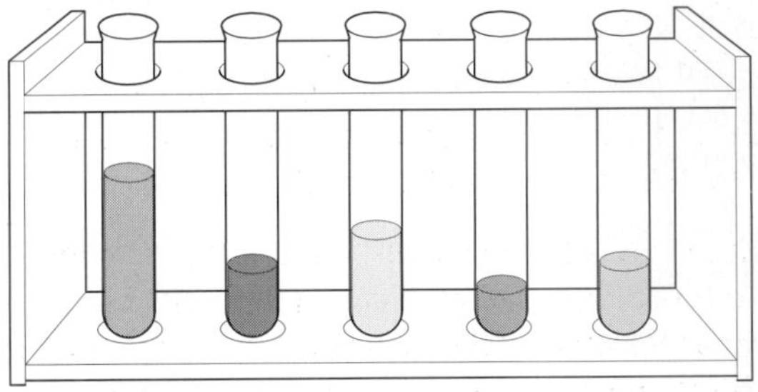

Science isn't just about what you find in test tubes. It's how people study, not what they study, that makes them scientists.

CRIT THINK CRIT THINK CRIT THINK CRIT THINK CRIT THINK CRIT THINK

A SOCIOLOGIST RECEIVES THE AMERICAN NATIONAL MEDAL OF SCIENCE

The recognition that sociology is a science gained considerable momentum in 1994 when the sociologist, Robert Merton, received America's highest scientific honour, the National Medal of Science. Read the extract below, which describes this important event:

'On 19 December 1994, eight of America's most brilliant scientists were en route to the White House where they were to receive from President Clinton the nation's top accolade for scientific achievement: The National Medal of Science. There were two biologists, two chemists, two physicists, a mathematician and a sociologist. During the journey, the sociologist, Robert Merton, commented on the sociologically predictable character of their behaviour. This, told in his own words, is what transpired:

> I remarked to my fellow medalists, "You remember that Newton thought of time as *quantitatively* and uniformly flowing. And he thought of space as absolute. Well, we sociologists think of time and space in terms of *qualitative* social time and social space. And those different kinds of social spaces lead people to engage in different behaviors. Notice, for example, how your behavior has been changing as we approach the sacred symbolic space of the White House, almost as though you were approaching a cathedral. Your voices have become more muted and your pace of walking has slowed." I got no further because one of my companions interrupted: "By God, you're right. That's just what we've been doing! We've been treating this as sacred ground."'

(Adapted from Schultz 1995)

Robert Merton's case that natural science deals with quantitative data and social science deals with qualitative data is put in fairly complex language.

1 Try to tease out the essence of his argument.

2 Is it appropriate that a sociologist should receive a National Medal of Science?

CRIT THINK CRIT THINK CRIT THINK CRIT THINK CRIT THINK CRIT THINK CRIT

Social science

Social science is the empirical study of the social or behavioural world. Its main sub-disciplines are economics, psychology and sociology. The distinctions made above shouldn't be pushed too far. There is overlap. For example, natural science isn't just about inanimate objects and animal behaviour. Biologists study human brains, chemists study the influence of drugs on human behaviour, and physicists study the physical aspects of human perception. Nevertheless, social scientists generally explain social behaviour on the basis of other social phenomena. For instance, your social behaviour in a classroom could affect the social behaviour of your peers. Similarly, the social behaviour of individuals is, in part, influenced by the social groups to which they belong and by the social conditions that impinge upon them.

In those contexts, sociologists might, for example, investigate the interplay of ethnicity, middle-class position and life chances upon the behaviour of African–Caribbean barristers. Being black could mean strong identification with a distinctive ethnic culture, and also the experience of discrimination; being upper middle-class (as barristers clearly are) has probably involved an immersion, through professional socialisation, into 'white upper middle-class' values. A sociologist might hypothesise that, owing to the social forces impinging upon them, black barristers are more likely than black manual workers to adopt the mannerisms at work of their white professional peers.

Using appropriate social scientific methods – a combination of interviews and observation of black barristers and black manual workers – it becomes possible to test this hypothesis against empirical evidence. If the investigation supports the hypothesis, further research can be conducted to see if the results are confirmed beyond one case study. If there is confirmation, it's important to realise that these social scientific findings are likely to be more tentative than the findings reported in the natural scientific world. People aren't as predictable as non-human animals and inanimate materials. Nesting birds, for example, exhibit pre-programmed nest-building behaviours that, once identified, are known to be repeatable. Acids are chemicals that have very distinctive and replicable properties. But with humans, the best we can do is to anticipate what kinds of social context typically generate certain behaviours.

We know from empirical research, for example, that being disabled in the UK is an accurate predictor of poverty, and that being a black male in the USA carries a heightened risk of suffering death by gunshot wound. However, we are talking the language of 'likelihoods' and 'increased chances' rather than certainties and '99 per cent probabilities'. Social science has human social behaviour as its field of study, not birds or chemicals in a laboratory. Social scientists present their best evidence of cause and effect, but they can't categorically say that 'A causes B'. That's why sociologists are obliged to remove 'law-like' statements from their scientific vocabulary. For to speak of scientific laws of human social behaviour, is to exaggerate the claims of sociology, as well as to deny the capacity of people to shape their own history. And here's where the sparks really fly in the debate about whether sociology is a science. On the one side, are the positivists who claim it is; on the other side, are the interpretivists who (well, at least most of them!) say it's not.

Positivists and interpretivists

Positivists believe that it's possible to discover regularities in social phenomena, and to predict these regularities with scientific rigour. For example, high levels of unemployment have been found to be associated with increased rates of property crime. Tell a positivist the unemployment rate and some other important details (for example, whether there's a strong social welfare safety net), and she or he will be well placed to make some reliable measurements of crime trends. To jog your memory, the word, 'positivist' was coined by the French philosopher, Auguste Comte (see Chapter 1, page 2). Positivists use scientific methods to study 'positive phenomena' (namely, things that can be discovered through the use of our senses, or, put another way, empirical data).

Interpretivists take a different view of things. According to them, social phenomena exist on the sufferance of wilful individuals. There are no unyielding rules or laws here. People socially construct the world in which they live. For example, interpretivists are likely to question the argument that high levels of unemployment necessarily lead to increased crime rates. They don't accept that official statistics should always be taken at face value because figures, say interpretivists, reveal as much, if not more, about the perceptions of the people who compile them as they do about the things they supposedly measure. How unemployment is interpreted in a society (does it, for example, include women who do unwaged work as mothers, but who don't enter paid employment?) affects what comes to be reported as being out of work.

Some interpretivists reject the view that sociology is or should be a science, preferring instead to see it as an almost journalistic, sometimes even a literary, humanities subject. But not all interpretivists go down this road. For example, the interpretivist sociologist, Laud Humphreys – whose ethnographic (a 'going native', observational method) study of homosexual behaviour is examined in some detail later (page 97) – described himself as a scientist.

Much of the debate between positivists and interpretivists centres around the issues of subjectivity, objectivity and value-freedom. For positivists, objectivity is the goal of social science, even though it's accepted that total objectivity is almost impossible to achieve. Better, however, to be as objective as possible than being a long way from it, say the positivists. This means minimising subjective intimations and trying hard to avoid the distorting intrusions of value-judgements. Some positivists would go so far as to say that sociologists are pure scientists who should confine themselves solely to reporting what is, not what ought to be. This rather orthodox positivist position holds that:

- sociology should strive to be value-free, which means that sociologists should adhere to the principle of value-neutrality, disengaging subjective opinion, and personal convictions from their research
- value-judgements should be reserved for social policy-makers, philosophers and moralists.

At the other extreme, sociologists who adopt a strongly interpretivist position argue that:

- value-neutrality is unattainable and undesirable. Sociologists should disclose their inevitable biases openly and honestly
- sociologists should use their knowledge to make society a better place.

Between these two positions, many positivists and interpretivists adopt a more conciliatory view, accepting that keeping one's personal values on the back-burner (value-neutrality) should generally apply to the research process, but not to what should be done, in an applied sense, thereafter. We agree with that position. Who's got it right: the positivists or the interpretivists?, you might reasonably ask. That's for you to make a judgement on, but heed the following exam tip.

> **EXAM TIP**
>
> Positivism, like functionalism, has sometimes been construed as the 'bad guy' defending a rearguard action against a 'knight in shining armour' called interpretivism. This is an unfortunate and an inaccurate portrayal. Being a positivist or an interpretivist at heart – or perhaps a bit of both – is fine, provided you apply your preferred method appropriately, and that you argue your position sociologically.

Most sociologists have a leaning towards either positivism or interpretivism, but most of them also believe that sociology needs both approaches. That said, it's helpful to consider the arguments for and against the view that sociology is a science, and to acknowledge that the strongest proponents of the 'for' view are nearly always positivists, and that the proponents of the 'against' view are most often interpretivists.

On balance, and here is where we, the writers, stand:

- Positivism, provided it recognises the important differences between the natural and social worlds, is a good methodological orientation. It rightly argues that anything short of empirical evidence isn't admissible for sociologists. Otherwise, assertions become subjective opinions rather than objectively verifiable facts
- Interpretivism correctly reminds sociologists that human social behaviour can't be accurately measured with the same tools as those of the natural scientist. Unlike rocks and reflex actions, people have opinions and they talk back. To get deeper insights into the human social condition, we need to cultivate empathy, thereby acknowledging that sociologists don't always know better than the people they study
- The best sociology is one that selects from the best features of the above perspectives rather than adopting an 'either/or' position. This doesn't imply some 'wishy washy' compromise. It means using positivistic methods when things can be measured in a conventional scientific way (for example, the statistical correlation between social class and infant mortality rates), and interpretivistic methods when it's necessary to 'reach the parts' statistics don't reach (for example, the feeling of what it's like to be a member of a gang). Sometimes it's a good idea to integrate positivistic and interpretivistic methods, as for example, did R. Emerson Dobash and Russell P. Dobash (1979) in their study, *Violence Against Wives*. The precipitating events leading to assaults on wives by their male partners were quantifiable (for example, a wife doing something that made a male partner think she might be seeing another man *commonly* led to an assault). At the same

SOCIOLOGY IS A SCIENCE

FOR

+ Human social behaviour is patterned and predictable, thereby being very amenable to scientific study. Most social behaviours are learnt and repeated in familiar contexts, and this measure of 'order' means that sociology can and should be scientific.
+ What counts, as far as evidence is concerned, isn't the intuitive, subjective feelings of the people sociologists study, but the sharply honed, objective scientific skills of the professional social scientist.
+ If sociology's claim to have privileged knowledge about society is to be accepted, it must support its assertions with reliable, scientific evidence. Through its rigorous use of quantitative methods, this allows other social scientists to conduct repeat 'tests', thereby making objective arbitration the judge of its assertions.
+ Social science appeals to reason, not ideology or personal experiences. In that sense, 'favourite' beliefs and anecdotal hunches don't figure in the systematic and public accumulation of empirical evidence of the scientific sociologist.
+ Scientific sociology is a powerful reminder that 'common sense' and 'homespun wisdom', though alluring, don't offer an accurate set of systematic criteria (i.e. empirical methods) for adjudicating between rival claims to truth about the nature of society. Your 'common sense' might be right, but until proven so, it remains untested opinion. Sociology is different: it bases its assertions on a rational appeal to impartial evidence.

AGAINST

– Much of what sociology studies, is insufficiently common to be described in the language of law-like scientific regularity. Human social behaviour isn't predictable: anything can happen because people are wilful. Moreover, positivism hasn't always been able to produce the triumph of prediction that it has promised.
– How people perceive, make sense of and socially construct their experiences and their shaping of society, is precisely what sociologists need to understand. People know better about what 'makes them tick' than professional sociologists, so empathy rather than objective detachment is the proper goal.
– Advocates of sociology as a science act as though they have privileged access to knowledge, whereas, in reality (literally!), the multiple complexities of the social world require lots of different ways of looking and understanding.
– Scientific sociology, say some feminists, is a male preoccupation. It promotes a 'masculine' ideology: keeping a distance between observer and observed, and treating subjective issues as though they were outside the realm of hard scientific inquiry.
– Positivists are guilty of 'physics envy': they want the social world to be mathematically structured and scientifically measurable because then they can be like 'real' scientists. Note though that modern-day positivists rebut this charge, arguing that they use 'social', not 'natural' scientific methods.

time, the women's perceptions of living with a male assailant, provided illuminative, qualitative insights into that very painful experience.

In summary, sociologists who, like Dobash and Dobash, use a 'mixed toolbag approach' (or 'triangulation', as it's sometimes awkwardly termed) get a multi-faceted anchorage on what they study. That said, there are times when one tool does the job better than two. For example, a study of the distribution of income and wealth is best conducted using positivistic methods. What we need to know here can only be discovered using quantitative, scientific measures. By contrast, an investigation into what it feels like to be on the receiving end of homophobic discrimination requires interpretivistic methods that allow those who are discriminated against to tell their story. Human language rather than raw statistics has much more resonance here.

QUESTIONS

1 Define 'objectivity' and 'subjectivity', and give examples of three objective and three subjective statements, explaining your choices on sociological grounds.
2 Compare (i.e. identify similarities between) and contrast (i.e. identify differences between) the characteristics of natural science and social science.

> ***EXAM TIP***
>
> Show the examiner you know that science has more to do with *how something is studied* than whether what's studied is a natural or a social phenomenon.

Theories and methods

In Chapter 4, you read about sociological theories. By way of a memory jog, you'll recall that there are two general perspectives in sociology, each of which contain two main theories. These are:

- *structural perspective* (main theories: consensus/functionalist and conflict/generally marxist)
- *social constructionist perspective* (main theories: interactionism, ethnomethodology and phenomenology).

The theory that a sociologist adopts reveals something of the way she or he looks at the social world. Sociologists who define that world as an objective, 'out-there', shaping environment, are often functionalists or marxists. Sociologists who regard the social world as an 'in the eyes of the beholders', negotiated, shaped as much – if not more than – shaping environment, are usually interactionists or ethnomethodologists. Given that people choose tools that the environment they work with requires, it's understandable that there's a relationship between theories and methods. In that context, functionalists and marxists tend to favour hard-cutting, number-crunching methods, while interactionists and ethnomethodologists often prefer intuitive, qualitative methods. Surveys and 'experiments' are typically used by structuralists, as is the quantitative content analysis of existing sources. Social constructionists often prefer participant observation and in-depth – almost conversational – interviews. They also employ content analysis, but are more concerned with letting the content tell its own story than with the extraction of mathematical patterns.

Structural theories and positivism

At the heart of structural theories of human social behaviour lies the belief that the basis for truth must be found through scientific methods. It's not what people believe about how they behave that explains their behaviour, it's how they've been shaped by social phenomena that is the underlying cause. Here, functionalist and marxist theorists are in agreement, and here they reveal their positivistic orientations. For both believe that how people behave is caused by the social forces that impinge upon them. Functionalists point, for example, to the moulding function of schooling on the beliefs and actions of students, noting how this social force tends to bind people to common values. Marxists acknowledge the same process, even though, unlike some functionalists, they locate the origins of 'educational socialisation' in the attempts of upper-class people to control the hearts and minds of their 'subordinates'.

It's commonly stated that marxists also differ from their structural cousins, the functionalists, because they recognise (and applaud!) the fact that human beings sometimes stand up to the social forces that make them what they are. Perhaps the most famous expression of this is Karl Marx's assertion that people make their history, but not in circumstances of their own choosing. But, while marxists probably place more emphasis on the struggles between human agency (i.e. 'free will') and the social forces that constrain us, it's important to recognise that even the most ardent of twentieth-century functionalists, Talcott Parsons, recognised that some people (for example, artists) resist the social structures that otherwise limit their hopes and desires.

Structural theorists argue that individuals aren't born ready to participate in society. On the contrary, they're born into an already existing culture. As they grow, they begin to internalise the rules of the particular culture(s) which they share with other human beings. We're not talking instinct here, but learning. Human beings have no instincts that prepare them to be members of a social class, followers of particular styles of music, speakers of Japanese, lawyers, plumbers, firefighters. This isn't to say that our 'biologies' and our 'sociologies' don't bounce off each other. They do. It's very likely, for example, that the psychological and social processes involved in learning our native language actually change the biological structure of our brain. Take the Japanese language, for example. Japanese adults can't distinguish between the sounds of the letters 'l' and 'r'. Yet all babies, worldwide (including Japanese babies), can tell these sounds apart. Therefore, if Japanese adults cease to be able to make this distinction, then the brains of Japanese-speaking adults probably differ from the brains of non-Japanese speaking adults. It's up to biologists and other natural scientists to try to identify and measure what these probable physiological differences are. Similarly, it's up to sociologists and other social scientists to seek to locate and to ascertain the impact of social forces on the language we speak and come to know.

Sociological research into language acquisition has revealed, for example, that working-class children are less likely than middle-class children to speak in an abstract, 'intellectual' manner. This has nothing whatsoever to do with instincts, but everything to do with the way they're brought up. Moreover, how these children speak has consequences for their future life chances. The linguistic 'cultural capital' of middle-class children is more highly valued by selective schools and universities than the language of working-class children. This explains, in part, why proportionately fewer working-class than middle-class children go to university. And here we encounter the structural sociologist's interest in measurement. To what extent is language use affected by the social class to which one belongs? How, in turn, are different language uses likely to influence one's chances of entering higher education, becoming a member of a profession, earning a good income, etc? These are the kind of questions positivists like to ask, to research and to measure.

The accent and dialect that this child will eventually acquire will be more contingent on social than on biological factors.

Because structural sociologists regard the process of socialisation as an amalgam of social forces by which all of us, in varying degrees, are shaped, they use methods that seek to measure the relationship between these forces and the way people behave. Measurement requires precision and clarity, and a structured research tool. In the questionnaire, for example, a method frequently used by 'structural/positivistic' sociologists, great care is taken to ensure that the questions are unambiguous, that they encourage or require standardised responses, and that the resulting data is amenable to quantification (for example, *95 per cent of the respondents* reported that they *strongly support* the right of citizens to have access to official data about their personal lives). Just as a natural scientist takes a thermometer to a substance and records the result, so does a social scientist take a questionnaire to a respondent and measures the outcome. But instead of coming back with a temperature reading, the sociologist returns with reliable knowledge of the respondent's true opinion. She or he might also seek to explain a strongly held conviction on the basis of its association with other variables (for example, the age, ethnicity, sex, and social class of the respondent).

Given, for example, that black people in the UK encounter discrimination more often than white people in the criminal justice system (see Chapter 16), a sociologist might hypothesise that black Britons are more likely than white Britons to fear the police. This hypothesis could be tested against empirical evidence by interviewing representative samples of black and white Britons in the UK. One of the questions asked of respondents might be:

> Do you worry about being stopped by the police for no good reason?
> A lot [ ]
> Sometimes [ ]
> Rarely [ ]
> Never [ ]

If research shows that significantly more black than white people reply, 'A lot', then we can infer that there is a *causal relationship* between being black and being afraid of the police. We can proceed to study the origins of this fear in the prior experiences and the socialisation patterns of black people. Once again, we're looking at *cause and effect relationships* – television portrayals of white police officers and black youths 'cause' young black people to become wary of the police, etc. As you can see, if your theoretical outlook disposes you to see people's attitudes and behaviour as being shaped by social phenomena, it's very likely that you'll adopt a method or methods that are designed to measure (often in statistical terms) the relationship between the 'shaper' and the 'shaped'.

Because structural sociologists believe that all of us face an external world of brute social facts that can't be negotiated away in some social constructionist imagining, they regard social facts as real, and as understood to be real by both the sociologist and the researcher. In that respect, when a respondent says she or he worries a lot about being stopped by the police, the structural sociologist accepts this reply as a literal fact rather than something that might contain some hidden meaning to be teased out through interpretivist methods. Moreover, the structural sociologist accepts that the extent of this fear can be scaled, as in the fixed-response options contained in the question above.

This statistical representation of human social characteristics makes social constructionists recoil in horror. For, unlike structural theorists, they don't believe in an external, 'out there', social world whose nature is amenable to quantifiable measurements. Rather, social constructionists adopt the interpretivist view that the social world we inhabit is what we define it to be. Gone is the notion that the task of sociology is to measure something that lies above and beyond what people believe to be real. Sociologists need to concern themselves with empathy instead of objectivity. It's getting on the same wavelength of those whom they study and reporting what they find on this wavelength faithfully, that sociologists must do, say the social constructionists.

Social constructionist theory and interpretivism

Social constructionist theorists repudiate the positivistic view that the social world is a predictable universe where human social behaviour is patterned and generalisable. Instead, they argue that it's very difficult, perhaps impossible, to discover 'laws' of human social behaviour. Some social constructionists (notably, ethnomethodologists and phenomenologists) claim that all human social behaviour is 'situated' and 'unique'. By this, they mean that what people do is 'determined' by each particular situation they find themselves in, and, therefore a series of 'one-off', singular events. This invalidates structured research methods (notably questionnaires) because people might think and do one thing today and something completely different tomorrow. Turning people's opinions and behaviours into operational categories, like 'strongly agrees' and 'votes Labour', yields only a partial – and possibly, a distorted – reading of the issues under investigation. Better to go for a qualitative approach to data collection, letting the received information tell its own story. This is why social constructionists often quote large verbatim chunks of respondents' dialogue instead of turning what people say into tables and graphs. In that respect, they believe that qualitative data puts the human detail and the texture back into sociological research.

Not surprisingly, given their theoretical belief that social life is tentative and negotiable rather than 'permanent' and structured, social constructionists prefer methods that enable sociologists to obtain intuitive understandings of the things they study. In that context, participant observation, whereby the sociologist steps into the shoes of the observed by doing what they do, as well as watching them, is prized by social constructionists. This relinquishing of the 'not-getting-involved', detached researcher role, commonly associated with positivistic methods, tells us that the 'interpretivist-social constructionist' doesn't claim access to privileged scientific knowledge. Indeed, she or he admits to an inherent lack of certainty about being able to accurately explain social phenomena. The best that sociologists can do is to seek to experience the social world of those whom they observe, and to thereby share knowledge of it. 'Telling it like it is' is the byword of these sociologists, which is why they prefer qualitative accounts to number-crunching methods.

But what is a qualitative account? Sometimes the words we use make it difficult to understand what we're trying to convey. For some readers, the word 'qualitative' might conjure up the notion of something that is 'high quality'. No doubt, all sociologists, however, would like to think that the data they produce – whether qualitative or quantitative – is high quality stuff! What qualitative means, in a sociological sense, is that the 'inherent essence' (i.e. the 'authentic quality') of social phenomena is captured in the concepts and terms that sociologists use to describe them. So instead of placing the anxiety experienced by a battered wife on a mathematical scale, I let her actual words and her facial expressions convey their 'authentic quality' by letting you hear and see what she has to say and how she says it on a videoed interview.

Where the structural sociologist sees an ordered world of predictable regularities, the social constructionist sees an underlying disarray and a wide range of behaviours that can't be foreseen. It's therefore of little or no concern if the sociologist uses methods that can't be replicated and tested by other sociologists to check their reliability. For each and every study is a 'case study', and the only thing which counts is that what is found is faithfully recorded and reported. Some commentators would argue that *validity* (using methods that accurately capture what they set out to obtain) is more important to social constructionists than *reliability* (using methods that allow repeat tests to be conducted). This view is, however, a simplification. For one thing, 'validity' isn't the sole preserve of either interpretivists or positivists. It would be as invalid, for example, to report infant mortality rates in qualitative terms as it would to quantify an Irish person's description of how it feels to suffer discrimination in the UK.

Validity says much more about using the right tool for the right job than it does about anything else. As for reliability, in the strict sense of being able to check an assertion by running the same test as the first researcher, the quantitative sociologists, arguably, have the upper hand. Nevertheless, it is possible to conduct repeat ethnographic studies of, for example, a local community. Provided such studies are conducted within an approximately similar time frame, and provided the ethnographers use the same kinds of method, then *qualitative reliability* is attainable. For ethnographers can and do produce qualitative categories that are comparable: 'tightly-knit communities', 'rural lifestyles', 'fatalistic orientations', etc.

They're also able to spell out what these words mean, so that other researchers can compare like with like in a meaningful kind of way. Of course, the purists among the interpretivists and social constructionists would argue that these words and elaborations might mean different things to different people, and aren't really comparable. That said, the 'not quite so purists' would probably concede that the categorisations of a particular community, provided they're carefully defined, do convey a common knowledge of its inherent nature. The assumption here is that identical words can mean the same things to different people. It's an assumption that's more likely to be held by an interactionist than an ethnomethodologist or a phenomenologist, because the first is not so far along the social constructionist continuum as the other two.

Although structural theorists tend to favour quantitative methods and social constructionists often prefer qualitative methods, such distinctions shouldn't be over-stated. For most sociologists, whatever their theoretical preference, use multiple methods. Even so, structural sociologists pack more quantitative instruments into their admittedly mixed toolbag, and social constructionists carry more qualitative instruments when they do their work. There are times, however, when qualitative and quantitative data just emerge as research proceeds, without this being anticipated by a particular theoretical orientation. Consider the positivist who wants to measure the impact of social class on health, and finds, during her pilot (testing the water) structured interviews that some respondents say much more than her pre-empted tick boxes ever contemplated. Faced, for example, with the question:

> How many days have you had off sick from work over the past year?
> None [ ]
> 1–4 [ ]
> 5–9 [ ]
> 10–15 [ ]
> 16–20 [ ]
> 21 or more [ ]

a respondent might reply:

> 'None of those numbers fit my experiences. I often do my work from home if I don't feel up to going into the office – and I don't count that as "being off sick". Perhaps my boss, though, looks at matters differently. Who knows?'

Think too of the interpretivist who, in an ethnographic study of men's locker room cultures, finds that some of the 'just watch and listen' techniques reveal quantifiable themes. It might be that talking about women takes up most of the time, with cars coming in a close second. If that's the case, we're already into quantification. So whatever their theoretical leanings, sometimes sociologists have just got to let the data show itself before deciding whether to make sense of it in a quantitative, a qualitative way, or a quantitative and a qualitative way. Increasingly, it seems, structural and social constructionist sociologists appear to be doing exactly that. We think this is good news.

Generational change

	% women uneducated	
	Aged 45–49	**Aged 20–24**
Sudan	86	42

Sometimes the quantitative and qualitative flavours of human social experience can be captured in the way in which social scientists present their data. This is illustrated in this extract from a UNICEF publication, which imparts both statistical and real 'flesh and blood' characteristics.

(UNICEF 1995: 43)

QUESTIONS

1 Why do social constructionists tend to prefer qualitative research methods, and why do structural sociologists tend to prefer quantitative research methods?
2 Why does the above question contain the word 'tend' two times?

> ***EXAM TIP***
>
> Avoid making the over-generalised assertion that positivists only use quantitative methods and interpretivists only use qualitative methods.

Can and should sociology be value-free?

What does it mean to be value-free? It means not to let personal values, however worthy they might be, get in the way of an objective evaluation of the evidence. In that respect, it's rather like not being subjective. However, a subjective statement might or might not contain a value. For example, the subjective opinion that Beethoven was a better composer than Mozart displays a clear value-judgement. Such is not the case, though, in the subjective hunch that a new medication might cure duodenal ulcers. Values imply personal preferences and/or moral commitments. And, unless one adopts the view that humans are robots, it must be accepted that sociology and sociologists can't be completely value-free. This doesn't mean that sociology can't be objective, for, as Max Weber rightly asserts: 'An attitude of moral indifference has no connection with scientific objectivity' (cited by Lee and Newby 1986: 172).

Nor can natural science distance itself from value-judgements. Nor should it! A physicist makes a value-judgement, for example, when she chooses to specialise in cosmic physics instead of another area. So does a biologist, when he researches eagles rather than seaweed. Both scientists *value* one field of study over another. So it is too with the social scientist who undertakes a participant observation study of religious cults in preference to a content analysis of men's magazines. Put simply, what a scientist, of the natural or social world, chooses to study is itself to exercise a value-judgement.

But what happens once this selection has been made? Do scientists then bring value-judgements into their investigation of scientific phenomena? They probably do, but it's important that they try their very best to minimise such intrusions. For at the investigative stage, it's essential to be as detached and as objective as is humanly possible. The crucial goal here is to limit the intrusion of values into scientific analysis. Once that analysis has started, values become an encumbrance to objective research, and they must therefore be vigorously discarded. Imagine, for example, that you're a feminist social scientist who is studying the extent, if at all, to which the 'glass ceiling effect' hampers the promotion prospects of female officers in the Police Force. You've made a value-judgement already by making this issue a subject worthy of study. However, now you've got to study the facts dispassionately, and to report what you find openly and honestly.

Let's pretend that you don't find evidence to support the hypothesis that the West Yorkshire Police Force discriminates against its female officers. If that's the case, you mustn't cook the books by falsifying the evidence in line with what you might expect to find, but actually haven't. To resist that temptation is, of course, very difficult and, because you're only human, some biased observations (for example, 'seeing' sexist behaviour when it isn't really present) might creep into the proceedings. However, if you're a good social scientist, such bias will be minimal and it mustn't be conscious. Otherwise, the value-neutrality that is so vital to objective social scientific research will be seriously compromised, and your findings will be gravely flawed. As the marxist sociologist, John Westergaard, pointedly puts it: 'Priorities in social science cannot be free of influence from value judgements, though the latter must then be tamed by respect for facts' (Westergaard 1995: 11).

We're not suggesting that the 'glass ceiling' does or doesn't hold back talented female officers in the Police Force. The simple truth is that we don't know. What we are saying, however, is that although the selection of a research issue rightly involves the making of a value-judgement, once the study is up and running, values must be put to one side. Value-neutrality makes for the best scientific research. For the intensity of a conviction that your original hypothesis is true has no bearing whatsoever on whether it's found to be true.

So how can you stop your values from confounding your scientific rigour? You must report only *what you find*, not what you might want to find or assume is the case.

For an exponent of scientific sociology, this means:

- being rigorous in the adherence to strict, exact procedures (for example, using a fixed-response, quantifiable questionnaire)
- regarding only those facts which accord with or 'fit' reality as valid (i.e. truthfully reflecting what's there).

For an interpretivist sociologist, this means:

- letting things unfold: going with the flow rather than adhering to systematic rules of scientific procedure
- being more concerned with capturing the 'lived experiences' of the observed than with assuming there exists an 'out-there' reality. Validity, say interpretivists, is being able to tell things like they are, empathetically

(i.e. portraying the perceptions of the people who are observed).

Not needing to re-visit ground that's already been covered in detail, we reiterate, concisely, what we said earlier: the scientific (essentially positivistic) and the interpretivist approaches provide, in combination, a more rounded and therefore a more accurate reading of the situation than either approach does on its own. We don't play favourite to any one particular method here.

And so, finally, having considered the stages of selection of topic to study and the conducting of the research, we arrive at the third and final stage: what to do with our findings. There are lots of things that can be done here, but all necessarily involve making a value-judgement. This also holds true for those social scientists who might decide that it's not their job to take matters any further, perhaps handing their data over to inspectors of prisons, politicians, trade union officials, etc. For the very act of deciding not to follow through one's research personally in an applied sense is the exercising of a value-judgement. However, when social scientists want to use the knowledge they have discovered, these are some of the more important options:

- extending the frontiers of knowledge in order to foster intellectual understanding in its own right (for example, finding interpretivist insights in the works of a renowned sociologist who has hitherto been regarded as a strict positivist)
- verifying, falsifying, modifying or discovering a theory (for example, discovering a theory that convincingly unites individual behaviour with social structure)
- solving social problems (for example, implementing a school buildings programme that's designed to meet the needs and the rights of students and staff who are disabled)
- identifying and extending examples of best practice (for example, finding types of non-custodial regime that are more effective than imprisonment in reducing the risk of re-offending, and applying these insights widely).

OVER TO YOU

Find other examples of 'applied sociology' for each of the above options.

These and other applications of sociological knowledge aren't necessarily mutually exclusive. They can and do occur simultaneously. For example, making more use of non-custodial sentencing might reduce the social problem of burglary. What is important to recognise is that the uses to which sociological knowledge are put are linked to the values of particular sociologists. Those of a conservative disposition, for example, might undertake research that helps politicians who favour traditional methods of teaching in schools. Those who are in sociology to make lots of money might sell their research on consumer preferences to advertisers. Those who take an option for the poor and oppressed in society might investigate ways of reducing poverty and democratising decision-making in local communities.

QUESTIONS

1 To what extent, if at all, is it possible for sociology to be value-free?
2 Compare and contrast the relationship between values and research in the natural and the social sciences.

Choice of topic

What a sociologist chooses to study is influenced by a range of considerations. Among the more notable are:

- what the sociologist considers is worthy of researching
- who the funder of the research is
- the extent to which researching a particular issue, irrespective of its inherent value, might advance the professional career of a sociologist.

Taking the matters of worthiness, funding and career aspirations in turn, consider these examples.

The Japanese sociologist, Kazuko Ohtsu, has chosen to study the economic and social aspects of the banana trade between the Philippines and Japan because it's a trade that highlights the huge inequalities between a poor and a rich country. Moreover, she's written a book for Japanese high school students that gets them to reflect on the ethics of this trade, in the hope that they'll become principled consumers who buy fairly-traded rather than market-priced fruit. Fair trade means that the poor farmers who grow bananas in the Philippines become a little more prosperous than if their produce is sold to transnational corporations who are more interested in big bucks than social justice. Ohtsu has made a value-judgement: the banana trade is worthy of study because the injustices that it throws into relief might prompt tomorrow's consumers to buy fairly traded fruit.

On the matter of funding, we'll turn to the USA for our illustrative example. Criminological research there receives generous federal support, but the government has a say in which projects get funded. Eric Dowdy (1994) notes that federal funding is more likely to support studies that have an individual rather than a structural focus. For example, studies that relate individual family circumstances to delinquent behaviour (for example, delinquent children from lone-parent families) will probably attract federal dollars. However, research that highlights the potentially damaging effects of unemployment on levels of crime will have less chance of government backing. A big danger here is that biased government funding can distort the very realities social scientists need to study. In that context, models of 'knowledge' that fit the agendas of funding agencies can usurp the important quest for empirical evidence.

As for how choice of research topic might be linked to furthering one's own professional ambitions, it would be churlish to name sociologists who study issues less out of interest than out of a desire to pursue their own careers. But it would be naive to think that there aren't sociologists who do just that. When, for example, a particular subject is in vogue (for example, ethnomethodology was a hugely popular issue in the 1970s, as is postmodernism in the 1990s), it pays – literally – to get on the research and publishing bandwagon. Lucrative academic posts and publisher royalties are widely sought prizes, and those who want to obtain them are sometimes likely to place the current concerns of academics before other considerations. One sure-fire winner is to become an expert in so-called 'defence' matters. Arms dealers and governments are lining up to promote the professional careers of both social and natural scientists who can deliver in this area. Providing the military with research-led guidance on how to persuade soldiers to kill when under fire (many are reluctant to kill the 'enemy'), or to increase the 'kill potential' of high-tech rifles are examples that come to mind.

Natural scientists have chosen to engage in research that increases the technological kill potential of this soldier. Would it be ethical for social scientists to unravel his childhood socialisation, and persuade him that using his formidable armoury on another human being is ethically acceptable?

Choice of method(s)

In an earlier section, we examined the relationship between the theoretical approaches of sociologists and the methods they use in their investigation of society. Besides theoretical considerations, there are other factors that influence choice of methods. Among the more important are:

- *The funding body may decide what methods are to be used*. For example, in the criminological research it funds, the UK Home Office seems especially fond of large-scale, quantitative surveys. This might be because it's keen to monitor research into crime prevention strategies, like the effectiveness of close circuit television (cctv) in car parks. The monitoring of this and other crime prevention measures is heavily reliant on statistical analysis (for example, the decline in car theft after the implementation of cctv).
- *Costs and time factors are important considerations*. Postal questionnaires, for example, are usually cheaper and faster than interviews. On the other hand, if time and money are available in abundance, sociologists might, for example, use longitudinal surveys and interviews (for example, studying the lives of ex-prisoners over a number of years, interviewing them on a half-yearly basis).
- *Whether or not existing data is available*. Why engage in extensive field investigations if the data you want to collect has already been collected by someone else? If, however, what's available is insufficient or irrelevant, sociologists will have to carry out primary research, namely, the deployment of pro-active methods, like questionnaires and interviews.
- *The kinds of issue to be investigated*. For example, a postal questionnaire would be an insensitive and an inappropriate method for investigating the effects of bereavement on surviving spouses. A more humane and a more effective method would be a 'conversational interview'. Similarly, the use of participant observation to obtain reliable information on the number of women who are university professors would be unsuitable.

Conduct of research

How sociologists carry out research is governed by a number of important principles. In the UK, for example, the British Sociological Association (BSA) has its own code of practice for the researching sociologist – the Statement of Ethical Practice. This is referred to in Chapter 3, which deals with how to conduct research as an optional part

Funding bodies (for example, the governments of these two African presidents) sometimes decide which methods are used in social scientific research.

of the A-level Sociology exam. Even if you don't take the coursework option paper, please read the BSA statement because it contains much that is relevant to this section – factors influencing the carrying out of research. One of the provisions is:

'Sociologists have a responsibility to ensure that the physical, social and psychological well-being of research participants is not adversely affected by research.'

So no tricks or shocks that cause distress and consternation, please! Such an admonition is well-received by most sociologists. However, some are prepared, where public interest demands otherwise (for example, the exposure of corrupt practices), to let this obligation weigh less heavily on their research considerations.

To some extent, the choice of a method and the choice of how to conduct research overlap. For example, the ethical objection against deception might prompt you not to choose covert participant observation, and not to conduct research if the freely-given permission of those who are studied hasn't be sought. That said, the conducting of research is more about the execution of a method than the decision to choose it. So our focus here will be on the factors that affect the doing part rather than the choice of method. We'll begin with ethical issues before moving on to practical considerations.

The matter of whether it's morally acceptable to lie to respondents or to deceive them is vexed. Most sociologists, we think, are opposed to lies and deception. Not only is such conduct intrinsically wrong in a moral sense, it's also likely to undermine public trust in social science. As Alex Thio puts it:

'Suspecting social scientists of being tricksters, subjects may lie to the researcher, pretend to be naive, or do what they think the investigator expects them to do. If deception escalates, we may reach a point where we no longer have naive subjects, but only naive researchers, cranking out bogus data.'

(Thio 1989: 47)

There's also the important consideration that unethical practices during the conduct of research might do harm to the respondents. In that context, a famous (some would say infamous!) study by the social psychologist, Stanley Milgram (1974), deserves mention. Milgram told his respondents that he was conducting tests on the effects of punishment on learning. He lied. He was actually carrying out research on obedience to authority. After asking each of the respondents to assist in the research by adopting the role of 'teacher', Milgram introduced him or her to another alleged respondent who was playing the role of 'student'. In reality, the 'student' was Milgram's research associate.

Then Milgram instructed the teacher to punish the student with an electric shock each time the student gave the wrong answer to a question. Whenever the teacher obeyed this command by pressing the electric shock button, the teacher heard the student screaming in pain. Of course, this was faked, for no real electric shock was actually administered, and the screams were also faked. Nevertheless, the teachers were led to believe that everything they did and heard were real. In response to this incorrect but felt assumption, the teachers sweated, trembled and showed other signs of stress when 'punishing' the student. Despite this, a large majority continued to follow Milgram's orders. This led Milgram to conclude that ordinary people will follow inhuman orders if they believe they come from a legitimate authority – much in the way that German concentration camp guards committed atrocities against Jews, disabled people, homosexuals and socialists when they were told to do so by their leaders. But were these German people merely following orders, as Milgram's thesis might suggest? 'No!', says the American historian, Daniel Goldhagen (1996), who, on the basis of extensive – mainly document analysis – research, concludes that the tens of thousands of ordinary Germans, who willingly and zealously murdered Jews, did so out of racist hatred.

Whatever the merits of Goldhagen's passionately argued case, we can still probably learn a lot from Milgram's research. There are some people who do what they're told to do, even when they know it's wrong. If our aim is to stop this from happening, we can encourage our children, through schooling and other means, that it's never right to do what's obviously wrong, whoever gives the order. To be sure, that inner strength would be difficult to instil, given that brave individuals who put principle above instructions from above often seem to be in short supply. Nevertheless, the decision to make human rights education a part of every student's schooling would surely be a noble goal. Indeed, it's a principle already advocated by the Council of Europe (Ian Lister 1984). But is it ethically right to come to this knowledge by using unethical and potentially harmful forms of research conduct? Lies and deception aside, imagine, for example, the stress that the respondents suffered during the research. Some actually pleaded with Milgram to let them stop administering 'electric shocks', but still they were told to continue. Imagine too how the respondents who didn't refuse to carry out the 'punishments' (the vast majority) must have felt when they afterwards found out the truth of the research – pretty low, we suspect!

Another ethically controversial piece of research was conducted by the social psychologist, Philip Zimbardo (1972). He set up a mock prison in a university basement. Then he recruited student volunteers to take part in a research project on the effects of imprisonment. Some of them were told to play the role of prison guards, and the others of prisoners. After only six days, Zimbardo had to call a halt to proceedings. The 'guards' had become very cruel, and the 'prisoners' had become so depressed that they would have become mentally ill had they not been 'released'. There wasn't any deception here – all respondents knew that the whole exercise was a fake – but some of the guards turned into sadists, and some of the prisoners reached psychological breaking point. While Zimbardo's work warns us not to be complacent about the potential cruelty that exists in the 'normal, average person', people got hurt in order to make this point.

OVER TO YOU

Evaluate the ethical arguments for and against research similar to that conducted by Milgram and by Zimbardo.

There are also important practical factors that influence the conduct of social scientific research. For example, in their research into the experiences of battered women, Rebecca Dobash and Russell Dobash (1979), for ethical and practical reasons, used female interviewers. It would have been potentially very upsetting and impractical (if, for example, respondents wouldn't co-operate) to have used male interviewers when talking to women in a safe house where they were protected from male violence. Similarly, when William Labov (1969) conducted research into the speech patterns of black children from New York's Harlem district, he sensitively and sensibly used a black interviewer. In a society where white adults might frighten some black children, he made the right choice.

Another important practical consideration is gaining access to the subjects one wishes to study. When Bill Whyte (1981, first published 1943) studied a 1930s Boston slum and when Laud Humphreys (1970) investigated homosexual behaviour in 1960s USA, they both used co-operating confederates in order to enlarge their research pool. Whyte gained the confidence and the co-operation of a gang leader called 'Doc', who, in turn, introduced the sociologist as 'my friend Bill' to other members of the community. During the initial stages of his research, Humphreys told a friendly potential respondent that he was a sociologist conducting research. This calculated risk paid off. The respondent got Humphreys invited to cocktail parties before an annual 'drag ball', thereby giving him a point of entry into gay subculture.

Some social scientists take very drastic measures to ensure that their research isn't impeded by practical problems. Consider J. H. Griffin (1964), for example. He wanted to study what it felt like to be a black American on the receiving end of racial discrimination. There was, however, an important practical consideration – Griffin was white. To remedy this problem, he artificially darkened his skin and successfully passed as a black American in the Deep South state of Alabama. In this very inventive manner, Griffin was able to experience unprovoked rudeness from a female bus company ticket clerk, a 'hate stare' from a middle-aged, well-dressed white man, and a refusal to use a washroom from a custard stand owner.

It also helps if sociologists possess the practical skills of some of the people they associate with during their investigations. That's why being an accomplished jazz pianist was useful when Howard Becker studied marijuana use in jazz clubs. It was also useful that Ned Polsky was a good pool player when he conducted research into poolroom hustling. In both cases, blending into the background was superbly accomplished by the possession of these skills.

QUESTIONS

1. Give some examples of factors that affect choice of topic, method(s), and how research is conducted.
2. Examine how sociologists gain access to the research they want to carry out.

Social policy: Social science in applied form

What's the point of studying any science, natural or social, if its findings aren't put to good use? One might reasonably argue that the pursuit of knowledge is an important goal in its own right. We would agree. That said, we also believe that whenever knowledge can help us to build a better society, the opportunity should be seized upon. Sometimes mere fact-finding isn't enough. Sometimes we really do have to ask, 'Knowledge for what?' If, for example, natural scientists discover more effective ways of preventing malnutrition among children in poor countries, it would be immoral to let that knowledge lay idle. Similarly, if social scientists find more effective ways to integrate children who are disabled into mainstream schools, it's our responsibility to make that knowledge work.

This isn't just about ethics. Policy-oriented research in the social sciences makes good sense, because it provides factual data upon which policies can be more reliably formulated. Before such policies can take shape, however, it's first necessary to further our understanding of social reality so that we know what we're dealing with. If, for example, we're seeking to find ways of effectively integrating people who are disabled into mainstream society, we need to find out about the existing lay of the land. Thereafter, we will be in a better position to apply that understanding to the development of policy. In short, the rigorous investigation of the current situation must precede the issuing of guidelines for practical decision-making.

While it's true that value-judgements enter social policy decisions (for example, to prioritise poverty reduction policies rather than extra leisure centres), once such decisions have been made, the best ways to implement them can and should be determined scientifically. This requires the sociologist to judge dispassionately which of several alternative strategies of achieving specific goals is likely to be the most appropriate and the most effective.

Consider, for example, our example above about integrating children who are disabled into mainstream schools. Suppose the local city council commissioned you and a team of social scientists – sociologists, psychologists, economists, etc. – to make this begin to happen in a particular local education authority area.

Your task is likely to be costed and time-framed, so account must be taken of budget and schedule. You'll also need to consider existing arrangements. Do the current mainstream schools have building design features (wide doors, lifts, etc.) that would enable children who use wheelchairs to enjoy unimpeded mobility, or are structural modifications required? What about learning resources? Are voice-command computers needed so that blind children can use information technology without the need for keyboards, or would the allocated money be 'better' spent on employing teacher assistants to give these children extra support? And what about in-service training for mainstream teachers who have little or no experience in working with children who have special needs? These and other important questions confront the social scientist-as-researcher, and they need to be addressed in a rational, evidence-driven, systematic manner. Even so, it's right to concede that, when faced with alternative policy options, the exercise of moral choice invariably plays some role. Imagine, for example, that you're advising health authorities on how to prioritise limited government funding for kidney transplants. Who gets a kidney and lives? Who doesn't and dies? There are medical and social considerations here, but clearly there are moral decisions to be made too.

OVER TO YOU

How would you design a research project whose aim is to investigate and provide policy directions to a local education authority which wants to 'mainstream' all special educational needs provision? Pay particular attention to the methods you would use and why.

It's now widely accepted that social science has something to offer, because scientific knowledge makes for better policy decisions. But don't think this is just a present-day view. As early as the nineteenth century, Auguste Comte envisaged sociologists providing governments with reliable social scientific knowledge that might be used to improve society. Comte and other positivists believed that the only effective way to manage social problems was to win over the social environment through the systematic application of scientific knowledge. More recently, Americans elected a president who had studied sociology – Ronald Reagan. In these instances, advocacy and precedent – for better or worse – both exist for the view that sociologists can and should occupy key policy-making roles (Paul Stephens 1996). Moreover, sociology exists on the sufferance of people in society. There must be a pay-back. Some good must flow from the discipline to society. What better way than for sociologists to advise governments and other organisations on:

- how to measure and eliminate (let's avoid the unambitious 'reduce') homelessness
- how to identify the emergence of racist, sexist, disablist and other negative '-ism' attitudes in children, and to set in motion effective interventionist policies
- how to channel overseas aid in a manner that targets the most needy among the poor of the majority world?

And one can add to the list.

OVER TO YOU

Add to the list above – think of other social problems on which sociologists could advise governments and other organisations.

While social science is superbly placed to inform and develop effective social policies, prevailing political sentiments sometimes ride roughshod over the important insights it offers. In the USA, for example, when politicians can win votes for getting tough on drugs, some of them don't want to hear that 'A dollar's worth of drug treatment is worth seven dollars spent on the most successful law-enforcement efforts to curb the use of cocaine' (Joseph Treaster 1994, cited by Jay Livingston 1996: 495). Yet this finding has been reported by Rand, a Californian research organisation that has worked closely with the US Federal Government. The organisation's research into how to curb cocaine use was partly funded by the White House. However, once the findings were published, the White House immediately rejected the main points. It would appear that some politicians don't want to endorse social scientific research proposals which support social policies that might cost them votes.

In the UK, there is evidence that politicians sometimes don't pay much attention to social scientific evidence if it points to proposals that they think might cost too much money. For example, the Black Report (1980), commissioned by a Labour Government and submitted to a new Conservative Government, found that the lower a person's social class, the less healthy the person is likely to be and the sooner she or he can expect to die. The report, which contained evidence from the sociologist, Peter Townsend, also pointed out that the children of working-class parents are at a greater risk of injury, illness and death. The general message was that the health problems of British working-class people were probably linked more to their standard of living than to what the health system could or couldn't do for them. In that context, for example, a doctor might cure a bout of food poisoning, but the problem is likely to persist if the patient is so poor that she or he returns to eating scraps from public bins.

The findings of the Black Report embarrassed a government whose policies were implicated in lowering the living standards of certain vulnerable members of society. It received a frosty reception, and the government sought to bury it. Ministers don't appear to have heeded the report's proposals, for the living standards of the very poor have continued to fall into the 1990s. But governments are prepared to act on social scientifically-generated advice that they consider 'safe'. Illustrative of this is some criminological research that was commissioned by the Home Office into prison parole decisions and undertaken by John Copas, John Ditchfield and Peter Marshall (1994). The task of these social scientists was to help prison parole boards to make 'release' or 'continued detention' decisions on the basis of statistical data. By looking at a range of factors (sex of prisoner, past 'form', etc.), the social scientists calculated the probability that particular types of prisoner would re-offend within definable time frames were they to be paroled. The object of the research, the findings of which were put into practice, was to provide parole boards with predictions of 'low risk', 'medium risk' and 'high risk' re-offence profiles.

To illustrate what has been said, here are two examples of how offender characteristics are, according to the researchers, related to re-offending probability:

- *Example 1* A male prisoner aged 20 at conviction with 13 prior convictions, of which two resulted in youth custody sentences, who is serving a sentence for theft, has a re-offending probability (for any offence) of 48 per cent within one year after discharge.

- *Example 2* A male prisoner aged 39 at conviction with no prior convictions with an offence of violence would have a re-offending probability (for any offence) of 5 per cent within one year after discharge.

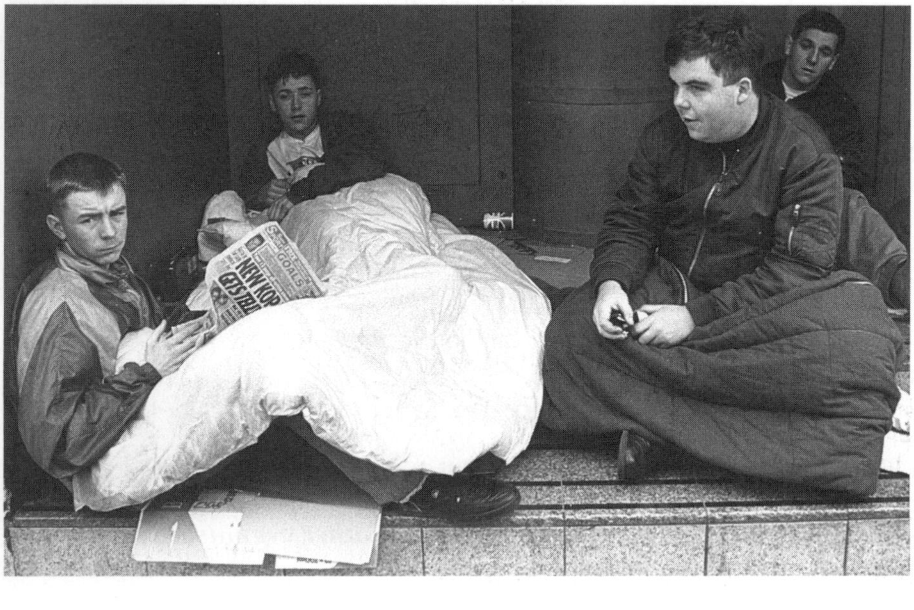

We have the social scientific knowledge to curb, perhaps even eliminate, all kinds of problem, including substance abuse and homelessness. What is more problematic is for this knowledge to be harnessed to a nation's political will.

The two examples above (extended to a two-year after-discharge period) are represented in the graph below.

QUESTION

Looking at the graph below, what's the probability of any re-offending for:

a the prisoner described in Example 1, 18 months after discharge?

b the prisoner described in Example 2, two years after discharge?

It's important to add that the above and other predictions are for the 'average' offender whose profile fits a particular category. It's recognised, of course, that each offender has additional individual characteristics that need to be taken into account by a parole board before a release or detain decision is made.

Some sociologists would argue that the kind of research described above fails to get at the root cause of why some people commit crimes in the first place, offering a 'quick-fix' rather than a longer term solution. Thus one might argue, for example, that government measures which reduce unemployment are more likely to cut overall rates of property crime than the dispensing of advice and guidance to parole boards. On the other hand, social scientists who support government policies are more sceptical of the argument that impoverished social conditions necessarily cause crime. What about the many poor people who don't turn to crime? is one retort. 'New Right' sociologists are more likely to support educational reforms that get 'back to basics' and promote the teaching of 'moral values' as panaceas against juvenile delinquency and later adult crime.

Moreover, some right-wing think tanks command considerable influence over previous Conservative policies. A key figure in that context was Sheila Lawlor, former deputy director of the Centre for Policy Studies, and, more recently, founder of another think tank, Politea. She has long influenced the teaching of subjects in schools, and supports a strong right-wing moralist agenda. The 'New Left' also has its policy think tanks. The Secretary of State for Education and Employment, for example, is mindful of the advice he receives from a team of academics and researchers headed by the social scientist, Professor Michael Barber. It's reputed too that Tony Blair sometimes heeds the wise 'counsel' of sociologist Professor Anthony Giddens, who is Director of the London School of Economics and Political Science.

On the left side of the political spectrum, one very famous sociologist who looked to social science in the pursuit of a 'better' society was Dr Martin Luther King. Having graduated in sociology at Morehouse College, Atlanta, he resolved to put his social scientific knowledge of American society to good use. While noting that African–Americans had at last been 'spared the lash of brutality and coarse degradation', Dr King also pointed out that 'the absence of brutality and unregenerate evil is not the presence of justice' (King 1969: 13). Summoning an impressive array of social statistics, he (1969) revealed that black people in 1960s USA suffered huge inequalities:

- Half of all black people lived in sub-standard housing.
- Black people had half the income of white people.
- Twice as many black people than white people were unemployed.

Probability of reoffending during specified period

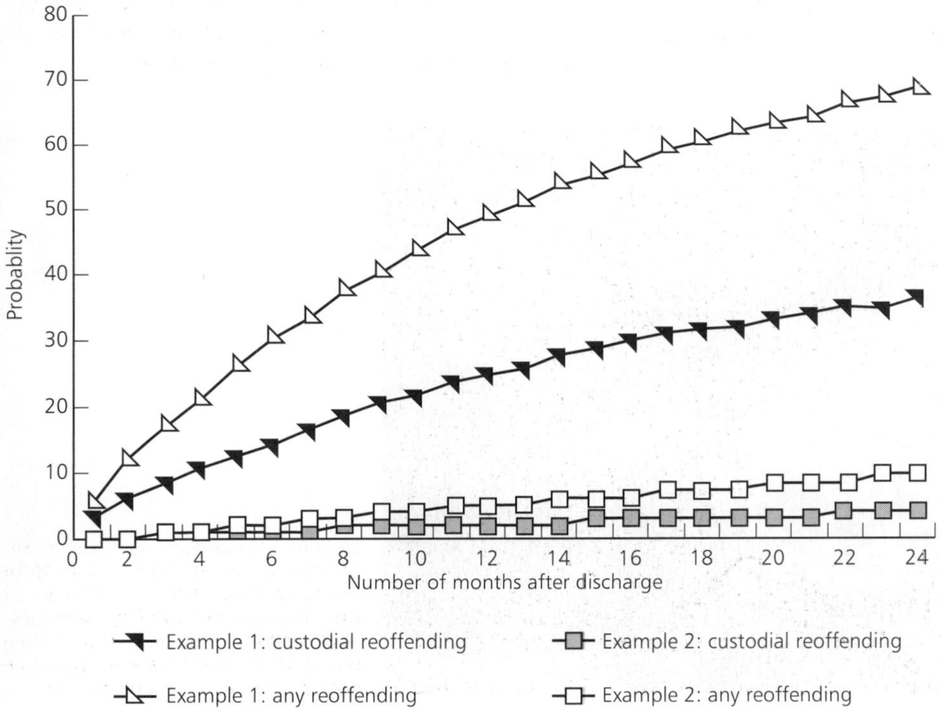

(Copas, Ditchfield and Marshall 1994: 34)

- Of employed black people, 75 per cent had menial jobs.
- The rate of infant mortality among black people was double that among white people.
- Twice as many black people were combat soldiers in Vietnam compared to white people at the beginning of 1967.

Recognising that this and other quantitative data helped to get a purchase on 'the size of the problem' (1969: 15), Dr King also acknowledged that 'The personal torment of discrimination cannot be measured on a numerical scale . . .' (1969: 17). Some of his most eloquent oratory expressed that torment, as well as his hope for a better future:

'Pity is feeling sorry for someone; empathy is feeling sorrow with someone . . . I doubt if the problems of our teeming ghettos will have a great chance to be solved until the white majority, through genuine empathy, comes to feel the ache and anguish of the Negroes' daily life.'

(King 1985: 22)

'We can never be satisfied as long as a Negro in Mississippi cannot vote and a Negro in New York believes he has nothing for which to vote.'

(King 1985: 43)

Dr King fused a sociologist's awareness of the size and dimension of a problem with a civil rights leader's resolve to put things right. For, 'Ultimately a great nation is a compassionate nation' (1969: 169–70). The solution to society's ills, claimed Dr King, was in a radical redistribution of a nation's wealth: 'True compassion is more than flinging a coin to a beggar; it understands that an edifice which produces beggars needs restructuring' (1969: 178). In that spirit, he contended that, through compassionate social policies:

'There is nothing to prevent us from paying adequate wages to school-teachers, social workers and other servants of the public to insure that we have the best available personnel in these positions which are charged with the responsibility of guiding our future generations. There is nothing but a lack of social vision to prevent us from paying an adequate wage to every American citizen whether he be a hospital worker, laundry worker, maid or day laborer. There is nothing except shortsightedness to prevent us from guaranteeing an annual minimum – and livable – income for every American family.'

(King 1969: 179)

Some 30 years on, politicians and social policymakers are implementing legally enforceable minimum wages in the European Union. It's a measure that Dr King, were he alive today, would be proud of.

EXAM TIP

We hope you've noticed that these topics – whether sociology is a science; value-freedom and value-neutrality; choice of method and topic; conduct of research; and social policy – all bounce off each other. From a revision standpoint, it's a case of 'all for one and one for all'!

Dr Martin Luther King graduated from Morehouse College, Atlanta, with a BA in Sociology, in 1948. He put his social scientific knowledge of American society to good use by identifying and tackling the roots of racism and other forms of social injustice.

QUESTIONS

1 Why does it make good sense to undertake policy-oriented social scientific research?

2 Give an example of a policy-oriented disclosure.

Methods in social science

We've said quite a lot about methods, but without going into specifics. In this section, we'll look at the principal research methods used by sociologists when they study social phenomena. There are four basic methods in sociology:

- the survey
- observation
- the analysis of existing (also called 'secondary') data
- the experiment.

We'll examine each in turn.

Surveys

Surveys are the most commonly used method of data collection in sociology. Most surveys gather information through written questions (questionnaires) and/or oral questioning (interviews). Questioning takes many forms. Among the most common are:

- self-administered questionnaires, delivered and collected personally by the sociologist
- self-administered questionnaires that are mailed to prospective respondents
- face-to-face interviews
- telephone interviews.

Contrary to the impression that some people seem to have, surveys can be quantitative, qualitative, or a combination of the two. However, it's fair to say that most surveys are largely quantitative.

Sampling

To conduct a survey, sociologists first have to select a *population* – the people they want to study. In sociology, a population doesn't have to be (nor rarely is) a national population. Generally, all populations have some things in common. For example, a population might consist of all the residents of Leeds, or all teachers in the UK, or even – in the case of the ten-yearly census – all people in the UK. It's rare though that a sociologist will approach and question all members of a given population, More usually, a *sample* of the population (a small number of people taken from the whole population) is selected. The sample, however, must be *representative*, that is, it must accurately represent the population from which it is drawn. Otherwise, the information obtained from the sample cannot be generalised to the population. Failure to ensure this could produce misleading conclusions.

Selecting a sample will never be as accurate as getting in touch with an entire population. Nevertheless, just as I might invite you to sample a piece of my pumpkin pie without expecting you to scoff the lot before you give an opinion of the pie, so might I invite you, as a school or college sociology student, to tell me how difficult or easy you find the A-level course without having to interview all A-level sociology students in the country. It's essential, though, that I make sure you and the other students I select are representative of A-level sociology students in general. It wouldn't do just to talk to the first 100 sociology students I come across. Imagine, for example, if I went to Eton public school to interview their sociology students. If 90 per cent said they found it moderately easy, could I infer that 90 per cent of A-level sociology students in the country thought the same? No, of course I couldn't, because Eton students have characteristics that are markedly different from sociology students in general (most come from very privileged social backgrounds).

If a sample is to be representative, all members of the population must have the same chance of being selected for the sample. Put another way, and in the language of social science, the selection must be *random*. That's why a representative sample is also called a *random sample*. One way to do this, would be to count and put the names of, say, all Manchester firefighters into a giant hat, 'shake it all about', and pluck out, 'at random', a 10 per cent (or whatever per cent you want) sample. Incidentally and importantly, a print-out list that contains all the names of a particular population (in this case, all Manchester firefighters) is called a *sampling frame*. Using your sampling frame, you could also do your random selection by giving each firefighter a number (say, 1, 2, 3, etc. up to the actual number of firefighters), and then 'instructing' a computer to randomly select 10 per cent of these numbers. The above sampling techniques produce what's called a *simple random sample*.

Another random sample technique is called the *systematic sample*. To select a systematic sample, you need to follow these steps:

1 Identify or construct a sampling frame. Let's stay with our Manchester firefighters, and let's pretend there are 1,000 such persons in that city.

2 Compute what's called a sampling fraction. This is the number of the sampling frame (1,000) divided by the number of the chosen sample (say, 100). In this example, the sampling fraction is 1,000 divided by 100, which equals 10.

3 Randomly select (for example, the 'numbers in a hat' method) a number between 0 and the sampling fraction, namely, between 0 and 10. Let's assume 5 is this number. Five then becomes your first number.

4 Keep adding 10 to the first number (in this example, resulting in 15, 25, 35, etc.) until you either arrive at the number that represents the size of the sampling frame (here, 1,000) or to the last number up to but not exceeding 1000 to which 10 can be added. In our firefighter sampling frame, this number would be 995.

5 The names on the sampling frame that correspond to the numbers drawn above, constitute your *systematic random sample*.

Both simple random and systematic random samples can, to use another specialist term, be stratified, thereby producing *stratified random samples*. This is sometimes done when the population in question can be divided into various strata (groups), such as females, males, people who live in towns, people who live in villages, etc. To draw a stratified random sample, you need to know what percentage of the population falls into each of the strata used. Then you must select a random sample from each strata whose number is in exactly the same proportions as in the population. Suppose we know that the population of students in a school is 52 per cent female and 48 per cent male. Then our stratified random sample should also be 52 per cent female and 48 per cent male. The strength of stratified random sampling is that it enables the sociologist to obtain a high degree of representativeness among all groups contained in a target population. In that respect, it's a reliable fine-tuning instrument.

OVER TO YOU

Select a random stratified sample of the students in your year group, for example, all Year 12 students, ensuring that your sample represents the same proportions of females and males as in the entire year group. You might, with your teacher's permission, be able to use class registers as your sampling frame. You might also, when you've read this chapter, consider asking your sample to answer a questionnaire that you've constructed (for example, a political opinion poll).

There is a variety of other types of random sample (all random samples, by the way, are also called *probability samples*). Of these, one of the most important is the *multi-stage sample*. In this method, a sequence of samples is drawn from already selected samples, but only the last sample is studied (the so-called *final stage sample*). For example, suppose you wanted to study the views of all Londoners on the hospital bed shortage in that city. You could divide the city into its different boroughs, and then randomly choose, say five suburbs in each borough. Then you might identify all the streets in each of the five suburbs, thereafter selecting five streets, at random, from all the streets. Now it's time to identify the households on each of the chosen streets. Let's say that we end up with 1,000 households. From this sample, we could select a random 10 per cent final stage sample of 100 households, and then interview everyone aged 16 and above, as appropriate, in those households.

The advantage of the multi-stage sample is that, with each successive stage, the sample becomes more specific and more relevant to the research question. For at each stage, we're ensuring that as high a representation of respondents from as many appropriate categories (in this instance, residents of different London boroughs) as possible end up in the final stage sample. This enhances representativeness.

As well as random (probability) sampling, sociologists can also employ *non-random (non-probability) sampling*. This kind of sampling doesn't – indeed, can't – claim representativeness, which is, of course, a big drawback from a scientific point of view. Nevertheless, there are circumstances when non-random sampling is the only option. If, for example, a sociologist wanted to study a sample of bank robbers, she or he is hardly going to be able to locate a suitable, ready-made sampling frame, or to construct one. Even if one were able to get hold of a list of convicted bank robbers known to the police, what about the many other ones who have never been caught, let alone convicted?

Among the more widely used non-probability sampling methods are:

- *Accidental sampling* Also known as 'grab sampling', this is when large numbers of respondents, whom the sociologist comes into contact with during a certain period, are asked to take part in a survey. The researcher might stand outside a church after Sunday service, on the pedestrian precinct of a shopping mall, in the entrance foyer of a night club, etc., and ask any number of people if they would agree to be interviewed. Sometimes certain defining characteristics will be looked for (for example, all people who appear to be aged 18–24 leaving a church after a service). Accidental samples are easy to construct, and are fine when non-representativeness isn't an issue.
- *Purposive sampling* Here, the sociologist purposely chooses people who are considered relevant to the research aim. For example, I (Stephens 1997) selected a purposive sample of secondary school student teachers whom I was supervising in order to find out, through semi-structured group interviews, how they were finding the school-based part of their professional course. My findings can't claim to be representative of student teachers in general, but they do yield suggestive insights that could lead to further research which might use representative sampling.

- *Quota sampling* A very popular technique, it's actually a type of stratified sampling. However, instead of dividing a population into strata from which a number of respondents are randomly drawn, it operates on 'quotas' that are set in advance by the researcher. Suppose, for example, I know that a company contains 520 female employees and 480 employees, I could ask a researcher to interview two quotas: any 52 females and any 48 males. That would give me a 10 per cent, non-representative, stratified sample, whose proportions of females and males are the same as in the whole company. Quota sampling is relatively inexpensive, can be completed in a fairly short time span, and is often very 'representative', even though it's not a genuinely representative technique. It's especially 'representative' in political opinion polls, when interviewers are instructed to select quotas that represent the demographics (for example, age, ethnic, sex groups, etc.) of an area or even a nation.
- *Snowball sampling* In this technique, the sociologist begins with one or a few respondents who have characteristics appropriate to the study (for example, night-club goers in Manchester), and who agree to take part in the research. These respondents are requested to ask other people (usually, their acquaintances) to join in too. If these people agree to take part, they're asked to recommend other people, and so the process gathers pace until recruits dry up or the sociologist calls a halt. This is a good method to use when there's no readily available sampling frame. It doesn't require a great deal of prior preparation, and, provided things really start rolling and get bigger (hence the snowball metaphor), it's a fairly easy way to get hold of a sizeable sample.

Having examined some of the main kinds of sampling method, it's now time to look at the two most common research tools used in surveys:

- questionnaires
- interviews.

Questionnaires

The overriding characteristic of the questionnaire is that it's offered to the respondent with minimal interference on the part of the sociologist. If, for example, you receive a mailed questionnaire asking for your views on discrimination against people who are disabled, it's quite possible that the only contact you'll have with a sociologist is via the instructions she or he includes on the questionnaire. This minimises the risk that you might, for example, give the answers you think the sociologist wants to hear if you met him or her face-to-face. The way people dress, talk, etc. can and do influence how we respond to them.

It's important to realise that issues such as content and type of questions and the response options (notably, open-ended or fixed-response) are as relevant to interviews that use questionnaires (also called structured or formal interviews) as they are to self-administered questionnaires. Some students seem to think that questionnaires aren't questionnaires if they're administered by interviewers – they are!

As far as response options are concerned, in:

- *open-ended questions*, the respondents are free to answer in their own words (for example, *What is your occupation?*, followed by empty writing space, lets the respondent reply as she or he sees fit)
- *fixed-response questions* (also called closed-ended or pre-coded questions), the respondents are expected to choose one or more, as appropriate, of the given options (for example, *Which of these categories best describes your occupational status? Circle one option: manual/professional/managerial/pensioned/student/unwaged homemaker*, restricts the respondent to a pre-specified choice range).

Each type of question has its advantages and disadvantages, summarised in the tables below and on page 90.

Advantages and disadvantages of open-ended questions

Advantages	Disadvantages
Respondents get to express their thoughts in an unimpeded manner (especially important when complex issues are involved).	Respondents sometimes drift from the issues under consideration, providing 'irrelevant' information.
Respondents are able to offer an abundance of detail.	Respondents sometimes provide huge amounts of information, which requires considerable expenditures of time and effort to interpret.
Respondents sometimes come up with thoughts that haven't been pre-empted, perhaps not even considered, by the researcher.	Respondents offer replies that can be very difficult, sometimes impossible, to codify and make statistical sense of, thereby making standardised comparisons with other respondents hard to achieve.

Advantages and disadvantages of fixed-response questions

Advantages	Disadvantages
Respondents are likely to keep on track because there's no room for drifting.	Respondents aren't allowed to digress, even if this is how they want to express their feelings.
Respondents provide the amount of information that's pre-set by the fixed response format, so the researcher can quickly and accurately make sense of the data.	Respondents aren't able to provide sufficient information because the fixed responses only permit restricted answer options.
Respondents' replies are easy to codify, quantify, and compare.	Respondents' replies are literally 'boxed in by tick boxes', thereby restricting creativity and expressiveness.

QUESTIONNAIRES

FOR

+ They're often quite inexpensive to produce and distribute (especially mailed questionnaires), and, when self-administered, interviewers aren't required – which eliminates the possibility that respondents might, for example, say what they think the interviewer wants to hear.
+ They usually produce quick results that can often be speedily and accurately interpreted using computer software. This is particularly true with fixed-response questions.
+ They provide respondents with a real sense of anonymity. Imagine how reluctant many people would understandably be to discuss intimate sexual matters in a face-to-face, or even a telephone, interview.
+ They give sociologists a consistent, stable and uniform measurement tool, thereby enhancing reliability by allowing accurate replication. For example, if I conduct a questionnaire survey of political attitudes in a local village, you can do a follow-up study in the same village using the exact same questionnaire.
+ When self-administered, they give respondents the time to ponder their replies and to give considered answers.
+ They offer the prospect of wide geographical distribution via surface, air, and electronic mail.

AGAINST

– Unless the researcher is to hand, they don't allow respondents the chance to seek immediate clarification of things that aren't understood, thereby increasing the likelihood that some questions will be guessed at or not answered.
– They don't always attract a sizeable response. This is a real problem with mailed questionnaires. Too few returns compromise representativeness on at least two counts: the sample of respondents becomes too small to generalise from, and the respondents might exhibit unrepresentative characteristics simply because, unlike the majority, they actually completed and returned the questionnaires.
– Unless the researcher watches the respondent filling in the questionnaire or fills it in on the respondent's behalf, there's no way of being certain that someone else didn't complete the questionnaire.
– They restrict respondents to the questions they contain. In that context, they sometimes say more about the issues that sociologists think are important than the priorities of the respondents. Moreover, in the case of fixed-response questions, respondents don't have the chance to elaborate on their replies.
– The filling-in of a questionnaire places the respondent in an artificial setting that is removed from her or his lived experiences.

Interviews

Together with questionnaires, interviews are the typical methods of the survey. In that usage, interviews are usually *structured*. This means that the interviewer uses a questionnaire (also called an *interview schedule*) which she or he reads out to the respondent, thereafter filling in the replies. It's a systematic approach which allows no freedom to make any adjustments or improvisations to the content, order and wording of questions. The interviewer adopts the role of a neutral collector of information. She or he adopts the same appearance, and uses the same probes and prompts, while simultaneously showing no personal interest in the research topic, when interviewing the respondents. If you wear a pair of 501 jeans and sneakers while interviewing one respondent, and a tailored skirt and court shoes while interviewing another, don't be surprised if you get replies that, in part, reflect the respondents' reactions to your appearances.

In those cases when interviews aren't used in survey research, they're commonly *unstructured*. This means that the interviewer, while normally 'guiding' the questioning towards certain issues, adopts an almost conversational approach in the ensuing discussion. There are no restrictions about the content, order or wording of questions, and much levity is granted to the interviewee to stay on or off a particular track. Nevertheless, to say an unstructured interview is totally unstructured is a bit of an exaggeration. For, if that were so, there would be total drift and no direction.

Somewhere between structured and unstructured interviews, lie *semi-structured interviews*. The degree to which these interviews are more or less structured depends on the kind of research that's being conducted, as well as on the theoretical orientation of the researcher. The well-known functionalist, R. K. Merton, was a pioneer of semi-structured interviews in the 1940s. He believed they were very helpful research tools in the study of propaganda, and in the analysis of mass communication. Some sociologists refer to semi-structured interviews as 'focused interviews'. This is because such interviews focus on specific issues, which respondents are asked to discuss. The emphasis though is on 'discuss' rather than on giving 'fixed-response replies'.

Quite often, researchers who use semi-structured interviews provide a stimulus related to an article, a film or a situation that interviewees are familiar with, and then discuss the issues with them. A good example of this is provided by the research of Philip Schlesinger, Rebecca Dobash, Russell Dobash and Kay Weaver, reported in their book, *Women Viewing Violence* (1992). Drawing upon group interviews with women who have experienced violence and women who have not, these social scientists uncovered the complex responses to television's depictions of men's violence against women. Using carefully selected programmes that include scenes of domestic and sexual violence, the research offers qualitative and quantitative analyses of how women reacted to watching this material. Here are some examples of the guiding questions that one of the interviewers used in a semi-structured group interview of women who had just watched an episode of the British soap series, *EastEnders*, in a comfortable setting provided by the researchers. The 30-minute episode included a violent domestic incident when the clenched fist of one of the characters, Matthew (a white, muscular 'Englishman') is thrust into the face of another character, Carmel (a slender woman of African–Caribbean origin).

GUIDING QUESTIONS FOR DISCUSSION

EastEnders

(i) General discussion of programme:
- immediate reactions (gauge familiarity with programme)
- perceived purpose of programme
- gratifications from programme
- entertainment values
- realism and storyline . . .

(v) Specific reactions to the violence:
- at what point did the violence begin to become apparent?
- reactions to inclusion of this violence
- what is the value, if any, of including the violence?

As you can see, part (i) is fairly open, seeking to elicit the initial reactions of the women. As the semi-structured interview proceeds, however, the discussion is intended to become more focused, guided by a series of questions (some exemplified in part [v]) that are posed by the interviewer.

Semi-structured interviews have a long pedigree in sociology, and, originally, they were often employed in group situations. These days, they're used in both group and one-to-one settings. A great advantage of the method is that it encourages the discussion to go beyond the priorities of the interviewer, thereby maximising the opportunity of obtaining information that the interviewee regards as important. However, this carries with it the risk that too much freedom might lead the interview into 'irrelevant' areas. But, then again, 'Who's to say what is and what isn't relevant?' would be the interpretivist's rejoinder! Unlike positivists, who definitely prefer more structured interviews, interpretivists argue that 'going with the flow' yields more valid (i.e. authentic, 'like it really is') data.

OVER TO YOU

Have a go at setting up a semi-structured interview on the issue of private health care, and conduct it with another student or with a teacher as the interviewee. If you prefer, conduct a group interview. If permission is given by the interviewee(s), record the interview, using an audio cassette tape recorder. Then see if you can interpret the data, by focusing on the key themes that arose during the discussion.

INTERVIEWS

FOR

+ There's usually a high return rate because the presence of an interviewer means that data is collected straightaway.
+ Respondents aren't usually required to read lengthy and sometimes complex instructions, which increase reluctance to co-operate and/or the risk of error.
+ The researcher has the chance to observe and note non-verbal cues (unless, of course, the interview is conducted on the telephone).
+ The researcher can help, by way of clarification, if the respondent doesn't understand particular questions.
+ When the order in which questions are asked is important, the interviewer can ensure that this ordering is maintained.
+ When spontaneous responses are needed, the interview fares better over the self-administered questionnaire (where pondering can occur).
+ Interviewers are normally able to ensure, in the case of structured interviews, that all the questions are addressed and answered.

AGAINST

– Interviews are often more costly and sometimes more time-consuming than other methods (for example, self-administered questionnaires).
– The presence of the interviewer can bias the responses of the interviewee. For example, respondents might seek to gain the approval of the researcher by giving answers they think she or he wants to hear.
– Interviews are sometimes unsuitable when sensitive issues are involved. For example, a respondent might prefer to fill in a questionnaire than to talk about a past criminal record. On the other hand, unstructured interviews can help some people to 'open up' when they're discussing sensitive issues.
– Interviews take place in contrived – and therefore artificial – settings. In that respect, they differ from the more natural surroundings available to the ethnographic (in the field) observer.

An example of a survey

We've looked at the two main tools of the social survey, the questionnaire and the interview. Now it's time to look, in some detail, at a real survey. That way, you'll get a much better purchase on what sociological research actually entails.

The survey in question was conducted by Von Bakanic (1995), and it investigated racial attitudes in the American Deep South. Bakanic employed structured interviews (i.e. interviewer-administered questionnaires) to a random sample of residents from two Mississippi towns: Philadelphia (not the Pennsylvania one) and Meridian. Mailed questionnaires were also used in some cases (see below). Given that Mississippi, especially in the above two communities, has a violent history of race relations, and that Deep South white Americans are generally portrayed as more racist than other white Americans, this study was particularly important. For it would either confirm that things were pretty much the same, or that the violent racist past was literally a thing of the past.

Von Bakanic and his co-researchers randomly drew 722 phone numbers from the 1988–9 phone listings for the two communities. The vast majority of Americans have telephones, so the sample was reasonably representative. In June and July of 1989, the sociologists contacted and completed 365 interviews. Three callbacks were attempted for telephone numbers that were busy or not answered. The researchers later mailed questionnaires to non-respondents. Of the 357 non-respondents, they were unable to obtain mailing addresses for 22. Moreover, 43 questionnaires were returned by the US Mail as undelivered. Another 37 questionnaires were completed and returned, but four were discarded because the respondents were minors (under 21 years old, in Mississippi). The final number of respondents was 398 – a 55 per cent return.

The main aim of the survey was to compare responses to open-ended questions on racism in Mississippi from black and white people who supported segregation (i.e. that black people should live in separate communities to white people) and from those who didn't.

Respondents were asked:

- whether they supported segregation
- whether race relations had changed in their communities
- how they perceived the treatment of black people
- how they responded to press coverage their communities had received as a result of two recent films (*Mississippi Burning*, and *Murder in Mississippi*) based on the notorious civil rights murders that occurred in Neshoba County, Mississippi, in 1964
- in more general terms, about racial attitudes, and the changes they observed in the status of black people in Mississippi and in the USA as a whole.

A comparison was also made between the attitudes of Mississippi respondents and respondents who were involved in national surveys that asked about racial attitudes.

An important goal of the research was to investigate the gap between the results of the fixed-response and the open-ended replies. The respondents were asked three fixed-response questions about racial segregation, to which they could select one of: Strongly agree, Agree, Disagree, Strongly disagree:

1. White people have a right to keep blacks out of their neighbourhoods if they want to, and blacks should respect that right.
2. Black people have a right to keep whites out of their neighbourhood if they want to, and whites should respect that right.
3. Do you think white students and black students should go to separate schools?

These three questions provided a scale of support for segregation, as indicated in the pie chart below.

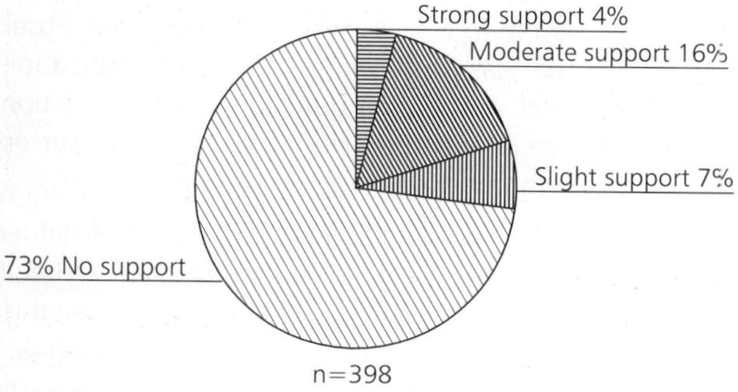

Support for segregation

(Von Bakanic 1995: 71)

As seen, the majority of respondents said they didn't support segregation. But before taking this as evidence that old-style Mississippi racism is on the wane, it's relevant to note this finding. When asked how black people were treated, 74.7 per cent of white respondents in the Mississippi sample indicated 'the same as whites', compared with 27.1 per cent of black respondents who believed they were treated 'the same as whites'. That's why it was necessary to go beyond the fixed-response data to look at what the respondents said in their own words.

Based on their replies to the fixed-response questions, the respondents were separated into four attitude groups:

- strong support for segregation (16 of 398 respondents, two of whom were black)
- moderate support (64 respondents, nine of whom were black)
- slight support (29 respondents; no information given on black/white ratio)
- no support (289 respondents, 78 of whom were black).

When asked to elaborate on their opinions, the respondents' answers often didn't address the questions they were asked. They spoke about race relations in general, but content analysis (cross-checked by different researchers, and yielding a large degree of agreement on interpretation) of the verbatim comments, revealed three major themes:

- whether to remember or suppress Mississippi's racially troubled history
- how those memories should be reconstructed
- whether changes in race relations should be encouraged or feared.

There was diversity within these three broad themes, and people didn't just fall into neat little boxes. But that's one of the strengths of open-ended questions: people express themselves more freely.

In elaborating on their replies to the earlier fixed-response questions:

- The white strong supporters tended to express concern over how their community or state was being unjustly maligned, but, curiously perhaps, there were no racist slurs or overtly racist opinions expressed by anyone. One of the black respondents chose not to comment, and the other one, elderly and disabled, expressed a wish for her 'race' to be 'left alone': 'We done suffered enough. Leave us be . . . I done seen so much that the Lord had mercy and took my eyes.'
- The white moderate supporters were mainly concerned about suppressing negative accounts of their communities' racially troubled pasts, and were worried about the impact of bad publicity. Again and again, people said that the 'truth' hadn't been told. Compared to the strong supporters, this emphasis on 'truth' was paramount. They were also more defensive than the strong supporters, and felt that somehow their views on race were in need of justification.
- The slight supporters wanted to ignore the past rather than suppress the racial strife of bygone years. Fear that trouble might be 'stirred up' was a recurrent theme. In contrast to the wary attitudes of white respondents about racial turmoil, black respondents wanted to forget.
- The non-supporters were, by far, the largest group. There were more racist terms (even though this was quite rare) among these respondents than among the supporters of segregation. There was also a great deal of diversity of opinion among the non-supporters. That said, a strong, recurring concern with the accuracy of the media portrayal of their communities and state was evident, but there was less of a readiness to regard this portrayal as completely false. Moreover, there was a willingness to learn from the mistakes of the past. Fear of racial trouble, although expressed, wasn't as frequent as among the supporters of segregation.

Opinions weren't necessarily 'liberal'. The paramount belief of black respondents was that the racial turmoil of the past should be remembered. Black respondents also had some optimism that race relations had got better and would continue to improve.

In replying to open-ended questions, Von Bakanic noted that respondents didn't appear to censor their comments nor adopt 'politically correct' attitudes for the sake of social acceptability. This contrasts with the risk, noted below, in fixed-response racial attitude surveys for people to say what they think is socially acceptable rather than what they might actually believe. Another feature of open-ended responses is that they permit respondents to give much fuller expositions of their views. In that context, it's important to note that some of the respondents who opposed segregation (as indicated in their fixed-response replies) held racially prejudiced views that were teased out when they answered open-ended questions. Nevertheless, the fixed-response data suggest a lot more tolerance these days, and Mississippians' responses are similar to those reported in other surveys throughout the USA. The open-ended responses revealed somewhat less tolerance. Both types of response suggest that black people and white people in Mississippi still hold different views about race relations.

Bakanic recognised that there's a problem with research about racial attitudes. What respondents say about their racial attitudes isn't always consistent with how they actually behave. There's a large research literature which shows that there are overwhelmingly tolerant responses to fixed-response questions on racial issues, but ample evidence of continuing racial discrimination. If one were simply to rely on fixed-response attitude surveys, one would come to the erroneous conclusion that discrimination and prejudice have significantly diminished. The problem is that this simply doesn't fit the growing racial tensions in American cities and schools.

This is why quantitative methods need to be supplemented with 'dig deeper' qualitative methods. For, as Bakanic says, 'While respondents may wish to express socially acceptable responses, most do not sustain attitudes adopted for social approval when asked to expound upon their opinions' (1995: 69). Bakanic's important point is this: people sometimes censure their real attitudes when asked to respond to tick box questions, but are more likely to tell it like it is when they're given the chance to express their attitudes in their own words.

QUESTIONS

1 Compare and contrast the uses of random and non-random sampling methods.
2 Outline the role of questionnaires and interviews in social scientific research.

The survey is the favourite tool of the positivistic sociologist. Interpretivists sometimes conduct surveys, but not nearly as often as they use observation.

EXAM TIP

When you're studying questionnaires, you're also studying structured interviews, because a structured interview uses a questionnaire. It's important to recognise, of course, that self-administered questionnaires don't involve an interview.

Observation

Observation is a means of empirical data collection that uses the sense of vision as its main vehicle. There are various kinds of observational technique, the most important in sociology being *participant observation* and *non-participant observation*. In the first type, sociologists get involved in the action that they study. For example, a sociologist studying night club life in a north England city might also be an MC, as well as carrying out observations. In the case of non-participant observation, sociologists watch and record but keep out of the action. An example would be observing children in a nursery school at play through one-way vision glass.

The extent to which observation is open (*overt*) or hidden (*covert*) depends on the kind of study that is being undertaken, and also – very importantly – on the ethics of disclosure. Many sociologists won't engage in covert observation, even if it might be the most suitable method, because it's deceitful and doesn't obtain the informed consent of the people who are being observed. Even so, some sociologists claim that undercover observation is necessary if natural behaviour is to be noted, and if injustices (for example, discrimination against people who are disabled) are to be exposed. There are also some circumstances where ethical considerations really don't have a bearing on the matter. Is it, for example, really necessary or, indeed, even possible, to declare oneself openly as a sociologist when conducting an observational study of the behaviour of audiences at rock concerts? Nevertheless, the ethics and the practicalities of overt versus covert observation do play a prominent role in current debates. So does the important issue of validity. These are issues we'll return to later.

Some types of observation are structured. For example, if you were watching to see how many female and male motorists jumped red traffic lights, you might use a checklist observation schedule with one column for female traffic violators and one for males. Other forms of observation are unstructured. For example, if you were observing young people 'hanging out' on street corners in Leicester, you might decide simply to watch things unfolding, writing up your observations later in a field diary. It's possible, of course, that you might mix and match a bit of structured with a bit of unstructured observation – though rarely simultaneously.

> ### *OVER TO YOU*
>
> ***When might it be useful to employ both structured and unstructured observations in the same research? Explain your answer.***

A very important consideration for any observer is how to obtain access to the people she or he wants to observe. In a study of female witches in America, Wendy Griffin (1995) was invited to a witches' coven by one of her students. Laud Humphreys (1970) often just turned up at male public toilets in the US in his undercover study of homosexual behaviour. Some aspects of human social behaviour are, of course, beyond the sociological gaze: intimate relations between spouses, bank robberies, church confessionals, etc. Most sociologists only use observation when it's appropriate and – importantly – ethical to do so.

Overt participant observation

This is an 'up-front' method. The sociologist gets in on the action, but admits to being an observing social scientist. This makes the method ethically acceptable, because there isn't the deceit associated with undercover observation. However, we're talking degrees of honesty here, because sociologists who are overt observers tend to be open only in their dealings with key respondents. Bill Whyte, for example, in his famous ethnographic study of community life in a 1930s Boston slum, confided to a gang leader called Doc that he was a writer, and left it at that. Ken Pryce, who studied black culture in 1970s Bristol, was an overt observer some of the time and a covert one on other occasions.

In a much more recent overt participant observation (OPO) study of feminist witches in the US, the social constructionist sociologist, Wendy Griffin (1995), used observation and in-depth interviews to collect her data. Like many OPO sociologists, she gained access to the witches through – as indicated earlier – a co-operating acquaintance: one of her students. The student belonged to a coven of feminist witches, and she invited Griffin to attend one of their religious rituals. Griffin accepted the invitation, and attended the ceremony with a colleague. Thereafter, they sought and received permission from the coven to conduct OPO, using a mixed toolbag of methods, including:

OBSERVATION

FOR

+ In terms of getting up and running, it's often a quick procedure: no time-consuming questionnaires to plan and prepare, and, often, no lengthy sampling techniques to develop and implement.
+ It sometimes offers data when 'respondents' are unwilling and/or unable to co-operate or to provide information (for example, covert observation of football fans using cctv; watching children at play instead of getting them to fill in questionnaires that they can neither read nor understand).
+ It often allows social scientists to study people in natural environments (on the street, in clubs and pubs, etc.) rather than in the contrived environments of experimental laboratories, interview rooms, and so on.
+ It offers first-hand, up-front data that doesn't rely on the findings and interpretations of other researchers.
+ It provides very rich, illuminative data. This is especially so in participant observation, because the observer becomes immersed in the action and comes to know it as both a watcher and a doer.
+ Except in cases where elaborate equipment and props are used (for example, cctv and one-way vision glass), it's a relatively inexpensive method. That said, long-term observational studies of an ethnographic type (where the observer 'goes native') can be quite costly.

AGAINST

– It's often inappropriate and/or impossible to conduct when very large numbers of people are being studied.
– It's difficult directly to study attitudes through observation.
– Certain forms of behaviour are usually out of bounds for the observer (for example, psychiatrist–patient interactions).
– What the observer 'sees' is liable to be influenced by her or his personal biases, selective perception, and selective memory.
– Except in very controlled conditions (for example, laboratory observation of people's reaction speeds after consuming alcohol), it's not really possible to exactly replicate an observed event to check the reliability of initial findings.
– It sometimes exposes the observer to the risk of getting drawn into deviant behaviour. This is especially so in participant observation, but more so in covert than in overt forms.
– Covert observation sometimes runs the risk that one's cover might be blown, with unforeseen and possibly dangerous outcomes.
– Covert observation is, arguably, unethical because it doesn't seek nor obtain the informed consent of the observed parties.

- written and tape-recorded fieldnotes on all events they were permitted to attend
- when possible, original photographs and video tapes
- semi-structured (i.e. focused but flexible), in-depth, recorded interviews.

The functions attended included both private and public (open) rituals, camping weekends, planning meetings, several religious services that marked significant life events for specific individuals, and occasional social gatherings. Griffin and her co-researcher collected data for a year and a half from this group – which they named the Coven of the Redwood Moon. While they were accepted as peripheral (on the edge) members, they didn't join the coven, nor did they ask to be apprenticed into its rituals. After this period, the co-researcher moved elsewhere, and Griffin started to conduct individual research on a local 'goddess group' that she called Womancircle. She returned to Redwood Moon only occasionally for public rituals.

As with Redwood Moon, initial contact with Womancircle was made on the campus where Griffin worked. She used the same *triangulation* (a term for 'mixed toolbag') of methods as previously. Overtures were made to Griffin encouraging her to participate as a core member of Womancircle, but she discouraged them, deciding instead to remain as a researcher. That's one of the advantages of being an overt researcher. Those whom you study know that's the primary role, and are less likely to put pressure on you to do things that you don't feel comfortable about. It's much more difficult, of course, to be selective in a participating sense if you're working undercover. All the women in both groups identified themselves, at one time or another, as feminist witches. Moreover, the women appeared to accept uncritically that there were pre-historical (very ancient indeed!) 'goddess cultures', where women and women's values were pivotal to society's values.

One of the differences between qualitative and quantitative research is that the former usually is more concerned with words than numbers. Illustrative of that point, here's a very richly detailed, almost literary, description from Griffin's fieldnotes, where she describes a public ritual involving a woman called Hypatia (Dianic witch and priestess in Redwood Moon) in which the sociologist participated, along with some 60 other women:

'The second night out was a full moon and we waited impatiently for the moon to crest the tall pines so that the ritual could begin. Finally, we saw two flames winding down the mountain path. As they neared, we saw that these were torches, held by priestesses in silver gowns which caught the light from the flames and glittered like pieces of the moon herself. The priestesses paused in the south, and then I noticed the enormous shadow thrown against the hill. It is Diana who comes behind them. Rationally, I know it is Hypatia, but I also "know" it is Diana. A heavy green cape is swept over her shoulders and matches her baggy pants. Her huge breasts are bare, and her chest is crossed with the leather straps that hold her cape and the quiver of arrows on her back. She carries a large bow and her face is hidden behind a mask of fur and dried leaves. Deer horns spring from her head. There is no face, not a human one, anyway . . . The Goddess pauses between the torches and fits an arrow to the bow. She draws it back and with a "twang" shoots it into the darkness. The sound is a catalyst. We are released like the arrow and begin to cheer. (24 August 1991)'

(Griffin 1995)

One senses, even though Griffin is keen not to be a participating witch, that she's actually got quite involved with this particular ritual. That's sometimes how it is with participant observation. Being so close to – indeed, being a part of – the action can lead to a personal engagement that would have our resolutely objective, quantifying positivists deeply exasperated.

> **OVER TO YOU**
>
> ***Check out these participant observation studies, summarise their findings, and consider their strengths and weaknesses:***
>
> 1. ***H. J. Parker,* View From the Boys *(a study of car radio theft in Liverpool)***
> 2. ***Ned Polsky,* Hustlers, Beats and Others *(a study of, among other 'shady practices', pool hustling in the US)***
> 3. ***Bill Whyte,* Street Corner Society *(a study – and a real classic – of gang life in 1930s Boston, US).***
>
> ***Full details of these are given in the References section on page 108.***
> ***See if you can find some other, more recent, OPO studies and report back on them to your class.***

Covert participant observation

This is an undercover method. It involves the sociologist participating in the action she or he observes without telling the other participants that they're being watched. It's an ethically controversial method because the informed consent of the people who are being studied is neither sought nor provided. There are also a number of risks associated with covert participant observation (CPO). Supposing you're posing as a pool room hustler in order to become more intimately acquainted with the culture of pool room life. You might easily get drawn into illegal activities if the other participants think you're one of them rather than a professional social scientist.

There's also the very real prospect of getting mixed up in pool room brawls. If, however, like the sociologist, Ned Polsky, who actually studied American pool rooms, you're honest about who you are, there's considerably less risk of getting drawn into behaviour that you'd prefer to watch rather than copy. Polsky didn't disguise the fact that he was researching as well as playing pool. Nor did Howard Parker in his ethnographic study of boys and young men in an inner city Liverpool neighbourhood who stole car radios. Yet the undercover sociologist, Laud Humphreys, got into all kinds of difficulty when he decided to study homosexual behaviour in American public toilets, including being arrested by the local police department.

Humphreys' CPO study was a classic of its kind, and because, in so many ways, it underscores some of the major advantages and disadvantages of covert research in the social sciences, we're going to look at it in some detail.

Laud Humphreys wrote a book in 1970 called *Tearoom Trade: A Study of Homosexual Encounters in Public Places*. It was based on his CPO study in the mid-1960s of 90 public toilets (so-called 'tearooms') in the parks of an American city (which, to protect the identity of his respondents, he kept anonymous). These toilets provided the setting for homosexual encounters between American men, 50 of which were systematically observed by Humphreys in his guise as a gay voyeur (someone who gains sexual pleasure by watching, in this case, live sexual encounters between men).

Humphreys' interest in homosexual behaviour, at the time a crime in the USA, derived from his work as a trainee priest in what was called Chicago's 'queen parish'. This was, as Humphreys put it, 'a place to which the homosexuals could turn for counsel, understanding priests, good music, and worship with an aesthetic emphasis' (Humphreys 1970: 23). He later served parishes in Oklahoma, Colorado and Kansas, twice working as an Episcopal (similar to Church of England) campus chaplain. Joined by his wife, he counselled hundreds of homosexuals 'over the coffee pot for many a night' (1970: 23).

As well as being a priest, Humphreys was also a sociologist who wanted to gain entry to the 'deviant subculture' of homosexual behaviour, thereby being able 'to listen to sexual deviants with a scientist's rather than a pastor's ear' (1970: 23). We hasten to add that his use of the term 'sexual deviants' is probably more in keeping with the norms and values of 1960s USA than with Humphreys' own views. For, as he put it, lots of homosexuals sought his counsel, 'Because I was considered "wise" and did not attempt to "reform" them . . .' (1970: 23).

Noting that homosexuals had developed defences against the intrusions of outsiders, Humphreys, 'had to enter the subculture as would any newcomer and to make contacts with respondents under the guise of being another gay guy' (1970: 24). His reticence in telling them his true identity was, in part, prompted by being told by a gay friend that homosexuals in the community were wary of sociologists, supposedly because a graduate student hadn't disguised the names of bars and respondents in a master's thesis on homosexuality.

Humphreys wasn't going to make the same mistake. Nor was he going to advertise the fact that he was an undercover social scientist:

'In the first place, I am convinced that there is only one way to watch highly discreditable behavior and that is to pretend to be in the same boat as those engaging in it. To wear a button that says "I Am a Watchbird, Watching You" into a tearoom, would instantly eliminate all action except the flushing of toilets and the exiting of all present.'

(Humphreys 1970: 25)

He also believed that CPO would make it possible to study the '"onstage" behavior of social actors' (1970: 26) rather than behaviour that might otherwise be distorted if people knew they were being observed by a sociologist.

While he did reveal his true identity and ostensible role to about 12 of the participants whom he had come to know well, for the rest, Humphreys adopted the persona of a 'voyeur watchqueen'. This was a recognisable role in the homosexual community. It was adopted by gay men who derived sexual pleasure from watching the homosexual behaviour of their peers, but who also kept an eye out for vice cops and other 'intruders'. In that sense, Humphreys could be fairly certain that his watching brief wouldn't interfere with the 'normal' action, because 'voyeur watchqueens' were part and parcel of the gay scene. Adopting that role, said Humphreys, meant that:

'I was able to move around the room [toilet where homosexual activity occurred] at will, from window to window, and to observe all that went on without alarming my respondents or otherwise disturbing the action.'

(Humphreys 1970: 28)

Humphreys employed a 'mixed toolbag' approach to methods. CPO was prominent, and was largely based on 50 systematic observations made and written down by Humphreys between March and August 1967. Numerous informal observations he had made previously, as well as 30 systematic observations made by a co-operating respondent, served as a helpful (and a generally confirming) check against the 50 observations. On page 98 is an example of one of the 50 systematic observation sheets, some parts filled in by Humphreys in his own very bad handwriting. Being teachers, we know a thing or two about bad handwriting! So this is what we make of the portions that contain Humphreys' handwriting:

Weather and temp. 80 degrees – partly cloudy – beautiful
Number and type of people in parks: moderate number; few ?, most engaged in sports
Estimated volume of gay activity: heavy 8 in 35 minutes
Time began: 3:20 (Encounter A)
Time ended: 3:30
Participants: X: 40 – black hair, pants and shoes – pink sport shirt – towel
Y: 45 – balding – tall, dark pants, blue and tan checked sport shirt

Others: A – Negro*, tan slacks – white sport shirt

* 'Negro' is a 1960s term. 'African–American' or 'black' are the preferred terms these days. Some black Americans also call themselves 'people of colour'. The term 'coloured', however, is offensive.

Humphreys supplemented observational methods by:

- 'talking with the few men I could involve in conversation' (1970: 29)
- scrutinising automobile licence plate data (Humphreys secretly noted down the licence plate numbers of many of the men who drove to the 'tearooms' for gay sex), which enabled him to trace addresses and, thereafter, obtain marital and occupational details of the participants
- conducting follow-up interviews, under the guise of a health survey (with Humphreys in physical disguise!), with 50 of the men who had been traced.

At all times, Humphreys made strenuous and, it appears, successful efforts to keep the identity of his respondents anonymous. He even allowed himself to be jailed rather than alert the police to the nature of his research, thereby avoiding the incrimination of respondents by their homosexual behaviour. Moreover, he kept the list of respondents to be interviewed in a safe-deposit box, and he changed his appearance, dress and car from the days he posed as a voyeur so that the respondents wouldn't recognise him.

By using multiple methods, and a considerable amount of undercover stealth (some of his critics call it downright deceit!), Humphreys delved deep into homosexual subculture, and he came up with some unexpected findings:

- 54 per cent of his research subjects were married men living with their wives
- 60 per cent were veterans of the armed forces, especially ex-navy men
- the more popular 'tearooms' were all located near major commuter routes through the city, easily accessible to 'the young white-collar bachelor or the working class husband in transit to his home' (1970: 152).

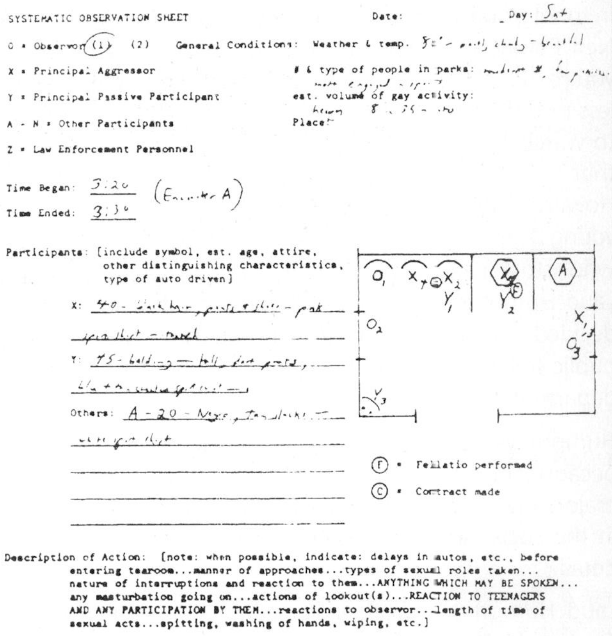

SYSTEMATIC OBSERVATION SHEET Date: Day: Sat

O = Observor (1) (2) General Conditions: Weather & temp.

X = Principal Aggressor # & type of people in parks:

Y = Principal Passive Participant est. volume of gay activity:

A - N = Other Participants Place:

Z = Law Enforcement Personnel

Time Began: 3:20 (Encounter A)

Time Ended: 3:30

Participants: [include symbol, est. age, attire, other distinguishing characteristics, type of auto driven]

X:

Y:

Others: A – 20 –

Ⓕ = Fellatio performed

Ⓒ = Contract made

Description of Action: [note: when possible, indicate: delays in autos, etc., before entering tearoom...manner of approaches...types of sexual roles taken... nature of interruptions and reaction to them...ANYTHING WHICH MAY BE SPOKEN... any masturbation going on...actions of lookout(s)...REACTION TO TEENAGERS AND ANY PARTICIPATION BY THEM...reactions to observor...length of time of sexual acts...spitting, washing of hands, wiping, etc.]

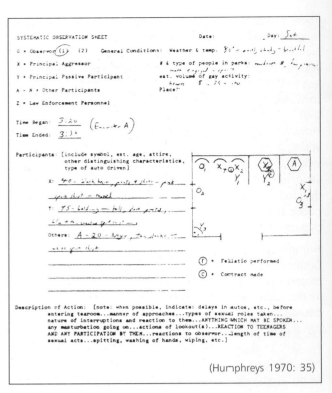

(Humphreys 1970: 35)

An example of one of Humphreys' observation sheets

Humphreys' study is a helpful corrective to anyone who might imagine that all offenders are the same as the ones who are arrested. The 1960s stereotype of the American man who sought gay sex in public toilets was of a lonely, unmarried individual. Yet Humphreys' study – while it can't be taken as necessarily statistically representative – reveals a majority of married, presumably heterosexual men seeking an additional sexual outlet that was quick, uncomplicated and undemanding. Fully committed homosexuals were less commonly observed.

Moreover, while courtroom accounts of indecent approaches made to police officers portray a picture of aggressive washroom homosexuality, Humphreys' research suggests things might be otherwise. He found that fairly overt and mutually understandable sexual signals typically preceded sexual approaches. Another common and perhaps misinformed image of homosexual behaviour is that people who engage in it must be homosexuals. While Humphreys' work can't and doesn't claim representativeness about homosexual behaviour in general, it does suggest that some of this behaviour is engaged in by married men who live with their wives and children. If such is still the case (remembering that Humphreys's study is over 25 years old), this has serious implications for research into the transmission of HIV and AIDS. For, if 'straight men' are more 'bisexual' than we think, there's a heightened risk that the virus(es) responsible for these diseases are more prevalent among heterosexual people than previously thought.

OVER TO YOU

Check out these two covert participant observation studies, summarise their findings, and consider their strengths and weaknesses:

1. ***J. H. Griffin*, Black Like Me**
2. ***James Patrick*, A Glasgow Gang Observed.**

Full details of these studies are given in the Reference section on page 108.

Overt non-participant observation

If you want to observe people with their consent and knowledge but don't wish to participate in the event, then this is the method to use. Sociologists often use overt non-participant observation when they're monitoring interactions in organisations, like factories, offices and schools. Typically, the sociologist sits at the back of the classroom or workplace with a lap-top computer, and keys in what she or he observes. Sometimes a systematic checklist is used (for example, time taken for a manager to close a telephone sales deal; number of teacher questions directed at girls in a physics class, etc.). Alternatively, or as a supplement, the sociologist lets things unfold without pre-empting what to look out for.

One overt non-participant observation study is so famous that it has a phenomenon named after it: the Hawthorne effect. It was conducted by Elton Mayo in the 1930s at the Hawthorne plant of the Western Electric Company in Chicago: a city that has witnessed a number of path-breaking social scientific studies in the twentieth century. Mayo wanted to find out what kinds of incentive and work condition would encourage employees to work harder. He first initiated a series of systematic changes: the coffee breaks, the lighting, the lunchbreak hours, etc. To his astonishment, whatever change he made resulted in increased productivity. When they were given two or three coffee breaks, employees worked harder, but when they were allowed no coffee breaks, they still worked harder. Similar effects were recorded when the lights were brightened and then dimmed, and for other changes.

Bemused at first, Mayo later realised that the increased work rates were due to all the attention the workers were getting from the overt non-participant observer. He was the critical factor, the independent variable, if you will! The workers felt they were important people in the eyes of the researcher – after all, he was observing them all the time – and they reciprocated by increasing their output. This impact of a researcher's presence on respondents' behaviour, to return to our initial theme, became known as the 'Hawthorne effect'. While it may have been a profitable effect, as far as the bosses of the electric plant were concerned, social scientists are generally keen to minimise its intrusion into the research process. For when people play to the gallery of the researcher, what they do ceases to be natural and normal behaviour, and therefore produces invalid data.

This doesn't mean that sociologists have to give up on any form of overt research. If they make allowances for the fact that sometimes what they see is influenced by their presence, and if they are adept at blending into the background, sociologists can still produce valid research findings. It would be crazy though to imagine that one could, for example, accurately study the cultures of 'singles bars' by sitting on a bar stool in a white coat, punching data into a laptop computer as couples interact! As in all areas of observational research, a genuine sensitivity towards one's surroundings, coupled with a research technique that is minimally intrusive, is guaranteed to enhance the validity of what the researcher is able to observe and record.

Quite often, sociologists who use overt non-participant observation also employ participant observation. For example, David H. Hargreaves (1976) adopted both methods in his 1960s study of a north England secondary modern school for boys. Sometimes, as a non-participant observer, he sat at the back of the class during lessons. This, however, led to certain teachers perceiving him in the role of an inspector. Hargreaves was at pains to avoid this, and he counteracted the perception by adopting a more participatory stance in other situations:

> 'Through constant participation in the informal social activities of the staff and the consequent initiation and acceptance into the informal relations, cliques and private jokes and quarrels, I could to a large extent shed the Inspector-role.'
>
> (Hargreaves 1976: 198)

It's clear that Hargreaves wanted to be regarded more as a participating than as a non-participating observer. His sociability and his previous teaching background, coupled with the fact that he was to spend a third of his time in the school teaching classes, helped Hargreaves to be seen as one of the staff by teachers and students.

His role as an observer who slipped in and out of being a participant and a non-participant isn't uncommon in social science. The renowned social anthropologist, Margaret Mead, also adopted both roles in her now-classic study of children growing up on a New Guinea island. Displaying her penchant for mixing participant and non-participant observation (both overt and covert forms), Mead writes:

'In my large living-room, on the wide verandas, on the tiny islet adjoining the houses, in the surrounding lagoon, the children played all day and I watched them, now from the midst of a play group, now from behind the concealment of the thatched walls. I rode in their canoes, attended their feasts, watched in the house of mourning and sat severely still while the mediums conversed with the spirits of the dead. I observed the children when no grown-up people were present, and I watched their behaviour towards their parents.'

(Mead 1970: 16)

The next section examines the kind of monitoring that takes place, 'from behind the concealment of the thatched walls' – covert non-participant observation.

Covert non-participant observation

This is how social scientists study people's behaviour without getting in on the action, and without the people knowing. Sometimes this is done through one-way view windows. You've probably seen these if you've watched TV police shows like *NYPD Blue*. The suspect is in an interrogation room being questioned by two detectives, while, unknown to her or him, the captain of detectives is watching the proceedings from an adjoining room through a disguised viewing panel. A similar strategy is sometimes used by social scientists (especially, psychologists) when they monitor human social behaviour (children at play in a 'laboratory' that's transformed into a 'playroom' is a particular favourite) unobtrusively and without participating in the interaction. Undercover investigative journalists and motorway police are also regular users of non-participant covert surveillance, typically employing hidden cameras in order to monitor 'discreditable behaviour': crack-dealing in a dimlit street, driving recklessly on a motorway, etc. Closed circuit television is now commonly used in car parks and in pub and club city centres, and for the many unsuspecting citizens who don't know the cameras are there, this is also a form of covert non-participant observation.

While it's used in many different contexts and for lots of different reasons, sociologists rarely employ covert non-participant action. There are a number of reasons why this is, notably:

- Like any form of covert research, the informed consent of those who are studied is neither sought nor (except when people agree to co-operate after being told that they've been secretly observed) obtained. This makes the practice deceitful and therefore unethical.
- Those sociologists who argue that it's sometimes acceptable to be deceitful (when, for example, in exposing racist behaviour) usually need to get close to – even 'involved' in the action – as participating observers to get a full picture of what's happening.

However, social psychologists seem less concerned than sociologists about the ethics and, perhaps also the practicalities, of covert non-participant observation. Illustrative of this is a study by Martin S. Remlanc, Tricia S. Jones and Heidi Brinkman (1995) who employed the method when they researched interactions between people in public places. Naturally occurring interactions between pairs of people (dyads) in England, France, the Netherlands, Italy, Greece, Scotland and Ireland were secretly videoed. The film tape was then coded and analysed to study the effects of culture, gender and age on the physical distance people keep between themselves, body orientation, and touch.

A Zenith VHS-C camcorder with a 6X zoom lens was used to record the interactions in each country. When recording the dyads at an unobtrusive distance, the camera was pointed in their direction, and the interaction was recorded through a raised viewfinder, so that the researcher didn't directly look at or orient her or his body towards the interacting pair. On the rare occasions when they were spotted by the people they were watching, the observers excluded those pairs from the data analysis.

Once they'd finished filming, the social scientists used very quantitative approaches to data analysis. Interpersonal distance between observed pairs was measured, for example, in inches between the individuals' heads and torsos, and body orientations were coded based on geometrical angles (side by side: 180°, etc.). Touching was coded on the basis of, for example, spot touched by hand lasting less than two seconds, and so on. Age estimates of the pairs were also made. Thereafter, lots of mathematical calculations were computed: the percentages of pairs from different countries who touched each other, touching percentages based on whether pairs were female/female, male/male and mixed, the average distances between pairs based on the country they were from, etc. Important and interesting findings emerged:

- Irish and Scottish pairs stood closer than did English, French, Greek, and Italian pairs.
- Greek and Italian pairs used touch during their interactions more often than did English, French, and Dutch pairs.
- Mixed pairs touched more than male pairs, but male pairs didn't touch less than female pairs.
- Men in the over-60 age group seemed to maintain more direct body orientations than did women in either the same age group or women in the 40 to 50 age group.
- Greece and Italy were revealed as contact cultures, compared to more northern European countries.

Aside from the obvious ethical objection that this covert research doesn't tell people they're being watched, it seems to adopt the extreme positivistic view that 'if it moves, measure it'. But can we really infer that contact cultures can be measured in inches and degrees of geometric angle? Of course, these social scientists would reply that contact cultures are essentially defined by distances between torsos and angles of body tilt. Their point is well taken, but, surely, their measurements are only a start. Human social behaviour is complex and intricate. Trying to measure and, more importantly, to make sense of it on the basis of mathematical calculations doesn't give a complete picture. Perhaps more needs to be done to encourage quantitative and qualitative researchers who use observation to pool their resources and their talents. Then we really will be better informed in an all-round kind of way.

It's important to recognise that observational studies can be quantitative (like Remland *et al.*), qualitative (like Wendy Griffin's) or a combination of quantitative and qualitative (like Humphreys'). We emphasise this point because some students seem to think that observation is an exclusively qualitative method, used only by interpretivists and avoided, at all costs, by positivists. Such isn't the case. Observation is employed by all kinds of sociologist.

> **EXAM TIP**
>
> Don't make the mistake of assuming that observation is only used in qualitative research. While sociologists who use observational techniques tend to adopt qualitative approaches, other social scientists (notably, social psychologists) sometimes use observation in a very quantitative way.

QUESTION

What are the four main types of observation in social science? Give one real-life example of each.

Analysis of existing data

Don't imagine that all sociologists collect their data out in the field. One of the most important, pathbreaking studies ever undertaken in sociology, Emile Durkheim's *Suicide* (1897), was largely based on the analysis of existing data. It's a study that is examined in Chapter 16, so we won't dwell on it here. Suffice it to say, that Durkheim's *magnum opus* was largely based on official statistical publications on mortality (especially suicide) rates. From the analysis of existing data, Durkheim produced findings that endure even to this day: divorced adults are more likely to commit suicide than married adults who live together, prisoners more than free people, to name but two examples.

More recently, a team of sociologists (Augustine J. Kposowa, K. D. Brealt and Gopal K. Singh 1995) in America have also examined official suicide statistics. Using existing data from the 1979–85 National Longitudinal Mortality Study, these social scientists investigated risk factors associated with suicide mortality among white males in America. The sociologists only considered white males aged 15 and older. Suicide rates among other 'race' groups and among women were too small to permit meaningful analysis. In that context, it's relevant to note that suicide deaths among white males account for nearly 75 per cent of all such deaths in the US.

Before looking in more detail at this American study, we'll first take note of some of the different kinds of existing data used by sociologists:

- *other official documents:* government reports, parliamentary debates (see Paul Stephens, page 103), Home Office research findings, etc.
- *mass media content:* advertising, cinema, cyberspace, newspapers, magazines, television, etc.
- *personal documents:* diaries, home videos, letters, photo albums, scrapbooks, etc.

One of the great advantages of existing data is that it's already there. If they're also available to sociologists (we don't, for example, go around reading people's diaries, unless we have the writer's permission, or when they're in archive or published form), it saves us lots of time and money. There are, of course, other good reasons to use existing data:

- They provide great opportunities for the content analysis of documents that offer a window onto the behaviours, attitudes and perceptions of their compilers (for example, how coroners 'make sense' of suicides) and the people who figure in them (for example, how US congresswomen respond to the abortion debate).
- In the case of some documents, the people behind them aren't available for comment (for example, they're dead, or, if living, can't or won't be interviewed).
- Some material is only available to a researcher as secondary (another name for 'existing') data (for example, television news bulletins; even real-time reporting is 'secondary' data to the viewer).
- Sometimes sociologists are able to glean new knowledge from existing data that wasn't apparent before rigorous analysis (for example, patterns in statistics that reveal associations between poverty and suicide).
- With the advent of cyberspace, existing data can be exchanged and downloaded in seconds via the Internet. Some of the data in this book was taken from cyberspace databases in different parts of the world.

There are, however, at least two major disadvantages with the uses of existing data:

- The data might not be relevant to what the sociologist is looking for, having been assembled for very different purposes (for example, if you wanted to find out about female 'breadwinners' in UK households, it would be of little help if existing data only reported on male 'breadwinners').
- Without lots of detailed information, which mightn't be available, you don't always know how reliable and valid existing data are. If you're looking at social scientific journals, hopefully, the methodology of the authors will be explicit and checkable. However, if, for example, you're looking at data that's been collected by a pressure group (for example, the Fieldsports Society or their opponent, the League Against Cruel Sports), how can you be sure that bias hasn't crept in?

Once they've decided on the existing data, sociologists then have to analyse them:

- *Content analysis* is the preferred tool when the data are qualitative.
- *Statistical analysis* is more often employed when the data are quantitative.

That said, there's considerable overlap between the two kinds of analysis.

Content analysis

We're all content analysts. When, for example, we listen to radio news, watch televsion commercials, and read magazine articles, we 'make sense' of the content from these data. Social scientists also use content analysis, but in a much more systematic way. As a method of social scientific data collection, content analysis provides a rigorous qualitative and/or quantitative 'fine toothcomb' sifting and categorisation of the content of existing data. Among the documents that have come under the social scientist's scrutiny are children's books, women's magazines, television commercials, news bulletins, and a whole lot more. As a qualitative method, it can be directed towards the extraction of subjective information, such as the attitudes and motives of journalists. In a quantitative usage, it might be employed to draw out objective data, such as the most common forms of female behaviour that typically precede a wife-battering assault.

These are the most common steps in content analysis:

1. The selection of the research topic (for example, the extent to which female actors play high status occupational roles in US police series).
2. The operationalisation of the categories to be used (for example, high status occupations might be defined as police lieutenant and above, attorney, doctor, coroner, judge, corporation manager/boss, etc.).
3. The design of the research (for example, the nature and size of the sample – perhaps the two most popular police series broadcast between 1997–8 – and the methods for recording and analysing the data).
4. The collection of data (for example, the recording of the above series).
5. The analysis and interpretation of data (for example, noting the frequency of women actors who play top job roles, and 'making sense' of this).

OVER TO YOU

Using each of the steps identified above, conduct a content analysis of the frequency with which women appear in high-status roles in television commercials screened on Channel 4 between 8 p.m. and 9 p.m. over a period of five consecutive (Monday–Friday) weekdays.

The content analysis of television series, like the very popular ER, *helps sociologists to ascertain the extent to which women are portrayed in 'top jobs' on prime time broadcasting channels.*

Statistical analysis

Analysis of quantitative data (for example, infant mortality rates) provide sociologists with facts and figures that enable them to make statements about the significance of their findings. The most common statistical representations of this kind of data is in the form of distributions, graphs and tables. Opposite is *part* of a table that Kposowa *et al.* (1995) produced from their statistical analysis of existing quantitative data on suicide in America.

Hazards estimates of the effects of social factors on white male suicide in the US, 1979–85

Social factor	**Risk factor***
Marital status:	
Married	1.00
Single	1.61
Divorced/separated	2.65
Widowed	1.97
Social isolation:	
Lives with others	1.00
Lives alone	2.36
Education:	
< 12 years	1.00
12 years	0.78
13+ years	0.84
Occupation:	
Professional	1.00
Non-professional	1.24
Unemployment/outside labour force	1.32

*Where 1.0 represents the reference group for comparison, for example, 2.00 would be twice the risk of 1.00; 0.50 would be half the risk of 1.00.

(Adapted from Kposowa *et al.* 1995)

Staying with the above study, we'll now look at it in a little more detail. In this research, the *dependent variable* (a social scientific term which means the 'effect' or 'outcome') was the risk of suicide mortality. The *independent variables* (a social scientific term which means the 'cause') were mainly:

- age
- education
- family income
- nativity (whether US-born or otherwise)
- occupation
- residence (urban, including city centre and suburban, or non-urban)
- social integration (measured by marital status and social isolation, i.e. living alone or otherwise).

A complicated-sounding statistical test called the Cox Proportional Hazards Model was used to estimate the effects of social integration factors (mainly the ones indicated above) on the risk of suicide mortality. Simplifying all this, the sociologists used a statistical analysis of existing data to see whether or not factors such as living 'down town' or out of town, being married or single (not counting under 18-year-olds), residing alone or with another/others, etc., were either likely to increase or reduce the risk of suicide among white males.

This is pure, unadulterated positivism *a là* Durkheim. The official statistics on suicide rates are taken largely at face value without going into how coroners and other officials come to define what deaths should be interpreted as suicides and what shouldn't – more about that in Chapter 16. This, in summary, is what the sociologists found:

- The suicide risk for the divorced and separated was 2.65 times greater than for the married. Moreover, being single (not including under 18 year-olds) was associated with a significantly higher risk of suicide.
- The suicide risk for the persons living alone was 2.36 times greater than for those living with other(s).
- The suicide risk for those aged 55 or older was 2.2 times greater than for those aged 25–34 years. Moreover, those in the 25–34 age group had a significantly lower risk of suicide than those aged 15–24 years.
- The suicide risk for those who were US-born was 2.33 times greater than for those who were born outside the US.
- Compared to non-urban residents, those living in central city areas of metropolitan districts were 50 per cent more likely to commit suicide. Interestingly, this finding, note Kposowa *et al.* (1995: 323), 'can be taken as support for Durkheim's theory as many authors . . . see the central city as less socially integrated than nonurban areas.'

The researchers rightly conclude that 'much more work needs to be done' (1995: 324), but they, nevertheless, show us that the rigorous statistical analysis of official data is a crucial tool of sociological research.

Not all studies of official documents, of course, focus on statistics. For example, in his research on the nineteenth-century landed ruling class in England, Paul Stephens (1987) conducted a longitudinal (over a time-span) content analysis of published parliamentary debates on working-class schooling from 1806–33. By focusing on the stated intentions and the acknowledged motives of 'landed aristocrats' who made their views on this issue 'public' in parliamentary debates, Stephens was able to identify a number of important and recurrent themes.

Contrary to the received view that landed aristocrats generally opposed the education of poor children, he discovered that the majority view in parliament was actually pro-, not anti-education. Stephens also found that debates on 'popular education' disclosed evidence of conservative and liberal thought within the ruling class. This internal ideological contest manifested itself in the respective educational visions adopted by two main aristocratic groups. On the one hand, was a traditionalist group: conservative, cautious, Anglican, rooted in the land, not against educating the poor, but wary of the 'wrong kind' of education. Against them, was a reformist group: forward-looking, adventurous, sympathetic to religious 'Dissent', inclined to curry favour with captains of industry, and anxious to relate schooling to the new realities of coal and steam.

Reformist opinion in aristocratic quarters eventually won the day, and it was a government of aristocrats, not of the middle class, who in 1833, issued the first parliamentary grant for the education of the English poor. By looking anew at existing data, Stephens was able to show that, far from being the 'diehard' opponents of educational reform – as they have so often been portrayed – members of the English ruling class, 'were the neglected architects of an educational revolution' (1987: 20).

The above two studies both made use of existing official data, one looking at fairly recent statistical data on suicide in contemporary America, the other at historical 'written word' data on the ruling class in nineteenth-century England. There are, to be sure, many more kinds of existing data available to sociologists – a point that has been made earlier. Some of the most exciting research in this field during the 1990s is being carried out by a team of sociologists at the University of Glasgow. Since the 1970s, the Glasgow University Media Group have been conducting a content analysis of television broadcasts on important issues like the 1984 Coal Miners' Strike, the 1982 Falklands/Malvinos War and the 1992 Gulf War. The work carried out by this famous team is examined in Chapter 15. So feel free to fast-forward now if you wish!

QUESTIONS

1 Examine the strengths and limitations of the analysis by social scientists of existing data.
2 How does the statistical analysis of existing data help sociologists to measure social phenomena?

EXAM TIP

When answering exam questions on the analysis of existing data, be sure to draw upon the numerous studies that use this technique which feature in other areas of the syllabus: content analysis of print and electronic mass media, statistical analysis of crime, content analysis of schoolbooks, etc. Note too that data *are* plural.

Experiments

The experiment, as stated earlier, is the principal method of the scientist. But whether it's a method that works as well in social science as in natural science is fiercely debated. Natural scientists have the advantage of being able to study phenomena in the artificial setting of a laboratory without that artificiality necessarily distorting the results. Such isn't often the case in the study of the social world. Think about it. If you're investigating the effect of a stain remover on a fabric, it doesn't much matter, as far as the chemical reaction is concerned, whether the experiment takes place in a laboratory or anywhere else, provided certain key conditions (for example, temperature, humidity, etc.) are kept the same. On the other hand, if you're studying the effect of nursery schooling upon later educational achievement, placing young children and teachers in a 'social scientific lab' might make them behave differently. A nursery school teacher might, for example, put on a bit of a show if he knows he's in an experimental group being monitored by a 'white-coated' researcher.

Some social scientists would retort, 'Fair point, but . . .':

- experiments don't have to take place in a laboratory. They can be conducted in natural settings, like real nursery schools
- certain forms of human social behaviour aren't significantly affected by a laboratory setting. Social psychologists can create very realistic 'laboratories' (for example, a children's 'playcentre' with a one-way viewing panel for researchers).

We think it's also important to recognise that even the natural world isn't always best studied in a laboratory. How, for example, would it be possible to study, in a laboratory setting, the effect of sulphur dioxide emissions from UK factories on Swedish forestland, or the impact of tourism on marine life in the Florida Keys? Sometimes experiments just aren't the right tool for the job, and that can apply to natural, as well as social phenomena.

There are, of course, circumstances when the experiment is an excellent choice of method. In the social sciences, however, this is more likely to happen, especially in the case of laboratory experiments, in social psychology than in sociology. Society is hard to squeeze into a laboratory, but the behaviour of a relatively small number of individuals (typical in social psychology experiments) is a more manageable proposition. Whether you're a sociologist or a psychologist, however, these are the steps you'll need to take if you want to carry out an experiment into the causes of human social behaviour:

1 Select the respondents to ensure that there is an experimental and a control group (see the earlier section on science for an explanation of these terms). Perhaps you want to study the effects of an innovative teaching method on student progress in maths. You'd first need to ensure, through appropriate bench-mark testing, that your experimental and control groups are at approximately the same level of mathematical ability.

2 Introduce the experimental group to an appropriate stimulus, and keep things the 'same as usual' for the control group (for example, self-study programmes in algebra using a computer for the first group, and 'common garden variety' lectures for the second group).

3 Measure the effect of the independent variable (the stimulus) by computing the difference between the bench-mark maths scores and the post-stimulus math scores for the experimental and control groups. If there's a significant improvement in the scores of the experimental compared to the control group, it can be inferred that the self-study programme induces more progress than conventional lectures.

In the above experiment, part of it could be conducted in a laboratory (perhaps a seminar room converted for the purpose of the bench-mark testing), and part of it could be conducted in the field (i.e. in students' own homes and real lecture halls). There are, of course, some experiments that are totally laboratory-based (for example, reactions to films screened in universities by researchers), and others that only occur in the field (for example, reactions to television films that are viewed in the respondents' own homes).

Whether it occurs in an artificial or a natural setting (or in both), experimentation is only ethically acceptable when measures applied to the experimental group don't harm them, and when measures that are deliberately not provided for the control group don't cause them ill-effects. In that context, it's apposite to refer back to the hypothetical but very unethical experiment referred to earlier (page 70) in the section on science. There we have an example of how being a member of the control group would result in a denial of very real benefits. In some cases, there could also be directly harmful effects for a control group. This actually happened in a very controversial field experiment in the US. Robert Rosenthal and his colleague, Lenore F. Jacobson (1968), wanted to test the theory of the self-fulfilling prophecy – people will behave according to the expectations other important people in their lives have of them. In applying this theory to an elementary school, they hypothesised that teachers' expectations affect students' performances. Put simply, if teachers expect some students to be low achievers, the students will 'live down' to that expectation. The opposite holds true for students who are considered high flyers.

To test this hypothesis experimentally, Rosenthal and Jacobson gave all the students in a particular elementary school an IQ test. Subsequently, and without consulting the test results, the researchers randomly selected a small number of children and told their teachers, falsely, that these students had achieved very high test scores. The intention was to encourage the teachers to expect these allegedly very 'bright' students (the experimental group) to show remarkable progress during the coming year. Thus this experimental group was exposed to a stimulus (artificially-induced high teacher expectations), while all the other children constituted the control group (to which no such stimulus was applied). Eight months on, the researchers administered another test to all the children. They found that the experimental group out-performed the control group. They therefore concluded that teacher expectations (the independent variable) caused high student performance (the dependent variable).

We hope you'll agree that this experiment is not only under-handed (teachers were deliberately deceived by the researchers), but also potentially damaging to the children in the control group. Those children are more likely than their experimental peers not to get the teacher attention and time they deserve. They're also more likely to be on the receiving end of negative labelling, which can induce a negative self-fulfilling prophecy spiral. This important theme is picked up in Chapter 9 on education. It's message is simple and powerful – expect people to do 'badly' and that often 'causes' the anticipated behaviour.

Arguably, it would be worse, of course, if the stimulus to an experimental group caused its members harm. Imagine, for example, a physician giving an experimental group of patients a trial drug that was likely to produce very serious side-effects, in order to gauge how dangerous the drug was. Even if the people who formed the experimental group knew the hazards and agreed to take the product, this would still be an unethical experiment. One can think of parallels in social scientific research, for example, inducing heightened prejudice, encouraging violent behaviour, fostering feelings of worthlessness, etc. We think this is wrong, but there are some people who adopt a different view. They would argue that sometimes to reach a noble goal, it's necessary to make people suffer, in the interests of science, along the way. What do you think?

QUESTIONS

1 Compare and contrast the use of the experiment in natural and social science.

2 What are the respective advantages of laboratory and field experiments in social scientific research?

> ***EXAM TIP***
>
> Make the examiner aware that you know experiments are more likely to be used by social scientists who are psychologists than by social scientists who are sociologists.

Concluding remarks

Whatever method or methods a sociologist decides to use in the investigation of social phenomena, it's this readiness to test assertions against the evidence, that makes him or her different from the commentator who just makes unsubstantiated statements. While the social constructionists remind us not to go overboard with quantification, that doesn't make them any less concerned with truth than structural theorists. Maybe they just find it harder to figure out what truth actually means. Both the quantifying positivist and the interpretivist who opts for the qualitative approach, want to be closer to the truth than further from it.

Even the positivists – these days! – are less inclined to talk about certainty and more of probability. Interpretivists might be construed by some sociologists as being just a bit more modest about owning up to how difficult it is to achieve razor-sharp precision in sociological research. We shouldn't be too concerned that some of them prefer to be called ethnomethodologists rather than social scientists. What they bring to the sociological enterprise – empathy, intuition, receptiveness, sensitivity – are important and helpful. So too are the contributions of the scientific sociologists – a dispassionate commitment to hard evidence, and a rigorous concern with identifying cause and effect in the social world. In the 1970s, it was fashionable to draw the battlelines between different theoretical and methodological approaches, and to declare as winner the one who, faced with the toughest assaults, survived intact. Such, thankfully, isn't any longer the case. We now recognise the need to acknowledge high calibre sociology for what it has to offer rather than to dismiss it outright when it doesn't fit our own pre-conceived views.

Social scientists and natural scientists have colluded in research that has been used for military purposes. One needs to ask whether they've done this out of conviction or in the pursuit of selfish financial and professional gain.

Once social scientists have chosen what to study and how to carry it out, they mustn't duck the crucial question of what to do with their findings. Even if they choose simply to pass the findings to someone else (for example, a politician) without further comment, this is a decision, and, by default, it's a value-judgement. So value-judgements do enter the sociological arena. It's our view that this is cause for celebration rather than concern. For sociology is an emancipatory social science. It has the capacity to both study the society in which we live and, if its counsel is acted upon, to make that society a better place. As with any science, however, the uses to which sociology is put can be for better or for worse. It's not only physicists who provide our political and military 'leaders' with the capacity to destroy the planet; sociological findings can also be placed at the disposal of warlords and the like.

In 1964, for example, the US army recruited social scientists for what was called Project Camelot, a $6 million research venture into the causes of social change in Latin America. About six months later, the social scientists discovered the real purpose of the project – to obtain data that would enable the US army to learn how to prevent revolutions against repressive governments. After the project was begun in Chile, many social scientists voiced their objections to it, and Project Camelot was cancelled within a year. By co-operating in such a research exercise, social scientists would have colluded with the United States in an effort to interfere in the internal affairs of other nation states. For many of these social scientists, that was clearly unethical.

Although value-judgements are an integral part of all social scientific research, their intrusion into the methods we use must, for the sake of objectivity, be minimised. In practice, this means that the sociologist should 'own up' to having values. At the same time, she or he must place more 'value' in the impartiality of the research method than in her or his ethical and political values. For if the sociologist gets sidestepped in the investigative process by personal values there's a great danger that bias will falsify later findings. If, for one moment, research becomes sloppy, all that follows, however clever and sophisticated, won't enable us to produce objective knowledge. Alex Thio alerts us to this problem when he quotes the psychiatrist, Thomas Szasz, who once observed that when you put on a shirt, 'if you button the first buttonhole to the second button, then it doesn't matter how careful you are the rest of the way' (Thio 1989: 47). Szasz is right. If, on the other hand, we button the first buttonhole to the first button, then we can be confident that our findings are trustworthy.

Glossary of key terms

Accidental ('grab') sampling As its second name suggests, a non-representative method that involves 'grabbing' any individuals who are willing to take part in a study

Content analysis A method of studying existing (typically, written, spoken or visual) data to discover their meaning

Covert observation Observation in which the identity and aim of the sociologist aren't disclosed to the people who are observed

Dependent variable The effect caused by the action of an independent variable on something (*see* Independent variable)

Empirical evidence Data that are known and confirmed by the senses (for example, observation, smell, touch)

Ethnography An interpretive method of data collection that involves the sociologist living in the setting (for example, an island community) that she or he studies

Existing data Data that already exist; also called secondary data

Experiment A scientific method that typically studies 'cause and effect' under controlled conditions

Field experiment An experiment that's carried out in the 'field' (i.e. in a natural as opposed to an artificial setting) where some control of variables is, nevertheless, usually sought

Fixed-response questions Used in questionnaires and interviews, these questions require the respondent to choose between pre-determined responses

Hypothesis An educated guess that needs to be tested against empirical evidence

Independent variable A thing that causes something to happen

Interpretivism The use of methods that are very empathetic and which, typically, produce qualitative findings

Interview A method of data collection that asks questions and elicits replies in verbal form

Laboratory experiment An experiment that's set up and conducted in a laboratory, with a very high degree of control

Non-participant observation Observation that involves the sociologist as one who watches but who doesn't take part in the observed action

Objectivity Knowledge that's based on empirical evidence

Observation A method of data collection that primarily uses the sense of vision

Open-ended questions Used in questionnaires and interviews, these questions let respondents answer in their own words

Overt observation Observation in which the identity and aim of the sociologist are openly disclosed to the people who are observed

Participant observation Observation that also involves the sociologist as a participant

Population The entire group of people to be studied (for example, all Irish people, all Amnesty International members in the UK)

Positivism The use of methods that are very scientific and which, typically, produce quantitative findings

Primary data Data that are generated in the process of research. Once they're published, though, they become secondary data to other people who study them

Purposive sampling Used by sociologists who purposely choose people who are relevant to their research aim. It's non-representative

Qualitative methods Methods that analyse and present social phenomena in a manner that conveys their inherent quality (for example, a suicide note)

Quantitative methods Methods that analyse and present social phenomena in statistical terms (for example, crime rates)

Questionnaire A method of data collection that asks questions and elicits answers in written form

Quota sampling A technique in which the population is divided into strata and non-random samples are taken from each stratum

Random multi-stage sampling In this method, a sequence of random samples is taken from already selected random samples, but only the last sample is studied (for example, a random sample of cities is taken, from which a random sample of districts is taken, from which a final random sample of hospitals is taken)

Reliability Knowledge that's confirmed through repeat-testing

Representative Reliability across groups (for example, a representative sample contains the same characteristics as the larger sample from which it's drawn)

Sample A group of individuals selected from a population

Sampling A method of choosing samples

Sampling frame An existing list of people from which a sample is drawn (for example, all members of the National Union of Mineworkers)

Science Knowledge that's based on the reliable and valid analysis of empirical evidence

Semi-structured (focused) interview An interview that doesn't use questionnaires but which employs fairly focused guiding questions and probes

Simple random sample A lottery-style sampling method that employs probability theory (persons selected have the same probability of being selected as other persons in a particular population)

Snowball sampling Similar to 'grab sampling', but the individuals who are initially selected, extend the 'grabbing' by asking their acquaintances to co-operate in the research. Hence the sample gets bigger and bigger like a snowball

Social policy The application of social scientific knowledge for the purpose of improving society

Statistical analysis Numerical production and/or analysis of data

Stratified random sample A technique in which the population is divided into strata and random samples are taken from each stratum

Structured (formal) interview An interview that employs a questionnaire (also termed an 'interview schedule')

Subjectivity Preferences and viewpoints that haven't (in some cases, yet) been confirmed by empirical evidence

Survey A method of data collection that typically uses questionnaires and/or interviews to obtain information about a population

Systematic random sample Like simple random sampling, but the selection is made by picking every 'nth' (for example, every tenth) person from a sampling frame

Theory A systematic body of knowledge that has been repeatedly supported by empirical evidence; a collection of hypotheses that have 'graduated'

Triangulation A 'mixed toolbag' of different methods that are employed in the same study in order to obtain a better, all-round understanding of social phenomena

Unstructured (informal) interview An interview that's conversational and minimally 'structured' in character

Validity Knowledge that's obtained by ensuring that the best and most suitable methods are employed

Value-judgement Saying what should be rather than what is

Value-neutrality Saying what is rather than what ought to be

References

Bakanic, Von (1995) I'm not prejudiced, but . . .: A deeper look at racial attitudes, pp 67–86, *Sociological Inquiry*, Vol. 65, No. 1, Winter

Copas, John, Ditchfield, John and Marshall, Peter (1994) Development of a new reconviction prediction score, pp 30–7, *Home Office Research and Statistics Department Research Bulletin, Special Edition: Prisons and Prisoners*, No. 36

Dobash, R. Emerson and Dobash, Russell P. (1979) *Violence Against Wives*. London: Open Books

Dowdy, Eric (1994) Federal funding and its effect on criminological research: Emphasizing individualistic explanations for criminal behavior, pp 77–89, *The American Sociologist*, Vol. 25, No. 4, Winter

Durkheim, Emile (1968) *Suicide*. London: Routledge & Kegan Paul

Goldhagen, Daniel Jonah (1996) *Hitler's Willing Executioners*. London: Little, Brown and Company

Griffin J. H. (1964) Black like me, pp 479–86 (excerpts), in Worsley, Peter (ed.) (1972) *Problems of Modern Society*. Harmondsworth: Penguin

Griffin, Wendy (1995) The embodied goddess: Feminist witchcraft and female divinity, pp 35–48, *Sociology of Religion*, Vol. 56, No. 1, Spring

Hargreaves, David H. (1976) *Social Relations in a Secondary School*. London: Routledge & Kegan Paul

Humphreys, Laud (1970) *Tearoom Trade*. London: Gerald Duckworth & Co. Ltd

King, Martin Luther (1969) *Chaos or Community?* Harmondsworth: Penguin

Kposowa, Augustine J., Breault, K. D. and Singh, Gopal K. (1995) White male suicide in the United States: A multivariate individual-level analysis, pp 315–25, *Social Forces* Vol. 74, No. 1, September

Labov, William (1969) The logic of nonstandard English, pp 21–66, in Keddie, Nell (ed.) (1978) *Tinker, Tailor . . .* Harmondsworth: Penguin

Lee, David and Newby, Howard (1986) *The Problem of Sociology*. London: Hutchinson

Lister, Ian (1984) *Teaching and Learning About Human Rights*. Strasbourg: School Education Division, Council of Europe

Livingston, Jay (1996) *Crime and Criminology*. Upper Saddle River, New Jersey: Prentice Hall

Mead, Margaret (1970) *Growing up in New Guinea*. Harmondsworth: Penguin

Milgram, Stanley (1974) *Obedience to Authority*. New York: Harper & Row

Parker, H. J. (1974) *View From the Boys*. Newton Abbott: David & Charles

Patrick, James (1973) *A Glasgow Gang Observed*. London: Eyre Methuen

Polsky, Ned (1967) *Hustlers, Beats and Others*. New York: Adline

Pryce, Ken (1979) *Endless Pressure*. Harmondsworth: Penguin

Remland, Martin S., Jones, Tricia S. and Brinkman, Heidi (1995) Interpersonal distance, body orientation, and touch: Effects of culture, gender, and age, pp 281–97, *Journal of Social Psychology*, Vol. 135, No. 3, June

Rosenthal, Robert and Jacobson, Lenore F. (1968) Teachers' expectancies: Determinants of pupils' IQ gain, in Insel, Paul M. and Jacobson, Lenore F. (eds) (1975) *What Do You Expect? An Inquiry into Self-Fulfilling Prophesies*. Menlo Park, California: Cummings Publishing Company

Schlesinger, Philip, Dobash, R. Emerson, Dobash, Russell, P. and Weaver, C. Kay (1992) *Women Viewing Violence*. London: British Film Institute

Schultz, Ruth W. (1995) The improbable adventures of an American scholar: Robert K. Merton, pp 68–77, *The American Sociologist*, Vol. 26, No. 3, Fall

Stephens, Paul (1987) The landed interest and the education of the English working class 1807–1833: A sociological study of aristocratic debate and policy. Ph.D. thesis, University of London

Stephens, Paul (1997) Student teachers' concerns and accomplishments on main school placements: What school mentors can learn from them, pp 56–66, *Mentoring and Tutoring*, Vol. 5, No. 1, Summer

Thio, Alex (1989) *Sociology: An Introduction*, Second Edition. New York: Harper & Row

UNICEF (1995) *The Progress of Nations 1995*. New York: UNICEF House

Westergaard, John (1995) *Who Gets What?* Cambridge: Polity Press

Whyte, William Foote (1981) *Street Corner Society*, Third Edition. Chicago: University of Chicago Press

Zimbardo, Philip G. (1972) Pathology of imprisonment, pp 4–8, *Society*, Vol. 9, No. 6, April

Exam practice: Theory and methods

As indicated in Chapter 4, Theory also features in this exam practice.

Data response question

Item A

The Economic and Social Research Council's 16–19 Initiative was launched in 1986 to investigate the wider social and psychological implications of youth's new conditions. A representative sample of over 5000, drawn from four parts of Britain (Kirkcaldy, Liverpool, Sheffield and Swindon), was surveyed by mailed questionnaire in 1987, 1988 and 1989. In each area, sub-samples were studied in greater depth through home interviews, and further ethnographic fieldwork was undertaken in Sheffield and Kirkcaldy.

(Adapted from *Young Citizens* in *Social Science Teacher*, 20.2 Spring 1991, Ken Roberts)

Item B

Eichler's 'Non-sexist Research Methods' can be thought of as a handbook describing how every practicality of research can be sexist and how this can be avoided. The examples which are most readily recognised concern the construction of questionnaire items. In many ways, the art of writing good questions is a matter of constructing them in down-to-earth language. One drawback of this is that it becomes all too easy to pull in the sexism which resides in everyday talk. The classic example of this is when question-writers use 'he' when they are inquiring about persons-in-general. As an example, consider the following question on racial attitudes:

"If someone wanted to make a speech in your community claiming that blacks are inferior, should he be allowed to speak or not?"

(Adapted from *Feminist Methodology in Developments in Sociology*, Vol. 8 Ray Pawson)

Item C

Intensive, informal interviewing is another characteristic method in qualitative research. Respondents whose social situation or behaviour is the object of study are selected, and they are questioned at length. Instead of using the structured, pre-coded type of interview schedule, such interviews use many more open-ended questions and may be more conversational in character. Dennis Marsden's study 'Mothers Alone' tried to make the interview as much like a conversation as possible; while in Frank Coffield et al's case study of four deprived families, the research began with unstructured interviews and developed into something akin to a friendship, though with the research purpose explicit throughout. This is unusual for intensive interviewing, but completely different from the conventional large-scale survey interview, involving one visit to ask largely pre-structured questions.

(Adapted from *Social Science and Social Policy*, Martin Bulmer)

(a) Suggest **two** reasons why the researchers in **Item A** might have wanted to carry out home interviews with sub-samples of the original 5000 respondents. *(2 marks)*

(b) Re-write the question on racial attitudes in **Item B** so that it avoids 'the sexism which resides in everyday talk'. *(1 mark)*

(c) Assess the usefulness of mailed questionnaires as a method of sociological research (**Item A**). *(8 marks)*

(d) (i) What do sociologists mean by 'representative samples' (**Item A**)? *(2 marks)*

(ii) How far do you agree that samples should always be representative? *(4 marks)*

(e) With reference to information from the Items and elsewhere, assess the strengths and weaknesses of the **two** different types of interview identified in **Item C**. *(8 marks)*

(From Summer 1994 AEB A Level Sociology Paper 1 © 1994 AEB)

Essay questions

Not for students taking coursework:

1 Compare and contrast Marxist and functionalist theories of social change. *(25 marks)*

2 Assess the influence of feminist perspectives on sociological research. *(25 marks)*

(From Summer 1996 AEB A-level Sociology, Paper 2, © 1996 AEB)

Not for students taking coursework:

3 "All sociological theories are selective, and as such, provide a biased view of social reality." Explain and evaluate this statement. *(25 marks)*

(From June 1992 AEB A Level Sociology Paper 2 © 1992 AEB)

4 Critically examine the relationship between interactionism and qualitative methods of research. Illustrate your answer with reference to appropriate sociological studies. *(25 marks)*

(From Summer 1997 AEB A-level Sociology, Paper 2, © 1997 AEB)

Only for students completing coursework:

5 Discuss the influence of ethical issues on the methods chosen by sociologists. *(10 marks)*

(From Summer 1997 AEB A-level Sociology, A Soclgy 3, © 1997 AEB)

6 Culture and identity

Topics covered in this chapter
- *Defining culture and identity*
- *Theories of culture*
- *Culture and identity in relation to social class, gender, ethnicity, age and region*
- *Types of culture*

I was in south London recently. The people there speak with a London accent, but the people with the strongest cockney accents come from London's East End. It struck me, however, that the speech of the people around me was as cockney as any East Ender's. I was puzzled.

Then I found out why these south London people spoke like the people on the north-east side of the river. After the Second World War, lots of East End families whose homes had been bombed were re-housed on a big council estate in the part of south London where I found myself. Today's inhabitants of the estate were first, second and third generation 'East Enders'. The first generation – grandparents now – had passed on their accents and other aspects of East End *culture* to their children and – through them – to their grandchildren.

Culture, of which language is a very important vehicle, is the defining quality of our humanity. It's a heritage of norms, values, beliefs and tastes that we obtain through socialisation from our society and from our locality. It's a social thing, but it shapes our *identity*. You readers who come from Yorkshire are both Yorkshire *people* and Yorkshire *individuals*. You *share* a liking for Yorkshire *culture,* but your private *self* is also engraved with a Yorkshire *identity*. On the other hand, it's probable that your sense of being *Yorkshire* isn't as pronounced as that of your parents and grandparents. They were born when people's sense of who and what they are was heavily bound up with region, class, gender, ethnicity and age. In this so-called *post-modern* world we're said to inhabit, those categories, although still important, are more intermingled than previously.

This chapter explores the ways in which cultures are defined and experienced in identities, and how cultures and you get on – or not, as the case may be – with each other.

Defining culture and identity

Culture is a way of life, not instinct or simple imitation. It's learned, incorporated, adapted and contested, but its imprint is always there. Talk to a Catholic who no longer attends Mass, or a Jew who doesn't eat kosher food, and you'll still find vestiges of Catholic and Jewish culture in their lives. The wearing of a cross, for example, or a Star of David medal means that their personal identities still connect, however tenuously, with Catholic and Jewish traditions. *Identity is how I see myself in relation to an inner me that connects with my culture, as well as my individuality.* In practice, the cultural and the individual sense of self are intertwined, such that all identities are socially situated rather than free-floating. Our identities are therefore *cultural identities.*

Culture and identity meet 'at the point of suture' (Stuart Hall 1996a, in Hall, Held and McGrew 1996: 25) between society and the individual. When an individual asks the question, 'Who am I?', she or he is pondering this interface. For example, when I say, 'I'm a researcher', I identify with what I think society expects a researcher to be, and with what I think a researcher ought to be. My identity as a researcher thus contains an attachment to social convention and an individual wilfulness. In that respect, to understand culture is to understand the relationship between the individual and society – the connectedness between the two.

The popular television soap, EastEnders, *creates a 1990s version of working-class culture in London's East End.*

This bond between us and our culture is what makes us belong to a human society. Some biologists portray human beings as mere carbon-based life forms whose destiny is to preserve 'selfish' molecules called genes. But, dare we say it? – yes, we dare – sociologists know better. The scientific vision of Marie Curie, the artistic genius of Michaelangelo, the musical talent of Jimmy Hendrix, add up to more than molecules. These people were products of their time and place – of their cultures. Their creativity and genius can't be understood purely on the level of biology. Society is part of the equation.

This isn't to diminish the importance of genes. As the functionalist sociologist, Talcott Parsons, notes, 'Every empirical analysis of action presumes biologically given capacities' (Parsons 1964: 9). Of course, our biological make-up is important and affects our lives. But it doesn't forge nor does it transmit our culture. Society does that. All of us come from a common gene pool, but how we think and behave is more linked to culture than to genetic make-up. This is demonstrated by the fact that people who have the same genetic heritage – all of humankind – have different cultures. As Peter L. Berger and Thomas Luckman put it: 'the ways of becoming and being human are as numerous as man's [*sic*] cultures. Humanness is socio-culturally variable' (Berger and Luckman 1975: 667).

So what is this thing we call culture? In the *Oxford Universal Dictionary Illustrated* (1965: 437), culture is defined, in its early sixteenth-century usage, as 'improvement or refinement by education and training'. This image has endured in middle- and upper-class circles, and is often associated with ballet, film, literature, music, painting, scholarship, sculpture and theatre. However, as Raymond Williams argues, culture has 'a range and overlap of meanings' (Williams 1976: 80). Thus, for example, a sub-culture is a 'culture of a distinguishable smaller group' (1976: 82). You might reasonably argue that the so-called 'high' culture of the upper class is also a sub-culture because the upper class is a small group. However, upper-class people exercise powers that are greater than their size as a group might suggest. Through the ownership and control they exercise in 'culture industries' like cinema and theatre, they can make their definitions of good taste stick.

The sociological concept of culture

The American sociologist, Henry L. Tischler, describes culture as 'a blueprint for living in a particular society' (Tischler 1996: 70). That's a good starting point for a concept which is quite hard to define. *Culture is what we as human beings learn to know and live out*. Beyond sociological circles, the term is sometimes used to describes the lifestyle of 'cultivated' upper-class people. But sociologists don't make this value-judgement. For them, all human beings have a culture, even if society privileges certain cultures above others. Sociologists try to understand culture by making sense of it through theories.

Sociologists maintain that culture is acquired, not inborn. To quote Berger and Luckmann, 'The individual . . . is not born a member of society', but 'becomes a member of society' (Berger and Luckmann 1975: 149). This becoming social is what sociologists term *socialisation*. Put simply, *socialisation is the process whereby people learn to become social human beings. Primary socialisation* is the first part of the 'lesson'. It begins at birth, typically in the family, and carries on through childhood. *Secondary socialisation* is the icing on the cake: it's 'a subsequent process that inducts an already socialized individual into new sectors of the objective world of his [*sic*] society' (Berger and Luckmann 1975: 150).

During socialisation the individual *internalises* – that is, takes in – the image of society that is mediated to her or him by the people 'in charge' of socialisation – the *significant others*. Parents usually figure prominently among significant others. Through *identification* with the significant others, the child takes on their culture and makes it part of her or his own. In this way, the individual acquires a self – a sense of subjective identitity. For example, a boy whose significant others give him toy guns to play with might begin to see himself as an 'intitiate warrior'. In this sense, the self takes on the expectations of significant others.

Culture imparts *values* (what people are committed to) and *norms* (how people behave), and it defines their *status* (social position) and *role* (expected conduct attached to statuses).

However, don't think of cultural transmission as an assembly line where all the products end up the same. People don't always like what society tries to make them. They sometimes resist convention by doing the exact opposite of the 'respectable' – by investing their identity in punk, new age or other forms of alternative culture, for example.

Nor do human beings always accept the view of the world portrayed by the media. Thus, for example, Rosalind Brunt has documented the resistance of a group of unemployed people who regularly met at a community centre to discuss the media:

'"We enjoy a good argument," they said, interrupting, all speaking at once, in unabashed "fighting talk" in which "the media" were constantly and triumphantly caught in the act of bias and fortunately revealed as part of an all-embracing "they" intent on doing "us" down.'

(Brunt 1992, in Grossberg, Nelson and Treichler 1992: 72)

The 'us' and 'them' dichotomy is the language of the contender. It reminds us that the 'culture industries' don't always succeed in creating a mass culture.

Culture becomes inscribed on our personalities in a way that makes our internal world more than just a physical thing. To be sure, our brains are physically wired, but the wiring responds to our cultural preferences. If, for example, you've been socialised into a particular music culture, listening to your favourite track can trigger brain functions which are experienced as inner pleasure. But cultural identities can be changed, especially during times, like now, of sweeping economic and social change. In that context, it's important to emphasise that how people see themselves in relation to social class, gender, ethnicity, age and region is undergoing transformation.

EXAM TIP

Avoid getting into lengthy discussions about biological influences on human behaviour in the exam. You're studying sociology, not biology.

QUESTIONS

1 Briefly, define these terms: culture, identity, socialisation (primary and secondary), significant others, values, norms and roles.
2 What is the relationship between culture and identity?
3 How do we know that the way people think and act is more linked to culture than biology?
4 How do people resist prescribed cultural forms?

Theories of culture

In this section, we'll examine seven important theories of culture:

- functionalism
- marxism
- social constructionism
- modernism
- postmodernism
- structuralism
- poststructuralism.

All of them feature in sociology, but the last four theories, in particular, are widely used by philosophers, anthropologists and literary critics. Chapters 1 and 4 have already looked at functionalism, marxism and social constructionism. There's no need therefore to re-visit these theories in detail. Instead, we'll concentrate on what they have to say about culture.

Each of the seven theories will be critiqued in terms of 'For and against' arguments.

Functionalist theory of culture

The '"structure of culture" consists in patterns of meaning', says Talcott Parsons (1967: 141). By this, he's referring to how meanings are attached to things. What meaning, for example, do you attach to a painting by Vincent Van Gogh, a red telephone box, an album by Nirvana, a bag of fish and chips? Things British perhaps to the second and fourth items, 'high fine art' to the first, and the Seattle grunge scene to the third. The patterns to which Parsons alludes are the predictable associations between perceptions and objects. People who like grunge music, for example, perceive that style in bands like Nirvana and Sound Garden. Saying the words 'fish and chips' conjures up for many an immediate association with Britain, just as 'Coca Cola' evokes images of America.

These cultural forms are transmitted through institutions – the family, education, the media, etc. People acquire them through socialisation. In that sense, culture is a shaping force because it exercises a strong influence on how individuals make sense of their own identities and the society they inhabit. But people are also producers of culture. As Parsons maintains, 'Culture . . . is on the one hand the product of, on the other hand a determinant of, systems of human social interaction' (1964: 15). Put simply, we make culture and culture makes us. You've come to like Oasis, REM and Blur because you've decided to give their music a try. But, in the first instance, your friends persuaded you to buy their albums. Now it's your turn, in conjunction with your friends, to influence other people by suggesting that they give these bands a go. Here we have an individual decision influenced by social factors, and then a new social force as you and your friends seek to shape the musical tastes of other people.

In its extreme form, functionalism argues that people are the raw material with which culture works. In that sense, the *function* of culture is to socialise us into the value system of the society we inhabit and to define our identities for us in terms of the roles we're expected to play. Of course, as biological mortals, we lead finite lives, but culture is timeless. It faces us when we're born and continues when we die. Its form changes, but it endures as a social force. This model of culture as a shaping thing is, to be sure, deliberately over-stated. Like caricature in art, it exaggerates in order to draw attention to key features. Functionalists recognise that the degree to which culture shapes people and the degree to which it is shaped by people varies. In a big city, like Manchester, where difference is celebrated, individuals embody, enact their own cultural styles. In a small country town, like Kiltimagh in Ireland, where collective sentiments are cherished, individuals adhere to a communal culture.

While Parsons and other functionalists recognise that cultures embody ideologies, there's a tendency to regard ideology primarily as 'the belief system shared by the members of a collectivity' (Parsons 1964: 331) rather than by a dominant class. Functionalists might point to the many examples of shared values that are held by most people in society, but they perhaps underestimate the extent to which consensus is engineered by the rich and powerful. Instead of looking for conspiracy theories, functionalists tend to see modern culture as playing a civilising and enlightening role.

Thus, for example, S. N. Eisenstadt contends that the cultural outlook of modernisation:

> 'has been characterized by an emphasis on progress and improvement, on happiness and the spontaneous expression of abilities and feeling, on individuality as a moral value, and concomitant stress on the dignity of the individual and, last, on efficiency.'
>
> (Eisenstadt 1966: 5)

While critics can point to the very undignified character of nazi Germany, also a product of the modern age, Eisenstadt regards that episode as a regressive aberration, out of kilter with the generous spirit of genuine modernism. He actually referred to German nazism as a 'trend toward complete demodernization' (1966: 160).

FUNCTIONALIST THEORY OF CULTURE

FOR

+ People are shaped by the culture of the society they inhabit. Your accent is what it is because your culture has fashioned it in that way. Functionalism reminds us of a simple but easily overlooked fact – we're largely products of our culture, and our sense of self, of personal identity, is culturally defined.
+ Functionalism, as its name implies, properly emphasises the *function* of culture in society. Culture is the cement that holds the structure of society together. It's the value system that people acquire and later transmit to other generations, without which society would crumble and fall.
+ Functionalist sociologists document the impressive cultural legacy of the modern age, especially in relation to its optimistic quest for improvement and progress, and its respect for human dignity.

AGAINST

– While it acknowledges that individuals play a role in creating culture, functionalism actually underplays this fact and exaggerates the extent to which culture has a life over and above the people who help to construct it.
– Functionalism doesn't pay enough attention to the crucial question of whose particular interests culture serves most. It over-emphasises collective interests, and underestimates the ways in which dominant groups perpetuate ideologies through cultural forms.
– Its optimistic appraisal of the alleged civilising effect of modern culture doesn't square with all the facts. There are lots of examples of so-called modern cultures which oppress working-class people, people who are disabled, women, gay people, and minority ethnic groups.

Even if Eisenstadt's description of the nazi period as a form of 'demodernization' is an accurate one, modern culture isn't without its drawbacks. The process of 'western' modernisation involved empire-building, slavery and economic exploitation. It celebrated white male power and oppressed black people and women. The development of science was harnessed to the technology of warfare. These are aspects of modernisation that must feature in the overall picture. Otherwise, we obtain an unbalanced and distorted version of events.

OVER TO YOU

Which aspects of culture have had a strong influence on your attitudes and behaviour?

The main propositions of functionalist theory of culture

- Culture comprises patterns of meanings that are transmitted through institutions, like the family, education, and the media.
- People acquire these meanings through socialisation. For example, British people attach the meaning 'Emergency Services' to the numbers '999', whereas, for Americans, '911' evokes that association.
- Culture is a shaping force because it exercises a strong influence on how individuals make sense of the society they inhabit and how they identify themselves in terms of roles. While functionalists are often accused of representing culture as a totalising force, they accept that people also produce culture.
- Modern culture generally reflects widely-held values in society, and usually plays a civilising and enlightening role.

The marxist theory of culture

Marx believed that people have to attend to economic needs before they can participate in culture. You need food in your belly before you can enjoy poetry or sport. There's an element of chicken and egg (which came first?) here, but Marx's argument is more one of emphasis than of absolutes. Think about it. People do have to take care of basic needs – food, warmth, shelter – before other things. In that respect, Marx has got it right. Where, however, he becomes very controversial is with his next proposition – that the economic system shapes the cultural system.

What Marx means by this is that the richest and most powerful people in society create and sustain cultural institutions that promote their economic interests. For example, capitalists send their children to elite schools so that they'll be socialised into a leadership culture. On reaching adulthood, these children will have acquired the cultural capital (upper-class knowledge, values, tastes, etc.) that will help them to prosper economically. Moreover, the ruling class also presides over important cultural institutions – notably, schools and the media – which convey 'appropriately' scaled-down beliefs and tastes for the general population. For example, largely public school-educated political elites enact policies that affect the education of those 93 per cent of British children who attend state schools.

Like the functionalists, marxists contend that humankind is the controlled product of culture. Marxists, however, believe that culture in capitalist society is oppressive because it conveys the belief system (i.e. the ideology) of the ruling class rather than promoting the well-being of all people. Louis Althusser, a structuralist (see page 123) and a marxist, argues that the ruling class uses schools and other cultural institutions to propagate its ideology. Thus, for example, the school 'drums into them [children] . . . a certain amount of "know-how" wrapped in the ruling ideology' (Althusser 1971: 147). In that way, the school chains the identity into a submissive sense of self.

The majority of people, claim marxists, are born into a world which isn't theirs, and they're expected to align their identities with the system. It's a world whose design is constructed by the rich and powerful. Marxists don't like this. They want something different. The majority of the people don't have to submit to the cultural ascendancy of the dominant class. Instead of accepting a 'hand-me-down' culture, they can forge a working-class identity, and through collective struggle, can make a popular socialist culture the prevailing one. As the marxist, Antonio Gramsci, says, 'History is at once freedom and necessity' (1919, in Gramsci 1977: 75). The will to freedom, maintain marxists, exists on an international as well as a national level. That's why they urge poor countries to remove what they term the yoke of 'western' capitalism which has exploited – and continues to exploit – them in the modern age and beyond.

Marxists, as idealists and as social scientists, contend that there's no such thing as unalterable structure – tough, yes, resilient, maybe, but fixed – never!

OVER TO YOU

To what extent, if at all, have you experienced culture as something imposed upon you by powerful people?

The main propositions of marxist theory of culture

- People have to meet their economic needs before they can have a culture. In practice, powerful people create and sustain cultural institutions which promote their own economic interests.
- Like functionalists, marxists argue that humankind is the controlled product of culture. Marxists add, however, that culture in capitalist society is oppressive because it protects the interests of the ruling class rather than promoting the well-being of all people.
- Marxists contend that culture isn't unalterable, and that oppressive cultures should be contested by 'the people', especially through their identification with and engagement in class struggle.

The social constructionist theory of culture

In his book, *Moving Culture*, Paul Willis says:

'it's high time we started from where young people are rather than from where traditional arts or youth policies think they ought to be. In order to do this we need to pose different questions.

Not exclusively, "how can we bring 'the arts' to youth?" but "in what ways are the young already in some sense the artists of their own lives?"

Not exclusively, "why is their culture not like ours?" but "what are their cultures like?"

Not "how can we inspire the young with Art?" but "how are the young already energised in ways which we can re-inforce?"'

(Willis 1990: 9)

By recognising that Art and other cultural identities are created by young people rather than just simply offered to them, Willis – a marxist theorist – here adopts a social constructionist approach. The affinity of marxism with social constructionism is at its closest in the discussion of *human agency*, that is, when individuals choose to make decisions. Unlike marxism, however, social constructionism doesn't see choice as something which occurs only at critical moments, as in the marxist notion of revolutions – those no-turning back points when individuals seize the historical moment and topple old power structures. Voluntarism (i.e. the capacity to be wilful) doesn't have to wait, say the social constructionists. You can express your cultural identity, for example, by designing your own clothes, composing your own music and writing your own poetry.

In that way, you're a maker of culture. To be sure, you'll also select some of your cultural preferences from a menu of cultural forms – grunge or classic, the *Sun* or the *Guardian*, 501s or a skirt. In that sense, your choice is affected by the available cultural forms. There's a recognition too among social constructionists that culture,

MARXIST THEORY OF CULTURE

FOR

+ Marxism helpfully identifies the link between material factors and cultural forms. People have to eat before they can create or participate in cultural life. Moreover, cultural forms often serve economic aims (for example, a public school culture perpetuates elite self-recruitment).
+ Related to the preceding point, marxism shows that culture is less an amalgam of societal beliefs and values than the embodiment of ruling-class ideology. In that respect, marxists rightly remind us to ask the question: '*Whose* culture are you talking about?'
+ Marx argued that the ruling ideas are the ideas of the ruling class, but – importantly – he made it clear that this didn't have to be so. There is a wilfulness in individuals which, when galvanised in combined and concerted action, can successfully challenge cultural 'indoctrination', and introduce new cultural identities.

AGAINST

– Marx exaggerated the extent to which culture is shaped by economic forces. There are 'stand-alone' aspects of culture that people engage even without taking account of economic factors. Consider, for example, the *free* and extensive use of public libraries.

– Marx invokes conspiratorial theory when he proposes that the cultural tastes of the ruling class express their ideology. The appreciation and enjoyment of Shakespeare, for example, doesn't make an upper-class person a manipulator of other people. Shakespeare's plays are widely read and watched by people from wide-ranging backgrounds because his work is outstanding in itself, not because the ruling class say so.

– The intimation that different cultures can't peacefully co-exist is evident in Marx's strong emphasis on conflict. However, the locking of horns between 'high' and 'low' culture is only one possible outcome. Lots of cultural preferences can exist alongside each other within an atmosphere of mutual toleration.

especially in the period of early socialisation, has a profound influence on the formation of identity. Thus, for example, the social constructionists, Peter L. Berger and Thomas Luckmann, note that:

'the developing human being not only interrelates with a particular natural environment, but with a specific cultural and social order, which is mediated to him [*sic*] by the significant others who have charge of him.'

(Berger and Luckmann 1975: 66)

As people get older, however, their autonomy grows and their dependence upon prescribed norms and values loosens. This is especially apparent in the transitional phase from youth to adulthood, when individuals are often very eager to do their 'own thing'. The American sociologist, Alvin Gouldner, captures this mood when he writes:

'For, when cultural patterns fail to satisfy the individual in a specific environment . . . he [*sic*] may and does modify them; that is, the embodied individual can extricate himself from conventional beliefs'

(Gouldner 1972: 225)

If such weren't the case, culture would be frozen in its tracks and society wouldn't change. People would simply learn and repeat the cultures of preceding generations *ad infinitum*. There are, of course, some societies where change is much slower than in others. But all societies change, whatever the pace of the process. It's also important to emphasise that human agency transcends (i.e. breaks through) ruling-class ideologies. People who choose and create their own cultural styles aren't the robotic dupes of other people's cultures. They're themselves and they make their own statements.

OVER TO YOU

In which aspects of your musical and other tastes do you sense a tension between your own and other people's views. How can this tension be resolved? Try to use sociological language.

The main propositions of social constructionist theory of culture

- Culture and cultural identity are created by people rather than just simply offered to them.
- The relationship of the individual to culture is an interactive one. People make culture but they also select cultural forms from what's already on offer.
- During early socialisation, culture profoundly shapes identity, but maturity brings more autonomy, giving adults the confidence to contest and change existing cultural forms.

SOCIAL CONSTRUCTIONIST THEORY OF CULTURE

FOR

+ It strikes the right balance between social influences and individual wilfulness. People are socialised into a culture – or cultures – and their attitudes and behaviours reflect this. They also, particularly as they move out of childhood, step off the cultural treadmill and experiment with new cultural identities.

+ Social constructionism accounts for cultural change because it recognises that all individuals have a measure of personal autonomy above and beyond the society they inhabit. This wilful energy enables them to prise free from existing social structures and to change the *status quo* through innovative behaviour.

+ Social constructionist theorists remind us that ruling-class ideology isn't as powerful as individual wilfulness. People respond to the tastes of the ruling class in different ways. Some people think they know best; others have a different vision upon which they act.

AGAINST

– It overstates the extent to which people are able to act and think autonomously. Culture is a powerful shaping force. The ability to prise free of it is generally a temporary youthful blip. As adulthood responsibilities beckon, daughters and sons often become as conventional as their parents.

– The same individualism that social constructionists describe is, in large measure, that level of independence which culture 'allows' people to have. Thus, for example, in the US, a certain amount of wilfulness is permitted and even encouraged by American culture. Indeed, making one's distinctive mark is highly prized in the US.

– Social constructionism doesn't pay sufficient attention to the power differentials between different social classes. Ruling-class people exercise cultural power (hegemony) over other classes because they own and control culture industries. In their political capacity, they also influence the content and form of schooling.

Modernism and postmodernism

'The truth is out there', as any *X-Files* fan will know. Special Agent Dana Scully uses all her scientific skills to get at it. Her professional partner, Special Agent Fox Mulder, is more drawn to paranormal theories. When Mulder re-opened the X-files, the FBI's cases concerning unexplained phenomena, the powers who wanted to keep those cases out of the public eye teamed him with Scully. They hoped that Scully, a doctor turned FBI agent, would discredit Mulder's paranormal beliefs, thereby leading to the closing of the X-files once and for all. But Scully disappoints them.

Her scientific culture tells her to accept only what the hard empirical evidence reveals. Scepticism of things paranormal, however, is gradually tempered when Mulder's unorthodox ideas shed plausible insights on things unseen and unexplained. Heartened by his partner's new-found open-mindedness, Mulder remarks, 'In our investigations you may not always agree with me, but at least you respect the journey' (*The X-Files: The Movie*, 1996). Later, after court officials pour scorn on one of his oddball theories, Mulder enquires of Scully, 'Do you think they would have taken me more seriously if I wore the grey suit?'

Mulder's question highlights the difference between the *modern* and the *postmodern* outlook:

- *Modernists* espouse conventional, tried and tested arguments.
- *Postmodernists* are suspicious of the 'obvious' and debunk old 'certainties'.

Scully and Mulder: doctor-turned-FBI agent with modernist leanings, and FBI agent-cum-paranormal investigator with postmodernist inclinations

You might be thinking that modernists, by definition, can't be proposing old arguments. However, postmodernists are even 'newer' than modernists. Modernists were around in the seventeenth century when science challenged superstition. Postmodernists are twentieth-century thinkers who are taking on science. This isn't to say that modernism and postmodernism can't or don't co-exist in the same society. They can and they do. Modernism, for example, is still very entrenched in the way British scientists study the universe. However, there are clear postmodern themes in the way that some British thinkers are blurring the hard and fast boundaries between heterosexual and homosexual identities.

In necessarily simplified terms, we can understand the essential difference between a modernist and a postmodernist view of the world by asking an advocate of each approach to look at a potato and write down what they see. The modernist writes down 'potato', because that word provides a fairly accurate mental representation of what she or he sees. The postmodernist doesn't write anything, because a word can't convey a mirror image of what she or he sees – the one thing is a round-shaped vegetable, the other a series of letters. The modernist believes we can reasonably accurately describe a real thing in written (or spoken) language because we share common understandings rooted in culture. The postmodernist believes we can't describe 'reality' – whatever that might be – because a word is not the same as the thing it describes, and can mean different things to different people.

Modernism

Sociology started its life as an academic discipline in the nineteenth century. It was, and in many ways still is, a product of the so-called modernist perspective. Modernism was sparked by the work of scientists during the period known as the Enlightenment. Galileo (1564–1642) and Newton (1642–1727) are among the better known of the Enlightenment scientists. These two physicists set about unlocking the mysteries of the universe. In that quest, they rejected the superstitious culture of the 'ancients' and replaced it with the *enlightened* culture of *modern* science.

Their aim was to conquer the forces of nature through scientific knowledge. If, for, example, you measure the physical force of gravity, you might be able to build a roof that can withstand the impact of a falling tree. In that way, you conquer the force. Similarly, the positivist sociologist, August Comte (1798–1859), sought to measure the social forces that shape human behaviour and shape cultural identities in order better to turn and tilt these forces in a direction which helps society. In that respect, knowledge is applied to moral purpose. For instance, if we find that property crimes increase under the impact of unemployment, we can use that knowledge to tackle the causes of crime.

Reason, in the service of humankind, has profound emancipatory potential. This is why modernist sociologists like Jurgen Habermas are suspicious of postmodernism and its rage against the promise of the Enlightenment. Habermas persistently argues against the postmodernist suspicion of reason because, as Anthony Giddens puts it, 'The modern world for Habermas *is* more enlightened than the primitive' (Giddens 1987, in Bernstein 1987: 100). But let's allow Habermas to speak for himself:

'Over and over again, the necessary conditions for a "good life" are carelessly and arbitrarily violated. It is from this experience that the tradition of thought that unites Marx and Freud draws its inspiration.'

(Habermas 1987, in Bernstein 1987: 216)

In alluding to Marx and Freud, Habermas is placing his trust in their efforts, through the ethical application of reason and science, to make a more just and a happier world. In his last philosophical encounter with the famous philosopher and social scientist, Herbert Marcuse, his scholar friend told him that the most basic value judgements are rooted in compassion, in a sense for the suffering of other human beings. For Marcuse, this is an incontestable moral truth. Like him, Habermas believes that humanitarian and moral arguments could and must become vital cultural forces. Habermas also puts his faith in certain universal empirical truths, for example, that the earth is approximately spherical in shape – whether or not you or I think otherwise. This is a key feature of the modernist perspective because it challenges the postmodernist notion that truth is simply in the eyes of the beholder. Accepting that it's right to show compassion to a neighbour and that the earth approximates to a sphere are unconditional truths.

Habermas doesn't overstate the claims of science. He accepts that when there are disagreements about scientific claims, the modern spirit lives 'in the expectation of *future* resolutions' (1987, in Bernstein 1987: 194). The point is to be able to distinguish between good arguments which endure and those which are fads of the moment. This isn't to claim absolute, perfect knowledge. Rather, it's to say that some claims to knowledge are more reliable than others. If, for example, social scientific evidence suggests that pre-school education helps to reduce later juvenile delinquency, that evidence should be taken as more trustworthy than a personal opinion about this.

In distinguishing between the modern and postmodern mood, it's important to take account of more than just different perspectives. The settings in which the perspectives are located are just as important. In his book, *Myth and Meaning*, Claude Levi-Strauss puts his finger on this when he says:

'What threatens us right now is probably what we may call over-communication – that is, the tendency to know exactly in one point of the world what is going on in all other parts of the world. In order for a culture to be really itself and to produce something, the culture and its members must be convinced of their originality . . . We are now threatened with the prospect of our being only consumers, able to consume anything from any point in the world and from every culture, but of losing all originality.'

(Levi-Strauss 1978: 20)

In a modern world, culture is familiar, well-rehearsed, and original, and the self knows its place in a familiar setting. In a postmodern world, culture is elusive, hard to grasp, and variable, and the self becomes a process rather than a fixture. Levi-Strauss is right to point out that globalism is eroding distinct national cultures. Take, for example, the increasing 'europeanisation' of nation states like the UK, France, Germany and other EU countries. The prospect of a European currency beckons, and people eat English breakfasts in Spain and drink Spanish wine in London. This inter-mixing of different cultural forms demonstrates that globalisation doesn't necessarily replace national standardisation with global standardisation.

It's possible to act locally and globally in lots of different ways. Sometimes there's an obvious connection between the two, as, for example, when one marches in London against the use of torture worldwide. Here we have an example of local democratic rights being exercised in pursuit of global human rights. On other occasions, without contesting each other, local and global behaviours don't have to converge. For instance, Irish people can celebrate their cultural roots in music, and also advocate the rights of all children to proper nutrition, good health care and decent education.

While it's true that modernity, like postmodernity, comes in different shapes and sizes (i.e. it's not possible to pin down one specific type of modern society), it's also the case that modernists prefer to explain social phenomena in fairly singular terms. The discourse of science is especially favoured, while more literary and intuitive arguments are often treated as 'fables'. Science makes great claims about its ability to get it right when it describes and analyses the world. It speaks a big triumphalist language – a *metanarrative*. It's precisely this 'know-all' posture that bugs the postmodernists. That's why their approach, the postmodern one, is best defined, to quote the postmodernist Jean-Francois Lyotard, 'as incredulity toward metanarratives' (1984, in Hall *et al*. 1966: 356).

The main propositions of modernist theory of culture

- There is a universal truth and it can best be known and understood through reason and objective evidence. At the end of the day, the force of a better argument must be recognised and acknowledged.

MODERNIST THEORY OF CULTURE

FOR

+ Reason and empirical evidence – hallmarks of modern culture – are more reliable than superstition and hearsay – features of the pre-modern age. In that sense, modernity represents progress. Myth might declare the earth to be flat, but science knows otherwise. Modernism offers the promise of a better understanding of the world in which we live. What we need is more *enlightenment*, not less.
+ Modernism has played and continues to play an emancipatory role in society. The application of science and reason were integral to the making of the modern world. Consider, for example, the medical advances that the application of modern knowledge has produced. Who do you trust to treat you when you're ill – a doctor or a magician? Nobody's suggesting that science and reason are perfect, but they're surely more trustworthy than superstition and ignorance.
+ Our experience tells us there is a world outside our bodies. We bump into it every day, sometimes literally! Parts of that world are physically real (for example, even if we think a brick wall isn't real, we can't walk through it), and parts are socially real (for example, we might imagine that ethnicity is a mere illusion, but try telling that to a human being who has been assaulted because she or he is Irish).
+ It's important to accept that there are at least some universal standards against which justice can be measured. Otherwise, anything goes. While there are areas of contention about what's right or wrong, there are some principles that endure across cultures and over time. For example, the conviction that we should treat other people in the way we want them to treat us is a self-evidently decent moral code. It holds true for all humans, of any or no religion.

AGAINST

– The modernist outlook has 'know-all' tendencies. To be sure, it's scientific approach is an advance on superstition, but science doesn't have all the answers. For example, we still haven't found a cure for all cancers. It's therefore important that scientists adopt a more modest stance when they make claims based on empirical evidence alone. Life is too complex to be understood on just one level of analysis. Other ways of looking are also important.

– While the application of modernist thinking has led to progress, it's also led to the oppression of people with different cultures. The science of navigation, for example, made us realise the earth isn't flat. But this knowledge helped unscrupulous sea captains ship human cargo – slaves – from Africa to the Americas. Modernism brought science but it didn't always insist on the use of scientific knowledge in humanitarian ways.

– Modernists adopt the somewhat culturally 'elitist' view that objective knowledge is superior to subjective knowledge. This leads to the putting up of an artificial barrier between the world and the individual. The relationship between these two phenomena isn't 'either/or'; it's interactive. My subjectivity isn't just an opinion. It's very real to me, and it's worthy of investigation.

– Modernists don't attach sufficient importance to human wilfulness, instead seeing people as the generally complicit subjects of social structure. In that respect, modernism tends to see the relationship between the individual and society as one in which the individual 'discovers' social laws rather than 'creating' them. What can be overlooked here is that people make the structures that later 'imprison' them.

- The privileging of reason above superstition underpins cultural, economic and technological progress. Placing reason in the service of humankind is emancipatory and profoundly moral.
- Sociology and other sciences must trust objectivity more than subjectivity. If, for example, a doctor tells me her data strongly links smoking to a higher incidence of lung cancer, she's referring to data that's independent (i.e. free-standing) of my personal opinions.

Postmodernism

According to Stanley J. Grenz, 'Postmodernism was born in St Louis, Missouri, on July 15, 1972, at 3:32 p.m.' (Grenz 1996: 11). At that precise moment, a housing estate in St Louis, originally hailed as a landmark of modern architecture but hated by its low-income inhabitants, came crashing down – blown up by dynamite. Grenz is actually referring here to the assertion by Charles Jencks – arguably, the single most influential advocate of architectural postmodernism – that this event pronounced the death of modernity and the birth of postmodernity.

So what has the deliberate demolition of a building got to do with this rite of passage from one age to another? The housing estate was built by people who believed it was a technological 'masterpiece' – the application of modern, scientific design in the quest for better living conditions. The people who lived on the estate were unimpressed, and 'vandalised' it. The 'high' culture of the architects who thought they knew best was pitted against the 'low' culture of the inhabitants who knew they knew better. And here we have the spirit of the postmodern age – postmodernism marks the end of a single, all-encompassing, universal worldview. It replaces this with a celebration of the multiple, the particular, and the local. In that respect, following the philosopher, Friedrich Nietzsche (1844–1900), postmodernists claim that 'reality' takes different forms.

While modernists think that conventional science, with its emphasis on empirical measurement, provides the closest we can get to irrefutable knowledge, postmodernists are sceptical. Instead of seeing human energy as a quantifiable force, the French postmodernist, Jacques Derrida, urges us to look inwards to a humanity that can't be measured in quantifiable terms. Thus, in his book, *The Gift of Death,* he writes:

> 'Force has become the modern figure of being. Being has allowed itself to be determined as a calculable force, and man [*sic*], instead of relating to the being that is *hidden under* this figure of force, represents himself as quantifiable power.'
>
> (Derrida 1995: 37)

In an earlier book, *Of Grammatology*, Derrida's disdain for 'done and dusted' empirical pronouncements is revealed in his reference to 'all the "empiricist" or nonphilosophical motifs that have constantly tormented philosophy throughout the history of the West' (Derrida 1982: 19). Postmodernists rebut the modernist claim that the empirical search for knowledge will lead to objective understanding of the world in which we live. Rather, they claim that we participate in this world, and that reality is what we make it through our cultural identities. In that sense, truth is sometimes what our hearts, not our minds, tell us.

While postmodernists are anti-measurement in the sense that they don't trust positivism, they don't rule out the possibility of measuring things altogether. Thus, for example, the postmodernist, Jean-Francois Lyotard, recognises that money can be used in a measuring context when he writes:

> 'it remains possible and useful to assess the value of works of art according to the profits they yield. Such realism accommodates all tendencies, just as capital accommodates all "needs", providing that the tendencies and needs have purchasing power.'
>
> (Lyotard 1983, in Docherty 1993: 42)

Nevertheless. postmodernists challenge the notion that self-styled, 'high culture' experts have a more privileged access to knowledge than anybody else. In that sense, the scientist and the philosopher, for example, must enter a 'conversation' with non-experts in which everyone has a voice and a right to be heard. The postmodernist philosopher, Richard Rorty, endorses this argument when he writes:

> 'If we see knowing not as having an essence, to be described by scientists or philosophers, but rather as a right, by current standards, to believe, then we are well on the way to seeing *conversation* as the ultimate context within which knowledge is to be understood.'
>
> (Rorty 1979: 389)

Rorty's concluding sentence in his book, *Philosophy and the Mirror of Nature*, reiterates this conviction:

> 'The only point on which I would insist is that philosophers' moral concern should be with continuing the conversation of the West, rather than with insisting upon a place for the traditional problems of modern philosophy within that conversation.'
>
> (Rorty 1979: 394)

In simple language, Rorty is saying that everyone, not just philosophers, should join in deciding what is worthy of discussion and debate. His argument accords with the postmodern view that what counts as truth is often linked to what powerful people say it is. Knowledge is thus *situated* (i.e. linked to particular cultural contexts) rather than *universal*. Another way of putting this is to say that knowledge is *historicised*, namely, located within an historical age and culture. Alternative medicine is an example of the postmodern perspective because it challenges the historically entrenched assumption that *all* health matters are the province of conventional medicine.

Postmodern influences extend beyond the realm of science to embrace art, fashion, literature, media, morality, music, and lots more. Grunge, for example, represents a different voice to classical music, a voice that says, 'Your tastes aren't ours'. The same is so with new art forms that refuse to be set on a lower level than traditional 'fine art' – a different level maybe, but certainly not an inferior one. Postmodernism heralds, as Stanley Grenz puts it, a:

> 'moving away from the mass culture of modernity, which offered a few styles that changed with the seasons, toward a fragmented "taste culture", which offers an almost endless variety of styles.'
>
> (Grenz 1996: 19)

This emphasis on pluralism controversially characterises the postmodern stance on morality. Suspicious of universal claims to justice, equality and freedom, postmodernists celebrate different views and alternative cultures. In some contexts, this might be interpreted as tolerance, but an 'anything goes' approach to morals makes it impossible to discern right from wrong. This point is forcefully argued by the phenomenologist sociologist, John O'Neill, who writes:

> 'It is a conceit of postmodernity that it stands on a point of the highest morality achieved through the erosion of

all previous moral institutions. Today we are told to jettison the old fashioned belief in unique values that cannot be exhausted by their practice . . . It is not the masses who have sickened of the injustice and exploitation that grinds their lives . . . it is not these people who have abandoned idealism, universalism, truth and justice. It is those who already enjoy these things who have denounced them on behalf of the others.'

(O'Neill 1995: 1)

Strong stuff! O'Neill is clearly disturbed by the contemplation that an intellectual post-modernist elite, who claim not to accept that any one view is more valid than another view, should be making pronouncements about morality. By contrast, postmodernists claim that conventional morality has become a discourse which oppresses those who are victims of the 'naming game' of the rich and the powerful. People who are called 'criminals', 'looney lefties', 'aggressive beggars' and such like are

POSTMODERNIST THEORY OF CULTURE

FOR

+ Postmodernism restores a human touch to an over-mechanised modernist portrayal of the world. It teaches us to reflect on our inner selves and to act on our informed beliefs, instead of adopting the view that society programmes us in a robot-like fashion. In that way, it forces us to consider the human autonomy that resides outside of 'cultural systems'.
+ Postmodernism highlights the extent to which science and reason have been used in the service of elites, and often against 'weaker' members of society. Foucault, for example, identifies dominant and subjugated knowledges (i.e. knowledge considered true because the ruling class say so, and knowledge deemed untrue because the subservient aren't heeded).
+ The metanarratives ('big canvas' theories) of society are losing their authority. Triumphalist universal truths overstate the global and understate the local. Thus, for example, self-styled 'western' experts who tell poor countries that the 'west knows best' about population control don't understand that, from the cultural perspective of a poor family, lots of children means more hands to raise crops.
+ The postmodern outlook encourages people to become more aware and more tolerant of social differences and more accepting of multi-culturalism. Its refusal to accept that a self-appointed intellectual and moral elite have access to superior knowledge and higher ethical principles, gives a voice to those groups in society who remain outside charmed and privileged circles.

AGAINST

− The postmodernist tendency to regard lots of different assertions as equally valid leads to a lack of resolution in moral and empirical affairs. Issues are left dangling because no argument, however compelling, is privileged above contesting views. Thus, for example, the empirical fact that poverty is associated with ill-health is treated as mere opinion. It's this loss of certainty that makes it difficult to confront real problems as though they were real. Moreover, why should we take postmodernism seriously when, by its own admission, postmodernist views are just 'any other' arguments?

− Postmodernists have 'double standards'. They lead their lives 'as if' the world is real, but, on an abstract intellectual level, they contest the notion that what's real is actually knowable. When, for example, they visit the doctor, they treat that person as an expert. In that respect, they privilege certain forms of knowledge because it makes good sense to rely on a doctor's diagnosis. They also adopt commonly accepted notions of right and wrong in everyday life. Yet they say morality is a matter of opinion.

− Postmodernism claims to be against privileged cultural forms. Yet postmodernists don't communicate their ideas in a way that's easily understood by ordinary people. As John O'Neill (1995) argues, postmodernists are an intellectual elite who enjoy idealism, universalism, truth and justice while denouncing these things on behalf of 'ordinary' people.

− It succumbs to conspiratorial theory when it argues, following Nietzsche, that claims to truth are claims to power. Objective truth isn't anyone's ideological prop. It's a stand-alone statement based on evidence about the real world. Science and ideology are inimical to each other. The one is based on empirical data, the other on value judgements. Being objective means telling it like it is, even if that upsets people in power.

denounced by these labels and they suffer the consequences of them. Isn't it appropriate, inquire the postmodernists, that we listen to their side of the story, their moral values rather than accepting that the elite knows better?

The main propositions of postmodernist theory of culture

- There's no absolute certainty, no irrefutable objective fact, no singular correct perspective, no universal morality. There are as many kinds of knowledge and morality as there are different cultural identities, and we should be wary of the claim that some cultures are better than others.
- Postmodernism is generally suspicious of empirical measurement and other aspects of scientific culture. Rather than envisaging a single measurable reality, postmodernists, adopting the perspective of the philosopher, Friedrich Nietzsche, emphasise that reality is rich and varied.
- Postmodernists contest the view that self-styled experts have a more privileged access to knowledge than anybody else. They urge academics to enter a 'conversation' with non-academics, to tune into 'the people's' culture, and to listen as well as speak.

Structuralism

Structuralism and modernism tend to go hand in hand, but there are also some similarities between structuralist and postmodernist ideas. Like modernists, structuralists believe that culture *structures* (i.e. shapes) our beliefs and behaviours. In that respect, culture is construed as an objectively real force which fashions our identities. The task of the structuralist is to locate that which all cultures have in common, even though surface appearances often suggest lots of differences. British people who shake hands and French people who kiss exhibit behaviours that are outwardly different. Dig a little deeper though, and we find an underlying structure which impresses upon all people the need to display open affection towards friends. It's how the display manifests itself that differs, not the sentiment.

Like modernists, structuralists also claim that it's possible to distinguish between truth and untruth. Thus, for example, the marxist structuralist, Louis Althusser, believes that the primary task of philosophy is '"to draw a dividing line" between the true ideas and false ideas' (Althusser 1971: 23). As exponents of the belief that structures are real, structuralists are, of course, bound to make this distinction.

The affinity between structuralists and postmodernists – and we emphasise that the two perspectives are generally dissimilar – is perhaps most apparent in literature. Take a famous writer, like William Shakespeare. Structuralists don't see an individual genius behind his plays. Instead, they envisage a man who was a product of his culture. His culture is the author; he is but the tool. This takes away from Shakespeare the notion of literary gravitas which derives from Enlightenment-inspired, modernist notions of 'great writers'.

The idea of individual greatness, whether in literary or other fields, is a powerful feature of the Enlightenment celebration of the 'self'. However, in the structuralist outlook, the great writer, the genius scientist or whatever, fade into the social structure of which all of us are a part. The famous French anthropologist and structuralist, Claude Levi-Strauss, even goes so far as to almost deny his own sense of personal identity:

> 'I never had, and still do not have, the perception of feeling my personal identity. I appear to myself as the place where something is going on, but there is no "I", no "me".'
>
> (Levi-Strauss 1978: 34)

Levi-Strauss says that he doesn't have the feeling that he writes his own books. Rather, he reports, 'I have the feeling that my books get written through me' (1978: 3). The parallel with postmodernism is apparent here – elevated, so-called canonical literary works, path-breaking scientific discoveries, and, in the case of Levi-Strauss, mighty anthropological findings, are transformed into more modest enterprises. Shakespeare, Newton and Levi-Strauss become the mere carriers of prevailing cultural trends.

The view that culture is more powerful than individual self-expression lies at the heart of Levi-Strauss' structuralism. In his analysis, the self is just a surface flicker because all human brains are similar. Strip away the masks that give the appearance of human difference, and you find we're all pretty much the same. As Levi-Strauss puts it:

> 'It is probably one of the many conclusions of anthropological research that, notwithstanding the cultural differences between the several parts of mankind [*sic*], the human mind is everywhere one and the same and that it has the same capacities. I think this is accepted everywhere.'
>
> (Levi-Strauss 1978: 19)

By way of illustration, Levi-Strauss (1949; in Coser and Rosenberg 1969: 80) notes how the act of giving food and drink is underpinned by a core value system even though the transaction differs in its manifest form. Thus, for example, an old bottle of wine 'calls for shared consumption', because to consume such a fine drink alone stirs feelings of guilt. Similarly, in Polynesian culture, '"to eat from one's own basket"' is considered inappropriate behaviour. In both cultures – a 'western' and a South Pacific island one – sharing is the norm. At the heart of structuralism is what Levi-Strauss terms an attempt 'to reach the invariant property of a very complex set of codes . . . The problem is to find what is common to all of them' (Levi-Strauss 1978: 9). The issue is about 'trying to find an order behind what is given to us as a disorder' (1978: 11), that is, seeking for the structural similarities behind different cultural forms.

The marxist structuralist, Louis Althusser, is also interested in the analysis of deep-lying structures in society. In capitalist societies, contends Althusser, these structures are oppressive, but they lurk behind seemingly benign institutions, like schools. Closer investigation reveals schools for what they really are: cultural institutions that reproduce the existing power structure. Each social class is tutored into its future role. Althusser's argument is supported by empirical research in Britain and the USA (see Chapter 9, Education). Schools and other ideological institutions receive back-up from tougher agents of social control – the military, police forces, prisons, etc. Once again, the power structure is behind the work of these bodies.

Structuralism is also an important approach in literary criticism. Structuralists believe that books reflect not so much the ideas of their authors, but more the ideas of society. In that sense, some structuralists are said to have proclaimed the 'death of the author'. The themes of love and death, for example, manifest themselves in everything from ancient Greek tragedy, through Shakespeare, Grimm's *Fairy Tales* and James Bond. These and other important themes are deeply embedded in the structures of all cultures, and they rise to the surface in written works. That's why readers recognise them almost instantly. As for the writer who 'says he [*sic*] has worked without giving any thought to the rules of the process, he simply means he was working without realizing he knew the rules.' (Umberto Eco 1994: 11). Eco, a novelist (he wrote the medieval detective story, *The Name of the Rose*) and a literary critic, is, of course, a structuralist.

More conventional literary critics lament the tendency of structuralists to reduce the status of great writers to mere carriers of culture. Harold Bloom, for example writes:

'Shakespeare criticism is in full flight from his aesthetic supremacy and works at reducing him to the "social energies" of the English Renaissance.' (Bloom 1995: 2)

For the structuralist, the individual genius of Shakespeare is transformed into the product of an age. Bloom takes strong exception to this. Focusing on 26 writers (among them, Chaucer, Milton, Goethe, Walt Whitman, Tolstoy, Freud, Joyce and Kafka), he ranks Shakespeare as the greatest of the 'western' canon. (Canon means those texts which are deemed to be the most eminent in a culture.) These writers, says Bloom, have qualities that make them 'authoritative in our culture' (1995: 1). He adds that 'William Shakespeare wrote 38 plays, 24 of them masterpieces, but social energy has never written a single scene' (Bloom 1995: 37).

That might be so, but it's important to heed the argument of the structuralist, Ferdinand de Saussure, that to use a language isn't just to express individual and original thoughts. It also involves cueing into and activating meanings that are embedded in a culture which pre-exists the individual author and endures after her or his death. As Saussure noted:

'the language is . . . a "<u>social product</u>" . . . [It] is quite independent of the individual; it cannot be a creation of the individual; it is essentially social; it presupposes the collectivity.'

(de Saussure 1910, in Komatsu and Harris 1993: 7a–8a)

Shakespeare, for example – like any other great writer – tapped into the metaphors, puns and other linguistic devices of his day. In that respect, his individual genius found expression in the systems of meaning that existed in sixteenth-century England.

Consider a favourite writer. When that author uses words that appeal to you, she or he is dipping into a cultural resource that you each share – language. The nice turn of phrase only works because you and the writer understand what it *means*. In a structuralist sense, it's this affinity of understanding between the writer and the reader that makes reading enjoyable. So if you get on with Roald Dahl because his sense of fun and yours are similar, then you'll judge his books as good. On the other hand, one of Shakespeare's comedies mightn't be your cup of tea if you don't like his kind of humour.

Structuralism thus undermines claims to the canon because it denies that great works are the product of individual genius, and accords a similar status to the tastes of the general reader as it does to the literary critic. The argument that some popular choice might be more important than canonical status was recently brought to the forefront when the Waterstones bookshop chain in the UK conducted a national readership survey in 1997. Asked to rate their favourite books of the century, 25,000 customers came up with some choices that surprised the 'critics'.

The top five books were:

1 *The Lord of the Rings,* by J. R. R. Tolkien
2 *1984,* by George Orwell
3 *Animal Farm,* by George Orwell
4 *Ulysses,* by James Joyce
5 *Catch 22,* by Joseph Heller.

Compare this with the more canonical preferences of Dr Nicholas Tate, Chief Executive of the Qualifications and Curriculum Authority:

1 *Remembrance of Things Past*, by Marcel Proust
2 *Speak, Memory*, by Vladimar Nabokov
3 *The Four Quartets*, by T. S. Eliot
4 *Collected Poems* of Jorge Luis Borges
5 *Collected Poems* of John Betjeman.

Among the national 100 favourites in the Waterstones bookstore 1997 poll were Delia Smith and J.R.R. Tolkien.

CRIT THINK CRIT THINK CRIT THINK CRIT THINK CRIT THINK CRIT THINK

IS THERE SUCH A THING AS GOOD LITERATURE?

Read this extract from an article by Judith Judd.

'Popular culture, revealed in the choice of *The Lord of The Rings* as the book of the century, is a threat to educational standards, Chris Woodhead, Chief Inspector of Schools, said yesterday. He said the success of the BBC comedy *Only Fools and Horses* and the big vote for JRR Tolkien's *Lord of the Rings* from a bookstore's customers were both examples of that danger. At a London lecture he asks: "What does this really say about our attitude towards quality in the arts?" Later he said: "I am sometimes pessimistic about cultural expectations and the extent of support for teachers doing a difficult job." Mr Woodhead, a former English teacher, said the view of Tolkien that was revealed [it was voted Greatest Book of the twentieth century in a Waterstone's book chain poll] . . . militated against the work of English teachers across the country. "They are trying to develop discrimination in their pupils and an understanding of literature. *The Lord of the Rings* is an immensely readable book but it is not the greatest work of the century." . . . Anne Barnes, General Secretary of the National Association for the Teaching of English, said: "It is ridiculous to say that certain books shouldn't be read in schools. Schools are there to help children read what interests them. And to give them the opportunity to discuss why a book is enjoyable." She said that Tolkien's *The Hobbit* was sometimes used in schools by teachers who were Tolkien enthusiasts. *Lord of the Rings* was rarely taught.'

(Judith Judd, The *Independent*, 22 January 1997, page 3)

1 *What suggests that Chris Woodhead, Chief Inspector of Schools, is adopting a canonical approach to literature? How is the canon sometimes at odds with popular culture?*

2 *How would you characterise the approach adopted by Anne Barnes, General Secretary of the National Association for the Teaching of English? Whose culture is she an advocate of?*

3 *Referring to the passage and elsewhere, what are the arguments for and against the view that some written works deserve canonical status and others don't. Think about the important questions, 'Says who?' and 'Whose culture?', when you address these arguments.*

CRIT THINK CRIT THINK CRIT THINK CRIT THINK CRIT THINK CRIT THINK CRIT

STRUCTURALIST THEORY OF CULTURE

FOR

- **+** It convincingly highlights the deep-lying structures that underpin all human social behaviour. Social scientific research and literary criticism reveal that these structures are evident in seemingly different cultural practices and in language.
- **+** It reminds us that even individual genius is embedded within a social structure. Great writers, for example, dip into the cultural pool of the society they inhabit. The famous physicist, Isaac Newton, is reputed to have said that his own fame rested on the shoulders of other great thinkers.
- **+** In its marxist usage – notably, in the works of Louis Althusser – structuralism cautions us not to take all benign appearances at face value. His argument that cultural forces, like education, reproduce social class inequalities is supported by empirical evidence in the UK and the US.

AGAINST

- **–** The structuralist assumption that all surface appearances have deeper meanings is speculative. Sometimes what you see is what you get. Even in those cases when this isn't so, it's disingenuous for structuralists to imagine that they know what the undercurrents are.
- **–** While society plays a powerful formative role in the acquisition of culture, genius and the canonical scholarship it produces are rare and therefore strikingly individual. Suggesting, for example, that Shakespeare is just a product of his age, diminishes his real and unique greatness.
- **–** Marxist structuralism ascribes sinister roles to people like teachers and other cultural workers. The implication is that they are the complicit or naive agents of the ruling class, and 'teach' working-class students to accept a subordinate position in society. This doesn't square with the attempts of many teachers to give their students – all of them – better futures through education.

The main propositions of structuralist theory of culture

- ◆ Culture *structures* our beliefs, behaviours and identities. In that respect, culture is regarded as an objectively real force.
- ◆ It's possible to distinguish between truth and untruth through rigorous scholarship (for example, through anthropology, literary criticism and philosophy).
- ◆ Language is a social product, so claims to individual literary greatness and canonical works are misguided.
- ◆ The analysis of deep-lying structures in capitalist societies reveals oppressive forces masquerading as benign institutions.

Poststructuralism

Poststructuralists generally accept the main arguments of postmodernism. Their particular interest, however, is with language. They claim that language doesn't convey a mirror image of the world. For example, the word 'beautiful' means different things to different people. It requires their interpretation. In that respect, as the saying goes, 'beauty is in the eyes of the beholder'. Importantly, poststructuralists remind us that words have to be *deconstructed*, that is, broken down in order to find the cultural meanings that language *signifies*.

This is all very complex stuff, so let us illustrate what we mean with a further example. Take the word 'politician'. At face-value, this word signifies an elected representative of the people. However, if we keep interrogating the word, lots of other meanings might rise to the surface – for example, an oppressor of the people, a power-seeker, a member of the ruling class, etc. The task of deconstruction is thus to take apart – to *deconstruct* – the common-sense understanding of the word 'politician', and to reveal it as a social construction.

If people understand that common-sense notions of words like 'politician', 'judge', 'general', 'businessman' and so forth are socially constructed (and talked up) in positive ways, they might, through the process of deconstruction, begin to perceive a different 'reality'. The respected 'businessman' who gets a knighthood for selling arms to oppressive regimes suddenly becomes a 'monster', not a model worthy of imitation. Of course, words that have negative connotations (for example, sexist representations of women) can also be deconstructed to obtain a better understanding of whose interests they promote and whose interests they subvert. Much work has been done in this area by feminist writers who have shown how gendered uses of language in patriarchal culture oppress girls and women.

Applying the ideas of Derrida, the postmodernist, Joan W. Scott shows how certain words are culturally privileged in contrast to their opposites. Says Scott:

'the generalized opposition male/female serves to obscure the differences among women in behavior, character, desire, subjectivity, sexuality, gender identification, and historical experience.'

(Scott 1988, in Seidman 1994: 295)

Put simply, there isn't such a thing as a typical woman. Women are individuals, and they can't be defined and categorised under such umbrella (and typically demeaning) categories as 'acting like a female'. Some women conform to that expectation. Others forge identities that actively disengage from chauvinistic cultural stereotypes. One can think of lots of instances to support the claim that many dominant words derive their socially constructed pre-eminence from the suppression of their opposites. 'White' is considered pure, 'black' sinister; 'man' strong, 'woman' weak; 'soldier' noble, 'terrorist' evil.

OVER TO YOU

Add to the above list of pairs, and discuss the meanings contained in the words you select. Then look up the words 'black' and 'white' in a dictionary and discuss what you find.

In Chapter 18, World Sociology, we contest the notion that terms like 'First' and 'Third Worlds' should be taken at face-value. Clearly, these words convey a sense of superiority and inferiority. This hierarchical privileging in language of the 'western' world (commonly understood as the First World) can be taken as the 'west's' own justification of its global domination and cultural superiority. As Zygmunt Bauman maintains:

'The era of modernity had been marked by an active superiority; part of the world [the west] constituted the rest as inferior – either as a crude, still unprocessed 'raw material' in need of cleaning and refinement, or a temporary extant relic of the past.'

(Bauman 1994, in Seidman 1994: 189)

The postmodernist, Michel Foucault, takes this debate further by applying poststructuralist analysis to 'discourses'. A *discourse* refers to a cultural *representation* of the world. Psychiatry, for example, is a *discourse* that *represents* certain mental conditions as illnesses. Once they've objectified these conditions (i.e. made them real), psychiatrists are empowered in certain cases to hospitalise individuals who exhibit 'disordered' behaviours. Here we see that a discourse can be linked to power. The people in society who define what constitutes mental

POSTSTRUCTURALIST THEORY OF CULTURE

FOR

+ Poststructuralism cautions us not to assume that everyone interprets a word or words in the same way. Take, for example, the word 'justice'. For some people, it means having a forgiving nature, for others exacting revenge for a wrong. Postructuralists admit they don't have all the anwers, but they refuse to take the easy option of assuming that words are mirror-images of real things.
+ Poststructuralist analysis, particularly, the use of deconstruction, reveals how language can be used to oppress. For example, Foucault's work on the discourses of the powerful alert us to the danger and the injustice of labelling language that demeans the dignity of people who don't conform to the standards set by elites.
+ Poststructuralism shows how disadvantaged groups in society can obtain empowerment through language. Women gain more prominence when 'she or he' is used instead of the catch-all 'he'; replacing the term 'the handicapped' with 'people who are disabled' draws attention to and provides scope to challenge the fact that they *are* often disabled by society; African–Caribbean people who choose to be described as 'black' obtain a self-respect that 'coloured' doesn't convey.

AGAINST

− Poststructuralism exaggerates the extent to which people attach different meanings to the same word. Without a common understanding of what words mean, communication would be impossible. If, for example, you and I speak and understand the same language, we're generally likely to associate the same meanings with the same words. Of course, there'll be some differences of interpretation, but not so many as to prevent meaningful communication.
− Poststructuralism, particularly, the kind engendered by Foucault's work on discourses, attributes ulterior motives to institutions like hospitals and schools. By suggesting that these institutions reproduce elite ideologies, poststructuralists overlook the cultural resistance that occurs within the medical, nursing and teaching professions towards politicians and other dominant groups.
− Poststructuralism has an egalitarian rhetoric, but its dialogue too often takes place within charmed and privileged circles. The same intellectuals (Paolo Freire is a notable exception) who uncover and attack elite discourses, create their own 'ivory tower' discourses, and exhibit a tendency of speaking on behalf of the poor rather than with them.

illness have certain powers to remove from circulation those who are judged to be seriously mentally ill. Similarly, when government officials introduce a new vocabulary of unemployment, calling jobless people job-seekers, the people so defined who don't conform to the label might be denied their benefits.

Foucault is very interested in the disciplinary institutions that control individuals in society – barracks, factories, hospitals, prisons and schools. In his book, *Discipline and Punish* (1979), he shows how prisons developed in the later modern age to signify the rational, not spiteful, disapproval of society towards crime and the criminal. Out goes the bloody spectacle of public torture, and in comes an 'example . . . now based on the lesson, the discourse, the decipherable sign, the representation of public morality' (Foucault 1979: 110). The discourse has moved from terror to an educative process: 'the punishments must be a school rather than a festival; an ever-open book rather than a ceremony' (1979: 111).

However, the alternative to a sinister discourse is an emancipatory one. Language has been used to oppress people, but it can also be used to liberate them. As the Brazilian educator, Paulo Freire (1972), notes, the ruling class who oppress the poor use words like 'bandit' and 'conspirator' to describe the hero who challenges an oppressor. This is done to entice 'the people' into the discourse of the ruler. But Freire teaches the poor to divest their cultural identities of ruling-class hegemony, to learn another language – the language of liberation. When poor people describe those who seek to free them as heroes rather than bandits, they discover new routes to freedom because they too can be heroes.

There's a clear message here. When people enter into dialogue with language, they begin to understand their own authentic culture better. They find out too that it sometimes tells a different 'truth' to the one they were led to believe by those in power. They find a road to freedom.

The main propositions of poststructuralist theory of culture

- Words have to be *deconstructed*, that is, broken down in order to decode the cultural meanings that language *signifies.*
- Elite discourses are privileged above other forms of language, and are sometimes used to as the 'official' definitions of deviance, leading to the oppression of those so defined.
- When people enter into dialogue with language, they obtain a better understanding of their own authentic culture and a resolve to live it.

Modernism, postmodernism, structuralism and poststructuralism: Pulling the threads together

These are difficult concepts, so don't worry if you're a bit confused. Things will eventually fall into place. We'll try to make things a little clearer by referring to parts of a televised discussion (reported by Paul Rabinow 1987, adapted by and with added commentary from us) between a famous modernist-structuralist, Noam Chomsky, and an equally renowned postmodernist-post-structuralist, Michel Foucault. Try to understand their different views. That way, you'll be able to grasp some of the main differences between modernism/postmodernism and structuralism/poststructuralism.

Chomksy adopts the structuralist view that there is a human nature. For without it, scientific understanding is impossible. Chomsky raises the question of how, on the basis of a limited set of fragmentary experiences, humans in every culture are able to learn language and use it creatively. He believes there's only one possible answer – there must be a physical structure underlying the mind which enables all people to achieve this. This structure isn't a social construct, but a real thing. That's a very modernist assertion. The structure exists, whether or not we, you or anybody contests its existence. In that sense, it's independent of culture, even though culture works with it as raw material. Chomsky has devoted his scientific career to uncover this structure. His quest is to find a testable mathematical theory of the mind. Chomsky's perspective is a mix of modernism and structuralism

Foucault rebuts Chomsky's scientific view of human nature. Instead of asking what human nature is, he addresses, as a poststructuralist, the issue of how the discourse of human nature has been used in society. Foucault believes that at different times in history society has changed its view of human nature. Physical structures can't explain this. Culture, not science, is the key factor here. Foucault doesn't take a stand on whether there is or isn't a human nature. Instead, he asks another question: how does culture influence what scientists claim to be true? He's implying here that science can be used as ideology, and thereby invoking the postmodernist argument that science shouldn't be privileged above other knowledge. The science of psychiatry isn't always a real science. Sometimes it's a convenient weapon of social control. If, for example, a psychiatrist declares that you're seriously 'sick', it then becomes permissible for society to use force in order to try to make you 'normal'. Foucault's aim is to understand society without looking for universal physical structures. His perspective is a mix of postmodernism and poststructuralism.

These different outlooks affect the ways in which Chomsky and Foucault respond to the interviewer's questions on the television programme.

- When asked why they're interested in politics, *Chomsky* says he thinks there's a universal human need for creative work and free inquiry, which is stifled by an oppressive society. Work, for example, is often alienating and monotonous. There must therefore be a political will to overcome oppression. This requires a vision of a better society in which creativity and knowledge prevail. It's important to use the creative potential of human nature as a standard against which to judge society. An unjust society thwarts this potential. A just one nurtures it.
- *Foucault* refuses to say why politics interests him He shifts the 'why' in the interviewer's question to a 'how' – how am I interested in politics? Not, he says, by imagining an ideal social model of a society based on science or technology. Foucault contends that western political philosophy has been devoted to first principles and utopias. But, he says, these abstract models have distracted us from asking how power actually operates in society. Foucault thinks the real political task is to criticise institutions which appear to be neutral and independent so that the political violence which has covertly been exercised through them will be unmasked, and thereby opened to challenge. There are echoes here of Althusser's structuralist theory of ideological and repressive state apparatuses. Given that Foucault is a poststructuralist, it's apparent that structuralism and poststructuralism share some common ground.
- Asked about why it's important to fight against political violence, *Chomsky* says we must struggle against injustice in the name of a higher goal – justice. Unless we have a guiding principle, says Chomsky, we have no possibility of judging the actions of others. Think about this. If we can't agree on basic principles, like all children have a right to proper nourishment, how can we begin to speak of morals? Chomsky argues that a revolution might turn out to be worse than the regime it replaces. Unless we can have fixed and rational criteria for judging what constitutes a better society, we're lost. This doesn't mean, adds Chomsky, that we have to achieve a perfect enactment of the good society. However, unless we have a sense of what the good is, we can't act or judge. Chomsky's point is clear – we may not be able to attain perfection, but if we know what we're aiming for, we might get close.
- *Foucault* disagrees with Chomsky. He says it seems to him that the idea of justice is something which has been invented as a tool of a certain political and economic elite or as a weapon against that elite. Words like justice aren't the real issue. The object is to do battle, not to engage in conversation. The point is to change power relations, not to talk about them. Foucault is incredulous towards claims about justice and other first principle rhetoric. He wants to know how those discourses are used rather than what they are.

EXAM TIP

Point out to the examiner that:

- functionalist, marxist, modernist and structuralist theories tend to emphasise the shaping power of society
- social constructionist, postmodern and post-structural theories tend to emphasise human wilfulness (as does certain elements of marxist theory).

QUESTIONS

1 Very briefly, and taking each in turn, what are the main propositions of these seven theories of culture: functionalism; marxism; social constructionism; modernism, postmodernism, structuralism, and poststructuralism?

2 In summary form, critique the arguments for and against the above seven theories.

Culture and identity in relation to social class, gender, ethnicity, age and region

Our identity is our self-image, but it's attached to our culture. In that respect, social class, gender, ethnicity, age and region represent varying degrees of anchorage. As indicated earlier, identities are formed during interaction with other people whom we regard as important in our life – *significant others*. The image we have of ourselves is to a large extent based on how these people respond to us. If they make us feel good about ourselves, we develop a positive identity, but the opposite occurs if they constantly criticise us. Thus, for example, if a girl who does well in Technology is encouraged by her teacher to become an engineer, her investiture in that identity gets a confidence boost. On the other hand, a harsh word from a parent that boys don't cry, might make a boy feel wanting as a *son*. Throughout our lives, especially as we grow to adulthood, our culture is mediated to us through the processes of approval and disapproval.

OVER TO YOU

What are the things that other people in your life do and say that make you feel good about yourself? What role do teachers play in this process?

According to Stuart Hall, 'Identity, in this sociological conception, bridges the gap between the "inside" and the "outside" – between the personal and the public world' (Hall 1996a: 276). The process of socialisation teaches us to align our personal identity with the cultural identity that society expects of us. In early childhood, my as yet 'unfinished' personal identity might have been one that got its way through tantrums: 'I'm so important, all I have to do is scream and shout and people will give me what I want'. Most of us grow out of this into an identity that recognises some 'give and take' between the 'inner me' and the 'outer society'.

The alignment of a personal identity with a cultural identity is accompanied by strong feelings of belonging, best summed up as, 'My face fits in this group'. If your face doesn't fit, you either re-align your identity in accordance with group expectations, or you keep your identity and remain an outsider. Sometimes, of course, because of racist and sexist attitudes, an outsider status is ascribed, irrespective of what an individial does.

In stable societies, identities are fairly clear-cut, and socialisation into them proceeds routinely. However, in societies undergoing rapid change, people often get confused about who they are or who they are meant to be. Consider Nelson Mandela. Twenty-five years imprisoned on Robben Island, some of it spent breaking rocks, makes even the strongest man realise he's a *prisoner*. Then, in the early 1990s, he's released, apartheid is dismantled and Nelson Mandela becomes *president* of a new, democratic South Africa. From prisoner to president – what a dramatic change in identities!

Think too about a Jewish doctor in 1930s Germany. Her identity as a physician is secure and intact. Then Adolf Hitler becomes Chancellor, and German society changes rapidly. A racist, nazi 'culture' takes hold, and the doctor's licence to practise medicine is revoked by fascist officials. Some of her former patients spit at her in the street. She's a strong woman, but her self-respect is challenged at every juncture, and her personal identity as a doctor is under threat, and might, understandably be shattered.

It's this cultural de-stabilisation, for better or worse, which produces the *postmodern individual*. Nothing stands still long enough for people to settle into an identity because, identities are constantly on the move, 'in relation to the ways we are represented or addressed in the cultural systems which surround us' (Hall 1996a: 277). Identity isn't a stable, 'rest of my life' thing. I change; you change; we all change. Identities have become particularly less settled in relation to class, gender, ethnicity, age and region. Incidentally, we suggest you read the section in Chapter 15, Mass Media (pages 457–68), on media representations of class, gender, ethnicity and age.

Social class

Class is not as visible these days as it was when workers wore flat caps and managers had bowler hats. While it's true that upper-class people still retain a fairly distinct cultural style, birthright no longer guarantees them a superior cultural identity. Moreover, the widespread occupational fragmentation that has been occurring within the middle and working classes (see page 246) sometimes makes it difficult – and inappropriate – to differentiate between middle- and working-class cultural types. The UK is becoming like America, where a person's identity is based more on merit than on birth. An extract from Richard Hoggart's *The Way We Live Now highlights* how things are changing:

'Visit the Stock Exchange . . . Go down into the places where the tough dealing is done and you are as likely to find a cockney voice, and that a young woman's, as that of a public-school man. Those places must respond to the need for new, technologically competent talent. But the predominantly male public-school products elsewhere in the building? The old boy network is still operating to a fair extent? Yes, will be the answer, but nowadays we can't "carry" such people if they prove to be incompetent, whatever their family connections.'

(Hoggart 1996: 203)

In the past, a cockney who made it to the Stock Exchange (few did) would have had to hide his (it was a male institution) accent and cultivate an 'upper-crust' one. The shedding of his cultural roots and the donning of a 'respectable' identity would have been essential. Nowadays, in this postmodern world of ours, individuals are more inclined to construct new identities through community and popular cultures without feeling that the only acceptable culture is the one prescibed by the upper class.

OVER TO YOU

Do you have a social class identity, a sense of belonging to a social class? Ask that same question of your parents and grandparents, and make a note of your findings and reflections.

Gender

Moving to gender, we find that dominant cultural forms generally have a masculine imprint, and that this is represented as a universal – as 'good enough' for everyone. Yet, as Joan W. Scott argues:

'We need theory that will let us think in terms of pluralities and diversities rather than of unities and universals. We need theory that will break the conceptual hold, at least, of those long traditions of (Western) philosophy that have systematically and repeatedly construed the world hierarchically in terms of masculine universals and feminine specificities.'

(Scott 1988, in Seidman 1994: 282)

Her point is that women are culturally marginalised. It's very much a case of those word opposites mentioned earlier. In this instance, masculine is privileged and denotes the dominant term, whereas feminine is debased and becomes a residual term. Put another way, the discourse is that 'it's a man's world'. The alternative to this oppositional use of language isn't, says Scott, sameness. Her contention is that women are different but not inferior. She also wants to see the idea of difference within the sexes emphasised. Not all women are the same. Neither are all men. This point also needs to be borne in mind when white women and white men assume that black women and black men aspire to white outlooks.

Like all negative '-isms', sexism is learned rather than inevitable. Its hold on cultural identities thereby lies in its routine character. As Jack Levin notes:

'we shouldn't necessarily look for sexism in the most pathological, most deviant members of our society. Instead, sexism is conventional; it often originates in the mainstream, rather than at the margins, of a society.'

(Levin 1996: 256)

It's important, from a feminist standpoint, to emphasise that a woman's identity doesn't have to surrender to sexist stereotypes about how women ought to be. On the contrary, in its refusal to privilege macho imagery and through its resolve to change patriarchal (male-dominated) culture, feminism offers women an alternative sense of womanhood.

Postmodernist feminists like Angela McRobbie (1994) find a way out of this mainstream label by questioning the notion of the 'real me'. Postmodernity, says McRobbie, signals new discourses about the positioning of the self. In that context, women are encouraged to rephrase the gender discourse in a manner that expands the notion of what it means to be a woman.

Ethnicity

When we look at the issue of ethnicity, we find that some cultures in society are considered 'unworthy' of mainstream status. Says Michael Brake, when slaves were shipped to the Caribbean and United States, 'Attempts were made to obliterate African culture' (Brake 1985: 116). Yet while African names and language were prohibited, 'the subversive element of African music remained, combining the West African rhythms of work songs with religious and folk music of the New World' (1985: 117). American blues and jazz are the cultural expression in music of the early sorrow of being black, of having that identity, in a white racist nation. More recently, some black rap music revives the sorrow and urges black people to hit back at the society that oppresses them.

The black sociologist, Stuart Hall, argues that the task of cultural studies, its moral mission, so to speak:

'is to mobilize everything that it can find in terms of intellectual resources in order to understand what keeps making the lives we live, and the societies we live in, profoundly and deeply antihumane in their capacity to live with difference.'

(Hall 1996b, in Storey 1996: 343)

Once we know why some people believe that an English cultural identity only connects with Anglo–Saxons and Yorkshire puddings, we might be able to persuade them to accept that there are also multi-cultural conceptions of what it means to live in England.

This doesn't imply a multi-culturalism of exotica, whereby the beliefs, values and tastes of minority ethnic groups are paraded in a fashion show for the liberal white onlooker. The hope is that being black will no longer be seen as inimical to being fully British. This is why new cultural identities such as black British and African–British are displacing labels which assign people from minority ethnic groups an outsider status – terms like 'coloured' and 'Negro'. Even the word 'minority' is falling out of favour, as more black people begin to contest the idea that they play a 'minor' role in society.

Age

In his book, *Moving Culture* (1990), Paul Willis seeks to broaden restricted and traditional ideas about 'the arts' by arguing that young people already have a rich culture in activities that aren't conventionally recognised as 'cultural': music, room and personal decoration, magazines, radio, television. Their baby-boomer parents – born in the late 1940s and the 1950s – were no different when they were young. They too looked for anti-establishment cultural identites in bands like Aerosmith, the Grateful Dead, Pink Floyd and the Rolling Stones. The revival of interest by young people today in these cultural icons of the past suggests perhaps that younger and older generations have more in common than they think.

It's important, however, to note that young people today sometimes re-work the cultural meanings of 'old' songs by changing the original message. Angela McRobbie (1994), for example, describes how the 'Thus the Was Not' remix of the soul classic, 'Papa was a Rolling Stone', has Papa's children rapping back at him for not fulfilling his parental obligations, and for leaving Mama to work for her family. Youthful subcultural resistance articulates a defiant pleasure in telling adults that they're not as moral as they like to believe. Adults hit back by labelling young rebels as deviants, a theme richly explored in Stanley Cohen's *Folk Devils and Moral Panics* (see pages 507–8).

Just as young people have to face negative age-related stereotypes about youth in general, old people also have to contend with cultural representations that demean their dignity. In hard-hitting words, Jack Levin writes:

'one of the most offensive olfactory images is that of elderly citizens – especially nursing home residents – who are too often stereotyped as reeking from incontinence, indifference, and the ravages of age.'

(Levin 1996: 29)

Depressingly, Levin notes that studies of age stereotyping conducted over the last 50 years show that negative images of ageing are widespread. In the 1950s, for example, American research into the attitudes of graduate psychologists revealed that most perceived old people as set in their ways, slow walkers, poorly co-ordinated, bossy and likely to doze. A 1988 study by William C. Levin (reported by Jack Levin 1996) found that Americans characterise older people as less active, attractive, competent, creative, educated, energetic, flexible, intelligent, reliable, wealthy, and socially involved than younger people.

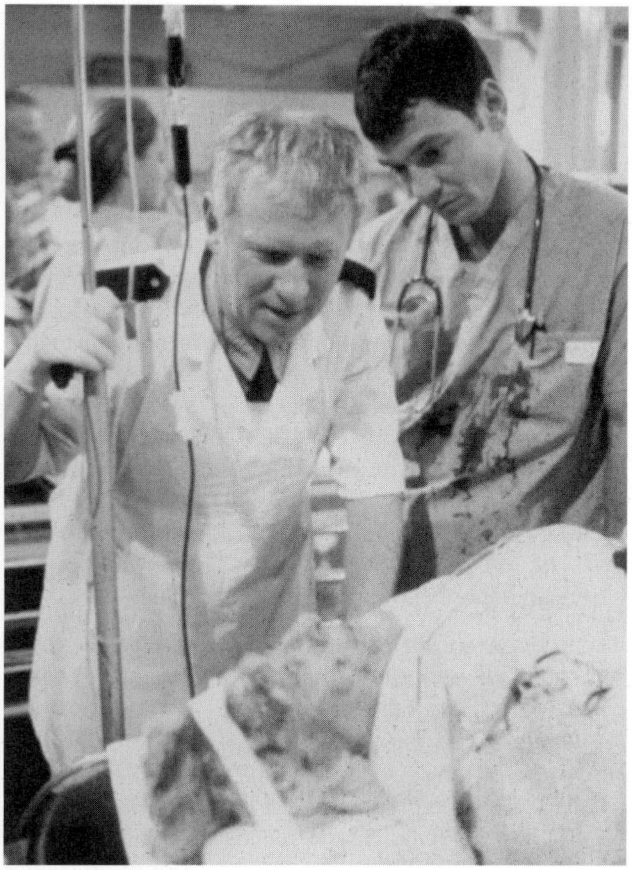

Research suggests that ER staff try harder to resuscitate younger than older patients.

Another stereotype in the US – different but hardly less flattering – portrays older people as a drain on medical and welfare resources. Whether or not old people contest this negative image doesn't necessarily mean that younger people will re-align their prejudicial views. Says Jack Levin (1996), research has even shown that emergency room personnel tend to put greater effort into resuscitating younger patients.

OVER TO YOU

***To what extent, if at all, is the above tendency apparent in television depictions of emergency room work, such as in* Casualty, ER *and* Chicago Hope?**

Region

When we consider region, it's apparent that dominant regional identities are not so firmly embedded in people's minds as before. In the UK, Englishness – a southern-based, white culture which tries to represent itself as the core British culture – has that claim contested by Scottish, Welsh, Irish and other regional cultures. Films like *Braveheart*, with Mel Gibson, and *Michael Collins*, with Liam Neeson, stir the Celtic spirit of Scots and second-generation Irish, thereby undermining the imperial mind-set. On a larger scale, the so-called Euro-sceptic politicians, with their exaggerated sense of Englishness, are increasingly regarded – even within the Conservative Party – to be out of kilter with a European outlook.

The process of Europeanisation encourages people to think locally and to act globally – to cherish their culture and to respect the cultures of others, to have a local voice without suggesting that other voices are inferior, to replace nationalism with internationalism. Globalism challenges the sociological orthodoxy of single-society analysis. Indeed, according to Anthony McGrew, 'In effect, globalization raises the prospect of the "end of the nation-state" as the primary container of modernity' (McGrew 1996: 64). The emergence of a global consiousness doesn't, as indicated, mean the end of locality and region. For example, people from Newcastle can retain their local ways, as well as appropriating some of the cultural styles of other places. British football (Newcastle United included) is fiercely local in home matches, but international in the range of players and styles exhibited on the field.

QUESTIONS

1 How might a cultural identity be infiltrated by negative stereotypes?
2 Describe and analyse some of the different ways in which culture and identity connect with class, gender, ethnicity, age and region.

Types of culture

In rather complex language, J. Clark, S. Hall, T. Jefferson and B. Roberts write:

'The singular term, "culture", can only indicate, in the most general and abstract way, the large cultural configurations at play in a society at any historical moment.'

(Clark *et al*. 1976, in Thompson 1996: 31)

What they mean is that the notion of one culture is a shorthand way of describing national characteristics. Many Britons, for example, love a cup of tea, even though their tastes differ in lots of other respects. They live British national culture insofar as they incorporate aspects of it, but they also cue into other cultures when they exhibit regional, minority ethnic, class and other preferences. The melting pot and the mosaic co-exist.

Richard Hoggart, formerly Director of the Centre for Contemporary Cultural Studies at Birmingham University, makes a similar point regarding the need sometimes to generalise about culture when he writes:

'Yet one may fairly make generalizations about attitudes without implying that everyone in the working-classes believes or does this or this about work or marriage or religion.'

(Hoggart 1992: 22)

While cultures contain internal differences, it's also important to recognise that they designate boundaries. This is particularly highlighted in the sociological critique of high and low cultures and subcultures, and folk, mass and popular cultures.

High and low cultures and subcultures

The notion of *high culture* conjures up, as Donald Horne writes, a setting 'in which the world of the intellect, of scholarship and the arts is regarded as being a minority, specialist concern' (Horne 1986: 183). In similar manner, Willis says we might refer to the people who attend the traditional performing-arts as '"the 3-M audience" – middle class, middle-aged and minority' (Willis 1990: 10). The cultural studies theorist, Lawrence Grossberg, wants to demystify this elite aura, and to re-connect scholarship with the people. Thus:

'The *popular* defines a necessary focus and commitment of cultural studies. As a political commitment, it is anti-elitist; it demands that we not separate ourselves entirely from the masses.'

(Grossberg, in Storey 1996: 184)

According to Grossberg, academics are part of the people.

Another scholar of culture, Joel Pfister, is less convinced that intellectuals are just ordinary folk. Those who practise cultural studies in the US, insists Pfister, are of 'the academic wing of the professional-managerial class' (Pfister 1996: 287). Their language and their concepts, he intimates, are those of an elite rather than a popular forum. Even the deservedly respected Stuart Hall writes in a style, suggests Pfister, that often veers into language which is only familiar to academics. Moreover, not all of them understand the complexities of 'cultural studies-speak'. When his own friends expressed an interest in reading an essay by Pfister on cultural studies, they first asked him if they'd be able to understand it!

John Fiske (1992) links *high culture* to empowered people and *low culture* to disempowered people. He's not making a personal judgement here, but stating a fact. Powerful people are able to make their culture dominant because they own and control the 'culture industries'. They don't, however, invite '*low culture* people' to the '*high culture* banquet'. Instead, they infiltrate *low culture*, hooking it onto values that ruling-class people want working- and middle-class people to have – patriotism, a fondness for venerable traditions, and, of course, respect for the ruling class! By contrast, people who have very little power can't force their own authentic tastes on the whole of society.

In describing the characteristics of *high* and *low culture*, Fiske argues that 'distance' is a key component of the former, and 'no distancing' of the other. He means that socially advantaged groups place a distance between art and everyday life. Art is revered; everyday life is common. Sometimes the distancing occurs between the spectator and the work of art, as when the onlooker treats the object as something above and beyond her or him. *Low culture* is altogether different: 'popular art is part of the everyday, not distanced from it' (Fiske 1992: 154). It's interesting that Fiske here equates *low culture* with *popular culture*. He's right to do so, and 'popular' is a more generous term than 'low'. In power terms, the people are the 'low' class – the disempowered – but theirs is the majority culture, the 'popular' one.

It's among 'the people' that one also hears of *subcultures*. The term is rarely used to describe variations within *high culture*. A *subculture* is a culture that typically occupies a subordinate position outside of mainstream culture – at least, in the eyes of the dominant elite. *High* and *low culture* individuals are different but 'respectable'. The subcultural individual is subversive. This is especially emphasised in the context of predominantly male subcultural forms among teddy boys, mods and rockers, hippies, skinheads, punks and Rastafarians.

In that context, it's important to point out that the sociological study of *subcultures* has often marginalised the experiences of girls and women who don't identify with mainstream views. Even rave subculture is a largely male representation, perhaps though, as Angela McRobbie contends, because girls seem less involved than their male counterparts in its cultural products – from the flyers, to the events, to the MCs. Says McRobbie, rave 'provocatively places working-class masculinity shirtless, sweating, *en masse*, in the vast hangers of the rave party' (McRobbie 1994: 168). In this encounter, continues McRobbie, the trope of masculinity is friendly rather than laddish. While acknowledging that males are at the forefront in rave culture, McRobbie importantly argues that dance is where girls have always been found in subcultures, and that rave – where dance is a powerful motivating force – retains this prominence.

Nevertheless, as indicated, the sociological study of female subcultures is still comparatively rare, a point also taken up in Chapter 16, Deviance.

Folk, popular and mass cultures

In their article, 'From Marx to Man. City' (1996), Bill Sugrue and Calvin Taylor map the history of the concept of popular culture from its identification as *folk culture* in the nineteenth century, through its conversion into *mass culture* in the first half of the twentieth century, on to its reigning position, say postmodernists, as the culture of the late twentieth century. In this respect, *popular culture* is an umbrella term that describes the culture of the majority of people, expressed at different times as *folk culture*, *mass culture* and *the culture*.

This latter term seems to suggest that *popular culture* has wrested control from *high culture* to become, as its name implies, *the culture* – a sort of 'anything goes' *mélange*. We think another much more feisty culture should be appended to the somewhat quaint nineteenth-century notion of folk culture – that of a *working-class culture*. Here we have in mind the culture of an urban-dwelling, factory-employed, trade-unionised class of people who set up their own schools and engaged in political struggle against a class of factory owners who over-worked and under-paid them. It's also important to bear in mind, as Stuart Hall (1986) reminds us, that the evolution of *popular culture* is an 'evolution' with quotation marks around that word. This suggests that *popular culture* is essentially a series of 'snapshots' over time which has breaks and discontinuities, as well as continuous, uninterrupted phases.

Referring to Peter Burke's contention (1988, cited by Sugrue and Taylor 1996: 3) that *popular culture* is the culture of 'the majority, for whom popular culture was the only culture', Sugrue and Taylor add that:

> 'The key feature of this culture (which attracts the title *folk*) is the sense that it was made by the people, for the people, and transmitted down the generations through the community.'
>
> (Sugrue and Taylor 1996: 3)

'Folk' has its origins in the Old English meaning of 'people', and it was generally used as a friendly term to denote people in general – irrespective of social rank. It's often associated, however, with the habits and beliefs of 'ordinary poor folk' who lived in the kind of pre-industrial society described by Emile Durkheim that was based on mechanical solidarity (see Chapter 4, Sociological Theories, page 51). The setting envisaged by Durkheim was distinctively rural, and was sustained through local folklore, including holidays, fairs and wakes.

Folk culture was bounded and parochial – as depicted in the moors pub visited by two Americans in the film, *American Werewolf in London*. When these unsuspecting tourists stepped into the bar, there was a deadly hush. The locals shunned outsiders and were reluctant to acquaint unwelcome guests with their own beliefs and practices. While pockets of *folk culture* still persist to this day – often of the kind 'attenuated into a last few souvenirs' (Horne 1986: 184) – the industrial revolution ushered in a new era of clocks and factory whistles. Productivity and efficiency were in. Seasonal work and 'rural idleness' were out. Not that one should necessarily lament the passing of the old ways. As the marxist historian, E. P. Thompson, reminds us, the customs of 'merrie England' were not all quaint or romantic:

> 'The unmarried mother, punished in a Bridewell, and perhaps repudiated by the parish in which she was entitled to relief [i.e. "social welfare"], had little reason to admire "merrie England". The passing of Gin Lane, Tyburn Fair, orgiastic drunkenness, animal sexuality and mortal combat for prize-money in iron-studded clogs, calls for no lament.'
>
> (Thompson 1968; cited by Sugrue and Taylor 1996: 4)

Industrialism forged a new urban culture. But it didn't happen overnight, nor was it uncontested by former rural dwellers. Writing in the 1950s of his nineteenth-century-born grandmother, Richard Hoggart said that while she learned to become a city dweller, her house was never really urban:

> 'Newspaper-packets of home-dried herbs hung from the scullery ceiling; a pot of goose-grease lay always on the shelf there, in case anyone "got a bad chest".'
>
> (Hoggart 1992: 25)

The cultural incompleteness of the impact of industrialisation in English society was documented by Durkheim (1933: 282), who highlighted the co-existence of 'Great industry and commerce' with 'the autonomy of local life and the authority of tradition'. But incompleteness doesn't mean that things didn't radically change. They did. The nineteenth century witnessed the gradual replacement of rural *folk culture* with new patterns of living in towns and cities. Festivals and revelry weren't encouraged by factory owners, who wanted their employees to tend the cotton gin rather than swig the liquid variety.

That said, it would be wrong to think that the majority of the people – the working class – yielded to the demands of the capitalist class. A strong and enduring popular culture of resistance, *a working-class culture* – more 'political' than 'folksy' – resonates throughout the nineteenth century. This is evidenced by the various parliamentary restrictions imposed by the upper class on the spread of 'popular' political tracts in the early part of that century. Tom Paine's *Rights of Man* was burned; public reading rooms were shut, and licences were revoked from coffee houses and taverns in receipt of working-class newspapers. But the genie was out of the bottle – education was here to stay. So too was a wilfulness among the poor to wage a political struggle for better wages, better working conditions, and the right to vote.

While muskets and sabres were sometimes used to quell working-class unrest, softer means of social control were also favoured. This explains, in part, the attempts of the propertied classes – landed and industrial – to silence working-class agitation by schooling working-class children in the ways of capitalism. Elementary schools were thus imposed on working-class culture by people from different classes. This is what the historian, Thomas W. Laqueur (1976, cited by Stephens 1987: 70), calls 'the supply side of the equation', that is, the supply of so-called 'popular education' as a cultural weapon of the rich and powerful.

Interestingly, Laqueur turns the equation around and looks at 'popular education' in terms of popular demand rather than elite supply. Says Laqueur, many working-class parents purchased an elementary education for their children in the open marketplace. The eagerness of working-class parents to provide an education for their children had earlier been reported by James Mill in the *Edinburgh Review*, a nineteenth-century Whig journal:

'Even around London, in a circle of fifty miles radius . . . there is hardly a village that has not something of a school; and not many children of either sex who are not taught, more or less, reading and writing. We have met with families in which, for weeks together, not an article of sustenance but potatoes had been used; yet for every child the hard-earned sum was provided to send them to school.'

(Mill 1813, cited by Stephens 1987: 71)

While, of course, the middle and upper classes tried to control the content and thus the culture of future generations of workers, the 'people' had their agendas too, especially 'the "earnest minority" among working-class people', who had 'an influence on their group out of all proportion to their numbers' (Hoggart 1992: 318). Hoggart has in mind people like those who, often at great personal sacrifice, supported trade unionism during its early days and who were connected with the co-operative movement. Out of their efforts and energy, came the birth of the Labour Party. There were also a number of middle-class intellectuals who, parting company with the bourgeois inclinations of their own class, urged working people to become popular agitators. Most noteworthy among these middle-class intellectuals was the German-born, London-residing philosopher and social scientist, Karl Marx.

Working-class culture, in its self-affirmative political form, has always threatened the ideological interests of the capitalist class. The capitalist ideology defended the payment of low wages, and the untrammelled workings of a 'free market'. Working-class socialists – some marxist, some not – struggled for better pay and the provision of public services. During the twentieth century, however, this working-class consciousness was gradually tamed (at least, in part) by the imposition of a so-called mass culture. While some commentators regard *mass culture* as one form of popular culture, Robert L. Root Jr makes the interesting point that '"Mass", rather than "Popular", implies faceless anonymity and the loss of identity that comes from being part of the masses' (Root 1987: 4).

It also implies a lack of voice. *Mass culture* is produced for the general public, but it expresses the interests of an elite. It's what the elite deems as appropriate not for them but for the 'masses'. Mass culture therefore comes in what Paul Willis (1990: 11) terms 'provided commercial forms'. By this, he means that advertising, music, films and other marketed tastes and styles are designed to appeal to as many consumers as possible in order to sell rather than improve or educate. This providing of a pre-packaged culture by an elite is the defining feature of mass culture. It's provided *for* the masses, not created *by* 'the people'.

Who are this elite? They're the people who own and control the 'culture industries' – advertising, the press, radio, television, etc. In this manner, to use Gramsci's term, they exercise *hegemony* over 'the people'. Hegemony refers to the management of consent through culture rather than through force. As indicated, the media play a crucial role here. Thus, for example, by what Stuart Hall (citing the first Director-General of the BBC, J. W. C. Reith) terms 'The brute force of monopoly' (Hall 1986: 40), the consent and confidence of the people are solicited through broadcasting.

The important theme of ideological propagation through the media is taken up in Chapter 15, Mass Media. However, we don't want to end this section by giving the impression that mass culture and mass media are the defining features of British cultural life. Some people do 'need' and demand what the media give them. But 'the people' are more varied and complex than the term 'mass' implies. Their cultures are characterised by extraordinary diversity, as is their investiture in a wide range of cultural identities.

QUESTIONS

1 What are the main features of: high culture, low culture, subculture, folk culture, popular culture and mass culture?
2 How does working-class culture express popular sentiments?

EXAM TIP

When answering questions on culture and identity, as appropriate, make it clear to the examiner that there is still a lack of resolution in sociology about all the issues. More study and more research are vital.

Concluding remarks

This has been a difficult chapter to write, and we suspect it contains some concepts that are difficult to grasp. Postmodernism and poststructuralism, for example, are very elusive theories. Don't be despondent. The most recent debates on culture and identity take sociology into uncharted areas. But the questions sociologists ask are familiar ones:

◆ How much do individuals make culture as well as being influenced by culture?
◆ What happens at the intersection of the individual and society?
◆ Which perspective(s) is(are) best for illuminating these crucial questions?

In keeping with the spirit of this book and the sentiments of the authors, we respect Agent Mulder's emphasis on the importance of the intellectual journey, but we endorse Agent Scully's view that 'old' theories sometimes help us find new destinations.

Glossary of key terms

Canon A standard of excellence against which other things are measured. For example, Shakespeare is a writer whose works represent a canon

Culture A *way of life* is the most concise definition of this complex term. A culture is an amalgam of beliefs, knowledge, norms, values and tastes which individuals learn and acquire through life-long socialisation

Deconstruction In relation to language, this refers to the rigorous interrogation of the meaning of words. In a wider sense, deconstruction also refers to the demystification of knowledge, namely, its removal from the assumed and 'precious' possession of intellectuals

Folk culture A culture made by the people, for the people, and typically transmitted through a rural community

High culture The culture of elites, often premised on the view that the arts and the classics confer taste and wisdom

Identity The inner me which is formed and modified in continuous dialogue with the culture(s) I experience and the *significant others* who impart it(them). In that sense, my identity is at the interface between my individuality and society. In practice, the cultural and the individual sense of self are intertwined, such that all identities are socially situated rather than free-floating. Our identities are therefore *cultural identities*

Low culture A culture imputed to the majority of the people by an elite rather than fashioned by themselves; hence the derogatory label, 'low'. Assumed by the elite to be not of the arts, but of popular, everyday pleasures

Metanarrative A grand discourse ('big story') that proclaims privileged access to truth. Science is one of the most important metanarratives of the modern age

Modernism An outlook that rejects traditional superstition and which embraces philosophy and science in a quest for moral, social and technological improvement. Its legacy is the Enlightenment

Norms How people behave; prescribed codes of conduct

Popular culture An umbrella term that describes the culture of the majority of people, expressed at different times as *folk culture, mass culture* and *the culture*. Popular culture is essentially a series of 'snapshots' over time which has breaks and discontinuities, as well as continuous, uninterrupted phases

Postmodernism An outlook that has gained rapid momentum in the 1980s and 1990s, and which rejects the modernist search for universal moralities and truths. Postmodernism celebrates relativism and pluralism, emphasising that people need to 'work through' who they are in lots of different ways rather than 'finding out' who they are on the basis of science and moral absolutes

Poststructuralism An outlook which generally supports the arguments of postmodernism. Poststructuralists are particularly interested in language. They claim that language doesn't convey a mirror image of the world. Words have to be deconstructed, that is, broken down in order to find the cultural meanings that language *signifies*

Self A sense of subjective identitity. For example, a boy whose significant others give him toy guns to play with might begin to see himself as an 'initiate warrior'. In this sense, the self takes on the expectations of significant others

Roles Expected conduct attached to statuses

Significant others The people 'in charge' of socialisation – parents, sisters, brothers, friends, teachers, etc.

Status Social position (standing) in society

Socialisation The process whereby people learn to become social human beings. *Primary socialisation* – typically, in the family – begins the process, and *secondary socialisation* – typically, in the later stages of schooling and through, for example, the media – rounds it off

Structuralism A perspective which claims that culture structures (i.e. shapes) our beliefs and behaviours. In that respect, culture is construed as an objectively real force which fashions our identities. The task of the structuralist is to locate that which all cultures have in common

Values What people are committed to

Working-class culture The way of life of working-class people. Its legacy is of an urban-dwelling, factory-employed, trade-unionised class of people who engage in political struggle and self-education

References

Althusser, Louis (1971) *Lenin and Philosophy and Other Essays*. London: NLB

Bauman, Zygmunt (1988) Is there a postmodern sociology?, pp 187–204, in Seidman, Steven (ed.) (1994) *The Postmodern Turn*. Cambridge: Cambridge University Press

Berger, Peter L. and Luckmann, Thomas (1975) *The Social Construction of Reality*. Harmondsworth: Penguin

Bloom, Harold (1995) *The Western Canon*. London: Papermac

Brake, Michael (1985) *Comparative Youth Culture*. London: Routledge & Kegan Paul

Brunt, Rosalind (1992) Engaging with the popular: Audiences for mass culture and what to say about them, pp 69–80, in Grossberg, Lawrence, Nelson, Cary and Treichler, Paula (eds) (1992) *Cultural Studies*. New York: Routledge

Coser, Lewis A. and Rosenberg, Bernard (eds) (1969) *Sociological Theory*, Third Edition. London: The Macmillan Company

Derrida, Jacques (1982) *Of Grammatology*. Baltimore: The Johns Hopkins University Press

Derrida, Jacques (1995) *The Gift of Death*. Chicago: The University of Chicago Press

de Saussure, Ferdinand (1910), in Komatsu, Eisuke and Harris, Roy (eds) (1993) *Saussure's Third Course of Lectures on General Linguistics (1910–1911) – From the notebooks of Emile Constantin*. Oxford: Pergamon Press

Eco, Umberto (1994) *Reflections on The Name of the Rose*. London: Minerva

Fiske, John (1992) Cultural studies and the culture of everyday life, pp 154–73, in Grossberg, Lawrence, Nelson, Cary and Treichler, Paula (eds) (1992) op. cit.

Foucault, Michel (1979) *Discipline and Punish*. Harmondsworth: Penguin

Giddens, Anthony (1987) Reason without revolution? Habermas's Theorie des kommunikativen Handelns, pp 95–121, in Bernstein, Richard J. (ed.) (1987) *Habermas and Modernity*. Cambridge and Oxford: Polity Press in association with Basil Blackwell

Gouldner, Alvin W. (1972) *The Coming Crisis of Western Sociology*. London: Heinemann

Gramsci, Antonio (1977) *Selections from Political Writings 1910–1920*. London: Lawrence & Wishart

Grenz, Stanley J. (1996) *A Primer on Postmodernism*. Grand Rapids, Michigan: William B. Eerdmans Publishing Company

Grossberg, Lawrence (1996) The circulation of cultural studies, pp 178–86, in Storey, John (ed.) (1996) op. cit.

Habermas, Jurgen (1987) Questions and counterquestions, pp 192–216, in Bernstein, Richard J. (ed.) (1987) op. cit.

Hall, Stuart (1986) Popular culture and the state, pp 22–49, in Bennett, Tony, Mercer, Colin and Woollacott, Janet (eds) (1986) *Popular Culture and Social Relations*. Milton Keynes: Open University Press

Hall, Stuart (1996a) The question of cultural identity, pp 273–325, in Hall, Stuart, Held, David and McGrew, Tony (eds) (1996) *Modernity and its Futures*. Cambridge: Polity Press in association with the Open University

Hall, Stuart (1996b) Race, culture, and communications: Looking backward and forward at cultural studies, pp 336–43, in Storey, John (ed.) (1996) op. cit.

Hoggart, Richard (1992) *The Uses of Literacy*. London: Penguin

Hoggart, Richard (1996) *The Way We Live Now*. London: Pimlico

Horne, Donald (1986) *The Public Culture*. London: Pluto Press

Levin, Jack (1996) *Sociological Snapshots 2*. Thousand Oaks, California: Pine Forge Press

Levi-Strauss, Claude (1978) *Myth and Meaning*. London: Routledge & Kegan Paul

Lyotard, Jean-Francois (1983) Answering the question: What is postmodernism?, pp 38–46, in Docherty, Thomas (ed.) (1993) *Postmodernism: A Reader*. New York: Harvester Wheatsheaf

Lyotard, Jean-Francois (1984) The postmodern condition: A report on knowledge (extracts from), pp 356–60, in Hall, Stuart, Held, David and McGrew, Tony (eds) (1996) op. cit.

McGrew, Anthony (1996) A global society?, pp 61–102, in Hall, Stuart, Held, David and McGrew, Tony (eds) (1996) op. cit.

McRobbie, Angela (1994) *Postmodernism and Popular Culture*. London: Routledge

Mill, James (1813) Education of the poor, *Edinburgh Review*, Vol. XXI

O'Neill, John (1995) *The Poverty of Postmodernism*. London: Routledge

Parsons, Talcott (1964) *The Social System*. London: The Free Press of Glencoe, Collier-Macmillan Ltd

Parsons, Talcott (1967) *Sociological Theory and Modern Society*. New York: The Free Press

Pfister, Joel (1996) The Americanization of cultural studies, pp 287–99, in Storey, John (ed.) (1996), op. cit.

The Oxford Universal Dictionary Illustrated (1965) Vol. 1. Oxford: The Clarendon Press

Root, Robert L. Jr (1987) *The Rhetorics of Popular Culture*. New York: Greenwood Press

Rorty, Richard (1979) *Philosophy and the Mirror of Nature*. Princeton, New Jersey: Princeton University Press

Scott, Joan W. (1988) Deconstructing equality-versus-difference: Or, the uses of poststructuralist theory for feminism, pp 282–98, in Seidman, Steven (ed.) (1994) op. cit.

Stephens, Paul (1987) The landed interest and the education of the English working class 1807–1833: A sociological study of aristocratic debate and policy. Ph.D thesis: University of London

Storey, John (ed.) (1996) *What is Cultural Studies?* London: Arnold

Sugrue, Bill and Taylor, Calvin (1996) From Marx to Man. City, pp 2–6, *Sociology Review*, Vol. 6, September

Thompson, Kenneth (1996) *Key Quotations in Sociology*. London: Routledge

Tischler, Henry L. (1996) *Introduction to Sociology*, Fifth Edition. Fort Worth: The Harcourt Press

Williams, Raymond (1976) *Keywords*. London: Fontana/Croom Helm

Willis, Paul (1990) *Moving Culture*. London: Calouste Gulbenkian Foundation

Exam practice: Culture and identity

Data response question

Item A

The first known case of a human infant living in social isolation was Anna. She was discovered hidden away in an attic room, bound to a chair. There she had stayed deprived of essential human contact for five years, because of her illegitimate status.

Kingsley Davis (1940), an early sociologist, travelled to see the child and found that she was completely unresponsive as if the world around her did not exist. She was unable to speak, only making grunting noises, couldn't feed herself and could hardly walk.

During the next year Anna made some progress as she experienced the humanising effect of socialisation. She showed greater interest and responsiveness to other people, developed human expressions and even smiled with pleasure. However, she was almost ten years of age before she showed signs of using language; but she remained very limited in her expression, which seemed to be related to her earlier social isolation.

(Adapted from John J. Macionis, *Sociology 5th ed* (Prentice Hall) 1995)

Item B

People ache to believe that we human beings are vastly different from all other species, and they are right! We are the only species that has an *extra* medium of design preservation and design communication: culture . . . other species have not developed culture to the take off point the way our species has. We have language, the primary medium of culture, which has Darwinian origins too! Human cultural transmission can operate many magnitudes faster than genetic evolution and carry *memes* [units of cultural transmission = ideas] forward, leaping through design space at a fast forward speed.

What we are is very much a matter of what culture has made us, it is the deciding factor of human survival. But, there is considerable competition among the memes for entry into as many minds as possible, thus creating an infosphere where cultural evolution occurs. Speaking, hearing, writing and reading are the underlying technologies of cultural transmission and replication, often generated via print of electronic borne communication.

The theory of evolution by natural selection is like a universal solvent, it leaves nothing untouched . . . it eats through every other explanation for culture . . . the reductionist finale! . . . but that which survives the acid test . . .

(Adapted from D. Dennett, *Darwin's Dangerous Idea* (Penguin) 1995)

Item C

Mass culture as we know it is a product of the twentieth century. It is the foreseeable result of advanced communications technology, the general low level of education, available time and disposable income for a great body of ordinary people in the more highly developed societies. It is the processes of capitalism which bring all these together for profit through persuasion.

Mass culture has a very short breath, it has to be successive, to move on always and restlessly, it can rarely stay with one subject. It has to be predatory, like a small creature with a limited capacity, it can and must rapidly digest small items and quickly void them. Its impulse is to be seductive at all times.

Processing demands something to process, so mass culture is parasitic. As some new form of popular art appears, with its own particular and attractive elements, when this *becomes* popular, it is only a matter of time before the machines of mass culture take it over, create a simulacrum of it and flood the market. Mass culture processes experiences so that consumers can easily digest the watered-down, smooth-edged commodity. The products of mass culture must at first glance seem like the real thing, but this surface form or stylised image is only a synthetic creation which stands for the reality it claims to be.

This raises the question of what people actually *do* with mass culture. People are not empty vessels into which anything can be poured, neither is their whole being mirrored in the conventional sentimentalities of the time. People do not accept such processing passively, but as individuals already deeply imbrued within their culture, whatever that culture may be. This protects them from a naked radiation of ideas and attitudes from the mass media.

(Adapted from R. Hoggart, *The Way We Live Now* (Pimlico) 1995)

(a) With reference to **Item A**, give one example of:

(i) the 'humanising effects of socialisation' on Anna during her *first* year of social contact.

(ii) the effect of 'earlier social isolation' on Anna. *(2 marks)*

(b) Drawing on the information presented in **Item A**, and elsewhere, give *three* reasons why sociologists emphasise the importance of the 'humanising effects of socialisation' in becoming a member of society. *(3 marks)*

(c) With reference to **Item B**, explain what is meant by 'memes' and 'infosphere', using examples to illustrate your answer. *(4 marks)*

(d) Evaluate Dennett's claim in **Item B**, that culture is merely competing ideas jumping from one mind to another, without thought for person, time or place within human societies. *(8 marks)*

(e) Using the information in **Item C**, critically evaluate to what extent mass culture is *the* dominant culture in a consumer driven advanced industrial society. *(8 marks)*

7 Social stratification

Topics covered in this chapter
- *Defining social stratification*
- *Social class*
- *Ethnicity (and 'race')*
- *Gender*
- *Age*

The black civil rights leader and sociologist, Dr Martin Luther King, made discrimination and poverty the focus of his non-violent campaign. As his wife, Coretta Scott King, eloquently said:

'He spoke out sharply for the poor in all their hues, for he knew if color made them different, misery and oppression made them the same.'

(King 1969: Foreword)

In that one sentence, Coretta Scott King captured the spirit of Dr King's resolve to wage a peaceful struggle against class and racial injustice. It was a cause for which he willingly gave his life, struck down by an assassin's bullet in Memphis on 4 April 1968.

In 1960s USA, Dr King looked around him and didn't like what he saw: 'grim ghettos [that] contradict the fine language of the legislation' (1969: 19); of employed black Americans, 75 per cent holding menial jobs; and millions of Americans (black, white and Native American) 'smothered in poverty in the midst of opulence' (1969: 83). What he saw, in sociological terms, was a social and economic pyramid with rich and relatively prosperous people in the top and middle portions and the less prosperous and abjectly poor at the bottom. He also noted that black people were heavily concentrated at the base of the pyramid.

This multi-layered cake is an example of what sociologists call *social stratification*. Each layer (stratum) in the cake represents economic groups called *social classes*. Moreover, each class is further *differentiated,* containing its own layers. For example, middle-class women usually earn less than middle-class men, Irish working-class people less than white working-class Britons, etc. Some sociologists – usually of a marxist disposition – believe that class is the bedrock of stratification, arguing that economic security (the basis of class) is more important than being a woman or a man, black or white, old or young. Other sociologists – notably weberian in outlook – claim that all forms of stratification are potentially as important as each other. What all sociologists are agreed on, however, is that stratification leads to inequality. Whether that should be something to lament or to merely describe and understand remains debatable. What do you think?

Defining social stratification

'I'm middle class now', said the Deputy Leader of the Labour Party, John Prescott, in 1996. Some commentators in the UK reckon that we're all middle class now – with a tiny rich minority at the top and an 'underclass' minority at the bottom. If this assertion is correct, out goes the pyramid model to be replaced by a diamond, bulging in the middle and sharply tapered at its peak and base. But what do sociologists have to say about the matter? In answering that question, we'll first look at theories of social class, and then at some important empirical evidence. Later, we'll address the issue of three other kinds of social stratification in society, namely, the different social and economic *life chances* of females and males (*gender*), of black (and other minority ethnic) people and white people (*ethnicity*), of children, youths, working-age adults and retired adults (*age*). We'll also consider the *differentiation* that occurs within these groups. Social classes, for example, aren't simply *en bloc* categories; there are differences within each class: middle-class women, middle-class men; skilled workers, unskilled workers, etc.

Quite often, sociologists make a distinction between *social class* (which refers to an individual's economic position) and *social status* (which refers to the amount of esteem an individual has). In relation to the four aspects of stratification considered in this chapter, one refers to class groups and the other three (age, ethnicity and gender) refer to status groups. In reality, of course, the distinction isn't always cut and dry – as the following examples demonstrate. Working-class people enjoy a high status in the eyes of some trade unionists – their class defines the amount of esteem they have, not just their economic position. Women are paid lower wages than men by some employers – their status group defines their economic position, not just the amount of esteem they have.

> ***EXAM TIP***
>
> Examiners give top marks to candidates who recognise that social stratification groups don't exist in splendid isolation. People who belong to a class, for example, also belong to other groups: female/male, black/white, etc.

Before moving on, we need to define two key terms:

- *Social stratification* is the division of society into different social strata (social layers) in such a way that people in some social strata have better life chances than people in other social strata.
- *Life chances* are opportunities for living a good life.

Social class

In every society, material rewards are distributed unequally. As a result, people are divided into different social classes, each class containing individuals whose command or lack of command of economic resources are relatively similar. In that respect, classes are groups of people who share the same kind of economic (and related) life chances. For example, people on low wages struggle to make ends meet, whereas profit-rich corporation bosses lead lavish lifestyles. In between the poor and the rich, the rest of us fall. Here we have three classes: the upper class, the middle class, and the lower class. Some sociologists – usually the ones who are influenced by Max Weber – adopt this model of social stratification. Other sociologists – typically the ones who agree with Karl Marx – say there are just two *main* classes: people who 'work for a living' and people who 'live off the backs of workers'.

Theories of class

You'd expect Marx and marxists to be controversial, and indeed they are. For them, the discovery of social inequality isn't just an issue of identification and measurement. It's also one of exposing injustice and fighting for a more equal society. Weber and weberians are, arguably, less controversial and more concerned with establishing the facts of social inequality than with passing social commentary. There are, of course, some weberians who bemoan the fact that life chances are very unevenly distributed. They're less likely, however, than marxists to bring politics into social science, being more inclined to describe *what is* than in saying what ought or ought not to be. The tension inherent in trying to be scientifically objective about social inequality, while not getting righteously angry about it at the same time, is eloquently expressed by the American sociologist, Melvin Tumin:

> 'As social scientists, we are bidden to press for the greatest possible amount of value-neutrality and objectivity in our professional work. The political and moral implications of social inequality are issues on which my personal predilections [Tumin is quite 'left-wing' and morally opposed to inequality] are reasonably well-known.'
>
> (Tumin 1967: vi)

Like many sociologists, Tumin doesn't fit neatly into the either/or categories of marxist/weberian. He's influenced by both perspectives, as well as by the most dominant perspective in 1960s American sociology: functionalism. You see, not all functionalists are inherently conservative!

Functionalist sociologists, of course, also have things to say about class. Talcott Parsons, for example, defined a class as 'an aggregate of kinship units of approximately equal status[1] in the system of stratification' (1964: 172). Putting this rather complex language into simpler terms, a class is a group of people and their families who have the same kind of social standing in society. Thus, for example, people who are employed in a steel factory and who live in a steel town share a common social position in the community. That social position defines their location within a system of stratification, relative to the social positions of other people. Steelworkers and coalminers have similar levels of prestige, power and income, and may be said to belong to the same class. Architects and engineers are part of another class whose members collectively enjoy higher levels of social advantage than manual workers.

Some functionalists have suggested that the hierarchical arrangement of society into occupational classes (with the higher classes 'deservedly' earning better life chances) performs the useful function of ensuring that talent rises to the top. This polemical argument was proposed by

[1] Some sociologists use status to refer to the *amount of esteem* (or *lack of esteem*) people have. Parsons and like-minded functionalists employ the term more widely to refer to *overall social standing* in relation, for example, to occupation, esteem held, power exercised, etc.

two students of Parsons – Kingsley Davis and Wilbert Moore – in 1940s USA, and is still influential in certain 'right-wing' circles. Don't think, however, that all forms of hierarchy are endorsed by functionalists. Parsons for example, in his critique of 'conservative' German society, wrote disapprovingly of its 'authoritarian family structure, in which the wife was carefully "kept in her place"' (1964: 193).

There are then three main theories of class:

- marxist
- weberian
- functionalist.

Marxist theory of class

In a fragment from his unfinished *opus magnum* (great work!), *Capital, Volume 3*, Karl Marx came as close as he ever did to identifying 'social classes':

'The owners of mere labor-power, the owners of capital, and the landlords, whose respective sources of income are wages, profit and ground-rent, in other words, wage laborers, capitalists and landlords, form the three great classes of modern society resting upon the capitalist mode of production.'

(cited by Coser and Rosenberg 1969: 379)

Having said earlier that marxists envisage the existence of two main classes in society, how can we square this assumption with Marx's three-class model? Not with too much difficulty, actually. The English society that Marx lived in and wrote about was one in which a land-owning ruling class was gradually being eclipsed by a factory-owning ruling class. To be sure, the 'landed aristocrats' enjoyed a long 'Indian summer' at the helm of political power, but by 1880 Parliament was represented for the first time with a majority comprised of businessmen and industrialists.

Thenceforth, one can justifiably make the marxist distinction between a ruling (or upper) class of industrial capitalists and a 'proletariat' of manual and non-manual workers. However, there's an important caveat here. The distinction is the one that marxists and weberians both agree exists between employers and employees, but the weberians place much more emphasis than the marxists on the differentiation within these two groups. As will be seen later, weberians regard the non-manual branch of the marxist 'proletariat' as a class in its own right – a 'middle class'.

Much more concerned with defining the 'fault lines' between the two major classes than with the differences between types of worker, Marx emphasised the importance of people's relationship to the 'means of production'. Before going any further, we need to define this important term. The *means of production* are the machines, land, banks, etc., that enable goods and services to be produced. For example, in the nineteenth-century England that Marx lived in and wrote about, a 'cotton gin' produced rolls of sheet cotton, farmland produced corn, and banks produced financial services. One's relationship to these and other means of production, said Marx, was either that one owned them or that one didn't. Marx claimed that the most powerful owners of the means of production in late nineteenth-century England were factory owners. They owned the machinery that had fuelled England's 'industrial revolution'.

But do such stark cleavages between a ruling class of employers and a working class of employees exist in the UK today? And has the middle class disappeared? We'll address these important questions after we've considered the weberian theory of social class.

> **EXAM TIP**
>
> Some candidates write that Marx only envisaged two classes. In fact, he envisaged two *main* social classes.

Weberian theory of class

The first thing to say about Weber and weberians is that they agree with Marx and marxists about class being an essentially economic category. They place more emphasis than the marxists, however, on the differentiation that exists within classes (for example, the income and status difference between an unskilled manual worker and a skilled manual worker). For marxists, the main division between classes is the one that separates the people who work for a living and the people who do the hiring. It doesn't much matter to a marxist if the person who works for a living is a construction worker or an astronomer – what counts is that they sell their labour power. Weberians, however, while recognising – like marxists – that it's important and helpful to distinguish between employers and employees, also highlight the differences that exist within these two groups. For the weberian sociologist – and, it has to be said, for the majority of sociologists in the UK – occupation is the single most important tool for classifying people into different classes. American sociologists also recognise the usefulness of occupation as a general-purpose classification tool, but they tend more often than their British counterparts to use multi-dimensional scales (for example, a person's occupation, her income, and her education might be included in the overall class equation).

Writing about class in the early part of this century, Weber noted that:

'We may speak of a "class" when (1) a number of people have in common a specific causal component of their life chances, in so far as (2) this component is represented exclusively by economic interests in the possession of goods and opportunities for income, and (3) is represented under the conditions of the commodity or labor markets.'

(cited by Coser and Rosenberg 1969: 388)

Confused? So were we when we read this very complex definition. After some thought and reflection, we managed to put Weber's definition into simpler terms:

A class is a group of people who share the same kind of life chances because they occupy the same kind of economic position in society.

Thus, for example, they might own the same kinds of house, car and other material possession, receive similar incomes, and work in comparable occupations (or be employers). Their similar economic positions provide them with similar life chances: to be in good physical and mental health, drink connoisseur coffee, enjoy excellent working conditions, fly business class – or, of course, the converse on all counts. In short, these common characteristics mean they belong to the same class.

OVER TO YOU

Describe the economic and life chance profiles of three imaginary individuals, one from the upper class, one from the middle class, and one from the lower class.

EXAM TIP

Be sure to refer to the similarities as well as the differences between marxist and weberian theories.

Functionalist theory of class

Functionalists pay less explicit attention to class than marxists and weberians. When they do write about class, it's typically in the style of Talcott Parsons, who used the term to denote general social standing in the community and society at large. For Parsons, economic position is only one part of this equation, for one's standing is a measure of more than just material trappings. It embraces such factors as where one went to school, one's family background, one's neighbourhood – indeed, anything that a particular society takes account of in its evaluation of an individual's place within the social hierarchy. In that respect, the parsonian concept of class is essentially interchangeable with what Weber termed social status (namely, socially-defined esteem or honour).

Strongly leaning in the same direction as Parsons, the American sociologists Kingsley Davis and Wilbert Moore (1945) envisaged stratification as the ranking of individuals based on the extent to which they embodied valued qualities and performed worthwhile functions in society. According to Davis and Moore, in order to function effectively, society must ensure that its most important positions are occupied by the most qualified people. Healers must be registered doctors, legalists qualified lawyers, etc. Society must also provide sufficient rewards to these important people to induce them to perform their essential functions. Otherwise, they wouldn't be motivated to undertake the lengthy education and training necessary to competently discharge their duties. For this reason, the most important occupations in society are the best paid, and the more important one's occupation, the higher one's class and attendant prestige.

The most famous attack on the Davis–Moore critique came in 1953 from another American sociologist, Melvin Tumin, who argued that manual workers are just as indispensable to the successful operation of a factory as engineers. He added that there are many inducements for motivating people to perform important functions, of which high pay is just one. Nor, said Tumin, was it functional (i.e. useful) for society to perpetuate the preferred distribution of material rewards offered to the most talented people to their children. For this would mean that inherited inequality took precedence over 'meritocracy' – the idea that each generation afresh rises, stays put, or falls on the basis of its own merits. Contrary to being functional, social inequality is *dysfunctional*, contends Tumin – it does more harm than good.

To be fair to Davis and Moore, they did concede that what comes to be judged as functionally important varies from society to society. Being a lawyer in American society might carry lots of prestige and attract high earnings, while being a priest in Renaissance Rome might have equivalent kudos. Nevertheless, it needs to be said that even in societies where an occupational role is generally agreed to be very important, it isn't automatically highly paid. Firefighters, in anybody's estimation, are brave people who do important work, but they're relatively low paid in the UK and the US.

EXAM TIP

It's over-simplistic to claim that the functionalists are conservatives who support hierarchical class systems. Some do, some don't. Moreover, describing a hierarchical class system which exists doesn't mean that one likes what one sees.

These firefighters do functionally important work for much less pay than advertising executives. Who do you think does more to help society: a firefighter or an advertising executive – or is that an impossible question to answer?

Models of class today

Marxist and weberian influences on present-day conceptions of class are strong and helpful. Functionalist ideas on class, however, are much less influential. In part, this results from strong antipathy against the inherent conservatism of the Davis–Moore critique. But it's also the case that marxist and weberian sociology focuses much more on the issue of class than functionalism. However, modern-day marxists and weberians don't employ the theories of Marx and Weber in an uncritical manner. Circumstances have changed since Marx (who wrote in the nineteenth century) and Weber (who wrote in the early twentieth century) formulated their models of class. Better to cherrypick the ideas that endure than to transplant the entire theories in a dogmatic fashion. We've much to learn from Marx and Weber, but we must never assume that they bequeathed sociology with an infallible legacy of untouchable and untamperable concepts.

What does endure from their work is the important notion that class can be defined and measured by social scientists. Most sociologists adopt this so-called *objective approach to class*. The defining process typically involves the sociologist in setting a number of attributes (occupation, level of education, residence, etc.), and then assigning people to groups (classes) whose members generally share the same attributes. Taking a look at what this means in real terms, examine the table of classes in the US below.

Like their American counterparts, British sociologists recognise that occupation, education and children's

Social stratification in the United States by occupation

Class	Occupation	Education	Children's education
Upper class	Corporate ownership; upper-echelon politics; honorific positions in government and the arts	Liberal arts education at elite schools	College and postcollege
Upper-middle class	Professional and technical fields; managers; officials; proprietors	College and graduate school training	College and graduate school training
Lower-middle class	Clerical and sales positions; small-business owners; semi-professionals; farmers	High school; some college	Option of college
Working class	Skilled and semi-skilled manual labor; crafts people; foremen; non-farm workers	Grade school; some or all of high school	High school; vocational school
Lower class	Unskilled labor and service work; private household work and farm labor	Grade school; semi-illiterate	Little interest in education; high school dropouts

(Tischler 1996: 254, adapted from US Bureau of the Census, *Statistical Abstract of the United States: 1981*, Washington DC Government Printing Office, 1981)

education are useful indicators of class position. However, they rarely single out education (neither the incumbent's, nor her or his children) in official classifications of class, preferring instead to use occupation as a catch-all composite of other attributes – education among them. In that respect, British models of class are strongly influenced by weberian theory. Take, for example, the *Standard Occupational Classification* (*SOC*). Among the most recent and, increasingly, a very widely used model in the UK, the SOC regards occupation as the bedrock of class – hence its weberian legacy. It's now the official class category used by the Office of Population Censuses and Surveys (OPCS).

The SOC identifies and aggregates occupations into distinct groups in relation to the similarity of qualifications, training, skills and experience commonly associated with the competent performance of work tasks – echoes here of functionalist theory! For example, people who are in a 'professional occupation' (for example, doctors, teachers, lawyers) typically have a degree or equivalent qualification, and some jobs in this group require postgraduate qualifications and/or a formal period of experience-related training. As you may have noted, education is treated as one of the defining features of occupation rather than identified as a category in its own right.

Unlike the scientifically flawed – and very sexist practice – adopted in the recent past (and sometimes even today) of placing a wife in the same social class as her husband (on the basis of *his* occupation), the SOC classifies people according to their own occupation. Prior to 1991, official definitions of class were typically based on the occupation of the so-called 'head of household'. In most cases, this was a male, and his wife and children were treated as though they belonged to his class. This very 'malestream' – to borrow a term from Pamela Abbott and Claire Wallace (1997) – convention is rapidly becoming obsolete in modern social science.

In the new SOC model, people are judged to be in an occupation if they're 'economically active', which means that they're in paid employment, or currently looking for or available for paid employment. Occupation is generally defined as the current *main* job a person does, but for persons not currently employed, it's defined as the most recent – or most recent *main* – job. While SOC is increasingly becoming the standard measure of class in social science, there are other classifications that require brief mention. The predecessor of SOC is the *Registrar General's social classes* (RG). Dating from 1921, the RG classification has, until recently, been the most commonly used measure of class in the UK. It's a 'head of household' (read male) occupational classification (i.e. weberian) which, since 1971, has been based on six classes. The following table identifies these classes and provides typical occupations in each class.

Typical occupations[1] of each social class (RG80)

I PROFESSIONAL, ETC.
Accountant, architect, chemist, company secretary, doctor, engineer, judge, lawyer, optician, scientist, solicitor, surveyor, university teacher, veterinarian.

II INTERMEDIATE
Aircraft pilot or engineer, chiropodist, farmer, laboratory assistant/technician, manager, proprietor, publican, member of parliament, nurse police or fire-brigade officer, schoolteacher.

IIIn SKILLED NON-MANUAL
Auctioneer, cashier, clerical worker, commercial traveller, draughtsman, estate agent, sales representative, secretary, shop assistant, typist, telephone supervisor.

IIIm SKILLED MANUAL
Baker, bus driver, butcher, bricklayer, carpenter, cook, electrician, hairdresser, miner (underground), policeman or fireman, railway engine driver/guard, upholsterer.

IV PARTLY SKILLED/SEMI-SKILLED
Agricultural worker, barman, bus conductor, fisherman, hospital orderly, machine sewer, packer, postman, roundsman, street vendor, telephone operator.

V UNSKILLED
Chimney/road sweeper, kitchen hand, labourer, lift/car park attendant, driver's mate, messenger, railway stationman, refuse collector, window/office cleaner.

1 In alphabetical order. These are mainly basic occupation titles; foremen and managers in occupations listed are allotted to different classes.

(Reid 1989: 56, devised from *Classification of Occupations* (1980), pp 1–89 and appendices B1 and B2)

Each of the six classes in the table above is based, as far as is possible, on the grouping together of heads of household who have similar levels of occupational skill. In sociological shorthand, classes I, II and IIIn are 'middle class' (i.e. non-manual) employees, and classes IIIm, IV and V are 'working class' (i.e. manual) employees. So where's the upper class? you might properly ask. The simple answer is that they don't feature in the RG classification. Weberians aren't too troubled about this because they tend to place more emphasis on occupation than on employer/employee distinctions. Marxists, however, regard the omission as a serious shortcoming of the RG classification. For them, the fundamental class divisions in society are between employers and workers.

CRIT THINK CRIT THINK CRIT THINK CRIT THINK CRIT THINK CRIT THINK

CHALLENGING THE 'MALESTREAM' PERSPECTIVE

The following extract is adapted from *An Introduction to Sociology: Feminist Perspectives* by Pamela Abbott and Claire Wallace. As the title suggests, the book offers a feminist way of looking at issues like social stratification.

'There's increasing empirical evidence which suggests that the social class position of women can't be ignored or treated as the same as their husbands' or fathers'. Not only do those assumptions fail to explain women's social and political behaviour, they often lead to incorrect conclusions about men's social mobility [i.e. movement up or down the social class ladder], and the way British society is structured for women and men. For example, women's readiness to "have a job" rather than a career is important in explaining male mobility, because more often than not the man has a career and the woman fits her work around the demands of that male career. Moreover, a wife's unpaid labour at home helps many men to pursue their occupations in earnest, and most upward mobility is arguably dependent on the woman being able to adapt to a "higher" lifestyle.

The examination of women's social class convinces us of the importance of studying family members in their own right, and of avoiding common-sense assumptions about shared family norms and interests or shared social experiences. It might be the case that shared interests and experiences occur in families and that class is a more important form of stratification than gender in our society. That this might be so, however, must be demonstrated, not taken for granted in the untheorised way of malestream sociologists. For this, we need adequate tools and unblinkered theories so that women are fully incorporated into sociological research.'

(Abbott and Wallace 1997: 68)

1 *Using books, newspapers, experiences and other appropriate sources, find out if the evidence supports the following assertions made by Abbott and Wallace:*

- *'There's increasing empirical evidence which suggests that the social class position of women can't be ignored or treated as the same as their husbands' or fathers'.'*
- *'Women's readiness to "have a job" rather than a career is important in explaining male mobility, because more often than not the man has a career and the woman fits her work around the demands of that male career.'*

2 *What kind of 'adequate tools and unblinkered theories' are needed in sociology to ensure 'that women are fully incorporated into sociological research'?*

CRIT THINK CRIT THINK CRIT THINK CRIT THINK CRIT THINK CRIT THINK CRIT

Nor are feminist sociologists impressed with the RG model. They rightly point out that its 'malestream' assumption marginalises the class position of women by treating it as derivative from the class of their husbands, or – in the case of girls – their fathers.

Class as an objective category

The SOC and RG classifications of class are treated as objective. Sociologists establish the criteria that define each class, and assign individuals to a particular class on the basis of the criteria. The individuals aren't asked for their views on the matter. If, for example, I'm a plumber and consider myself upper class, my subjective opinion wouldn't make a dent on the sociologist's determination that I'm actually working class. A parallel procedure in biology is when natural scientists determine what constitutes a female and a male human being, and then assign to either category individuals whose biologies fit the scientific criteria. While there are some 'biological females and males' who might feel they belong to the opposite sex, the biologists' criteria are generally treated in the scientific community as more reliable.

The big advantage of objective concepts of class is that it's a precise scientific tool which identifies and measures real (especially, economic) differences between different groups of people in society. Linked to this advantage is the one that sociologists can easily obtain scientifically agreed upon (OK, there are some differences of opinion here, but not so many as to obviate a fair degree of scientific consensus) data on objective class criteria – occupation, income, education, etc. On the negative side, the opinions of individuals as to how they define their class positions (if, indeed, they do assign themselves to classes) is largely ignored. It follows from this, argue interpretivist sociologists, that so-called objective concepts of class are privileged above other concepts merely because positivistic sociologists think they know best. Now that, say the interpretivists, is pure professional arrogance!

Class as a subjective category

Interpretivists claim that the concerns of social scientists are rarely as straightforward as the concerns of other scientists. The fact that classes exist at all is because they're perceived to exist by people in society. In that respect, classes are socially constructed rather than objectively 'out there', and are thereby inherently subjective. If, for example, my parents both work in low-paid manual occupations, but I become a well-paid architect, the fact that I feel working class might be much more real to me than being told by a sociologist that I'm objectively middle class. My subjective perception has all the more cadence if it affects the way I think and act. This important point has been noted by William Form (1982, cited by Alex Thio 1989), who points out that if self-employed American car mechanics, electricians and plumbers consider themselves upper class, they can be expected to have politically conservative views, and to vote Republican – just like 'real' upper-class Americans.

The main advantage of the subjective approach to class is that it echoes the felt convictions and experiences of ordinary people. If they feel working, middle or upper class, then that's the reality of their lived world, and it's a reality that interpretivist sociologists always treat with the utmost respect and seriousness. Allied to this advantage is the usefulness of the subjective classification in understanding and predicting attitudes and behaviours of people who think and act on the basis of their self-proclaimed class – those Republican-voting car mechanics come to mind. On the downside, if sociologists 'trusted' the subjective class evaluations of everyone in society, they'd have no common benchmarks against which to measure objective indicators of class – income, occupation, and such like. For, however little importance some individuals might attach to these indicators, they are real and they have real consequences. Another disadvantage of subjective opinions is that, at least in the US, when asked what class they think they belong to, most Americans tend to say middle class. This can be highly misleading, because, as Alex Thio astutely remarks:

'Both "upper class" and "lower class" have connotations offensive to democratic values. To call oneself upper class is to appear snobbish. To call oneself lower class is demeaning, because it implies that one is a loser in this supposed land of opportunity. As a result, many high-status people such as doctors and lawyers would call themselves middle rather than upper class; meanwhile, many low-income and lower-status Americans such as maids and laborers would also say they were middle class.'

(Thio 1989: 218)

Combining objective and subjective concepts of class – worth a try?

Although most sociologists, including the writer of this chapter, attach more credence to objective than to subjective concepts of class, it's possible, and arguably better social science, to take account of both dimensions. And here, perhaps surprisingly, is where Marx joins the debate. When he defined the working class – the proletariat, as he called them – in the nineteenth century, Marx combined objective (a class in itself) and subjective (a class for itself) considerations. A 'class in itself', said Marx, is a group of people who share a common economic position in society. A 'class for itself', he believed, have inter-subjectively (i.e. collectively) sensed and recognised this common position and forged a common cause. Thus, for example, a class of nineteenth-century underpaid, underfed wage labourers who know they are collectively exploited might unite in protest or revolution against their perceived oppressors.

While Marx properly acknowledges that a class which exists both in itself and for itself is a category that fuses objective and subjective elements, he controversially assumes that he, the social scientist, knows which class people belong to. It follows from this assumption that working-class people are 'expected' to recognise subjectively that Marx has got it objectively right all along. Moreover, when he speaks of a class both in and for itself, he seems to do so only with working-class people in mind, thereby neglecting other classes. There is, of course, a political agenda here: Marx wanted the proletariat to unite in common cause against the ruling class. The notion that workers might become a class for themselves was clearly a call to action. Can Marx therefore be trusted on a social scientific level, or is he just another 'politician'? Now there's a tricky question! Consider and discuss it with each other and with your teacher.

The class structure of present-day society

Having looked at and evaluated alternative ways of conceptualising class, it's now time to examine the class structure of present-day society. Here we adopt the marxist and – it needs to be emphasised – the weberian perspective that the gulf between the proprietor upper class and the rest of society is very significant. We also take the more singularly weberian view that there are real and meaningful differences between different groups of employees, namely, the middle and working classes. Our model then is a three-class one, based on economic and social distinctions between the upper class, the middle class, and the working class. Each of these three classes, as will be seen below, has its own fairly distinctive life chances.

The upper class

Comprising about 1 per cent of the population in the UK, this small but very powerful class are mainly big property owners. Their incomes largely derive from capital assets and shares. The richest 500 of their number were worth upwards of £35 million each in 1996 (Philip Beresford and Stephen Boyd 1996). This figure refers to estimates of their minimum wealth (notably, significant public company shares, property, land, racehorses and art treasures). The select few who make up the richest 500 people in the UK are worth at least £70.5 billion, their average wealth being around £140 million. This is an average, and the actual range runs from £37 million to a staggering £2,880 million. If you go to your fridge and open a carton of milk or fruit juice, chances are it'll have a Tetra Pak logo on it. Tetra Pak is a food packaging company owned by two Swedish brothers, Gad and Hans Rausing, one of whom (Hans) lives in the UK. Hans is worth £2,880 million, which makes him the richest person in the country.

It's 'new money' rather than aristocratic incomes that rules the roost at the top. While this comes in different shapes and sizes – manufacturing, entertainment, banking, publishing, etc. – the big rollers are in retailing and commerce, accounting for 148 (nearly 30 per cent) of the richest 500. Though the 'landed aristocracy' no longer dominate the upper class, they'll still be around for several generations. Their vast collections of 'old master' paintings ensure their continued existence. As Beresford and Boyd note, 'it simply takes the auction of one £5m painting to provide enough liquidity for some years of house repairs and general living expenses' (1996: 4).

Although it's sometimes said that 'purist' marxists only regard the big owners of *productive property* (i.e. property that begets goods and services – factories, hotels, and the like) as belonging to the upper class, Marx anticipated that a minority of top managers would become almost as one with their bosses. His forecast proved correct. Today, top-ranking executives might be 'employees' in name, but they wield *de facto* power on a par with their owner-bosses. Some of them make just as much money too.

The lifestyles and life chances that go hand-in-hand with the massive incomes, as well as the vast wealth (*income* is a cash flow asset, *wealth* is property) of the upper class, are well-documented (see, for example, Malcolm Hamilton and Maria Hirszowicz 1993). They move (and marry) within the same social circles and exhibit a high degree of social cohesion, marked by such things as lavish entertainment and travel, membership of prestigious London clubs, private education (public schools and 'Oxbridge' feature prominently) and healthcare, attendance at hunt balls, Ascot, the Henley Regatta and the 'London season', and grandiose residences. They're very disproportionately over-represented – often through *elite self-recruitment* – in the top positions of business and finance, and – directly or indirectly – they hold considerable sway in politics.

The middle class

Orthodox marxists don't concede that the middle class are indeed a class, preferring to see them as the non-manual branch of the working class. For if the working class is regarded as all employees whose work contributes to profit creation, but who don't share in the profits, then this class must include manual and non-manual workers. The argument has merit if one considers the similar life chances and pay levels of the better paid manual workers and the less well-off, non-manual workers. These days, for example, a skilled electrician enjoys a similar standard of living to a teacher. Compare though the economic positions of a city lawyer with those of a garbage collector. The gulf is enormous, not just in income terms, but also in the lifestyles and 'cultures' that invariably accompany big differences in pay levels. It's in this context that marxist orthodoxy becomes stuck in dogma rather than convincingly addressing the reality of the society in which we live. Some marxists (for example, John Westergaard 1995) are beginning to recognise this, and are reconciling their differences with weberian sociologists.

That said, the recognition of the middle class as a class in its own right, and the description of its characteristics remains very much a weberian accomplishment.

Sociologists commonly identify two groupings within the middle class:

- *the 'old middle class'* (sometimes called the 'petite bourgeoisie') of relatively well-to-do proprietors – either self-employed (for example, a barrister) or employers of only a small number of employees (for example, a country practice vet). Though their numbers are probably down these days, the reference to 'old' doesn't mean the members of this grouping are in retreat. Rather, it suggests that they occupy positions in society that have a long lineage
- *the 'new middle class'* of non-manual employees. Their 'new' adage principally refers to their large, still growing numbers. There's wide diversity within the 'new middle class': the NHS heart surgeon, the school teacher, the office worker. The better-paid employees rub shoulders with some members of the upper class. The worst paid earn less than skilled manual workers, and might accurately be described by both weberians and marxists as the non-manual section of the working class proper.

The life chances and lifestyles within the middle class vary enormously. Those in the higher level – top lawyers and other elite professionals, politicians, senior managers, generals and ambassadors – are located in what John Westergaard eloquently describes as 'the foothills surrounding peak privilege and power' (1995: 128). They do very well indeed, having life chances and lifestyles similar to those of the upper class. The middle section of the middle class – intermediate professionals, 'ordinary' managers, etc. – enjoy decent salaries, good health and education, and long lives, and participate in an affluent culture. But the lower middle class (predominantly female, 'routine white-collar' employees) do considerably less well incomewise, often earning no more than manual workers. Some of them might aspire to a 'middle-class lifestyle', but unless they 'marry upwards', they're unlikely to acquire the cultural or the material capital to accomplish this.

The working ('lower') class

The term 'working class' is conventionally used by British sociologists to describe what their American counterparts generally refer to as the 'lower class'. There's something rather pejorative, however, about the adjective 'lower'. It suggests inferiority and subservience, which both insults and misrepresents people who earn relatively low incomes. We'll stick with the term 'working class'.

Like the classes 'above' them, working class people belong to a class that contains various groupings. Before looking at this internal differentiation, it's first helpful to consider what the working class has in common. These characteristics (and please note the changing trends) are:

- typically not having any formal education beyond school-leaving age (currently 16). There is, however, a discernible trend in the 1990s for more working-class children to stay on at school to age 17 or 18, and, increasingly, to enter higher education (particularly, the 'new' universities)
- working in a manual occupation doing jobs that are often physically demanding and sometimes dangerous (for example, construction). These days 'hard-hat' heavy industries are in decline, and working-class people (especially women) are moving into routine, low-paid service sector work (for example, retailing and office employment).

In structural terms, sociologists often make a distinction between two main groups within the working class:

- *skilled or semi-skilled employees* (for example, carpenters, computer operators) who earn about the same as lower middle-class employees (for example, nurses, social workers), but who still retain an essentially working-class outlook on life (for example, vote Labour, value community, etc.)
- *unskilled employees* (for example, cleaners, kitchen porters) and non-working people on low fixed incomes (for example, long-term unemployed, pensioners, 'rough sleepers') who are becoming increasingly pauperised and marginalised from mainstream society.

Most manual working-class people lead reasonably healthy, relatively prosperous, happy lives. But if and when things do go wrong, working-class people are more likely to be on the receiving end than middle-class people. For example, more working-class children die at birth or during childhood, and manual employees are more at risk of ill-health (sometimes as a result of occupational hazards and diseases) and less likely to receive, on a needs basis, adequate health care than non-manual employees. Such differences, however, are more stark when one compares the life chances of the 'upper middle class' with those of unskilled manual workers.

As far back as the 1950s, a number of commentators were suggesting that the lifestyle of the working class was becoming increasingly middle class. This, the inappropriately termed 'embourgeoisement thesis', was put to the test in the 1960s by John Goldthopre, David Lockwood, Frank Bechhofer and Jennifer Platt (1973), who found it wanting. They discovered that affluent workers (the most likely, if the thesis were true, to adopt middle-class norms and values) hadn't been, nor wanted to be, assimilated into middle-class culture. Nevertheless, they detected the signs of a 'new working classness', manifested in large part, by the desire for a 'privatised' rather than a community-based lifestyle. During the 1980s, Fiona Devine (1994) re-visited the location of the Goldthorpe team study – Luton – to find if traditional working-class community life had been eclipsed by the rise of privatised lifestyles. She found little evidence of this, instead discovering a network of sociability involving kin, neighbours and 'fellow' workers. It seems that the 'Essex Man' ethos hasn't arrived in Luton!

> **EXAM TIP**
>
> When writing about modern classifications of class, it's very important to highlight the limitations of models which assume that a woman belongs to the class of her father or husband/partner.

The 'underclass'(?)

While the working class today certainly contains quite a wide range of life chances and lifestyles within its ranks, some sociologists make a distinction between working-class people who lead reasonably prosperous lives and those who suffer deep and persistent material inequalities. This second category – which includes the non-working people described above – is sometimes controversially referred to as the 'underclass'.

Whatever deprivation indices you care to consult – housing, income, health, etc. – the 'underclass' are at the bottom of the pile. In that sense, the term accurately describes the position of the poorest people in our society: the homeless, pensioners on low fixed incomes, workers on poverty wages, black unemployed youths who are victims of racism, people who are disabled, and so forth. Perhaps 'underclass' is a useful catch-all phrase to describe the plight of these people. Even Marx identified a nineteenth-century 'underclass', whom he called a 'lumpenproletariat' of 'vagabonds', 'ruffians', and the like.

However, most modern-day marxists contest the 'underclass' concept, pointing to the obvious lack of common identity that exists between very diverse groups who only have in common the fact that they're poor. If 'class' refers not just to an economic category but also to a sense of oneness and common purpose (a 'class in itself'), how then can it be helpful to describe, for example, an unemployed young black male in south London and a pensioned single woman in Newcastle as part of the same class? Their social worlds are poles apart. To use sociological language, such people are 'socially heterogeneous', even though their lives are materially impoverished. Another objection to the use of the term 'underclass' is that it insults, degrades and 'pathologises' those whom it supposedly describes. To quote Ruth Lister, 'it is the language of disease and contamination . . . it stigmatises' (1991: 194).

If one were to use the term – or better still, a non-derogatory alternative – to describe very poor individuals whose lives were lived and experienced in a similar social universe (for example, unemployed former steel workers), the 'underclass' might prove to be a more relevant concept. One might even extend the concept to include marginalised low-paid, often casual or part-time, workers of the kind described by Gosta Esping-Andersen, who tread 'a relatively closed, dead-end career road, from which improvement is unlikely and in which life-chances are strongly pre-ordained to be poor . . . ' (Esping-Andersen 1993: 229). This 'underclass' is perhaps more likely to be female than male, because the UK's post-industrial 'service proletariat' (centred around low-end clerical and sales work) is predominantly female.

> ***EXAM TIP***
>
> It's always a good idea to put inverted commas around the term 'underclass'. This signals to the examiner that you're aware of the problematic nature of the term.

This description of classes has made some important references to the link between class and life chances, an issue that we will now examine a little further.

Class and life chances

In very dramatic but accurate terms, the American sociologist Alex Thio noted the impact of class on life chances when the ocean-going liner, *Titanic,* sank in the Atlantic in 1912. Fifteen hundred lives were lost, but 'social class was a major determinant of who survived and who died' (Thio 1989: 223). Of the females on board, 3 per cent of the first-class passengers drowned, compared to 16 per cent of the second-class and 45 per cent of the third-class passengers. All passengers in first class were given the opportunity to abandon ship, but third-class passengers were ordered to remain below deck, some of them at gunpoint. Less dramatic but equally worrying, people in 'lower' classes generally live shorter and less healthy lives than those higher up the social ladder. For class is still a good predictor of how people get on in life – of their life chances.

People who earn poverty wages, who look for 'sale' items in charity clothes shops, who eat one meal a day so their children can eat two, who suffer industrial injuries, who bed down for the night in a shop doorway, are rarely, if ever, found in the middle and upper classes. They're at the lower end of the working class, and their class position is the 'cause' of their diminished life chances. Significantly better life chances – longer life expectancies, higher incomes, superior housing, etc. – go hand in hand with being middle and upper class.

A number of important class-linked life chances have already been referred to in the description of the three classes. Here are some other examples to consider:

- Unemployment during the Thatcher years was heavily concentrated in the working class, and – within this class – among people who were disabled, sick, old and young (A. H. Halsey 1995).
- A construction worker is ten times more likely than a lawyer to be made redundant (Carey Oppenheim and Lisa Harker 1996).
- Eight out of ten people in the 'managerial classes' took a holiday in 1991, compared to half of the unskilled workers (A. H. Halsey 1995).
- Life expectancy at birth is about seven times higher in social class I (professional, etc.) than in social class V (unskilled workers) (Department of Health 1995, cited by Oppenheim and Harker 1996).
- In secondary school education, despite an overall improvement in achievement, working-class students still do less well, on average, than middle-class students (Kenneth Roberts 1996).

OVER TO YOU

Using the most up-to-date sources you're able to locate, add to the above list of class-linked life chances.

Social mobility and changes in class structure

Nobody's life chances are permanently and immutably fixed. At various points in our lives we experience changing fortunes, for better and for worse. For many of us, this is related to ascending or descending the social ladder – to *social mobility.*

Social mobility refers to movement from one class to another. If your mum and dad are middle class and you become upper class, you're upwardly socially mobile. If you become working class, you're downwardly socially mobile. If you remain middle class, you're socially immobile. The preceding forms of social mobility/immobility are referred to as *inter-generational*. They describe mobility or immobility between generations – between, for example, father and daughter. Another form of social mobility/immobility is *intra-generational*. This refers to movement up or down the occupational ladder during a person's own working life or, of course, just staying put! Today, you're a construction worker; tomorrow you're a journalist: that's intra-generational social mobility. Inter-generational social mobility generally receives far more attention from sociologists than intra-generational social mobility because it enables them to plot long-term trends. Nevertheless, the fact that people change their jobs much more often these days than in the past cautions us not to overlook social mobility patterns of the intra-generational kind.

One of the most recent studies of social mobility in the UK is by A. H. Halsey. In his book, *Change in British Society* (1995), Halsey focuses on inter-generational social mobility. He does so by addressing the important question of whether people whose lives will be lived mainly in the twenty-first century have more or less equal chances of becoming rich or professional or unskilled or unemployed, compared with past generations. Combining empirical evidence with a weberian theoretical orientation, Halsey asserts 'that in industrial society the anatomy of class is displayed in the occupational structure' (1995: 33). It's in their jobs that most Britons differ from each other, rather than whether or not they own factories and other productive property.

In that respect, Halsey finds that the long-run tendency in British society over the past century has been one of a loosening class structure, with more opportunities for upward social mobility, and – in some cases – for downward social mobility. At the beginning of the twentieth century, he notes, over three-quarters of employed and self-employed Britons were manual workers. In 1911, 28.7 per cent of these were skilled, 34.3 per cent semi-skilled, 9.6 per cent unskilled, and 1.8 per cent were self-employed artisans. On the next rung up was a professional and white-collar class, and above them a ruling class of a few thousand individuals. By the mid-twentieth century, the proportion of manual workers had fallen below two-thirds. Since then, it's fallen to about a third.

By the 1970s, the class structure was more differentiated, but also more balanced. In the middle, there were three main occupational groups of roughly similar size, each accounting for about one-fifth to one quarter of the total workforce: the semi-skilled manual workers; the skilled manual workers; and the clerical and sales workers. Below and above these three groups were three smaller groups, each between 7 and 15 per cent of the total workforce: on the lower side, the unskilled workers, and, on the other side, the professional and technical workers, and the administrative, managerial and supervisory staff. At the top, were an 'upper class' of employers and proprietors, numbering about 8 per cent of the economically active population.

Although Halsey identifies an important trend towards a more 'open' society (i.e. people aren't as 'closed out' from upward social mobility as they were in the past), he correctly acknowledges that some class differences still endure. Thus in the post-war period up to the 1970s, he notes this combination of continuity and change:

- The typical English working-class male was born, and remained, working class.
- The number of English 'middle-class' sons who moved into the 'lower middle class' or working class was nearly the same as those who stayed in the class they were born into.
- Of 'middle-class' English males, two out of three had been born into another class.

Focusing on the changing aspects of the class structure, Halsey likens them to a shift from a pyramid to a light bulb. The pyramid contains a tiny apex of rulers, a widening middle section of professionals, and a further widening, very large section of manual workers. The light bulb contains . . .

OVER TO YOU

What does the light bulb contain? Draw diagrammatic representations of the pyramid and the light bulb class models.

Halsey identifies in these structural adjustments a movement away from a 'proletarian' society, a transformation that has gained additional pace in the 1980s and 1990s. Thus, for example, the proportion of employed manual workers fell from 51 per cent to 36 per cent between 1964 and 1987. The driving force behind this structural change is economic transformation. Out goes heavy industry and the 'hard-hat' worker. In comes an expansion of service sector occupations and the 'white-collar' worker: some, especially women, in low paid office-style work; others in relatively well-paid, career-ladder administrative and technical employment.

It's in this structural transformation from blue-collar to white-collar employment that the main explanation for increased upward social mobility in British society lies. Put simply, the working class has contracted and the middle class has expanded because there has been a decline in the number of working-class jobs and an increase in the number of middle-class jobs. There has subsequently been, as John Goldthorpe (1980, cited by Malcolm Hamilton and Maria Hirszowicz 1993: 206) puts it, increasing 'room at the top'. At the same time, even though the chances of working-class boys moving into the middle class (including its upper reaches) during their adult lives has significantly improved, the prospect of boys from 'upper middle-class' backgrounds retaining their advantaged position has been enhanced to an even greater extent (Hamilton and Hirszowicz 1993).

So what about girls, and women? you might reasonably ask. Social mobility statistics have long been distorted and disgraced by the non-inclusion of females. Things are beginning to change here, and much is owed, in that context, to the pioneering work of Pamela Abbott and Claire Wallace (1997), whose research into women's mobility has revealed the following trends in the UK:

- On the whole, women are more likely than men to be downwardly mobile, and less likely to be upwardly mobile, because of the prevailing labour market – an excess of jobs for women at the bottom of the non-manual class, and at the bottom of the manual one.
- Daughters are somewhat less likely than sons to obtain the same occupational levels as their fathers if this were a high level, and less likely than men to be countermobile (i.e. to bounce back up and even go further up the ladder after an initial drop in occupational level).
- For working-class women, their experience of upward social mobility is largely confined to movement into routine non-manual occupations.

Particularly striking in the changing social structure has been the increased entry of women into the paid workforce. While the number of men in paid employment has remained relatively stable in recent decades, the number of women has grown by about one million since the mid-1980s. It will continue to grow until, by 2001, women will comprise about 45 per cent of the civilian paid workforce. The number of men and women entering non-manual employment is increasing, but men are more likely than women to obtain higher professional and managerial positions. Women, by contrast, are more likely than men to fill the fast expanding array of routine white-collar jobs, especially in relatively unskilled sales and service sector employment. Importantly, this places a question mark over the assumption that women from working-class backgrounds who enter routine, non-manual employment are actually upwardly socially mobile. Indeed, it's probably more accurate to say that they simply move sideways from blue-collar to 'white-collar proletarianism'. As for men who work in the unskilled service sector, they aren't very mobile, and if they do move, it's unlikely to be in an upward direction. Typically, it will be into manual work.

Taking an historical view of things, women's paid employment has increased from about one tenth at the beginning of the twentieth century to about one half today. Even so, women still tend to regard paid employment as additional to retaining the main responsibility for domestic work. Moreover, the female labour market is typically intermittent, part-time and less well-paid than the male labour market. In that sense, it often constitutes what sociologists call a *secondary labour market* – one that lies outside of the predominantly male *primary labour market*. This is why the most common 'head of household' – measured by the size of the pay packet – is a male. It's also important to recognise that although both sexes today are more upwardly mobile than their parents and grandparents, men are generally more upwardly mobile than women.

QUESTIONS

1. Compare and contrast marxist and weberian theories of class.
2. Assess the contribution of functionalism to the sociological understanding of class.
3. What's the difference between objective and subjective conceptions of class?
4. Describe three life chances each for: the upper class; the middle class; the working class.
5. Assess the arguments for and against the view that the UK has an 'underclass'.
6. Briefly, and taking account of gender, describe the chief patterns of social mobility in British society.

Ethnicity (and 'race')

Racist chants and much worse reverberate in the Germany of the 1990s some 50 years after the nazi Third Reich came tumbling down at the end of the Second World War. While the worst excesses of racism are undoubtedly the result of crimes carried out by a minority of white Germans – neo-nazis, racist skinheads and the like – racist attitudes are widespread in Europe. In the UK, for example, a survey for BBC Radio Five Live in 1996 found that about a third of white, Asian and black people think racism has worsened. Sixty-one per cent of white people thought prejudice existed against Asians, while 49 per cent of black people and 31 per cent of Asian people believed there was a great deal of anti-Asian prejudice. White people and black people agreed there was significant anti-black prejudice (55 per cent and 49 per cent, respectively). Sixty per cent of black people and 40 per cent of Asians said they had suffered physical attacks.

Theories of 'race' and ethnicity

Although there are only very small biological differences between Asian, black and white people, racism negatively exaggerates 'racial' differences. While, for example, a young, black, male 100-metre track sprinter has the same skin colour as an older arthritic black male, he's got much more in common, biologically speaking, with a young, white, male athlete: similar weight, muscle-to-fat ratio, cardio-vascular performance, etc. Yet racists only look, literally, skin-deep. They see different skin colours and they invent other differences – the alleged intellectual superiority of white people, the purported criminal tendencies of black people, and so forth.

Most social scientists have concluded that it makes little sense to talk about 'race', preferring instead to concentrate on *ethnicity*, namely, the cultural significance people attach to their national origin – to their 'roots'. After all, according to biologists, we're all descended from a common gene pool – a single group of humans who originated in Africa, and lived there until about 100,000 years ago, when humans first started to migrate northwards. As they moved to different parts of the world, different migrants developed different physical characteristics in response to the physical environments they settled. For example, inuit (so-called 'eskimo') people have relatively thick layers of fat under the skin of their eyes, and other parts of the body, which serve as good insulation against the icy cold of Arctic regions. The black skin of African people offers a measure of protection against the fierce sun of tropical regions. If you're white and go brown in the sun, the chemical in your skin that helps you to bronze – melanin – is a legacy from your original black ancestors. Even today, about 20 per cent of white Americans have at least one relatively recent black ancestor, and about 70 per cent of black Americans have some recent white ancestry. It's also relevant to note that of the approximately 60,000 genes that humans have, only about six are responsible for differences in skin colour.

Given that a significant genetic difference between different 'racial' groups hasn't developed, 'race', from a sociological perspective, is socially constructed. It's simply the perception by some people that they're biologically different from other people. People are thereby assigned to different 'races' not on the basis of science, but because of prevailing opinions that exist in society. Such opinions are typically moulded by majority ethnic groups who have a tendency to ascribe themselves a superior 'racial status' to minority ethnic groups. Sometimes this assumed superiority is based on the discredited theory that the 'white race' are biologically more advanced than black people, Jewish people, 'gypsies', and other allegedly inferior 'bloodlines'. This, the so-called eugenics theory, has a long and sordid history, but no basis whatsoever in scientific evidence. Nazis aside, who used the theory to 'justify' their extensive acts of genocide in the 1930s and 1940s, there are modern proponents of the view that racial genetics affect educational achievement, criminal tendencies, etc.

Some pseudo 'academics', for example, suggest that black people are genetically predisposed to be less intelligent than white people. They base this erroneous assumption on the unconvincing argument that black people allegedly have lower IQs than white people. Yet, recently, a group of 50 leading professors in the fields of behavioural genetics, cognition, individual differences, and intelligence have (as reported by Drew Westen 1996) found that members of different 'racial' and ethnic groups are found at every point on the IQ distribution. While there are some differences between the mean (average) IQ scores of these groups (for example, Jews and East Asians tend to have the highest IQs), we, the writers of this book, believe such variations are better explained by sociological factors than biological ones. For example, Jewish and East Asian cultures place a very high premium on scholarship, and this has a strong self-fulfilling prophecy effect. Moreover, IQ tests are often culturally loaded in ways that favour white middle- and upper-class conceptions of intelligence.

This last point was persuasively made by the African–American psychologist, Robert L. Williams, who, at age 15, was advised to become a bricklayer after scoring 82 (very low) in an IQ test. Sensibly and courageously rejecting the advice, Williams became an academic, obtained a Ph.D., and developed the Black Intelligence Test of Cultural Homogeneity. The test incorporated vocabulary more familiar to black than to white Americans, and, not surprisingly, black people tended to obtain higher scores than white people on it. Even though Williams's test isn't offered as a serious alternative to standard IQ tests, it makes a telling point: there's no such thing as an unbiased IQ test! Nor is there an IQ gene. Indeed, given that only one quarter of 1 per cent of basic human genetic information can be attributed to 'racial' differences, it's more sensible to conclude that there's only one human race (Christopher Hitchens 1994).

Sociologists note that sometimes apparently 'racial' explanations for educational and other behavioural differences are actually linked to social factors. Many black and Bangladeshi Britons, for example, receive low pay because of racial discrimination. This means that people from these minority ethnic groups are disproportionately represented among the poorer sections of the working class. They consequently suffer the many educational disadvantages of working-class children from low income households: inadequate facilities for home study, greater risk of peer group pressure to identify with counter-school cultures, etc. Marxist sociologists, in particular, emphasise how what at root is a class-based problem often masquerades as a minority problem. Weberian sociologists accept this point, but argue that a person's ethnic status can, by itself, be very significantly implicated in diminished life chances. Thus, for example, in the USA, some black students fear being ridiculed by their pals if they do well at school because this is construed as 'acting white'. For weberian sociologists, no single aspect of stratification – class, ethnicity, etc. – is automatically more or less consequential for an individual's future prospects. Each situation has to be judged according to prevailing circumstances.

From the preceding paragraphs, we can distil three sociological theories of ethnicity:

- *the social constructionist perspective*, which says that perceptions of ethnicity are socially manufactured. In a racist sub-culture of neo-nazis, for example, the dominant socially-constructed perception of Jews is negative. In a non-racist subculture of human rights activists, the dominant perception of Jews is positive. Social constructionists rightly remind us that what is perceived and acted upon is real in its consequences. Jews are persecuted at the hands of neo-nazis, but are respected by civil rights activists
- *the marxist perspective*, which says that people from minority ethnic groups often encounter class oppression and racial discrimination. Marxists point out that certain minority ethnic groups (notably, of African–Caribbean, Bangladeshi and Pakistani origin or ancestry) are disproportionately represented among the poorest section of the working class. Although this is often linked to racism, it's in their pockets – in their *class position* – that their suffering is at its worse. Marxists also argue that the minority of black Britons who are 'middle' or upper class are to some extent shielded from racism by their high class position
- *the weberian perspective*, which says that people from minority ethnic groups suffer the consequences of a low status (one's status defines the extent or lack of prestige which one has in society) as much, if not more than, the effects of their relatively low class position. For weberians, minority ethnic status must be considered in its own right, not just in relation to class. Status and class are both important, but they don't always operate in concert.

> ***EXAM TIP***
>
> Use the term 'race' only when absolutely necessary. Generally, sociologists prefer to use the term 'ethnicity'.

Ethnicity and life chances

Black and Asian people in the UK are disadvantaged on most economic and social indicators, according to an official report published in 1996 by the Office for National Statistics. The report, *Social Focus on Ethnic Minorities*, found that while some groups – notably, Indians – do relatively well in areas like education and home ownership, minority ethnic groups generally fare much worse than white people in relation to unemployment, pay and housing, and as crime victims. The graphs on page 154 highlight these relative disadvantages.

Adding to the depressing picture of bleak life chances for minority ethnic groups in the UK, Carey Oppenheim and Lisa Harker write:

'Every indicator of poverty shows that Black people and people from other minority ethnic groups are more at risk of unemployment, low pay, poor conditions at work and diminished social security rights. Their poverty is caused by discriminatory immigration policies which have often excluded people from abroad from access to welfare; employment patterns which have marginalised Black people and other minority ethnic groups into low-paid manual work; direct and indirect discrimination in social security; and the broader experience of racism in society as a whole.'

(Oppenheim and Harker 1996: 132)

Unemployment rates for black people and other minority ethnic groups in the UK have been about double that for white people since 1984. In 1994, the male unemployment rate for black and other minority ethnic groups was 25 per cent, more than double that for white men, which was then 11 per cent. Differences in unemployment rates for women were also marked: 16 per cent compared to 7 per cent. Even well-qualified black people and members of other minority ethnic groups encounter greater risks of unemployment, due to discrimination. As for those people from these groups who have a job, they're more likely than white Britons to receive low wages, and to experience poor working conditions (for example, more shift work).

As the marxist sociologists, Stephen Castles and Godula Kosack, write:

'In objective terms, immigrant workers belong to the working class. But within this class they form a bottom stratum, due to the subordinate status of their occupations.'

(Castles and Kosack 1973: 67)

Ethnic Britain

Crime

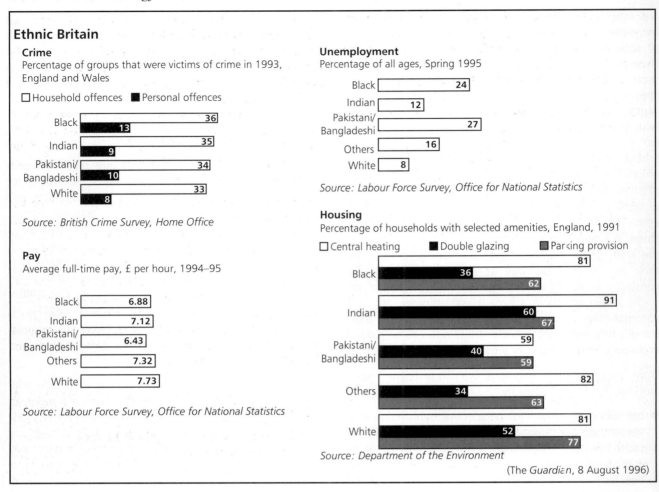

Percentage of groups that were victims of crime in 1993, England and Wales

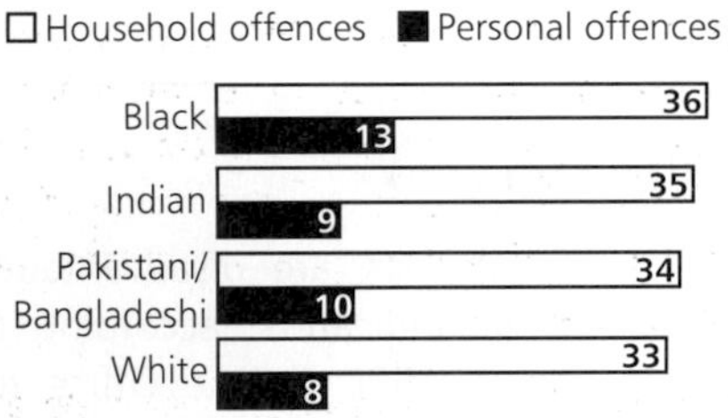

Source: British Crime Survey, Home Office

Pay

Average full-time pay, £ per hour, 1994–95

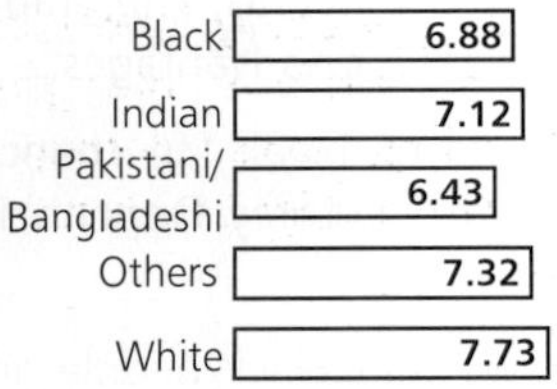

Source: Labour Force Survey, Office for National Statistics

Unemployment

Percentage of all ages, Spring 1995

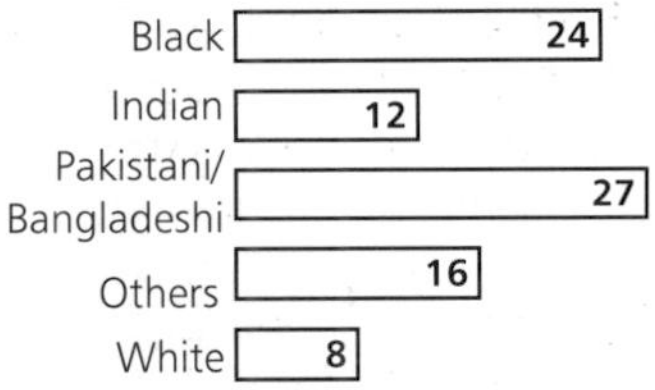

Source: Labour Force Survey, Office for National Statistics

Housing

Percentage of households with selected amenities, England, 1991

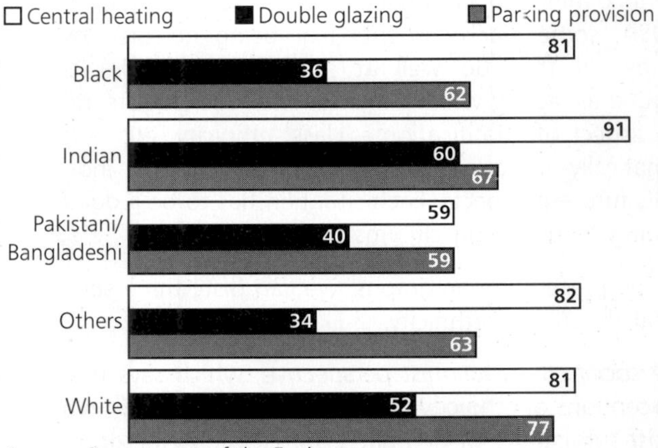

Source: Department of the Environment

(The *Guardian*, 8 August 1996)

It's in these circumstances, contend Castles and Kosack, that some minority ethnic groups in Europe suffer the double blows of class oppression and racial discrimination. Echoing this point, C. Blackburn remarks, 'Black people share the disadvantages of white working-class people and more' (Blackburn 1991, cited by Culley and Dyson 1993: 27). While being black, Bangladeshi, Pakistani, or Irish and working class deals a doubly bad hand, middle-class members of minority ethnic groups commonly encounter discrimination too.

Nevertheless, it's important not to put all minority ethnic groups in the same general category. In that context, it's relevant to note that Indian households are less likely than white households to be on gross incomes of less than £200 per week. It's also important to recognise that middle-class people from Indian and other minority ethnic households enjoy better life chances than their ethnic peers who are on low incomes. This point is noted by marxist sociologists who argue that, despite the damaging effects of racism, class is the bedrock predictor of overall life chances. Weberian sociologists, however, argue that in some cases (notably, heightened risk of unemployment), inequality of opportunity experienced by minority ethnic groups is better explained by racism than by class position.

It has been shown by numerous studies (noted, for example, by Steven Hunt 1995) that Caribbean and Asian groups are more likely than white Britons to experience poor housing and associated detrimental conditions. This has dire consequences for the health of people from minority ethnic groups. Damp, cold, overcrowded living conditions adversely affect physical and psychological health. However, while the low paid in society – among whom members of minority ethnic groups are disproportionately represented – suffer poverty-linked ill-health, it would be overly simplistic to suggest that all medical conditions are caused by low pay. Take, for example, diseases of genetic origin that are related to particular racial groups. Sickle-cell disease is a group of genetically linked disorders of the haemoglobin in the red blood cells. The disease mainly affects black people. Even so, genetic factors have a limited influence on overall health patterns, racism and low class position being generally more important.

Yet despite these obstacles, it would be a mistake to imagine that progress isn't being made. According to the 1991 Census, more than a quarter of the UK's African–Caribbean population were in managerial, professional or technical jobs. That's a slightly lower proportion than other ethnic groups, but it makes for a very visible inroad into the middle class. There's also an increasing black presence in parliament, local government, trade unions, the Church, senior media posts, arts and sport. 'Little wonder', noted Gary Younge in the *Guardian* on 20 March 1995, 'most black people believe that, on balance, things have improved in the past 10 years.' In the same article, Younge also captures the diversity that exists within the black community:

'Stand long enough on Brixton High Road, the main street in the capital of black Britain, and the entire cross-section of the country's Afro-Caribbean community will pass before your eyes. Alongside nurses, sales reps, barristers and students are the retired, the unemployed and the never-employed. You will see rastas, rappers, ravers and raggas; dreadlocks, flattops, beaded braids and curly perms; middle-aged women with bibles, young women with babies, young men with mobile phones and school-children with attitude. All in a spectrum of skin tones from darkest black to lightest beige.'

(Younge 1995)

Younge's observations caution us not to regard black people as belonging *en bloc* to an 'underclass'. While in both British and American society, we're still some way from Martin Luther King's dream that his 'four little children will one day live in a nation where they will not be judged by the colour of their skin but by the content of their character' (1963, in King 1985: 95), we're getting there. As a species there's no objectively grounded problem of 'race'. What we still have is racism and racists, and those are the fundamental problems we need to tackle in order to make Dr King's inspired dream a reality.

QUESTIONS

1 What's the difference between ethnicity and 'race'?
2 How does social constructionist theory help sociologists to understand the concepts of ethnicity and 'race'?
3 Briefly outline the ways in which belonging to a minority ethnic group affects an individual's life chances.

Gender

Females account for half of the inhabitants on the planet. Yet, compared to males, who make up the other half, they generally have less power, less prestige and fewer material possessions.

The paid labour market, for example, is and has long been differentiated along unequal gender lines. Today, unskilled sales and service sector employment is largely female-segregated, just as domestic service was for previous generations of women. Moreover, the many women who work in this rapidly expanding sector are badly paid. Nor do many of them have good opportunities of moving forward in career terms, typically because of 'domestic' responsibilities. The relative disadvantages of girls and women, compared to boys and men, are sometimes attributed to differing biologies and psychologies. But sociologists argue that the roles which females and males have in society are not biologically or psychologically inevitable. There are, of course, some anatomical and, perhaps, some psychological differences between the sexes. However, what's important is the way in which those differences are perceived and acted upon in society. For what girls and boys become in relation to gendered roles is largely the result of sociological processes; and here, nothing is inevitable!

Sex refers to the biological differences between male and female humans, while *gender* describes how those biological differences are responded to on a social and psychological level. If, for example, a father believes his young son is biologically destined to be a tough guy (which he isn't), he might actively socialise the boy into patterns of behaviour that are exaggeratedly 'masculine': encouraging him not to cry if he falls over, giving him toy guns, etc. Believing that biology is also destiny for his young daughter, the same father might seek to turn her into a very 'feminine' girl.

OVER TO YOU

How might a girl be socialised into becoming 'feminine'?

Gender refers to the social construction of behaviour deemed appropriate for males (masculine behaviour) and for females (feminine behaviour). And who decides the 'deeming appropriate'? you might reasonably ask. The expected behaviour of boys and girls is typically defined, encouraged and reinforced by adults with whom they come into contact, and other agents of socialisation: their age group peers, brothers, sisters, mass media, etc. Moreover, in most societies such expectations are largely based on male ideology (namely, ideas that support male supremacy). In that context, to quote the feminist sociologists, Pamela Abbott and Claire Wallace:

'The exclusion of women from positions of power and from the production of knowledge has . . . meant that male ideology has been able to present itself as universal knowledge.'

(Abbott and Wallace 1997: 9)

Increasingly, these ideologies have been and are being contested by some women, some men, and by some social scientists. The challenge contains both moral purpose and scientific rationality. Why should girls and women be socialised into a world in which they are forced to endure sexist prejudice and discrimination from men (and sometimes from other women)? Moreover, why should people believe that 'boys will be boys' and 'girls will be girls' when social scientific research shows that 'masculinities' and 'femininities' are learnt rather than biologically programmed?

Theories of gender

Most sociologists adopt the feminist view that the subordination of girls and women must be intellectually questioned and morally challenged. In that sense, it's true to say that sociological theories about gender are, these days, largely informed by feminist insights. Occasionally one comes across a 'last vestiges of ultra-conservative functionalism' suggestion that a woman's place is in the home and a man's in the workplace. But real events and new ways of thinking have all but overtaken this view. Moreover, it's important to recognise that not all functionalists accept that the subjugation of women by men is natural, inevitable, and functionally desirable. Describing and analysing a set of gendered roles that generally make life much easier for men than for women doesn't mean that one likes what one sees. Moreover, the functionalist sociologist, Emile Durkheim, wrote of societies where:

'female functions are not very clearly distinguished from male . . . where the woman mingles in political life. That has been observed especially in the Indian tribes of America . . . we very often observe women accompanying men to war . . . and even taking a very active part. In Cuba, in Dahomey, they are as war-like as the men and battle at their side.'

(Durkheim 1964: 58, first published 1893)

Even so, functionalism, as a theory of gender, doesn't enjoy a favourable reputation in sociological theory today, because it's assumed – often wrongly – that functionalists are misogynists. The simple truth is that some are, some aren't – and that holds true for marxists, interactionists, and even for some who declare themselves feminists.

Nevertheless, feminism holds sway in gender theory. It accurately describes real differences in the life chances of females and males, where, in most (but not all) circumstances, males get an 'unfair' headstart. This is a premise generally shared by all who describe themselves as feminists. However, even though feminist theory is united in its identification of and opposition to the oppression of girls and women, there are different 'feminisms' within the theory. Abbott and Wallace (1997) identify a series of feminist perspectives, four of which we consider below (we've added our own interpretations and examples, as appropriate):

- *Liberal/reformist feminism* Proponents of this perspective argue that women and men are innately equal, but socialisation mitigates against this by discouraging women from regarding themselves as equal to men, and by making men either happy with or complacent about this. Liberal/reformist feminists advocate the passing of anti-sexist legislation to protect women's inherent rights to be treated as equal. Liberal/feminists tend to adopt a positivistic position towards research, arguing for impartial, unbiased methods, and evidence-based assertions. Unlike radical feminists, they're probably more sympathetic to the view that some boys and men are also victims of gender inequality, though less so because of girls and women and more so because of dominant males. Consider, for example, the harmful impact upon boys who are encouraged by adult males not to cry when they really need to do so, as well as the common 'masculine' expectation that 'real' men should be prepared to fight physically for what they want. Their readiness to let the evidence tell its tale makes liberal/reformist feminists good social scientists. But do they have that fire in the belly which unites a concern for empirical scholarship with a commitment for practical social justice?
- *Marxist feminism* Proponents of this perspective contend that capitalism oppresses women and men, but women fare worse. They're expected both to reproduce biologically the future labour force, and to 'reproduce socially', in their role as child-raisers, willing and submissive generations of future workers. Moreover, their 'domestic' role is, by and large, a form of unpaid labour, the main beneficiary being the capitalistic system which gets new and disciplined workers without incurring any costs to itself. Those women who do enter paid work (more and more these days) also do capitalism an unwitting favour because they generally receive lower pay than men. Marxist feminists adopt, of course, a marxist approach to research. In that context, two priorities stand out: exposing social injustice through empirical research, and getting rid of the injustice through political struggle. Is marxist feminism then a form of reliable and morally committed social science, or is it an approach that only looks at one side of the picture and says too much about what ought to be than what actually is?
- *Radical feminism* While there's quite a lot of variation within this perspective, radical feminists assert that gender inequalities are largely the result of *patriarchy*, namely, male domination which oppresses women. These feminists advocate a revolutionary movement for the emancipation of women. Women are encouraged to celebrate their femaleness and to unite as sisters. Citing the same logic that made black slaves keep white masters out of their liberation movements, some radical feminists advocate keeping men outside of women's affairs. Radical feminists are suspicious of so-called science, which they regard as male-defined and male-benefiting knowledge. Consider, for example, 'biological' arguments which controversially suggest that male brains are 'superior' to female ones. These feminists encourage women to adopt reflective,

social constructionist approaches to the study of gender, thereby enabling them to understand intuitively their own womanhood and to re-construct their lives in affirming ways. Have radical feminists uncovered the root cause of the oppression of half of the inhabitants of this planet: the subjugation of females by males? Or have they underplayed the extent to which other forms of stratification affect life chances, and overplayed the extent to which all men are oppressors? And what about the injustices suffered by low-paid male workers who are employed by female employers?

- *Socialist feminism* Proponents of this perspective claim that age, class, ethnicity and gender all play a role in shaping the oppression of women, but the degree to which each of these components comes into play varies. In that sense, socialist feminists aren't exclusively concerned with the damaging effects of patriarchy. They also take account of the divisive impact of capitalism, especially the low pay of female employees relative to male employees. Socialist feminists are often described as dualist theorists: they recognise that both patriarchy and capitalism create injustices for women. They often adopt the same research methods and a similar commitment (though perhaps quite not so fervent) as marxists to using the insights of social scientific research in order to build a more just society. While their adherence to a political agenda might lead to bias in selecting which issues are deserving of research, as well as to an ideologically rather than a scientifically based view of the uses of social science, unlike their marxist cousins, socialist feminists take much more account of patriarchy. Have they struck the right balance between radical/revolutionary feminism on the one hand and marxist feminism on the other, or are they fence-sitting?

OVER TO YOU

Answer the questions raised in the preceding sections on different kinds of feminist theory. Are your replies based on hard evidence, personal conviction, or both?

Gender and life chances

Economic security is arguably the most important predictor of good life chances. In the UK today, women are more likely than men to be poor, and they generally earn less than men in paid employment. In 1990, women's hourly earnings in the UK were 76.6 per cent of men's, much as it had been during the previous decade. Furthermore, because women work a shorter paid week, their gross weekly earnings are a lower proportion: 68 per cent. A major reason for this shorter week is that as much again, if not more or most, of women's work takes place in the home. Such 'domestic' work is, of course, rarely paid. It's therefore not surprising to find that women's access to an independent income from the labour market is significantly associated with not having dependent children. While men work at home too, proportionately more of their work is of the 'paid employment elsewhere' type.

Women are, however, making some headway on the occupational front, compared to their mothers and grandmothers. These days, women comprise around one in three of administrators and managers, and about four in ten of professionals. But they have to work much harder at securing promotion than men, often hitting what's termed the 'glass ceiling' when they seek to get to the top of the career ladder. Job discrimination against women commonly occurs in three ways:

- When they're hired, they're often given jobs that are less prestigious than male recruits who have the same qualifications.
- They generally find it harder than men, as indicated above, to secure promotion.
- If they eventually obtain the same job descriptions as male employees, they frequently receive less pay than the men for equivalent work.

Discrimination against women in very prestigious occupations can be very subtle. Thus, while a top consultant heart surgeon who is a woman is unlikely to be paid less than her male equivalent, the simple fact is that there are very few female consultant heart surgeons. The Hansard Society report, *Women at the Top*, disclosed that 'in any given occupation, and in any given public office, the higher the rank, prestige or influence, the smaller the proportion of women' (cited by Gillian Pascall 1995: 3). Women are especially under-represented in the criminal justice system. In 1993, for example, out of 91 High Court judges, only five were women, and out of 496 circuit judges, just 28 were female.

Having already noted that there is some improvement in women's employment prospects, it needs to be added that girls have now caught up and overtaken boys in relation to school achievement. Males still have a bit of an edge though in higher education. These and other related point are made more fully in Chapter 9, pages 215–17, so feel free to fast-forward if you want to look at the specific details. The changing fortunes of girls at school bode well for the career prospects of the next adult generation. Indeed, a common concern these days is with the under-achievement of boys relative to their female age peers in public exams. Some commentators might say that the boot is now on the other foot, but most sociologists and most teachers would support policies that are designed to ensure that all young people

– girls and boys – reach their maximum potential in academic terms.

Writing about the changing fortunes of women, John Williams (1996) cautions against over-optimism, reminding us that 'this change is coming very slowly.' Noting that in 1975, when the Sex Discrimination Act was introduced in the UK, women earned, on average, 71 per cent of the average male earnings, Williams, reports that by 1993 women earned 79 per cent of male pay: not much to shout about, is it? Women still don't get an even break with men, and, as Williams further adds, 'In the UK, the search for the "new man" at home continues to look a little forlorn'.

QUESTIONS

1 What's the difference between gender and sex?
2 How does social constructionist theory help sociologists to understand the concept of gender?
3 Briefly outline the ways in which being female and male affect life chances.

Age

All sociologists recognise that ageing involves important biological processes. As we get older, we gradually find it more difficult to fight off disease. Yet while ageing has deteriorating effects, few older people become physically disabled. This doesn't, however, stop the social construction of negative stereotypes about old people. For some old people, this ageist labelling creates far more hurt than the physical effects of ageing. And it's here that sociology rightly points out that the social effects of ageing are society's doing, not biology's. Sociologists have also demonstrated that the way the old and other age groups are treated varies from society to society. In that sense, it's probably true to say that the dominant sociological perspective or 'theory' of age is social constructionism.

Sociological theorising about age

Making a very important sociological point, Jane Pilcher writes:

'societies tend to group persons together on the basis of their similar age, and by the typical behaviour patterns and social roles culturally expected to be associated with that age . . . Age may, therefore, be used as an index to locate an individual's likely position in the "life course", in a socially-defined "timetable" of behaviours deemed as appropriate for particular stages within any one society.'

(Pilcher 1995: 12)

Her astute points combine both a functionalist standpoint – roles are assigned to similar age groups – and a social constructionist one – the roles are socially defined. For example, in the UK, reaching the chronological age of 18 ushers in the adult role of being a voting citizen. But this role expectation exists on the sufferance of society and the socially manufactured nature of 'adult responsibilities'. It's a role expectation that has consequences for as long as society allows it to. So, if at some stage in the future, the government decides that adulthood and adult roles begin at age 16, this would become the new socially constructed reality.

Even childhood, argues the social constructionist historian, Philippe Aries (1973), only exists if society says so. Medieval society didn't say so, claims Aries (a view contested, incidentally, by some commentators) because the concept of 'childhood' didn't exist during the Middle Ages. For example, children's dolls in that period typically

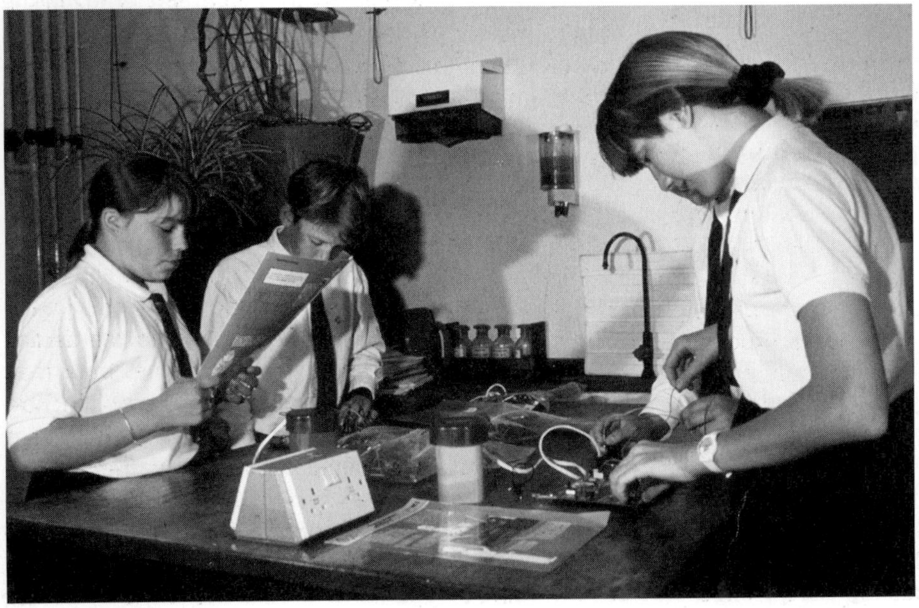

Things are changing for girls, not least because they're beginning to outperform boys at school. This might enhance the career opportunities of women in the near future, but what about the boys? Some people might say they're getting a taste of their own medicine. Most sociologists, however, would say that all children, irrespective of sex, should have the same educational opportunities.

depicted miniature adults. According to Aries, children were assumed into the adult world shortly after infancy, being thenceforth regarded as 'little grown-ups'. While Aries's argument is probably over-generalised, he did make a significant contribution to the social constructionist view of age – that it is as much, if not more, about how people define chronological age than mere biology. Past societies also held different conceptions of old age. In pre-industrial societies, old people were often highly esteemed, and their experience greatly valued. Even in this century, notes Alex Thio (1989), the old of the African peoples of the Igbo and the Bantu are regarded as deserving of respect, as are older people in Thailand and rural Mexico. Indeed, on the Pacific island of Samoa, old age is considered the best time of life. This respect is based on an emphatic regard for old age, and on a very positive social construction of the later years of life.

Yet the same chronological old age is often perceived in very negative terms in 'western' societies, and also in other societies whose cultures are succumbing to the 'western' way of life. Says Alex Thio of the most 'western' of 'western' (no pun intended!) countries, the USA:

> 'Today it sometimes seems as if we expect the elderly to do nothing but wait to die. There is no prestige attached to being old; it is generally seen as a handicap. This is why older people tend to lie about their age.'
>
> (Thio 1989: 295)

Father and son: but will 'junior's' adulthood be socially constructed and experienced by him in the same way as his dad's? Conceptions of age vary across societies and across time.

OVER TO YOU

When does 'old age' begin in the UK? Explain your answer, using sociological language. What kinds of perception do people of your age have of old people? In both cases, consider how class, ethnicity, and gender interact with 'old age'.

Although sociological theorising of age is, today, largely based on social constructionism, the documentation of the relationship between age and life chances is typically couched in positivistic terms – in hard statistics. There needn't, of course, be any tension between social constructionism and positivism because how the age status of people is perceived and constructed has real statistical consequences for them. The fact, for example, that in Washington DC, some police officers are very suspicious of young, black males who drive expensive cars, undoubtedly leads to them being stopped more often by traffic cops. Here, the social construction has statistical outcomes. More about that in Chapter 16.

Age and life chances

While, like other aspects of stratification, the life chances of different age groups are affected by class, ethnicity and gender, a person's age in itself does affect her or his opportunities. Take, for example, young people in the UK. The dramatic changes in employment and unemployment over the past 20 years have hit them hard. At the time when the school-leaving age was last raised (from 15 to 16 in 1972), almost two-thirds of all young people left school as soon as they could, and the great majority obtained employment more or less immediately. Yet, by the early 1990s, less than one in ten 16-year-olds were leaving school and starting work. As Kenneth Roberts (1996) pointedly puts it, 'Britain's young workers of the 1970s have been replaced by the young unemployed, students and youth trainees'.

Although many more young people are staying on at school or going to college than in the past (about two thirds are in full-time education these days), young people have been victims of high unemployment. School leavers today are much less likely, owing to the decline of heavy industry, to enter unskilled manual work than their predecessors some 25 years ago. For those that stay on at school because work isn't available, one might argue that this is a good thing. Yet much depends on what kind of post-16 education the 'stay-ons' receive. Those who end up on vocational courses and vocational training aren't faring too well, because employers still tend to favour applicants who have done academic courses: A-levels rather than GNVQs. To be sure, GNVQs have been 'talked up' by politicians a lot lately, and have even been called 'vocational A-levels'. Yet, as Paul Stephens notes:

'Vocational education is still regarded by some teachers as suitable for students who have "failed" academically. The culture that underpins this assumption must be successfully challenged if GNVQs (at all levels) are not to be regarded as "second best".'

(Stephens 1993: 11)

Stephens' assertion is supported by evidence provided by social scientists from the National Foundation of Educational Research (NFER). In their study, *Sixth Form Options* (cited in the *Times Educational Supplement*, 7 June 1996), Sandie Schagen, Fiona Johnson and Claire Simkin of the NFER, reported that parity of esteem between academic and vocational courses was a long way off. Many teachers gave a clear message to their students that GNVQs were 'second best'. Vocational students at many of the 22 schools visited by the NFER team complained that they were sidelined, with A-level students being the centre of attraction.

Nor have 'non-academic' young people who have entered the Youth Training Scheme (YTS) lived up to the politicians' high expectations. It seems that some employers have viewed YTS recruits as 'failed young people' who were unable to get 'proper' jobs, and have treated them accordingly – retaining the best and discarding the rest after 'try out' periods. To quote Kenneth Roberts, 'Youth Training [has] become another expensive failure' (Roberts 1996: 28). Academic education still accounts for the majority of post-16 enrolment in full-time education, and still the best passport for future career success: for girls, boys, working-, middle- and upper-class students, for black and for white students. Unless society as a whole begins to regard vocational courses and vocational training as equal but different to the academic pathway, the employment and career prospects of young people who tread a vocational path seem bleaker than their academic age group peers.

Moving to the other end of the age range, how do older people fare in society today? While later life is often portrayed as a time of poverty, poor health and dependency, Jay Ginn and Sara Arber write that:

'there are wide differences among elderly people in their access to the key resources which promote independence and enable full participation in desired activities.'

(Ginn and Arber 1992: 6)

In particular, they note, older women fare less well than older men, for 'ageing is a gendered process' (1992: 6).

The proportion of the population in the UK aged over 65 is now around one in five, compared with about one in 20 in 1900. This demographic revolution is mainly a consequence of lower birth rates, and, to some extent, increased life expectancy. Women account for two-thirds of people aged over 65. Moreover, the financial disadvantages they incur, relative to men, in their 'working lives', continue into later years through their lower income from occupational and private pensions. This state of affairs, as Ginn and Arber maintain, is a result of sex segregation in the labour market, and the impact of women's 'domestic' role on their employment histories (having part-time jobs in order to be a mother, means lower occupational pensions). Even though Ginn and Arber found that 'higher class' women had better pension provision than 'lower class' women, within each class men did better than women.

Ginn and Arber conclude that the position of older women in the UK today has not been helped by the right-wing political climate of the 1980s and 1990s. The attendant emphasis on personal responsibility and individualistic self-interest has allowed, they write:

'the constraints of poverty, ill-health and dependency to bear hardest on those who already lack resources because of their previous labour market position, that is, on elderly women and working-class elderly women. The current attack on the welfare state is likely to exacerbate elderly women's disadvantage in maintaining their independence.'

(Ginn and Arber 1992: 10)

OVER TO YOU

How might social scientific research help government ministers to enhance the life chances of older women?

In between the young (here, taken to mean youths) and the old lie 'young adults' and 'middle-aged adults'. The documentation of their life chances has received little explicit attention from sociologists – perhaps because their lives have been described more in relation to their class position, their ethnicity, and their gender rather than their age. Given that they're much more likely than the young and the old to be in paid employment, it's arguable that these other aspects of stratification are much more in the frame than their age, insofar as economic opportunities are concerned. On a general level, we can expect and we find that 'young adults' and 'middle-aged adults' are financially better-off than the old and the young who aren't yet adults. Male incomes usually rise as they get older, with peak earnings commonly obtained in the forties and fifties. For single women, this is probably also the case. However, the employment histories of most 'working women' are typically punctuated by their 'domestic' roles. Some of them probably earn more (taking account of changes in the cost of living) in their early twenties as full-time employees than in their thirties as full-time mothers and part-time employees. Moreover, as children grow up, it's much harder for women than for men to climb the career ladder.

Even though the adult, pre-pension age group generally has a relatively enhanced material lifestyle, age discrimination in some employment fields is a common problem for people in their forties (in some cases, even earlier). Research into age discrimination among UK employers has been highlighted by the Institute of Employment Consultants. In a study which it carried out in 1995, this body found that a majority of employers still stipulate age limits when seeking to recruit new staff. The most common reason given for doing this was the aim of maintaining age consistency across the workforce. Age discrimination in a society where the workforce is ageing, unless perhaps curbed by anti-ageist legislation (already in place in Australia, New Zealand, Canada, and the US), will increasingly blight the employment prospects of more and more people.

OVER TO YOU

What do you think? Should the UK introduce laws to prevent discrimination by employers on the grounds of age? Such legislation already exists to protect the rights of women and minority ethnic groups.

Is it also appropriate and right to protest the rights of children more robustly in law? Patrick McNeill seems to address, perhaps controversially, this and other important issues in the hard-hitting opening paragraph of his 1989 article, 'Growing up: Children's rights' (reproduced in his book, *Society Today*):

'Which group of people in our society is not allowed to choose where to live, to dispose of its own property, to consume alcohol or to smoke, to take a full-time job, to drive, or to engage in sexual activity? Which group can be physically assaulted, even in public, without the law necessarily being involved, and can legally be confined to a building for seven hours a day?' [His answer is unequivocal:] 'children.'

(McNeill 1991: 153)

While most of these prohibitions are ostensibly implemented to protect children from their own inexperience, McNeill claims that 'some aspects of some children's experience suggest that what they need protection from is adults' (1991: 153). He argues that where there's a gulf of power such as exists between children and adults, there's also the risk of the abuse of power, in short, the risk of child abuse by adults. At its worse, this abuse is manifested by the fact that the age group most at risk of homicide are babies. On a less serious, but still important, level, children are often routinely treated with adult authoritarianism verging on rudeness during those seven hours a day when they 'can legally be confined to a building', as McNeill puts it. That building is, of course, school. Contemplating the ways in which some teachers frighten children into submissiveness in schools where punitive back-up is readily available, one of the writers of this book urges intending teachers to:

'Show the same kind of courtesy to young people as to adults. Otherwise, it's easy to fall into the bad habit of using a "sliding scale" model of dealing with people, whereby increasing age somehow merits more courtesy. Reflecting on this matter . . . I recently stopped doing something that I now consider inexcusable: jumping the canteen dinner queue. When I started queuing up behind children, a 12-year-old boy said "Thank you".'

(Stephens 1996: 74)

The life chances of the 'very young' (babies, children and infants) are generally linked to the class position of their parents than most other factors. The argument that lone parenthood is associated with lack of educational achievement and emotional problems in children is rebutted by Anna Coote, Harriet Harman and Patricia Hewitt (1990, cited on the back cover page of *Sociology Review*, September 1991, Vol. 1, No. 1). They claim that poverty and the *quality* of relationships between children and divorced or separated couples are the important issues here. Given though that lone parenthood is a powerful predictor of low income, children who are raised in lone-parent households are more at risk than children who are brought up by two parents to suffer the many disadvantages associated with poverty.

QUESTIONS

1 What's the difference between biological age and socially constructed age? Illustrate your answer with concrete examples.
2 Compare and contrast the life chances of different age groups in British society.
3 How do gender and old age interact, and with what effects?

EXAM TIP

While not having revised a topic thoroughly isn't an excuse for bad work, it's probably fair to inform the examiner, if context permits, that age is a relatively neglected research area in the sociology of stratification.

Concluding remarks

Human society is very unequal. Some individuals have much better life chances than others, based on their position within the social 'pecking order' sociologists call social stratification. But is inequality between different age groups, classes, ethnic groups, women and men inevitable, and is it desirable? Some mid-century functionalists (notably, Kingsley Davis and Wilbert Moore 1945) have suggested that inequality is necessary and beneficial because society must select different people to fill different roles, and must then reward the occupants of the most important positions. But who decides what jobs are more important than others? asked Melvin Tumin, in his rebuttal of the Davis–Moore critique. Who is to say that a firefighter does a less worthwhile job than a lawyer, who is far better paid?

Yet the functionalist argument, in its Davis–Moore variant, does seem to strike a chord with some people. We live in a society where individuals are expected to be motivated by material rewards, and, if everyone got equal pay, the most talented people wouldn't have the incentive to get to the top. For people who have right-wing values, this is a plausible moral argument. Even functionalist sociologists who hold left-wing opinions might concede that Davis and Moore describe real, if unpalatable, circumstances. All functionalists, moreover, recognise that some things in society can be *dysfunctional* (i.e. impede rather than promote 'desirable' outcomes). Thus, for example, a dysfunctional consequence of social inequality is that people who are less well off are more likely to become ill. Aside from the distress this causes individuals and families, the fact that sick people have time off work doesn't serve a useful function.

Marxists, in particular, rebut the argument that some people need to be higher up the social ladder than others if society is to function properly. Not only is this dysfunctional because greed is less reliable than moral purpose – would you trust a doctor who provided shoddy treatment to poor patients and excellent care for rich patients? – it's also unfair and unjust. Weberian sociologists, though sometimes less inclined than marxist sociologists to mix social science with morals and politics, recognise and document inequality without applauding it. They place more emphasis than marxists on the various ways in which stratification is manifested, arguing that statuses like age, ethnicity and gender have potentially equally strong impacts on people's lives, as does their position within the class structure.

Whereas functionalists, marxists and weberians focus on the structural aspects of stratification (i.e. the relatively permanent features of inequality), social constructionists highlight the ways in which social groups in society are perceived to be at different levels on the social ladder. Their insights offer pessimistic and optimistic alternatives. For example, women are perceived to be less reliable than males by some sexist employers, who consequently discriminate against them, but feminists have helped to restore women's right to protest for right. Similarly, black people are regarded as 'sub-humans' by racist white supremacists who therefore persecute them, but scientists have demonstrated that all humans have a common gene pool, thereby persuading reasonable people to celebrate their common humanity. In these examples, one discerns the inter-meshing of socially constructed stereotypes and consequent discriminating behaviours on the one hand, and of contending interpretations and their resultant 'fighting back' actions on the other.

> ***OVER TO YOU***
>
> ***This is a tough one, but how do you think the last sentence shows how social constructionist and structural theories in sociology can work together rather than against each other?***

Feminists also make important contributions to stratification theory and research. They argue that patriarchy enhances the life chances of boys and men, and diminishes the life chances of girls and women. They summon impressive empirical evidence to back up these claims. Feminists describe and analyse gendered inequalities, and make it quite clear that they don't like what they see. In that sense, like conventional marxist sociologists, they're open to the charge of placing value-judgements before social scientific detachment. But also like conventional marxists, they reply to that charge by arguing that being objective in one's research doesn't require one to be indifferent about what one does with one's findings.

One final thought. Sometimes one hears people saying that equality, even if desirable, is unattainable. Our reply to that is that it's better to get closer to an ideal than to remain a long way from it. Take the position of women, for example. The inequalities they suffer in the UK are worse than those encountered by women in certain other countries – in Norway, for example. Ask a British women if she'd prefer more equality to less equality, and we think you'll find she'll say, 'Yes'.

Glossary of key terms

Age group A group of people whose age lies within a similar chronological range, and whose age status is socially constructed. The term thereby contains both biological and sociological connotations

Ethnic group A status group of people who share a common cultural identity typically based on a collective sense of 'racial' and/or 'country of origin' roots

Femininity Socially defined and prescribed characteristics and behaviours that are deemed appropriate to females

Feminist theories of gender While there are a number of variants here, feminist theories of gender stress the socially constructed nature of gender roles, emphasising how male-dominated societies socialise males into dominant roles and females into subordinate roles. Feminists don't like what they find, and seek to 'de-construct' and 're-construct' gender roles in ways that promote equality and justice between and for females and males

Functionalist theory of social class While not spelling out how many classes there are in society, this theory argues that the higher the class one belongs to, the more important the function one performs. Engineers, for example, would belong to a higher class than street sweepers because – allegedly – engineers perform more important tasks than street sweepers. Most functionalists, these days, would accept that 'considered more important' is a better description than 'are more important' of the work roles deemed to be in the higher range

Gender group A status group of people who share the pyschological and social characteristics that are socially defined as appropriate for females (femininity) and males (masculinity)

Inter-generational social mobility Movement of individuals up or down the social stratification ladder between generations (for example, the son of a middle-class mother becomes upper class during his lifetime)

Intra-generational social mobility Movement of individuals up or down the social stratification ladder within one generation (for example, a job-hopping individual moves in and out of different classes during a lifetime)

Marxist theory of ethnicity While conceding that members of minority ethnic groups are often persecuted by members of majority ethnic groups, marxist theory emphasises the primacy of class in the social stratification system. Marxists do, however, acknowledge that black people, for example, often encounter the double blows of class oppression (by being over-represented in the poorer sections of the working class) and 'racial' discrimination

Marxist theory of social class A two-class model comprising the ruling class of big property-owning employers and the working class of wage-earning employees. Marxists accept that there's a manual/non-manual divide within the working class, but are reluctant to describe this as a working/middle-class divide. The main fault-line between different classes lies, according to marxists, between an exploitative employer class and an exploited employee class. 'Middle-class' people are essentially the non-manual branch of the working class

Masculinity Socially defined and prescribed characteristics and behaviours that are deemed appropriate to males

Meritocracy A system of social stratification where the most meritorious obtain the higher positions in the hierarchy and the least meritorious the lower positions

Minority ethnic group An ethnic group who constitute a minority in a given society and who typically suffer discrimination at the hands of some members of the majority ethnic group (for example, African–Caribbeans who are attacked by white racists)

Objective classification of class A group of people who share common characteristics, as defined in advance by social scientists (for example, individuals who work in non-manual occupations that require degree-level education and training are middle class)

Patriarchy A system of social stratification based on male domination of females

Racial group A group of people who share minor but sometimes quite 'visible' biological characteristics that are most commonly based on skin colour

Racism The activation of prejudice leading to discrimination, based on the negative perception of 'racial' characteristics

Sex group A group of people who share either the biological characteristics of being female or of being male

Social class A group of people who typically share similar economic life chances and similar lifestyles

Social constructionist theory of age An explanation of age based on the belief that different societies interpret and construct age according to prevailing beliefs and values. For example, 'old age' generally has a low status in the UK but often a high status in rural Mexico, even though older people in these societies are in the same chronological age range

Social constructionist theory of ethnicity The notion that ethnicities are defined by society in relation to how ethnic groups are 'supposed to behave'. Skin colour, although of little overall biological significance, is usually important in social perceptions of 'anticipated' behaviours

Social constructionist theory of gender The notion that gender roles (femininities and masculinities) are defined by society in relation to how females and males are 'supposed to behave'. There are therefore no inherent, universal gender roles because different societies socially construct lots of role variants. Most individuals learn to behave in socially defined and prescribed 'feminine' or 'masculine' ways through socialisation

Social mobility Movement of individuals up or down the social stratification ladder, typically from one class to another. Thus a working-class woman who becomes middle class is *upwardly socially mobile*, whereas a middle-class man who becomes working class is *downwardly socially mobile*

Social status The amount of esteem an individual or a group has in society. Age groups, ethnic groups, and gender groups are commonly referred to as status groups

Social stratification The arrangement of people into different and unequal groups

Subjective classification of class An individual's self-defined class position (for example, I feel I'm upper class)

Weberian theory of ethnicity This theory treats ethnicity as a social status whose impact on people's lives is potentially as important as any other aspect of social stratification

Weberian theory of social class A three-class model comprising the ruling class of big property owners, the middle class of non-manual employees, and the working class of manual employees. Weberian sociologists generally steer clear of terms like 'exploitative' and 'exploited' in their descriptions of classes, preferring to document rather than to judge

References

Abbott, Pamela and Wallace, Claire (1997) *An Introduction to Sociology: Feminist Perspectives*, Second Edition. London: Routledge

Aries, Philippe (1973) *Centuries of Childhood*. Harmondsworth: Penguin

Beresford, Philip and Boyd, Stephen (1996) The eighth annual Sunday Times survey of Britain's rich, published with the *Sunday Times*, 14 April 1996

Coser, Lewis A. and Rosenberg, Bernard (eds) (1969) *Sociological Theory: A Book of Readings*, Third Edition. London: Collier-Macmillan Ltd

Culley, Lorraine and Dyson, Simon (1993) 'Race', inequality and health, pp 24–7, *Sociology Review*, Vol. 3, No. 1, September

Davis, Kingsley and Moore, Wilbert (1945) Some principles of stratification, pp 242–9, *American Sociological Review*, Vol. X, No. 2, April

Devine, Fiona (1994) 'Affluent workers' revisited, pp 6–9, *Sociology Review*, Vol. 3, No. 3, February

Durkheim, Emile (1964) *The Division of Labor in Society*. New York: The Free Press

Esping-Andersen, Gosta (1993) Mobility regimes and class formation, pp 225–41, in Esping-Andersen, Gosta (ed.) (1993) *Changing Classes*. London: Sage Publications Ltd

Goldthorpe, John H., Lockwood, David, Bechhofer, Frank and Platt, Jennifer (1973) *The Affluent Worker in the Class Structure*. London: Cambridge University Press

Halsey, A. H. (1995) *Change in British Society*, Fourth Edition. Oxford: Oxford University Press

Hamilton, Malcolm and Hirszowicz, Maria (1993) *Class and Inequality*. Hemel Hempstead: Harvester Wheatsheaf

Hitchens, Christopher (1994) Let's lose the race, p. 24, *New Statesman & Society*, 25 November

Hunt, Steven (1995), The 'race' and health inequalities debate, pp 28–32, *Sociology Review*, Vol. 5, No. 1, September

King, Coretta Scott (ed.) (1985) *The Words of Martin Luther King*. London: Fount

King, Martin Luther (1969) *Chaos or Community?* Harmondsworth: Penguin

Lister, Ruth (1991) Concepts of poverty, pp 192–5, *Social Studies Review*, Vol. 6, No. 5, May

McNeill, Patrick (1989) Growing up: Children's rights, in McNeill, Patrick (1991) *Society Today* 2. Houndsmills, Basingstoke: Macmillan Education Ltd

Office for National Statistics (1996) *Social Focus on Ethnic Minorities*. London: HMSO

Oppenheim, Carey and Harker, Lisa (1996) *Poverty: The Facts*. Third Edition. London: Child Poverty Action Group

Pascall, Gillian (1995) Women on top?, pp 2–6, *Sociology Review*, Vol. 4 , No. 3, February

Parsons, Talcott (1964) *The Social System*. New York: The Free Press of Glencoe

Reid, Ivan (1989) *Social Class Differences in Britain*, Third Edition. Fontana Press

Roberts, Kenneth (1996) Youth and employment in modern Britain, pp 25–9, *Sociology Review*, Vol. 5, No. 4, April

Stephens, Paul (1993) GNVQs: A guide to the new terminology in education, p. 11, *Timetable*, 19 November

Stephens, Paul (1996) *Essential Mentoring Skills: A Practical Handbook for School-based Teacher Educators*. Cheltenham: Stanley Thornes

Thio, Alex (1989) *Sociology: An Introduction*, Second Edition. New York: Harper & Row

Tischler, Henry L. (1996) *Introduction to Sociology*, Fifth Edition. Fort Worth: The Harcourt Press

Tumin, Melvin (1953) Some principles of stratification: A critical analysis, pp 415–27, in Coser, Lewis A. and Rosenberg, Bernard (eds) (1969) op. cit.

Tumin, Melvin (1967) *Social Stratification*. Englewood Cliffs, New Jersey: Prentice-Hall

Westen, Drew (1996) *Psychology: Mind, Brain and Culture*. New York: John Wiley & Sons, Inc.

Westergaard, John (1995) *Who Gets What?* Cambridge: Polity Press

Williams, John (1996) Is feminism dead?, back cover page, *Sociology Review*, Vol. 5, No. 3, February

Younge, Gary (1995) Black in Britain, *The Guardian*, 20 March

Exam practice: Social stratification

Data response question

Item A

Giddens argues that class relations are shaped by such factors as the division of labour in production, authority relations in employment organisations, and patterns of consumption. These all help to determine the 'structuration' of classes – the degree of consciousness, solidarity and cohesion which they can achieve. The development of the division of labour, for example, has tended to sharpen the distinction between manual and non-manual workers – between working class and middle class. This sharpening has been reinforced by the involvement of non-manual workers in the exercise of authority over manual workers on the behalf of the owner and controllers of businesses. Consumption patterns, similarly, reinforce class relations by creating for example a residential, neighbourhood segregation of middle class and working class 'communities', each with their particular and distinct styles of life and patterns of living.

(Adapted from *Social Stratification*, John Scott (Development in Sociology Vol. 7))

Item B

Marx sees a particularly strong connection between class and culture. Marxists often use the term 'class culture' to refer to a way of life – physical and mental – and behaviour typical of a given class . . . Weber did not think that culture was quite so closely connected with class as do Marxists. Indeed, he often used the term 'life-style' rather than culture, which has a deliberately more individualistic sound to it. For him, the working class person with middle class values, friends and leisure pursuits is a relatively common exception requiring no special explanation. People develop their own cultural habits which can easily cut across class lines. Functionalists, including Durkheim, tend to regard it as the major role of culture to unite rather than divide society. In particular, Durkheim was concerned to bridge the rift between capitalist and worker.

(*A New Introduction to Sociology*, Mike O'Donnell (Harrap))

Item C

Mrs Thatcher was on record as saying there was no such thing as society – only individuals. Her successor as Prime Minister, Mr John Major, had a different opinion. On taking office, he spoke of Britain as moving towards a 'classless' society – a society of opportunity based on merit and effort. He said, "what people fulfil will depend upon their talent, their application and their good fortune". This vision is well known to sociologists as the 'meritocracy' concept. Mr Major came from a grammar school background and left school at 16. His rise to the top job in the land illustrates the possibilities.

(*Sociology Update 1991*, Martyn Denscombe)

(a) What does Giddens mean by 'the structuration' of social classes (**Item A**)? *(1 mark)*

(b) To what extent do sociologists agree that manual workers and non-manual workers are still sharply distinct (**Item A**)? *(7 marks)*

(c) Using material from the **Items** and elsewhere, assess the evidence for the existence of class cultures in modern Britain. *(8 marks)*

(d) How far does sociological evidence support the idea that Britain is a 'meritocratic' society (**Item C**)? *(9 marks)*

From Summer 1993 AEB Paper 1 A Level Sociology

8 The family

Topics covered in this chapter

- *Defining the family*
- *What is the family for?*
- *Theoretical perspectives*
- *Historical perspectives*
- *Current family patterns and demographic trends*
- *Relationships within families*
- *Current issues*

You only need listen to the conversations taking place around you on the bus or in the local shops, or think about what you talk about with your co-students, to be made aware that the minutiae of our daily lives are tremendously important to us. We all have tales to tell about our own families and often have strong opinions about both our immediate experience and what we see happening in the world around us. Small wonder, then, that stories about family life feature so prominently in the media and that family policy has become a central tenet of any government's overall strategy.

In listening to these conversations you will have tuned into one of the most fundamental questions for sociology: the paradox that we're all individuals yet, at the same time, we are social beings. What's the balance between being separate and unique, and also being a member of society? The family is generally acknowledged as playing a pivotal role in making these links.

Quite an unusual family. Identical twins, married to brothers, and their baby daughters, born within three weeks of each other.

This chapter will explore what sociologists have to say about that role.

First, we'll consider what you might already know about the family and how you should use this knowledge.

The family is frequently chosen as the starting point for sociology courses, and it's easy to see why. Most of us have some experience of living in a family situation, (which we'll define later), and are therefore likely to find this area of study more accessible and 'real' than some other parts of the syllabus.

OVER TO YOU

Before we go any further, ask yourself the following questions:
a What is a family? How would you define it?
b What is the purpose of the family?
Make a note of your answers. We'll return to these questions later.

Did you find these questions easy to 'answer'? Did you all agree? It's understandable that we tend to start by drawing upon what we already know, but there are risks in this. Sociology isn't an agglomeration of anecdotes and personal opinions. Sociology is all about making sense of life in society; it's about asking questions and looking for explanations. It's also about realising that there's no one 'right' answer. Sociology is also about looking for patterns and structures. They do exist and, as you become more skilled in thinking sociologically, you'll learn how to use your personal insights and inspirations as a springboard for a more systematic study of social institutions.

Pamela Abbott and Claire Wallace highlight the interplay between the 'individual' and the 'social' when they write:

'Sociology is about understanding the relationship between our own experiences and the social structures we inhabit.'

(Abbott and Wallace 1997: 5)

Peter and Brigitte Berger say that everyone knows what the family is and also warn us of pitfalls that are associated with the study of the family:

'the family is an essential component of almost everyone's taken-for-granted world. It is all the more necessary to gain some distance from this taken-for-granted perspective if one is to understand what the institution is all about . . . Familiarity breeds not so much contempt as blindness . . . Sociology tries to introduce a sufficient element of artificial strangeness into what is most familiar to us in order that we may be able to describe the familiar in clearer ways.'

(Berger and Berger 1976: 93–4)

The quote from Berger and Berger should also have alerted you to the question of appropriate methodologies for studying the family. As you progress through this chapter you should pay particular attention to the research methodologies which are used in the various studies. They may not always be stated openly, but they're always there, built into the work Don't be afraid to ask the most basic questions and don't take anything for granted. (There's more on this theme at the start of the section on demographic trends.)

Defining the family

We asked you to define the family and, to be honest, assumed that you would quickly run into difficulties. You'll have realised that the term 'family' is used to denote many different types of domestic (i.e. living) arrangement. Your discussions will also have indicated the wide range of meanings attached to the use of the term. We should now explore the ideas behind the words and move towards developing a definition of the family which can accommodate the variations which you'll have noted.

The early sociologists were intent on developing a science of society, of discovering the laws which govern society. We've also said that in sociology we're often looking for patterns, but is this the same as seeking to discover the laws of society?

Both sociology and social policy are predicated on the assumption that it's possible to discern patterns in human behaviour, to identify causes and thereby to effect some changes. Diana Gittins argues for a very cautious set of analytical frameworks which focus primarily on the European experience (remember this when we consider later the criticism that [male-dominated] sociology has ignored non-white, non-European experiences):

'First, we need to acknowledge that while what we may think of as families are not universal, there are still trends and patterns specific to our culture which, by careful analysis, we can understand more fully. Second, we can accept that while there can be no perfect definition, it is still possible to discover certain defining characteristics which can help us to understand changing patterns of behaviour and beliefs. Finally, and most important, we can "deconstruct" assumptions usually made about families by questioning what exactly they mean.'

(Gittins 1993: 70–1)

Exploring the use and meaning of words

We can learn a lot from the linguistic study of terms such as 'the family'. It can give us a clue to earlier social structures and also make us more aware of how they might still exert some subconscious influence over us.

Raymond Williams' book, *Keywords* (1988), is a very useful source of such information. From him we learn that the word 'family' came into usage in the English language in the late fourteenth century from the Latin *familia*, meaning household or servant. This household consisted of 'either a group of servants or a group of blood relations and servants living together in one house'.

The adjective 'familiar' described situations of friendship or intimacy, such as those which would be experienced by 'people living together in a household, in close relations with each other and well used to each other's ways'.

At this time (i.e. the late fourteenth century) the word 'family' is being used synonymously with 'household', to denote a group of people who may or may not be kin, all living under the same roof. In the Bible, this large kin-group is often used as the equivalent of tribe.

Family/household/community

Traditional farming communities of South Asia are based upon a patriarchal, extended family system. The male head of the family and his wife, their sons and their wives, their grandsons, their wives and children, all typically live in one household and run the family farm. The community is often regarded as an extension of this family, with close relationships between families. There's a similar pattern in traditional Chinese society.

In her study of Samoa, Margaret Mead describes yet another form of household:

'A Samoan village is made up of some thirty to forty households, each of which is presided over by a headman called a matai . . . the composition [of these households] varies from the biological family consisting of parents and children only, to households of fifteen and twenty people who are all related to the matai or to his wife by blood, marriage, or adoption, but who often have no close relationship to each other . . . Such a household is not necessarily a close residential unit, but may be scattered over the village in three or four houses.'

(Mead 1969: 38)

Here again, we have a description of a family structure which is closely interwoven with that of the wider community. Both this family structure and the community seem to be long-established and stable.

In the literature there are innumerable examples of types of household, for example, in the work of Gittins (1993). Whilst you may feel that 'household' provides you with a more satisfactory framework within which to place your analysis of the family, you should also heed Gittins' caveat:

'There is no hard and fast rule, much less a definition in universal terms, that can be applied to household in terms of domestic activities . . . Household is thus in some ways just as nebulous a term as family, although it lacks the ideological implications that "family" carries.'

(Gittins 1993: 61)

It's between the seventeenth and nineteenth centuries that we see the conceptual shift towards using 'family' to mean small kin-group, which we typically describe as the 'nuclear family' and which is now established in 'western' thinking as the family form. There's a more detailed analysis of this shift in meaning and usage in a later section of this chapter.

The question of continuity and change constantly surfaces in the analysis of family forms. Juliet Mitchell tells us:

'For though the family has changed since its first appearance, it has also remained – not just as an idealist concept but as a crucial ideological and economic unit with a certain rigidity and autonomy despite all its adaptations.'

(Mitchell 1971: 153)

She's picking up on points which we've already encountered. The family has changed over time and yet, despite these changes, there seem to remain some common, long-standing elements. Furthermore, the family remains important in terms of what it seems to represent.

We describe the family as an 'institution', not made of bricks and mortar like a prison or a hospital, but just as real none the less. In our search for a definition we're trying to identify these core elements, to construct something tangible, like an institution.

So far we've considered the family as:

- a household
- a large kin-group
- a tribe.

We've also seen that family/household/community are frequently intermingled. I'm sure you will sympathise with Gittins' comment that 'families are not clear-cut, but are highly complex and often confusingly fluid social groupings' (1993: 4).

There are other interesting current uses of 'family' words. 'Family' can be used to denote traceable lineage, for example, 'he comes from a long-established family'. It can have distinctly upper-class associations, for example, 'the family is in residence'. 'Family' is often specifically used to mean children, for example, 'my wife (or husband) and family'. To be 'in the family way' means to be pregnant. Newly-weds are often asked when they intend 'to start a family'.

Thus, in addition, we have family as:

- traceable lineage (pedigree!)
- children.

OVER TO YOU

Where would criminal subculture 'families', such as the mafia or triads, fit in our analysis?

You shouldn't assume that the use of the term 'kin' indicates a blood or biological relationship, but rather you should view 'kin' as a social construct. There are many examples, across both time and cultures, of family terminology being liberally interpreted and applied beyond strictly blood relationships. In Shakespeare's plays the term 'cousin' is used to indicate close friendship. In Hindu communities it's regarded as disrespectful for youngsters to address adult family friends by their first name and so the epithet 'auntie' or 'uncle' is used. This is described as *fictive kinship*.

These next two quotes explore further the question of kinship. Firstly, Rayna Rapp notes:

'Since family is supposed to be more reliable than friendship, "going for brothers, for sisters, for cousins", increases the commitment of a relationship, and makes people ideally more responsible for one another. Fictive kinship is a serious relationship.'

(Rapp 1980: 292)

Secondly, this is what Gittins has to say:

'Kinship . . . is a way of identifying others as in some way special from the rest, people to whom the individual or collectivity feel responsible in certain ways. It is a method of demarcating obligations and responsibility between individuals and groups.'

(Gittins 1993: 65)

Family and ideology

In much established sociological thinking there's an inherent tendency to ignore the experiences of anyone who isn't a white, middle-class, European male. 'Western' culture is dominated by familial ideology (an explanation of this term is given shortly) and all too readily we fall into the trap of assuming that the nuclear family is the only, the ideal, family form. Certainly, if you'd been studying the sociology of the family 20 years ago, you would have been presented with a range of texts which concentrated on very different issues. Conspicuously absent was any serious treatment of gender or cultural diversity. This is an argument substantially developed in the writings of Abbott and Wallace:

'Sociologists concentrated on the public sphere of government and the workplace and ignored the private sphere of the home and domestic relationships. This was at least in part because the division of labour between the public sphere (men) and the private shere (women), was seen as natural – that is, as having a biological basis.'

(Abbott and Wallace 1997: 7)

Again, we draw upon the work of Abbott and Wallace, this time to explore further the issue of ideology:

'Familial ideology presents the nuclear family – of mother, father and dependent children living as a household, with the man as economic provider and the woman as carer in the domestic sphere – as a natural (biologically based) and universal institution . . . By 'ideology' we mean a pattern of ideas (common-sense knowledge) – both factual and evaluative – which purports to explain and legitimate the social structure and culture of a social group or society and which serves to justify social actions which are in accordance with that pattern of ideas . . . Ideologies, especially dominant ones, also serve to construct certain aspects of the social world as natural and universal, and therefore unquestionable and unchangeable.'

(Abbott and Wallace 1997: 9)

Just as we've done before with quotations which contain a lot of possibly difficult ideas, we suggest that you should read this quote very carefully. The writers:

- give us one definition of the *nuclear family*
- raise the issues of *biological determinism* and *universality*
- give us a definition of *ideology*.

You should use these pointers to clarify in you own mind the meaning of these terms.

Don't panic if you find the concept of ideology difficult to grasp; both the meaning and the use of the term continue to arouse fierce political and academic debate. You'll find that a good sociology dictionary will help.

Anthropology and the family

We can discern another angle on the impact of ideology when we look at how the family used to be studied and taught. The antidote to the European nuclear family was often provided by citing anthropological examples from 'primitive' societies. In the introduction to *Coming of Age in Samoa*, Mead explains that:

'anthropologists choose to study simple peoples, primitive peoples, whose society has never attained the complexity of our own . . . A study of the French family alone would involve a preliminary study of French history, of French law, of the Catholic and Protestant attitudes towards sex and personal relations. A primitive people without a written language present a much less elaborate problem.'

(Mead 1969: 14)

It's interesting that Mead identifies precisely those factors which today we regard as essential components of any study of the family, namely history, law and religious beliefs. Do anthropologists still regard 'primitive' societies as simple societies? Do you, for that matter?

Feminists argue that we need to question and analyse that which was previously 'hidden from history' (Sheila Rowbotham 1973).

One of the many interesting developments in family study has been the more widespread application of anthropological techniques in a 'western' setting. The development and acceptance of a broader range of research methodologies reflect the impact of feminist thinking. Sociology no longer tries to duck the kinds of 'problems' which Mead anticipated with a study of the French family.

Again, we've raised the question of appropriate methodologies for studying the family.

More definitions, a framework and a summary

It's possible to think of families in terms of:

- structure
- relationships.

You also need to know the terminology applied to forms of marriage. You'll notice a considerable degree of overlap and repetition as we move from one category to another.

Families as structure

- *The nuclear family* This typically consists of two adult partners (one female, one male) and their dependent children. They live comparatively independently of their wider kinship network and local community.
- *The extended family* This consists of several generations of one family who live either under the same roof or in close proximity to each other. They offer mutual support and have close links with their local community.
- *The reconstituted or blended family* This is formed when two previously separate families come together. Implicit in this situation are the legal issues of divorce and step-parenting.
- *The lone-parent family* The term is usually taken to mean a mother living with her children. There are also male lone parents. Whilst this family unit now comprises only one adult, in the majority of cases this will previously have been a two-parent family.
- *Same-sex couples* They may or may not have children living with them.

Families as relationships

- *Patriarchal* Authority in relationships and also financial and legal power is vested in the adult male. Inheritance and lineage is passed down through the male heirs. Ralph Linton (1936) uses the term 'consanguine' to denote the same relationship.
- *Matriarchal* Authority in relationships, and also financial and legal power, is vested in the adult female. Inheritance and lineage is passed down through the female heirs.
- *Symmetrical* Willmott and Young (1973) use this term to describe the kind of relationship which they believe now exists between a couple. The domestic division of labour is becoming more equitable, reflecting the greater equality of roles experienced by both men and women in the wider society. Linton uses the term conjugal to describe the equal partnership between couples.

Forms of marriage

- *Monogamy* This is marriage between one man and one woman.
- *Serial monogamy* This is where the person is married more than once, the preceeding marriage having been ended by divorce or widowhood.
- *Polygamy* This describes the concurrent marriage of one person to two or more members of the opposite sex. This is the generic term to cover all multiple marriages although it is often also, incorrectly, used when the man has more than one wife. Be careful how you use it.
- *Polygyny* This is the concurrent marriage of one man to two or more women.
- *Polyandry* This is the concurrent marriage of one woman to two or more men. This is a rare form of marriage.

What is the family for?

We now need to develop a coherent way of structuring the welter of ideas and issues relating to the family which we have generated so far. This is no simple task, and when you look at the relevant literature it often seems as though every writer approaches this in a different way.

Ways of thinking about the family

We've already seen how the family is both an individual experience and also a societal institution. It's possible to think of the family from the standpoint of:

- the individual looking outwards
- society looking into the family.

When you were first asked to think about the purpose of the family, you probably produced something like this:

The family is for:

- *practical care of all of its members*
  - *the young*
  - *the elderly*
- *emotional support of all of its members*
- *preparation of children for adulthood.*

This kind of list reflects our individualised perspectives of the family as experienced from the inside; this is what the family means to us.

The Bergers develop this personal perspective approach. They start with the family as the world:

'The family is, for the child, an entire world of people and meanings of very great significance . . . In the beginning, of course, it is the only world . . . For almost everyone, the family is, as it were, the home port from which the individual starts out on his [*sic*] lifelong journey through society.'

(Berger and Berger 1976: 92–3)

From there, we move to the family as a place of waiting:

'As the child becomes aware of the large structures that loom in the background of his [!] everyday life, he begins to see his own family as the circumscribed vantage point from which he views and relates to these larger structures . . . The family is the place in which he waits for the larger world.'

They also identify the family as a place of refuge, particularly for adult members; more about this later.

The Bergers make the link from the individual to the wider society through the legal framework which surrounds the family:

'It is the family that generally provides the individual with a name and determines his [!] basic legal standing. This not only makes it possible to reckon the individual's descent (which has far-reaching economic as well as legal implications) but also provides the basic means by which individuals can be identified and located in the social order.'

(Berger and Berger 1976: 95)

Perhaps the most frequently quoted definition of the family is that of George Murdock:

'The family is a social group characterised by common residence, economic co-operation and reproduction. It includes adults of both sexes, at least two of whom maintain a socially approved sexual relationship, and one or more children, own or adopted, of the sexually cohabiting adults.'

(Murdock 1949: 1)

The basis of these socially-approved sexual relationships varies considerably from society to society. We'll be looking in greater detail at current trends in the UK in a later section.

Anthony Giddens uses this definition of the family:

'A family is a group of persons directly linked by kin connections, the adult members of which assume responsibility for caring for children.'

(Giddens 1993: 390)

In these two definitions from Murdock and Giddens you have a very clear illustration of the close link between the definition of the family and its purpose. Both of these definitions also span the individual–social divide. Let's have a closer look at what they're saying about the family.

Firstly, here are the defining characteristics:

- Murdock highlights:
  - common residence
  - economic co-operation
  - reproduction/adoption of children
  - heterosexual adults
  - socially-approved sexual relationship between adults.
- Giddens highlights:
  - kin connections
  - children.

A question you should immediately ask is whether the absence of, or variation from, any of these characteristics means that a particular domestic arrangement does not constitute a family?

Secondly, what do these two definitions have to say about the purpose of the family?

- Murdock cites:
  - economic co-operation
  - reproduction
  - regularising sexual activity.
- Giddens cites responsibility for child care.

OVER TO YOU

Compare these definitions with your original definition. Give reasons for any differences.

We now examine in more detail the various elements of the family debate.

Sexual activity and procreation

The Bergers identify three basic human activities, namely:

- sexuality
- procreation
- primary socialisation.

They claim that all human sexual relations are structured through family forms:

'The family provides a typology of others in terms of their degree of relationship to the individual, and it is this typology which determines the permissible partners for sexual relations. In view of the very great strength of sexuality as a motive for human conduct, it is clear that this institutional patterning is of great importance for any human society.'

(Berger and Berger 1976: 94)

By the regularisation of sexual activity, commentators are referring to two different, but linked, aspects of sexual behaviour. Firstly, there's the issue of confining sexual activity within a legally-defined relationship, typically marriage. Thus, it's important to ensure celibacy before marriage and also fidelity within marriage. Secondly, there's the question of defining appropriate sexual and marriage partners. In 'western' society, marriage isn't permitted between first cousins; other cultures have different mores with regard to this. In small-scale, stable, traditional communities, comprising perhaps half a dozen extended families, the range of suitable marriage partners will be limited. Incest is very much frowned upon, but that doesn't mean that it doesn't occur.

Murdock also clearly placed much emphasis on the need to regularise sexual activity. Procreation is also specifically identified as a core function of the family.

The novelist, George Orwell, in *Nineteen Eighty-Four*, gives us a slightly different perspective on the same issues:

'The aim of the Party was . . . to remove all pleasure from the sexual act. Not love so much as eroticism was the enemy, inside marriage as well as outside it. All marriages between Party members had to be approved by a committee appointed for the purpose . . . The only recognised purpose of marriage was to beget children for the service of the Party. Sexual intercourse was to be looked upon as a slightly disgusting minor operation, like having an enema . . . All children were to be begotten by artificial insemination (artsem, as it was called in Newspeak) and brought up in public institutions.'

(Orwell 1954: 56)

Is Orwell's world completely far-fetched or is he perhaps highlighting elements which are present in our own experience?

Biology: Motherhood

You'll remember being alerted to the question of the family as a biological imperative. This is what the Bergers say on the matter:

'The biological fact which underlies the patterning of procreation is the duration of human pregnancy and of the helplessness of the infant after birth. Not only is the mother relatively incapacitated during the pregnancy, but the human infant is completely helpless at birth and would die unless social arrangements are made for its care and protection. The family as an institution has provided patterns of conduct surrounding the biological process of procreation and allowing it to proceed with greatly diminished danger.'

(Berger and Berger 1976: 94–5)

No one would argue with the assertion that we must reproduce in order to survive and that the new-born babe is very vulnerable, but does everything else that we currently associate with the family have to automatically follow suite? Contrast the Bergers' view with that of Gittins:

'That women conceive and bear children is a universal phenomenon; that they do so by instinct is a fallacy. So is the notion that they always raise them. From the moment of birth motherhood is a social construction.'

(Gittins 1993: 67)

Here we have a description of Tahitian society, from Felicity Edholm:

'In Tahiti young women often have one or two children before they are considered, or consider themselves to be, ready for an approved and stable relationship. It is considered perfectly acceptable for the children of this young woman to be given to her parents or other close kin for adoption . . . The girl can decide what her relationship to the children will be but there is no sense in which she is forced into "motherhood" because of having had a baby.'

(Edholm 1982:170)

OVER TO YOU

What does Gittins mean by her statement that motherhood is 'a social construction'?

EXAM TIP

To develop your response to the question on the family as a biological imperative, you need to gather information on the social arrangements which are made for the care of the infant from a variety of societies and cultures.

More questions about parenting:

We've raised the question of whether children and families have to go together. Let's now look at this link from some different perspectives.

Couples seeking assisted conception often say that they don't feel like a proper family because they don't have any children. What about couples who choose not to have any children? Do the adults have to be heterosexual? There are many adults who have children from a heterosexual relationship but who are now in 'gay' relationships. There are 'gay' couples, both male and female, who want to have children. What exactly is a 'socially-approved sexual relationship'? (to quote Murdock). Who should be a parent?

Consider the issues raised by Russell Conlon and his partner Stephen:

'Russell Conlon, 39, and his partner Stephen, 32, are seeking a lesbian couple prepared to enter a surrogacy arrangement to provide them with a baby, after being turned down as foster carers by their local social services department. In return they say they would provide the sperm for the lesbian couple to have a baby of their own . . .

Mr Conlon, who "married" his gay partner last year in a ceremony blessed by a priest after an on/off relationship lasting 10 years, told the Independent yesterday of his lifelong desire for a child . . .

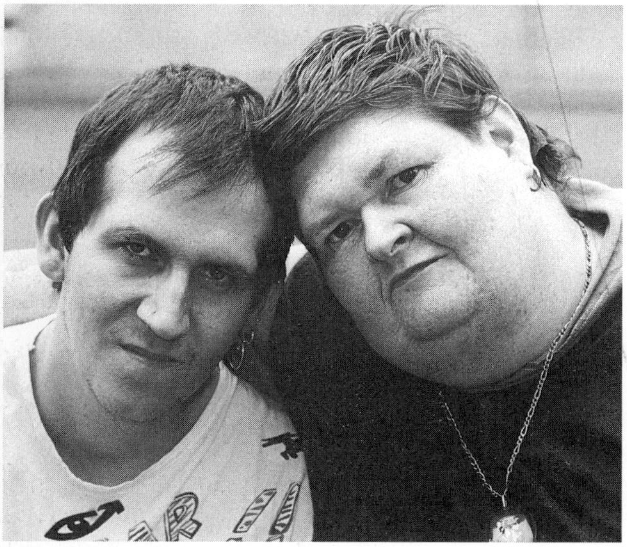

"We can give a child as much love, care, understanding and discipline as any heterosexual couple can. We are married in the eyes of God, we have a marriage certificate, we wear rings and our marriage was blessed by the church . . . If we could share a baby with a lesbian couple that could be just as good. They could have it three or four nights a week and we could have it two or three nights. Then we would go through the midnight feeds and changing nappies that are part of what having a baby is about."

Valerie Riches, Director of Family and Youth Concern, argues for the need to tighten surrogacy law to exclude gay couples:

"The situation has got completely out of hand. They don't seem to be thinking of the rights of the child to be born to a man and a woman so he or she has got a solid base to start from."'

(The *Independent*, 28 May 1997)

OVER TO YOU

1. ***This gay couple have had their relationship blessed in a church, so does this mean that society approves of their relationship?***
2. ***Valerie Riches stresses the importance to the child of having both male and female parents. Is this the most important part of parenting? Or can other adults make the same sort of contribution to the child's upbringing?***

The need for stability

How important is stability and continuity for human beings? Certainly, throughout time it seems that writers on family and society have stressed this as a basic human need.

How important is physical, practical continuity and stability of residence if society is to acknowledge and approve family/domestic arrangements? Is it essential for the 'family' members to always share the same roof? Many people, for a variety of reasons, have to work away from home, often for extended periods. Where do long-distance lorry drivers, seasonal workers and astronauts, for example, fit in this scenario?

In black Caribbean Sociey, it is the norm for the father to be absent for long periods of time while he is away working. Despite his physical absence, he remains the family figurehead in both an emotional and a financial sense.

There's the same pattern of dispersal within many first generation immigrant families in the UK. Typically it's the young men who are admitted first, because they're able to make a defined contribution to the economy. Often it may take years before the whole family can be united. We say the whole family, but of course that can never completely be the case. There are always uncles, cousins, parents, grandparents, who remain in 'the old country' and with whom powerful and significant links remain. These links are strong, even for the children of these first generation immigrants.

Does the domestic/family roof have to be a static one in order for it to qualify under Murdock's criteria? What about travellers, whether traditional or New Age? What about nomadic peoples in 'traditional', non-industrialised societies?

Is continuity of parenting important?

In particular, how important is it for the mother to have close contact with her child during its infancy?

Across time and across cultures we see many variations in the arrangements made for child care. We also see how these arrangements are frequently determined by economic necessity. In *The Midwife's Tale*, Nicky Leap and Billie Hunter record the oral histories of women in pre-NHS/Welfare State Britain. Edie M. attributes the death of two of her babies to returning too quickly to work after the births:

'There was nothing else for it. You had to work unless – well, I s'pose you could stay at home and manage on bread and marg or something . . . '

During the war, Edie placed some of her children in a creche, but that arrangement was not entirely trouble-free:

'The creche closed for the holidays, so I used to put him in a little box beside me in the kitchen, and we used to keep putting his dummy into syrup or something. And that's how we got over the week or fortnight's holiday when the creche was shut.'

(Both quotes: Leap and Hunter 1993: 134–5)

Ellen Ross describes the arrangements which women in early twentieth-century Lambeth made:

'Neighbours and indeed neighbourhoods functioned as auxiliary parents . . . a large group had formal childcare arrangements with neighbours and a still larger group with no formal plans for their children may well have relied on informal supervision by women living nearby. Another survey of London working women, made a few years earlier, found that half left infants with relatives, thirty percent with neighbours. Landlords, and especially landladies . . . in exercising general superintendence over renters, kept a casual eye out for children as well as for old people living in the house.'

(Ross 1983: 12)

These arrangements can be interpreted in different ways. Some would argue that such casual, informal provision for child care was indicative of parental negligence and an abdication of responsibility. Others would celebrate such a system as representing all that was good about the cohesion of traditional communities.

Today, parents with young children still have the same child-care dilemmas to resolve and frequently make the kinds of arrangements described by Ross and by Leap and Hunter.

In the kibbutzim in Israel, we have perhaps the apotheosis of ideals of community living and community care. Each kibbutz, which can comprise anything from 50 to 2,000 members, functions as a single household, with all members participating in the economic activity (usually agriculturally-based) of the kibbutz. Child care is the responsibility of the whole commune and, in some instances, the children live separately from their parents, in special homes.

The family and socialisation

There's an implicit assumption in much of the popular and political rhetoric about the family that it's 'a good thing' and the absence of it is somehow a 'bad thing'. Much of the current 'moral panic' about the family broadly adopts the stance that many of the ills in our society can be explained by shortcomings in current family structures, by the disintegration of the 'traditional' family, whatever that might be.

You'll have encountered frequent use of the term 'socialisation'. This is the definition given in the *Oxford Dictionary of Sociology*:

'Socialisation is the process by which we learn to become members of society, both by internalising the norms and values of society, and also by learning how to perform our social roles (as worker, friend, citizen, and so forth).'

(Marshall 1994: 497)

This is a definition which looks out from the family towards the wider society.

Giddens gives us a definition which treats the process very much more from a personal, experiential, perspective:

'Socialisation is the process whereby the helpless infant gradually becomes a self-aware, knowledgeable person, skilled in the ways of the culture into which she or he is born. Socialisation is not a kind of "cultural programming" in which the child absorbs passively the influences with which she or he comes into contact . . . Socialisation connects the different generations to one another . . . Although the process of cultural learning is much more intense in infancy and early childhood than later, learning and adjustment go on throughout the whole life-cycle.'

(Giddens 1993: 60)

It's interesting that Giddens focuses on cultural learning, in its broadest sense, whereas Marshall cites, as the first social role, that of worker. All of these aspects of social learning are typically described as being key purposes for the family.

You'll have realised by now that both the term and the process of 'socialisation' cover a wide range of different tasks. The social learning, the *primary socialisation*, is that which typically occurs, in its most concentrated form, during infancy and early childhood. This is how and when you learn social graces, like not putting your knife in your mouth, like shaking hands with someone when you're introduced.

Primary socialisation also includes all the earliest aspects of what later will become more formal learning – the development of language, awareness of size and shape, self-expression, interpersonal relationships, knowledge of immediate environment, avoidance of danger.

Much of the current 'panic' about family life seems to operate on the assumption that this primary socialisation must take place within the family, and moreover, a very specifically defined form of family. There also tends to be an assumption that this learning must be transmitted by the mother. For example, our native language is called the 'mother tongue'.

In 'traditional', non-industrialised societies primary socialisation would have encompassed all aspects of the preparation necessary for adult life. All adults are expected to be able to provide for their own survival and that of any dependants. Their survival into adulthood is taken to indicate success in this most basic human requirement and puts them in the position of being the experts. In a world which is seemingly static, unchanging, what they know will be equally relevant to the next generation. How very different from the balance of inter-generational relationships today.

In the past, primary socialisation covered both the transmission of general social mores and culture (as today), and also the specific elements of education and training. There would have been no clear lines of demarcation between the two strands. Then, as now, the acquisition of particular skills and knowledge was essential for economic functioning and therefore to basic survival. Then, this education and training occurred almost exclusively through the family/domestic/community structure, and would have happened on an informal basis, alongside other aspects of daily life. Family life would have been virtually synonymous with the whole of one's experience of life.

Today, the balance of the situation is very different, with sharply defined components for both the public and the family spheres. We stress the value of ensuring that young children are given early learning opportunities at home. We also seek to develop home–school partnerships once a child begins formal education. For the most part, however, it's assumed that parents don't have the level of expertise required for the complete education and subsequent training of their children. This has now been almost entirely taken over by the formal education system. The rosy picture of the child sitting at the feet of a revered elder, hanging on his every word, has now been replaced by the techno-wizz youngster mocking the parent who cannot cope with pre-setting the VCR.

The family as an economic unit

Just as we must procreate for the human species to continue, so we must also labour in some way to provide ourselves with the food and shelter necessary for our survival.

In non-industrialised societies the family was, of necessity, an economic unit. It was essentially self-sufficient, based almost invariably on some form of subsistence farming. Everybody had a role to play, everybody mucked in. The children could perform the lighter tasks, the adults could supervise them and also carry out the heavier work. There was some demarcation of roles, both in terms of the farming work and also with regard to child care, the care of older and infirm family members, and other domestic duties. Nevertheless, since everything took place within the same fairly confined location, our present experiences of the sharp division of labour were not a practical possibility.

Within this set-up, children learned from their parents or other adults in the community. If there were a large number of children, too many to sub-divide the family holding between, some would have been sent away to live and to work. Typically, the boys would be apprenticed to a master craftsman while the girls would be sent into service with a wealthy local family. Notice how all of these other arrangements were still based on a household setting – apprentices lived with the family of the master, domestic servants 'lived in'.

The Industrial Revolution heralded both the breakdown of the agrarian-based economy and radical changes in the ways in which the family could operate as an economic unit. In the early days, the 'putting out' system allowed established family patterns to continue. Even with the move to factory-based production, there was a period during which the whole family was employed as a unit by the factory owner and the father typically performed the role of family foreman. As the machines became larger and more sophisticated, it became impossible to continue with this form of labour employment and organisation. It's at this point that we see the fracturing of the link between family and work, and when individuals became employees. This is also the point at which we see a separation between work and family life and all that entailed for the care of family members.

Today we now have an almost exclusive emphasis on the family as a unit of consumption rather than of production. In white, 'western' societies, it's unusual for children to work in the family business. Indeed, how many family businesses are there in these days of multi-national corporations? In many respects we regard the exercise of the family option with disfavour and expect children to make their own way in the world, unaided by any advantage which family connections might bring. This is not the case with all cultures, with Asian families providing us with perhaps the most familiar alternative example.

The family as a place of emotional experience

During the course of the twentieth century we've witnessed the separation of the public and private spheres of our lives and the development of the notion of family life as a separate and identifiable experience. Now that the responsibility for many elements of our lives, for example, education, training and health care, has shifted to the public sphere, there has been a commensurate increase in the emphasis now placed on the family as a place for personal succour and fulfilment. This is very different from the way things were in the past. When the daily routine was determined by the need to ensure personal survival, notions of leisure, privacy, spending 'quality' time with one's family would have been complete anathema. There simply would not have been time for such indulgencies.

We must be careful about applying current frames of analysis and expectation to very different social situations. We can know something about the structure of daily life and the overall pattern of an individual's life-course. We can, however, know very little, from this distance, about how people felt about, how they experienced, their lives. It's part of familial ideology to romanticise family life in the past, to portray it through rose-coloured glasses. We have this vision of everyone living in stable and harmonious relationships and, for good measure, living in thatched cottages with roses entwined around the door. This representation has been challenged by studies such as that by Phillipe Aries' *Centuries of Childhood* (1973). You don't need me to point out that family life isn't automatically an experience of unalloyed joy.

QUESTIONS

1. Are the needs of the individual the same as those of society?
2. Are there situations when the needs of society conflict with the needs of the individual?
3. How could such conflicts be resolved?

Theoretical perspectives

An alternative title might be: 'Who is the family for?'

So far the material in this chapter has been presented in a mainly descriptive fashion, quite deliberately so, in order to build up gradually a more detailed presentation of the whole issue. Now we look explicitly at the application of sociological theory to the study of the family. The previous section, 'What is the family for?', was written largely from the stance of looking outwards from the individual experiences of the family. Moving into a theoretical mode also shifts us to a point outside the family, from where to establish a degree of distance and analysis.

Firstly, we'll set out a number of theoretical perspectives. You need to remember that each of these is *one* way of organising the information in order to derive causal explanations of social phenomena. You'll no doubt develop a preference for one over others, but in your work you'll be expected to review narrative material from a number of different perspectives.

These strands of sociological theory are presented in a broadly historical sequence. Sociology as a discipline has been continuously changing and developing since its inception, and the kinds of concerns which it seeks to address are always the product of a particular moment in time. Theory does have a longer-term shelf-life, but nevertheless you should always be able locate it within its original context.

Sociology, as an identifiable academic subject, is very much the product of the Industrial Revolution. Across Europe 'traditional' ways of life, 'traditional' communities and social structures were changing rapidly. Suddenly, the evidence and effects of social change were everywhere and inescapable. Older academic disciplines such as philosophy and political economy lacked the conceptual frameworks to adequately explain these massive changes – hence the emergence of sociology.

Auguste Comte

Auguste Comte (1798–1857), who is generally regarded as the founding father (*sic*) of sociology, identified the foci of sociological enquiry as:

- economic life
- ruling ideas
- religion
- the division of labour
- forms of individuality
- family structure
- language.

In this chapter we'll examine how each of these have an impact upon 'the family'. It's interesting to note that Comte includes family structure, a very specific element of social analysis, amongst his otherwise more abstract foci for sociological enquiry. By this, he is signalling clearly the importance he attaches to family structure in the overall life of any society.

Also relevant to our analysis is the distinction which Comte draws between 'social statics' (the prerequisites for social stability) and 'social dynamics' (forces for social change). We've already seen the importance of stability for both family and community structures.

Comte was writing in response to the cataclysmic changes of the early Industrial Revolution. This was a time of rapid population growth, a radical shift of population from rural to urban living and the transformation of the economy from one based on farming to large-scale industrial production. These changes aroused great anxieties from a number of quarters and for many different reasons. Undoubtedly in the UK there was genuine concern about the vast numbers of people living in the appalling conditions of the rapidly growing industrial towns of the midlands and the north. Certainly there was genuine concern about the apparent breakdown of traditional social networks of support and a humanitarian desire to moderate the worst excesses of unregulated capitalism. There was also a real fear that the spirit of revolution would cross the Channel from France, take root amongst the urban masses in England and thereby threaten the established order. The influence of these various fears and concerns is reflected in the preoccupations of early sociological theory.

Remember that sociology was conceived of as a science of society; the aim was to identify the laws of human behaviour and thereby exert some control. Social analysis was conducted at a macro level and produced very abstract conceptualisations of human life. This is all a far cry from ethnomethodology, phenomenology and postmodernism. Hence, you also need to remember that the early sociologists did not lower their gaze sufficiently to look in detail at the family. They did, however, give us some theoretical frameworks which we can use in our analysis.

Ferdinand Tonnies

Ferdinand Tonnies (1855–1936) drew a distinction between *Gemeinschaft* (community) and *Gesellschaft* (association) (see Chapter 17). Gemeinschaft characterises a small-scale, stable society, in which the family and the church play key roles in ensuring continuity and social order. The family is clearly located within a co-operative and supportive village community. With the division of labour, we witness the breakdown of these traditional, supportive relationships and social mores. *Gesellschaft* relationships characterise large-scale, impersonal organisations. In such a society the ideals of competition and individualism come to dominate.

Emile Durkheim

A continuous thread through all of the work of Emile Durkheim (1858–1917) is his interest in morality and moral authority, which is most directly developed in his writings on religion. His work is underpinned by an abiding concern with the impact of industrialisation, and with a constant questioning of the relationship between the individual and society. With his typology of *mechanical* and *organic solidarity* (see Chapters 4 and 17), we see close parallels with Tonnies' Gemeinschaft and Gesellschaft. Traditional, pre-industrial societies are characterised by mechanical solidarity, a society held together by shared ideals and values which are transmitted through social institutions such as the family, the tribe or the clan. In this society, there are no clear lines of demarcation between the individual and social institutions. In contrast, modern, industrialised society, which is held together by organic solidarity, stresses the importance of individualism. The division of labour fosters the development of higher levels of skill and the development of specialist institutions, such as hospitals and schools. This aspect of industrialisation could be regarded as 'progress', as making a positive contribution to the overall quality of life for that society's citizens. However, it brings in its wake the fracturing of traditional forms of social stability and integration, and the unleashing of anti-social excesses.

Durkheim was working within a model of human nature which regarded humans as having no innate mechanism which would curb their desires. The necessary regulation of these desires and instincts comes from the social structure. The overall health of the social body was assured through the mechanical solidarity of traditional society. However, there were dangers if the process of economic change, the division of labour and its attendant dislocation of the social structure occurred too quickly. The forms of moral regulation in an organically-structured society would not be able to adapt sufficiently quickly to keep pace with the social effects of economic change. In such circumstances, we would see the development of an *anomic* or abnormal division of labour. ('Anomie' is derived from a Greek word which means 'without law'.) In Durkheim's view of human nature, we see the precursor of Murdock's emphasis on the need to regulate human sexuality.

This work on anomie is further developed by Durkheim in his work on suicide. He charted the coincidence of increased rates of suicide with periods of economic depression. From this he argued that it was during such periods of downturn in the economy that people would feel less committed to society and its mores. It's at this point that their most basic desires would be unleashed. They would drift into a state of meaninglessness and confusion. Durkheim regarded the act of suicide as both the most individual of actions yet simultaneously a social fact, an action 'caused' by social circumstances. This approach echoes the observation made earlier that the family is both an individual, personal experience and also a social institution.

Durkheim is frequently characterised as an exponent of *consensus* (functionalist) *theory*. There's a bias in his work towards lauding the principles of stability which are inherent in his account of mechanical solidarity. There's also quite a strong sense of the weight of society as a whole bearing down upon the individual, who is seemingly rudderless if left to her or his own devices.

Karl Marx

Karl Marx (1818–83) was again centrally concerned with analysing the processes of social change instigated by the Industrial Revolution, and from this analysis he developed his concept of *alienation*. Put at its simplest, alienation is the estrangement of individuals from one another or from the social structures around them. Throughout time humankind has become alienated from her or his true self, and it will only be within a communist society that individuals will again be able to find themselves. Alienation attains its ultimate form in the capitalist system which is predicated on the division of labour, the exploitation of the proletariat and the creation of wage slaves.

Marx would not have described himself as a sociologist, but rather a social theorist, and as such he operated at the level of grand theory. For him the family was a bourgeois institution which would automatically disappear with the overthrow of the bourgeoisie and the advent of true communism. He didn't examine in detail the nature of relationships within the family nor did he concern himself specifically with gender inequalities, whether in the home or in the wider society.

Subsequent marxist theorists have applied some of these very broad ideas more specifically to the family. They argue that capitalism has exploited the family and forced it to be structured in a way which meets the needs of the capitalist society. It's in this light that social reforms introduced in the latter part of the nineteenth century can be interpreted. For example, the legislation which restricted the employment of women and children, promoted on humanitarian grounds, did also have the effect of confining women to the home and ensuring their economic dependence on their male, presumably employed, partners. The health education measures introduced by the last Liberal government (1906 onwards) stressed the necessity of educating women to become good mothers. They should stay at home, give due attention to ensuring the general health of their partner and children and thereby support a productive workforce.

Talcott Parsons

The previous section, 'What is the family for?' assiduously avoided using the term 'function' as applied to the family. Sociological thinking has long been dominated by functionalist theory, in particular that of Talcott Parsons (1902–79). Functionalist theory is based on a consensus view of society, that the various social institutions serve to ensure stability and continuity. Within this framework the family is a key component.

Let's spell out the main points of functionalist theory on the family:

- The family is a universal form of social organisation.
- It's based on biological necessity.
- Biology determines gender roles.
- The process of industrialisation led to the development of the nuclear family type as that most functionally appropriate to the demands of a complex 'modern' society.
- The economy requires a mobile, fit, well-disciplined and full-time work force (instrumental needs).
- Society as a whole requires that both adults and children experience security and love and are well cared-for (expressive needs).

- The nuclear family is ideally constructed to satisfy both these instrumental and expressive needs.

The emphasis is on the dominance of society over the individual. There's some room for the occurrence of social change, but the initial impetus for this will come from the wider social structure. For example, changes in employment patterns, such as increased work opportunities for women, or the trend towards part-time, flexible employment, will have an impact on domestic roles and relationships. There nevertheless remains the perennial dilemma of functionalist theory, which is: how to reconcile the inbuilt emphasis on stability and continuity with the recognition that social change does occur? Can the *status quo* and consensual social change exist side by side?

Social constructionist theorists

Social constructionist theorists bring a different perspective to the processes which actually occur when the individual encounters this wider society. Here we see an emphasis on the negotiation which takes place, through the process of socialisation, between individual social actors and society. Socialisation is not simply social programming, but is a process of negotiation. To what extent the two main players meet as equals is undoubtedly an issue which you need to debate. This interaction, this negotiation, this resolution of conflicting forces takes place both within the family and also as the individual acts in the wider social forum. Such a formulation of action allows for the occurrence of social change and for the individual actors to have more power over their individual circumstances.

Feminist theorists

Feminists have generated the most radical shift in theoretical approaches to the family, yet at the same time there's no uniform feminist perspective. At a general level they identify a number of key issues. The family:

- has a key role to play in the relationship of the individual to the wider society
- was significantly affected by the process of industrialisation and the division of labour
- is the fundamental site of the exploitation and oppression of women, both within the family itself and in relation to society.

Through all of this we see that the family is being placed centre-stage in sociological thinking. We've clearly established the important links between the personal, the private, and the public, the social. Over a prolonged period women have been systematically excluded from public life and confined to subordinate roles within the home. Sociological theory reflected this marginalisation of whole areas of women's experiences and now all of this is coming under scrutiny.

Just as all men don't have a common theoretical 'line' on the family, so women also have a variety of perspectives. Also, don't presume that all women are feminists.

Marxist feminists stress that the exploitation of women in the home serves the needs of capitalism, whereas radical feminists stress that this exploitation is based on patriarchy. Even though they adopt different labels, their views are not a million miles apart.

Barrie Thorne (Thorne and Yalom 1982) identifies four main strands to the feminist alternative to established 'malestream' approaches to the family:

- Family forms are not based on biological imperatives, but are socially constructed.
- Family members experience family life in different ways. What can be a good experience for some can be very bad for others. In this respect, they point to exploitation based on gender and also on age.
- The family shouldn't be left as a private sphere of experience, another 'secret garden', to use a phrase originally coined to describe the state of education in the mid-1970s.
- The family should be a central area of sociological analysis.

To summarise many of the points made in this section we have outlined the main points for and against the functionalist perpective on page 181.

> ***EXAM TIP***
>
> You'll be expected to analyse material on the family in terms of the following concepts:
>
> socialisation — theory
> social change — power
> social differentiation — identity.

Historical perspectives

Why do we study history? No doubt, there've been times in your academic career when you've muttered darkly about the value of learning about the fall of the Roman Empire or the diet of Cistercian monks. Why do we want to know what happened in the past? Why, in particular, should any sociologist be interested in what happened in the past?

At a most fundamental level, all social analysis can be described as exploring certain core, recurrent themes:

- the sources of stability

FUNCTIONALIST PERSPECTIVE OF THE FAMILY

FOR

+ With the work of Parsons and Murdock we have for the first time in sociological theory an acknowledgement of the central importance of the family. The early sociologists largely took the family for granted and did not systematically analyse either what happened within the family or the ways in which the family related to the wider society. It's interesting that Karl Marx, whose political writings are all about social change, presumed that the family, as a bourgeois institution, would automatically wither away with the overthrow of the capitalist system. The functionalists certainly did not want society to undergo revolutionary change and explicitly highlighted the role of the family in ensuring social stability.

+ Functionalist theory gives us the first clear exposition of the roles of family members, especially those of parents. These roles are clarified both in terms of the life within the family itself and also with regard to the roles which family members play in the wider society. This lowered horizon, in comparison with the meta-theory approach of many early sociologists, allows for the detailed examination of the role of the man in society and in the family; similarly for the woman. There's an awareness that society is comprised of different spheres and that we operate in a number of them.

+ Parsons focused on the importance of women's domestic role, an aspect which has subsequently found favour with some feminists. In functionalist theory, the structure and the function of the family is based on a particular view of the world. This is a world in which the man is able to go out to work because his wife stays at home to look after the children. Society needs men to contribute to the economy and society needs women to fulfil this servicing role for the man. The two roles are necessary and complementary.

AGAINST

− Functionalist theory is based on a consensus view of society, one which presumes that all the members of society are working towards the same goals, all experience society in the same way. The goals of stability and continuity are paramount and regarded as basic human needs. Such a view of society cannot accommodate social change and yet the evidence that societies are constantly changing is all around us. Conflict is seen as dysfunctional because it's de-stabilising.

− Functionalist theory is based on the efficacy of the nuclear family and regards all other family forms as dysfunctional or deviant. There are many other family forms both in 'western' society and elsewhere. These families do manage to 'function' and their societies do survive. Functionalist theory does not easily accommodate these variations.

− Functionalist theory presumes that families are good for all its members. The realities of family life, at least for some people, are very different. Feminists criticise functionalist theory for sanitising the unequal distribution of power within society and condoning the ways in which this is replicated within family life. Women generally play a subservient role, both in society and within the family. The unequal distribution of power and economic resources can lead to extremes of domestic violence and abuse, none of which is recognised within functionalist theory.

- the threads of continuity
- the causes of social changes
- the consequences of social change
- the interrelationship between these elements.

Sociologists want to develop an understanding of the processes of change, of cause and effect. That information is used to anticipate the future, to take action, and is the basis of all social policy.

Much of our thinking about societies is implicitly coloured by notions of 'progress', of linear development from the simple to the complex, from the primitive to the advanced, from the traditional to the modern. We tend to think of the past as a prelude to the present. Certainly, much of the early work on the sociology of the family could be 'found guilty' of making this assumption.

We need to be very careful about how we use terms such as traditional or advanced. On the one hand, we tend to regard earlier forms of social organisation in a pejorative light: they're primitive, simple, backward. At the same time, we indulge in a glorification of the past as being some mythical golden age. The writing of Tonnies on Gemeinschaft and Gesellschaft epitomises this approach. Before the 1960s much of the work on the sociology of the family was also cast in the same mould.

In the past, so we've been led to believe, families were large, supportive and caring. There were no latch-key kids and no abandonned grannies. Communities were stable; there was no crime or vandalism. You could leave your windows open in summer and your back-door unlocked all night. The basis of this 'golden age' was the extended family. The coming of the Industrial Revolution caused the break-up of these traditional communities and family structures. Instead we had the development of the nuclear family, a totally self-contained unit, each living in a small house and completely estranged both from its wider kinship network and the community in which it is located.

The work of functionalists such as Parsons and Murdock is founded on the assumption that the nuclear family and industrialisation go hand in glove. For them, the nuclear family is ideally constructed to serve the needs of a modern, complex society, whereas the extended family could be regarded as an unnecessary encumbrance which would hinder economic growth.

Recent research by historians and demographers has shown that, in fact, family structures in pre-industrial 'western' society more closely resembled the nuclear family then was previously thought. From a number of different sources, the consensus now seems to be that the average family size was about 4.75 people, living in what we would regard as a nuclear family. For example, Peter Laslett (1965) found that in the period 1564–1821 only about 10 per cent of households could be described as conforming to the extended family model. Michael Anderson (1983) quotes work on household listings for the period 1650–1749 which suggests a mean conjugal group of 3.4, although the mean household size rises to 4.4 once servants and other residents are included.

Looking at the argument another way, Anderson again quotes recent research which estimates the mean household size in England in 1970 at 2.9, with the mean nuclear family size at 2.8. Again in 1970, about 8 per cent of households contained three or more generations.

In other words, it's a gross distortion to represent the extended family as the norm in pre-industrial society, and it's an equal distortion to deny the existence of the extended family in contemporary society. The figures for the extended family are virtually identical in each case: 10 per cent and 8 per cent respectively. What we do have to be careful about is applying the same label, whether it's 'nuclear' or 'extended', to what may be very different forms of social organisation and relationships.

These various statistics all give the lie to the notion that the Industrial Revolution caused radical changes in the size and composition of households and family structures.

Whilst we're constrained by the quality of information available to us about family patterns and structure in the past, social demographers and historians are building up a more complex picture.

Lawrence Stone (1977, cited in Gittins 1993: 7) proposed a different way of tracing the development of family forms over time and identifes three main types of family:

- *the open lineage family* – common from medieval times until the early sixteenth century; characterised by lack of privacy, extensive kin ties, lack of close relationships between parents and children
- *the restricted patriarchal nuclear family* – from about 1530 to 1640; declining loyalties to lineage, kin and community and increasing loyalties to state and Church; emergence of father as unquestioned authority-figure
- *the closed domesticated nuclear family* – 1640 onwards; coincided with the rise of 'affective individualism', privacy within the home, close bonds between parents and children, strong sense of individualism.

Frederick Le Play (1806–82) distinguished between four family types:

- patriarchal
- unstable
- particularist
- stem.

Of these, the patriarchal family is to be found typically in communities based on agriculture and characterised by stable, long-standing traditions of land-holding. The stem family is a more flexible version of the patriarchal type, still based on the inheritance of property, and consisting typically of six or seven adult members who were labourers or farm tenants.

In both the work of Le Play and Stone we can see how the structure of the family is closely allied to the relationships which characterise these structures. We can also clearly see that the functionalist dichotomies between nuclear and extended, pre-industrial and industrial, simply cannot be substantiated by the evidence.

In comparing the past with the present the differences which do emerge are attributable to other variables:

- the later onset of puberty and therefore of physical maturity
- the later age of marriage
- the higher incidence of infant mortality
- the generally shorter life expectancy.

The causes of all these factors are many and complex. Again, this illustrates the way in which all aspects of the family are interwoven with the wider society.

We now come more or less up-to-date, and yet somehow remain in the past.

In the 1950s, Young and Willmott (1962) researched the working-class communities of Bethnal Green in East London. They described in detail the strong, supportive local communities which were based on extended kinship ties. This family structure was fostered by their geographical concentration in the rows of nineteenth-century terraced housing which had been built around the local factories. Young and Willmott likened these extended family networks to the kinship networks which were believed to have characterised pre-industrial, agrarian society.

Young and Willmott then followed families from Bethnal Green who were rehoused on a new estate 30 miles away at Greenleigh, in Essex. They reported on the changes in family structure which accompanied the move, describing the new family as 'privatised'. Cut off from their extended family networks, the families which had moved focused more on home-based leisure activities and were less involved with the immediate locality.

Research by Michael Anderson (1983) has dug deeper into the myth of the prevalence of extended families in pre-industrial society. He found that, in fact, the extended family network came into particular prominence in the development of the industrial towns and cities. At that time there was no Welfare State, no services to support women with young children, no unemploment or sickness benefit, no housing officers to help you with accommodation. All of this was, of necessity, provided through informal networks. These traditional working-class communities were then preserved in aspic, as housing policies at that time prevented families moving out of the areas where they had initially settled. Young and Willmott had captured something held in a time warp and reified it into an ideal. The stability which was so prized by political commentators had in reality been imposed on these families by external circumstances.

Those external circumstances changed again after the Second World War. Throughout the UK there was a massive house building programme, aimed at clearing the nineteenth-century slum dwellings, a process started by the bombing of these same areas during the war. This is the time of Macmillan's 'you've never had it so good'; when post-war austerity measures were being relaxed and when the notion of consumer spending on non-essential items begins to emerge. It's also the time of David Lockwood and John Goldthorpe's work on 'the affluent worker', and the dominance of the embourgeoisement thesis. We were all becoming middle class, all ensconced in our neat semis with 2.4 children.

Willmott and Young published further research on the family in 1973 – *The Symmetrical Family*. In this they argue that the development of the family in the UK can be traced through three stages:

1 the pre-industrial family

2 the early industrial family

3 the privatised nuclear family.

In stages 1 and 2 family structure and function were focused around economic survival, whether on the farm or in the factory. In stage 3 the focus has shifted towards the family as a unit of consumption, and we see the development of concepts of family life and leisure activities. Within this privatised nuclear family, conjugal roles have become more equal, reflecting the greater employment opportunities for women in the wider employment sphere.

Willmott and Young further argue that stage 3 developed as the result of *stratified diffusion*. This is the process whereby ideas on family form have filtered down from the upper classes through the social strata to the lower classes. As general levels of prosperity have increased and as working people have benefited from shorter working hours, they're able to concentrate more on their home life and are less dependent on the informal support networks of the extended family system.

Taking the stratified diffusion argument a stage further, Willmott and Young then posit a fourth stage in family life; the *asymmetrical family*. In this form, the man is highly involved with his work and leads a life very separate from that of his wife, who has sole responsibility for running the home. This model of family life bears a strong resemblance to the model aspired to by the upper middle classes in the nineteenth century.

Their work has been criticised from a number of quarters, most notably the feminists who challenge their assertion that conjugal roles and relationships are becoming more symmetrical. They also challenge the assumption that what happens to the upper and middle classes today will trickle down to the working classes tomorrow.

QUESTIONS

1 In what way does social class have an impact on family structure?

2 Is Willmott and Young's thesis about the symmetrical family substantiated by the current evidence on conjugal roles?

Current family patterns and demographic trends

We now examine the current situation by concentrating on demographic (i.e. population) trends. In a text such as this, it's impossible to present a fully comprehensive review of family forms or to give a complete set of all the relevant data. At best it can offer a few examples and encourage you to gather more specific data to substantiate your own particular needs and interests.

The material in this section will inevitably be mainly statistical, presented in a range of formats, and supplemented by some comments intended to aid your understanding. In reading any text, there's always a tendency to look at the pictures and skip the tables. Pictures are attractive because it's possible, with the minimum of effort, to read so much into them. Lists of numbers and pie charts contain just as much information, but you perhaps need some guidance on how to read them, how to extract the information. This is both a general observation on your learning strategies and also a reminder that you'll be given questions in the examination which require you to be able to use statistical information.

What questions should you ask of any set of data?

- How accurate are the figures? Do the figures add up? Have they been rounded up or down?
- How were the figures obtained?
- What questions are they in response to?
- Why were these questions asked?
- Were these the right questions to ask in order to gain access to the issues raised?
- Which questions weren't asked?
- Why were they omitted?
- Would their inclusion have produced a very different picture?
- Are there differences in apparently identical data from different sources? If so, how can these differences be explained?

. . . and so on. No doubt you've got the general idea. The essential point to remember is that we all tend to accept statistics as the ultimate truth, when in fact they can be interpreted and applied in a variety of ways.

In spite of these warnings about the validity and reliability of statistics, it's still possible to discern overall demographic trends in family structure. These trends can be summarised as follows:

- Fewer people are getting married.
- There's been a big increase in divorce rates.
- Cohabitation is increasing.
- More cohabiting couples are having children outside marriage.
- There's a significant rise in the number of lone-parent families.
- Women are having fewer children on average and they also are having them later in life.

Now we'll to flesh out these generalisations.

Types of household and family composition

As the most general observation, the 'married couple with children' family type is not the most common family form in Britain today. In 1993 the General Household Survey found that less than one quarter of all households comprised two adults with one or more dependent children. This compares with a figure of 31 per cent in 1979. We know that the 1993 figure includes cohabiting couples with children, but the exact composition of the 1979 figure isn't clear. Perhaps the question on marriage wasn't asked in 1979.

The pie chart 'Households and family composition' gives us some more detailed information on the recent picture. But what isn't clear from this information is the marital status of the couples. Also, there's no separate breakdown of the information for same sex couples, yet we know that this is a developing trend. How many of these kinds of situation are subsumed within other categories?

We can obtain a longer-term perspective from the table 'Households, by type of household and family'.

QUESTION

What trends can you pick out from the information in the table? In other words, what has been happening in the period 1961–1995/6?

Yet more information on marriage and cohabitation:

- In 1979, 74 per cent of women aged 18–49 were married. In 1993 the figure was 59 per cent. (*The General Household Survey*)
- Of the unmarried 16–59-year-old men and women in Britain in 1992, nearly one in five were cohabiting. (*Social Trends 24*)

The pie charts 'Living with partners' present the same kind of information in a different way. Apart from the data relating to marriage and cohabitation, there are two other elements of which you should be aware:

- The figures exclude anyone over the age of 59. We know that we have a generally more aged population. Their experiences of widowhood, single living and/or remarriage are not included in this picture.
- The pie chart gives us information on the number of people who live alone, a demographic trend to which we'll return shortly.
- In 1995, official estimates indicated that 70 per cent of women lived with their future husband before marriage. This compares with 5 per cent in the mid-1960s.
- In the mid-1990s, 51 per cent of all weddings took place in register offices; 32 per cent took place in Anglican churches. (*Population Trends*, 1995)

Households

By type of household and family, percentages

	1961	1971	1981	1991	1995/6
One person					
Under pensionable age	4	6	8	11	13
Over pensionable age	7	12	14	16	15
Two or more unrelated adults	5	4	5	3	2
One family					
Married couple					
No children	26	27	26	28	29
1–2 dependent* children	30	26	25	20	19
3 or more dependent children	8	9	6	5	4
Non-dependent children only	10	8	8	8	6
Lone parent					
Dependent children	2	3	5	6	7
Non-dependent children only	4	4	4	4	3
Two or more families	3	1	1	1	1
All households (millions)	16.3	18.6	20.2	22.4	23.5

*Dependent children means all those under 16 or 16–19 in full-time education

(The *Guardian*, 10 June 1997)

House holds and family composition, based on data for Great Britain, 1991

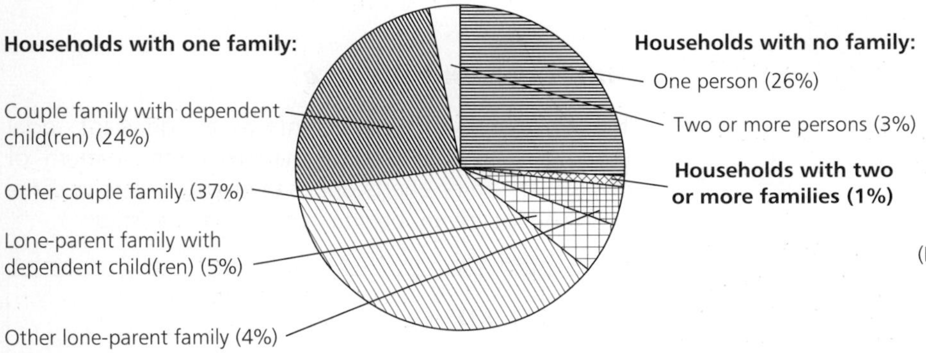

(Denscombe, *Sociology Update*, 1995: 3, using figures from Household and Family Composition, OPCS Monitor, September 1994)

Living with partners: Proportions of people living with or without a partner, ages 16–59

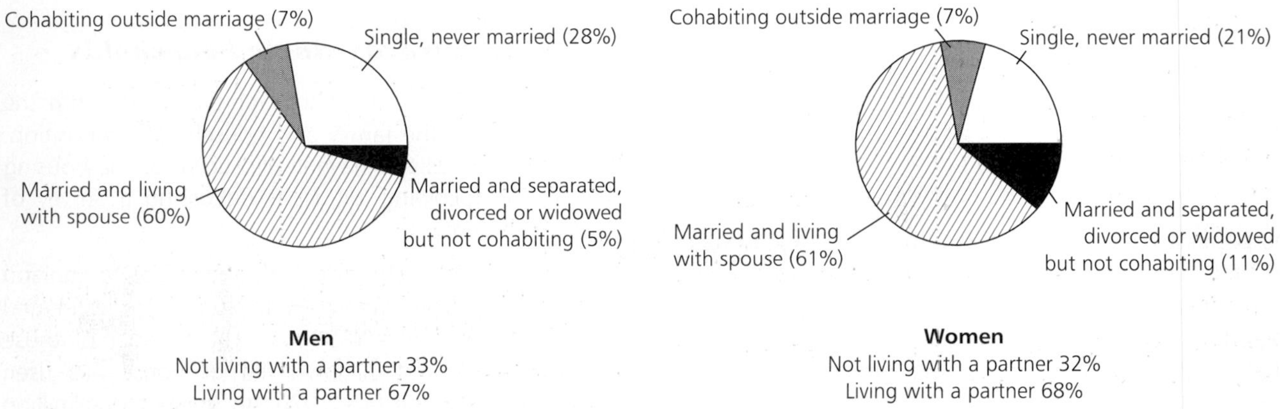

(Denscombe, *Sociology Update*, 1996: 11, using figures from *Population Trends 81*, 1995)

Parenting

- Between 1982 and 1992 the number of births outside marriage has more than doubled (to nearly 1:3). However three-quarters of these were registered to both parents.
- By 1991 there were 7 million mothers with dependent children in Britain. Of these mothers over one million were lone parents. (*Social Trends 24*)
- In 1991 there were half a million stepfamilies with dependent children (which represents 1:15 of all families with children).
- Over one million children live in stepfamilies (which means that about 1:12 of all children live in stepfamilies). (*Population Trends*, June 1994)

Lone parents

The graph 'Lone-parent families' gives us the general picture, both currently and also how it's developed since 1971.

Lone-parent families, as a percentage of all families with dependent children

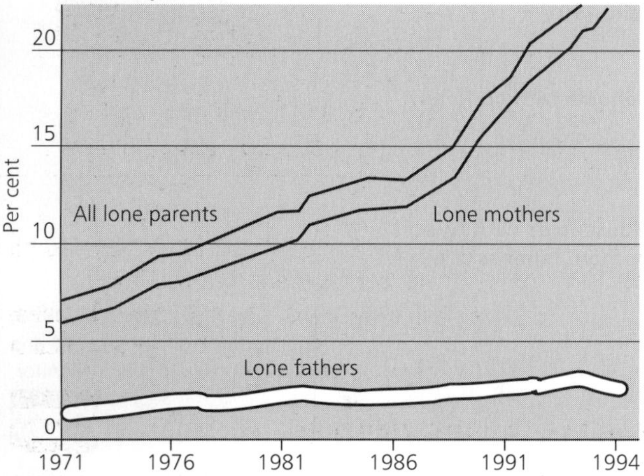

(The *Guardian*, 10 June 1997, using figures from *Social Trends 27*)

Clearly, there's been a significant increase in lone parenting during the last 20+ years. The pie chart 'Types of lone-parent families' tells us more about the composition of this potentially heterogeneous group.

The populist conception of a lone parent is of a teenage girl who has deliberately become pregnant in order to jump the council housing queue. Whilst this pie chart does not tell us the ages of the 'single lone mothers', what is clear is that by far the greatest proportion of single parents have at some time been in a couple relationship.

Types of lone-parent family

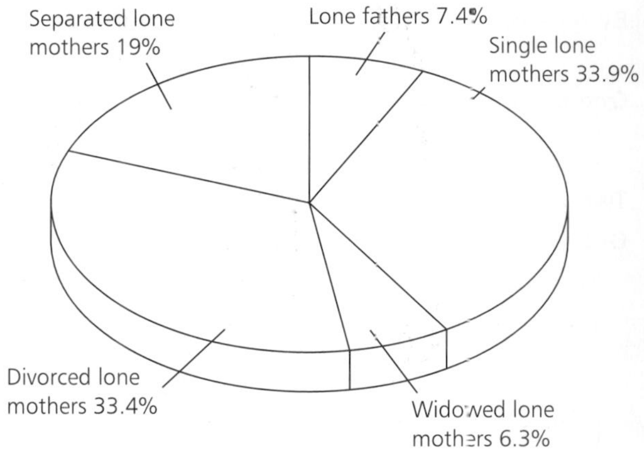

(The *Guardian*, 11 January 1994)

> **OVER TO YOU**
>
> ***Use the earlier work on family ideology to prepare a critique of this data and the prevailing attitudes towards the lone parent. Your analysis could include an assessment of the Child Support Agency.***

Marriage and divorce

The emergence of lone parents as a significant social group is linked in part to changes in the pattern of divorce. The three charts opposite give us access to some of the social trends behind the divorce statistics.

> **EXAM TIP**
>
> Take particular note of the charts opposite – this is the kind of exam question you need to prepare for.

The trend towards single households

So far we've looked at demographic changes from the point of view of the family and household composition. These same trends also have implications for the housing market. The following extract is discussing a Survey of English Housing:

'Since 1971, the total number of households in England has expanded from nearly 16 million to an estimated 20.5 million this year [1997] . . . The number of those who live alone in their own flat or house has risen from 370,000 in the late 1970s to at least one million today . . .

Patterns of marriage and divorce

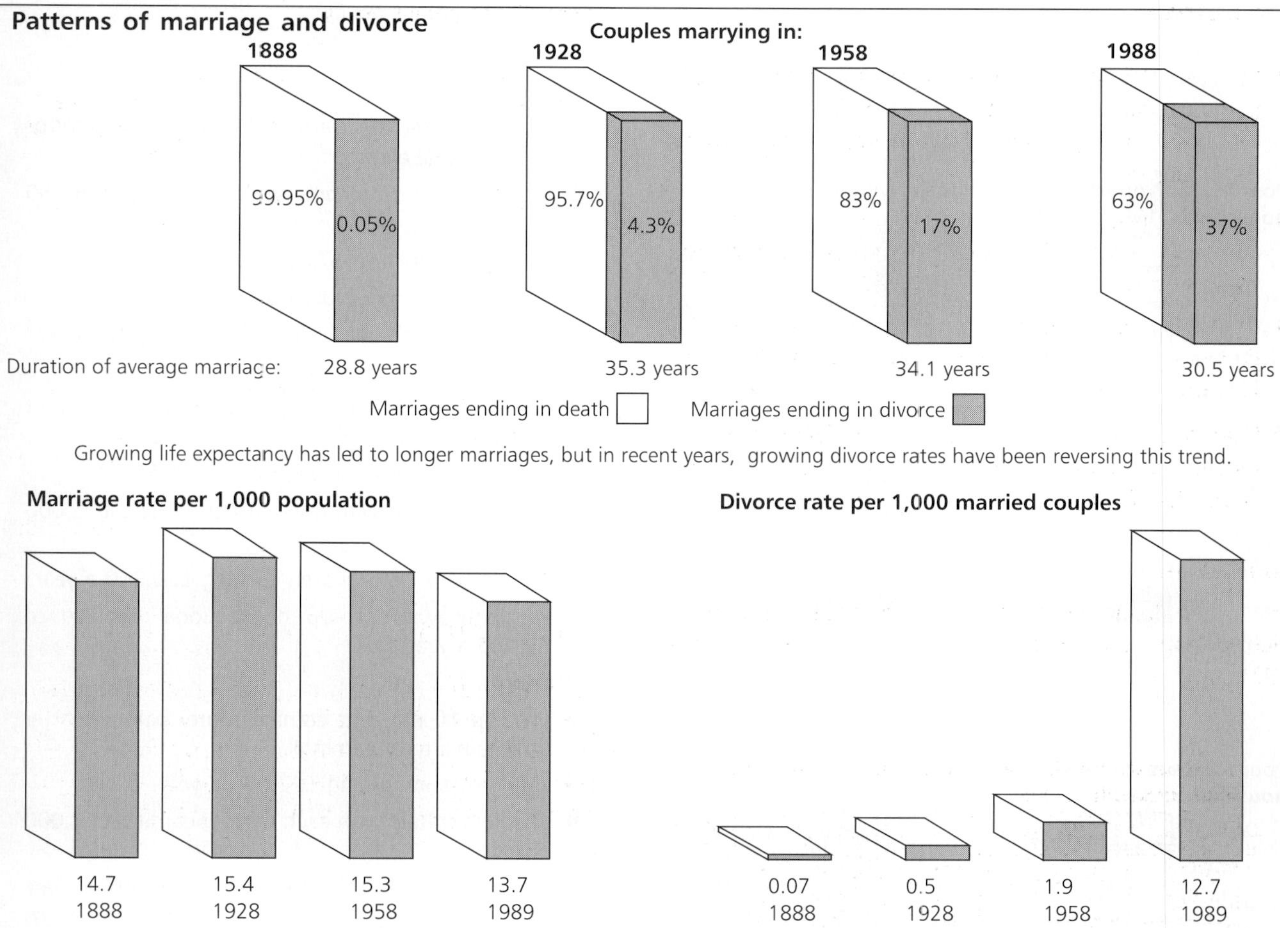

(AEB A-level examination paper, 1993, adapted from the *Observer Magazine*, June 1991)

The change is believed to be due to higher divorce rates, the decline in extended families, the later age at which couples get married, and growing affluence allowing individuals to afford their own homes . . . The increase of openly gay and lesbian individuals may also be having a marginal impact . . .

Single trend: Changes in households, UK

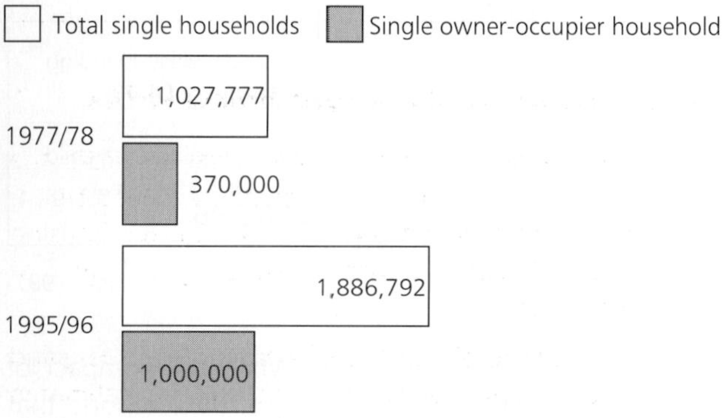

Most of the increase has been among those in their late twenties and thirties. Last year there were more than six times as many owner-occupiers who had never married, were not cohabiting and aged under 45 compared to 1977–78, when such figures were first collected.'

(The *Guardian*, 9 May 1997, figures in chart from Office for National Statistics)

Parenting and poverty

27:47

In the previous section we saw the effect of rising income levels on housing demand amongst single people. There's also emerging evidence from a number of sources on the link between parenting and poverty.

The chart 'Poor living' (page 188) looks at the incidence of poverty across the whole European Union. The figures are for individuals living in poor households. To quote from the same *Guardian* article:

'In 1979, the number of people living below half average income – the official poverty line – was 5 million; by 1992-3 it had almost trebled to 14.1 million.'

(The *Guardian*, 28 April 1997)

Another set of figures published at around the same time paints an even bleaker picture. The Households Below Average Income (HBAI) figures show that 13.7 million people are living below the poverty line. The HBAI statistics also show that 31 per cent of British children now live in households where no one is in full-time employment, compared to 18 per cent in 1979 (see the chart 'Poor children').

Poor living: Proportion of individuals living in poor households, 1993

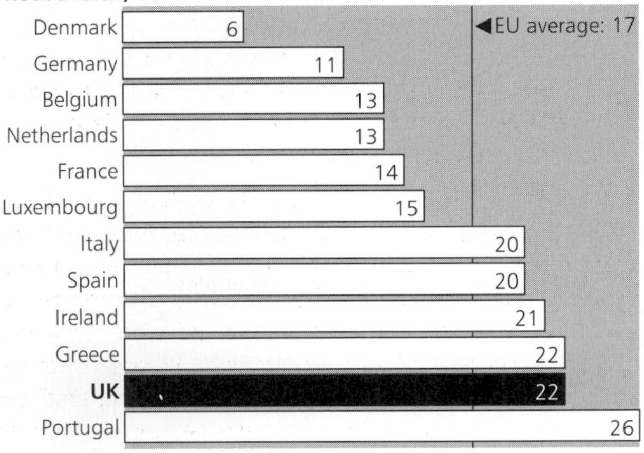

(The *Guardian*, 28 April 1997, using figures from *Eurostat*)

Poor children: Proportion of children living in poor households, 1993

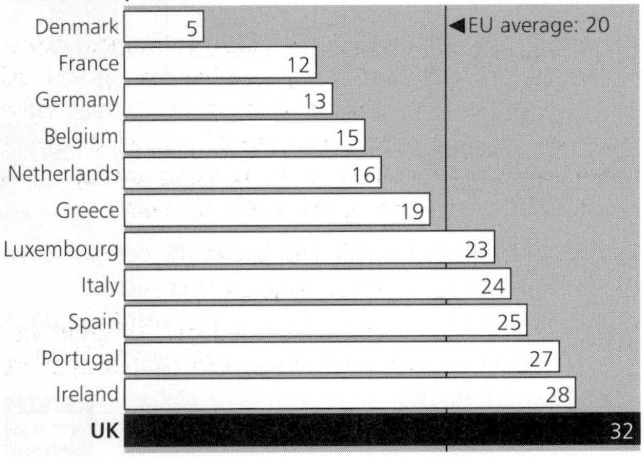

(The *Guardian*, 28 April 1997, using figures from *Eurostat*)

Figures published by the Institute of Fiscal Studies at the end of July 1997 (shown in the chart 'Rich or poor?') highlight the growing gap between rich and poor in British society and also provide further confirmation of the particular concentration of families with children among the poorest members of society.

'Families with children now make up more than half of the poorest decile (10%) group, compared with only around a third three decades ago.'

(The *Guardian*, 28 July 1997)

Just what are the costs of bringing up a child?

Look at the chart 'The price of a child'.

Rich or poor?

The Poor

- Bottom 10 per cent earning less than 3 per cent of Britain's total earnings.
- Single person on income support of less than £50 per week.
- Childless couple on £73 per week.
- Couple with two children on £122 per week.
- Pensioner on the basic pension of £59 per week.

The Average

- The middle 20 per cent earning 15 per cent of Britain's total earnings.
- Single person earning £8,500 a year.
- Childless couple with one partner earning £15,000 a year.
- Couple with two children earning £20,000 a year.
- Pensioner with top-up occupational pension of £5,000 a year.

The Rich

- The top 10 per cent earning more than a quarter of Britain's total earnings.
- Single person earning £22,000 a year.
- Childless couple with each partner earning £17,000 a year.
- Couple with two children earning £50,000 a year.

(The *Guardian*, 28 July 1997)

The price of a child: Average weekly spending on a child, £

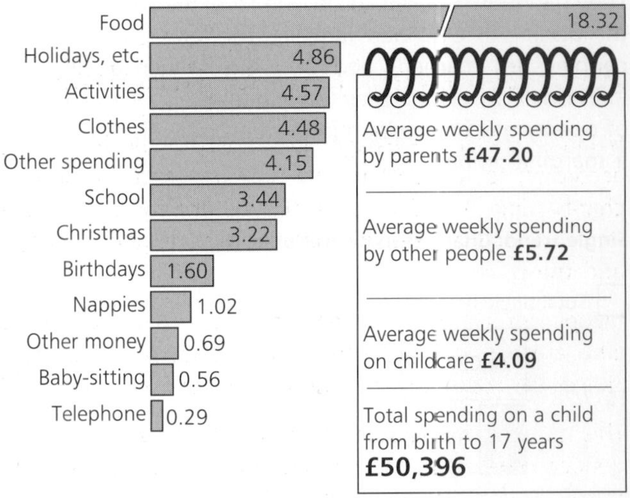

(The *Guardian*, 10 July 1997)

Why does this matter so much? What is the impact of poverty upon children? Lingxin Hao (1996) reports that poverty rates among children have increased in the United States from less than one sixth of all children in 1980 to more than one fifth in 1990. To quote from his article:

'Economic well-being of families with children is an important factor affecting children's outcomes . . . Children who live in poverty, especially persistent poverty, suffer significant disadvantages in physical and mental development and socio-economic attainment when they reach adulthood. They have relatively high mortality rates, poor nutritional status, impaired cognitive development, disturbed cognitive and socio-economic development, and low socio-economic attainment in adulthood.'

(Hao 1996: 269)

Many parents shield their children from the full impact of household poverty. In July 1997 the Joseph Rowntree Foundation published a study of the cost of bringing up a child. They report that as many as 85 per cent of mothers said they sometimes went without clothes, shoes, holidays or entertainment to provide for their children. One in 20, particularly lone mothers on Income Support, sometimes went without food to ensure their children had enough to eat. Half the parents defined by the study as 'poor' had children who were not poor by the Foundation's definition.

The variations in family patterns which we observe reflect differences in social class, in economic circumstances, in geographical location, in gender and sexuality and in age. They also reflect the cultural diversity of our society. Any analysis of the family in contemporary British society must acknowledge the existence of these variations. Remember that what constitutes 'normal' has always to be located within its own particular cultural and social context. Remember also that sociologists have a particular social and cultural context which will inevitably influence their work.

Relationships within families

Is family life and marriage good for your health? 'Yes', according to a report by the marriage and partnership charity, One Plus One. In 1995 the charity published a report, based on research data from throughout Europe and the USA:

'People who are unmarried are more likely than those who are married to die from heart disease, to die from cancer, to commit suicide and to suffer fatal accidents.'

This isn't the whole story, however. There are significant gender differences in the putative link between good health and marriage. Family life can act as a buffer against stress and anxiety, but men seem to benefit from this more than women. In relation to mortality, marriage also seems to confer greater benefits to men rather than women. Conversely, married women experience considerably higher rates of mental illness than single women. It's not clear whether this disparity is caused by their domestic role *per se* or because they're increasingly expected to fulfil both a domestic and an economic role. In playing this dual role they're subjecting themselves to much greater physical and psychological stress.

Is family life and marriage a good experience for the individual? The correlation which we have just noted between the incidence of mental illness in women and being married would seem to suggest otherwise. Much of the early, male-dominated, conventional work on the sociology of the family has tended to be based on two unquestioned premises. Firstly, that the family 'is a good thing'. Secondly, that all the members of a family experience family life in the same way. We've been developing a more critical view of these assumptions.

This section focuses on the realities of family life from the perspectives of women and children, or rather of *some* women and children. Whilst this may seem to be confirming the separation of these two groups from the wider society, that is certainly not the intention. However, it does reflect the influence of feminist research thus far upon the prevailing focus of family studies. Comparatively little research has been done on the experiences of family life from a male perspective. After all, men have traditionally looked towards the outside world of work and have not regarded the private world of the family as worthy of attention. Male house-husband sociologists take note!

The advice columns in the magazines and tabloid newspapers tell us that relationships within families are all about give and take. Sociologists couch these same processes in terms of the exercise of power, of dominance and of subordination. In working through this section you need to think about the following:

- Who holds power within the family?
- What's the source of that power?
- What's the balance of the relationships? (Willmott and Young claim that contemporary family relationships are more symmetrical.)
- What are the experiences of each member?
- In what ways can power be abused?
- In what ways do the balance of power and the experiences of family life vary for the individual over time? (For example, from childhood, to adulthood through to old age?)

Some reference has already been made to attitudes towards older people, both in 'western' and other cultures. The care of older people, and all the complex issues which current demographic trends pose for politicians and society as a whole, are covered more substantially in Chapter 12, Health.

The adult partners: Being a wife and a mother

'Behind every successful man there's a good woman.' How's this for a novel spin to this old adage:

'On Friday June 20th Jonathan Aitken dramatically withdrew his libel action against the Guardian and Granada TV after it emerged that he had lied to the High Court about his trip to the Paris Ritz.

He now faces a legal bill of £1.8 million and moves to strip him of his status as a Privy Counsellor . . .

His mother, Lady Aitken, blamed Aitken's wife, Lolicia, for his downfall, saying she had not looked after him. "She doesn't cook for him – I don't think she even knows what a saucepan looks like – and she spends most of her life in health farms or at airports," she said.'

(The *Guardian*, 23 June 1997)

What does a statement like this tell us about expectations placed on wives?

Jacky Fleming has a way with pen and ink as the cartoon opposite shows.

CRIT THINK CRIT THINK CRIT THINK CRIT THINK CRIT THINK CRIT THINK

LEARNING GENDER ROLES

Perhaps Lady Aitken would be more approving of the way in which Ge Youli was brought up in Shanghai. Although Ge Youli was born in post-Revolutionary China the old ways were still very influential:

'"I lived with [my grandparents] and a grand aunt who had remained single all her life. Naturally, these two older women shouldered the responsibility for making me a 'real girl'. My grandmother taught me by example. She took on all the household chores without complaint: waking up at four o'clock in the morning to line up to buy food; coming home after six o'clock with a big basket of goods; preparing breakfast for the entire family; then doing the laundry, the cleaning the cooking, and the dishwashing. My grandfather, then retired, stayed idly at home, doing almost nothing to help her other than managing the family finances. But my grandmother never uttered one word of complaint . . . My grandaunt gave explicit instructions about what behaviour was appropriate. Sometimes feeling too restrained, I would venture to ask her, 'why don't you subject my older brother to your discipline?' She would answer me coldly, 'Because you are a girl' . . . When feeling wronged, I would again ask her loudly, 'why do you treat me like this?' She replied, frigidly, 'because when you grow up you'll get married.'"

Ge Youli then went back to live with her mother whom she describes as an optimistic, independent woman. School education in the 1950s gave her the confidence that "'women can hold up half the sky' . . . Mum often says to me confidently, 'as long as you work hard, women are equal to men.' At that time, she really believed that the country had created all possible conditions for the equality of men and women. The rest was up to the women themselves. As a mother, she gave me the physical and spiritual freedom to escape the inhibitions of my childhood."'

(Feminist Studies 1996: 502)

This is a long quotation, which raises many key issues.

1 *Using the information given in the extract and also your own extrapolations from it, develop a more complete picture of a 'real girl'. What would its counterpart, a 'real boy', be like? Your 'picture' could be presented in a variety of ways:*
   - *as a piece of writing*
   - *as a spoken piece*
   - *as a mini-drama*
   - *visually, perhaps a collage of images from magazines.*

2 *Education can be used to reinforce behaviour and attitudes, and also to effect change. How successful have equal opportunities initiatives in education been in altering the lives of women in the UK?*

3 *In the extract Ge Youli used the phrase, 'At that time, she [her mother] really believed that . . . ' Do you think that she still has the same beliefs? What do you think might have happened?*

4 *What are the sociological explanations for the processes illustrated here of socialisation, of factors contributing to social stability and also to social change?*

CRIT THINK CRIT THINK CRIT THINK CRIT THINK CRIT THINK CRIT THINK CRIT

(Fleming 1991 [© Jacky Fleming])

This quotation from Carol Buswell succinctly combines two important dimensions of family analysis:

'Women and children have for centuries been defined in terms of their relationship to the kinship system whilst men have typically been described in terms of their place in the occupational system.'

(Buswell 1989: 21)

The status attached to these two roles, the domestic and the economic, are very different. Status within our society is closely tied to economic function. When we first meet someone our opening question is likely to be: 'What do you do for a living?' Teenage girls squirm with embarrassment when their father quizzes a new boyfriend about his financial circumstances. Conversely, how many times have you heard a woman write herself off by saying that she doesn't work, that she's 'just' a housewife? Taking this line of argument still further, how many men are comfortable describing themselves as 'house husbands'?

Lydia Morris reports on how one couple responded to a ten-month period of unemployment for the husband:

'During the period in which Mrs D. held two jobs and Mr D. remained unemployed, Mrs D. worked mornings until about 2.00 p.m. and evenings from 5.00 p.m. until 8.00 p.m. The children had their mid-day meal at school and Mrs D. would prepare their tea before leaving for work at 4.45 p.m., leaving the dishes for her husband. She would then return from work to cook an evening meal for herself and Mr D.

Although in theory Mr D. took on the task of keeping the house clean . . .

"He doesn't like housework anyway. I suppose he thinks it's not manly. He'd dust and tidy downstairs but he won't do upstairs because no-one sees it and he won't clean the front windows in case the neighbours see him . . . "

Mr D's view of the situation was thus:

"A 'housewife' means just that. She's supposed to stay at home . . .

When I was out of work I felt I wasn't playing a part in things, ashamed that I wasn't keeping my family."'

(Morris 1985: 406–7)

Feminist theory covers a very broad spectrum. All argue that women are oppressed, but they differ in their explanation of the causes of this oppression and the strategies that should be adopted in order to overcome it.

Marxist feminists focus on the role of women as carers, thus ensuring that the economically active members of the family are well-supported at home. Capitalism and patriarchy are closely interlinked.

'Wages for housework' has long been a rallying cry for many women, avowedly feminist or not. But how can we cost such activities? The Office for National Statistics is currently attempting to build an economic model for the value of domestic labour. Their deliberations will have to negotiate a feminist minefield! Some of the questions they will have to resolve will include things like:

- How to categorise activities such as gardening, DIY or dressmaking? Whilst all of these undoubtedly contribute to the economy of the family, they're also significant leisure activities. Is shopping 'work' or leisure?
- How much economic value can be ascribed to an hour's cleaning? If the going rate for externally employed cleaners is £4 per hour, should all housewives be 'paid' that amount for the cleaning which

they do? This is called the 'substitute wage' approach. On this basis, the New Economics Foundation calculates (in 1997) that the value of domestic labour is equivalent to £2,368 per head of the population, or £130 billion a year.

- Should the calculation be based on opportunity cost? If the housewife doing the cleaning is also a highly paid professional, such as a barrister, should she be paid at that, much higher rate, in acknowledgement of the earnings which she foregoes whilst doing the cleaning? There are pitfalls in this approach – men typically earn more than women in the labour market and so, if the house husband were to use the opportunity cost argument, he would be a more expensive option than the woman. Mothers contribute 70 per cent of domestic labour, but only 50–60 per cent of the value of domestic labour.

Men also make certain that their domestic travails are noticed . . . Jacky Fleming strikes again.

(The *Guardian*, 10 July 1997 [© Jacky Fleming])

Radical feminists see the family founded on patriarchy as the key locus of the oppression of women. Women are oppressed through sexual slavery and forced motherhood – through male control of women's bodies. This oppression is experienced by all women, irrespective of the economic basis of society.

Marxist feminists point to the interlinking between economic roles in the wider society and roles within the family. Applying this link to contemporary UK, it could be argued that changes in employment patterns are altering the division of labour within the home. There has been a big increase in the number of women who now work outside the home, in both part-time and full-time jobs. What impact has this had on the relationships between men and women, and also on the allocation of tasks involved in running a home and bringing up children? Look at the table opposite.

The more critical of you will immediately point out that these figures are ten years old. Does that mean that the situation they apparently describe has radically altered? Think back to what Ge Youli had to say about the older women in her family and the longevity of their attitudes which had persisted despite the Cultural Revolution.

Violence towards women

The nature of power relationships in the private sphere of the home means that differences of opinion are not just about who should do the washing up or change the baby's nappy. We're all too familiar with stories such as this:

'*Family of four found dead at home*

All four members of a family have been found dead at their home in west London, Scotland Yard said last night. Members of an ambulance crew called to the house in Greenford were traumatised by the gruesome discovery and are receiving counselling.

The bodies of a man and woman together with a boy and a girl aged less than 10 years are believed to have suffered knife wounds.

Detectives are working on the theory that the man killed his family and then himself. The family has not been formally identified and post mortems will take place today. Scotland Yard said the deaths were being treated as murder.'

(The *Guardian*, 24 June 1997)

Until very recently, the police would not routinely intervene in what they called 'a domestic'. Such an attitude is a clear example of what it can mean in practice to treat the family as a 'private' sphere of life. And yet it also contradicts what police officers will readily tell you; namely, that nearly 70 per cent of murders are committed by close relatives.

Household division of labour: by marital status, 1987 (Great Britain, percentages)

	Married people[1]						Never-married people[2]		
	Actual allocation of tasks			Tasks should be allocated to			Tasks should be allocated to		
	Mainly man	Mainly woman	Shared equally	Mainly man	Mainly woman	Shared equally	Mainly man	Mainly woman	Shared equally
Household tasks (percentage[3] allocation)									
Washing and ironing	2	88	9	–	72	27	–	57	41
Preparation of evening meal	6	77	17	–	55	42	–	42	55
Household cleaning	4	72	23	1	45	52	1	35	62
Household shopping	7	50	43	1	33	65	–	22	77
Evening dishes	22	39	36	11	18	69	9	14	74
Organisation of household money and bills	32	38	30	22	14	62	24	15	59
Repairs of household equipment	82	6	8	74	1	23	64	–	34
Child-rearing (percentage[3] allocation)									
Looks after the children when they are sick	2	67	30	–	47	51	–	40	58
Teaches the children discipline	13	19	67	10	5	83	17	2	80

1 983 married respondents, except for the questions on actual allocation of child-rearing tasks which were answered by 421 respondents with children under 16.
2 234 never-married respondents. The table excludes results of the formerly married (widowed, divorced or separated) respondents.
3 'Don't knows' and non-response to the question mean that some categories do not sum to 100 per cent.

(Jowell *et al.* 1988)

The response of the courts to domestic killings has attracted much adverse comment. Firstly, here is a case reported in the *Guardian*:

'Mary stabbed her violent (second) husband to death after six years of abuse. A white working-class woman in her forties, with grown-up children, Mary suffered sexual, psychological and physical violence from her husband before killing him as he was attacking her. She was so traumatised following the years of abuse, and in particular that fatal incident, that she cannot yet give a clear version of events about the stabbing. (She remembers him attacking her and has the strangulation marks around her neck to substantiate this.) . . . Mary has recently discovered that the Crown's main strategy is to discredit her as a woman. They have been approaching potential witnesses to give evidence that she is "less than a saint".'

(The *Guardian*, 11 June 1997)

Compare the treatment of Mary to that of David Swinburne:

'On Tuesday, the High court in Edinburgh sentenced David Swinburne to 200 hours community service – "for atonement". Swinburne had admitted stabbing his wife, Margaret, to death after she had told him she was leaving to live with her lover. Lord Prosser, summing up, told the defendant that he saw no public need for a custodial sentence and that he "recognised the stresses involved." Swinburne's defence rested on two aspects: i) that his wife had insulted him by deserting him for another man; ii) that she had ceased to behave in the manner of a proper woman. While her husband was working away from home, the court heard, she had begun to drink heavily and to neglect her children. She took a lover. She was living, the defence said, "what can only be described as a riotous lifestyle".'

(The *Guardian*, 10 July 1997)

Yet again, we have this notion of a 'proper woman'.

Violence towards children

It's been estimated that 90 per cent of violent attacks in the home take place in front of children or with children in the next room. Says Professor John Collings, an independent Leeds psychologist:

'All children experience their parents arguing. It is part of normal family life. Children have to know that relationships go up and down, but they are normally resolved and a child does not feel threatened. But when you are talking about abuse or violence, this can have a huge effect on them. Children need to feel secure. Their world is built around their parents.'

(*Yorkshire Evening Post*, 1 July 1997)

A statement like this raises all sorts of questions:

- Just what is 'normal' family life? (It's that word 'normal' again.)

- How can a child know when something isn't normal?
- Where does anyone, whether adult or child, draw the line between normal and abnormal?
- Just what kind of behaviour towards children does occur within the home?
- What kind of impact does this behaviour have on the children themselves?

Everyone would probably agree that child abuse is 'a bad thing'. Beyond that there's no agreement on the causes of abuse or on the definition of abuse. There are disagreements over the meaning and nature of abuse claims and also about the means whereby they are generated. Furthermore, there is confusion amongst professional workers about how to respond to allegations of abuse.

In America, child abuse didn't receive much attention until the 1960s. Beckett (1996) reports that:

'it was pediatric radiologists with X-rays documenting extensive damage to children's limbs who catapulted the issue of physical child abuse to the front pages. In the late 1940s doctors attributed children's broken bones, bruises and other injuries to "internal medical causes" but by the early 1960s they were diagnosed as evidence of battered child syndrome.'

(Beckett 1996: 59)

Legislation to deal with such abuse would have to identify causes and this was no easy path to tread. Again to quote from Beckett:

'The passage of the federal Child Abuse Prevention and Treatment Act in 1974 depended upon a "classless" construction of the child abuse problem. Senator Mondale warned that any effort to link the issue to social problems such as poverty and unemployment would lead to the bill's demise. Similarly, policy-makers were careful not to construct the problem as one of unequal power within the family.'

(Beckett 1996: 59)

What's your response to the imposition of such analytical blinkers? How, for example, is it possible to square such an assertion with the activities of these parents which were reported in the *Guardian*?

'A couple who made pornographic videos and sexually assaulted their young daughters were jailed yesterday . . . The attacks on the children had taken place for more than three years.

The man, aged 34, was jailed for life at Swansea Crown Court for the rape of two of his daughters. His wife, aged 33, who was said to be addicted to hardcore porn and had joined in acts of sexual and physical torture, was jailed for 15 years . . . The court heard they made videos of their eldest daughter, who was raped weekly from her twelfth birthday and was given £1 each time . . . The court heard that the children were kept in squalid conditions to ensure their co-operation.'

(The *Guardian*, 11 April 1997)

Whilst this is undoubtedly an extreme example, it also does show how the process of socialisation works by using a combination of the stick and the carrot.

Many writers have stressed the role of marriage and the family in controlling sexual behaviour. These particular instances give a very different angle on this issue. The family does not only exist to control sexual behaviour, but sometimes also to provide a forum for sexual practices. Because the family has come to be regarded as a private place, these practices have gone largely undetected and certainly not regulated by the wider social structure. Only very belatedly, through the involvement of the police and the courts, is social control eventually established.

All of this seems a far cry from the Bergers' cosy descriptions of the family as 'the world' and 'as a place of waiting'. Are we all living on the same planet? How can sociology help you to make sense of these very different world views?

QUESTION

What is the sociological explanation for the kinds of domestic behaviour which has been described in this section? Take the following perspectives in turn:

a marxism
b functionalism
c feminism.

Current issues

It can be argued that the persistent 'moral panic' about the family is generated by the mismatch of familial ideology with the wide variations in family organisation actually to be found in contemporary British society. This familial ideology gives us a clear statement of how things ought to be and yet we also know that the reality around us is very different. It's then easy to take the step from this observation into assuming that something is going 'wrong' and we must 'do' something about it.

We've repeatedly seen how issues of family structure and community structure are closely interwoven. If terms such as household, family, kin and clan are to be understood fully, they have to be set within this wider social context. Many politicians and the press would have us believe that we live in a society which is rapidly disintegrating. There seems to be a melting pot into which has been thrown a mix of run-down housing, poverty, unemployment, vandalism, crime and broken or distressed families. The 'blame' for all of this is variously laid at the feet of parents, changing work and leisure patterns, failing schools and teachers, urban decay . . undoubtedly, you could add to the list.

We're now going to look in some detail at a range of issues about children and youth. This doesn't mean that we subscribe to the (populist) view that this is where all the problems lie – far from it. However this deliberately limited focus does enable us to deal more fully with one aspect of life in contemporary society and hopefully give you greater insight into how a number of factors impinge upon each other.

Attitudes towards children and childhood

In part, this issue relates to the massive changes which have taken place, both in the recent past and cumulatively over a much longer period, in the ways in which we conceptualise the whole life-course. When the family was primarily an economic unit, based on subsistence farming, the concept of childhood (or retirement for that matter) would have been totally lacking from the experience of any individual. Life was hard and all about survival. Children were expected to contribute, in whatever way possible, to the family economy almost as soon as they could toddle. The time of infancy was the time when the child was nothing but a burden on the family, unable to contribute anything in its own right and also inhibiting the contribution which its parents could make. You have to wonder when, in those so-called halcyon days, did any child have the opportunity to skip through the golden cornfields, skim stones across a pond or sit on grandfather's knee?

During the eighteenth and nineteenth centuries there were a number of different attitudes towards children, all of which can be traced through to the present day:

- There was the view that children are inherently bad and need to be saved from themselves. The hell-fire and brimstone rhetoric of nonconformist hymns was used in Sunday schools to quell the natural exuberance of children. This is an argument substantially developed by E. P. Thompson (1968). Toddlers were taught to sing that they were 'by nature and by practice too, a wretched slave to sin'.

  There's not a sin that we commit,
  Nor wicked word we say,
  But in thy dreadful book 'tis writ,
  Against the judgement day.

  (Thompson 1968: 412–13)

  We worry today about the impact of violent TV programmes on young children. What kind of psychological impact would words such as these have made upon a four-year-old?

- In complete contrast we have the Romantic poets. They were influenced by the work of Rousseau and regarded childhood as a time of innocence. This is an extract from a poem written by William Wordsworth in 1802:

The images of children from the past show them depicted as mini-adults. There would seem to be no separate state of childhood. (This is Portrait of a Child with a Rattle, *1611, attributed to Paul van Somer. c.1577–1621.)*

  To H.C. Six Years Old
  O blessed vision! happy child!
  Thou art so exquisitely wild, ...
  Thou art a dewdrop, which the morn brings forth,
  Ill fitted to sustain unkindly shocks;
  Or to be trailed along the soiling earth;
  A gem that glitters while it lives, . . .

Perhaps you're put off by the flowery language, but no doubt you still get the message it conveys. Both extracts illustrate the ways in which a young mind can be influenced.

OVER TO YOU

You'll be familiar with the Victorian precept that 'children should be seen and not heard'. What attitudes towards children and childhood prevail currently in our society? You'll need to substantiate your views and also be able to account for the origins of these attitudes.

Who is to blame?

The concept of 'blame' has already been introduced. The two favourite whipping boys (girls?) seem to be the family/parents and schools/teachers. How can such a consensus be explained?

Amitai Etzioni provides us with a useful conceptual framework. He identifies, firstly, a libertarian approach in which one blames conditions in society for ill-conduct. In contrast, social conservatives start from the assumption that people are by nature sexually and physically aggressive and must therefore be restrained. (You're already very familiar with these philosophical approaches.) Etzioni then argues for a third, communitarian, position: 'Infants are born without values but, given the proper moral infrastructure, they can acquire values'.

What is this infrastructure based upon? Etzioni identifies families, schools and communities as the cornerstones of society (writing in the *Guardian* in July 1997, prior to the publication of *The New Golden Rule: Community and Morality in a Democratic Society* [Etzioni 1997]).

Small wonder then, when we as a society are confronted with the apparent breakdown of law and order amongst young people in particular, that the blame for this is placed squarely at the door of the family and/or the school. The current political rhetoric is couched very much in terms of 'failing' schools and 'failing' parents. What constitutes 'failing'? Parsons would have probably talked in terms of dysfunction. In essence, they're all identifying the same social phenomenon; there's an ideal, a well-functioning state which is not being achieved and whilst society is in this situation, then its stability, its success is threatened.

The family and education

Many demands and expectations are placed on teachers and schools, a clear indication of the pivotal role played in society by the education system; a pivotal role, moreover which is matched by that of the family. Mention has already been made of the push towards including within the school curriculum lessons on good parenting. This is certainly not the first time that it's been advocated. With the introduction of compulsory elementary education in the UK in the late nineteenth century, government ministers saw this as an opportunity to promote the virtues of good housekeeping and family values, amongst the working classes at least. Girls would be taught domestic science and homemaking skills, whilst the boys learned vocational skills such as woodwork. Yet again, we have this reinforcement of the domestic/economic gender divide. More recently, during the 1980s the then Minister of Education, Sir Keith Joseph, advocated that teenage bad behaviour and delinquency could best be tackled by teaching young people how to be better parents.

Parents now are also being exhorted to make a more specific contribution to their child's progress in the early years of education. The value of parents' involvement with reading programmes has long been recognised, but now we are apparently moving towards a formalisation of this hitherto pleasurable, private activity. At the end of July 1997, the government published proposals whereby the parents of primary age children will be asked to sign an undertaking to read to their children for 20 minutes each day.

'"The parental reading pledge will be included in home-school contracts setting out teachers' responsibilities and parents' contributions towards good behaviour, attendance and punctuality which will be expected of the children." The Minister, Stephen Byers, gave an assurance. "They [the contracts] will not be legally binding and there is no intention of parents being sued if they do only 19 minutes of reading with their children . . . A lot of parents are looking for clear guidance about what is expected of them and they will find this helpful . . . There would always be a small minority who failed to discharge their responsibility."'

(The *Guardian*, 29 July 1997)

The family and youth crime

5:02

There have been other recent indicators of the shifting boundary between home and social responsibility, particularly with regard to the 'need' to tackle youth problems. There's much talk of imposing youth curfews, of 'tagging' young offenders, of lowering the age of criminal responsibility. Whilst the proposals are still not on the statute book, they do give a clear indication of the way the tide is moving. Magistrates would have the power to force parents to keep their children in at night. Parents who failed to ensure this could be fined up to £1,000, made to do community service or ordered to pay for the damage caused by their children.

Certain kinds of family and parent emerge from all of this as the guilty parties, and not just in the UK. Here we have Jerold Heiss (1996) writing about America:

'A perpetual part of the "conventional wisdom" is the belief that non-mainstream family structures (i.e. female-headed households or mother-only households) are at the root of many contemporary American problems . . . It seems that every urban disturbance, each increase in drug use or crime, and most examples of individual failure are attributed to "family disintegration".'

(Heiss 1996: 246)

Nicholas Davidson certainly subscribes to this view:

'Fifteen million American children . . . are growing up today without fathers. This is the greatest social catastrophe facing our country.

It is at the root of epidemics of crime and drugs, it is deeply implicated in the decline of educational attainment, and it is largely responsible for the persistence of widespread poverty despite generous government support for the needy.'

(Davidson 1990: 40)

The family, housing and community structures

The important links between family life and family structure, housing provision, and thereby the 'health' of the whole community has long been recognised. There's a long tradition of using housing policy as a tool of social engineering. We're familiar with the various model villages built by nineteenth-century industrial philanthropists, such as Saltaire, built by Titus Salt on the fringes of Bradford, or Bournville, now a suburb of Birmingham, built by the Cadbury family. In the twentieth century we've had Hampstead Garden suburb, Welwyn Garden city, Milton Keynes, and so on.

There have been significant differences in recent years between the approach adopted by the UK government and by, for example, the French. Francois Mitterand's *Politique de la Ville* aimed to encourage the development of new forms of social solidarity.

John Pitts reports on a piece of transnational research which compares the relative merits of housing policies in Mantes la Jolie, an industrial suburb to the west of Paris, and Tower Hamlets, London:

'Mantes: Housing policy aims to locate the children and relatives of local residents in local accommodation in order to strengthen ties of friendship and kinship, stabilise the community and strengthen indigenous sources of social control. As a result, however, many apartments are overcrowded, being unsuitable for the many large families on the estate. Nonetheless, crime in general and violent crime in particular has not risen in recent years.

Tower Hamlets: The housing department operates a qualified first-come first-served system and, by and large, the size of accommodation is matched to the size of families. However, this has meant that "disruptive" tenants, those who don't pay their rent regularly, the homeless, often young single-parent families, and successive waves of refugees are allocated to the estate surrounding the school on this basis. This is producing a less stable neighbourhood with few ties of kinship or friendship. One of the consequences of this has been that the neighbourhood now has one of the highest levels of racial attacks in the borough.'

(Pitts 1995: 4)

Deciding on the balance between responsibility and blame is always contentious and there will never be a definitive answer. We're currently living through a radical review of many of our post-war/Welfare State attitudes towards the responsibilities of the state and the individual. As the location of responsibility is being shifted so it's necessarily matched by a process of allocating blame.

In Bradford the local council is proposing to put 50p a week on the rent of tenants who live on estates which have a widespread problem of theft, vandalism and drug-related crime. The revenue raised from the tenants will pay for two additional beat officers on each of the main council housing areas.

We often hear that the child is the father of the man. In van Somer's Portrait of a Child with a Rattle *(page 195) we see a vision of the adult that child is mirroring. Looking at this picture of a child on a Bradford estate, what picture of adulthood do we get? Are there alternatives to the Bradford model?*

OVER TO YOU

What does such a proposal tell us about:
a the identified causes of social problems?
b the identified solutions to such problems?

The 1994 EU conference on the Family in Europe in the Year 2000 'commended a broader view of the family as an evolving and increasingly complex set of relationships which must be supported by the state in order to maximise its positive potential to enhance the chances and choices of children'.

E. Currie writes in a similar vein about America. He proposes an:

'"active family policy": a comprehensive package of child and family interventions which prevent child abuse by supporting families to cope with "real-world" stress in their neighbourhoods; provide high-quality pre-school education; and a comprehensive youth strategy which offers "changed lives" and extended possibilities for young people.'

(Currie 1991, cited in Barrett 1997: 156)

Both of these examples give us a very different slant on the question of responsibility and blame.

Concluding remarks

In this chapter we've begun to explore the vast and diverse subject area of the family. We've traced how the subject boundaries themselves have been substantially redefined, due in no small part to the impact of feminist thinking upon the whole of sociology. Now the study of the family is located centre-stage.

One of the prevailing themes in this chapter has been the continually shifting boundary between the individual, the 'private' world of the family and the wider society. Throughout time, and in all societies, the same issues are raised and the same juggling act has to be performed. By now you should have concluded that there is no 'answer' to this. What you should also realise by now is the importance of locating social institutions within their own time and space. We cannot understand any element of society if it's removed from its context. Unlike the natural sciences, we cannot isolate social phenomena, smear them on a glass slide and examine them under a microscope.

Our study of the family throughout this chapter has stressed the link between the family and the wider community. This is a link first highlighted by the functionalists and one certainly to the forefront of current political thinking. Practical sociology goes hand in glove with the formulation of social policy. We need to understand more about how society works, how it functions, in order to intervene and make changes in people's lives.

The kinds of issues and problems which make the headlines in the UK today are the same as those faced by every country to varying degrees. Issues such as youth unemployment, disaffection, homelessness and urban decay are all of major social concern and all impinge upon family life. We're going through a fundamental restructuring of the Welfare State and the NHS, and this in turn will initiate a significant realignment of the boundary between the family and the state. We have an ageing population who will have to be cared for, either by the state or by the family. We now have the mantra of 'care in the community', particularly for people who are mentally ill who previously received institutional care.

As a general principle, we can see the state clearly shifting back onto the individual much of the responsibility for care. In the past, the burden of care whether in the community or within the family, has been shouldered by the women. All social policy is based on a specific conceptualisation of the structure of society and the roles played by its members. The policies of successive governments in the nineteenth and twentieth centuries have been based on the assumption that the adult male of the family is the breadwinner and that he is supported in that role by his female partner. During this century we've seen many changes to the role and status of women in 'western' society.

In May 1997 a Labour Government was elected. They claim to offer a new vision and a new set of answers. Whatever policies they introduce, you can be sure that the family will feature prominently. These are very interesting times for the sociologist.

Glossary of key terms

Agrarian Based on farming, agriculture. Usually applied to a society or an economy

Alienation The estrangement of individuals from one another or from the social structures around them. Marx depicts capitalist society as the most alienating form of social organisation

Anomie The breakdown or absence of norms in society. A term most closely associated with the work of Emile Durkheim

Apprentice Someone who is learning a trade, a craft, a skill. Before industrialisation and the establishment of formal training, the apprentice learned from the master and lived in his home as a member of his family

Clan A kin group which claims descent from a common ancestor and is often represented by a symbol, such as the Scots' tartans

Cohabitation (literally means) Two people living together. Usually used to indicate that they're living as husband and wife even though they are not legally married

Conjugal Based on marriage

Consanguine Based on ties of blood, birth

Demography The statistically-based study of human populations, their growth, decline, changes, population movements, etc.

Division of labour Individuals specialise in doing one task or job, on the assumption that other people in the organisation or society will also be concentrating on doing other, different jobs. All of these activities have to be co-ordinated and there is a system of exchange

Extended family Several generations of one family living together

Gemeinschaft Relationships based on close, emotional ties, founded in stable, well-ordered communities. Typically associated with pre-industrial societies

Gesellschaft Describes those relationships typically found in urban, industrialised societies which are characterised by mobility and impersonality

Heterogeneous Composed of different elements

Heterosexual Attracted to members of the opposite sex

Homogeneous Composed of elements of the same kind

Homosexual Attracted to members of the same sex

Ideology Ideas and culture which are linked to the sources of power in society

Kin In everyday usage often regarded as synonymous with a 'blood' relationship. Some anthropologists regard it as a highly variable and flexible social construction of relationship

Lineage Usually used to indicate a biological connection, ancestry

Lone-parent family Typically, but not necessarily, a mother and her children

Mechanical solidarity The form of integration in traditional societies. Social structure is comparatively simple and the clan or tribe are important sources of values and social cohesion

Monogamy The marriage of one man to one woman

Nuclear family Spouses (partners?) and their dependent children. Comparatively independent of their wider kinship network and community

Organic solidarity Typifies modern, complex societies, with the emphasis on individualism, specialisation and differentiation

Polyandry The concurrent marriage of one woman to two or more men. This is a rare form of marriage

Polygamy The concurrent marriage of one person to two or more people of the opposite sex

Polygyny The concurrent marriage of one man to two or more women

Procreation Producing offspring

Reconstituted or blended family The coming together of two previously separate families

Secular Concerned with the non-religious

Self-sufficiency An individual or a group who are able to provide for all of their material needs. Typically used to describe the kind of society before industrialisation when each family unit combined farming with some kind of trade. Such a society has a very low level of specialisation and, in theory, no need for money as a means of exchange

Serial monogamy When one person is married more than once during the course of their lifetime, the previous marriage having been ended by divorce or widowhood

Single-parent family *see* Lone-parent family

Socialisation The processes through which the child learns the 'rules' of society

Symmetrical family Identified by Peter Wilmott and Michael Young in the early 1970s. The domestic division of labour is evenly balanced with both partners sharing in all the tasks involved in running the home and bringing up any children. It is linked to a growing emphasis on the importance of home and family life, especially for men

Traditional A term applied to a variety of non-industrial societies; often counter-posed with modern or advanced

References

Abbott, Pamela and Wallace, Claire (1997) *An Introduction to Sociology: Feminist Perspectives*, Second Edition. London: Routledge

Anderson, Michael (1983) What is new about the modern family? p. 69 in Drake, M. (ed.) (1993) *Time, Family and Community*. Oxford: Oxford University Press/Blackwell

Aries, Phillipe (1973) *Centuries of Childhood* (trans. R. Baldick). London: Peregrine

Barrett, David (ed.) (1997) *Child Prostitution in Britain*. London: The Children's Society

Beckett, David (1996) The case of child sexual abuse, p. 59, *Social Problems*, Vol. 43, No. 1

Berger, Peter L. and Berger, Brigitte (1976) *Sociology: A Biographical Approach*. Harmondsworth: Penguin

Buswell, Carol (1989) *Women in Contemporary Society*. Basingstoke: Macmillan

Davidson, Nicholas (1990) Life without father; America's greatest social catastrophe, p. 40 in *Policy Review*, 51.

Denscombe, Martyn (1995) *Sociology Update 1995*. Leicester: Olympus Books

Denscombe, Martyn (1996) *Sociology Update 1996*. Leicester: Olympus Books

Edholm, Felicity (1982) The unnatural family, in Whitelegg, Elizabeth *et al.*, *The Changing Experience of Women*. Oxford: Martin Robertson

Etzioni, Amitai (1997) *The New Golden Rule: Community and Morality in a Democratic Society*. Profile Books

Feminist Studies (1996) No. 22, Feminist Studies, Inc.

Fleming, Jacky (1991) *Be a Bloody Train Driver*. London: Penguin

Giddens, Anthony (1993) *Sociology*. Oxford: Polity Press

Gittins, Diana (1993) *The Family in Question*. Basingstoke: Macmillan

Hao, Lingxin (1996) Family structure, private transfers, and the economic well-being of families with children, p. 269, *Social Forces*, September, The University of North Carolina Press

Heiss, Jerold (1996) Effects of African American family structure on school attitudes and performance, *Social Problems*, Vol. 43, No. 3

Jowell, Roger, Witherspoon, Sharon and Brook, Lindsay (eds) (1988) *British Social Attitudes: The Fifth Report*. Gower

Laslett, Peter (1965) *The World We Have Lost*. London: Methuen
Leap, Nicky and Hunter, Billie (1993) *The Midwife's Tale. An Oral History from Handywoman to Professional Midwife*. London: Scarlet Press
Linton, Ralph (1936) The Study of Man: *An Introduction*. New York/London: Appleton-Century
Marshall, Gordon (ed.) (1994) *The Concise Oxford Dictionary of Sociology*. Oxford: Oxford University Press
Mead, Margaret (1969) *Coming of Age in Samoa*. Harmondsworth: Penguin
Mitchell, Juliet (1971) *Woman's Estate*. Harmondsworth: Penguin
Morris, Lydia (1985) Renegotiation of the domestic division of labour in the context of male redundancy, in Roberts, B. *et al*., New Approaches to Economic Life. Manchester: Manchester University Press
Murdock, George (1949) *Social Structure*. New York: Macmillan
Orwell, George (1954) *Nineteen Eighty-Four*. Harmondsworth: Penguin
Pitts, John (1995) Public issues and private troubles: A tale of two cities, *Social Work in Europe*, Vol. 2, No. 1
Rapp, Rayna (1980) Family and class in contemporary America: Notes towards an understanding of ideology, *Science and Society*, Vol. 42
Ross, Ellen (1983) Survival networks: Women's neighbourhood sharing in London, *History Workshop Journal*, Issue 15
Rowbotham, Sheila (1973) *Hidden From History*. London: Pluto Press
Social Trends 24 (1994). London: HMSO
Social Trends 27 (1997). London: The Stationery Office
Thompson, E. P. (1968) *The Making of the English Working Class*. Harmondsworth: Pelican
Thorne, Barrie and Yalom, Murilyn (1982) *Rethinking the Family*. London: Longman
Williams, Raymond (1988) *Keywords*. London: Fontana
Willmott, Peter and Young, Michael (1973) *The Symmetrical Family*. London: Routledge & Kegan Paul
Young, Michael and Willmott, Peter (1962) *Family and Kinship in East London*. Harmondsworth: Pelican

Exam practice: The family

Data response question

Item A

Rapoport identifies five types of contemporary diversity in the family: organisational, cultural, class, life-course and cohort.

Families today organize their respective individual domestic duties and their links with the wider social environment in a variety of ways. The contrasts between 'orthodox' families – the woman as 'housewife', the husband as 'breadwinner' – with dual-career or one-parent families, illustrate this diversity. Culturally, there is greater diversity of family beliefs and values than used to be the case. The presence of ethnic minorities (such as West Indian, Asian, Greek or Italian communities), and the influence of movements such as feminism, have produced considerable cultural variety in family forms. Persistent class divisions, between the poor, skilled working class, and the various groupings within the middle and upper classes, sustain major variations in family structure. Variations in family experience during the life course are fairly obvious.

(Adapted form *Sociology*, Anthony Giddens, (Polity Press))

Item B

The idea of 'the family' or 'nuclear family' is an idea with remarkable strength and power – it is something which just about any member of our society can define and which many powerful lobbies (political, moral, religious) claim to support and revere. The image of 'the family' is quite clear.

Our traditional family model remains central to all family ideology. This is a model of a married heterosexual couple with children, and a sexual division of labour where the husband as a breadwinner provides economic support for his dependent wife and children. While the wife cares for both husband and children.

I propose that there is no such thing as 'the family' and in reality, no such things as 'normal families'. The simplest approach is at the statistical level of counting how many families do correspond to the clear image of 'the family'. Work on the 1981 Census suggested that few households correspond to the image.

(Adapted from *The Family in Question*, Jon Bernades (Social Studies Review 1990))

Item C

Preliminary results of the 1989 General Household Survey by the Office of Population Censuses and Surveys show continued increases in the number of single-parent families. The proportion of such families rose from 8 per cent in 1981 to 17 per cent in 1989, of which lone mothers were 15 per cent and lone fathers were 2 per cent.

At the same time, the proportion of households containing only one person rose from 17 per cent in 1971 to 25 per cent in 1989, with only 26 per cent of households in 1989 comprising a married or cohabiting couple and children.

(Adapted from *The Guardian*, David Brindle, (October 1990))

a) State the increase in the percentage of lone-parent families between 1971 and 1989 (**Item C**). *(1 mark)*

b) Identify one way in which the presence of ethnic minorities has contributed to the 'contemporary diversity' in the family (**Item A**). *(1 mark)*

c) How far do you agree with the idea expressed in **Item B** that the 'traditional family model remains central to all family ideology'?
Support your argument with appropriate examples. *(6 marks)*

d) Using information from the items and elsewhere, to what extent does sociological evidence support the idea that there is a 'contemporary diversity in the **structure** of the family? *(8 marks)*

e) With reference to any of the issues raised in the Items, assess the contribution of feminist perspectives to an understanding of contemporary family life. *(9 marks)*

From Summer 1993 AEB Paper 1 A Level Sociology

9 Education

Topics covered in this chapter
- *Sociological theories of education*
- *The relationship between education and social mobility*
- *Educational achievement*
- *School curriculums*
- *Teachers and students*

'He tried to kick me, in fact he did kick me, and his mother then came to school and abused me . . . '

You might think that comment came from a teacher at the 'infamous' Ridings School in Halifax, where, we're told by the media, such unruly, disruptive behaviour was a common occurrence before the arrival of a new headteacher in late 1996. In fact, it's an extract from a school logbook for the year 1884 (cited by Mick McManus 1996: 58).

While it's true that the number of students excluded from school has risen quite significantly in recent years, it's also very important to make the sociological point that most students, according to their teachers, behave well in class. Getting that sense of proportion is what distinguishes rigorous social scientific evidence from hearsay media sensationalism.

In this chapter, we're going to look at sociological theorising about and sociological investigations of key educational issues. In that context, the way students think, behave and learn are crucially important. For education is a powerful shaping process, the experience of and the outcome of which varies quite considerably between different people. Girls outperform

This teacher is helping a student to read. Reading is a key skill in society. It's also an important vehicle of culture.

boys at GCSE and, to some extent, at A-level. Asian minority communities contain some of the highest and the lowest achieving students. White boys who misbehave are more often treated with greater leniency by teachers than black boys who misbehave. Middle- and upper-class students are more likely than working-class students to go to university – but things look set to change here.

These are just some of the issues that sociologists seek to understand, and explain. Good understanding and valid explanations of educational processes help us to improve education for everybody. It's important that sociologists play a significant role in that endeavour. For education, perhaps more than anything else, is the most vital social and economic investment any society can make in the quest for a better today and an even better tomorrow.

Sociological theories of education

Education has a high profile in British society. Politicians and the mass media have put it on the national agenda. As a sociology student, you'll be examining an educational system which has recently undergone a transformation. The government, through its introduction in 1988 of the National Curriculum, has wrested control from schools and town halls. Politicians now decide what children are taught. But they haven't been able to control educational outcomes. Social class, gender and ethnicity are still powerful predictors of how well students perform at school.

In this chapter, you'll explore what goes on in schools and what comes out of schools. Unlike politicians and journalists, however, you'll be bringing social scientific evidence to bear on the conclusions you arrive at.

Education as socialisation

Societies endure because they transmit their cultures and knowledge to new-born members through *socialisation*. The process of socialisation typically begins in the family (*primary socialisation*), but it branches out as the child grows to include other institutions – peer groups, mass media, schools, etc. (*secondary socialisation*). Much of what goes on during socialisation involves values, norms, language, shared meanings and customs soaking into us without the need for formal instruction. However, education, as Emile Durkheim points out, consists 'of a systematic socialization of the young generation' (Durkheim 1956a, in the School and Society Course Team at the Open University 1973: 92). It is, as he puts it, 'the influence exercised by adult generations on those not yet ready for social life' (1956b: 71).

In every human being, notes Durkheim, there's an individual being and a social being. The individual being is a mental state that constitutes a person's unique personality. The social being comprises the beliefs and behaviours that express a person's awareness of being a member of society. You, for example, have certain unique mental qualities that define your individuality. You also have a social side that expresses, among other things, your sense of being African–Caribbean, English, Irish, Scottish, Welsh, European, or whatever. It's this social side that socialisation imparts and shapes, and 'To constitute this being in all of us is the end [i.e. the aim] of education' (Durkheim 1956a, in the School and Society Course Team at the Open University 1973: 92).

While some education takes place in families, places of worship, among friends, watching television and in other settings, schools are the main transmitters of formal education and, in that respect, of formal socialisation. By formal, we mean the directed learning of things that are deemed as 'proper' attitudes and behaviour, and 'relevant' knowledge.

OVER TO YOU

What attitudes and behaviour of its students does your school or college deem to be 'proper' and what knowledge 'relevant'? How does your school or college seek to socialise you into the things it values?

What is very interesting about schools is that, for most people, they're a relatively modern phenomena. Even though they existed in ancient times, schools were attended by a very small percentage of the population. Only in the last 100–150 years have they become compulsory and common. In pre-industrial societies, the process of cultural transmission through the generations didn't need schools to hammer people into shape. Village life was characterised by common values, imparted by family, church and community without specialised help from schools. In industrial and post-industrial societies, things have changed. People lead more individualistic lives, and schools are expected to forge a common adherence to societal values.

What kinds of socialisation they impart and for whose benefit are the subjects of vigorous debate in sociology. Should schools, for example, create a melting pot national culture from lots of diverse elements? Or is it the role of schools to promote cultural diversity and mutual toleration? To be well-informed about these and other important issues, we need to return to the three main sociological theories, and to examine their application in the context of education. We'll first consider functionalist theory, then marxist theory, and, finally, social constructionist theory.

Functionalist theory of education

Functionalism examines institutions in relation to the functions they perform in society. Functionalists don't necessarily condone what institutions do, but they document what happens. Thus, for example, the functionalist sociologist, Emile Durkheim, didn't say that schools *should* have the function of educating people in relation to societal needs. He simply noted that this was how schools tended to function. Given therefore that education is one of the means by which society perpetuates itself, 'the moral organization of the school must reflect that of civil society' (Durkheim 1904–5: 105). The school, in turn, immerses the child into its norms and values. Durkheim emphasised this point when, in reference to Jesuit schooling, he remarked that:

'The child's moral environment followed him [*sic*] wherever he went; all around him he heard the same ideas and the same sentiments being expressed with the same authority.'

(Durkheim 1904–5: 102)

Because most children turn into relatively law-abiding adults, it seems reasonable to assume that education promotes consensus and keeps disorder at bay.

As well as inculcating morals, education helps society to ensure that its members are equipped with the knowledge and skills to work. The functionalist sociologist, Talcott Parsons, makes these points explicit when he writes:

'experience in the course of formal education is to be regarded as a series of apprenticeships for adult occupational roles.'

(Parsons 1964: 239–40)

He continues:

'There is, then a sense in which the school system is a microcosm of the adult occupational world, and experience in it is a main field of operation of the second stage mechanisms of socialization, the specification of role-orientations.'

(Parsons 1964: 240)

Incidentally, don't worry if you find Parsons' language rather difficult to understand. He even has that effect on professors of sociology! His main point is that schools, as part of *secondary socialisation* – *primary socialisation* beginning in the family – teach and prepare students for their work roles in adult life.

Functionalists tend to emphasise the positive contributions of education to the smooth functioning of society. In that context, they argue that education helps to integrate young people into their adult roles as loyal citizens and competent workers. Society thereby uses education in order to make people in its own image. As Durkheim puts it:

'The man [*sic*] whom education should realise in us is not the man such as nature has made him, but as society wishes him to be; and it wishes him such as its internal economy calls for.'

(Durkheim 1956b: 122)

During the 1950s and 1960s, functionalism was the main player in sociological thinking about education. From the 1970s onwards, however, functionalist theory was largely eclipsed by a shift towards marxist and social constructionist theories, both of which looked more searchingly at the question, 'Whose interests does education serve?' The 'new sociology of education', as it was called – a hybrid of marxist and social constructionist propositions – wasn't satisfied with the rather bland reply: society. It dug deeper and looked further, and concluded that education generally served the interests of the rich and powerful – and also exploited the working class.

It would be a mistake, however, to think that functionalism looks unfavourably on working-class children. Indeed, as Robert Burgess notes, functionalism is a theory:

'whereby education was seen in terms of its function to provide a literate and adaptable workforce . . . coupled with an interest in the wastage of working class ability.'

(Burgess 1986: 12)

The two main functions of education, according to functionalist theory, are to:

- transmit norms and values from one generation to another, thereby promoting social stability
- provide children with the knowledge and skills that create tomorrow's workforce, thereby meeting society's economic needs.

Looking at what these functions mean in relation to schooling in the UK, we find that students are encouraged and helped to acquire and value a 'British way of life'. In this manner, children from a wide range of social and ethnic backgrounds are immersed within a curriculum that cherishes and promotes British history and English literature. Whatever their origins, they're socialised into and thereby prepared for 'responsible' citizenship. It's also evident that schools are designed to equip students with appropriate knowledge and skills. In that respect, society's economic needs are paramount. For without an education system that is able to provide future workers with the technological expertise to discharge their occupational roles, society would come to a standstill.

Writing in the 1960s, Burton Clark, a notable contributor to the sociology of education in the US, noted that:

'Greater schooling for greater numbers also has brought with it and evidently implies, a greater practicality in what the schools teach and what they do for students.'

(Clark 1962, cited by Karabel and Halsey 1977: 9)

Present-day politicians also embrace this classic functionalist argument when they call for, and implement, school curriculum reforms that are geared to labour market needs. They have a strong argument. Contemplate, for example, a UK without doctors, refuse collectors, scientists, engineers, paramedics, and so forth. Seen in this light, functionalism envisages the school as both a provider and a selector of skill potentials. The aspiring medical student requires a good grounding in basic sciences, the would-be mechanical engineer will have to focus on design and technology, and so forth.

While each will study the National Curriculum, they'll also need to embellish this with carefully chosen options, and specialist post-16 courses. This is where education functions as an assessor and a provider for different types of talent. If you haven't already done so, it would be very helpful at this stage for you to read the section on the functionalist theory of social stratification in Chapter 7, especially the parts that deal with Davis and Moore (page 142). Without going over too much of the same ground, this theory proposes that education helps to ensure that the most suitably qualified people 'deservedly' tend to get the most important and the best paid jobs. It's that 'deservedly' tag which grinds with critics of the Davis and Moore thesis. 'Deservedly, says who?', they ask.

In reply to that question, one might argue that people who defer employment in order to undergo lengthy university and postgraduate training – doctors and lawyers, for example – would be less likely to do so if they didn't anticipate a lucrative payback at the end of the day. On the other hand, it's also arguable that university life is far more agreeable than dull, low-paid employment. So where do we go from here? The short answer is we try to ensure that our theories describe *what is* rather than *what ought* to be.

Although functionalism has its critics, even they have to concede that the pathbreaking scholarship of functionalist sociologists like Durkheim and Parsons laid the foundation for the sociology of education. It seems appropriate therefore at this point to consider the principal arguments for the functionalist theory of education (see below) before looking at its main limitations.

Marxist theory of education

Marx sometimes went hungry to pay for the education of his three daughters, who were brought up in nineteenth-century London. But he was sceptical of compulsory education, such as existed in Prussia and America, because he believed it transmitted ruling-class ideology. Here we see a radically different concept of national education to that held by functionalist sociologists. Far from serving the useful function of transmitting moral values from one generation to the next, Marx

FUNCTIONALIST THEORY OF EDUCATION

FOR

+ Its wide-lens perspective brings to the surface issues that might remain concealed or remote when analysis doesn't, as sometimes happens in social constructionist theory, go beyond the level of the classroom or the individual school.
+ Linked to the preceding point, it accurately links what goes on in schools and other educational institutions with the 'systemic' needs of the wider society. In that respect, the biological analogy of the school as an 'organ' whose function is to serve the 'body', that is society, is a helpful one – provided we remember that it *is* an analogy.
+ It properly identifies the school as a transmitter of knowledge, norms and values, and as a selector, through its assessment system, of post-school role allocation in further and higher education, and/or employment. While it's true that some functionalists (for example, Davis and Moore) seem to regard this as a useful function, as a theory, functionalism posits rather than judges.

AGAINST

– It overstates the extent to which education serves the common good, and understates the extent to which schools promote the interests of dominant groups in society, thereby tending to 'take the side' of the *status quo*.
– Being a macro-approach, functionalism doesn't get as close as it might do to the different ways in which students and teachers make sense of their educational experiences. There's a bit too much 'sociologists know more than you guys' happening here.
– It exaggerates the influence of education by placing too much emphasis on the power of schools to shape attitudes and behaviour, and too little emphasis on the ways in which some people contest and overcome social forces.

feared that schools would help the rich and powerful to indoctrinate working-class children into early submission. As he cogently put it in a lecture he gave at a German Working Men's Association in 1847, 'by moral education the bourgeois understands the drumming into the head of bourgeois principles' (in Saul K. Padover 1979: 205). Marx added, in deliberately ironic tone, that:

'The actual meaning of education in the minds of the philanthropic economists [the intellectual defenders of capitalism] is this: Every worker should learn as many branches of labour as possible, so that if, either through the application of new machinery or through a changed division of labor, he [*sic*] is thrown out of one branch, he can easily be accommodated in another.'

(cited by Padover 1979: 205)

Although marxists, like functionalists, recognise that schools provide different job opportunities to different people, they pointedly add that employers use education to filter out:

- for middle- and upper-class entrants to their own ranks, people who have been 'educated' into knowledge and culture that primes them for the top jobs and positions
- for working-class entrants to the lower ranks, people whose schooling has provided knowledge suited to manual and routine non-manual work, and which has instilled a respect for the carriers of 'high culture'.

The above two propositions constitute two closely related marxist theories: the *theory of social reproduction* and the *theory of cultural reproduction*. These theories propose that the education system reproduces the respective social and cultural rankings of different classes over generations. The people at the top get an education that equips them with leadership know-how and 'style', and the people lower down the ladder learn more basic skills and how to be compliant to their managers and bosses. In that respect, schools provide a social and cultural training ground and a rite of passage into adult work roles. Moreover, each class is helped to self-recruit from among its own.

The theory of social reproduction theory is very much associated with the work of the American social scientists, Herbert Bowles and Samuel Gintis (1976), and the theory of cultural reproduction with the work of the French sociologists, Pierre Bourdieu and Jean-Claude Passeron (1977). Bowles and Gintis state their argument as follows:

'The educational system, basically, neither adds to nor subtracts from the degree of inequality and repression originating in the economic sphere. Rather, it reproduces and legitimates a preexisting pattern in the process of training and stratifying the work force.'

(Bowles and Gintis 1976: 265)

Using even more complex sounding language, Bourdieu and Passeron contend that:

'The School today succeeds, with the ideology of natural "gifts" and innate "tastes", in legitimating the circular reproduction of social hierarchies and educational hierarchies.'

(Bourdieu and Passerson 1977: 208)

OVER TO YOU

Try to put the two preceding quotes, from Bowles and Gintis and from Bourdieu and Passeron, into simple, straightforward language.

Incidentally, Bowles and Gintis (1976) sometimes refer to the theory of social reproduction as the *Correspondence Principle* because what goes on in school corresponds to what later goes on at work – teachers command, as do managers, for example.

Bowles and Gintis don't stop at the identification of a problem. They propose a solution: socialism. Defining this political creed as:

'a system of economic and political democracy in which individuals have the right and obligation to structure their work lives through direct participatory control,'

(Bowles and Gintis 1976: 266)

they argue that socialism will liberate education, enabling it to promote personal development and equality. However, while they reject the conventional power relationship between teachers and students as a dress rehearsal for future work roles, they anticipate that teachers would impose reasonable constraints on students in a socialist society. Invoking a rather functionalist-sounding justification for this, they point out that the teacher, any teacher, 'is delegated by society to mediate the passage to adulthood' (1976: 266).

The argument that education in capitalist society is a tool of ruling-class ideology underpins marxist theory. Arguably, the strongest adherent of this position is the French structuralist sociologist, Louis Althusser (1971). Structuralism is a very deterministic perspective. It regards individuals as the 'effects' of social structure – literally as 'subjects' who are 'subjected' to the structure that is society. According to Althusser, this 'subjection' is accomplished the 'hard way' or the 'easy way' – through force or persuasion. These two forms of social control are exercised through what Althusser calls the Repressive State Apparatus (whose agents – soldiers, for example – predominantly use violence) and the Ideological State Apparatus (whose agents – teachers, for example – predominantly employ enticement). In shorthand, these two apparatuses are often referred to as the RSA and the ISA.

Like Bowles and Gintis (1976) and Bourdieu and Passeron (1977), Althusser regards the function of ideology as: 'to reproduce the social relations of production' (1971, cited by Stuart Hall 1996: 12) – namely, to recruit students into dominant and subordinate social classes. He also envisages tough back-up in the form of the RSA, the most powerful element of which is:

'the army, which (the proletariat has paid for this experience with its blood) intervenes directly as a supplementary repressive force in the last instance, when the police and its specialized auxiliary corps are "outrun by events".'

(Althusser 1971: 131–2)

OVER TO YOU

a *Using Althusser's concepts of ISA and RSA, under which of those headings do you think he would have placed the following elements of the apparatuses?*

Legal system	*Political parties*
Religion	*Family*
Trade union	*Army*
Police	*Mass media*
Civil service	*Government*
Workplace	*School*
Pressure group	

Culture (for example, literature, art, sport)

b *Taking each element in turn, how might they discharge a repressive or ideological role on behalf of the ruling class? Might any of these elements oppose the ruling class?*

c *Does the teaching of A-level sociology transmit ruling-class ideology? Apply this question to other school subjects.*

Another important marxist sociologist, Ralph Miliband (1969), argues, like Althusser and other cultural and social reproduction theorists, that education consolidates and reinforces the power of the dominant economic class. In that context, Miliband believes that schools play a role of 'political socialisation'. Private schools do this overtly, and state schools do it covertly. The upshot is that education is out of touch with working-class culture, confirms the alleged inadequacy of most working-class students, and instils the semblance of a consensus that serves the interests of the dominant economic class.

You might think that the theories of social and cultural reproduction/ISA sound a bit conspiratorial. They seem to suggest that school teachers 'conspire' with the ruling class to ensure that some children are primed for leadership and others for servitude. Speaking as teachers, we don't regard our role as one of colluding with the rich and powerful in an attempt to provide different learning cultures for future leaders and servants. On the contrary, Paul Stephens, for example, reported that his aim as a teacher was to 'enhance the life chances of school students by providing them – all of them – with opportunities to maximise their credentialised learning outcomes' (Stephens 1996: 25).

In seeking to do that, he set up a 'shared gatekeeping' role between teachers at his school and admission tutors at a local university to help give 'socially disadvantaged' high school students a better chance of going to university. On a personal level, at least, we reject the 'charge' that we're complicit agents of some ruling class-orchestrated process of social and cultural reproduction.

Another example of a teacher who isn't an agent of white, upper-class, male ideology is referred to by Saeeda Cahanum:

'Molly Somerville [who teaches at Bradford Muslim Girls' School], a charismatic white woman, dressed in a *shalwaar-kameez* and wearing earrings shaped like the continent of Africa, teaches French and the Christian element of religious studies. The only presence of Islam in the French lesson is the press cuttings of the three French Muslim Alchaboun sisters involved in the campaign to allow them to wear the *hijab* (veil) to school. In the afternoon the same classroom doubles as a room for religious studies. Today the girls are learning about leprosy. They are told to look it up in the Bible and the Koran and compare the two. The girls then discuss modern-day equivalents of outcasts. Suggestions made include people with AIDS, the homeless and people with disabilities.'

(Cahanum 1992, in Giddens 1992: 210)

Even if some schools and some teachers, consciously or otherwise, transmit aspects of ruling-class ideology, we mustn't forget that some students, as Michael Apple contends, offer 'resistance' by 'acting in ways that often contradict . . . expected norms and dispositions which pervade the school' (Apple 1982: 95). In this way, authentic working-class culture (students who resist typically come from this class) strikes back in heroic fashion at an imposed middle-class curriculum. The important issue of student resistance will be examined more fully in the section on teachers and students (pages 220–5).

While, as teachers, we contest the idea that we're active agents of the ISA, as sociologists, we recognise – as, no doubt do most proponents of social and cultural reproduction theories – that people's actions sometimes have unintended consequences. As Stuart Hall remarks, 'Change in Education takes place because the Capitalist system "requires" it, not as a consequence of the "activity of men [*sic*] in pursuit of their ends"' (cited in Blackledge and Hunt 1985: 159).

Thus, for example, in our teaching roles we've invariably become sorters of different children's abilities because society requires us to do this. Those Year 7 students whose work one of us judged to be at Level 4 in History, for example, gained an academic and, potentially a 'cultural' edge on the students whose work he graded at Level 3. Such gradings, whether or not we like it, have consequences for the educational and, eventually, the occupational futures of our students. It's on this macro, wider than the individual, level that the marxists have a strong case. For education does shake and sift students into different tracks, even though many individual teachers conscientiously strive to help all their students obtain good life chances.

In summary, the two main functions of education according to marxist theory are:

- to indoctrinate the working class into accepting the authority of the ruling class, thereby promoting the appearance of consensus and social stability
- to ensure that working-class people are equipped with menial skills, thereby serving the economic interests of capitalists.

Interestingly, although functionalist and marxist theories of education come at their quarry from different angles, both are macro-approaches and both draw their arguments from broadly similar empirical sources. Where, however, functionalists emphasise the snug and mutually compatible fit between family, school, and work, marxists lament what they see as the transmission of social inequalities through the same three institutions.

Social constructionist theory of education

Unlike functionalism and marxism, the social constructionist theory of education is much more 'grounded'. By this, we mean that it's *grounded* in the empirical evidence out of which it arises. For example, suppose we find, from observing one particular classroom, that disaffected middle-class students 'mess around' there just as much as disaffected working-class students. We might then propose a micro-theory about that setting which prompts other sociologists to look at other classrooms. This would take the debate on counter-school cultures further. In that sense, the theory is a bit like a micro-climate – it's very situational, very specific to the circumstances from which it issues, but it also signals the need to look further afield.

The social constructionist theory of education – with distinctive marxist undertones – came to be called the

MARXIST THEORY OF EDUCATION

FOR

+ As a macro-perspective with a strong penchant for 'detective work', it roots out and documents the extent to which the school curriculum ('official' and 'hidden': see the section on curriculums on pages 217–20) is shaped and sustained by the actions of powerful groups in society. Given that these groups typically occupy and benefit from high class positions in an unequal society, it's likely, as the marxists suggest, that they will continue to use education to maintain inequality.

+ It unmasks the unstated agenda of the school by flushing out the hidden curriculum, especially, those aspects of it that undervalue working-class and minority ethnic cultures and which seek to intimidate students into early submission. In relation to social class, marxist theory also highlights the debilitating effects of low income and poverty on educational achievement.

+ In its emancipatory form, and also in combination with some of the insights it shares with social constructionist theory, it documents an optimistic and a realistic struggle by working-class students and other oppressed groups against the negative labelling they encounter at school, and against a culture that is often at odds with their own.

AGAINST

– In its orthodox form, it exaggerates the extent to which working-class students are socialised into docility towards authority figures – notably, teachers, and later, bosses and managers – and also the degree to which they uncritically accept low-paid, spirit-breaking work.

– It downplays the involvement of lots of stakeholders in the development of educational policy and curriculum initiatives by singling out and exaggerating the influence of the middle class and, especially, of the upper class. In that respect, it's a conspiratorial theory.

– It intimates, in the context of educational practices and ideals, that working-class culture is heroic, honest and relevant, and that middle- and upper-class cultures are manipulative, self-serving and out of touch with the interests and values of most students. In those respects, marxist theory is value-judgemental.

'new sociology of education' in the Britain of the 1970s. Very much associated with the work of Michael F. D. Young (1971), it attracted this name because it heralded a departure from the earlier domination of functionalism in educational sociology. Rather than taking the content of education as an uncontested given, Young and his followers regarded the crucial question of '"what counts as educational knowledge" as problematic' (Young 1971: 3).

There are echoes here of the German philosopher Friedrich Nietzsche's (1844–1900) proposition that claims to truth are merely claims to power. A key figure behind the postmodernist way of looking at the world, Nietzsche contended that what counts as knowledge isn't about truth, but about the power that some people have to make their version of reality stick. Thus teachers, for example, have the power to force their definitions of knowledge on unwitting students, as do other powerful players, like political and military elites. As R. Meighan remarks, 'the technological knowledge to effect moon landings was produced in two societies when the political and military needs were established' (Meighan 1981: 101) .

While the 'new sociology of education' helpfully extended thinking in British sociological circles from just the function of the school to who determines what happens in classrooms, we have misgivings about the word 'new'. Like the term 'postmodern', the word carries a burden of completion which is contradicted by the fact that society is constantly renewing itself. Moreover, while social constructionism might have gathered momentum in the 1970s, the insights of that theory had a bearing on the sociology of education long before then, especially in the US.

Illustrative of this, an article by the interactionist sociologist, Howard Becker, published in 1952, revealed that social backgrounds of students were classified and reacted to by teachers. On this basis, the teachers socially constructed three categories of student: a bottom stratum, a middle stratum, and an upper stratum. While these terms refer to teacher classifications, Becker adds that they're probably equivalent to: the 'lower-lower' and parts of the 'upper-lower' class, the 'lower-middle' and parts of the 'upper-lower' class, and the 'upper-middle' class, respectively.

After interviewing 60 Chicago teachers, Becker disclosed that:

'Children of the lowest group, from slum areas, are characterized as the most difficult group to teach successfully, lacking in interest in school, learning ability, and outside training'. Said one teacher, 'Of course it's not their fault; they aren't brought up right . . . parents in a neighbourhood like that really aren't interested . . .

Ambivalent feelings are aroused by children of the middle group [probably, notes Becker, equivalent to "lower-middle class" and parts of the "upper-lower class"]. While motivated to work hard in school they lack the proper out-of-school training.' [As one teacher put it] 'They want to work and do well . . . Of course, they're not too brilliant . . . But they are very nice children'

(Becker 1952, in the School and Society Course Team at the Open University 1973: 120)

Becker notes, 'In definite contrast are the terms used to describe children of the upper groups'. He quotes a teacher who said, 'In a neighbourhood like this there's something about the children, you just feel like you're accomplishing so much more. You throw an idea out and you can see that it takes hold (Becker 1952: 120).'

But not everything goes the upper group's way. Becker is a very astute sociologist who probes deeply. Although he found that the 'slum' children most offended the teachers' sense of moral correctness, Becker also picked up on certain middle-class attitudes and behaviours which irritated teachers. He thus noted that, 'Children from the "better" neighbourhoods are considered deficient [by their teachers] in the important moral traits of politeness and respect for elders' (Becker 1952: 123). A teacher, for example, informed Becker that if they drop a piece of cloth on the floor, 'they wouldn't think of bending over to pick it up. That's janitor's work to them.' These students were also considered to transgress what teachers defined as moral boundaries in relation to smoking and drinking. Given that most later sociological research into negative teacher perceptions of student types focuses heavily on working-class 'traits', Becker's insightfulness cautions sociologists to look beyond the 'seemingly obvious'.

OVER TO YOU

Using up-to-date social class terminology (refer, for example, to Chapter 7), how would you describe Becker's 'lower-lower' and 'upper-lower' class, 'lower-middle' class, and 'upper-middle' class?

The preoccupation of the social constructionist theory of education is with the classroom. Where functionalists and marxists see the school as an institution that is responsive to things that go on outside of schools, social constructionists turn the spotlight on what goes on between teachers and students. Teachers do, of course, as Becker's research shows, take account of their students' social backgrounds. But it's how they make sense of this in the classroom, and how students make sense of what teachers do that interests the social constructionist. It's here that the so-called 'new sociology of education' comes into its own.

A very important study of the classroom from the 'new sociology' stable was conducted by Nell Keddie (1971) in a large girls and boys' comprehensive school with a fairly mixed social class intake. Her study focused on the humanities department which, in 1969–70, introduced an exam course based on history, geography and social science to Year 10 (then known as fourth year) students. Influenced by Becker's concept of the teacher's 'ideal' student (typically, though not in all respects, from the middle and upper strata defined by him earlier), Keddie found, through observation, tape-recording and questionnaire, that 'the A stream academic and usually middle-class pupil' (Keddie 1971: 137) generally fitted the bill. Says Keddie:

'There is between teachers and A pupils a reciprocity of perspective which allows teachers to define, unchallenged by A pupils, as they may be challenged by C pupils [typically from working-class backgrounds], the nature and boundaries of what is to count as knowledge.'

(Keddie 1971: 155–6)

When teachers label students from different backgrounds as 'ideal' or as 'awkward customers' (as many of the C stream pupils studied by Keddie were designated, 1971: 142), there are consequences. Tell students that they're badly behaved and of low ability, and they might believe this, and act and perform in accordance with the expectation. The opposite might hold true for students whom teachers label as well behaved and intelligent. Research generally confirms that the recipients of negative teacher labelling are black, male, and working-class, and that students whom teachers look more favourably upon are white, female, and middle- or upper-class. There are, however, variations here. For example, a black middle-class boy might attract more positive responses from a teacher than a white working-class girl.

The notion 'that one's expectations for another's behavior can actually affect that other's behavior in such a way that the prophecy is more likely to come true simply for its having been made' (Rosenthal 1975: vi) is called the *self-fulfilling prophecy*. So important is this concept in the sociology of education, that a pioneering but very controversial experiment by Robert Rosenthal and Lenore F. Jacobson (1968) is considered in some detail in the section on teachers and students (pages 220–5). The same section also considers the way in which some negatively labelled students, for example, African–Caribbean girls, contest the labels.

In the preceding sections on functionalist and marxist theories, we summarised the propositions of those perspectives in terms of the *functions* education serves. However, it's not as appropriate to use the term 'functions' when considering the social constructionist perspective. Unlike the two former approaches, social constructivism doesn't view society as a structure with functions, but as a series of constructed and re-constructed social settings. For a functionalist or a marxist, any classroom has generally the same function – the transmission of culture. For a social constructionist,

SOCIAL CONSTRUCTIONIST THEORY OF EDUCATION

FOR

+ It takes things as it finds them rather than assuming that education serves the common good or vested interest groups. The starting point for the social constructionist is the question, 'What's happening here?' From thereon, it's for the evidence to illuminate the event.
+ It gets closer to the lived experiences of real people by focusing on how teachers and students socially construct their educational encounters, and demonstrates how they have the power to affect educational outcomes. It reminds us that not everything is 'caused' by a student's social background.
+ With its astute use of labelling theory, it reveals the negative and the positive stereotypes that students from different class, ethnic and gender groups encounter during their day-to-day experiences in school, and it highlights the effects these stereotypes have on students' life chances.

AGAINST

– Its close-lens orientation sometimes makes it difficult for social constructionist theory to get beyond the micro level of the classroom or individual school. In that respect, it tends to lose sight of the influence on education policy of politicians and other powerful people.

– Related to the last point, social constructionist theory doesn't place enough emphasis on the impact of out-of-school factors, like poor housing, low income, and poverty. Such factors can't be spirited away by what just goes on in classrooms. They do have a measurable effect.

– It sometimes overestimates the influence of negative labelling on students who are judged, on the grounds of 'low' social class, of African–Caribbean, Bangladeshi or Pakistani origin, and in some cases being a boy, in others, being a girl, to be low achievers. Not all students take this kind of stereotyping lying down. It's known, for example, that some African–Caribbean girls successfully challenge such negative labelling.

different classrooms have the potential to *make* and/or *transmit* cultures – or to reject them.

So instead of saying these are the two main functions of education according to social constructionist theory, we'll say these are the two main *understandings* of education based on that theory:

- What counts as knowledge isn't fixed and permanent. It's constantly contested, sometimes retained, sometimes ditched, during social interaction, especially the interaction that occurs between teachers and students in classrooms.
- In that process of interaction, teachers are generally the more powerful players. How they define knowledge and what they regard as acceptable behaviour, carries the authority of society, and is therefore hard, but not impossible, to challenge successfully.

QUESTIONS

1 What role does education play in socialisation?
2 Outline and evaluate the strengths and weaknesses of:
  a the functionalist theory of education
  b the marxist theory of education
  c the social constructionist theory of education.

The relationship between education and social mobility

One of the most famous studies of the relationship between education and social mobility is by Ralf Turner (1958), who, in his paper, 'Sponsored and contest mobility and the school system', contrasted the then American education system with its then British counterpart. As a functionalist, Turner believed that society was primarily concerned with maintaining order, and with that end in mind, 'the most conspicuous control problem is that of ensuring loyalty in the disadvantaged classes' (1958: 77). The American and British education systems approached this problem in radically different ways. American education, reported Turner, was characterised by a *contest norm*, and British education by a *sponsored norm*. The table below, adapted from Turner's work, clarifies these different types.

QUESTION

Unpack the differences between *contest norms* and *sponsored norms* in the table below. Then give some examples of how educational selection still continues in the UK. In that context, consider how people who occupy an elite position in society are able to use education to protect that position and recruit their children into it.

You might argue that Turner's model, at least as far as the UK is concerned, is outdated, now that we've had comprehensive schools nationwide for over 30 years. But the grammar schools that characterised the so-called tripartite (three-part) system of post-war schools (the other two being secondary modern and technical schools) are still around in some parts of the country. Moreover, 7.1 per cent of children receive an education in elite, independent schools like Eton and Harrow (an actual increase of 1.2 per cent since 1979–80: DfE 1995), and the 'old boy network' (male-dominated, as its name implies) heavily recruits future members of the 'establishment' from public schools. In that manner, *elite self-recruitment*, whereby the elite chooses from amongst its own, still endures in British society.

Historically – and things are only recently beginning to change here – the study of education and social mobility has neglected mothers and daughters and focused on fathers and sons. Pick up almost any study of education and social mobility before the 1990s, and chances are you'll find a male inter-generational (between male

Ralf Turner's typologies of American and British education systems

American education system	**British education system**
Contest norm	**Sponsored norm**
• All start equal; thereafter status is achieved through contest.	• People are born into their status which is thereby ascribed; thereafter, the elite are sponsored for the 'best' education.
• All students receive equal treatment based on comprehensive education.	• People from different backgrounds are selected onto different educational paths at an early age. The elite go to the 'top' schools.
• The hope of upward social mobility is alive, and the elite survives because people are loyal to a system where anyone can make it from a log cabin to the White House.	• Education segregates people into an elite and the 'masses'.
• The elite is controlled because everyone knows it can be displaced by others.	• The elite is socialised into 'caring' for the rest of society, and, through public service, is encouraged not to abuse its position.

(Adapted from Turner 1958)

generations) analysis of how closely or otherwise the education and class destinations of men correspond with their and their fathers' original social origins.

EXAM TIP

Point out to the examiner that a major limitation of sociological research into the relationship between education and social mobility has been its marked tendency to marginalise the experiences of girls and women.

In their extensive interview-based study of the social origins and educational destinations of about 10,000 adult men – a representative sample of men living in England and Wales in 1972 – A. H. Halsey, A. F. Heath and J. M. Ridge tackled a crucial question of 'whether education can change society' (Halsey *et al.* 1980: 1). The oldest of these men entered school just after the First World War, and the youngest entered in the mid to late 1950s. Based on the evidence obtained, Halsey *et al.* concluded that 'school inequalities of opportunity have been remarkably stable over the forty years which our study covers' (1980: 205).

They reported that the service (i.e. middle) class has had roughly three times the chance of the working class of obtaining some type of selective secondary education (i.e. grammar type or private). Only at age 16 was there any significant reduction in relative class chances. Yet even here, the absolute gains have been greater for the service class. The idea that the UK had become a *meritocracy* in the 1970s – that is, a society where educational opportunity is based on merit rather than class, gender, ethnicity or other ascribed positions – isn't supported by Halsey's evidence.

The research by Halsey *et al.* (1980) addresses an important issue in the sociology of education: equality of educational opportunity. In sociological terms, *equality of educational opportunity* refers to the prospect of equal access to a good education irrespective of one's background. It's not the same as *equality of educational condition*, which describes equally good educational outcomes for all people. The first is about starting a race on the same starting line and competing on the basis of merit alone, even thought the final outcome usually involves losers and winners. The second means that everyone obtains an equally good final outcome. Most sociologists would concede that equality of educational opportunity is a reasonable goal. However, equality of educational condition is a much tougher proposition. Some sociologists would like to see it happen. Others probably regard it as a fanciful pipedream.

In a later book, *Change in British Society*, A. H. Halsey re-iterated the point that:

'we have been forced to the depressing conclusion that over the first three-quarters of the century, the unequal relative educational chances of boys from different class origins were remarkably stable, and that the conventional picture of a steady trend towards equality was an optimistic myth.'

(Halsey 1995: 156)

Noting that educational reform has moved on since the 1970s, Halsey (1995) nevertheless reports that a general tendency towards inequality of educational achievement still continues. The proportions of students from manual, working-class families entering higher education, for example, has hardly shifted in comparison with students from managerial and professional backgrounds, says Halsey. He adds: 'Class, gender, and ethnicity are now the three giants in the path of aspirations towards equity . . . ' (1995: 162). However, while gender inequalities still persist, Halsey contends that they've decreased rapidly during the past two decades. He qualifies this though with the observation that the entry of more women into higher education is characterised by 'a skewed distribution towards the less prestigious courses and institutions' (1995: 164).

Pamela Abbott and Claire Wallace (1997: 94) claim that girls generally do better than boys in school exams – GCSEs and A-levels. While what they say is true for GCSEs, they're probably mistaken about A-levels. Very recent research by Jannette Elwood and Chris Comber (1996) at the Institute of Education, University of London, reveals that during the period 1990–4, male students outperformed female students in all A-level subjects except physics and geography, and were ahead overall. It should be noted, however, that in relation to A-level physics, the researchers found that there were small groups of female entrants of high ability.

Nevertheless, the relatively high overall performance of females isn't matched by their position in the labour market. Paradoxically, for example:

'the academic hierarchy remains very firmly masculine . . . the higher up the academic ladder we go, the more dominated it becomes by men. Primary and infant schools are more likely to have women teachers and women heads. At the other end of the spectrum, there are far fewer women professors than male ones and hardly any female vice-chancellors or college principals.'

(Abbott and Wallace 1997: 94)

Analysis of female social mobility, note Abbott and Wallace (1997), suggests that it's very different from men. Women are much more likely to be in what they term 'service' occupations (for example, librarian, nurse, teacher) than in 'professions' (for example, chartered accountant, doctor, lawyer). Women are also concentrated in routine office work and shop work. Moreover, there's some evidence, continue Abbott and Wallace, that women are less likely than men to be regarded as 'promotable', and that they're recruited on the understanding that they won't seek promotion.

Things are likely to change, however. The sheer momentum of well-qualified women leaving school today makes that almost inevitable.

QUESTIONS

1 What are the main differences between an educational system based on *contest norms* and one based on *sponsored norms*?
2 What are the key findings of Halsey *et al.*'s and Halsey's (on his own) research into education and social mobility, as reported in 1980 and 1995, respectively?
3 Briefly define these terms: *equality of educational opportunity*, *equality of educational condition*, and *meritocracy*.
4 How does gender connect with education and social mobility?

Educational achievement

Don't believe that your intellectual destiny just lies in your genes. If that were so, social factors wouldn't be associated with educational achievement. However, social factors – as this section will demonstrate – are powerful predictors of what different people achieve. Genes provide the biological material and, perhaps, a potential for learning, but society has a huge impact on attainment. Sociology provides compelling evidence here, especially in relation to the documented association between educational achievement and class, gender and ethnicity.

Social class

Just because the Conservative Party and New Labour talk about what Mairtin Mac An Ghaill (1996a: 163) refers to as 'the classless, genderless, investor citizen', this doesn't mean that class and gender are dead. Both are important predictors of educational outcomes. In the 1950s, 1960s and 1970s, the link between class and achievement was the prime concern of educational sociology. Countless studies confirmed that middle-class students outperformed their working-class counterparts. Among the more important of these studies – most of which, it must be emphasised, only focused on males – were those of:

- D. V. Glass (1954; reprinted 1963), who was the leading light in a team of social mobility experts based at the London School of Economics and Political Science in the 1950s. Glass reported that for the sons of skilled manual and routine non-manual workers who went to grammar schools or their equivalent there was a rise from 2.2 per cent for boys born before 1890 to 10.7 per cent for boys born in the period 1920–9. Referring, however, to the 1950s, Glass wrote that:

  'the general picture so far is of a rather stable social structure, and one in which social status [here referring to occupational ranking] has tended to operate

This advertisement for Book Tokens ran in late 1996 in the national press and a wide selection of (mainly women's) magazines. It was designed to reflect the heights that reading can take you to. The headline 'Who knows where a Book Token might lead' encapsulated the important message that giving someone a Book Token enables them to choose whatever book they want. In this case, the girl at a young age has chosen a book that has sparked her interest to become an astronaut.

within, so to speak, a closed circuit. Social origins have conditioned educational level, and both have conditioned achieved social status.'

(Glass 1963: 21)

- J. E. Floud, A. H. Halsey and F. M. Martin (1958), who conducted research into the relationship between class and educational opportunities in England in the 1950s. They found that the chances of boys getting into grammar schools at that time was more closely linked than ever before to measured ability than to social origins. Even so, they also reported that:

  'the probability that a working-class boy will get to a grammar school is not strikingly different from what it was before 1945, and there are still marked differences in the chances which boys of different social origins have of obtaining a place.'

  (Floud *et al.* 1958: 142–3)

  In 1953, the proportion of working-class boys who entered grammar school in one Yorkshire borough was 12 per cent, and in a Hertfordshire district 14 per cent. Importantly, however, Floud *et al.* found that:

  'what are often taken to be characteristically "middle-class" attitudes and ambitions in the matter of education are, in fact, widespread among parents much lower in the occupational scale.'

  (Floud *et al.* 1958: 87)

  They also drew attention to the material plight of children of 'poor but educationally well-disposed parents' (1958: 145).

- David Hargreaves (1967), whose case study research in a boys' secondary modern school revealed that the teachers there 'constantly under-estimated or were ignorant of the power of the peer group in regulating the behaviour of pupils' (Hargreaves 1967: 183). Hargreaves found that boys who were placed in low-ability streams were associated with a sense of status deprivation at school. But boys in these streams often had no desire to be promoted into a higher stream, and sometimes actively avoided this. High-stream boys, by contrast, had a fear of demotion. Thus, as Hargreaves put it: 'One of the most important results of the segregation of the pupils into streams at Lumley School was . . . that the boys in one subculture perceive the other subculture as a major negative reference group' (1967: 186). This kind of stand-off between academic and anti-academic school subcultures was documented by Paul Willis in his celebrated study, *Learning to Labour: How Working-Class Kids Get Working-Class Jobs* (1978) – see below.

- J. W. B. Douglas (1968), whose pioneering longitudinal study – which began in 1946 – of a large representative sample of children living in England, Wales and Scotland, found that, for middle-class children, primary school and family environments tended to positively reinforce each other, and for working-class children negatively. Douglas discovered that parental encouragement was an important predictor of children's success in picture, reading, vocabulary and arithmetic tests. In that respect, middle-class parents were generally found to take more interest than working-class parents in their children's progress at school. However, Douglas also noted that some working-class parents had 'middle-class standards . . . in their expectations of grammar school awards' (Douglas 1968: 84).

- Nell Keddie (1971), who, through observation, questionnaire and discussion, found that teachers in the humanities department of a mixed comprehensive school tended to see students from the top stream as displaying middle-class, conforming behaviours and students from the bottom stream as having working-class, noisy behaviours. Says Keddie, 'Clearly, A stream pupils' definition of appropriate behaviour in the situation was taken over from or coincided with that of the teachers' (Keddie 1971: 143). By contrast, 'C stream pupils are often seen to lack those qualities which are deemed by teachers desirable in themselves and appropriate to school'. The B stream students were left in the middle and tended to shift around in the teachers' perceptions.

- Basil Bernstein (1973), whose oral and other research revealed that working-class speech wasn't as valued by teachers as middle-class speech, thereby placing working-class children at an educational disadvantage to middle-class children. When working-class children encounter middle-class language – as they tend to do from teachers – Bernstein discovered that they're sometimes left puzzled, because 'The working-class child has to translate and thus mediate middle-class language structure through the logically simpler language structure of his [*sic*] own class to make it personally meaningful' (Bernstein 1973: 47). Failure to do this, leads to confusion and misunderstanding. Bernstein isn't making a personal judgement about working-class language. He's documenting society's judgement.

- Samuel Bowles and Herbert Gintis (1976), whose empirical research and theoretical arguments led them to conclude that working-class and some minority ethnic students in America attend schools where they're subject to very repressive regimes that prime them for the oppressive hierarchies they will later encounter in employment. A more liberal ethos, however, prevails in middle-class schools, which prepare their students for future leadership roles in the world of work. In this way, schools socially reproduce inequalities across generations – from whence derives the theory of social reproduction.

- Paul Willis (1978), whose interviews with working-class boys – the 'lads' – in a Midlands secondary school exposed a subculture among them that rejected academic values and subverted the authority of teachers. They equated manual work with success and intellectual work with failure. For them, achievement was measured in terms of resistance to teachers and ascendancy over 'ear'ole' swots. Yet, while they may have won the battle in the classroom, these working-class rebels lose the war by ending up in low-paid, dead-end jobs.

- Paul Corrigan (1979), whose ethnographic study of working-class boys in Sunderland revealed that they experienced secondary school as oppressive and rallied together against its power. Defining teachers as 'big-heads' who pushed them around, the boys played up, 'to continue their normal way of life despite the occupying army of the teachers and the power of the school' (Corrigan 1979: 58). School for them was an imposition, and therefore something to be vigorously challenged.

Mac An Ghaill (1996a) argues that the sociology of education needs to re-connect with class. He's right. When, for example, one of the authors of this book revealed how difficult it is for relatively low-achieving, working-class school-leavers to gain admission to sociology degree courses at 'old' UK universities (Paul Stephens 1995), a professor of sociology, Geoff Payne, reminded him of 'a shift of intellectual concern among many sociologists from class to other forms of social division!' (Payne 1995: 20). Although the 1980s and 1990s have seen these 'other forms of social division' – notably, gender and ethnicity – moving to centre stage in the discussion of differential educational achievement, class has still remained a very important predictor of educational outcomes.

Referring to a nationally representative study of exam performance scores in 1985 for students arranged by class (professional, intermediate, manual), ethnic background (African–Caribbean, Asian, white) and gender, David Gillborn and Caroline Gipps point out:

'Social class is strongly associated with achievement regardless of gender and ethnic background: whatever the pupils' gender or ethnic origin, those from the higher social class backgrounds do better on average.'

(Gillborn and Gipps 1996: 17)

This point is clearly illustrated in the chart below.

Stephens' argument that working-class students still find it hard to get to university is vindicated by evidence submitted by the Committee of Vice-Chancellors and Principals of the Universities of the United Kingdom in a report entitled *Our Universities Our Future*. The Committee said:

'If higher education is to support social cohesion – as we believe it should – universities will need to address the persistent social class imbalance in their intakes. Social classes I (professional) and II (intermediate) still dominate the student population: among home entrants to full-time undergraduate courses, 61% in 1994 were

Average exam scores by ethnic origin, gender and social class, England and Wales, 1985

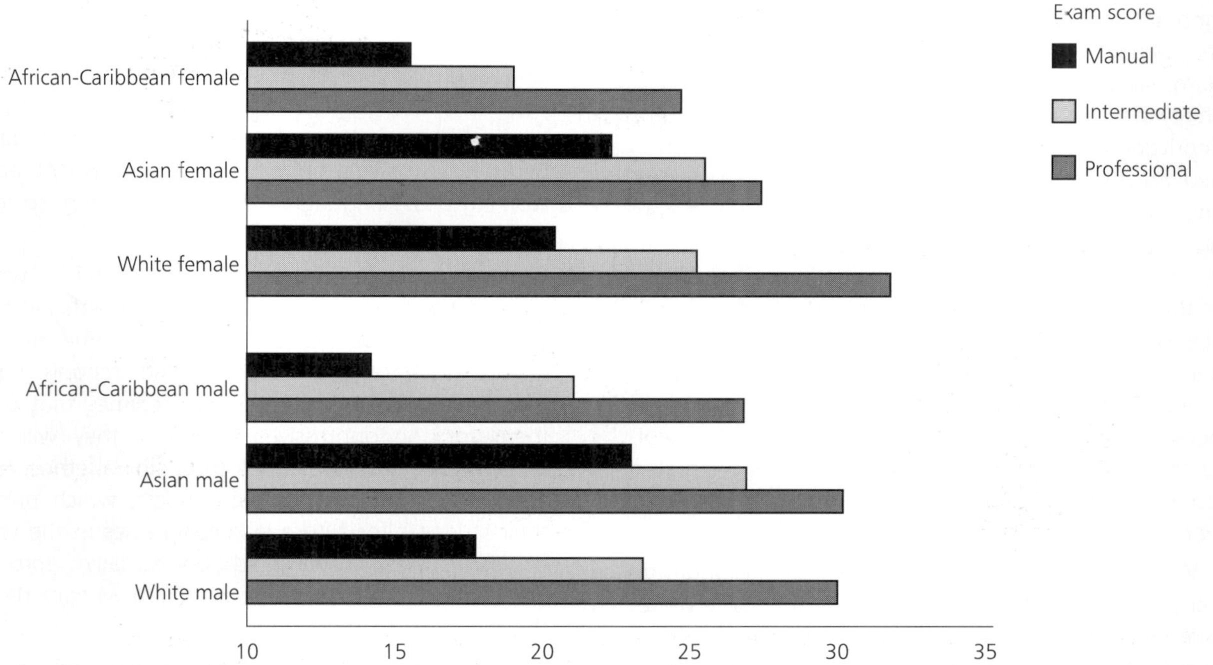

(Gillborn and Gipps 1996: 17, adapted from Drew, D. and Gray, J. (1990) 'The fifth year examination achievements of Black young people in England and Wales', p. 114, *Educational Research*, Vol. 32, No. 3)

from these two classes, despite the fact that they represent only 37% of the economically active population.'

(Committee of Vice-Chancellors and Principals of the Universities of the United Kingdom 1996: Part 2, Point 13)

The relative educational 'disadvantages' of working-class students start long before they might contemplate going to university. A study by Pamela Sammons (1995) confirms that social class has a profound influence on the reading progress of primary school children in the UK. Children from semi- or unskilled manual backgrounds made 'less progress, attaining poorer results than predicted, given their prior reading attainment and taking account of the impact of other factors' (Sammons 1995: 473).

The impact of class on educational achievement still endures, as can be seen from the pie charts below, which link qualifications to socio-economic groups (i.e. social classes).

QUESTION

This exercise will test your skills of *interpretation* and *application*.

Referring to the data below, summarise the main features of the relationship between socio-economic groups and levels of educational qualification in Great Britain from 1992–3.

> ***EXAM TIP***
>
> This kind of exercise frequently features in the education data response question in Paper 1 of AEB A-Level Sociology.

Gender

In the first chapter of his book, *Schooling the Smash Street Kids*, Paul Corrigan acknowledges that his study:

'follows the male-dominated sociological line of researching only into male adolescent activity . . . girls . . . suffer a series of multiple oppressions which are beyond my experience and, like being adolescent in a black ghetto, need researching and writing about by someone who has experienced those oppressions.'

(Corrigan 1979: 13–14)

Corrigan is sincere, and it's true that people who are oppressed are better qualified to document their suffering than those who lead less troubled lives. Nevertheless, it really is indefensible that girls and women have been relatively ignored by sociologists for so long, especially in the area of social mobility research. Girls

Highest qualification shown as percentage of each socio-economic group, Great Britain, 1992–3

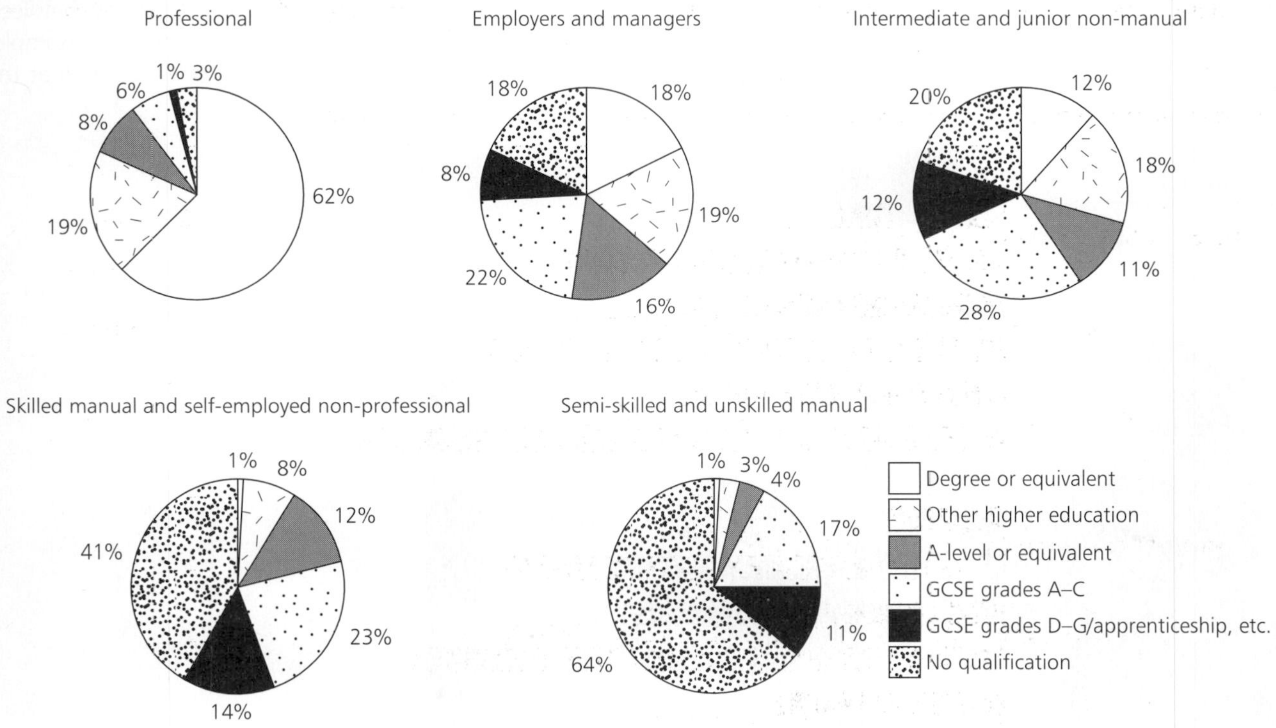

Note: The figures for 'Intermediate and junior non-manual' and for 'Semi-skilled and unskilled manual' each combine two OPCS categories; people with qualifications other than those above (e.g. from abroad) are omitted; the sample is confined to economically active people aged 25–69, not in full-time education.

(Mackinnon *et al.* 1996: 185, adapted from OPCS [1994] *General Household Survey 1992*, London: HMSO, Table 8.3a)

have a high media profile now because they're generally outperforming boys, and those in the higher reaches of the educational hierarchy – mainly white, middle-class males – are getting worried that boys aren't keeping pace. Arguably, that's the wrong reason for social scientists to start taking the educational experiences and achievements of girls and women more seriously. Females deserve that recognition because they constitute half the people on this planet. Sociologists should be mindful of that simple, but compelling, statistic when they compile their research agendas. Aside from the moral issue, it's bad social science not to provide a balanced picture of events.

Recent research reported by the Office of Her Majesty's Chief Inspector of Schools and the Equal Opportunities Commission (1996), based on OFSTED and HMI inspection and EOC casework, reveals a clear link between gender and educational achievement. Specifically:

- Girls out-perform boys at ages 7, 11 and 14 in National Curriculum assessments in English, but achievements in maths and science are broadly similar.
- At GCSE grades A* to C, girls either out-perform or are as broadly successful as boys in almost all major subjects. They are achieving success in subjects conventionally regarded as 'boys' subjects' – design and technology, computer studies, maths, chemistry, and combined science. However, their performance is usually relatively less good in these subjects than in others.
- The only major subject in which girls perform significantly less well than boys is GCSE physics.
- At A- and AS-level, boys gain very low or very high point scores more often than girls. For any given GCSE score, female candidates seem less likely than male candidates to achieve high A- or AS-level scores. This is more noticeable among candidates with high GCSE scores. For example, among candidates with GCSE points scores of 60 or more in 1992, 32 per cent of male candidates and 22 per cent of female candidates achieved A- or AS-level scores of 30 or more in 1994. The pattern of differences in the performances of female and male students in the various subjects at GCSE is thus not continued at A- and AS-level.

The most troubling aspect of gender patterns in sixth-form study, says the report, is that, despite their success in maths, science and technology at GCSE, relatively few young women take A-level courses that are wholly mathematical, scientific or technological. They are thereby denying themselves certain career opportunities in engineering, science and technology.

As in any consideration of the relationship between a social group and educational achievement, it's very important not to look at one factor – in this case, gender – in splendid isolation. Thus, for example, even though girls generally out-perform boys at school, middle- and upper-class boys are more likely to obtain better exam results than working-class girls. The interplay between gender and ethnicity is also significant. For example, David Gillborn and Caroline Gipps (1996) report that the

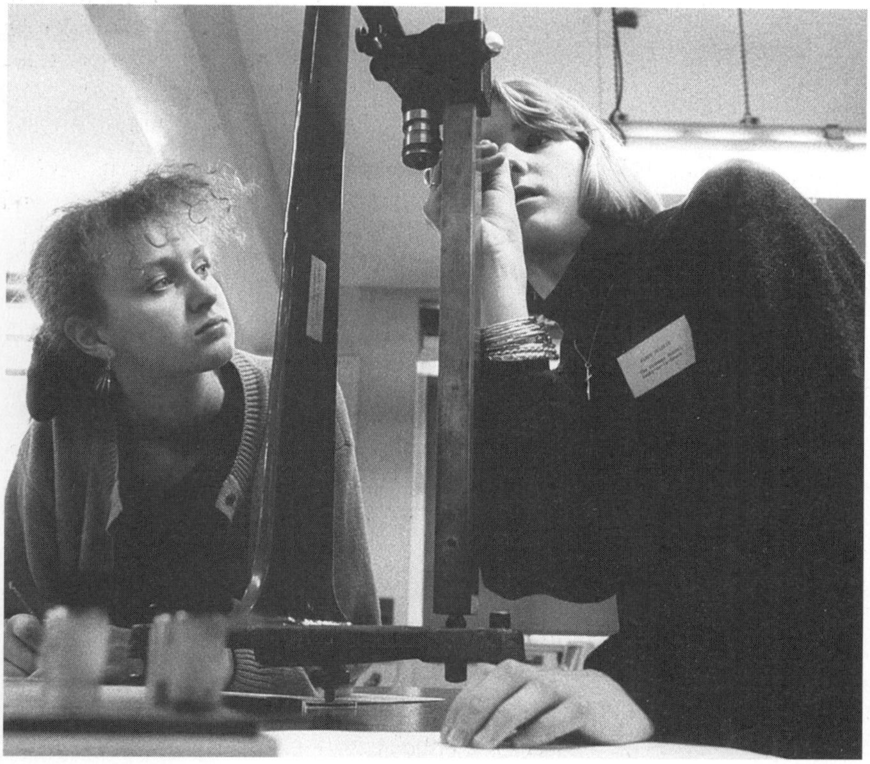

At GCSE, girls are achieving success in subjects conventionally regarded as 'boys' subjects', such as chemistry and combined science. Giving them a taste of university science might persuade them to go further in these fields.

pattern of girls out-performing boys in 1985 (based on the findings of a nationally representative sample) was only uniformly true for white students. It didn't apply to Asian students in any social class, and only applied to African–Caribbean students from manual backgrounds.

On the subject of ethnicity, it's now time to consider the relative achievements of students from different ethnic groups.

Ethnicity

In their major review of the educational achievements of ethnic minority students in the UK, Gillborn and Gipps (1996) provide a comprehensive summary of what the social scientific research shows. Here are some of their key findings.

Achievement in the early key stages

- Evidence on the performance of infant and junior school students doesn't paint a clear picture. On average, African–Caribbean students appear to achieve less well than white students, although the situation is reversed in recent data from Birmingham.
- A more consistent pattern of lower average attainment of Bangladeshi and Pakistani students in the early primary school is evident. This may reflect the importance of levels of fluency in English, which is strongly associated with performance at this stage.

At the end of compulsory education

- In GCSEs at age 16, results show that, irrespective of ethnic origin, students from more economically advantaged backgrounds achieve the highest averages. Girls tend to do better than boys from the same social classes.
- Indian students consistently appear to achieve more highly, on average, than students from other South Asian backgrounds.
- Indian students achieve higher average rates of success than white students in some – but not all – urban areas.
- There's no single educational achievement pattern for Pakistani students, but they achieve less well than white students in many areas.
- The relative achievements of Bangladeshi students are often less than students from other ethnic groups. Bangladeshi students have, on average, less fluency in English and tend to experience greater levels of poverty than other South Asian people. However, in one London Borough, very significant improvements in achievement have been recorded – here Bangladeshi students are now the highest achieving of all major ethnic groups.
- African–Caribbean students haven't shared equally in the increasing rates of educational achievements. In many local education authority areas, their average achievements are significantly lower than other ethnic groups. The achievements of young African–Caribbean men are a particular cause for concern.

The above data reveal that it's important not to look at the relationship between educational achievement in terms of just two broad categories: what white students achieve and what minority ethnic students achieve. There's quite considerable variation between and within different ethnic groups.

QUESTIONS

1 What are the main relationships between educational achievement and:
  a social class?
  b gender?
  c ethnicity?

2 Why is it important that sociologists take account of the *interplay* between the above factors and educational achievement?

School curriculums

That which a school teaches constitutes its curriculum. Sociologists usually distinguish between an *overt or official curriculum* of subjects, like maths, English, sociology, etc., and a *hidden or unofficial curriculum* that conveys the ethos of a school, like corridor posters, use or not of school uniform, gendered aggregation of girls and boys in registers, etc. Given the often very 'up-front' procedures that go on in schools, we sometimes wonder if the adjective 'hidden' is really appropriate. Nevertheless, that's the term conventionally used by sociologists and, having raised our 'objection', we'll stick with it.

This section looks at the factors which shape the official curriculum, the functions of the hidden curriculum, and the students who encounter both of them.

The 'official' curriculum

According to Patrick McNeill:

'The school curriculum is the result of a process involving the production, selection and ranking of knowledge. When this knowledge has been transmitted, pupils are assessed on their ability to demonstrate what they have learned.'

(McNeill 1987, in McNeill 1991: 3)

The knowledge that McNeill refers to is the *official curriculum*. But who decides what this knowledge is? Who has the power to shape the curriculum?

In England and Wales, the short answer to this question is the government. They gave themselves this power in

1988 when the Education Reform Act introduced a statutory *National Curriculum* into all state schools. About 93 per cent of students attend such schools. This curriculum occupies most – but not all – of what these students learn during compulsory schooling – namely, between the ages of five and 16. Scotland doesn't have a statutory curriculum.

Prior to the Education Reform Act, things were very different. For more than 40 years after the 1944 Education Act, the government had no official role in determining school curriculums, other than the requirement that one subject – religious education – was compulsory. However, individual students weren't obliged to attend religious education classes if their parents objected. Otherwise, the curriculum was deemed the responsibility of local education authorities, and in practice left largely to headteachers (in association with school governors after the 1986 Education Act). Even though, in theory, a headteacher could choose, if she or he wanted, to divide the curriculum up into just religious education and American football, the reality was otherwise.

While there was no set curriculum as such, any school that neglected to offer subjects that parents and teachers regarded as necessary – science, maths, English, etc. – wouldn't have got very far. In secondary schools, the universities exercised (and often still do) quite considerable control over the content of the secondary (especially the grammar) school curriculum – because they largely ran the GCE O- and A-level exam boards. They also set the entrance requirements for students who wanted to study at university. To a large extent, the universities still exercise these powers.

An important feature of the National Curriculum is its emphasis on a common knowledge entitlement for all children. This challenges the older notion that some students weren't up to academic subjects and others were too good for vocational subjects. Although there is quite a lot of scope for vocational choices after the age of 16, most students before that age are expected to follow a fairly academic regime with some vocational aspects. There is, however, a resurgence of interest in vocational education, commonly referred to as the 'new vocationalism'. Whether this turns out to be a matter of old wine in new bottles remains to be seen. It will be that if some students, mainly of working-class origin, are placed on predominantly vocational programmes, and others, mainly of middle- and upper-class origin, are selected for largely academic courses. That adds up to social reproduction! It won't be if all students are required to study a mix of academic and vocational subjects, and are taught to value both kinds of knowledge.

As for valuing the academic and the vocational as equal but different forms of scholarship, the government is committed to this principle. Paul Sharp (1996), for example, points out that the government wants to remove the barriers to parity of esteem between academic and vocational qualifications in the 16–19 age group. This is one of the main recommendations of the review of 16–19 education carried out by Sir Ron Dearing, published in 1997. This report identified three different but equally valuable 'families' of qualifications: work-based vocational qualifications (NVQs); school or college-based general vocational qualifications (GNVQs); and school or college-based academic qualifications (AS/A levels). The difficulties arise in the detail of where parity lies and how 'transparent' the boundaries are between the three families.

The jury is also out on what will happen about conventional and degrading stereotypes of girls, women, people from minority ethnic groups and people who are disabled, which are widespread in schoolbooks and other curriculum material. Kate Reynolds (1991), for example, has noted that feminists still highlight the continued sexist stereotypes in books. She adds, however, that many people who are concerned with education and gender have welcomed the 'equal access' that girls have to the 'core' subjects of English, maths and science.

The current compulsory curriculum is made up of a National Curriculum determined centrally by government and a religious education whose content may be decided locally. Since the 1993 Education Act, sex education (including education about HIV and AIDS) has a statutory status rather like that of religious education, though in secondary schools only. Sex education is required by the Act to have regard to moral issues and to the values of family life. Schools are supposed to be able to offer some non-statutory curriculum studies (for example, GCSE Sociology) to students aged 5–16, but not all decide to do this.

Today, through the powers of the 1988 Education Reform Act, politicians decide what our students will learn for most of the time they're at school. Despite the large influx of female MPs after May 1997, most MPs are still middle- and upper-class white males, and lots of them, especially Conservative politicians, are ex-public schoolboys. There's a certain irony here. Ministers, who didn't attend state schools and whose children generally don't either, have enacted legislation that determines what state school children must learn, but which students who attend private schools don't. In practice, private schools often enter their students for GCSEs (in keeping with the statutory curriculum), but they aren't required to do so.

It would be too simplistic, however, to leave the analysis here. Even though, in a strictly legalistic sense, politicians hold sway over what most students have to study at school, the trail of influence is longer. Politicians have legislative powers, but their ideas about what constitutes appropriate knowledge aren't just formed in parliamentary circles. They solicit the opinions of other stakeholders: friends and acquaintances, constituents, parents, teachers, headteachers, professors of education, OFSTED inspectors, the Qualifications and Curriculum Authority (QCA), heads of industry, examining boards, and so forth.

The power of these different stakeholders to shape the curriculum – or more accurately, perhaps, parts of it – varies. Examining boards, for example, probably carry more weight in the eyes of education ministers than teachers. Writing of the influence of examining boards in the 1970s, Michael F. D. Young made it clear that secondary school teachers were largely under the sway of these bodies:

'One way in which [the passivity of the teacher] is displayed is the way outside bodies such as University Exam Boards are able, almost without question, to define what counts as knowledge in the schools. Even bodies such as the CSE boards and the Schools Council are, more often than not, felt as external constraints on the work of classroom teachers.'

(Young 1975: 187)

Getting back to the present, since the merger of the former Schools Curriculum and Assessment Authority (SCAA) and the former National Council for Vocational Qualifications (NCVQ) in October 1997, the new body, QCA, exercises huge influence over all the examining boards. Like the government, to whom it's answerable, QCA is dominated by powerful white males. Together, the mainly middle- and upper-class white males of both these institutions make the decisions that have major consequences for what our students learn at school. They shape the official curriculum.

The 'hidden' curriculum

While the official curriculum conveys subject knowledge, the *hidden curriculum* instils attitudes and promotes behaviours. It cultivates incidental learning within a sort of 'this is how it's done' framework. The emphasis is more on procedure than subject content. If, for example, students are expected to stand when a teacher enters a room, that procedure impresses upon them the need to show respect for people in authority. When this respectful attitude and its corresponding deferential behaviour is duly installed, the student is expected to show the same kind of obedience towards other authority figures – notably, in later life – managers and bosses at work. Conversely, of course, schools that encourage a non-authoritarian ethos – like Summerhill (an ultra-progressive British school) – invoke a hidden curriculum which celebrate equality. Students and teachers relate to each other more as equals than as 'inferiors' and 'superiors'.

Summerhill and other seats of liberal learning aside, many sociologists who write about the hidden curriculum bemoan its generally anti-egalitarian messages. Perhaps not surprisingly, this is certainly the line adopted by most marxist social scientists. Bowles and Gintis, for example, contend that the internal procedures of schools prepare different types of student for different social class roles:

'The rule orientation of the high school reflects the close supervision of low-level workers; the internalization of norms and freedom from continual supervision in elite colleges reflect the social relationships of upper-level white-collar work. Most state universities and community colleges, which fall in between, conform to the behavioral requisites of low-level technical, service, and supervisory personnel.'

(Bowles and Gintis 1976: 12)

Returning to an earlier observation by Michael W. Apple (1979) that the teacher is a kind of first 'boss' to the student, this is deeply embedded in the taken-for-granted culture of most schools. Therein lies its strength – it's a settled, undisputed matter. Even students who take a rise out of teachers seem to cultivate a studied kind of 'insolence' which, in most cases, stops short of direct confrontation.

Bowles and Gintis highlight the different social relationships that prevail among and within schools for different types of student. Thus black and other minority students:

'are concentrated in schools whose repressive, arbitrary, generally chaotic internal order, coercive authority structures, and minimal possibilities for advancement mirror the characteristics of inferior job situations. Similarly, predominantly working-class schools tend to emphasize behavioral control and rule-following, while schools in well-to-do suburbs employ relatively open systems that favor greater student participation, less direct supervision, more student electives, and, in general, a value system stressing internalized standards of control.'

(Bowles and Gintis 1976: 132)

Patrick McNeill develops the theme of how the hierarchies of schools inculcate a sense of subordination by describing how conventional classrooms, with teachers at the front, controlling the chalkboard and able to see all that's going on, encourages students 'to internalise a view of themselves as inferior and subject to those more powerful' (1990, in McNeill 1991: 160).

OVER TO YOU

What do you think? Do the procedures at your school or college make you feel inferior to teachers, or is this notion just marxist propaganda?

McNeill also makes the important point that the hidden curriculum makes its presence felt in the official curriculum. Subjects at school, says McNeill, reflect an elitist, male and ethnocentric view of what constitutes worthwhile knowledge. Thus, for example, literature courses that only focus on 'dead white males' might suggest that African and Asian writers and female writers aren't worthy of serious attention. Moreover, the government's aim of ensuring that history places England at the centre of the world stage devalues the heritage of other countries.

The relationships that prevail between teachers and students when the official curriculum is being taught also brings the hidden curriculum to the fore. When, for instance, maths teachers ask boys more questions (and more challenging questions) than girls in class, the unstated assumption that boys are better than girls at maths can hinder girls' progress in the subject. Similarly, if white teachers pay less attention to black students than to other students, this can adversely affect how the black students perform in the official curriculum. It doesn't help matters either if the official curriculum is bereft of black role models.

Both these points were highlighted in a study published by the Scarman Centre at the University of Leicester ('Education Matters: African–Caribbean people and schools in Leicestershire', cited in the *Times Educational Supplement*, 23 August 1996, page 7). The research found that black children, especially boys, who fail at school do so largely because of racism and stereotyping. African–Caribbean children said they felt left out because teachers gave more attention to Asian and white students. One student said: 'There's nothing about black people in any of the lessons. I think that is wrong especially as we have to learn things about everyone else'. On a bleak note, the sociologist, Professor John Benyon, Director of the Scarman Centre, reported that the findings reflected the national picture.

The relative absence of black culture in the school curriculum raises a crucial question which has been put by John Rex. Should minority parents:

> 'insist upon education in their own values and thereby allow their children to receive differentiated and possibly inferior treatment? Or should they accept what education has to offer by way of improving their children's life-chances at the expense of their losing their own culture?'
>
> (Rex 1986: 72)

By 'inferior treatment', Rex doesn't mean that black culture is less valuable than white culture. What he's implying is that (white) society has defined what counts as important knowledge, and black students need access to this privileged knowledge if they're to get on in adult life.

While the official curriculum in England and Wales is largely shaped by politicians, and the hidden curriculum, say the marxists, serves employers' interests, the imparting of these curriculums is the task of teachers.

QUESTIONS

1 Briefly define these terms: official curriculum; hidden curriculum; national curriculum; 'new vocationalism'.

2 What's the difference between 'academic' and 'vocational' education?

Teachers and students

Students aged 5–16 in the UK are the captive audiences of teachers for 11 years. Indeed, the teacher, as Michael W. Apple (1979: 84) succinctly puts it, is 'a child's first "boss".' Thereafter, some two-thirds of them 'elect' to remain a 'voluntary' audience for a further year or two while they study for A-levels and GNVQs.

Teacher expectations of 'success' and 'failure'

Students tend to live up to high teacher expectations and to live down to low teacher expectations. Sociologist refer to these outcomes as *self-fulfilling prophecies*. The outcomes are fulfilled because they're believed in by those who do the prophesying and by those who are prophesied about.

One of the best known studies of the self-fulfilling prophecy effect was carried out in the US by Robert Rosenthal and Lenore F. Jacobson (1968, in Insel and Jacobson 1975).

Rosenthal, a Harvard University psychologist, wondered whether students might learn better when expected to do so by their teachers. His curiosity was soon to be satisfied. He received a letter from an elementary school principal from California, Lenore F. Jacobson, suggesting it was high time to conduct an experiment to test whether teacher expectations might affect students' intellectual development. Rosenthal agreed, and the two of them set up an experiment in what they called Oak School, an elementary school in the South San Francisco Unified School District. To avoid the risk of letting it be thought that some students could be expected to perform poorly, they established only the anticipation that some students might show 'superior' performance.

At the beginning of the experiment in 1964, Rosenthal and Jacobson told the teachers at the school that additional proof was needed for a new kind of test designed to predict intellectual gain in children. In reality, they used a standard intelligence test which was quite new and not familiar to the teachers. In May of that year, the teachers administered the tests to all the children then in the kindergarten and in years 1 to 5. Before Oak School opened the following September, about 20 per cent of the children were defined as potential academic 'spurters'. There were about five such students in each class. Their names were conveyed to the teachers in a deliberately casual manner: '"By the way, in case you're interested in who did what in those tests we're doing for Harvard . . . "' (Rosenthal and Jacobson 1968: 64).

The names of the 'spurters' weren't based on test results at all, but were selected at random. Thus:

'The experimental treatment of the children involved nothing more than giving their names to their new teachers as children who could be expected to show unusual intellectual gains in the year ahead. The difference, then, between these children and the undesignated children who constituted a control group was entirely in the minds of the teachers.'

(Rosenthal and Jacobson 1968: 64)

True to form, the ensuing artificially-induced high teacher expectations generally led to excellent learning progress. As Rosenthal and Jacobson said, 'The results indicated strongly that children from whom teachers expected greater intellectual gains showed such gains' (1968: 64). At the end of the 1964–5 school year, the teachers were asked to describe the classroom behaviour of their students. The students from whom marked progress was expected were described as having a better prospect of being successful in later life, and as being happier, more curious and more interesting than the other students. There was also a tendency for the 'spurters' to be regarded as more appealing, better adjusted, more affectionate, and less in need of social approval. These findings were especially marked among the first-year children.

By contrast, when teachers were asked to rate the students who hadn't been designated as potential high-flyers, many of whom had also gained in IQ during the year, 'The more they gained, the less favorably they were rated' (Rosenthal and Jacobson 1968: 65). Incredibly, teachers were looking upon children who made intellectual gains when no such gains were expected 'as showing undesirable behavior' (1968: 66).

Paul Stephens and Tim Crawley (1994) have identified the main recipients of positive and negative self-fulfilling prophecies. The principal beneficiaries of the positive ones are:

- middle- and upper-class students
- male students, notably, in relation to high expectations of their abilities in maths, physics and technology
- students from ethnic groups whom some teachers tend to consider as highly motivated, particularly, those of African black, Chinese, Indian and white origin.

The main 'casualties' of the negative ones are:

- working-class students – especially if they're expected to leave their authentic culture at the school gate and pick it up on the way home
- female students, notably, in relation to low expectations of their abilities in maths, physics and technology
- students from ethnic groups whom some teachers expect to under-achieve or only excel in limited ways, particularly, those of Caribbean black, Bangladeshi and Pakistani origin.

This isn't to say that teacher expectations are the sole determinant of successful or failing learning outcomes. Life is much more complex than that. Some students, for example, successfully challenge and resist negative stereotypes. Studies of African–Caribbean young women, in particular, note Gillborn and Gipps (1996), provide evidence of students who regard academic success as a means of ensuring self-independence after school, fighting stereotypes in constructive rather than self-defeating ways. Moreover, while stereotypes exist of South Asian women as facing restricted opportunities

CRIT THINK CRIT THINK CRIT THINK CRIT THINK CRIT THINK CRIT THINK

A SOCIAL SCIENTIFIC EXPERIMENT IN THE CLASSROOM

Based on this last finding above, Rosenthal and Jacobson concluded, 'It would seem that there are hazards in unpredicted intellectual growth' (1968: 66). Re-read the above summary of the Rosenthal and Jacobson research, and explain what you think they meant by this conclusion. Then do the following tasks.

1 *Explain what is meant by an experimental and a control group, and identify who was in each in the experiment conducted by Rosenthal and Jacobson.*

2 *Which teacher-attributed qualities of students in the above experiment form part of the official curriculum and which form part of the hidden curriculum?*

3 *Discuss the ethics of the experiment. Was it justified? Did it have any beneficial and/or harmful effects?*

4 *Compare and contrast this social scientific experiment with an experiment of the natural scientific kind.*

CRIT THINK CRIT THINK CRIT THINK CRIT THINK CRIT THINK CRIT THINK CRIT

because of assumed community traditions, the proportion of white women who remain in full-time education is less than the figure for all major minority ethnic groups.

It's not just female students from minority ethnic backgrounds who have to contend with prejudices that potentially close down educational opportunities. With some exceptions, black males in particular are vulnerable to teacher expectations that they're of low ability and potentially disruptive. Thus, for example, while Gillborn and Gipps report that:

'African Caribbean girls are often described as "boisterous" and "noisy", it's their male peers who are typically seen as presenting the most serious threat to teachers' authority and who are likely to experience more severe sanctions within school.' (Gillborn and Gipps 1996: 59)

This heady mix of 'masculine' and 'racial' stereotypes may make it hard for some young black men to avoid getting caught up in cycles of increasingly severe criticism and punishment.

It would be inaccurate and unfair to accuse teachers of being consciously racist. Some – a very small minority – probably are. The vast majority almost certainly aren't. Illustrative of this, in his study of a co-educational comprehensive school in the Midlands in the mid-1980s, David Gillborn (1990, cited by Gillborn and Gipps 1996) found that most of the teachers appeared genuinely committed to equality of opportunity. However, observations, interviews with students of all ethnic backgrounds, and an analysis of school punishment records each suggested that black students of both sexes were disproportionately criticised by white teachers.

Subsequent ethnographic research in the late 1980s and early 1990s generally reveals that relationships between teachers and African–Caribbean students are fraught with conflict and suspicion. Irrespective of teachers' conscious intention to help all students equally, many black students tend to experience school in ways that are significantly more confrontational and less positive than their peers – regardless of ability. It seems therefore that some teachers 'expect' problems from black students even though the same teachers aren't deliberately racist.

Although some students, against the odds, succeed despite low teacher expectations, it's clearly potentially damaging to the learning experiences and self-esteem of any student to be made to feel a 'failure'. In that context, an HMI inspection of 'Boys and English' (1993, cited by the Office of Her Majesty's Chief Inspector of Schools and the Equal Opportunities Commission 1996) found that secondary age boys tend to have more negative attitudes than girls towards reading and writing. They often have more restricted experiences of fiction, write more predictably, and find the affective aspects of English difficult. But – and this is important in relation to expectations and outcomes:

'Their learning improves when the teaching convinces them of the value of what they are doing, and gives them a clearer understanding of the variety of language use.'

(Office of Her Majesty's Chief Inspector of Schools and the Equal Opportunities Commission 1996: 16)

Working-class students also tend to have more difficulties with teachers than students from higher classes. To be a teacher means to be middle-class, and this often means that teachers and middle-class students are on similar cultural wavelengths. Even teachers with working-class origins have arrived at a different destination to many of their schoolday peers. True, they probably have sympathies with students from low-income backgrounds, but they're statistically more likely, the way schools are run, to encounter disaffection from working- than from middle-class students. There's an important lesson to be learned here – perhaps teachers should become more like their students. This doesn't mean that an adult becomes a child. Rather, the adult becomes more positively responsive to the child's culture. The social constructionist, Nell Keddie, makes this point when she writes:

'It would be more sensible to consider how to make teachers more bicultural, more like the children they teach, so that they can understand forms of English which they do not themselves use as native speakers.'

(Keddie 1973:10)

Most young teachers today, compared to those who were trained in or before the decade when Keddie was writing, have undergone courses in multi-cultural awareness, and are probably more attuned than older teachers to the language needs of students from different backgrounds. There's also a great deal of emphasis in the 1990s on school effectiveness research and school improvement strategies. Whereas in the 1960s and 1970s, a fairly common sociological view was that schools and teachers couldn't do much for students from working-class backgrounds, it's now demonstrable, as Michael Barber (1996) argues, that schools can and do make an important difference to how well any child performs.

Barber cites a study by Pam Sammons, Sally Thomas and Peter Mortimore (1995) – one of the world's leading teams of social scientists in this field – of 94 secondary schools in eight inner-city local education authorities. They found that the difference between the most and least effective schools was more than 12 GCSE points for an average student. This is the equivalent of obtaining six grade Bs as opposed to six grade Ds in the GCSE exams. Schools with similar social class intakes can and do perform very differently. Therefore something other than social class accounts for this.

So what are the characteristics of effective schools? A review of school effectiveness research by Pam Sammons,

Josh Hillman and Peter Mortimore (1995) found that 11 key factors were commonly associated with effective schools. The table below summarises their findings.

While the evidence strongly suggests that schools matter, no one is suggesting that social class isn't important. On the contrary, social class matters a lot. But teachers who give up on working-class children, and who impute lack of parental interest from working-class homes are doing a great disservice to these children and their parents. It would certainly be wrong to infer, as perhaps J. W. B. Douglas' study did, that middle-class parents are more concerned than working-class parents with their children's schooling. Indeed, at least one study has shown that parental involvement can be *more effective* in schools that enrol more poor or working-class students (P. Hallinger and J. Murphy 1986, cited by Sammons *et al.* 1995). All parental encouragement, whatever the class of the parents, helps children do well at school.

Student cultures

'Nationally almost half of all pupils say that others often make fun of pupils who work hard.'

(Barber 1996: 76)

The theme of disdain for academic endeavour and for students who are academic, as well as resistance towards teacher power, is vividly portrayed in Paul Willis' (1978) account of white working-class boys who poked fun at 'swots' and engaged in contrived insolence towards teachers.

Another study of disaffected working-class boys was conducted by Paul Corrigan, who explored 'the problems of secondary education as experienced by bored 15-year-old working-class boys' (Corrigan 1979: 7) in two schools in Sunderland. In both schools, Corrigan discovered that it was 'the structure of perceived compulsion' that made school 'such an oppressive experience' (1979: 15). In

Eleven factors for effective schools

1	Professional leadership	Firm and purposeful A participative approach The leading professional
2	Shared vision and goals	Unity of purpose Consistency of practice Collegiality and collaboration
3	A learning environment	An orderly atmosphere An attractive working environment
4	Concentration on teaching and learning	Maximisation of learning time Academic emphasis Focus on achievement
5	Purposeful teaching	Efficient organisation Clarity of purpose Structure lessons Adaptive practice
6	High expectations	High expectations all round Communicating expectations Providing intellectual knowledge
7	Positive reinforcement	Clear and fair discipline Feedback
8	Monitoring progress	Monitoring pupil performance Evaluating school performance
9	Pupil rights and responsibilities	Raising pupil self-esteem Positions of responsibility Control of work
10	Home–school partnership	Parental involvement in their children's learning
11	A learning organisation	School-based staff development

(Sammons *et al.* 1995)

particular, the 'Smash Street Kids', as Corrigan termed them, resented and resisted 'big-head' teachers who pushed them around. Explaining this derogatory description of teachers, one of the boys said:

'Well, some are [big-heads] because they think, Ah, they're a teacher and they think that they can rule you in school and tell you what to do and where to go and all that.'

(Corrigan 1979: 54)

Much more recent work by Mike Collison (1996), based on the recorded biographical narratives of a group of young male offenders at Stoke Heath Young Offenders' Institution in the UK, revealed a similar disdain towards teachers. Nearly all of those interviewed admitted some school truancy, and resistance to authority was very apparent:

'" . . . couldn't cope with school, teachers always gave me a hard time, but I gave the teachers a hard time . . . " (20-year-old).

" . . . I'm not f***ing thick, but it just didn't interest me. When I was in school, I was the kind of person who just used to disrupt a class, if I was in class I'd disrupt it, I don't know what it was with me. I'd always be getting sent home, always getting detention, always be getting suspended . . . " (21-year-old).'

(Collison 1996: 437)

What distinguishes Willis' 'lads', Corrigan's 'Smash Street kids' and Collison's young offenders from the low-achieving American high school students described by Bowles and Gintis is that these 'rebels' are wilful, but the American students tend not to be. For example, while Willis' 'lads' chose to join their brothers and dads on the factory shop floor, the American students described by Bowles and Gintis were generally socialised into accepting their lot as manual workers. In the first instance, we have agency (wilfulness), in the other passivity (submissiveness). To be fair to Bowles and Gintis though, they did recognise that while the 'authoritarian classroom does produce docile workers . . . it also produces misfits and rebels' (Bowles and Gintis 1976: 12).

One mustn't, of course, generalise from Willis' very small unrepresentative sample of white working-class boys to working-class students in general, not all of whom exhibit the wilful rebelliousness of the 'lads'. Illustrative of this important point is a fascinating American study conducted by Jay MacLeod (1987, cited by Hugh Mehan 1992). MacLeod studied two groups of working-class high school boys who lived in the same American housing projects, attended the same school and experienced the same environment where success was uncommon. One group – the 'Brothers' – were predominantly black; the other – the 'Hallway Hangers' – predominantly white. Despite the similarity of their environment, however, the boys responded differently to their circumstances. The 'Hallway Hangers' responded in a manner that was reminiscent of Willis' lads – cutting classes, playing up in the few classes they attended, dropping out, smoking, drinking, taking drugs and committing crimes. In short, they opposed the school regime and resisted its achievement ethos. By contrast, the 'Brothers' tried to conform to socially approved expectations – attending classes, following rules, studying hard, rejecting drugs and playing basketball.

While the reactions of the 'Hallway Hangers' vindicates the 'Willis Thesis', the behaviours of the 'Brothers' can't be explained by that thesis. Other factors, notably ethnic and family ones, did. The 'Brothers' thought that racial inequality had been curbed over the years, and they believed in equality of opportunity. They recognised that effort hadn't been rewarded in their parents' generation, but anticipated that it would be in their own because of the civil rights movement and affirmative action. Family factors were also important. The parents of the 'Brothers' wanted their children to enter professional careers, and expected them to perform well at school. Violations of these academic aspirations were punished, and the punishments stuck. The parents of the 'Hallway Hangers', however, gave their sons free rein, and didn't monitor their schoolwork. So when these boys rejected the achievement ethos, there was little or no comeback from parents.

The fact that these two groups responded to similar social structures in different ways, cautions sociologists to be sensitive to diversity and variability among working-class students. There is a tendency in sociological research to treat working-class students and also black students as unitary undifferentiated groups. MacLeod's study demonstrates the limitations of this approach and poses a strong challenge to overly undifferentiated theories (like those of Willis).

OVER TO YOU

The last sentence refers to 'a strong challenge to overly undifferentiated theories (like those of Willis)'. What does this mean?

A more recent study of student behaviours was conducted in the UK by Kay Kinder, Alison Wakefield and Anne Wilkin (1996). Based on extensive interviews with 160 young people, nearly all of whom had a history of truancy and/or 'disruption', these social scientists found that the students reported peer and friend influence as the cause or stimulus of their anti-conformist behaviours. Girls aged 8–16 referred to this more than boys. For some students, 'joining in with or imitating others' behaviour' offered 'a source of social fun or even a sense of solidarity or self-esteem'. Disaffected behaviour was also:

'explained as a way of conforming to (or blending in with) peer expectations, thus averting possible teasing or harassment, or the threat of banishment from certain friendship groups.'

(Kinder *et al.* 1996: 7)

There are echoes here of Paul Willis' 'lads' who ridiculed conformist 'ear-oles'.

However, in a society where white working-class, low-achieving boys who, as Mairtin Mac an Ghaill (1996b: 384) puts it, 'have deep investments in older forms of masculine work that have disappeared', more complex and wider forms of 'masculinity' beckon. In research he conducted in a secondary school, Mac an Ghaill (1995; cited by same 1996), identified a range of male peer groups that, while including traditional working-class anti-school 'Macho Lads' and upwardly-mobile 'Academic Achievers', also featured middle-class 'Real Englishmen' and working-class 'New Enterprisers'.

There is also, as research by Kinder *et al.* (1996) signals, a need to look more closely at female cultures in schools. Scott Davies (1995) notes that 'resistance theorists', following Willis, emphasise how a defiant masculinity ignites school rejection. Those who have developed 'feminised' versions of the Willis Thesis, says Davies, suggest that girls' counter-school cultures are less confrontational than those of the 'lads'. According to this view, continues Davies, girls' opposition to school is claimed to be expressed through two forms of gender traditionalism:

'Girls accentuate their femininity in exaggerated displays of physical maturity and hyper-concerns with "romance" on the one hand, and prioritize domestic roles such as marriage, child-rearing and household duties over schooling on the other hand.'

(Davies 1995: 663)

Applying analysis of existing data to a large representative survey of students in 60 Ontario high schools conducted in 1984–5, Davies put the Willis Thesis to the test. He didn't find much evidence to support it in these Canadian schools. Rather than class being the most important predictor of resistance to school values, Davies discovered that gender and the students' immediate school situation were more important. Males, for example, were more likely than females to plan for a job. Difficulties with school were notable here, which perhaps does seem to support Willis' finding that male school rejection is linked to preparation for labour.

Females who resisted school tended to contemplate marriage, devalue education, perceive schooling as useless, and espoused traditional gender roles. Among males, the main forms of resistance were linked to expecting early marriage, devaluing education, perceiving teacher bias, and espousing traditional gender roles. Although there is some crossover here between the female and male anti-school students, it's important to realise that the living out of traditional gender roles between females and males are radically different. On the one hand, there's 'exaggerated femininity', and on the other 'exaggerated masculinity'.

It's important to add that Davies' research suggests that schools in Ontario probably aren't overloaded with dissension. Indeed, he argues that:

'Prevailing depictions of resistance tend to ignore the majority of working-class youth . . . who are pragmatically instrumental towards school. Rather than engage in rebellion, it is likely that most students subtly disengage from school.'

(Davies 1995: 681)

We mustn't, of course, be dismissive of the Willis Thesis. As Davies himself concedes, Canada isn't the UK. He also notes that the process of de-industrialisation might mute conventional class-linked student responses, i.e. masculine manual labour of the type in 1970s UK wasn't as prevalent in mid-1980s Canada. On the other hand, Davies' findings demonstrate that case study work of the kind conducted by Willis can only be treated as suggestive, not as exhaustive. For in Ontario, it seems that gender rather than class is a more durable predictor of different student responses to school.

EXAM TIP

Don't just talk about resistance cultures in relation to white, working-class males. Extend the discussion to girls and other issues. Get up-to-date with the research findings.

We hope you don't think that the sociology of education is a discipline that can't make up its mind. That isn't so. Case studies like those of Willis, for example, are *valid* in terms of the particular cases they describe and analyse. Representative samples, like the one examined by Davies, are *reliable* and allow us to infer that what's discovered in a slice of a population is likely to be found further afield.

OVER TO YOU

What differences, if any, have you noticed between the ways female and male students resist teachers and school values? Does what Paul Willis (1978), Paul Corrigan (1979) and Scott Davies (1995) found in their research have any bearing on what you've seen in your school?

QUESTIONS

1 How do teachers' expectations of 'success' and 'failure' affect students' learning?
2 Identify as many kinds of student subculture as you can.
3 What are the strengths and limitations of the Willis Thesis?

Concluding remarks

Education imparts knowledge and values. Functionalists, marxists and social constructionists are agreed on this. Where they sometimes differ is on the matter of who decides what to impart and how this affects people's lives. Functionalists are pluralistic in outlook. They claim that a consensus about the proper role of education arises from consultation between lots of stakeholders. Marxists are inclined towards 'conspiracy theory'. They contend that the ruling class use education to control working-class and, to some extent, middle-class people, and to socialise their own children into future leadership roles. Social constructionists believe in human wilfulness. They argue that education is what happens when people interact in ways that involve learning and teaching. Some marxist sociologists (for example, Willis) emphasise this same point by revealing that what counts as useful knowledge is sometimes contested by students and teachers. The upshot, say the social constructionists and the marxists, is that sometimes people become what they are, not because they have to, but because they choose to.

By drawing on the combined insights of the three theories, and by gathering empirical evidence, sociologists obtain a sound knowledge and a good understanding of educational processes. What they've found is that nobody is born a genius or a fool. Biology isn't destiny. All of us have the potential to reach our potential. The journey is shaped by the social circumstances we encounter and the wilfulness we act upon.

Glossary of key terms

Correspondence principle Associated with the work of the marxist social scientists, Herbert Bowles and Samuel Gintis (1976), the notion that school hierarchies between teachers and students *correspond* with work hierarchies between managers and managed

Cultural reproduction theory A marxist theory which claims that the culture of the school is *reproduced* (i.e. repeated) in the dominant culture of society

Education A form of socialisation that involves the deliberate, directed and systematic imparting of knowledge and culture

Equality of educational opportunity Equal access, irrespective of background, to the same educational courses

Equality of educational condition Parity of educational outcomes for all people

Functionalist theory of education The theory that education has the generally useful functions of: transmitting norms and values from one generation to another, thereby promoting consensus; and providing children with the knowledge and skills that create tomorrow's workforce, thereby meeting society's economic needs

Hidden curriculum The norms and values of the school that aren't explicitly taught through subjects, but which either rub off in an incidental way or are instilled through rewards and punishments

Ideological state apparatus (ISA) Based on the theory of the French marxist sociologist, Louis Althusser, the institutions in society that promote a ruling class ideology. Schools are among these institutions

Marxist theory of education The theory that education helps to indoctrinate the working class into accepting the authority of the ruling class, thereby promoting the semblance of social stability; and ensures that working-class people are equipped with menial skills, thereby serving the economic interests of capitalists

Meritocracy A system (real or sought) where educational opportunity is based on merit, not birth

National Curriculum Enacted by the 1988 Education Reform Act, this is what the government says must be taught and assessed in schools in England and Wales for students aged 4–16. If you add religious education – which also must be taught in most cases, but whose content can be locally decided – to the National Curriculum, you end up with the *compulsory curriculum*

Official curriculum The subjects students study at school: English, maths, science, sociology, etc.

Self-fulfilling prophecy An outcome (for example, educational achievement) that's fulfilled because it's believed by the people (for example, teachers) who do the prophesying and by the people (for example students) who are prophesied about

Social constructionist theory of education The theory that educational processes are socially constructed during interactions between educators and learners, and that educational outcomes reflect the tilts and turns of these encounters

Social reproduction theory A marxist theory which claims that the power relations between teachers and students are *reproduced* (i.e. repeated) in the social relations between bosses and workers

Student subcultures Generally used by sociologists to refer to anti-school values that unite some students in concerted opposition to teachers. While certain sociologists would argue that students who have a pro-school outlook are part of a different subculture, other sociologists would question this on the grounds that conformity endorses mainstream culture

References

Abbott, Pamela, and Wallace, Claire (1997) *An Introduction to Sociology: Feminist Perspectives*, Second Edition. London: Routledge

Althusser, Louis (1971) *Lenin and Philosophy and Other Essays*. London: New Left Books

Apple, Michael W. (1979) *Ideology and Curriculum*. London: Routledge & Kegan Paul

Apple, Michael W. (1982) *Education and Power*. London: Routledge & Kegan Paul

Barber, Michael (1996) *The Learning Game*. London: Victor Gollanz

Becker, Howard S. (1952) Social-class variations in the teacher–pupil relationship, pp 119–25, in the School and Society Course Team at the Open University (1973) *School and Society*. London: Routledge & Kegan Paul

Bernstein, Basil (1973) *Class, Codes and Control*. St Albans: Paladin

Blackledge, David and Hunt, Barry (1985) *Sociological Interpretations of Education*. London: Croom Helm

Bourdieu, Pierre and Passeron, Jean-Claude (1977) *Reproduction in Education, Society and Culture*. London: Sage Publications Ltd

Bowles, Samuel and Gintis, Herbert (1976) *Schooling in Capitalist America*. London: Routledge & Kegan Paul

Burgess, Robert (1986) *Sociology, Education and Schools*. London: Batsford

Cahanum, Saeeda (1992) Finishing school: Asian girls in the British educational system, pp 210–13, in Giddens, Anthony (ed.) (1992) *Human Societies: A Reader*. Oxford: Polity Press

Collison, Mike (1996) In search of the high life: Drugs, crime, masculinities and consumption, pp 428–44, *British Journal of Criminology*, Vol. 36, No. 3, Special Issue

Committee of Vice-Chancellors and Principals of the Universities of the United Kingdom (1996) *Our Universities Our Future* (1996: http://www.cvcp.ac.uk/dearing/parttwo.htm, Part 2, Point 13)

Corrigan, Paul (1979) *Schooling the Smash Street Kids*. London: The Macmillan Press Ltd

Davies, Scott (1995) Reproduction and resistance in Canadian high schools: An empirical examination of the Willis Thesis, pp 662–87, *British Journal of Sociology*, Vol. 46, No. 4, December

Department for Education (DfE) (1995) *Education Facts and Figures England 1995*. London: Government Statistical Service

Douglas, J. W. B. (1968) *The Home and The School*. London: Panther

Durkheim, Emile (1904–5) L'evolution pedagogique en France (from a series of lectures given by Durkheim at the Sorbonne University in Paris), English translated excerpt entitled 'On education and society', pp 92–105, in Karabel, Jerome and Halsey, A. H. (1977) (eds) op. cit.

Durkheim, Emile (1956a) Pedagogy and sociology, pp 91–5, in the School and Society Course Team at the Open University (1973), op. cit.

Durkheim, Emile (1956b) *Education and Sociology*. New York: Free Press

Elwood, Jannette and Comber, Chris (1996) Gender differences in A-level examinations: New complexities or old stereotypes?, pp 24–8, *British Journal of Curriculum & Assessment*, February

Floud, J. E. (ed.), Halsey, A. H. and Martin, F. M. (1958) *Social Class and Educational Opportunity*. London: William Heinemann Ltd

Gillborn, David and Gipps, Caroline (1996) *Recent Research on the Achievements of Ethnic Minority Pupils*. London: HMSO

Glass, D. V. (ed.) (1963) *Social Mobility in Britain*. London: Routledge & Kegan Paul

Hall, Stuart (1996) Introduction: Who Needs 'Identity'?, pp 1–17, in Hall, Stuart and du Gay, Paul (eds) (1996) *Questions of Cultural Identity*. London: Sage Publications

Halsey, A. H., Heath, A. F. and Ridge, J. M. (1980) *Origins and Destinations*. Oxford: Clarendon Press

Halsey, A. H. (1995) *Change in British Society*, Fourth Edition. Oxford: Oxford University Press

Hargreaves, David H. (1967) *Social Relations in a Secondary School*. London: Routledge & Kegan Paul

Karabel, Jerome and Halsey, A. H. (eds) (1977) *Power and Ideology in Education*. New York: Oxford University Press

Keddie, Nell (1971) Classroom knowledge, pp 133–60, in Michael F. D. Young (ed.) (1971), op. cit.

Keddie, Nell (ed.) (1973) *Tinker, Tailor . . . The Myth of Cultural Deprivation*. Harmondsworth: Penguin Education

Kinder, Kay, Wakefield, Alison and Wilkin, Anne (1996) *Talking Back: Pupil Views on Disaffection*. Slough: NFER

Mac an Ghaill, Mairtin (1996a) Sociology of education, state schooling and social class: Beyond critiques of the New Right hegemony, pp 163–76, *British Journal of Sociology of Education*, Vol. 17, No. 2, June

Mac an Ghaill, Mairtin (1996b) 'What about the boys?' Schooling, class and crisis masculinity, pp 381–97, *Sociological Review*, Vol. 44, No. 3, August

Mackinnon, Donald and Statham, June, with Hales, Margaret (1996) *Education in the UK: Facts & Figures*, Revised Edition. London: Hodder & Stoughton in association with the Open University

McManus, Mick (1996) The needs of teachers of disruptive pupils, pp 57–73, in Smith, Colin J. and Varma, Ved P. (eds) (1996) *A Handbook for Teacher Development*. Aldershot: Arena

McNeill, Patrick (1991) *Society Today 2*. Basingstoke: Macmillan Education

Mehan, Hugh (1992) Understanding inequality in schools: The contribution of interpretive studies, pp 1–20, *Sociology of Education*, Vol. 65, No. 1, January

Meighan, R. (1981) *A Sociology of Educating*. London: Holt Education

Miliband, Ralph (1969) *The State in Capitalist Society*. London: Weidenfeld & Nicolson

Office of Her Majesty's Chief Inspector of Schools and the Equal Opportunities Commission (1996) *The Gender Divide: Performance Differences Between Boys and Girls at School*. London: HMSO

Padover, Saul K. (ed.) (1979) *The Essential Marx: The Non-Economic Writings*. New York: The New American Library, Inc.

Parsons, Talcott (1964) *The Social System*. London: The Free Press of Glencoe

Payne, Geoff (1995) Whose side are we on? A reply to Paul Stephens, p. 20, *Social Science Teacher*, Vol. 25, No. 1, Autumn

Rex, John (1992) *Race and Ethnicity*. Milton Keynes: Open University Press

Rosenthal, Robert and Jacobsen, Lenore F. (1968) Teacher expectations for the disadvantaged, pp 60–8, in Insel, Paul M. and Jacobson, Lenore F. (eds) (1975) *What Do You Expect? An Inquiry into Self-Fulfilling Prophecies*. Menlo Park, California: Cummings Publishing Company

Rosenthal, Robert (1975) Foreword, pp vi–viii, in Insel, Paul M. and Jacobsen, Lenore F. (eds) (1975) op. cit.

Sammons, Pamela (1995) Gender, ethnic and socio-economic differences in attainment and progress: A longitudinal analysis of student achievement over 9 years, pp 465–85, *British Educational Research Journal*, Vol. 21, No. 4, September

Sammons, Pamela, Hillman, Josh and Mortimore, Peter (1995) *Key Characteristics of Effective Schools*. London: Institute of Education

Sharp, Paul (1996) Lecture notes handout: 'Recent Developments in the 16–19 Curriculum', School of Education, University of Leeds, November

Stephens, Paul and Crawley, Tim (1994) *Becoming an Effective Teacher*. Cheltenham: Stanley Thornes

Stephens, Paul (1995) University Admissions Tutors: Whose side are they on?, pp 17–18, *Social Science Teacher*, Vol. 24, No. 3, Summer

Stephens, Paul (1996) *Essential Mentoring Skills: A Practical Handbook for School-based Teacher Educators*. Cheltenham: Stanley Thornes

Turner, Ralph H. (1958) Sponsored and contest mobility and the school system, pp 71–90, in Hopper, Earl (ed.) (1971) *Readings in the Theory of Educational Systems*. London: Hutchinson & Co.
Willis, Paul (1978) *Learning to Labour: How Working-Class Kids Get Working-Class Jobs*. Farnborough, Hants: Saxon House
Young, Michael F. D. (ed.) (1971) *Knowledge and Control*. London: Collier-Macmillan Publishers
Young, Michael F. D. (1975) Curriculum change: Limits and possibilities, pp 185–91, in Dale, Roger, Esland, Geoff and MacDonald, Madeleine (eds) (1979) *Schooling and Capitalism*. London and Henley: Routledge & Kegan Paul in association with the Open University Press

Exam practice: Education

Data response question

Item A

Percentage of the working-age[1] population with a qualification[2]: by gender and ethnic origin, Spring 1995

Great Britain
Percentages

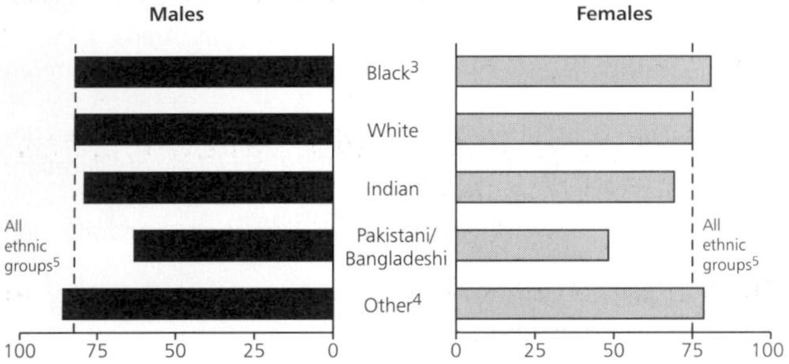

1 Males aged 16 to 64 and females aged 16 to 59.
2 Includes those obtained at school, college, work and from government training schemes.
3 Includes Caribbean, African and other Black people of non-mixed origin.
4 Includes Chinese, other ethnic minority groups of non-mixed origin and people of mixed origin.
5 Includes ethnic group not stated.

(Department for Education and Employment, from *The Labour Force Survey*, 1995)

Item B

Qualifications[1] attained: by gender (percentages)

	Males			Females		
	1980/81	1990/91	1993/94	1980/81	1990/91	1993/94
England						
3 or more GCE A levels[2]	10	13	14	8	14	15
1 or more GCE A levels[2]	16	21	21	15	23	23
5 or more GCSE grades A–C[3]	24	36	39	26	44	48
1 or more GCSE grades A–C[3]	50	63	64	55	73	75
1 or more GCSE grades A–G[3]	87	95	91	90	95	93

[1]Or equivalent. See Appendix, Part 3: Qualifications.
[2]Students at school aged 16 to 18 at start of academic year as a percentage of 17 year old population.
[3]Pupils aged 15 at start of academic year as a percentage of the 15 year old school population.

(*Social Trends 26*, 1996)

Item C

Nuttall et al's ILEA study on ethnic background and examination results in 1989, explored the existence or otherwise of a 'school effect'. In 140 secondary schools, the attainment of Afro–Caribbean pupils could differ by as much as one 'high grade' O level pass when the full range of school differences was considered. Amongst Pakistani pupils the differences could amount to as much as two 'high grade' passes. This study provided some support for the view that schools make some difference. But to what extent do minority ethnic group pupils attend less effective schools than their white counterparts?

Drew and Gray (1991) are not convinced that this evidence is an indicator of a school's contribution to the existence of the black–white gap in achievement. Schools certainly differ to some considerable extent in their effectiveness, but whether they are the major contributing factor remains unclear. A wider study with a sufficient number of pupils and schools, covering a sufficient range of variables, with a nationally representative sample is required to answer the questions posed in the Swann Report, 1985.

(Adapted from *New Community* 17(2), January 1991)

Item D

There has been an increasing influence from feminist and anti-sexist approaches since the 1970s. Although many feminists would argue that not enough progress has been made, research into gender inequalities does seem to have had a greater influence on education policies than has research into social class inequalities.

The Sex Discrimination Act 1975 can be clearly associated with an equal access approach to equal educational opportunities. The National Curriculum also emphasised equal access, by tackling the problem of gendered subject choice. Tests of 7 year olds have, since 1992, shown that girls achieve better grades than boys in English, Maths, Science and Technology. However, these results have come as no surprise to some educationalists. It has long been claimed that boys are expected to catch up at a later stage.

(Adapted from *Making Sense of Society: An introduction to sociology*, Ian Marsh et al (Longman) 1996)

(a) What percentage of Pakistani/Bangladeshi males in the working-age population has a qualification? **(Item A)** *(1 mark)*

(b) Describe the general pattern of qualifications attained by gender, as illustrated in **Item B**. *(3 marks)*

(c) Suggest two reasons why people of the Pakistani/Bangladeshi ethnic origin are the least likely to have an educational qualification. **(Item A)** *(4 marks)*

(d) To what extent do you agree that a school is the most significant 'contribution to the existence of the black–white gap' in educational achievement? **(Item C)** *(8 marks)*

(e) With reference to the **Items** and elsewhere, what explanations have sociologists offered for the differential educational performance of boys and girls? *(9 marks)*

10 Work, organisations and leisure

Topics covered in this chapter

- *Technological change*
- *Work satisfaction, work dissatisfaction and conflict*
- *Work, non-work and leisure*
- *Unemployment*

Para-medic: 'Two-year-old found unresponsive in cot. We couldn't get an IV.'

ER doctor: 'What did you find on arrival?'

Para-medic: 'Cyanotic, no spontaneous resps, pulse faint at 200. It was scoop and run.'

ER doctor: (*turning to one of the parents*) 'What happened?'

Parent: 'She stopped breathing.'

ER doctor: 'Was she sick?' (*Parent shakes head*) 'Any medications; recent trauma?'

Parent: 'No, nothing.'

ER doctor: 'Laryngoscope; Magill forceps.' *(The doctor extracts an earring, and the child gasps.)* '3.5 ET tube. Hyperventilate her. Blood sugar?'

Nurse: 'Twenty.'

ER doctor: 'Hand me a 14 gauge. I'm going in interosseus.'

(. . . *then a movement. The baby takes a breath, cries. The doctor smiles.*)

(Adapted from the television series, *ER*)

There's lots of work going on in the Emergency Room, and lots of organisation too. The ER doctor is in control, but she's also a team player. Who is she accountable to? The patient? Yes. The parents? Yes, too. The hospital? Surely, yes. But who owns the hospital and its life-saving technology – a private

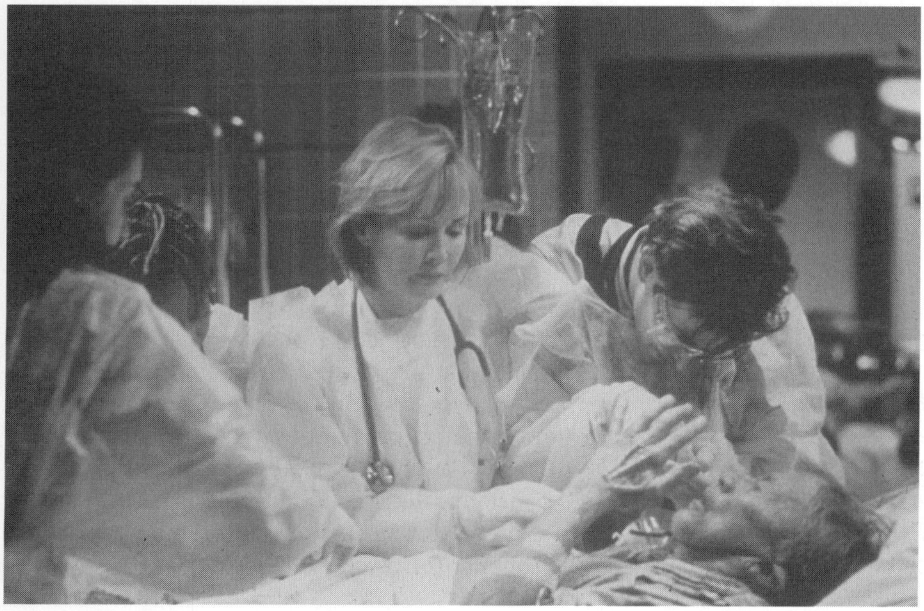

It might seem confusing to an outsider, but this medical team know exactly what they're doing and where each of them fit into the overall action. This is an example of effective organisation.

corporation or the people? This question has implications for accountability too.

Some individuals are fortunate to have jobs where leisure and work go hand-in-hand – but not paramedics, doctors and nurses. Things look set to change though. New technology is increasingly taking the drudgery out of boring routine office tasks, the danger out of heavy manual work, and the stress out of complex technical procedures. The question is, will this lead to more opportunities to 'mix business and pleasure', to more affordable leisure, or to enforced low-quality 'leisure' of the kind created by unemployment?

Today, most people work in organisations. Effective organisations thrive on teamwork, like the emergency room depicted in the television series, *ER* – on people working together rather than individually. Many modern organisations owe their legacy to the Industrial Revolution. The transformation on a large scale and at a relatively rapid pace of a society based on agriculture to one based on industry had a profound impact on the organisation of work. Mass production, the defining feature of industrialisation, gave rise to the quintessential organisational form of the Industrial Revolution: the factory.

In this chapter, we'll first look at the *impact of technological change* on the organisation of work tasks. This involves a consideration of different types of organisation, including the development of the factory system, the characteristics of bureaucracy, and the alternatives to bureaucracy envisaged by management theory. We'll also investigate changes in the ownership and control of technology. Second, we'll examine the issues of *work satisfaction, work dissatisfaction and conflict*. Third, we'll concentrate on the relationship between *work, non-work and leisure* in terms of age, class, gender and ethnicity. Finally, we'll discuss the causes and effects of unemployment.

Technological change

'The hand-mill gives you society with the feudal lord: the steam-mill, society with the industrial capitalist.'

(Marx, cited by Thompson 1975: 208)

When technology changes, so does the rest of society. When factories and machines replaced fieldwork and farm horses during the English Industrial Revolution, people stopped *doing jobs* and *got a job*. This transition from being a multi-task 'parent-cum-teacher-cum farmer' to being a specialist factory hand has been expertly documented by Durkheim (see pages 50–1). Put simply, society became industrialised, and people moved from villages to towns. The impact of technological change on the organisation of working people's lives was huge. Gone was a sense of seasonal tasks, punctuated with periods of non-work and leisure. In was an awareness of being on time at the factory gate, and a job all-year-round. To be sure, all of this didn't happen overnight, but it was, nevertheless, a driven, no-turning back process – a definite 'march of history'.

People responded to technological change in different ways. Some landlords, farmers and agricultural labourers fought it, often for different reasons. The landlord relied on rent from tenant farmers; the farmer on rent and work from labourers; and the labourer on produce and wages from the farmer, as well as charity from the village squire. Landlords used the most powerful institution in the land – parliament – to further their cause. Farmers turned to their local landlords, many of whom were also magistrates, for support. Some agricultural workers formed loose alliances with farmers and landlords. Others united in common cause with like-minded workers against the intrusions of the new machinery, some of which – in the hands of certain 'capitalist-minded' farmers and landlords – was beginning to replace manual labour.

The forces of 'tradition' and 'progress' clashed resolutely, and, when the dust had settled, the society which emerged was a capitalist industrial one. A new ruling class of industrialists emerged victorious. Those landlords who had moved with the times retained many of their privileges. A middle class of bankers and professionals also made a good living. The rest, at least, the majority of them, formed an increasingly industrial working class. This class was at the forefront of popular agitation during the first half of the nineteenth century. Steam power and the cotton mill – the epitome of industrialisation – heralded a new, and an increasingly organised, working class. True, there was popular unrest in earlier periods, but, says E. P. Thompson, 'Almost every radical phenomenon of the 1790s can be found reproduced tenfold after 1815' (1975: 209). By 1832, strong, politically conscious working-class institutions – trade unions, educational and religious movements, friendly societies, and more – flourished.

This forging of a collective consciousness is expertly mapped in E. P. Thompson's, *The Making of the English Working Class* (1975, first published 1963). Referring to 1800 onwards, Thompson writes:

'In the mills and in many mining areas these are the years of the employment of children (and of women underground); and the large-scale enterprise, the factory-system with its new discipline, the mill communities – where the manufacturer not only made riches out of the labour of the "hands" but could be seen to make riches in one generation – all contributed to the transparency of the process of exploitation and to the social and cultural cohesion of the exploited.'

(Thompson 1975: 217)

So how did this new technology – these steam-driven machines – stir people to collective action in trade unions and other organisations? The machines and the appalling conditions of the 'dark, Satanic mill' intensified the collective suffering of working people under one roof. People who had previously exercised a level of independence in craft and field-work were thrown together in dangerous, dirty, noisy factories where the pace and organisation of work was dictated by the speed of the machine. They were treated by factory owners as mere instruments of mass production. They laboured for others instead of cultivating food for their families. Their 'reward' was the *extrinsic* (outside them) one of low wages rather than the *intrinsic* (inside them) one of creative satisfaction. This sense of not being connected to the product of one's labour is called *alienation*. It's a very important concept in sociology, and is considered in more detail in the section dealing with work satisfaction, work dissatisfaction and conflict (pages 240–4).

EXAM TIP

E. P. Thompson is a marxist who writes in a manner that is openly sympathetic to the working class. This makes some of his observations polemical and, dare we say, subjective. Nevertheless, his book is probably the most thorough critique of working-class history in its formative years, 1780–1832. It's a massive but very readable work, and we strongly recommend that you dip into it regularly.

The Industrial Revolution represented a turning point in the history of humankind, and its heritage endures. Modern trade unions and factory inspectors have ensured, however, that the conditions of factory work are far less grim than in the nineteenth century. Now we're on the verge of yet another technological revolution. Heavy industries have been in decline over the past several decades, and light industry production methods and a burgeoning service sector have become the norm. This is but the prelude to a new age, a twenty-first century where '9 to 5' is being replaced by much more flexible employment patterns in an information-based economy. Electronic technology has turned our world into what management guru, William Bridges, describes as 'a great electronic spider web, where footsteps anywhere are felt by individuals everywhere, so that today we experience hundreds of . . . thousand changes' (Bridges 1996: 17). Rapid and numerous changes require faster decisions which old-style bureaucracies – with their rigid hierarchies – can't handle. The upshot is a shortening chain of command, self-managing teams, and more autonomy for innovative employees.

Organisation of work tasks

In the Seattle corporation of the computer software giant, Microsoft, these organisational changes are very apparent. Far from being a conventional organisation where distinct tasks are parcelled out into individual jobs and where 'workers' and 'managers' know their place in the overall hierarchy, people are accountable to project teams of which they're a part. There are no regular hours, and buildings are open to employees 24 hours around the clock. People decide when and for how long they want to work. No one keeps account of their hours, but everyone watches their productivity. Within their project teams, individuals are always given a bit more than they can handle to encourage constant collaboration with co-workers. Microsoft trusts its employees to do what they can already do, lets them loose to troubleshoot problems, and helps them when they get stuck.

The new technology relies much more on brain power than on physical exertion: leave that last part to the gym after work! Even the assembly line is being taken over by robots. The human element in continuous flow production (for example, car manufacture) is increasingly more one of monitoring than of turning wrenches. Some workers are also moving into positions where they're becoming *pro-active* (i.e. initiators of ideas) rather than *reactive* (i.e. reacting to orders from above). Frank Blackler has described this trend – using very complex language – as 'a shift from dependence on the embodied and embedded knowledge towards embrained and encultured knowledge' (Blackler 1995: 1029). What he means is that individual craft (embodied) skills and uniform, factory-type (embedded) productivity are yielding ground to individual creative (embrained) problem-solving and team-based (encultured) empowerment. Of these four models, the last one – encultured organisation – appears to be the one to which many organisations are moving.

What kind of organisation would you like to work in? This question gets right to the heart of the issue of job satisfaction? Do you want to work *for* a company where work is broken down into small, standardised, measurable tasks, where everyone knows their place? Or would you prefer to work *with* an organisation where your knowledge and ideas are respected and where you're largely left to your own devices? I have no hesitation in saying I wouldn't like to work in the first kind of organisation, and that I would like to work in the second type.

Contrast my preferred workplace, however, with its polar opposite: the bureaucratic organisation.

Bureaucracy

The German sociologist, Max Weber, provided the first detailed sociological study of the nature of bureaucracy. A bureaucracy is an hierarchical institution for administering the organisation of work tasks. Think of a big car

CRIT THINK CRIT THINK CRIT THINK CRIT THINK CRIT THINK CRIT THINK CRIT THINK

MODELS OF REALITY

Blackler presents his four models in the following diagrammatic form.

Organizations and Knowledge types (Arrows summarize trends suggested in the knowledge work literature)

	FOCUS ON FAMILIAR PROBLEMS	FOCUS ON NOVEL PROBLEMS
EMPHASIS ON COLLECTIVE ENDEAVOUR	**(ii) Knowledge-Routinized Organizations:** *Emphasis on knowledge embedded in technologies, rules and procedures.* Typically capital, technology, or labour intensive. Hierarchical division of labour and control. Low skill requirements. *Example:* 'Machine Bureaucracy' such as a traditional factory. *Current issues:* Organizational competencies and corporate strategies. Also, the development of computer integrated work systems.	**(iv) Communication-Intensive Organizations:** *Emphasis on encultured knowledge and collective understanding.* Communication and collaboration the key processes. Empowerment through integration. Expertise is pervasive. *Example:* 'Ad hocracy', 'innovation mediated production'. *Current issues:* 'Knowledge creation', dialogue, sense-making processes. Also, the development of computer supported cooperative work (CSCW) systems.
EMPHASIS ON CONTRIBUTIONS OF KEY INDIVIDUALS	**(i) Expert-Dependent Organizations:** *Emphasis on the embodied competencies of key members.* Performance of specialist experts is crucial. Status and power from professional reputation. Heavy emphasis on training and qualifications. *Example:* 'Professional Bureaucracy' such as a hospital. *Current issues:* Nature and development of individual competency. Also, computer displacement of action skills.	**(iii) Symbolic-Analyst-Dependent Organizations:** *Emphasis on the embrained skills of key members.* Entrepreneurial problem solving. Status and power from creative achievements. Symbolic manipulation is a key skill. *Example:* 'Knowledge-intensive-firm' (KIF) such as a software consultancy. *Current issues:* Developing symbolic analysts, the organization of KIFs. Also, information support and expert systems design.

(Blackler 1995: 1030)

Using interesting resources (for example, an OHP), prepare a simplified presentation on one of the models described in the diagram.

Bring the model to life by referring to real organisations – especially ones you're acquainted with – whose operation contains some of the features it contains. For example, you might work in a labour-intensive (i.e. people do lots of the tasks) pizza takeaway, which is a characteristic of the Knowledge-Routinized Model.

You could do this as a group activity. Divide into four groups, with each group taking responsibility for presenting one of Blackler's models to the rest of the class.

CRIT THINK CRIT THINK CRIT THINK CRIT THINK CRIT THINK CRIT THINK CRIT

parts company with a managing director who has overall control, assisted by middle manager underlings who ensure that her or his decisions are carried out by blue-collar workers on the shop floor – and there you have an example of bureaucracy. Weber developed an *ideal type* (see page 60 for a definition of this important concept) model of bureaucratic organisation by defining the key features of bureaucracies in general. These – in abridged and simplified form – are the characteristics of the archetype bureaucracy he highlighted:

- Work tasks are clearly and officially defined so that everyone knows their particular job. Weber referred here to 'the principle of fixed and official jurisdictional areas' (in Coser and Rosenberg 1969: 447).
- People in the higher reaches of the hierarchy are thoroughly and expertly trained managers whose duty is to the company before all else.
- These high-ranking officials supervise people in the lower reaches of the hierarchy.
- Office workers do the paperwork (some sociologists, though not Weber, refer disparagingly to this task as the 'red tape' aspect of bureaucracy).

OVER TO YOU

Describe any present-day organisation whose working arrangements are the same as or similar to those described in Weber's ideal type bureaucracy.

Weber, himself, had ambivalent views towards bureaucracy. As a German, he seems to have been influenced by the nineteenth-century Prussian idea that bureaucracy represented the ultimate in organisational efficiency. But he didn't like all that he saw. During one of his lectures on bureaucracy, he even managed to sound quite marxist when he lamented a consequence of the 'bureaucratisation' of economic enterprises:

'By it [the rational calculation that issues from bureaucracy], the performance of each individual worker is mathematically measured, each man [*sic*] becomes a little cog in the machine and, aware of this, his one preoccupation is whether he can become a bigger cog . . . it is . . . horrible to think that the world could one day be filled with nothing but those little cogs . . . '

(in Coser and Rosenberg 1969: 455)

While Weber probably regarded bureaucracy as better than the 'seigniorial' leadership of pre-industrial society because of its reliance on management skills rather than noble blood (merit rather than birth), it's clear that he lamented its depersonalising impact on people's lives. Weber's concern here was echoed by one of his colleagues, Robert Michels. In his famous analysis of the bureaucratisation of socialist political parties (1915), Michels notes how 'mechanism' rather than people's ideals becomes the primary goal – more about Michels in Chapter 13 on power and politics.

Despite the depersonalising tendencies of bureaucracy, the American sociologist, Philip Selznick (1943), discovered that people who work in bureaucratic organisations rediscover their personal autonomy by 'doing their own thing' – even if this doesn't square with the official regime. In this way, organisations create informal structures which take care of workers' 'own felt needs' (Selznick 1943: 47). For, as Selznick points out, 'in the real world of living organizations there is always the possibility of counter-pressure, of devising techniques for blocking the bureaucratic drift' (1943: 54). What Selznick means by this is that employees develop informal cultures based, for example, on joking, ridicule, avoidance techniques, etc. which give them control over their own social space. The British sociologist, Paul Willis (1978), found evidence of a similar informal culture among boys in a Midlands secondary school and, later, in their workplace. Not liking the rules, regulations and hierarchy of the school and the factory, the boys subverted these things by creating a counter-culture which poked fun at conforming people and took a rise out of authority figures. See pages 213–14 of Chapter 9 on education for more about Willis' study.

Bureaucracies still exist, especially in organisations where hierarchy is deemed very important – schools, police stations, the military, some corporations – but it isn't looked upon favourably in modern management theory.

While his book was written in the late 1940s and updated in the 1950s, Robert K. Merton (1957) highlights the important dysfunctions (disadvantages) of bureaucracy. Examples to illustrate his points have been provided by the authors. To maintain the flow of the narrative, the 'against' arguments precede 'for' arguments on this occasion.

Despite the points in its favour, bureaucracy is generally considered by contemporary management theorists to be an out-moded and a dysfunctional form of organisation. One of today's most famous experts on management, the American, Tom Peters, is scathing in his criticism of bureaucratic organisation:

BUREAUCRACY

AGAINST

- Bureaucrats sometimes arrive at a position of 'trained incapacity', a term first used by the sociologist, Thorstein Veblen, in the 1920s. This occurs when actions based on prior learning don't move with the times. For example, a manager who adheres to the old-fashioned maxim that management shouldn't consult with 'subordinates' won't get very far in a company culture that encourages all staff to have a say in policy decisions. By contrast, a manager who actively consults and acts upon staff opinion is unlikely to remain stuck in a rut.
- Over-conformity by bureaucrats to their pre-defined scripts becomes exaggerated and intensified to the extent that the following of set procedures becomes an end in itself, even when this leads to irrational decisions. For example, an excess of 'red tape' in a department store over customer refund entitlements can result in customer dissatisfaction and a fall in sales revenue. One of the reasons for the success of stores like Marks & Spencer is their 'no fuss', no 'red tape' policy on customer refunds.
- Bureaucrats are trained not to get personal with their clientele. Rather, they're encouraged to minimise individual differences and to maximise abstract categorisations. Instead of, for example, thinking this customer's needs are different and require special handling, the bureaucrat looks for a rulebook answer to the client's problems. Here, once again, 'red tape' rears its unhelpful head.
- Irrespective of her or his position within the bureaucratic hierarchy – whether junior clerk or senior manager – the bureaucrat is taught to be a representative of the power and prestige of the entire organisation. This often leads to a domineering approach towards clientele. Take, for example, a customer who calls a telephone company which is run on bureaucratic lines (no pun intended!) to complain of slight over-charging for calls made. Instead of exercising sensible, independent judgement and writing off the alleged excess, the bureaucrat informs the customer that *company regulations* call for a full and thorough investigation before any refund can be considered. Don't be surprised if the customer takes her or his business elsewhere.

To summarise Merton's points, the unintended and negative consequence of the over-zealous drive for bureaucratic efficiency, is inefficiency in other quarters. The question must then be asked, does bureaucracy have any advantages? Yes, it does. These are the main ones:

FOR

+ Merton, for example, claims that 'The chief merit of bureaucracy is its technical efficiency, with a premium placed on precision, speed, expert control, continuity, discretion, and optimal returns on input' (1957: 196). He then adds that 'Bureaucracy maximises vocational security' (i.e. gives job security).
+ It places rationality above mere traditionalism. The maxim, 'That's how it was always done', gives way to a more scientific approach to organisational decision-making.
+ Merit replaces birth as the recruitment and the promotion criteria for people who work in bureaucratic organisations. This enhances efficiency because talent is more reliable than blood.
+ By treating its clients and customers as 'equals' in relation to their bureaucratically defined entitlements, personal favouritism is replaced with an unbiased commitment to playing it by the rules.
+ By establishing and rigorously defining clear chains of command, bureaucracies are, in their own way, very efficient organisations. Each person knows and is trained to perform their respective role, and the muddle and confusion occasioned by not knowing who is responsible for what don't arise.

'But I've come to realize that, in this madcap world, turned-on and theoretically empowered people (not to mention genius management strategy makers, even if strategy making did make sense) will never amount to a hill of beans in the vertically oriented, staff-driven, thick-headquarters corporate structures [i.e. bureaucracies] that still do most of the world's business. Empower until you're blue in the face.'

(Peters 1993: 13)

Peters goes so far as to dedicate one of his books – *Liberation Management* (1993) – to among other people, 'Percy Barnevik, who abhors bureaucracy'. Peters' opposition to bureaucracy is based on his belief that tomorrow's 'organisations' will be conjured up anew each day rather than set in marble. Incidentally, his antipathy to the very word 'organisation' is why it's placed in inverted commas. What Peters is saying is that pre-established procedures – especially of the bureaucratic 'rules and regulations' kind – get in the way of spirited imagination and innovation. He's not just a conviction exponent, but also a follower of real trends. Citing the Danish corporation, Oticon – the world's market share leader in hearing aids – Peters describes an 'organisation' whose work practices are inimical to bureaucracies. At Oticon, after a quick scan of the on-line project listings, employees decide what to work on and whom to work with. This is a corporation where curiosity, initiative and autonomy take precedence over following orders in an uncritical manner.

'Boss management' doesn't make for good management. Managers who exercise power vested in position alone seldom gain respect. As A. H. Halsey puts it, 'Rigidly hierarchical forms of industrial authority produce at best the solidarity of the resentful' (Halsey 1995: 232). A happy workforce makes for a happy organisation – and a productive one. But how is this achieved? Social scientists have long studied different ways to obtain optimum organisational efficiency within an environment that's also conducive for human growth. The umbrella term conventionally used for their area of interest is 'management theories'.

Management theories

Says A. H. Halsey:

'Work relations in the past have given low discretion and low trust to subordinates *vis-à-vis* their superiors. This was the triumph of the so-called scientific management which reached its most extreme form in the modern factory assembly line.'

(Halsey 1995: 231–2)

Scientific management was initiated towards the end of the nineteenth century by Frederick Winslow Taylor. Scientific management breaks down work into its simplest elements and seeks to improve workers' performances in each of the elements. Its 'scientific' label derives in large part from the notion that worker output is visible (i.e. empirically verifiable) and measurable. Teach a construction worker to erect scaffolding in a step-by-step logical and efficient manner, give the worker time to learn the ropes, and watch productivity rocket! Those are the basic principles behind scientific management, or 'Taylorism' or even 'Fordism' (based on its application in the Ford motor company) – to call it by its other popular names.

Scientific management theory

The idea that work should be scientifically studied by people who 'manage' it, rather than by people who perform the tasks has been traced by the marxist sociologist, Harry Braverman (1974), to the middle of the seventeenth century in England. What Taylor did was to develop and present a practice that had earlier origins, giving to a series of initiatives in England and elsewhere a coherence and a name. Himself the son of a well-to-do Philadelphia family, Taylor dropped out of Harvard University, and took the unusual step of starting a craft apprenticeship in a firm whose owners were friends of his parents. After completing his apprenticeship, he took a job as a labourer in the Midvale Steel Works, also owned by family friends. Within a few months, he rose to the position of gang boss in charge of the lathe department. Before long, he began a series of experiments into ways of improving worker productivity at the steel works. The experiments lasted 26 years! He argued that managers know more about organisation than workers. It was therefore up to managers to figure out ways to improve productivity by making workers adopt rational, time-saving behaviours (getting pig iron, for example, from A to B in the quickest, most efficient manner). He also believed in offering workers financial incentives to work harder.

Together, these elements add up to the *theory of scientific management*: namely, the assumption that managers should increase productivity by maximising the efficiency of the workforce. The 'carrot' here is an extrinsic reward – better pay. For workers who don't live up to management expectations, there's also the 'stick' – discipline and punishment.

Taylor regarded gang bosses ('foremen') as the 'sergeants' of the shopfloor. It's vital, he said of the gang bosses, to:

'nerve and brace them up to the point of insisting that the workmen shall carry out the orders exactly as specified on the instruction cards. This is a difficult task at first, as the workmen have been accustomed for years to do the details of the work to suit themselves, and many of them are intimate friends of the bosses and believe they know quite as much about their business as the latter.'

(cited by Braverman 1974: 120)

Quite a lot of modern managers still use Taylor's principles. However, some of them go overboard on the 'stick' side of the equation. Look around you, and you'll understand what we mean. Consider organisations like the army, schools and fast-food outlets, for example. In the first, you have the 'kick butt and put 'em through their paces' management of soldiers; in the second, the 'take names and do that homework' management of students; and in the third, the 'get those fries on time or you're out of here' management of fast order cooks!

> **OVER TO YOU**
>
> ***Extend the three examples in the preceding paragraph, and explain how they're all linked to the principles of 'scientific management'. Do you like what you see in these examples?***

Very few management experts would openly declare their allegiance to 'Taylorism' today. Nevertheless, its heritage is everywhere to be seen – well, perhaps not everywhere. There are alternative management theories, some of which have, slowly but surely, gained ground. We'll take you on a 'Cook's tour' of what's on offer soon, but before that, consider the case for and against scientific management theory.

Author of one of the most widely read and most often quoted books – *The Human Side of Enterprises* – on management theory, Douglas McGregor (1960) identifies two distinct starting points for managing workers: Theory X and Theory Y. Theory X assumes that people don't like work, and are lazy. Therefore they must be driven to work through measured doses of threat and reward. The belief here is that workers can't accept responsibility for their own actions, but must be monitored and controlled by managers. Theory Y, by contrast, assumes that people have a psychological need to work, and thrive on achievement and responsibility. While McGregor presented these two theories as options and 'feigned' impartiality, it's clear that he favoured Theory Y.

In an approximate sense, Theory X corresponds to scientific management theory, and Theory Y accords with what's termed *human relations theory*. We've already considered the first of these theories. Now it's time to look at the other one.

Human relations theory

This theory is, like scientific management, a 'control' theory, but it's less directly manipulative than the former school of thought. Most closely associated with the work of Elton Mayo, an Australian who settled in America, human relations theory proceeds from the premise that when a 'hand' is hired, the whole person comes with it. Mayo argued that workers needed more than money

SCIENTIFIC MANAGEMENT THEORY

FOR

+ It represents an advance on the 'hit and miss see what'll happen' style of 'management', because its proposals for increasing productivity are research-led.
+ It recognises, at least in the context of America and countries like it, that workers need financial incentives, as well as good management, if they're to become more productive.
+ It offers managers the time and the space to manage, and workers the same opportunities to accomplish their roles. This division of labour ensures that each group become experts in their own right.

AGAINST

– Its scientific aspirations are clouded by its tendency to see things in relation to owner and manager viewpoints. Says Harry Braverman, 'It [scientific management] investigates not labor in general, but the adaptation of labor to the needs of capital. It enters the workplace not as the representative of science, but as the representative of management masquerading in the trappings of science' (1974: 86).

– Financial incentives aside, it doesn't hold out much prospect of advancement for manual workers. Their role is confined to simple tasks, whereas the role of the manager is to study how those tasks are executed. Not having dirtied their hands on the shopfloor (Taylor was an unlikely exception here), managers are removed from the object of their study.

– It pays too much attention to financial incentives and 'boss management' and too little to other motivators of increased productivity. Workers are assumed to work hard based on carrot and stick strategies, on what Douglas McGregor (1960) calls 'Theory X' (see above).

incentives; they needed to enjoy their work, to find it psychologically satisfying. The human relations theory of management is based on the assumption that managers should offer workers intrinsic rewards – notably enjoyable working conditions – as well as decent pay, because happy workers are productive workers. 'Indulgent persuasion' rather than 'carrot and stick' is the primary management tool.

Mayo based his contentions on a series of experiments conducted by him and a Harvard University research team from 1927 to 1932 (see page 99). These were carried out at the Hawthorne Works of the Western Electric Company in Chicago. Mayo wanted to find out why there was so much dissatisfaction among many of the 30,000 employees who worked at the Hawthorne plant.

Originally, he thought that the problem lay in the factory's lighting system. Change the lighting, he figured, and workers would become less discontented and more productive. Sounds a bit like 'Taylorism', doesn't it? But Mayo went further than this. After discovering that groups of workers who were placed in either darkened or more illuminated conditions both increased their productivity, Mayo realised he was on to a different trail – but he didn't yet realise where it would lead. Subsequent experiments involving a selected group of female employees over a period of five years revealed startling results. Whether they had one or two breaks, normal or earlier finishing times, productivity tended to go up or remain the same.

Mayo concluded that tampering with lighting, breaks, finish times, and such like didn't influence output rates. The independent variable – the cause – of increased productivity was the presence of the research social scientists in the electric company. The dependent variable – the effect – (for example, greater output) was the social psychological response of workers to being involved with researchers in a meaningful experiment: the human relations side of things. Being observed – not so much being checked up on, more to do with being involved in a collaborative research exercise – heightened the workers' sense of importance and well-being. It was this rather than crude 'time and motion' techniques that led to a resolve to want to work harder.

Out of Mayo's pioneering work in human relations management have developed most forms of modern management theory. It would be wrong, however, to imagine that these new ideas have got rid of pyramid structures altogether. While the pyramids are arguably becoming flatter than before, directors and managers occupy positions higher up the slope than routine technicians and shopfloor workers. Certainly, modern management theory envisages a more flexible chain of command, but it doesn't favour equality between the 'suits' and the 'overalls'. It does, however, recognise, as Paul Lillrank argues, 'the need to get bottom-up initiatives flowing in a hierarchical organization' (1995: 985). What Lillrank means here is that people at the lower part of the hierarchy get the chance to have their ideas listened to and acted upon by management. One way to achieve this is to develop, as has happened in Japan, a so-called parallel organisation – a pyramid on one side and a satellite next to it. The pyramid represents the management hierarchy. The satellite represents a workers' think tank – a Quality Control Circle – that passes its ideas into and up the pyramid. In Japan, this is known as a *Kaizen organisation* (see the diagram below).

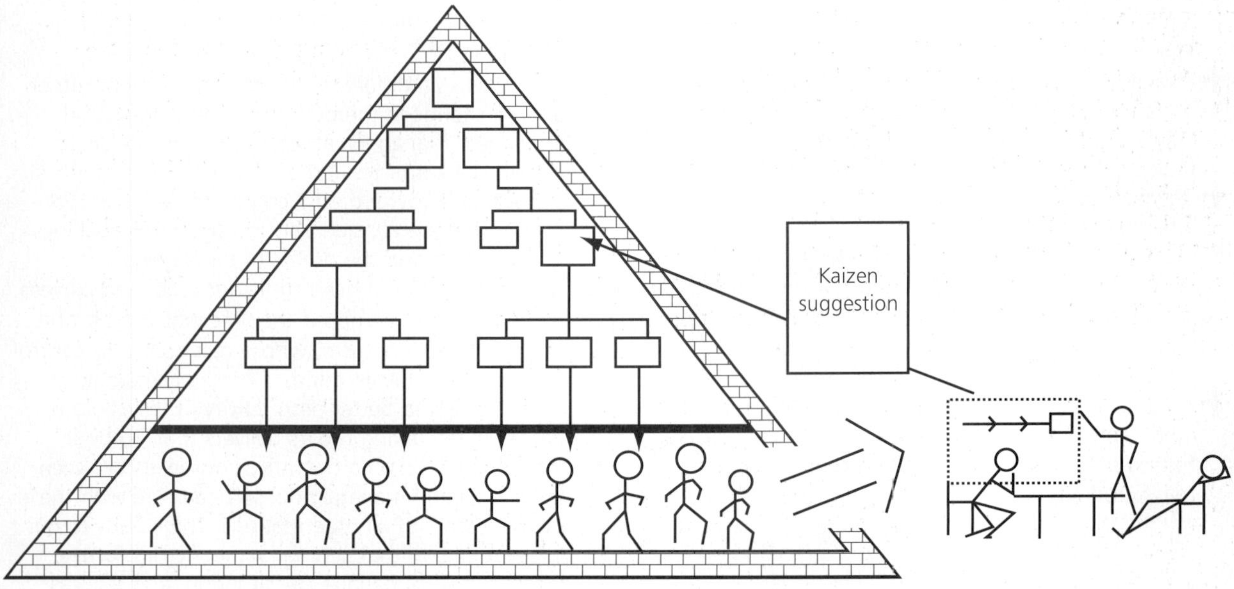

(Lillrank 1995: 983)

The QC circle bypasses the formal organisation.

The Kaizen is very much rooted in Japanese culture, which is hierarchical and buttressed by stylised rituals, like bowing to 'social superiors'. The Quality Control Circle bypasses this system without offending the 'social superiors'. Suggestions merely flow from workers to management without names and personalities being referred to. In European and American companies, where hierarchies have often been flattened out, the Quality Control Circle tends to be more integrated within the organisational structure. Put simply, there isn't the need for a satellite outside a pyramid. The satellite becomes a part of the pyramid, usually through teamworking that involves both blue-and white-collar employees.

Even Japan, with its very hierarchical notions of status differentials in the wider society, has come to realise that managers have to work with, not against, factory floor operatives. The 'do what you're told' ethos of scientific management has been superseded there and elsewhere by the human relations school of management, which solicits workers' voices. The expression of 'voice' in the decision process can, as W. Chan Kim and Renee A. Mauborgne note:

> 'make one feel wanted or worthy, or a group member, or treated with dignity. Consequently, organizational members can be expected to feel a strong allegiance toward the decision system as a whole. Through their deep-rooted allegiance, employees can be expected to defend and support the decisions resulting from that decision system.'
>
> (Chan Kim and Mauborgne 1996)

Don't imagine though that managers who adopt a human relations outlook are no longer interested in control. They are, but they seek the co-operation of those over whom they exercise authority rather than forcing unwilling and often resented obedience. Whatever their strategy, managers are inherently in the business of managing subordinates. Under 'Taylorism', they were used to doing this in a climate of antagonism between 'suits' and 'overalls'. Human relations management hasn't really removed this underlying conflict. However, it has often kept discord at bay by 'humanising' the relations between the manager and the managed. In that regard, as Braverman pointedly puts it, 'the practitioners of "human relations" and "industrial psychology" are the maintenance crew for the human machinery' (1974: 87). They've become 'amenable coaxers' instead of 'sergeant majors'.

We've said quite a lot about managers in relation to the approaches that inform their relations with more junior employees. But we mustn't forget that managers are themselves answerable, ultimately, to owners.

Who owns? Who controls?

There are two main kinds of ownership:

- ◆ public ownership (for example, the BBC)
- ◆ private ownership (for example, British Airways).

The post-war Labour government embarked upon a public ownership programme – called 'nationalisation' –

HUMAN RELATIONS MANAGEMENT THEORY

FOR

- + It takes the social scientific study of work beyond the mere mechanical and pay considerations of 'Taylorism', by paying more attention to the human relations between management and staff.
- + It's more in line with current trends in organisations, where doing what the manager says is becoming replaced with greater autonomy for 'junior' employees to show initiative and make decisions. This is especially the case in the organisational cultures of knowledge (for example, computer software) companies.
- + It's a more humane form of management. Employees aren't conceived as cogs on a wheel whose task is to fit into the impersonal and often brutal demands of mass production.

AGAINST

- – It advocates a different style of management rather than a change in the positions of managers and managed. Managers, at least in the private sector labour market, are still the 'lieutenants' of capitalist bosses, and 'lower grade' employees still work for wages that are considerably lower than the salaries of managers and the profits of employers.
- – The participation it gives to 'lower grade' employees in being consulted about their feelings is a bit of a sham, a false liberalism, whose real goal is to control rather than cultivate minds. Ultimately, managers want more and better productivity. If 'psychology' rather than barking orders delivers that, so be it.
- – Its emphasis on a co-operative consensus between managers and managed doesn't coincide with the requirements of all organisations. Think back to our *ER* example. In that setting, someone has to take charge, has to manage the situation, and tell less qualified people what to do.

of major industries and services over which some form of public regulation was considered necessary. The National Coal Board (now gone with the shrinkage and privatisation of the coal industry) and the National Health Service (still going, but increasingly influenced by 'quasi-private' initiatives) are two examples of publicly-owned developments. Public sector management permits quite a lot of operational control to managers on a day-to-day running basis, but the public – represented by government – are both the owners, and, at the level of overall policy formation, the controllers.

> ***EXAM TIP***
>
> Be sure to make the distinction between publicly-owned and privately-owned concerns. Some candidates seem to assume that private capitalists own everything – they don't!

In the private sector, managers are more accountable to individual owners – typically, big shareholders – than they are to the public. Things weren't always like that. During the English Industrial Revolution, the owners of cotton mills (the defining technology of that age) were often the controllers of their factories. They were owner-managers. As industrialisation proceeded, however, some owners delegated control to relatively well-paid employees who were just managers. Here we have what sociologists refer to as a *divorce between ownership and control*. This cleavage was actually documented by Marx, who distinguished between 'a mere manager, administrator of other people's capital, and of the owner of capital . . . a mere money capitalist' (cited by Maria Hirszowicz 1981: 125). Here, noted Marx, we have, 'private production without the control of private property' (cited by Hirszowicz 1981: 125).

The divorce between ownership and control arguably gathered pace during the twentieth century. For example, Adolf Berle and Gardiner Means (1932, cited by Hirszowicz 1981) drew attention to the fact that American corporations were becoming increasingly owned by multiple shareholders, thereby eclipsing the control of a single owner and strengthening the power of business administrators. In an American study published some 40 years later (J. Larner 1970, cited by Hirszowicz 1981), Berle and Means' argument was given added weight when it was found that 84 per cent of the 200 biggest non-financial organisations, and 70 per cent of the next 300 were controlled by managers rather than owners. Similar trends have occurred in the UK, where managers have a very prominent control function. In a society where an increasing proportion of company shares are owned by institutions – pension fund bodies, unit trusts, etc. – it's difficult to pick out individual capitalists. However, managers who exercise operational command are very prominent.

The first sentence of the preceding paragraph contains the word 'arguably'. It's a word which suggests that the issue of ownership and control has more than one interpretation. Berle and Means, and Larner, as well as a number of other social scientists (for example, Tom Burns and G. M. Stalker 1961; Ralf Dahrendorf 1972) take a very literal view of the purported 'divorce', and argue that it has ushered in a new powerful class of managers. Some sociologists, however, (for example, T. Nichols 1969; John Westergaard 1995) contend that managerial 'control' is conducted according to the rules of owner capitalists. In a forceful rebuttal of the argument that control has passed from owners to managers, Westergaard maintains that real control lies with owners. Acknowledging that 'Business power has . . . become more impersonal and 'anonymous' than it was', he points out that:

> 'the power . . . is still exercised by, and to large money gains for, small numbers of high executives and directors, top advisers and key dealers, quite often members of family groupings with extensive financial connections.'
>
> (Westergaard 1995: 126)

To be sure, there'll be some senior managers with quite large shareholdings – 'manager-owners' – in this group, but there'll also be powerful capitalists who either individually or as a consortium are the majority shareholders and the behind-the-scenes controllers.

Rather than pitting the proponents and opponents of the divorce between ownership and control thesis against each other, it's better to concede that both make important contributions to our understanding of who owns and who controls. Some companies employ managers who are dominated by owners. Others employ managers who exercise operational control and who sometimes even buy into the ownership cake.

QUESTIONS

1. Briefly describe the impact of technological change on working people's lives during the English Industrial Revolution.
2. What are the defining features of a bureaucratic organisation?
3. Summarise the main advantages and disadvantages of bureaucracies.
4. Compare and contrast scientific management theory and human relations management theory.
5. What are the strengths and limitations of:
   - **a** scientific management theory?
   - **b** human relations management theory?
6. What is meant by the divorce between ownership and control? Is it a helpful concept?

Work satisfaction, work dissatisfaction and conflict

When people consider whether they like their job, they don't just think about pay. Whether or not the job is a satisfying experience in itself is a very important issue. Recently published research in the UK (Roger Penn, Michael Rose and Jill Rubery 1994) showed that being able to use one's own initiative is very highly valued. The research also found that job dissatisfaction was associated with lack of autonomy and of decision-making. Some sociologists, however – notably, those of a marxist leaning – argue that job satisfaction can never be fully realised in a society where one class of people – workers – are exploited by another class of people – employers. Based on this argument, capitalism creates the illusion of happiness by giving workers token concessions, 'under the banner of job enlargement [i.e. swapping job tasks to relieve tedium] and the humanization of work' (Braverman 1974: 37).

According to marxists, conflict always exists between workers and capitalists, even if the former are lulled into thinking this isn't the case. The mission of the marxists is thus one of unmasking the hidden agenda of the ruling class: to create 'happy robots' who will obey their 'superiors' and remain satisfied with a very meagre portion of the economic cake. Such contentions are considered by non-marxist sociologists to be fanciful and unscientific. Whether workers are satisfied or otherwise is more related, they argue, to the jobs people have to do than whether or not they work in a capitalist society.

Robert Blauner (1964), for example, found that workers on a car assembly line found their job very tedious and dissatisfying, whereas workers in a chemical plant derived satisfaction from the control they had over complex automatic machinery. Both factories were in America, which is a strongly capitalist society. Yet it's the technology they use that makes workers happy or unhappy, not whether or not they work in a capitalist society. That said, Blauner did recognise that car plants had a 'tendency to use the workers as "means", as commodities in the classic Marxist sense' (1964: 180). In this respect, he acknowledged the important debt sociology owes to Marx's recognition of the powerful alienating tendencies in factory technology. Blauner simultaneously added, however, that some kinds of technology can actually promote worker satisfaction – even if the machines are owned by capitalists!

Work satisfaction and dissatisfaction

In the 1970s, the American marxist sociologist, Harry Braverman, wrote, 'Almost every major periodical in the United States has featured articles on the "blue-collar blues" or "white-collar woes"' (1974: 31). Car assembly lines, in particular – echoing Blauner's findings – were cited as a prime example of job dissatisfaction. In 1969, for example, the Ford assembly plant on the outskirts of Detroit had an 8 per cent 'quit rate' each month. At the Chrysler Corporation's Jefferson Avenue plant in Detroit, a daily average 6 per cent absentee rate was reported in 1971, as well as an annual average turnover close to 30 per cent. Chrysler reported that during 1969, almost half its workers didn't complete their first 90 days at the job. In routine white-collar work things were also rather grim. Braverman reports that the greatest job dissatisfaction in America was among young, well-educated workers employed in low-paid, dull clerical positions. That was the US – according to Braverman – a quarter of a century ago, a place where pride in one's work had been replaced by the dull monotony of *de-skilled*, routine labour.

> **EXAM TIP**
>
> Show the examiner you're aware of sociological subtleties by highlighting Blauner's recognition that car plants in capitalist society tend to be exploitative in a 'classic marxist sense'. This adds a little intellectual flourish to the otherwise largely correct interpretation that Blauner's work is generally non-marxist in orientation.

These days, however, things are quite a bit different at Chrysler. As will be seen later, the company has radically redesigned its shopfloor practices in an effort to enhance job satisfaction. Closer to home, a major study of the relationship between skills and work attitudes in Britain by Roger Penn, Michael Rose and Jill Rubery (1994) contends that the evidence of the 1980s reveals a society much at odds with the 'de-skilled' and 'degraded' portrayals of work by the likes of Braverman and other marxists. Penn *et al.* found that many employees in their survey reported very high levels of *intrinsic* (to do with feelings about one's work) job satisfaction. However, levels of satisfaction were generally lower in relation to *extrinsic* (to do with pay and conditions) job satisfaction. A very interesting and, it must be said, surprising finding, was that women who worked part-time expressed higher overall job satisfaction than women and men in full-time employment.

Could it be that Braverman was right in his analysis of the then US and that Penn *et al.* are right in their representation of 1980s Britain? Yes, it could be. On the other hand, it might be more accurate to suggest that Braverman's marxism makes it very difficult for him to imagine that workers can ever be truly happy in their work in a capitalist society. Liberal-minded managers might make the drudgery of work a bit more palatable, but, ultimately, workers are mere instruments of capital. It's true that Braverman summons statistics on job turnover and absenteeism to support his 'unhappy worker' thesis. However, one suspects he can't imagine that workers will attain fulfilment in a society which seeks to acclimatise them to working for capitalist bosses. Like most marxists, Braverman seems to think he knows better than workers themselves whether they're happy or not.

As for Penn *et al.*, they place more credence on the self-reported experiences of workers. They asked employees to rate their job satisfaction on a 0–10 point scale. While Penn *et al.* recognised that some employees might not display true feelings to an outsider, the fact that workers were expected to make their own judgements about levels of satisfaction suggests that the researchers didn't presume to know better. In that respect, Penn *et al.* adopt a similar position to Blauner. Both studies suggest that what makes people happy or unhappy in their work has more to do with how they find their job rather than whether they work in a capitalist society. Boring work is boring work; satisfying work is satisfying work – period!

Alternatively, one could argue that sociologists like Braverman alert us to the clever manipulations of labour relations 'experts' who give workers an illusory sense of job satisfaction while denying them the chance to share the fruits of their labour. In that sense, the sociologist – in an overtly value-judgmental way, to be sure – shows the worker that 'happy robots' are still only 'robots'. The up-front horrors of work conditions during the Industrial Revolution have merely been veneered today with a thin sugar coating. Scratch the surface and the injustice and inhumanity become very apparent.

OVER TO YOU

Can sociologists ever 'know better' about the people they study than the people themselves? This is a difficult but important question.

A key concept in the debate about job satisfaction and dissatisfaction is that of *alienation*. The term has already been alluded to, but hasn't yet been properly defined. We'll return to Blauner for a comprehensive definition of this important concept:

'Alienation exists when workers are unable to control their immediate work processes, to develop a sense of purpose and function which connects their jobs to the over-all organization of production, to belong to integrated industrial communities, and when they fail to become involved in the activity of work as a mode of personal self-expression.'

(Blauner 1964: 15)

Blauner's definition, while embracing a number of strands, owes its legacy to Marx's claim that alienation represents a fundamental lack of connectedness between a human being and what she or he produces. If, for example, you worked in a Lancashire cotton mill in the nineteenth century, you would, we suspect, have found it well-nigh impossible to 'connect' in any kind of enriching way with the stultifying toil that would have been your lot. Alienation is the most powerful expression of job dissatisfaction. People who are alienated can't invest creativity and purpose in their work because their job causes them suffering.

This all sounds very grim. However, Blauner argued that the portrayal of work in modern society (the 1960s was the decade referred to) as alienating isn't generally supported by evidence. Blauner's dated, but important, study of the attitudes of manual workers in car assembly line, chemical, printing and textile occupations found that the extent to which alienation was experienced varied between these different jobs. He described the experience of alienation as feelings, varying in form and intensity, of powerlessness, meaninglessness, isolation and self-estrangement. The proportion of workers who found their work alienating, noted Blauner, was a low 4 per cent in the printing industry, rising to 11 per cent in the automated chemical industry, to 18 per cent in the textile industry, and to 34 per cent in the car industry.

Blauner was forthright about the limitations of his research, and such intellectual honesty adds to his integrity as a social scientist. Importantly, he acknowledged that his case studies weren't necessarily representative of firms in general: 'many of the generalizations that emerge from this research are only suggestive rather than conclusive' (Blauner 1964: 14).

Today, employee knowledge in organisations is increasingly centring around what Thomas H. Davenport, Sirka L. Jarvenpaa and Michael C. Beers term, 'know-what, know-how, know-why, and self-motivated creativity' (1996: 54). If Blauner's thesis that more autonomy equates with more job satisfaction is right, this bodes well for the twenty-first century workforce. The traditional, menial, repetitive job, exemplified by Blauner's 1960s car assembly line worker, diminishes autonomy and heightens alienation. Nowadays, things are very different. New technology is rapidly replacing the assembly line. Instead of each worker having one small task to perform as a part-built vehicle passes her or his station, employees work in teams and build cars from start to finish. In that way, they do connect with what they produce because they see the finished product before their very eyes, rather than some fleeting skeleton of a car frame on its way to a distant destination at the other end of the plant.

Even where the assembly line remains a part of the production process, automation does the dull and dreary stuff. Thus, for example, in the spotlessly clean Honda plant close to the Japanese town of Kashiwabara, workers push buttons and watch finished fuel tanks, welded by automatic machines, roll off the conveyor belt. It's a very different world to the American car plants lamented upon by Braverman 20 years earlier. There, workers hunched over assembly lines that echoed with the clanging of metal, and they were stifled by the heat and smoke of heavy welding torches. In the modern car industry, workers wear crisp, clean uniforms, maintain and repair their own machines, set and monitor their own quality control, and switch jobs regularly to avoid boredom.

Nor has the American car industry stood still. When, for example, Chrysler restructured its vehicle design process, it introduced a so-called 'platform team' that brought together engineers, manufacturers, accountants, and others. The onus became teamwork, and individual performance became linked to the overall vehicle success. Moreover, the detailed tasks and steps in new vehicle development were left to each new car development team. Employees were trusted to develop collectively the skills needed to do the job. Whether they 'feel' happier than their predecessors of the 1960s Chrysler plant described by Braverman remains a moot point. If they reported a sense of job satisfaction, it's likely that sociologists like Penn *et al.* (1994) would pretty much take them at their word. Braverman, however, would probably describe such management tinkerings with the organisation of work tasks in the language he used some 20 years earlier:

'They represent a style of management rather than a genuine change in the position of the worker. They are characterized by a studied pretense of worker "participation", a gracious liberality in allowing the worker to adjust a machine, replace a light bulb, move from one fractional job to another, and to have the illusion of making decisions by choosing among fixed and limited alternatives designed by a management which deliberately leaves insignificant matters open to choice'.

(Braverman 1974: 39)

Strong words – but are they ideological rather than factual? What do you think?

Whatever your response, don't imagine that post-industrial automation and enlightened management necessarily represent the end of worker discontent. That remains to be seen, and much more research is needed before we can begin to address this important issue. Industrialisation, especially in its earlier gritty and grimy forms, certainly played a part in creating an alienated workforce, but the end of industry doesn't guarantee that all will be well henceforth. Even people whose work experience has always remained outside of industry often encounter job dissatisfaction. In that context, the *Guardian*'s reader survey on attitudes to work, 'Powerful people' (Kingston 1996), revealed that academics are considerably more demoralised than people in other jobs. Challenging the popular notion that conditions of work in academic settings are more congenial than most, it found that academics suffer as much stress and worry as the rest of the workforce. They're also just as likely to dream about changing jobs. Just over half the professors and lecturers in the survey reported that their job caused them stress all or most of the time. Says Peter Kingston:

'Professors and lecturers appear to be as prone as anyone else to dreams of chucking it all in for something else. One in five admit they think about this on a daily basis and the same number again consider hanging up their gowns for good once a week.'

(Kingston 1996: vi)

The reasons for discontent include: being on a short-term employment contract and the resultant job insecurity; bad pay; feelings of being less valued in their job than other workers; and bad management.

The findings of the survey, based on the results of a self-completion questionnaire which ran in the newspaper from 22–27 June 1996, are presented in the chart below, where the work attitudes of professors and lecturers are compared to the work attitudes of the total sample workforce.

Owing to the fact that the *Guardian*'s reader survey was a survey of only the readers of that newspaper, and only those readers who decided to fill it in when they read about it (i.e. it isn't a random sample), the findings can't be treated as statistically representative Given, however, that many lecturers and professors probably read the *Guardian*, the views of those who responded might be fairly 'representative' of their colleagues.

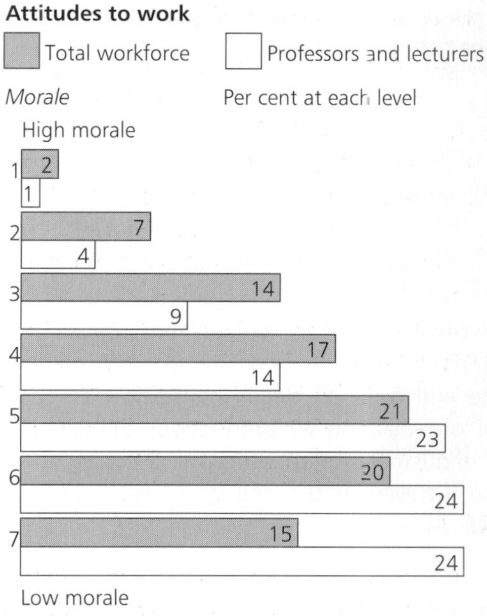

(Kingston 1996: vi)

OVER TO YOU

But what about the views of the total sample workforce in the Guardian survey (i.e. those readers who responded, whether professors/lecturers or in other occupations)? What do you think are the dangers of inferring representativeness here?

The extent of worker dissatisfaction today compared to the past continues to be debated. In some respects, the new information technology of service sector employment has liberated working-class people from dangerous, dirty, noisy work, offering a more congenial work environment. Moreover, de-industrialisation and the rise of service – often office-based – work has led to a reduction in the size of the working class, and an increase in opportunities for middle-class employment. Yet, despite the striking expansion of non-manual employment, some sociologists (for example, Braverman 1974) claim that such work has become increasingly routinised and mechanised and, in that respect, 'de-skilled'. Thus, for example, the traditional skills of the craftperson are replaced with the modern drudgery of the keyboard employee.

Even upward social mobility into the professional middle class doesn't guarantee a stress-free life so far as work is concerned – as indicated by the findings of the *Guardian* survey of middle-class lecturers and professors reported above. Probably a more accurate representation of events is that technology has made life better for some people, and worse or no better for others. Consider, for example, the difference between a car assembly line worker who has been 'up-skilled' into a design engineer, with a former printer who has been 'de-skilled' into a fast-order cook in a pizza take-away.

One thing is clear: whether the problem has got better or worse, job dissatisfaction still occurs. When, for example, I returned in late August 1996 on a flight from Stockholm to Manchester, I discovered that the train service from Manchester Airport to York was temporarily discontinued because of strike action by railway workers. Around the same period, I remember too that postal services were hit by selective strike action on the part of workers in that sector. Clearly, railway and post office workers were sufficiently dissatisfied to stop working. Some months previously, British Airways pilots were threatening strike action too, and industrial action was only averted when their demands for better pay were met.

Conflict

In Chapter 4, you'll have come across Marx's claim that there's an inherent conflict between capitalists and workers. Capitalists want to maximise their profits, so they try to keep wages down. Workers want decent pay, so they seek to keep wages up. It was during the nineteenth century that Marx advanced his argument and that workers began to get increasingly organised through trade unions in their bid for better pay (and better conditions). Today, about 42 per cent of the British labour force are trade union members. In Sweden, the figure is as high as 90 per cent.

In the twentieth century, as in the nineteenth century, governments have sought to curb the legal rights of unions. The Combination Acts of 1799 and 1800 made the meetings of organised worker groups illegal. The Trade Union Act of 1984 took away the right of certain civil servants to belong to a union. There's little doubt that a general decline in union influence and in membership is a phenomenon of recent years. Moreover, strikes – the most powerful weapon of unions in the arena of conflict at work – have considerably diminished during the 1980s and 1990s. That said, strikes still do occur, as illustrated by my anecdotal experience at Manchester Airport reported earlier. Not all strikers are union members, but strikes which are backed and organised by unions generally represent a stronger show of force than those that aren't.

Evidence (Richard Hyman 1989) suggests that when workers experience sufficiently acute deprivations, unrest will be expressed in some form or another. Absenteeism, quitting, sabotage (for example, breaking a machine to slow down a breakpoint pace), go-slows, overtime bans, and, of course, strikes, are among the different ways that workers deal with grievances against their employers. While, as Peter Turnbull, Julie Morris and David Sapsford note, 'for most workers, striking is a rare event' (1996: 692), the strike is a very cohesive and visible show of employee force. It represents a temporary stoppage of work in pursuit of clear objectives, notably, better pay and conditions. In Britain, strikes have been particularly concentrated in mining, metal industry and transport. In the case of the first two sectors, it's likely that the occupational communities one finds in pit villages and steel towns help develop the resolve to react to common problems through collective action. During the 1984–5 coal miners' strike, for example, in a pit in the Rhondda Valley, South Wales, pickets weren't even deployed. So unified were community sentiments in defence of strike action, that no miner seemed even to contemplate a return to work until a settlement had been agreed.

The explanation for the strong united front of coal miners when they go on strike is, suggest C. Kerr and A. Siegal (1954, cited by Hirszowicz 1981), linked to their deep immersion in working-class communities. In a now dated but still a classic study of the proneness to strike in different industries in leading industrial countries, Kerr and Siegal found that miners had a high propensity to strike. They explained this in terms of the relative isolation of miners from mainstream society and their socialisation into remote but tightly cohesive communities. In such settings, miners develop a strong sense of *esprit de corps* based on physically tough elemental work and an epic tradition of heroism and struggle. When conflict erupts between them and their employers, it goes beyond local grievance over pay and conditions. It becomes a rebellion against people at the top in society, an 'us' and 'them' affair. In that respect, it embraces the marxist concept of class struggle. Here, there's a theoretical and an empirical meeting. Marxists theorise that the root cause of conflict is between the working and ruling classes. Kerr and Siegals' findings highlight the sense of taking on the establishment which galvanises industrial action in mining communities.

A weakness of the marxist position, however, is that it pays more attention to grievances by strikers against power centres in society than it does to the more unique predisposing factors that account for individual strikes. In their analysis of British dock strikes, Turnbull, Morris and Sapsford (1996) recognise that factors like occupational solidarity can predispose (or deter) workers to engage in strike action. But they also point out that such factors:

'account for no more than the general characteristics of the time and place which must be combined with a detailed and particular analysis of the different patterns of conflict and accommodation that are produced and re-produced at the workplace.'

(Turnbull *et al.* 1996: 720)

Illustrative of this, they noted 'the persistent militancy of dockers in the major ports', in contrast with 'the relative quiescence of their comrades in the majority of smaller ports' (1996: 721). In short, not all dockers, at least not those in the smaller ports, are swayed by the political will to take on the establishment.

QUESTIONS

1 What do marxist sociologists mean by 'happy robots'?
2 How is technology linked to job satisfaction and job dissatisfaction?
3 Compare and contrast marxist and non-marxist explanations of conflict at work.

Work, non-work and leisure

These three seemingly uncomplicated terms are not as easy to define as might appear.

> **OVER TO YOU**
>
> ***Define the terms work, non-work and leisure yourself. Then under each of the three headings, write down some real-life examples of what, in your own life, constitutes work, non-work and leisure.***

Leisure and work for this musician are virtually indistinguishable.

What did you come up with? Perhaps you regard that part-time job at the local store as *work*, and what remains as *non-work*. Maybe you regard the portion of the non-work time when you go clubbing, watch television, and otherwise entertain yourself as *leisure*. But what about your study of A-level Sociology? Isn't that work too? As you can see, the boundaries between the three terms are quite hard to pin down. Maybe they have more to do with how people define their experiences than with what sociologists have to say on the matter. Consider musicians, for example. When does work stop and leisure start for them – or do the two merge into each other? And what about women's continued responsibility for family care? It's work, but it's not the kind that generates income.

Defining work, non-work and leisure

Despite the complexities, and allowing for the different ways of looking at these issues, it's necessary to make some observations about the more common features of work, non-work and leisure:

- *Work* is generally defined as an activity that produces goods and services (for example, making furniture and parenting).

- *Non-work* is activity or non-activity that occurs before work is undertaken (for example, childhood experiences), during the time that remains when work is completed (for example, relaxing after a hard day at the office), and after work is no longer undertaken (for example, unemployment and retirement).
- *Leisure* is recreational activity that typically occurs during non-work time (for example, clubbing on the weekend).

These three spheres are interrelated. For example, coal miners do work that has a high probability these days of becoming non-work in the form of unemployment as pits are continuously shut down. Firefighters often enjoy leisure together because their job creates strong bonds based on supporting each other during tough, arduous, and dangerous work. Influences can also flow from what people do during non-work time to what they do at work. For example, certain individuals choose to work in bookstores because reading is their favourite leisure activity. There are also some people who do temporary work so that they can travel the world in-between jobs.

Sociological research has generally focused on the relationship between work and that portion of non-work when people engage in leisure. Moreover, much of the emphasis has been on the experiences of working- and middle-class, adult white males. This a serious shortcoming, and even though the research focus is much wider these days, a lot more needs to be undertaken in relation to the experiences of women, black people, people who are disabled, and people of different ages.

> **EXAM TIP**
>
> Where sociology has neglected to study the experiences of the groups just referred to, emphasise this in your exam answers. Pointing that out demonstrates an awareness of sociology's own evaluation of itself.

While it's now usually quite easy to distinguish leisure from work, such wasn't always the case. Kenneth Roberts (1981), for example, notes that modern leisure, in the sense of being a distinctive package, is a product of industrialism. Pre-industrial people, he points out, occupied a world in which work and leisure spilled over into each other. Factory bosses, however, didn't permit this intermingling. They insisted that work was work, and leisure was what took place outside the factory gate. In this way, work and leisure became separate activities. Denied the right to indulge their pleasures while they worked, factory hands demanded other rights – the right to relax and the right to be entertained.

These considerations were firmly in mind on the other side of the Atlantic too. On 2 December 1889, hundreds of American trade unionists paraded through the streets of Worcester, USA, with a banner held high by local carpenters proclaiming: 'Eight Hours for Work, Eight Hours for Rest, Eight Hours for What We Will' (Rosenzweig 1985). In the eighteenth and early nineteenth centuries, notes Rosenzweig, American workers interweaved work with drink-induced leisure. In the shoe shops of Lynn in the 1820s, he relates, a half pint of 'white eye' was an expected part of the daily wage. Similarly, for the mostly Irish immigrants who toiled from sunrise to sunset building America's canals and railroads, five or so breaks for a 'jigger' of whiskey was a daily routine. Things began to change, however, as the nineteenth century progressed. The development of mechanised industry heralded the implementation of workplace discipline, and whiskey was relegated to the saloons. In this way, the distinctiveness of work time and leisure time became sharpened.

Roberts (1981: 9–10) highlights two aspects of leisure: 'spare or free time' and 'play'. The first dimension refers to the time left when work has been completed and physical needs (for example, sleeping) have been met. The second dimension focuses on what we do in that non-work time in terms of recreation. As to the extent to which work affects leisure, Roberts raises a critical question: 'How strong is the long arm of the job?' (1981: 53). He accepts that there is a work effect on leisure, but he cautions against exaggerating this association. On the effect side, Roberts refers to a study by G. Friedman (1961) who found that routine, boring work encourages some people to:

- indulge in hobbies which require skills denied expression at work. Roberts refers to this kind of leisure as *compensatory* because interesting leisure activities compensate for work-based drudgery
- use leisure to escape into fantasy worlds and amusement, thereby reducing the awareness of unhappiness at work
- carry over the same 'couldn't care less' attitude at work into leisure, in a manner that generates a sense of indifference towards life in general.

Roberts (1981) also cites C. Wright Mills' (1956) finding that the sense of status attached to white-collar work encourages people so employed to emulate 'upper-middle' class lifestyles in their leisure pursuits.

The relationship between work and leisure with regard to different social groups

Social class

As indicated earlier, much of the literature on the relationship between work and leisure emphasises the link this relationship has with *social class*. Middle-class leisure, for example, is often characterised by what Roberts (1981) calls an *extension* type. Illustrative of this, lawyers sometimes attend social functions in order to *extend* their professional contacts. Other examples of extension leisure include business executives using a computer room at home as an extended office, and salespeople playing golf to add to their client lists. The extension pattern is succinctly defined by Stanley Parker in his dated but important book, *The Future of Work and Leisure*:

> 'Briefly, the *extension* pattern consists of having leisure activities which are often similar in content to one's working activities and of making no sharp distinction between what is considered as work and what as leisure.'
>
> (Parker 1971: 101–2)

Working-class leisure, however, is more likely to be of the kind described by Roberts (1981) as compensatory. Parker (1971) characterises this work–leisure relationship as an *opposition* pattern. In this model, leisure and work are polar opposites. Consider, for example, the sober, sharp wits of distant water fisherman while at sea with the explosive hard drinking that ensues during shore leave. Illustrative of the stark contrast between work and beer, Paul Willis describes the British pub as:

> 'a social environment which announces immediately that here is a place which is about relaxation, leisure and pleasure – polar opposites to the formal qualities of work.'
>
> (Willis 1990: 43)

Parker (1971) also identifies what he terms a *neutrality* pattern, whereby leisure activities are generally different from work ones but not deliberately so. People who display this pattern (clerical workers are an example) are neither so engrossed in their work that they want it to follow through into leisure, nor so damaged by it that they adopt a hostile attitude towards it.

These class-related differences are arguably less clear-cut today than they were in the past. When heavy industry was the economic backbone of the British economy, there was a discernible divide between manual and non-manual occupations. 'Hard hat work' forged a recuperative camaraderie between men, which spilled over into nights out 'with the boys' in pubs and clubs. Non-manual employment was more likely to be characterised by the extension and neutral patterns than by this compensatory type. In the 1990s, however, in the age of service sector expansion and manufacturing decline, the cleavage between the middle and working class is more likely to occur between different types of non-manual employment. On the one hand, there are low-paid, low-status workers who perform routine non-manual tasks (for example, secretaries who are also usually women) and, on the other, there are high-paid, high-status workers whose skills involve problem-identification and problem-solving (for example, software consultants who are also usually men).

It's likely that the high-status workers will adopt or continue extension type leisure. The burgeoning female-dominated, routine non-manual sector offers little scope, however, for this kind of pattern. Many women workers have considerably less non-work time than their male counterparts in which to pursue leisure.

Gender

For many such women, what Roberts in the 1980s referred to as 'the double shift of paid employment followed by domestic work' (Roberts 1981: 81) is still a common experience. Even when watching the television, these woman are often 'on duty' as mums and wives. Moreover, as relatively low-paid workers, their opportunities to engage in leisure outside the home is often restricted.

In the UK women are still paid less than men on average, despite 20 years of equal pay legislation – a fifth less according to the Equal Opportunities Commission which reported its findings in 1996. After a lengthy study, the Commission reported that in her early twenties, a woman earns 91 per cent of a man's hourly pay. In her thirties, this drops to 87 per cent, in her forties to 75 per cent, and in her fifties to 72 per cent. For women who work part-time, the picture is even bleaker. They earn less than 50 per cent of what men earn in full-time employment.

Given these income differentials, men are more likely than women to have more money available for out-of-home leisure. Younger women, however, are beginning to close the wages gap, and their active participation in club and pub leisure is very visible. Rosemary Deem (1986) found in research she conducted in Milton Keynes that women in better-paid secretarial jobs, administrative jobs and caring professions tended to have quite a lot of outside recreation. Many of them also informed Deem that they had developed new leisure pursuits because of people whom they met at work and the facilities available. Nevertheless, it seems that female participation in recreation outside the home is generally less than that of men. Roberts (1981) notes that one explanation for this is that they're less likely than men to have access to cars. This could be linked to low income, but there's also the patriarchal phenomenon of men exercising 'first claim' on the family car. Roberts adds that, in some communities, there are cultural pressures on women not to go out for leisure except with their families or to visit relatives.

Deem has also highlighted the impact of male employment on women's leisure. Her research found that most married or cohabiting women whose partners were employed had their 'free time' adversely affected by the nature and timing of their partners' work. This ranged from having to cook two evening meals – one for children, the other for a late-returning partner – to having to wash work clothes. Deem cites a study conducted by

R. Dixie and M. Talbot (1982) in the working-class neighbourhood of Armley in Leeds which found that male work roles and patterns of employment had a significant impact on women's leisure, especially women not in paid employment. They reported that:

'Daily life for housewives in Armley revolves around the routine of the breadwinner . . . the work patterns of men are accommodated . . . "Most days he's out (to work) at half past seven at the latest and God knows when he'll be back . . . " The husband's work role sometimes caused conflicts of interest, whether it was because work was brought home . . . or because the husband needed to switch off to recuperate . . . either way the wife was excluded.'

(Dixie and Talbot 1982, cited by Deem 1986: 113)

Ethnicity

In her study, Deem (1986: 139) also makes the important point that was alluded to earlier: 'ethnicity has by and large been absent' in leisure research. While specifically referring here to women's leisure and the marginalisation of black experience by 'white feminism', Deem's contention applies to the experiences of minority ethnic people in general. It's as if their leisure is either assumed not to be sufficiently different from white people's leisure or too insignificant to merit detailed consideration. While more is now written on the subject than previously, much more research is needed on the relationship between work and leisure from the perspective of minority ethnic communities. Certainly we mustn't conclude, as Roberts reminds us, 'that the minorities would wish to emulate middle-class white's leisure habits, if granted equal opportunities' (Roberts 1983: 149).

Some Asian people, for example, notes Roberts (1983), have no concept of leisure. He adds that even apparently identical leisure activities, like participation in sports, can have very different meanings for black people and white people. Other Asian people are prepared to work very long hours in order to obtain periodical extended holidays in their countries of origins. Roberts (1983) refers to Bangladeshi textile workers in Lancashire who choose work schedules with long hours, on whatever shifts available, in order to maximise earnings to pay for air tickets 'back home'. Given that some of these people have migrated to Britain without their families, such sacrifices help pay for home visits that sometimes last from between six and 12 months.

This emphasis by Roberts on the need of Bangladeshi people to work long hours in order to enjoy home visit leisure, highlights the fact that they receive low rates of pay. Members of minority ethnic groups, as was documented in Chapter 7 (pages 153–4), generally receive lower pay than white Britons. This has clear implications for the disposable income they have available to lead an active leisure life. Moreover, in some Asian minority ethnic communities, it's considered frivolous to attach value to pursuits that offer mere personal pleasure when social and economic obligations to family (including extended family) ties are considered of paramount importance. While, for example, going to the pub is a popular leisure activity for many young white men, it's much less common, as Paul Willis (1990) reveals, for most young Asians.

Age

Another factor that has an important bearing on the relationship between work and leisure is age. Children and old people are generally disadvantaged in labour market terms because children haven't started working and old people have stopped working. That gives both groups lots of non-work time in which to pursue leisure. However, other important intervening variables like social class and gender impinge upon the actual opportunities to participate in leisure. For example, Jay Ginn and Sara Arber (1992) have drawn attention to the disadvantages older women experience relative to older men regarding access to resources that permit full participation in desired activities. Women in this age group generally have less money than their male counterparts to spend on leisure.

After children (not forgetting the by-proxy economic advantages and disadvantages they obtain from parents) and old people, the next most disadvantaged age group in earnings terms are young people who are just beginning work, and older workers who are at risk of redundancy. 'Later young adulthood' and middle age represent positions in the life course when financial advantage in relation to employment and leisure is generally at its best.

While it's true that people who are starting work are generally entering more prosperous futures than those who are preparing for retirement, it's also important to recognise that younger employees face a shorter working life than their parents. Moreover, many young people enter employment at a later stage than their parents first did. In the early 1970s, nearly two-thirds of young people left school as soon as they could, and most school leavers entered employment straightaway. In the early 1990s, less than one in ten 16-year-old people were leaving school and entering full-time employment. Roberts describes this change in concise terms: 'Britain's young workers of the 1970s have been replaced by the young unemployed, students and youth trainees' (Roberts 1996: 25).

It's these young people whose leisure activities, especially if they involve substance misuse and other illegal activities, are causing so much concern among politicians today. When young people can't get work (or decently paid work), some of them turn to illegal means of making a living and a leisure culture that prizes law-breaking. This theme is taken further in Chapter 16.

To conclude this section on work, non-work and leisure, it should be emphasised that most sociologists are agreed that there *is* a relationship between the three spheres. The agreement rests on the sensible assumption that, for most people, the time they spend working directly affects the amount of non-work time they have in which to engage in leisure. As I'm sitting here writing this chapter, I'm conscious that I also want to watch a video that I rented today. The writing is work, and when I get time to stop writing, viewing the video will be a leisure activity. For leisure is often like that, a chunk of time snatched to do something which will bring rapid, short-lived pleasure. Chris Rojek makes this same point when he writes: 'popular leisure activity seems to thrive on fragmentary, contrasting and fleeting experience' (1993: 213). That's what the video is going to offer me – some short-lived mental recuperation from my intellectual labour!

While, however, as Roberts notes, 'Few uses of leisure completely escape the shadow of work experience' (1981: 56), he also cautions that one single factor – in this case, occupation – doesn't necessarily account for what people choose to do in their free time. It's only in 'cultural' interests like theatres and concerts that a marked white-collar/blue-collar divide is apparent. Roberts (1981) draws upon a study by J. R. Kelly (1978) who, after studying three American communities, concluded that leisure was independent of all social predictors. While relationships existed between his respondents' jobs and their use of leisure, Kelly found that the association was far from watertight. The respondents said that their jobs weren't relevant to how they spent their leisure time. Roberts adds that 'Many leisure interests straddle occupational and social class lines' (1981: 65). In that context, he notes that watching television is a major leisure interest across all social groups, and that alcohol accounts for a substantial proportion of money spent on leisure. For good measure (again, no pun intended), he reports that even within the same occupational groups, there are wide variations in leisure patterns.

An important type of non-work that affects millions of Britons but which hasn't yet been considered in detail is unemployment. Some people imagine – and *imagine* is an apt word here – that unemployment is a condition of limitless leisure. The next section, in the best sociological tradition of harnessing empirical evidence, explodes that myth.

QUESTIONS

1. Define the terms: work, non-work and leisure.
2. How are the above three spheres interrelated in relation to:
   - **a** class?
   - **b** gender?
   - **c** ethnicity?
   - **d** age?

Unemployment

Most people who are unemployed aren't out of a job through choice. They either can't get one when they leave school, or are made redundant, or have to stop working because of ill-health. Some people – a small minority – become voluntarily unemployed. Most of them are sufficiently well-off to make this decision.

Being employed in the contracting heavy industry sector today increases the risk of becoming unemployed.

Working-class young people are more likely than their middle- and upper-class counterparts to be among the involuntary unemployed or among trainee groups. For males, this trend is related to the major occupational restructuring of old heavy industries by new light service sector employment. Sons are much less likely than previously to follow their fathers into mining, shipbuilding and other 'hard-hat jobs' because those industries are either obsolete or in decline.

Among students, middle-class young people still account for the majority at university. However, the conferring of university status on large numbers of higher education institutes in the early 1990s could change the demographics here. In particular, more working-class young people than previously are likely to study for degrees at these so-called 'new universities'. Then, like their middle-class counterparts, they'll be able to defer entry into employment 'with prospects' until after graduation.

'Later young' and middle-aged adults are more likely than members of other age groups to be in employment. However, younger adults will increasingly work in temporary employment, compared to their older peers. The notion of a job for life in one company or even employment for life in one occupation is fast becoming an unrealistic proposition. Companies and public sector employers now assign short-term contracts to temporary employees more than ever before, a trend that looks set to continue in the flexible employment practices of an information-based economy. Says Lance Morrow:

'America has entered the age of the contingent or temporary worker, of the consultant and subcontractor, of the just-in-time work force – fluid, flexible, disposable.'

(Morrow 1993, cited by Bridges 1996: 1)

The same trends are evident in the UK and in other post-industrial societies.

The young worker and the future worker are entering a new age. This doesn't mean that you won't have to work when you finish full-time education. What it means is that you will probably work part-time, will probably do a fair bit of freelance work, and will probably do a little of this and a little of that. The setting is one in which you and other young people will be doing different things for different people without being able to describe everything under the heading of 'one job'. Not all young people are entering or will enter this new world. Old jobs will still linger – for a while – and some people – though markedly fewer than in previous decades – will have a job for life with one employer in one job field. Certainly, middle-aged people and people approaching retirement age, if they have such a job already, will probably be able to 'hang on in there'.

It's you, the reader of this book, who will have to get used to the idea of replacing the notion of a 9 to 5, 12 months a year job and a pension at 65 with something radically different. This needn't be a bleak future. Provided you learn to ride the crest of this wave of change by adapting to and 'learning' the ways of the new technology, you'll do well and prosper. On the other hand, young people who enter – or don't enter – the labour market without good qualifications and realistic versatility risk grim prospects. In a post-industrial Britain wracked by unemployment, it's particularly working-class young people who, notes Frank Coffield:

'are struggling to form new identities without reference to work; and fashionable theories of social reproduction will have to be abandoned because there is no longer a working class to be reproduced.'

(Coffield 1995, cited by Pilcher 1996: 167)

OVER TO YOU

What does Coffield mean when he claims that 'fashionable theories of social reproduction will have to be abandoned because there is no longer a working class to be reproduced'?

It was the awful prospect of that plight, which urged one of the authors, as a comprehensive school teacher in a former mining community in Leeds, to persuade his students to stay at school for as long as possible and to leave well-qualified. A coal mine not far from the school was shut down in the early 1990s, so sons could no longer follow their fathers into mining. Nor were the prospects for less well-qualified girls very encouraging. The options were either poorly-paid service sector work or unemployment. The school admitted some of its students from one of the poorest areas of Leeds, where, curiously it seems, uncarpeted dwellings and satellite dishes co-existed. However, when people are unemployed, as many still are in that area, watching MTV or a Sky movie makes a bleak life a bit more bearable. The £22 or so monthly subscription to the satellite company works out at about 70p a day – hardly a lavish indulgence, but it probably means going short on some food or heating. Many unemployed people are housebound because most of them are poor. Unable to afford to go to the pub, club or cinema, 'They watch a lot of television, smoke too much and have to spend too much money on launderettes, pay phones, food from the corner shop and electric fires' (Harris 1984: 88). If his students entered this kind of world when they left school, the author felt that he hadn't done his job well.

Measuring unemployment

High levels of unemployment have persisted. In August 1995, the UK unemployment rate was 8.1 per cent:

nearly 2.3 million people. This figure contrasts starkly with the unemployment rate in 1979 which stood at 4.1 per cent: nearly 1.1 million people. These are *official* statistics. However, measuring the actual rate of unemployment is difficult and often very controversial. The UK government uses what's called the 'claimant count'. This is the number of unemployed people who receive benefits or who 'sign on' to receive credited National Insurance contributions. The government has changed the method of 'counting' the unemployed about 35 times since 1979. New changes, for example, were introduced in 1996 with the introduction of a Jobseeker's Allowance.

Changes that affect how many people are officially defined as unemployed are of four main types:

- *statistical changes*, like only counting people on benefits or contribution credits
- *benefit rule changes*, which then automatically translate into changes in the number of people who are officially considered unemployed
- *administrative changes*, such as making people accept work that they're not suited to by tightening up the 'availability for work' rules
- *temporary work and training schemes*, which can create short-lived 'employment blips'.

According to the Unemployment Unit, the real experience of unemployment is much more widespread than the official version. It estimates that the unemployment rate in August 1995 was *really* 11.6 per cent: nearly 3.5 million people. Even the Royal Statistical Society has criticised the government's use of the claimant count as an inaccurate measure of unemployment. Just consider, for example, those unemployed people who don't know how to make a claim or decide not to make a claim. They're unemployed, but they don't appear in the official statistics. In that respect, the statistics are to some extent socially constructed – that is, they reflect, in part, the ways in which the government decides to categorise unemployment.

Causes of unemployment

What are the causes of unemployment? No, they don't have anything to do – at least, not in the vast majority of cases – with people being lazy. Most people who are unemployed want a job, though some of them, understandably, aren't prepared to accept a job for which they're unsuited, one that pays a very low wage, or one that breaches decent standards of health and safety. The causes of unemployment are many and varied.

In the UK, a rising trend in unemployment was very evident in the 1970s. The main cause of this was an increasing workforce that wasn't met with an equivalent demand for labour. Added to this, was the decline of heavy industry (such as coalmining and shipbuilding), and the rise of high-tech production processes that rely less on human labour. The legacy of these continuing trends is that older (mainly male) workers are increasingly at risk in the 1990s of becoming redundant in the contracting industrial sector. Moreover, school leavers (especially young men) don't get the chance to do the jobs their parents did. One million jobs, note Adrian Sinfield and Brian Showler (1981), were lost in the 1970s to 'deindustrialisation'. In 1993, unemployment rates were three times higher for those previously in manual jobs as for those in non-manual jobs (Oppenheim and Harker 1996).

While the above paragraph maps the main 'whole society' causes of unemployment, there are other 'causes' that explain why some people are more at risk than others of being unemployed. The principal ones are:

- *Being disabled, prone to ill-health, or having suffered injuries* (often work-related). Accidents in construction work, for example, are high. Disabled people, say Sinfield and Showler (1981), find it very hard to get back to work once they've lost a job, and so they're particularly prone to long-term unemployment.
- *Having limited skills and few or no formal qualifications*. In that context, notes Kenneth Roberts (1996: 28), 'It still makes as much sense as ever before, in career terms, for young people to continue in mainstream academic education for as long as they are able to progress'. Given that there's a shrinking worldwide demand for unskilled manual workers and an expanding demand for highly skilled people, my efforts to persuade students to stay on at school make good sociological sense!
- *Belonging to a minority ethnic group*. Unemployment rates for black and other minority ethnic groups have been about double that of white people since 1984 (Oppenheim and Harker 1996). Black people and people from other minority ethnic groups who are well qualified are at greater risk than other people of unemployment because of discrimination.

Looking at the causes of unemployment is, of course, just one part of the story. We have to consider the effects too.

The effects of unemployment

In his very moving book, *Unemployment*, Jeremy Seabrook (1983) lets unemployed Britons talk frankly about their experiences. The people who are the statistics – women, men and school-leavers – are given a voice. In the emptied towns where once men worked in coal, steel and construction, Seabrook documents among the unemployed a deep-seated sense of despair, feelings of lack of self-worth and of wasted potential. He concludes that the experience of prolonged unemployment is for most people a profoundly destructive experience.

Adrian Sinfield, while recognising that different people react to unemployment in a variety of ways, writes:

'Active distress may be greater among those forced by disability, declining health or lack of demand for their experience and skills to look for less rewarding and lower-status jobs or to contemplate many years of passing their time on the dole until they can claim the established status, and higher benefits, of retirement.'

(Sinfield 1981: 153)

Whatever differences exist in how people who are out of work perceive unemployment, Carey Oppenheim and Lisa Harker put the main objective effect in clear, stark language: 'Unemployment means *poverty*' (1996: 49). They also refer to research by Bill Daniel (1990), who found that the effect of unemployment, however brief, was hardship and trauma. Asked about their experience of unemployment, people generally ranked it as close to the worst life event they'd ever endured. Asked about the worst things about being out of work, 78 per cent of them reported lack of money or not being able to afford goods or activities. Sixty per cent of them identified boredom or not having anything to do. A substantial minority spoke of depression and shame. So much for the myth that unemployed people enjoy boundless leisure!

Another important effect of unemployment is that if a married man becomes out of work, there's a strong risk that his wife will give up paid work as well. This, note Oppenheim and Harker (1996), is because of the benefit rules. If a family is living on Income Support, most of a wife's earnings is offset pound for pound against the benefit. This means that the woman would need to earn a high wage to make it worthwhile for the family to come off benefit. The upshot is often that a two-earner family has no earners at all. Oppenheim and Harker's findings are supported by research from a study by Bill Jordan and Marcus Redley (1994). Noting that 'When their partners were out of work, it was not "worth it" for them [women] to stay in employment', Jordan and Redley illustrate this point:

'"Then me husband lost his job so we had to go on social security and they would only let me earn 4 pound. They only let me keep 4 pound out of 20 pound that I earned [laughs]. So I soon jacked that in." (Mrs Parrett, catering worker)'

(Jordan and Redley 1994: 164)

Importantly, Jordan and Redley challenged the notion that the unemployed necessarily surrender to the material challenges of poverty. Rather than seeing themselves as drifting and vulnerable, some unemployed people develop survival strategies and cultures of resistance. Among men who were on the margins of society – unemployed or in low-paid work – Jordan and Redley uncovered 'a thriving trade in animals, birds and fish; stocks could be built up in more prosperous periods, and run down in bleaker times. One unemployed man used his dogs for hunting at night to catch "rabbits, hares, foxes, deer, I get it all"', which he then sold (1994: 170).

Suggesting that people sometimes develop coping strategies when they become unemployed isn't to say that they don't suffer hardship. In most cases, they do. There are, however, a small number of people who voluntarily choose to stop working in order to improve their quality of life. In America, this phenomenon of 'downscaling' – whereby people exchange simple for lavish lifestyles – is becoming increasingly popular among the middle class. The process typically means voluntary early retirement or swapping a high-paid executive position for a self-employed job or work that's low on pay but high on satisfaction. Contemplate, for example, a stress-ridden, mid-career accountant who turns her back on corporate employment, and settles for a beachside home where she paints pictures for pleasure – and, if possible, also for sale.

One term used to describe this change in working habits is 'voluntary simplicity'. It's all about finding peace and happiness on a slower track. Out goes the 40-hour week – a largely post-Second World War invention. In comes a downscaled, sustainable lifestyle with an emphasis on thrift-store shopping, job-sharing, telecommuting, cycling and car-pooling. This kind of lifestyle is, of course, only possible if one can afford to 'retire' early. So it assumes a relatively prosperous employment profile prior to the decision to 'chuck it all in' and live off the proceeds. Few of us are able to afford that – dare we say? – enticing option!

QUESTIONS

1. How is unemployment measured, and what are the problems associated with compiling unemployment statistics?
2. Outline the main causes of unemployment, pointing out the most vulnerable groups.
3. What are the principal effects of unemployment on people's lives?

Concluding remarks

Most of the issues raised in this chapter are crucially linked to the ownership and control of technology. In a society where machines are owned and controlled by capitalists, technology is the servant of company profits. People who can't afford to pay for private medical care have to wait for treatment. Workers whose jobs are taken over by computers get laid off. In the kind of society envisaged by Marx, where the machines are owned and controlled by the people, technology serves community interests. Patients are treated on a needs basis, and workers are offered leisure without financial penalty when information technology does their job.

While Marx would surely approve of the National Health Service, his vision of a mass leisure society, say his critics, is a fanciful pipedream. We in the UK live in a capitalist society where most adults work for a living. Sociologists must deal with that reality. Even so, it's not a reality that everyone is happy with. There's widespread dissatisfaction among the British public, for example, about the private ownership and control of water. On the other hand, industrial disputes that lead to strike action are on the wane. Doesn't this suggest that capitalism is quite secure?

It's not for us to tell you how to answer these questions. However, what we can and do say is, be mindful of the sociological evidence and arguments that will help you to arrive at considered judgements.

Glossary of key terms

Alienation The sense of being disengaged from one's work, a lack of job-satisfying connectedness

Bureaucracy An hierarchical institution for administering the organisation of work tasks

Claimant count The number of unemployed people in the UK who receive benefits or 'sign on' to get credited national insurance contributions. These are the 'official unemployed'

De-skilling Very much associated with the work of the marxist, Harry Braverman (1974), this is the process whereby work tasks that once required craft skill have succumbed to mechanised routines

Division between ownership and control The process whereby owner-capitalists devolve operational control to managers

Downscaling More a middle- than a working-class prerogative, replacing lavish with simple lifestyles, typically by switching to part-time or less well-paid work, or becoming voluntarily unemployed

Extrinsic job satisfaction Deriving material satisfaction from the 'by proxy' sense of enjoyment obtained from a well-paid job

Human relations management theory The belief that managers should offer the workforce intrinsic rewards – notably, enjoyable working conditions – as well as decent pay, because happy workers are productive workers

Industrial Revolution The fairly rapid transformation of society from an agricultural to an industrial economy

Intrinsic job satisfaction Deriving satisfaction from the inner sense of enjoyment obtained by doing a job that one likes

Job-enlargement Having multiple job tasks within the same organisation in order to relieve boredom.

Kaizen organisation An organisational structure that incorporates a workers' think tank – a Quality Control Circle – that passes its ideas into and up the management pyramid. The kaizen is very popular in Japan

Leisure Recreational activity that typically occurs during non-work time

Non-work Activity or non-activity that occurs before work is undertaken, during the time that remains when work is completed, and after work is no longer undertaken

Scientific management theory The belief that managers should increase productivity by maximising the efficiency of the workforce. Extrinsic rewards – notably, financial incentives – are paramount, buttressed, as appropriate by discipline and punishment. The theory was developed by Frederick Taylor, and is sometimes called 'Taylorism', and also 'Fordism'

Strikes Temporary stoppages of labour in pursuit of employee goals. Strikes are usually symptomatic of intense conflict between employers and employees

Technology The tools that enable us to produce goods and services

Unemployment Being out of work, usually not through choice. In the UK, the method for counting unemployed people is the 'claimant count'

Work An activity that produces goods and services

References

Bernhardt, Annette, Morris, Martina and Handcock, Mark S. (1995) Women's gains or men's losses? A closer look at the shrinking gender gap in earnings, pp 302–28, *American Journal of Sociology*, Vol. 101, No. 2, September

Blackler, Frank (1995) Knowledge, knowledge work and organizations: An overview and interpretation, pp 1021–46, *Organization Studies*, 16, Issue 6

Blauner, Robert (1960) Work satisfaction and industrial trends in modern society, pp 117–22, in Worsley, Peter (1972) (ed.) *Problems of Modern Society*. Harmondsworth: Penguin

Blauner, Robert (1964) *Alienation and Freedom*. Chicago: The University of Chicago Press

Braverman, Harry (1974) *Labor and Monopoly Capital: The Degradation of Work in the Twentieth Century*. New York: Monthly Review Press

Bridges, William (1996) *Jobshift*. London: Nicholas Brealey Publishing

Davenport, Thomas H., Jarvenpaa, Sirkka L. and Beers, Michael C. (1996) 'Improving knowledge work processes', pp 53–65, *Sloan Management Review*, Summer

Deem, Rosemary (1986) *All Work and No Play*. Milton Keynes: Open University Press

Ginn, Jay and Arber, Sara (1992) Gender and resources in later life, pp 6–10, *Sociology Review*, November

Halsey, A. H. (1995) *Change in British Society*, Fourth Edition. Oxford: Oxford University Press

Harris, Martyn (1984) How unemployment affects people, pp 88–90, *New Society*, 19 January

Hirszowicz, Maria (1981) *Industrial Sociology*. Oxford: Martin Robertson

Hughes, Karen D. (1996) Transformed by technology? The changing nature of women's 'traditional' and 'non-traditional' white-collar work, pp 227–50, *Work, Employment & Society*, Vol. 10, No. 2, June

Hyman, Richard (1989) *Strikes*, Fourth Edition. Houndsmills, Basingstoke: Macmillan

Jordan, Bill and Redley, Marcus (1994) Polarisation, underclass and the welfare state, pp 153–76, *Work, Employment & Society*, Vol. 8, No. 2, June

Kim, W. Chan and Mauborgne, Renee A. (1996) Procedural justice and managers' in-role and extra-role behaviour: The case of the multinational, pp 499–515, *Management Science*, Vol. 42, No. 4, April

Kingston, Peter (1996) Powerful people, p. vi, The *Guardian Higher*, 29 October
Levin, Jack (1996) *Sociological Snapshots*. Thousand Oaks, California: Pine Forge Press
Lillrank, Paul (1995) The transfer of management innovations from Japan, pp 971–89, *Organization Studies*, 16, Issue 6
McGregor, Douglas (1960) *The Human Side of Enterprises*. London: McGraw-Hill
Merton, Robert K. (1957) *Social Theory and Social Structure*. New York: The Free Press
Michels, Robert (1958) *Political Parties*. Glencoe, Illinois: The Free Press
Oppenheim, Carey and Harker, Lisa (1996) *Poverty: The Facts*, Third Edition. London: Child Poverty Action Group
Parker, Stanley R. (1971) *The Future of Work and Leisure*. MacGibbon & Kee
Penn, Roger, Rose, Michael and Rubery, Jill (eds) (1994) *Skill and Occupational Change*. Oxford: Oxford University Press
Peters, Tom (1993) *Liberation Management*. London: Pan Books
Pilcher, Jane (1996) Transitions to and from the labour market: Younger and older people and employment, pp 161–73, *Work, Employment & Society*, Vol. 10, No. 1, March
Roberts, Kenneth (1981) *Leisure*, Second Edition. London: Longman
Roberts, Kenneth (1983) *Youth and Leisure*. London: George Allen & Unwin
Roberts, Kenneth (1996) Youth and employment in modern Britain, pp 25–9, *Sociology Review*, Vol. 5, No. 4, April
Rojek, Chris (1993) *Ways of Escape*. Houndsmills, Basingstoke: Macmillan
Rosenzweig, Roy (1985) *Eight Hours For What We Will*. Cambridge: Cambridge University Press
Seabrook, Jeremy (1983) *Unemployment*. St Albans: Granada
Selznick, Philip (1943) An approach to a theory of bureaucracy, pp 47–54, *American Sociological Review*, Vol. 8, No. 1, February
Sinfield, Adrian and Showler, Brian (1981) Unemployment and the unemployed in 1980, pp 1–26, in Showler, Brian and Sinfield, Adrian (1981) (eds), *The Workless State*. Oxford: Martin Robertson
Sinfield, Adrian (1981) Unemployment in an unequal society, pp 122–66, in Showler, Brian and Sinfield, Adrian (1981), op. cit.
Thompson, E. P. (1975) *The Making of the English Working Class*. Harmondsworth: Penguin
Turnbull, Peter, Morris, Julia, and Sapsford, David (1996) Persistent militants and quiescent comrades: Intra-industry strike activity on the docks, 1947–89, pp 692–727, *Sociological Review*, Vol. 44, No. 4, November
Weber, Max (original date not provided) Characteristics of bureaucracy, pp 447–54, in Coser, Lewis A. and Rosenberg, Bernard (1969) (eds), *Sociological Theory: A Book of Readings*, Third Edition. London: Collier-Macmillan Ltd
Weber, Max (original date not provided) Some consequences of bureaucratization, pp 454–55, in Coser, Lewis A. and Rosenberg, Bernard (1969) (eds), op. cit.
Westergaard, John (1995) *Who Gets What?* Cambridge: Polity Press
Willis, Paul (1978) *Learning to Labour: How Working-Class Kids Get Working-Class Jobs*. Farnborough, Hants: Saxon House
Willis, Paul (1990) *Moving Culture*. London: Calouste Gulbenkian Foundation

Exam practice: Work, organisations and leisure

Data response question

Item A

Population of working age[1]: by gender and employment status, Spring 1996 (millions)

	Males	Females	All
United Kingdom			
Economically active			
In employment			
Full-time employees	10.8	5.9	16.7
Part-time employees	0.8	4.5	5.3
All employees	11.6	10.4	22.0
Full-time self-employed	2.2	0.4	2.6
Part-time self-employed	0.2	0.4	0.5
All self-employed	2.4	0.7	3.1
Others in employment[2]	0.2	0.2	0.4
All in employment	14.2	11.3	25.4
ILO unemployed	1.5	0.8	2.3
All economically active	15.7	12.0	27.8
Economically inactive	2.9	4.9	7.8
Population of working age	18.6	17.0	35.5

[1]Males aged 16 to 64, females aged 16 to 59.
[2]Those on government employment and training programmes and unpaid family workers.

(From: *Labour Force Survey*, Office for National Statistics 1996)

Item B

Unemployment rates[1]: by gender and age (percentages)

	1991	1992	1993	1994	1995	1996
United Kingdom						
Males						
16–19	16.4	18.6	22.0	20.9	19.6	20.6
20–24	15.2	18.9	20.3	18.3	17.0	16.2
25–44	8.0	10.5	10.9	10.2	9.0	8.7
45–54	6.3	8.4	9.4	8.6	7.4	6.4
55–59	8.4	11.2	12.3	11.6	10.2	9.9
60–64	9.9	10.2	14.2	11.6	9.9	8.9
65 and over	5.9	4.9	4.6	3.7	..	4.1
All males aged 16 and over	9.2	11.5	12.4	11.4	10.1	9.7
Females						
16–19	12.7	13.6	15.9	16.0	14.8	14.6
20–24	10.1	10.2	11.8	10.7	10.6	8.9
25–44	7.1	7.3	7.3	7.0	6.7	6.3
45–54	4.6	5.0	5.0	5.0	4.5	4.1
55–59	5.5	4.5	6.0	6.5	4.7	4.2
60 and over	4.4	3.1	3.9	2.9	..	..
All females aged 16 and over	7.2	7.3	7.6	7.3	6.8	6.3

(Source: *Social Trends 27*, 1997)

Item C

Only a minority of jobs in Britain now fits our idea of a 'normal' or 'real' job. Since the late 1970s the labour market in the UK has undergone more radical changes than occurred in the previous half a century.

Less than 50 per cent of the working population in Britain has a full-time, long-term job with a traditional employment contract. There has been a sharp rise in the variety of ways in which work is organized. We cannot describe it as 'the way people are employed' because many of these expanding forms of working arrangements (subcontracting, franchising, self-employment) break the link between work and employment.

The story is one of increases in almost every form of work – except the traditional full-time, long-term job. One million people have more than one job. Part-time work has more than doubled in the last fifteen years and so has self-employment. Temporary employment and fixed-term contracts have significantly increased. And new working arrangements, such as job-sharing and annual hours contracts, have been established. These changes are now in all forms of working.

(Adapted from Chris Brewster in Anthony Giddens, *Sociology: Introductory readings* (Polity Press) 1997)

Item D

Employees' say in decisions affecting their work

	1985 %	1987 %	1989 %	1991 %	1993 %
% having a say	62	51	50	54	52
% saying:					
Should have more say	36	46	44	45	52
Satisfied with the way things are	63	53	54	54	47

A disturbing trend is towards increasing discontent among employees about their involvement in decisions affecting them.

Moreover, there appears to be a relationship between levels of consultation and positive attitudes to management. Of workers who think they would have no say in a decision affecting their work, less than one in five believe their workplace is very well managed. And half of those who would have a great deal of say believe it. It would be facile to conclude from this evidence that reduced levels of consultation have been the cause of the deterioration in management–worker relations – it could well be the other way round – but they may have played a part.

(British Social Attitudes, the 11th report, Social and Community Planning Research, 1994)

(a) What is the total number of people economically inactive of working age in the population? **(Item A)** *(1 mark)*

(b) Describe the trends, as shown in **Item B**, of unemployment rates. *(3 marks)*

(c) Define the following working arrangements: 'subcontracting, franchising and annual hours contracts'. **(Item C)** *(3 marks)*

(d) With reference to the **Items** and elsewhere, outline the main changes that have taken place since the late 1970s, in work and leisure patterns. *(9 marks)*

(e) With reference to **Item D** and elsewhere, assess the argument that a 'deterioration in management–worker relations' has taken place in the workplace. *(9 marks)*

11 Wealth, poverty and welfare

Topics covered in this chapter
- *Defining and measuring poverty*
- *The extent of poverty*
- *Disparities between the rich and the rest*
- *The causes of poverty*
- *Welfare social policy: A solution to poverty?*

Switch on the television, turn the pages of a newspaper, and a dominant theme is that the world beyond our immediate experience is one of suffering. Poverty and hunger figure prominently. Much of the suffering is caused by disputes between competing power blocs in an unequal world. While the extent of inequality varies between nations, it is universal.

Differences in wealth and poverty between the rich and poor worlds are absolute. In the UK, few people starve to death. In the Sudan, many do. Within a nation, however, differences are often relative. I earn a reasonable income, which means I'm relatively well-off compared to some people and relatively less well-off compared to others.

Like many Britons, however, in my kind of 'average' economic position, I aspire to something better. So I play the Lottery. As I write this chapter, I'm considering what numbers I should select for this week's bonanza prize. The jackpot might be £40 million. Why am I doing this when the odds against me winning are so great? I guess it's the tantalising, if remote, prospect that, from being just an average person today, I could become a millionaire tomorrow.

Win or lose, my income isn't so low that I have to rely on welfare benefits. For then I would be poor. Not only is Income Support very meagre, many poor people in the UK live below the Income Support level. Poverty isn't just about low income. It's also:

'about rights and relationships; about how people are treated and how they regard themselves; about powerlessness, exclusion and loss of dignity. Yet the lack of an adequate income is at its heart.'

(*Faith in the City* 1985, cited by Oppenheim and Harker 1996: 7)

Some people are ground down by poverty and have a shorter life-span than other citizens. Are they relatively or absolutely poor – or both?

Read on!

Defining and measuring poverty

On Christmas Day 1994, according to the *Guardian*, six men drank their way through 12 bottles of the Dorchester Hotel's most expensive claret, £960 a bottle. A little less than a year later, the *New Left Review* (September/October 1995) reported that ten million people in the UK earn less for a whole year's work than that half dozen people spent on the connoisseur wine.

In a relative sense, the ten million people are poorer than the claret drinkers. But are they in *absolute poverty*? An absolute definition of poverty assumes it's possible to identify a benchmark level below which people have sunk. That level is typically regarded as the one needed to obtain basic physical needs – food, water, clothing and shelter. In the UK, some politicians and economists argue that absolute poverty, in this stark sense, doesn't exist. However, Amartya Sen proposes a compelling argument for the use of the concept of absolute poverty in any society:

'Poverty is not just a matter of being relatively poorer than others in the society, but of not having some basic opportunities of material well-being – the failure to have certain minimum "capabilities". The criteria of minimum capabilities are "absolute" not in the sense that they must not vary from society to society, or over time, but people's deprivations are judged absolutely, and not

Are the situations depicted in these two scenes from Beirut illustrative of absolute or relative poverty?

simply in comparison with the deprivations of others in that society. If a person is seen as poor because he [*sic*] is unable to satisfy his hunger, then that diagnosis of poverty cannot be altered merely by the fact that others too may also be hungry . . . it is a question of setting certain absolute standards of minimum material capabilities relevant for that society. Anyone failing to reach that absolute level would then be classified as poor, no matter what his relative position is *vis-à-vis* others.'

(Sen 1985: 669–70)

This kind of definition appears to be adopted by the general public (Oppenheim and Harker 1996). In 1990, for example, 95 per cent of Britons agreed that poverty was about living below minimum subsistence. Only 25 per cent of Britons thought that poverty was being relatively less well-off than others.

So whose got it right – the absolutists or the relativists? We'll look at their respective arguments in turn. First though, we'll briefly put the debate into its historical context.

Pioneering research into poverty

In 1886, Charles Booth investigated the extent of poverty in London. His was the first systematic sociological study of poverty in the UK. The results, a massive 17-volume report presented in 1902–3, documented the living and working conditions of the London poor. Adopting a *relative* approach to poverty – defined as inability to meet the usual standard of life – Booth estimated that the level at which poverty set in for a family of two adults and three children was 21 shillings per week (£1.05 today). He offered no detailed justification for this poverty line, although it's suggested that it was derived from the minimum wage (21 shillings) needed to meet the 'usual standard of life'. Booth estimated that 30.7 per cent of London's total population were in poverty.

Taking the investigation of poverty beyond the capital, Seebohm Rowntree investigated the state of the poor in the city of York in 1899. Adopting an *absolute* perspective, he highlighted a minimum standard of living which fulfilled people's biological needs for food, water, clothing and shelter. This is also referred to as the *subsistence level*. People whose lives fell below this minimum standard were unable to eat enough, clothe themselves or live in shelter. Rowntree subsequently drew up a list of those minimum personal and household necessities required for survival. He then established two categories of poverty:

- *primary poverty* – the person is unable to acquire the minimum necessities, also known as *absolute poverty*
- *secondary poverty* – a portion of the person's total earnings is absorbed by other useful or wasteful expenditure such that it's not possible to maintain the minimum standard.

Rowntree constructed a list of necessities costed weekly. From this, he drew up a poverty line using the help of expert dieticians' estimates of what a family needed to survive on. Rowntree calculated a *primary poverty line* based on the minimum income necessary to maintain physical sustenance. For a family of man and wife and three children, this was calculated at 17 shillings and 8 pence (about 88 pence today), which he broke down as follows:

- 12 shillings and 9 pence for food (about 64 pence today)
- 2 shillings and 3 pence for clothing (about 11 pence today)
- 1 shilling and 10 pence for fuel (about 9 pence today)
- 10 pence for household and personal sundries (about 4 pence today).

A family whose income fell below 17 shillings and 8 pence – the primary poverty line – was considered to be in a state of primary poverty.

In 1899, Rowntree calculated that 15.45 per cent of the working population were in primary poverty in York. Later studies by Rowntree documented a fall to 6.8 per cent in 1936 and to 2.77 per cent in 1950. However, in the 1936 study, he admitted that socio-economic conditions had changed greatly, the average family size was smaller, and great medical progress had been made. In that same year, Rowntree set a minimum level necessary for maintenance of 53 shillings and 3 pence per week (about £2.66 today) for an urban worker, wife and three children. Three shillings and 6 pence (about 18 pence today) was built in for other contingencies, like beer and amusements. He believed the 53 shillings and 3 pence represented a scientifically objective benchmark. However, this is rather fanciful because it was based on Rowntree's subjective judgement.

OVER TO YOU

Discuss the sociological implications of the last two sentences.

As for secondary poverty, Rowntree set out to find the average sum spent weekly by families on 'drink, gambling or other wasteful expenditure and to ascertain also whether the wife was a thrifty house keeper or the reverse' (Rowntree 1901: 115).

Notwithstanding these moralistic overtones, Rowntree concluded that 27.94 per cent of York's working population experienced secondary poverty. He did, however, accept that the immediate causes of secondary poverty were the inevitable consequences of life in the slums in absolute poverty. One can imagine, for example, that desperately poor people might turn to drink to anaesthetise their despair.

We can see then that Booth adopted a relative measure of poverty, and Rowntree used an absolute concept.

OVER TO YOU

Who do you think got it right: Booth or Rowntree, or perhaps both in their different ways?

Now it's time to consider each measure of poverty in turn. The section on relative poverty is the much longer of the two, because this measure is more commonly used today in rich countries like the UK.

Absolute poverty

Although the absolute poverty principle still strikes a chord with the British public and also with various influential institutions (including the World Bank), it was given short shrift in 1976 by former Conservative Secretary of State for Social Services, Keith Joseph. Said Joseph:

> 'An absolute standard of means is defined by reference to the actual needs of the poor and not by reference to the expenditure of those who are not poor. A family is poor if it cannot afford to eat . . . By any absolute standards there is very little poverty in Britain today.'
>
> (cited by Oppenheim and Harker 1996: 8)

In 1989, John Moore, the then Secretary of State for Social Security, went further. He claimed that the economic success of the UK had put an end to absolute poverty. The concept of absolute poverty has also been criticised by Oppenheim and Harker (1996). Whilst recognising the extensive and damaging effects of poverty in the UK today, they contend that it's hard to define an 'adequate' minimum need because perceptions of what constitutes a reasonable subsistence level change over time (and generally, in progressive societies, change upwards). Absolute concepts don't properly take account of cultural and social needs. As Pete Alcock discloses, 'different people need different things, in different places, according to differing circumstances' (Alcock 1993: 60). His relativist stance suggests that the adequate minimum standard of living is itself defined by what society judges as socially-acceptable – a point returned to later.

On a rather polemical note, Sean Stitt asserts that the absolute view:

'corresponds with the liberal conscience to help the poor, but not at the unacceptable cost of imposing any restrictions upon the wealth-accumulation activities and privileges of others.'

(Stitt 1994: 59)

Stitt's argument suggests that well-off people won't eradicate subsistence poverty without tackling the root cause of the problem – the unequal distribution of material advantages. Liberal tinkering – a little more benefit here, a little less tax there – only scratches the surface. The best way to get rid of poverty – absolute or relative – is to forge a more genuinely equal society. That means taxing big profits and huge earnings much more stringently.

While some commentators think the absolute definition of poverty is a bit out-dated, we beg to differ. Our objection is based on the social scientific premise that many people still try to eke out a living below subsistence levels. To be sure, this is generally more commonplace in poor countries, but lest we become complacent, there are also cases closer to home. In the UK, for example, some older people suffer – even die – from the cold because they can't afford to heat their homes.

Relative poverty

The relative definition of poverty gained prominence in the post-war period as a response to the alleged achievements of the Welfare State in eradicating absolute poverty. The work of Brian Abel-Smith and Peter Townsend in the 1960s referred to the relative nature of poverty. They said that:

'People are poverty-stricken when their income, even if it is adequate for survival, falls markedly below that of the community. Then they cannot have what the larger community regards as the minimum necessary for decency.'

(Abel-Smith and Townsend 1965: 252)

ABSOLUTE CONCEPT OF POVERTY

FOR

\+ There's clarity of conceptual definition. The poor are people whose income is insufficient to buy the food and shelter necessary to keep them healthy. Anyone in this situation is in absolute/primary poverty. That's self-evident. Sure, there are degrees of poverty even amongst the absolutely poor, but all hungry and homeless people suffer absolute poverty.

\+ Rowntree's notion of primary (i.e. absolute) poverty, although an ideal type construct (a sociological approximation of reality), had a compelling resonance with the grim reality of poverty in York. In that respect, it was an excellent concept – it fitted the reality it analysed and described. Even for some Britons today – rough sleepers, for example – the concept of primary poverty accurately describes their situation.

\+ Rowntree's (and similar) studies carry strong moral force. When people don't have enough money for food, that's wrong by anyone's standards. Much of the work of organisations like Oxfam and Christian Aid today are premised on the argument that absolute poverty is morally unacceptable and requires redress.

\+ Rowntree's pioneering research pre-empted the Welfare State because it highlighted what the basic needs were to survive. Thereafter, it was the mission of others to eradicate absolute poverty through welfare policies. Initiatives include the Unemployment Assistance Act (1934), the Beveridge Report (1942), Supplementary Benefit (1966), and Income Support (1986), all of which are based on a poverty line measurement.

AGAINST

– Measures of absolute poverty don't take adequate account of the cultural settings in which perceptions of poverty are generated. People's expectations change over time because 'Adequate minimum and necessary goods' (as defined by Rowntree) are socially-constructed terms. Not having an inside toilet these days, for example, is a sure sign of poverty, but such wasn't the case in Victorian times.

– It's difficult to define a minimum standard of living because time doesn't stand still. Changes in living standards and expenditure patterns, for example, occurred between the years of Rowntree's different studies. He pays insufficient attention to these trends. Moreover, the assumption by 'experts' that they know where the poverty line is might be construed as somewhat presumptuous.

– It focuses on physiological needs and pays insufficient attention to social and psychological needs. This isn't to deny the real physical pain of hunger and poverty-induced disease. However, the experience of poverty operates on all three levels. Omitting two of them, gives an incomplete, sociologically inadequate picture.

– The concept of absolute poverty has some resonance in the poor majority world. However, in the rich nations, absolute poverty has largely been relegated to the historical dustbin. Few Britons are so poor that, like their Sudanese counterparts, they starve to death. The relative measure of poverty is generally more valid in relation to the 'western' experience.

This approach doesn't see poverty as a subsistence line/level determined by individual need, but as relative to the general standards of living in the country as a whole. Peter Townsend contends that individuals, families and groups are in poverty when:

'they lack the resources to obtain the types of diet, participate in the activities and have the living conditions and amenities which are customary, or at least widely encouraged or approved, in the societies to which they belong.'
(Townsend 1979: 31)

The above definition takes poverty beyond abject material want to one where people are excluded from participating in the customs of society, from being full stakeholders in society. Social exclusion takes many forms – not being able to go to the cinema, to take children to the seaside, to buy a colour TV, etc. This isn't to suggest that absolute poverty no longer exists in the UK. The very visible presence of rough sleepers in towns and cities across the country contradicts any such assumption. These people are very poor, absolutely poor. But the ranks of the poor contain more than them. Britons who can't afford to buy new clothes are clearly poor by popular consent, even though the wearing of second-hand clothes doesn't constitute the absolute poverty of going without food.

The concept of relative poverty isn't new. The economist, Adam Smith, remarked in the eighteenth century that:

'A linen shirt, for example, is strictly speaking not a necessity of life . . . But in the present time . . . a creditable day labourer would be ashamed to appear in public without a linen shirt.'
(Smith 1776: 691)

This relative viewpoint is probably the one most widely held by social scientists in relation to the discussion of poverty within industrial and post-industrial nations. As indicated earlier, however, absolute poverty measures are commonly used in 'majority world' (previously called 'Third World') countries. But how is a relative term to be measured objectively? Alan Walker (1988: 33) says the matter isn't about scientific calculation, but about the minimum income necessary to participate in a range of 'roles, relationships and consumptions'.

The two approaches most closely linked to the objective measurement of relative poverty are both based on deprivation indexes:

- the *expert-compiled index*
- the *social consensus-compiled index*.

These are lists of items whose lack provides evidence of relative poverty.

The expert-compiled index

This is based on Peter Townsend's work. In that sense, he's the expert compiler. Townsend constructed a deprivation index – ultimately, a list of 12 key items (for example, not having a household fridge) – the lack of which indicates relative poverty. Not having a fridge at home wouldn't have been an indicator of poverty in the 1940s. But it is these days because, *relatively speaking*, it indicates that one is much less well-off than the average Briton.

Townsend's first use of the deprivation index in a real setting was in 1979, when he conducted a survey of 2,000 households in the UK against 60 indicators of lifestyle. These included diet, clothing, fuel and light, home amenities, housing, family support, recreation, education and health. Townsend was aware that many of the items only applied to some sections of society, but he sought to 'ensure that all the major areas of personal, household and social life were represented' (Townsend 1979: 251). From his findings, he compiled a deprivation index which covered major aspects of dietary, household, family, recreational and social deprivation.

The table on page 260 shows the 60 forms of deprivation devised by Townsend, and the table on page 261 shows his deprivation index, which represents those forms most 'highly suggestive of deprivation'.

Townsend champions the idea that poverty is relative, yet can be objectively determined and measured. He found that over 40 of the 60 indicators revealed a close correlation between deprivation and income. He claimed that there was a 'threshold of deprivation (a poverty line) for certain types of household at low levels of income' (1979: 271), and this threshold was at levels higher than the government's supplementary benefit standard, especially for families with children and households with disabled people.

Importantly, Peter Townsend, Paul Corrigan and Ute Kowarzik recognise that poverty involves 'material' and 'social' dimensions:

'People may not have the material goods of modern life or the immediately surrounding material facilities or amenities. On the other hand, they may not have access to ordinary social customs, activities and relationships. The latter are more difficult to establish and measure, and the two sets of conditions may be difficult in practice to separate.'
(Townsend *et al.* 1987: 127)

Economic privations clearly have social consequences. People whose lives are blighted by economic hardship become socially-excluded from lifestyles that other people take for granted. Going out with friends, dating, participating in sports, and such like, all require money. Not having funds often leads to social isolation.

Townsend's findings are disputed by, among others, David Piachaud (1981), Amartya Sen (1985) and Joanna Mack and Stewart Lansley (1985). They think

Townsend's multiple deprivation indicators

Form of deprivation	
Dietary	1 At least one day without cooked meal in last two weeks
	2 No fresh meat most days of week
	3 School child does not have school meals
	4 Has not had cooked breakfast most days of the week
	5 Household does not have a Sunday joint three weeks in four
	6 Fewer than three pints of milk per person per week
Clothing	7 Inadequate footwear for both wet and fine weather
	8 Income unit buys second-hand clothes often or sometimes
	9 Income unit misses clothing club payments often or sometimes
	10 (Married women) No new winter coat in last three years
Fuel and light	11 No electricity or light only (not power)
	12 Short of fuel sometimes or often
	13 No central heating
	14 No rooms heated (or only one)
Household facilities	15 No TV
	16 No refrigerator
	17 No telephone
	18 No record player
	19 No radio
	20 No washing machine
	21 No vacuum cleaner
	22 No carpet
	23 No armchair
Housing conditions and amenities	24 No sole use of four amenities (indoor WC, sink or washbasin, bath or shower, and cooker)
	25 Structural defects
	26 Structural defects believed dangerous to health
	27 Overcrowded (in terms of number of bedrooms)
Conditions at work (severity, security, amenities and welfare benefits)	28 Works mainly or entirely outdoors
	29 Stands or walks at work all the time
	30 Working 50 or more hours last week
	31 At work before 8 a.m. or working at night

Form of deprivation	
Conditions at work (severity, security, amenities and welfare benefits)	32 Poor outdoor amenities of work
	33 Poor indoor amenities of work
	34 Unemployed for two weeks or more during previous 12 months
	35 Subject to one week's entitlement to notice or less
	36 No wages or salary during sickness
	37 Paid holidays of two weeks or less
	38 No meals paid or subsidized by employer
	39 No entitlement to occupational pension
Health	40 Health poor or fair
	41 Sick from work five or more weeks last year
	42 Ill in bed 14 days or more last year
	43 Has disability condition
	44 Has some or severe disability
Educational	45 Fewer than ten years' education
Environmental	46 No garden or yard, or shared
	47 If garden, too small to sit in
	48 Air dirty or foul smelling
	49 No safe place for child (1–4) to play
	50 No safe place for child (5–10) to play
Family	51 Difficulties indoors for child to play
	52 Child not had friend in to play in last four weeks
	53 Child not had party last birthday
	54 Household spent less than additional £10 last Christmas
Recreational	55 No afternoons or evenings out in last two weeks
	56 No holiday in last 12 months away from home
Social	57 No emergency help available, e.g. illness
	58 No one coming to meal or snack in last four weeks
	59 Not been out to meal or snack with relatives or friends in last four weeks
	60 Moved house at least twice in last two years

(Townsend 1979: 1173–6)

Townsend's deprivation index

Characteristic	**% of population**
1 Has not had a week's holiday away from home in last 12 months	53.6
2 *Adults only.* Has not had a relative or friend to the home for a meal or snack in the last four weeks	33.4
3 *Adults only.* Has not been out in the last four weeks to a relative or friend for a meal or snack	45.1
4 *Children only* (under 15). Has not had a friend to play or to tea in the last four weeks	36.3
5 *Children only.* Did not have a party on last birthday	56.6
6 Has not had an afternoon or evening out for entertainment in the last two weeks	47.0
7 Does not have fresh meat (including meals out) as many as four days a week	19.3
8 Has gone through one or more days in past fortnight without a cooked meal	7.0
9 Has not had a cooked breakfast most days of the week	67.3
10 Household does not have a refrigerator	45.1
11 Household does not usually have a Sunday joint (3 in 4 times)	25.9
12 Household does not have sole use of four amenities indoors (flush WC; sink or washbasin and cold-water tap; fixed bath or shower; and gas or electric cooker)	21.4

(Townsend 1979: 250)

he set himself up as the expert on what a deprivation indicator, or needs of society, should be without empirical evidence to support this. For example, Item 9 from the index, 'has not had a cooked breakfast most days of the week', might be contested by health-conscious Britons who eat a high-bran cereal instead of bacon and eggs.

That said, Piachaud (1987) confirms the general point that deprivation increases as income falls. What remains unproved is where the poverty threshold occurs. As Piachaud argues:

'the combination of two factors – that there is diversity in styles of living, and that poverty is relative – mean that you would not, in fact, expect to find any threshold between the poor and the rest of society.'

(Piachaud 1981: 421)

Townsend, however, argues that:

'People can experience one or more forms of deprivation without necessarily being in poverty. People with the same resources may display a different relationship to forms of deprivation.'

(Townsend 1987: 130)

For example, low-paid people who aren't exactly 'poor' might go without certain 'treats' which other people can afford. It's also the case that an individual who earns the same as her or his neighbour might regard such 'treats' as extravagant, while the neighbour thinks they should be affordable. Here we enter that tricky domain of the subjective.

Allowing for these differing opinions, it's nevertheless important to emphasise that people who experience severe forms of deprivation are, almost without exception, on low incomes and have minimum resources. Townsend highlights this correlation by comparing the top 5 per cent of households with the bottom 5 per cent – whom he considers to be the richest and poorest groups in society (see the table on page 262). The comparisons are based on the combination of income and wealth-generating assets.

Most of the differences are as one would expect. Nearly nine-tenths of the poor are in manual occupations. Only a few poor people own their homes. The poorest 5 per cent obtain their income from low earnings or benefits. The rich, by contrast, have a range of assets – both income and wealth.

In a later study by Peter Townsend, Paul Corrigan and Ute Kowarzik (1987), these social scientists distinguished between the measurement of deprivation in different areas and the kind of people experiencing that deprivation, by identifying different forms of material and social deprivation. Taking a random sample of 2,700 of the adult population in all 755 wards of Greater London, they selected 77 deprivation indicators. The indicators were used to avoid subjective notions, such as the inclusion of attitudes and beliefs. Instead, they reflected conditions, relationships and behaviour.

The people in the sample were asked to denote which of the indicators in the table on page 263 were 'necessary to them as individuals'. In so doing, they were highlighting things that are fundamental in terms of contemporary living standards.

The aim of the study was to measure the extent of multiple forms of deprivation using 13 types of deprivation and 77 indicators, to a maximum total score of 94.

The findings reveal a high concentration of unemployment throughout London, coupled with growing disparity in standards of living between the rich and poor. Three hundred thousand people were found to be living below the government's Income Support standard. A further 600,000 received Income Support; and another 900,000 had incomes on the margins – 1.8 million

Richest and poorest households compared

Characteristic	Richest 5%	Poorest 5%
Household resources		
1 Mean value of assets	£28,185	£31
2 Mean net disposable income	£2,934	£420
3 Mean income net worth	£4,976	£423
4 Principally dependent for income on earnings	69%	27%
5 Overdraft facilities	17%	0%
Household characteristics	*Percentage of households*	
6 Owner-occupiers	87	7
7 Council tenants	0	45
8 Sometimes or often short of fuel	0	22
9 No garden or too small to sit in	12	37
10 Large garden	56	5
11 Not got sole use of four household facilities	5	39
12 Fewer than 6 of 10 selected consumer durables	7	64
13 Head of manual status	12	88
14 Either chief wage-earner or housewife or both say they are working class	19	72
15 Either chief wage-earner or housewife or both say they are middle class	81	28
16 Have dependent children	20	26
17 Have one-parent families	3	14
Individual characteristics	*Percentage of individuals in such households*	
18 Under 15	20	38
19 40–59	34	10
20 65 or more	16	25
21 Not born in United Kingdom	7	5
22 Non-white	3	6
23 Scoring 1 or more on disability index	22	37
24 Adults of 25 or over with more than 10 years education	56	5
25 Unemployed one or more weeks in year (among those available for employment)	2	16
26 Employed or self-employed	52	20
27 Receiving Supplementary Benefit	0	35
28 Eligible for Supplementary Benefit but not receiving	1	22
29 Feels poor sometimes or always (among chief wage-earners and housewives only)	4	59
30 Little or no support routinely or in emergencies from family	34	24
31 Severe social deprivation (scores of 6 or more on social deprivation index)	10	58
32 Member of one or more types of social minority	39	70
33 Not had holiday away	29	79

(Townsend 1979: 358–9)

people in total. Importantly, the study also highlighted the increasing feminisation of poverty:

'A disproportionate number of these [on the margins or in poverty] are women: women who look after children or other dependants unpaid and receive insufficient income; lone women with children, whether or not in paid employment; elderly pensioners, especially women living alone; and women with low earnings in households where total income is low.'

(Townsend *et al.* 1987: 83)

They also note that:

'the "tail" of the distribution of poverty is getting longer. There are instances of people living far below the poverty line. Examples are unemployed people not getting benefit . . . , single unemployed people confused and harassed (by the DSS), homeless people, and recent (officially approved) immigrant families . . . There is evidence that the system itself has become less lenient and in many places has gone sour . . . . The experience of poverty is not however simply a matter of how much money is made available. It is also about how it is made available.'

(Townsend *et al.* 1987: 50)

The authors of the study advocate the abolition of excessive wealth and income, along with a redistribution of resources. Townsend, in an earlier context, had argued for 'innovations in public ownership, industrial democracy and collaboration instead of hierarchical work structures' (1979: 926). They also believe that without full employment and a reasonable minimum wage, poverty will continue.

The social consensus-compiled index

This approach is particularly associated with the work of Joanna Mack and Stewart Lansley (1985). Like Townsend, they study the extent to which the poor are excluded from customary and reasonably expected lifestyles. Rather than devising their own index, however, Mack and Lansley solicit the views of 'ordinary' laypeople. In that respect, they develop an approach that:

'aims to identify a minimum acceptable way of life not by reference to the views of "experts", nor by reference to observed patterns of expenditure or observed living standards, but by reference to the views of society as a whole. This is, in essence, a consensual approach to defining minimum standards.'

(Mack and Lansley 1985: 42)

Survey of poverty and the London labour market 1985–6

Material deprivation

1 *Dietary deprivation:*
- i At least one day in last fortnight with insufficient to eat
- ii No fresh meat or fish most days of week (alternative formulation for vegetarians)
- iii No special meal or roast most weeks
- iv No fresh fruit most days
- v Short of food on at least one occasion in last 12 months to meet needs of family

2 *Clothing deprivation:*
- i Inadequate footwear for all weathers
- ii Inadequate protection against heavy rain
- iii Inadequate protection against severe cold
- iv No dressing gown
- v Fewer than three pairs of socks/stockings in good repair
- vi Bought second-hand clothing in last 12 months

3 *Housing deprivation:*
- i No exclusive use of indoor WC and bath
- ii External structural defects
- iii Internal structural defects
- iv No electricity
- v All rooms not heated winter evenings
- vi Housing not free of damp
- vii Housing not free of infestation
- viii Poor state of internal and/or external paintwork and decoration
- ix Poor access to accommodation
- x Overcrowded (fewer rooms – excluding kitchen and bathroom – than persons)
- xi No spare room for visitor to sleep

4 *Deprivation of home facilities:*
- i No car
- ii No television
- iii No radio
- iv No washing machine
- v No refrigerator
- vi No freezer
- vii No electric iron
- viii No gas or electric cooker
- ix No vacuum cleaner
- x No central heating
- xi No telephone
- xii Lack of carpeting in main rooms

5 *Deprivation of environment:*
- i No garden
- ii Nowhere for children under five to play safely outside
- iii Nowhere for children aged five to ten to play safely nearby
- iv Industrial air pollution
- v Other forms of air pollution
- vi Risk of road accidents around home
- vii Problem of noise from traffic, aircraft, building works

6 *Deprivation of location:*
- i No open space (like part or heath) within easy walking distance
- ii No recreational facilities for young people or older adults nearby
- iii No shops for ordinary household goods within 10 minutes journey
- iv Problem of litter in local streets
- v Doctor's surgery or hospital outpatients department not within 10 minutes journey

7 *Deprivation at work*
- i Poor working environment (polluted air, dust, noise, vibration and high or low temperature – maximum score of 9)
- ii Stands or walks about more than three-quarters of the working day
- iii Works 'unsocial hours'
- iv Either poor outdoor amenities of work or poor indoor amenities at work (maximum score of 10)

7a *Alternative series on deprivation at work:*
(for people not answering questions applying to paid employment and who have shown they undertake at least 20 hours unpaid work altogether caring for children, sick or disabled or elderly persons in the household or elsewhere):
- i Repeat the total score for housing deprivation (items 3 above – maximum score of 11)
- ii No central heating (4 x above: repeat score if necessary)
- iii No telephone (4 xi above: repeat score if necessary)
- iv Worked 50 or more hours in last week (unpaid work but also including any paid work)
- v Air pollution (items 5 iv and 5 v above)
- vi Repeat the total score for locational deprivation (item 6 above – max. score 5)

Social deprivation

8 *Lack of rights in employment:*
- i Unemployed for two weeks or more during previous 12 months
- ii Subject to one week's termination of employment or less
- iii No paid holiday
- iv No meals paid or subsidised by employer
- v No entitlement to occupational pension
- vi Not entitled to full pay in first six months of sickness
- vii Worked 50 or more hours previous week

9 *Deprivation of family activity:*
- i Difficulties indoors for child to play
- ii If has children, child has not had holiday away from home in the last 12 months
- iii If has children, child has not had outing during the last 12 months
- iv No days staying with family or friends in previous 12 months
- v Problem of the health of someone in family
- vi Has care of disabled or elderly relative

10 *Lack of integration into community:*
- i Being alone and isolated from people
- ii Relatively unsafe in surrounding streets
- iii Racial harrassment
- iv Experiences discrimination on grounds of race, sex, age, disability or sexual orientation
- v In illness no expected source of help
- vi Not a source of care or help to others inside or outside the home
- vii Moved house three or more times in last five years

11 *Lack of formal participation in social institutions:*
- i Did not vote at last election
- ii No participation in trade union or staff association, educational courses, sport clubs or associations, or political parties
- iii No participation in voluntary service activities

12 *Recreational deprivation:*
- i No holiday away from home in last 12 months
- ii Fewer than five hours a week of specified range of leisure activities

13 *Educational deprivation:*
- i Fewer than 10 years education
- ii No formal qualifications from school or subsequent educational courses or apprenticeships

Material and social deprivation; Total indicators or groups of indicators: 77 (with a maximum total score of 94).

(Townsend *et al.* 1987: 91–4)

As indicated earlier, Rowntree also based individual needs on 'public opinion'. So this isn't a completely new approach.

Using public opinion surveys, Mack and Lansley (1985) found there was a general consensus about what constitutes a minimum standard of living. They therefore argue for a measure of poverty based on the social perception of needs. Say Mack and Lansley:

'there is no such thing as an "objective" as opposed to a "socially perceived" measure: items become "necessities" only when they are socially perceived to be so . . . These . . . are themselves determined by social conditions, in particular by the distribution of resources and of living standards, but also by other factors such as the distribution of power.'

(Mack and Lansley 1985: 38)

Mack and Lansley note that deprivation among the poor surfaces in different ways according to particular circumstances. The effect on the individual will depend on how she or he perceives it. Thus, Mack and Lansley define poverty 'in terms of an enforced lack of socially perceived necessities' (1985: 39). The attraction of this definition is that it no longer remains a privileged 'expert' concept. It extends the discussion to laypeople, taking proper account of their perceptions.

Mack and Lansley used a quota sample of 1,174 respondents aged 16 and over who were interviewed in their homes in 80 sampling points across Great Britain in 1983. The sample was designed to include a large number of poor households, although the results were adjusted to be representative of national attitudes and opinions. In 1990, a second phase of research – carried out by Harold Frayman (*Breadline Britain 1990s: The Findings of the Television Series*, 1991) – investigated subsequent poverty trends. The results of the 1983 and 1990 studies were reported in two television documentaries called *Breadline Britain* during the 1980s and early 1990s. The 1983 study found a high degree of consensus among respondents over what constitutes necessities. Of the 35 items responded to by the household sample, the ranking showed a considerable degree of agreement on what were regarded as necessities, as can be seen from the table below.

Mack and Lansley believe the findings of their 1983 survey gave strong backing to a relative view of deprivation:

'The Breadline Britain findings clearly show that people make their judgements about the necessities for living on the basis of today's standards and not by some historical yardstick. Their definition of necessity goes wider than

The public's perception of necessities

Standard-of-living items in rank order	% classing item as necessity
1 Heating to warm living areas of the home if it's cold	97
2 Indoor toilet (not shared with another household)	96
3 Damp-free home	96
4 Bath (not shared with another household)	94
5 Beds for everyone in the household	94
6 Public transport for one's needs	88
7 A warm waterproof coat	87
8 Three meals a day for children[a]	82
9 Self-contained accommodation	79
10 Two pairs of all weather shoes	78
11 Enough bedrooms for every child over 10 of different sex to have his/her own[a]	77
12 Refrigerator	77
13 Toys for children[a]	71
14 Carpets in living rooms and bedrooms	70
15 Celebrations on special occasions such as Christmas	69
16 A roast meat joint or its equivalent once a week	67
17 A washing machine	67
18 New, not second-hand clothes	64
19 A hobby or leisure activity	64
20 Two hot meals a day (for adults)	64
21 Meat or fish every other day	63
22 Presents for friends or family once a year	63
23 A holiday away from home for one week a year, not with relatives	63
24 Leisure equipment for children e.g. sports equipment or a bicycle[a]	57
25 A garden	55
26 A television	51
27 A 'best outfit' for special occasions	48
28 A telephone	43
29 An outing for children once a week[a]	40
30 A dressing gown	38
31 Children's friends round for tea/a snack once a fortnight[a]	37
32 A night out once a fortnight (adults)	36
33 Friends/family round for a meal once a month	32
34 A car	22
35 A packet of cigarettes every other day	14

Average of all 35 items = 64.1

[a] For families with children only.

(Mack and Lansley 1985: 54)

subsistence . . . For all the differences in people's styles of living, the concept of "socially established" necessities does in practice have meaning.'

(Mack and Lansley 1985: 59)

This is confirmed by the fact that the top five necessities from the table opposite were judged to be the same by all social classes. The degree of agreement here adds weight to the concept of 'socially perceived necessities and a set of nationally sanctioned standards' (Mack and Lansley 1985: 65).

The views expressed in the 1990 survey generally echoed the findings of the 1983 one. However, in terms of necessities, there was a substantial increase in the number of people in 1990 who regarded two meals a day, a meat meal (or vegetarian equivalent) every other day, a refrigerator, and children's toys as essential. A telephone, best outfit, entertainment and outings for children also became recognised as necessities. John Scott (1994) argues these changes point to fluctuating standards and social expectations. People were seen as deprived if they were unable to enjoy 'comforts', as well as necessities for survival.

Both surveys also investigated the question of choice. A poor woman may go without an annual holiday because she can't afford it. However, an affluent man might not have a holiday because he doesn't want one. Therefore, even though it may be significant that large numbers of the population are 'lacking' one necessity, this doesn't imply they're poor. Mack and Lansley did find that choice was a significant factor among those who lacked one or two necessities but, for those who lacked three or more necessities, the deprivation was not about taste or preference but was overwhelmingly unavoidable. In the case of low-income families, one in five households lacked six

RELATIVE CONCEPT OF POVERTY

FOR

+ It attempts to measure poverty objectively by discovering which 'necessities' are lacking by households and linking this with the personal income of families. This keeps the discussion within clearly defined quantitative limits.
+ It's based on a public consensus of essential necessities rather than the views of 'experts' and politicians. 'Ordinary folk' (among whom there are more likely to be poor people than among 'experts' and politicians) get to have their say.
+ Townsend's work and the Breadline Britain studies isolate specific personal and social activities from which the poor are excluded and present a compelling moral argument that a redistribution of income and wealth should occur to ensure a minimum standard of living for all.
+ Relative studies reveal changes in the forms of deprivation over time, as well as changes in the income levels when deprivation occurs. The government is thereby kept informed of the changing cost of living, and can examine and adjust Income Support rates accordingly.

AGAINST

– Townsend is criticised by John Veit-Wilson (1987) because he assumes the privileged status of 'poverty expert'. Who is to say that his indicators of poverty are any more valid than those of other people? To be fair to Townsend, his more recent research does take account of what people think is the income level below which, for them, poverty cuts in.
– A social consensus approach implies agreement about what is a necessity. Yet Mack and Lansley don't comment on the criteria that people employ in deciding whether an item is a necessity or a non-necessity? Are such judgements based on experience or hearsay? Ultimately, irrespective of what people might agree constitutes relative poverty, Sen (1983, cited by Oppenheim and Harker 1996) rightly notes that there's a stark irreducible core of absolute poverty.
– It's difficult to convert the selected items of necessity into levels of consumption, expenditure or income. Is a household poor if its members can't afford necessities, but actually buy non-necessities? Without an understanding of the margin allowed for non-necessities, it's hard to envisage how the social consensus approach can move from a list of necessities to a determination of the income necessary to obtain them
– It's debatable how far the relative approach has demonstrated there is a 'threshold level' at which a clear shift occurs, with deprivation increasing as income falls. If there's diversity in styles of living and poverty is relative, it becomes arbitrary trying to set a line between the poor and the rest of society, which leaves Townsend's attempt to present an objective poverty line in disarray.

or more necessities. Based on the benchmark of lacking three or more necessities, Mack and Lansley argued that 7.5 million (22 per cent) of the British population were in or on the margins of poverty in the early 1980s. The 1990 study revealed an increase to 11 million (approximately 32 per cent) of the population.

Mack and Lansley also investigated whether it was possible to identify a minimum income level below which a household's risk of going without necessities dramatically gathered pace. The two groups most at risk of poverty through low income, as identified by Mack and Lansley, were the unemployed and lone parents. The authors were attempting to discover whether there was an income line – what Townsend had called the 'threshold level of deprivation' – separating the poor from the non-poor. Townsend (1979) had suggested this 'threshold level' of income should be set at 150 per cent of the Supplementary Benefit level.

In social policy terms, the clear implication is that the income of families needs to be raised well above the present benefit levels. Mack and Lansley found that by increasing the minimum income level to one equivalent to 150 per cent, the numbers of people in poverty would plunge from 7.5 million to 1.5–2 million, only about 3 per cent of the population. Said Mack and Lansley:

'In summary, the evidence suggests not just that supplementary benefit is too low , but that it is considerably too low . . . [and] to move towards "solving" the problem of poverty would require raising the incomes of those on supplementary benefit (or equivalently low incomes) by some 50% . . . although it would be a long way indeed from solving all their problems.'

(Mack and Lansley 1985: 196)

Indeed, their findings (1985: 197) have revealed that many people, who are not amongst the most deprived, still fall below what can be described as a 'minimal acceptable way of life'.

The Breadline Britain surveys have advanced the study of poverty by investigating the 'customary social expectations that define the normal and acceptable standard of life for those who enjoy the status of full citizenship' (Scott 1994: 105). Jonathan Bradshaw (1992) has taken this approach further by attempting to establish a link between people's perceptions of necessity and the level at which Income Support is provided to families. Bradshaw sought to move to a relative viewpoint, whilst also measuring basic subsistence on the basis of customary expectations.

As is often the case in social science, instead of pitting two ways of looking at an issue against each other, it's often better to distil the best of both perspectives. This is what the so-called Budget Standards approach does.

EXAM TIP

On their own, neither relative nor absolute concepts of poverty offer a complete definition of poverty. Emphasise to the examiner that it's important to capitalise on the advantages of both definitions. In practice, most attempts to define and research poverty do combine both, as with the Budget Standards approach below.

The budget standards approach

The budget standards approach defines poverty by incorporating features of both the absolute and relative concepts. The model has been developed in Britain and a range of other countries (in particular, the US), and draws from Rowntree's absolutist tradition of a list of necessities and Townsend's relativist notion of deprivation indicators which define customary lifestyles.

Says Pete Alcock:

'Budget standards approaches to defining poverty are based upon attempts to determine a list of necessities, the absence of which can then be used as a poverty line below which, people should not be permitted to fall.'

(Alcock 1993: 63–4)

These approaches have clear absolutist leanings, but budgets can also represent socially-defined needs. Budget standards definitions are usually derived from a basket of goods and services:

'and although normative judgements of technical "experts" from a variety of fields including nutritional science are still used, these are increasingly supplemented by legal and government standards and by evidence derived from expenditure and consumer surveys.'

(Bradshaw *et al.* 1987: 168).

There are, however, problems with the use of a basket of goods to define a socially-determined standard for a family. Can we rely on the imposition of arbitrary and unrealistic 'expert' judgements in relation to what needs to be spent on food, clothing, transport and housing, when the experts are unlikely to have any experience of living on benefits? Surely it would be preferable to turn to the real experiences of the poor?

In that spirit, the work of Bradshaw and the Family Budget Unit at York University (now based at King's College, London) during the 1990s has used data from the real-life experiences of families. With the assistance of expenditure patterns and the weekly budgets of people living on Income Support, the team have determined a 'modest but adequate' budget for a British family. With 13,680,000 of the population on or below Income Support (based on Low Income Families Statistics 1995), it's important that these people are consulted about whether benefits paid to them are adequate. Bradshaw submits that the budget standard has the potential to examine whether the Income Support rates are adequate because it's based on the premise that poverty is quantifiable.

However, Norman Fowler, in his former role as Secretary of State for the Department for Health and Social Security (in 1993, the department became two departments: Health and Social Security), presented the then Conservative government's position in a White Paper purported to be the most substantial review of social security since the Beveridge Report of 1942. Said Fowler:

'There have been many attempts to establish what would be a fair rate of benefit for claimants. But it is doubtful whether an attempt to establish an objective standard of adequacy would be fruitful.'

(DHSS 1985: 21)

Yet the Department for Social Security still use an objective measure.

The table below shows the benefits available for people on Income Support, as determined by the then Conservative government.

Watts (1980, cited by Bradshaw *et al.* 1987: 170) suggests that budget standards have four different uses. They can:

- provide standard of living norms for a given family type
- be used to derive standardised comparisons of living standards (equivalence scales) for different family types

Income Support allowances (as from April 1995, per week)

Single people		
16 and 17 years old		£28.00
16 and 17 years old with good reason for living away from home		£36.80
16 and 17 years old entitled to disability premium		£36.80
18 to 24 years old		£36.80
18 years old and over and bringing up a child on their own		£46.50
25 years and over		£46.50
Couples		
Both under 18		£55.55
With at least one of the couple 18 or over		£73.00
Special rules apply if one of the couple is under 18		
For each child in the family		
Under 11		£15.95
11 to 15 years old		£23.40
16 to 17 years old on a full-time course not above A-level/OND standard		£28.00
18 years old on a full-time course not above A-level/OND standard		£36.80
Premiums		
Special additions are given to help with the extra needs of certain groups		
Family (paid if the customer has at least one dependant child)		£10.25
Lone parent (paid if the customer is bringing up one or more dependant children on their own)		£5.20
Disabled child (paid for each dependant child receiving DLA or registered blind, and the child has less than £3,000 savings)		£19.80
Long-term sick or disabled:		
Disability	Single	£19.80
	Couple	£28.30
Severe disability	Single	£35.05
	Couple	£70.10
People aged 60 or over – Pensioner:		
Paid if the customer or their partner are 60 to 74 inclusive	Single	£18.60
	Couple	£28.05
Enhanced, if the customer or their partner is aged 75 to 79	Single	£20.70
	Couple	£30.95
Higher pensioner, if the customer or partner is aged 80+, or aged 60+ and disabled	Single	£25.15
	Couple	£35.95

People who receive Income Support and who are responsible for housing costs may also get help in two ways:
1 Housing Benefit payments (for example, rent, council tax, hostel charges)
2 Housing cost payments (for example, mortgage interest payments, interest on loans to the home)

(Adapted from DSS 1995: 119–29)

- be used to compare living standards over time
- be used to compare living standards between areas.

In practice, the budget standards have rarely been used by local or national government in guiding policy-making, but they have been used for evaluating policy and examining living standards.

The Family Budget Unit drew up a 'modest but adequate' budget standard for different household types. This budget was compiled by a panel of experts drawn from consumer groups using expenditure figures. The Family Budget Unit only includes items in their 'modest but adequate' budget standard if over half the population have them or regard them as essential necessities in public opinion surveys. On this basis, the Family Budget Unit's average weekly household expenditure for a 'modest but adequate' budget (based on 1993 prices) for a couple with two children was calculated at £278.38 per week, after housing costs.

As Oppenheim and Harker point out:

'The modest but adequate budget standard can be seen as representing a level of income which allows people to participate fully in society rather than simply exist.'
(Oppenheim and Harker 1996: 42)

The Crit Think exercise gives you the opportunity to make your own judgement.

In considering the budget standard for households, as shown in the table opposite, it's clear that many people forego many items that the majority of society would take for granted (for example, taking a holiday abroad and having spectacles). The starkness of poverty becomes even more apparent when one compares the poverty lines represented by Income Support, 50 per cent of an average family income after housing costs, and the modest but adequate budget standard, as shown in the table below.

A comparison[1] of the modest but adequate (MBA)[2] budget with the Income Support (IS) and 50 per cent of average income poverty lines (£ per week, 1995 prices)

	Single man		**Couple**		**Lone mother + 2 children[3]**		**Couple + 2 children[3]**	
Housing (tenants)	35.33	36.46	33.61	34.69	46.34	47.82	46.34	47.82
Council tax	5.29	5.46	7.05	7.28	6.17	6.37	8.23	8.49
Fuel	5.82	6.01	8.36	8.63	14.74	15.21	16.26	16.78
Food	28.09	28.99	41.33	42.65	40.52	41.82	60.92	62.87
Alcohol	8.48	8.75	14.54	15.01	6.06	6.25	14.54	15.01
Tobacco	0.00	0.00	0.00	0.00	0.00	0.00	0.00	0.00
Clothing	6.99	7.21	14.95	15.43	22.91	23.64	29.86	30.82
Personal care	3.93	4.06	9.25	9.55	8.04	8.30	11.45	11.82
Household goods	8.99	9.28	13.86	14.30	22.88	23.61	24.46	25.24
Household services	4.02	4.15	5.79	5.98	4.37	4.51	6.33	6.53
Motoring	36.13	37.29	36.16	37.32	36.67	37.84	39.10	40.35
Fares	3.41	3.52	5.70	5.88	5.43	5.60	11.18	11.54
Leisure goods	6.21	6.41	8.49	8.76	15.20	15.69	15.43	15.92
Leisure services	11.98	12.36	22.96	23.70	13.08	13.50	19.45	20.07
Child care[4]	0.00	0.00	0.00	0.00	69.60	71.83	28.79	29.71
Trade union dues	1.31	1.35	2.60	2.68	1.27	1.31	1.95	2.01
Pets	0.00	0.00	3.65	3.77	6.04	6.23	6.04	6.23
Total for tenants		**171.30**		**235.63**		**329.53**		**351.21**
Less housing costs[5]		134.84		200.94		281.71		303.39
IS poverty line		46.50		73.00		93.85		115.15
% of MBA budget met		35%		36%		33%		38%
50% average income poverty line		65.00		118.00		113.00		166.00
% of MBA budget met		48%		59%		40%		55%

Notes:
1 After housing costs.
2 The MBA budget has been updated to 1995 prices using the all items retail prices index (this is a slightly different methodology from that used by the Family Budget Unit – see source).
3 Boy aged 10 and girl aged 4.
4 Includes childcare/babysitting costs which are not incurred by everyone.
5 Housing costs are deducted for the purposes of comparison with the poverty lines which are after housing costs.
The MBA budgets are based on model families.

(Family Budget Unit, *Modest but Adequate Summary Budgets for Sixteen Households*, 1995, cited by Oppenheim and Harker 1996: 43)

CRIT THINK CRIT THINK CRIT THINK CRIT THINK CRIT THINK CRIT THINK

IS INCOME SUPPORT ADEQUATE?

The Family Budget Unit's average weekly household expenditure for a 'modest but adequate' budget (based on 1993 prices), for a couple with two children is £278.38 per week, after housing costs.

Read the following family descriptions and complete the questions which follow:

Family A
A couple, 22 and 24 years of age, with one disabled child, 9 months old, and one child, 3 years of age. The husband has been unemployed since 18. They live in a council property.

Family B
A retired married couple aged 77 and 82. They have a daughter aged 55 living with them, and she doesn't work. They have paid off their mortgage on a bungalow.

Family C
A lone mother, aged 29, with two young children, aged under 4. She is unable to work due to child care responsibilities. They live in a two-bedroom council flat.

1 *Using the Income Support allowances table on page 267, calculate the maximum financial support available for families A, B and C.*

2 *If you were the local Benefits Officer (the person who is employed by the Department for Social Security to decide whether people are entitled to any benefits) what other information would you require before being able to provide any financial assistance (for example, Income Support) to these families?*

3 *Compare the Family Budget Unit's average weekly household expenditure of £278.38 (after housing costs) for a couple with two children with the Income Support available from the government for families A, B and C. Then calculate for each family:*

- **a** *the amount of money that should be budgeted for transport, clothing, food and housing per week*
- **b** *the other costs which may be incurred by the families during the week.*

4 *Do you think the assistance available through either Income Support allowance or through the 'modest but adequate budget' is sufficient for families A, B and C to participate fully in society rather than simply exist?*

5 *Obtain the most recent Income Support allowance details available. Is there a significant improvement today on the 1995 allowances for people in receipt of benefit?*

6 *Study the table below. This is a summary of standards for households from the 'modest but adequate budget' as used by the Family Budget Unit in November 1992. These are the items regarded as either necessities or non-necessities by over half the population in the public opinion survey. Do you agree with the Family Budget Unit's findings?*

Summary budget standards for six households

Examples of items included	**Examples of items excluded**
Basic designs, mass manufactured furniture, textiles and hardware	Antiques, handmade or precious household durables
Prescription charges, dental care, sight test	Spectacles, private health care
Fridge-freezer, washing machine, microwave, food-mixer, sewing machine	Tumble-dryer, shower, electric blankets
Basic clothing, sensible designs	Second-hand, designer and high fashion clothing
TV, video hire, basic music system and camera	Children's TVs, compact discs, camcorders
Second-hand 5-year-old car, second-hand adult bicycle, new children's bikes	A second car, caravan, camping equipment, mountain bikes
Basic jewellery, watch	Precious jewellery
Basic cosmetics, haircuts	Perfume, hair perm
Alcohol – men 14 units, women 10 units (⅔ HEA safety limit)	Smoking
One week annual holiday	Holiday abroad
Walking, swimming, cycling, football, cinema, panto every two years, youth club, scouts/guides	Fishing, water sports, horse-riding, creative or educational adult classes, children's ballet/music lessons

(Family Budget Unit, November 1992, cited by Oppenheim and Harker 1996: 42)

CRIT THINK CRIT THINK CRIT THINK CRIT THINK CRIT THINK CRIT THINK CRIT

As you can see, at no time do the poverty lines set by Income Support or 50 per cent of average family income reach the standard of assistance set by the modest but adequate budget. This means that lots of people are going without many of the most basic essentials, such as a healthy and varied diet, new but basic clothing, and money for leisure activities. Social scientists who support a more equitable distribution of income argue that the poverty level should be set at an income which enables households, following their ordinary expenditure patterns, to have sufficient money left for necessities. However, this proposition doesn't solve the problem of defining what a necessity is, or the relative issue of what is 'acceptable' non-necessary expenditure.

QUESTION

With reference to the table on page 268, calculate the modest but adequate budget standard for:

a a couple
b a lone mother with two children (£ per week).

The budget standard approach isn't confined to just one method of calculation. Bradshaw, Mitchell and Morgan (1987), for example, identify and have trialled three types of calculation in employing the technique. These are:

- the *New York Budget Standard*, which is employed by the New York Community Council and is their own variant of standards used in the UK. With this technique, each consumption item (for example, food, clothing, fuel, recreation and transport) are costed. A comparison of the prices of the same commodities in different countries is then calculated using the foreign exchange system. Bradshaw, having translated the New York budget into British terms item by item, is then able to compare it with the Income Support rates for a family. He found with every family type that the budget exceeded the Income Support provided by the government
- *statistical techniques for fixing budget standards*, which are used to reduce the normative judgements of 'experts' in drawing up budget standards. The statistical techniques employed fix the level of expenditure that should be devoted to a consumption item. This, in effect, moves towards the use of income levels as a proxy (or substitute) for a budget standard or expenditure patterns. A variety of this technique was employed by the American social scientist, Molly Orshansky (1969), to measure poverty. She compared the expenditure patterns of families at different income levels to ascertain what proportion of their income was spent on necessities. She found that as the family income increased, they spent a greater proportion of their money on non-necessities. Therefore, concludes Orshansky, a reliable indicator for a poverty line is the average expenditure devoted to necessities. She suggests that a household is in poverty when they spend more than 30 per cent of their budget on food. Bradshaw *et al.* (1987) argue that this technique can pinpoint the Townsend 'threshold level' – where choice replaces need for most household types of expenditure (for example, food, clothing and fuel);
- *the consumption of families on Income Support*, which is a technique developed by Bradshaw and Morgan (1987), following David Piachaud (1981). Piachaud assessed the adequacy of the benefits system in supporting dependent children by drawing up a schedule of requirements necessary to maintain a modest lifestyle. Like Piachaud, Bradshaw and Morgan employ a basket of goods limited to what people actually spend their money on. Based on a sample of 76 low-income families (comprising a couple and two children aged 5 and 10) receiving Supplementary Benefit of £74.88 per week (February 1986), they applied this income to 94 commodities as used by the Family Expenditure Survey in 1982. The table below represents the results of the families' expenditure compared with

Weekly expenditure (less housing costs) devoted to each commodity group (two adults and two children), February 1986

Family expenditure survey expenditure code	Commodity	Family on Supplementary Benefit £ p	Average family £ p
6	Housing repairs	0.82	5.89
7–11	Fuel	11.46	12.26
12–43	Food	30.50	45.20
44–46	Alcohol	2.47	8.69
47–49	Tobacco	6.59	4.95
50–59	Clothing and footwear	3.55	16.64
60–67	Durable household goods	3.13	19.56
68–76	Other goods	5.69	16.53
77–82	Transport	4.40	30.46
83–93	Services	4.78	25.04
94	Miscellaneous	0.45	1.47

(cited by Bradshaw *et al.* 1987: 178)

the average household expenditure of families of the same type.

Bradshaw *et al.* note that:

'living standards of families on supplementary benefit is harsh: the food component is short on calories and even that diet is only achieved with the most determined of self control in purchasing only the cheapest items and avoiding all waste. Furthermore, it is achieved at the expense of expenditure on all other commodities. We have shown this with clothing but in addition the family cannot afford a holiday away from home – only a day outing a year – cannot afford a newspaper every day and has no money for books and magazines, never go to the cinema, cannot afford to buy bicycles or run a car, cannot maintain a garden, can afford one haircut a year.'

(Bradshaw *et al.* 1987: 179)

The bleak lifestyle depicted by Bradshaw and Morgan's findings are graphically illustrated by the example below of a mother who only spent 94 pence per week on clothes and shoes to ensure there was enough food for her family.

Bradshaw and Morgan drew up a wardrobe based on the mother's level of expenditure, suggesting:

'She can afford one coat lasting 15 years, one nightdress lasting ten years, one bra every five years, one dress every five years, three pairs of knickers every year, one pair of shoes every one and a half years and a handbag every ten years. The number and range of items may be feasible but the lifetimes are not.'

(Bradshaw *et al.* 1987: 179)

EXAM TIP

Whilst sociological research should be as objective as possible, human responses to research findings invariably engage values, and, in the case of the mother below, should stir much concern.

Bradshaw and Morgan recognise that the quality of people's lives isn't solely represented by the goods they acquire. However, the budget standard approach does attempt to establish a list of necessities, the absence of which can then be used as a poverty line, a standard and level people should not fall below. The budget approach is a hybrid, absolutist in structure, but also representing socially-defined needs as recommended by the relative approach. Supporters of the approach see it as leading to a more considered review of how we treat people on Income Support and how inadequate such so-called support is.

QUESTIONS

1 Why is it difficult to arrive at a universal definition of poverty?
2 Summarise the key findings from the studies of Rowntree, Townsend, Mack and Lansley, and Bradshaw *et al.*

Clothing budget for mother in 1986

Number	Garment	Price £ p	Expected lifetime in weeks	Cost per week in pence
1	Coat	39.95	780	5.1
1	Sweater	9.99	520	1.9
2	Dress	39.98	260	15.4
4 pairs	Tights	1.65	10	16.5
1 pair	Shoes	16.99	78	21.8
3 pairs	Knickers	3.60	52	6.9
1	Petticoat	4.50	520	0.9
2	Bra	7.88	260	3.1
1	Nightdress	9.99	520	1.9
1	Skirt	9.99	520	1.9
2	Blouses	17.98	208	8.6
1	Swimming costume	9.99	520	1.9
1 pair	Gloves	2.99	520	0.6
1 pair	Slippers	2.99	52	5.8
1	Handbag	9.99	520	2.0
			Total cost	94 pence

(Bradshaw *et al.* 1987: 179)

BUDGET STANDARDS APPROACH TO POVERTY

FOR

+ As Watts (1980) suggests, it provides a model of living norms for a given family type which can be used to derive standardised comparisons of lifestyles over time and between areas.
+ It fuses the strengths of the absolute and relative definitions of poverty, thereby distilling the combined wisdoms of both. By using the two concepts, we get to look at the bigger canvas rather than arguing about which concept is the 'better' one.
+ It sets out a range of costed necessities based on scientific, nutritional information (for example, the Family Budget Unit), or on statistical calculations (for example, the Orshansky method). Such quantitative data provide reliable indicators of poverty, and make it easier for policymakers to develop clear poverty reduction targets.
+ Linked to the last point, it encourages government agencies to consider their claimants' budgeting patterns. This has led to the creation of a Social Fund which is a budgeting loan to a family who are unable to make ends meet.

AGAINST

– The following questions aren't adequately addressed by this approach: Who defines what is a necessity? Will the needs identified be equally applicable to each family type? How are non-necessities (for example, alcohol and smoking) incorporated into the expenditure budget of an ordinary person's living pattern? The relative issue of how much 'unnecessary' expenditure is acceptable, for example, to run a car or for children's hobbies, also arises. Bradshaw would respond by arguing that budget standards are representations of real family needs and expenditures.
– The budget standard is nothing more than a composite method devised by so-called 'experts' which sheds light on the cost of certain items (if you can shop at the cheapest places!). It fails to offer a clear and comprehensive poverty line.
– The costing of the minimum requirements still exceeds the Income Support levels provided by government. Arguably, the budget standard is more useful as a political tool than as an adequate measure of poverty.
– The real-life needs of people can't be adequately represented in budgets that are just based on statistical techniques. Statistics are important, but qualitative data is necessary too in order to give a more rounded and a more human picture.

The extent of poverty

Poverty is a contested concept, so it's not surprising that measuring it is a problem as well. Says Meghnad Desai:

'Measuring poverty is an exercise in demarcation: lines have to be drawn where none may be visible and they have to be made bold. Where one draws the line is itself a battlefield.'

(cited by Golding 1986: 1)

Social divisions and poverty: Who are the poor?

Unlike some countries (for example, the US), a Conservative government abandoned the British official subsistence definition based on Social Assistance (called Supplementary Benefit, and later replaced by Income Support) levels in 1985. Previously, the original definition had shown the number of people on incomes equivalent to this Social Assistance rate. This was the government's measure of those living on the poverty line. The level was called the *benefit poverty line*. From 1985 onwards, there has been no one government-approved method of measuring or analysing the changing number of people in poverty. In fact, there's no official recognition that poverty exists. It could be argued that this is to avoid having to acknowledge the extent of the problem.

The House of Commons Social Security Committee (an all-party representative committee) weren't happy with this state of affairs, and subsequently commissioned the independent Institute of Fiscal Studies to produce documentation (first published in 1993) on the numbers of people living below, on or just above the Income Support level (benefit poverty line). The numbers are published in the Low Income Families statistics and are used by the Child Poverty Action Group (CPAG) as a proxy (i.e. substitute) for the poverty line. This Income Support level was set each year by parliament and was intended to function as a 'safety net' for the poor.

The next table shows the poverty line (in £) for those living on, below and up to 140 per cent of Income Support during the period 1992 to 1996. For a detailed breakdown of the 1995/6 Income Support figures, see page 267.

The poverty line using Income Support rates

Family type	Income Support rates April 1992–March 1993[1]	April 1995–March 1996[1]
Non-pensioners		
Single person: aged 18–24	£33.60	£36.80
aged 25+	£42.45	£46.50
Lone parent with 1 (child aged under 11)[2]	£71.05	£77.90
Couple[3]	£66.60	£73.00
Couple with 2 children[4] (aged under 11)	£105.00	£115.15
Pensioners (aged 60–74)		
Single person	£57.15[5]	£65.10
Couple	£88.95[6]	£101.05

Notes
1 These figures are the levels of benefit that were paid at the time (i.e. they are cash figures which are not adjusted for inflation).
2 Lone parent is aged 18 or over.
3 At least one member of the couple is aged 18 or over.
4 See note 3.
5 This figure relates to payments between April and October 1992. After October 1992, the Income Support rate for single pensioners increased to £59.15.
6 This figure relates to payments between April and October 1992. After October 1992 the Income Support rate for couple pensioners increased to £91.95.

(Adapted from the *National Welfare Benefits Handbook 1992/3* and *1995/6*, CPAG)

The Child Poverty Action Group defines all people who are on Income Support as being in poverty. Those living on an income up to 40 per cent above the Income Support level (140 per cent of Income Support) are on the margins of poverty. The bar chart shows that the total number of people living on the margins of poverty has increased since 1979. Of even greater concern is the fact that the number receiving or living below the Income Support level has continued to increase since 1989.

These figures reflect a sharp rise in unemployment – although this is now in decline – which has led to an increase in Income Support claimants. Associated with this problem is the heightened risk that a child will grow up in a poor family. Recent official statistics (HMSO 1995) show that 35 per cent of all children (4,530,000) are living in a household which is either in, or on the margins of poverty.

In 1988, the then Conservative government introduced a series of statistics called *Households Below Average Income*. These replaced the Low Income Family Statistics – although they're still produced under the auspices of the Social Security Committee. The statistics represent official figures about people living on low incomes (in relation to the incomes of the rest of society) and don't indicate an obvious Income Poverty Line. They focus on the living standards of people in the lower half of the income distribution, after housing costs. These days, sociologists and social policy analysts tend to use a poverty line which is 50 per cent of average income because it's comparable with Income Support (and is also after housing costs). The poverty line derived from the

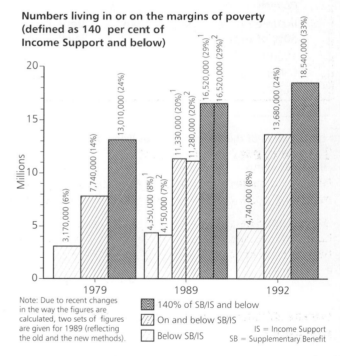

Numbers living in or on the margins of poverty (defined as 140 per cent of Income Support and below)

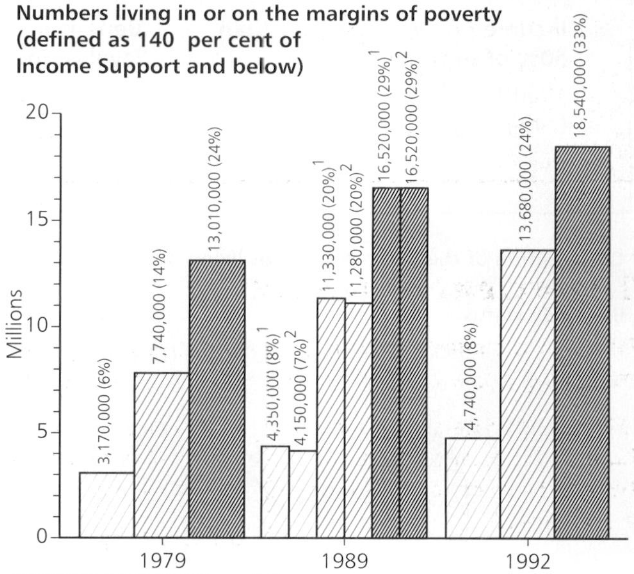

Note: Due to recent changes in the way the figures are calculated, two sets of figures are given for 1989 (reflecting the old and the new methods).

(Department for Social Security, Households Below Average Income, A Statistical Analysis 1979–1992, HMSO, 1995)

Department of Social Security's statistical analysis in 1995 is as indicated in the table.

The 'households below average income' measure reveals that 14.1 million people were living in poverty in 1992–3 – that is, below 50 per cent of average income and without housing costs. It reveals that a wide range of

Households below average income: The poverty line in 1992/93 and expressed in 1995 prices: defined at 50 per cent average income (after housing costs), £ per week

	1992/93	1995 prices
Single person	£61	£65
Couple	£110	£118
Couple with three children (aged 3, 8 and 11)	£183	£196
All family types	£110	£118

(Adapted from Oppenheim and Harker 1996: 33)

groups are at risk. Those at greatest risk are the unemployed, couples with children and 'other', as can be seen in the pie charts below.

Another measure of poverty in the UK has been provided by Mack and Lansley (1985) and Frayman (1991), who took a national sample of households and looked at the number whose members lacked 'essential items'. It's based on the social consensus approach (see earlier). The measure is sometimes referred to as the Basic Essentials Poverty line. Based on statistical tests, Frayman (1991) found that over 11 million people in Britain in 1990 lacked three or more essential items. This showed a marked increase in poverty on 1983.

Significantly, irrespective of which device is employed to measure poverty, the number of households living in or on the margins of poverty has increased. Moreover, each device charts similar figures for *households* living in poverty, as demonstrated by Jane Millar's (1993) table below.

The previous Conservative government responded to criticism over its initial failure to provide up-to-date poverty figures. This provision was expedited, as already said, when, from 1988, the Department of Social Security produced annual figures on Households Below Average Income and, from February 1995, also provided information on the household incomes of families with children,

Poverty in Britain: The early 1990s

Income poverty line (less than 50% of average income)	Benefit poverty line (at or below level of Income Support)	Basic essentials line (lacking 3 essentials)
1990/1 13.5 million (24%)	1989 11.3 million (20%)	1990 11 million (20%)

(Adapted from Millar 1993, in Sinfield 1993: 12–14)

Composition of the poor (defined as living below 50 per cent of average income after housing costs) in 1992/3

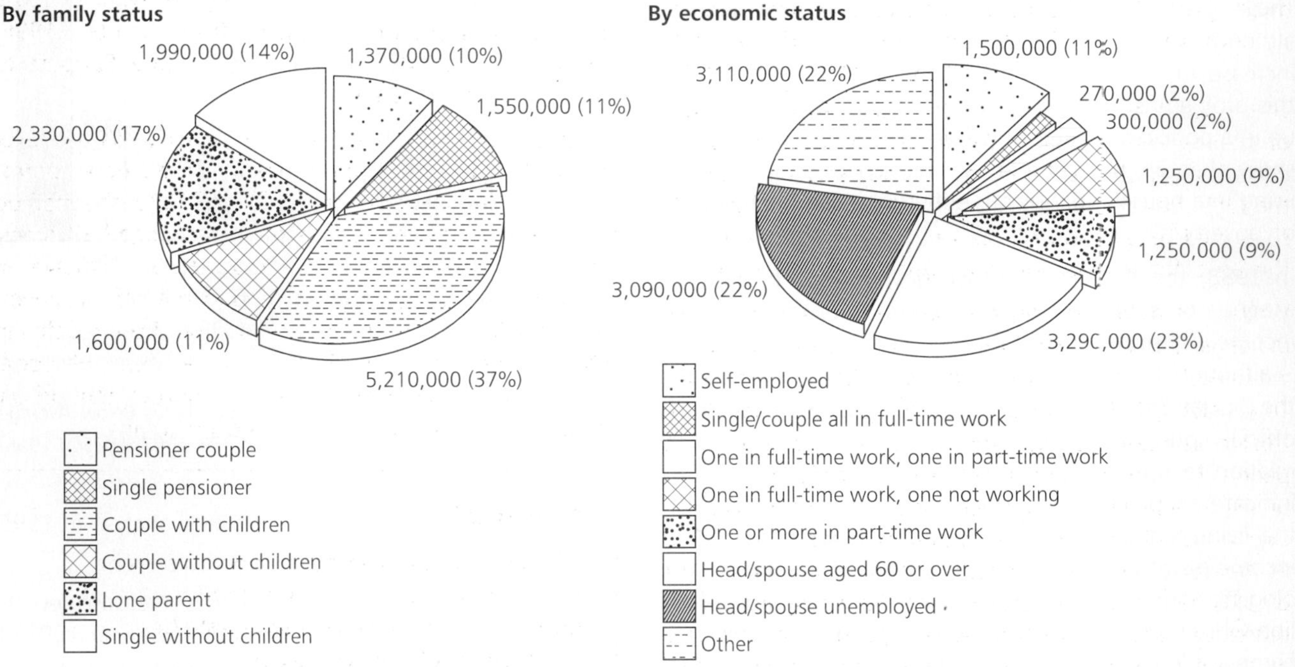

(*Households Below Average Income*, 1995, as cited by Oppenheim and Harker 1996: 35)

unemployed people, older people, sick/disabled people, and of people of different ethnic origins. The findings are reported yearly in the Family Resources Survey.

At this point, it's important to focus in more detail on which groups in society are more prone to poverty. It's crucial to emphasise that poverty isn't always the consequence of a 'bad break' or isolated misfortune, but often a combination of many factors. For example, an older black woman in receipt of a low fixed income (for example, an old age pension) is very likely to be poor. It's important to recognise that the risk of poverty is affected by unemployment and low pay (generally, indicators of 'low' social class), gender, ethnicity, age and disability.

So what does the evidence show about the relationship between these factors and the incidence of poverty?

Unemployed people and low-paid workers

The report from the Commission on Social Justice, published on the 24 October 1994, collected evidence from individuals and organisations on poverty throughout the UK. Its remit was to present policy recommendations promoting social and economic opportunities. Its broad principles included:

- the view that employment is the quickest and most effective route out of poverty
- a commitment to full employment as being fundamental to any labour market strategy
- a jobs, education and training strategy to get the long-term unemployed and lone parents back to work
- the need for family-friendly employment practices
- the introduction of a minimum wage
- the promotion of equal opportunities in employment.

(Adapted from CPAG's response to the Commission on Social Justice Report, Insert in CPAG [1995])

The report clearly recognises the scale and complexity of poverty and inequality. Access to a good job, with a decent salary should be central to any strategy, but, as the Child Poverty Action Group (CPAG 1995) points out, so should recognition of the value of unpaid work and the need for security for those unable to find work.

Whilst unemployment figures published in August 1997 indicated the lowest level of unemployment for 17 years, we need to be circumspect about statistics like this. Peter Townsend (1979) argues that unemployment can't be treated as a discrete phenomenon. By this, he means that people of working age aren't sharply divided into the unemployed and the employed. At one end of the continuum are the long-term unemployed who want work, and at the other end are those with continuous experience of employment and little prospect of this changing before retirement age. Between these groups are the part-time and seasonal workers, those with recurrent experience of unemployment, the workers in fear of redundancy, and those who are exploited by low wages but need the employment in order to support their families.

It's also pertinent to point out that unemployment is probably more than double the 1.7 million jobless (6.2 per cent of the working population) previously reported by the last Conservative government. This is because, according to the HSBC (in the *Independent on Sunday*, 13 April 1997, page 1), parent company of Midland Bank, the then government ignored categories like: people working part-time because they can't get a full-time job, young people on training schemes, and people who have gone on to sickness or disability benefit rather than the dole. The UK jobless rate, say the HSBC, could have been as high as four million people (14 per cent).

Clearly, there's a link between the likelihood of poverty and period of time unemployed, but there are substantial pay differences between occupations. In some cases, the low paid may find themselves only a few pence better-off than the unemployed, and just as likely to experience poverty. Mack and Lansley (1985) confirm that the majority of low-paid workers are on the margins of poverty or below the poverty line. But it was unemployed people who suffered the most extreme levels of deprivation (lacking seven or more necessities). The economic recession of the 1980s intensified their experience of acute deprivation, a reflection of a temporary and unstable employment world.

The official statistics on unemployment don't, as indicated above, tell the whole story. There's a 'dark figure' of unemployment, a hidden number of people who don't figure in the statistics. This is because the Department of Education and Employment's unemployment figures are based solely on those registered as unemployed. It's called the 'claimant' count. This figure includes those claiming Unemployment Benefit (from October 1996, called the Jobseeker's Allowance), Income Support or National Insurance credits.

Constant haggling between the political parties over the 'real' figure for unemployment shows how controversial measurement devices are. Since 1979, the method for counting unemployed people has changed 33 times. The latest introduction of the Jobseeker's Allowance in 1996 has made it appear as though the official unemployment figures are down. Here we see how redefining what counts as unemployment is a form of social construction. Each new definition conveys the official interpretations of civil servants and politicians.

EXAM TIP

Official statistics, whether on unemployment, crime, homelessness, etc., mustn't be taken at face-value. The statistics often mask the assumptions of their compilers.

The distinction between the employed and unemployed is further obscured by economically inactive people exceeding the numbers officially recognised by the government as unemployed. One third of those who move out of unemployment become economically inactive. This can be explained by an increased preference for early retirement and changes in the demand for types of labour. The composition of the workforce is constantly changing. Moreover, as the following data show, unemployment patterns are crucially linked to social class, age, sex, ethnicity and region.

- The *Employment Gazette* (November 1995) reported that 2,292,300 people were registered as unemployed. This accounts for 8.1 per cent of the potential working population.
- Unemployment rates are three times higher for those previously in manual jobs.
- Long-term unemployment (without work for more than one year) is most often experienced by older workers who are close to retirement age, those people prone to illness, and people without any skills or qualifications.
- Unemployed women number 1,467,400 (Labour Force Survey, Autumn 1994) – 43 per cent of the total unemployed.
- Twenty-five per cent of male minority ethnic groups are unemployed, compared to 11 per cent of white men. This is even more severe for young black men aged 16–24, of whom 37 per cent are unemployed (*Employment Gazette*, June 1995).
- Higher rates of unemployment occur in those regions which were centres of the manufacturing industry, for example, the North (10.6 per cent), the Midlands (8 per cent), North West (8.8 per cent), and Yorkshire and Humberside (8.9 per cent). The new service industries have been more pronounced in the South East and South West, which has helped to maintain the reality of a 'North–South' divide.

According to Oppenheim and Harker (1996), a further (hidden) factor in the poverty debate is low wages and poor working conditions. The gap in pay for those at the top and at the bottom is now greater than at any time since 1886. Employment rights for the low-paid have weakened with the abolition of the Wages Council in 1993, which protected the pay of workers in low-waged industries. Employers now have a large pool of cheap labour to draw from and no minimum wage to abide by until the European Social Chapter is fully implemented in the UK. The *New Review*, the journal of the Low Pay Unit discloses the wages for the ten best and ten worst paid jobs in Britain in 1996, based on the New Earnings Survey of 1996 in the tables below.

It's a man's world: The ten best and ten worst paid jobs in Britain in 1996 (according to the government)[1]

The ten best paid jobs	Men (£/wk)	Women (£/wk)
General manager, large company/organisation	£1,733.30	n/a
Treasurer/company finance manager	£935.80	£605.60
Assistant secretary and above, national government	£902.90	n/a
Medical practitioner	£852.70	£706.90
Underwriter/claims assessor/broker/investment analyst	£790.90	£464.50
Legal professional	£727.30	£517.30
Organisation and methods works study manager	£725.10	n/a
Police inspector and above	£700.20	n/a
Education officer/school inspector	£683.10	n/a
Bank/building society/post office manager	£661.80	n/a

The ten worst paid jobs	Women (£/hr)	(£/wk)	Men (£/hr)	(£/wk)
Childcare assistant	£3.69	£152.50	n/a	n/a
Bar staff	£3.76	£152.60	£4.18	£186.60
Kitchen porter/kitchen hand	£3.82	£142.90	£3.95	£164.40
Waiter/ress	£3.87	£158.00	n/a	n/a
Hairdresser	£3.93	£150.90	n/a	n/a
Shelf filler	£3.97	£161.40	£4.86	£206.80
Catering assistant/counterhand	£4.08	£162.90	£4.08	£176.10
Cleaner/domestic	£4.10	£166.10	£4.52	£201.50
Laundry worker/dry cleaner/presser	£4.13	£162.30	£4.32	£182.90
Checkout operator	£4.27	£165.20	£4.27	£167.70

[1] Average hourly pay for bottom tenth and average weekly pay including overtime for bottom and top tenths of earners in these jobs.

(Adapted from *The New Review of the Low Pay Unit*, No. 42, November/December 1996, page 19, based on the New Earnings Survey, 1996)

QUESTION

Summarise the main findings in the preceding tables in relation to the highest and the lowest paid people.

The Council of Europe's decency threshold is £228.68 a week or £6.03 an hour. Comparing this with the ten worst paid jobs above, none come anywhere near that figure, even with overtime. According to the Labour MP, Michael Meacher (cited by the *New Review of the Low Pay Unit*, November/December 1996), in the UK there are:

- 9.9 million working adults (48.1 per cent) earning less than this decency level
- 6.3 million of these are women
- 4.4 million of low-paid employees work part-time and most of these are women.

The Low Pay Unit report that low pay is the single most important cause of poverty in the UK, and 4.6 million of the 13.1 million people in poverty are in households where the family head is in employment. In response to this, the Trades Union Congress (TUC) has launched a campaign for a minimum rate of pay of £4.00 an hour. The Confederation for British Industry (CBI) reckon that if a minimum hourly wage of £4.10 were introduced, the national wage bill would rise by 1.5 per cent, to approximately £4.5 billion, and 150,000 jobs would be lost. The last Conservative government claimed that up to 800,000 jobs would have to go.

More recently, in 1996, the Channel 4 Poverty Commission, under the Chair of Peter Townsend, travelled around the UK for four months interviewing a sample of 100 people. The Commission suggested that by imposing a statutory minimum wage of £4.26 and a maximum wage no more than 10–25 times the wage of the lowest-paid, more people could be employed on better wages. The Commission reported that:

'Low wages are the single most important cause of poverty in the UK with one third of those suffering from poverty in households where one person is working. More than 60 per cent of full-time workers earn less than male average earnings of £375 per week.'

(cited by Glenda Cooper, in 'Maximum wage will end poverty trap', the *Independent*, 12 October 1996)

The Benefits System is also of little or no real assistance to the low-paid for whom there are no social security benefits on the whole, although help is given on housing and council tax. Family Credit (introduced by the 1986 Social Security Act) is paid to families in low-paid work, with children, but claimants then lose out on free school meals for their children, Housing Benefit and Council Tax Support, and receive no help with mortgage interest payments. As Oppenheim and Harker note, 'This pushes some families into the unemployment trap because they are better off on Income Support than Family Credit' (1996: 54).

There's also a potential poverty trap in the system because, as a family raises its earnings, they're taken away through increased tax, National Insurance and reduced benefits. According to the Social Security Departmental Report, *The Government's Expenditure Plans 1995/6 to 1997/8* (1995), 640,000 families stand to lose between 70 pence and 99 pence out of every extra £1 they earn.

Gender

Poverty amongst women has been largely 'invisible', say Caroline Glendinning and Jane Millar (1992), because the predominant focus on household and family income has obscured the true extent of poverty for women. Women are regarded as wives of poor unemployed or low-paid men rather than poor women. Even when they're the family breadwinners, they're still discriminated against or disadvantaged in the labour market.

According to the Department of Social Security's figures in 1995, 3,935,240 women relied on Income Support. This accounted for 59 per cent of the female adult population on Income Support. In an analysis of 'Women's incomes: Past, present and prospects', Stewart Webb (1993, cited by Oppenheim and Harker 1996) discovered that Income Support was the principal source of income for lone mothers and women pensioners. Married women's access to the labour market was also affected by the age of their children and the economic activity of the spouse. Women who faired the best in the labour market were those without dependent children (married or single), as Webb discloses in the table on page 278.

The consideration of gender and poverty has raised the important issue of the 'feminisation of poverty'. This, says Henry L. Tischler, refers:

'to the disproportionate concentration of poverty among women. If present trends continue, 60 per cent of all children born today will spend part of their childhood in a family headed by a mother who is divorced, separated, unwed or widowed. There is substantial evidence that women in such families are often the victims of poverty.'

(Tischler 1996: 260)

Although Tischler is referring to American society, what he has to say is relevant to the British experience. Female-led households are more likely to be poor because of 'the feminisation of work, income maintenance or family and household resource distribution' (Stitt 1994: 117). All of these forms of inequality lead to greater poverty for women, but, more importantly, are the product of a male-dominated, patriarchal society where women are seen as economically dependent upon men.

According to the Labour Force Survey (1995), the number of women in part-time employment between 1987 and 1995 had increased by 12 per cent to 5.2 million

Independent income of women, 1991, by source and by family type

	Non-pensioners				Pensioners		
Income source (£ per week)	**Single with children**	**Married with children**	**Single no children**	**Married no children**	**Single**	**Married**	**All women**
Earnings	37.00	54.70	92.40	90.60	4.20	6.10	53.40
Self-employment	4.70	5.10	2.70	7.10	0.20	0.40	3.80
Social security	61.50	16.40	12.20	3.50	57.40	30.40	23.40
Investments	2.80	5.00	6.70	13.10	18.90	18.20	11.00
Pensions/annuities	2.60	0.20	2.10	1.50	19.70	6.50	4.90
Other	15.20	3.80	4.10	3.40	0.80	0.60	3.40
Total	123.80	85.10	120.00	119.10	101.20	62.20	99.90

(S. Webb, *Fiscal Studies*, Vol. 14, No. 4, Institute for Fiscal Studies, 1993, cited by Oppenheim and Harker 1996: 93)

and by 8 per cent in full-time employment. However, women employees are still clustered in occupations which reflect the 'caring' roles they carry out within the home. The biggest sector for women employees remains in public administration, education and health, as the bar chart from the Labour Force Survey below testifies.

Part-time workers also make up the substantial majority of low-paid workers, exposing a further gendered division of labour. The abolition of the Wages Council in 1993 is likely to have had a further detrimental effect on women's wages, as can be seen in the New Earnings Survey (1995) produced by the Department of Employment:

- 52 per cent of women full-time workers in clerical and secretarial occupations
- 72 per cent of women full-time workers in personal and protective services
- 73 per cent of women full-time workers in sales occupations all earned below £220 per week.

Based on this wage rate, it would take a woman 50 hours a week to earn an average income in line with the Council of Europe's decency threshold of £228.68 weekly. *Family Credit Quarterly Statistics by Job* (July 1995) confirm these low wages. Some 626,300 families now depend on an earnings top-up to survive. Of these claimants, nearly 58 per cent work in clerical, catering, cleaning, hairdressing, and other personal services – all traditionally 'women's jobs'.

OVER TO YOU

Give three examples of female occupations in the personal and protective services.

The position of women in the labour market is compromised by 'interruptions' from work due to childbirth, child care and caring for sick, old or other dependants.

Employees by gender and occupation, UK, Spring 1995

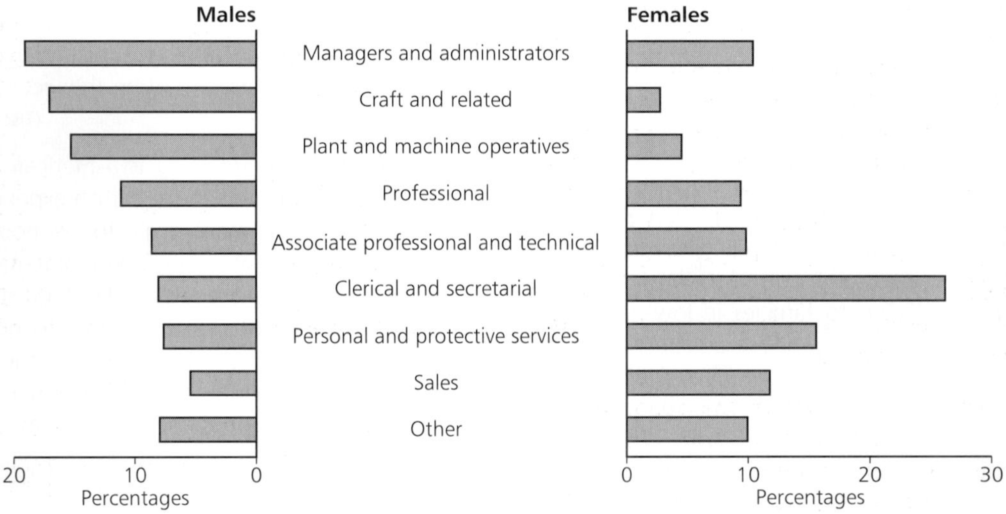

(Labour Force Survey, Central Statistical Office 1995)

The time women spend supporting other people and generally trying to achieve a given standard of living has in the past largely been neglected in discussions on poverty. The 1997 Conservative Party Manifesto proposed a £1.2 billion tax so-called 'give-away' to married women. Worth up to £17.88 a week, it envisaged that mothers at home looking after children or an older relative could transfer their £4,045 tax allowance to their husband.

In response to the Conservative policy proposal, the Director of CPAG, Sally Witcher, said:

'This is clearly designed to promote one particular type of family rather than make a real difference to the largest group of "have nots", namely children in poverty. If the intention was to tackle child poverty and improve mothers' choices, an increase in child benefit would be more effective. The measure will be of no benefit to lone parents, unmarried couples or families out of work.'

(The *Mirror*, 4 April 1997, page 3)

Heather Joshi (cited by Glendinning and Millar 1992) suggests that a mother with two children would lose an average £202,500 in foregone earnings over a lifetime if she took on a full-time caring role rather than enter paid employment. The British Household Panel Study in 1991 found that 41 per cent of women spent over 50 hours a week caring for someone living with them (for example, a child or older relative). Clearly, many mothers would opt for employment and longer working hours if suitable and affordable child care were provided by the state or by employers. However, this wasn't a priority of the previous Conservative government. The then government's publicly-funded child-care provision was the lowest in the European Union.

With the shift of the labour market from industry to service sector work, the increase in part-time work and the expansion of the 'flexible' labour market, women are becoming the most important source of labour power in the UK. The Employment Rights Act of 1996 goes some way – though, arguably, not far enough – towards reducing the disadvantages experienced by full-time and part-time women workers by, for example, protecting women from dismissal when pregnant, improving maternity rights, and safeguarding part-time women workers against unfair dismissal and/or redundancy when working less than 16 hours per week (if continuously employed for two years). All of these changes are vital because a woman's income is often of the utmost importance in shielding a family from poverty. Indeed, it's recognised that seven out of every ten families need two family incomes to pay the mortgage.

As a consequence of their dependency on low-paid and part-time work, careers disrupted by child care, and the risk of unemployment and changes in family patterns (notably, the increase in female lone-parent families), women have a greater reliance on the social security system. The system, however, isn't designed to offer them maximum support. For example, irregular working patterns and low wages often mean that women haven't paid the required National Insurance contributions. In 1995–6, over 2.3 million women were in this position. Consequently, they had to rely on means-tested benefits or lower-rated contributory benefits. An update of Ruth Lister's research for the Equal Opportunities Commission in 1992 which was published in *Hansard* (25 May 1995) highlights this reliance on different benefits (see the table below).

One specific group of women who rely to a great extent on benefits are lone parents. Significant changes have taken place during this century in terms of family patterns. One in three births now occur outside marriage. Lone parents are economically disadvantaged compared to two-parent families. A recent study by the Policy Studies Institute on changes in lone parenthood (1989–93) found that 40 per cent of lone parents survive on less than £100 per week, compared to 4 per cent of two-parent families. Furthermore, over half of lone parents experienced severe financial hardship and, in 15 per cent of the cases, ill-health suffered by themselves or their children meant they were unable to work.

Percentage of social security claimants, by sex. Great Britain 1993–4

Benefit	**Men** %	**Women** %
Industrial injury disablement benefit	86	14
Invalidity benefit	73	27
Maternity benefit	nil	100
Non-contributory retirement pension	20	80
Retirement pension	35	65
Sickness benefit	58	42
Unemployment benefit	76	24
Widow's benefit	nil	100
Reduced earnings allowance	81	19
Attendance allowance	29	71
Child benefit	3	97
One-parent benefit	9	91
Invalid care allowance	31	69
Mobility allowance	52	48
Severe disablement allowance	38	62
Family credit[1]	43	57
Income support	48	52
Disability living allowance	52	48
Disability working allowance	60	40

1 Figures based on sex of main earner

(cited by Oppenheim and Harker 1996: 97, using figures from House of Commons, *Hansard*, 25 May 1995, cols 695–7)

For lone parents, employment is often another area of disadvantage. Combining the role of sole carer and bread-winner is a heavy burden. Almost 70 per cent of lone parents have to claim Income Support. In 1994, according to the Department of Social Security, this represented 1.097 million people, of whom 658,000 had been on Income Support for more than two years. Their position isn't generally one of choice, but more likely a consequence of the high cost of child care alongside low wages. The majority of lone parents are caught in a benefits trap.

Yet some commentators, particularly, those of a New Right persuasion, contend that state support is over-generous to lone parents, and that the system encourages them to rely on social security instead of looking for a job. Even New Labour seem to have come to a similar conclusion. However, according to the Child Poverty Action Group (1995), the most common reason for being a lone mother is divorce.

The most common reason for being a lone mother is divorce.

Even in households comprising men and women with apparently adequate incomes, the distribution of resources may leave many, usually women, experiencing poverty. It mustn't be assumed that resources are shared equally among family members. In lower-income families, for example, the male often assumes the traditional role of breadwinner and provides what he decides is an acceptable housekeeping allowance to the female. She's then often solely responsible for the management and budgeting of the household tasks with what may be an inadequate share of the family income.

The *Eighth British Social Attitudes Report* in 1991/2, confirmed that such tasks included main responsibility for shopping, cooking meals, cleaning, washing, ironing and child care. Women appear to take on much of the burden of poverty within households, making sacrifices so that ends meet. Lydia Morris (1989) found that, where women are in paid employment, they typically use their money to subsidise shortfalls in the housekeeping budget. From a feminist viewpoint, Pamela Abbott and Claire Wallace conclude that:

'women's poverty can be understood only in the context of gender inequalities that persist throughout life. Ideologies of women's "natural" abilities and "natural" roles structure women's opportunities to take on paid work and the type of jobs that are offered to them. The realities of women's lives, structured by these ideologies and state policies, also limit their opportunities to take on employment and the range of types of employment they can take on. Furthermore, the assumption that men support their wives means that much female poverty is hidden . . . Women also have to suffer the stress, the lack of opportunities for fulfilment and the feelings of insecurity that go with being poor.'

(Abbott and Wallace 1997: 281)

Ethnicity

Kaushika Amin and Carey Oppenheim note that:

'Poverty is not even-handed. The chances of experiencing poverty are far higher for people from ethnic minorities than for white people. Moreover, the way in which poverty is experienced by ethnic minority communities may be more acute, as low income is compounded by discrimination and exclusion.'

(Amin and Oppenheim 1992: 1)

This statement isn't surprising. There is significant evidence that black and other minority ethnic communities suffer disproportionately compared to the majority population in the UK.

In view of the economic hardships that many members of minority ethnic groups suffer, one might think it easy to draw links between poverty and them. But, as Pete Alcock says:

'given their experience of racism, it is quite understandable that black people in Britain should be wary about research which attempts to determine their ethnic origin in order to relate this, for instance, to their employment, housing or benefit status.'

(Alcock 1993: 144)

The upshot is that evidence is in scarce supply. However, a variety of sources are now becoming available, such as the Department of Social Security's Family Resources Survey, which provides official statistics on income, social security benefits and ethnic origin, the annual Labour Force survey by ethnic origin from the Policy Studies Institute, the 1991 Census which, for the first time, included a question on ethnic origin, and small-scale local studies focusing on unemployment and poverty.

So what are the facts of the poverty experienced by minority ethnic groups?

- Unemployment rates for black and other minority ethnic groups have been about twice that of white people since 1984.
- Sixteen per cent of ethnic minority women are unemployed, compared with 7 per cent of white women.
- Black men (33 per cent), Pakistani/Bangladeshi men (29 per cent), and Pakistani/Bangladeshi women (24 per cent) suffer the highest unemployment rates.
- Six out of ten black people who are unemployed are long-term unemployed.
- Even with qualifications, minority ethnic groups are still more likely to experience unemployment because of discrimination.

The table illustrates some of the above points, and also provides some additional information.

What these figures confirm is that black and other minority ethnic groups experience a higher rate of unemployment. For younger people, the unemployment rates are even greater. One in two young black men are unemployed. A local survey by Chris Hasluck (1991) in the Calderdale and Kirklees areas of West Yorkshire showed that the proportion of West Indian and Asian people who were long-term unemployed was double that of white people. In Kirklees, 75 per cent of Asians had been unemployed for more than three years. Also revealed in the study was a greater risk of unemployment for minority ethnic groups compounded by their lack of work experience and training.

Unemployment rates are more complex than they first appear, being influenced by factors like ethnicity, sex and region. Spitalfields, a Bangladeshi community in East London, is part of the Docklands Development Scheme. There has been rapid industrial and economic change in this area, but the skills of the community could not be matched to the jobs on offer. The Local Economic Policy Unit Survey (1991) found that 22 per cent of the community were economically inactive. Of those, 79 per cent were women. Few of these Bangladeshi women worked outside the home for cultural reasons. Moreover, housework and child care were seen as strenuous and demanding enough. Participation in the paid labour market was out of the question.

Racism clearly affects employment prospects. Research conducted by the Commission for Racial Equality and the Policy Studies Institute in the 1980s found black employees concentrated in low-paid, low status and part-time jobs. Black people are also especially vulnerable to recessions and to the decline in UK manufacturing industries.

Many of the industries where minority ethnic groups are concentrated pay very low wages. The 1993 Policy Studies Institute Report and the 1994 New Earnings Survey by the Department of Employment revealed that:

- 22 per cent of minority ethnic men worked in the distribution, hotels and catering sector, and 26 per cent of these earned less than £170 per week

Unemployment rates by sex, age and ethnic origin, Spring 1994, Britain (%)

	Men		**Women**	
	All aged 16 & over	**16 to 24**	**All aged 16 & over**	**16 to 24**
White	11	18	7	12
Ethnic minority groups:				
All	25	37	16	27
Black	33	51	18	41
Indian	16	30	12	*
Pakistani/Bangladeshi	29	34	24	*
Mixed – other origins	22	*	16	*

People who describe themselves as Black Caribbean, Black African and Black other (which includes Black British) are grouped together.
* Sample too small

(Department of Employment, *Employment Gazette*, June 1995, cited by Oppenheim and Harker 1996: 116)

- 14 per cent of minority ethnic men worked in manufacturing, and 27 per cent of these earned less than £170 per week
- 22 per cent of minority ethnic women worked in the distribution, hotels and catering sector, and 35 per cent of these earned less than £130 per week
- 22 per cent of Pakistani women worked in manufacturing (mainly clothing and footwear), and 33 per cent of these earned less than £130 per week.

People from minority ethnic groups who have a job are often employed on lower skill levels. Only 21 per cent of minority ethnic men fall into the category of professional/manager/employer, compared with 27 per cent of white men. This category comprises only 12 per cent for African–Caribbean, Pakistani and Bangladeshi men. Twenty-three per cent of minority ethnic men fall into the semi-skilled manual category, compared with 15 per cent of white men. Sixty-five per cent of Bangladeshi men are in this category, as are 45 per cent of Pakistani women.

A 1990 survey commissioned by Leicester City Council on the earnings and working conditions of white and Asian workers revealed a similar picture to the one presented by the then Department of Employment. Asians were more likely to be low paid and to have worse conditions at work (for example, to work irregular and long shifts). Furthermore, Irene Bruegel, in her study of the London labour market in 1989, found there were also hidden aspects of the labour market, such as homeworking, family employment in shops, and domestic work, which were associated with minority ethnic work. Homeworking was the most acute example of poor pay and working conditions.

Amin and Oppenheim document the plight that many members of minority ethnic groups find themselves in:

'The broad patterns of inequality are clear – people from ethnic minorities are more likely to work in sections of the economy with greater risk of low pay, doing shift work, with longer hours of work and with less access to training and occupational benefits . . . The overall inequality in employment . . . is affected by the particular ethnic minority, by gender, by region and by whether the industry is in the public or private sector.'

(Amin and Oppenheim 1992: 14)

There's also a relationship between ethnic origin and dependency on the social security benefits system. High levels of unemployment and low pay are bound to lead to more state dependency, as are the higher proportions of lone-parent families amongst African–Caribbeans. Moreover, aspects of the social security system sometimes discriminate both directly and indirectly against people from minority ethnic groups, leaving some of them exposed to economic and social hardship without the protection of benefits.

Thus, for example, the contributory principle doesn't favour minority ethnic groups. People receive National Insurance benefits (for example, Jobseeker's Allowance and retirement pension) in return for contributions made during employment. In 1997–8, anyone earning below £62 per week didn't make any contributions. Many people in ethnic minorities earn below this minimum and are forced to apply for means-tested support which carries with it conditions of residence for entitlement.

Residence rules often work against people from minority ethnic groups. Many such people, note Oppenheim and Harker (1996), maintain family links involving visits abroad. These visits frequently incur breaks in contributions, leading to reductions in or exclusions from contributory benefits in later life. Moreover, non-contributory benefits have residence and/or presence conditions attached to them, which, historically, have been very tough. Non-contributory benefits like Child Benefit were specifically aimed at people living in the UK. Often people from minority ethnic groups who live in the UK still support family members in their countries of origin. These obligations aren't recognised by the UK social security system, which can result in people having to survive on considerably reduced incomes.

The residence issue in relation to minority ethnic groups was raised in the 1980s by Norman Fowler, the then Secretary of State for Health and Social Security:

'we are concerned that the present conditions can allow too ready access to help by those who have no recent links with this country. Claimants will therefore need to satisfy a presence test; that is, the claimant will need to have been in the country for a set period to qualify for income support.'

(Department of Health 1985: Paragraph 2.87)

Oppenheim and Harker contend that, for many immigrants to the UK (not forgetting that many black people these days are British-born), the means-testing system appears to be an extension of immigration control: 'Passport checks on black claimants – whether or not they were born in the UK – have become a frequent occurrence at Benefit Agency offices' (1996: 128).

Black people are thus sometimes confronted by a set of conditions which have to be fulfilled in order to obtain benefits. This often leads to a low level of benefit take-up by minority ethnic families. Oppenheim and Harker (1996) also examined means-testing as part of the 1988 Social Security Act and how it affected ethnic minority claimants. They reported that:

- Income Support was removed for most 16–17-year-olds, which indirectly discriminates against black people and other minority ethnic groups who are over-represented in this age group and who are also unemployed.

- No right of appeal existed against Social Fund (a repayable hardship loan) claims.
- Date of arrival in the country was added to the Income Support form.
- The State earnings-related pension scheme was based on a lifetime's earnings.
- Inducements into private pension schemes didn't benefit the majority of minority ethnic groups.
- Family Credit rules asked for greater detail on employment history. Many people from minority ethnic groups were in low-paying sectors where employers were reluctant to provide information on National Insurance contributions and tax.

Low benefit take-up by minority ethnic groups also has cultural dimensions. Dependency on 'hand-outs' is sometimes seen as a sign of weakness, of not using the family and community support networks available, and an internalisation of inferior status. Gary Vaux and David Divine (1988) highlight too the difficulties minority ethnic families face when they seek to negotiate the complicated benefits claim system. Some people in the Bengali community, for example, have limited understanding of English.

Poverty isn't just about money. It also embodies access to housing, health and education. If you recall the Breadline Britain surveys of 1983 and 1990, 'a damp free home' came top of the ranking regarded as a 'necessity'. The study found that around 10 million people were living in squalid housing. Although they didn't specifically analyse the experiences of ethnic minorities and housing, it's well documented elsewhere that many live in overcrowded, unheated and damp properties in the private rented sector.

Access to housing is a significant source of inequality and deprivation in relation to ethnicity. Trying to get a home is often a harrowing experience for many minority ethnic groups. This includes the direct racism of landlords and the indirect racism of local authorities who put 'residence' conditions on the allocation of council homes. Minority ethnic groups are often 'channelled' towards the less desirable, poorer quality housing in run-down, inner-city areas. Interestingly, an important consequence of this residential segregation insofar as minority ethnic groups are concerned is that as 'people are forced to live together, communal ethnic ties will be strengthened by daily interaction' (John Rex 1992: 71).

In recent years, the housing conditions of minority ethnic groups have changed, and sometimes for the better. These days, less (11 per cent) live in private rented accommodation (*Social Trends* 1987–1990). People of Asian origin are more likely to be owner-occupiers, although this varies amongst Asian groups. Forty-two per cent of the African–Caribbean community, however, live in council accommodation. Moreover, as Alcock writes:

> 'deprivation in housing, health and education add significantly to the financial inequality of black people in Britain, and they have remained important despite the introduction in the 1960s of race relations legislation designed to prevent discrimination.'
>
> (Alcock 1993: 155)

Poverty and racial injustice take many forms, as demonstrated by Amin and Oppenheim (1992) in the chart below. Notice how the main components of poverty perpetuate vicious circles and spirals.

Race and poverty: Vicious circles and spirals

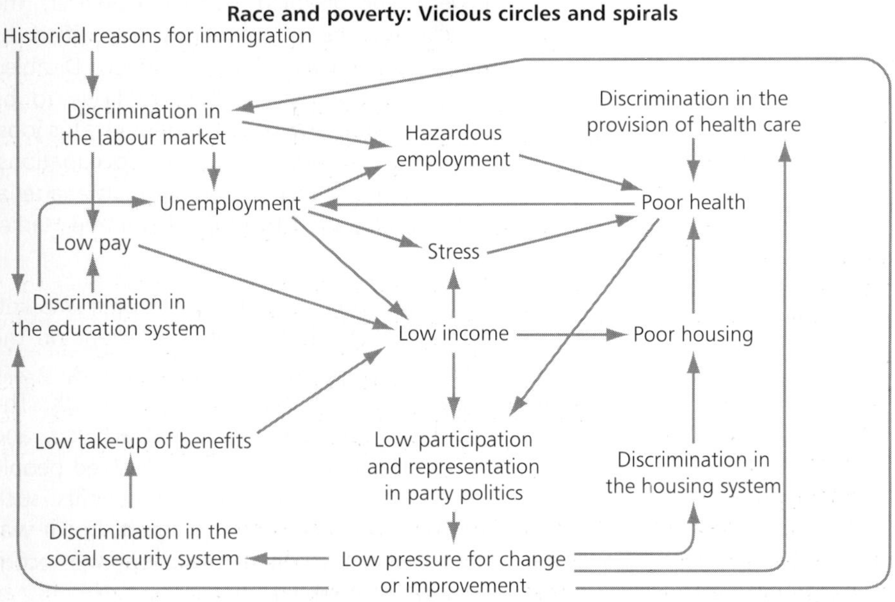

(Amin and Oppenheim 1992: 29)

Age

Many studies of poverty have revealed that the risk and extent of it varies with age. What is consistent with all patterns of life cycle inequality is the decline in income in old age. Booth's studies of poverty in London in 1892 and 1894 revealed higher levels of poverty amongst older people than in the rest of the population. Rowntree, in his studies of York in 1901 and 1941, identified three high risk periods of poverty: childhood, parenthood and old age. Townsend (1979) found that older people comprised 36 per cent of the poor, and that 64 per cent of older people were in receipt of under 140 per cent of the Supplementary Benefit entitlement, which was roughly equivalent to his definition of poverty. Mack and Lansley (1985) discovered that 37 per cent of pensioners on Supplementary Benefit lacked three or more necessities because they couldn't afford them.

What is also evident is that inequalities experienced in working life are taken through to old age. At one extreme, there are homeless old people on Income Support, with no private pension or savings. Next to them, are the old who live in council homes whose income is also low and who have no or little savings. At the other extreme, there are those who had well-paid jobs and have secured a 'nest egg' for retirement, and often a good occupational pension. Of the 10.6 million older population, women make up around two-thirds, and are more likely to be poor pensioners due to lower previous earnings, interrupted working careers, and greater life expectancy. The Family Expenditure Survey (1994/5) confirmed that 51 per cent of household income for retired people came from the benefits system, and there were five times as many women claimants as men.

There are other factors which reduce the income of older people. In theory, some older people should benefit from savings made over their lifetime, especially in the case of insurance policies or private pensions, but over long periods of time, these can be severely affected by inflation. The last government's record on state pensions is mixed. It increased the pension more than benefits for the working population, but, in 1980, pensions were adjusted annually with the rise in prices (rather than by earnings, or whichever was highest). If earnings had been the guiding measure, pensions would, in 1994, have been £20.30 per week higher for a single person and £33.05 per week higher for a couple (based on Department for Social Security statistics, October 1994). On the other hand, the then government might have argued that they did increase the means-tested benefits for pensioners by over £1.2 billion per year, since 1988.

However, successive Conservative governments have promoted the incentives for people to take out private personal pension plans, whilst simultaneously weakening the state earnings-related pension scheme. This was based on the assumption that the burden of pension payment would become too great for the rest of the population to afford. So, currently we have a large number of older people on inadequate pensions struggling to maintain even a very modest standard of living.

Rising costs are also a significant cause of poverty among older people. As a consequence of their generally lower finances, a greater proportion of their weekly income is being spent on the spiralling costs of housing, water rates, council tax, transport, and charges for care and essentials, such as food, fuel and clothing. This leaves less for luxury items and consumer durables which enhance the quality of life. Costs are partly covered by Income Support and Housing Benefit, but older people are unlikely to offset price hikes by taking part-time work or extending their retirement date. Being old in the UK today isn't easy.

Disability

'To be disabled . . . is also to be disadvantaged. It means regularly being unable to participate in the social and economic activities which most people take for granted. It means confronting the negative attitudes of others.'

(S. Lonsdale 1990, cited by Oppenheim and Harker 1996: 57)

Says Dulcie Groves, 'Poverty is disability's close companion' (1988: 171). Poverty resulting from being disabled is also closely linked to age. Half of the disabled in poverty are over pensionable age (Dalley 1991). The Office of Population, Censuses and Surveys (1988) revealed that 6.2 million adults (14 per cent of adults) and 360,000 children (3 per cent of children) were disabled. A later Policy Studies Institute investigation in 1993 found that 47 per cent of disabled adults were living in poverty.

Low income and benefit dependency are the major causes of poverty for disabled people. However, the receipt of a low income is frequently intensified by the extra costs associated with being disabled. Disabled people who are employed are still more likely to be concentrated in low-paid, low-skilled and low status jobs. Thirty-one per cent are in low-skilled manual occupations, and only 12 per cent are in professional or managerial positions (RADAR 1993, cited by Oppenheim and Harker 1996: 58).

With their relative exclusion from the labour market, disabled people have to rely to a greater extent on the benefits system. Benefit provision for people who are disabled has had a chequered history in the UK. The policy changes have been piecemeal and *ad hoc*, and this has led to inconsistencies in the way disabled people are treated. They're able to claim ordinary benefits, such as a retirement pension and Income Support, but it was only after 1970 that extra benefit provision was recognised as necessary for disabled people.

These included an Invalidity Benefit, Severe Disablement Allowance, and Additional Mobility and Attendance Allowances. However, after the 1988 Social Security Act, disability and severe disability premiums were introduced, with the result that many disabilities were excluded, such as a child with chronic asthma. In 1995, a new Incapacity Benefit was introduced to tighten up the medical test and control procedures. This will reduce the recipients of this benefit by about 220,000.

The 1993/4 Family Resources Survey found that 64 per cent of households with a sick or disabled person received no income from employment. Essential care and additional expenditure of time in caring for a disabled family member by others in the household or wider family network subjects the carers to a greater risk of poverty. The incapacity benefit offers the opportunity for the carer to claim support, but this is dependent on the severity of the disability. As Alcock notes:

'The ironic twist is the interrelationship of dependency between carer and cared for, which because of the lack of other forms of support extends the risk of poverty associated with disability beyond both the disability itself and the person suffering from it.'

(Alcock 1993: 187)

This may be experienced as a dependency trap, reinforced by exclusion from the labour market.

QUESTIONS

1 Outline the main links between the risk of poverty and: unemployment, low pay, gender, ethnicity, age and disability.
2 How far is the risk of poverty increased when people don't have access to well-paid employment?

Sources and levels of income and wealth

Income and wealth distribution

Income and wealth both refer to access to resources, but the two words denote different things:

- *Income* is a money flow. In the UK, wages and salaries are by far the largest source of income for most people.
- *Wealth* is a fixed asset. Homes are the most common example of wealth in the UK.

Income and wealth are very unevenly distributed in the UK, which is another way of saying that we live in a very unequal society. Some sociologists think that's unfair. Others think it's fair. The first job of the sociologist, however, is to say what *is*, rather than what ought to be. So let's look at the figures before we start getting into value judgements.

Income

People receive income from lots of different sources. Wages and salaries from paid employment are, as already indicated, the largest source. People who don't have a job get most of their income from their parents if they're children (pocket money is an example), from Income Support and Jobseeker's Allowance benefits if they're out of work or unable to work, and from state retirement pension benefits if they're old. Increasingly, more and more old people also receive occupational pensions

OVER TO YOU

What other sources of income can you think of? Discuss this.

The table on page 286 summarises the main sources of household income in the UK from 1971 to 1995.

Although wages and salaries are still the largest source of household income, the proportion fell by 12 percentage points (68 minus 56) between 1971 and 1995. During the same period, the proportion of income from private pensions and annuities, etc., more than doubled (from 5 per cent to 11 per cent). This, in part, reflects the growing numbers of older people and the increased likelihood that they'll have occupational pensions.

Earnings from employment have outpaced increases in retail prices over the past 15 years or so. This means that the real value of earnings has increased. If, for example, you earned £100 a week in 1990 and paid £2 then to go to a film, and you earn £200 in 1998 and pay £3 for the same entertainment, you're relatively better-off now even though the ticket price has gone up.

Most government income is obtained through direct and indirect taxes, and social security contributions (for example, National Insurance). In turn, government spending provides benefits to many households (for example, Child Benefit). Some people are taxed more than they receive back in benefits. Others receive more benefits than they pay taxes. This is the principle of the redistribution of income.

Earnings between occupations differ very markedly. In 1996, for example, solicitors earned more than three times the pay of cleaners (see the graph at the top of page 287).

The proportion of people with incomes below half average income rose from 8 per cent in 1982 to 19 per cent in 1993.

One of the most graphic (literally!) representations of the distribution of earnings in the UK appeared in an article by Charles Leadbeater, 'How fat cats rock the boat', in the *Independent on Sunday* on 3 November 1996. It

Household income, UK

Source of income	1971	1976	1981	1986	1991	1995
	Percentages					
Wages and salaries[1]	68	67	63	58	58	56
Self-employment income[2]	9	9	8	10	10	10
Rent, dividends, interest	6	6	7	8	9	7
Private pensions, annuities, etc	5	5	6	8	10	11
Social security benefits	10	11	13	13	11	13
Other current transfers[3]	2	2	2	3	2	3
Total household income (=100%)(£ billion at 1995 prices[4])	314	365	398	472	573	599

1 Includes Forces' pay and income in kind.
2 After deducting interest payments, depreciation and stock appreciation.
3 Mostly other government grants, but including transfers from abroad and non-profit making bodies.
4 Adjusted to 1995 prices using the consumers' expenditure deflator.

(Adapted from *Social Trends 27*: 90, using figures from the Office for National Statistics)

shows, among other things, that the nation's half a million or so ambulance drivers earn about £200 per week, and the footballer Alan Shearer earns . . . Look at the chart opposite (centre) and work it out.

Another important income inequality occurs between women and men. At nearly all ages, women earn less on average than men, as indicated in the bar chart opposite.

The gap between average female and male earnings has remained fairly constant in real terms since 1971. The largest difference for people occurs in their forties, where the gap is more than £140 per week. Under age 18, however, women earn a bit more than men of the same age. The peak earning age for women is in their thirties, and for men in their forties. Home-making duties are implicated in the relatively lower earnings of women: having children, caring for them, and sometimes for older relatives. Starting and raising a family mean for many women an interruption of their employment pattern. A career break, a switch to part-time work, or a change in job are common.

Although women earn on average less than men, female earnings are a very important part of family incomes. This is true for many couples, not just the wives of relatively well-paid men. In fact, during the 1980s, the share of family income from women's earnings increased most rapidly for the wives of low-paid men – but not for those with no earnings (Hills 1996). This is why women's earnings shouldn't be seen as mere 'pin money'. Without the contributions of women's earnings, poverty rates for some couples would be much higher.

Since the late 1970s, the living standards of people in the bottom two- or three-tenths of the income league table haven't risen significantly. Income earners at the top of the table, however, have gained much more rapidly than the average (Hills 1996).

Wealth

Wealth is even more unequally distributed than income.

There are two main kinds of wealth:

- *marketable wealth* – assets that can be sold or cashed in (for example, homes and shares)
- *non-marketable wealth* – assets that can't be sold or cashed in or are hard to do so (for example, occupational and state pension rights).

The value of personal wealth (mainly owned by individuals, but including unincorporated private businesses, life assurance and pension funds) in the UK in 1994 exceeded £2,500 billion. Most people hold the biggest part of their wealth (between 40 and 60 per cent) in the form of their homes. Only individuals whose wealth is above £500,000 (about 1 per cent of the population) hold more of their wealth in shares than in other assets. While many Britons are shareholders (about 10 million in 1993), most of them only own a very small portion of the cake. It's the big shareholders who, in marxist terms, constitute the upper (or ruling) class.

The table on page 288 shows the distribution of wealth in the UK from 1976 to 1993.

QUESTION

Study the table on page 288 on the distribution of wealth in the UK from 1976 to 1993. What are the main trends?

The very wealthy in the UK can be narrowed down to 500 individuals who between them are worth close

Real[1] gross earnings[2]: by selected occupation[3], Great Britain

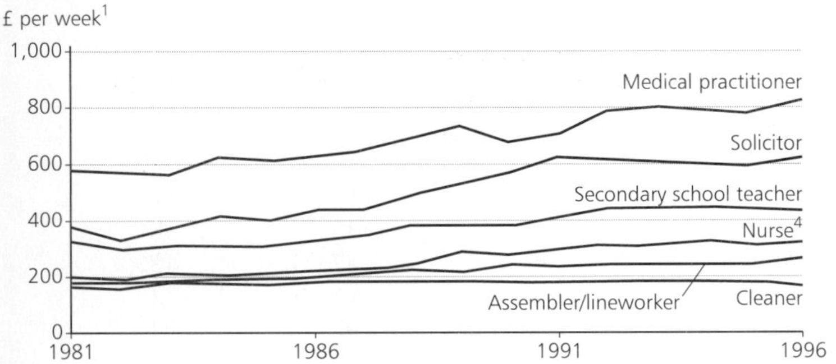

1 Adjusted to April 1996 prices using the retail prices index.

2 At April each year. Full-time employees on adult rates whose pay was not affected for the survey period by absence. Before 1983 average earnings are for men aged 21 and over and females aged 18 and over only.

3 The definitions of some of the occupations shown experienced minor changes when the Standard Occupational Classification was introduced in 1990.

4 National Health Service nurses and midwifery staff.

(*Social Trends 27:* 92, using figures from the New Earnings Survey, Office for National Statistics)

Who really earns what: Distribution of gross weekly earnings, with examples (Great Britain)

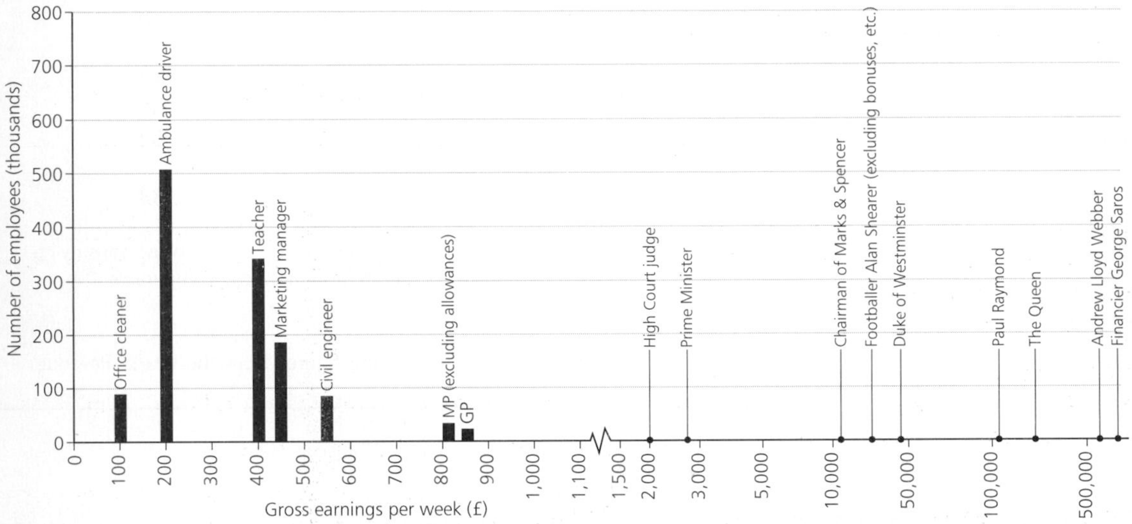

Note: The horizontal scale has been compressed after £1,500 to accommodate the highest earners. The graph represents gross earnings of people in full-time employment, but does not take into account any benefits (social security or company bonuses) that may also be received. Metropolitan, thirty-something, private-sector professionals may think a salary of say £25,000 (£480 a week) is about average. In fact, as the graph shows, it is roughly twice average earnings. According to the the 1995 New Earnings Survey, the bulk of full-time workers are on £150 – £350 a week.

(Adapted from the *Independent on Sunday*, 3 November 1996, using figures from the Office for National Statistics and the Income Data Service)

Gross weekly earnings[1]: by gender and age, UK, April 1995

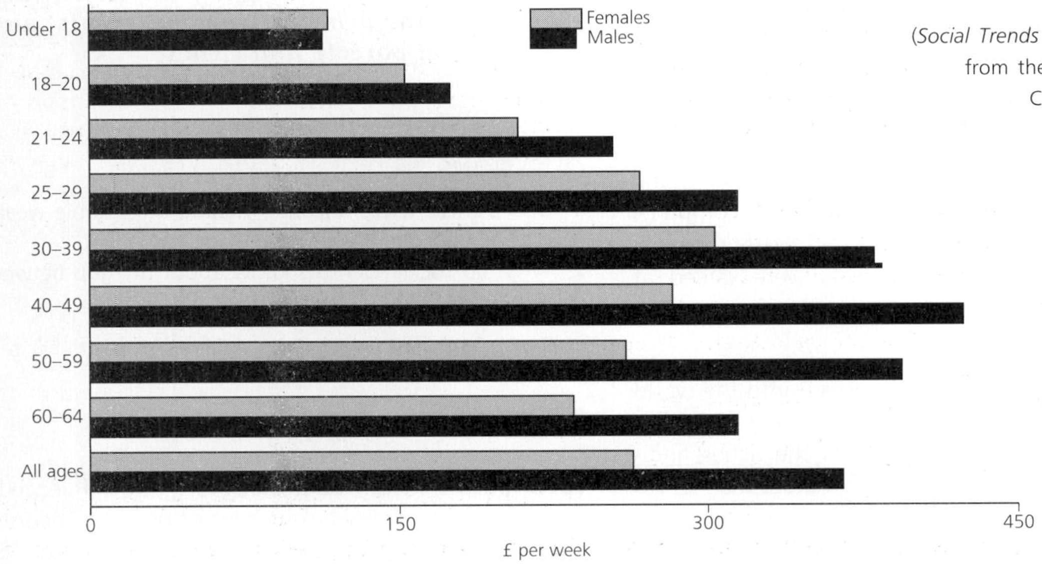

(*Social Trends 26*: 103, using figures from the New Earnings Survey, Central Statistical Office)

1 Full-time employees on all rates whose pay was not affected for the survey period by absence.

Distribution of wealth[1], UK

	1976	1981	Percentages 1986	1991	1993
Marketable wealth					
Percentage of wealth owned by:					
Most wealthy 1%	21	18	18	17	17
Most wealthy 5%	38	36	36	35	36
Most wealthy 10%	50	50	50	47	48
Most wealthy 25%	71	73	73	71	72
Most wealthy 50%	92	92	90	92	92
Total marketable wealth (£ billion)	280	565	955	1,711	1,809
Marketable wealth plus occupational and state pension rights					
Percentage of wealth owned by:					
Most wealthy 1%	13	11	10	10	10
Most wealthy 5%	26	24	24	23	23
Most wealthy 10%	36	34	35	33	33
Most wealthy 25%	57	56	58	57	56
Most wealthy 50%	80	79	82	83	82
Total marketable wealth (£ billion)	472	1,036	1,784	3,014	3,383

1 Applies to adult population aged 18 and over. Estimates for 1976, 1981, 1986 and 1991 are based on the estates of persons dying in those years. Estimates for 1993 are based on estates notified for probate in 1993–94. Estimates are not strictly comparable between 1993 and earlier years.

(*Social Trends 26*: 111, using figures from the Inland Revenue)

to £90 billion. At the top of the list – in April 1997 – was Joseph Lewis, a 60-year-old financier who plays the world currency markets from a vast computerised dealing room in his Bahamas villa. He's personally worth about £3 billion. Hans Rausing, the Swedish food packaging magnate who lives in the UK, was second, with a personal wealth rating close to £3 billion (Beresford 1997).

Only 155 of these 500 super-rich people inherited their fortunes in one form or another. 'Old money' is in decline at the top of the wealth hierarchy, as enterprise culture takes centre stage. Fortunes are being made today faster than ever. Brian Souter and his sister, Ann Gloag, the founders of the fast-growing rail and bus company, Stagecoach, are prime examples of rapid entrepreneurial wealth creation. In 1996, their assets were valued at £220 million. In 1997, these two Scots are worth £500 million.

As wealthy as they are, no Briton makes it into the world top ten, which is dominated by American entrepreneurs. Bill Gates, the founder of Microsoft, is the richest individual American. In 1996, he was worth more than £11.5 billion. That's 'modest', however, compared to the Sultan of Brunei. His oil-fuelled fortune makes him worth a cool £30 billion!

OVER TO YOU

We've documented the bold outlines of income and wealth patterns in the UK. What have you to say about the issue of income and wealth distribution in relation to social justice? Is it right for sociologists to engage the debate about the 'rights' and 'wrongs' of poverty and riches?

QUESTIONS

1 Define these terms: income; wealth; marketable wealth; non-marketable wealth.

2 What do social scientists know about the gap between average female and male earnings?

The causes of poverty

Social policies which address poverty are influenced by the conceptions policymakers have of poverty. Theoretical approaches to welfare policy and poverty differ. Each theory, notes Townsend:

'presupposes a different conception of the problem, different operationalization and measurement, and different explanation. Any statement of policy to reduce poverty contains an implicit if not explicit explanation of its cause.'

(Townsend 1979: 64)

We'll now consider the main explanations that have been offered as causes of poverty under the two umbrella headings:

- individualistic theories
- structural theories.

Individualistic theories

Individualistic theories identify the main causes of poverty within individuals themselves. Social and cultural factors aren't entirely discounted, but more emphasis is placed on inappropriate individual behaviours. Moreover, the socio-cultural dimension is typically framed in terms of 'faulty' socialisation leading to individual 'bad habits'. There are three main types of individualistic theory:

- orthodox economic theory
- minority group theory
- subculture of poverty theory.

Orthodox economic theory

This theory proposes that poverty can be explained by the economic deficiency of the individual. Harold Lydall (1968) argues that the general abilities of men in the labour force determine the distribution of incomes. These abilities are allegedly created by genetic, environmental and educational factors. In short, the problem of poverty resides in the poor. To reduce poverty, policies need to target individuals' own value systems, to develop their own personal qualities in a manner that makes them more attractive to future employers. The individual is poor because *he* hasn't maximised *his* true potential in the labour market. This approach is clearly very 'malestream', failing to recognise the gender/class/ethnic divisions within society and in the labour market.

Minority group theory

Minority group theory (not to be confused with minority ethnic groups) originated from the earliest studies of poverty based on the findings of Booth (1897) and Rowntree (1901). These pioneering social scientists didn't attempt to discover the causes of poverty, merely the characteristics of certain groups of poor people. Rowntree, for example, identified a cycle of poverty – children, young married couples with children, and old people running the highest risk of entering into poverty. Rowntree hypothesised that families would experience poverty at particular stages of their life. This was most likely to occur during early childhood, early adulthood, when married with dependent children, and during old age.

Minority group theory has therefore largely constructed its explanation for poverty through examining the characteristics of the poor – for example, being old, being married with dependent children, etc. That said, the theory goes beyond such demographic indicators also to implicate alleged 'faulty' human characteristics. Holman, for example, notes that the theory is based on the belief that:

'[individuals] are wholly responsible for their behaviour, morals and conditions. Consequently, their poverty is explained in terms of individual failure. If society sees the poor as a group . . . unwilling through free choice or incapable through pathological weakness to avoid poverty . . . poverty relief should be no more than a poverty line existence.'

(Adapted from Holman 1978: 54–5)

This classification of 'at-risk' groups has prompted policymakers to implement a benefit system to ensure that the most basic of needs are met, without encouraging idleness and apathy. The poverty policies of successive governments have often been informed by minority group theory.

Subculture of poverty theory

Subculture of poverty theory is derived from a number of anthropological and sociological studies, particularly, the work of Oscar Lewis (1965). Lewis suggests that the poorest section of society forms a subculture which is distinctive and self-perpetuating. His research focuses on the location of poverty within the personality characteristics of individuals (hence the individualistic leanings of subculture of poverty theory) and the associated social environment in which they live. So-called 'problem' families, 'problem communities', inner cities and, more recently, the 'underclass' become the focus of attention in this theory. It's a perspective which proposes that a subculture of poverty exists amongst the most socially and economically deprived.

Referring to the experiences of children in poverty, Lewis notes that 'It is a way of life, remarkably stable and persistent, passed down from generation to generation along family lines' (1965: 24).

As part of an unskilled labour force, the children studied by Lewis suffered from unemployment, under-employment and low wages, which meant a shortage of cash, little food, and overcrowded, impoverished, living areas. Lewis did stress that this subculture of poverty wasn't the same as poverty. It was a response by people to their marginalised position in a stratified-class society. One can see here that Lewis isn't making a moral judgement about the habits of the poor. Indeed, he seems to be suggesting that individual behaviours are linked to social conditions.

A version of the subculture of poverty theory has emerged in right-wing circles. The Conservative politician, Keith Joseph, for example, referred to a subculture of poverty in the UK as a cycle of deprivation:

'by which problems reproduce themselves from generation to generation ... among the children of this generation there are some doomed to an uphill struggle against the disadvantages of a deprived family background. Do we not know that many of them will not be able to overcome the disadvantages and will become in their turn the parents of deprived families?'

(Speaking at a Pre-school Playgroups Association Conference in 1972)

Joseph suggested that people who experience this cycle of deprivation are poor because they have been unable to take advantage of the opportunities that have come their way. Thus, they are 'deprived' of mainstream cultural values that would keep them out of poverty. The policy response of successive Conservative governments has been to encourage the culturally 'deprived' individual to break out of her or his family values and adapt to the system and opportunities offered by 'normal', wider society. That's a tough expectation, given that early socialisation patterns are hard to break. It's also a pathologising view because it implies that certain families are lacking in socially-approved cultural habits. The important question here is, 'Who says what is culturally approved?'

OVER TO YOU

Represent the ideas of the cycle of deprivation in diagrammatic form.

Ken Coates and Richard Silburn (1970) found that the poor of the St Ann's district of Nottingham responded to the same values as wider society, but were taking a realistic appraisal of their position – no job opportunities, shrinking benefits and little power to change things. Similarly, Ruth Lister and Peter Beresford (1991), in a forum called 'Working together against poverty', met representatives of the poor who described hardship, stigma and a lack of confidence as factors which inhibited them from full involvement in society.

They were well aware of their circumstances, but felt powerless to escape them. The stigma attached to being poor meant that they barely admitted their poverty to themselves, let alone voice their opinions to the rest of society in a way that would force politicians to do something about it. Says Alcock: 'To identify oneself as poor is to identify oneself as having a problem, and in need of help' (1993: 212).

The culture of poverty thesis is a form of 'blaming the victim'. Many sociologists reject it, and instead argue that structural changes are required in society if we are to get rid of poverty.

Structural theories

Structural theories explain poverty on the basis of structural (i.e. whole society) factors. There are two main kinds of structural theory:

- functionalist theory
- marxist theory.

Functionalist theory

The functionalist theory of inequality and poverty was developed by Talcott Parsons and his students, Kingsley Davis and Wilbert Moore, during the 1940s. They point out that every society has people with different social status and 'functional' positions in society. In order to ensure that all positions are filled in society, it's necessary to differentiate incentives and rewards. The greater the material inducement, the higher the occupational and social status and personal motivation of these individuals. (Look back to the section on the functionalist theory of stratification in Chapter 7, page 142.)

Poverty is, therefore, functional by reinforcing the foundations upon which social structures of inequality are built. Robert Holman (1978) takes this point further by proposing that there are three ways in which poverty functions in a hierarchical society:

- It justifies poverty and wealth – the poor are solely to blame for their own lowly position through fecklessness, idleness and exploitation of the benefits system (there are clear links here with individualistic theories of poverty).
- It lessens prospects of change – the poor are a sizeable growing minority, but the categorisation of society now consists of various sub-classes, all with their own motivations. Thus, the poor will receive no special attention or sympathy by those who are 'above them'.
- It relies on 'dirty workers' – every stratified society requires by its nature unpleasant jobs and tasks to be completed. The poor help to ensure that these jobs get done.

Herbert Gans (1972) reflected at some length on the functions of poverty which help to maintain the social divisions in society. This is what he came up with (his is a commentary, not a personal view)

The positive functions of poverty

1 Poverty helps to ensure that dirty, dangerous, menial and undignified works gets done.
2 The poor subsidize the affluent by saving them money (for example, domestic servants, medical guinea pigs, and the poor paying regressive taxes).
3 Poverty creates jobs in a number of professions (e.g. drug pedlars, prostitutes, pawnshops, army, police).
4 The poor buy shoddy, stale and damaged goods (e.g. day-old bread, vegetables, second-hand clothes) which prolongs their economic usefulness, and similarly use poorly trained and incompetent professional people, such as doctors and teachers.
5 The poor help to uphold the legitimacy of dominant norms by providing examples of deviance (e.g. the lazy, spendthrift, dishonest, promiscuous).
6 The poor help to provide emotional satisfaction, evoking compassion, pity and charity, so that the affluent may feel righteous.
7 The poor offer affluent people vicarious participation in sexual, alcoholic and narcotic behaviour.
8 Poverty helps to guarantee the status of the non-poor.
9 The poor assist in the upward mobility of the non-poor. (By being denied educational opportunities or being stereotyped as stupid or unteachable, the poor enable others to obtain the better jobs.)
10 The poor add to the social viability of non-economic groups (e.g. fund-raising, running settlements, other philanthropic activities).
11 The poor perform cultural functions, like providing labour for Egyptian pyramids, Greek temples and medieval churches.
12 The poor provide 'low' culture which is often adopted by the more affluent (e.g jazz, blues, spirituals, country music).
13 The poor serve as symbolic constituencies and opponents for several political groups (being seen either as the depressed or as 'welfare chiselers').
14 The poor can absorb economic and political costs of change and growth in American society (e.g. reconstruction of city centres, industrialization).
15 The poor play a relatively small part in the political process and indirectly allow the interest of others to become dominant and distort the system.

(Gans 1972, cited by Townsend 1979: 85–6)

Gans asserts that, because poverty is beneficial to the advantaged classes, it will continue to thrive. He denies, however, that poverty should persist. Certainly, a list of functions like those above suggest there is a range of groups who do very well in a society with a vested interest in perpetuating poverty.

Marxist theory

Marxists contend that capitalism is the main cause of poverty. Capitalism places the ownership and control of the labour market in the hands of private individuals and groups. The upshot, said Marx, is that many people are poor. Capitalists aim to invest their profit and capital to create wealth, whilst the workers negotiate in the labour market to obtain a reasonable income and provide themselves with an acceptable standard of living. Unfortunately, workers' wages are not necessarily at a high enough level to ensure that they don't fall into poverty. Workers have little choice: they either sell their labour power at a level determined by the capitalist, or they live on inadequate welfare income.

Marx argued that the capitalist system couldn't survive without an adequate supply of labour power. Therefore capitalist owners required a surplus of working-class labour, both active and reserve. Commenting on the reserve portion of the equation, Marx wrote:

'Taking them as a whole, the general movement of wages (and thus poor relief levels) are exclusively regulated by the expansion and contraction of the industrial reserve army.'

(cited in Stitt 1994: 39)

By this, he means that the capitalist system is based on economic inequality. The reserve army of labour, subsisting on inadequate welfare benefits, is ready and willing to replace the active labour force if they don't accept low wages. Thus poverty in capitalist society is premised on a back-up army of unemployed people.

In order to understand Marx's perspective on poverty, it's also necessary to analyse his views on the state and its policies. Marx believed the state buttressed the economic and ideological interests of the ruling class, thereby helping to maintain an exploitative system. While the state might seek to reduce poverty, its primary role is to uphold the power of the capitalist system and the accumulation of profit. Illustrative of this, Marx argued that actions by capitalist governments to reduce poverty were forms of prudential state charity which might ameliorate certain social problems, but which would leave the *status quo* intact. The social security system today might be seen in this light – at least, from a marxist view.

Often these days referred to as *labour market theory*, the marxist explanation of poverty proposes that the main cause of poverty is to be found in the changing needs and demands of the labour market. The *dual labour market* explanation of poverty suggests that the labour market has split into two separate entities – the primary and secondary markets. The *primary labour market* contains the best jobs – the ones which have career prospects, secure full-time employment, decent pay and good conditions, and generous pension arrangements. Not so the *secondary labour market*. Here we find little or no chance of advancement, tenuous part-time jobs, poverty pay, poor – often dangerous – conditions, and basic or no pension provision.

The level of access to the primary market is influenced by employers' requirements. Employers will invest in workers with the requisite skills and work ethos by providing quality in-service training, paying high wages, offering job security, and good working conditions. In return, they expect their workers to remain loyal, reliable and hard-working. The secondary labour market provides a very different setting, one that's characterised by mundane, low skill work, and little confidence by employers that employees are capable of working at a higher level. The workers in the secondary labour market constitute a 'reserve army' of labour that can be hired or fired as the supply and demand of the market determines. People from minority ethnic groups, women, people who are disabled, and unskilled and semi-skilled working-class manual workers are over-represented in the secondary labour market.

If unemployment is a dire experience because benefits don't provide a decent standard of living, any opportunity to escape this poverty will be attractive. This may mean taking on a job in the secondary labour market which, though exploitative, is sometimes seen as better than being out of work.

An interesting model within dual market labour theory is *segmentation theory*. This posits that further segmentation takes place in the primary labour market sub-divided on the basis of class. The labour market is divided into a subordinate or routinised layer and an independent or creative stratum. Further divisions occur based on gender and ethnicity. These different sub-divisions are characterised by their own entry qualifications, methods of recruitment, working conditions and pay.

Employers shape the sub-divisions in order to promote their own self-interests through manipulating and controlling the differently 'created' social groups. The desire for appropriate workers for the different layers of the market is met by offering differentiated incentives. Says Townsend, segmentation theory is only 'a tentative step towards what has been termed "radical" economic theory. This draws heavily on the Marxist tradition' (1979: 78).

Also drawing upon aspects of marxism, is *class structuration theory*. This theory suggests that 'poverty results from some groups being prevented from gaining access to a wide range of resources (not just cash income) by the various systems of distribution in any society.' (Alan Walker 1990, in Haralambos 1990: 63). These systems of distribution are the wage and salary system, the benefits system, and the tax system.

Townsend's work on poverty is influenced by marxist theory. He proposes that people's economic position and status in society closely correspond to their general command over material resources. However, inconsistencies between economic position and status may arise, says Townsend, 'from the fact that the command over resources is not always conspicuously symbolised in style of living' by some people (1979: 83).

Townsend refuses to isolate individual traits, subcultures or labour market developments. Instead, he argues that the causes of poverty are located in the unequal structures of society. The solution to this inequality will only be solved by reforming the economic and social systems in order to re-distribute income and wealth and to challenge the values which perpetrate an unequal society. Arguing along similar lines, John Kincaid contends that:

'Poverty cannot be considered as a residual, historically determined effect of an otherwise fair society, but as an integral element that helps support a competitive social order.'

(Kincaid 1973: 23)

What's obvious, is that the causes of poverty are contested. Individualist and structural theories make this point. One of the most controversial concepts, however, in current considerations of poverty is that of the 'underclass'. The 'underclass' are the very poor, the people on the economic and social margins of society. They're a mixed bunch, which arguably invalidates the use of the suffix 'class' in the term. A class is a group of people who share lots of similar characteristics: outlook, income, type of job, etc. The 'underclass' have only this in common: they're right at the bottom of the income ladder. That apart, they count among their number such diverse social groups as young, unemployed black men, disabled people, older white women, people ill with mental disorders, and homeless people of all ages and of both sexes.

The 'underclass' debate

As the social processes of exclusion and polarisation increased in the 1980s, the question was raised as to whether the poorest and most excluded represented a permanent 'underclass'. This issue figured prominently in the social policy forums of successive New Right governments, particularly, during the Thatcher era. New Right thinking explains poverty on the basis of social 'pathology', depicting the so-called 'undeserving poor' as a 'diseased', isolated group in society. This approach has been very influential in post-war American society.

In the USA, New Right thinking has demonised many poor people. Its concept of the 'underclass' is often synonymous with poor, black Americans. Underclass theory – the notion that some poor people are permanently excluded from mainstream economic, cultural and social life because of their own bad habits – is strongly enjoined by Charles Murray, a right-wing political scientist at the Manhattan Institute for Policy Research. Murray argues that welfare benefits help to create a *culture of dependency* which draws some people into an underclass position. He particularly identifies young female lone parents as those who have chosen parenthood and dependency on welfare benefits rather than committing themselves to the responsibilities of marriage.

In 1989, Murray was invited to the UK by the Conservative-supporting *Sunday Times* newspaper to discover if there was an 'Emerging British Underclass' (the title of the ensuing article). He concentrated on three phenomena that are considered to be early warning signs of the emergence of an 'underclass': illegitimacy, violent crime, and a high drop-out rate from the labour force. Kirk Mann interprets Murray's perception of the underclass as 'criminally violent bastards who refuse to work' (1992: 106). Murray's findings were published by the right-wing policy group, the Institute of Economic Affairs, in 1990. His conclusion was that things were not quite as bad in the UK as in the USA, but that a new 'underclass' was looming:

'If illegitimate births are the leading indicator of an underclass and violent crime a proxy measure of its development, the definitive proof that an underclass has arrived is that large numbers of young, healthy, low-income males choose not to take jobs. (The young idle rich are a separate problem.) This decrease in labour force participation is the most elusive of the trends in the growth of the British underclass.'

(Murray 1990: 17–18)

Murray draws attention to the 'economically inactive' people who manage to qualify for benefit even though they allegedly have no desire to return to a job or have just given up. The 'black economy' (Murray's term, not ours) in which people are working for cash but not reporting their income to the authorities is another issue he addresses. The question facing the UK, according to Murray, is how contagious is this 'disease'? Is it going to spread indefinitely, or will it be self-containing? Murray believes the 'culprits' behind the trends reflect part of a 'decay in moral standards, the perverse incentives of welfare policy and the coddling of criminals' (1990: 25). The solution, says Murray, is that:

'Central Government [should] stop trying to be clever and instead get out of the way, giving poor communities a massive dose of self-government, with vastly greater responsibility for the operation of the institutions that affect their lives – including the criminal justice, educational, housing and benefit systems in their localities . . . Money isn't the key.'

(Murray 1990: 34)

Essentially, Murray blames the poor for their poverty because they supposedly 'decide' to act in inappropriate ways or, 'at best', are socialised to do so by the Welfare State.

Alongside the New Right individualistic approach (also called the behavioural approach), a structural discourse on poverty has developed which also acknowledges the existence of an 'underclass' but locates the causes in the social structure of society. According to the African–American academic, William Julius Wilson, it's the social isolation of the poor and materially-deprived inner-city families that has created an underclass:

'The social transformation of the inner-city has resulted in a disproportional concentration of the most disadvantaged segment of the urban black population, creating a social milieu significantly different from the environment that existed in these communities several decades ago.'

(Wilson 1987: 58)

Wilson calls this the 'tangle of pathology' in the inner city. Black poverty in the US has its foundations in several interrelated factors: the move from commodity production to service provision which resulted in the loss of many millions of unskilled jobs; the historical discrimination which has led to the concentration of a black 'underclass' in inner-city areas; and the legacy of 'white flight' (migration from the inner-city areas of white working- and middle-class families) which compounded the problems faced by isolated, poor black people.

In the UK, John Rex and Peter Tomlinson (1979) arrived at a similar conclusion in their study of Handsworth, a Birmingham suburb where many black people live. They concluded that minority ethnic groups formed an 'underclass' based on an inferior position in relation to housing, employment and education. As structural sociologists, however, they don't impute blame to these people. They adopt the sociological view that inequalities in society are to blame, not individuals.

In 'Britain's underclass: Countering the growth', the now Minister for Welfare Reform, Frank Field, said that, 'Britain does now have a group of poor people who are so distinguished from others on low income that it is appropriate to use the term 'underclass' to describe their position in the social hierarchy' (Field 1990: 37). Field maintains that the 'underclass' doesn't just comprise poor black people. Black people are in the ranks of the poor because they occupy some of the most vulnerable positions in British society. However, in areas of

Birkenhead (which Field represents as an MP), where there are very few black people, the 'underclass' consists largely of poor white people.

Field emphasises the importance of the structural position of the 'underclass', noting that it's composed of three main groups – frail older pensioners, lone parents with no chance of escaping welfare under existing rules and prevailing attitudes, and long-term unemployed people. His response to the New Right insinuation that poor people somehow 'choose' to become members of the underclass is unequivocal: 'No-one in their right mind believes that [the underclass] has volunteered for membership' (1990: 39).

What to do about the 'underclass' is crucial to current political debates about poverty and anti-poverty policies. The Right argue that welfarism promotes a culture of idleness. The Left claim that poverty has to be understood as a problem of inequality and requires state intervention to redistribute resources more fairly across society. This requires higher taxes on the rich.

To end on a conceptual note, many sociologists don't use the term 'underclass', because it conveys moral disapproval of the poor rather than of poverty, and conjures up a derogatory image. The only usefulness of the term in our view is as a catch-all description of the poorest of the poor – the human beings at the bottom of the economic and social pile. We prefer the term 'very poor' to 'underclass', and, in that context, are mindful of the views of a poor person on the underclass debate which was published on the Letters to the Editor page of the *Independent*:

'Sir: My class is as good or bad as yours, or Mr Mandelson's, and "under" neither . . . If I am "socially excluded" it is because I do not have the money to participate in such a society as we still have, which is built upon money and the inequality of its distribution. I and millions like me – pensioners, disabled, unemployed – do not need clever phrases to disguise us from all but ourselves. We need some relief from persecution by the debt collector and the council bailiff. We need to be lifted out of poverty by a booming economy, and we need the reordering of social priorities, so that real attempts can be made to help us rather than to penalise us for being poor.'

(The *Independent*, 16 August 1997)

QUESTIONS

1 What are the differences between the individualistic and structuralist approaches to poverty?
2 Evaluate the claim that the poor have themselves to blame for their poverty.

EXAM TIP

Make it clear to the examiner that it's inappropriate for sociologists to make moral judgements about people in poverty. The task of the sociologist is to identify the causes of poverty, and to put forward social scientific solutions to the problem.

Welfare social policy: A solution to poverty?

Social policy, as a discipline, draws on sociology, economics, politics and other social sciences. Its focus is on the development and implementation of policy measures in order to influence the social circumstances of individuals. In this spirit, social policy doesn't just analyse society; it puts forward proposals about how society should be.

Social policy in the UK is crucially linked to the issue of the Welfare State, which was launched in the wake of the Beveridge Report on Social Insurance and Allied Services of 1942. The Welfare State is a massive form of national social security. Its advent ushered in reforms designed to reduce the extent of poverty and inequality across the whole population, and to bring about a return to full employment. This intervention took the form of services provided by the state, using resources collected from the working population in the form of taxation.

Three features stood to the fore in the role of the new Welfare State:

- development of public social services (for example, the National Health Service, state education and a National Insurance scheme)
- nationalisation of major industries (for example, coal and steel industries were run by state-appointed managers)
- commitment to full employment (for example, employment protection rights).

The development of the Welfare State, says Alcock:

'is not only the product of the attempt to remedy the failings of a capitalist economy but also of the recognition of new ways in which this economy might be maintained and developed.'

(Alcock 1996: 45–6)

Ideas about what the Welfare State should do bring us, of course, into the area of welfare ideologies.

Welfare ideologies

The Welfare State incurs a large amount of public expenditure. The money is mainly spent on education, housing, health, social services and social security. However, the Welfare State can no longer be seen as a modern, rational mechanism for meeting the needs of the poor. What has occurred in the field of 'new' social policy is a range of competing 'ideologies' or 'models' of welfare. By ideology, we mean a shared outlook, in this case, one that adopts a particular perspective towards welfare policy.

Commentators often link welfare ideologies to political standpoints (for example, New Right versus left-wing positions). One of the most influential studies of social policy and political ideology is by Vic George and Paul Wilding (1976). They suggested that there are four main ideological positions – those of the:

- anti-collectivists
- reluctant collectivists
- Fabian socialists
- marxists.

Anti-collectivists

(Also termed New Right, Neo-Liberals, *Laissez-Faire* or Market Liberals.)

This group are opposed to state welfare provision above a basic minimum. They maintain that state intervention interferes with individual freedom, and they look to the family and the local community to provide traditional support roles. Their anti-collectivist sentiments are clearly of the kind that contest whole society solutions to poverty, but they approve of more micro collectivities, like families. The anti-collectivist ideology is endorsed in the UK by right-wing think tanks such as the Institute of Economic Affairs (IEA), the Centre for Policy Studies (CPS), and the Adam Smith Institute (ASI). The main argument of these institutions is that welfare assistance isn't desirable because it wastes human and capital resources, creates administrative inefficiency, and undermines a work ethos.

In economic terms, advocates of anti-collectivism want little interference with the free working of the market. Otherwise, great strain will be placed on the public purse

Reluctant collectivists

(Also termed Political Liberals, the Middle Way.)

Reluctant collectivists occupy the political middle ground of the Conservative, Liberal-Democrat and Labour parties. They embrace an ideological perspective similar to the one which informed Beveridge in his recommendations for social and economic reform during the post-war period. They're committed to the welfare system and its ability to protect all citizens. Reluctant collectivism was formed out of pragmatism, recognising the social needs of the public and the opportunity for a market to have private investment and economic growth. There's also an endorsement of the belief that individual freedom is central to a democracy – hence the *reluctant* collectivism

Fabian socialists

(Also termed social democrats.)

The position of the Fabian socialists is to the left of the Labour Party. It has two central propositions: total commitment to the democratic process, and unequivocal support for social welfare. It's an ideology that strongly believes in social justice within a capitalist economy which can be achieved through the introduction of state welfare services, redistributive tax, and benefit policies. A 'new Fabianism' has arisen in the 1990s as a response to the failure of the Welfare State to recognise the importance of consumer and citizenship rights, and partnerships between the state, market and other welfare sectors. Le Grand and Estrin (1989) calls it market socialism. Others call it New Labour. The Borrie Commission of Social Justice (1994), established by the then – now late – Labour Leader, John Smith, after the party's 1992 election defeat, advocates a 'new Fabian' approach. The commission recommended strategies on welfare, some of which have been adopted by the current Labour government

It's Social Exclusion Unit has a remit to rescue the UK's so-called 'underclass' from the twin dangers of unemployment and social exclusion. The unit is headed by the Prime Minister, Tony Blair, within the Cabinet Office. Poverty pressure groups, however, have dismissed the venture as a public relations gimmick. Even a former deputy leader of the Labour Party, Roy Hattersley, although welcoming the initiative, warns that there has to be an improvement in benefit rates if the worst levels of poverty are to be tackled.

Arguably, the unit isn't paying enough attention to the economic and social needs of people for whom employment mightn't be an option: the severely disabled, the fragile elderly, those with serious mental disorders, etc. These people often live in abject poverty, and their special circumstances generally don't connect with 'welfare-to-work' programmes. Critics of the government argue that the poor voted Labour because they believed it would help to bring them out of poverty. Yet this government seems to have adopted the view that the poor have to remain in poverty – at least, for the time being – because Labour was elected on the understanding that it wouldn't raise income tax.

In responding to these kinds of criticism, Peter Mandelson, Minister Without Portfolio, claims that the anti-poverty drive will be achieved through many different routes, not just the redistribution of money from rich to poor. He makes it clear that he wants to see more money in the pockets of poor people when economic circumstances and the re-ordering of public expenditure makes this possible. Mandelson also specifies who the most needy are:

- the five million people in workless homes
- the three million residents on the nation's 1,300 worst council estates
- the 150,000 homeless families
- the 100,000 children not attending school.

New Labour wants to remove welfare dependency. It's seeking, for example, to prevent unemployed school-leavers from becoming dependent on welfare by a welfare-to-work programme. The terms of the programme require young people to take up job training, or work on an environmental project, or for a voluntary organisation. Where the government has got it wrong, say the 'Old Labour' commentators, is in exaggerating the number of people who can be got off welfare into a job. Old people, for example, have 'done their bit', have put in a working life's labour in the home, the factory or wherever. Not for them, the need for a back-to-work scheme, but instead, a pension which provides genuine economic security.

A 'welfare-to-work' programme that offers decent pay and a brighter future for people whose circumstances realistically allow them to enter paid employment does make good sense. But the fact remains that the only way to get rid of poverty once and for all is to narrow, largely, through redistributive taxation, the gap between the rich and the poor. This is not political ideology but social scientific fact. In that context, it's important to note Labour MP, Roy Hattersley's remark that 'The press office at No. 10 will argue that 1,000,000 *Sun* readers are worth 100 professors'. What he's saying is that empirical evidence is a better guide to poverty reduction policy than tabloid populism. He's right

OVER TO YOU

We've mentioned people who are severely disabled and people who are very old as vulnerable poor people who are unable to work. What do we know about the problems these people face? Do a bit of research here. You might want to contact organisations like Help the Aged, Mencap and Scope. Find out what other groups of people might be unable to work (and we don't mean babies and children, of course!)

Marxists

Marxism is an ideology (orthodox marxists would contest this because they regard ideology as a 'dirty' word) on the far left of the political spectrum. Marxists regard the Welfare State as an ineffectual palliative which attempts to reduce the inequalities perpetuated by capitalist society. Only by overturning capitalism and replacing it with authentic socialism will the needs of all people be met. However, many marxists accept that some form of welfare is necessary as a temporary prop on the journey to an equal society. With the advent of equality, of course, welfarism will disappear because people will be attended to on the basis of need, not in terms of how much money they have.

Marxist ideologies – or visions, to indulge their preferred term – are quite varied, but are all essentially anti-capitalistic. Alcock (1996), for example, identifies *New Radicals* whose views appeal to such groups as feminists, anti-racists, disability awareness groups, environmentalists and green politics groups, and the anti-nuclear movement. Alcock suggests that an ideological shift in awareness has occurred to address the more diverse range of social divisions in society.

The quite wide appeal of New Radicalism has led some commentators to link it with so-called *new social movements*. However, Alcock points out the inadequacy of this latter term to cover such a divergent range of political and ideological problems under one heading.

Ideological disagreements on the development and implementation of social policy remain, and are further enjoined by postmodernist suspicions of self-styled policy experts. Postmodern theory (read the section on this in Chapter 6, Culture and Identity) essentially argues that:

'as societies have become even larger – and thus more complex, diverse and fragmented – the broad political movements and wide ranging ideological perspectives . . . have been replaced by a much more extensive range of more diffuse perspectives representing smaller social groups and narrower social interests.'

(Alcock 1996: 123)

If postmodernists are correct, the future problems for social policy are more diverse and complex, and are not simply resolved by reducing or extending state welfare.

The central role of the state, say the postmodernists, is being displaced by a range of organisations, allegiances and agencies. Power is being decentralised throughout society, and the self-indulgent discourse of civil servants and politicians is being knocked off its pedestal.

> **OVER TO YOU**
>
> ***Discuss the role that government should play in the funding of state education. This could be the subject of a class debate. Choose two competing perspectives from the anti-collectivist, reluctant-collectivist, Fabian socialist, and marxist ideologies.***

Sociological studies of the Welfare State

The modern Welfare State didn't exist during the lives of classical sociologists, Herbert Spencer and Emile Durkheim. However, these early functionalists did consider social policy indirectly through their work on social order and social solidarity. *Functionalists* see social policy as a necessary advance in response to the changing demands of industrialisation. The Welfare State is the institution that serves to integrate society, and maintains harmony and solidarity. It provides a range of services to the whole population that ensures they're protected from the threats of poverty and ill-health.

Ramesh Mishra (1981) is critical of the functionalist view of welfare. He argues that social policies favour one group over another. Poverty, disparities in income and wealth, racism and sexism don't point to harmony, stability and value-consensus in society. Alcock (1996) adds that we are all subject to the same policy developments and legal rights, but society is complex because divergent social needs have to be met. The Welfare State is unlikely, in practice, to be able to meet all these needs. As Fiona Williams (1989) states, there is now clear recognition that society is divided. Social policy must recognise this. The Welfare State was set up to provide 'for all', and so the policies must acknowledge this diversity.

As indicated earlier, *marxists* don't believe that the Welfare State keeps the inequalities of capitalism at bay. Welfarism is viewed as a sop to a citizenry who are – in most cases – taken care of in a superficial kind of way. Moreover, the ruling class is permitted to take a by-proxy, at-a-distance responsibility for welfare recipients whilst not yielding any of their power.

In British society, the size and composition of social classes is constantly evolving. Social mobility in the hierarchical occupational structure and the gaps between the social classes have become a major focus in social policy development. The introduction of welfare provision is intended to reduce the inequalities of social class. Social security is supposed to prevent the formation of an 'underclass'. The National Health Service is supposed to provide medical care on a clinical needs basis. State education is supposed to give every student the chance to reach her or his potential.

However, these goals haven't been attained. Le Grand (1982) reveals that universal services are more widely accessed by the middle class, and so aren't effective in ensuring equality across the classes. Marxists aren't surprised by this, pointing out that rich, powerful people aren't inclined to support welfare policies which radically redistribute wealth and income.

The *feminist* analysis on social policy and the Welfare State focuses on how it has been largely created by men to shape the lives of women: a form of patriarchal control. Feminist analyses of the Welfare State emphasise the great power and privilege men hold over women. Issues relating to the particular welfare needs of women have been marginalised in mainstream social policy debate, notes Elizabeth Wilson (1977). Gender inequalities remain sizeable and significant. Women earn 71 per cent of men's average rates of pay, only 37 per cent of women have company/private pensions, and many women have low pay and low status jobs. They're also more likely to be unemployed, but constitute a minority of the official unemployed because they're less likely to be entitled to the benefits, especially when their husbands work. Women are expected to support men and children, both as secondary wage earners and as unpaid workers in the home.

Jennifer Dale and Peggy Foster (1986) note that Beveridge's assumption that women would make 'marriage their sole occupation' has influenced access and use of the welfare services. Feminists advocate the need for active campaigning to improve or restructure welfare provision and establish services specifically in the interests of women. Examples of the reforms they endorse are Well Women Clinics, safe houses for victims of male domestic violence, maternity provision, and health screening.

Sociologists who study minority ethnic groups note that people from these communities are, like women, often marginalised in high-level discussions about the Welfare State. Racism is at the heart of this, and it's apparent too in the discrimination many black and Asian people encounter in the welfare system. Differences in ethnic and cultural background aren't properly addressed in social policy. As a result of the often inadequate welfare provision they receive, members of minority ethnic groups are at greater risk of poverty. As said earlier, discrimination is fuelled by suspicion of illegal immigration and the racist ideology that the Welfare State wasn't intended for black and Asian people – so why should they benefit from it?

Discrimination by Welfare State agents has restricted the provision of public sector housing and access to social security benefits for minority ethnic groups. The National Health Service has given little attention to diseases that are more prevalent among black people, such as sickle-cell, rickets and hepatitis. People from minority communities have responded accordingly. Excluded by the welfare system, such communities have developed their own provision (for example, Asian women's refuges, black housing associations, and black-parent-only adoption schemes).

Turning to *sociological research on age*, it's important to say that age discrimination in social policy has differing dimensions to problems associated with class, gender and ethnicity. On the whole (excluding the possibility of class mobility), the last three categories are relatively fixed and immobile. Black people, for example, are black all their lives. Ageing, however, is a staged process. During those stages, young and old people are especially vulnerable to discrimination. Children are unable to fend for themselves, and require the support of adults. On a welfare level, this support comes through family welfare policy.

We've already referred to the number of young people who live in low-income families on the margins of or in poverty. Child Benefit is paid as a direct subsidy to the family to meet the extra expenses incurred by having children. But the dependent young person who has left school at 16 is now excluded from benefit, and often has to turn to her or his family for financial support. Moreover, between 18 and 25 years of age, young people on benefits receive lower levels of support. Through no fault of their own, but by being unemployed and unable to pay National Insurance contributions, they suffer the consequences of this policy.

The discrimination faced by older people is often even more severe. There's a fear amongst the policy makers that the growing numbers of older people are placing an increasing burden upon the rest of society. This expansion in the number of older people is largely the result, say the Family Policy Studies Centre, of better nutrition, living and working conditions, and health care: cause for celebration one would think, not lament.

The changing size and structure of the older population from 1901 projected to 2021 is illustrated in the table below.

If the projection is accurate, we're going to have growing numbers of very old people. But surely this is a good thing? It means that the life expectancy of the population is going up as a consequence of the success of social policies and improved living conditions. Social policy experts shouldn't moan about this. They should design new policies that will meet the changing needs of a growing older population. While the old do consume a larger share of health and personal service spending (McGlone 1992), it's important to add that over half of people over 65 years of age are 'givers' too, through part-time employment and voluntary work. They've also given a great deal to the nation over the years in paid employment and as homemakers.

As for *what sociologists know about people who are disabled*, by and large, they report that the needs of these citizens have been neglected by policymakers. Discriminating practices (for example, excluded on the grounds that the disability isn't severe enough) deny them proper service provision. Definitional issues as to what is a disability have caused great debate in the world of social security. At present, the degree of disability determines the amount of benefit and mobility and care allowance disabled people receive. Clearly, disability is a major issue for social policy, with over 10 per cent of the population experiencing a disability.

The social security system does identify the specific needs of disabled people by paying out higher benefits to those who are chronically sick and disabled, but these levels are still inadequate. There has been a move in the 1990s to provide Care in the Community, allowing disabled people to take more control over their lives. However, this policy has been implemented on the cheap. With a reduction of resources to the public services, it has

Age structure of the elderly population of Great Britain 1901–2021 (by thousands)

	65+	% *	75+	% *	85+	% *
1901	1734	4.7	507	1.4	57	0.15
1971	7140	13.2	2536	4.7	462	0.86
1981	7985	15.0	3052	5.7	552	1.03
1991	8795	15.9	3844	6.9	757	1.4
2001	8656	15.3	4082	7.2	1047	1.9
2011	8911	15.7	4053	7.1	1187	2.1
2021	9956	17.2	4401	7.6	1230	2.1

* of total population

(Adapted from Population Projections 1981–2021 by the Government Actuary and from OPCS Census data 1901–1981) increased the pressure and reliance on the informal providers, 'further accentuating the family pressures that many disabled people and their caring relatives experience' (Alcock 1996: 246).

Welfare services

In this section, we examine the main welfare service providers, and the role they play in raising the socially-accepted minimum standards for individuals and families in society. Recent right-wing Conservative governments have been committed to a reduction in Welfare State provision, but most people support the existence of a Welfare State. Welfare services may be desirable in both economic and social terms, but they still have to be funded. The same budget can be spent in different ways, and this can lead to arguments over priorities. Which, for example, is more important when there's £30,000 left in the local council pot – a new school roof or a paramedic vehicle?

At present, 90 per cent of state expenditure for welfare services is raised through government taxation. Twenty-five per cent of this is then spent by local governments throughout the country. The balance between central and local government expenditure has created much conflict in recent years. Many local governments complain that they're unable to maintain the local welfare provision because state funding is too low. Indeed, a substantial number of Labour-controlled councils have resisted centrally-imposed cutbacks on welfare services. The then Conservative government responded with the 1984 Rates Act which gave Westminster the power to 'rate cap' (impose strict spending limits) these councils.

Movement towards the privatisation of services also created conflict between successive Conservative central governments and Labour local governments. The selling off or tendering of public services to generate revenue was central to this conflict. The New Right defended privatisation on the grounds that the extra revenue raised was necessary to fund the increased expenditure required by the Welfare State. Labour councillors retorted by pointing out that the Welfare State is a public responsibility.

Social welfare expenditure has remained at around a quarter of total government expenditure in the last 15 years or so. As John Hills (1993: 10) notes, 'there has been neither inexorable growth nor decline in the relative scale of the welfare state in recent years'. However, as Robert Page (1993) points out, the Welfare State has become increasingly resilient despite modest initiatives in private health care, sale of council housing and private pension provision. It has continued to act as a safety net – albeit, a very basic one – for people in poverty.

Welfare providers are varied, and it's now time to look at the main ones, beginning with social security.

Social security

A central plank of anti-poverty policy is the redistribution of resources – usually income. In fiscal (tax) terms, this is based on the Robin Hood policy of 'robbing' from the rich (i.e. taxing them until their buttons pip) to 'give' to the poor. Social security is another important means of redistributing income. The Department of Social Security is the largest social service provider, with an annual budget of over £90 billion. However, despite extensive social security provision, poverty persists in the UK.

The Social Security Act of 1986 introduced major changes to social security. Income Support replaced Supplementary Benefit, Family Credit replaced Family Income Supplement, and Housing Benefit, while remaining intact, was significantly reduced. A Social Fund was created to provide a range of grants and loans, and the use of means-testing was increased. Occupational and private pension schemes were introduced. The then Conservative government argued that the Social Security Act would simplify the administration procedures and speed up payments. So much for the rhetoric. In reality, the social security system is one in which, as Norman Johnson notes:

> 'the poor are treated as second class citizens, excluded from full participation by the low level of benefits and subjected to stigmatising attitudes and procedures. The system is not based on rights, and the notions of equality and fairness are absent.'
>
> (Johnson 1990: 65)

Alternative strategies have been examined, for example, the targeting of additional resources on a local basis to poor communities in order to help them escape both poverty and dependency on benefits. In 1996, the then Secretary of State for Social Security, Peter Lilley, outlined a programme to reform radically the social security system. He called it the 'Change Programme' – a shake-up in the way the benefits agency operated, better use of information technology to improve efficiency, and a drive to reduce cost (£750 million over a period of three years). At the heart of the scheme was direct involvement by the private sector. The impact on claimants and service needs will have to be monitored but, according to the Child Poverty Action Group (1997), in the short-term, the outlook isn't good for the people who are on benefits.

Health

A comprehensive National Health Service (NHS) was set up in 1948 based on legislation passed in 1946. It was to be funded from general taxation and was to include a range of services, such as the provision of General Practitioners (GPs), the establishment of state-run local hospitals, and the promotion of health. It was based on a curative rather than a preventative model – an 'illness' rather than a 'health' service.

Some 40 years on, Elim Papadakis and Peter Taylor-Gooby (1987) maintained that the NHS remained the most popular component of the Welfare State. Even its faults are generally attributed to government spending cuts rather than to the nurses and doctors who work within the service. Successive Conservative governments have, however, courted the prospect of private medical care. The biggest boost to private practice came in 1980 when hospital consultants were able to engage in private work without losing the advantages of working within the NHS. Some consultants now earn a considerable portion of their gross salary from private practice. Other areas of growth in private medicine have included private health insurance schemes, private beds in NHS hospitals, private hospitals, and the training of private sector nurses and medical staff on NHS courses.

In February 1988, the Department of Health urged health authorities to explore new ways of raising funds. Eight hundred and twenty-seven income-generating projects were suggested by the then government. They included leasing of hospital space to fast food chains, retail outlets, newsagents and hairdressers. At the same time, the government promoted increased competition within the internal markets of the NHS. Some hospitals and areas were able to specialise. Individual hospitals, whilst remaining in the NHS, were able to become independent of the local health authority and form self-governing hospital trusts. GPs were able to become more entrepreneurial. They could now fix budgets free from government restraint, and could buy treatments for their patients from hospitals. Many GPs employed business managers to run their budgets profitably.

Moreover, as Stephen Birch (1986) points out, 'backdoor privatisation' was also taking place. By this, he means that patients were now paying for an increasing proportion of the cost of their own treatment. Charging arrangements have increased dramatically in the last few years. Today, it's now commonplace to pay for prescriptions and ophthalmic and dental services. This has led to the concern that some patient charges will put people off using what are often preventative health services. For example, an eye test can show up the early signs of conditions such as glaucoma, which leads to blindness if left untreated. Although free eye tests are available for people with the disease and their immediate families, some people will suffer from this initially symptomless disease because they can't afford a diagnostic eye test in the first place.

Studies by, for example, Peter Townsend, Nick Davidson and Margaret Whitehead (1988), have shown that health charges have not impacted equally on all people in the UK. Middle-class people make greater and more successful use of the NHS and other available services. Social policy planners must therefore address the problem of securing services for all in the NHS if they're to be used by those who need them the most.

Education

Education in the UK is based on a state-run comprehensive school service alongside a private sector of so-called independent schools. A radical overhaul of state education occurred in 1988 with the passing of the Education Reform Act. Norman Johnson notes that 'the House of Commons spent 215 hours on the Bill, including ten days on the floor of the House and twenty-two days in Committee, and the House of Lords devoted over 150 hours spread over sixteen days' (1990: 98). This demonstrates how important the Act was in the eyes of politicians.

The Act saw the beginning of the demise of the local authority monopoly over schools. All schools were given much more control over the management of their own budgets. The then Conservative government also dangled attractive monetary incentives to schools if they opted out of local authority control and received direct funding from central government. But 50 per cent of parents on a ballot have to agree to the proposal before a transfer to a grant-maintained status can be accomplished. Few schools did opt out.

Opposition to the opting out principle has been strong among education associations, trade unions and local education authorities. The Secondary Heads Association (The *Guardian*, 9 September 1987) claimed that opting out wouldn't improve schools, especially when managed by inexperienced governing bodies. The National Union of Teachers (The *Guardian*, 21 November 1987) believes it was a way of introducing the elitist direct grant schools, run on the lines of old grammar schools, under the guise of increasing parental choice. The union also fear that all 'opted out' schools would become selective and fee paying.

Obviously, the effect of opting out on local educational provision will depend on the number of schools taking that particular route in a given area. The option has generally been adopted by a relatively small number of schools in Conservative-controlled councils, those schools threatened with closure or losing their sixth form, and grammar schools. The last Conservative government had hoped that left-wing councils would lose their control over schools, but this hasn't really happened.

At the same time, there has been more support for the private sector of education. State-financed (assisted) places have received greater funding – grants to assist able students from less well-off social backgrounds to attend private school. The current Labour government, however, is phasing out the assisted places scheme. City technology colleges have been set up with private industry funding, and they follow a curriculum that connects more closely with the needs of industry. Fifty per cent of the timetable is devoted to maths, science and technology. Opponents of city technology colleges claim they're socially divisive, and object to the fact that over 80 per cent of their capital comes from public funds.

Expenditure on non-educational services in schools has also been reduced by central government or tendered out completely to private contractors. Such services include school meals, free milk, subsidised clothing and cleaning.

The Education Reform Act (1988) introduced the National Curriculum, which contains a core of English, maths and science, and a range of foundation subjects. Changes were also made to the content of each subject and on the appropriate levels of attainment at each stage. Many of the imposed changes were opposed by teachers. In particular, there has been much controversy over assessment and testing. Teachers have expressed concern about the added stress on both the students and themselves to achieve success.

The introduction of school performance league tables has resulted in comparisons between schools, allowing parents to select the 'best' schools. Given that schools only receive funding if parents send children to them, some schools have turned to public relations experts in order to boost recruitment. Schools who can't or won't compete in the battle to secure healthy student numbers risk going to the wall.

The further and higher education sectors have suffered at the hands of central government. Funding has been cut dramatically, even though the demand for education provision in these sectors is greater now than it has ever been in the past. As Alcock says, 'the balance between central and local control, and between public and private provision, remains a controversial issue within policy debate' (1996: 29). Demand is up, but inequalities in participation and achievement still exist and continue to be of importance. One area where participation in further and higher education has been affected by reduced funding is with the student maintenance grant. This has been eroded continuously to the point where many students have to rely on full contributions from parents or on student loans.

What's clear is that the education system is under-resourced. There's a shortage of teachers, inadequate funding for books and equipment, and buildings require refurbishment and investment. The reshaping of the education system (post-1988) incorporates many central Conservative party policies such as privatisation and reduction in local authority control. The institutions of the education system are now part of the marketplace competing with each other. Labour's promise to make education its central policy plank is exciting. Now they're in government, only time will tell if they deliver on the commitment.

OVER TO YOU

Since coming to office in May 1997, what, if any, significant changes in educational policy have the Labour government implemented? Are we witnessing a radically new phase, or a continuation of Conservative initiatives?

Personal social services

Peter Alcock reports that:

'Despite the existence of a range of general provisions for welfare, there are nevertheless some groups of the population who have special needs resulting from their individual or social circumstances.' (Alcock 1996: 30)

He's referring to children, older people, people who are disabled, and people who have learning difficulties, as the main recipients of these personal services. Personal services, up to the 1980s, was a term which usually referred to community-based as opposed to institutional services.

Such services are now increasingly associated with the term 'community care', which includes both formal and informal care. *Formal care* (also called *a formal service*) is given by the health service and social services. It includes the services of doctors, district nurses, health visitors, social workers, home care assistants, support for people who are disabled, meals-on-wheels, and day-care provision. *Informal care* (also called *an informal service*) is given by family, friends and neighbours, usually to older people in the community. Many people who aren't able to support themselves require the help of the state social services, the voluntary sector (for example, charitable organisations) or private service (for example, commercial businesses) provision. However, the development of more formal provision has been an essential part of the growth of the welfare services.

In the 1940s, social workers were based in the voluntary sector agencies but, by the early 1950s, the majority had been transferred to public social services departments in local authorities. They had a general responsibility to assess needs and provide the services to all in need of care and support. Field social workers were employed in specific settings, such as residential homes. However, with the Disabled Persons Act 1986 and the Children Act 1989, extra statutory duties were placed on local authorities. Social work departments were asked to spend more time with those groups at greatest risk. Work with children and people ill with mental disorders became the highest priority.

The 1980s saw an intensification of interest in community care. However, there seemed often to be a discrepancy between sentiments of support for community care and practical action to implement it. Thus, for example, the New Right's support for the family as the pillar of society wasn't just a moral stance. Families provide a cheap way of providing care in the community, thereby reducing public expenditure. The New Right also support private provision and the voluntary sector. By contrast, the Fabian socialist ideology emphasises the role of the state in meeting identified needs. Crucial in that context is a strong commitment to improved financing of the health services and personal social services.

Chris Phillipson (1982) argues that, in times of economic crisis, the capitalist state will spend money on services such as education, health and housing to ensure the workforce is healthy and educated rather than on older people. The task of caring invariably falls to women, to what the Family Policy Studies Centre describe as the Welfare State's 'forgotten army'.

The previous Conservative government's intention in relation to community care was to make use of private and voluntary sectors. The statutory sector would play an important role in backing up, developing and monitoring private and voluntary care facilities, providing services where this was the best way of meeting these needs. This shifting balance of welfare provision away from local authorities is called the *mixed economy of welfare* approach or *welfare pluralism*.

If local authorities are to provide less funding, the informal, voluntary and commercial sectors will need to provide more. The informal sector means care by families – especially nuclear families. Population projections indicate that the number of potential dependants is increasing and, at the same time, the number of carers is declining. One of the most significant reasons for the decline in carers has been the increasing numbers of women who enter paid employment. The last Conservative government's policy on community care seriously underestimated the significance of this change, assuming that women would continue to accept a carer role.

Informal support from family, friends and neighbours is, of course, important and helpful. But it shouldn't be taken for granted, nor should it be seen by government as a cheap alternative to public funding of necessary personal services. One way forward might be to provide income in the form of social security benefits for informal carers, even though their work overlaps with support from the state or private sector.

Johnson (1987) lists five categories of social service performed by informal providers:

- personal care (for example, washing, dressing, feeding)
- domestic care (for example, cooking, cleaning)
- auxiliary care (for example, gardening, odd jobs)
- social support (for example, visiting, companionship)
- surveillance (for example, keeping an eye on vulnerable people).

Family members may provide services in all five categories, while friends or neighbours might only provide support in the latter three. What's significant about this informal care-networking is that it will be affected by changes and developments within the formal welfare sectors. If funding is reduced by the state, the burden is increased on family and friends. In the last two decades, there has been an emphasis on community care provision which has meant greater reliance on the informal care sector. Gillian Parker (1990) estimates that 14 per cent of all adults provide informal care. This is a significant proportion, and it's likely to continue to grow. What now needs to occur, as Julia Twigg (1989) points out, is policy planning for informal care that is constructed around the carers, not only the cared for.

The voluntary sector will also need to be extended if it's to meet increased welfare demands. The Wolfenden Committee (1977) estimated that voluntary activity in the UK was equivalent to the work of 400,000 full-time workers. Thus, the voluntary sector plays an important role in the development and provision of welfare services, but it's a complex and diverse role. Voluntary organisations vary considerably in size and shape, from small toddler groups to international aid organisations like Oxfam. They're not part of the state provision of services, either at central or local level, because they're not motivated by profit and try to avoid charging for their services.

However, some have an organisational structure which is similar to commercial companies. As David Billis (1989), Director of the Centre for Voluntary Organisations at the London School of Economics, has indicated, voluntary sector organisations have overlapping boundaries with government bureaucracy, business bureaucracy and the personal world (informal sector). A voluntary organisation may, for example, secure grant funding from the local authority or central government to fulfil a community service. In practice, though, voluntary organisations receive funding from more than one source, and the balance of these sources is ever-changing.

Alcock outlines the various classifications of voluntary organisations in the table opposite.

OVER TO YOU

Give definitions for each of the structures in the table opposite. Then research in detail the role of one local-based protective, representative, campaigning or service voluntary organisation.
You could do this in groups and report your findings back to the class.

Classification of voluntary organisations

Structure	**Level** **Community**	**Local**	**National**	**International**
Protective	LETS	Credit union	Friendly society	World Health Organisation
Representative	Music Collective	Gingerbread	Trades union	International Labour Office
Campaigning	New bypass opposition	Local transport campaign	CPAG	Greenpeace
Service	Lone parent group	CABs	WRVS	Oxfam

(Alcock 1996: 89)

In the early 1990s, general restrictions on the local authority welfare expenditure have threatened the grant funding on which many new community-based organisations rely. However, with the development of policies for community care, there continues to be a move towards contracts between the state and the voluntary sector. The voluntary sector is varied, flexible, non-bureaucratic, accessible and cheap, says Alcock (1996), but it's also unpredictable, and future welfare provision must recognise this.

Housing

Housing differs from other services because homes are durable assets. They're the biggest single item of expenditure in the budget of most households, and the housing market is dominated by an extensive and powerful private sector (Johnson 1990). But housing is also importantly linked to welfare. Nothing is more significant to a person's welfare than having somewhere to live. There are considerable differences in housing, and a wide gap exists between the majority of the population who are well-housed and the rest who live in poor accommodation or are homeless.

Changing policy initiatives by successive Conservative governments on housing tenure (ownership) have been central to this increasing polarisation. During the early twentieth century, the majority of housing was provided through private sector rental. However, through state intervention, the private rented sector has declined to less than 10 per cent of the market, whilst owner-occupation now extends to two-thirds of the population. In the case of council property, past Conservative government policies have encouraged existing tenants to buy their rented homes. This has become easier with the availability of mortgages to potential owners.

There have been some attempts by central government to control and improve the quality of housing and to provide accommodation for the homeless. This has included slum clearance, improvements to the standards of existing fittings in dwellings, grants to existing owners to improve their homes, and the use of hotel rooms, hostels and houses for homeless people. But the problems of the homeless have, by and large, not been prioritised in housing policy.

What has happened is that successive Conservative governments have relied heavily on privatisation. There have been drastic cuts in public investment in housing, and local authority housing stocks have become depleted with the reduction in building programmes and the sale of council homes. In 1988, the then Conservative government also brought Housing Action Trusts (HATs) to take over run-down estates from local councils. The HAT becomes responsible for improving housing and the environment. Occupants of homes taken over by HATs become secure tenants, although higher rents are charged after improvements. When the estates have been improved, the homes are sold to new landlords. The landlords can be, for example, councils, private companies, private individuals, housing associations or co-operatives.

The 1988 Housing Act allowed for the transfer of council and new town property to private landlords, housing associations or tenants' co-operatives. This change of landlord scheme is another example of the previous government's drive towards privatisation. Conservative social policy has basically distrusted local authorities, especially Labour-run ones. This is particularly apparent in housing, where previous Tory policy has intensified housing inequalities. As Johnson points out, 'council estates become ghettos for the very poor, the unemployed, elderly people, single person households and young adults with young children' (1990: 157).

The most serious indictment of the last government's housing policy is the increase, under its administration, in the number of homeless people – a telling and tragic legacy.

QUESTIONS

1. What evidence is there in this section to support/dispute the argument that recent Conservative governments have been committed to a reduction in Welfare State provision?
2. How far has the Welfare State created a form of 'dependency culture' rather than eliminated poverty?

Concluding remarks

The future of the Welfare State?

'The definition of poverty and, as a consequence, the income required to overcome it in most Welfare States is a minimum subsistence one', claims Alan Walker (1991: 71). But this kind of absolute poverty definition is a limited one. It's generally accepted by the British population that people require an income which allows them access to the resources necessary to play an active role in society. It seems therefore ironic that the Welfare State wasn't devised to abolish relative poverty, only to provide minimum security against absolute poverty. It certainly wasn't intended to remove inequalities in income and wealth. But neither was it meant to perpetuate them.

John Hills (1993) suggests that the UK has a series of choices about the future of the Welfare State. Two influential reports by the Commission on Social Justice (CSJ) (1994) and the Commission on Wealth Creation and Social Cohesion (CWCSC) (1995), respectively, illustrate the New Labour approach to the reform of the Welfare State. Sponsored by the Labour Party, the CSJ endorses an investor's strategy. It fuses economic and social policy in order to bring about a regeneration of society. In terms of social policy, the development of an 'intelligent' Welfare State, which provides opportunities for self-improvement and self-support is deemed to be vital. In the case of social security, this would mean less emphasis on poverty relief and, instead, the creation of economic independence through paid work.

The broad principles contained in the CSJ report are set out on pages 305–7.

QUESTION

One of the underlying themes of the CSJ report is reconnecting welfare rights with personal responsibility. An example is that people seeking work should be expected to accept offers for training and work rather than subsist on social security benefits. What other parts of the extract on pages 305–7 link welfare rights with personal responsibility, and how do these connect with current Labour government policy?

The CSJ wants to reduce injustice and inequality by providing all citizens with the opportunity to be in paid employment. The same aspiration is echoed in the CWCSC, set up by Paddy Ashdown, the leader of The Liberal Democrat Party. This commission stressed the importance of income tax as a source of government revenue. By raising extra revenue, it can then be used in those areas of the Welfare State in need of desperate financial help, for example, the education system, the NHS and the social security system. In the run-up to the 1997 General Election, of the three main parties, the Liberal Democrats was the only one to say that an effective Welfare State needs higher income tax.

One of the major problems identified by both commissions is the difficulty in creating well-paid and secure forms of employment. Even if a great number of jobs were created, individual rewards will still vary enormously. The Joseph Rowntree Foundation Inquiry into Income and Wealth (1995) demonstrated this increasing inequality in society. Robert Page further argues that if 'income and wealth does not trickle down from rich to poor social fragmentation is inevitable' (Page 1996: 123).

The solution to this inequality, argues Peter Townsend (1995), is increased public-sector and labour-intensive forms of private employment, as well as a fairer distribution of income and wealth. In combination with anti-discriminatory legislation and practice, Townsend believes the measures he proposes could 'halt and then reverse social polarization, impoverishment and unemployment' (1995: 150). Page (1996) argues that Townsend's approach is unrealistic given the advance of deregulated capitalism (by this we mean the removal of many rules and restrictions on industry across Europe), which makes it difficult for a country to adopt a generous social protection package when out of line with its European Community Colleagues.

Will Hutton, editor of the *Observer* and a supporter of New Labour, maintains that the:

> 'state in the name of deregulation and privatisation has apparently brought efficiency gains through aggressive rounds of lay-offs and redundancies.'
>
> (Hutton 1997: 15)

More serious, are the consequences of this competitive economic climate. Freedom, choice and independence are the vocabulary of deregulation, but with this comes inequality at a post-war high.

Also, says Hutton, 'social integration, family life and community are all diminished' (1997: 27). Fear of job redundancy leads to a low motivated workforce who have little desire to improve their qualifications or acquire new skills because they may be laid off at any time. The upshot is a low-waged, low-skilled workforce who will find it increasingly more difficult to provide for themselves, and more likely to rely on the Welfare State for assistance.

Hutton suggests that inequality can be controlled by introducing a minimum wage and a tax increase to redistribute income from the rich to the poor, ensuring a reasonable standard of living in relation to the average person. The tax revenue could also be used to finance state public welfare services, such as education and health. Here we find Hutton talking the same language as the Liberal Democrats.

During their 18 years in office from 1979 to 1997, successive Conservative governments have encouraged the development of private markets to provide welfare on a commercial basis. This market-based provision has

COMMISSION FOR SOCIAL JUSTICE: STRATEGIES FOR NATIONAL RENEWAL (extract)

Broad principles

The Commission:

- identifies three types of policy approaches: 'deregulators', characterised by their belief in the free market; 'levellers', who advocate the redistribution of income; and 'investors', who argue for the redistribution of opportunity as well as income – this last being the Commission's preference
- views employment as the quickest and most effective route out of poverty
- sees strong families as vital social institutions and a key requirement for social justice.

Beyond benefits

Employment

The Commission:

- sees commitment to full employment as being fundamental to any labour market strategy
- proposes a Jobs, Education and Training (JET) strategy to get the long-term unemployed and lone parents back to work
- recognises the need for 'family-friendly' employment policies
- supports the introduction of a minimum wage (a figure of no lower than £3.50 was suggested)
- stresses the need for policies to combat discrimination and promote equal opportunities (including equal pay) in employment.

Nursery education/child care

The Commission:

- notes the need for a government-led strategy and proposes a coherent, comprehensive and integrated approach
- proposes free nursery education for 85% of three-year-olds and 95% of four-year-olds by the year 2000
- recommends the extension of out-of-school/holiday care for under-11s
- suggests considering a fee relief scheme for child care, with nationally-set relief scales and charges starting at a 'reasonable wage'.

Education and training

The Commission:

- proposes literacy and numeracy targets for seven-year-olds and recommends a 'British Baccalaureat' at secondary school level, offering a broader mix of academic and vocational study based on a credit-based system
- suggests employers should invest a minimum proportion of their total payroll in training and pay a 'training wage' to young workers
- proposes a national, means-tested grant to help 16- and 17-year-olds stay in on full-time education and training. Recommends a new university education funding system: three possible repayment schemes are examined whereby students reimburse education costs immediately they enter employment or once they reach a certain level of earnings
- proposes a Learning Bank offering the equivalent of three years' education and training beyond A-level to all, to which employers and individuals would contribute.

Parental leave

The Commission:

- sets a long-term aim of 12 months parental leave (taken by either parent and inclusive of 29 weeks of maternity leave), funded via the social insurance scheme
- recognises that an earnings-related element to parental leave is important to encourage fathers to take parental leave.

Child Benefit

The Commission:

- recognises the importance of Child Benefit in supporting children and promoting the redistribution of resources from those without to those with children
- recommends reverting to the previous system of paying Child Benefit at the same rate for all children
- suggests using some or all money saved from abolishing the married couple's tax allowance and taxing the Child Benefit of higher earners to pay for an increase in Child Benefit.

Taxation

The Commission:

- suggests raising personal allowance to take as many people as possible out of income tax *or* introducing a new low tax rate of 10%
- for the time being recommends retaining the requirement to pay National Insurance contributions on all earnings once the lower earnings limit is reached and raising the upper earnings limit in line with prices rather than earnings
- proposes cutting employers' National Insurance contributions after the introduction of a minimum wage
- proposes introducing a new top rate of income tax for higher earners, either at five times average earnings or in relation to the top 1 or 2% of taxpayers, as well as introducing a 'minimum' tax bill for high earners and a 'maximum' of no more than 50% of total income to reinforce a commitment to fair taxation
- supports phasing out of certain tax allowances, such as the married couples allowance and mortgage interest tax relief.

Social security

Social insurance

The Commission:

- supports a central role for social insurance but recognises the need to make the system more inclusive by being available to more part-time and low-paid workers
- considers possibilities for a part-time unemployment benefit to enable people to continue earnings with benefit
- suggests incorporating invalid care allowance and the severe disablement allowance into the social insurance system and rethinking provision for sickness and disability
- proposes reversing the changes to be introduced with Jobseekers' Allowance
- proposes a requirement for more parents to be 'available for work' for at least part-time employment, particularly lone parents and parents with an unemployed partner who have school age children. Recommends that child-care assistance should be in place first.

Means testing

The Commission:

- envisages a residual role for means-tested benefits
- proposes that Income Support recipients should be able to accumulate earnings ignored in calculation of benefit and that the full costs of childcare and part of maintenance costs should be disregarded in benefit calculation. It recommends that 16- and 17-year-olds should be entitled to Income Support.
- suggests Income Support should be paid while Family Credit is calculated and that individuals should be automatically re-entitled to Income Support if their job ends within a specified period. Passported benefits (such as free school meals) should be available to those on Family Credit for up to two years
- in the longer term proposes replacing Income Support and Family Credit with a single means-tested benefit
- endorses a three-tiered system to replace single discretionary payments and loans under the Social Fund, with regular one-off payments to help with larger costs

- suggests a two-tier housing benefit scheme as a way of meeting housing costs and reducing poverty traps. It proposes that support for mortgage costs should be provided to low-income families up to a specified limit, with a gradual taper thereafter.

Child support

The Commission:

- criticises the practice of the current Child Support Agency, while agreeing with the principles of the scheme
- proposes that the maintenance element for the parent with care should be transformed into an allowance towards child-care costs, and that this allowance should be partly disregarded when eligibility for means-tested benefits is assessed
- suggests that £15 of maintenance should be ignored in calculating entitlement to Income Support
- suggests that the retrospective application of the child support formula should be removed
- proposes that the Child Support Agency should act as a 'guarantor' for maintenance payments to ensure that the parent with care has a secure income.

(cited in CPAG 1995)

continued to expand alongside voluntary sector activity. Social services provision now consists of a 'welfare mix' rather than a Welfare State, being funded not only from direct taxation (which translates into public expenditure), but also from private sources. What concerns many left-wing commentators is that greater emphasis is being placed on independent providers at the expense of adequate state funding.

Effective welfare policy must address the social differences amongst service users. Policy-makers need to be more aware of the needs of people in relation to age, ethnicity, disability, and so forth. In particular, it's imperative that much more support needs to be targeted on the most in need – so-called 'bottom-up' social policy.

In addition, and of increasing importance, is the significance of the UK's position in Europe. British social policy isn't just a Whitehall and Westminster affair, but is also affected by policies from Brussels and Strasbourg. The European Social Chapter, for example, contains legislation on minimum wages which now, under Tony Blair's government, is coming on stream in the UK.

As we move into the twenty-first century, we'll see social policy occupying a central place on the political agenda. As Alcock puts it:

'At all levels (national, local and supranational) policies for the future of economic growth and development are now automatically placed alongside policies for social integration, social regeneration and social justice.'

(Alcock 1996: 302)

Current policymakers face an enduring legacy of growing social inequalities and increasing poverty within a divided society. The need for a strong Welfare State and a redistribution of income and wealth that support an option for the poor pose a pressing challenge for New Labour. Will they rise to the occasion?

Glossary of key terms

Absolute poverty A level of poverty that is typically regarded as the one needed to obtain basic physical needs – food, water, clothing and shelter. In the UK, some politicians and economists argue that absolute poverty, in this stark sense, doesn't exist. People who live on the streets disagree!

Budget standards approach A measure of poverty that incorporate features of both the absolute and relative concepts. It's based upon an attempt to determine a list of necessities, the absence of which are used as a poverty line below which people shouldn't be permitted to fall, as well as on relative deprivation indicators which define customary lifestyles

Expert-compiled deprivation index This is based on Peter Townsend's work. In that sense, he's the expert compiler. Townsend constructed a deprivation index – ultimately, a list of 12 key items (for example, not having a household fridge) – the lack of which indicate relative poverty

Income A money flow. In the UK, wages and salaries are by far the largest source of income for most people

Individualistic theories of poverty These theories identify the main causes of poverty within individuals themselves. Social factors aren't entirely discounted, but more emphasis is placed on inappropriate individual behaviours

Marketable wealth Assets that can be sold or cashed in (for example, homes and shares)

Non-marketable wealth Assets that can't be sold or cashed in or are hard to do so (for example, occupational and state pension rights)

Relative poverty A level of poverty that represents an inability to meet the usual standard of living in a particular community or society

Social consensus-compiled deprivation index A relative approach to poverty that identifies a minimum acceptable standard of living by reference to the views of society as a whole – hence, a *social consensus index*

Structural theories of poverty These theories explain poverty on the basis of structural, i.e. whole society, factors

Underclass A controversial concept, often associated with New Right thinking, which denotes people who are economically- and socially-excluded from mainstream society. Arguably, a better and a more accurate term is *the very poor*

Wealth A fixed asset. Homes are the most common example of wealth in the UK

References

Abbott, Pamela and Wallace, Claire (1997) *An Introduction to Sociology: Feminist Perspectives*, Second Edition. London: Routledge

Abel-Smith, Brian and Townsend, Peter (1965) The poor and the poorest, occasional paper in *Social Administration*, No. 17, London: G. Bell & Son Ltd

Alcock, Pete (1993) *Understanding Poverty*. Basingstoke: Macmillan

Alcock, Pete (1996) *Social Policy in Britain: Themes and Issues*. Basingstoke: Macmillan

Amin, Kaushika with Oppenheim, Carey (1992) *Poverty in Black and White: Deprivation and Ethnic Minorities*. London: CPAG

Becker, Saul and MacPherson, Stewart (eds) (1988) *Public Issues and Private Pain: Poverty, Social Work and Social Policy*. London: Insight

Beresford, Philip (1997) The Sunday Times Rich List, *Sunday Times*, 6 April

Billis, David (1989) *The Theory of the Voluntary Sector: Implications for Policy and Practice*. London: Centre for Voluntary Organisation, London School of Economics

Birch, Stephen (1986) Increasing patient charges in the National Health Service: A method of privatizing primary care, pp 163–84, *Journal of Social Policy*, Vol. 15, No.2

Bradshaw, Jonathan, Mitchell, Deborah and Morgan, Jane (1987) Evaluating adequacy: The potential of budget standards, pp 165–81, *Journal of Social Policy*, Vol. 16, No. 2

Bradshaw, Jonathan and Morgan, Jane (1987) *Budgeting on Benefits*. London: Centre for Family Policy Studies

Brown, John (1995) *The British Welfare State: A Critical History*. Oxford: Blackwell

Bruegel, Irene (1989) Sex and race in the labour market, *Feminist Review*, No. 32

Clarke, Kenneth (1995) *The New Review of The Low Pay Unit*, No. 33, May/June

Coates, Ken and Silburn, Richard (1973) *Poverty: The Forgotten Englishmen*. Harmondsworth/New York: Penguin

CPAG (1995) *Poverty 91*, Journal of the Child Poverty Action Group, Summer

Dale, Jennifer and Foster, Peggy (1986) *Feminists and State Welfare*. London: Routledge & Kegan Paul

Dalley, Gillian (ed.) (1991) *Disability and Social Policy*. London: Policy Studies Institute

Department of Health and Social Security (1985) *Reform of Social Security*. London: HMSO

Department for Social Security (1995) *Benefits Information Guide*. London: HMSO

Field, Frank (1990) Britain's underclass: Countering the growth, pp 37–41, in Murray, Charles (1990) op. cit.

Frayman, Harold (1991) *Breadline Britain 1990s: The Findings of the Television Series*. London: LWT

Gans, Herbert (1972) The positive functions of poverty, pp 85–6, in Townsend, Peter (1979) op. cit.

George, Vic and Wilding, Paul (1976) *Ideology and Social Welfare*. London: Routledge & Kegan Paul

Glendinning, Carol and Millar, Jane (eds) (1992) *Women and Poverty in Britain, the 1990s*. London: Wheatsheaf

Golding, Peter (ed.) (1986) *Excluding the Poor*. London: CPAG

Groves, Dulcie (1988) Poverty, disability and social services, pp 171–80, in Becker, Saul and MacPherson, Stewart (eds) (1988) op. cit.

Hasluck, Chris (1991) *People and Skills in Calderdale and Kirklees: An Audit of the Education, Training and Work Experience*. Calderdale and Kirkless TEC

Hills, John (1993) *The Future of Welfare: A Guide to the Debate*. York: Joseph Rowntree Foundation

Hills, John (ed.) (1996) *The Changing Distribution of Income and Wealth in the UK*. Cambridge: Cambridge University Press

Holman, Robert (1978) *Poverty: Explanations of Social Deprivation*. London: Martin Robertson

Hutton, Will (1997) The state to come, exclusive extracts enclosed in the *Observer*, 20 April

Johnson, Norman (1987) *The Welfare State in Transition: The Theory and Practice of Welfare Pluralism*. London: Harvester Wheatsheaf

Johnson, Norman (1990) *Reconstructing the Welfare State: A Decade of Change 1980–1990*. London: Harvester Wheatsheaf

Kincaid, John (1973) *Poverty and Equality in Britain*. Harmondsworth: Penguin

Le Grand, Julian (1982) *The Strategy of Equality: Redistribution and the Social Services*. London: Allen & Unwin

Le Grand, Julian and Estrin, Saul (1989) *Markets, Welfare and Equality*. Oxford: Clarendon

Lewis, Oscar (1965) *The Children of Sanchez*. Harmondsworth: Penguin

Lister, Ruth and Beresford, Peter (1991), *Working Together Against Poverty: Involving Poor People in Action Against Poverty*, Open Services Project and the Department of Applied Social Studies, University of Bradford

Local Economic Policy Unit (1991) *Change in Spitalfields*. London: South Bank Polytechnic

Low Pay Unit (1995) *The New Review of the Low Pay Unit*, No. 35, September/October

Lydall, Harold (1968) *The Structure of Earnings*. Oxford: Clarendon

Mack, Joanna and Lansley, Stewart (1985) *Poor Britain*. London: Allen & Unwin

Mann, Kirk (1992) *The Making of an English Underclass? The Social Divisions of Welfare and Labour*. Milton Keynes: Open University Press

McGlone, Francis (1992) *Disability and Dependency in Old Age: A Demographic and Social Audit*. London: Family Policy Studies Centre

McLellan, David (1983) *Karl Marx: The Legacy*. London: BBC

Mishra, Ramesh (1981) *Society and Social Policy: Theories and Practice of Welfare*. London: Macmillan

Morris, Lydia (1989) *The Workings of the Household*. Cambridge: Polity Press

Murray, Charles (1990) *The Emerging British Underclass*. London: Institute of Economic Affairs Health and Welfare Unit

Oppenheim, Carey and Harker, Lisa (1996) *Poverty: The Facts*, Third Edition. London: CPAG

Orshansky, Molly (1969) How poverty is measured, pp 37–41, *Monthly Labor Review*, Vol. 92, February

Outram, Steve (1989) *Social Policy*. London: Longman

Page, Rovert (1993) Social policy, pp 92–120, in Haralambos, Michael (ed.) (1993) *Developments in Sociology*, Vol. 9. Ormskirk: Causeway Press

Page, Robert (1996) Social policy, pp 107–29, in Haralambos, Michael (ed.) (1996) *Developments in Sociology*, Vol. 12, Ormskirk: Causeway Press

Papadakis, Elim and Taylor-Gooby, Peter (1987) *The Private Provision of Public Welfare: State, Market and Community*. Brighton: Wheatsheaf

Parker, Gillian (1990) *With Due Care and Attention: A Review of Research on Informal Care*. London: Family Policy Studies Centre

Phillipson, Chris (1982) *Capitalism and the Construction of Old Age*. London: Macmillan

Piachaud, David (1981) Peter Townsend and the Holy Grail, *New Society*, 10 September

Piachaud, David (1987) Problems in the definition and measurement of poverty, pp 147–64, *Journal of Social Policy*, Vol. 16, No. 2

Report of the Joseph Rowntree Foundation Inquiry into Income and Wealth (1995), 2 volumes. York: Joseph Rowntree Foundation

Rex, John (1992) *Race and Ethnicity*. Milton Keynes: Open University Press

Rex, John and Tomlinson, Sally (1979) *Colonial Immigrants in a British City: A Class Analysis*. London: Routledge & Kegan Paul

Rowntree, Seebohm (1901) *Poverty: A Study of Town Life*. London: Macmillan

Sen, Amartya (1985) A sociological approach to the measurement of poverty: A reply to Professor Peter Townsend, pp 669–76, *Oxford Economic Papers*, No. 37

Scott, John (1994) *Poverty and Wealth: Citizenship, Deprivation and Privilege*. London: Longman

Sharkey, Peter (1987) The sociology of welfare, pp 135–58, in Haralambos, Michael (ed.) (1987) *Developments in Sociology*, Vol. 3. Ormskirk: Causeway Press

Sinfield, Adrian (ed.) (1993) Poverty, inequality and justice, *New Waverley Papers, Social Policy Series*, No. 6, University of Edinburgh

Smith, Adam (1776) *An Inquiry into the Nature and Causes of the Wealth of Nations* (edited in 1892), London: Routledge

Social Trends 26 (1996). London: HMSO

Social Trends 27 (1997). London: The Stationery office

Stitt, Sean (1994) *Poverty and Poor Relief: Concepts and Reality*. Aldershot: Averbury

Tischler, Henry L. (1996) *Introduction of Sociology*, Fifth Edition. Fort Worth: Harcourt Brace College Publishers

Townsend, Peter (1954) The meaning of poverty, *British Journal of Sociology*, June

Townsend, Peter (1979) *Poverty in the United Kingdom: A Survey of Household Resources and Standards of Living*. Berkeley: University of California Press

Townsend, Peter (1985) A sociological approach to the measurement of poverty: A rejoinder to Professor Amartya Sen, pp 659–68, *Oxford Economic Papers*, No. 37

Townsend, Peter (1987) Deprivation, pp 125–46, *Journal of Social Policy*, Vol. 16, No. 2

Townsend, Peter (1995) Persuasion and conformity: An assessment of the Borrie Report on Social Justice, pp 137–50, *New Left Review*, 213, September/October

Townsend, Peter, Corrigan, Paul and Kowarzik, Ute (1987) *Poverty and Labour in London*. London: Low Pay Unit

Townsend, Peter, Davidson, Nick and Whitehead, Margaret (eds) (1988) *Inequalities in Health: The Black Report and the Health Divide*. Harmondsworth: Penguin

Twigg, Julia (1989) Model of carers: How do social care agencies conceptualise their relationship with informal carers?, pp 53–66, *Journal of Social Policy*, Vol. 18, No. 1

Vaux, Gary and Divine, David (1988) Race and poverty, pp 208–19, in Becker, Saul and MacPherson, Stewart (eds) (1988) op. cit.

Veit-Wilson, John (1986) Paradigms of poverty: A rehabilitation of B.S. Rowntree, pp 69–101, *Journal of Social Policy*, Vol. 15, No. 1

Veit-Wilson, John (1987) Consensual approaches to poverty lines and social security, pp 183–211, *Journal of Social Policy*, Vol. 16, No. 2

Veit-Wilson, John (1989) House of Commons Paper 509, pp 74–95

Walker, Alan (1988) Poverty: Social analysis and policy, pp 29–47, in Haralambos, Michael (ed.) (1988) *Developments in Sociology*, Vol. 4. Ormskirk: Causeway Press

Walker, Alan (1990), Poverty and the underclass, pp 55–77, in Haralambos, Michael (ed.) (1990) *Developments in Sociology*, Vol. 7. Ormskirk: Causeway Press

Walker, Carol and Walker, Alan (1994) Poverty and the poor, pp 43–66, in Haralambos, Michael (ed.) (1994) *Developments in Sociology*, Vol. 10. Ormskirk: Causeway Press

Walker, Robert (1987) Consensual approaches to the definition of poverty: Towards an alternative methodology, pp 213–26, *Journal of Social Policy*, Vol. 16, No. 2

Watts, H. (1980) *New American Family Budget Standards: Report by the Expert Committee on Family Budget Revisions*. Wisconsin: Institute for Research on Poverty, University of Wisconsin

Williams, Fiona (1989) *Social Policy: A Critical Introduction: Issues of Race, Gender and Class*. Cambridge: Polity Press

Wilson, Elizabeth (1977) *Women and the Welfare State*. London: Tavistock

Wilson, William J. (1987) *The Truly Disadvantaged*. Chicago: University of Chicago Press

Wolfenden Committee (1977) *The Future of Voluntary Organisations*. London: Croom Helm

Exam practice: Wealth, poverty and welfare

Essay questions

1 'The Welfare State has failed to help the poor.' Discuss the arguments and evidence for this view. *(25 marks)*

2 'The definition and measurement of poverty are more influenced by the values of the researcher than by the practical difficulties of defining and measuring poverty.' Critically examine this statement. *(25 marks)*

(From Summer 1997 AEB A-level Sociology, Paper 2, © 1997 AEB)

3 The claim that 'the poor are themselves to blame for their poverty' is a feature of some explanations of poverty. Critically examine the sociological arguments for and against this statement. *(25 marks)*

(From Summer 1991 AEB A-level Sociology, Paper 2, © 1991 AEB)

4 'Despite many sociological studies on poverty, it is not possible to define a "poverty-line" which will be supported by all.' Critically examine the argument for and against this view. *(25 marks)*

(From Summer 1994 AEB A-level Sociology, Paper 2, © 1994 AEB)

12 Health

Topics covered in this chapter
– Defining health
– Models of health
– Sociological perspectives on health
– Disability
– Mental health
– Health chances
– Expectations of health
– The provision of health care

Scan the television schedules or peruse the shelves in the newsagents. You'll find that one of our national 'obsessions' is health. TV bosses can confidently assume an insatiable appetite for matters medical. They respond by serving up a mixed diet of hospital-based soaps, fly-on-the-wall documentaries, phone-in discussions, doctors' advice columns, keep-fit magazines, and more.

This prolific media coverage reflects the concerns of our popular culture and indicates deeper factors at play. Health is also a key issue on the political front, and the formulation of health-care policy is an area of rapid development and controversy.

There are a number of overarching questions which you should continuously pose as you work through the material in this chapter:

- How should we define health, illness and disability?
- What attitudes prevail in society towards health?
- What expectations do we have about health?
- What factors contribute to health?
- Where is power located in the giving and receiving of health care?
- Where does responsibility for health lie?

Although these are listed separately you'll quickly realise that the boundaries between them are fluid. The content of each is constantly being redefined and, in addition, there's a high level of interaction between them all. The analysis of disability is a good example of this continuous process of redefinition and realignment.

Defining health

19:10

Having already said that there's general agreement on the importance of health, it would seem reasonable to assume that we all know what health is, that we all recognise the goal we're striving to achieve. But is that the case?

OVER TO YOU

Write a definition of health.
You could discuss your definition with other students in your group. Do you all find it easy to agree? Do you find yourselves wanting to qualify your basic statement? What are the key variables which emerge from your discussions?

Having completed this preliminary sortie into the field of the sociology of health, don't despair! Linda Jones (1994: 3) tells us that health is a state of being that is subject to wide individual, social and cultural interpretations; it's produced by the interplay of individual perceptions and social influences.

In this section we're going to examine these individual, social and cultural factors which influence our definitions of health. Here we treat them separately to help you clarify the relevant issues, but you'll quickly realise that they overlap in actual situations.

Individual factors

How do people define their own health and respond to the circumstances in which they find themselves? Firstly, here's some anecdotal, qualitative data from Mrs Brown, an 80-year-old woman:

'I've lived in the village all my life and there's rarely a day when I haven't been out . . . You can see the hills from my window, we're the last house down the lane, you just step outside. Walking keeps you warm, getting around, that's what I call being well. I've never felt the cold except in the really bad weather, but now I can't walk like I used to, I need a stick. I always have the fire on and keep busy doing my jobs, tidy the house, cook the tea, but my legs go stiff and I have to stop, and then I do feel the cold.'

(Jones 1994: 3)

This description clearly reflects Mrs Brown's age and personal circumstances. Some women, irrespective of their age, link energy and vitality with the ability to undertake tasks associated with running a home. A teenage boy would probably focus on very different factors, most typically the ability to participate in sports.

David Watts, former *Guardian* journalist, offers us an extreme, and incredibly stoical, positive, perspective on his own health (he has a brain tumour):

'Mine is a story of good fortune which I write in the hope it may bring hope to others. Here are the facts: I cannot use my right eye, so I wear a patch; I cannot use my left leg and am mostly wheelchair-bound; I cannot use many of the muscles in my face so I cannot smile or talk properly; I cannot use half the muscles of my throat, so I choke and splutter a lot.

So far, so bad. But I am alive and what I can do far outweighs the cannots.

I can play and laugh with my children and my wife.
I can gossip and have a few drinks with friends.
I can take myself out in an electric chair.
I can swim . . . well, sort of.
I can dress myself, slowly.
I can eat most good food.
I can still do fulfilling work at a computer.
I could go on . . . '

(The Guardian, 9 September 1996)

The Health and Lifestyle Survey presents a more quantified approach to these individual definitions of and responses to health, in the table below.

Concepts used in the attempt to describe what health is

	Males			**Females**		
Concept of health used for describing someone else	**Age 18–39**	**40–59**	**60+**	**18–39**	**40–59**	**60+**
	Percentage					
Never ill, no disease, never see a doctor	26	39	37	45	51	37
Fit, strong, energetic, physically active	46	28	13	30	21	11
Able to do a lot, work, socially active	13	16	22	14	18	20
Has healthy habits (e.g. not smoking, taking exercise, taking care of health)	24	18	14	27	17	14
Psychologically fit (e.g. relaxed, dynamic, contented, able to cope)	9	9	6	11	8	5
In good health for their age (applied to an older person)	2	8	15	3	8	17
Mean no. of concepts used	1.2	1.2	1.1	1.3	1.3	1.1
Concept of health used for describing what it is to be healthy oneself						
Never ill, no disease, never see a doctor	15	17	16	12	10	11
Fit, strong, energetic, physically active	25	18	12	36	28	14
Able to do a lot, work, get out and about	18	18	27	18	23	31
Feel psychologically fit (e.g. good, happy, able to cope)	55	60	54	58	62	54
Can't explain, or don't know what it is to be healthy	8	7	8	6	6	10
Mean no. of concepts used by those offering any	1.3	1.3	1.2	1.4	1.4	1.3
Base = 100%	*1668*	*1240*	*997*	*2150*	*1596*	*1352*

Multiple answers possible

(Cox *et al.* 1987, cited by Jones 1994: 4)

In the table, there are specific, objective elements, such as age and gender, but the interpretation of the various categories is still inherently personal and individualistic. For example, no group of people, even if apparently homogeneous, would ever achieve exact agreement on the definition of 'psychologically fit' or being 'socially active'. Lay beliefs about health and illness are well-documented by Mildred Blaxter (1990), who discusses in detail the findings of the 1987 Health and Lifestyle Survey. You could also look at the work of Steve Taylor and David Field (1993).

Social factors

Health and illness are very individual experiences, yet we also live in society. It's our interaction with that wider society which mediates and, to a significant degree, defines our personal experiences. To be ill is not simply a biological or physical state. It has implications for the way in which people feel about themselves and also their ability to participate in social interaction.

When we feel unwell, there's a range of actions open to us. The precise path chosen by any individual will be the result of a combination of factors. It's very likely that they'll discuss their symptoms with others, probably family members or close friends. They may refer to the plethora of medical reference books now aimed at the lay person. Then they must decide what to do next.

They may decide to consult with a health-care professional. Most typically, in 'western' society, that would currently be the family doctor. Choosing this option is a reflection of the current dominance of the *medical model of health* (see page 319); however this model has not always been paramount and still isn't universally adopted.

We all carry in our heads a complex picture of what constitutes legitimate illness and the acceptable responses to that condition. At what point does a heavy cold, treatable with non-prescription remedies from the chemist or a stiff drink, become sufficiently serious to warrant a visit to the doctor? Even more fraught, in the current political-economic climate, are you well enough to get to the surgery, or could you ask for a home visit?

Michael Calnan (1987) highlights the complex pattern of thought engaged in before the decision is made to consult a doctor. As Stimson and Webb (1975) found, even when actually in the consulting room, there remains a further distinction between a person's private comments on their own ill-health and what they choose to tell their doctor. Jocelyn Cornwell (1984) explores the ways in which East Londoners differentiate between whether illnesses are 'normal' (infectious diseases), 'real' (disabling and life-threatening diseases) or 'health problems which are not illness' but which are linked to natural processes such as ageing or reproduction. J. Donovan (1986) studies the links for African–Caribbean and Asian people between health responses, diet, their cultural beliefs and religious practices.

Irving Zola (1973) presents a model (see below) of decision-making about health and illness which takes account of both the complex set of variables which apply at any one moment in time (for example, the initial physical symptoms) and also accommodates the social processes which exert their influence over a longer period of time (for example, the impact of these symptoms on work activities or personal relationships).

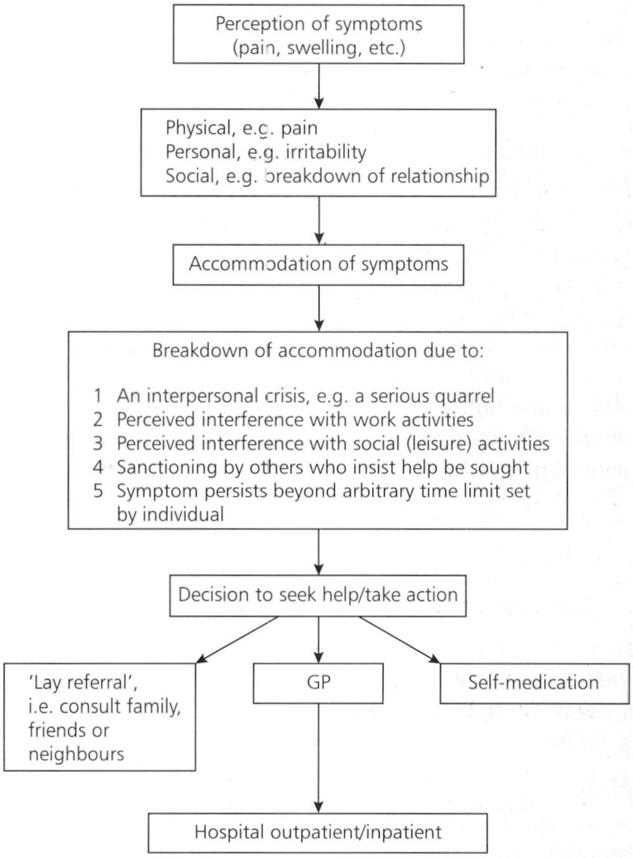

(Zola 1973, cited in Taylor and Field 1993: 107)

A model of the help-seeking process

Zola's model further illustrates the ways in which illness and sickness are, to a significant degree, socially-defined. They're not the simple objective conditions you might originally have thought them to be.

Before we proceed any further we need to define illness, sickness and disease:

- *Illness* is the state of feeling unwell. You might feel ill after eating or drinking too much, or after spending too long sunbathing in the back garden.
- *Sickness* is reported illness. This is when your illness becomes official, usually as the result of going to the doctor. It will become even more official if you come out of the surgery with a sick note.

- *Disease* is a specific medical condition with recognised symptoms. You've got chicken pox, including the spots to prove it.

Cultural factors

Here again, we're in the realm of the non-objective. Culture is mediated and communicated to us all through language. At a very deep level, the words which we use, the meanings which we attach to them and the ways in which we use those words affect our perceptions of and our responses to social phenomenon. But this operation of culture isn't a one-way transaction. Culture isn't 'out there', separate from the people in society. The meaning attached to words is a sensitive barometer of popular culture.

In your preliminary attempts to define health you may have referred to a dictionary; they always provide a good starting point for a new piece of work. A thesaurus is a rather unconventional dictionary. You won't find in it a slick, quick definition of a word. What it does give you is a range of words which have a similar meaning to the one you're looking up. This is an excellent way to gain a deeper understanding of the way in which we use words, and you'll develop a much more rounded picture of the cultural meanings attached to words. This is the abbreviated entry for 'Health' in *Roget's Thesaurus*:

'*health*, healthiness, good constitution, health and strength. *Vitality*; fitness, condition, bloom, rosiness; well-being. *Healthy*; healthful, wholesome, hygienic, sanitary. *Salubrious*; fat and well-looking, eupepic, euphoric, fresh, blooming, ruddy, rosy, florid, hale, hearty, sound, fit, well, fine, bobbish, full of beans, never ill, robust, hardy, *stalwart*; fighting fit, in condition, sound as a bell, fit as a fiddle, getting well, convalescent

be healthy, look after oneself, feel fine, bloom, flourish, wear well, keep fit; have a clean bill of health, have no mortality; convalesce.'

I'm sure that you now know what health looks like.

Immediately below is the entry for 'Ill-health and disease':

'*ill-health*, bad h., delicate h., failing h.; delicacy, weak constitution, unhealthiness, weak; illness, infirmity, debility. *weakness* seediness, loss of condition, manginess, morbidity, indisposition, cachexia, chronic complaint; allergy; invalidism, valetudinarianism, hypochondria, medicine habit, *illness*, loss of health, deterioration, affliction, disability, handicap, infirmity. *weakness*; sickness, ailment, complaint, complication; condition, history of; bout of sickness, attack, acute a.; breakdown, collapse, prostration, last illness, decease, sick-bed, deathbed.'

Again, you'll now have a very clear idea of what ill-health and disease is all about, at least in the mind of Jo(sephine) Bloggs.

You should note in particular the very clear divide between the positive attribute of health and all the negative connotations of ill-health. Your immediate response to this last point might be to say, 'So what? It's obvious, isn't it? Health is good, illness or disability is bad'. Note also the inclusion of disability and handicap within ill-health and disease.

OVER TO YOU

As you consider the implications of these definitions, draw up a list of those kinds of people who 'pass' the health test and those who 'fail'. Which is the longer list?

Look at the two pictures opposite. Are they 'pictures of health'?

We're still teasing out the meaning and usage of health-related words, so it's back to the thesaurus. Look at the entry under 'Vitality':

'*vitality*, *health*; liveliness, *life*; animal spirits, *cheerfulness*; virility, red blood, *manliness*, *male*; physique, muscularity, muscle, biceps, sinews, beef, brawn. *athletics*, sport; athleticism, gymnastics, feats of strength, callisthenics *exercise*; acrobatics, aerobatics; agonism, *athlete*, gymnast, acrobat; circus animal, performing flea; *contender*; wrestler, *wrestling*; heavy-weight, pugilist; weight-lifter, strong-man; he-man. *male*; strong-arm man, bully, bruiser, *desperado*; chucker-out, bouncer, ejector; amazon, virago; matador killer.'

In this definition there's a heavy emphasis on so-called male attributes. There's a clear association between maleness and athleticism. Interestingly, there are also connections made with less positive attributes, such as bullying and man as a killer. Feminists challenge the male-oriented definition of health which implicitly portrays women as weak and abnormal (see, for example, Abbott and Wallace 1997: Chapters 2 and 7; and Jones 1994: Chapter 7).

EXAM TIP

All of these definitions reflect patriarchal norms and values and are also heavily white and Eurocentric. You're expected in the exam to demonstrate an understanding of the social construction of health based on an analysis which encompasses gender, cross-cultural and historical dimensions.

Jeanne Calment, aged 122, was, until her recent death, officially the world's oldest person.

Official factors

At an official level we're offered two rather different resolutions of the dilemma of how to define health.

The first definition is from the World Health Organisation. In 1974 they defined health as:

'not merely the absence of disease, but a state of complete physical, mental, spiritual and social well-being.'

(cited in Jones 1994: 5)

This definition was welcomed because it represented a move away from the definition of health as the absence of disease. However, it was also criticised for apparently establishing Utopian goals (Seedhouse 1985). How could anyone achieve a state of complete health? How would we know when we had achieved this ideal state?

In 1984, the World Health Organisation Working Group report on health promotion presented a more comprehensive and practicable definition of health:

'Health is seen as a resource for everyday life, not the objective of living: it is a positive concept emphasising social and personal resources as well as physical capabilities.'

(Cited in Jones 194: 6)

The key element here is the emphasis on health as a resource for living, and it would seem to come closest to the individual accounts from Mrs Brown and David Watts, quoted earlier.

A second, and rather different, approach to the definition of health is apparent in UK government policy documents. We now live in a political culture which seeks to set targets for all aspects of public life and thereby to raise standards. The Conservative government's strategy for the health service – *The Health of the Nation* (Department of Health, 1992) – identified five key areas for improving health (see the table on page 316).

The overall emphasis is on reducing and preventing disease and sickness. It's easy to understand the attraction of such an approach; if these targets are attained they carry with them the implication that the overall objective, that of improving health, will have been achieved.

QUESTIONS

1 Why is it difficult to define health?
2 Do you think it's important to have a definition?
3 How are such definitions used in our society?

The Health of the Nation main targets

Coronary heart disease and stroke[1]

To reduce death rates for both CHD and stroke in people under 65 by at least 40% by the year 2000 (*Baseline 1990*)

To reduce the death rate for CHD in people aged 65–74 by at least 30% by the year 2000 (*Baseline 1990*)

To reduce the death rate for stroke in people aged 65–74 by at least 40% by the year 2000 (*Baseline 1990*)

Cancers[1]

To reduce the death rate for breast cancer in the population invited for screening by at least 25% by the year 2000 (*Baseline 1990*)

To reduce the incidence of invasive cervical cancer by at least 20% by the year 2000 (*Baseline 1986*)

To reduce the death rate for lung cancer under the age of 75 by least 30% in men and by at least 15% in women by 2010 (*Baseline 1990*)

To halt the year-on-year increase in the incidence of skin cancer by 2005

Mental illness[1]

To improve significantly the health and social functioning of mentally ill people

To reduce the overall suicide rate by at least 15% by the year 2000 (*Baseline 1990*)

To reduce the suicide rate of severely mentally ill people by at least 33% by the year 2000 (*Baseline 1990*)

HIV/AIDS and sexual health

To reduce the incidence of gonorrhoea by at least 20% by 1995 (*Baseline 1990*), as an indicator of HIV/AIDS trends

To reduce by at least 50% the rate of conceptions amongst the under 16s by the year 2000 (*Baseline 1989*)

Accidents[1]

To reduce the death rate for accidents among children aged under 15 by at least 33% by 2005 (*Baseline 1990*)

To reduce the death rate for accidents among young people aged 15–24 by at least 25% by 2005 (*Baseline 1990*)

To reduce the death rate for accidents among people aged 65 and over by at least 33% by 2005 (*Baseline 1990*)

[1] The 1990 baseline for all mortality targets represents an average of three years centred around 1990.

(Department of Health 1992, cited in Jones 1994)

Models of health

The dominance of the medical, or bio-medical, model in 'western' culture is of comparatively recent origin. Nevertheless, it has fostered the belief that we've progressed in a straight line from a position of ignorance to one of knowledge. It's important that you have a broader historical and cultural perspective on this whole question.

Thomas Kuhn (1962) gives us an analysis of the scientific community which is equally apposite to the study of health. He shows how the scientific community establishes a dominant 'paradigm' – a framework of thinking which sets the boundaries for 'normal' scientific activity. At the outset, there is much to be learned, many questions to be asked and experiments to be conducted, in order that the fine detail of this paradigm can be ascertained. All of this 'leg work' is the 'normal' scientific activity which then ensues. The boundaries of the dominant paradigm determine which experimental results are acceptable, those which are not and those which are due to faulty procedures or the use of impure materials. No doubt, you'll remember the rules you have to follow when conducting science experiments at school. However, by its very nature, this paradigm can only ever provide a partial explanation for natural phenomena. The limitations of the paradigm will generate a power struggle within the scientific community, the result of which will be the establishment of a new dominant paradigm.

This conceptualisation locates scientific activity firmly within its wider social context, rather than leaving it unquestioned and inviolate upon some remote pedestal. It also introduces to scientific activity the concept of power. The switch from one paradigm to another is a revolutionary event, the product of a power struggle between competing factions within the scientific community.

The work of Michel Foucault (1973) also explores issues of power and the organisation of knowledge. He argues that 'discursive formations', that is, structures of knowledge or epistemes, represent power and they also exert that power over social objects, including human bodies. He applied his philosophy to studies of madness, medicine, the body and prisons, to show how new 'regimes of truth' determine our knowledge, the categories which we employ, our systems of belief and our practices. This all sounds very similar to Kuhn's dominant paradigms and also takes us back to our earlier exploration of language.

Put in its broadest perspective, there's always been, at both a practical and also at a deeper philosophical level, a very close interrelationship between medicine, religion and magic. All systems of belief seek to provide us with a means of understanding the world in which we live. They all offer explanations of where we came from, for the events that occur to us whilst in this world, and of what will happen to us when we die. Our interest is not simply passive and philosophical but carries with it the practical desire to learn more, to find ways of intervening, of controlling and possibly altering these apparently externally determined processes.

Traditional societies

From the very earliest times, humankind has attempted to exert some influence over these life cycle processes. We know, for example, that cranial surgery (known as trephinning) was frequently performed in prehistoric times and not merely to repair a fractured skull. Some 'primitive' contemporary societies still do the same operation to let evil spirits out of the head.

Australian Aboriginal medicine comprised two key components. For the treatment of everyday ailments and injuries, the aborigines developed a wide range of simple but effective remedies based on their close knowledge of the natural world. However, some illnesses had no obvious cause or didn't respond to common-sense remedies. These, the Aborigines believed, were caused by the influence of evil spirits and had to be treated by other, non-medical means.

The pyramids are evidence, in the most monumental form, of the Egyptian belief systems. Doctors and priests worked together in the preparation of bodies for embalming, prior to being entombed in these pyramids.

'First they take a crooked piece of metal and with it draw out some of the brain through the nostrils and then rinse out the rest with drugs. Next they make a cut along the side of the body with a sharp stone and take out the whole of the contents of the abdomen. After this they fill the cavity with myrrh, cassia and other spices and the body is placed in natron for 70 days.'

(Herodotus, Book 2, Chapter 86)

The heart was usually left inside the body, but the other internal organs were removed, treated with preserving spices, and placed in a canopic jar which was taken to the tomb with the mummy.

The level of medical knowledge which Egyptian doctors gained from such activities was strictly limited by their religious beliefs and practices. The Egyptians believed in life after death, and so the body and its organs were preserved in this way. The doctors who participated in the removal of internal organs must have learned a great deal about human physiology. However, because of their cultural beliefs in an afterlife and the necessity of preserving the body and its constituent parts undamaged, they were forbidden to dissect further or to examine either the corpse or the organs.

OVER TO YOU

In what ways do religious beliefs and practices affect health and health-care issues in contemporary society? Gather information about different cultures and religions, rather than concentrating exclusively on your immediate experience. (An excellent reference source for this kind of information is Schott and Henley 1996.)

Hippocrates and other Greek doctors believed that the art of the physician should be separated from the cult of the priest. Such a separation would not have been achieved easily, given the power of the priests in Greek society. Greek doctors always worked on the assumption that diseases had natural, not supernatural, causes, and these causes could be ascertained by 'clinical observation'. Their underlying belief system on the causes of disease was based on the theory of the four humours and their relationship to the four basic elements, shown below.

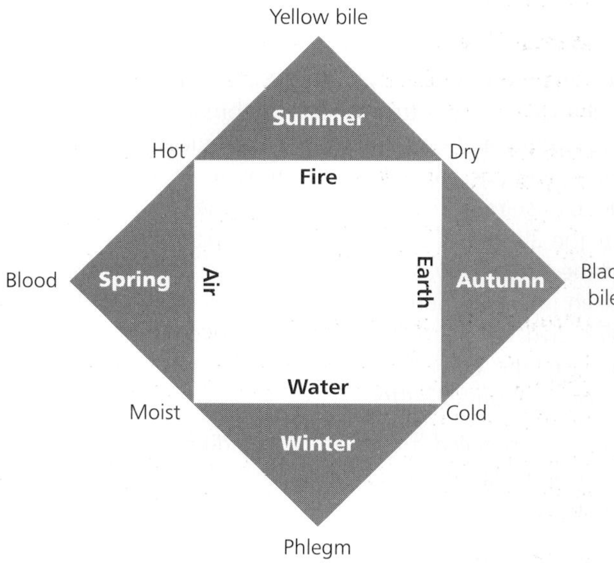

The theory of the four humours and their relationship to the four basic elements

This quotation explains the thinking behind such a diagram:

'Man's body . . . has blood, phlegm, yellow bile and melancholy bile [black bile]. These make up his parts and through them he feels illness or enjoys health. When all these elements [humours] are truly balanced and mingled, he feels the most perfect health. Illness occurs when one of these humours is in excess, or is lessened in amount or is entirely thrown out of the body . . . When one of these elements [humours] is isolated so that it has no balance . . . the particular part of the body where it is supposed to make balance naturally becomes diseased.'

(From *On the Constitution of Man*, section 4)

Greek doctors were convinced that nature itself was the best healer and that, whenever possible, they should not interfere with this process. The emphasis of their medical practice was on maintaining and restoring the balance of the four humours.

The history of medicine and health care is that of a continually shifting relationship between what can be explained and treated and what currently cannot. Thus, the roles of the doctor, the priest, the witch doctor or shaman are both complementary and conflicting. In traditional cultures there's frequent recourse to methods of placating the spirits who are the cause of any manner of ailments. In the Christian faith there's frequent reference to the will of God, particularly as a means of coping with personal tragedy.

Let's look a little more closely at this 'marriage' of medicine and spiritualism. The Romans set great store by the healing properties of water. They frequently dedicated springs to a minor deity, a nymph or a goddess of fertility or healing. In medieval times, Christian wells were dedicated to various saints and martyrs. Each disease or group of diseases was the responsibility of a particular saint. So, the waters at Little Walsingham in Norfolk were efficacious in the treatment of stomach disorders; the Old Spring at Great Malvern was dedicated to St Ann, the encourager of fertility. Pilgrims to St Tecla's Well in Denbighshire circled it three times, then laid an offering on the shrine. A cock or a hen, depending on the sex of the sufferer, was also carried round the well and then taken into the church by the pilgrim for the night. If the bird died before dawn, it was assumed that St Tecla's disease, the falling sickness, had been transferred to it from the human sufferer.

(A more detailed treatment of traditional explanations of health, disease and illness can be found in Aggleton 1990: Chapter 3.)

The weakening of tradition and the development of medical science

Throughout the history of medicine there's the continuous thread of the power struggles that ensue between various kinds of health practitioner. The emphasis within Greek medicine was to separate medical practice from the cult of the priest. In Europe, during the Middle Ages, in addition to establishing the primacy of a secular approach to medicine, the emphasis was also upon establishing the dominance of men in the provision of health care. From the thirteenth century onwards, women were excluded from European universities and thereby denied access to developments in scientific medical knowledge. Medical guilds helped to define health-care practice as the use of medical skills, the preserve of males, rather than as the intuitive, holistic approach used by women (Hockey 1993).

Not only were women denied access to learning, they were also often vilified as witches and subsequently killed. Barbara Ehrenreich and Dierdre English (1974) argue that there's a link between the campaigns against witches that occurred in Europe between the fourteenth and seventeenth centuries and the suppression of female healing. The effectiveness of these witch hunts was variable; not all women healers were regarded as witches during this period, and there's also evidence that unqualified women healers continued to practise until the nineteenth century.

This next quotation gives us a very clear indication of the way in which women were regarded, by one man at least:

'Everywhere the man strives to rid himself of women by objectifying it. "It is not", he says "that I dread her, it is that she is malignant, capable of any crime, a beast of prey, a vampire, a witch, insatiable in her desires. She is the very personification of what is sinister".'

(Karen Horney [1885–1952] quoted in Mills 1991: 263)

Ann Oakley (1976) writes:

'Etymologically and historically, four words or roles have been closely related. [Etymology is the study of the formation and the use of words; what we were doing earlier with the extracts from the thesaurus.] These are woman, witch, midwife and healer . . . In Europe medicine emerged as a predominantly male professional discipline and the traditional female lay healer was suppressed . . . Women have a long history as community healers in pre-industrial Europe and colonial America. The "good woman", "cunning woman' or "wisewoman" was the person to whom people turned in times of illness . . . Practising wisewomen midwives had a generally respectable and sometimes high, status among the people they served. The negative appellation "witch" was fostered by the medieval Church to whom disease was a god-given affliction, and thus a phenomenon which had to be under strict religious control.'

(Oakley 1976: cited in Mills 1989: 263)

During the eighteenth century there was an increasing trend for middle-class women to give birth in a lying-in (maternity) hospital rather then at home. This was part of the general trend towards the division of labour and the separation of the economic sphere from the domestic sphere. Previously, male participation in childbirth had been taboo, but this move towards the hospitalisation of childbirth allowed the emergence of male domination in this hitherto exclusively female preserve. The location of childbirth within a hospital setting also fostered the view that childbirth was a medical problem rather than an entirely natural process (Hilary Graham and Ann

Oakley 1981). This 'problem' required medical intervention, now almost entirely in the hands of men. (This argument is developed within a contemporary context in Oakley 1993.) Since a woman's natural processes have thus become defined as inherently problematic, it's a short step in the argument to portray all women as innately weak and unhealthy.

Quite clearly, there's been a radical shift in the balance of power and also in the very definition of the situation with regard to childbirth. With women as the traditional carers in childbirth, the emphasis is on everyone supporting and sharing in the process. Once hospitalisation occurs, and in particular when under the aegis of male doctors, the relationship becomes that of the expert exercising his authority over the weak and ignorant patient. Lesley Doyal and Imogen Pennel (1979: 30) argue that scientific medicine is 'curative, individualistic and interventionist', it treats patients as objects and ignores 'their status as social beings'. Oakley, in her essay, 'Technologies of procreation: Hazards for women and the social order?' (Oakley 1993), examines what she describes as the three themes which fire the reproductive technology debate: fertility, science and gender. At a micro level, she describes the form and function of the technologies; at the macro level, she looks at the context in which these technologies are used as a means of social control. Jalna Hanmer, in her essay, 'Women and reproduction' (Hanmer 1993), reviews much of the contemporary theory and practice in the same area.

The changes in female health care which have taken place since the late Middle Ages were part of a much wider process through which what is generally described as the medical model of health emerged as the dominant paradigm in 'western' health care.

Health care has traditionally been located primarily within the domestic or communal sphere, and is very often the domain of the women in the community. It's the mothers who typically provide care for their children and for older people. It's the women who typically assist at childbirth and the laying out of the dead. Women have accumulated a wide knowledge of lay medicine and this knowledge and skill has been passed down from generation to generation.

We think of the period since the early nineteenth century as a time of spectacular advances and discoveries in medicine, the accumulation of medical knowledge and the eradication of disease. There's no denying the significant contribution to our well-being of scientists such as Edward Jenner, Louis Pasteur, Joseph Lister and Paul Ehrlich – the names are legion. The names are also clear evidence of the male domination of science and medicine by the nineteenth century. Anne Witz (1985) examines these developments in terms of social closure and demarcation. By social closure, she means the measures taken to exclude women from practising medicine. Demarcation is the process whereby the (male) doctors defined what was medical and what was ancillary work, this latter to be carried out by female nurses and midwives.

The medical model of health

The dominant medical paradigm of our time is based upon the positivist (i.e. ultra-scientific) research techniques used by medical scientists in the nineteenth and twentieth centuries. They're all working in the tradition which dates back to the time of Hippocrates, who stressed the importance of clinical observation.

Taylor (Taylor and Field 1993: 42) presents the medical, or bio-medical, model thus:

- Health is the absence of biological abnormality.
- The human body is likened to a machine to be restored to health through treatments of one sort or another which arrest, or reverse, the disease process.
- The health of society is seen as largely dependent on the state of medical knowledge and the availability of medical resources.

The emphasis is on understanding disease and finding cures. The goal of complete health is out there and will be attained by the accumulation of medical knowledge.

A more detailed elaboration of the medical model is given in Jones (1994: 12).

A question for you to consider at this point is whether the methodology of clinical observation gives the doctor all the information necessary for a complete picture of the health of the patient.

A critical analysis of the medical model

The preceding account has already indicated two substantive areas of criticism levelled against the medical model:

- its reliance on allopathic medicine (the use of drugs to counteract the symptoms)
- the power relationships which ensue from the formalisation of health care.

Whilst the intention isn't to denigrate or devalue the great strides in medical knowledge which characterise this period, the omnipotence of this paradigm is increasingly being questioned. You'll need to weigh up the significance of this mounting tide of criticism: are the issues being raised the means whereby an essentially sound, theoretical framework will be further refined and adjusted to take account of a continually evolving set of circumstances? Alternatively, do they represent fundamental problems of theoretical structure which can only be resolved by a medical/scientific revolution?

Re-acquaint yourself with the WHO definitions of health (page 315) which offer a much more comprehensive working paradigm than the single-focused medical model.

Jones argues for a *social model of health*:

'Health is seen as being produced not just by individual biology and medical intervention, but by conditions in the wider natural, social, economic and political environment and by individual behaviour in response to that environment.'

(Jones 1994: 12)

A former Canadian Minister of Health and Welfare, Marc Lalonde, developed the *health field concept* (see below) and in his work stressed the necessity of acting simultaneously on all four 'fields'.

Human biology	Lifestyle
Environment	Health-care organisation

(Lalonde 1974, cited in Jones 1994: 13)

Lalonde's health field concept

Whilst the specific terminology used in Lalonde's model reflects the contemporary situation, there are also clear parallels between this model and that of the four humours. Both models stress the necessity of achieving an overall balance in a person's way of life. Both models stress the importance of the interaction between the individual and their environment. In Ancient Greece, that environment was determined solely by the seasonal round; today we interpret environment to particularly encompass human impact upon the natural world, for example, acid rain or damage to the ozone layer.

In order to bring about improvements in health the social model places a significant emphasis on health promotion, on broader structural and strategic interventions (Jones 1994: 34). The implications for the working practices of health-care professional are spelled out in some detail in the table opposite.

Now we have a much more complete picture of the range of factors which affect the health of the individual. We also can see very clearly the ways in which these various elements impinge upon each other. In order to take action which will have an impact upon health, it's this enormous range of factors which have to be taken into account, whether by health professionals or politicians responsible for the formulation of social policy initiatives.

When you look carefully at the table you'll see that the sequence of arrows runs from left to right. In reality, anyone working in the field of health care is most likely to start in the middle column, the one headed 'Possible health outcomes'. These are the symptoms that a patient is likely to present with. Like so many aspects of social life, the symptoms are perhaps the small tip of a much larger iceberg. If you follow the arrows, both to the left and right, you'll get a sense of the extent of this iceberg, and the range of interventions required to deal with it in its entirety.

Thomas McKeown (1976; 1979) has demonstrated conclusively that medical intervention played little part in the decline of many infectious diseases. For example, the incidence of TB, scarlet fever, whooping cough and measles was declining long before effective medical treatment was generally available. On the other hand, we mustn't overlook the fact that immunisation programmes against smallpox, polio and diphtheria can be directly correlated with a decline in these diseases.

The general improvements in life expectancy in the second half of the nineteenth century and continuing well into the twentieth century are largely attributable to public health measures rather than specific medical interventions. McKeown argues that measures such as improved water supply and public housing programmes ensured that people were generally better able to resist infectious diseases.

Here again, in this critical argument, we have an emphasis on the contribution of environmental factors to general levels of health. The Romans were fully aware of the importance of a good water supply and built aquaducts to ensure that water was brought into all their towns. They also provided public bath houses and latrines for the use of everyone, rich and poor alike. Not only did they value cleanliness for their personal comfort, bathing also formed an important part of their medical practice. When the Roman Empire collapsed, so much of this knowledge about medicine and the environment was then lost for centuries.

It could be argued that the preventative approach embodied in the public health measures fits very well within the rationale of the medical model of health. This is a model based on establishing a causal link between two factors and it's dependent upon being able to intervene in order to achieve a specific outcome. So, the gradual improvements in sanitary arrangements in nineteenth-century industrial towns can be seen to have had a marked effect on health outcomes.

There are, however, political factors which have to be brought into the overall picture. It requires a degree of public organisation and finance to ensure that public health measures are implemented. The problems in the early part of the Industrial Revolution had arisen precisely because there was no effective government machinery, at either a local or national level, to ensure that drains

Health problems and health work interventions

'External' influences	→ Issue/'problem'	→ Possible health outcome	Implications for health work interventions → Work with family	→ Work outside family
– Socialisation patterns and cultural influences – Standardised 'nuclear' family style housing – Close relationship of housing size and cost	→ – Large family → – Overcrowding – Inadequate housing	→ For example: Respiratory diseases Mental health problems 'Backwardness' of children	→ – Contraceptive advice (prevention) – Try to get family rehoused/ get improvement grants, etc.	→ – Liaison with local schools over sex and health education – Campaign for improvement in local housing/pressure to build adequate sized houses – Publicise evidence showing links between overcrowding and respiratory disease
– Growth of low wage sector of economy and casual working – High levels of unemployment – Low wages of women workers – Great inequality in distribution of income (and wealth)	→ Man, breadwinner, brings in sole family income → Family poverty	→ Possible problems from inadequate diet For example: Obesity Undernutrition Low resistance to disease (immune system impaired)	→ – Help with family budgeting – Try to get all benefit entitlement paid to family	→ – Plan local 'take up' campaign for low earners – Campaign for local crèche/ nursery facilities – Join with other health workers to publicise evidence on 'social costs' to NHS of low wages
– Cultural influences and socialisation patterns – Class influences – Impact of work patterns, conditions, environment	→ – Parenting influences – 'Unhealthy' lifestyle	→ Effect on infant feeding and health attitudes and smoking For example: Diet Alcohol consumption and so on	→ Giving knowledge and advice to immediate family circle (parents and grandparents)	→ – Campaign for government action on Health Divide, and NACNE reports/for tougher laws on drink – Set up self help groups – Produce your own health education literature geared to your clients' own priorities and defined needs in a locality

(Jones 1994: 35)

were laid, that sewage was properly disposed of, and the like. With a few notable exceptions, such as Titus Salt who built Saltaire on the outskirts of Bradford or the Cadbury family who built the Bournville estate in Birmingham, private builders and entrepreneurs didn't take a broader, socially responsible view of the whole issue. It's not altogether surprising that they were only interested in building lots of houses, close to their factories, as quickly and cheaply as possible. Roman society was organised around the needs of the military, and the large-scale provision of public facilities was achieved by using conscript labour. In nineteenth-century Germany, Bismarck made similar decisions in the national interest. Their rail network was laid out according to a national plan which would ensure the rapid movement of troops.

The UK doesn't have the same tradition of centralised decision-making. In histories of medicine Britons flag up the achievements of individuals, such as Pasteur or Fleming, and give much less prominence to the unspectacular work of those who laid water pipes or paved the streets. Even though public health measures have a greater impact on health outcomes, and are certainly cost-effective, they're not as glamourous or spectacular as specific medical discoveries and advances. Today, there's still the same imbalance in the allocation of resources, with preventative public health initiatives being allocated a tiny fraction of the overall budget for health care.

Setting targets: Using statistics

The *Health of the Nation* targets represent an essentially bio-medical approach to achieving improvements in health. Specific medical conditions have been selected, such as coronary heart disease and major cancers, as well as more socially-rooted factors such as suicide rates and accidents to children. In the current political climate we cannot fail to be aware that the setting of targets is always accompanied by the allocation of resources. The subsequent publication of league tables is done partly as a means of showing that society has received value for money.

The mix of political will, funding and a system of public accountability can give rise to some significant distortion of the ensuing statistics. John McKinlay (1996) reports on the 'social production of a health statistic'.

McKinlay argues that medical sociologists tend to give disproportionate attention to the behavioural factors that affect the social production of statistics, those denoted on the left-hand side of the diagram below, while overlooking the significance of the health system/provider responses indicated on the right of the diagram. Three separate system influences are spelled out in some detail. They include 'governmental or state policies, organisational priorities and provider behaviours'.

McKinlay examines in detail the response of doctors to women who present with symptoms of heart disease. There's a general view, amongst lay people certainly and also apparently amongst doctors, that women are less prone than men to heart disease. Many doctors were apparently blinkered by their preconceptions about the relative incidence of heart disease in men and women, which then resulted in them making a delayed diagnosis about the true nature of any particular referral.

Foucault (1973) also talks of distinctive 'ways of seeing' and 'ways of knowing' in the sometimes conflicting conceptions of what health is.

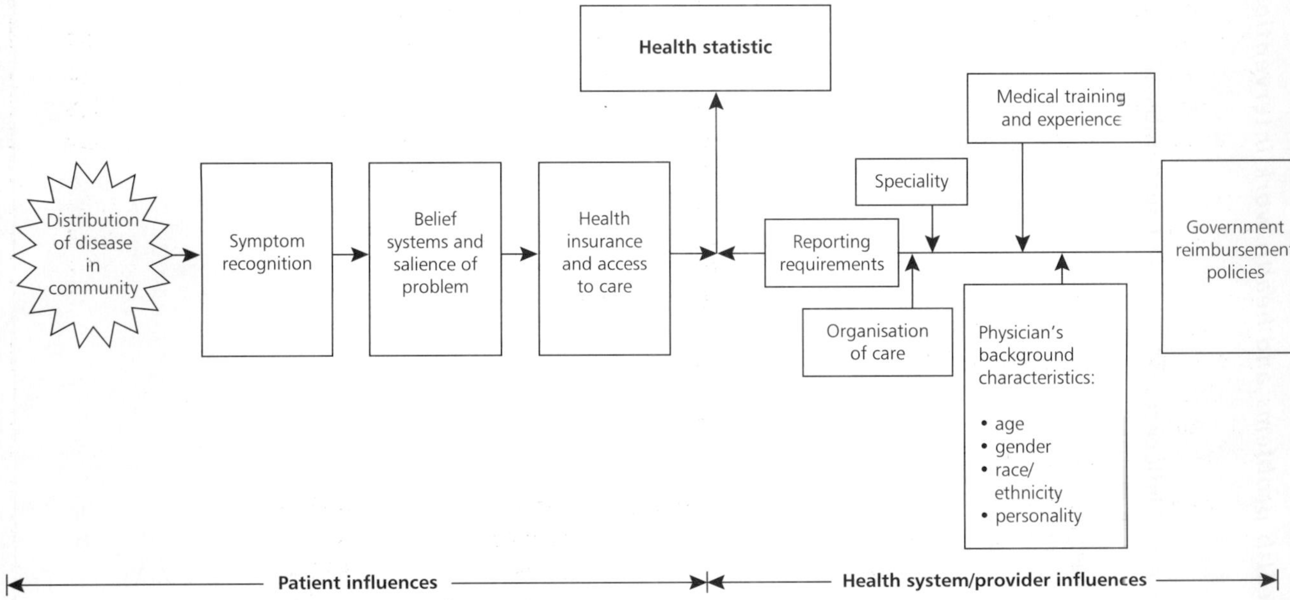

(McKinlay 1996)

Simplified model of the derivation of a health statistic

These's nothing new in the potential for doctors, or anyone else for that matter, to see only that which they have been trained to see. Medical statistics have always been fallible.

Below is some information about the deaths which occurred in London during 1665, a plague year. We can learn a lot from such a table of figures (not least, how rules for spelling have changed over the last 300 years).

Here we can read of a fantastic range of illnesses , some completely unknown to us and, conversely, find little mention of our current major causes of death. What is tissick, rissing of the lights or Kings Evill? Is cancer essentially a modern disease or was it present, but classified differently? To what extent did the plague account for many deaths which might otherwise have been differently attributed, given modern autopsy procedures?

Clearly, when we return to McKinlay's work on the incidence of heart disease amongst women, misdiagnosis could have fatal consequences.

Not only does McKinlay's model consider the impact of medical training, it also encompasses the wider political and economic environment in which those doctors work. The requirement to produce statistics, to report treatments in terms of outcomes and to be accountable for the use made of public funds, all encourage a particular construction of health statistics.

The bill of mortality for London 1665

Abortive and Stilborne	617	Kings Evill	86
Aged	1845	Leprossie	2
Ague and Feaver	5257	Lethargy	14
Appoplex and Suddenly	116	Livergrowne	20
Bedrid	10	Meagrom and Headach	12
Blassted	5	Meassles	7
Bleeding	16	Murthered and Shot	9
Bloudy Flux, Scowering and Flux	185	Overlaid and Starved	45
Burnt and Scalded	8	Palssie	30
Caleniure	3	Plague	68596
Cancer, Gangrene and Fisstula	56	Plannet	6
Canker and Thrussh	111	Plurissie	15
Childbed	625	Poyssoned	1
Chrissomes and Infants	1258	Quinssie	35
Cold and Cough	68	Rickets	557
Collick and Winde	134	Rissing of the Lights	397
Conssumption and Tissick	4808	Rupture	34
Convulssions and Mother	2036	Scurvy	105
Disstracted	5	Shingles and Swine pox	2
Dropssie and Timpany	1478	Sores, Ulcers, broken	
Drowned	50	and bruissed Limbes	82
Executed	21	Spleen	14
Flox and Smal Pox	655	Spotted Feaver and Purples	1929
Found dead in sstreets, fields	20	Stopping of the Stomack	332
French Pox	86	Stone and Strangury	98
Frighted	23	Surfet	1251
Gout and Sciatica	27	Teeth and Worms	2614
Grief	46	Vomiting	51
Griping in the Guts	1288	Vvenn	1
Hanged and made away themsselves	7		
Headmouldsshot and Mouldfallen	14		
Jaundies	110		
Imposstume	227		
Kild by sseveral accidents	46		

Chrisstened	Males	5114	Buried	Males	48569
	Females	4853		Females	48737
	In all	9967		In all	97306
				Of the Plague	68596

Over-medicalisation

According to Eliot Friedson (1970) health work has been confirmed as a formal, professionalised area of expertise. R. Taylor (1979) claims that 'medicine has become a malignant technology which is out of control'. There's increasing concern about the issue of doctor-caused (*iatrogenic*) disease: adverse reactions to prescribed drugs, the excessive use of interventionist technology, particularly in childbirth, complications following surgery, wrong diagnosis and inappropriate treatment.

Many women, and not just card-carrying feminists, have long railed against the excessive use of interventionist technology in childbirth. There's been a marked increase in the use of drugs to induce labour and also of caesarian sections if the imminent birth might be problematic. Thirty years ago the controversy focused on the drug Thalidomide. This had been widely prescribed to counter morning sickness in pregnant women, and then many of their babies were born with terrible abnormalities. It seems that this spectre has come back to haunt us. In August 1997 research was published which suggests that the effects of Thalidomide on DNA can be inherited:

'So far, 11 of the 380 children born to designated Thalidomide victims in the UK have been identified with congenital limb defects – at least five times more than the usual rate for the population as a whole . . . If the effects are proved, it would make Thalidomide the first drug in history to jump the generation barrier.'

(The *Birmingham Post*, 11 August 1997)

We all take antibiotics. We can't imagine how we'd cope with tonsillitis without them. Our GPs are criticised for sometimes prescribing them too readily; in reply, they claim that patients are disappointed if they leave the surgery empty-handed. In France you can buy antibiotics over the counter without a prescription. Did you know that there are also antibiotics in the food we eat? What effect are these drugs having upon us?

Ivan Illich (1990) extends the concept of clinical iatrogenesis and applies it to the whole of the medical establishment. His analysis is part of a fundamental critique of large-scale industrial societies in which the individual is dehumanised and, as a result, loses the ability to control the most fundamental aspects of her or his life. He identifies both *social iatrogenesis* – the bureaucratic and commercial domination of the provision of health care – and *cultural iatrogenesis* – the increasing medicalisation of all aspects of the human condition. By cultural iatrogenesis Illich means, for example, our intolerance of the impact of normal bodily reactions and functions. We automatically take a tablet when we've got a headache or medicine when we've got stomach ache. It's perfectly natural for our moods to vary, in response to a wide variety of factors, yet increasingly we resort to drugs to counter these changes rather than being in tune with our metabolisms. We've lost the ability to understand what is happening and to 'go with the flow'. Currently, many women going through the menopause are prescribed Hormone Replacement Therapy (HRT). Many doctors also favour it because it reduces the risk of osteoporosis. Some regard HRT, and also Frozac, as wonder drugs, others are more sceptical.

Vicente Navarro (1975) shifts the focus of 'blame' away from the health-care professionals themselves. They're not, *per se*, responsible for the over-medicalisation of health care, but rather they're responding to the commercial pressures within the capitalist system which encourages consumerism. The real *bêtes noires* are the pharmaceutical companies and private health-care providers.

MEDICAL OR BIO-MEDICAL MODEL OF HEALTH

FOR

+ It's established a framework of rigour in medical practice and the scientific investigation of disease. A massive body of knowledge has grown about a wide range of issues relating to health.
+ Huge advances have been made in the treatment of many diseases. There's been a positive impact on general levels of health and in increased longevity.
+ It's freed the study and practice of medicine from many of the inhibiting rules associated with religion and also from the influence of magic and spiritualism.
+ Medical practitioners have a high status, which is in part based on their high level of training and professional competence.

AGAINST

– The dominance of the medical model has been achieved at the expense of other forms of 'holistic' medicine. Many of these more ancient skills have been either lost or significantly devalued.
– Health isn't just about the treatment of disease. Good health is the result of the interaction of many factors, not all of which are apparent to the medical practitioner and not all of which are treatable with conventional medicine.
– Treatment of symptoms rather than underlying causes won't necessarily achieve a complete 'cure'.
– The over-dependence on drugs has caused us to lose touch with our bodies and not fully understand the natural rhythms of our metabolisms.

Much comment has already been made about the excessive focus, within 'western' medicine, on the treatment of disease. The human body is treated as a machine which has to be tinkered with and 'fixed'. The various forms of 'alternative' medicine adopt a more holistic approach to treatment and the person. We're seeing a massive revival of interest in 'alternative' medicine. This has been generated by a combination of factors. More people are beginning to question the efficacy of conventional medicine and this is coupled with a growing awareness that there are other ways of doing it. We live in a multi-cultural society; we're all part of the 'global village' and, thanks to modern technology, we're much better informed about how other people look after their health.

The field of alternative medicine is vast, and a text such as this cannot even begin to offer a comprehensive account of them all. You should, however, investigate them and, in so doing, seek answers to a number of important questions.

QUESTIONS

With particular regard to specific alternative therapies:

1. What's their basic philosophy and what do they claim to do?
2. How readily available to the general public are the therapies?
3. What's the response of the established medical profession to them?
4. Do you think they should be classified as 'alternative'?

Sociological perspectives on health

We've already looked at some aspects of sociological theory and health, particularly from a feminist perspective. As you now work through this section, you should refer back to this earlier material and incorporate the issues raised into your developing understanding and application of theory.

Typically, sociological theories are presented in pairs, very often as opposites. So we have, for example consensus/conflict.

The differences between the theories are real, and yet presenting them in such a stark fashion isn't necessarily the most illuminating approach when we come to 'sociology in practice'. Firstly, it's important to remember that none of the categories are mutually exclusive. We're not talking about a crude either/or analysis, but rather the location of any particular approach somewhere along a continuum. For example, we saw in Chapter 4 that consensus and conflict theories do share some common ground.

In addition, we invariably find that more than one theoretical perspective is combined in the analysis of a specific issue. For example, feminist theory can be variously located within conflict and social constructionist models, assuming, of course, prior acceptance of what Abbott and Wallace term the 'malestream' parameters of theorising.

There's a further overlay which you must take into consideration. Positivism and interpretivism both connect with theory, but they essentially denote types of research methodology. Very broadly, a positivist approach will be accompanied by the use of quantitative, empirical research methods, whereas interpretivists favour a qualitative methodology. Quantitative data are based on statistics, on so-called 'hard' information. Qualitative data are regarded as 'soft', based more on interviews and establishing an understanding of the subject matter.

EXAM TIP

You need to ask the same questions of all theoretical perspectives:

- What is the link between theory and method?
- How are they applied in the analysis of any particular issue?

Sociology, as a recognised and separate discipline, is very much the product of the Enlightenment and the Industrial Revolution. The Enlightenment is characterised by the emerging dominance of rationality and the growing secularisation of society. Whether we're looking at medicine, the natural sciences or sociology, they all share an underlying philosophy, namely that it's possible to classify and explain all aspects of the natural world, including the behaviour of human beings. When we study the development of sociological theory, and as we chart the emergence of the bio-medical model of health, we can tell a parallel story. This is the story of the challenges to traditional sources of authority and belief in society, such as the Church, and of the emergence of patterns of male domination. As we approach the end of the twentieth century, the fortunes of these three disciplines, medicine, sociology and the natural sciences, are still moving in tandem. They're all experiencing and responding to fundamental societal forces which may generate, in Kuhn's terms, the adoption of a new overarching paradigm.

The influence of the natural sciences has long been apparent in the primacy of empirical methods in sociology (particularly 'malestream'). Scientific method is based on the formulation of an hypothesis and the testing of that hypothesis against evidence. There are in-built assumptions to this approach: that there are 'facts', whether social or scientific, 'out there' to be studied; and that what is visible constitutes the real and whole manifestation of that phenomenon. Here also we see clear parallels with the bio-medical model of health, with its emphasis on the treatment of external symptoms.

Fabians, such as Sydney and Beatrice Webb, argued that social problems, such as unemployment or poverty, could be solved by the intervention of the state. This approach is based on the assumption that it's possible to measure social phenomena, that it's possible to establish causation and thereby to effect changes. All of this work must be empirically-based, from the initial observation, to the allocation of inevitably scarce resources, through to the monitoring of their effectiveness.

Much of the early work done in the social policy tradition was conceived of as being value-free. Social policy was based on an empiricist study of the provision of welfare. According to Richard Titmuss, the establishment of the Welfare State in the UK represented the 'end of ideology', thus re-iterating the supposed neutrality of social policy. The final section of this chapter will examine the detail of the underpinning issues relating to the current provision of health care.

The early sociologists and health

C. Wright Mills has argued that the motivation behind all classical social analysis was a concern with 'urgent public issues and insistent human troubles'. The generally recognised 'founding fathers'(!) of sociology (who would not necessarily have described themselves as sociologists, for example, Karl Marx) responded to the massive social changes of the Industrial Revolution at what we would describe as the level of grand theory. Their search for general, scientific laws of human behaviour led them to concentrate on the analysis of society at an overarching, abstract level, rather than focusing on particular issues within that society. Thus, in the writings of Karl Marx and Max Weber you'll find little direct reference to questions of health, although much has subsequently been written on health by those working within a marxist or weberian framework.

It's within his analysis of industrial capitalism that Marx gave consideration to its impact on the lives and health of the proletariat. He related the unequal incidence of illness and disease, for injuries and premature death, to the economic imperatives of capitalism. He also highlighted the impact of poor housing conditions, low wages and poor diet, as well as the absence of adequate health-care provision for the workers. Engels, in his seminal work, *The Condition of the Working Class in England in 1844* (1847) presented a graphic description of the impact of industrialisation, and as such was giving voice to the widely-held concerns of the time.

Weber's contribution to sociological theory is exemplified by his work on ideal types. In this we have perhaps the ultimate abstraction, but, nevertheless, one which is intended to give insight into the workings of real social institutions. In this respect, his work on organisations and bureaucracies is still influential in current analyses of the power relationships in health-care organisations.

Of the early sociologists, Durkheim is the one who gave particular attention to some aspects of health, namely that of mental health and suicide. This is covered in some detail later in this chapter.

Talcott Parsons

The work of Talcott Parsons held a dominant position in medical sociology for much of the immediate post-war period. He's often maligned for his alleged conservatism. Nevertheless, he can be credited with providing the impulse which shifts the focus of sociological parameters away from the macro and the impersonal, towards the roles of the players within the social system.

But first, what about Parsons' general theory? He adopted concepts from the field of medicine, most notably those of homeostasis and equilibrium, and applied them to the analysis of society. His work also has resonance with that of Durkheim on organic solidarity. The Greeks emphasised the need to maintain balance in the four humours. Parsons' equivalent 'humours' are the social, cultural, psychological and organic mechanisms of society. These have to be maintained in a state of equilibrium to correct deviance and to preserve social order. Within this social order everyone has an allotted role which must be maintained to preserve the smooth functioning of society. Conflict is dysfunctional and destabilising; the sources of conflict and instability (such as those which gave great cause for alarm in the nineteenth century) must be eradicated. This is why individuals must be maintained in a state of functional good health. Presented in such a manner, it's easy to see why Parsons has attracted such a bad press. All of this has a distinctly Orwellian ring to it.

In contrast with Marx's work on the capitalist system, Parsons places the role of medicine centre-stage in his social analysis. Society is a system which has both instrumental and expressive needs, and the role of medicine in society is of paramount importance. Illness will prevent an individual from making a practical contribution to the normal functioning of that society, most typically because they're unable to work. In addition to the loss of that person's economic contribution to society, they're also now withdrawn from normal social discourse. Whilst they're in that state, they constitute a potentially destabilising factor for the wider society. The function of medicine is to maintain health and to restore the sick to full health as quickly as possible, thus ensuring their reintegration into the mainstream of society.

Although, in Parsons' conceptual framework, we do have the presence of individuals, these individuals are portrayed very much as the minor adjunct of the social whole. Society is conceived of as separate from the individuals of which it is comprised. Society has needs which those individuals must satisfy. The direction of the relationship is all one way, with no question of interrelationship. Within this framework medicine is very much a form of social control; only those who are fit can participate in that society.

It is within this framework that Parsons developed his 'sick role' theory (Parsons 1964) The role of the patient comprises certain obligations and privileges. The patient:

- must want to get better as quickly as possible
- must be in need of care and unable to get better by her or his own efforts
- should seek professional medical advice and co-operate with the doctor
- will be released from (some of) her or his normal obligations (for example, going to work, housework).

The counterpart of the patient's sick role is the doctor's professional role. The doctor is expected to:

- bring a high degree of skill and knowledge to his(?) work
- be motivated by concern for the patient and the community, rather than seeking personal gain
- be objective and emotionally detached
- be bound by rules of professional conduct.

In return that doctor can expect to be granted:

- the right to examine physically the patient and to enquire into intimate areas of their physical and personal life
- considerable personal autonomy in their professional practice
- a position of authority *vis-à-vis* the patient.

Marxist analyses

All sociological theory revolves around questions of power relations in society. Using a classical marxist framework, power is directly related to the economic base of society – economic determinism – and all other relationships within society stem from the supremacy of this economic base. In health terms, the most important

PARSONS' SICK ROLE MODEL

FOR

+ Parsons draws attention to the social dimensions of sickness. For example, he explores the social negotiations involved and the changed social relationships that ensue when someone is sick. He also highlights the disruptive aspects of being sick, for both the individual and society. You'll know from your own experience what the ramifications of sickness can be. If you're ill, you can't honour your own obligations; perhaps you've arranged to go to the cinema with friends and they're dependent on you driving them there. If you're very unwell, then perhaps another member of your family has to take time off work to look after you. If they don't go to work, they may lose income. In addition, their workplace will not have the benefit of their work input. Perhaps as a result of their absence, mistakes are made in an important order and the firm subsequently loses the custom of that customer. See how the snowball gathers momentum.

+ Parsons' work in general spells out many aspects of the mechanics and consequences of living in a complex society. He shows how the components of society interlink and are interdependent.

+ Another significant area of Parsons' work focuses on the professions and the processes of professionalisation. In this respect, his work on the medical profession is part of this wider scenario.

AGAINST

– Parsons' model works most successfully with specific and tangible medical conditions, for example, appendicitis or a broken leg. Then the patient is clearly immobilised and forced to accept the medical interventions of the doctor. However, many medical conditions don't fit so tidily, especially long-standing conditions such as asthma or depression. In these cases diagnosis and treatment is much less clear-cut. In addition, the patient is likely to develop a greater level of knowledge and personal understanding about their condition, to the extent that the professional will find themselves working in collaboration with the patient.

– The model assumes that the patient will seek professional advice for her or his condition and in so doing make the transition from being ill to 'officially' sick. Parsons acknowledges the social dimensions of being sick, but doesn't give equal attention to the social forces which determine this prior stage.

– Some people enjoy the attention which they receive when they are sick or possibly want to prolong their time out of the daily hurly-burly. Again. Parsons' model presumes that everyone will want to get out of the sick role as quickly as possible.

consideration for the capitalists was to have an efficient workforce, and thus any measures undertaken to combat ill-health would be motivated by this overriding economic necessity. If this sounds like an unacceptably harsh and cynical interpretation of their motives, or perhaps one which was only appropriate to the early days of the Industrial Revolution, consider this report on health-care initiatives published in February 1997:

'The symptoms are alarming: British companies lose 175 million days and £10 billion a year through sickness and absenteeism, says the Confederation of British Industry – about eight working days per employee . . .

"We want to highlight the suffering and cost of employee absence and promote our beliefs that a healthy workforce will enhance the wealth of companies." (Ina Barker, executive director, Association of Insurance and Risk Managers)

It can cost £500 per head to provide health insurance for 300 top employees, but only £125 per person to insure a workforce of 2,000 because the risk for the insurer is spread across a wider pool.'

(The *Guardian*, 8 February 1997)

Neo-marxists widen their analysis to encompass the role of culture and ideology within people's behaviours and beliefs. Antonio Gramsci focused on the ability of capitalist society to reproduce a dominant ideology which gained hegemony, and thereby determined the basis of relationships and actions within that society at any particular historical time. Within such a social model, it's possible for very different groups to form an alliance, using the dominant ideology as a vehicle to pursue their own individual agendas. Such an alliance could be said to have developed around the formation of the Welfare State in the immediate post-war period.

Friedson argues that the medical profession has established its monopoly over health care through the exclusion of 'lay' practitioners. By taking this action on exclusion, the medical profession has also taken control of the social definitions of health and illness.

Lesley Doyal (Doyal and Pennel 1979) examines the way in which health and illness operate within a social and economic context. Whilst not wishing to deny the general improvements in health care which have resulted from the establishment of the National Health Service, it's by no means a 'socialist health service'. Rather, the NHS is the result of a compromise between the demands of the economy and of the workers (echoing Gramsci's work on hegemony). There are still gross inequalities in the health experiences of patients, inequalities which are rooted in class, gender and ethnicity. Furthermore, it's these same groups, typically black, working-class women, who are at the bottom of the occupational structure in the health service.

The emphasis on curative medical interventions serves to mask the role of the capitalist system as the underlying source of socially-produced ill-health. McKinlay (1984) argues that health has become commodified, an item for sale like any other product. Vicente Navarro (1975) also develops this theme of consumerism. Capitalist societies are dependent on generating an ever-increasing demand for health-care services and medical goods. Illich (1990) argues that we have lost the ability to cope with the normal aches and pains of human existence and expect to have them all smoothed away with some form of medical treatment.

Both Friedson and Doyal argue that medicine serves as an instrument of social control, serving the interests of the ruling class rather than society as a whole. We've come to regard medicine as an entirely neutral activity; in reality it's a source of ideological domination.

Feminist theories

Whilst there are differences of emphasis, all feminist theory takes as its starting point the analysis of society based on patriarchal domination. There are at least two ways in which feminists have made a significant impact upon the study of health:

- Their perspective has resulted in the focus on particular aspects of the health field.
- They've had an impact upon the methodologies employed in those studies.

Sheila Rowbotham (1973) has argued that, hitherto, male intellectual domination had resulted in much of women's experiences being 'hidden from history'. As much of the material presented in this chapter indicates, this situation is changing.

Feminist theorists tend to be very open and explicit about their choice of research methodology, arguing against the much-vaunted value of objectivity in sociology. As we've frequently stressed, health is both a subjective and an objective experience. Its complexities can, arguably, be more comprehensively studied using the range of broadly interpretivist methodologies favoured by many feminists. It's no random coincidence that the study of health has gained considerable academic momentum simultaneously with the emergence of clear feminist perspectives in sociology. They've highlighted issues which are of particular concern to women and have begun to explore the subjective, experiential aspects of health. Overall, both in the choice of methodologies and in the overarching epistemologies, the intention is to empower women, to validate their lived experiences and to liberate them from the dominant patriarchal relations in society.

How do male readers in particular react to this apparent exercise of a female monopoly over the study of health?

Isn't health an important, personal, subjective experience for both men and women? Aren't men also victims of patriarchal relations in society?

We started this section by talking about grand theory. As the discussion has progressed we've seen how these overarching explanations of human action have been increasingly challenged as they fail to account satisfactorily for the complexities of life in contemporary society. Postmodernists argue that it's no longer possible to construct a 'grand theory'. Modern society is characterised by ever greater diversity, fragmentation, pluralism and shifting sources of conflict. More appropriate methodological approaches are to be found in Weber's concept of *verstehen* (understanding) and also in hermeneutics, which means 'interpretation'. Now the focus of theorising is shifting onto the individual and the social action engaged in by that individual.

Foucault's theory of the fabrication of the human body could be regarded as the very antithesis of grand theory because it focuses clearly on the individual, albeit whilst still locating that individual within wider political structures. Foucault argues that our current conceptualisation of the body is a product of the powerful social and political forces which accompanied the rise to pre-eminence of rational scientific activity. The emphasis on clinical observation, of measuring and recording, the methods of bio-medicine, generated particular conceptions of what was normal, healthy and sane. Foucault argues that the human body as we know it has been constructed through a 'clinical gaze'; this is only one way of thinking about the body and may be replaced in the future by another:

'For us the human body defines.. a space whose lines, volumes, surfaces and routes are laid down . . . by the anatomical atlas. But this order of the solid visible body is only one way – in all likelihood neither the first nor the most fundamental – in which one spatialises disease. There have been, and will be, other distributions of disease.'

(Foucault 1973)

Keep these ideas in mind as you now come to consider aspects of disability.

Disability

Until recently the study of disability has been very much on the periphery of mainstream academic work. It was conducted in isolation from other disciplines, such as education, health, or other aspects of social welfare.

This academic neglect mirrors the general marginalisation of people with disabilities. The standard response to disability was to put people in institutions, and those institutions were usually located well away from the rest of the community. Disabled people were physically separated from society and that society was largely ignorant of them. A. Miller and G. Gwynne, in their study of residential homes (1972), conclude that the committal of people to such institutions was tantamount to defining them as 'socially dead'.

The climate is changing. Within education, many special schools have been closed and whenever possible children with special educational needs are taught in mainstream schools. This ground swell is now making itself felt in new employment legislation, such as the Disability Discrimination Act 1995, and in the general emphasis on care in the community. What was once hidden, ignored and forgotten is now much more visible and demanding of our attention.

You're coming to a study of disability at an exciting time. You may find only scant coverage of disability in the established texts on the sociology of health. However, if you like a challenge and are prepared to look a bit harder to find the relevant materials, you'll be directly contributing to the development of knowledge and theory in this subject.

What is disability? What are the prevailing attitudes towards disability?

As you'll have come to expect already, definitions have to be our starting point. And, as you know from experience, definitions are never simple or clear-cut. We'll be considering at least three broad sources of definition, all of which merge and interact with each other. We've chosen to 'cut the cake' in this particular way as a means of grouping the relevant points. You may eventually find that a different set of categories is more useful. In particular, one of the debates centres around whether or not it's actually helpful to treat disability as an organising category within health. Many of the arguments and issues around disability have resonance with those applied to stratification elements, such as gender and ethnicity. The theoretical study of disability is still in its infancy and we're all in the position of having to wait and see how the debates develop. Don't be alarmed by this uncertainty, but rather use this as an opportunity to test the established theoretical paradigms in sociology (remember Kuhn?).

The three broad perspectives adopted for this discussion of disability are:

- the common-sense, everyday usage of the term, conventionally by those who do not regard themselves as disabled
- medical/official definitions
- sociological perspectives.

We've already seen how definitions and attitudes exist in a symbiotic relationship with each other. It's important therefore that woven into our consideration of disability will be an examination of the attitudes which underpin these definitions. The selection of particular definitions also has implications for the allocation of resources, a key element in all aspects of health-care provision.

One of the interesting factors in the disability 'equation' is the political influence currently being exerted by disabled people themselves (for example, through the work of the British Council of Organisations of Disabled People). Whereas in the past people with disabilities were the passive elements in the situation, objects of study, now they're contributing directly to those studies and debates. Their vociferous presence is generating a radical realignment of all the long-accepted definitions and boundaries. Their input should possibly constitute a fourth heading under definitions of disability and their perspectives are presented at the end of this section.

When we were looking earlier at general definitions of health, you were alerted to the importance of socio-linguistic theory. Linda Jones reminds us of the issues:

'Much of the construction of common sense categories and understanding proceeds through language. Language conveys the symbolic meanings and images which influence our understandings and responses.'

(Jones 1994: 334)

This process of constructing common-sense categories is crucial with regard to the current study of disability.

The everyday use of terminology

Start, as before, with a word association game. What springs immediately to mind from the word 'disability'? What kinds of disability? In what kind of situation? How old is that person? What gender? What ethnicity?

The likelihood is that your first thoughts were of someone with a visible physical disability, possibly in a wheelchair and that person was a white male.

Refer again to the earlier definitions of health and also go back to the thesaurus. Disability is listed alongside impotence and illness. To be disabled is to be weak and helpless. With disability comes disqualification, disentitlement, lack of control. Without exception, all of these words have negative connotations.

Our earlier examination of concepts of health indicated that, depending upon which model is adopted, everyone could be doomed. None of us is born perfect and as we progress through life we become even less so. Such a perspective might lead you to argue:

- that we're all dis-*abled* in some way. It's not helpful to set up opposing categories of ability and disability, categories which, moreover, probably carry with them the implicit notion that ability comes at the top of the pile and disability is at the bottom.

Alternatively, the World Health Organisation's emphasis on fitness for purpose and the relative qualities of health could lead you to argue:

- that we're all variously abled in some way.

We all need to be careful about the terminology which we use. There's a fundamental difference between describing someone as a disabled person, or as a person with a disability. By using the former label we are saying that their disability defines their whole being, whereas the latter presents them first and foremost as a person, who also happens to have a disability. What meaning do we intend?

The issue then becomes one of examining the processes whereby some kinds of ability or health become stigmatised and thereby excluded from mainstream society. Goffman's work on stigmatisation (1990) has been particularly influential. He highlights three main sources of stigma:

- 'abominations of the body'
- 'blemishes of individual character'
- 'race, nation and religion'.

The diagram below charts the process of exclusion from social interaction which results from this stigmatisation.

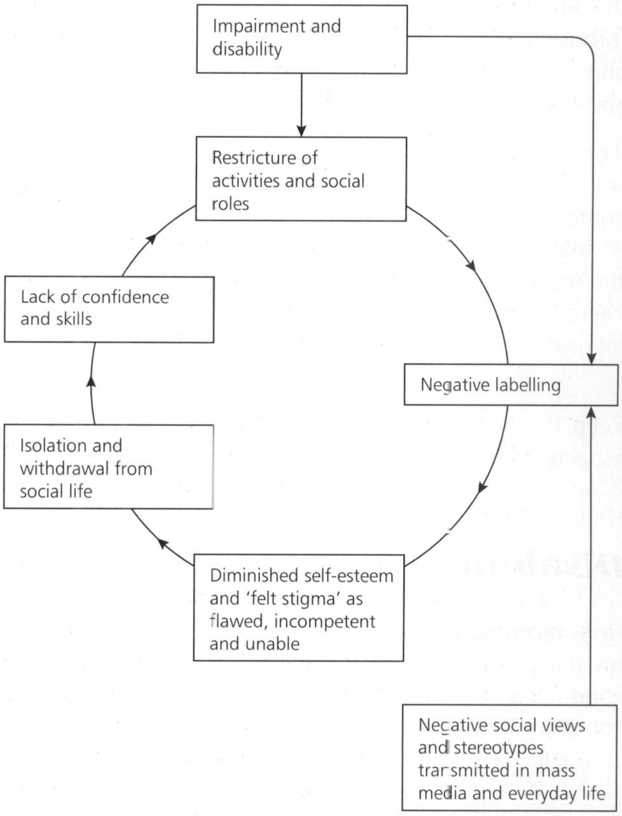

(Taylor and Field 1993: 128)

Not only is the disabled state a negative state, it's one which frequently attracts much pejorative language. A common form of abuse is to describe someone as a 'spaz' or 'spastic'. There are many derogatory terms which refer to intellectual functioning, for example, dumbo, drongo, nerd. Some people use them glibly, the current colloquialisms tripping off the tongue without any thought for the hurt they can cause.

Visual images are equally powerful. Here are two quotations which set out some of the issues. Firstly, from Colin Barnes:

'Stereotype assumptions about disabled people are based on superstition, myths and beliefs . . . They are inherent to our culture and persist partly because they are constantly reproduced through the communications media. We learn about disability through the media and in the same way that racist or sexist attitudes, whether implicit or explicit, are acquired through the "normal" learning process, so too are negative assumptions about disabled people.'

(Barnes 1992: 10)

Secondly, Darren Newbury:

'Photography, like language, provides a powerful means of defining individuals and social groups. Photographic images are intimately bound up with knowledge of the self in modern societies, providing a repertoire of self-images to which people aspire . . . The kind of exchange photography sets up between public and private meanings, particularly of the body, suggests that it can be understood as a pervasive and powerful means of socialisation. For people with disabilities, photography is especially important in that disability is most often conceptualised visually in terms of the body.'

(Newbury 1996: 349)

To explore further the issues of visual representation of disability, look at the work of David Hevey (1992) and Tom Shakespeare (1994). This particular aspect of disability study connects directly with Foucault's theory of the body.

It was a visual image that you were asked to conjure up in the initial word association exercise. Our heads are full of such images which we have accumulated from literature and the visual media.

Almost without exception, images of people with disabilities are used to emphasise particular negative or socially-unacceptable traits or behaviours. We're encouraged to fear people with physical deformities, viz. the Hunchback of Notre Dame, Quasimodo, and so on. No doubt you can think of other examples. The use of colour is, again, a common device. Snow White represents purity, the Wicked Witch is a stooped old woman, dressed in black, with a prominent hooked nose. Even being left-handed is often regarded as an abnormality which needs to be corrected. The Latin for 'left' is *sinister*, again indicating inherent attitudes to this particular ability.

Disability: An umbrella term

By now you'll have realised that the term 'disability' is applied to a wide variety of conditions. In fact, disability overlaps with three adjoining areas of analysis:

- chronic illness
- mental disorder
- ageing.

You'll also have realised that these various medical, psychological and intellectual conditions occur across the whole population. You may even be coming to the conclusion that disability is too broad a category to be of any real analytical use. It's undoubtedly a catch-all category and we need to disentangle the relevant perameters.

The two charts on page 332 are helpful, firstly, in identifying the types of disability and, secondly, in highlighting the age differentials in types of disability.

Variations in the ways in which disability is defined make it difficult to present firm statistics on its incidence. However, there's a general consensus that:

- there're over 6 million disabled adults in Great Britain – 3.5 million women and 2.5 million men
- there are about 360,000 disabled children, of whom there are more boys than girls.

The table 'Three patterns of physical disability' further illustrates the relationship between types of disability, causation and age.

Three patterns of physical disability

Type of onset	Age at onset	Typical conditions
At birth or infancy	0–5	Cystic fibrosis Spina bifida Down's syndrome
Sudden and unexpected	Teenage and young adult	Spinal cord injury
	Middle age	Coronary heart attack
	Old age	Stroke
Slow and gradually worsening	Middle and old age	Arthritis Respiratory diseases Parkinson's disease

(Adapted from Taylor and Field 1993: 125)

The estimated prevalence of disability, by type of disability, among adults in Great Britain

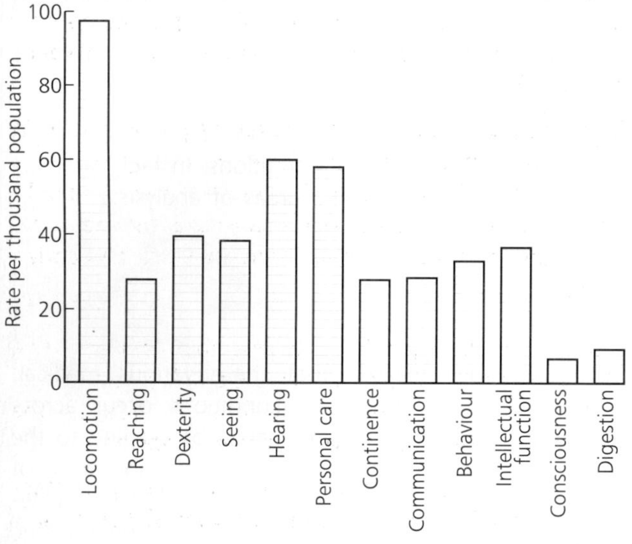

The estimated prevalence of disability, by type of disability, among children in Great Britain

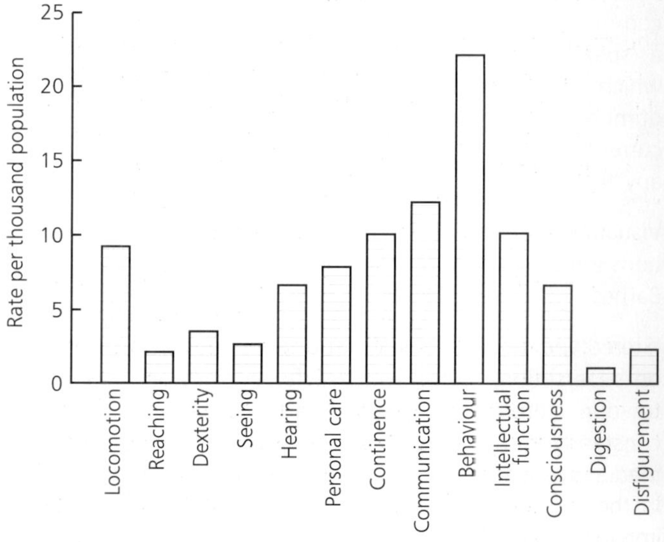

(Both graphs: Taylor and Field 1993: 119, based on data from Martin *et al.* 1988 and from Bone and Meltzer 1989)

It's very difficult to come up with water-tight generalisations about disability. However, we can highlight some broad features.

Age

Levels of chronic illness and disability increase with age. In adults the most common forms of disability are linked to mobility, typically arthritis, followed by disabilities in sight, hearing and personal care. With children, the most prevalent form of disability identified is behavioural, then speech, movement and intellectual functioning.

You might wonder why there's this difference in the incidence of behaviour-based disability between children and adults. M. Bone and H. Meltzer suggest that:

'it is likely that the very different questions asked about behaviour in children and adults are responsible for at least part of the difference.'

(Bone and Meltzer 1989: 24)

(Remember the earlier comments about the social production of health statistics.)

Social class and income

There's a strong correlation between social class and the incidence of both chronic illness and disability. Blaxter (1976) tells us that not only are people from lower social classes more likely to experience chronic illness and disability as a result of their lifestyle, occupation, housing conditions, and so on, they also have less access to the necessary support systems which could alleviate their condition.

Irrespective of social class, disability tends to bring with it a decline in income, partly as a result of reduced earning power and also because of the increased living costs which people with disabilities have to bear. Barnes makes this point very succinctly:

'Britain's six and a quarter million disabled people experience a lifestyle characterised by poverty and dependence.'

(Barnes 1992: 9)

For further information on the financial circumstances of adults with disabilities, see, for example, the work of Martin and White (1988).

Gender

Women are likely to have a double experience of disability and chronic illness. Firstly, they typically fulfil the role of unpaid carer for other family members. Secondly, since they tend to live longer than men, they're more likely to become either chronically ill or disabled themselves in later life.

Ethnicity

The impact of ethnicity is manifest in a number of different ways. In the bio-medical sphere, there's the link between 'race' and the incidence of particular medical conditions; for example, sickle cell disease within the African–Caribbean population. At a cultural level, there's the question of diet and health; for example, the high incidence of coronary heart disease in the Asian communities which is often attributed to their high-fat diet.

The minority ethnic communities have their own ways of defining and responding to chronic illness and disability. You need to be aware that there's a complex relationship between these deep-rooted cultural traditions and their dealings with the wider, essentially white, communities in which they're located.

The medical model and official responses

The medical, or bio-medical, model of health conceptualises the body as a machine in which all the parts function together in order to ensure health. If part of this machine malfunctions, it's the job of the clinician to intervene, treat and 'fix' it. Such a model carries with it very clear parameters of normality, and any deviations from these norms are regarded as pathological.

The emergence of such a conceptualisation of the human form and its functioning occurred simultaneously with the development of capitalism and its emphasis on individual enterprise and achievement. Within such a system, there's no room for those who cannot perform and meet the economic targets. Disability becomes synonymous with dependency, both of which, if unchecked, will be an unacceptable burden, in capitalist terms, on the economically active.

These two, rather bald, paragraphs contain within them the essence of 'western' attitudes and responses to disability that have developed since the Industrial Revolution. The argument is that bio-medicine and capitalism are mutually sympathetic and supportive. Wherever possible, the disability should be fixed or at least eased, which will presumably ensure a better quality of life for the individual and certainly enable her or him to be more economically productive. Until very recently, the policy was to put people with severe disabilities in institutions, ostensibly as the means of providing the specialist care which they required, but arguably also as the means whereby those people who didn't conform to prescribed standards of social functioning could best be dealt with. During the nineteenth and early twentieth centuries those institutions were the workhouses, deliberately providing only the bare minimum of care and comfort in order to discourage poor people from presuming that the state would make provision for them.

Whilst the workhouses have gone, it seems that their psychological legacy lingers, both in the mind of the general public and also for those who formulate public welfare policy. Through the media we are beset by a continuous campaign against those who apparently scrounge on welfare, we are urged to inform on our neighbours, and doctors are castigated for classifying too many people as 'chronic sick' when really they're work-shy. This mix of attitudes towards poverty, sickness and disability, the extent to which individuals have brought their misfortune upon themselves and the extent to which they are in some way a burden or supernumary to the rest of society, this mix is very complex and runs very deep in our collective psyche.

Reference has already been made to the current statutory position with regard to the payment of welfare benefits to the long-term sick and disabled (changes to the Disability Living Allowance made in 1992). This legislation gives us one official definition of disability and the attitudes which underpin it. Hahn expresses possibly the most extreme position with regard to the significance of policy formation:

'Fundamentally, disability is defined by public policy. In other words, disability is whatever policy says it is . . . The fact that disability is basically determined by public policy, moreover, seems to demonstrate the need for careful investigations of definitions that are embedded in existing policies.'

(Hahn 1985: 294)

In December 1996 the Disability Discrimination Act came into force and is intended to increase employment opportunities for people with disabilities. It includes the following guidance on how to define disability:

'a physical or mental impairment which has a substantial and long-term adverse effect on your ability to carry out normal day to day activities.'

At the time of writing the Act has not been tested in the courts and so we can only speculate about the issues which will arise as employers and potential employees begin to implement it.

There's a significant area of debate around the whole question of how to change attitudes and behaviour and the extent to which legislation leads or follows in this process. There are clear parallels with the introduction of equal opportunities and anti-racist legislation. In her essay on young people and education, Deborah Cooper explores some of the issues surrounding the introduction of new legislation:

'Legislation is a most powerful way of affecting people's lives in practice because it can open the door to services and close the door to undesirable activity.'

(Cooper 1996, in Hales 1996: 135)

Cooper's essay is a useful source of detailed information about the legislation passed since 1944 which affects the education of people with disabilities. The essay by Ken Davis in the same collection gives an overview of legislation on disability in both Britain and elsewhere in the world.

A sociological perspective

In the late 1960s, the Office of Population Censuses and Surveys (OPCS) conducted a national survey on the incidence of disability (Harris 1971). The survey was underpinned by a threefold classification of disability which has had a significant influence on the thrust of much subsequent work on disability. Certainly within official and medical circles the notions of impairment, disability and handicap have gained general acceptance. The following chart sets out in some detail the way in which these three categories are used to organise the various aspects of disability.

Impairment	*Disability*	*Handicap*
language	speaking	
hearing	listening	orientation
vision	seeing	
skeletal	dressing, feeding	physical independence
	walking	mobility
psychological	behaviour	social integration
disfigurement		social integration

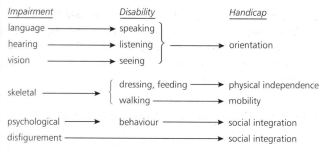

(Taylor and Field 1993: 117, based on data from Martin *et al.* 1988)

The relationship between impairment, disability and handicap

This approach to the study of, and also the provision of resources for, disability is increasingly being criticised. The original OPCS survey was commissioned because the government wanted to provide more services for people with disabilities. Vic Finkelstein (1980) argues that this approach to disability has focused on the individual as the cause and the source of disability. It leads to the conceptualisation of disability as a 'personal tragedy' (Oliver 1993: 50) and emphasises the dependency of disabled people upon society as a whole.

Mike Oliver (1993: 64) proposes three ways of defining disability:

- as an individual problem
- as a social construction
- as a social creation.

The individualisation of disability has already been referred to. A social constructionist view of disability can also be regarded as an interpretivist approach. Here the emphasis lies with the social processes, the attitudes behind the social definitions of disability, with the inherent implication that if the attitudes of able-bodied people are changed then the problems of disability will disappear.

A. Borsay (1986) argues for a structural account of disability; disability is 'a problem created by the institutions, organisations and processes which constitute society in its totality' (cited in Oliver 1993: 65). Certainly it's an analysis at this level which disabled people themselves are increasingly vocal in advocating. This is Ken Davies' view: 'our disability is caused not by the state of our bodies, but by the state of our society' (1996: 124).

It's impossible, in a short section, to do justice to the wide range of issues and conditions which are subsumed under the heading of disability and disability studies. Oliver (1993) argues for a working alliance between academic researchers and disabled people . . . watch this space!

QUESTIONS

1 Notwithstanding the almost complete omission of disability from established sociological perspectives on health, what do they have to say that's of relevance to the study of disability?

2 Labelling theory is strongly associated with theories on crime and deviance. How useful is it as a means of understanding responses to disability?

Mental health

There are considerable areas of overlap between the study of disability and of mental disorder. Firstly, many of the theoretical issues and perspectives are equally applicable in either area. Secondly, there's substantial overlap in the kinds of condition under consideration.

Defining mental disorder

It's possible to identify three broad kinds of mental disorder:

- that which is physiological, biological, for example, Down's syndrome or Alzheimer's disease. You might prefer to call these kinds of condition mental disability, although that's also a term fraught with problems. It's interesting to note that, whilst these forms of mental disorder do have an organic basis and therefore would seem to fit nicely within the bio-medical model of health, they're actually the least amenable to medical treatment
- behavioural problems, such as eating disorders or solvent abuse. Here you have to consider whether the behavioural problem identified, for example, glue sniffing, is symptomatic of an underlying problem or whether the behaviour causes the deeper problems. To continue with the example of glue sniffing: why do some kids sniff glue in the first place? Having done so, what physiological damage does it then cause which may result in more behavioural problems?
- specific mental disorders, such as depression or schizophrenia. Here again, the same kind of issues are debated. Is schizophrenia a disease or a behavioural problem?

The medical study of mental disorder and disability is beyond our brief as sociologists and we won't even pretend to understand in detail the complex functioning of the brain. However, as sociologists, you do need to know which are the relevant questions to ask. This is where sociological theory will provide you with the necessary framework of analysis.

The causes and treatment of mental disorder and mental disability

We've identified three broad types of mental disorder and inevitably we want to know what causes these conditions. We want to know about causes, firstly, so that we can perhaps offer some kind of treatment; secondly, so that we might be able to prevent such conditions either recurring in that individual or developing for the first time in someone else. This is the bio-medical model of health and treatment.

Whilst we've already indicated that those conditions which have the clearest organic causes are currently those which we're least able to treat medically, it's possible to argue that this failing will be remedied in time. For example, as we learn more about genetic engineering, we may be able to eradicate Down's syndrome. We do, of course, already have one way of treating this condition. Women who are deemed to be at risk of having a Down's baby are offered an amniocentesis test and then a termination, if the test is positive.

This particular example immediately takes us into non-medical areas. You'll be very aware of the powerful moral arguments which are put forward by the anti-abortion lobby. Whilst the medical profession seems to be urging more and more antenatal testing, many women feel that the knowledge thus gained about their pregnancy creates impossible moral dilemmas for them. We return to moral issues and the use of medical technology in a later section.

To continue with the theme of identifying the causes of mental disorder and thereby being able to effect some treatment, many forms of mental disorder have been treated with a wide range of medical interventions such as drugs, surgery and ECT (electro-convulsive therapy). Critics of these methods argue that we don't know enough about the functioning of the brain to use these safely. At best their use is ineffective, and at worst they can cause untold damage.

Many forms of mental disorder are believed to be the result of experiences in either early childhood or adolescence:

- Psycho-analytical theory focuses on the formative experiences of the very young child and particularly on relationship with parents. Psycho-analytical therapy aims to provide the patient with insights into her or his childhood and thereby begin to resolve the present problems.
- Cognitive psychology focuses on the importance of developmental stages. If something occurs to prevent the child from experiencing each of these developmental stages, then psychological problems may emerge in adult life. Cognitive therapy aims to challenge the patient's distorted behaviour patterns, to remedy the gaps in the childhood learning sequence and to establish more rational forms of behaviour.
- Experiences in later childhood, for example where conflict between parents may put the child under enormous pressure, are often cited as a cause of schizophrenia. Treatment of the individual patient will often also involve other members of the family.

These approaches to the various forms of mental disorder and the links made between causes and treatment are all based within conventional, medical definitions of medical illness. All focus on the mind or the body of the individual and attempt to 'put it right'. It's also very substantially grounded in Parsons' work on functional and dysfunctional families.

The social responses to mental disorder and disability

We focus on causes in order to instigate treatment. We also link cause with effect, and it's in this area that we can learn more about the particular significance of mental disorder from a societal point of view. We're back to definitions and the drawing of boundaries. T.J. Scheff (1966) argues that being mentally ill isn't a disease but a label applied to people who exhibit a wide range of behaviours. The key factor in being so labelled lies in the reactions of others to that behaviour.

We need to look carefully at the processes whereby someone is categorised as being mentally ill. What kinds of behaviour are deemed to be normal, socially acceptable, whilst others are not? What levels of intellectual functioning are necessary to enable the individual to be regarded as a fully competent member of society? What sorts of people typically fall into these categories?

When we look at a range of societies, and when we look back over time, we can clearly see that there are no simple or uniform answers to these questions. In the past we tolerated and accommodated 'the village idiot'. If someone was a bit eccentric or behaved unpredictably, we knew to give them a wide berth, but nothing more. Now, we have to intervene and treat everyone, seemingly to make them conform to a very specific model of normality. The example of antenatal screening is most apposite. Everyone hopes to give birth to a 'normal' (whatever that means), healthy baby, but in the past the actual outcome was left far more to fate. Many miscarriages in the early stages of pregnancy are caused by the body naturally rejecting an imperfect foetus. We now work very much harder to prevent miscarriages and perhaps are interfering too much with nature. (Remember the arguments about iatrogenic medicine.) Just what are the issues with regard to the birth of a less-than-perfect baby? Is the response motivated by concern for the life which the baby itself will be able to lead, or does it reflect the rejection of that baby by society?

Sociological theory

Labelling theory gained momentum from Edwin Lemert's (1967) distinction between primary and secondary deviance. By primary deviance he meant any initial 'deviant' behaviour, however generated; secondary deviance refers to what happens next, the ways in which the 'deviant' individual is treated by the wider society and the further behaviour which she or he then engages in. Howard Becker took the argument a stage further:

'Social groups create deviance by making the rules whose infraction constitutes deviance and by applying those rules to particular persons and labelling them as outsiders . . . Deviant behaviour is behaviour that people so label.'

(Becker 1963)

Just as beauty is in the eye of the beholder, so is deviance.

When this principle is applied to defining mental illness we can see the key role played by society, or, more to the point, by the medical professionals who have the power to create and perpetuate particular definitions. Labelling theory highlights issues of power, in this case of the medical professionals, counterposed by the powerlessness of the individual patient. This power has frequently been used and abused to impose political and social correctness. The Russian novelist, Alexander Solzhenitsyn, had personal experience of this in the mid-1950s when it was commonplace for political dissidents to be hospitalised and treated for non-existent illnesses. In the UK, there was recently a case of a woman who, because she refused to have a caesarian birth, was sectioned under the Mental Health Act and then forced to have her baby delivered surgically.

Once the label has been applied it tends to stick. Goffman (1990) highlights the way in which this label is used to devalue the person to whom it's applied. There's enormous stigma attached to 'mental illness', especially in 'western' society. This stigma is likely to result in the person continuing to be confined within this category even when it's no longer appropriate. It may also inhibit people from seeking the help they need because they're fearful of the long-term consequences. Some employers are often very wary of taking on anyone with a history of mental disorder, just as they're reluctant to employ someone who has a criminal record.

Criminality, mental disorder and other forms of deviance are often thrown into the same melting pot. We have Special Hospitals, such as Rampton and Broadmoor, where the criminally insane are sent by the courts. This is regarded by some as a more humane way of dealing with those who cannnot be held responsible for their criminal actions. In applying the label of mental disorder to certain kinds of deviant behaviour, society can be said to be medicalising its response to eccentricity.

The work of Durkheim (1964, first published in 1893) gives us two major inputs to the debate on mental illness. Firstly, his concept of anomie. Anomie is defined as a state of normlessness and breakdown which occurs most commonly during times of rapid social change. Traditional societies are held together by mechanical solidarity. Individuals are supported and protected by the family and strong community structures. When those forms of social support are disrupted, the individual is cast adrift. This shifts the 'blame' for deviant behaviour away from the individual and locates its cause more centrally within particular kinds of social structure and organisation.

This then leads into Durkheim's work on suicide (1968, first published in 1897). The act of commiting suicide was described by Durkheim as both the most intensely personal of deeds and yet simultaneously a social fact. Suicide as an individual action represents the failure of social solidarity and the absence of effective social bonds. In making this link Durkheim is exploring one of the most fundamental issues which pervades all sociological theory, namely, the interrelationship of the individual with the wider society.

CRIT THINK CRIT THINK CRIT THINK CRIT THINK CRIT THINK CRIT THINK

SUICIDE: A SOCIAL FACT?

A major area of criticism levelled at Durkheim's work on suicide highlights the difficulty of defining a death as suicide and of compiling reliable statistics. One of the *Health of the Nation* targets is to reduce rates of suicide:

'◆ to reduce the overall suicide rate by at least 15% by the year 2000 (Baseline 1990)

◆ to reduce the suicide rate of severely mentally ill people by at least 33% by the year 2000 (Baseline 1990).'

(Department of Health 1992)

How likely is it that this target will be achieved? Develop a critique of this particular health target.

Here are some questions to help you structure your work:

- *How do you define suicide?*
- *What are the social causes of suicide?*
- *How can you research and quantify suicide?*
- *What are the most appropriate ways to reduce suicide?*
- *(Why) should we reduce suicide?*

CRIT THINK CRIT THINK CRIT THINK CRIT THINK CRIT THINK CRIT

The thrust of Durkheim's work on anomie and suicide is very much towards the maintenance of social order, of the value of preserving the *status quo*. In contrast, his work on deviance (1895) takes him into the area of social change. He argues that every society needs deviance, at least the kind of deviance that represents a challenge to the established order; the deviance which poses awkward questions and will not conform. The power of the deviants' alternative vision of the social world provides the impetus to move on. Under the apartheid regime in South Africa, Nelson Mandela was incarcerated for years in prison on Robin Island. He was released in 1990 and has subsequently become established as one of the most respected statesmen on the world stage. His rapid transformation from deviant criminal to political demi-god provides us with the most remarkable illustration of Durkheim's thesis.

The patterning of mental disorder

As with all the other aspects of health which we have examined, there are patterns to the incidence of mental disorder and disability.

Age

The incidence of Alzheimer's disease is strongly correlated with advancing years. Whilst Alzheimer's disease does have an organic basis, it's often mistakenly applied to old people who are mentally confused. This confusion may be due to a variety of causes other than Alzheimer's. For example, the old person may be house-bound and lack the frequent social contacts which would keep her or him mentally alert. They may be taking medication for other conditions which has the side-effect of impairing her or his mental functioning. If they're put into some form of residential accommodation with others in a similarly confused state they are likely to slip quickly into the kind of behaviour which will confirm their classification as 'senile'.

Gender

At a superficial level of analysis, the statistics suggest that women are more prone to mental disorder than men. But that statement begs a lot of questions. Are women really more susceptible to mental disorder?

Do cultural definitions of maleness and femaleness affect the extent to which women are prepared to seek professional help for their mental state? Women are expected to be emotionally expressive, whereas men are expected to be strong and unemotional. The other side of the coin is the way in which the medical profession responds to male and female patients. Not only are women more likely to consult a doctor about a mental health problem, they're also more likely to be classified by the doctor as mentally disordered. There's a huge area of controversy around the medical responses to 'women's problems': premenstrual tension, postnatal depression, the menopause.

Do men and women respond differently to the same condition? It's culturally more acceptable for men to go to the pub and drown their sorrows in a few pints, whereas if a woman behaved in the same way a lot of alarm bells would start to ring. Graham (1984) argues that some working-class women with young children smoke cigarettes as a coping mechanism.

Ethnicity

Overall the incidence of mental illness among African–Caribbeans and among some Asian groups is higher than for the general population. The explanation for these patterns is complex and not entirely reliable:

- In part, causes for the incidence of mental disorder among minority ethnic groups are to be found in their experiences of migration and the racism and discrimination which they encounter in the UK.
- To some extent the various ethnic groups have different cultural definitions of acceptable and appropriate behaviours. When these do not conform to 'western' medical ideals, they may be classified as deviant or as symptoms of mental disorder.
- The overall picture is further complicated by the reluctance of many minority ethnic groups to 'go public' about a particular condition. There's a strong tradition of dealing with behavioural problems within the family, and this introversion is likely to be compounded by barriers of language and mistrust.

Social class

The incidence of diagnosed mental disorders is highest among the lower social classes and lowest among the upper classes. There's an argument that poor health causes downward social mobility (a variation on the survival of the fittest theme), but it's more likely that this pattern reflects the greater material hardships experienced by people in the lower classes. There are also class-based differences in the kinds of treatment given to people who are mentally ill. Someone from a working-class background is most likely to receive hospital-based treatment, whereas someone from a middle-class or upper-class background is much more likely to remain at home and have some form of psychotherapy.

Whilst the dimensions of the patterning of mental disorder have been presented as separate categories, in reality there's likely to be a pattern of multiple disadvantage.

The provision of care

In the past, people who experienced a mental disorder or who were disabled were invariably put into some kind of institution. The rationale for this move was to ensure that the patient received the appropriate specialist care. There's undoubtedly justification for this action in some cases, but there were certainly many other instances when people were institutionalised for social rather than medical reasons. The recourse to institutionalisation is a convenient way of removing from sight people who make us feel uncomfortable or whose behaviour we cannot cope with.

This exclusion of people from the mainstream of society means that we become ignorant about their condition and this ignorance compounds our fears and apprehensions.

The National Health and Community Care Act 1990 has heralded a major change in the provision of care for people who experience mental disorders. Many of the large hospitals have been closed and the emphasis now is on the provision of care in the community. This can and does mean many different things. Care in the community can mean that:

- care is provided in smaller units located within the community (rather than geographically isolated, as was frequently the case in the past)
- care is provided by the community, most typically by families and primary care facilities
- the individual is able to be reintegrated into the community.

There are problems associated with all three options:

- Applications to open local care units frequently meet with objections from local residents. They argue that they may be put at risk if people who are 'mentally ill' are housed within their community. They argue that property values will fall. The current terminology for such reactions is NIMBYism – not in my back yard. The fear and the ignorance about mental disorders which was fostered by the confinement of 'mentally-ill' people in large institutions will take a long time to counteract.
- In part, the shift towards care in the community was part of a cost-cutting exercise within the NHS. Resources which previously had supported the large hospitals were not redirected into the community. In practice, care in the community often means care by the family and, more specifically, care by the woman of the family.
- There are innumerable stories of people being discharged from mental hospitals and being left to fend for themselves, sometimes with tragic consequences. Significant numbers of people now sleeping rough on our streets have been discharged from mental hospitals, are unable to find either work or accommodation, and rapidly drift into situations which are likely to lead to a recurrence of their original problems.

QUESTION

To what extent is the medicalisation of mental illness a response prompted by the desire to provide the most appropriate form of care for the individual, or does it reflect the demands of society to be protected from those who are regarded as being mentally ill or deviant?

Health chances

Any analysis of health chances presumes that we can establish cause and effect in human behaviour. It presumes that we know how to achieve particular health outcomes. (Much official-speak these days is couched in terms of outcomes and outputs.) In essence, this is the bio-medical model of health in operation. By now you'll be sufficiently experienced in the analysis of health to respond with a degree of scepticism; would that it were so simple.

One of the general questions posed at the beginning of this chapter was: Where does the responsibility for health lie? In this section we're tackling that question head on. How much control does anyone have over their health? Health education programmes are aimed directly at the individual and presume that behaviour can be changed for the better. In our current political climate the question has acquired an even sharper relevance. One of the underpinning tenets of the Welfare State has been its promise to provide for the needs of all. That's proving to be a very expensive promise and one which is increasingly being qualified by the argument that some people, because of their alleged irresponsible behaviour, might no longer be automatically eligible for such benefits. For example, we read reports of smokers being denied expensive heart surgery. It could be argued that a heavy smoker is less able to withstand the rigours of a major operation and should not therefore be exposed to such a high level of risk. Equally it could be argued that the smoker has caused their own fate and should not expect society to pay the bill. A complex situation with no simple answer. The issue of smoking is dealt with in more detail later.

The diagram below succinctly presents a wide range of factors which all bear upon health chances.

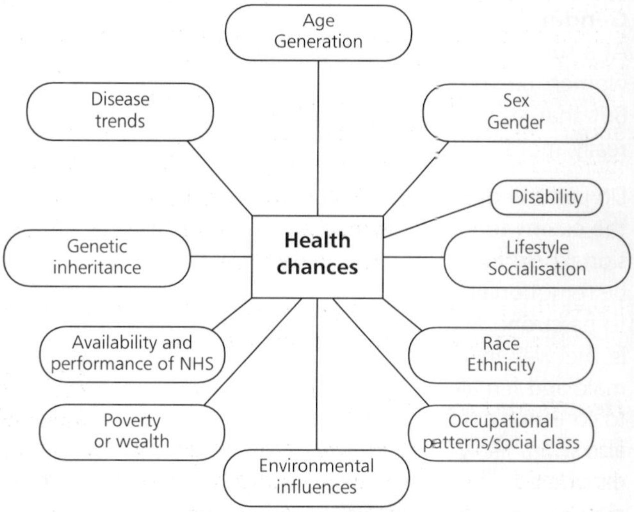

(Jones 1994: 18)

The diagram illustrates just how many factors there are to be considered. We're going to organise these under three broad headings:

- structured inequalities
- lifestyle
- the wider environment.

As with every other aspect of health, the boundaries between these headings aren't neatly replicated in real situations.

What do each of these categories mean?

Structured inequalities

By structured inequalities we mean those elements of social life which are built into the very fabric of the social structure, for example, class, gender, ethnicity, age and disability. The use of the word 'structure' leads us to believe that these are solid, tangible factors, and indeed that's certainly the case with ethnicity, gender and age. We've absolutely no control over when we're born and so we've no control over our age. Day by day we get older. Similarly, for gender and ethnicity; that's what we are and that's what we're stuck with. Some of these defining, structural elements, such as social class or disability, are extremely fluid. We've seen how the disability lobby argues very strongly that the 'problem' with disability lies within the structure of society, not with the individual people who have disabilities.

There's a strong social dimension with many of these structural inequalities, and that's what makes them so hard to get to grips with. The social part relates to the way in which society responds to these various factors. Why does one's skin colour or gender have such a profound impact on the way in which we experience life? We know that the structural factors listed have an impact on all aspects of our lives, in education, in employment opportunities, and not just in health. This is what makes them structural. They're not directly related to health, to education or to employment and yet they're consistently identified as determining elements in the overall equation. Remember also that we started with a question about responsibility. If structural inequalities have a marked effect on health chances, where does the responsibility for these lie? What kind of action needs to be taken in order to remedy health inequalities which are rooted in these structural inequalities?

In addition, we need to be aware that many of these factors combine to produce multiple disadvantage.

Health and social class

Post-war British society was permeated by a euphoric expectation that we were moving towards a more classless society. Greater economic prosperity and the cumulative effects of the Welfare State would result in the eradication of poverty. Harold Macmillan's assertion in the 1950s that we'd 'never had it so good', followed by the heady optimism of the 'Swinging Sixties', then gave way in the seventies to oil crises, rising unemployment and the rediscovery of poverty. In the late 1970s, Sir Douglas Black chaired a working party to examine inequalities in health and to make policy recommendations.

The Black Report was published in early 1980 and highlighted a number of measures of health inequality. Most significant was the strong correlation between occupational class and the incidence of disease. As an extreme example, the death rate for adult male unskilled workers was twice that for adult male professional workers. Other key contributory factors identified were those of ethnicity, gender, locality and type of household.

A second major survey, carried out by Margaret Whitehead and published as *The Health Divide* in 1987, confirmed the findings of the Black Report and investigated further differences in health chances and access to health care. Both of these studies produced evidence which seemed to be saying that the Welfare State was 'failing'. Whilst there had been a general improvement in the health of the population as a whole, the health of the lower occupational groups had actually deteriorated. Far from eradicating differences, the gap seemed to be widening.

In all of this we have ample illustration of the complexities of social class and its wide ramifications. Social class correlates with occupation, with poverty and with poor health. Throughout the 1980s researchers continued to investigate the many dimensions of health status and inequalities, developing more sophisticated social indicators and exploring the link between poverty or deprivation, however defined, and poor health.

Health and ethnicity

The Black Report (1980) acknowledged that black and minority ethnic groups experienced economic and social disadvantage. However, because official statistics did not specifically record data based on ethnic origin, it was very difficult to chart the impact of these disadvantages. In August 1997 the Policy Studies Institute published what it claims is the most comprehensive health survey ever conducted amongst the UK's ethnic minorities (Nazroo 1997). (There has been research on various aspects of health and ethnicity, but you have to ask why it's taken so long to respond to the omissions first highlighted in the Black Report.)

The overriding message in the Policy Studies Institute report is that members of some minority ethnic groups are 50 per cent more likely to suffer ill-health than the white majority. However, this huge disparity in health outcomes is the result of poverty, not innate biological differences.

The chart below indicates the differing incidence of two major killer diseases for six minority ethnic groups and for white people.

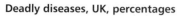

Deadly diseases, UK, percentages

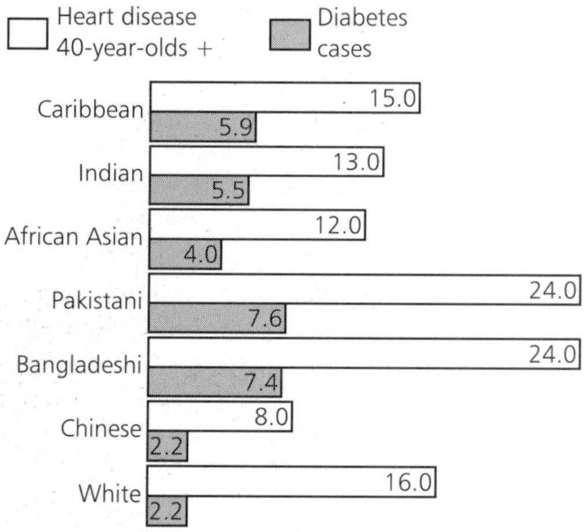

(The *Guardian*, 5 August 1997, using data from the Policy Studies Institute 1997)

The report found that Pakistani and Bangladeshi peoples were 50 per cent more likely to suffer ill-health than whites, and Caribbeans 30 per cent. Pakistanis and Bangladeshis had the highest risk of heart disease and diabetes, while people of African–Caribbean origin had the highest rates of hypertension and respiratory problems.

The report's author, James Nazroo gave his explanation for these trends:

'Poor health is associated with poverty. Some ethnic minority groups are among the poorest people in Britain and they have the worst health. They also appear to be receiving poorer quality health care than whites.

The differences in health were the result of economic status not biological factors. In addition, ethnic minority patients were not getting a good deal from the health service. For example, a significant number of south Asians and Chinese in the survey had seen doctors but had not understood the language that was being used.'

(The *Guardian*, 5 August 1997?)

Access to health care is a long-standing issue for ethnic minority groups. Language is an obvious barrier. Other barriers, based on prejudice and discrimination, are much harder to identify and overcome.

A three-year American study of 700 patients by Columbia University's School of Public Health (reported in the *Guardian*, 7 August 1997) found that whites were far more likely than people of colour to have access to the medicines that have revolutionised AIDS treatment. Their results showed that 33 per cent of whites said they had used a cocktail of drugs including those now recommended in federal guidelines. Only 12 per cent of black patients and 19 per cent of Latinos reported using them.

To give you some idea of the disparity of take-up, one in five Americans infected with HIV lives in New York, and two-thirds of them are people of colour.

Health and geography

The diagram on page 338 contains no specific mention of geography. We know that health-care resources are not uniformly distributed across the UK. We also know that the incidence of some diseases is geographically patterned, although the reasons for this are not yet fully understood. The two maps show the distribution of two forms of cancer.

Over the past 30 years, northerners have been less likely to die from cancers of the breast, ovary, brain, skin and non-Hodgkin's lymphoma. Southerners are less prone to cancers of the mouth, pharynx, stomach, rectum, cervix and kidney.

In seeking to find some explanation for these variations, we need to draw upon a combination of causal factors; for example, the impact of social and cultural dietary practices, environmental pollution, access to specialist hospital facilities. How can you allocate responsibility here?

In August 1997 the Joseph Rowntree Foundation published the results of research conducted by geographer, Dr David Dorling (Dorling 1997). It seems likely that his research will have an impact on a par with that of the Black Report in the 1980s. The report is entitled 'Death in Britain: How local mortality rates have changed: 1950s to 1990s'. A strong correlation was found between premature mortality and the most economically disadvantaged districts, measured by poverty indicators in the Census. The figures are based on death rates between 1990 and 1992 and present information on death rates for infants, adolescents and adults by sex throughout England, Scotland and Wales. Here are some of the findings:

- Glasgow residents were 66 per cent more likely to die prematurely than people living in rural Dorset, and 31 per cent more likely than those living in Bristol.
- A baby girl born in Leeds is more than twice as likely to die in the first year of life than an infant girl growing up in a town in Dorset.
- Death rates for baby boys in Blackburn, Halifax and Preston are almost double the national average.
- Eight times as many boys aged one to four died in Manchester between 1990 and 1992 as died in rural Gloucestershire.
- Early childhood mortality rates for boys in Dewsbury, Bethnal Green, Manchester and St Helens have doubled since 1981.
- There's been an increase in deaths among pre-school girls in Birkenhead, Manchester and the Isle of Wight.

Melanoma of the skin, Women, England

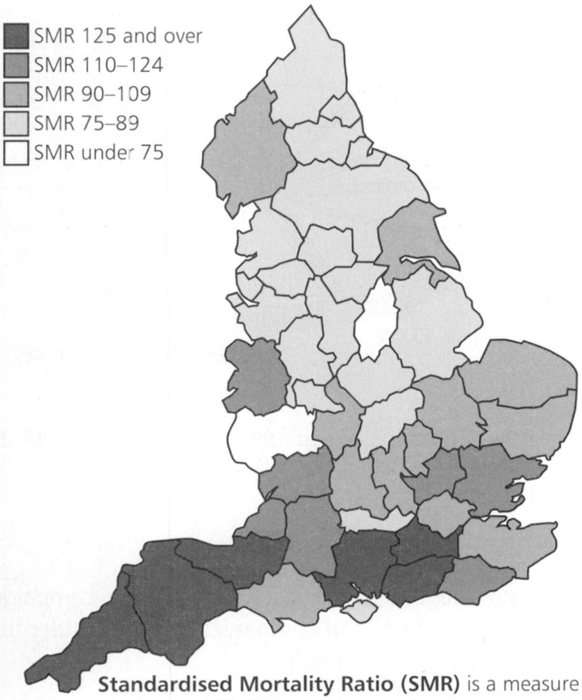

Standardised Mortality Ratio (SMR) is a measure of deaths per 100,000 in the population in a year: 100 is t average. Anything above indicates a higher than norma risk; lower rates indicate a reduced risk.

Cancer of the testis, England

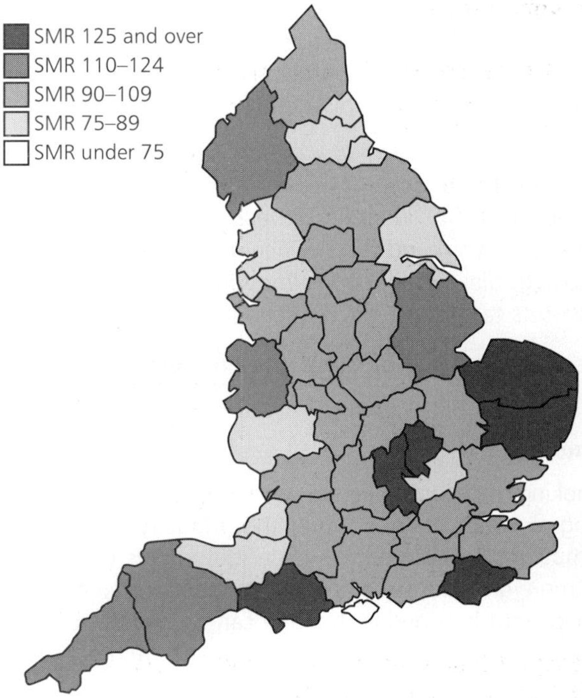

(The *Guardian*, 12 December 1995)

In commenting on the report's findings, Dorling said:

'This study does not seek to speculate on the reasons why divisions between different parts of the country have become so pronounced. However, it does seem that the trend has happened too quickly to be explained simply by a changing distribution of wealth, changing causes of death, or as a reflection of past health inequalities. There have to be other explanations. Income inequality is certainly part of it, as is long-term unemployment, but the factors need further investigation.'

(The *Guardian,* 11 August 1997)

Overall, this report seems to indicate that health inequality is at its worst for at least 50 years. Both the Black Report and the Whitehead survey were seized upon as evidence that the Welfare State was failing. A decade on and the same cry is going up. It's too soon to know what the longer term effect of this latest report will be. Some of the initial reactions seem to have fallen into two camps:

- those who argue that the NHS and the Welfare State promised equality of access, not equality of outcome
- critics of the recent changes in the whole structure of welfare provision, who point to the need to tackle health from a much more broadly-based perspective, targeting unemployment, bad housing, environmental pollution, and the like.

OVER TO YOU

A new Labour Government was elected in May 1997. Monitor the development of this debate on health outcomes and the overall structure of welfare provision.

Lifestyle

23:20

Lifestyle covers a wide variety of factors; you could call them a 'multitude of sins'. It's things like the food we eat, whether and how much we smoke and drink, how we spend our leisure time, how much stress we're under. This is the area of health-related behaviour which attracts the most attention from the personal responsibility lobby. But even here, once you start to examine the issues more carefully, you come to realise that there are many powerful social forces which affect our individual choices.

We're all very familiar with health education programmes which urge us to adopt more healthy lifestyles: the Christmas anti-drink-drive campaigns; the government health warnings on cigarette packets; the deluge of low-fat, no-salt, no-sugar products on the supermarket shelves. To what extent does such a programme of health education, which focuses on the individual, actually achieve the desired result?

Making changes in personal behaviour is very difficult. How many of you have tried to give up smoking? How often have you resolved to give up something for Lent or abandoned a New Year's resolution by 2 January? What explanation can you give for the high level of self-discipline which Muslims display in the observing of Ramadan?

The *Health of the Nation* document (Department of Health 1992) identifies several aspects of individual behaviour which do have a negative effect on health – smoking, diet, alcohol consumption and drug use – and then sets targets for the reduction of these 'risk' factors.

Let's look at some of these in more detail.

What's for tea? Children's food market sales by sector, 1995

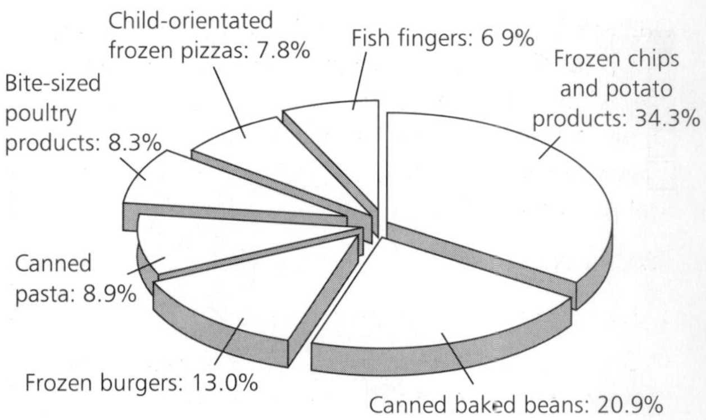

(The *Guardian*, 6 August 1996, using figures from Mintel)

Smoking

Smoking has long been a target of health education programmes. At one time the industry's advertising campaigns proclaimed the beneficial effects of smoking, claims which now seem quite incredible in the face of our current knowledge. No one can be any doubt about the risks to health which smoking causes and yet people continue to smoke. Why?

Part of the answer lies in the politics and economics of the tobacco industry. Nicotine is now acknowledged to be addictive and, furthermore, it's claimed by some health experts that nicotine levels in cigarettes were deliberately controlled to ensure addiction and thus preserve the demand for their product.

Again we pose the question about responsibility for individual health. Should the patient needing heart surgery be denied that treatment simply because she or he is a smoker? It could well be that they have been deliberately manipulated into that situation. Targeting individual lifestyles, when those individuals do not have the means at their disposal to alter their circumstances, can look very much like blaming the victim. Should the tobacco companies pay compensation to their customer/victims?

Diet

Mothers who've attempted to exercise some control over their children's eating habits know just how difficult that task can prove to be. The results of a survey by the market analysis group, Mintel, published in the *Guardian* in August 1996, formalises the meal-table tussles familiar to many (see the pie chart).

'Nearly half the country's parents fear they are losing the fight to resist their children's demands for crisps, cakes and sweets . . . Four fifths of the 500 mothers questioned said they tried to ensure their children had a balanced diet . . . One in five said the children refused to eat fresh vegetables. Parents of teenagers were especially worried.'

(The *Guardian*, 6 August 1996)

When you see the sophisticated advertising campaigns mounted by the fast-food companies, it's no wonder that kids hanker for a Macdonalds.

The old adage tells us that we are what we eat. Half of all adults are overweight or obese. In case you have any doubts about the long-term effects of eating habits developed in childhood, consider the risks of obesity summarised opposite. There are also, of course, serious risks attached to under-eating.

Why do we eat the food that we do? This question takes us from the realms of individual choice and responsibility and into the wider, social arena. Jeanne Calment, at 122 the world's oldest woman (until her recent death), and whose photograph you saw on page 315, attributed her longevity to the Mediterranean diet she had always enjoyed. In her case she favoured fish and local fresh produce, all cooked in olive oil.

We all eat the food that is most readily available to us. Our parents, our friends, the wider social community to which we belong, all play a major part in determining our diet. If we live on a large housing estate with very few shops available within walking distance, the likelihood is that we won't eat much fresh fruit and vegetables. There is an hypothesis that outbreaks of meningitis tend to cluster in areas where fresh produce isn't readily available. Apparently a local delicacy in parts of Glasgow is a Mars bar deep fried in batter. Remember how Glasgow topped the poll in the Rowntree study for premature mortality rates?

Alcohol consumption

There's growing concern about the increase in the number of young children with drinking problems. Drinkline Youth, a telephone helpline for children with

Obesity: when you've gone too far

OBESITY is currently defined by your body mass index (BMI) which is your weight in kilograms divided by your height in metres squared. A BMI of more than 35 is obese; normal or ideal BMI is 20–25. Some health risks begin to climb when your BMI goes over 25.

Obese people are:

- More likely to die prematurely
- 50 times more likely to develop diabetes; four times more likely to develop osteoarthritis

Obesity affects all the major body organs as follows:

- *Head and brain*: stroke; depression, anxiety, low self-esteem
- *Lungs:* under-breathing, interrupted breathing, particularly in sleep
- *Heart and circulation:* hypertension, ischaemic heart disease, blood clots
- *Gut:* gallstones, fatty liver, colon cancer, diabetes
- *Reproductive system:* infertility, heavy periods, hypogonadism
- *Joints:* osteoarthiritis, gout
- *Skin:* hirsutism, excessive sweating

(The *Guardian*, 17 September 1996)

drinking problems, says much of the blame lies with the drinks industry itself:

'"Alcopops are making it much easier for children with immature taste buds to get into drinking alcohol. The drinks industry is targeting young people, although it denies it." Sarah Berger, director of Drinkline'

The wider social forces in this case include the marketing strategies of the drinks industry, just the same process that we saw with the tobacco industry. Whilst it's the individual who has a drink, the results of that behaviour spread much wider.

'"Alcohol is itself a strong, addictive drug and its misuse increases the risk of accidents, alcohol poisoning, unprotected sex, unwanted pregnancies, crime and violence." Wendy Robinson, manager of Drinkline'

The wider environment

The term 'environment' can be used in at least three separate but interrelated senses:

- the immediate social and cultural environment in which we live, our family, friends, peers, our workmates, our neighbours
- the wider political and economic environment, the structure of our society
- the physical environment, the air we breathe, the water we drink.

We've already considered many examples of how these three forms of environment overlap with and affect each other.

Our physical environment is increasingly being harmed by the activities of industry against which individuals seem to have almost no redress. Often these activities have fatal consequences:

'A woman was struck down by a cancer as a result of living and playing in the asbestos-filled streets of Armley, Leeds, as a child, more than 50 years earlier . . . Edith McGuinness, 67, died from mesothelioma, a lung cancer caused by exposure to asbestos from the notorious and now closed J. W. Roberts factory in Armley . . . She played in the streets and walked past the factory to get to Armley Park School and remembered seeing extractor fans with a "snow-like substance" on the grills.'

(The *Yorkshire Evening Post*, 9 November 1996)

On 3 December 1984, there was a leak of poison gas from the Union Carbide factory in Bhopal, India. No one knows exactly how many were killed on that night. The official death toll is 5,325 but, according to the Bhopal Medical Appeal, the true figure may be nearer 15,000. Union Carbide didn't even issue an alert until two hours after the leak began and, to this day, the company has never revealed exactly what gas was leaked.

QUESTIONS

1. What are the issues of power which emerge from the work on health inequalities?
2. Where does the responsibility for the health of the individual lie?
3. What actions can be taken to redress persistent inequalities in health?

More detailed information about health inequalities can be found in:

- Townsend *et al.* (1988), which contains both the Black Report and the Health Divide report
- Bhat *et al.* (1988), which deals with racial and ethnic health inequalities in the UK
- Graham (1985), which deals with gender inequalities
- OPCS data published by the Stationery Office (formerly HMSO)
- General Household Survey information, published annually by the Stationery Office
- *United Nations Demographic Yearbook*, published annually, which provides international data.

Expectations of health

In your work on health you may often have found yourself pondering the simplicity of nailing jelly to a wall in comparison with trying to arrive at a satisfactory definition of health. In this section the analogy now becomes one of shifting goal-posts or even the absence of any goal-posts whatsoever! You already know that the parameters of health are determined by factors such as age, social class, occupation and cultural background. We're going to examine yet more relevant parameters, namely:

- changing demographic structure
- advances in medical science
- ethical/religious issues.

Running as continuous threads through much of this are questions about the allocation of resources and the increasing cost of health care.

Demographic factors

We all know that life expectancy in the west is increasing. We all expect greater longevity than our parents and grandparents. The graph below indicates the extent of this improvement during the twentieth century.

Life expectancy, UK, 1901–2021

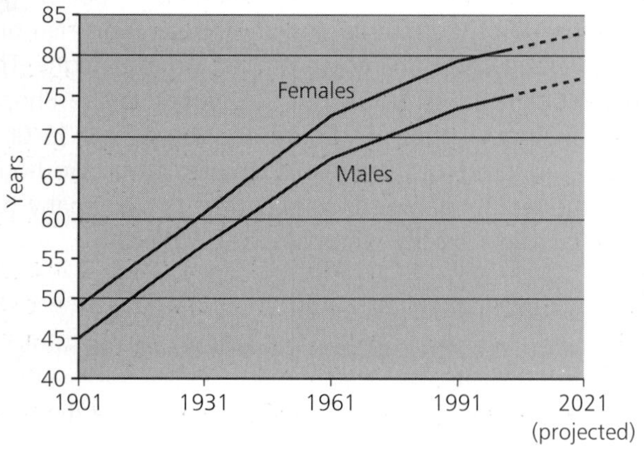

(*Social Trends 25*)

Let's put a little more flesh on the bones of the above graph. (Forgive the pun.) Firstly, some vital statistics.

Vital statistics for the UK, 1994

	1994(est.)	**1971**
Population	58 million	56 million
Life expectancy (men)	74 years	69 years
Life expectancy (women)	80 years	75 years
Births	760,000	902,000
Deaths	638,000	645,000
Migration	+45,000	-55,000
Age under 15	11.4 million	13.5 million
Over retirement age	10.7 million	9.1 million

(*Population Trends* No. 77, Autumn 1994)

Now, some further elaboration:

- The life expectancy of people born in 1992 is 73 years for males and 78.5 years for females. In 1980 the comparative figures were 70.4 years for males and 76.6 years for females. This is about 30 years longer than the Victorians could expect to live. For those who live until they are 70, men have a life expectancy of a further 11.6 years and women a further 14.6 years. (*Sociology Update* 1993)
- In Britain, 18.7 per cent of the total population are pensioners. (Census 1991)
- In 1991 there were about 4,400 people aged over 100 in England and Wales. Of these, over 80 per cent were women. (OPCS May 1994)
- The number of older people will rise by 6 million over the next 40 years, 2.5 million of whom will be over 75 years of age. (Department of Health 1995)
- The ratio of older men will rise from 1:3 to 1:2 over the next 30 years. (Department of Health 1995)
- Currently nearly 5 million households (25 per cent) contain only pensioners. (Deparment of Health 1995)

At first glance, all of these figures seem to indicate that it's life expectancy in old age which is increasing. Look again at the breakdown of figures in the table of vital statistics for the UK in 1994. It's indisputable that, for a variety of reasons, we have an ageing population. However, it's not merely that, in absolute terms, the number of older people is increasing, but also that, as a proportion of the total population, they're becoming a more statistically significant group. This means that the overall balance of population structure is changing, a trend which has major implications for all aspects of welfare provision.

The same table of figures gives us two more indices of this trend. Between 1971 and 1994 the number of births in the UK fell by 142,000; in the same period the under 15 population fell by 2.1 million. Whilst there have been important changes taking place which affect the adult/older population, there have been equally significant changes occurring at the beginning of the human life cycle. Birth rates have generally been declining since the 1850s.

There's also been a general reduction in the rates of infant mortality, as the graph opposite illustrates.

Demographic trends are the result of many complex factors which can only be hinted at in such a short section. You do need to be aware of two key points:

- *Changes in birth rates*. These will continue to make their effects felt for many generations to come, but not necessarily in a straightforward or predictable way. For example, immediately after (or rather, from nine months after) the end of the Second World War there was a sharp rise in the birth rate. These 'baby boom'

Infant mortality rates, England and Wales, 1846–1982

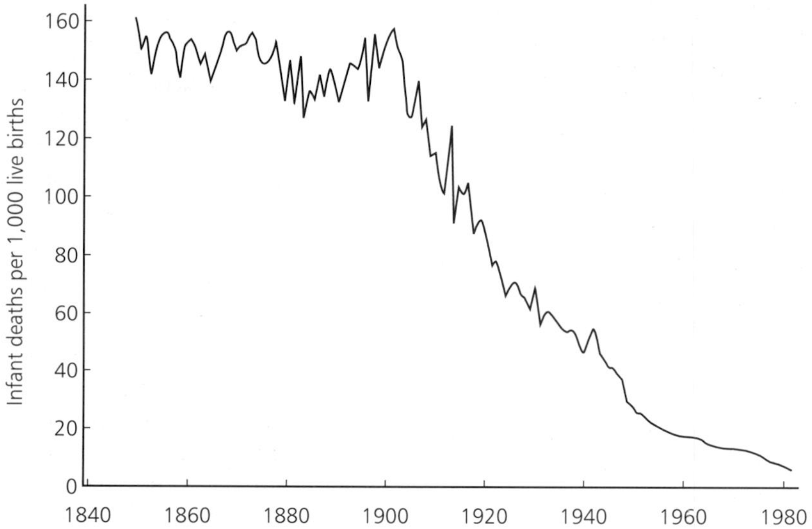

(Jones 1994: 99)

babies required nursery, then school provision, went on to fuel the expansion in higher education provision under Robbins in the 1960s and are now contemplating early retirement. Their 'bulge' will certainly further stoke up the trend towards an ageing population which was outlined above. You might expect that these post-war babies would have repeated the baby boom as they became parents themselves. However, this was also the generation which had the benefit of the contraceptive pill, and which developed very different attitudes towards marriage, child-bearing, women's role in the home and the workplace. All of these factors have affected the birth rate since the 1960s.

◆ *The significance of the overall structure and balance of the population*. It's the relationship between the economically active and the dependent groups which is so important. Our whole structure of welfare is predicated on the notion that those in work support those who are too young, old or infirm to support themselves.

When we examine apparently simple life expectancy figures and set them in the broader context of demographic and social trends, what we get are ripples of effect which are operating at all stages in the life cycle of the individual. These separate ripples can combine to accentuate a potential trend or can conflict and possibly nullify a potential development.

We've concentrated so far on aspects of increased life expectancy in infancy and old age; remind yourself of the *Health of the Nation* targets which seek to tackle various factors which affect life expectancy between these two polar points. Take, for example, coronary heart disease and stroke:

'Coronary heart disease (CHD) accounted for about 26 per cent of deaths in England in 1991. It's both the single largest cause of death, and the single main cause of premature death. Strokes were responsible for approximately 12 per cent of all deaths in 1991.

TARGETS

◆ To reduce death rates for both CHD and stroke in people under 65 by at least 40% by the year 2000 . . .

◆ To reduce the death rate for CHD in people aged 65 to 74 by at least 30% by the year 2000 . . .

◆ To reduce the death rate for stroke in people aged 65 to 74 by at least 40% by the year 2000.'

(Department of Health 1992)

If these targets are achieved they'll have a significant and almost immediate impact on the structure of the older population; another 'bulge' to work its way through the system. In addition, the mere setting of these targets plays an important role in shaping an individual's expectations for their own health.

Advances in medical science

We've already seen how from the very earliest times humankind has attempted to influence and control the body's functioning. Where the twentieth century differs from previous ages is in the pace and extent of the developments in medical knowledge and technology which have occurred. It's in this arena that our expectations are most rapidly expanding and are seemingly limitless. This isn't the place to present a comprehensive history of medical advances, but rather to indicate a few key developments and issues as illustrations of the overall argument.

In 1966 England won the World Cup. It's become one of those seminal dates in our collective consciousness, due in no small part to the continuing attention focused on the event by the media. In December 1967 Dr Christiaan Barnard performed the world's first heart transplant operation on Louis Washkansky. That event too attracted the attention of the world's media. For those of us who were alive at the time, whilst we may not remember the precise date, we certainly remember the name of the surgeon, the hospital and possibly also the patient. The important point about all of this is that, after the first operation, we knew that in theory such operations could be successful. The basic techniques were sound, and it was just a matter of time before the problems associated with organ matching and rejection were resolved. With that one operation our expectations of what was possible took a quantum leap forward.

Transplant surgery today has become commonplace and rarely makes the headlines. We're all urged to carry donor cards, and the notion of spare part surgery seems to have gained general acceptance. Here we have a very clear illustration of the conceptualisation of the body as a machine. For both technical and philosophical reasons, heart transplants are particularly spectacular, but we now also have the ability to transplant or replace many other parts of the human anatomy, for example, kidneys, liver, lungs, cornea, bone marrow, skin grafts, rebuilding fingers from toes. Blood transfusions have been successfully carried out for many years and indeed are the cornerstone of all major surgery.

Not only is it possible to replace one human organ with another from a human source, we also have the ability to construct artificial body parts and insert those. Joint replacement operations benefit many, both young and old, heart pacemakers are fitted to control a poorly functioning heart. Just look (below left) at what is now possible in order to restore someone's sight. Osteo-odontal keratoprosthesis has been performed in the UK for the first time. The technique involves extracting one of the patient's teeth to make a frame for a plastic lens which is then inserted inside the eyeball.

The demand for transplant surgery is outstripping the supply of donor organs, a clear illustration of the impact of rising expectations on health and the provision of health care. For some time there have been experiments in the use of animal organs for human transplant purposes (Xenotransplants), and the first such successful operation has been carried out in India (December 1996). The diagram below right gives some indication of the medical techniques involved and also highlights the many ethical and medical issues which have still to be resolved.

An extreme example of rising expectations can be seen in the issue of cryogenics. The body is frozen at the point

A cure for blindness?

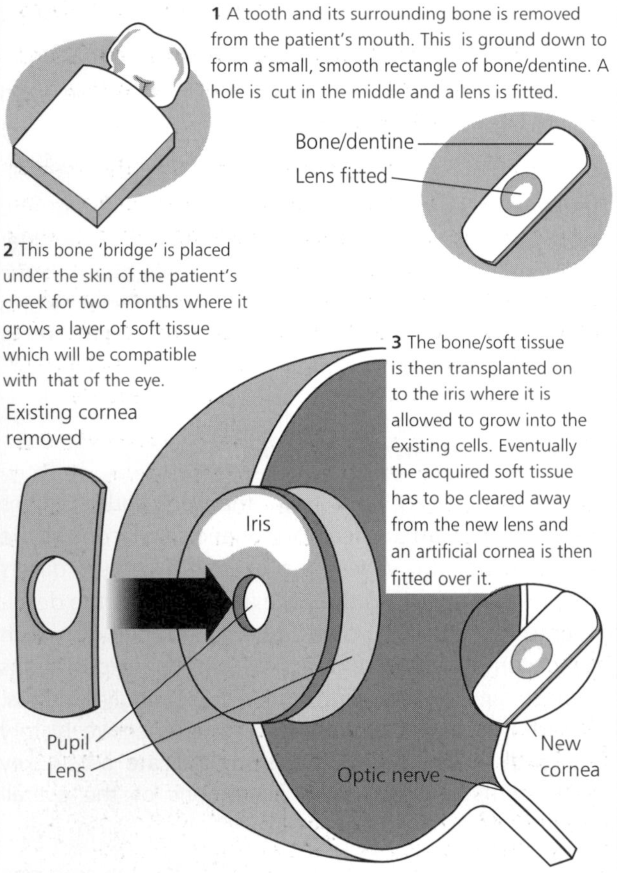
1 A tooth and its surrounding bone is removed from the patient's mouth. This is ground down to form a small, smooth rectangle of bone/dentine. A hole is cut in the middle and a lens is fitted.
Bone/dentine
Lens fitted
2 This bone 'bridge' is placed under the skin of the patient's cheek for two months where it grows a layer of soft tissue which will be compatible with that of the eye.
Existing cornea removed
3 The bone/soft tissue is then transplanted on to the iris where it is allowed to grow into the existing cells. Eventually the acquired soft tissue has to be cleared away from the new lens and an artificial cornea is then fitted over it.
Iris
Pupil
Lens
Optic nerve
New cornea

(The *Guardian*, 2 December 1996)

Pig transplant carried out in India

Surgeons have carried out the first successful heart transplant operation from a pig to a human, amidst widespread concern about the possible introduction of infectious animal diseases. The patient's body was tricked into not rejecting the transplanted organ using genetic engineering techniques.

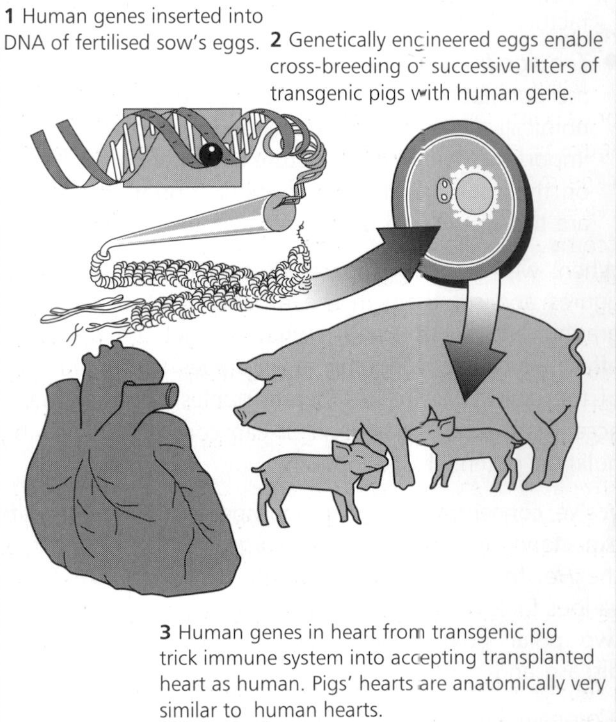
1 Human genes inserted into DNA of fertilised sow's eggs.
2 Genetically engineered eggs enable cross-breeding of successive litters of transgenic pigs with human gene.
3 Human genes in heart from transgenic pig trick immune system into accepting transplanted heart as human. Pigs' hearts are anatomically very similar to human hearts.

(YEP, 18 December 1996)

of near-death and then kept in a state of suspended animation until such time as a cure has been found for the disease which would otherwise have caused the death of that person. The individual will then be thawed out and enabled to benefit from this advance in medical knowledge. Early volunteers include Walt Disney who is frozen in a metal casket somewhere in California.

Ethical and religious considerations

The desire to know and understand more about the functioning of the human body has been with us since the earliest times. The same question has always been posed: At what point do you stop and say 'no more', this constitutes 'unnatural' interference? It's hard to come to terms with one's inevitable mortality, and the human race has developed a range of philosophical frameworks within which to make sense of our ultimate fate. Criticism of the apparently inexorable march of medical technology comes from many sources.

The notion of expectation is a multi-edged sword. We expect to be treated and hopefully cured. We're also expected to avail ourselves of these various treatments and can be regarded as irresponsible if we reject them. Here we have to recognise the multitude of religious, cultural and personal factors which will determine an individual's response to what medical science has to offer. For example, Jehovah's Witnesses refuse blood transfusions. Some cancer patients decline chemotherapy and prefer more holistic forms of treatment. There have been a number of high-profile court cases about defining the precise point of death (persistent vegetative state); the issue of euthanasia continues to arouse vehement debate.

Advances in medical science have also given us greater control over the creation of life. There are a range of techniques to assist conception, many of which are celebrated in the media. Think, for example, of the rosy portrayal of *in vitro* fertilisation, of the media circus which often accompanies a multiple birth. We're used to seeing advertisements for donations of male sperm or female ova. Yet also be aware that the ethical boundaries for all of the issues relating to conception are fervently contested; for example,controversy currently surrounds the question of surrogacy and also of the right of a woman to conceive using the sperm of her dead husband.

'Any technology is developed and utilized by one group of people for use on, or by, another group. It is not democratically selected, nor democratically distributed . . . Every technology in its mode of development and use will reproduce the power relations of the culture.'

(Oakley 1993: 172)

In February 1997 a report by the National Childbirth Trust claimed that some pregnant women were being forced to have antenatal tests, with health professionals making assumptions that screening was needed and that an unhealthy foetus would automatically be aborted. As reported in the *Guardian*, one woman said that during her antenatal visit the consultant commented: 'If there's something wrong with the baby, we just get rid of it.' The antenatal tests most routinely performed were for conditions such as Down's syndrome or spina bifida. The NCT report concluded:

'Women should have a right to choose or refuse each test or scan. Health professionals should not make assumptions about what is in the best interest of parents. They should never put any pressure on parents.'

This report from the NCT clearly connects with issues of disability, the exercise of power in the sphere of medicine and feminist analyses of health.

QUESTIONS

1 Where would you draw the line between natural and unnatural intervention in the development of medical science?
2 What role does religious belief play in the application of medicine in our essentially secular society?

A sociological critique

Critical evaluation of medical models has been woven into all aspects of this chapter. It's appropriate to remind you of two in particular in the context of expectations:

- Illich (1990) argues that we have become too dependent on health professionals to provide us with a remedy for every ache and pain.

  We've lost sight of the ebb and flow, the normal processes of the human body. People 'unlearn the acceptance of suffering as an inevitable part of their conscious coping with reality and learn to interpret every ache as an indicator of their need for padding and pampering'. For Illich, this critique is part of a much more fundamental analysis of the dominance of science and medicine in an industrialised society.

- Navarro (1975) locates the causes of over-medicalisation and iatrogenesis in the capitalist system, which is based on the need to generate continuous and unnecessary consumption, in this case of health-care goods and services.

OVER TO YOU

The drug companies play a significant role in the politics of health. Monitor newspaper reports, especially in the business sections, to generate an interesting portfolio of work from which you could more fully explore Navarro's thesis.

The provision of health care

The provision of health care is a political 'hot potato'. In the UK we're witnessing the introduction of fundamental changes to the structure of the welfare provision, the Welfare State, which was established in the post-war period.

Whilst the situation in the UK is the prime focus of this chapter, you also need to be aware of the situation in other countries. All modern industrialised countries have developed systems for the provision of health and welfare. (Does this confirm the marxist thesis that the capitalist system will invest in health care to a level that will thereby ensure a fit and efficient workforce?) In all of these industrialised countries, the same heated debates are taking place about how to structure and fund such provision. The main area of difference between them is in the extent to which the state assumes responsibility for making the provision. (It's that word 'responsibility' again.)

A text such as this can provide you with an appropriate theoretical framework within which to place current developments. However, you should also read the papers and keep abreast of reports in the media generally. Listen to the speeches of politicians and carefully analyse what they're saying about new policy initiatives. One thing you can be sure of: in the coming months and years they'll have plenty to say about the provision of health care. It's changing and will continue to change. The changes will be driven by underlying philosophies which you need to be able to locate within a broader sociological framework.

There are important questions to be asked here about the nature and role of social policy. At the most fundamental level, social policy represents one particular resolution of the relationship between the individual and society. We know that this is the key question which runs through all sociological theory. Within a social policy framework the needs and concerns of both the individual and the wider society are identified. From this initial analysis, measures are then introduced which are intended to meet both sets of needs and resolve both sets of concerns. It sounds perfectly straightforward and logical when presented in such terms, but we know that reality is always messy and refuses to stay within neat analytical boxes.

Social policy emerged as a distinct area of academic study in the UK in the early twentieth century, very much influenced by Fabians such as Sydney and Beatrice Webb. They argued for the necessity of state provision of welfare services, and the establishment of the Welfare State after the Second World War can be regarded as the apotheosis of their philosophy. Thomas H. Marshall (1963) argued that, prior to 1945, a person's access to social resources was dependent upon their income. The ultimate indicator of a civilised society was the provision of welfare benefits to all citizens, irrespective of their ability to pay for them. This was the guiding principle behind the Welfare State. The clear aim was to counter existing patterns of inequality through the provision of a universal health service, pensions and state education. In the immediate post-war period there was general optimism about the ability of the newly-established Welfare State to solve the social problems of the day and to bring about social justice. So much was riding on this. We've all been brought up within the Welfare State and cannot really imagine what life must have been like for ordinary people before its inception. We cannot really appreciate the hopes which it inspired because we've been in the fortunate position of taking many aspects of our welfare society for granted.

The National Health Service is one of the main planks of the Welfare State. Whatever other shortcomings it may have, the one feature which distinguishes the NHS from all other welfare systems is the principle of the provision of services to the patient which are 'free' at the point of use.

Other countries have developed different ways of resolving the balance of the relationship between the individual and the state. In the USA health care is controlled by private and occupational insurance schemes, with the state playing no direct part. The same can be said of Japan. In Western Europe there are systems of health care which combine both state and privately-run insurance schemes. In some respects the mix of private and state provision resembles that which currently operates in the UK, although there are significant differences in terms both of balance and of the administration of the various systems.

We've now studied health sufficiently to realise that health and politics are inextricably linked. By politics we don't mean just party politics, although the Thatcher era was undoubtedly characterised by a clear political philosophy. We mean politics in its broadest sense, the exercise of power. Any system of health-care provision represents one combination of theory and practice, of political philosophy and economic/political reality. The French and Germans don't seem to have any difficulty in acknowledging this link. In both the French and German languages the same word is used for both 'policy' and 'politics': *politique* in French and *politik* in German. There would seem to be no suggestion here that the formulation of social policy is a neutral activity. We could be accused of being much more naive in the UK. By the 1960s it was being argued by Richard Titmuss (1968) that the British Welfare State represented the 'end of ideology'. This kind of statement is more understandable when it's located in its historical context. In 1959 Harold Macmillan was telling us that we'd 'never had it so good'. In the early 1960s Lockwood and Goldthorpe were studying Luton car workers and developing the thesis of the affluent worker and embourgeiosement. The world of the late twentieth century is a very different place.

The origins of the current system of health-care provision

There are a number of reasons why it's important to give some consideration to the historical dimension. No system ever starts with a completely blank sheet, and that which had existed before to some extent will determine the structure of any new system. Inevitably we will have a pragmatic resolution of underlying political theory and its practical implementation.

Developments during the nineteenth century

The link between poverty and ill-health had long been widely acknowledged, although there was no consensus on the causes of poverty. Dating from the Middle Ages, there had been some charitable communal care for the most needy, but this was by no means universally available. In the early part of the nineteenth century at least, there was little support for the principle of state intervention or the state provision of welfare. The dominant philosophy of *laissez-faire* (leave alone) governed official policy. The Victorians believed that most poverty was the result of personal irresponsibility, an unwillingness to work and a failure to make adequate provision for sickness and old age.

Confronted by the effects of uncontrolled industrialisation upon the living conditions of the growing mass of urban poor, the government did gradually adopt a more interventionist approach towards the hitherto totally private spheres of the family and the workings of the economy.

Under the Poor Law Amendment Act of 1834 destitute, old and infirm people could receive 'indoor relief', but only if they went into the workhouse. Conditions in the workhouse were deliberately made worse than the worst conditions to be found outside, to deter anyone from making demands upon the public purse for relief unless they really were destitute. The aim was to reduce public expenditure and to encourage the able-bodied to take any work, however poorly paid. Those who couldn't work – people who were old, infirm, very young, or disabled – were labelled as paupers, the residuum.

Many of these workhouse buildings still survive within our modern hospital complexes. Not only do the buildings survive physically, it can also be argued that it's in the workhouse system that we find the origins of our present hospital-based system of health-care provision, our deep-rooted attitudes towards poverty and the unequal distribution of access to particular kinds of health care.

Public health

The 1848 Public Health Act established the principle of local authority provision of better water supplies and sewerage disposal. The 1872 Public Health Act formalised and standardised a range of public health measures and requirements which had developed over the previous hundred years. Local authorities were now required to ensure minimum standards of street paving, lighting, housing and drainage. Medical Officers of Health and Sanitary Inspectors were appointed.

Personal health

Better standards of housing, water supply and sanitation had a significant impact on the levels of hygiene it was possible to achieve in individual homes. After 1880 it was compulsory for children to attend school up to the age of ten, and it then became possible to implement health education programmes to increase awareness of the importance of personal hygiene.

McKeown (1976) has shown how the significant reduction during the nineteenth century in the incidence of potentially fatal infectious diseases, such as tuberculosis, cholera, typhus, typhoid, measles, etc., was the result of general improvements in both public and private hygiene. (The widespread use of antibiotics and immunisation programmes didn't begin until the mid-twentieth century.)

Towards a state system of provision

The Liberal government, elected in 1906, introduced a range of social welfare measures which in many respects can be regarded as laying the foundations of the Welfare State.

The poor health of army recruits during the Boer War had generated concern about the health of children and, therefore, a number of initiatives were introduced to remedy this situation. As part of their Children's Charter, provision for school meals was introduced in 1906, and a school medical service in 1907. Health visiting was also established as a local authority service in 1907.

In 1911 the National Health Insurance Act established the principle that employees, employers and the government should jointly fund a system of health insurance and also unemployment benefit, through the payment of weekly contributions. We still pay our National Insurance contributions today.

In introducing a National Insurance scheme, the Liberals were responding to pressure from the trade unions and the nascent Labour Party. They took as their model both the system of welfare insurance already introduced in Germany by Bismarck and the range of provision already available in Britain through the friendly societies and the trade unions.

There was much opposition to Liberal policy initiatives. Tories urged the workers 'to resist the deductions from their wage as a monstrous oppression by the government'. Doctors were opposed to the idea of having panel patients. (All insured persons were obliged to join a doctor's panel in order to receive GP care.)

These initiatives, whether from local or central government, can be variously analysed and interpreted, from:

- *a 'social conscience' perspective*. In the late nineteenth century there were a number of major studies of poverty, for example by Charles Booth and Seebohm Rowntree, which could be said to have generated the benevolent, paternalist approach to welfare which has been a significant feature of the British system
- *a functionalist perspective*. It's important to maintain industrialist capitalist society through 'system integration' and 'social integration' (look back to the earlier coverage of Parsons' work)
- *a marxist perspective*. The capitalist system requires a healthy and productive workforce and, therefore, measures are introduced which ensure minimum and necessary levels of health without also generating a major redistribution of wealth and power
- *a feminist perspective*. Upper-middle-class women played a significant role in the growth of social work in the late nineteenth century. Many of their 'good works' were motivated by the aim of remoralising the poor, but involvement in these social movements was also an expression of growing feminism. The various measures which were introduced by both the 1906 Liberal government and under the Welfare State are based on particular definitions of the role of women, the structure of families and their contribution to the wider labour market.

Establishing the National Health Service

The pre-war system of health-care provision was based primarily on a system of insurance which had proved less than completely satisfactory.

During the Second World War, the government had moved towards a nationally-funded health system, initially for members of the armed services only. Gradually this was expanded to include others directly involved in the war effort. From this was born the concept of a peace-time, state-funded public health service, 'free' to all at the point of use.

The National Health Service which was founded in 1948 represented a compromise between the political intentions of the Labour government and the insistence of the medical profession that they should retain a high degree of autonomy. Doctors were given a major role in the allocation of resources within the NHS and always retained their status as independent professionals, rather than becoming salaried employees.

The basic structure of the National Health Service was built on the following principles:

- the service was to be controlled mainly by the medical profession, accountable to a central Ministry of Health
- General Practitioners were to remain as 'independent contractors' to the NHS
- a three-tier system of health-care provision was established:
  - hospital
  - general practice
  - community
- the service was to be funded mainly through taxation, not insurance.

This structure has remained essentially unchanged since its introduction. As we've already seen, the structure of the NHS represents a compromise between powerful political and medical lobbies. In particular, GPs have always retained their contractual independence and private medicine has always co-existed alongside state provision in NHS hospitals. There was a time when a lot of political fury was directed against private medicine, but we're now in a new political climate. The Conservative government elected in 1979 was committed to the expansion of the provision of private health care and also to the introduction of market forces in the public sector. Here they were making a clear political statement.

The reforms to the NHS which were subsequently introduced were in response to a number of inescapable trends. The costs of health care are spiralling ever-upward, partly because of advances in medical technology and partly because of the impact of an ageing population. There was also growing criticism of the management of the NHS and its financial efficiency.

In 1991 the NHS and Community Care Act came into effect. The aims of this legislation were to:

- increase managerial control over health professionals
- make health-care organisations more accountable for the resources they use
- introduce more competition within the NHS.

This Act signalled the Conservative government's intention to challenge the autonomy of health professionals by making them more publicly accountable. This initiative has to be coupled with the setting of targets within the *Health of the Nation* document. With medical costs increasing rapidly, it was becoming imperative to introduce some forms of financial constraint. GPs were encouraged to become fundholders and were freed to make financial contracts with a range of health-care providers. Care in the community was also flagged as a means of providing more cost-effective and appropriate health care for many patients who previously were cared for in large and expensive institutional settings.

It's against this political and financial backdrop that we have to locate the current debates about personal responsibility for health and health care. There's now much talk about the need to ration health care. The example of the smoker who needed heart surgery was quoted earlier, but there are plenty of other examples. At what age is one too old to have a hip replacement operation? (Unless one is the Queen Mother, of course, when age limits do not apply.) Many local health authorities now ration *in vitro* fertilisation treatment. Should a drug user be entitled to a liver transplant?

We were told that the Welfare State would take care of us from the cradle to the grave. This no longer holds, it seems. It's generally recognised now that the state pension will be insufficient to meet our needs in old age, and so it's become incumbent on us all to make some private provision for pensions. Private health care used to be the preserve of the very rich, but now increasing numbers are subscribing to private health-care plans, again a recognition that state provision cannot be fully comprehensive.

There's some debate about the extent to which we are witnessing a fundamental change in British health policy. The public and private sectors have always co-existed, and the NHS retains a near-monopoly of health service provision. What we are currently experiencing is a realignment of all those elements in the provision of health care, in conjunction with a reassessment of the role of the state in providing either residual or institutional health care. Whether we're talking about Ancient Rome, medieval England or late twentieth century Europe, the questions and the dilemmas remain the same. The component of the jigsaw may have different names, but they all have to be fitted together somehow. The diagram below sets out the current scenario for us.

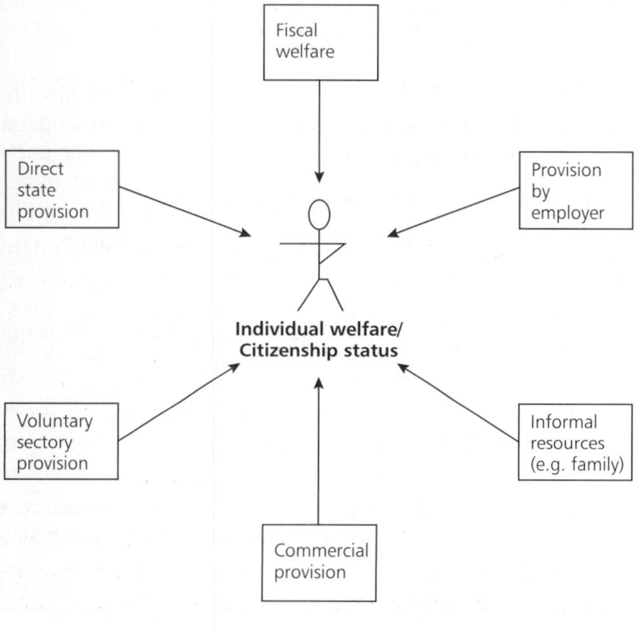

(Ackers and Abbott 1996: 4)

QUESTIONS

1 On what basis are financial resources within the NHS being allocated?
2 Do you consider that the introduction of market forces in the provision of health care is compatible with action on health inequalities?

Concluding remarks

We started this chapter by asking the question 'What is health?' A short question to which you now realise there's no short answer. We've also posed the question of why issues of health are so important, both to the individual and for the wider society. The whole focus of this chapter has been to examine many of the theoretical debates and the statistical information which relate to this question.

Not so very long ago, the cry used to be 'why can't we keep politics out of education?' By now you should also have realised that health is also an intensely political issue, possibly to the extent that it no longer seems to be about medicine at all. Throughout this chapter extensive use has been made of newspaper extracts. This alone should have alerted you to the necessity of keeping abreast of current developments. Change in all aspects of our lives is happening so quickly that you cannot expect any textbook to be completely up-to-date. In traditional societies, change happened only very slowly and depended on word of mouth to spread the news of any developments. That word of mouth was probably carried on foot. Today, we still rely on word of mouth, but now we have access to information via all forms of electronic media. We can have news from around the world 24 hours a day. We can surf the Internet and access web sites across the globe to learn more about developments in any field of activity.

Technology increasingly dominates all aspects of our lives and, in some respects, we're expected to welcome with open arms all the possibilities which this technology seems to offer us. At the same time, there's a growing scepticism about the wisdom of proceeding ever further down this road. In the health field, we're seeing a resurgence of interest in 'alternative' medicine, prompted in part by the evident shortcomings of allopathic medicine and informed by the knowledge which we have all gained from living in a multi-cultural society. Durkheim pointed to the value of deviance in moving a society on. Kuhn talks about scientific revolutions and paradigm shifts. Currently many alternative therapies are labelled as cranky, as deviant, but could they become the basis for a whole new approach to health? It will be interesting finding out.

Glossary of key terms

Allopathic The treatment of disease with drugs having the opposite effects to the symptoms – the orthodox practice within the bio-medical model, for example, the taking of pain killers to counteract a headache

Anatomy The study of the structure of the body, based on the skeleton

Anomie The breakdown or absence of norms in society. This term is most closely associated with the work of Durkheim

Birth rate/death rate The number per 1,000 of the whole population

Chronic illness/sickness/disease Serious, likely to last a long time

Demography The statistically-based study of human populations, their growth, decline, changes that occur, population movements, etc.

Disease Specific medical condition, with recognised symptoms, can be diagnosed

Division of labour When individuals specialise in doing one task and thereby develop some expertise. Whilst they are concentrating on this one task, they cannot be doing the other things, necessary for their survival; therefore someone else in the organisation or society must be doing them. The whole system requires a high level of co-ordination in order that all individual and societal needs are met. It also requires some system of exchange

Empirical Based on 'facts', on the results of experiments, observation, the collection of statistical data

Fecundity The ability to conceive, related to health, diet, etc.

Hegemony The representation of the ideas and interests of the ruling class as being for the benefit of the whole of society

Homeopathy Based on the principal that like cures like. Small doses of a drug cure symptoms like those which larger doses would cause

Homeostasis The maintenance of balance in the physical and chemical conditions within the body

Homogeneous Comprising elements of the same kind; for example, a group based on age or gender or race

Iatrogenesis Doctor-caused disease; caused by unnecessary interventions or the inappropriate use of medication

Ideal type A sociological concept developed by Weber. It doesn't mean 'perfect'. It's based on examples found in the real world, but consists of more than the combination of these examples. It's intended to highlight the key features of the social phenomenon and to be used as a tool for analysis

Ideology Ideas and culture which are linked to the sources of power in society

Illness The state of feeling ill or unwell

Impotence Specifically, the inability of the man to have successful sexual intercourse; also used to denote general powerlessness

Infant mortality rate Deaths in the first year of life (per 1,000 live births)

Lay Specifically means non-clerical, not ordained; for example, a lay preacher. Lay has a wider meaning of non-professional, not formally trained

Mechanical solidarity The form of integration in traditional societies. Social structure is comparatively simple. The clan, family or tribe are important sources of values and social cohesion, as is the system of religious beliefs

Morbidity Illness rate, derived from a number of sources; for example, medical records, claims for sickness benefit, social surveys

Mortality Death rate, age-group specific. Always available only as official statistics

Neonatal mortality rate Deaths in the first 28 days of life (per 1,000 live births)

Organic solidarity This form of social organisation typifies modern, complex societies. There's an emphasis on individualism, specialisation and differentiation

Paradigm A framework which determines the boundaries of thinking and analysis. Most closely associated with the work of Thomas Kuhn on the history and philosophy of science

Pathology The study of abnormal functioning of the body

Perinatal mortality rate Stillbirths and deaths in the first week of life (per 1,000 live births)

Physiology The study of the function of living organisms and their different parts

Procreation Producing offspring

Qualitative Based on understanding, an emphasis on meaning. Generally associated with interpretivist methodologies

Quantitative Based on statistical data. Generally associated with positivist methodologies

Secular Concerned with the non-religious

Self-sufficiency An individual or a group who can provide for all their material needs. The term is typically applied to the basis of society before industrialisation, when each family unit combined farming with some form of trade. Such a society has a very low level of specialisation and in theory no need for money as a means of exchange

Sickness Reported illness

Traditional A term applied to a variety of non-industrial societies; often contrasted with modern or advanced

References

Abbott, Pamela and Wallace, Claire (1997) *An Introduction to Sociology: Feminist Perspectives*, Second Edition. London: Routledge

Ackers, Louis and Abbott, Pamela (1996) *Social Policy For Nurses and the Caring Professions*. Buckingham: Open University Press

Aggleton, Peter (1990) *Health*. London: Routledge

Barnes, Colin (1992) *Disabling Imagery and the Media*. Halifax: Ryburn Publishing

Becker, Howard S. (1963) *Outsiders: Studies in the Sociology of Deviance*. New York: Free Press, and London: Collier-Macmillan

Bhat, Ashok, Carr-Hill, Roy and Ohri, Sushel (1988) *Britain's Black Population*. Aldershot: Gower

Black, Douglas (1980) *Report of a Research Working Group*. London: DHSS

Blaxter, Mildred (1976) *The Meaning of Disability: A Sociological Study of Impairment*. London: Heinemann

Blaxter, Mildred (1990) *Health and Lifestyles*. London: Tavistock/Routledge

Bone, M. and Meltzer, H. (1989) *The Prevalence of Disability among Children*. London: Office of Population Censuses and Surveys/HMSO

Borsay, A. (1986) *Disabled People in the Community*. London: Bedford Square Press

Calnan, Michael (1987) *Health and Illness: The Lay Perspective*. London: Tavistock

Cooper, Deborah (1996) Legislation: A practical example – Young people and education, p. 136, in Hales, G. (ed.) op. cit.

Cox, B. D. *et al.* (1987) *The Health and Lifestyles Survey: Preliminary Report*. London: The Health Promotion Research Trust

Cornwell, Jocelyn (1984) *Hard-Earned Lives*. London: Tavistock

Davis, Ken (1996) Disability and legislation: Rights and equality, p. 124, in Hales, G.(ed.) op. cit.

Department of Health (1992) *The Health of the Nation*. London: HMSO

Donovan, J. (1986) *We Don't Buy Sickness, It Just Comes*. Aldershot: Gower

Dorling, David (1997) *Death in Britain: How Local Mortality Rates Have Changed: 1950s to 1990s*. York: Joseph Rowntree Foundation

Doyal, Lesley and Pennel, Imogen (1979) *The Political Economy of Health*. London: Pluto Press

Durkheim, Emile (1964) *The Division of Labour in Society*. New York: The Free Press

Durkheim, Emile (first published in 1895) *The Rules of Sociological Method* (publication details not available)

Durkheim, Emile (1968) *Suicide*. London: Routledge & Kegan Paul

Ehrenreich, Barbara and English, Deirdre (1974) *Witches, Midwives and Nurses: A History of Women Healers*. London: Glass Mountain Pamphlet No. 1

Engels, Friedrich (1847) *The Condition of the Working Class in England in 1844* (publication details not available)

Finkelstein, Vic (1980) *Attitudes and Disabled People*. New York: World Rehabilitation Fund

Foucault, Michel (1973) *The Birth of the Clinic: An Archaeology of Medical Perception*. London: Tavistock

Friedson, Eliot (1970) *Profession of Medicine: A Study of the Sociology of Applied Knowledge*. New York: Dodd Mead

Goffman, Erving (1990) *Stigma: Notes on the Management of Spoiled Identity*. Harmondsworth: Penguin

Graham, Hilary (1985) *Health and Welfare*. Basingstoke: Macmillan

Graham, Hilary and Oakley, Ann (1981) Competing ideologies of reproduction, in Roberts, H. (ed.) *Women, Health and Reproduction*. London: Routledge & Kegan Paul

Hahn, H. (1985) Disability policy and the problem of discrimination, p. 294, *American Behavioural Scientist*, Vol. 28, No. 3

Hales, Gerald (ed.) (1996) *Beyond Disability*. London: Sage Publications

Hanmer, Jalna (1993) Women and reproduction, pp 224–49, in Richardson, D. and Robinson, V. (eds) (1993) *Introducing Women's Studies*. Basingstoke: Macmillan

Harding, S. (1987) *Feminism and Methodology*. Milton Keynes: Open University Press

Harris, A. (1971) *Handicapped and Impaired in Great Britain*. London: Office of Population Censuses and Surveys/HMSO

Hevey, David (1992) *The Creatures Time Forgot: Photography and Disability Imagery*. London: Routledge

Hockey, Jenny (1993) Women and Health, p. 258, in Richardson, D. and Robinson, V. (eds) (1993) *Introducing Women's Studies*. Basingstoke: Macmillan

Illich, Ivan (1990) *Limits to Medicine: Medical Nemesis: The Expropriation of Health*. London: Penguin

Jones, Linda J. (1994) *The Social Context of Health and Health Work*. London: Macmillan

Kuhn, Thomas S. (1962) *The Structure of Scientific Revolutions*. Chicago: University of Chicago Press

Lemert, Edwin (1967) *Human Deviance, Social Problems and Social Control*. Prentice-Hall

Marshall, Thomas H. (1963) *Sociology at the Crossroads and Other Essays*. London: Heinemann

Martin, J., Meltzer, H. and Elliot, D. (1988) *The Prevalence of Disability among Adults*. London: Office of Population Censuses and Surveys/HMSO

McKeown, Thomas (1976) *The Modern Rise of Population*. London: Arnold

McKeown, Thomas (1979) *The Role of Medicine*. Oxford: Blackwell

McKinlay, John B. (1984) *Issues in the Political Economy of Health Care*. London: Tavistock

McKinlay, John B. (1996) Some contributions from the social system to gender inequalities in heart disease, p. 2, *Journal of Health and Social Behaviour*, Vol. 37, No. 1

Martin, J. and White, A. (1988) *The Financial Circumstances of Disabled Adults Living in Private Households*. London: HMSO.

Miller, A. and Gwynne, G. (1972) A Life Apart. London: Tavistock

Mills, Jane (1991) *Womanwords*. London: Virago Press

Navarro, Vicente (1975) The industrialisation of fetishism and the fetishism of industrialisation: A critique of Ivan Illich, *International Journal of the Health Services*, Vol. 5

Nazroo, James (1997) *Ethnicity and Mental Health*. London: Policy Studies Institute

Newbury, Darren (1996) Reconstructing the self: Photography, education and disability, p. 349, *Disability and Society*, Vol. 11, No. 3

Oakley, Ann (1976) *Housewife*. Harmondsworth: Pelican

Oakley, Ann (1993) *Essays on Women, Medicine and Health*. Edinburgh: Edinburgh University Press

Oliver, Mike (1993) Redefining disability: A challenge to research, p. 64, in Swain, John., Finkelstein, Vic, French, Sally and Oliver, Mike (eds.) *Disabling Barriers – Enabling Environments*. London: Sage Publications

Parsons, Talcott (1964) *The Social System*. London: Routledge & Kegan Paul

Rowbotham, Sheila (1973) *Hidden From History*. London: Pluto Press

Scheff, Thomas J. (1966) *Being Mentally Ill: A Sociological Theory*. Chicago and London: Aldine Publishing Co.

Schott, Judith and Henley, Alix (1996) *Culture, Religion and Childbearing in a Multi-racial Society*. Oxford: Butterworth-Heinemann

Seedhouse, D. (1985) *Health: The Foundations for Achievement*. Chichester: John Wiley

Shakespeare, Tom (1994) Cultural representation of disabled people: Dustbins for disavowal? *Disability and Society*, Vol. 9, No. 2

Social Trends 25 (1995). London: HMSO

Sociology Updates (ed. Martyn Denscombe) are published annually by Olympus Books, UK

Stimson, G. and Webb, B. (1975) *Going to See the Doctor*. London: Routledge & Kegan Paul

Taylor, R. (1979) *Medicine Out of Control*. Victoria: Sun

Taylor, Steve and Field, David (eds) (1993) *Sociology of Health and Healthcare*. Oxford: Blackwell

Titmuss, Richard (1968) *Commitment to Welfare.* London: Allen & Unwin

Townsend, Peter, Davidson, Nick and Whitehead, Margaret (1988) *Inequalities in Health and the Health Divide*. Harmondsworth: Penguin

Whitehead, Margaret (1987) *The Health Divide*. London: Health Education Authority

Witz, Anne (1985) Patriarchy and the labour market: Occupational control strategies and the medical division of labour, in Knights, D. and Willmott, M. (eds) *The Gendered Labour Process*. Brighton: Gower

Zola, I. K. (1973) Pathways to the doctor – From person to patient, pp 677–89, *Social Science and Medicine*, 7

Exam practice: Health

Essay questions

1 'The unequal distribution of good health reflects wider patterns of inequality in society.'
Assess this view in the light of sociological arguments and evidence. *(25 marks)*

2 Evaluate sociological contributions to an understanding of the relationship between health care and gender. *(25 marks)*

(From Summer 1997 AEB AS Sociology, Paper 2, © 1997 AEB)

3 Evaluate sociological approaches which have challenged medical explanations of the social distribution of health. *(25 marks)*

4 Critically examine the relationship between mental illness and social control. *(25 marks)*

(From Summer 1997 AEB A-level Sociology, A/SOCY/3 Module Paper 3, © 1997 AEB)

13 Power and politics

Topics covered in this chapter

- *Sociological theories of power*
- *The modern state*
- *Political parties, political ideologies and political decision-making*
- *Pressure groups and decision-making*
- *Voting patterns*
- *The role of mass media in politics*

A new era began on 1 May 1997. Voting either for Labour or tactically against the Conservative Party, British voters elected a Labour government. It was an historic Labour landslide, and a spectacular Tory rout. The UK that Margaret Thatcher shaped since 1979 had become richer but more unequal. The British electorate had decided it was time for a change.

The ensuing victory was so colossal (Labour won 419 of the House of Common's 659 seats – a 177 seat majority), Prime Minister Tony Blair has been given a mandate for change no other incoming government has had in the second half of the twentieth century. The once all-powerful Conservative fighting machine that thought of itself as the natural party of government held just 165 seats. Not since the Duke of Wellington was defeated by the Whigs in 1832 have things been so bad for the Tories. The third party, the Liberal Democrats, increased their seats significantly, taking 46 in total. In share of the vote terms (turnout was 71.3 per cent), Labour obtained 44.4 per cent, Conservative 31.4 per cent, Liberal Democrats 17.2 per cent, and other parties 7 per cent.

Importantly, Blair's re-moulding of the Labour Party has struck a chord with the so-called 'Middle England' that was frightened off by Neil Kinnock in 1992. Henceforth, no political party can dare to assume that it owns anyone's vote. The old ideological gulf between parties of the business and trade union power blocs has been bridged. Even Blair expressed surprise over the collapse of the Conservative Party's assumption that it always gains a substantial portion of the vote.

The Prime Minister might have been surprised, but the social scientists did pretty well on this occasion. The percentage share of the vote predicted by the final poll of polls (with actual results in brackets) was: Labour 47 (44); Conservative 31 (29); Liberal

After 18 years of Conservative rule, a Labour Prime Minister enters Number 10 after the May 1997 General Election.

Democrats 16 (17); Others 16 (13). Several months after the election, another poll, reported in the *Observer* (5 October 1997), disclosed that four out of five voters thought Conservative Party leader, William Hague, was 'weak', whilst 90 per cent thought Prime Minister Blair was 'strong'.

Labour have made a spectacular comeback. The signs are that they'll be in office for at least two terms. But I read somewhere that a week is a long time in politics!

Sociological theories of power

Power comes from many things: the barrel of a gun; the position of corporate president; the bench of a red-robed judge; the four gold bands on an airline captain's jacket; the scalpel of a heart surgeon. *Power* gives those who wield it the capacity to do things that affect other people's lives. Often, it doesn't matter whether or not these people give their consent. A bank robber gets what she or he wants by threatening to shoot the cashier. A corporate president hires and fires because bosses are allowed to do that. Although some people contest and resist the powers of others, 'Different people', as Zygmunt Bauman points out, 'have different degrees of freedom' (1992: 113). Powerful people are able to act more freely than people who have little or no power.

The rich and mighty are also able to restrict the freedom of others. This means that even brave resistance might fail to achieve its goal. Georg Simmel says that 'the desire for domination is designed to break the *internal* resistance of the subjugated' (Simmel 1950, in Coser and Rosenberg 1969: 135). With a tinge of optimism though, he adds that, under the most severe forms of oppression, there's scope for a lot of personal freedom. Consider, for example, a brave mother who stands in a Latin American city square with a picture of her unjustly imprisoned son, daring a corrupt and cruel regime to release him. She exercises the freedom of a hero, and her *élan* carries great moral power.

Power, authority and ideology

Power on its own is raw, and often relies on the threat or use of violence or other unpleasant sanctions. *Legitimate power*, however, carries – indeed, becomes – *authority*. It rests on the acceptance of the people under its sway. *Legitimacy* is a claim to power that people accept. Naked power is often that of the bully or tyrant, legitimate power of the authorised holder of office. In most societies, a balance is struck between the use of coercion and persuasion, and, in that respect, force is the armour plating rather than the norm. Moreover, force is only permissible if it's used according to law.

Authority is an effective form of 'power' because it gains the consent of those who are subject to it. In capitalist societies marxists are wary of this. Used by corporate bosses and politicians, authority can be a soft form of social control, a gentle subjugation that uses *ideology* (the collective outlook of a social group) to coax rather than to cajole. There are, of course, in any society – capitalist or otherwise – types of authority that no marxist would object to: the authority of an authentic socialist, the authority of a dedicated paramedic, the authority of a good parent.

People who have lots of power, says the American sociologist, C. Wright Mills, 'are in positions to make decisions having major consequences' (1973: 4). All of us have some power, but few of us exercise the kind of power Mills has in mind. Contrast, for example, the power of teachers to detain students after school, with the power of the US military to detonate an atomic bomb over Hiroshima. Accepting that degrees of power exist, it's nevertheless helpful to define power in general. Here we turn to the German sociologist, Max Weber, who writes:

'By *power* is meant that opportunity existing within a social relationship which permits one to carry out one's own will even against resistance and regardless of the basis on which this opportunity rests.'

(Weber 1968: 117, first published in 1913)

These British police officers, who are removing Greenpeace activists protesting oil exploration in the Atlantic, must only use the force that the law allows.

Power becomes more palatable when it's exercised as authority rather than as brute force. Weber made this clear when he introduced the notion of legitimacy. Put simply, *legitimate power is authority*. A charismatic leader, for example, possesses authority in the eyes of her or his followers because of emotional surrender to the leader's will. Legitimacy might also derive from a rational belief in the binding validity of law, as when people accept the decision of a judge. We'll say more about Weber's theory of power and authority later.

The link between authority and ideology is important. People who exercise power on its own do so through the use or threat of coercion. Getting people to accept that one's power is legitimate, however, involves an act of persuasion. The vehicle for obtaining consent is often ideological control – or *hegemony* as it's also called. The marxist social scientist, Antonio Gramsci, argues that a ruling class sustains power by passing off its way of looking at things as the norm for the rest of society. Its ideology is thereby internalised and accepted by subordinate classes. This isn't to say that subordinates are expected to think and behave like rulers. Rather, they're socialised into attitudes and behaviours that the rulers deem appropriate for the 'lower' classes.

Power is complex. It manifests itself in different ways. There are, however, general categories. Herbert Goldhamer and Edward A. Shils (1939, in Coser and Rosenberg 1969: 145) distinguish three main types of power in relation to the kind of influence exercised by an individual over another:

- *force*, when she or he 'influences behavior by a physical manipulation of the subordinated individual (assault, confinement, etc.)'
- *domination*, when she or he 'influences behavior by making explicit to others what he [*sic*] wants them to do (command, request, etc.)'
- *manipulation*, when she or he 'influences the behavior of others without making explicit the behavior which he [*sic*] thereby wants them to perform' (propaganda and the undermining of confidence are examples of manipulation).

OVER TO YOU

Which, if any, of the three types of power described by Goldhamer and Shils correspond to authority? This is a tricky question.

Now that we've introduced the concept of power and highlighted its connection with authority and ideology, it's time to consider five key sociological theories of power:

- functionalist–pluralist
- marxist
- weberian
- elite
- postmodern.

Functionalist–pluralist theory of power

Functionalists and pluralists adopt a similar approach to power, which is why we've joined functionalist and pluralist with a hyphen. Some commentators might suggest that, because functionalists emphasise *consensus* and pluralists emphasise *difference*, the two theorists are at odds with each other. This isn't really the case. Functionalists and pluralists both recognise that consensus and difference co-exist in society. They also note that people who have different views often agree to disagree. In a pluralist society, there *is* a consensus about the need for tolerance.

Functionalists and pluralists argue that power is diffused rather than in the hands of rulers. The functionalist sociologist, Talcott Parsons, contends that:

'Power may, for the present purposes, be conceived as the capacity of the society to mobilize its resources in the interest of goals, defined as positively rather than permissively sanctioned by the system as a whole – goals that are "affected with a public interest".'

(Parsons 1967: 224, first published in 1959)

This is complex language. In simpler terms, Parsons is proposing that power is what people allow politicians to do in the public interest. Tony Blair's remark that government is the servant of the people echoes this point.

Adopting the weberian concept of legitimate power (i.e. authority), Parsons proposes that the most important holders of power in society are members of the government. Contesting the argument that power is control over others, he (1967: 225) sees 'power as capacity to get things done', irrespective of resistance or not. Parsons adds that power engages 'the capacity of a social system to get things done in its collective interest' (1967: 225). Power is thus envisaged as the property of society rather than of a privileged minority. Parsons proposes that responsible political leadership protects personal freedom and property, ensuring justice and order, and promoting the general – the plural – welfare.

In a critique of his fellow American, C. Wright Mills (see the section on elite theory, page 367), Parsons (1960, in Parsons 1969) argues that Mills over-exaggerates the extent to which power in American society is concentrated in the hands of the very rich. Noting that Mills seems to overlook the series of checks and balances of the sort that keeps monopolistic power blocs at bay, Parsons is sceptical of the argument that a power elite has been freed from the historic constraints of American society. It's apposite that America has never had a titled ruling class of the kind previously found in the UK. Americans are wary of ascribed status, fiercely championing the principle of achieved status. In such a society, it becomes well nigh impossible for one social group to achieve overall command. The original captains of industry and their heirs have thus failed to gain overall cumulative advantage.

The notion of an absence of cumulative advantage by one or a few groups is crucial to the concept of *pluralism*. It underpins the work of the pluralist theorist, Robert A. Dahl. Says Dahl of democratic societies, pluralism refers 'to the existence of a plurality of relatively autonomous (independent) organizations (subsystems) within the domain of a state' (Dahl 1982: 5). He concedes though that no actual regime ever achieves democratic pluralism. The ideal criteria are too demanding. Even so, countries whose political arrangements most closely approximate the criteria may be considered as having pluralist systems. This is a fair and reasonable point. Human endeavour rarely, if ever, obtains perfection. But if it gets fairly close, that's good enough for purposes of sociological classification.

The participatory ideal of pluralism – whereby everyone becomes a political decision-maker – is, of course, unattainable in large nations. Dahl acknowledges this. He also accepts that marxism is correct in emphasising the strong tendencies in society towards domination by ruling groups. But these tendencies aren't inevitable and, even when they do arise, they can be countered by independent organisations that help to curb concentrated power. Pressure groups, like trade unions and charities, can sometimes be very effective in this context. Consider, for example, the work of Amnesty International in persuading certain governments to show more respect for human rights.

Parsons (1960, in Parsons 1969) advances the functionalist–pluralist argument that power in society, while in some cases disproportionately concentrated among certain groups, is also quite widely dispersed. Responsibility in American society, he contends, has been carried by business and military elites, politicians, lawyers, economists, journalists, educational professionals, political scientists, natural scientists and 'upper class' people in more than the purely economic sense. He also highlights 'non-political' government officials who influence policy decisions.

Maybe power is more scattered than elite theorists like Mills would have us believe. However, lorry drivers, nurses, coal miners and unemployed people don't feature in the circles of power and influence to which Parsons refers. Nor has power filtered to any significant degree through to women, to people who have disabilities, or to minority ethnic groups. Nevertheless, politicians do take account of 'ordinary people'. In 1997, for example, the Labour government decided to set up a 5,000-strong focus group to gauge public reaction to existing and new policies and to the performance of public services.

The 'people's panel' – expected to come on stream by 1998 – will sit for at least a year, and will be quizzed on various issues and policies. Ministers believe the

In a pluralist society, the people make their opinions known to government. There's no guarantee that politicians will act on what the people demand. But if popular views are ignored, there's no guarantee that the people will return them to power at election time.

panel will narrow the gap between politicians and voters, and make government more accountable. The pluralistic ethos of the Labour government was also highlighted in the Queen's Speech (which sets out government policy plans) in 1997 shortly after it had won the election. The agenda was an ambitious one. It included:

- a Scottish parliament
- an authority for Wales
- a strategic authority for London (the 'people's voice' in the capital was lost when Margaret Thatcher abolished the Greater London Council)
- a commitment to incorporate the European Convention of Human Rights into UK law
- a promise of a white paper on freedom of information to enable consultation of the proposed legislation.

New Labour is also considering an alternative to 'first-past-the-post' voting. The 1997 General Election – in which about 44 per cent of the people's votes put Labour MPs on two-thirds of parliament's seats – highlights the deficiencies of this system. There's already a promise to introduce proportional representation (PR) for elections of British MPs to the European Parliament. Even closer to home – with Celtic and European parliaments elected by PR – Westminster, says the *Observer*'s political columnist, Andrew Rawnsley, 'would look strikingly anomalous, the last rotten borough of democracy' (13 July 1997, page 25). If Labour keeps to its pledges, things look set to move in a pluralist direction.

FUNCTIONALIST–PLURALIST THEORY OF POWER

FOR

+ 'Western' societies are democratic, which means that 'people power' does exist. Not only is this power manifested in the ballot box, but also in pressure groups, the media, and so forth. The people have otherthrown monarchs, dictators and presidents. They've also played important roles, through referendums, in policy decisions. It's likely, for example, that UK citizens will be able to decide if they want the country to join a common European currency. This is precisely the kind of consensus that functionalists point to.

+ Functionalist–pluralists don't go overboard with their claims. Dahl, for example, acknowledges that marxists are right to emphasise strong tendencies towards minority group domination. At the same time, Dahl and other pluralists point out that checks and balances help to keep oligarchy at bay because no one single group is usually able to obtain absolute power. From Dahl, we also learn the important point that concentrated power and dispersed power don't have to be seen as 'either/or' issues. Both can and do co-exist, but rarely if ever does an oligarchy gain the upper hand.

+ The functionalist–pluralist claim that power is dispersed and consensus prevails seems to fit the reality of the consensus politics promoted and practised by the New Labour government. Its readiness to listen to voices from all sections of society – industry, professionals, trade unions, the 'people's panel', fox hunters – suggests that politicians intend to bring a wide spectrum of opinion into government policy. While it's true that listening isn't the same as acting upon what one hears, it's relevant to note that President Clinton in the US has incorporated the opinions of voter panels into political policy.

AGAINST

– The notion that politicians are the servants of the people, and act on plural rather than singular interests, is an article of faith rather than an empirical reality. To be sure, some politicians are altruistic and public-spirited. Others, however, are greedy and corrupt. Yet others, while not necessarily corrupt, are more interested in furthering their political careers than taking a serious interest in serving their constituents. Functionalist–pluralist theorists are rather naive if they place too much emphasis on the view that politicians have the common good in mind.

– Although they probably wouldn't admit it, functionalists–pluralists are quite ideological. By regarding power, 'responsibly' devolved and executed, as the benevolent guarantor of social cohesion, they implicitly approve the continuation of the *status quo*. This makes them – with some notable exceptions – inclined towards conservative ways. Arguably, such a 'political' orientation compromises their efforts to remain objective. Even though functionalists–pluralists are rarely as 'up-front' about their values as marxists, they can't pretend not to have ideological leanings.

– The functionalist–pluralist notion of checks and balances in society, whereby one group's power cancels out another's, doesn't take full account of the inequalities of power that exist between different groups. The presence of ascendant and subordinate groups (for example, politicians and unemployed people) suggests that, far from there being a balance of power, there's a huge imbalance. When 'unstoppable force' meets 'immovable object', a negotiated compromise is the only realistic outcome. But when either of these power blocs encounters a weaker obstacle, it usually knocks it out of the way or halts its momentum.

The Queen's Speech in 1997 signalled the Labour government's commitment to give more of a voice to the people.

Marxist theory of power

Marx contends that power is concentrated in the hands of an economic class that rules politically – a ruling class. The landed aristocracy which presided over government and other strategic command posts in nineteenth-century England was such a class. For much of the nineteenth century, the landed aristocrats (titled and non-titled) dominated both Houses of Parliament. The basis of political ascendancy was property. As Robert A. Nisbet remarks:

'Economic ownership and political power coalesced almost perfectly. This was to seen not merely in the overwhelming number of Parliamentary seats that went to members of the landed class and in the astonishing degree of consensus that reigned among them, but in the monopoly they held of administrative functions in local and county government.'

(Nisbet 1970: 114–15)

Minimum landed credentials for entry into parliament had been established by law in 1710, and so the owners of land derived from it not only wealth but the right to govern. As late as 1868, landowners supplied two-thirds of MPs, and it wasn't until 1880 (three years before Marx's death) that parliament was represented for the first time with a majority of the new ruling class of capitalists. Before taking centre-stage in politics, however, the capitalists had to work through landowners patrons. Writing of the landed Whigs, Marx reported that they:

'are the aristocratic representatives of the Bourgeoisie, of the industrial and commercial middle class. Under the condition that the Bourgeoisie should abandon to them, to an oligarchy of aristocratic families, the monopoly of government and the exclusive possession of office, they make to the middle class, and assist it in conquering, all those concessions which in the course of social and political development have shown themselves to have become unavoidable and undelayable.'

(Marx 1852, cited in Bottomore and Rubel 1975: 201)

By the late nineteenth century, the *bourgeoisie* (Marx's term for the economically powerful capitalist class) had monopolised and was using the state to pursue its own interests. At this crucial moment, the new barons of steam and coal had also became a dominant political class – a ruling class. But, according to Marx, they were destined to be the last ruling class. Pauperised by low wages, workers would eventually unite in common cause and overthrow their rulers – peacefully or violently, depending on circumstances – and usher in a classless, egalitarian society based on communism. In such a society, power differentials would disappear.

Though not quite so close-fitting as it was in the nineteenth-century world, Marx's model of power is an approximation of what happens in capitalist societies today. John Scott, for example, claims that:

'Britain is ruled by a capitalist class whose economic dominance is sustained by the operations of the state and whose members are disproportionately represented in the power elite which rules the state apparatus. That is to say, Britain does have a ruling class.'

(Scott 1992: 151)

Even those capitalists who don't actively participate in politics, are part of the ruling class, because crucial political decisions are taken on their behalf by their 'representatives' in government. In the UK, for example, cabinet members regularly confer with the business community and act upon its counsel. Marx actually considered parliament and other state institutions to be the 'committee rooms' of the bourgeoisie.

On the other side of the Atlantic, the sociologist, William Domhoff (1979), notes that today's American ruling class – at most, 0.5 per cent of the population – ensure that they obtain 'access' to the politicians who are elected to office. Ralph Miliband, also American, notes that business leaders exercise political influence and sometimes determine state intervention in economic affairs. He adds, however, that only rarely is there 'direct and sovereign rule by businessmen as such' (cited by Scott 1992: 29). Nevertheless, a fusion clearly occurs between economic position and political influence, even when this happens indirectly.

The Italian marxist and political prisoner, Antonio Gramsci (1891–1937), also highlights the way in which capitalists look to government to support their interests. During the early part of the twentieth century, for example, the Italian capitalist class relied on the political support of the Liberal Party. Says Gramsci of the party:

> 'It is the governing party of the capitalist class: through the effects of competition, it aims to industrialize the whole of society's organized labour and to mould the entire property-owning class on the model of its economic client, the capitalist industrialist.'
>
> (Gramsci 1977: 167, first published in 1920)

Another marxist, Nicos Poulantzas, contends that the capitalist state represents the interests of a power bloc of dominant classes and fractions (sub-groups within classes). While, however, he recognises that 'the state is the centre of the exercise of political power' (1973: 115), Poulantzas argues that this doesn't mean that the state is a mere instrument of social classes. It has its own autonomy. Unlike some of the classical marxists,

MARXIST THEORY OF POWER

FOR

+ In the nineteenth century, the English society Marx experienced, studied and wrote about contained a ruling class of big property owners who either exercised direct political rule or flexed economic muscles to ensure that parliament largely did as they bid. Despite his tendency to get righteously angry about social arrangements he personally disapproved of, Marx's concept of an economic class that rules directly or strongly influences political decisions closely fits this empirical reality.
+ Allowing for changes in the power structure over the past 100 or so years, Marx's emphasis on the links between economic power and political rule is still a helpful concept. Many Conservative MPs are capitalists. The 'City' and New Labour enjoy a close, cosy relationship. The Prime Minister, Tony Blair, and the Chancellor of the Exchequer, Gordon Brown, take account of 'City' opinion when they make important political decisions. Even though many Labour MPs don't have a business background, the fact that New Labour is keen to cultivate a good relationship with the capitalist class lends support to Marx's notion that government is the committee of the bourgeoisie.
+ The marxist concept of hegemony demonstrates that marxist thought itself has matured as time has gone by. Orthodox marxists arguably exaggerated the extent to which the ruling class consciously controlled the working class. Hegemony is a more subtle and a more plausible notion. It shows how instruments of social control are weaved into taken-for-granted norms and values. Direct propaganda is a blunt instrument and, although it exists to some degree in British society, marxists acknowledge that ruling-class ideology is more often mediated rather than 'injected'.

AGAINST

– Marx mixed social scientific rigour with personal opinion. While, for example, he understood that capitalist behaviours were shaped by prevailing social circumstances, he displayed profound hostility towards capitalism and capitalists. Nor were aristocratic landowners, especially Whigs (whom he saw as collaborating with factory owners and bankers), immune from his scathing commentaries. Marx referred to Whigs as corrupt and deceitful. His work is a mixed bag of social science and rage. Even in his more dispassionate moments, one wonders to what extent his objectivity might have been affected by his intense dislike of the capitalism he described.

– Marx's belief that classes and power differentials would vanish under communism is wishful thinking rather than empirical fact. The strength of his conviction has no bearing on the likelihood of the predicted outcome. Conviction aside, no social scientist – Marx included – is in a position to make pronouncements about the future of political systems. This is crystal ball gazing, not sociology. The best that marxists can do, in social scientific terms, is to make modest suggestions about possible developments based on current trends. By attempting to do more than this, they overstate their case.

– Marxists exaggerate the extent to which the ruling class exercises power over other classes. Politicians and capitalists aren't immune from the collective power of voter opinion and trade union action. The Conservative leadership found that out to its cost when Labour won a landslide victory in the 1997 General Election. In the same year, British Airways also discovered that the Transport and General Workers Union wasn't prepared to be browbeaten by bosses during an industrial dispute. The union managed to negotiate a settlement with the airline on terms agreeable to its members.

Poulantzas doesn't assume that political power is contingent on economic muscle. Thus, for example, a dominant political class that loses economic sway doesn't necessarily lose its pre-eminent position in government. The reverse is also the case. Indeed, there are endless permutations.

Take, for instance nineteenth-century Britain. Landowners continued to govern even when their economic wealth was surpassed by rich industrialists. On the flip side of the coin, some industrialists possessed massive economic power, but failed to gain entry to parliament.

Marxist sociologists – and Marx himself – are agreed that ruling-class power relies on more than just coercion. Marx notes that ruling-class ideas saturate society and become part of the people's culture. This assertion is echoed by Gramsci, who contends that the rule of one class over the rest of society is based less on brute force than on cultural ascendancy (*hegemony*). Gramsci argues that for a class to be dominant, it has to pass off its own values as the values of the whole of society. In that way, it achieves the ideological predominance of hegemony, of control obtained by the 'consent' of subordinate classes.

Hegemony is exercised through cultural institutions, such as schools. The hegemony of the ruling class permeates everyday norms and values, such that people imbibe the leaders' ideology without being aware of this. The more that leaders have to rely on force to keep opposition at bay, the less likely they are to succeed in the long term. Coercive regimes tend to have a short shelf-life, because violence often provokes a strong backlash from the subjugated class. Hegemony is such a potent cultural weapon precisely because it coaxes rather than cajoles obedience. In that respect, it converts naked power into authority.

There's an interesting parallel here with Weber's concept of legitimation, which was discussed earlier and is considered further in the next section.

Weberian theory of power

Unlike Marx, who argues that power is essentially class-based, Weber contends that power is distributed between three main groups:

- *social classes* – economic groups whose members share similar market situations and therefore similar material and social benefits
- *status groups* – social groups whose members share similar levels of prestige, and who typically place restrictions on how other people may interact with them
- *parties* – political groups whose members influence the actions of the state. Weber's use of the term 'parties' is fairly flexible, and includes pressure groups (for example, animal rights activists) and trade unions (for example, the National Union of Mineworkers), as well as political parties (for example, the Liberal Democrat Party).

People usually belong to more than just one of these groups. For example, a coal miner is working class, belongs to a status group of skilled workers, and is a member of a 'party' in the form of a trade union. Each of these groups is involved in an attempt to obtain power in society. Although the exercise of power ultimately relies on the use or threat of force, Weber reminds us that most power relationships involve obedience. The people over whom power is exercised usually accept the authority of the power-holders. Such acceptance, notes Weber, is typically based on three kinds of authority:

- *legal-rational* – resting upon rules that are rationally enacted (for example, the authority of an official, like a school inspector)
- *charismatic* – resting on extraordinary personal qualities (for example, the authority of an inspirational hero, like a civil rights leader)
- *traditional* – resting on what has actually or allegedly always existed (for example, the authority of a parent, like a mother).

> **EXAM TIP**
>
> Charismatic people aren't necessarily good people. Some are; some aren't. Martin Luther King and Adolf Hitler both had charismatic qualities, even though the first struggled for justice, and the second committed acts of terrible injustice.

Legal-rational authority

Weber regarded legal-rational authority as a key feature of the modern world. People who possess it appeal not to magic or personal qualities, but to correct procedure. Law is the most obvious manifestation of legal-rational authority. It's literally legal, and it's rational. Law requires the compliance of everyone, and its rules are applied rationally and consistently. What's obeyed is the law, not a person. There are, however, makers and enforcers of laws. These people are office-holders, and their authority is defined within the limits of the law In that sense, legal-rational authority isn't arbitrary or capricious. If, as an officer of the law, I arrest you, my action must be lawful. The authority of British MPs is also of the legal-rational type. The holders of political office have authority, not as individuals, but as officers of parliament. They're bound by its conventions and procedures.

Charismatic authority

This kind of authority rests on the exceptional attributes of the power-holders. Charismatic leaders obtain these extraordinary characteristics in lots of different settings. Charismatic leaders range from religious prophets, through generals, to politicians. Examples in each of these categories (and there are, of course, other categories) are Jesus Christ, Napoleon Bonaparte and John F. Kennedy. In these and in other cases, authority is granted by advocates and supporters because they believe in their leaders' missions. In a 'pure' charismatic setting (which rarely occurs in the real world), the charismatic leader exercises power without organisational back-up. Jesus didn't have to rely on any organisation to inspire his followers. However, this kind of 'solitary' charisma seldom lasts. Over time, the great leader's teachings often become 'corrupted', not least by organisations which become carriers and also distributors of the original message. Weber speaks here of the routinisation of charisma. The authority lose its brio and becomes routine rather than special.

Traditional authority

This kind of authority resides in the power of convention. Weber identified three types of traditional authority:

- gerontology (rule by elders)
- patriarchalism (rule by head of household, typically, as the name implies, by males)
- patrimonialism (rule by despots, again, usually males).

Rule by elders is commonly found in small pre-industrial communities. One might add, however, that some nation states have their 'elder statesmen' (and they usually are men). The Russian president, Boris Yeltsin, is an example. Patriarchs, say feminists, are commonplace even in the 1990s, because a head of household status role is often adopted by men. The tradition was also enshrined in the principle of primogeniture among English aristocrats, which meant that the first-born son inherited the country

WEBER'S THEORY OF POWER

FOR

+ Weber notes that *different* groups in society exercise *different* types of power. He takes the discussion beyond social class to include political and status groups. His is a sociological model that looks to the evidence rather than assuming that economic muscle is the only or predominant fount of power. This isn't to say that Weber ignores the importance of class. He doesn't. But nor does he privilege one power group over another. There's no second-guessing with Weber. His concepts of power are drawn from but never replace empirical reality.

+ Weber refines the concept of power by describing its legitimate forms in terms of types of authority: charismatic, traditional and legal-rational. His model of legal-rational authority approximates more closely than any other concept to the reality of authority in the modern 'western' world. That said, people today are arguably less in awe of persons whose authority rests on legal-rational authority than in the past. Given his resolve to be guided by empirical evidence, Weber would have refined or augmented his types of authority in line with current developments – were he alive today, that is.

+ The avoidance of value judgements is a recurrent theme in Weber's analysis of power. Privately, he might have been angry about the greed of certain capitalists (he had socialist leanings), but he doesn't allow his personal politics to cloud his sociological judgement. He recognises that values arise when sociologists decide what to study, but, once the study is underway, he seeks to keep value-judgements at bay. This makes for excellent sociology. When one reads Weber's work, one knows that social science, not polemic, is at the forefront.

AGAINST

– Weber arguably underestimates the importance of economic power in society. While power can independently come from other sources, notably, status and politics, economic clout usually lies behind high status and political influence. It's rare to find, except in a moral sense, high levels of esteem among the poor and oppressed. Nor do many people from low-income households exercise significant political influence. Nobody is saying that all authority derives from economic position. However, perhaps more comes from that source than Weber might allow.

– The trend towards postmodern culture requires an even more sophisticated analysis of authority than Weber's three types achieves. Postmodernists contend that legitimacy in all its forms is severely strained by an increasingly sceptical public. In the UK, for example, electors are increasingly distrustful of politicians, imposition from above, and the assumption that 'Whitehall is the expert'. The setting up of people's panels suggests that voter authority needs to be taken into account. Weber's model needs updating.

– The avoidance of value-judgements in sociological analysis makes for a social science that eschews advocacy in favour of science. To be fair to Weber, he disapproved of an indifferent sociology, but his insistence on objectivity has arguably influenced some sociologists to focus more on method than on social justice. Moreover, placing social science above polemic, and empiricism above conviction is itself a value judgement. Values always enter the picture. Better to accept this and adopt the right values rather than imagine they can be kept on the back-burner.

estate. Patrimonial leaders, said Weber, are typically exemplified by sultanates. Similar forms of authority also existed in medieval Europe (for example, barons).

In the real world, different types of authority tend to blend into each other. Even within an institution where one type predominates, some individuals might have authority that rests on another type. Illustrative of this, the American president, JFK, was at the pinnacle of a power structure that rested on legal-rational authority. Yet the president was widely regarded as a charismatic leader. Whilst charisma usually fades, there are exceptions. For example, the 'rebel charm' of the late Argentina-born doctor and revolutionary, Che Guevara, 'reaches beyond the grave to forge [a] popular new front', reports the *Observer* (4 May 1997).

OVER TO YOU

What other leaders today or in the past might be said to have charismatic authority? Justify your answer sociologically.

Weber's main interest was in the development of legal-rational authority in 'western' societies. Weber had a bit of a pluralist tendency. He rejects simplistic notions of domination, arguing that no group – capitalist class or otherwise – is assured of the automatic right to rule. Effective rule is grounded in authority – through custom, charisma or, in the case of modern societies, law and other rational procedures. Weber does, however, concede that the state can exercise a decisive political role, in part, because it holds a monopoly over the legitimate use of force. Importantly, he adds that the state isn't the puppet of any one group.

Even former US President, Richard Nixon, couldn't avert impeachment when his behaviour was judged to have breached correct procedure. People power can be formidable, as John Major found to his cost at the last general election. US president, Bill Clinton, acknowledges that 'There is no one more powerful than a member of a focus group'. Clinton is referring to representative panels of voters – like the UK People's Panel referred to earlier – who offer their opinions to politicians. Throughout his 1995 budget showdown with the Republican-led Congress, focus group data showed voters wanted a balanced budget, but not at the expense of public spending on health, education and the environment. Accordingly, Clinton promised fiscal restraint, but always exempted those key three areas. He won the budget stand-off and the 1996 presidential election.

It looks as though grassroots democracy and the 'voter authority' it bestows might add a fourth type of authority to Weber's trilogy.

Elite theory of power

Elites are 'superior' groups whose position is based on economic and/or other criteria. The 'and/or' part is important. A ruling class, for example, is, first and foremost, a powerful economic group, from whence it derives political domination. Marxists believe that economic power is the main fount of all other power. Elite theorists make no such assumption. They argue that an elite is an ascendant group whose dominance can come from any number of sources: superior education, better morals, military might, vast wealth, etc. In the case of vast wealth, of course, an economic elite might also be a political ruling class.

Among the most well-known elite theorists are:

- Gaetano Mosca
- Vilfredo Pareto
- Robert Michels.

The first two are Italian, the third German. Unlike Marx, who predicted the future collective rule of the people, Mosca, Pareto and Michels all believed that this vision would be confounded by an endless succession of minority ruling elites. Although the claims of these three sociologists differed in certain respects, they were all distrusting of a marxist utopia. They wrote in response to the popularity of socialist doctrines in early nineteenth-century Europe.

They argued that there were inevitable splits between the unorganised masses of the people and the organised minority of a dominant elite. Even when democratic values are officially adopted by political organisations, the tendency towards rule by *oligarchies* (elite minorities) is marked. Michels even spoke of an 'iron law of oligarchy'. All three sociologists adopt the pessimistic view that domination by a select minority – an elite – is inherent in large-scale society, and won't therefore vanish under socialism. We'll look at each of these three 'classical' – they wrote some time ago – elite theorists in succession. Then we'll turn the spotlight on a more recent elite theorist, the American sociologist, C. Wright Mills.

Gaetano Mosca

Mosca contends that societies are always ruled by oligarchies (powerful minorities):

'In all societies . . . two classes of people appear – a class that rules and a class that is ruled. The first class, always the less numerous, performs all political functions, monopolizes power and enjoys the advantages that power brings, whereas the second, the more numerous class, is directed and controlled by the first, in a manner that is now more or less legal, now more or less arbitrary and violent, and supplies the first, in appearance at least, with material means of subsistence and with the instrumentalities that are essential to the vitality of the political organism.'

(Mosca 1939: 50, first published in 1896)

Mosca distinguishes different types of oligarchy: military elites; priestly elites; hereditary elites; landowning elites; moneyed elites; and elites of merit. He also acknowledges that an 'elite' can emerge from the people. If discontented, the people might rise up and depose their rulers. In such an event, 'there would have to be another organized minority within the masses themselves to discharge the functions of a ruling class' (Mosca 1939: 51). This sounds remarkably like the marxist notion of the *dictatorship of the proletariat*: a transitional revolutionary ruling group which would unselfishly pave the way to its own demise, thereby allowing the emergence of a classless society.

The ruling minority – often referred to by Mosca as the 'political or ruling class' – justify their rule on the basis of principles that are accepted by the ruled majority. Marx would call these principles an 'ideology'. Mosca uses the term 'political formula'. He accepts that the formula isn't exactly truthful, but adds that it isn't a deliberate deception either. Controversially, Mosca also argues that members of the ruling minority are superior to the masses. This superiority can be gauged in material, intellectual, and even moral terms.

It's noteworthy that Mosca extends the discussion beyond purely economic issues. The marxist concept of ruling class is premised on the notion of an economic class that enjoys or strongly influences political rule. For Mosca, the ruling minority constitute an elite: the 'top' people, whether this ascendancy is based on military, economic, religious, educational, moral or other grounds. Not only did Mosca adopt a different theoretical argument to Marx, he also morally rejected the political vision of Marx. Said Mosca:

'As we have seen, a pernicious and effective propaganda of destructive hate between the social classes is developed in the pages of Marx's *Kapital*. It is also certain that to promote that hatred was one of the purposes that Marx set himself in his writings.'

(Mosca 1939: 479)

Espousing what sounds like a functionalist 'cause', Mosca says that 'Devotion to the national interests must always be stronger than devotion to class interests' (1939: 481). He laments, however, the tendency in modern representative systems (i.e. democracies) of relaxing the forces of moral cohesion 'which . . . constitute the cement without which any political edifice totters and collapses' (1939: 481). Clearly, Mosca is no believer in democracy. In fact, he regards 'the granting of universal suffrage as a mistake' (1939: 492). While he concedes that to go back on democracy would be a second mistake, it's clear that Mosca approves of the rule of the 'best' people, of a 'superior' elite. He doesn't approve of a greedy aristocracy though – rather one that is moral and intellectual. Do I hear you saying, 'Wishful thinking!'?

Vilfredo Pareto

Like Mosca, Pareto broadly distinguished between a 'superior' (notably, more talented) stratum and a 'lower' stratum. The former group are divided into two subgroups: those who directly or indirectly play a substantial governing role and those who don't. The elite thus contains a governing elite (also called a governing class or governing classes) and a non-governing elite.

Although he was a sociologist and therefore concerned with group behaviour, Pareto also highlighted the influence of strong human personalities on elite behaviour. Said Pareto:

'The notion that great historical occurrences are attributable to small personal causes is now almost wholly discarded, but it is frequently replaced by another error, that of denying the individual any influence at all on circumstances. Unquestionably, the battle of Austerlitz could have been won by some general other than Napoleon if this other had been a great battle commander. But if the French had been led by an incompetent general, they would have lost the battle well and truly.'

(1902, in Pareto 1976: 123–4)

Given that competence is generally associated with reason, it comes as a surprise to find that Pareto believes:

'a very large number of human actions are not the outcome of reasoning. They are purely instinctive actions, although the man [*sic*] performing them experiences a feeling of pleasure in giving them, quite arbitrarily, logical causes.'

(1902, in Pareto 1976: 124)

Inner urges are manifested by outward actions. These actions aren't as raw as instinct. They're modified and refined through experience, and are called *residues*. People, however, attribute a semblance of reason to residues. This 'justification' is called a *derivation*. Thus, for example, an aggressive urge might be manifested in military marching (a residue). The argument (derivation) to make this appear a reasonable action might be that it fosters the spirit of 'brothers in arms'.

Pareto does concede that some actions are genuinely logical. If he didn't, his remarks on the pivotal decisions of battle commanders would be disingenuous. The *interests* – in the sense of wants – that people have often give rise to logical reasoning. When people want things, they generally figure out ways to get them, thus behaving in logical, calculating ways.

According to Pareto, the residues that characterise a particular elite correspond to a particular form of government. Two general types of residue are noteworthy here:

- *combination (so-called class I) residues*, which include personality traits such as activeness, entrepreneurial spirit, innovativeness, originality and risk-taking
- *persistence (so-called class II) residues*, which include personality traits such as caution, legalism, patriotism, prudence and traditionalism.

Elites whose members have mainly class II residues are military types who obtain position through force. Once in power, they become patriotic traditionalists. Pareto refers to these elites as lions. Their counterpart, foxes, are elites where class I residues predominate. Foxes are cunning and secure office by stealth. Once the lions have settled into comfortable old ways, the foxes display innovative, risk-taking entrepreneurialism. Gradually, they outwit the conservative lions and take over. The circulation of elites continues though because a traditionalist backlash, accompanied by the threat or use of force, sweeps the lions back into power.

Unlike Mosca, who was quite openly against democracy, Pareto claimed that his own work was scientific, not subjective, and that he wasn't an opponent of democracy. Indeed, Pareto greatly admired Swiss democracy, which he regarded as the best government in the world. That said, he seems generally to have taken a rather dim view of the concept of democracy. In scathing terms, Pareto writes:

'A political system in which the "people" expresses its "will" (supposing it to have one, which is arguable) without cliques, intrigues, lobbies and factions, exists only as a pious wish of theorists. It is not observable in reality in the past or the present, either in the West or anywhere else.'

(1916, in Pareto 1976: 270)

What about Switzerland? one is minded to ask.

Although it might be argued that Pareto's emphasis on instinctual behaviour makes him a biological determinist, at the time he was writing, the term 'instinct' had a wider meaning than it has today. Instincts were seen by some early twentieth-century commentators – perhaps Pareto, among them – to comprise acquired and socially conditioned behaviours.

As indicated, Pareto is rather sceptical towards democracy. Nevertheless, he notes that the only way to protect the people from an elite is to strip the elite of its powers and to implement the checks and balances of a pluralist society.

Robert Michels

Michels, a contemporary and a friend of Max Weber, was fascinated by political parties. His extensive study of them led him to conclude that there is 'the inevitability of oligarchy in party life' (1958: vii, first published in 1915). Oligarchy refers to very concentrated power, the kind that is exercised by a tiny minority of leaders. Indeed, 'The most restricted form of oligarchy, absolute monarchy, is', notes Michels, 'founded upon the will of a single individual' (1958: 3).

The antidote to absolute monarchy is democracy, which, in theory, repudiates the right of this kind of despotic power. The *in theory* bit is significant. Says Michels:

'The democratic external form which characterizes the life of political parties may readily veil from superficial observers the tendency towards aristocracy, or rather towards oligarchy, which is inherent in all party organization.'

(Michels 1958: 13)

Michels is perplexed by the fact that the very tendency against which socialist and democratic parties declared war – oligarchy – actually develops in such parties. His study suggests why this happens. According to Michels, the state cannot be anything other than the organisation of a minority whose aim is to impose upon the majority a legal order. This is because the majority are always incapable of self-government. That authority has to be delegated to an oligarchy. The masses also have a tendency to venerate oligarchic leaders, and oligarchic leaders are inclined to be indifferent or apathetic to the needs of the masses. Echoing Weber, Michels also makes the important point that, in politics, the dilettante (the amateur) inevitably yields to professionalism. Put another way, rationalism eventually replaces the heroic dash of the idealist.

On a macro level, Michels supports the assertion of Mosca that no highly developed society is possible without a politically dominant class who are a minority. Michels also brings Pareto into the discussion, noting that Pareto sees socialism as a movement which is favourable to the creation of a new working class elite. Michels adds, however, that Pareto's theory of the circulation of elites must be accepted with considerable reserve. For in most cases, proposes Michels, there isn't a simple replacement of one elite by another, but a continuous process of intermixture whereby new elites get assimilated into old ones.

Michels disputes the marxist notion that the revolution of the working class against the capitalist ruling class will lead to a society in which the state (in marxist terms, the 'executive committee' of the ruling class) will eventually wither away. Marx said this would be preceded by a transitional period in which the revolutionary leaders would take command as 'benevolent socialist dictators'. These leaders would then usher in the stateless communist society in which all social divisions would disappear. Michels isn't convinced.

If such events were ever to transpire, he thought it likely that the working-class dictators, like any group of oligarchs, who would seek to retain their power rather than surrender it. He also predicted that the new 'egalitarian' society would need an extensive bureaucracy. Social (i.e. public) wealth couldn't be administered in any other way. Thus, says Michels, 'we are led by an inevitable logic to the flat denial of the possibility of a state without classes' (1958: 399). In a remarkably insightful manner, he writes:

'The administration of an immeasurably large capital, above all when this capital is collective property, confers upon the administrator influence at least equal to that possessed by the private owner of capital,'

(Michels 1958: 399)

In 1917, two years after Michels wrote these words, the Russian Revolution swept away absolute monarchy, and replaced it with an oligarchy of communist leaders, one of whom, Joseph Stalin, resolutely clung to power, eventually becoming an autocratic dictator. The new 'administrators' of the 'common property' of the people wielded massive political power, and some of them and their successors experienced lifestyles as resplendent as any capitalist.

C. Wright Mills

A more recent elite theorist is C. Wright Mills. In a famous study of the pinnacles of power in 1950s America, Mills identified a:

'power elite . . . composed of men whose positions enable them to transcend the ordinary environments of ordinary men and women . . . they are in command of the major hierarchies and organizations of modern society. They rule the big corporations. They run the machinery of the state and claim its prerogatives. They direct the military establishment. They occupy the strategic command posts of the social structure, in which are now centred the effective means of the power and the wealth and the celebrity which they enjoy.'

(Mills 1973: 3–4)

This quote discloses three key power bases: the economic, the political and the military, all of which interlock. When, for example, America dropped two atomic bombs on Japan during the Second World War, big decisions were made in the boardrooms of arms manufacturers, the Oval Office of the White House, and the airforce bases of generals. Each of these three domains were headed by economic, political and military elites. Acting in unison and collectively, the three elites converge to form what Mills calls 'the power elite of America' (1973: 9).

Mills broadly sees this power elite as a small, tightly knit 'upper class' who occupy the positions in society where major decisions are made. These decisions have a huge impact on society and on the world. Mills doesn't regard the power elite as an exclusively hereditary upper class. Some key decision-makers have inherited wealth, but others are self-made. Noting though that the members of the power elite count a disproportionate number of Ivy League 'old boys' (alumni of prestigious East Coast universities, like Harvard and Yale) within their ranks, Mills bemoans the fact that they're not representative of the population in general.

Unlike Mosca and Pareto, Mills endorses the principle of power to the people. Like the two Italian sociologists, however, Mills concedes that elites aren't at the top of the power pyramid just because they're rich. Warlords, for example, are professional executives rather than capitalists. Although not usually rich, 'They are inside an apparatus of prerogative and graded privilege in which they have been economically secure and unworried' (1973: 195). Top politicians – the members of what Mills terms the political directorate – mainly have a background in the corporate world – professionally, financially, or both. Many will have been businessmen or bankers or the salaried lawyers of big corporations or members of large law firms. A minority are professional politicians – party staffers and civil servants who've made it into politics proper.

Among the corporate rich, we find the major capitalists. The higher one goes into the upper reaches of the corporate rich, the more important is property and the less important is income from professional work. Those with big incomes receive them overwhelmingly from corporate property. While the 'corporate rich are a propertied rich', they also enjoy corporate perks, what Mills terms 'fringe benefits of the higher circles' (1973: 157). These include free medical care in an America where others have to pay, payments of exclusive club fees, company lawyers and accountants available for tax, private recreation areas, company automobiles, etc. Money also spells political influence. Not only do corporate fat cats help to fund political campaigns, more and more of them have entered government directly.

Importantly, Mills adds that American government isn't in any simple sense an extension of the corporate world. It's not the 'committee' of the ruling class. It's a network of 'committees' upon which 'sit' corporation bosses, politicians and military brass. Here we see that Mills is an elite rather than a ruling class theorist. He recognises that corporate clout enters and influences the political arena, but not just on its own. All three elites are involved in virtually every key decision. Which of the three elites takes the lead depends on the task at hand. Generals lead in the Pentagon, corporate bosses in the boardroom, politicians in Washington circles.

But there are crossovers. American capitalism has become military capitalism. There's a coincidence of interest between the owners of productive property and the leaders of warriors. The Washington military clique comprises, says Mills:

'a coalition of generals in the roles of corporation executives, of politicians masquerading as admirals, of corporation executives acting like politicians, of civil servants who become majors, of vice-admirals who are also the assistants to a cabinet officer, who is himself, by the way, really a member of the managerial elite.'

(Mills 1973: 278)

As we can see, the higher reaches of power can't be represented in simple terms. The reality of power is complex, and it's to his credit that Mills recognises this in the concepts he uses. At the same time, Mills doesn't fall into the trap of assuming that the power elite necessarily only represent the interests of upper-class Americans. Some members of elites, says Mills, 'may be ideological representatives of the poor and humble' (1973: 280). Probably many more, of course, represent the sectional interests of their own class. The point is, however, that we can't automatically infer from their social origins what their particular political psychology might be. In that context, it's apposite to note that there are notable examples of middle-class rebels who passionately fought for the rights of the poor and dispossessed: Mandela, King, Ghandi and Guevara, to name a few.

The cement that binds the power elite is the social interaction that occurs in upper circles. Members of the economic, military and political elites know each other as personal friends and even as neighbours. They mingle on the golf course, in the gentlemen's club, on ocean liners and transcontinental aeroplanes. In this manner:

'In the course of their lifetimes, the university president, the New York Stock Exchange chairman, the head of the bank, the old West Pointer – mingle in the status sphere, within which they easily renew old friendships and draw upon them in an effort to understand through the experience of trusted others those contexts of power and decision in which they have not personally moved.'

(Mills 1973: 282)

The higher members of the three elites are also readily able to take over each other's point of view, always

ELITE THEORY OF POWER

FOR

+ History is witness to the fact that in most cases societies divide into elites and non-elites. Not only does this occur in relation to government and people, but also within organisations, like political parties. Michels' point about the oligarchic tendencies of political parties is also corroborated by the reality of political life. New Labour, for example, is tightly policed by the people at the top of the party hierarchy, and it has surrendered many of the ideals of its more egalitarian founders.
+ Elite theorists don't get caught up in the dogmatic assertion that only ruling classes rule. A ruling class – a powerful economic group that makes major political decisions – is simply one kind of ruling elite. Others include military, priestly and intellectual elites, some of whom rule in unison, other of whom contest and replace each other. It's true that economic elites sometimes rise to the pinnacles of power, but there's nothing inevitable about this. Each elite must be described in relation to its particular characteristics.
+ Elites really do exist because, as Mills notes, decisions that have major ramifications are taken in the higher circles. Contrary to what the pluralists argue, the economic, military and political elites aren't held in responsible check by a plurality of citizen lobby groups. The people who decided to drop two atom bombs on Japan neither sought nor obtained popular consent. As members of the American power elite, their decisions didn't have to connect with opinions outside their own charmed and privileged circle.

AGAINST

– Pareto and Mosca assume that elites have superior qualities, and they take a rather dim view of the masses. Yet elites and the masses aren't *en bloc* groups each of which have separate and very distinct attributes. There's differentiation within each group. There's talent among elites and among the masses. Take the masses – working-class intellectualism played a significant role in the formation of the Labour Party. Moreover, a sizeable minority of very able Labour MPs have working-class roots.

– Mosca is anti-democratic. His politics express a personal view, not a sociological argument. Even on the level of value judgement, to be against democracy is to be at odds with what most Britons and other Europeans prize. Mosca's notion that a moral and intellectual elite is what society needs is fanciful. The evidence suggests that power corrupts or, at least, makes it difficult to act ethically. In that context, the disclosure of corruption and sleaze among certain British politicians seems particularly apposite.

– Parsons accuses Mills of engaging in 'a fiery and sarcastic attack on the pretensions of the "higher circles" in America' (1960, in Parsons 1969: 189). *The Power Elite*, says Parsons, although containing insightful exposition and analysis, represents an indictment of American society. Although his personal politics are different to Mosca's, like Mosca, Mills gets values entangled with sociological critique. This means that his work requires careful sifting in order to distinguish fact from opinion.

sympathetically, and often in a knowledgeable way too. In this way, social and psychological affinities intensify upper-class male bonding so that each can say of the other, 'He's one of us'. Of course, there are clashes in the higher circles. Democrats and Republicans fight each other through the proper channels. But more powerful than the clashes is the community of interest that binds the power elite on major issues.

Like Michels – but unlike Pareto – Mills emphasises the importance of elite self-recruitment in relation to the perpetuation of elite rule. Between the three elites, there's an interchangeability of position based on the assumption that executive ability is a transferable skill, and on the practice of co-opting within the charmed and privileged circle. Thus, for example, the corporate arms dealer becomes the Secretary of Defence, and the wartime general dons a civilian suit to enter government and then becomes a member of a corporation board of directors.

The existence of a power elite mitigates against a society in which power and influence are widely diffuse. There's little or no pluralism in a power structure where key decisions are made at the top, where the middle levels are more inclined to make demands than to exercise power, and where the rest have largely been transformed into a mass society, a citizenship in name only, but in reality increasingly powerless.

Postmodernist theory of power

Claims to truth, said Friedrich Nietzsche (1844–1900), are claims to power. Imagine, for example, that, as the leader of an island community, I persuade 'my' people that a leader needs twice as much food as anybody else. Once they accept that 'truth' and give me lots of their food, my claim to power has been accepted. A social construction has become a source of power.

Nietzsche's assertion underpins the postmodernist theory of power. He distrusted modernism and its enlightenment concept of truth. According to Nietzche, people don't discover truth, they create it. Motivated by a will to power, people devise conceptions of truth that best serve their particular purposes. One of Nietzche's postmodern heirs, Michel Foucault (1926–84), has taken this argument further. The belief systems of modernism, says Foucault, are claims to power. According to Foucault, there's a battle for truth between different contenders in society. This isn't about an inherent truth that needs discovering. It's about the rules according to which 'truth' is socially constructed.

The battle is about the status of truth and the role that high status knowledge plays in society. In that sense, powerful experts define truth as that which coincides with the ideological outlook of the dominant classes in society. When, for example, a medical doctor defines a particular behaviour as deviant, it becomes possible to confine and 'treat' the person who displays the proscribed behaviour. The expert judgement of the doctor becomes the accepted *discourse* – the taken-for-granted framework within which official decisions are made. The concept of the discourse features prominently in Foucault's work.

Discourses form a kind of cultural hegemony. They codify the assumptions of the establishment and its servants. They give legitimacy to the power of the politician, the civil servant, the lawyer and the doctor. They keep the rest of us in our place. Foucault also shows how the discourses of the modern period aren't as emancipatory as the architects of the enlightenment might like to believe. The same age of reason that banished ghosts and goblins also:

> 'confined the debauched, spendthrift fathers, prodigal sons, blasphemers, men who "seek to undo themselves", libertines. And through these parallels, these strange complicities, the age sketched the profile of its own experience of unreason.'
>
> (Foucault 1965: 65)

What Foucault is saying is that reason can sometimes be very unreasonable! It confines in prisons, asylums and other institutions those who would dare to disagree. Reason has become power: the power of the gaoler, the asylum director, alongside all those micro-powers – family, 'friends', neighbours – who are complicit in confining the 'deviant' and the 'mad' at the local level. Foucault extends the concept of power beyond the consolidated domination of one group or class over others.

Power circulates. It's not in anybody's hands. It weaves itself into the micro-fabric of everyday life, imprinting our routine social relations. There are echoes here of the pluralist theory of power. Indeed, Charles Jencks claims that 'The post-modern agenda is an intense concern for pluralism and respect for local cultures resisting modernisation' (1996: 77). Postmodernism contests and subverts dominant taste cultures. It gives rise to what Jencks calls a 'paraclass' of the new information society which cuts across old hierarchies. I guess Bill Gates, who owns Microsoft, must be at the pinnacle of this class, but its membership extends to all who have access to the World Wide Web.

The postmodern outlook confronts politicians head-on. Their claims to privileged knowledge are revealed for what they are – ideologies. Here we find an affinity between marxist and postmodern critiques of power structures. But there are important differences. Marxists are modernists. Their inspiration derives from the enlightenment belief that the quest for objective knowledge is inherently good. Postmodernists reject the notion that knowledge is objective, seeing it instead as the make-believe truths of powerful elites. So what about the knowledge that postmodernists produce? Is that knowledge privileged? They would have to say no, if they followed the logic of their own arguments.

But we mustn't be too harsh on postmodernists. They have a right to critique other ways of thinking, even if their own thinking often seems rather muddled. On the critique front, postmodernist argument has kindled a debate over the extent to which politicians and their scientific experts should be trusted to look after the natural environment. This point is discussed in the section on 'The postmodernist view of nature' in Chapter 17.

In essence, what writers like Ulrich Beck (a sceptical modernist with postmodernist leanings) and Brian Wynne (who uses postmodernist insights) argue is that rich nations have created environmental risks which politicians shouldn't be trusted to deal with. Having caused these problem, politicians then use public relations consultants to cloak blunders in the respectable language of science. The last government's handling of the BSE crisis over British beef is an example of this.

Though not strictly speaking a postmodernist, Noam Chomsky (1968, in Chomsky 1969) takes a postmodernist-style swipe at 'experts' who were in the pockets of the White House during the Vietnam War. The advocates of American expansionist policy – the 'New Frontiersmen', as Chomsky decries them – are called upon to provide a propaganda cover for US military aggression. Thus, for example, Arthur Schlesinger described the bombing of Northern Vietnam and the huge escalation of military commitment in early 1965 as based on a rational argument: as long as the Vietcong thought they were going to win the war, they wouldn't be interested in any kind of negotiation settlement. Bombing them to death would supposedly bring them to the negotiation table.

POSTMODERNIST THEORY OF POWER

FOR

+ The postmodernist critique of power reminds sociologists to consider the impact of discourses – the voices of the powerful. This alerts us to the concealed, but profound, influence of cultural hegemony. Unlike force, which is up-front, hegemony is a soft variant of control that beguiles by stealth. Its discourses aren't necessarily conspiratorial, but they become widely accepted because they saturate popular culture. Postmodernists reveal discourses for what they are – claims to power.
+ Postmodernists encourage outsiders to have an opinion and to regard it as important. The cult of the expert is de-throned and disclosed – whether or not it dresses itself in science – as an ideology. The postmodernist critique demystifies privileged knowledge, especially the kind that does countless damage in the name of science. It encourages a democratisation of knowledge, lending support to an important claim by Antonio Gramsci that we're *all* intellectuals.
+ Postmodernism reminds us of the complexity and the nuances of power. Things aren't as clear-cut as modernist theorists like Marx and Weber seem to imply. Power exists at lots of different levels and expresses itself in diverse forms. Marx's contention that political rule springs from economic power, and Weber's argument that power is expressed through class, status and political grouping don't exhaust the debate. Power is exercised between friends, within families and in lots of other everyday contexts.

AGAINST

– While some discourses represent claims to power, others represent valued expertise. It's disingenuous to imagine, for example, that the role of psychiatrists in society is to confine 'madness'. The main goal of psychiatrists is to cure mental disorders, not to keep people in hospital. Foucault exaggerates the control side of discourses and underestimates the role they have to play in advancing our understanding of the world we inhabit. The enlightenment isn't a tool of ruling-class rule. It emancipates reason and places it at the service of humankind.

– Related to the last point, the postmodernist disdain for the discourses of modern society isn't convincingly complemented with a better alternative. Postmodernist claims often amount to a rebuttal of other's claims to truth rather than the development of a better proposal. Postmodernists criticise other theories, but why should we treat their claims more seriously? Indeed, the discourse of postmodernism is an intellectual claim to power in its own right, and certainly one that's far removed from what most ordinary folk can understand and make sense of.

– Postmodernists exaggerate the extent to which power autonomously operates at different levels and in different forms. The micro-power zones of significant others (family, friends, teachers, etc.) are mediated through the hegemony of the ruling class. Teachers, for example, operate on a micro-level in their dealings with students, but they reproduce dominant cultural and social arrangements. When, for example, a child learns to respect the authority of a teacher, this becomes a dress-rehearsal for the deference the later adult is expected to show to the capitalist.

Says Chomsky of Schlesinger's statement, it's:

'less an example of deceit than of contempt – contempt for an audience that can be expected to tolerate such behaviour with silence, if not approval.'

(1968, in Chomsky 1969: 259)

No wonder Chomsky regards 'the cult of the expert [as] both self-serving, for those who propound it, and fraudulent' (1968, in Chomsky 1969: 271). Chomsky wants intellectuals to expose the lies of the powerful, and to seek the truth that lies behind the veil of ideology and class interest through which the events of current affairs are presented to the public.

QUESTIONS

1 Briefly outline and assess these theories of power: functionalist–pluralist; marxist; weberian; elitist; post-modern.
2 Compare and contrast any two of the above theories.

The modern state

Politics arose out of the need to control and reconcile diverse interests in society. The structure within which these functions occur is called a *political system*. The supreme law-making authority in modern (and post-modern) political systems is the *state*.

Types of state

Today, most nations claim to have *democratic* states (derived from and accountable to the people). The UK is a democratic society. Its multi-party MPs are elected by and represent the people. The People's Republic of China is a *totalitarian* society (ruled by one leader or one party). It's one-party communist state exercises total control over the people. Democratic and totalitarian regimes exist at either end of the spectrum of different political systems. In between are regimes which lean in one or either direction. There's also inevitable overlapping. Some of the emergent democracies of Eastern Europe, for example, probably still retain a few totalitarian tendencies.

Even in countries where either democracy or totalitarianism clearly predominates, differences exist within generic political systems. Like China, Saudi Arabia has a totalitarian state. Unlike China, however, it has no political party. The Saudi Arabian king rules by decree, and has total political sovereignty. He's an absolute monarch. Sweden and the UK are both democratic countries. In Sweden, parliament is elected by the people. Yet in the UK, voters elect politicians to only one part of parliament: the House of Commons.

The state is at the apex of most political systems. It comprises the political and administrative institutions having legal jurisdiction over the affairs of a nation. In the UK, these institutions are parliament and the civil service. Societies that have states are called *nation-states*. Such societies lay claim to territories which have their own laws, and are typically defended by military force. The UK is a nation-state, as are, for example, India, the US, Eire, China and South Africa. Each of these countries has law-making institutions, and civil servants who implement laws. They exercise jurisdiction, backed by military force, over defined territories.

The question as to what constitutes the best political system is a matter of debate. The 'west' prefers democracy, but its very recent history has contained totalitarian systems (for example, Nazi Germany and Fascist Spain). The former Soviet Union – totalitarian communist up to less than ten years ago – has now fragmented into a number of democratic nation-states: Russia, Poland, Hungary, a united Germany, etc. Essentially, communism now only exists in four nations: China, Laos, North Korea and Vietnam.

Development of the European democratic state

Although states existed in ancient times, the modern European state is a product of the sixteenth century onwards. It didn't significantly feature in medieval thought. But as the grip of medieval feudalism loosened, social thinkers like Thomas Hobbes (1588–1679), John Locke (1632–1704) and Jean-Jacques Rousseau (1712–78) considered that political rights and obligations might become concerns of a 'state' rather than of an absolute monarch. In that sense, the state was envisaged as the servant of public power. It would protect citizens from the arbitrary powers of royal oligarchs. It would be a democracy.

Hobbes argued that, left to their own capricious devices, human beings are profoundly selfish. They inhabit a world which is, says Hobbes, 'solitary, poor, nasty, brutish, and short' (1651, in Hobbes 1960: 82). The upshot is a constant struggle for survival. Hobbes poses an important question: How can people enter a bargain with one another such that they can protect their individual and common interests? His reply, in essence, is that they must hand over their right of self-government to a single authority – thereafter authorised to act on their behalf – provided every individual agrees to this social contract. That single authority is the state – a person or an assembly established as sovereign which represents the people.

Hobbes' argument doesn't necessarily imply democratic government. While he regarded *sovereignty* (the right of political command) as an authority conferred by the people, he also considered it to be ultimately absolute. The sovereign (for example, a queen or a parliament) is granted a right of command. Once they had granted their consent to a sovereign power, the people had better obey their ruler(s). This is less autocratic than the prerogative of royal birth, but it bestows enormous powers on the person or persons who obtain the mandate of the people.

Locke objected to the Hobbesian argument that individuals could only live in harmony if they were governed by a sovereign. It's not credible, argues Locke, that people who don't really trust each other would place their trust in an all-powerful ruler. Locke approved of the English revolution and settlement of 1688 which put constitutional limits on the authority of the Crown. He believes the state (which he essentially spoke of as the government) should defend the life, liberty and property of free citizens. Government by consent – such consent being removable if the public trust is violated – lies at the heart of his philosophy.

Unlike Hobbes, Locke doesn't think that the state of nature is inevitably one of 'dog eat dog'. It's a state of liberty, but not of licence to do as one pleases. That said, adherence to the ways of nature is confounded by individuals who don't fully respect the rights of others. Hence, it's necessary for individuals to bestow on government the wherewithal to pursue the rights of the governed. This doesn't mean that the rights of citizens are forfeited to the state. Rather, the state has the obligation to preserve the life, liberty and property of its citizens. It makes laws not as an independent lawmaker but as the agent of the people. The government is also bound by law, for, as Locke puts it, 'Wherever Law ends Tyranny begins' (cited by David Held, in Held *et al.* 1985: 13).

Like Hobbes and Locke, Rousseau is interested in the idea of legitimate government. He sides with Locke in his belief that in nature, human beings were free and happy. Also like Locke, he assumes that individual human weaknesses compromise this ideal. The fullest expression of liberty must therefore be protected by social contract. In Hobbes' and in Locke's notion of social contract, the people transfer sovereignty to the state and its ruler or assembly. For Rousseau, sovereignty comes from and stays with the people. His is one of the most thought-provoking advocacies of self-government – of genuinely direct democracy.

Rousseau applauds the idea of an active participatory citizenry who would meet together and make laws. In this vision, the affairs of the state become enmeshed in the affairs of ordinary citizens. Rousseau therefore argues in favour of a society in which the *legislative* (law-making) and *executive* (carrying out) functions of the state are demarcated. The people are the legislative assembly. The government or 'head' of state executes the people's laws. If, however, the executive doesn't fulfil the general will of the citizens, it must be revoked.

The writings of Hobbes, Locke and Rousseau address pre-industrial, agrarian societies. These political philosophers had no experience of industrial capitalism. Moreover, their ideas, while evocative and profound, are largely theoretical. It was left to other writers to address the reality of the state which emerged out of the smoke and bustle of the Industrial Revolution. Notable in that context, are the writings of Karl Marx.

The state, said Marx, is 'the official résumé of society' (1846, cited by Poulantzas 1973: 49). A résumé is a summary, a condensed version of something. In this sense, the state is a concentrated expression of ruling-class power. Marx did recognise that the state in capitalist society could represent interests other than the capitalist ruling class. For example, he commended the independent and principled judgements of factory inspectors who exposed inhuman work conditions, even if this did embarrass their political paymasters. He also applauded the democratic aspirations of the Chartists, and had great hopes (ultimately dashed) that the first enfranchisement of the English working class in 1867 would lead to democratic socialism. Nevertheless, in most of his writings, Marx regards the state as the bureaucratic instrument of the capitalists.

Supporting Marx's contention that the state is, by and large, the servant of the ruling class rather than of the people, Antonio Gramsci writes: 'In its [the state's] organs the power of the propertied class is centralized' (1919, in Gramsci 1977: 73). There's something perverse about a state, which is supposed to represent democratically public interests, protecting and preserving the ambitions of a minority dominant class. Marx laments this, but sees it as largely inevitable in capitalist society. He believes that the state is a 'superstructure' which rests upon the foundation of economic and social relations in society. In this manner, the state directly serves the interests of the ruling economic class. Marx makes this point forcibly when he writes: 'The executive of the modern state is but a committee for managing the common affairs of the whole bourgeoisie' (1848, in Bottomore and Rubel 1975: 138).

Engels echoes the same outlook by arguing that:

'the state arose from the need to hold class antagonisms in check, but because it arose, at the same time, in the midst of the conflict of these classes, it is, as a rule, the state of the most powerful, economically dominant class, which, through the medium of the state, becomes also the politically dominant class, and thus acquires new means of holding down and exploiting the oppressed class.'

(Engels 1884, in Held *et al.* 1985: 104)

Marx, Engels and Lenin envisaged that the capitalist state would be replaced by a temporary socialist one, a 'dictatorship' of the proletariat, which, during the transition from capitalism to communism, would signify the right of all people – not just a privileged minority – to administer the state. Once communism is introduced, the need for a state disappears because class antagonism ceases. There is therefore no longer any need for a state to act either as the upholder of a ruling class or to hold the ring between oppressor and oppressed. The state ends because class conflict ends. Communism is a political system that exists in a stateless society. It's also a pure form of direct democracy.

Lest marxism be regarded as fanciful utopianism, Lenin notes:

'We are not utopians, and do not in the least deny the possibility and inevitability of excesses on the part of *individual persons*, or the need to stop such excesses. In the first place, however, no special machine, no special apparatus of suppression, is needed for this; this will be done by the armed people themselves, as simply and as readily as any crowd of civilized people, even in modern society, interferes to put a stop to a scuffle or to prevent a woman from being assaulted.'

(Lenin 1917, in Held *et al.* 1985: 119)

Lenin believed that communism would end exploitation, and, in turn, crime and greed. There would no longer be a need for a state to keep these vices at bay. Says Lenin:

'Only in Communist society . . . "the state . . . ceases to exist", and "*it becomes possible to speak of freedom*". Only then will a truly complete democracy become possible and be realized, a democracy without any exceptions whatever.'

(Lenin 1917, in Held *et al.* 1985: 117)

His prediction, insofar as Russia was concerned, didn't happen. A totalitarian, one-party, communist regime took over, in which politicians enjoyed extravagant lifestyles and the poor stood in line to shop for meagre food. This isn't an indictment of communism, but of its corruption. Lenin, like Marx, had a dream of a genuine participatory democracy where the state had withered away and left the people to their own collective decision-making. Instead, the state remained, got stronger, became repressive and lavished its party officials with economic and political privileges.

Democracy today

Whilst soviet communism never attained the democracy that some of its founders anticipated, the 'western' version of democracy today would surely fill Lenin with disquiet. Although 'western' nations have representative governments elected by an electorate from the entire adult population whose votes are freely made and carry equal weight, 'people power' is a bit of a pipe dream, claim marxists. Democracies in countries like the UK and the US, they argue, serve the interests of the rich and powerful more than those of the majority of the people. In capitalist democracies, most of the members of the state assemblies and civil services are either capitalists or the 'servants' – witting or otherwise – of capitalists. British MPs, for example – especially Conservative ones – tend to come from relatively privileged backgrounds. Some of them are capitalists in their own right. Even New Labour contains its fair share of ex-public school boys, including Blair. Democratically elected it might be, but representative of the people it isn't!

Rousseau made a similar point in the eighteenth century when he attacked so-called representative democracy as a sham, stating that English citizens are only free to elect MPs, being enslaved thereafter. This is why we need to be cautious about 'western' claims to have the only real democracies. Definitions of democracy clearly differ, even though at the heart of each is a commitment to the interests of the people.

The 'western' model is a representative democracy in which citizens elect representatives to the legislative assembly – in the UK, to parliament. Yet some communists argue that democracy is about ruling the people in the interests of the people, even if this means there's only one party. Thus, for example, the communist Cuban president, Fidel Castro, has provided extensive health and social care for all Cubans, despite the absence of democratic elections.

Nearly all states now claim to be democratic, even though their respective political systems might be as different as the one-party regime that prevails in Cuba, and the multi-party system in the UK.

QUESTIONS

1. Define these concepts: the state; democratic political system; totalitarian political system.
2. Is it true to say that the British state is a 'committee' of the ruling class?
3. Why is it difficult to arrive at one all-encompassing definition of democracy?

Political parties, political ideologies and political decision-making

Political parties are central to democratic political systems. In most totalitarian regimes, parties either don't exist at all, or do so in the form of one-party states. Of the two main political systems – democratic and totalitarian – in the world today, democratic systems prevail. This section largely focuses on political parties, political ideologies,and political decision-making in a democratic nation-state: the UK. Be mindful, though, that the UK model of democracy is only one example of the different forms democracy can take.

Political parties

In the UK, parties provide the only source of entry to the House of Commons. It's rare that a non-MP (for example, a lawyer or an academic) is appointed to government positions. Normally, membership of the government is attained after a substantial period in party politics as an MP.

According to Bill Coxall and Lynton Robins (1994), parties affect the actions of government in the Commons in four ways, by:

- providing it with a political programme based on its election manifesto, and which provides a platform for the legislation it puts before the Commons
- supplying a team of key politicians who fill ministerial posts
- persuading most of its backbenchers (less senior politicians) to vote in line with government policy
- providing an extensive organisation to select parliamentary candidates, campaign on their behalf and, once elected, keep them up to the mark.

One could add to the above list, but it contains the main points. With its overall majority and the usual loyal support of its backbenchers, the party of government is able to govern. Normally, only one party is in government. The MPs of the non-governmental parties constitute an opposition which criticises the government of the day and seeks to replace it at general elections.

The two major political parties are the Conservative Party and the Labour Party. Between 1918 and 1997, the Conservatives were in government for 59 years – 75 per cent of the time – either as a single party or as the dominant partner in coalition. Despite the lead over Labour, this is in part attributable to a majority electoral system (first-past-the post), which often translates a minority of votes into a majority of seats. The Conservatives have only gained over 50 per cent of the vote on two occasions since 1918 (in 1931 and 1935). In their four election victories from 1979 to 1992, they haven't achieved over 44 per cent of the total share. Their latest showing in the General Election of 1997 was just 31 per cent of the vote (165 seats).

It remains to be seen if Labour will set a new trend. But it's going to be around for some time. To quote the political columnist, Philip Stephens: 'In winning by such an extraordinary margin, Mr Blair has all but assured himself of two terms in government' (*Financial Times*, 3 May 1997, page 16). In part, this might be because Blair has made Labour a party which 'middle England' is ready to accept.

Whilst the big political battles are largely fought between the Conservatives and Labour, minority parties can play an important role too. The Liberal Democrat Party is a substantial minority party, and multi-party politics (including other minority parties, like the Green Party and Plaid Cymru in Wales) are becoming much more prominent in British politics. Their fortunes have been buoyed by the success of the Liberal Democrat Party at the polls in 1997. The party more than doubled its representation in the Commons, taking Liberal Democrat seats up to 46 – even though the overall vote was down 1 per cent on the 18 per cent gained in 1992. It now seems possible that the Liberal Democrats will be able to close the chapter on their reputation as the party of the 'wasted vote'.

Political ideologies

In representative democratic societies like the UK, political parties compete for electors' votes. They set out their policies in documents called *manifestos*. These are a long established feature of British politics. The first party manifesto is usually credited to Robert Peel, who issued the Tamworth Manifesto in 1834 after his party (Conservative) had been elected. The manifesto set out Peel's main proposals for the next parliament. The growth of mass politics and universal enfranchisement, however, persuaded party leaders to publish their policy proposals and the beliefs which underpinned them before general elections.

Manifestos provide voters with a checklist of party ideologies. An ideology is a set of values that a group – in this case, a party – believes in. The term carries pejorative connotations in marxist circles because, according to marxists, an ideology is an adherence to ruling-class values in defiance of facts and values. However, most sociologists use the concept of ideology to denote any set of values that a group holds dear: Amnesty International, the Conservative Party or the Chicago Police Department!

Political ideologies typically prescribe an ideal, and then propose strategic advice on how to achieve it. In the 1997 Conservative manifesto, for example, we find that the Conservatives believe that 'Persistent juvenile offenders need to be properly punished'. In order to accomplish this, they propose, among other strategies, to 'give the courts the power to detain persistent 12–14 year old offenders in secure training centres once the places become available'.

Although the three main political parties each try to make a case in their manifesto for being different to and better than their opponents, all three share a fair amount of common ideological ground. Crucially, the Conservatives, Labour and the Liberal Democrats support capitalism and market economics. Despite their nods in favour of the Social Chapter and a minimum wage, Blairites, like yesterday's Thatcherites, believe that the UK should seek competitive advantage in the world market. They endorse

CRIT THINK CRIT THINK CRIT THINK CRIT THINK CRIT THINK CRIT THINK

MANIFESTOS AND IDEOLOGY

The following extract is from the 1997 Green Party Manifesto:

'Not simply defending ourselves

The UK fought the Gulf War to protect our supply of oil and discovered that the enemy were using western weapons. Against Argentina in 1982, we discovered that their military dictatorship had British weapons paid for by British loans! Each year the UK government gives £1 billion in subsidies to arms exporters (source: Campaign Against Arms Trade). UK Defence policies are making the world less safe.

In 1975, Indonesia illegally invaded East Timor. The UK has sold arms to Indonesia ever since, despite the massacre of 200,000 people and the subsequent condemnation in the United Nations.

> "Four of my cousins were killed in Hawk attacks near Los Palos . . . most people in East Timor know about the British Hawks."
>
> Jose Amortin, East Timorese citizen

New Labour wouldn't stop this trade, it would seem that morality is a dirty word.

It is important that we can defend ourselves effectively should the need arise. Despite the end of the Cold War, the UK maintains a predominantly *offensive* capability. In 1995, the Defence budget was over £22 billion, that's twice the Education budget. Defence policies are simply costing too much.

The UK has an expensive and unnecessary nuclear destructive capacity which does not make the world a more secure place. It is as pointless as it is immoral. Who exactly are these weapons pointed at? Our nuclear arsenal is a burden on our resources which we cannot afford.

An imaginative programme of arms conversion could use many of the skills and resources at present tied up in military use. Instead of making weapons we could fund public transport systems and energy conservation as well as appropriate technology for developing countries.

Promoting global security

- Our defence forces need to be restructured from their primarily aggressive orientation to a more defensive system.
- The UK Government should end involvement in the promotion of military exports and, in particular, close the Defence Export Services Organisation.
- All applications for export licences should be published in advance.
- The UK should end the export of military, para-military and police equipment to governments responsible for sustained human rights abuse, which are involved in armed conflict, or to countries in areas of tension.
- The Green Party supports immediate unconditional nuclear disarmament, promotion of the Non-Proliferation Treaty and a ban on the export of nuclear technology.
- A national audit of the resources used in military production would allow strategies for arms conversion to be developed. Help to establish civilian industries should be given to communities and be funded by cuts in defence spending.'

(Green Party Manifesto, 1997, page 13)

1. *Identify three ideological positions on defence that the Green Party support.*
2. *What strategic proposals do the Green Party seek to implement in order to achieve the three ideological aims you've identified?*
3. *Imagine you belong to a party called the Education Party. Compose a section of its manifesto which states its ideological views on either secondary school education or further education, and its proposed strategic plan. Before doing this, obtain and consult the manifestos of the Conservative Party, the Labour Party, the Liberal Democrat Party and, if possible, the Green Party. Look at what these parties have to say about education, but create your own manifesto on the issue.*

These tasks can be done in groups, reporting back to the whole class on completion.

CRIT THINK CRIT THINK CRIT THINK CRIT THINK CRIT THINK CRIT THINK CRIT

capitalist values, such as low labour costs, low levels of social protection and deregulated labour markets. The theme of common ground and points of departure in the ideologies of Blair and Thatcher is humorously parodied in the cartoon below.

In a content analysis of the text of the twelve major party election manifestos published from 1979 to 1992, Richard Topf (1994, in Heath *et al.* 1994) found that the issues of Citizenship, Economy, Environment and Welfare predominated in every one of ten identified domains. Even if consensus politics is more commonplace today, during the period studied by Topf, he did find different ideological underpinnings between the parties. Thus, for example, Conservative manifestos produced a consistently negative stance towards egalitarianism, and socialist and communitarian values, whilst producing null or positive results for traditionalism and *laissez-fair*ism. Topf's analysis also showed that, in its 1992 manifesto, Labour moved modestly towards the centre in ideological terms, whereas the Conservative manifesto for the same year was the most extreme of any party since 1979.

As indicated earlier, political party manifestos are ideologies. They denote in explicit terms the principal set of values that each party claims to hold. Before examining the manifestos of the three main parties, we'll first examine their ideological origins: conservatism, liberalism and socialism.

Conservatism

Modern conservatism began in the 1790s in opposition to the French Revolution. It favoured stability and tradition over change and radicalism. Conservatives – or Tories, as they were also called – were cautious, Anglican, rooted in the land, and wary of political and social reform. Believing that noble birth was the best credential for entering the ranks of the ruling class, they stubbornly resisted social assimilation. They had archaic impulses, and believed that the landowning ruling class should strive to continue with a minimum of concession to the Industrial Revolution.

Tories were more interested in honour than profit. When, for example, the Tory Duke of Wellington inadvertently purchased a farm at a price well below its market value, he instructed his steward to pay the seller the additional sum. Wealth that was manifested only by purchasing power was deemed socially disreputable; not so wealth that embodied itself in the ownership of soil. For the Tory, a landed estate, like war medals, servants and gun dogs, was the honorific measure of its owner's standing.

Even impoverishment didn't lower the prestige of an established county family. Indeed, *Burke's Landed Gentry* thought it quite proper to include in its august pages:

> 'men with pedigrees long or splendid, who have perhaps but one dilapidated and moated grange . . . left to them as a relic of former greatness, the value of which may not reach £50 per annum.'
>
> (cited by John Bateman 1883, in Bateman 1970: xv)

The conservative outlook was uneasy with the aggressive 'pushiness' of early industrialism. Nor was it comfortable with the associated gradual conversion of society to bourgeois liberal values and interests. It was especially disdainful of those members of its own class – most of whom were Whigs – who did deals with the industrial capitalist class.

The unyielding adherence of eighteenth- and nineteenth-century Tories to an aristocratic ideal pushed them into an ideological confrontation with the new barons of industry. Marx describes this encounter in a short but brilliant series of juxtapositions:

> 'Rent of land is conservative, profit is progressive; rent of land is national, profit is cosmopolitical; rent of land believes in the State Church, profit is a dissenter by birth.'
>
> (Marx 1852, in Bottomore and Rubel 1975: 199)

(The *Guardian*, 16 July 1997)

On the political front, Toryism was conspicuous for its neglect of capitalist interests (how unlike its twentieth-century heirs!) and for its antipathy towards any form of liberalism. As for aristocratic Whigs, the ultra-Tory Wellington regarded them as little better than revolutionaries. For Whigs were consorting with the enemy. They were class traitors, or, as Marx put it, 'the *aristocratic representatives* of the Bourgeoisie of the industrial and commercial middle class' (1852, in Bottomore and Rubel 1975: 201). Whigs wanted to replace the Tory tradition of *noblesse oblige* with the free trade principle of capitalism. So opposed were the Tories to the free market, they complied with community as opposed to market prices in determining the price of corn.

Toryism drew on old-fashioned values of rural paternalism, administering fair prices and charity in the face-to-face transactions of village life. Under the system of what E. P. Thompson (1971) termed the 'moral economy of the English crowd', the local landowners provided the immediate purchasers of corn – rural labourers – with purchasing privileges that were protected in an eroded body of statute law, as well as in common law and patrician custom. Corn prices were consequently set in accordance with a commonly-accepted notion of what constituted a fair price.

Much as they criticised the liberalism of Whigs, the Tories were eventually to find a liberal-minded member within their own ranks – Robert Peel. By accepting the repeal of the Corn Laws in 1846 – which meant opening corn prices to market forces – Peel had done the unthinkable. He had sided with the capitalist class. His actions split the parliamentary Conservative Party but, under Disraeli's leadership, cohesion was gradually rebuilt. By the time of the third major reform of the franchise in 1884, the skeleton of the present Conservative Party was apparent. There was a distinct and increasingly cohesive body of Tory MPs in the Commons, a National Union linking the constituency associations, and a professional party bureaucracy dealing with elections at Conservative Central Office.

More recently, although patrician impulses still exist in old-fashioned Tory circles, Thatcherism completed the earlier shift towards the endorsement of market capitalism started by Peel in the last century. Thatcher embraced the market with fervour. The ideology of *laissez-faire* liberalism, with its origins in industrial capitalism and Whig opportunism, now lies at the heart of Conservative Party thought. Words like 'freedom' (read free market), 'choice' (read market choice), and 'independence' (read private as opposed to public) capture the spirit of 1990s Toryism. They describe the 'political correctness' of the New Right.

Just as Peel's radicalism split the party in the 1840s, so has Thatcherism – particularly, its anti-European bias – fractured unity in the Conservative Party today. The real marketeers find it strange that the New Right of a party which stands for untrammelled international trade are so fiercely nationalistic. An economic ideology that encourages international investment (including 'foreign' ownership of British assets) balks at the idea of European citizenship.

Ironically, given its preference for *laissez-faire* principles, the New Right has had to build a strong state to impose 'market freedoms'. This has meant, for example, capping the budgets of local councils who are deemed by the mandarins in Whitehall to be over-spending. A curious mix of centralisation and privatisation ensued. Centralised education policies, for example, co-existed with delegated budgets for individual schools.

Having considered the shift in Tory ideology from its anti-capitalist beginnings to its current pro-free market principles, it's time to look at the main ideological agenda of the Conservative Party, as set out in its most recent manifesto – *You Can Only Be Sure With The Conservatives* (1997). In this document, the Conservative Party spells out its proposed vision for the UK:

- Tight control of public spending, aim for a 20p basic rate income tax, maintain inflation and mortgage rates at low levels
- Protect jobs by keeping the UK outside the European Social Chapter, build on falling unemployment, help get the long-term unemployed back to work, require people on benefit for some time to undertake work experience on a community project
- Support growth and investment, by keeping low taxes, pursuing the UK's global trade, curbing unnecessary regulations, reforming business rates to help small businesses, keep the UK ahead in future technologies, encourage new entertainment and information services, and use the Millennium Lottery Fund to give people access to new computers and information links in schools, libraries and other public places
- Reduce tax bills for families looking after dependent children or relatives, help family members with heavy caring responsibilities for a relative to take a much needed break, and encourage schemes to help employees become shareholders in the company they work for, alongside tax benefits for other savings schemes
- Transform pensions by providing all young people entering the workforce with a personal pension fund paid for by a rebate on their National Insurance contributions, while guaranteeing a state pension, and make it possible for people to afford care costs in old age without giving up their house and savings
- Guarantee school standards by intervening directly to raise standards when schools or local education authorities are letting children down, widen choice and diversity in schools, with more freedom for schools to develop their own character, more specialist schools, a

grammar school in every town where parents want this choice, and maintain the nursery voucher scheme offering a choice of places for parents of all four-year-old children

- Continue to increase resources committed to the National Health Service, enable all family doctors to provide a wider range of services in their surgeries and in practice-based cottage hospitals, thereby offering faster and more local treatment
- Continue to improve the standards and value for money of the UK's public services, providing users with more information and, where possible, wider choice, and introduce measures to protect the public against strikes which cause excessive disruption to essential services
- Support local police schemes to crack down on petty crime, continue funding TV security cameras in town centres and public places where they are wanted, give courts power to impose speedy sanctions on young offenders, including some recompense to the victim, continue the war on drugs, and ensure that persistent house burglars and dealers in hard drugs get mandatory minimum prison sentences
- Continue to regenerate towns and cities, especially through private capital going into the worst public housing estates, keep on protecting the countryside and heritage, use the National Lottery to help promote British art, culture and sports, maintain the UK's international leadership role in protecting the environment, and carry on improving air and water quality at home alongside good conservation of national wildlife
- Maintain the unity of the UK, preserve the stability of the nation through an evolutionary rather than a revolutionary approach to constitutional change, seek a partnership of European nation-states, not permit the UK to be part of a federal European state, and guarantee that the UK will not join a single currency in the next parliament unless the British people give their consent in a referendum.

As with all propaganda, the Conservative manifesto seeks to convey the most favourable impression. Notwithstanding this inevitable bias, it's a valuable sociological document because it sets out the official ideology of the Conservative Party.

> ### EXAM TIP
> Point out to the examiner that nineteenth-century conservatism is a far cry from its current version. Tories in the last century opposed *laissez-fair*ism. Today's Tories embrace it as a central philosophy.

Liberalism

The main opponent of the Conservative Party after 1867 until the end of the First World War was the Liberal Party. The forerunners of the Liberals were the Whigs, who supported, to the annoyance of their equally aristocratic Tory opponents, *laissez-faire* (free market) capitalism. In its nineteenth-century context, liberalism meant adopting a conciliatory approach to the new barons of iron and steam, courting favour with the Free Trade Movement, supporting the enfranchisement of the 'respectable' middle class, and championing social reform.

As the nineteenth century progressed, the heirs of the Whig party often adopted the continental term of 'liberal' to denote their common cause with other European parties who stood for free trade capitalism. It was argued by early liberals that the right of private property and the right to buy and sell in a free market were expressions of individual freedom. For this reason, liberalism – especially its Whig form – was severely denounced by Marx as bourgeois ideology. Liberal-minded aristocrats, however, were lords of land. By making timely concessions to the industrial bourgeoisie, they were facing up to economic realities, thereby ensuring the political survival of the landed class in a changing social structure.

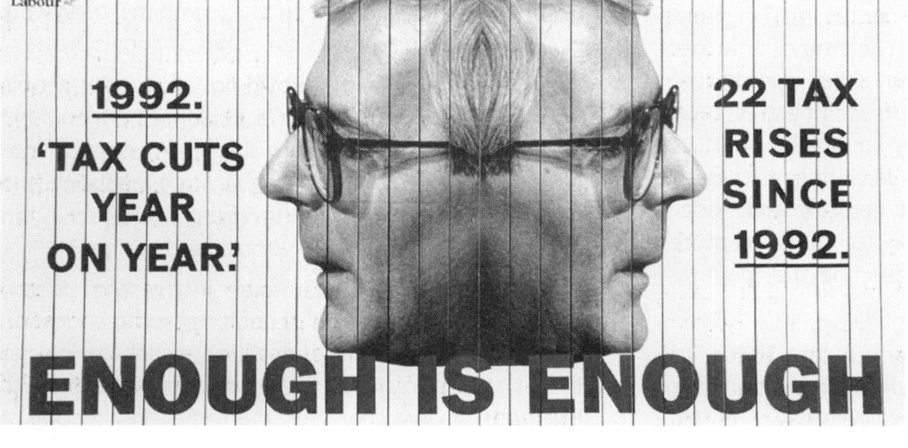

The British electorate didn't think much of the 1997 Conservative manifesto. Acting on the message contained in this Labour campaign hoarding, they threw the Tories out and returned a Labour government.

Such friendly overtures to factory owners provoked alarm in traditional Tory quarters. Solid landowners occupying the same notch on the social and economic ladder as other members of the aristocracy were seen to be challenging the authority of the *status quo*. Referring to a coalition of Whig, Radical and even Tory supporters of a 'new liberal system', David Robinson reported in the Tory *Blackwood's Edinburgh Magazine*:

'Various of its members and publications have called for the admission of foreign corn duty free; resistance to them is ignorance, and a desire to oppress the people. One portion or another of them, calls for universal suffrage – the abolition of all protecting duties – the abandonment of our colonies – the robbery of the church – the destruction of the aristocracy, &c &c; and opposition to it is illiberality, bigotry, intolerance, corruption, and hostility to improvement.'

(Robinson 1827: 431)

Despite the rage of diehard Tory rhetoric, the politics of compromise and concession was adroitly managed in liberal aristocratic circles, and its deployment helped lay the groundwork in law and other institutions for the development of an industrial society. It's significant that an unreformed house of landed aristocrats reformed itself in 1832 and that a parliament of landowners, under mounting capitalist pressure, repealed the Corn Laws in 1848.

Instead of making no concessions to the industrial age, the Whigs joined the bandwagon, moving – sometimes cautiously, often reluctantly, and always gradually – in the direction of social reform. By the end of the nineteenth century, these liberal aristocrats had avoided both outright war and unconditional surrender. The compromise was a merger of landed and business elites into a new ruling class of varied social origins and social aspirations.

Thereafter, moving into the twentieth century, liberal thought played a decisive role in reforms of a different kind. The so-called 'classical' liberals of the nineteenth century had come to accept *laissez-faire* capitalism. The social reforms they supported reflected this commitment. Educating the poor, for example, was intended to encourage them to stand on their own feet rather than rely on 'hand-outs' from the rich. The twentieth-century successors of classical liberalism struck out in a different direction. They loosened their attachment to *laissez-faire* individualism, and placed more emphasis on social justice. Thus, for example, the Liberal government of 1906–15 implemented important welfare measures – notably, the introduction of old age pensions in 1908.

It was therefore ironic at the end of the 1970s that a new Conservative prime minister, Margaret Thatcher, reverted to the free market ideas of the nineteenth-century liberals. This reawakening occurred despite the fact that the Liberal Party ceased to be a major political force after about 1918. In the 1920s, the social justice platform was essentially taken over by the Labour Party. By the 1950s, the Liberal vote in general elections was well under a million, but thereafter a revival occurred. In 1981, the Liberals entered an alliance with the newly-formed Social Democratic Party, and in the 1983 General Election, the Alliance gained the highest vote for a third party since the 1920s.

The Alliance lasted to 1988, to be replaced by the Liberal Democrat Party, a non-socialist reforming party of the centre, pro-European, environmentalist, in favour of proportional representation, supportive of both free enterprise and a strong Welfare State. Although the party didn't do too well in the 1992 General Election, it made up for lost progress in 1997. For 18 years prior to the 1997 General Election, the entire Liberal Party (now the Liberal Democrats) has fitted on a single Commons bench. These days the party needs a bit more space. Its total of 46 seats is the largest number for a third party since 1929, and more than double the 20 seats it won in 1992. It has become a medium-sized party sitting alongside a much depleted Tory opposition, and embracing what its leader, Paddy Ashdown, calls 'constructive opposition' to the Labour government.

With their new parliamentary strength, coupled with the fact that they're the second party of local government, the Liberal Democrats are well placed to make an important impression on constitutional reform. Labour and the Liberal Democrats have agreed a common approach here, including reform of the House of Lords and devolution. Blair has also promised a referendum on electoral reform within his first term. Paddy Ashdown, leader of the Liberal Democrat Party, isn't in a position to push his party's agenda too forcefully. The sheer size of the Labour majority mitigates against that.

A compilation of Liberal Democrat principles was published in its 1997 manifesto, *Make the Difference*. In summary, the manifesto proposes to:

- Endeavour to make the UK the world's foremost learning society by the year 2010, investing an additional £2 billion per year in education, funded by an extra 1p in the pound on the basic rate of income tax
- Seek to end the boom and bust cycle and equip the UK's economy to compete in the global marketplace, by maintaining economic stability, encouraging saving and promoting enterprise. The Liberal Democrat Party will raise the quality of the workforce through extra investment in education and training, and will shift the burden of taxation from employment to pollution and resource depletion
- Aim to make clean air, pure water and a good environment central priorities of government, saving energy, cutting traffic congestion, stopping the unnecessary destruction of the countryside, and stemming pollution

- Endeavour to give every person in the UK the security of a decent home in a safe, strong community, by adopting practical measures to rebuild community life, tackle the causes of crime, reduce homelessness, and make people feel safer at home and on the streets
- Strive to make year-on-year improvements in people's health and the quality of the National Health Service, by increasing funding for the NHS, maintaining it as a comprehensive service free at the point of need, and mainly funded from general taxation. The Liberal Democrat Party will make the NHS more accountable and initiate a long-term shift towards preventive medicine
- Venture to restore trust in British politics, by modernising outdated institutions, renewing democracy, and giving the UK's nations, regions and local communities more say in their own affairs
- Undertake to widen opportunities for everyone to make the most of their lives, by promoting self-reliance, strengthening equality for all in law and employment, and by working for a society that cherishes diversity
- Look to recast the UK's overseas policy and enable the country to play a leading role in shaping Europe and strengthening international institutions, by ensuring that the UK is at the forefront of democratising and buttressing Europe's work for prosperity, peace and security. With its world experience, expert armed forces and permanent membership of the United Nations Security Council, the UK has a unique role to play in reforming international institutions.

If this manifesto is taken as an accurate reading of what the Liberal Democrats would do in government, its ideology has shifted yet again. The party is now arguably more 'left-leaning' on certain issues – notably, its readiness to raise income tax to spend more on education – than New Labour. If New Labour eventually decides to introduce proportional representation in British elections – who knows? – the Liberal Democrats might get the chance to re-enter government.

Socialism

Socialism grew out of opposition to nineteenth-century capitalism and *laissez-faire* Whiggism. It also opposed classical Toryism. Its most famous nineteenth-century proponent was Karl Marx. Although he had little truck for Tories, Marx's disdain for Whigs was ferocious. He referred to Whigs as 'Grand Masters of corruption' (1852, in Bottomore and Rubel 1975: 203). Although they were the lords of land, and, in that respect, the 'natural' enemies of industrial barons, they cut deals with capitalists and other supporters of *laissez-faire* capitalism. Said Marx of the British Whigs, they are:

'Feudalists, who are at the same time Malthusians, money-mongers with feudal prejudices, aristocrats without point of honour, Bourgeois without industrial activity, finality men with progressive phrases.'

(Marx 1852, in Bottomore and Rubel 1975: 203)

The Whigs knew that Old England was on the wane and that it was prudent to be on good terms with capitalists. When the capitalist class gained political dominance (which occurred around Marx's death in the late nineteenth century), Marx anticipated that:

'the struggle against capital will no longer be distinct from the struggle against the existing Government – from that very moment will date the social revolution of England.'

(Marx 1852, in Bottomore and Rubel 1975: 206)

Describing the Chartists as 'the politically active portion of the British working class', Marx (1852, in Bottomore and Rubel 1975: 206) identified the architects of this revolution – a socialist party-in-waiting.

Marx thought the Chartists' bid for universal suffrage would:

'be a far more socialistic measure than anything which has been honoured with that name on the Continent. Its inevitable result, here, is the political supremacy of the working class.'

(Marx 1852, in Bottomore and Rubel 1975: 207)

The first enfranchisement of the working class in 1867 didn't fulfil Marx's expectation (see page 389). Nevertheless, in 1889, the Trades Union Congress decided upon independent political action. The following year, some trade unions joined with three socialist sects to form the Labour Representation Committee. By 1906, a separate and self-styled Labour Party gained 29 seats in the Commons.

Socialism, in its original Marxist form, believes in a society where goods and services are distributed on the basis of people's needs rather than on their class position. Marx's own path to socialism originated in his work as an investigative journalist. His friend, Engels, said he had:

'always heard from Marx that it was precisely through concentrating on the law of thefts of wood and the situation of the Moselle winegrowers, that he was led from pure politics to economic relationships and so to socialism.'

(cited by McLellan 1983: 19)

In his first major article in the newspaper, *Rheinische Zeitung*, Marx vented his anger, arguing that more than five-sixths of all prosecutions in the Rhineland dealt with wood. The fate of human beings had become determined by timber which had now become a commodity. Marx's later exposure of widespread poverty among the Moselle winegrowers eventually led to the suppression of the newspaper. His proposed solution to the exploitation of winegrowers and other workers lay first in 'transitional socialism', and thereafter in 'full socialism' (communism). The first stage would take the means of production (land, machines, etc.) into social ownership and the state would continue as an administrative body. Eventually, the state would wither away, and a pure democracy based on 'people power' equality, and no politicians would emerge.

This is, of course, a utopian vision. One shouldn't, however, assume that an ideal is beyond human endeavour. Marx envisaged struggle. And even if perfection were an unrealistic goal, getting close would suffice. The best hope of this lay in the newly-founded Labour Party.

According to Coxall and Robins (1994), there have been three major influences on Labour Party socialism:

- the ethical commitment of the Independent Labour Party (1893) based on altruism and co-operation
- the collectivism of the Fabian Society, which endorsed the inevitability of 'gradualness' and equated socialism with state intervention
- the trade unions, which committed the Labour Party to the pursuit of working-class interests.

Until very recently, the Labour Party did contain a genuinely socialist goal in its constitution – a pledge to the public ownership of the means of production, distribution and exchange. This was the famous Clause IV, now defunct. The decision of a special conference in April 1995 to remove Clause IV from Labour's constitution was a watershed turning point. Says Mark Garnett, it was a decision that was 'the most potent of Blair's determination to change his party's ethos' (1996: 7).

No longer would the Labour Party reassert its post-war advocacy of massive state intervention in economic affairs. Shortly after the 1997 Labour victory, the Chancellor of the Exchequer, Gordon Brown, made this new position a reality. He gave the Governor of the Bank of England a power that once belonged to politicians – the right to set and change interest rates. The City is very comfortable with this new arrangement, and Brown has become popular with capitalists, even though he seems to personally favour a more equitable redistribution of income and wealth.

Blair's victory was partly based on adopting policies of Thatcher's and Major's Conservative governments and re-packaging them in a more palatable form. Two days after he entered 10 Downing Street, the *Financial Times* (3 May 1997) reported that the remarkable extent of Blair's transformation of Old into New Labour was shown by the market response to the Labour landslide: UK gilts and equities rose, and sterling hardly wobbled. In times past, a Labour victory would have spelt a fall in stocks and shares, and in the pound.

On 2 July 1997, the first Labour budget in 18 years demonstrated that Labour wants to please capitalists and socialists. The day after the budget, which included the announcement of a cut in corporation tax, saw the 100 Shares Index soar to a record high, and the pound rose too. The 'City' was impressed. However, huge one-off taxes on privatised utilities (including water companies and British Telecom) and big cash injections into state schools and the National Health Service confirmed that New Labour is still committed to the Welfare State. By taking on the utility 'fat cats', Blair and Brown – depicted in the cartoon below – showed they're sometimes prepared to do battle with powerful capitalists. And the mice did get the cheese on this occasion!

(The *Independent on Sunday*, 18 May 1997)

The readiness of New Labour to talk and practise 'consensus politics' rather than return to the rhetoric of left and right, of socialist and capitalist, reverberates in the party's 1997 manifesto, *New Labour Because Britain Deserves Better*. These, based on the manifesto, are the core commitments and promises of the party:

- Education is the Labour Party's number one priority, and the share of national income spent on education will increase as the bills of economic and social failure decrease.
- There won't be an increase in the basic or top rates of income tax.
- Labour will provide stable economic growth with low inflation, and promote dynamic and competitive business and industry at home and abroad.
- Two hundred and fifty thousand young unemployed people will be taken off benefit and found work.
- The NHS will be rebuilt, spending on administration reduced, and spending on patient care increased.
- Labour will be tough on crime and on the causes of crime, and halve the time taken to bring persistent young offenders to court.
- Labour will build strong families and strong communities, and lay the foundation for a modern Welfare State in relation to pensions and community care.
- The environment will be safeguarded, and an integrated transport policy will be developed to fight congestion and pollution.
- Labour will clean up politics, decentralise political power in the UK, and place the funding of political parties on a proper and accountable basis.
- Labour will give the UK the leadership in Europe that the UK and Europe need.

These ten statements are ideological – they state what the Labour Party says it will do over the five year period of a Labour government.

Political parties and decision-making

British political parties work within a parliamentary system wherein decision-making operates at a number of levels. Parliament consists of two houses – the Commons and the Lords. Although legislation – the making of laws – is enacted by 'the Queen in Parliament', the notion of the sovereignty of parliament (especially of the Commons) is well-established.

Legislation is first passed by the Commons, and then by the Lords, before obtaining the 'royal assent' from the Queen. The most powerful figure in parliament is the Prime Minister, who is chosen, by convention, from the majority party in the Commons, and is usually the leader of that party. Most candidates for election to the Commons as Members of Parliament stand in the name of a party, and are subject to its discipline. The Commons is the democratically-elected House of Parliament, and it contains 651 MPs. Each MP is elected in a single-member constituency on a first-past-the post basis. Most seats go to Conservative and Labour, with a sizeable minority going to Liberal Democrats. The rest are shared between small parties and independent MPs, like Plaid Cymru and the former TV journalist, Martin Bell.

Decision-making is more the prerogative of the party or parties of government than of those in opposition. As Coxall and Robins write:

> 'opposition policy is no more than a set of aspirations about what the party thinks it might do if in office, whereas Government policy is operational since it is generally implemented.'
>
> (Coxall and Robins 1994: 352)

Coxall and Robins make a distinction between what to do (policy-making) and how to do it (decision-making). In practice, however, the two merge. Opting for a policy or not is, in itself, a decision. Resolving how to implement a policy or to explain why a policy wasn't adopted also involves a decision. At the heart of political power in the UK is the Cabinet. It's the apex of government, the nation's top executive committee. It's where decisions are made that have far-reaching consequences. The Cabinet usually consists of 20–22 members, who are typically white, male and middle- or upper-class.

There are power differentials within the Cabinet. The most powerful figure is the Prime Minister, followed by the Chancellor of the Exchequer. The Foreign Secretary is also in the inner circle, as is the Deputy Prime Minister. In the current (1997) Labour cabinet, this inner Cabinet group form what the *Observer* (11 May 1997, page 19) describe as 'The Power Steering Committee'.

The Power Steering Commitee
(an inner Cabinet group)

Tony Blair
Prime Minister

John Prescott Deputy Prime Minister	*Gordon Brown* Chancellor of the Exchequer
Robin Cook Foreign Secretary	*Alastair Campbell* Press Secretary
Peter Mandelson Minister without Portfolio	*Ann Taylor* Leader of the House
Nick Brown Chief Whip	*Jonathan Powell* Chief of Staff

(Adapted from the Observer, 11 May 1997, page 19)

Most Cabinet members are heads of departments of state. These departments include the Home Office, the Foreign Office, the Ministry of Defence, the Department of Education and Employment, and the Department of Health. The heads of these departments – commonly referred to as ministers or secretaries of state – are often assisted by junior ministers.

Below the ministerial team are civil servants headed by a permanent secretary. The permanent secretary is a key policy adviser to the minister and, in that respect, wields considerable influence. This is an important point. Some sociological descriptions of power structures give the impression that high office is tantamount to unbridled power. The reality in democratic societies is usually different. In the UK, for example, most decisions within the cabinet system are taken by Cabinet committees. This is because the sheer complexity and volume of government business make it impossible for the Cabinet alone to handle. The Prime Minister and senior Cabinet ministers chair the most important of these committees, and committee decisions have the status of Cabinet decisions. Only if a consensus isn't arrived at in committee are decisions referred to the 'Cabinet proper' for resolution.

Coxall and Robins (1994) helpfully reproduce a diagram (see below) from Burch (1990) which shows how the Cabinet, while centrepiece, is part of a bigger canvas.

Some of the experts who advise certain current (1997) Labour cabinet members are given in the diagram on page 384.

Politicians, although democratically elected, don't have similar socio-economic profiles to the electorate at large. As said earlier, among the political decision-makers there's a preponderance of white middle- and upper-class males. Nevertheless, today's MPs are recruited from a wider base than capitalists, financiers and landowners. This applies especially to the Labour Party. The last time Labour came to power in 1974, there were plenty of lawyers and academics among the party's MPs. There were also 16 miners, five railway workers, 27 engineers, and 13 other manual workers.

While the 1997 Labour intake is probably more white-collar than the last Labour administration, its MPs are still generally employees rather than employers. The diagrams and table on page 385 (which also contain data on age, gender and education) reveals the occupational backgrounds of Labour MPs in 1997.

In a helpful snapshot summary, Byron Criddle observes that the 'average' member of Labour's new intake of MPs is 'Forty-five years old, state schooled and red brick educated, public sector employed, on the local council, and in many cases simply surprised' (*Financial Times*, 3 May 1997, page 11).

It's also important to note that many more women are in parliament than previously. Of the 419 Labour MPs, 101 are women, and other parties add a further 59 female MPs.

Clare Short, the Minister for Overseas Development, reckons that the doubling of women MPs is bound to

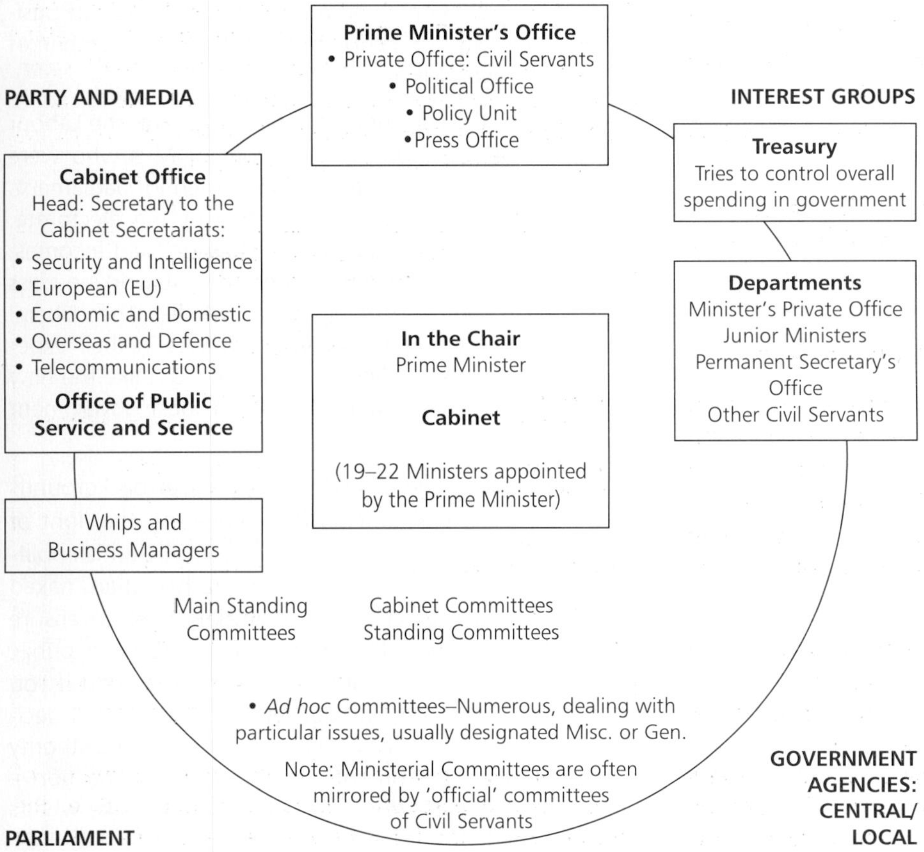

(Burch 1990, in Coxall and Robins 1994: 356)

The policy-making process

Minister	Expert
Harriet Harman (Secretary of State for Social Security)	**Frank Field** Labour MP for Birkenhead, former chairman of the Commons Select Committee on Social Security and author of numerous books and pamphlets on poverty.
Margaret Beckett (President of the Board of Trade)	**Dan Corry** A single currency-supporting economist who worked as a prolific writer at the Institute for Public Policy Research.
	Sir David Simon Former BP Chairman recently recruited to government by Blair, despite massive salary cut.
Jack Straw (Home Secretary)	**Norman Warner** A former civil servant and health specialist who has known Straw for nearly 20 years.
Robin Cook (Foreign Secretary)	**David Clark** Robin Cook's special adviser on Europe for three years. A young moderniser and sceptic.
Gordon Brown (Chancellor of the Exchequer)	**Ed Balls** Gordon Brown's chief economic adviser and a former FT economics specialist.
Lord Irvine (Lord Chancellor)	**Robert Hazell** No direct influence over Lord Irvine, but as Director of the Constitution Unit has compiled the most thorough work on Labour's massive constitutional agenda.
David Blunkett (Secretary of State for Education and Employment)	**Michael Barber** Resigned as Director of Initiatives at London University's Institute of Education to help implement many of his ideas on standards, literacy and relationships between local education authorities and schools.

(Adapted from the *Observer*, 11 May 1997, page 19)

The experts behind the new Cabinet (1997)

change the male 'yah-boo' culture of the Commons. Harriet Harman, Secretary of State for Social Security, added that the higher number of women MPs will drive forward policies on child care and opportunities for women at work, and create a new balance between home and work.

New Labour became, in 1997, the most socially diverse parliamentary force ever assembled in the UK. Women make up almost a quarter of its MPs. More black (four) and Asian (five) Labour MPs have been elected than ever before. There's still plenty of room for improvement though. Black and Asian Labour MPs are conspicuous by their absence from senior Cabinet seats, even though there are no shortage of well-qualified candidates to fill the posts. The party counts a youthful contingent (eight of the new intake are under 30) which is unprecedented this century. Blair is in his mid-forties, very young for a prime minister. Significantly, as Andrew Rawnsley writes:

'Labour people swim in different social pools to Tories. The influence of bankers and brokers begins to wane; that of doctors and teachers starts to wax.'

(The *Observer*, 4 May 1997, page 21)

Looking at the social composition of the Commons before the 1997 General Election, Coxall and Robins (1994) reported that:

- Over three-fifths of the Tories were educated in public schools, and the vast majority of Labour MPs went to state schools.
- Over 60 per cent of Conservative graduates went to Oxford or Cambridge, and more than 70 per cent of Labour graduates attended other universities.
- Conservatives contained a sizeable proportion of businessmen (38 per cent), but a very small number of working-class MPs.

Even though the current party of government, the Labour Party, contains a substantial number of MPs who were public sector professionals before entering parliament, the party isn't socially representative of the electorate. There are no poor Labour MPs on low or fixed incomes, and proportionately fewer of them are of working-class origin than adult Britons as a whole. The Liberal Democrats are closer to the Conservatives in their experience of private schooling and business. But like the new Labour intake, many of them have a local government background.

Notwithstanding the often different social backgrounds of MPs and the constituents they represent, the right of parties in parliament to make decisions in the British political system is based on authority rather than naked power. In that respect, British politicians seek to ensure that their decision-making role is premised on a public acceptance of their authority. This isn't to say that if you vote Liberal Democrat, you approve of Labour policy decisions. However, it's likely that you accept the authority of the elected government – single party or coalition – to exercise decisions even if you don't always like what's been decided.

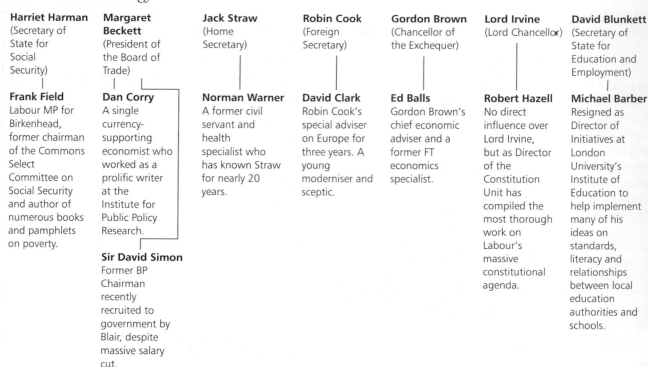

New Labour's parliamentary make up, 1997

Age of Labour's MPs

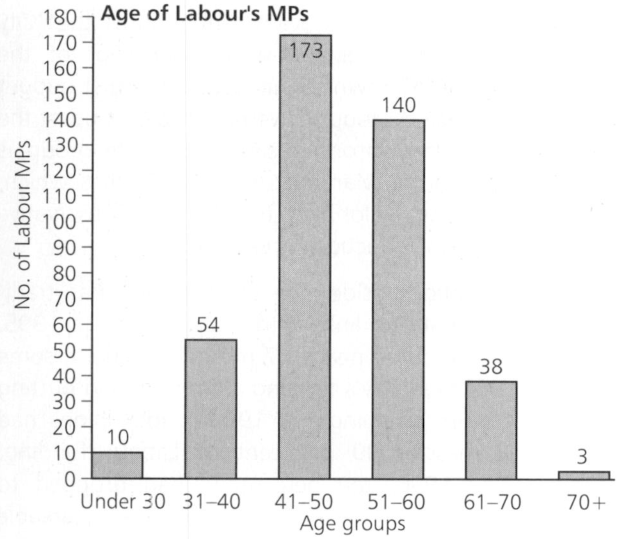

The occupations of Labour's MPs

Occupation	No. of Labour MPs
Academics/lecturers	55
Teachers	49
Journalists	32
Trade unionists	28
Barristers	16
Company directors	16
Solicitors	12
Social workers	12
Mineworkers	7
Dockers	2
Taxi driver	1

Gender of Labour's MPs

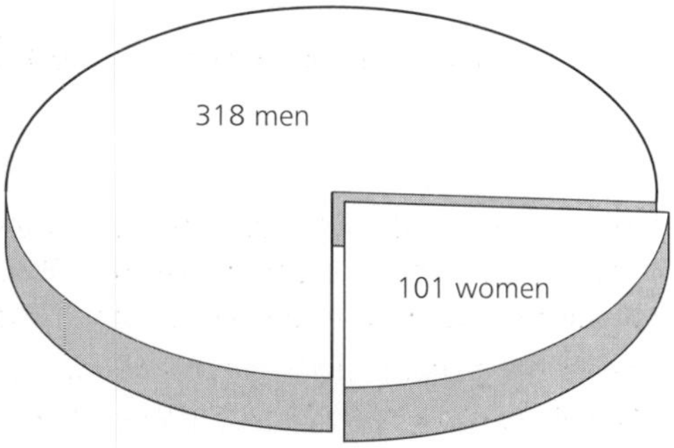

Education of Labour's MPs

Out of the 419 Labour MPs:

239 went to university

of whom 68 went to Oxford or Cambridge

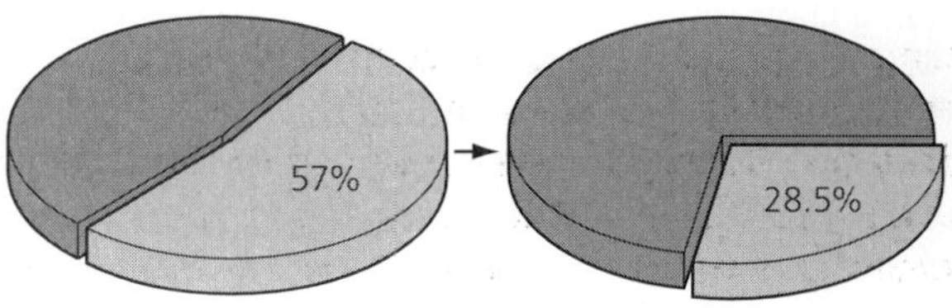

(Adapted from the *Observer*, 4 May 1997, page 21)

Of the 419 Labour MPs elected in 1997, 101 are women.

The 'powers' conferred on MPs are permissions to do things only within the authority granted. Politicians are not despotic individuals. Every act of government is performed not by an individual or a party, but by a servant of the state who derives her or his authority from parliament. This might sound a little unconvincing, given that the people who elect the servants of the state ultimately yield to their 'servants'. Yet the principle does set limits on what individual politicians and parties are permitted to do. The UK constitution (the set of conventions that provide the authorisation and the limits of political power) upholds the sovereignty of parliament and seeks to ensure that it's not damaged or overruled by individuals or parties.

> ### OVER TO YOU
>
> ***How does Max Weber's model of legal-rational authority correspond with the authority of the British parliament?***

QUESTIONS

1. In ideological terms, how does late twentieth-century Conservatism differ from nineteenth-century Toryism, Whig liberalism from Liberal Democrat liberalism, and Marx's socialism from New Labour 'socialism'?
2. How are Cabinet decisions arrived at?
3. What kinds of people become MPs, and why is this question sociologically important?

Pressure groups and decision-making

A *pressure group* is a group that has enough influence on central government to put pressure on politicians to advance the group's goals. Examples include Greenpeace, the Confederation of British Industry and the Trades Union Congress. Pressure groups are more likely to influence than to make decisions on a national policy level. It's very likely, for example, that Robin Cook's (the Foreign Secretary) resolve to stop selling British-made arms to countries that don't respect human rights is influenced by Amnesty International campaigns against torture.

Some pressure groups have a fairly direct relationship with political parties. Indeed, the Labour Party originated from a decision in 1900 of representatives of a number of pressure groups – socialist societies and trade unions – to seek working-class representation in parliament (see page 380). These days though, it's rare for pressure groups to seek direct parliamentary representation.

They're more likely to forge mutually supportive links with MPs than to join them in Westminster. Business groups, for example, have long enjoyed close relations with the Conservative Party. The 'City' is a collection of powerful capitalist pressure groups whose interests are typically represented through trade associations like the British Bankers' Association. No government ignores the 'City view'. Even the relatively left-wing Chancellor of the Exchequer, Gordon Brown, ensured that the first budget of the newly elected Labour Government didn't upset the 'City'. A particularly strong business pressure group is the Society of Motor Manufacturers and Traders which, in 1992, successfully lobbied the pro-car Conservative government for a reduction in car tax.

'City' considerations aside, the Labour Party has traditionally enjoyed strong links with trade unions. In 1995, the unions contributed nearly £7 million to Labour, some 54 per cent of the party's funding. That said, and putting a different gloss on things, in 1990, trade unions had provided a massive 90 per cent of Labour funding. Moreover, by 1996, the percentage had dropped to 33 per cent. Nowadays – and this really is a remarkable turnabout – the main source of Labour funding is individual donations from businessmen.

Nevertheless, a number of Labour MPs are sponsored by unions. The *TUC Directory* for 1966 lists under each union the MPs they sponsor. The Transport and General Workers Union, for example, sponsored 38, including the then Shadow Chancellor, Gordon Brown. This system no longer applies though because union money now goes straight to the party centrally for distribution to constituencies to assist running costs and election expenses.

The table on page 387 shows the links between five powerful trade unions and the Labour Party.

Notwithstanding the traditionally close links between Labour and the trade unions, things look set to change. Since 1992, the Labour Party has been distancing itself from the old relationship. John Smith, who took over the leadership of the party after Neil Kinnock's 1992 election defeat, introduced increased union democracy by insisting that unions vote on a 'one member, one vote' basis rather than *en bloc* at Labour conferences. The unions once controlled 90 per cent of the vote at Labour conferences, but this has been reduced, first to 70 per cent, and later to just under 50 per cent. Having a diminished influence on conference voting translates, in wider terms, into less influence on political decision-making.

There are two main kinds of pressure group:

- *sectional groups* (also called *interest groups*), which typically promote the activities and aspirations of occupational and business groups (for example, the National Union of Mineworkers and the Confederation of British Industry)
- *cause groups* (also called *promotional groups*), which, as the name implies, are more likely to fight for causes. Amnesty International and Oxfam are good examples.

There is overlap between sectional and cause groups. The British Medical Association, for example, acts as a sectional group when it seeks better employment conditions for doctors, and as a cause group when it seeks an independent inquiry into the clinical effects of boxing.

The strategies used by pressure groups vary considerably. Some groups, like the civil rights groups led by Martin Luther King in the 1960s, are prepared to break unjust laws.

Other groups, like the National Union of Mineworkers, are ready to go on strike to advance their goals. Less combative approaches are used by groups such as Shelter, who appeal to public and political opinion through publicity campaigns. Some pressure groups offer opportunities for popular involvement in politics. Greenpeace, for example, probably has more supporters than the Labour Party. Environmental pressure groups are extremely influential these days. The surge of publicity that turned Swampy, the environmental protester, into a media celebrity in 1997 has also put the spotlight on members of a network of perhaps thousands of committed individuals throughout the the UK who are campaigning for a better environment.

Montgomery, Alabama 1958. Not knowing who he is, two police officers arrest the civil rights leader, Dr Martin Luther King, for 'loitering'.

Environmental and other advocacy pressure groups (for example, Friends of the Earth, Traidcraft and Oxfam) realise that 'western' consumers have a lot of power to influence not only politicians, but also big business. In that context, ethical shopping has grown rapidly in recent years. The micro level work of these organisations in promoting the idea that paying poor workers a fair price for their produce makes good ethical and economic sense is moving into mainstream. Pressure for the potential wearer of a Bangladeshi-produced cotton shirt can make Marks & Spencer, Burton, and other retailers, pay more attention to the rights of workers in their suppliers' factories.

Oxfam and Christian Aid have each launched campaigns to improve labour conditions in poor countries by persuading supporters in the UK to lobby British retailers. The business world realise that they can't take anything for granted about the sourcing of their products and the conditions that prevail in their suppliers' factories. The battle to introduce ethics into trade has also moved from the high street to the boardroom. Pressure can be applied at annual meetings of companies who don't engage ethical practice, and also through major shareholders. The aid charity and pressure group, Aid on Want, is pursuing this avenue by calling on people who favour an option for the poor to lobby their pension funds to exert moral pressure on companies in which the funds are invested.

A number of companies want to be seen to be doing the right thing, and respond to the pressure. That's one of the reasons you can buy fairly traded coffee, tea and

The big five: How the top five unions line up in support of the Labour Party

	No. of members	**1996 donation**	**Labour NEC members**	**Share of conference vote**
GMB	740,000	£3.48 million	Mary Turner, Diana Holland and Steve Pickery	9.5%
MSF	446,000	£483,000	Margaret Wall	2.4%
T&G	900,000	£2.67 million	John Mitchell	9.5%
UNISON	1.3 million	£6.28 million	Maggie Jones, Christine Wild	9.5%
ASLEF	15,700	less than £130,000	None	0.2%

(Adapted from the *Guardian*, 4 April 1997, page 13)

PRESSURE GROUPS AND DEMOCRACY

FOR	AGAINST
+ *Participation and political access* Pressure groups increase participation and access to political system, thereby enhancing the quality of democracy. They enable the *intensity* of feeling on issues to be considered, opinions to be weighed as well as counted.	– *Sectionalism and selfishness* Pressure groups improve participation, but unequally, benefiting the well-organised but disadvantaging the weakly organised. They benefit 'those who shout loudest' against the rest.
+ *Improvement of government* Consultation with affected groups is the rational way to make decisions in a free society: the information and advice provided by groups helps to improve the quality of government policy and legislation.	– *Anti-parliamentary democracy* Secret, behind-the-scenes consultations between government and groups enables covert 'deals' to be made thereby detracting both from open government and the legitimate influence of elected legislators in parliament.
+ *Social progress* Pressure groups enable new concerns and issues to reach the political agenda, thereby facilitating social progress and preventing social stagnation.	– *Pluralistic stagnation* Group opposition can slow down or even block desirable changes, thereby contributing to social immobilism.
+ *Pluralism* Pressure groups are a product of freedom of association, which is a fundamental principle of liberal democracy: its obverse is autocratic or tyrannical suppression of interests. Freely operating pressure groups are essential to the effective functioning of liberal democracy: they serve as vital intermediary institutions between government and society, assist in the dispersal of political power and provide important counterweights to undue concentration of power.	– *Elitism* Group system only *apparently* functions on 'level playing field'; in practice reinforces existing class and power structure – 'in the pluralist heaven the heavenly choir sings with a strong upper class accent' (Schnattschneider, 1960, cited Grant, 1989, p. 26).
+ *Social cohesion* Pressure groups increase social cohesion and political stability by providing 'safety-value' outlet for individual and collective grievances.	– *Social disharmony and dislocation* Inegalitarian operation of groups increases social discontent and political instability by intensifying sense of social frustration and injustice felt by disadvantaged and excluded sections of the population.
+ *Opposition* Pressure groups assist surveillance of government by exposing information it would rather keep secret, thereby reinforcing and complementing work of official opposition through political parties.	– *Failure of opposition* True in theory but only to limited extent in practice; in contemporary Britain, groups and parties combined are unable to mount effective opposition to government policies because often lack adequate information.

(Adapted from the original table in Coxall and Robins 1994: 296)

chocolate in British supermarkets. This translates into poor growers getting a decent price for what they produce. The Co-op and Sainsburys are even developing fair trade codes which might lead to all their buying being conducted on fair trade principles. In the face of consumer power, clothes retailer, GAP, and sports shoe manufacturer, Reebok, have adopted tough codes of practice towards their suppliers. Among the issues GAP checks its suppliers on are child labour, discrimination, environmental responsibility, the right to join a trade union and working conditions. Suppliers who don't meet these conditions are subject to termination of contract.

The extent to which pressure groups promote or hinder democratic processes is debated. Trade unions and business groups, for example, might promote sectional interests that don't represent popular opinion. On the other hand, the anti-poll tax lobby that forced the Conservative government to scrap this very unpopular tax struck a chord with the British public.

Helpfully, Coxall and Robins have produced a For and Against table of arguments (opposite) on the debate about whether or not pressure groups are good for democracy.

While the actions of pressure groups in society do make a difference, the extent of their impact on major decision-making is less certain. Pressure groups that have the ear of business and political elites are probably more likely to influence policy decisions than those that haven't. Thus, for example, the 'high-level lobbying' of trade and professional associations enables middle-class people to connect and click with the people at the top. At the lower end of the power structure, the impact of working-class trade unions on party politics has dwindled.

QUESTIONS

1 Define the term 'pressure group'.
2 Give three examples of pressure groups, and show how they influence political decision-making.

Voting patterns

Things ain't what they used to be! On the 1 May 1997, business tycoons and coal miners alike voted for Tony Blair. As we write, the figures on the latest general election voting patterns are still being compiled and assessed. But we can give some general pointers, and we can also look at past trends. Throughout the 1950s and 1960s, note Anthony Heath, Roger Jowell and John Curtice (1985), about two-thirds of non-manual adults voted Conservative and about two-thirds of manual adults voted Labour. These relatively stable and enduring attachments to one or other of the major parties tend to develop during the early formative years. If mum and dad vote Labour, chances are the children will follow suit.

Social class and voting

In the 1950s and 1960s, there was only a limited amount of *partisan dealignment* (generally used to denote cross-class voting) – whereby traditional working-class Labour voters switched to Conservative, and traditional middle-class Conservative voters went over to Labour. Individuals tended to retain their *partisan alignment* (generally used to denote class-based voting) over time, voting the same way in successive elections.

> ### *EXAM TIP*
> In relation to cross-class voting and class voting, *class dealignment* and *class alignment* are sharper terms than partisan dealignment and partisan alignment. Strictly speaking, a partisan position can refer to more than just a class position.

'Natural' class voting (i.e. workers vote Labour; bosses vote Tory) remained at least as high in 1966 as it was in 1945. There was a bit of a dip in working-class support for Labour in 1959, but it recovered in 1964. So common was it for working-class people to vote Labour and for middle- and upper-class people to vote Conservative, that any deviations from this pattern were treated by some commentators as literally deviant! The point shouldn't, however, be pushed too far. Robert McKenzie and Allan Silver (1968) note that the urban working class, first enfranchised in the late nineteenth century, has been the dominant section of the British electorate since 1885. Importantly, they add that from that date to the 1960s, the Conservatives have ruled the UK alone or in coalition for about three-quarter of the time.

According to McKenzie and Silver (1968), this achievement is explained in considerable part by the success of the Conservative Party in winning at most general elections at least one-third of the working-class vote. McKenzie's and Silver's findings indicate that the debate on class dealignment is complex. Their working-class Tories seemed to have seen the Conservative Party as a 'natural' party from the outset rather than crossing over from left to the right. The legacy of the working-class Tory is a long one. From the first enfranchisement of the working class in 1867, the left were waiting for the day when the sleeping giant would sweep socialism into parliament. They were in for a surprise. After scrutinising the results of the first general election that followed in 1868, Engels expressed his exasperation in a letter to Marx:

'What do you say to the elections in the factory districts? Once again the proletariat has discredited itself terribly . . . It cannot be denied that the increase of working class voters has brought the Tories more than their simple percentage increase; it has improved their relative position.'

(cited by McKenzie and Silver 1968: 14)

Ninety years and 23 elections on, a section of the 'big battalions of the poor and unprivileged' – as Peter Shore (1952, cited by McKenzie and Silver 1968: 14) called them – were still 'discrediting' themselves. Labour was ejected from office in 1951, confounding the expectation that universal suffrage would make socialism the natural party of government. McKenzie and Silver conclude that the exercise of the right to vote:

'has by no means completely eroded the social and political deference of ordinary people; in fact, deference continues, one hundred years later, to sustain the political loyalties of a very considerable proportion of working class Conservatives.'

(McKenzie and Silver 1968: 240–1)

In addition to the 'deferential voter', McKenzie and Silver also identified the pre-cursor of the 1980s Tory-voting 'Essex Man', whom they dubbed a 'secularised voter'. The 'secularised voter' supported the Conservatives on the basis of a conditional commitment linked to the voter's continuing evaluation of different parties' performances and the prospects of future benefits. Self-interest figures prominently here. Significantly, McKenzie and Silver reported evidence of deference being displaced by the more calculated outlook of the 'secularised voter'. They also noted that 'secularism' was most often found among the younger and better-paid working-class people and, within this group, among men.

McKenzie and Silver then put their finger on a trend that has since gathered momentum – *voter volatility*. They predicted that working-class support for the Conservatives might become less reliable, being more likely to respond pragmatically to political events. These days, voter volatility affects all the main parties. The pollster company, Gallup, conducts monthly surveys on voter behaviour. Responses to their question on party identification show that this fluctuates quite markedly from month to month.

It's now quite widely argued that class-based voting has weakened over the years, and that the UK has therefore experienced class dealignment. A number of reasons are given to explain this alleged trend:

- Social classes are becoming more similar in political and ideological outlooks.
- The growth in affluence, education, and social and geographical mobility in the post-war period has reduced social cohesiveness and class identity.
- Class isn't as important as it once was in relation to individual and collective political action (for example, trade unionism has declined).
- Political parties are becoming more centrist, becoming less concerned about income and wealth distribution, and more concerned with 'quality of life' issues.

The first three of these propositions support a dealignment thesis based on the argument that left–right issues no longer strongly divide classes. It's a position supported, for example by T. N. Clark and S. M. Lipset (1991, cited by Evans *et al.* 1996), who maintain that traditional class hierarchies have declined and new differences have emerged. They conclude that politics is now less influenced by class and more by other loyalties. The argument that parties are moving towards the centre insinuates a dealignment thesis based on the assertion that left–right issues no longer strongly divide parties. It doesn't contradict but rather complements the class dealignment thesis.

Signs of a marked decline in class voting behaviour are apparent since 1966, argue proponents of the class dealignment thesis. By 1983, it's suggested that perhaps fewer than half of voters were supporting their 'natural' class party. This is based on the assumption that the Liberal and Social Democratic parties weren't class parties. If, however, say Heath *et al.* (1985), these parties are treated as a non-manual party alongside the Conservatives, the decline in class voting becomes less striking – but still evident. Although analysis of voting behaviour in the 1970s seems to suggest that cross-class voting had increased, Heath *et al.* point out that relative class support for Conservative and Labour was as high in February 1974 as it was in 1950.

In general, say Heath *et al.*, the period from 1945 to 1974 reveals no consistent trend. There are ups and downs, but these are more linked to changing political events (for example, the parties' programmes, their success in office, etc.) than with underlying class factors. Even the apparent drop in relative class voting in 1979 and 1983 might be no more than a temporary fluctuation as a result of specific political events. That said, Heath *et al.* think the assumed drop is almost wholly spurious (false), being based on shaky manual/non-manual classifications compiled by researchers. The dichotomy between manual and non-manual voters risks confusing class dealignment with changing class sizes. For example, self-employed manual workers are considerably less likely to vote Labour than the working class proper. However, they've been increasing in number in recent years, whereas the working class proper has been contracting:

> 'The internal composition of the manual category as a whole has thus changed, and its declining relative propensity to vote Labour will be, at least in part, a consequence of this change in composition.'
>
> (Heath *et al.* 1985: 34)

Put simply, Labour's 'natural' class base has been shrinking not because class and politics are no longer important, but owing to the de-industrialisation of the UK. The decline of heavy industry has meant fewer working-class jobs, and therefore fewer working-class voters. Similar factors might explain why the Conservatives won the 1992 General Election – its most recent victory at the polls. David Butler and Dennis Kavanagh (1992) note that there were significant social changes in the 1980s, many assisted by the Thatcher government. These included the growth in self-employment highlighted by Heath *et al.*, greater prosperity for the majority of people in work, a steady shift of jobs from manufacturing to services, and a growth in home ownership.

Two statistics, propose Butler and Kavanagh, make the point. In 1950, there was 29 per cent home ownership; in 1990, the figure was 67 per cent. In 1950, manual workers accounted for 68 per cent of the labour force. By the end of the 1980s, the figure was 48 per cent. In blunt terms, say Butler and Kavanagh, 'The working class was a new minority' (1992: 3). These structural trends in the composition of the working class, coupled with social trends like a decline in trade union membership and increased home ownership, meant that the predominantly Conservative-voting social groups were increasing and the Labour-voting ones were in decline.

Geoffrey Evans, Anthony Heath and Clive Payne (1996, in Rallings *et al.* 1996) retain the earlier scepticism of Heath *et al.* (1985) towards the class dealignment thesis. Taking into account the 1992 General Election, Evans *et al.* conclude that 'The strength of association between class and vote in Britain has remained basically unmoved for over 20 years' (1996: 170). They disclose, for example, that what's thought to be class dealignment can turn out to be class realignment. By this, they mean that changes of voting within a class can sometimes be mistaken for cross-class voting. As an example, they refer to the fact that in the 1964 General Election, support for Labour as opposed to Conservative was stronger in the skilled working class than in the semi- and unskilled working class. In the 1992 General Election, however, the position was reversed.

Even though class is still probably an important predictor of voting behaviour, it's not the only influence. In the UK, voting patterns are typically linked to:

- social class and other background factors involved in the voter's political socialisation
- political and other attitudes that reflect and reinforce that socialisation
- evaluations of government performance (both altruistic and selfish) and of prospects under different parties
- assessments of party leaders
- campaign effects.

It's likely that the strength of an individual's identification with a party over time is related to one or more of the above factors. Thus, for example, the typical Labour supporter (notably, of working-class background, and with a strong sense of community) is more likely than a voter from another background to identify with that party for a long time. Similarly, the archetypal Conservative supporter (notably, upper-middle or upper class, and committed to an ethos of self-help) is likely to remain loyal to that party even when it's in decline.

Research by R. J. Johnston and C. J. Pattie (1997), however, suggests that the strength of British voters' identification with the three main political parties is liable to a lot of fluctuation. Citing data from the British Household Panel Study (a longitudinal study that tracks small-scale social change among a target of about 5,000 British households – *c.*10,000 individuals), they found that of 7,131 individuals who were fully interviewed from 1991–4:

- the number of very strong and fairly strong party identifiers fell over the four years
- the number of not very strong party identifiers substantially increased over the same period.

This makes for a more volatile electorate, and one whose voting intentions are harder to predict. We're now in an era a long way from the 1960s and 1970s, when millions of Britons remained anchored to one political party for very long periods of time. In the 1997 General Election, voter volatility was very apparent. The swing to Labour was huge – the equivalent of three million voters changing allegiance since the previous election five years earlier. Dealignment was concentrated in regions where it did the Conservatives most damage – the Midlands, the South and London, and, importantly, among middle-class voters. Here, at least, there does seem to have been some class dealignment. John Major also suffered from tactical voting, with voters going for the candidate best placed to beat the Tory one.

Peter Kellner (*Observer*, 18 May 1997, page 24) writes that as many as 3.2 million people who voted Conservative in 1992 switched to a different party in 1997: 1.4 million to Labour, 1.2 million to Liberal Democrat, 400,000 to the Referendum Party, and 200,000 to nationalists and other minority parties. By contrast, the Tories only gained 500,000 votes from other parties. The chart on page 392 outlines the gains, losses and switches.

Even among the rich and the powerful, there has been a change of the guard. The Tory old guard counted among its supporters people like Lord Sterling, Sir Tim Bell, Lord King, Lord McAlpine, Lord Gowrie and Lord Hanson. They were the natural followers of the Conservative Party. The new guard, many who support New Labour, are much more varied in make-up and less likely to be titled. They include businessmen Sir Terence Conran and Richard Branson, actors Imogen Stubbs and Alan Rickman, and lawyers Lord Irvine and Helena Kennedy QC.

Since the election of Tony Blair as leader of the Labour Party, the party has had a significant opinion poll lead over the Conservatives. In fact, the lead has been around 25 per cent for a very long time. The pollsters got it right when Blair took the premiership in 1997, but were wrong in 1992. Then, they predicted a Labour win, but the Tories polled 7.6 per cent more. Ivor Crewe (cited by Garland and Rowe 1996b) suggests this error might have been the result of the so-called 'shame factor' – a tendency for Conservative voters to deny their intentions when surveyed. There could also have been a late swing in the Tories' favour, for as much as 8 per cent of voters made their minds up during the final 24 hours before the election day.

It's too early yet to determine whether the 1997 General Election indicates an increase in class dealignment. An exit poll conducted by NOP for the BBC (cited by Curtice 1997) indicates that support for Labour in this election was higher amongst voters in working-class occupations than amongst those in middle-class jobs. That said, the rise in Labour's support compared with 1992 was about the same in each of these social classes. It's significant that, despite some inevitable dealignment, many Tories still stuck with their party. This is easy to forget in the flurry of statistics which proclaimed a Labour landslide. Even after its impressive campaign to capture the heart and soul of 'Middle England', Labour's share of the final poll was less than the polls some months before the election, which gave it well over half the 'intended' votes of the electorate. As in 1992, the final result in 1997

How Britain's votes moved 1992–97

(All figures shown in millions)

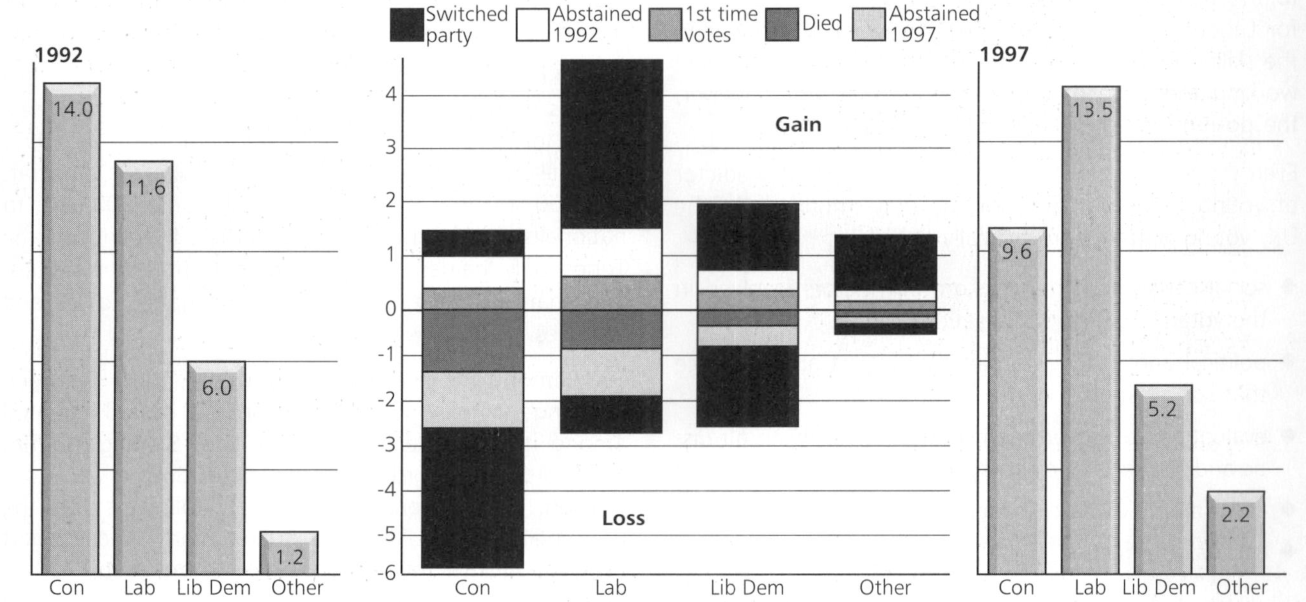

(The *Observer*, 18 May 1997, page 24)

indicates that quite a few people who voted Conservative told a different story to the opinion pollsters. Labour has a huge majority, but it knows that a majority of the electorate actually voted against it.

That some class dealignment has occurred isn't disputed. The extent to which it has occurred is. Against the argument that class dealignment is widespread, we must remember, as well as the points made by Evans *et al.* (1996), the powerful influence upon adult human behaviour – including voting – of early socialisation. In their analysis of the loyalties of voters, Richard Rose and Ian McAllister (1990, cited by Coxall and Robins 1994: 258), explained how a lifetime of learning steadily shapes voting behaviour. Habits are laid down in childhood, when children develop attitudes towards the authority of

(The *Independent*, 28 April 1997, page 18)

This time the compilers of the late polls got it right in predicting the outcome of the 1997 General Election. So did this cartoonist in his depiction, three days before the election, of a smiling Tony Blair on John Major's doorstep.

Voting intention by social class, 1995

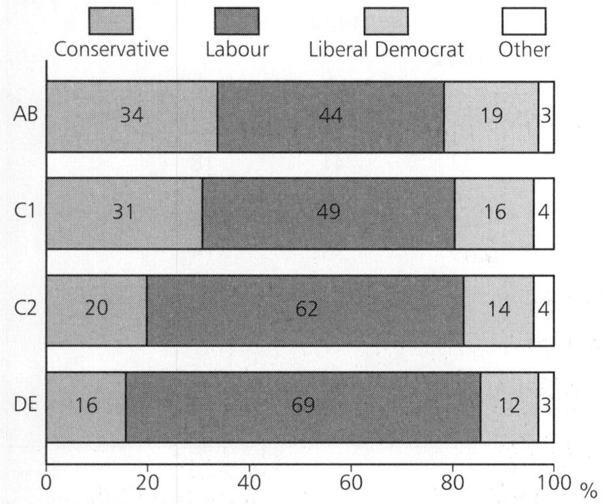

(Garland and Rowe 1996a, using data from MORI, August 1995)

their parents and other significant others. Families are in turn located within different social classes, and often reproduce and reinforce class-based attitudes and behaviours – including those connected with voting.

While class still remains a predictor of voting intentions, it's worth noting that, in 1995, as the chart above indicates, the Labour Party enjoyed considerable support among all classes, ranging from 69 per cent among class DE (very low income groups, including unemployed people), to 44 per cent for the ABs (middle to high income groups, including top professionals).

If we go back to firmer but earlier ground and look at the relationship between class and actual, as opposed to intended, voting, we find class voting alive and well in both the 1987 and 1992 General Elections, as indicated in the table below.

Interestingly, John Gray (cited by Williams 1995) thinks recent polling trends indicate a reversal of the 'bourgeoisification thesis' (the notion that we're all becoming middle class). In the wake of increasing job insecurity, segments of the British middle class have found common cause with the working class in their concern about the erosion of public services. Some have also become disillusioned with Thatcherism and Majorism, and have sided with 'left/green' campaigns on transport and animal rights. Before, however, jumping to the conclusion that the middle class is defecting *en bloc* from Conservative to Labour, we should be mindful of Evans *et al.*'s (1996) argument that class voting still endures.

It does sometimes appear that class is all and the rest minor detail in the sociological analysis of voting behaviour. But other factors, notably age, gender, ethnicity and region, are also important – if not perhaps so extensively researched.

Age, gender, ethnicity and region in relation to voting

Age

It's noteworthy that disillusionment with parties in general is high among 18–24-year-olds. The rate of non-voting in this age group increased from 31 per cent in 1987 to 43 per cent in 1992. Shortly before the 1997 General Election, only about 49 per cent of 18–24-year-olds said they were certain to vote, according to MORI. That's 10 per cent fewer than at the same stage in the run-up to the 1995 election.

At the time of writing, we're still waiting for more detailed data on the 1997 General Election. However, we do know that, since the vote was granted to 18-year-olds in 1970, Labour has performed better amongst

Voting patterns by occupational class in the 1987 and 1992 General Elections (row percentages)

	1987[1]			**1992**[2]		
Occupational class	**Con.**	**Lab.**	**Lib. Dem.**	**Con.**	**Lab.**	**Lib. Dem.**
Professional/managerial (AB)	52	15	31	56	20	21
Routine non-manual (C1a)	54	21	23	49	28	20
Skilled manual (C1b/C2)	38	41	20	39	40	18
Unskilled manual (D/E)	31	47	22	30	51	14

1 The 1987 figures (N = 3204) are taken from Crewe *et al.* 1991.
2 The 1992 figures are calculated by averaging the breakdowns reported in the Harris exit poll (N = 4701) and the Gallup postelection survey.

All figures exclude 'don't know's and 'refused to say' from the percentage base.

(Adapted from King *et al.* 1993: 189)

Voting patterns by age in the 1987 and 1992 General Elections (row percentages)

	1987[1]			1992[2]		
Age	**Con.**	**Lab.**	**Lib. Dem.**	**Con.**	**Lab.**	**Lib. Dem.**
Under 25	36	40	22	38	35	22
25–34	38	36	25	37	41	18
35–44	44	28	26	38	38	21
45–64	47	29	22	44	35	19
Over 65	49	27	23	49	33	14

1 The 1987 figures (N = 3204) are taken from Crewe *et al.* 1991.
2 The 1992 figures (N = 1880) are taken from the Gallup postelection survey.

All figures exclude 'don't know's and 'refused to say' from the percentage base.

(Adapted from King *et al.* 1993: 189)

18–24-year-olds than amongst the electorate generally. In general, the young are more inclined to vote Labour, and the old are more likely to vote Conservative. An NOP/BBC exit poll at the 1997 General Election found that Labour's support was 19 points higher than five years earlier for voters aged 18–29. But it was two points lower amongst the over-65s (Curtice 1997).

The table above shows voting patterns by age in 1987 and 1992.

Gender

David Sanders (1993, in King *et al.* 1993) notes that between 1964 and 1979, the Conservatives consistently enjoyed more support from women than men. During the 1980s though, this gap gradually disappeared, so that in the 1983 and 1987 General Elections there was little gender difference in party support. Yet in the 1992 General Election, the traditional gender divide was restored, with support for the Conservatives around five percentage points higher – and support for Labour three points lower – among women than among men. Sanders says that the precise reasons why the gender gap reappeared is difficult to specify. The fact that 48 per cent of women compared with 42 per cent of men thought the Conservatives had the best leaders may, he says, have had some role to play. In the 1997 General Election, Labour overcame its previous deficit amongst women voters (Curtice 1997).

The table 'Vote by gender' opposite provides a longitudinal analysis of male and female voting patterns from 1963 to 1987.

It will be interesting to see if, when more 1997 General Election data are published, a gender gap still exists in female and male voting patterns. What do you think?

Ethnicity

Ethnicity also plays a significant role in voting behaviour. 'Those blacks who vote', reports the leader column of the *Guardian* (22 July 1997, page 16), 'already overwhelmingly vote Labour'. Earlier research tends to corroborate this finding. In its study of the October 1974 General Election, for example, the Community Relations Commission (1974, 1975, cited by Coxall and Robins 1994), drew four conclusions about minority ethnic group voting:

- Minority ethnic groups swung more to Labour than the electorate as a whole.
- Members of minority ethnic groups were five times more likely than white people in the same area not to be registered to vote.
- Although minority ethnic groups tended to conform with their social class position in voting Labour, other parties could attract their support if efforts were made.
- Minority ethnic groups played an important role in determining the outcome of the election.

A later study by the Harris Poll (1987, cited by Coxall and Robins 1994) showed that Labour was still holding on to its support from the minority ethnic communities. The table opposite analyses the black vote in relation to social class.

Survey data for the three general elections in 1979, 1983 and 1987 suggests there has been remarkable stability in black support for Labour.

Region

Looking at region, differential voting patterns are discernible. According to Gillian Peele (1995), regional factors played a significant role in the voter volatility that confounded predictable trends in the 1974 General Election. The election was called by Conservative Prime Minister Edward Heath in an attempt to defeat a miners' strike. Heath lost the election to Labour, and more voters than usual switched parties. A notable feature of this election was the emergence of distinct regional variations in voting patterns. Although some of the variations were linked to economic factors, especially differences in

Vote by gender (%)

Men

	1963[1]	**1964**	**1966**	**1969[1]**	**1970**	**Feb. 1974**	**Oct. 1974**	**1979**	**1983[2]**	**1987[2]**
Party voted for:										
Conservative	32.1	40.2	36.3	56.2	42.7	37.4	34.6	45.3	45.5	44.0
Labour	53.4	47.4	54.3	33.8	47.5	41.6	44.9	37.7	29.8	31.2
Liberal	14.2	11.7	8.7	8.0	7.0	17.5	15.6	14.7	23.4	23.5
Other	0.3	0.7	0.7	2.0	2.8	3.5	4.8	2.3	1.3	1.3
Total	100.00	100.00	100.00	100.00	100.00	100.00	100.00	100.00	100.00	100.00
No. of respondents	787	735	741	461	688	989	973	750	1494	1528

Women

	1963[1]	**1964**	**1966**	**1969[1]**	**1970**	**Feb. 1974**	**Oct. 1974**	**1979**	**1983[2]**	**1987[2]**
Party voted for:										
Conservative	41.0	43.1	40.9	56.4	48.3	38.6	37.4	48.5	44.9	44.2
Labour	46.3	46.5	50.9	28.7	42.0	39.8	40.0	37.5	27.7	30.9
Liberal	12.6	9.8	7.8	12.9	7.7	20.5	20.4	13.0	26.0	23.4
Other	0.0	0.6	0.4	2.0	2.0	1.1	2.2	1.0	1.4	1.4
Total	100.00	100.00	100.00	100.00	100.00	100.00	100.00	100.00	100.00	100.00
No. of respondents	965	843	829	495	773	1078	982	808	1711	1674

1 No general election was held in 1963 or 1969. For these two years, the data refer to vote intention, not actual vote. It's interesting to note that, in 1969, the percentage of women and men who said they intended to vote Conservative was almost identical: 56.4 per cent of women, and 56.2 per cent of men

2 In 1983 and 1987, the Liberal Party contested the election in alliance with the Social Democratic Party (SDP). In these two years, Liberal voters include those who voted for the SDP or the Alliance

(Crewe *et al.* 1991: 6)

Party support by class among black voters (%)

	AB	**C1**	**C2**	**DE**
Conservative	33	30	14	10
Labour	54	52	78	84
Liberal-SDP Alliance	13	17	9	5

(Coxall and Robins 1994: 264, using data from the Harris Poll, May 1987, published in *Talking Politics*)

employment prospects, Peele contends that simply being in an area where one party was strong might have had an influence on voters who may otherwise have voted differently.

Says Peele, 'Thus, from 1974 what seems to have been emerging is a "culture of place", which has acted as an independent variable on voting' (1995: 297). For example, living in a region where Scottish National Party representatives were prominent may have 'caused' more people than usual to vote for them. From 1974 onwards, the most obvious regional variations were in Scotland and Wales, where significant nationalist parties emerged, and where the Conservatives were increasingly marginalised. Labour stayed strong in both areas. In England, the Conservatives lost ground to Labour in the north and to Liberals (later Liberal Democrats) in the west. Labour found it harder to retain votes in the southern part of the country.

Up to – and to some extent beyond – the 1997 General Election:

- ◆ Labour strongholds were prominent in the north, Wales, and Scotland
- ◆ the south-east was a bastion of Tory voters
- ◆ Cornwall and Devon proved popular for the Liberal-Democrats.

In 1997, of course, certain aspects of the political map changed. After Blair's victory, the Tories had no seats in Scotland, and none in any big English cities except London, where they only won 12 out of 72 seats. Given that the Conservatives no longer have control of any urban councils, they've become the party of suburban and rural England. By contrast, Labour now draws its support from all over the country, including many seats in core Tory territory, such as Hove and St Albans. In broad terms, Labour have strengthened their north England and Scottish representation, and have made some successful raids on some prime Tory seats in south England. The west has continued to support the Liberal Democrats. Tory safe seats still endure in the countryside and affluent southern areas, but have otherwise suffered the consequences of regional dealignment in favour of other parties.

QUESTIONS

1 Briefly define these terms: class alignment; class dealignment; partisan alignment; partisan dealignment. Why is it sometimes more appropriate to refer to *class* rather than to *partisan*?
2 Briefly evaluate the claim that voting behaviour has shifted from class alignment to class dealignment.
3 How do age, gender and region affect voting?

The role of mass media in politics

Early days

For as long as the mass media have been around, politicians and political writers (including Marx) have used them. In the early nineteenth century, for example, radical working-class newspapers were openly political, opposing Whig, Tory and factory owner alike. It was against this 'pauper press' and other radical publications that parliamentary restrictions were imposed by the ruling class. Tom Paine's *Rights of Man* was burned; licences were withdrawn from coffee houses and taverns in receipt of working-class newspapers; and duties were levied on educational materials.

The Tory writer, Southey, lamented the political mischief of weekly radical newspapers that found their:

'way to the pot-house in town, and the ale-house in the country, inflaming the turbulent temper of the manufacturer, and disturbing the quiet attachment of the peasant to those institutions under which he and his fathers have dwelt in peace.'

(Southey 1812: 347)

Tories didn't only attack the working-class press, but also radical members of their own class. When, for example, the Whig politician, Henry Brougham, co-wrote an article in the *Edinburgh Review* (1808) praising the Spanish Revolution, some members of the ruling class were deeply offended. There was a well-publicised story about Lord Buchan solemnly placing the offending number of the *Edinburgh Review* on his hall floor and kicking it into the middle of the street.

Despite such internecine skirmishes in privileged circles, as well as the journalistic fury of Marx towards all Whigs and Tories, the prominent London newspapers in the nineteenth century generally supported ruling-class ideas. Marx recognised this when he noted that the nation's rulers were able to influence press coverage because they owned leading newspapers and had political and social connections with important editors (see the section on 'Ownership and control of mass media', Chapter 15). The *Times*, *Punch*, the *Morning Post* and the *Morning Advertiser* were all, said Marx, in the pockets of the nation's rulers.

Notwithstanding the immense influence of the London press, newspapers that addressed a working-class readership (for example, the *Poor Man's Guardian* and the *Northern Star*) still struggled on. The last successful bearer of working-class views on political issues of the day, notes Wagg (1989), was the *Daily Herald*. It was launched in 1912, and again after the First World War. At one time it outsold the *Mail* and the *Express*, but between the 1940s and 1960s, it went into decline. It closed in 1964, but reopened shortly thereafter as the *Sun*. In 1969, it was bought by its present owner, Rupert Murdoch.

Political partisanship

In the February 1974 General Election, the *Sun* switched to the Conservatives, becoming a politically partisan, populist tool of the capitalist class. From thereon, it spoke for what Wagg terms 'an imaginary "common person", representing the populace at large' (1989: 21). This person was, in crude terms, a jingoistic, sexist, 'little Englander' who voted Conservative and showed little or no tolerance towards beggars, 'foreigners' and toffs. Such figures, were, of course, reviled by the paper. By contrast, the *Sun* revered self-made figures – chat show hosts, Richard Branson types, football players and – at the top of the list – Maggie Thatcher.

In the run-up to the 1997 General Election, the *Sun* re-invented itself as the paper of New Labour, throwing its weight firmly behind the premier-to-be, Tony Blair. A series of meetings between Blair and the *Sun* owner, Murdoch – as well as a long-standing association between Blair's press secretary, Alastair Campbell, and the *Sun* editor, Stuart Higgins – set things rolling. Once a subtle series of pronouncements made it clear that Murdoch's holding company, News International, had nothing to fear under Labour, the *Sun* was won over.

'It's the Sun wot swung it', proclaimed the paper on the day after the election, adding that, 'Jubilant Tony Blair praised the Sun last night for helping to clinch his stunning General Election victory' (The *Sun*, 2 May 1997, page 2). A perusal of its leader column, 'The Sun Says', on the same day reveals why the paper switched to Labour: 'Blair has transformed Labour into a free-market political force, the people's choice' (The *Sun*, 2 May 1997, page 6). In other words, Blair has made Labour the party of popular capitalism, which is exactly what the *Sun* stands for. It must be hard though for the paper to come to terms with Blair's 'toff' background – he attended a public school. That can be forgiven though, provided his party stands up for *Sun* values.

And that's not hard to do. The Labour Party has so fundamentally changed, it now seems comfortable with a trade union-opposing tabloid like the *Sun*. For its part, the popular tabloid's backing for Labour during a time of huge Tory unpopularity might be a clever way of stealing some readers from its arch-rival and long-standing Labour supporter, the *Daily Mirror*. In that context, it's noteworthy that the Tory-supporting *Daily Mail* seriously misjudged its readers in the 1997 General Election. At the previous general election in 1992, when the *Daily Mail* strongly backed the Conservatives, well over 60 per cent of its readers supported Major at the polls. This time round, research by the pollster company, MORI, suggests that a little over 40 per cent voted Conservative, with Labour and the Liberal Democrats getting more than half the readership.

The *Daily Mail*'s former editor, Sir David English (now chairman and editor-in-chief of the paper's parent company, Associated Newspapers), and the paper's proprietor, Lord Rothermere, had both courted Blair. However, they counselled caution in the paper's handling of the election. The paper, under the editorship of Paul Dacre, backed the wrong horse. Dacre was given free reign to indulge his ferocious anti-Europeanism in the *Mail*, and launched his 'Battle for Britain' crusade against a single European currency.

Rothermere has made questioning noises, and it seems unlikely that Dacre will be given quite so much levity in future. Shortly after Blair's victory, Rothermere announced that henceforth he would be supporting Labour. However, he hasn't shown any signs of wanting to fire Dacre. On the contrary, he reckons Dacre is the best editor in the UK. It seems he's not the kind of proprietor whom orthodox marxists describe as the 'puppet master' behind the editorials. There might be the odd nudge here and there, but no direct control over what his editor prints.

The Tory-supporting *Daily Telegraph* didn't break ranks. About a week before the election, the paper chose to run the Labour-supporting *Guardian*'s ICM opinion poll which showed Labour's lead falling – despite the *Telegraph*'s own Gallup poll indicating an increasing Labour lead!

Political parties do their best to persuade journalists to write stories that support them and knock opponents. The party 'spin doctors' – notably, Charles Lewington for the Conservatives, and Peter Mandelson for Labour – brief journalists on how they want their press conferences reported in the media. They also provide journalists with copies of their leaders' keynote speeches with an appropriate 'spin' which highlights issues which it's hoped will be splashed on tomorrow's headlines.

What happens next is open. Pluralists contend that journalists exercise professional freedom and write stories how they see fit. The reality is sometimes different. Journalists who don't respond to the spin often get cold-shouldered by party activists, which can lead to their sources drying up. Parties also feed stories to favoured newspapers.

As the 1997 election run-up gained momentum, both Labour and the Conservatives engaged in very English nostalgia. Labour paraded Fitz the bulldog, and Major delivered a Churchillian lecture to the nation. These were just two of the 'propaganda' events monitored by Peter Golding and David Deacon of Loughborough University's Communication Research Centre prior to election day. In a fascinating piece of research (see the tables on page 398), Golding and Deacon (reported in the *Guardian*, 21 April 1997, page 11) coded press and television coverage which were unambiguously favourable in tone or content to one of the three main parties. They found, for example, that:

- the broadsheets maintained an approximate balance of positive stories across the main parties
- the *Sun* did the same, despite its turnabout declaration for Labour
- the *Mirror* (Labour), the *Mail* (Conservative) and the *Express* (Conservative) retained their long-established partisanship, but without the trenchant certainty of 1992
- television broadcasts generally favoured the Conservatives.

OVER TO YOU

The Express is now owned by the Labour peer, Clive Hollick. Conduct a content analysis of the paper's political coverage of the Labour government over any one week. What did you find?

You could do this in groups and report your findings to the rest of the class. Compare your results with those of other groups. Are they the same? Why is this question important in relation to reliability?

The tables on page 398 put the above points in more precise statistical terms.

Despite the cosy relationship that exists between some politicians and certain sections of the media (for example, between Blair and the *Daily Mirror*), it would be over-simplistic to imagine that media personnel are simply the ideological servants of the ruling class. In their functionalist–pluralist critique of American politics and the mass media, Parsons and Winston White point out that:

'Contrasted with the ascriptiveness of tradition is the range of alternative sources of communication output, newspapers, magazines, books, broadcasting stations and programs. This is far from unlimited, but unless restricted by totalitarian types of policies, far wider than in any traditional system.'

(Parsons and White 1960, in Parsons 1969: 249)

Framing the debate: Percentages of stories which are clearly positive about each main party[1]

Media	Pro Conservative	Pro Labour	Pro LDem	% neutral stories or with unclear bias
Times	28	22	6	34
Guardian	20	19	5	50
Telegraph	22	21	4	48
Independent	17	25	10	41
Financial Times	21	28	1	44
Sun	35	35	0	25
Mirror	18	50	1	29
Star	30	34	2	32
Mail	35	17	1	45
Express	32	12	3	49
BBC 9 O'Clock News	14	11	7	57
ITN News at Ten	14	14	9	61
Newsnight	14	4	4	73
Channel 4 News	13	10	5	71

1 Excludes stories positive to other parties

Framing the debate, by media type: percentage of stories which are clearly positive about each party[1]

Media type	Pro Conservative	Pro Labour	Pro LDem	% neutral stories or with unclear bias
Broadsheets	22	23	5	43
Tabloids	30	28	1	37
Broadcast	14	9	5	64

1 Excludes stories positive to other parties

(Both tables adapted from the *Guardian*, 21 April 1997, page 1, based on research by Loughborough University's Communications Research Centre)

They also claim that there's a wide range of content choice for the prospective consumer of mass media. Parsons and White do acknowledge that concentrations of media sources, especially with reference to broadcasting and the press, can and do occur. But they see this as a malfunction which doesn't really fit the American experience. Countervailing forces rather than monopoly control prevail, according to the functionalist–pluralist perspective. The ensuing plurality of media perspectives means that no one dominant ideology is able to take hold.

Even the historical ideological bias in the British press towards the Conservative Party hasn't prevented Tory newspapers from criticising the Conservative Party and Conservative governments. No party can assume it has a newspaper, television or radio company in its pocket. Journalists have their own agendas, and aren't averse to catching politicians out and eagerly reporting political gaffes. Jeremy Paxman, who presents BBC 2's *Newsnight*, says that a broadcaster's attitude towards politicians should be the degree of respect that a dog gives to a lamppost! Underlying this sentiment is the belief that journalists should give politicians a hard time rather than acting as their supporters.

There have been a number of skirmishes between the media and politicians when the government has sought to 'manage' the news. One of the most well-known of these was the battle that took place between politicians and broadcasters over the 1988 Thames Television programme, *Death on the Rock*. The events are documented in Bob Franklin's (1994) book, *Packaging Politics*. Produced by the This Week team, the programme chronicled the shooting of three IRA members in Gibraltar who were subsequently found to be unarmed. The conclusions of *Death on the Rock* challenged the official version of events. The government tried to prevent its showing in the UK on the grounds that it would allegedly constitute trial by television. Thames Television eventually commissioned a special inquiry into the programme.

The ensuing *Windlesham/Rampton Report on Death on the Rock* vindicated Thames Television, finding that it didn't compromise due impartiality. Downing Street issued a statement announcing that the then Prime Minister rejected the findings of the report. Three years on, when Thames Television were refused the renewal of their franchise to broadcast, Peter Kellner described the process of allocating the new television licences as 'an exercise in ideological vengeance' used by the government 'to punish the company that made *Death on the Rock*' (The *Independent*, 18 October 1991, cited by Franklin 1994: 78).

The relationship between the media and the political establishment is complex. There are examples of partisanship (especially in tabloid papers), but journalists work for newspaper and television companies, not for political parties. Moreover, there's no guarantee that what they report and how they report it will influence what the public think about politics.

Media effects

The extent to which media coverage of election campaigns and other political issues actually sways voter opinion is very hard to ascertain. Given that political socialisation starts early and that deeply ingrained habits and attitudes tend to endure, it seems unlikely that most committed Conservative, Labour, Liberal Democrat or any other voters will be persuaded to switch party allegiance on the basis of what they read and see in the media. On the other hand, the individual who is undecided or prone to dealign might be more influenced by the media.

In the early part of the twentieth century, American research into media effects suggested that the public were quite gullible and could be easily swayed by the media (see the section on media effects in Chapter 15). In response to this, post-Second World War studies in the US played down direct effects theory (*hypodermic syringe theory*, as it's popularly termed), and proposed theories of mediated and minimal effects – *two-step-flow theory* and *uses and gratifications theory*, respectively. Research since the 1970s has essentially arrived at a position which balances the best arguments of all three theories, integrating them into an approach called *cultural effects theory*.

This newer perspective proposes (and here I draw upon the work of Pippa Norris 1996) that the media influence people through four main ways:

- enabling them to keep abreast of world affairs (learning)
- defining the major economic, political and social issues of the day (agenda setting)
- influencing who gets praised or blamed for events in the news (framing responsibility)
- shaping, through everyday social construction, people's attitudes and behaviours (hegemony).

According to William L. Miller *et al.* (1991; 1990, cited by Norris 1996), television coverage had little effect on agenda setting or perceptions of party credibility in the 1987 General Election. However, the press had a significant influence on voting choice and on party and leadership images. This research was based on a panel survey and content analysis. In her investigation of survey data from the 1992 British General Election Study, Norris (1996) came to the following conclusions:

- Watching television news does seem to influence people's levels of political knowledge, as well as levels of participation in and effect on the political process.
- Evidence concerning learning from television news isn't always consistent, and there's no support for the agenda setting effects that are often emphasised in American studies.
- Television may have had a modest effect on voting behaviour, because the most attentive viewers were slightly more likely to switch away from the Liberal Democrats between the 1987 and 1992 general elections.
- Overall, the preceding findings should be treated with caution because it's difficult, on the basis of survey data, to attribute detailed media messages to specific media effects.

Norris is an excellent sociologist. She looks to the evidence, and doesn't overstate her case. Much more research, as Norris freely acknowledges, is needed before sociologists can disentangle from the extensive factors that shape political socialisation, the particular ones that are linked to media effects.

QUESTIONS

1 To what extent do the media act in concert with and independently of politicians?
2 What does research reveal about the relationship between media effects and political outlooks?

Concluding remarks

After 18 years of Tory rule, a Labour government was elected on 1 May 1997. Shortly afterwards, the new Foreign Secretary, Robin Cook, said that human rights would figure prominently in British foreign policy. The new political elite says it won't supply military hardware to regimes that violate human rights. If it keeps its promise, the government will show that it's prepared to put ethics before profits.

This might be difficult. Sociologists of power remind us that political elites don't usually act independently of economic elites. The UK's defence industry is a formidable lobby group. It has prospered for years from government contracts in a global capitalist economy where political leaders are often reluctant to let human rights considerations get in the way of business.

As sociologists, you find yourselves in an exciting political era. Whether you or I agree with their judgement, on 1 May 1997, the British electorate decided it was time for a change. They voted in a Labour government whose campaign band, D-Ream, promised that 'Things can only get better'. Is this empty rhetoric? Will New Labour live up to their promise? Time will tell, but only if we sociologists get out there and do the research.

Glossary of key terms

Cabinet The Cabinet is the apex of government, the nation's top executive committee

Civil society The part of society that comprises social interactions between people which are based on agreed customs rather than law

Class alignment An alignment between the social class of the voter and loyalty to a particular party. For example, working-class people often vote Labour

Class dealignment A switch of alignment between typical class characteristics and loyalty to a particular party. For example, some working-class Labour voters switch to voting Conservative

Democracy A political system in which the people, rather than any privileged group, have the power to elect a government of their own choosing, which they then are expected to obey (refer to the main text for variants on this definition)

Discourse The taken-for-granted framework within which official decisions are made

Elite A minority group whose members possess 'superior' qualities (for example, military might, economic muscle, intellectual flair). An economic elite that enjoys political power is a ruling class

Executive The branch of government that implements and applies laws. In the UK, the executive includes the Crown and the Ministers of the Crown, and the Civil Service. The key institutions of the executive are the Cabinet and the Civil Service

Government The exercise of influence and control through law (including 'legitimate' force) over people in a designated territory (notably, a country)

Ideology A set of values that a social group (for example, a political party) believes in

Laissez-faire A capitalist ideology which believes in minimal intervention by government in the economic market

Legislature The part of the political system which makes and changes the law. In the UK, the legislature comprises the monarch, the Commons and the Lords. In the USA, it's composed of the President, the Senate and the House of Representatives

Parliament A term used for institutions (in the UK, the Commons and the Lords) of consultative government. Parliament has political sovereignty in the UK. In practice, this largely amounts to the sovereignty of the Commons because that House is empowered to override the decisions of the Lords

Partisan alignment An alignment between voter characteristics (notably, social class) and loyalty to a particular party. For example, working-class people often vote Labour

Partisan dealignment A switch of alignment between voter characteristics (notably, social class) and loyalty to a particular party. For example, some working-class Labour voters switch to voting Conservative

Pluralism A political system based on checks and balances wherein no single group gains the overall upper hand, and in which people don't infringe other people's right to hold a different opinion. In that sense there is consensus – the kind that agrees to disagree

Power elite A term used by C. Wright Mills to denote a fusion of economic, political and military elites. The leading men (and Mills refers to men) who are at the pinnacle of each elite come together and make decisions that have major consequences

Ruling class A powerful economic group whose members exercise direct or indirect political rule. For example, powerful politicians who are also big capitalists belong to a ruling class

Social class A group of people who share similar economic life chances and similar lifestyles

Society A relatively large group of people who normally inhabit a determinate territory and who typically interact in a predictable, systematic way

State The legal and political institutions that preside over a determinate territory

Totalitarianism A one-party political system where the state exercises total control over the people

References

Bateman, John (1970) *The Great Landowners of Great Britain and Ireland*, Fourth Edition. New York: August M. Kelley

Bauman, Zygmunt (1992) *Thinking Sociologically*. Oxford: Blackwell

Bottomore, Tom and Rubel, Maximilien (eds) (1975) *Karl Marx: Selected Writings in Sociology and Social Philosophy*. Harmondsworth: Penguin

Butler, David and Kavanagh, Dennis (1992) *The British General Election of 1992*. New York: St Martin's Press

Chomsky, Noam (1969) *American Power and the New Mandarins*. London: Chatto & Windus

Coser, Lewis A. and Rosenberg, Bernard (eds) (1969) *Sociological Theory: A Book of Readings*, Third Edition. London: Macmillan

Coxall, Bill and Robins, Lynton (1994) *Contemporary British Politics*, Second Edition. Basingstoke: Macmillan

Crewe, Ivor, Day, Neil and Fox, Anthony (1991) *The British Electorate 1963–1987*. Cambridge: Cambridge University Press

Curtice, John (1997) Anatomy of a non-landslide, pp 2–8, *Politics Review*, Vol. 7, No. 1, September

Dahl, Robert A. (1982) *Dilemmas of Pluralist Democracy*. New Haven, Connecticut: Yale University Press

Domhoff, G. William (1979) *The Powers That Be*. New York: Vintage Books

Evans, Geoffrey, Heath, Anthony and Payne, Clive (1996) Class and party revisited: A new model for estimating changes in levels of class voting, pp 157–74, in Rallings, Colin, *et al.* (eds) (1996) op. cit.

Foucault, Michel (1965) *Madness and Civilization*. New York: Pantheon Books

Franklin, Bob (1994) *Packaging Politics*. London: Arnold

Garland, Jon and Rowe, Michael (1996a) The centre ground in British politics, back cover, *Politics Review*, Vol. 5, No. 4, April

Garland, Jon and Rowe, Michael (1996b) Interpreting opinion poll data, back cover, *Politics Review*, Vol. 6, No. 1, September
Garnett, Mark (1996) Searching for 'the big idea', pp 6–9, *Politics Review*, Vol. 6, No. 2, November
Gramsci, Antonio (1977) *Selections from Political Writings (1910–1920)*. London: Lawrence & Wishart
Heath, Anthony, Jowell, Roger and Curtice, John, with the assistance of Field, Julia and Levine, Clarissa (1985) *How Britain Votes*. Oxford: Pergamon Press
Held, David *et al.* (eds) (1985) *States and Societies*. Oxford: Blackwell/The Open University
Hobbes, Thomas (1960) *Leviathan*. Oxford: Blackwell
Jencks, Charles (1996) *What is Post-Modernism?* Fourth Edition. London: Academy Editions
Johnston, R. J. and Pattie, C. J. (1997) Fluctuating party identification in Great Britain: Patterns revealed by four years of a longitudinal study, pp 67–77, *Politics*, Vol. 17, No. 2, May
King, Anthony, Crewe, Ivor, Denver, David, Newton, Kenneth, Norton, Philip, Sanders, David and Seyd, Patrick (1993) *Britain at the Polls 1992*. Chatham, New Jersey: Chatham House Publishers, Inc.
McKenzie, Robert and Silver, Allan (1968) *Angels in Marble*. London: Heinemann
McLellan, David (1983) *Karl Marx: The Legacy*. London: BBC
Michels, Robert (1958) *Political Parties*. Glencoe, Illinois: The Free Press
Mills, C. Wright (1973) *The Power Elite*. London: Oxford University Press
Mosca, Gaetano (1939) *The Ruling Class*. New York: McGraw-Hill
Nisbet, Robert A. (1970) *Tradition and Revolt*. New York: Vintage Books
Norris, Pippa (1996) Political communications in British election campaigns: Reconsidering media effects, pp 125–38, in Rallings, Colin, *et al.* (eds) (1996) op. cit.
Pareto, Vilfredo (selections from 1896-1921), *Sociological Writings*, selected and introduced by Finer, S. E. (1976) Oxford: Blackwell
Parsons (1967) *Sociological Theory and Modern Society*. New York: The Free Press
Parsons (1969) *Politics and Social Structure*. New York: The Free Press
Peele, Gillian (1995) *Governing the UK*, Third Edition. Oxford: Blackwell
Poulantzas, Nicos (1973) *Political Power and Social Classes*. London: NLB/Sheed & Ward
Rallings, Colin, Farrell, David M., Denver, David and Broughton, David (eds) (1996) *British Elections and Parties Yearbook 1995*. London: Frank Cass
Robinson, David (1827) The faction, Vol. XXII, *Blackwood's Edinburgh Magazine*, October
Southey (1812), Inquiry into the Poor Laws & c., *Quarterly Review*, Vol. VIII, December
Scott, John (1992) *Who Rules Britain?* Cambridge: Polity Press
Thompson, E. P. (1971) The moral economy of the English crowd in the eighteenth century, pp 76–136, *Past and Present*, No. 50, February
Topf, Richard (1994) Party manifestos, pp 149–71, in Heath, Anthony, Jowell, Roger and Curtice, John, with Taylor, Bridget (eds) (1994) *Labour's Last Chance? The 1992 Election and Beyond*. Aldershot: Dartmouth Publishing Company Limited
Wagg, Stephen (1989) Politics and the popular press, pp 17–22, *Social Studies Review*, Vol. 5, No. 1, September
Wagg, Stephen (1994) Politics and the media in postwar Britain, pp 29–33, *Sociology Review*, Vol. 4, No. 2, November
Weber, Max (1968) *Basic Concepts in Sociology*. London: Peter Owen
Williams, John (1995), Power and politics, back cover, *Sociology Review*, Vol. 5, No. 1, September

Exam practice: Power and politics

Essay questions

1 Critically evaluate the view that voting behaviour in the United Kingdom during the last 30 years has been increasingly influenced by factors other than social class. *(25 marks)*

2 Compare and contrast Marxist and New Right perspectives on the role of the state in society. *(25 marks)*

(From Summer 1996 AEB A-level Sociology, Paper 2, © 1997 AEB)

3 Compare and contrast Marxist and Weberian accounts of the ways in which power is exercised and legitimated. *(25 marks)*

4 'Post-war British politics have been dominated by two political parties whose ideologies and support are based on social class.'
Assess this statement with reference to sociological evidence. *(25 marks)*

(From Summer 1997 AEB A-level Sociology, Paper 2, © 1997 AEB)

14 Religion

Topics covered in this chapter

- *Defining religion*
- *Sociological theories of religion*
- *Religion: Conservative force and initiator of social change*
- *Churches, denominations, sects and cults*
- *The secularisation debate*
- *Religion in a changing society*
- *Religion and social position*

In statistical terms, the majority of Britons are Christians. I wonder if that's a nominal figure, or if most Britons would describe themselves as being religious? Writing on Boxing Day in 1993, Martin Wroe remarks:

'It was like an old-time revival but nobody noticed. Yesterday up to 15 million people – 35 per cent of the population – went to church in Britain. The trouble is, they were only there to pay their respects, to doff metaphorical caps at a Saviour in a crib they do not really believe in, a God incarnate they cannot really credit. It will be back to normal in many of Britain's churches today, rows of empty pews and empty prospects.'

(Wroe 1993: 19)

Are those 15 million people religious or just following a festive Christmas tradition? Do the empty pews on other days signify a decline in religion, or is religious experience a more private affair today? In our late-modernist or post-modernist age, do we adopt a 'pick and mix' approach to religion: a deity to fit a lifestyle, a bit of spiritualism, a touch of Buddhist meditation,

Mother Teresa's death in 1997 stirred religious sentiments worldwide. Her religious convictions were based on practical Christianity. Like the poor she cared for, Mother Teresa lived in poverty. Her sole possessions were the clothes on her back and a wash bowl.

a drop of faith healing, and attendance at an occasional evangelical concert? Are we moving from orthodox, institutionalised religion, to an age of religious pluralism?

This chapter explores the nature of religion, outlines important sociological theories of religion, considers the role religion plays in promoting both stability and change, investigates churches, denominations, sects and cults, addresses the changing nature of religious beliefs and institutions, and looks at religion in relation to age, class, ethnicity and gender.

Defining religion

Arriving at a universally accepted, 'all purpose' definition of religion is a fruitless quest. Max Weber highlights this dilemma by declaring his misgivings:

'To define "religion", to say what it is, is not possible at the start of a presentation such as this. Definition can be attempted, if at all, only at the conclusion of the study.'

(Weber 1971: 1, first published in 1925)

Weber's doubts about a packaged definition of religion should be taken seriously. But we have to start somewhere, if only to map the domain of sociological inquiry. We'll begin with the concise definition provided by the mid-nineteenth-century British anthropologist, Edward B. Tylor. Says Tylor: 'It seems best . . . simply to claim, as a minimum definition of Religion, the belief in Spiritual Beings' (1891, in Birnbaum and Lenzer 1969: 39). Using language and ideas to which serious exception would be taken by sociologists today, Tylor argues that religion begins among 'savages' in the form of animism (from the Latin word *anima*, meaning soul).

Animism refers to a belief in human souls and spirits. The most powerful spirits are worshipped as gods. Spirits are believed to affect people's lives on earth and in the hereafter. Human actions either please or displease the spirits. In some cultures, human sacrifices were made to keep the gods happy. The druids of Ancient Britain once sacrificed a man who had been raised for that specific purpose. Druid priests struck the unfortunate on the head with an axe, garrotted him, cut his throat and threw him into a pool. His dying in four different ways was intended to appease four Celtic gods who might then rally to help the druids overthrow the Roman invaders.

Tylor thinks that, in ancient times, people were fascinated by dreams, probably inferring that every human had 'two things belonging to him [*sic*], namely, a life and a phantom' (1891, in Birnbaum and Lenzer 1969: 42). The phantom gives rise to a belief in ghostly forms or personal souls. This seems plausible. People dream, and in their dreams they travel, as spirits, to different places. The spirit part is believed to live on when the body dies. Again, one can understand why this was believed. If, for example, a departed family member appeared in a dream, this was 'proof' that the soul lived on.

Adopting an evolutionary approach, Tylor charts the course of religious development from 'primitive fantasies' about the migration of the soul during dreams to more complex and sophisticated religious beliefs in modern times. He recognises that animism survives in modern religion. Again using polemical terms, he writes:

'The theory of the soul is one principal part of a system of religious philosophy, which unites, in an unbroken line of mental connexion, the savage fetish-worshipper and the civilized Christian.'

(Tylor 1891, in Birnbaum and Lenzer 1969: 49)

Tylor says that modern people are more rational and scientific than their forebears. They know from science, that their souls don't go 'a-walking' when they dream.

Another nineteenth-century British thinker – this time a sociologist – who, like Tylor, looked at religion in an evolutionary way, is Herbert Spencer. Spencer believes that ancestor worship is the root of all religion. He uses the term 'ancestor worship' quite widely, 'as comprehending all worship of the dead, be they of the same blood or not' (1877, in Birnbaum and Lenzer 1969: 51). According to Spencer, the inference that the soul survived death was sustained by the reappearance of the dead in the dreams of the living – a theme we've already discussed. Initially, says Spencer, superstitions are *ad hoc* and inconsistent. Over time, however, coherent beliefs develop, and concepts of the divine become clearer. These ghosts are the prototypes of the gods.

Ghosts are an important feature of traditional belief. Among the Native American Apaches, for example, the presence of an owl – whose hooting was believed to be the voice of a ghost issuing threats – was a serious matter. Says Donald E. Worcester (1992), there were no jokes or folk-tales about owls among the Apaches. It was even 'bad luck' to talk about them. People who heard and understood the 'words' of an owl were thereby exposed to 'owl', 'ghost' or 'darkness' sickness. This was likely to be fatal unless cured by a shaman ('medicine man') whose powers actually came from owls. By taking this power from the owl, it seems that the shaman could turn it to good rather than malevolent use.

The French sociologist, Emile Durkheim, whilst accepting that religion engages the sacred, rejects the notion that this has to entail a belief in the supernatural. Says Durkheim:

'A religion is a unified system of beliefs and practices relative to sacred things, that is to say, things set apart and forbidden, beliefs and practices which unite into one

single moral community called a church all those who adhere to them.'
(Durkheim 1912, in Pickering 1975: 123)

Durkheim takes issue with Tylor for failing to recognise that Buddhism (according to Durkheim) doesn't involve supernatural beliefs, but is still a religion. Not everybody would agree with Durkheim's interpretation of Buddhism as a non-spiritual faith. Moreover, some sociologists contend that a concept of religion which doesn't contain a belief in the supernatural is inadequate. Rodney Stark and William Sims Bainbridge, for example, think Durkheim has got it wrong. According to them:

'religions involve some conception of a supernatural being, world, or force, and the notion that the supernatural is active, that events and conditions here on earth are influenced by the supernatural.'
(Stark and Bainbridge 1985: 5)

In support of their contention that religion involves a belief in the supernatural, Stark and Bainbridge quote the anthropologist, Sir James G. Frazer, who wrote: 'religion consists of two elements . . . a belief in powers higher than man [*sic*] and an attempt to propitiate or please them' (1922, cited by Stark and Bainbridge 1985: 5).

Frazer believes that the age of religion was preceded by an age of magic. He doesn't know what led to the evolution from a magical to a religious phase. However, he hypothesises that when people found that magic couldn't deliver, they turned to higher powers. Thus:

'It was they (higher powers), as he (the human being) now believed, and not he [*sic*] himself, who made the stormy wind to blow, the lightning to flash, and the thunder to roll.'
(Frazer 1941, in Birnbaum and Lenzer 1969: 37)

The next stage – and here he sounds like August Comte (see below) – in Frazer's epic of human development is the scientific age. This occurs when people discover that nature is governed by scientific laws, not by gods. Interestingly, Frazer detects a similarity between the magical and the scientific stages. Both believe in cause and effect. The magician casts a spell to procure rain, and (sometimes!) the clouds pour forth. The scientist applies a force in one direction, and an equal force occurs in the other. The difference is that the magician's notion of cause and effect is based on false beliefs, and the scientist's is based on correct ones. In Frazer's three-stage evolutionary model, religion appears to come off as the least convincing, because it allegedly sidesteps cause and effect.

Having conducted a quick survey of some major thinkers, we're still left with the issue of saying what religion is: Weber warns us not to make prior assumptions; Tylor, Spencer, Frazer, and Stark and Bainbridge contend that religion involves a belief in the supernatural; and Durkheim settles for a belief in the sacred, whether or not this entails spiritual powers.

Recognising that defining religion isn't easy, we think the following definition captures the essential sociological character of the term:

Religion is a cultural belief system which provides a sense of reality grounded in the sacred, which in most but not all cases encompasses a belief in the supernatural.

Some sociologists are religious. Some aren't. But when they study religion, their job is to understand, not to judge whether people's beliefs are true or not.

Sociological theories of religion

'Religion', says Bryan Wilson, 'retains the imprints of long-persisting cultural imperatives and deeply felt commitments' (Wilson 1982: vi). This makes it a subject of abiding sociological interest. The classical sociologists recognised that religion played a powerful role in social development. Auguste Comte (1798–1857) believed that religion and science represented two different stages in social evolution. Emile Durkheim (1858–1917) showed how religion forged common values and a collective resolve in society.

Karl Marx (1818–83) claimed that religion was an otherworldly substitute for misery on earth, and a form of ideological control to keep the masses in their place. Max Weber (1864–1920) discovered a link between religious belief and capitalistic behaviour.

More recently, Talcott Parsons (although alive until 1979) continued in the classical tradition of Weber and Durkheim, and Rodney Stark and William Sims Bainbridge developed a new general theory of religion – based on the human need for supernatural compensation – in the 1980s. Approaching the study of religion in social constructionist terms, Peter Berger and Thomas Luckmann have also made a contribution to theory. However, theirs is less of a general theory than a theoretical insight.

In this section, we explore the works of important theorists of religion, beginning with the classical theorists, and then looking at the theories of Parsons and of Stark and Bainbridge. We'll also consider Berger and Luckmann's work.

Classical theorists were interested in the relationship between types of religious belief and types of society. Comte contends that animism characterises priest-led *theological society*. Durkheim says that animal and plant *totemism* (a belief that certain animals and plants have supernatural powers) is sacred in early aboriginal society. Marx claims that a belief in the hereafter compensates for exploitative relationships in capitalist society. Weber highlights an affinity between Protestantism and an economic outlook that embodies the 'spirit' of capitalism. These four thinkers are arguably among the greatest of the classical theorists of religion.

Auguste Comte

Comte believed that social facts could be studied objectively as things. He proposed that definite laws of society could be discerned. The human mind, said Comte, had evolved through three stages in its quest for knowledge. Each stage was a type of society, and each stage represented an evolutionary step towards 'Order and Progress':

1. *Primitive theological society* This stage is preoccupied with religious thought, especially animism. Theological society cherishes intuition and feeling, and places great emphasis on blood ties.
2. *Transient metaphysical society* This stage is characterised by a transition from believing in many gods to a belief in one God. Supernatural forces still feature in human thought, but in a more consistent, predictable way than in the previous stage.
3. *Final positive society* This stage is a secular scientific one, where a 'positive science of society' – sociology – addresses and answers the big questions in life instead of religion. In that sense, sociology becomes a 'secular religion' with its own 'priesthood' of sociologists.

Comte's third stage envisages the replacement of religious by sociological explanations. It removes God from the centre. Comte thus pits religion and sociology against each other as competing claims to truth. His posture is one of 'methodological atheism', to borrow a phrase from Peter Berger (cited by Wilson 1982: 4). By depicting the 'final positive stage' as the end of a long journey towards 'Order and Progress', he also implies that social science is superior to religion.

There's a resonance here with Karl Marx and Sigmund Freud, both of whom, as Wilson (1982) says, believed that religion wasn't just to be explained, but also 'explained away'. Comte regards religion as an inferior form of knowledge, Marx sees it as a form of false consciousness, and Freud considers it to be a mass neurosis.

Not all sociologists see an incompatibility between believing in God and in science. David Martin, for example, is a professor of sociology and an ordained Church of England clergyman. In his sociological role, he pursues dispassionate scholarship, honestly sifting the evidence, and guided always by the best empirical data. As a clergyman, he practises and preaches Christian beliefs. Peter Berger is a committed Lutheran, and also a famous sociologist of religion. His private religious beliefs and his sociological scholarship are separate

COMTE'S THEORY OF RELIGION

FOR

+ Comte's theory of the evolution of human thinking through three stages is an important forerunner of the secularisation thesis. His insights into the shift from theological to scientific thinking accord with historical evidence. The erosion of the supernatural as a central concern in life, or at least its separation from mundane, profane activities, has gathered pace. Today, we inhabit a world which is much less religious than societies of the past.
+ Related to the preceding point, modern people are generally less superstitious and more scientific in outlook than their forebears. Comte's argument that human society has moved on from magic and superstition to embrace the clarity and enlightenment of positivism rings true. These days, for example, physics is more relied upon than spirits to tell us what tomorrow's weather is likely to be.
+ Comte played a significant role, as a scientific modernist, in persuading people to accept that science offers the most reliable means of understanding society and nature. His commitment to the third stage – to the *final positive society* – is a powerful endorsement of the view that science goes beyond conjecture, hearsay, and half-truth to the weighing-up of evidence. Comte teaches us that science is the best we can know.

AGAINST

− Comte's supposition that science would relegate religion to the past represents a gigantic leap of the imagination rather than a fact. Religion flourishes in the world today, even though its forms do differ in many important respects from the past. There are also signs of religious revival (for example, Islam in Egypt and Turkey, and evangelical Christianity in the UK). Clearly, people haven't lost the capacity for belief in religion.

− Religion and science don't have to be pitted against each other, as Comte envisages. 'Science and technology have not made us atheists', says Steve Bruce (1996: 51). There are plenty of religious scientists around who don't see a contradiction between faith and empiricism. Some scientists believe that the laws of nature represent the divine will of God.

− Comte makes the value judgement that scientific knowledge is superior to theological knowledge. It's not the task of sociologists to do this. Their job is to study, understand, and explain belief systems. Comte's invention of a new 'religion' of humanity – scientific sociology – goes well beyond this remit. Instead of retaining a dispassionate, objective stance towards the processes of social change, one senses that Comte approves of what he says is happening.

domains. Bryan Wilson, on the other hand, is an atheist, but he thinks that religion is good for social cohesion, and mourns the decline of public worship.

Comte's suggestion that religious belief is untenable takes him beyond the remit of the sociologist. That said, Comte did contribute to the debate on the development of religion. It's therefore appropriate that we critique his work (see opposite) by first looking at its strengths.

QUESTIONS

1 What are the three Comtean stages?
2 How does Comte view religion and sociology?

Emile Durkheim

In *The Elementary Forms of Religious Life* (1912), Durkheim writes:

'Religious beliefs are *representations* which express the nature of sacred things and the relations they maintain with each other, or with profane things.'
(Durheim 1912, in Pickering 1975: 117)

The *sacred* refers to that which is consecrated or holy and which society holds in the highest esteem. Durkheim defines the profane in relation to its negative oppositeness to the sacred. Thus the *profane* is that which undermines the sacred.

Durkheim says that society elevates sacred things above what humans know through their senses. Conversely, the profane is the empirical world, the one that's conveyed through the senses. The sacred is extraordinary and mysterious, and engages awe and reverence. It stands out from the profane, which is commonplace and routine. The same object might, however, be regarded as sacred or profane, depending on how people define these things. Bread is profane in sandwiches, and sacred to Christians as a communion wafer.

Durkheim maintains that the most elementary form of religion is *totemism*. Totemism refers to animals and plants that are believed to have supernatural powers. Durkheim studied totemic tribes, focusing on an aboriginal people: the Arunta of central Australia. Among their totems were the lizard, caterpillar, rat, cockatoo and plum tree. For the aborigine, the totem symbolised two different kinds of thing: God and the clan. 'If, then, it is at once the symbol of god and of society, is this not because god and society are one and the same thing?' (Durkheim 1912, in Pickering 1975: 125).

Durkheim's question is rhetorical. He contends that a god is a being whom people imagine to be superior to themselves, and on whom they're dependent. Moreover, 'society is to its members what a god is to the faithful' (Durkheim 1912, in Pickering 1975: 125). Like a god, society 'imperiously demands our co-operation' (1912, in Pickering 1975: 125), requiring that we should become its servants. We're therefore obliged to follow social rules which are sometimes different to our most basic instincts. Society thereby gains the respect and the consent of the group.

In 'primitive' society, says Durkheim, people visualise the force of society in religious symbols, notably, the totem. The totem is society writ large. Believers, whether aborigines, crusaders or revolutionaries, all have their totems. The totem is revered during religious ceremonies. At these assemblies, the faithful express beliefs, which, if left to individuals, would otherwise atrophy. Religion therefore has a social function. It engenders an *esprit de corps*. The coming together in religious ceremony forges this sense of common purpose. Here we see a clear functionalist orientation in Durkheim's theory.

Religion involves ritual – rules of conduct that prescribe how people must behave in relation to the sacred. Some rituals involve pain. In the Arunta initiation rite, the initiate lies on a bed of leaves under which are live coals. The suffering that these and other rituals produce, says Durkheim, isn't arbitrary cruelty. Rather:

'it is a necessary school, where men [*sic*] form and temper themselves, and acquire the qualities of disinterestedness and endurance without which there would be no religion.'
(Durkheim 1912, cited by Pickering 1984: 331–2)

He adds that society is only possible at this price.

Ritual banishes the egoistic to the realm of the profane. Through ritual – the active component of religion – people rise above their own selfish interests, and embrace collective sentiments. The live coals rite is an example of what Durkheim calls a *negative ritual*. The function of rituals is to separate the spheres of the sacred and the profane, bringing home to the worshipper the undesirability of the profane. Thus a negative ritual purges anything that profanes the sacred.

Durkheim also identifies *positive rituals*. These, the more numerous, directly introduce the worshipper to the sacred. They're celebratory and are conducted in a state of enthusiasm and joy. Blood sacrifices are an example of positive rituals. There's no implied moral judgement here, by Durkheim or us, that the blood-letting of an animal or a person is good. But a sacrifice wasn't thought to be a sad affair. Typically, one animal or person suffered for the perceived sake of others.

Blood-letting, whether real or acted out, is conducted for different reasons. For example, the Native American Commanches would whip a slave who was supposed to represent a god, if it were thought that the god refused to respond to prayers and offerings. The hope here is that a timely chastisement of the god will restore the deity to a more sympathetic frame of mind. Similarly, in China, during periods of severe drought, people constructed a paper dragon representing the rain god, which they carried in solemn procession. If no rain came, they hurled abuse at the effigy, tearing it to pieces.

These examples suggest that humans don't always have a high opinion of gods. There are other rites of sacrifice, however, where the intention is to please the gods. The human sacrifice to the four Celtic gods fits this category. Another form is where the god is 'eaten' as a sacramental meal (for example, taking bread and wine in a Christian Church). By consuming Jesus, worshippers enter communion with God and obtain grace and strength from Him.

A key function of ritual, says Durkheim is participation in common activities:

'The only way of renewing the collective *representations* which relate to sacred things is to retemper them in the very source of the religious life, that is to say, in assembled groups . . . by the very fact of uniting, they (the assembled) are mutually comforted; they find a remedy because they seek it together. The common faith becomes reanimated quite naturally in the heart of this reconstituted group . . . After it has been restored, it easily triumphs over all the private doubts which may have arisen in individual minds.'
(Durkheim 1912, cited by Pickering 1984: 345)

Ritual celebrates and maintains social unity. The 'sacred' embodies moral feelings that become part of the collective conscience: the common value system. Just as gods and other totems serve as 'flags' around which collective sentiments rally, so do leaders become 'sacred'. Their virtual 'deification' expresses itself in similar actions towards a totem. Ordinary mortals keep their distance, and approach the leader with caution. The importance attributed by general opinion to the god, the lizard, the plum tree and the leader is a form of sanctification. The leader and the totem are 'god-like'.

The totem makes honour a social obligation. A regimental flag, for example, embodies the glory of the regiment, and will be defended to the death. Here we see a powerful social function at work. In material terms, the flag is just of piece of cloth. But in a 'religious' sense, it's sacred. Moreover, the 'powers' bestowed upon the flag act as if they were real, and affect human behaviour. Soldiers rally to a flag, they fight by it, and even die for it. Next to it, they become brothers in arms. In the sacred emblem of the flag, soldiers engage the social function it bestows: loyalty to the group. By venerating the totem, the soldier pays homage to the regiment. On a wider scale, religion is therefore the worship of an object that represents society.

OVER TO YOU

How might an Elvis Presley memento from Graceland embody an aura of the 'sacred', in the way that Durkheim defines this term?

The social function of collective ritual was touchingly displayed after the death of Diana, Princess of Wales in 1997. The number of floral tributes to the Princess, never mind the other makeshift shrines round London, is said to have passed a million. 'This week', reported the *Guardian* (6 September 1997), 'has provided the final proof that Margaret Thatcher was wrong: there is such a thing as society.' On the eve of her funeral, Kensington Gardens had become an open air 'temple' for people of all religions and for people with none. At four in the morning, people walked arm in arm between the thousands of impromptu candlelit shrines that were erected in every bowl of tree and on every crowd barrier. Atheists, agnostics, Buddhists, Christians, Hindus and Muslims placed offerings and lit candles. This was a celebration of the sacred such has rarely been seen in the UK for a long time.

The death of Diana, Princess of Wales, on 31 August 1997 led to mass mourning on a global scale. Unlike conventional aristocrats, she valued dash above protocol. Her death has engendered in the British 'collective conscience' a yearning for what she represented, a new, less stuffy Britain.

In this picture, the Princess' hearse nears its journey's end as it enters the gates of her ancestral home in Althorp, Northamptonshire. Her grave, reports the Observer (7 September 1997), will be a site of pilgrimage for people generally thought to have given up that kind of thing long ago.

As well as sanctifying supernatural and human life, society also sanctifies beliefs. The moment a belief is accepted by a social group, it becomes forbidden to challenge it. Even in modern times, says Durkheim:

'when we allow each other a great measure of freedom, a man [*sic*] who totally denies progress, who scoffs at the human ideal to which modern societies attach so much importance, would in effect be committing an act of sacrilege.'

(Durkheim 1912, in Pickering 1975: 132)

A belief in the sacred performs an integrative function. The believer is locked into a 'collective conscience', going with the social grain rather than against it.

Each society has its own notion of the sacred. This means, as W. S. F. Pickering notes, that 'anything can stand for the sacred and therefore anything can be "religion" or "religious"' (1984: 131). Durkheim accepted that religious institutions were losing their sway over people's beliefs. But he insisted that there was still a functional need for group values to be symbolised and celebrated. Whilst in the past, religious symbolism was largely rooted in collectivities, Durkheim anticipated that the sacred would become more individualised. There's some empirical evidence that this is happening today.

Individuality, provided it respects the rights and needs of others, needn't be anti-social. The kind of individualism that Durkheim has in mind imposes reciprocal obligations. Different people, working co-operatively, make for social stability. There's an organic analogy here with the biological functions of different organs working together for the good of the whole. Durkheim develops this theme in *The Division of Labour* (1893), where he argues that societies evolve from *mechanical solidarity* to *organic solidarity* (see page 51). Under conditions of mechanical solidarity, individual behaviour is strongly influenced by religious beliefs and practices. Religion stirs striking emotional excitement, engendering what Durkheim calls 'collective effervescence'.

When organic solidarity takes over, however, institutional religion has less sway over people's lives. The individual has more personal autonomy. More emphasis is placed on individual conscience, and powerful religious sentiments become less intense. Durkheim had no wish to re-establish strong religious beliefs. Indeed, he believed that the development of organic solidarity heralded the appearance of progressive collective sentiments which were more appropriate to the modern age. Organic solidarity shifts things around. Instead of focusing on the individual's duty to society, it centres on the rights that individual citizens have in society.

Although brought up in a Jewish rabbinical family, Durkheim described himself as an agnostic. He accepted, however, that religion played a crucial role in society. Religion brings out the social in people. It produces social cohesion because the power of beliefs held in common binds individuals. Durkheim also recognised that religion sometimes has a destabilising function. For example, during the early days of new religions, old habits and customs are confronted and contested. In that sense, the social cohesion of the *status quo* is disrupted by religion. Over time, though, new religions become settled religions and create alternative forms of social cohesion. Moreover, settled religions usually remain long enough to exercise a powerful socialising influence on people's lives, integrating them into common values.

Durkheim called the moral community which brings people together in shared beliefs and common practices a *church*. A religion without a church, he says, is never encountered in history. That said, churches do differ. Some are very nationalistic, others international, some embrace a whole people (for example, Ancient Romans, Ancient Greeks, Hebrews), whilst others include only a fraction of a people (for example, post-Reformation Christian groups). Durkheim notes that some churches are led by priests, and some are almost completely free from properly appointed leaders. He also identifies subgroups which he calls *cults*, but pointedly adds that 'such limited churches are in reality merely chapels in a far vaster church' (1912, in Pickering 1975: 120).

Interestingly, Durkheim notes that the church distinguishes religion from magic. In magic, there's no church. The magician has a clientele rather than a church. The individuals who consult a magician don't belong to a social group comparable to that of worshippers of the same god. They visit the magician as individual patients go to a doctor's surgery. A priest, by contrast, orchestrates social rituals in front of a congregation of believers. The idea that religion is inseparable from the institution of the church demonstrates, says Durkheim, 'the fact that religion must be a pre-eminently collective thing' (1912, in Pickering 1975: 123).

In the functionalist thinking that underpins Durkheim's approach, religion is a force which binds the individual to society. The mapping of this relationship is illustrated by Henry L. Tischler in the diagram on page 410.

Durkheim claims that the social functions of the sacred are essential to the maintenance of society. Even a secular society would need to substitute some system of shared values and beliefs in the form of ritual. The acceptance of a moral value system underpins cohesion and stability in religious and secular life. Durkheim and other functionalists note that religious institutions work alongside other social institutions to support behaviours which engage prescribed values. Religion, if it's accepted, is a particularly powerful guarantor of group norms because it appeals to a higher order: God. It also reminds believers that their actions have consequences. For example, in

Society, religion and the individual: A functionalist view

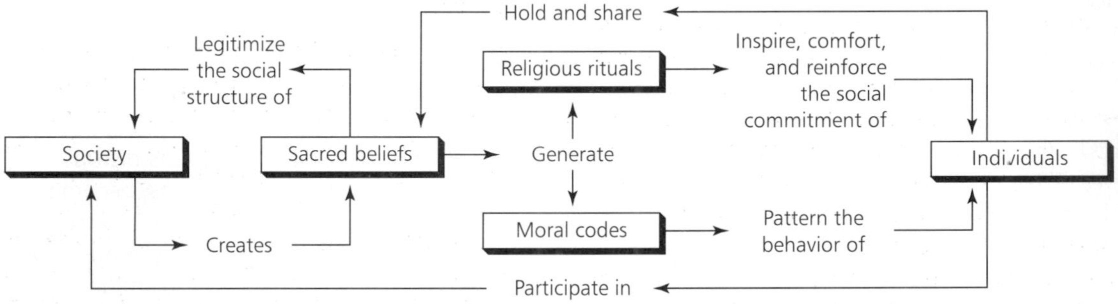

(Tischler 1996: 404)

the Hindu and Christian religions, adherence or non-adherence to holy teachings have outcomes in future reincarnations or life in the hereafter.

According to Pickering (1984), Durkheim regarded religion as the key to the understanding of society. Its eminently social quality helped him to understand the nature of the social bonds that make society itself. In religion, Durkheim saw society writ large. Religion is part of the social cement that holds the social structure of society together. It helps to create a strong sense of social obligation, even when the social becomes 'privatised' by more individualised forms of religious practice. People might practise religion without going to church, but their religiosity binds them to social obligations.

QUESTIONS

1. How does Durkheim define the sacred and the profane?
2. What is the social function of a totem? What social totems exist in society today, and how do they affect the way people think and behave?

DURKHEIM'S THEORY OF RELIGION

FOR

+ The sociology of religion owes much to the monumental and pioneering work of Durkheim. In this field of sociological inquiry, says Pickering, 'the advances that have been made have frequently been an extension of his theoretical ideas' (1984: 523). That's how it is with a big theory thinker like Durkheim. Even if parts of the total are flawed, there are enough flashes of profound insight (for example, the integrative functions of the sacred) to inspire further research.
+ Durkheim's argument that the 'sacred' in society is the emblematic carrier of group values rings true. Consider, for example, how, throughout history, people have rallied to flags, crosses and holy scripture in their affirmation of common goals. On a secular level too, the power of the 'sacred' to arouse strong group sentiments is apparent. Donning the red of Manchester United or the blue of Chelsea, for example, turns a *crowd* into *supporters*.
+ Although his background was Jewish, Durkheim wasn't a religious person. But he didn't let this get in the way of his study of other people's religious beliefs and practices. In that respect, he retained the objective distance of a sociologist. He made it his task to understand the origins and functions of religion, not to pass judgements on whether religious beliefs were inherently true or false.

AGAINST

− Durkheim's definition of religion is too broad. By including non-supernatural as well as supernatural beliefs, he makes it well nigh impossible to differentiate religious from moral, political and other convictions. This leads to interminable debates about where the demarcation of religious beliefs begins and ends. Restricting religion to beliefs in the supernatural creates clear, well-defined boundaries.

− In using religion as the starting point for the explanation of social life, Durkheim goes too far. The centrality of religion in society varies across cultures and over time. In British society, today, for example, pluralism has arguably replaced the universal standards of the Church. Secular values, as well as religious ones, impact upon the social, and which of the two have the bigger effect is a matter for empirical investigation, not general theory.

− Durkheim tends to focus on the positive functions of religion in society rather than looking at the negative consequences of religious beliefs and practices. Religion has been by used by Christian crusader knights to justify the extermination of Muslims, by the ruling class to keep the poor in their place, and by certain cults to encourage members to commit mass suicide. No doubt, one can add to this list of 'dysfunctions'.

Karl Marx

Marx's father was a reluctant convert from Judaism to Protestantism. He converted for reasons of job security. He told his son, Karl, that a simple faith in God provided a good basis for morality. These sentiments were repeated, discloses David McLellan (1987), in a set essay on religion which Marx wrote for his school-leaving exam. In the essay, Marx explained how the advent of Christianity was needed for full moral development. This early religiosity didn't survive long. In his doctoral thesis on ancient Greek atomic theory, Marx invoked the god Prometheus who, against the orders of a higher god, gave humanity the power of fire. The preface to the thesis contains these words:

'Philosophy makes no secret of it. The proclamation of Prometheus – "in a word, I detest all the gods" – is her own profession, her own slogan against all the gods of heaven and earth who do not recognize man's [*sic*] self-consciousness as the highest divinity. There shall be none other beside it.'

(cited by McLellan 1987: 9)

Marx was a materialist. He didn't believe in a supernatural realm. He asserted that 'man [*sic*] makes religion, religion does not make man' (1844, cited by McLellan 1987: 13). Marx argues that religion produces an ideological mystification of reality. In this way, religion sanctifies the established order. It proclaims that the political authority of the ruling class is ordained by supernatural authority. Marx's contention that religion serves the *status quo* is echoed in Bryan Wilson's argument that the role of the Church is to socialise each new generation in a repertoire of socially entrenched values which support social order. In that context, says Wilson:

'the Church counsels the rich and powerful to exercise mercy, and urges the poor and suffering to adopt attitudes of subservience and contentment with their lot. In all of this, the significance of the Church as an agency for social order and control is clear, supporting established authority (providing always that those authorities do not depart too radically or too abruptly from the canons of religious truth).'

(Wilson 1981: 224)

A belief in a better hereafter also serves as comfort and solace to the poor and oppressed. Says Marx of religion, 'It is the *opium* of the people' (1884, in Birnbaum and Lenzer 1969: 94). Through religion, argues Marx, the people are 'drugged' into accepting their lowly position in return for a superior afterlife. Religion thereby functions as a potent form of social control by keeping the poor in their place. Marx set out to strip away what he regarded as the illusory nature of religion, and to expose it for what he claimed it was: an ideological tool of the ruling class. The demolition of religious credibility was seen as an important precursor of 'scientific socialism'. People need to lay fantasy bare before they can think critically.

There's a parallel here with Comte's notion that science represents an evolutionary step beyond theology. Marx's main objective was to liberate the working class from the oppression of capitalism. Anything that served capitalist interests – including the social control function of religion – had to be critiqued, de-mystified, contested and, ultimately, got rid of. Religion in the hands of the ruling class celebrates the *status quo*. It legitimates a social order based on inequality, implying that this is ordained by divine will. Marx offered an alternative prospect: a humanist society based on socialism and, ultimately, communism.

Although an atheist, Marx was more against institutional religion than religion in its pure, unadulterated form. Indeed, his own socialistic leanings have much in common with authentic Gospel Christianity. Jesus said that when people fed and clothed the poor, they were behaving as true Christians. He also said it's harder for a rich person to enter the Kingdom of Heaven than for a camel to walk through the eye of a needle. This isn't the talk of a champion of the rich and powerful, but of a brother of the poor and oppressed. The nineteenth-century version of 'Christianity' that Marx wrote about and criticised was altogether different. The then Church of England has been described as the Tory Party at prayer. The clergy were usually members of the ruling class with vested interests in keeping the poor in their place.

Marx longed for the erosion of supernatural beliefs, and was convinced that secularisation would liberate people from mystified forms of social oppression. He and his co-writer and friend, Friedrich Engels, claimed that the poor were uninterested in any form of institutional religion. That said, Engels picks up on the sensitivity of religious belief when he writes:

'Although English workers reject religion in practice without much conscious thought, they nevertheless recoil from an open admission of their lack of faith. Hard necessity will force the workers to give up their religious beliefs. They will come more and more to realise that these beliefs serve only to weaken the proletariat and to keep them obedient and faithful to the Capitalist vampires.'

(cited in Scharf 1970: 85)

Engels' prediction that the English working class would become increasingly disillusioned was inaccurate. As David McLellan (1983) points out, religion and socialism weren't seen as incompatible. Christian socialism represented a powerful fusion of religious and political beliefs about social justice, and profoundly influenced the early Labour Party. On the other side of the Atlantic, Dr Martin Luther King rallied poor black Americans behind a Christian non-violent protest movement against white racism and capitalist greed.

There are instances of the use of religion by dominant elites to keep the poor in their place. But there's no sociological law that says this has to be so. Each situation must be judged dispassionately on the basis of the available evidence. Scharf's very plausible 'view that religions, except in isolated preliterate societies, do not stand in a close and regular relationship with social structure, in either their economic or political aspects' (1970: 86), challenges simplistic notions that the powerful have religion in their pockets.

To be fair to marxism on this point, Antonio Gramsci, a famous Italian marxist, recognises that religion has complex and multi-dimensional aspects to its relationship with society. As Gramsci puts it:

'Every religion, even Catholicism (in fact especially Catholicism, precisely because of its efforts to maintain a superficial unity and not allow itself to be fragmented into national churches or along class lines) is really a multiplicity of religions that are distinct and often contradictory: there is a Catholicism of the peasant, a Catholicism of the petty bourgeoisie and urban workers, a Catholicism of women, and a Catholicism of the intellectuals.'

(Gramsci 1966, cited by Carroll 1996: 232–3)

In this view, the religion of the ruling class is just one variant among many, and like other interpretations, it doesn't have an overriding influence on all social groups in society. In a recent context, for example, one can see that the liberation theology of Catholic priests who take an option for the poor and put themselves, sometimes quite literally, in the line of fire contests rather than supports a ruling-class ideology.

QUESTIONS

1 What is the social function of religion according to Marx?
2 Is Christianity a tool of ruling-class ideology?

MARX'S THEORY OF RELIGION

FOR

+ Marx's view that religion mirrors economic circumstances provides a helpful starting point for social scientific analysis. People need food in their bellies, clothes on their backs, and roofs over their heads before they can develop institutional religion. And the religion they adopt tends to reflect their economic position. For example, ruling-class people are more likely to favour hierarchical church religion (for example, nineteenth-century Anglicanism), whereas working-class people are sometimes more inclined to support egalitarian sect religion (for example, nineteenth-century Methodism).
+ Linked to the preceding point, in the context of nineteenth-century English society, Marx's argument that religion was a vehicle of ruling-class ideology has considerable resonance. Called by some commentators, the 'Tory Party at prayer', the Church of England supported a hierarchical notion of society.
+ Marx shows how institutional religion, in the service of powerful economic and political elites, can dampen the political consciousness of the oppressed. If the poor accept their lot in return for a better hereafter, they'll stop seeking social justice here on earth. They will, from a marxist perspective, imbibe 'spiritual gin' instead of putting food on the table. Marxism thereby offers an applied version of social science – the kind that helps the oppressed to understand the reality of their oppression and to fight for something better.

AGAINST

– Marx's hostility towards belief systems, including religion, which he didn't personally subscribe to, gets in the way of objectivity. Being dispassionate – the hallmark of good social science – didn't come easy to Marx. Instead of stepping back and scientifically studying religious beliefs, he turns religion into a conspiracy of the ruling class to keep the poor in their place. Marx represents religion as a form of 'spiritual gin' rather than finding out what a belief in God means to those who hold it.

– Marx's view that religion shifts earthly problems to a heavenly plane underestimates the extent to which religion is and has been used to promote social justice in the here and now. Christian theology is premised on the assumption that when people feed and clothe the least privileged of their sisters and brothers here on earth, they are doing the same for Jesus Christ. Embracing that belief and acting upon it is more like secular socialism than ruling-class ideology. When Christian religion becomes the bearer of the views of the rich and powerful, it becomes less Christian.

– Marx underestimates the extent to which religion exercises an autonomous influence on society. He tends to see it as a servant and reflector of a particular kind of society. Religion is a powerful mover of social change, as well as an institution that responds to transformations in society. As Weber has shown, nascent capitalism became vitalised because its economic habits bore the stamp of religious conviction.

Max Weber

In his personal life, Max Weber was a non-believer. However, his discussion of the sociology of religion proceeds from the assumption that a belief in the supernatural is universal. His analysis of world religions led him to conclude that 'breakthroughs' occur in an evolutionary process from 'primitive' to modern religious beliefs. The concept of breakthrough is crucial. Weber sees religion as an essentially dynamic force. To quote Talcott Parsons on this point:

'Weber's *primary* interest is in religion as a source of the dynamics of social change, not religion as a reinforcement of the stability of societies.'

(Parsons 1925, in Weber 1971: xxx)

> **OVER TO YOU**
>
> ***Why have we placed inverted commas around the term 'primitive'?***

Weber (1925, in Weber 1971) distinguishes between the social functions of magicians and priests as mediators between people and the supernatural. The magician's role is to cope with relatively *ad hoc* affairs and tensions. For, example, a bad harvest might be made not to repeat itself if the magician recites a magic formula. In this way, the magician makes magical forces serve human needs. The priest's role is largely independent of one-off catastrophes. It's more systematic, being organised into an institutional cult. The priest prays to God for divine intervention, for example, to request that the next harvest will be a good one. Magic cajoles and recites formulae; religion solicits and worships.

That said, all supernatural beliefs have both magical and religious aspects, though in widely varying proportions. But it's the religious prophet rather than the magician who is the primary agent of breakthroughs. 'Unlike the magician', says Weber, 'the prophet claims definite revelations, and the core of his [*sic*] mission is doctrine or commandment, not magic' (1925, in Weber 1971: 47). Prophets urge people to break with convention.

Weber identifies two kinds of prophet:

- *the exemplary prophet*, who embodies a high level of personal virtue and whom others can *choose* to follow. There's no implication that the prophet's ways are binding on others. The prophet is a vessel of the supernatural power, standing in some personal relation of identification with the divine. This kind of prophet is associated with pantheistic principles (God is everywhere and in all things) of divinity, as represented, for example in, the religious beliefs of India
- *the ethical prophet*, who imposes moral demands on other people such that it becomes their duty to follow the prophet's precepts. These precepts are less an emulation of the prophet's own lifestyle, and more a case of conforming with an impersonally defined moral code. The prophet is an instrument of a divine will, and has a mission to make others obey this will. This kind of prophet is associated with a transcendental God or gods (who stand outside and above the mortal world). Christianity, Islam and Judaism are examples of transcendental religions.

Christianity is the religion to which Weber devotes most attention. He was especially interested in an unadorned, severe form of muscular Christianity which found its fullest expression in Calvinism. As ascetic (puritan-minded) Protestants, Calvinists sought 'religious enfranchisement' for the individual believer from the 'corporate' structure of the Catholic Church. Theirs was a religion that strove for a bracing personal relationship with God. Naked before the divine, without the intermediaries of priests and bishops, Calvinists cherished self-help and hard work.

In that context, Calvinists believed that success in business demonstrated righteous living and therefore divine approval. There are biblical injunctions here, like, for example, the parable of the man who prudently invested his inheritance and reaped a generous return later in life. The notion that one should methodically demonstrate habits of self-reliance, thrift and hard work is, of course, perfectly suited to an entrepreneurial temperament.

Weber asserts that:

'Only ascetic Protestantism completely eliminated magic and the supernatural quest for salvation, of which the highest form was intellectualist, contemplative illumination. It alone created the religious motivations for seeking salvation primarily through immersion in one's worldly vocation.'

(Weber 1971: 269–70)

The idea of a task set by God – a *calling* – is central to the notion of a divinely ordained vocation. In its mandate to the believer that she or he should work in a definite field, Weber (1904–1905, in Weber 1974) regards the calling as a distinctly Protestant duty. It made the fulfilment of duty in worldly affairs, especially in business, the highest moral achievement. Protestantism scorned the monastic tradition of certain Catholic orders, seeing them as renouncing the duties of the earthly world. 'In contrast, labour in a calling appears to him [the protestant leader, Luther] as the outward expression of brotherly love' (Weber 1974: 81). For the Calvinist Protestant (whose Protestantism was more extreme than even the Lutheran version), 'brotherly' love is expressed in the obligation to perform daily tasks in an earthly world designed by God to be utilised by humans. This makes work in the service of utility an act that promotes the glory of God.

In the book in which Weber outlined and developed the above thesis – *The Protestant Ethic and the Spirit of Capitalism* (first published in 1904–1905) – he judged the likelihood of capitalism being caused by economic climates to be about the same in the European, the Chinese, and the Indian contexts. Given the profound differences in economic outcomes between these three civilisations, he had a strong case for arguing the importance of religious movements as differentiating influences – not total explanations – of economic change. In traditional China and India, industrial capitalism didn't take off like it did in Europe. Eastern religions, with their rejection of material values, put a break on capitalistic impulses.

European Protestantism – especially, Calvinism – had the opposite effect. It regarded material success as a sign of divine favour. Like believers of other salvation religions, the Calvinists longed for a better hereafter. They also believed in predestination: the notion that their fate on this earth and the hereafter was already known by God. This meant that whatever one does or doesn't do will make no difference. God predetermines everything, including whether one goes to heaven or hell. Understandably, not knowing one's destiny caused anxiety and apprehension. Calvinists figured that the best way to discover if they were among the elect was to obtain the assurance that comes from righteous living.

Among other things, this meant:

- carrying out religious duties (for example, worshipping and praying)
- being morally pure (for example, avoiding self-indulgence)
- working one's hardest (for example, keeping idleness at bay)
- striving to make money (for example, re-investing earnings).

The surest sign that one was leading a righteous life was to be successful in business. Idleness was considered a sin, and industriousness – its counterpart – a virtue. Thus, the pursuit of material success, considered wrongful in Catholic teaching, became charged with a sense of religious responsibility. As R. H. Tawney puts it:

'Baptized in the bracing, if icy, waters of Calvinist theology, the life of business, once regarded as perilous to the soul . . . acquires a new sanctity. Labour is not merely an economic means: it is a spiritual end. Covetousness, if a danger to the soul, is a less formidable menace than sloth. So far from poverty being meritorious, it is a duty to choose the more profitable occupation. So far from there being an inevitable conflict between money-making and piety, they are natural allies, for the virtues incumbent on the elect – diligence, thrift, sobriety, prudence – are the most reliable passport to commercial prosperity.'

(in Weber 1974: 2–3, Foreword)

> ***OVER TO YOU***
>
> ***To what extent does the Calvinist outlook, as outlined by Tawney in the preceding quote, connect with the economic and social policies of New Right – and, arguably – New Left governments?***

Protestantism, with its emphasis on individual struggle, was conducive to the rational self-help ethos of the business world. There was an elective affinity between a Protestant outlook and capitalist behaviour, such that the first gave rise to the other. This wasn't about greed. Even though they invariably prospered in material terms, Calvinists adopted a very negative attitude towards worldly pleasures. Says Weber of the Calvinist outlook, 'The world exists to serve the glorification of God and for that purpose alone' (1974: 108). He adds that:

'God requires social achievement of the Christian because He wills that social life shall be organized according to His commandments, in accordance with that purpose . . . [The duty of the individual in that context is to engage] labour in a calling which serves the mundane life of the community.'

(Weber 1974: 108)

You might think that Calvinists would harbour nagging doubts about whether predestination favoured their own individual fates. However, they were exhorted to have no such doubts. On the contrary, for the Calvinist it was an absolute duty to consider oneself among the chosen. Doubts were to be combated as temptations of the devil, lack of self-confidence being the consequence of insufficient faith and imperfect grace. Certainty of one's own election was to be found in the daily struggle of life. Thus, says Weber:

'are bred those self-confident saints whom we can rediscover in the hard Puritan merchants of the heroic age of capitalism and in isolated instances down to the present . . . in order to attain that self-confidence intense worldly activity is recommended as the most suitable means. It and it alone disperses religious doubts and gives the certainty of grace.'

(Weber 1974: 112)

It also creates the energy that lies behind pivotal social change. Unlike Marx, who regards religion as a conservative force, Weber regards it as a potential catalyst. Calvinism looked beyond the protection of Mother Church to an altogether hardier environment. It beckoned a new way of thinking and of behaving. Says Weber:

'[It] strode into the market-place of life, slammed the door of the monastery behind it . . . [and] did its part in building the tremendous cosmos of the modern economic order.'

(Weber 1974: 154, 181)

With its rejection of magic and superstition, Calvinism treated the natural world as a relatively 'neutral' place. The unintended consequence (or *latent function*, to coin a functionalist term) of this was to spark a process of rational disenchantment of the 'sacred', and a trend towards secular capitalism.

Weber's thesis suggests that religious beliefs have an impact on economic phenomena. You'll remember that Marx sees things the other way round – the direction of influence proceeds, by and large, from the economy to religion. Weber does concede, however, that events can be as Marx says. The ultimate test of this isn't theory. Only empirical evidence will tell. Weber's insistence that subjective points of view (for example, a religious conviction) must be taken account of doesn't mean that sociological interpretation becomes subjective. There are typical patterns of meaning which people in given social contexts attribute to their actions. For example, many Protestants interpreted success in business as a sign of divine favour. In that sense, subjective meanings are inter-subjectively shared.

In his critique of Weber's book, *The Sociology of Religion*, Parsons concludes that:

'this book is *the* most crucial contribution of our century to the comparative and evolutionary understanding of the relations between religion and society, and even of society and culture generally.'

(Parsons 1971, in Weber 1971: lxvii)

High praise, indeed!

WEBER'S THEORY OF RELIGION

FOR

+ Weber's thesis on the elective affinity between the Protestant ethic and the development of modern capitalism remains one of the greatest sociological works ever written. Ever-cautious not to overstate his case, Weber provides compelling evidence to show that instead of capitalism 'causing' religion, things tended to go in the other direction. Protestantism, particularly its Calvinistic version, produced exactly the kind of mind frame which encouraged capitalistic habits. Hard work, a sign of divine grace, had the unintended consequence of turning puritans into 'businessmen'.

+ Weber's theory is based on a vast amount of factual data and very extensive scholarship. His rich empirical data spans the world's great religions, providing a much wider canvas than the more limited research of scholars like Comte and Marx on religion. The breadth of his research makes Weber's claim that believing in the supernatural is a worldwide feature of human society all the more plausible. Moreover, as Parsons acknowledges, 'This view that belief in the supernatural is universal has been completely confirmed by modern anthropology' (1971, in Weber 1971: xxviii).

+ To quote Ephraim Fischoff, Weber's *The Sociology of Religion* displays an 'extraordinary combination of erudition in the social sciences, disinterested and impartial observation, and poignant yet scientifically cautious nostalgia toward religious phenomena of the past' (1971, in Weber 1971: xiii). Weber kept his own personal values on the back-burner when he conducted research into religious beliefs; not for him, the marxist habit of 'knocking' beliefs that didn't square with scientific socialism. Weber looks to the evidence, and evaluates it dispassionately.

AGAINST

– The English historian, R. H .Tawney (1938, cited by Collins 1990), argues that Weber has got the relationship between Protestantism and capitalism the wrong way round. According to Tawney, Protestant sects appeared in England in the 1500s and 1600s because the country was starting to become capitalistic. Protestantism, as Weber rightly suggests, fits psychologically with capitalism. However, economic factors create the mind set, not the reverse.

– Capitalism isn't just associated with Protestantism. It flourished in Buddhist/Shinto countries like Japan, and Catholic ones like Belgium. More recently, it is flourishing in countries with an atheistic legacy, like Russia. Whilst particular religious beliefs might act as catalysts to capitalistic growth, the real driving force behind capitalism isn't religion, but the concentration of productive technology in the hands of powerful economic classes. Weber, were he alive today, would probably say he didn't argue that capitalism in general was 'caused' by Protestantism. Rather, there was a relationship between Calvinistic Protestantism and the typical modern European version of capitalism.

– Weber arguably exaggerates the extent to which prophets are agents of social change. Divine qualities aside, prophets are shaped by social forces. Even their rebelliousness is linked to the 'deviant' subcultures they tend to move in. Taking on social structures and initiating a breakthrough is seldom a lonesome venture. Prophets work in concert, and are influenced by confederates. They might be the feather that breaks the camel's back, but the pre-topple weight on the camel has social origins.

QUESTIONS

1 How do prophets make religion a dynamic rather than a static force?
2 What are the elective affinities between Calvinism and capitalism?

Evaluation of classical theorists

A fairly consistent theme among the classical sociologists of religion is of increasing secularisation – of the continued erosion of beliefs in the supernatural. Comte thought that sociology would divest theology as the pre-eminent outlook; Durkheim anticipated that rationalisation would lead to the diminution of religious influence; Marx claimed that the march of scientific socialism would dispel pie-in-the-sky beliefs; and Weber intimated that religion strained intellectual credulity in modern society. The approach of these great thinkers, although differing in certain important respects, is essentially modernist. It envisages traditional society as religious and modern society as rational. It puts more faith in science than in religion.

Unlike their classical predecessors, sociologists today tend to focus on particular aspects of religion rather than proposing grand theories. Quite often their work, while located within a theoretical framework, has an empirical orientation. For example, Gene Burns (1996) uses the theoretical notion of religious pluralism to understand the political culture of Catholicism in the USA. As a theory, religious pluralism envisages that religion is the 'property' of subcultures rather than of an entire society. This fits the empirical reality of American history. For, unlike its older European variant, the American form of Catholicism was the religion of a persecuted immigrant minority. In much of Europe, it had been the central belief system of a universal sacred canopy. For the American Catholic, her or his religion was distinctive, forming a subcultural religious identity. In that context, Catholicism offered a rallying call to groups who were marginalised from Protestant circles of power.

Here we see theory and empirical evidence working in harmony. One of the shortcomings of earlier theorists was their tendency to speculate. Much of the speculation was of the creative, suggestive kind, but it wasn't always complemented with empirical rigour. This isn't to suggest that theorising is unhelpful. Sociologists like Durkheim didn't have modern computers and sophisticated statistical software. They had to make sense of the sometimes fragmentary, often incoherent and occasionally indecipherable data available. Faced with these limitations, they did a good job.

Before turning to the often more empirical, but generally smaller, brushstroke theories of contemporary sociologists of religion, we'll examine the work of three of the last of the great grand theorists: Talcott Parsons, and Rodney Stark and William Sims Bainbridge. Parsons believes that classical sociology confers past wisdoms. He distils the best ideas of the 'old masters', and adds his own profoundly insightful thoughts. Stark and Bainbridge develop a new general theory of religion. We'll also look at the relatively recent theoretical contributions of Peter Berger and Thomas Luckmann (who adopt a social constructionist approach) to the sociology of religion.

Talcott Parsons

'[B]elief in the supernatural is universal', says the functionalist sociologist, Talcott Parsons (in Weber 1971: xxviii). It's appropriate that Parsons makes this observation in his introduction to Max Weber's book, *The Sociology of Religion*. Although himself an original thinker, many of Parsons' thoughts on religion were derivative. He was particularly indebted to Durkheim and Weber, critiquing – in generally very complimentary terms – their pioneering work in the field. On Durkheim's contribution to the issue of social integration (i.e. how individuals become social beings), Parsons wrote, it 'can be said to have been nothing short of epoch-making' (1960, in Parsons 1967: 4). Religion plays a key role in social integration because, as Durkheim reveals, religious rituals reinforce social solidarity, making the individual feel part of society rather than a 'lone wolf'.

Parsons was equally complimentary of Weber's path-breaking work in the sociology of religion. Not only did he rate Weber 'as one of the principal founders of modern social science, in particular modern sociology' (1966, Introduction to Weber's [1922] *The Sociology of Religion*: xix), he also described Weber's *Protestant Ethic and the Spirit of Capitalism* (1904–1905) 'as one of the major landmarks of recent Western intellectual history' (ibid: xx).

Indebtedness to earlier greats aside, Parsons made important contributions in his own right. He defines religious beliefs as non-empirical answers to the problem of meaning in life. In that context, the moral implications of human action are significant. Religion makes one consider one's actions in relation to society and the cosmos. This is why religious beliefs function to bolster social morality. Respect for the sacred is a social thing. It fosters group sentiments, and discourages selfish preoccupation. Religion also functions to buoy people up when life gets difficult. The empirical world is a harsh, neutral universe. It doesn't offer the solace that a belief in something bigger – the supernatural – does.

What religion offers, says Parsons, is compensation. Unearned suffering on earth is compensated by a better afterlife. If people believe this, religion performs the function of maintaining social stability because individuals accept their lot. Parsons makes the important point that there's 'a correlation between a firmly insitutionalized belief in supernatural compensation and an ascriptive emphasis in the institutionalized value-system' (1964: 382–3). This is difficult sociology. Put more simply, Parsons is saying that when people believe that the 'last shall be first' in the hereafter, they're more likely to accept their birth-given status on planet earth.

One can see a parallel here with Marx's view that religion exploits the poor by offering the promise of spiritual rewards in exchange for material hardship. Unlike Marx, however, Parsons doesn't get into value-judgements. He describes the social functions of religion rather than approving or disapproving of them. Parsons notes that the credibility of compensation is a crucial issue. People won't take their medicine if they don't believe it will help them. Compensatory balance sheets ('If I put up with this, I'll gain that') are probably more likely to be found, thinks Parsons, in traditional societies. He cites the example of strongly institutionalised Catholic beliefs, recognising simultaneously that such official beliefs are periodically contested. The most notable challenge, of course, occurred during the Reformation.

A different kind of compensation occurs, says Parsons, when religion offers earthly solutions to earthly problems. In sceptical mood, however, he adds that future benefits 'almost inevitably must wait for full realization until after the lifetime of the current generation' (1964: 373). The promise of a utopian future for the next generation mightn't be enough to coax this generation to play by the prescribed rules.

Having a proper relation to the supernatural is a solid guarantor of social control. Obeying God's will, when His will is institutionally defined, means that individuals put social above personal considerations. People learn to accept that conformity with prescribed religious values are part of the very fabric of society. Adherence to these values, says Parsons, is institutionally expected, and departures from them are kept in check through sanctions. In this manner, '"Worldly interests", are thereby inevitably enlisted in the motivation of religious conformity' (Parsons 1964: 379).

By the same token, when religion is taken seriously, the church or its institutional equivalent acquires power and prestige in worldly as well as spiritual affairs. This, says Parsons, can lead to instability and challenges to church authority. Getting involved in secular issues leads to political engagement. Some Catholic priests, for example, argue that the church must play a decisive political role in protecting the poor from oppressive regimes. Here we see the potential for social change, and functionalist

PARSONS' THEORY OF RELIGION

FOR

+ Parsons keeps alive sociology's intellectual indebtedness to Durkheim and Weber. He dips deeply into their profound scholarship, and holds high their greatest achievements – notably, Durkheim's insights on the social functions of the sacred, and Weber's thesis on the elective affinity between Protestantism and capitalism.
+ Parsons keeps his personal values on the back burner. Whatever his own personal beliefs about religion, he comes to the subject as a sociologist. Whilst writing in the functionalist tradition, which sometimes tends to highlight the positive functions of religion in society, Parsons looks at what religion does rather than what it ought to do.
+ Parsons is a bold thinker. We need big thinkers. They look beyond the immediate and the mundane, and dare to venture into uncharted territory. Even though much of what Parsons says is based on theoretical ideas rather than empirical testing, he forces others to test his arguments against the evidence.

AGAINST

– Parsons' contention that religion is universal, requires refining. In China, for example, whilst there are undoubtedly some religious individuals, the ethos is essentially secular–atheist. The same was true in the former Soviet Union. Anthropological evidence might suggest that religion is a worldwide phenomenon, but how can we be sure of this? Not every society, historically and cross-culturally, has been under the intellectual scrutiny of 'western' social scientists. Perhaps, Parsons is overstating his case.
– Linked to the preceding point, and bearing in mind Parsons' grand theorising tendencies, he does over-generalise things. Parsons sees religion as a functional part of a big social system and, in that respect, his approach is deductive. In other words, he begins with big theoretical assumptions about the nature of society and the role of religion within it. Perhaps he should have been more inductive, by conducting lots of fieldwork on religion, and deriving conclusions about religion from the data.
– Parsons' functionalist approach to religion privileges the vantage point of the sociological theorist over the religious believer. It leaves little or no scope to let the believer tell things her or his way. In short, it thinks it knows better than the people whose beliefs and behaviours it studies. This is a common shortcoming of big canvas theories.

though he is, Parsons acknowledges that religion can and does promote change as well as stability. He also says that, once the dust has settled, revolutionary fervour typically creates a new belief system which subsequently becomes as equally ingrained as the one it overturned.

> ***EXAM TIP***
>
> Don't make the mistake of thinking that Parsons and other functionalists only see religion as a conservative force. They recognise that religion, in different cirmcumstances, can be conservative or radical.

Parsons (1963, in Parsons 1967) likens religious groups (up to a point) to the family. The family has lost many traditional functions and has increasingly become a sphere of private sentiments. Similarly, religion has largely become a private matter in which individuals decide to associate with groups of their own choice. In both cases though, a high sense of autonomous responsibility serves important social functions. Individuals are less tied than they were to the institutional 'policing' of families and churches, but have internalised the value of tolerance. Although the solidarity that tolerance builds – one based on mutual respect – is different to the solidarity fostered by social control – one based on dogmatic conformity – both types endorse social obligations.

Change happens, but religion adapts and continues to promote a sense of social duty. This is the legacy of Parsons' theory.

Rodney Stark and William Sims Bainbridge

Most sociologists today focus on issues rather than grand theories, but Stark and Bainbridge have, over the past ten years or so, developed a general theory of religion. Their theory has been hailed as a milestone contribution to the sociology of religion. Says Michael P. Carroll, writing in the prestigious academic journal, *Sociology of Religion*, 'If there is any one theory that is taking the sociology of religion by storm, this is it' (Carroll 1996: 225).

At the heart of the Stark–Bainbridge theory is the idea of a religious economy – a marketplace of different religions on offer to potential believers. The market nature of these often competing 'religious products' means that their promoters seek to give them maximum 'customer appeal'. People can pick and choose, and are likely to consume 'religious products' avidly. Religious participation therefore flourishes. By contrast, when the state 'coerces' people into accepting one particular kind of religious belief, priests don't market religion, and it becomes stale. Monopoly offers little or no choice to the religious consumer, so doctrines that might 'sell' aren't marketed.

Stark and Bainbridge argue that the religions which do 'sell' are those that offer other-worldly rewards to compensate a lack of this-worldly ones. In an unregulated religious economy – a pluralist market, if you will – clergy who offer this compensator are the most likely to drum up 'custom'.

Starting from the premise that 'Humans seek what they perceive to be rewards and try to avoid what they perceive to be costs', Stark and Bainbridge (1985: 5) contend that this human tendency confronts the fact that:

- rewards are scarce and unequally divided
- some intensely desired rewards (for example, immortality on this earth) don't seem available at all.

Faced with these problems, people place their faith in compensators. Stark and Bainbridge define a *compensator* as: 'the belief that a reward will be obtained in the distant future or in some other context which cannot be immediately verified' (1985: 6). The compensator provides an IOU, a promise that, in return for gratification deferred now, the desired rewards will eventually come. The perpetual quest for the ultimate compensator guarantees the eternal continuance of religion in society.

Stark and Bainbridge rebut Durkheim's argument that religion doesn't necessarily have to involve supernatural beliefs. According to them:

> 'When we examine human desires, we see that people often seek rewards of such magnitude and apparent unavailability that *only by assuming the existence of an active supernatural can credible compensators be found*. . . [Therefore] to accept that earthly suffering gains meaning as prelude to everlasting glory is to embrace the supernatural.'
>
> (Stark and Bainbridge 1985: 7)

The human concern with the supernatural seems to go back a long way. Stark and Bainbridge refer to archaeological evidence that our Neanderthal ancestors buried their dead with ceremony and with food and possessions for the next world. In more modern times, some commentators have disparaged such rituals as mere superstition. Indeed, says Bainbridge, 'Sociology has long acted as if religion were dying and deserved little notice' (1997: 403). Bainbridge doesn't agree. With his co-theorist, Stark, the two argue that, although individual religions are constantly born, change and die, religion in general is perpetual.

Stark and Bainbridge conclude that the future looks bright for religion, because 'All our work shows religion to be the direct expression of universal human needs' (1985: 18). Naturalistic faiths, like political creeds, can't compete with supernatural faiths, because only a belief in the supernatural can hope for the ultimate compensator – a supernatural reward after death. That's why politics isn't religion, and Christianity, Islam and Judaism are.

One of the strengths of the Stark–Bainbridge theory is that it explains a wide range of real empirical developments. For example, the dis-establishment of religion brought about by the American Revolution should have led to the pluralistic religious economy predicted in the theory. True to form, R. Finke and R. Stark (1992, cited by Carroll 1996) have shown that religious participation in America did increase from 1776 to the present. R. Stark and L. Iannaccone (1994, cited by Carroll 1996) also contend that, in a similar way, the deregulation of religion in Europe has led to more success for some Protestant sects, and will soon lead to an increase in overall levels of religious participation. Here again, the theory fits the pattern. Cities contain increasingly more competing churches, and are characterised by higher rates of religious participation.

On a less convincing note, the Stark–Bainbridge theory makes the controversial assumption that human behaviour is based on reward-seeking and cost avoidance. This sounds more like a market model of economic behaviour than a general theory of social action. It's an American enterprise culture notion of how people behave which is generalised beyond the American experience. There are plenty of examples of people in this world who embrace costs and shun reward-seeking. They're called heroes. Mother Teresa was one, as was Dr Martin Luther King, and President Nelson Mandela still is.

Notwithstanding this criticism, Stark and Bainbridge offer a theory that, even if it misses the mark in some instances, provides bold outlines which are supported by the latest evidence.

STARK–BAINBRIDGE THEORY OF RELIGION

FOR

+ The Stark–Bainbridge theory reminds us that human needs extend beyond mere material wants. It's an optimistic theory. People yearn for a greater good, for values that transcend money and property. They understand that material things are temporal, and are no guarantors of happiness and fulfilment. The anticipation of a better hereafter is the kind of aspiration that endures even if the forms religion takes change.

+ As a theory, it explains a lot of real developments. For example, because European cities are likely to contain more competing religions, these places should have relatively high levels of religious participation. And they do, just as the theory predicts. Similarly, the demise of the Established Church should, according to the theory, lead to the proliferation of different religions. This has happened in the UK, where religious pluralism is flourishing.

+ The Stark–Bainbridge theory forces a re-assessment of the common assumption that society is witnessing the 'twilight of the gods'. Religion is still a vibrant force in the world today. Sure, some religions have died out (for example, those of the ancient Greeks and of the Vikings), but new religious movements – commonly called NRMs – (for example, Scientology and the 'Moonies) are continually arriving on the scene.

AGAINST

– Who is to say that all people regard supernatural compensators as the most fulfilling form of deferred gratification? The theory is a celebration of the American respect of market forces projected onto a religious plane. As Michael P. Carroll puts it:

'the "America" that underlies the S/B theory-qua-cliché is . . . the idealized . . . entrepreneurial America of Henry Ford and Thomas Edison or better yet, of P. T. Barnum and Buffalo Bill; an America . . . fueled by the actions of rugged individualists who took charge of their destinies and sold large audiences on the products they were marketing.'

(Carroll 1996: 227)

It's an ideology, not an explanation.

– Like most grand theories – so-called meta-theories – it makes deductive claims that can't be assumed to be right until they've been tested. Whilst some events might give credence to the theory, others will undoubtedly disconfirm it. In this respect, the theory suffers from being too all-encompassing, too universal. It should be treated as a series of tentative hypotheses which need to be tested against empirical evidence.

– The prediction by Stark and Bainbridge that religion is forever is untestable. It's an assumption which goes beyond what social science is able to know. Although the development of new religious movements supports the Stark–Bainbridge contention that religion still endures, one can't provide evidence that this is eternal. The best that the Stark–Bainbridge theory can do is to look ahead a few decades, and make some tentative predictions on the basis of existing trends.

QUESTIONS

1 What are compensators, and how do they affect religious beliefs?
2 Why do Stark and Bainbridge argue that religion is eternal?

Peter Berger and Thomas Luckmann

Berger and Luckman, writing in the 1960s, argue that sociology must study what people define as social reality on a common-sense level. This doesn't mean that sociology itself is common sense. Rather, it studies common-sense notions instead of adopting a 'social scientist knows better' posture. Throughout human history, claim Berger and Luckmann (1963), religion has played a decisive role in how people make sense of the universe. In the past, religion was the authoritative voice in this venture. The process of secularisation, however, has led to a legitimation crisis.

Religion has to compete with other belief systems (for example, politics and science), each of which lays claim to legitimate truth about the universe. Beliefs have become less institutionalised and more privatised. In an isolated, rural community where people shared similar beliefs, it was easier for respected religious leaders to shape those beliefs. In the modern world, however, individuals are more discerning. Insofar as religion is concerned, commitment has moved into the private domain.

The 'common sense' people accept nowadays is more likely to be how they define it. Not for them the pre-packaged prescription of religious leaders. In a later study, Thomas Luckmann writes: 'Personal identity becomes, essentially, a private phenomenon' (1970: 97). Once religion becomes disembedded from institutions like churches, individuals are more free to choose from the assortment of 'ultimate' meanings. There are echoes of this argument in the Stark–Bainbridge theory. Luckmann doesn't rule out the importance of traditional religious social constructions. However, he notes that optional social constructions jostle for favour with official ones.

Luckmann concludes that 'The primary social institutions have "emigrated" from the sacred cosmos' (1970: 115). This means that religion is no longer in the hands of the rich and powerful. It's neither capitalistic nor communistic, says Luckmann. But he seems uncertain about whether this is beneficial:

'This liberation [of individual thinking] represents a historically unprecedented opportunity for the autonomy of personal life for "everybody". It also contains a serious danger – of motivating mass withdrawal into the "private sphere" while "Rome burns". On balance, is this good or bad?'

(Luckmann 1970: 117)

He doesn't answer his own question. What do you think?

QUESTION

What are private and official social constructions of religion?

Religion: Conservative force and initiator of social change

In this section, we distil from the preceding one those aspects of sociological investigation that emphasise the role of religion in relation to social stability and social change. We also throw in some other studies for good measure.

Religious influence must be understood in particular social contexts. This point is persuasively made by J. Milton Yinger (1971), who urges sociologists to give up notions of general 'laws' when investigating the extent to which religion is influenced by or influences social processes. In early nineteenth-century Britain, Church of England schools for poor children reproduced hierarchical conceptions of social order. Economic and social processes exercised strong influences over what was taught in these schools. In late twentieth-century South Africa, Catholic schools contested apartheid, and admitted black children, including one who eventually became the nation's first black president, Nelson Mandela. Here, religion was an independent force for change.

Yinger reminds us that 'Religion cannot be understood simply as a force that blocks or retards change – whether for good or ill' (1971: 514). There's no general formula. Sometimes religion promotes social stability. Sometimes it does the opposite.

Religion and social stability

Religion is often a conserver of existing values rather than an initiator of new ones. It doesn't stop social change, but can slow it down. It does this by exercising a regulating role – affirming existing values and forging common behaviours. When religion doesn't perform this function, says Durkheim, confusion and uneasiness result.

Taking account of particular contexts, these are the main ways in which religion promotes social stability:

- In traditional societies (for example, Australian aboriginal), totems harness an *esprit de corps*. People rally around the totem, paying collective respect to the sacred values it embodies. Although generally not as strong as in these settings, totems perform the same function in modern and postmodern societies.
- In hierarchical societies, religion sometimes reproduces the *status quo*. Thus, for example, claim marxist sociologists, the values of the Church of England often mirrored and supported the ideology of powerful economic and political elites in the nineteenth century.

- In close-knit communities (those whom Durkheim says are characterised by mechanical solidarity), religion socialises the individual through force and/or persuasion into accepting and acting upon established moral precepts. Once these values and norms have been internalised, habit takes over and is resistant to change.
- Insofar as it's accepted, Yinger argues, religion provides:

  'emotional support to the fundamental values of a society; it softens the hardness of the struggle for scarce values by emphasizing values that can be achieved by all (as, for example, salvation).'

  (Yinger 1971: 110)

  In this way, religion functions as a powerful stabilising and unifying force.

Religion and social change

Whether religion keeps change at bay or initiates change is a matter for empirical investigation. Once started, religious ideas gather momentum and can then exert an independent influence on social structure. For example, martyrdom can and does inspire some religious people to take on what they see as oppressive regimes.

Once again, being mindful of particular contexts, these are the main ways in which religion promotes social change:

- Some religions develop an outreach mission whose aim is to change the beliefs, values and practices of people that missionaries seek to convert. Missionary work in small, preliterate societies, notes Yinger, is especially likely to exercise a de-stabilising effect on established ways, increasing 'the wobble in various parts of the old order beyond the capacity of the homeostatic processes to handle' (1971: 528).
- Resistance to the prevailing *status quo* can be sparked by messianic movements. Stark and Bainbridge (1985), for example, refer to the role of messiahs in encouraging Native American resistance to the encroachments of white settlement. Sometimes the effects of these messiahs was to persuade Native Americans to return to pre-Columbian ways. This meant the rejection of liquor, woollen clothing and white medical techniques, and the initiation of new rites and prayers and the use of traditional spears and bows.
- Sects and cults represent a break with convention, even though, in the case of sects, there's a tendency to re-invent tradition along stricter lines. The Dead Sea scrolls show that early Jewish and Christian sects rejected society's self-indulgent pursuit of worldly pleasures and repudiated what was perceived as corrupt religious establishments. Some sects were persecuted, even martyred. This often steeled the resolve of other sect members, and, in the case of Christianity, led to anti-establishment fervour and social change. Cults are innovative religious groups whose departure from convention promotes novel beliefs and practices.
- Although sects are often thought to be more 'rebellious' than churches, the recovery of a protest element in churches also sometimes occurs. Robert Bocock (1993), for example, cites the development of Christian socialism earlier in the twentieth century, the development of liberation theology in Latin America in the last few decades, and the recent critique of Communism by the Catholic Church in Poland as protest movements.

QUESTIONS

1 Why is it unwise to apply a general formula when considering religion in relation to social stability and social change?

2 What are the main ways in which religion promotes social stability and social change? Use some examples other than those referred to above to illustrate your points.

Churches, denominations, sects and cults

The classical sociologists of religion were big thinkers. They liked working on a broad canvas, and produced grand theories. These theories concerned total societies and wide historical sweeps. The worlds which the early theorists studied were religious places. People didn't divide the natural and the supernatural into separate spheres to the extent that they do today.

In the late twentieth century, with some notable exceptions (for example, Parsons, and Stark and Bainbridge), sociologists tend to theorise on micro or middle range rather than on whole society levels. This tendency has led to what Thomas Luckmann rather ruefully describes as the new sociology of religion – 'church-oriented religiosity' (1970: 26). Linked to an interest in churches is a fascination with secularisation, 'typically regarded', laments Luckman 'as a process of religious pathology to be measured by the shrinking reach of the churches' (1970: 23). Luckmann made this observation in the 1960s, and, since then, the focus of the sociology of religion has undergone some changes. A great deal of attention today, for example, is devoted to the study of new age beliefs.

Churches, dwindling membership or otherwise, are nevertheless an important part of the sociology of religion. In this section, we examine *churches* and also the other main forms of religious organisation: *denominations, sects* and *cults*. The boundaries between all four organisations are often fluid. Therefore we generally avoid treating them under distinct sub-sections. To do that, would be to sacrifice reality for neat boxes. To help you, the more important references to each organisation are printed in **bold** text.

Mindful of Bainbridge's observation that 'Perhaps the cornerstone of the sociology of religion is church-sect theory' (1997: 38), we'll begin with churches and sects.

Weber is generally credited with introducing the notions of church and sect, and his student, Ernst Troeltsch, continued the study of them. Starting with the mentor before the student, Weber (1922, in Birnbaum and Lenzer: 318) characterised the church and the sect in ideal types. The *ideal type* is a conceptual tool which helps sociologists make sense of complex social issues. Thus, for example, when Weber identifies the key features of a sect, he produces a sociological caricature of its essence. The ideal type doesn't lay claim to being a mirror image of reality, but it aspires to get close.

Beginning with the **churches**, Weber's (1922, in Birnbaum and Lenzer: 318) ideal type describes a church as an institution with:

- 'a professional priesthood removed from the "world", with salaries, promotions, professional duties, and a distinctive way of life'
- 'claims to universal domination'
- 'dogma and rites (*Kultus*) . . . rationalized [and] recorded in holy scriptures . . . and turned into objects of a systematic education'
- 'all of these features . . . in some kind of compulsory organization'.

Weber adds that churches, unlike sects, consider themselves to be 'trust funds' of eternal blessings offered to all. As a rule, members are born into a church rather than joining it. In the full sense of the term, says Weber, churches have only arisen in Christianity, Islam and Lamaist Buddhism. In a more restricted sense, churches were also created by Judaism, Mahdism and, it seems, in the ancient Egyptian *hierocracy* (a system that enforces its values by giving or denying religious benefits).

A **sect** – among which he refers to Baptists and Quakers – is distinguished, according to Weber (1922, in Birnbaum and Lenzer: 320), by these characteristics:

- 'the principle of lay preaching and of every member's priesthood'
- '"direct democratic administration" by the congregation', whose clerical officials are 'servants of the congregation'
- 'endeavors to exist as a voluntary association of qualified believers'
- 'must advocate "tolerance" and "separation" of church and state'.

Following Weber, Troeltsch uses ideal types to identify the three main forms of Christian organisation: the church, the sect and mysticism. This last of Troeltsch's categories essentially corresponds to a **cult**. Says Troeltsch:

> 'The aim of the **Church** is to be the Church of the people and of the masses . . . it possesses an absolute directly divine truth and doctrinal authority over all subjects.'
>
> (Troeltsch 1912, in Birnbaum and Lenzer 1969: 311)

In bringing the message of salvation to the whole nation, it demands the co-operative power of the state (including the use of 'justifiable' force in the people's interest).

Sects, by contrast, don't want to be mass churches, but rather what Troeltsch describes as 'Christian denominations composed of "saints"' (1912, in Birnbaum and Lenzer 1969: 311). Sects are independent of state and the wider society. They're exclusive rather than universal. Like churches, they claim to have access to absolute divine truth. However, they don't force their interpretation of the Gospel on other people, and in turn, they demand religious toleration from the state. The truth they lay claim to isn't meant for the masses.

Insofar as mysticism (which, as indicated, is **cult**-like) is concerned, writes Troeltsch, 'the truth of salvation is inward and relative, a personal possession which is unutterable' (1912, in Birnbaum and Lenzer 1969: 312). Freedom of conscience is paramount. There's a sense, as the Quakers put it, of being 'moved by the Spirit'. Doctrinal authority is replaced by personal conviction. This can lead to problems because there's no final authoritative version of Christianity. Hence, organised groups can fragment into private ones of a personal kind. The development of what Troeltsch terms 'a comparative individualism' can occur.

Troeltsch's ideal types set in high relief the distinctive features of churches, sects and cults. However, his evidence was largely drawn from European medieval sect formation, and shouldn't be generalised beyond specific historical circumstances. Wilson (1982) has warned how the use of the ideal type can produce an artificial sense of timelessness, alluding here not just to Troeltsch, but also to the research into Christian sects of H. Richard Niebuhr. Niebuhr argues that sects began as radical protest groups, but, over time, the protest became attenuated. Says Niebuhr of sect members

> 'Rarely does a second generation hold the convictions it has inherited with a fervor equal to that of its fathers, who fashioned these convictions in the heat of conflict and at the risk of martyrdom.'
>
> (Niebuhr 1929, in Birnbaum and Lenzer 1969: 317)

Routinisation sets in, and sects become **denominational** (i.e. more churchlike) in outlook.

According to Wilson, Niebuhr overstates his case by paying insufficient attention to groups who retained a distinct sectarian stance. Mindful of his own argument that ideal types shouldn't hide the fact that religious groups develop in different ways, Wilson (1963, in Bocock and Thompson 1993) introduces a seven-fold classification of sects. His typology refines and broadens our understanding. Sects come in different shapes and sizes. They're not, as Niehbuhr tends to assume, all the same as the ones he observed.

Wilson's ideal types focus on each kind of **sect** in relation to its response to the world. Here's his seven-fold typology:

- *Conversionist sects* These are the typical sects of 'evangelical', fundamentalist Christianity. Their reaction towards the outside world is that it's corrupted because humans are. If people are changed, the world will change. Sect leaders use techniques of mass persuasion in an emotionally-charged atmosphere. In Christian sects, much emphasis is placed on an individual relationship with a personal saviour. Sect members tend to interpret scripture literally. The Salvation Army, in the initial stages of its development, the Assemblies of God and other Pentecostal movements, as well as independent evangelical sects, are examples of conversionist sects.
- *Revolutionary sects* Their posture towards the outside world is to be rid of the existing *status quo* – if necessary, by force. Members of these sects await a new order under God's direction, and it's they who will becomes God's representatives on earth. Prophetic religious texts are valued, and sect members compare sect predictions with unfolding events. Conversion is considered an occasional and gradual process, and permission to join the sect isn't freely given. God is viewed as a divine autocrat whose will is felt throughout the universe, and there's little sense of members feeling a direct relationship with Him. Jehovah's Witnesses, Christadelphians and the English seventeenth-century Fifth Monarchy Men are examples of revolutionary sects.
- *Introversionist sects* These sects expect neither to convert nor to overturn the world. Sect members retire from worldly things and cherish personal holiness. They express no interest in social reform, social revolution and individual conversion. Personal piety is paramount. However, Christian introversionist sects conceive of a divinity of the type of the Holy Spirit rather than of a more personalised form. The relationship between the divine and the human is akin to an outpouring and a receiving vessel. Typical introversionist sects are apparent among certain 'holiness movements', and in European pietist movements of the eighteenth century.
- *Manipulationist sects* Members of these sects accept the goals of the outside world, but claim distinctive knowledge. Often, they think they have a more spiritual version of society's goals, and sometimes teach members to lead culturally more fulfilling lives. This is why manipulationist sects are sometimes called **cults**. Assembly seems more about proclaiming the success of sect techniques than worship. The notion of a personal saviour isn't strong, and there's an absence of an emotional relationship with God. Anyone can learn the doctrine. The hereafter seems to be envisaged as an enhancement of earthly joys. Typical manipulationist sects are Christian Scientists, Unitarians, Psychiana, Scientology and Rosicrucians.
- *Thaumaturgical sects* These are movements which hold that the outside world can be changed through miracles. Members of these sects often call upon spirits and other powers to perform miracles, and frequently seek relationships with deceased relatives. When the members of thaumaturgical sects assemble, they form an audience which hopes for personal benefits or watches other receive them. Examples of thaumaturgical sects include the National Spiritualist Church and the Progressive Spiritualist Church.
- *Reformist sects* These seek to transform the outside world. Originally revolutionary, their outlook sometimes becomes introverted over time. The history of the Quakers is illustrative here. This type of sect studies the world and then engages it through good deeds. It has a strong social conscience. Whilst the reformist sect associates with the world, it also seeks to remain untainted by worldly things. The preferred religious texts are those which say that faith without good works is in vain. Members seem to place more emphasis on humanitarian concerns than on doctrinal dogma. The Christadelphians might eventually become transformed into this kind of sect.
- *Utopian sects* Such sects partly withdraw from the outside world, and partly want to remake the world to a better specification along communitarian lines. Some utopian sects set up colonies with a global mission. Others become communal in defensive response against the irreligion of the world. Favoured biblical texts of utopian Christian sects might be those in Acts which recount the setting up of the early Christian community in Jerusalem. Among Christian – or more or less Christian – utopian sects, one might single out the Tolstoyans, the Community of Oneida, the Bruderhof, and perhaps certain sections of Christian Socialists.

EXAM TIP

In the exam, don't go overboard on descriptive detail. Highlight the bold outlines, and display analytical rigour. For example, you might argue that Wilson's seven types remind sociologists not to treat all sects as the same.

In keeping with his view that ideal types should clarify social reality rather than setting it in marble, Wilson argues that 'Any typology of sects must point up, and not hide, the fact that sects pass through processes of change' (1963, in Bocock and Thompson 1993: 304). Wilson is mindful that his models are caricatures to be adapted in response to changes in the real world. Whilst being careful not to overstate common features of all sects, Wilson highlights a general feature that tends to distinguish sects from churches: 'Whereas the church has offered timeless truth, the sect has always canvassed timely truth' (1981b, in Wilson 1981a: 225).

This is an important distinction. The **church** values tradition. The **sect** debunks convention, and offers a new truth to be communicated *now*. Interestingly, though, as Stark (1985, in Hammond 1985) points out, the **sect** doesn't find a new faith. Rather, it seeks to revive or restore an earlier, more otherworldly version of the church from which it breaks away. Its new message is that the original teachings have drifted from their historic anchorage.

Church–sect theory envisages a set of religious institutions and movements in which an established church forms an alliance with the upper class, and small dissenting sects cut loose in social opposition and strong religious fervour. The process of breaking away is called a *schism*. Sect formation often resulted as a protest against ecclesiastical pomp and circumstance.

Churches are of two main kinds:

- *established* (for example, the pre-Reformation Catholic, Orthodox and Coptic churches, when one of these formed the established church – sometimes called an *ecclesia* – in a nation or a wider territory)
- ***denominational*** (for example, post-Reformation churches, including the three churches just mentioned when they co-exist with other churches).

Established churches were integrated into the societies over which they exercised religious domination. Some of them aspired to be universal churches. The Catholic Church almost achieved this status in the pre-Reformation Christian world.

In the UK and the US today, it's difficult to find any religious group that fits the ideal type definition of an established church. Even the Church of England is *de facto* a denominational church which co-exists with other churches – Methodist, Reform Jewish, Orthodox Jewish, Sikh, and many more. Like sects, **denominations** flourished in Europe after the Reformation. Reform spelt the disestablishment of Catholic 'universalism', and the proliferation of both sects and denominations. Unlike sects, **denominations** were churchlike even though they weren't churches in the classic sense. They often had a professional clergy, and a close affinity with respectable elites. People could choose to join, but were often born into a denominational church.

Denominations make more modest claims than established churches and sects (and, in some cases, cults), and are fairly tolerant of other religious beliefs. In Holland, for example, Catholicism – more a denomination there than a church – works jointly with other denominations. **Denominational churches** are part and parcel of pluralistic culture. There are few countries in the 1990s that have one single church which is the theological mouthpiece of all religious beliefs.

Of the four main types of religious organisation – churches, denominations, sects and cults – the **denominations** are the most tolerant in relation to theological claims to truth. They see their grasp of theological belief to be *pluralistically legitimate* (i.e. one among other beliefs). **Churches** and **sects**, by contrast, define their theological orientation as *uniquely legitimate* (i.e. the one definitive belief). **Cults** are generally quite tolerant of differing beliefs. There are, however, some notable exceptions here. Some cults insist they know better than other religious groups about the nature of the divine. On the other hand, as Bruce (1996a) points out, other cults are so 'liberal', they let their 'members' pick and choose from the 'ordained' beliefs.

In the table below, Roy Wallis makes a helpful distinction between the four religious organisations in relation to the internal conception they have of their own authority. He also highlights external conceptions (respectable or deviant) of society towards them.

Typology of religious collectivities

		External conception	
		Respectable	**Deviant**
Internal conception	**Uniquely legitimate**	Church	Sect
	Pluralistically legitimate	Denomination	Cult

(Wallis 1981, in Wilson 1981a: 119)

As indicated earlier, some **sects** 'graduate' into **denominations**, a process reported by Niebuhr. The development of Methodism fits this picture well, as do changes among Quakers in the nineteenth century. However, Bruce (1996a) follows Wilson in noting that some sects go down that road, and others don't. Thus, contends Bruce, 'The drift towards the denominational compromise is a common career but it is not inevitable' (1996a: 81).

Wilson (1970) notes that conversionist sects were more likely than others to become denominations. As their members became more respectable, their protest against mainstream culture declined. Revolutionary sects haven't shown so consistent a tendency. Jehovah's Witnesses, for example, have undergone some change, but not towards denominationalism. They're still an Adventist sect, and as vigorously single-minded in their doctrine as ever.

Whilst voluntary commitment is increasingly becoming the hallmark of religious belief, this doesn't threaten **sects** as much as churches. Sects have always operated on voluntary principles. People make conscious decisions to join them, and are expected to exhibit appropriate behaviours, like, for example, being 'born again' in adult baptism. Interestingly, sects often emphasise traditional religious values more fervently than churches.

In a recent analysis of the church–sect treatise, Bainbridge offers formal definitions of **church**, **sect** and **cult**. He groups **denomination** under the umbrella category of church:

'A *church* (or denomination) is a conventional religious organization. A *sect* movement is a deviant religious organization with traditional beliefs and practices. A *cult* movement is a deviant religious organization with novel beliefs and practices.'

(Bainbridge 1997: 24)

By 'deviance', Bainbridge doesn't mean 'bad', just a departure from convention.

Rather than placing churches and sects in distinct boxes, Bainbridge prefers to set religious organisations along a continuum. Noting that **established churches** (for example, the medieval Catholic Church in England) have been 'replaced' in many pluralistic societies with **denominational churche**s (for example, the Catholic and Episcopalian Churches in the US), Bainbridge places denominations at one end of the continuum and sects at the other end.

Bainbridge defines **denominations** as low tension and **sects** as high tension organisations. The term *tension* refers to the relationship a religion has with mainstream society. The tension, for example, between the Church of England and English cultural values is relatively low, compared to the tension between strict Baptist and mainstream orientations.

Like sects, cults are deviant, but their deviance is different. **Sects** seek to reclaim corrupted past wisdoms, and are revivalist. **Cults** offer new ideas and are innovative. They're also quite flexible. Although they're organised around common themes, cults – like denominations – are tolerant towards their own members. Indeed, says Bruce, the cult 'is so tolerant that it hardly has "members"; instead it has consumers who pick and choose those bits of its product that suit them' (1996: 82).

This internal pluralism can be the cult's undoing. Religious groups which are unable to guarantee the allegiance of members are prone to be short-lived. Although the process takes longer, even more traditional forms of religious organisation can find it difficult to command the obedience of members. The important issue of the extent to which religion still exercises a hold on people today is the subject of the next section.

QUESTIONS

1 Allowing for the often fluid boundaries between churches, denominations, sects and cults, what are the essential features of each of these groups?
2 In what ways do convention and deviance appear in religious groups?

The secularisation debate

It was remarked that during the first half of the twentieth century virtually every serious sociologist expected religion to vanish before the year 2000. Whilst this hasn't happened, the erosion of the supernatural seems to have gathered pace. *Secularisation* – 'that process by which religious institutions, actions, and consciousness, lose their social significance' (Wilson 1982: 149) – is on the march.

Wilson (1982) proposes an *all-encompassing theory of secularisation*. He contends that religion *in general* is in retreat. He claims that indicators of this include:

- the takeover by politicians of the property and facilities of religious agencies
- the shift from religious to secular control of various functions previously served by religion
- the decline in the amount of time, energy and resources which people devote to supernatural concerns
- the decay of religious institutions
- the supplanting of religious with technical criteria in relation to prescribed behaviours
- the gradual replacement of a religious consciousness (for example, charms, rites, spells, prayers and spiritually-inspired ethics) by an empirical, rational, practical outlook
- the abandonment of mythical, poetic and artistic interpretations of nature and society in favour of matter-of-factness and, related to this, the rigorous separation of emotion and science.

The main 'cause' of secularisation is modernism. The 'western' scientific and technical mood of the Enlightenment claimed that science knew better than religion. The attack took its toll. Religion wasn't defeated but, henceforth, competed with other claims to truth. Science has proved to be a formidable adversary. Earthquakes, for example, are explained on the basis of scientific causes, not because the 'gods' are angry. Moreover, many behaviours once condemned by religion are now considered a matter of choice.

In the twentieth century, Wilson (1966) believes that the churches recognise their increasingly marginalised position in society, and are coming to terms with changing moral values. Social fragmentation has ushered in cultural pluralism, with alternative beliefs competing for favour. Religions have also become more private and less public. The position can be summed up by saying that God no longer chooses us; we choose God.

Wilson (1982) contends that secularisation occurs in association with the process of social change from a communally-based to a societally-based system. He calls this development *societalisation*. Through societalisation, says Wilson, 'human life is increasingly enmeshed and organised, not locally but societally' (1982: 154). Because religion has its source in, and draws strength from, the community, societalisation has shorn religion of its former social control role.

There are times, however, when the Church (of England) plays a pivotal role. This was vividly illustrated in 1997, after the death of Diana, Princess of Wales. Her funeral service at Westminster Abbey was broadcast across the world. Elton John sang a rewritten version of the 1974 classic, *Candle in the Wind*, originally composed with Marilyn Monroe in mind.

The 1997 version of the song stirred patriotic and religious emotions, elevating Diana to English sainthood.

A few days after the funeral, Tony Blair addressed the Trades Union Congress. Before his speech, he alluded to the ceremony, and announced he was proud to be British. In mourning the death of the 'People's Princess', the Prime Minister and the British public have discovered that there is such a thing as society. They've also found that Britishness speaks in a more inclusive, tolerant voice. The playwright, David Edgar, captured this mood, when, writing of the mourners, he observed:

'Most people in Hyde Park and in the Mall have commented on the particular visibility of women, Afro-Caribbeans, Asians and gay men, those constituencies who were particularly excluded from the Thatcher feast.'
(The *Guardian*, 10 September 1997, page 17)

National religious ceremonies remind us that the sacred is still important. But such events are quite rare. Our world, say the secularisation theorists, is generally profane, leaving only occasional, sentimental contemplation of the supernatural. So are we seeing the final twilight of the gods? Stark and Bainbridge (1985) don't think so. Contesting the argument that religion is living on borrowed time, they believe the prediction of a religionless future is false.

Stark and Bainbridge accept that secularisation is occurring, but regard the process as a decline in church religion, *accompanied* by religious revival (sect formation) and innovation (cult formation). In short, secularisation *does not* mean a decline in religion in general.

Elton John sings at the funeral of Diana, Princess of Wales.

EXAM TIP

Emphasise that Stark and Bainbridge don't reject the secularisation thesis outright. They contest the assumption which commonly lies behind the thesis, namely, that secularisation is leading to religious extinction.

Stark and Bainbridge (1985) propose that religion has persisted, noting, for example, that:

- a third of Americans claimed to be born again Christians, and 90 per cent prayed regularly
- during the nationwide strikes in Poland, workers didn't hoist the red flag, but the blue banner of Our Lady
- the then Soviet press conceded that 70 years of intensive education in atheism and strict repression of religion were a resounding failure.

In his book, *The Sociology of Religious Movements*, Bainbridge concludes 'that religion will constantly renew itself through religious movements, indefinitely into the far-distant future' (1997: 395). According to Bainbridge, the followers of various religions don't seem to have contemplated the chilling prospect that their own denomination might someday disappear. The implication is that they know better than the sociologists, who have long acted as though religion were dying. Bainbridge is one of an increasing number of sociologists who contest the argument that the death of religious faith is inevitable. So influential has the counter-secularisation thesis become that Stephen Warner (1993, cited by Bainbridge 1997) calls it a New Paradigm (i.e. new model) in the sociology of religion.

Even the major religious traditions have staying power, insists Bainbridge (1997). Neither concentration camps nor totalitarian regimes have extinguished them. Moreover, new religions are constantly emerging. Bainbridge thinks only a tiny fraction of the new ones will become prominent, but out of these, he expects different traditions to emerge, replete with their own denominations. What will be our faith be like, more than 4,000 years ahead?, wonders Bainbridge. In responding to his own question, he writes:

'The images of carolers singing Christmas songs under the hurtling moons of Mars, and of a priest hearing confession on an outer satellite of Saturn, are faintly ridiculous. And yet, if humanity does move outward toward the stars, it will take its familiar religions with it. The line from Stonehenge to here extends onward to infinity, and the religious movement that quarried those stones, then dragged them miles to the site, will be born again on other worlds.'

(Bainbridge 1997: 422)

Dig below secularisation, and you find alternative or revised kinds of religiosity. People don't attend church as often as before, but lots of them pray. In his book, *The Invisible Religion*, the social constructionist theorist, Thomas Luckmann writes: 'The modern sacred cosmos legitimates the retreat of the individual into the "private sphere" and sanctifies his [*sic*] subjective "autonomy"' (1970: 116). Religion is taking on a more 'invisible', private face. It gets dislodged from mainstream, and becomes a matter of personal choice.

Empirical indicators of secularisation focus on the 'visible', public dimensions of religious behaviours. They're useful, but don't reach sufficiently into the 'invisible' subjective dimension. As indicated before, what it means to be 'religious' is hard to pin down. People think and act differently in relation to religious conviction. This makes it difficult to be precise about whether people are religious, and whether religion is in decline. Another potential difficulty in measuring 'religiousness' is that it expresses itself in different dimensions. Charles E. Glock (1958, in Birnbaum and Lenzer 1969) identifies four dimensions:

- *experiential* – feelings, perceptions and sensations experienced by an individual or defined by a religious group or society as involving some communication with the divine
- *ritualistic* – religious actions (for example, worship, prayer, church attendance), rather than feeling or thought
- *ideological* – what people believe about the nature of the divine or ultimate reality and its purpose, rather than what they feel
- *consequential* – what people do with the attitudes they have as a result of their religious beliefs, experiences and practices (for example, how people relate to other human beings in accordance with the religious principles they hold).

Glock accepts that these dimensions are interrelated, but sees them as useful ideal types. In order to measure the religiousness of an individual or a group, the social scientist must make clear the dimension she or he is referring to. One can see, for example, how an over-reliance on one indicator of religious behaviour (such as going to church) can lead to invalid conclusions. A non-church-going individual might be very religious in the consequential sense of behaving towards the poor as though they were Christ. Yet, this person might be defined as non-religious if we just focused on church-going.

Notwithstanding these and other methodological problems, Wilson (1982) thinks that the secularising impulse is almost universal. In the 'west', says Wilson, the decline in religion is associated with the growth of science and the development of the state. Echoing Weber, Wilson also notes that Protestantism was a reform of Christianity which encouraged a more rational approach to religion and everyday affairs. It accomplished this by reducing the extensive powers of the Catholic Church. 'Magical' intercessions, holy relics and shrines were demystified and rejected. In their place, individuals became keepers of their own consciences.

Even the Catholic Church has succumbed – albeit to a lesser degree than Protestantism – to the rationalising forces of modernisation. Its Latin liturgy and ritualistic masses have largely given way to the vernacular and the popular. However, secular culture still bears the imprint of religious history. Catholic community spirit, for example, surfaces in the strong group culture of southern European and Irish cultures. In the US, by contrast, the rugged individualism of puritanism awakens in the steely resolve of the self-made corporation boss. Such legacies might be in retreat. According to Wilson, 'generally it may be said that western culture lives off the borrowed capital of its religious past' (1982: 88).

Conceding that European culture may never have been devoutly religious, Wilson argues that the social significance of religion was greater in the past. Whilst most sociologists probably concur with the general proposition that secularisation is occurring, a number of sociologists (for example, Bainbridge 1997) contest the suggestion that the process is gnawing steadily at the roots of religious faith. Even though some forms of supernatural belief might succumb, the gap is filled by other religions.

The next two sections examine, respectively, the evidence in support of the secularisation thesis, and the challenges marshalled against it. Unless otherwise indicated, the secularisation thesis refers to its most common variant, namely, that religion in general is in decline. Opponents of this thesis (for example, Stark and Bainbridge 1985) usually concede that secularisation has affected some religions.

In support of secularisation

Stroll in any British city centre, advises Steve Bruce (1992), and count the churches and chapels that have been converted into carpet showrooms or sheltered housing or have just been left to rack and ruin. Note how the rural church of St John's with St Cuthbert in the Wold and St Martin's has brought what were three separate parishes under one roof. Ponder the decline in the status of clerics, whose members are low paid and sometimes part-time.

Anecdotal though Bruce's reflections are, there are lots of indicators of religious decline in the UK. In an admittedly very sketchy summary of religious trends in Britain, Bruce (1992) proposes that the evidence supports the pattern below:

- In medieval times, the Catholic Church was a powerful, hierarchical social institution, with a professional clergy. Many people were ignorant of the details of the religion into which they were baptised. However, they had a profoundly Christian outlook, which was overlaid on a view of a world pervaded by magic, spirits and witchcraft.
- With industrialisation, lay involvement in churches (note the plural in this post-Reformation age) increased, and individual beliefs and morals became more important.
- From a high point between 1860 and 1910, the churches declined rapidly until religion is now a pursuit of only a small minority of people.

However, Bruce is sceptical about 'inevitabilist' notions of religious decline. The picture is more complex. Churches and denominations are in retreat. But minority ethnic religions are popular, and supernatural beliefs and practices are common in sects and cults. Notwithstanding these differing trends, the statistics generally support the view that involvement in institutional religion is on the wane. We'll start with some figures on church membership.

Dwindling church membership

Grace Davie (in Haralambos 1989) discloses that only 15 per cent of supposedly Christians in the UK claim membership of a Christian church. In Britain, nominal allegiance (i.e. in name rather than devotional) is the most common form of religious attachment. No allegiance, however, is quite rare. Nevertheless, says Davie:

> 'The description of the Church of England as the church from which the English choose to stay away catches the religious mood of a significant proportion of the population.'
>
> (in Haralambos 1989: 77)

Membership of the principal Christian denominations in this country is declining. The rate of decline, however, seems to be decreasing, and Baptists have managed to halt the process. Whilst there has been a rapid growth in the Orthodox Church and in 'other churches' (for example, African/West Indian, Independent and Pentecostal), these churches are relatively small. Consequently, fast growth has limited impact on membership statistics of Christian churches as a whole. To some extent, the same growth pattern is apparent in non-Christian religions, where overall figures are quite low. But there are variations: the Muslim community has outgrown the Methodists, and the Jewish community continues to dwindle.

Putting some statistics to changes in church membership rates between 1800 and 1990, Bruce (1996) discloses that we're unlikely to be far wrong if we estimate that:

- about 18 per cent of the adult population of England were church 'members' in 1800
- the above figure rose to 27 per cent by 1850, declining slightly to 26 per cent in 1900.

Thereafter, church membership continued to decline, so that the corresponding figure for 1990 was about 14 per cent or less. Membership of the Protestant denominations – which until recently represented the vast majority of British Christianity – dropped from 22 per cent of the adult population in 1900 to just 7 per cent in 1990.

Patterns of religious affiliation vary hugely on an international level. For example, Anthony Heath, Bridget Taylor and Gabor Toka (1993), writing in *International Social Attitudes: The 10th British Social Attitudes Report*, say that in the Irish Republic and Poland substantial majorities of a sample reported they were regular church-going Catholics. In the former East Germany, by contrast, 64 per cent said they had no religion.

Reduced religious attendance

In the 1993 British Social Attitudes Survey, only one in every ten people said they attended church or related meetings once a week or more. Nearly a quarter said they never, or practically never attended church. In statistical terms, there's a lot of evidence to back the claim that the principal Christian denominations are struggling for members and active church attenders. Although there are disagreements about the precise pattern of church attendance over the past 200 years, it's generally accepted that there are far fewer church members and church-goers today than there were in 1800, 1850, 1900 and 1950.

There were numerous surveys of church attendance in the nineteenth century, notes Bruce (1996). Newspapers organised local surveys, churches collected figures and, in 1851, the national Census of Religious Worship was conducted by Horace Mann. The census, however, counted attendances rather than attenders, and many people went to church services more than once on a Sunday. Multiple attendance, itself an indicator of strong religious commitment, makes it hard to be precise about how many people attended church. Attendance at church represented 61 per cent of the Scottish population and 58 per cent of the population of England and Wales. Bruce (1996) reckons that one estimate puts the number of church-goers at about half of the attendances. In other words, it assumes that most church-goers attended twice on a Sunday. We can therefore guess that about one-third of Britons went to church on the census Sunday of 1851.

Like any snapshot survey, census data must be treated with caution. All kinds of things, weather included, affect church attendance. Bruce makes the point that church attendances on a particularly wet day in Cheltenham in 1882 was 47.7 per cent of the population. On a fine day one week later, the figure was 61.4 per cent. Adds Bruce, 'Not even bourgeois Cheltenham could now hope to exceed 12 per cent, no matter what the weather!' (1996: 30). A similar picture of institutional decline is apparent among the number of clergy in the main (so-called Trinitarian) UK Christian denominations (Anglican, Methodist, Catholic, etc.).

In the US, very recent research by Andrea Williams and James Davidson (1996) on Catholics' conceptions of faith shows that there has been a movement from an institutional to an individual notion of faith. Catholics have become more self-reliant rather than turning to priests. Williams and Davidson focus on events that have influenced the religious beliefs and practices of three generations of Catholics. The cohort which came of age in the 1970s and 1980s grew up in an era of political corruption (for example, Watergate), scientific and technological disasters (for example, the Chernobyl nuclear reactor meltdown) and increasing social problems (for example, AIDS, drugs, divorce, etc.). These strong secular experiences left some Catholics trusting only themselves. In this context, Williams and Davidson report a decline in confidence in religion as a social institution.

Drop in the number of clergy and churches

In 1900, there were somewhat over 20,000 Church of England clerics. The number had halved to just over 10,000 by 1984. Looking at a more compressed and recent period, between 1970 and 1987, the number of Trinitarian ministers as a whole had fallen from 43,000 to 39,000 – although this had stabilised by 1990 to 39,200. The clergy is an ageing profession. A large majority of clerics are over 45. Many are older than 65. Ordinations to the Catholic Church in England have now fallen below replacement levels.

According to Wilson (1974), the clergy share the growing anonymity of mobile urban populations. Even in stable moral communities, their importance is reduced. As demand for their service falls, so too does the supply of clergy coming forward for ordination. In the 1960s, the Anglican church held a special campaign in which the laity were urged 'to pray for your priest, pray for more priests'.

The decline in clerics is paralleled by a reduction in church buildings, as indicated in the table below.

Trinitarian church ministers and buildings: by denomination, UK (thousands)

	Ministers			Buildings		
	1970	**1980**	**1987**	**1970**	**1980**	**1987**
Anglican	17.4	14.7	13.8	20.3	19.4	18.7
Presbyterian	4.2	3.7	3.4	6.6	6.1	5.7
Methodist	4.5	3.9	3.7	10.0	8.6	7.8
Baptist	2.5	2.4	2.4	3.7	3.3	3.4
Other Protestant churches[1]	6.6	8.5	9.8	7.8	8.5	9.5
Roman Catholic	8.1	7.6	6.2	5.1	4.1	4.4
Total Trinitarian	43.2	40.9	39.3	53.5	50.0	49.6

1 Includes orthodox churches

(*Social Trends 20*: 165, using data from UK Christian Handbook 1989/90, MARC Europe)

Decline in religious and civil ceremonies

Calling upon churches to celebrate important social events is more popular than joining or attending a church. But, notes Bruce (1996), even here there are signs of decline. Take baptism, for example. In 1900, 65 per cent of live babies were baptised in the Anglican Church. In 1927, the figure was 71 per cent; in 1960, 55 per cent; in 1970, 47 per cent; and in 1993, 27 per cent. Church weddings are still popular, but less so than in the past. At the beginning of the twentieth century, almost 70 per cent of English couples married in the state church. This fell to 53 per cent by 1990. In early Victorian Scotland, nearly all weddings were religious ceremonies. For example, in 1876, 98.9 per cent of weddings were solemnised in church. In 1990, the figure was 57 per cent.

In Britain, of the 365,000 weddings in 1990, there were a fifth fewer than in 1970, and two-thirds of these couples were marrying for the first time. Marriages where one or both partners had previously been married were far more likely to be solemnised with a civil ceremony than those where both partners were marrying for the first time. However, the trend in society is for slightly fewer people to get married, with some preferring to live together and have children without first getting married.

The table below provides some statistics on religious and civil marriage ceremonies.

QUESTION

What is the broad sociological picture conveyed in the table below?

As far as baptisms and confirmations are concerned, it's difficult to obtain very up-to-date figures because statistics are no longer collected centrally by churches. Moreover, many children who are baptised when young don't necessarily attend church as they grow older. Confirmation statistics arguably give a more reliable reading of religious commitment because they're normally carried out when a person is older and able to make a more considered judgement. The figures here indicate a fall in commitment – most dramatically in the Church of England, but also in the Catholic Church.

Decline in religious belief

The annual British Social Attitudes Survey in 1991 reported a discernible decline in belief in a personal God over a period of 40 years (1947; 1957; 1987), as indicated in the table below.

What is God? Britain, 1947, 1957 and 1987

	1947	1957	1987
'There is a personal God'	45%	41%	37%
'There is some sort of spirit or vital force which controls life'	39%	37%	42%
'I am not sure that there is any sort of God or life force'	16%	–	–
'I don't know what to think'	–	16%	–
'Don't really think there is any sort of spirit/god or life force'	–	6%	–
Other/neither/don't know	–	–	21%

(Bruce 1995b, in Haralambos 1995: 4)

Marriages: religious and civil ceremonies, 1971 and 1990, Great Britain (thousands and percentages)

	1971	1990		
	All marriages	First marriages[1]	Second or subsequent marriages[2]	All marriages
Manner of solemnisation				
Religious ceremony:				
Church of England/Church in Wales	160	107	3	116
Church of Scotland	20	10	3	13
Roman Catholic	48	24	1	26
Other Christian	37	17	7	37
Jews and other non-Christian	2	1	–	1
Civil ceremonies	180	72	53	171
Total marriages	447	231	66	365
Civil marriages as a percentage of all marriages				
England and Wales	41	31	82	47
Scotland	31	30	68	43
Great Britain	40	31	79	47

1 First marriage for both partners
2 Remarriage for both partners

(*Social Trends 23*: 154, using figures from Office of Population Censuses and Surveys; General Register Office, Scotland)

Notwithstanding this decline, the table on belief actually reveals an increasing tendency over the 1947–87 period to believe in some kind of spirit or vital force which controls life.

Reduced coverage of religion on British television

Until 1993, BBC1 and ITV transmitted religious programmes on early Sunday evening simultaneously: *Songs of Praise* on BBC1, and *Stars on Sunday* and *Highway* on ITV. Sixty per cent of the television audience watched these programmes (approximately 14 million people), although there was little else and it was a prime time slot. The television companies found that the viewers were mainly church-goers (particularly older people and women), who didn't continue watching television for the rest of the evening.

In 1993, legislation removed the 'religious slot' requirement, although broadcasters were still required to feature religion. Nevertheless, religious programmes have been reduced significantly. This change in the nature of traditional religious broadcasting and the decline in the popularity of religious programmes are further evidence of secularisation.

It remains to be seen whether the new satellite televangelism programmes will take off in relation to British viewing rates.

Criticisms of the secularisation thesis

According to Bruce (1996), the secularisation thesis is accepted by most social scientists. As an all-encompassing theory, however, it's contested by some very respected sociologists, among them Martin (1981, in Wilson 1981) and Stark and Bainbridge (1985). Martin concedes that mainstream churches have a declining social influence, but notes too that new religious movements attract new members. Stark and Bainbridge contend that religion is here to stay because people need the solace of supernatural support.

These are just two of the rebuttal arguments against the secularisation thesis – in its *religion in general is in decline* form – which are considered below. We begin by taking another look at the statistics. If the secularisation theorists have misinterpreted these, their case is suspect.

Re-evaluating the statistics on religion

Despite the overall decrease in church membership, most people still believe in a deity. For a substantial minority, belief in God is unequivocal. When asked in the 1995 British Social Attitudes Survey, more than one in five people said they believed in God, with no doubts, as indicated in the table above.

Belief in God[1], 1995, Great Britain (percentages)

	1995
Do not believe in God	11
Do not know if God exists and cannot find evidence for God's existence	15
Believe in a higher power of some kind	12
Believe sometimes	12
Doubt, but believe	23
God exists, with no doubts	21
Can't choose/not answered	7

1 Respondents were asked which statement came closest to their belief about God.

(*Social Trends 27*: 224, using figures from British Social Attitudes Survey, and Social and Community Planning Research)

In the same survey, people were asked about their religious affiliation. Although two-fifths said they had none, just under a third said they were Church of England/Anglican, and a quarter reported they were affiliated to other Trinitarian churches. One in nine of those with a religious affiliation said they attended services or meetings associated with their religion at least once a week. But about half said they never, or practically never, attended.

Social Trends 27 concludes that 'Religious activities form an important part of many people's lives' (1997: 224). Noting that the pattern of membership of various religions and denominations in the UK has witnessed contrasting changes over the past quarter of a century (for example, Trinitarian churches have experienced a fall in membership, from 9.1 million adults in 1970 to 6.4 million in 1995), *Social Trends 27* adds that there have been increases in other religions. The Muslim faith, for example, experienced a big increase in membership between 1970 and 1995. The number of clergy is broadly mirrored in changing patterns of membership, with increasing numbers of clerics in non-Trinitarian and other religions and decreasing numbers in Trinitarian churches. However, the decline in Trinitarian clerics hasn't been as rapid as the decline in membership.

The table on page 432 (top) gives a more comprehensive picture of the trends referred to above.

There's an evangelical and non-Christian revival taking place which, in proportional if not absolute terms, challenges the claim of the secularisation thesis. The increasing popularity of NRMs suggests that some people, instead of relinquishing religion altogether, are turning to sects and cults in search of alternative religious experiences. Even within the major churches, we mustn't exaggerate the extent of decline in religious participation. For, as David Martin reminds us, 'The major

Church membership[1] and number of clergy, UK

	Membership (millions)		Clergy (numbers)	
	1970	**1995**	**1970**	**1995**
Trinitarian churches				
Roman Catholic[2]	2.7	2.0	9,239	7,645
Anglican	3.0	1.7	16,915	12,059
Presbyterian	1.8	1.1	4,082	3,015
Methodist	0.7	0.4	4,404	3,901
Baptist	0.3	0.2	2,520	3,030
Other free churches	0.5	0.7	4,718	9,341
Orthodox	0.2	0.3	114	208
All Trinitarian churches	9.1	6.4	41,992	39,199
Non-Trinitarian churches				
Mormons	0.1	0.2	110[3]	400[3]
Jehovah's Witnesses	0.1	0.1	7,050	14,200
Other non-Trinitarian	0.1	0.3	1,482	2,265
All non-Trinitarian churches	0.3	0.6	8,642	16,865
Other religions				
Muslims	0.1	0.6	900	2,900
Sikhs	0.1	0.4	80	200
Hindus	0.1	0.1	80	150
Jews	0.1	0.1	390	450
Others	0.0	0.1	289	1,792
All other religions	0.4	1.3	1,739	5,492

1 Adult active members
2 Mass attendance
3 Bishops

(*Social Trends 27*: 224, using figures from Christian Research)

churches still command the allegiance of millions in every Western country' (1981, in Wilson 1981: 43).

People do have the capacity for believing in things that aren't 'rational' or based on scientific proof or fact. The table below makes the point.

In rounding off this section, it's appropriate to heed the conclusion of the American sociologist, Andrew Greeley, who says that 'the British are more religious than they think they are' (1992: 69). Greeley adds that Stark, who commented on an earlier draft of Greeley's work, says they might even be more religious than they used to be.

Superstitions, Britain, 1991 (percentages)

Propositions	**'Definitely' and 'Probably' true**	**'Probably' and 'Definitely' false**	**'I can't choose' and 'No answer'**
Good luck charms sometimes do bring good luck	22	72	6
Some fortune-tellers really can foresee the future	40	53	8
Some faith-healers really do have God-given healing powers	45	45	10
A person's star sign at birth, or horoscope, can affect the course of their future	28	64	9

(Bruce 1995a: 54, using figures from the British Social Attitudes Survey 1991)

Reorientation rather than demise

Martin (1981, in Wilson 1981a) says that disorientations to mainstream religion are sometimes accompanied by reorientations to NRMs. He highlights the intensity and certainty that attract a proportion of the religiously committed public to new religions. The proportion is tiny, but the quality of commitment is impressive. Moreover, the revival of old religious beliefs and their recasting in line with late twentieth-century culture cast serious doubt on the notion that secularisation is inevitable. We have in mind here what Grace Davie calls 'the appearance on a large scale and across several continents of the type of religiosity normally associated with the word fundamentalist' (1995: 2). Fundamentalist beliefs are fervent and often public.

> **OVER TO YOU**
>
> ***With the help of your teacher, explore and define the essential features of fundamentalist religious beliefs. Illustrate your findings with some examples of fundamentalist creeds.***

In relation to more private forms of religious expression, Parsons (1960, cited by Beckford 1989) thinks these are an appropriate response to industrial society. But this doesn't mean, says Parsons, that religion has become secularised. Indeed, Martin goes so far as to propose that, '"real" secularization is not susceptible to measurement' (1969, in Worsley 1976: 545).

Some aspects of religiosity are certainly difficult to quantify. Figures on church attendance, for example, don't tell sociologists if the non-attenders are religious or not. Non-attenders who are religious might practise their religiosity in private and/or in non-institutional forms. Whilst quantitative investigation makes it possible to gauge the *extent* of religious belief, qualitative methods are arguably better research tools for teasing out issues surrounding the *nature* of religious belief.

The Archbishop of Canterbury's Commission on Urban Priority Areas – *Inner City God* (Ahern and Davie 1987) – found that a relatively large number of Britons who say that they believe in God are reluctant to express this in the form of church practice. However, the authors of the report observe that this finding begs other questions. What do different people think about God? Do they think about God at all? What do they envisage as 'the church'? Does hostility to the church imply hostility to the idea of God?

Most Britons still like the idea of religion. However, whether they believe in it seems largely a matter of preference, of idiosyncrasy. Sociologists can't therefore infer, on the basis of a decline in church membership, that people have given up on religion. Perhaps religious faith has moved into an area that statisticians find hard to reach – people's hearts.

> **OVER TO YOU**
>
> ***How might religiosity be expressed in private and/or in non-institutional forms?***

Looking beyond the British experience

Stark and Bainbridge (1985) argue that American society is conducive to religion. In response to unmet demands for supernatural compensators, they cite the vigour of evangelical Protestantism and the growth of the Catholic charismatic movement. They argue that many elements of the Christian–Judaic tradition have been disconfirmed by science, but note that new faiths don't carry this legacy. Mormonism, for example, appeared in the nineteenth century, and was compatible with scientific knowledge of that time.

Against the prevailing 'wisdom' of the conventional secularisation thesis, Stark and Bainbridge (1985) contend that the strength of religious commitment in faiths like Mormonism and the Unification Church (Moonies) is strong. Wilson (1975, cited by Stark and Bainbridge 1985) has elsewhere argued that the prevalence of new religions is part and parcel of secularisation. The modern world has produced, says Wilson, a supermarket of faiths, of relatively unimportant consumer items, which co-exist because society is so secular. Not so, retort Stark and Bainbridge:

> 'Simply to equate cults with religious trivia and to make them a symptom of secularization is to miss the opportunity to investigate the link between secularization and religious innovation. Surely it is to deprive the concept of secularization of coherent meaning if we describe persons deeply engrossed in supernatural belief and worship as secularized.'
>
> (Stark and Bainbridge 1985: 437)

Rather than seeing cults as the last whimper of religious belief, Stark and Bainbridge see them as a religious reaction to the secularisation of traditional religion. In this sense, they support the 'reorientation rather than demise' thesis referred to above. They conclude that:

> 'In the future, as in the past, religion will be shaped by secular forces but not destroyed. There will always be a need for gods and for the general compensators which only they can plausibly offer.'
>
> (Stark and Bainbridge 1985: 527–8)

Even the argument that traditional forms of religious allegiance are in decline sometimes overstates its case.

For, as Neil J. Smelser (1997) reveals, religion exercises a profound and a continuing influence in such places as Northern Ireland, Lebanon, Syria, the former Yugloslavia and other Balkan regions. In part, this is explained by the religious distinctiveness which is attached to cultural identity. The strength of the Catholic Church in Ireland, for example, owes a great deal to its historical role in promoting Irish identity.

There are also possibilities for the re-kindling of religion. In the former Soviet Union, for example, as Bainbridge (1997) points out, the liberation of Muslim portions is of crucial importance. No longer under the sway of an official atheistic regime, who knows what religious momentum might gather here? In the Arab world, the resurgence of Islamic fundamentalism has very obvious de-secularising tendencies. Indeed, it represents a reversal of disenchantment of the sacred. Like other forms of fundamentalist revival, it distils essential teachings of traditional religion and applies them in a twentieth-century context.

Closer to home, in Ulster, Protestantism forges a close sense of affinity with the UK. Everyday life is often dominated by the religious/ethnic divide between Protestants and Catholics. Attitude surveys show that people in Northern Ireland are most likely to hold religious views, and not break away from one of the two broad religious camps. Bruce suggests that in Northern Ireland 'each side sees doing God's will as being much the same as "representing my people"' (1995a: 64).

Cautioning against the over-generalising tendency of the secularisation thesis, Peter Beyer (1994) argues that modernisation and globalisation have had ambiguous rather than simply negative consequences for religion. Beyer identifies what he calls 'performance-oriented religio-social movements' (1994: 97). As the term implies, these movements fuse religion in an activist way with social concerns. Illustrative of this, the New Christian Right in the US seeks to recover public influence for religion in moral, political and educational affairs.

Bocock suggests that, by being involved in discourses, 'Religion is seen by most people as being especially relevant to the family, sexual behaviour and gender issues' (1993: 231). Christianity is importantly involved in the legitimation of social behaviour which contains notions of love, reconciliation, justice, equality, peace and joy.

The kinds of discourse referred to above seek a reaffirmation of traditional values. Religion can also power radical social causes. For example, black civil rights leaders emphasised practical Christian action in their struggle for equal rights in 1960s America.

Even if the relative secularisation of the UK is occurring, looking beyond our own shores forces us to consider whether the British (and Northern European) experience is exceptional rather than global.

The myth of a golden age

The conventional secularisation thesis is based on the argument that traditional worlds were religious places and modern/postmodern ones are not. But there's evidence of irreverence in the past. Bruce (1996) cites court records reporting peasants playing cards and firing off shotguns in church, for not attending church, and for taking part in pagan rituals. He qualifies these observations though by implying that church courts mightn't offer the most reliable evidence, and by pointing out that the records often complained about the wrong religion rather than irreligion. So although he yields a bit of ground to the 'myth of the golden age' argument, Bruce thinks it offers an unconvincing rebuttal of the secularisation thesis. Even among 'ungodly' medieval people, a fundamental supernaturalism was much more widespread than it is now.

Greeley also refers to the myth of the golden age. He says that it's 'usually assumed rather than proven, and the most recent historical research casts doubt on the assumption' (1992: 52). Greeley reports Butler's (1990) conclusion that Nonconformist religion declined rapidly after the end of the Cromwellian era from a high of no more than 5 per cent in 1670 to less than 2 per cent of the population in 1700. Says Greeley: 'The real religion of Britain at the time (and of the USA too) was, it may be argued, magic' (1992: 53). According to Greeley, high levels of religious observance in Europe are linked to rather recent developments.

As for bygone America, R. Finke and R. Stark paint a very irreligious picture of the 'Wild West':

> 'Everyone knows that the Wild West of the nineteenth century, towns such as Dodge City, Tombstone, and Deadwood were not filled with God-fearing, Sunday-go-to-meeting folks, but were wide open, lawless capitals of vice and violence. Why should it have been any different when the frontier boom towns were New York or Charleston?'
>
> (Fink and Stark 1992, cited by Carroll 1996: 235–6)

The image sounds a bit fanciful, shaped, no doubt to some extent, by Hollywood stereotypes. However, if nineteenth-century America was as secular and deviant as Finke and Stark imply, its present-day culture seems unlikely to be more irreligious.

Crystal-ball gazing

Crystal-ball gazing isn't good social science. If secularisation is occurring, it hasn't run its course, and sociologists can't scientifically predict final outcomes. There's a danger that historical trends are being extrapolated into 'done and dusted' conclusions about the future. Yet, as Anson Shupe and David G. Bromley (1985, in Hammond 1985) argue, perhaps the relatively linear pattern of secularisation will continue or perhaps a longer-term cyclical development will occur. Linear trends continue existing patterns; cyclical ones re-visit earlier epochs. Sociology is on safer ground when it sticks to the past, the present and the immediate future.

We shouldn't, however, forget that some opponents of the secularisation thesis also make untestable predictions. Stark, for example, states that 'although individual religions are constantly born, change, and die, religion in general is eternal' (1997: 404). How can he know this?

The limits of science

In the postmodern world, people are becoming disenchanted with science. Some scientists exhibit an anti-religious bias, arguing that their insights are more reliable than priestly ones. Yet, says Robert Wuthnow, 'Science is in fact a socially constructed reality and seemingly irrefutable scientific facts are really reflections of social experiences' (1985: 194).

Science is helpful, but so too is religion. When a loved one has a disease that the best science can't cure, some people turn to prayer. Religion provides personal and emotional support which science can't offer.

There's also a gendered dimension to the privileging of the rational above the emotional. Men are expected to be hard-nosed and logical, and women are assumed to be soft-hearted and intuitive. These stereotypes reinforce patriarchy.

CRIT THINK CRIT THINK CRIT THINK CRIT THINK CRIT THINK CRIT THINK

THE TWILIGHT OF THE GODS?

These are the arguments sociologists are having to consider, each expressed by an eminent professor of sociology, each with different views.

Steve Bruce, who supports the secularisation thesis, concludes that:

'Belief in the supernatural has not disappeared. Rather the forms in which it is expressed have become so idiosyncratic and so diffuse that there are few specific social consequences. Instead of religiosity expressing itself in new sects with enthusiastic believers, it is expressed through piecemeal and consumerist involvement in elements of a cultic world. To pursue Weber's music metaphor, the orchestras and mass bands with their thunderous symphonies have gone. Handfuls of us will be enthusiastic music-makers but, because we no longer follow one score, we cannot produce the melodies to rouse the masses.'

(Bruce 1996: 234)

William Sims Bainbridge, who contests the secularisation thesis, believes that:

'Religion is a prime component of the system of human life, that moves across all time and links the ancient past with the unimaginable future. Religion will undergo schism, innovation, and transformation, sending echoes throughout human society, unto the end of time. In describing his own impending death, whether in the Glastonbury zodiac or elsewhere, King Arthur gave us words to understand the constant renewal of faith through religious movements: "The old order changeth, yielding place to new; and God fulfils himself in many ways".'

(Bainbridge 1997: 422)

This exercise can be done as a class debate, with one group arguing the case for the 'prosecution' (i.e. for the secularisation thesis) and the other for the 'defence' (i.e. against the secularisation thesis). Your teacher can act as the jury and decide which group has made the most persuasive case.

If you cannot hold a debate, you can present it as a piece of written work, weighing up both sides of the argument, and coming to a considered conclusion.

1 *Read the two extracts carefully. Then put each one into more simple language.*

2 *Collect as much evidence as you can to support and rebut each argument. Anecdotal evidence is admissible, provided its limitations are honestly admitted.*

3 *Prepare, and if possible make, a presentation arguing the case for the 'prosecution' and/or the 'defence'. Provide evidence for your argument and use sociological language. Remember, this is not an argument about whether God exists or not. It's an evaluation of the arguments for and against the view that religion – in the all-encompassing sense of the secularisation thesis – is less important nowadays than in the past.*

CRIT THINK CRIT THINK CRIT THINK CRIT THINK CRIT THINK CRIT

Having looked at the secularisation thesis, considered its evidence and claims, and those of its critics, where do we stand? The honest answer is that the jury is still out. The Crit Think invites you to join the 'prosecution' and 'defence' teams, to weigh up the evidence and arguments, and to come to a considered and convincing conclusion.

QUESTIONS

1. What do sociologists mean when they talk of secularisation?
2. What is the relationship between rationality, science and secularisation?
3. What are the sociological arguments which support the secularisation thesis?
4. Which sociological arguments challenge and/or modify the secularisation thesis?

Religion in a changing society

Proponents and opponents of the secularisation thesis are generally agreed that, as societies become more industrial and post-industrial, religion holds less of a monopoly sway over culture. Where they differ is in their interpretation of what happens next. Secularisation theorists anticipate the eclipse of the sacred canopy. Opponents note the advent of a pluralistic religious 'marketplace'. There are lots of religions to choose from these days. Whether this diversity spells the twilight of the gods or a new vital re-enactment remains to be seen.

As we approach the twenty-first century, the major religions are still Buddhism, Christianity, Hinduism, Islam, Sikhism and Judaism. They're not as unified as they once were, but their devotees are still religious. Modernisation, argues Bruce (1996), has made church religion untenable. The 'universal church' has split into denominational churches. Denominations undermined the privileging of universal truth and created a climate for further schism. Sects moved into the social space thus created and developed religious subcultures. Some of these prospered, and still do (for example, Christian fundamentalist sects in America). Others created such a wide gulf between their views and mainstream culture that they attracted few converts. Their survival, says Bruce, is dependent on socialising their own children into the faith. Cults, the fourth main type of religious organisation, don't usually have a history of prior attachment to a 'parent religion'.

Cults are growing. Although, like sects, they're 'deviant' religious bodies, unlike sects they look forward rather than backwards. Sects, note Stark and Bainbridge (1985), claim to be authentic, purged and refurbished versions of the faiths from which they split. Cults, by contrast, add new revelations, and claim to be different. In some quarters, the term 'cult' has negative connotations, so sociologists often prefer the term *new religious movement* (NRM). But this term can be confusing because certain cults are old and certain sects are new. Stark has elsewhere suggested to Bainbridge that *new* religious movements should refer to *novel* religious movements.

Eileen Barker is an expert on the sociology of NRMs. She (1985, in Hammond 1985) notes that the majority appeared after the Second World War. Had they appeared earlier, says Barker, most would have been called cults or sects. New though these religious groups are, the basic ingredients have existed before. It's the way the ingredients are selected, and the rhetoric in which they're packaged, says Barker, that provide the novelty. Bainbridge (1997) similarly argues that the most successful NRMs tend to retain some of the basic concepts, symbols and practices of the religious tradition that's already popular, adding extensions or modifications of their own. This isn't a uniquely modern phenomenon. Christianity drew upon Jewish beliefs, and Islam drew upon them both.

More recently, says Bainbridge, all four of the really successful novel American NRMs – Seventh-day Adventism, Jehovah's Witnesses, the Church of Jesus Christ of Latter-Day Saints (Mormons) and Christian Science – remain Christian. Among the Hindu-based new religions, reveals Barker (1985, in Hammond 1985), are the Hare Krishna, Divine Light Mission Brahma Kumaris and the disciples of Bhagwan Rajneesh. In the Bhuddist tradition are various Zen groups and many movements from Japan. In addition to the Christian-based movements, identified by Bainbridge above, are the Family of Love and the Way International (both offshoots of the Jesus Movement).

Barker notes that a helpful way of classifying NRMs is according to the commitment they obtain. At one extreme is the demand for complete involvement and obedience, with members living in what sociologists call 'total institutions' – isolated communities cut off from the mainstream. The People's Temple (see below) fits this category. At the other end of the continuum are members who have just attended a weekend 'spiritual therapy' course, and left it at that. Somewhere between the two extremes are NRMs which are generally happy with what the world has to offer, and who embody a 'can do' optimism. Scientology and Transcendental Meditation exemplify this position.

The media tend to focus on the extreme cults. In new religions of these types, life-long commitment is expected. This can have tragic consequences. An extreme (and a violent) cult was the People's Temple, founded in 1956 by Jim Jones in Indianapolis, USA. Attracted by the marxist regime in Guyana, he sent followers there in 1974 to set up a utopian community. On 18 November 1978, members of the People's Temple murdered American congressman, Leo Ryan, who had been sent to Guyana to investigate the commune. There then followed the murder-suicide of 914 members, including 276 children, as well as Jones himself.

Although other violent episodes involving cults come to mind (for example, the 1993 Branch Davidian shoot-out at Waco, Texas), the vast majority of NRMs don't experience unusual violence. Even so, as Bainbridge (1997) points out, many Americans take the Waco catastrophe as further 'proof' that novel religions are dangerous and should be controlled or eradicated. Seventy-six bodies were found in the burnt-out ashes of the Branch Davidian cult compound after a strike force assault by agents of the Bureau of Alcohol, Tobacco and Firearms. Yet opinion polls reveal that Americans overwhelmingly supported the federal agents who besieged the Waco compound.

Their antipathy towards cults was further aggravated when, in 1997, 38 members of a UFO cult in San Diego, California, committed suicide with their leader, Marshall Herff Applewhite. This cult's mission was to meet up with a spaceship believed to be travelling behind comet Hale-Bopp. The cult members died in three squads. According to recipes near their bodies, they took alcohol and phenobarbitol with apple sauce, and were then suffocated with plastic bags. Despite evidence of forced killings in other mass suicides, officials insist this wasn't the case here.

Sociologists don't know how many NRMs there are in the world. Barker (1985, in Hammond 1985) thinks 3,000 is probably a conservative estimate in the 'west' (including Australia and New Zealand). It's more difficult to estimate the number of new religions in Africa and Asia. Membership of NRMs generally appear to be very small. There's also a higher turnover rate than media reports suggest.

Tabloid reporting of cults sometimes give the impression that they 'brainwash' their initiates. But Barker (1991) discloses that substantial research on the joining and leaving of NRMs has repeatedly shown that most people are very capable of rejecting the movements' overtures.

EXAM TIP

Avoid treating tabloid and other sensationalist claims as reliable social scientific evidence. When you make assertions, back them up with appropriate sociological findings.

Roy Wallis (1983) distinguishes between three types of NRM:

- *world-accommodating NRMs* (for example, Neo-Pentecostalism, and 'western' versions of Nichiren Shoshu Buddhism), who are reasonably happy with or indifferent to the world as it is
- *world-affirming NRMs* (for example, Human Potential Movement), who seek to help members to cope with the world and its values
- *world-rejecting NRMs* (for example, Unification Church), who expect the millennium to start soon, or the advent, guided by members, of a new, utopian world order.

The last category of cult is the one that normally grabs the headlines. But Wallis (1981, in Wilson 1981a) notes that world-rejecting cults can and do change, referring in this context to the Children of God (also called, like many other NRMs, The Family). Among the important changes in the group, says Wallis, is 'The rapprochement of substantial sectors of the movement with a society and social institutions formerly regarded with intense hostility' (1981, in Wilson 1981a: 97). Wallis tracked the development of this cult from its origins until the late 1970s.

The Children of God, reports Wallis, grew out of the Jesus People, an umbrella label describing a number of groups that emerged in the late 1960s on the US west coast. These groups offered an evangelical ministry to the young, and criticised traditional authority. Among the first was a small band consisting of two itinerant preachers, David and Jane Berg, some of their four married children and partners, and young people who travelled with them. Aware of the growing population of 'drop-out' youth living in the beach towns of Southern California, David Berg and his team went to Huntington Beach, witnessing to the lonely and the lost.

Berg's Teens for Christ, as they became known, acquired premises where they offered coffee, food and sympathy. They attracted a steady following, which gathered momentum after Berg attacked the American *status quo*, calling it the Whore of Babylon. He drew a sharp distinction between God and the world, between following God and the devil. Believing that the Lord will provide, Berg and his followers rejected conventional work and education. They considered themselves as a Revolution for Jesus against an ungodly, material world, expecting and at times welcoming persecution for their stand.

Eventually, Teens for Christ left Huntington Beach, splitting into groups which witnessed and demonstrated across America, warning of the coming of the Antichrist and of the return of Jesus Christ. Early in 1970, the cult settled on the Texas Soul Clinic Ranch. They had by this time adopted the name Children of God, and at the Ranch led a life according to their beliefs. Berg, now called Moses (or Mo), believed God's covenant with the Jews was still valid, and that the Jews would be converted before Christ's return. Mo headed off to Israel in late 1970, but found the country hostile to Christian missionary endeavour. Thenceforth, Mo would view his movement as 'gypsies', rather than a contemporary version of Old Testament Jews. The Children of God were now to follow what was seen as the habits of the early church and of the 'gypsies', scattering in small, decentralised colonies.

Early in 1972, Mo began to adopt a more conciliatory attitude to outsiders. In the wake of mounting hostility towards religious cults, the support of conventional members of society sympathetic to the Children of God would be advantageous. Mo, who considered himself as God's prophet, wrested control from 'old bottles' who were unable to take the 'new wine'. Mo's supporters moved to a position of greater accommodation with mainstream society – abandoning communalism, taking up jobs and placing their children in denominational or state schools. They even accepted that non-believers could do God's will, if only to a limited extent. Similar changes, notes Wallis (1981, in Wilson 1981a), are apparent in other world-rejecting movements.

Wallis has shown that even a very 'extreme' cult can shift its position over time. The Children of God started life as a vigorously anti-establishment movement, but has gradually begun to move cautiously in the direction of denominalisation. The end of this journey – becoming a denomination, like Methodism, for example – isn't, of course, guaranteed. The Children of God is still sufficiently 'deviant' to be considered a 'cult'.

What does the rise of NRMs imply for the future of religion? Proponents of the secularisation thesis reply, not much. The movements of the 1960s and 1970s, says Bruce (1996), were always small, and most members didn't stay in them long. The last 30 years have been particularly tough for the world-rejecting cults. Some of them have become less hostile towards the outside world, shifting towards a more accommodating position. Others were so against the prevailing world order that they committed mass suicide. Yet others have gone underground. As for the world-affirming movements, they've endured better. But even they have a tendency to come and go.

Coming and going doesn't, however, mean that NRMs are on the wane. Bainbridge (1997), whilst conceding that few NRMs will solidify into substantial denominations of the future, sees them as a formidable religious counter-culture. Provided they retain a 'medium tension' with the rest of society (i.e. by being moderate rather than extreme), they're off to a good start. They can be deviant, but not too deviant! The extreme cults tend to have a bumpier ride. If they can't handle stigmatisation and social exclusion, they tend to go to the wall.

Bainbridge (1997) contemplates the development of two trends in relation to new (or as he prefers to call them, novel) religious movements:

- The emergence of lots of small innovative movements, accompanied by increased toleration for alternative supernatural beliefs might lead to the re-paganisation of society. This doesn't imply the end of conventional churches, but rather the eruption of thousands of freshly created religions, each one with very little impact and limited membership Walk through Glastonbury in England or Rosicrucian Park in San Jose, California, and you'll get the picture, says Bainbridge.
- Novel religious movements might develop into major denominations, which, in turn, through schism and further innovation, will create new religious traditions comparable in strength and variety to today's great world religions. This would be a more challenging route than the former one of diffuse paganism. Referring to the former Soviet Union, Bainbridge notes that such a society is fertile ground for the development of NRMs. Some new religions being born right now in St Petersberg or Kiev may be exportable, he says, spreading throughout the world.

Bainbridge's anticipated futures brings us back once more to the secularisation debate. Has religion ceased to be an important part of the social fabric? Or have certain religions gone into retreat to be replaced by new movements? There are no straightforward answers to these questions. That said, the development and vitality of NRMs suggest that even if secularisation occurs in some parts of society, a countervailing religious consciousness flourishes elsewhere.

QUESTIONS

1. What are the key characteristics of NRMs that are: world-accommodating; world-affirming; world-rejecting?
2. How did the world-rejecting cult, the Children of God, become less world-rejecting over time?

Religion and social position

'Religious affiliation', says Tischler, 'seems to be correlated with many other important aspects of people's lives' (1996: 417). In that context, Tischler notes that direct relationships exist between people's religion and their politics, professional and economic standing, educational achievement, family life, social mobility and attitudes towards controversial social issues. Tischler illustrates this point in relation to ethnicity, so we'll start with that example of social position. Thereafter, we'll consider other links between religion and social position in terms of social class, age and gender.

Ethnicity

In the US, reports Tischler, Jews (both a religious group and, in relation to their cultural roots, a minority ethnic group), who represented only 2.5 per cent of the total population in the 1990 American census:

- are proportionately the best educated religious group
- have higher incomes than Christians in general

- are proportionately more likely to be in business and the professions.

Tischler adds, however, that despite their higher socio–economic and educational position, Jews – like Catholics – occupy relatively few of the top positions in the corporate world and in politics. These positions are typically filled by white Anglo–Saxon Protestants: so-called WASPS. Whilst mass scale immigration has turned the US into a religiously plural society, WASPS are still inclined to be rather cliquish. Indeed, according to Bruce (1996), immigration has had the effect of making the WASP community more aware of their 'Anglo–Saxon' origins. There's a 'class defence' posture here: a settled and privileged elite defending its Protestant heritage against Catholics, Jews and other 'social subordinates'.

For the immigrant, religion also has had a role to play. Migration is a socially unsettling experience. People leave their homes, but they don't forget their roots. This is why, in the US, the building of ethnic churches performs a crucial function in easing the transition from an old to a new home. Some immigrants (for example, Finns, Norwegians and Swedes), whilst all predominantly Lutheran, built their own churches. Migrants from Catholic countries (for example, Italy, Ireland and Poland) often attended ethnic parishes, even though most belonged to the same Mother Church. One often hears Catholic Americans describing themselves as Italian–American, Irish–American, and so forth.

Among African–Americans, many of whom lived in America long before nineteenth-century European emigrants moved there, religion has remained a potent source of ethnic identity. One of the most notable black preachers was Dr Martin Luther King. At Morehouse College in Atlanta, King studied sociology with Walter Chivers, who had done research on lynchings. Chivers taught him that racist injustice was inseparable from economic injustice, a lesson that King was never to forget. King embraced the teachings of the Social Gospel Movement, which taught it wasn't enough just to seek one's own salvation through prayer and worship.

In addition, the Christian had a duty to perform good works, to make self-sacrifice, and to struggle for social justice. King practised this belief by becoming a spokesperson and a martyr for all the poor – black and white. Interestingly, his doctrine combines elements of the Protestant notion of salvation obtained through faith in Christ and the Catholic belief that the just go to Heaven because they show kindness to the poor. One sees in the brand of Christianity practised by King and his followers a close affinity with liberation theology (see page 441). Indeed, it would be accurate to call King's efforts to forge a strong link between Christian belief and human rights activism as a form of liberation theology. Rather than being run by and for the rich and powerful, King saw the mission of the Church to become the 'church of the poor' and in their service.

The fusion of black African and Christian traditions has an important history in another 'New World' nation: Jamaica (Jamaicans were originally from Africa). The black scholar, Stuart Hall (Professor of Sociology at the Open University), charts the encounter between the two cultures in the nineteenth century (Hall 1985). Christian missions to the slaves met a Jamaican folk religion which included magical beliefs and behaviours. When Christianity arrived, it was assimilated into folk beliefs to form an Afro-Christianity which rethought the missionaries' religion in African terms.

Common features, reports Hall, were the use of ecstatic trances, night gatherings, processions led by a 'captain' accompanied by muffled drums, and Christian baptism in 'African' sacred waters. Even to the present day, this intermingling of Christian (typically, Protestant) and 'folk' traditions endures in Jamaica. In the more extreme mix, Protestant hymns and prayers co-exist with animal sacrifice and incantations to the dead.

The official Christian religion of the white slave owners was Anglican. But Anglican clergy didn't generally adopt a missionary role. That was largely left to dissenting sects, like the Baptists, who made wide use of black preachers. Black Baptism, reveals Hall, was commonly reviled by the white slave owners for allegedly fermenting slave revolt. The external form of black Baptism may have been European. However, the inner core was 'native', if not positively 'African', says Hall.

Afro-Christianity gave key biblical events high prominence. Thus, for example, the story of the Israelites, God's chosen people, being driven into servitude in Egypt and their subsequent liberation by Moses stirred the 'African' heart. Black people in Jamaica and the Americas spoke and sang fervently about Moses and the Promised Land. The notion of just struggle against the 'black wo(man's) burden' was powerfully articulated in the 1920s, when a diverse set of black Christian 'sect-churches' were founded, many of them Pentecostalist in orientation. These revivalist sects were, to some extent, part of a political movement whose aim was to return the children of slaves 'Back to Africa'.

This aim features in another black religion, the Rastafarian Movement. In 1914, the Jamaican evangelical preacher, Marcus Garvey, moved to the US, where, reports Hall, he preached a heady mixture of black nationalism and evangelical revivalism. It's interesting that in America, where Christian evangelicism tends to be associated with conservative politics, that black evangelists are strong supporters of the liberal social justice agenda (Olson and Carroll 1992).

Black people, said Garvey, were born free but were everywhere chained, having been forcibly abducted into bondage. They must return to the freedom of their homeland: Africa. Look to Africa, where a black king shall be crowned, counselled Garvey. Although Garvey's efforts failed, his mission to send his black brothers back to the Bible led to the foundation of the Ras Tafari brethren, whose teachings were based on the Book of Revelations. This part of the Bible refers to the Lion of Judah who loosed the seven spirits of God.

The Ras Tafari brethren found the 'Lion' in Emperor Haile Selassie I of Ethiopia, whom they at once pronounced as the reincarnation of Jesus, the Living God, King of Kings, Black Messiah, Redeemer: Jah. His mission was to deliver black men from Babylon. These days, Rastafarianism, although still male-oriented and male-dominated, contains followers who want to improve the way in which women are regarded and treated.

At the heart of Rastafarianism are two key themes:

- a strong identification with Africa, coupled with the belief that the Rastas are the lost ancient tribe of Israel, enslaved by Babylon. Babylon refers to the oppression of the chosen people. Oppressors vary from, for example, the 'brown' middle classes in Jamaica to the white rulers of America and the UK. Rastas believe that redemption from slavery and a return to the 'Promised Land' are one and the same. They employ a starkly polarised view of the cosmos: black/white; good/bad; Zion/Babylon, which helps them to make sense of the story of black oppression
- a belief in the divinity of Haile Selassie. Though Rastas invoke 'Jah' (an early form of Jehovah), he's not always literally identified with Haile Selassie. Some Rastas believe that Haile Selassie is still alive, but interpretations do differ here.

On the other side of the Atlantic, Rastafarianism first made an appearance in the UK in the late 1950s, becoming particularly visible in the late 1970s and early 1980s, reports Barker (1991), among black inner-city youths. Its growth was stimulated by the experiences of 'Babylon' through unemployment and low wages, and also by the popularity of reggae music. The songs of Bob Marley carried the Rasta message worldwide. The Rasta 'look' is distinctive. Coils of uncut hair (dreadlocks) are sometimes covered by tams knitted in the Rastafarian colours of red (representing the blood of Jamaican martyrs), black (the colour of African skin), green (depicting vegetation and victory over oppressive Babylon), and the gold of the Jamaican flag.

Although usually pacifist in outlook, some disaffected Rastas have occasionally resorted to violence. Says Barker (1991), this, coupled with a reputation for smoking 'ganga', the 'wild' appearance of dreadlocks, and the suspicion that Rastas were at least partly responsible for the Brixton riots in 1981, have contributed to them being represented as 'folk devils' in the media. On the other hand, the Catholic Commission for Racial Justice has proposed that Rastafarianism be recognised as a valid religion.

Of course, Rastafarianism isn't the only or the main religion of black Britons, even though it has high visibility. Bruce (1996) cites Peter Brierley's estimate that the African–Caribbean population of England is about 600,000. Of these, 17 per cent (one in six) attended a Christian church in October 1989 (the date of Brierley's census), which is a lot higher than the English norm of under 10 per cent.

Religion, whether among black Pentecostalists, orthodox Jews, Shi'a Muslims, Hindus or Sikhs, is a powerful carrier of ethnic identity. Moreover, for many minority ethnic groups, religion and struggle are inextricably tied. This reminds us yet again to be wary of the argument put forward by some marxists that religion keeps social change at bay. Oppressed people who see in religion the road to the Promised Land – however that aspiration might express itself in religious terms – long for and fight for change.

Social class

There's no simple relationship between social class and religion (or lack of religion). The ancient Jews believed that a Messiah would rise to crush tyrannical power. But in present-day America some Jews occupy high office. Bhuddism arose as a salvation doctrine among the privileged. Yet today its adherents come from all classes. Islam was the religion of a knight order of disciplined warriors. These days, its followers are found among the poor and the rich. Jesus told a rich man to give his possesions to the poor. Yet today, Christianity counts presidents, as well as paupers, among its followers.

Despite the above qualifications, there are documented instances of an affinity between class and religion. In the English Civil War, for example, the Established Church of England was a staunch supporter of the Crown and of the landed aristocracy, teaching that the monarch's power came from God alone. Among people of puritan inclinations, merchants and the poor were more prominent. Oliver Cromwell, however, blocked the economic and political aspirations of the 'lower classes', and their voice found expression in sectarian protest against their 'puritan masters'.

Civil War sectarians (for example, Levellers and Ranters) believed that the end of the world was nigh, being hastened by their efforts to bring down the elite – whether Cromwellian or Royalist. They had a strong social conscience, and felt betrayed when the new post-Civil War rulers fell back on comfortable old ways. This kind of dissent was also, to some extent, echoed in nineteenth-century English Methodism, which enlisted working-class support and gave preaching roles to lay people (including women!). Unlike their seventeenth-century sectarian predecessors, however, the Methodists were more concerned with personal salvation than social reform or revolution.

Like all religions of the oppressed, Methodism, contends Bruce (1996), offers comforts to the poor. The idea that 'the last shall be first' is a gospel message with obvious appeal to people who have nothing. It's a creed that also turns poverty into a virtue. Not being able to afford fancy clothes, drink fine wine, gamble on horses and eat rich foods are losses until one adopts a religion that says these excesses are sinful. From a marxist angle, of course, the asceticism of the Methodist are just what the factory owner wants – workers who keep away from liqueur and horses, and who turn in a hard day's work for a low wage!

Methodism began as a sect, breaking away from the Church of England, and later became a denomination, moderating its earlier 'radicalism'. Whilst Methodism and other sects often enjoyed the support of the 'lower classes', it would be too simplistic to imagine that sects only attract a working-class following. As Wilson (1981, in Wilson 1981a) discloses, in their initial stages, sect membership varied from case to case – the relatively poor, urban and industrial working-class of the Pentecostolists; the middle aged, middle-class, 'genteel', mainly female clientele of Christian Science and Vedanta; the lower middle-class, self-employed Plymouth Brethren; the rough sleepers to whom the Salvation Army took its Christian charity, and the small-town converts to Seventh-Day Adventism.

Nor should we assume that churches simply represent the 'Tory Party at prayer'. Today's Church of England regularly criticises governments for their failure to promote social justice. Moreover the Catholic Church repeatedly attacks class inequality. A particularly radical strand of Catholicism – liberation theology – openly encourages the poor and oppressed to challenge their rulers. Joseph H. Fichter, a Catholic priest and eminent sociologist of religion, was an exponent of this religious outlook. Passionately committed to human equality and social justice, Fichter pursued research he thought would promote human rights. He held the simple but profound belief that knowledge of inequality would somehow contribute to fighting it. At various times, Fichter took on the Klan, the New Orleans Police and the Catholic Church hierarchy.

Jeffrey K. Hadden (1996) has documented some of the counter-culture, anti-authority actions taken by Fichter. These include:

- integrating black and white students from Loyola and Xavier colleges in the 1940s
- setting up a Commission on Human Rights in New Orleans in 1949
- exposing brutality within the New Orleans Police Department
- joining feminists in defiance of the 'men only' policy of a bar in the Monteleone Hotel during the annual meeting of the American Sociological Society in New Orleans
- taking a high profile at Unification Church ('Moonie') meetings to express what he interpreted should be the ecumenical spirit of the Second Vatican Council, and to expose what he thought was a wave of bigotry in America.

Further south, in Latin America, another Catholic priest and sociologist, Camilo Torres, was involved in revolutionary activity against the Colombian ruling class in the 1960s. Swapping his priestly cassock for the combat gear of a freedom fighter, he sought to become 'more truly a priest' (1965, in 1973: 9). In 1966, Torres died in action, fighting for the freedom he believed in. Torres advocated a sociology committed to social justice and a Christianity that took up arms against oppression. His view of the Colombian ruling 'caste' was scathing:

'For more than a hundred and fifty years, this economic caste, the few families which own almost all of Colombia's riches, has usurped political power for its own benefit. It has used all the tricks and gimmicks to keep this power and fool the people.'

(Torres 1965, in Torres 1973: 419)

Another liberation theologist, a priest by the name of Salomon Bolo Hidalgo, was so shocked by the living conditions of the poor and by the unwillingness of the ruling class to do something about this, that he joined a clandestine liberation group. Jailed in 1965, Bolo was denounced by the Cardinal of Lima, Peru, for being a traitor or a communist and an advocate of violence, all of which meant he didn't love his 'fellow' human beings. From his prison cell, Bolo, replied to the cardinal in an open letter, part of which is reproduced here:

'If you, Mr Cardinal, loved your neighbour, you would have given your wealth to the poor, because Christ's order is specifically aimed at bishops and cardinals: "If thou wilt be perfect, go, sell what thou hast, and give it to the poor . . ." (Matthew 19:21) . . . Have you forgotten all this, Mr Cardinal, with your luxurious car, palaces, and regal train, with which we could dress the poor? . . . [Y]ou, Mr Cardinal, by your deeds, prefer one hundred superficial and exploiting families who organize balls while the people wail over their dead, who attend races, blessed by you, where the horses receive better care than the children of Peru.'

(1965, in Torres 1973: 21)

The crucial relationship between church and class, when such an association exists at all, is when a church stands for class interests. Even here, the picture is complex. The Church of England is a broad church in more ways than just its theological teachings. Undoubtedly, during the nineteenth century, when some of its parsons supported ruling-class interests, other clerics (probably some of whom 'defected' to Methodism) spoke up for the working class. Similarly, today, you will find exponents of all social classes among the major world religions. Even among the Hindu religion, with its belief in caste, one finds sects and cults that preach a more egalitarian message. Let's not forget that Ghandi was a Hindu.

Turning to the NRMs, Barker (1985, in Hammond 1985) reports that their composition varies. Whilst poor black people did follow Jim Jones (leader of the People's Temple), and Rastafarianism has a strong appeal among the black working class, Barker notes that movements disproportionately recruit from the middle class. Sufism, which keeps re-surfacing on the fringes of American religion, often attracts relatively well-educated recruits, notes Bainbridge (1997).

Age

Looking at the relationship between age and religion, the association is often clearer than that involving class.

Old people and young children are probably the most religious people. Children though tend to grow out of religion, and old people back into it. Older people, reports Davie (1994), are more religious than the young (and here we exclude the very young). This generational difference is reflected in church membership statistics, and is increasingly corroborated by studies of religious belief. *Social Trends 27* (1997) reports that, when compared with the size of the population in Great Britain, people aged under 15 and aged over 45 are over-represented among those who are active in their religion. Those aged between 15 and 44 are under-represented. It's not clear, however, from the way the *Social Trends 27* figures are presented if they apply to *females* or to both *males and females*. Probably, the latter is the case.

An earlier *Social Trends* report (1992) provides a useful chart (below) which indicates the relationship between age and church attendance in England in 1979 and 1989.

Percentage of the population attending church services: by age, 1979 and 1989, England

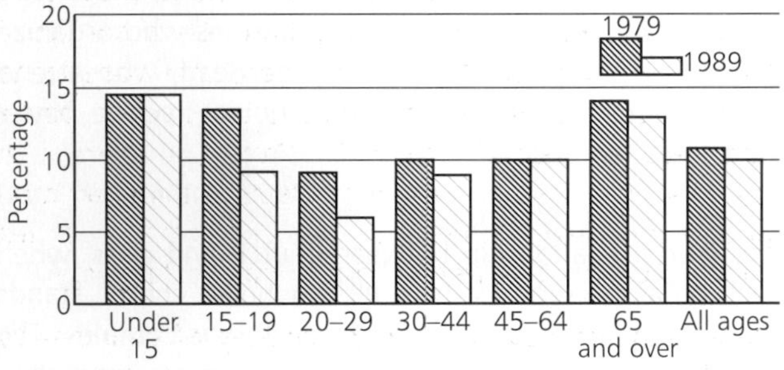

(*Social Trends 22*: 1992, using figures from the English Church Census, MARC Europe)

Among the findings over this period which are disclosed in the graph are these:

- The proportion of the overall population who attended church fell very slightly from 11 per cent to 10 per cent.
- The proportions of people aged under 15 and those aged over 30 were strikingly similar for the two years.
- The proportion of people aged between 15 and 19 who attended church fell from 13 per cent to 9 per cent.
- The proportion of people aged between 20 and 29 who attended church fell from 9 per cent to 6 per cent.

In the USA, Greeley (1992) reports that research on the relationship between religion and age provides persuasive evidence that religious faith and observance:

- begin to decline in the mid-teens
- reach bottom in the mid-twenties
- thereafter, slowly climb until levelling off in the mid-forties.

QUESTION

Look at the graph below. What happens next?

Belief in God, by age and gender

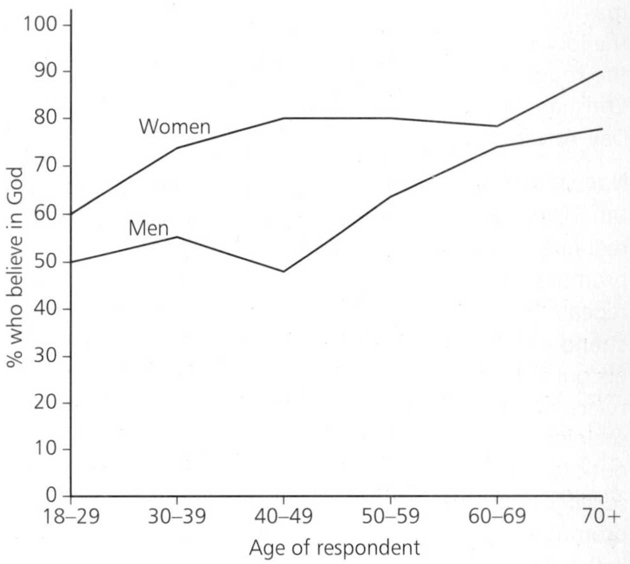

(Greeley 1992: 65)

Among the NRMs, Barker (1985, in Hammond 1985) reveals that people who become full-time members are usually young – in their early twenties – and without strong ties. But she also points out that there are many examples of couples and older people who surrender former lifestyles to follow new leaders. As is so often the case in sociology, we mustn't overstate things. Tendencies rather than trends is the preferred choice when we speak of age and NRMs.

Gender

According to Davie, 'sociologists of religion have, it seems, given a relatively low priority to matters of gender, and gender specialists appear equally unconvinced about religion' (1994: 118). That said, the studies which have been conducted in this area have consistently shown that women are more religious than men. Allan S. Miller and John P. Hoffmann (1995) report that women:

- are more likely to express a greater interest in religion
- have a stronger personal religious commitment
- attend church more often.

These patterns appear to hold true throughout life, irrespective of the kind of religious organisation (i.e. cult, sect or church membership) or religious belief (i.e. belief in astrology, magic, spirits, etc.). Miller and Hoffmann (1995) identify two main explanations in the sociological literature for such gender differences:

- *differential socialisation* – females are taught to be more submissive, passive, obedient and nurturing than males, and these traits are predictors of religiosity. By the same token, men who internalise these norms tend to be more religious than men who aren't. The same is true for women
- *differential roles* – females have lower rates of participation in paid work and higher rates of participation in child rearing. The first factor allegedly gives women more time for church-related activities, and more need for a source of personal identity and commitment (what about unpaid female labour?, we hear you asking!). The second factor increases religiosity because it correlates with a concern for family well-being.

Miller and Hoffman (1995) also introduce a third explanation. They argue that women are more religious than men because women are more likely than men to minimise risk-taking in life. Religious beliefs offer much to gain, and little if anything to lose. Applying the model of risk analysis in this context, Miller and Hoffmann propose two hypotheses:

- Females are more religious than males in part because they tend to be more risk-averse (i.e. averse to taking risks).
- Risk preferences (i.e. being risk-taking or risk-averse) influence religiosity *within*, as well as *between*, sexes. In other words, it's predicted that risk-averse males will be more religious than risk-taking males, and risk-averse females more than risk-taking females.

Hypotheses are clever hunches. Before they're accepted as admissible evidence, they have to be tested and found not wanting. Note too that the first hypothesis is cautious. It uses the words *in part* and *tend to be* in order not to overstate its prediction. Miller and Hoffmann checked their hypotheses against data obtained from a nationally representative annual American survey of high schools students conducted by the University of Michigan Survey Research Center. The survey is called *Monitoring the Future: A Continuing Study of the Lifestyles and Values of Youth*.

Risk preferences were measured by two questions which asked senior high school students to rank their attraction (or lack of) to risk and danger on a scale of 1 to 5 (known as a Lickert scale). The survey also contained questions designed to measure the religiosity of respondents on the basis of church attendance, and a subjective rating of the importance of religion in each student's life. Noting that the subjective dimension is a more reliable indicator of religion than going to church, Miller and Hoffmann use it as the *dependent variable* (i.e. the *effect* of risk preferences). They found that the analysis of the data supported the two hypotheses.

Another explanation for the more religious orientation of women is offered by Greeley. Says Greeley, women's religiosity is more like – though still different to – men's before they acquire a partner and children. But, 'Once you start "taking care" of people, perhaps, you begin implicitly to assume greater responsibility for their "ultimate" welfare' (Greeley 1992: 62). Greeley contends that women are more involved in caring than in practical responsibilities. Caring, it seems, tends to be associated with a more religious outlook.

The table on page 444 shows that women are undoubtedly more religious and devout than men. Only in terms of one of the eleven items, 'Intense experience', do we find a proximity between the two sexes.

The theme of gendered approaches to caring roles has been researched in the context of female clergy by Rita J. Simon and Pamela S. Nadell (1995). Simon and Nadell refer to their earlier in-depth interviews with 32 female Jewish rabbis. They asked, 'As a rabbi who is also a woman, do you think you carry out your rabbinical role differently than a male rabbi who is the same age as you are and who was ordained from the seminary?' Almost all the women rabbis said yes. These women described themselves as less formal, more approachable, more egalitarian, more inclined to touch and hug, less likely to intrude their egos, and less likely to seek centre stage. Some of them used the phrase 'Own the ritual', by which they meant they wanted ceremony participants to take charge of fulfilling rituals. Simon and Nadell also reported that 17 out of 27 Protestant clergy who were women described themeselves as less formal, more people oriented, more into pastoral care, and less concerned about power struggles than male clergy.

Whilst women have been the mainstay of churches for hundreds of years, the top positions in the major Christian churches in the UK, as in society generally, are dominated by men. It's appropriate, in this context, to

Women and men in relation to devoutness and religiosity

	All	Men	Women	Women: Working full-time	Women: Not working full-time
% believing in:					
God	69	60	76	69	79**
Life after death	55	47	61	65	60**
Religious miracles	45	40	50	49	51**
Affiliated with a denomination	64	58	69	57	73
Pray weekly	27	21	33	25	36
Attend service two or three times a month	16	12	19	17	20**
Intense experience	28	30	26*	27	25**
Feel close to God	46	38	52	47	54
Confidence in churches	58	53	62	57	65**
Churches have too much power	28	33	24	26	24**
In favour of school prayers	70	66	74	64	78

* Difference from men is not statistically significant

** Difference between women working full-time and women not working full-time is not statistically significant

(Greeley 1992: 63)

note Davie's (1994) remark that if they're asked to define the God in whom they believe, women focus rather more on the God of love, comfort and forgiveness than on the God of power, planning and control. It seems, says Davie, that men concentrate on the reverse.

Women's concerns and identities often obtain more expression (though not always the desired outcomes!) among the major religions today. In that context, it's appropriate to consider case study research by Charlotte Butler (1995) on the experiences of second-generation Asian Muslim women in Bradford and Coventry. Using semi-structured interviews of 15 young women and 15 young men, Butler found that all of the interviewees thought that Muslim women were becoming more independent in the UK. The interviewees also disclosed that Muslim women were better able to challenge, under Islamic law, some of the restrictions which aspects of their parent Asian culture imposed. This isn't to say that the women abandoned their parents' culture in favour of a 'British' lifestyle. Rather, says Butler:

'It would appear that the second generation are adept enough to adapt to both cultures, to gain a deeper understanding of their religion and to tailor their own culture around it.'

(Butler 1995: 21)

OVER TO YOU

What advantages, in a sociological sense, do case studies like this have? Why would it be inappropriate to generalise from Butler's case study findings to the outlook of the young Muslim population in the UK as a whole?

In terms of influence within religious organisations, we perhaps have to look to some of the NRMs for a more empowered female presence. One of the most robust female cults is (or *was* – it disbanded in 1993) Wildfire – a lesbian 'utopia-in-the-making' group, based in New Mexico, USA. Set up by Sonia Johnson, a radical feminist, Wildfire started off as an all-female sanctuary. Money was considered a corrupt tool of male sado-masochism, and all funds and property deeds were pooled. Johnson used a 'spirit woman' who danced in a trance-like state at meetings, and who 'channelled' decisions about day-to-day affairs at the Wildfire communal sanctuary. Although all but one follower eventually left the sanctuary, Johnson wants to create a female-owned, female-run town in which women would develop new community and economics principles.

A less strident feminist cult is the Goddess Movement, which seeks self-empowerment by 'naming' female experiences as divine, and by shunning patriarchal sexism. Indeed, says Jon P. Bloch:

'Goddess- or Dianic-based spirituality can be conceptualized as a cultural movement aimed at eliminating patriarchal biases through . . . a process of "carrying over" spiritual values across social domains.'

(Bloch 1997: 181)

Bloch notes that some women view the Goddess as a necessary half of a spiritual whole, and so include male imagery in their conception of the divine. Men, says Bloch, might view the Goddess as more nurturing or expressive than self-empowering. It's possible that the death of Diana, Princess of Wales, in 1997 will galvanise more female empowerment. She has already been 'canonised' in popular sentiment. It's particularly interesting that some 80 per cent of the people who signed condolence books after her death were female. Nor must we forget the powerful spiritual imagery of the Madonna in the Catholic religion. Being the Mother of God makes a woman very powerful!

QUESTIONS

1 Outline the main links between religion and: ethnicity, social class, age and gender.
2 How can religion become a force for social justice?

Concluding remarks

Most of the classical sociologists, whatever other differences separated them, agreed that religion would disappear. They regarded this development as the inevitable outcome of rationality and science. Yet, says Stark, 'although generations of social scientists have diagnosed terminal ailments in religion, the patient has been uncooperative' (1985, in Hammond 1985: 144). Stark is one of a relatively recent group of sociologists who don't equate the process of secularisation with the demise of religion. Unlike Wilson, who thinks religion in general is in decline, Stark maintains that some religions are in retreat, and others are on the move.

Religion's refusal to leave the stage has led to major re-evaluations of the standard secularisation thesis. The facts, says Mark Chaves (1994), aren't much contested. NRMs continue to arise; older religions such as Pentecostalism and Mormonism keep expanding; religious fundamentalism flourishes throughout the world; and, at least, in the US, substantial numbers of Americans continue to proclaim a belief in God, and participate in traditional organised religion. Religion is alive and kicking on lots of different fronts. The breadth and endurance of this staying power challenge the argument that new cults merely represent extreme religious conviction in an otherwise unbelieving world.

Sociology needs to reformulate its conception of secularisation rather than recycle the inherited model. In seeking to do precisely that, Chaves asserts that 'Secularization is best understood not as the decline of religion, but as the declining scope of religious authority' (1994: 750). Sociologists who argue that cults and sects constantly arise to take up the religious slack left by churches, seem to place too much emphasis on mere affiliation. In that sense, they perhaps exaggerate the extent of religious authority over affiliates' lives.

The issue of affiliation is also important in relation to the old religions. Talk to Jews and Catholics today, and you'll probably come across a sense of affiliation to their religious bodies, and perhaps a sense of loyalty to them. But will you find the same level of obedience to religious authority that their parents and grandparents displayed? We think not. The growth in inter-faith marriages, and the rejection by many Catholics of the Church's teaching on contraception are just two examples of the demise in the authority of the old hierocracies. One could, of course, bring in some counter-examples. For example, certain fundamentalist Muslims are probably no less obedient to the teachings of their mullahs than in the past. But in the other major religions (and, indeed, among more liberal Muslims), there does seem to be a trend towards individual conscience taking precedence over institutional authority

This doesn't mean that the 'Church' has become 'desacralised' in late modern society. Nor does it imply that people have given up on God. Far from it. What seems to have happened is that institutional religion has generally loosened its grip, and religious beliefs and behaviours have become more private.

Glossary of key terms

Animism A belief in human souls, and also in spirits. The most powerful spirits are worshipped as gods

Calling A vocational task set by God. Max Weber regards it as a distinctly protestant duty

Calvinism An ascetic (severe and unadorned) form of Protestant Christianity. Calvinists believe in predestination and that the elect are 'known' through their business acumen. Weber suggests that Calvinism provided the perfect cultural mind-set for the development of modern capitalism

Church Churches are of two main kinds: *established* (for example, the pre-Reformation Roman Catholic, Orthodox and Coptic churches, when one of these formed the established church – sometimes called an *ecclesia* – in a nation or a wider territory) and *denominational* (for example, post-Reformation churches, including the three churches just mentioned when they co-exist with other churches). Established churches were well integrated into the societies over which they exercised religious domination, some aspiring to be universal churches. The Catholic Church almost achieved this status in the pre-Reformation Christian world. Churches define their theological orientation as uniquely legitimate (i.e. the one definitive belief)

Compensator The belief that a reward will be obtained in the distant future or in some other way which can't be immediately proven. According to Rodney Stark and William Sims Bainbridge, the perpetual quest for the ultimate compensator guarantees the future of religion

Cult A deviant religious organisation with novel beliefs and practices. Cults are generally quite tolerant of differing beliefs

Denominations Denominations are tolerant about theological claims to truth. In other words, they see their grasp of theological belief to be *pluralistically legitimate* (i.e. one among other beliefs). *See also* Church

Ecclesia Essentially, an established church

Magic Reciting by a magician of formulas in order to make magical forces serve human needs The magician's role is to cope with relatively *ad hoc* affairs and tensions. For, example, a bad harvest might be made not to repeat itself if the magician recites a magic formula

New religious movement (NRM) A deviant religious organisation which offers alternative, 'new' beliefs and practices

Profane That which undermines the sacred

Religion A cultural belief system which provides a sense of reality grounded in the sacred, which in most but not all cases encompasses a belief in the supernatural

Sacred That which is consecrated or holy and which society holds in the highest esteem

Sect A deviant religious organisation with traditional beliefs and practices that are 're-discovered' and practised more fervently than the churches from which many sects defect from. The breakaway is called a *schism*

Secularisation In its all-encompassing sense, secularisation refers to the process by which religious institutions, actions, and consciousness, lose their social significance. Some sociologists use the concept in a more limited way to denote the reduced significance in people's lives of the major religions

Secularisation thesis In its all-encompassing sense, the argument that society has, by and large, seen – or is seeing – the 'twilight of the gods'. In a more moderate form, the thesis argues that the major religions are a dwindling social force, and the resultant slack isn't being amply filled by revived religions, nor by new religious movements

Totemism Refers to animals and plants that are believed to have supernatural powers

References

Ahern, Geoffrey and Davie, Grace (1987) *Inner City God*. London: Hodder & Stoughton

Bainbridge, William Sims (1997) *The Sociology of Religious Movements*. New York: Routledge

Barker, Eileen (1991) *New Religious Movements*. London: HMSO

Beckford, James A. (1989) *Religion and Advanced Industrial Society*. London: Unwin Hyman

Berger, Peter and Luckmann, Thomas (1963) Sociology of religion and sociology of knowledge, pp 410–18, in Birnbaum, Norman and Lenzer, Gertrud (eds) (1969) op. cit.

Beyer, Peter (1994) *Religion and Globalization*. London: Sage Publications

Birnbaum, Norman and Lenzer, Gertrud (eds) (1969) *Sociology and Religion*. Englewood Cliffs, New Jersey: Prentice-Hall, Inc.

Bloch, Jon P. (1997) Countercultural spiritualists' perceptions of the goddess, pp 181–90, *Sociology of Religion*, Vol. 58, No. 2 Summer

Bocock, Robert (1993) Religion in modern Britain, pp 207–33, in Bocock, Robert and Thompson, Kenneth (eds) (1993) op. cit.

Bocock, Robert and Thompson, Kenneth (eds) (1993) *Religion and Ideology*. Manchester: Manchester University Press in association with the Open University

Bruce, Steve (1992) The twilight of the gods: Religion in modern Britain, pp 11–14, *Sociology Review*, Vol. 2, No. 2, November

Bruce, Steve (1995a) *Religion in Modern Britain*. Oxford: Oxford University Press

Bruce, Steve (1995b) Religion and the sociology of religion, pp 1–16, in Haralambos, Michael (ed.) (1995) op. cit.

Bruce, Steve (1996) *Religion in the Modern World*. Oxford: Oxford University Press

Burns, Gene (1996) Studying the political culture of American Catholicism, pp 37–53, *Sociology of Religion*, Vol. 57, No. 1, Spring

Butler, Charlotte (1995) Religion and gender: Young Muslim women in Britain, pp 18–22, *Sociology Review*, Vol. 4, No. 3, February

Carroll, Michael P. (1996) Stark realities and Eurocentric/Androcentric bias in the sociology of religion, pp 225–39, *Sociology of Religion*, Vol. 57, No. 3, Fall

Chaves, Mark (1994) Secularization as declining religious authority, pp 749–74, *Social Forces*, Vol. 72, No. 3, March

Collins, Randall (1990) *Max Weber: A Skeleton Key*. Newbury Park, California: Sage Publications

Davie, Grace (1989) Religion, pp 73–100, in Haralambos, Michael (ed.) (1989) op. cit.

Davie, Grace (1994) *Religion in Britain Since 1945: Believing Without Belonging*. Oxford: Blackwell

Davie, Grace (1995) Competing fundamentalisms, pp 2–7, *Sociology Review*, Vol. 4, No. 4, April

Glock, Charles E. (1958) The religious revival in America?, pp 397–410, in Birnbaum, Norman and Lenzer, Gertrud (eds) (1969) op. cit.

Greeley, Andrew (1992) Religion in Britain, Ireland and the USA, pp 51–70, in Jowell, Roger, Brook, Lindsay, Prior, Gillian and Taylor, Bridget (eds) (1992) *British Social Attitudes: The 9th Report*. Aldershot: Dartmouth Publishing Company Limited

Hadden, Jeffrey K. (1996) One man warrior: Reflections on the life and agenda of Joseph H. Fichter, pp 351–7, *Sociology of Religion*, Vol. 57, No. 4, Winter

Hall, Stuart (1985) Religious ideologies and social movements in Jamaica, pp 269–96, in Bocock, Robert and Thompson, Kenneth (eds) (1993) op. cit.

Hammond, Phillip E. (ed.) (1985) *The Sacred in a Secular Age*. Berkeley: University of California Press

Haralambos, Michael (ed.) (1989) *Developments in Sociology*, Vol. 5. Ormskirk: Causeway Press

Haralambos, Michael (ed.) (1995) *Developments in Sociology*, Vol. II. Ormskirk: Causeway Press

Heath, Anthony, Taylor, Bridget and Toka, Gabor (eds) (1993) Religion, morality and politics, pp 49–80, in Jowell, Roger, Brook, Lindsay and Dowds, Lizanne, with Ahrendt, Daphne (eds) (1993) *International Social Attitudes: The 10th British Social Attitudes Report*. Aldershot: Dartmouth Publishing Company Limited

Luckmann, Thomas (1970) *The Invisible Religion*. London: The Macmillan Company, Collier-Macmillan Ltd

Martin, David (1981) Disorientations to mainstream religion: The context of reorientations in new religious movements, pp 43–58, in Wilson, Bryan (ed.) (1981a) op. cit.

McLellan, David (1983) *Karl Marx: The Legacy*. London: BBC

McLellan, David (1987) *Marxism and Religion*. Basingstoke: Macmillan

Miller Alan S. and Hoffmann, John P. (1995) Risk and religion: An explanation of gender differences in religiosity, pp 63–75, *Journal for the Scientific Study of Religion*, Vol. 34 No. 1

Olson, Daniel V. A. and Carroll, Jackson W. (1992) Religiously based politics: Religious elites and the public, pp 765–86, *Social Forces*, Vol. 70, No. 3, March

Parsons, Talcott (1960) Durkheim's contribution to the theory of integration of social systems, pp 3–34, in Parsons, Talcott (1967) *Sociological Theory and Modern Society*. New York: The Free Press

Parsons, Talcott (1964) *The Social System*. London: The Free Press of Glencoe, Collier-Macmillan Limited

Pickering, W. S. F. (1975) *Durkheim on Religion*. London: Routledge & Kegan Paul

Pickering, W. S. F. (1984) *Durkheim's Sociology of Religion*. London: Routledge & Kegan Paul

Scharf, Betty R. (1970) *The Sociological Study of Religion*. London: Hutchinson

Shupe, Anson and Bromley, David G. (1985) Social responses to cults, pp 58–72, in Hammond, Phillip E. (ed.) (1985) op. cit.

Simon, Rita J. and Nadell, Pamela S. (1995) In the same voice or is it different? Gender and the clergy, pp 63–70, *Sociology of Religion*, Vol. 56, No. 1

Smelser, Neil J. (1997) *Problematics of Sociology*. Berkeley: University of California Press

Social Trends 20 (1990). London: HMSO

Social Trends 22 (1992). London: HMSO

Social Trends 23 (1993). London: HMSO

Social Trends 27 (1997). London: The Stationery Office

Stark, Rodney (1985) Church and sect, pp 139–49, in Hammond, Phillip E. (ed.) (1985) op. cit.

Stark, Rodney and Bainbridge, William Sims (1985) *The Future of Religion*. Berkeley: University of California Press

Tischler, Henry L. (1996) *Introduction to Sociology*, Fifth Edition. Forth Worth: Harcourt Brace College Publishers

Torres, Camilo (1973) *Revolutionary Priest*. Harmondsworth: Penguin

Wallis, Roy (1981) Yesterday's children: Cultural and structural change in a new religious movement, pp 97–133, in Wilson, Bryan (ed.) (1981a) op. cit.

Wallis, Roy (1983) *The Elementary Forms of the New Religious Life*. London: Routledge & Kegan Paul

Weber, Max (1971) *The Sociology of Religion*. London: Social Science Paperbacks in association with Methuen & Co. Ltd

Weber, Max (1974) *The Protestant Ethic and the Spirit of Capitalism*. London: Unwin University Books

Williams, Andrea and Davidson, James (1996) Catholic conceptions of faith: A generational analysis, pp 272–89, *Sociology of Religion*, Vol. 57, No. 3, Fall

Wilson, Bryan (1963) A typology of sects, pp 297–311, in, Bocock, Robert and Thompson, Kenneth (eds) (1993) op. cit.

Wilson, Bryan (1966) *Religion in Secular Society*. London: Watts

Wilson, Bryan (1970) *Religious Sects*. London: Weidenfeld & Nicolson

Wilson, Bryan (1974) The Anglican Church and its decline, *New Society*, 5 December

Wilson, Bryan (ed.) (1981a) *The Social Impact of New Religious Movements*. New York: The Rose of Sharon Press, Inc.

Wilson, Bryan (1981b) Time, generations and sectarianism, pp 217–34, in Wilson, Bryan (ed.) (1981a) op. cit.

Wilson, Bryan (1982) *Religion in Sociological Perspective*. Oxford: Oxford University Press

Worcester, Donald E. (1992) *The Apaches*. Norman: University of Oklahoma Press

Worsley, Peter (ed.) (1976) *Problems of Modern Society*. Harmondsworth: Penguin

Wroe, Martin (1993) p. 19, The *Observer*, 26 December

Wuthnow, Robert (1985) Science and the sacred, pp 187–99, in Hammond, Phillip E. (ed.) (1985) op. cit.

Yinger, J. Milton (1971) *The Scientific Study of Religion*. London: The Macmillan Company, Collier-Macmillan Ltd

Exam practice: Religion

Essay questions

1 'The main function of religion in society is the control of weaker social groups by the more powerful.'
Evaluate sociological arguments and evidence both for and against this statement. *(25 marks)*

2 'Sociologists do not agree on the meaning of secularisation but they do agree that it is taking place.'
Critically discuss this statement with reference to relevant sociological evidence. *(25 marks)*

(Summer 1996 AEB A-level Sociology, Paper 2, © 1996 AEB)

3 'The growth of new religious movements is largely a response to deprivation.'
Evaluate the sociological arguments and evidence for and against this view. *(25 marks)*

(Summer 1997 AEB A-level Socgy/3 Module, Paper 3, © 1997 AEB)

4 Compare and contrast functionalist and Marxist explanations of the role of religion in society. *(25 marks)*

(Summer 1992 AEB A-level Sociology, Paper 2, © 1992 AEB)

15 Mass media

Topics covered in this chapter

- The structure and development of mass media
- Mass media and ideology
- Selection and presentation of mass media content
- Influence of the mass media
- Ownership and control of the mass media

A couple of centuries ago, the time it took for news of a riot in London to reach the town crier in York was the speed of the fastest horse between those two cities. Dick Turpin might have made the ride in 24 hours, but that doesn't come close to the almost real-time transmission speed today of a satellite report on a Californian earthquake from Los Angeles to London.

During the reign of Queen Victoria, *The Times* was read by the English middle and upper classes. Now, Bill Gates, the American founder and chairperson of Microsoft, presides over an information age empire that has global ramifications.

From one newspaper in Adelaide, Australia, Rupert Murdoch has transformed his News Corp Ltd into an enterprise that touches two-thirds of the planet's population.

The technology of mass media has undergone a revolution. Cyberspace, fibre optics and satellites mean global audiences, but 'narrowcasting' – lots of different kinds of media reaching many different audiences – is emerging alongside mass broadcasting. One of the most exciting developments in narrow-casting is 'telepresence surgery', whereby a surgeon sits at a computer console and operates through a video conference, her movements transmitted via radio waves to a robot that performs the surgery on the other side of the world. No wonder the US military is spending millions of dollars on this project in order to place surgical expertise on frontlines where, without immediate surgery, half of wounded soldiers bleed to death.

Lots of media doesn't mean lots of media owners. Bill Gates and the likes of Rupert Murdoch and Steven Spielberg are part of a very small, but powerful, group of proprietors who construct the worlds that lie beyond our immediate experiences.

We'll begin by defining two important words:

- *mass* refers to lots of people
- *media* refers to more than one medium, a medium being a conveyor of 'information'.

If Karl Marx were alive today, he could phone his stories through to his newspaper editor rather than rely on slower means of communication.

Putting the two words together, *mass media* are *conveyors of 'information' to lots of people*.

> **EXAM TIP**
>
> Mass media *are*; not mass media *is*.

The reason why we've put inverted commas around the term 'information' is that what passes for 'information' isn't always clear-cut. Some kinds of knowledge seem straightforwardly objective (such as real-time weather reports). Others are open to debate and interpretation (such as the findings of the 1996 *Scott Report* on arms sales from the UK to Iraq).

Denis McQuail (1987: 51) notes that the mass media differ from other 'information'-providers (for example, families, schools) in important respects:

- They act as general carriers for lots of institutions.
- They operate in the public domain.
- They reach more people than other institutions and for longer, 'taking over' from early socialisation processes.

In this way, the 'symbolic environment' (of beliefs, ideas and values, etc.) that we inhabit is, in part, known to us by the work that the mass media do. For they have an important input on what we 'know' and how we perceive the world that lies beyond immediate, personal experience. While, of course, we all have our own distinctive outlooks on a wide range of issues, it's also very probable that we share many common perceptions about the world in which we live. For example, we probably perceive that we live in a society where – in most cases – we have freedom of speech, and I expect, also, that we're pleased about this.

What we share in common is, in no small measure, partly related to our common exposure to mass media. For the media 'mediate' between the real world and what we come to define as that real world. We can know very little just from direct experience of our own society. Much of what we take for granted is gleaned from what we obtain (and how we interpret this) from the mass media. But can we trust what we receive from the communications industries? McQuail (1987) helpfully summarises a range of responses to this question, as follows.

The mass media are alternatively:

- an objective window on experience that accurately enables us to extend our gaze
- an interpreter that explains and makes sense of complex issues
- an interactive link that permits output from senders and feedback from receivers
- a signpost that points the way and gives guidance
- a filter that, deliberately or otherwise, selects what's 'newsworthy' and what isn't
- a mirror that reflects back, with some inevitable distortion, an image of society to itself
- a screen that conceals truth in the service of escapism or propaganda.

> **OVER TO YOU**
>
> ***Match each of the seven points above to actual examples of media output. For example, you might argue that Channel 4's* Right To Reply *programme is an example of the media as a mirror that reflects an image of how society 'thinks', via the views of the television-watching public.***

The structure and development of mass media

The physical structure of the mass media can be divided into two main parts:

- *print:* notably, books, magazines, newspapers
- *electronic:* notably, CDs, motion pictures, radio, television, videos and – increasingly – cyberspace superhighways.

These are the instruments of communication that reach mass audiences locally, nationally and worldwide. Most of the communication goes in one direction: from the media to the mass. The media communicate with us much more than we communicate with them. We hear you saying, 'What about Channel 4's *Right to Reply* programme (referred to above), the letters columns of newspapers and interactive television? The truth is that these 'let the audience have their say' conduits are very small indeed compared to the information that comes – in the opposite direction – from those who own and control the media.

So who are these owners and controllers? We'll consider that in more detail in a later section. Here we consider the structure of the ownership and control of mass media:

- *National broadcast systems*, for example, the BBC in the UK, are quasi-governmental organisations, funded (and, in that sense, 'owned') by the tax-paying public, but they're often influenced (and, in that sense, to some extent 'controlled') by their governments.
- *Private business broadcast systems*, for example, MTV in the US and, now, worldwide, are largely owned by profit-seeking shareholders, and controlled by the

biggest shareholders or, by proxy, through their managers.

So how is the structure of mass media (hereafter, for the sake of brevity, generally referred to as the media) developing in relation to technology and ownership and control patterns?

One of the major media players, Rupert Murdoch's News Corp, is extending its cable and satellite transmissions on a global scale. Looking slightly ahead to when homes will receive 100 or more cable or satellite channels, Murdoch believes there's going to be a lot more targeted broadcasting to rather specialised audiences. He's making an important point. In some respects, 'mass' media are actually becoming less 'massive' in relation to the size of the individual audiences they reach – even though the overall number of people in the world who are touched by the media is probably increasing. Back in 1978, for example, three American broadcasting systems (ABC, NBC and CBS) had a captive television audience: 90 per cent of prime-time television viewers tuned in to these stations. By 1989, the figure had dropped to 64 per cent, with independents (including Murdoch's Fox network) up to 24 per cent, and cable channels at 22 per cent. In 1989, about half of US households could choose from among more than 30 television channels.

A significant technological step towards so-called 'narrowcasting' (transmitting to multiple, specialised audiences) is anticipated when entire nations are wired with fibre optic cable. This development will open up many opportunities for sending and receiving individualised messages. New technology will also enable the consumers of media to become more interactive with what they view. But this doesn't mean that there will be equality between the 'owners and controllers' and the 'users' of media over what's transmitted. Users might get more autonomy but, unlike the media moguls, they won't be flexing corporate muscles. They'll just be exercising more audience choice than in the past.

But choice is tempered by the fact that much of what audiences worldwide are able to select has its origins in 'western' culture and ideology. The biggest entertainment company on the planet is American: Disney. The company that gave us *Pinnochio* and *The Lion King* is now poised to distribute its 'American apple pie' values to a vastly larger worldwide audience. Interestingly, notes Nancy Gibbs, 'Political regimes that might not welcome the independent political views of American broadcasts have no problems with cartoons or sports, two of Disney's strengths' (*Time*, 14 August 1995: 31). Yet cartoons and sports aren't neutral. They're carriers of a nation's culture, which, in an American context, often embodies a strong sense of individual enterprise and 'up and at 'em' competitiveness. The gritty determination of O'Malley the Alley Cat in *The Aristocats*, for example, epitomises the winner spirit of the all-American hero.

On a more sinister note, the US Pentagon is studying ways to take over the media of potential aggressor nations in what has been dubbed 'information warfare'. In the event of war, US planes jam the enemy's television broadcasts with propaganda messages designed to turn the people against their leaders. A similar strategy was actually used by the US in the 1990s when the Pentagon launched a propaganda campaign against Haiti's military regime to return deposed President Jean-Bertrand Aristide. The US Army showered hundreds of thousands of pro-Aristide leaflets upon Haiti's populace, and the former president was returned to office.

Controlling the hearts and minds of people is, of course, more effective than ruling them through terror. When the majority of a society internalise (i.e. take in and accept as truth) the values of a ruling class, there's no need for 'heavy-arm' tactics – which brings us onto the next section: the relationship between the mass media and ideology.

Mass media and ideology

This field is dominated by two broad theoretical approaches: marxism and pluralism. Both are macro-perspectives, that is, they examine and explain the relationship between mass media and ideology on the basis of whole-society models. Moreover, the empirical findings of marxists and pluralists generally support the view that the media exercise a powerful and persuasive influence on the way people think and behave. There, perhaps, the similarities end. Marxists argue that media promote a *ruling class ideology* (namely, a set of beliefs that characterises the social outlook of a powerful group) which persuades the people that their rulers know best. Pluralists claim that media are receptive to widely-held beliefs and values throughout society, transforming them into communication products, and offering them back to audiences. For pluralists, ideology isn't the peculiar province of those at the top of the social ladder. Any number of groups – feminists, political parties, animal rights lobbyists, fox hunters, Oxfam, etc. – have ideologies that define what they believe and promote.

In the marxist model, the media hold up a mirror to society that shows a one-sided, distorted picture. In the pluralist model, the mirror which is held up offers a faithful, multi-faceted reflection of reality. We'll now take a closer look at both perspectives, beginning with marxist theory.

Marxist theory

This perspective argues that the mass media are communication systems that enable the ruling class to pursue their interests. It's an approach that echoes Karl Marx's famous assertion in *The German Ideology* that:

'The ideas of the ruling class are in every epoch the ruling ideas: i.e. the class which is the ruling material force in society is at the same time its ruling intellectual force. The class which has the means of material production at its disposal has control at the same time over the means of mental production, so that thereby, generally speaking, the ideas of those who lack the means of mental production are subject to it.'

(Marx and Engels 1965: 61; first published 1846)

Sounds complicated! In simpler terms, classical marxism claims that the most powerful economic class in society shapes the *culture* (the lifestyle, opinions and values) of the rest of us, by using the mass media and other 'culture-producing industries' to actively promote their ideology (their idea of what's best both for 'them', i.e. to stay rich and powerful, and for 'us', i.e. to accept that our rulers know best). What's allegedly foisted upon the majority by the elite minority is, to quote D. MacDonald, a 'Mass Culture . . . integrating the masses into a debased form of High Culture and thus becoming an instrument of political domination' (1957, cited by Bennet 1992: 36). In this explanation, 'High Culture' describes the lavish lifestyle of the ruling class, who employ cultural technicians (journalists, etc.) to stupefy and subdue the rest of society by fabricating a popular 'Mass Culture' of entertainment and escapism.

It's a view put forward by the so-called Frankfurt School: the perspective adopted by marxist theorists like Theodor Adorno, Herbert Marcuse and Max Horkheimer, who were associated with the Institute for Social Research founded in Frankfurt in 1923. The Frankfurt sociologists argued that the ruling class uses the media to innoculate its own ideology against subversion. It does this by shaping and tutoring the consent of the people through its ownership and control of the media. This doesn't happen in some crude, direct way. The process of ideological control (*hegemony*) is more subtle – and therefore more effective – than that. The values of the rich and powerful permeate the whole of society, so that a particular interest becomes represented as a national interest. In that context, the media are seen to represent impartially what 'all decent citizens' know to be true and right: 'law and order' is good, our troops are peacekeepers/other armed groups are 'terrorists', the democratic process means that the people chose their 'rulers', etc.

As Stuart Hall notes, the media:

'to be impartial and independent in their daily operations . . . cannot be seen to take directives from the powerful, or consciously to be bending their accounts of the world to square with dominant definitions. But they must be sensitive to, and can only survive legitimately by operating within, the general boundaries or framework of "what everyone agrees" to: the consensus.'

(Hall 1992: 87)

The important point made by Hall is that journalists and broadcasters don't consciously spout the ideology of their ruling-class bosses. Rather, they engage in a discourse whose taken-for-granted logic contains uncritical assumptions about the nature of the world in which we live. For example, when a TV interviewer asks a striking firefighter why she's prepared to put the lives of the public at risk by refusing to work, the interviewer is asking a question that most 'reasonable' members of the public would expect to be asked, as well as echoing the assumptions of those at the top of the social hierarchy. Simultaneously and importantly, the interviewer is failing to ask the striking firefighter why she decided to go on strike in the first place. Her answer to such a question might, of course, implicate a government which doesn't pay firefighters a decent wage.

The theme of presenting what are often very controversial issues as though they were accepted wisdom has been the subject of extensive investigation by a marxist-oriented group of social scientists in Scotland: the Glasgow University Media Group. They've been studying this area for more than 20 years – they're still at it, and they're very good. The Glasgow Group's main focus is on the role of the media in shaping audience (especially television viewers') understandings of current events.

What's broadcast on television news bulletins as the 'official line' isn't the result of a puppet-controlling conspiracy whose strings are pulled by those in high places. The process is more subtle. Media personnel exercise a fair degree of professional autonomy in the work they do. However, they're more likely to turn to important people' than to the rest of us when they want to know and report about 'important news'. Who are the 'important people'? Typically, they're government ministers, senior civil servants and city economists. More to the point, they also have 'political' views on the issues they talk about: crime, homelessness, inflation, etc. Yet their views are sometimes presented by journalists as merely factual.

Thus, for example, the Glasgow Group found that the 'causes' of inflation were routinely reported on television news during the 1970s as 'high wages'. Journalists also linked this theme to the alleged need for wage restraint, and tacitly endorsed the then Labour Chancellor, Denis Healey's stern warning about the effect of wage-led inflation. It's not that the journalists were blatantly trumpeting a government view; rather, they were couching the reporting of inflation in terms that essentially reflected the logic of the Chancellor's argument. In that sense, the opinion from the top is presented as though it were 'common sense' and therefore unlikely to be challenged by the average viewer.

Advertisers too play on the 'common sense', reasonable values of the 'average' consumer. During the late 1980s, for example, the tobacco and food giant, Philip Morris (a corporation, not a person), conducted a robust $60 million celebration of the American Bill of Rights. On television and in newspapers, the corporation cited famous utterances on the written guarantees of every American's freedoms – from Thomas Jefferson to Martin Luther King. This sponsorship of heritage culture is, of course, linked to a familiar theme in tobacco advertising: the notion that smokers have a right to choose what they consume, a right that mustn't be infringed upon by the anti-smoking lobby. So incensed was the Public Citizen Health Research Group by Philip Morris' deal with the National Archives in relation to the celebration of the 200th anniversary of the Bill of Rights, they charged that the agreement 'smears the Bill of Rights with the blood of all Americans killed as a result of smoking Marlboro and other Philip Morris cigarettes' (cited by Conroy 1989: 426).

Some commentators suggest that Marx and marxists have adopted a 'conspiracy theory' approach to media. But Marx and marxists are far too clever for that charge to stick. Marx and his followers recognise that there are times when rich and powerful people bully their way into the headlines. However, they also know that this doesn't happen so often. More commonly, the ruling class gets over its views by proxy: ensuring its representatives are invited onto talk shows; buying shares in media industries and, thereby, influencing the selection of senior media personnel; procuring knighthoods for editors who run the right kind of stories, etc. The upshot is that members of the ruling class enjoy a disproportionate share of influence over media output, but they don't 'call all the shots' all the time. If they did, we would be living in an Orwellian-style society, and that isn't the case.

Indeed, there are times when even a cosy relationship between a ruling class and the media doesn't always serve the long-term interests of those at the top of the social hierarchy. Illustrative of this is a fascinating case study by James Lull (1995) of the role of the media in the downfall of Brazil's former President Fernando Collor de Meno, who, in 1992, was impeached from political office and indicted on 20 counts of racketeering, forging documents and peddling influence. The impeachment vote countdown was broadcast live from Brasilia on the national television network, TV Globo. Astoundingly, says Lull:

MARXIST THEORY

FOR

+ The marxist model, with its emphasis on social conflict between different groups in society, offers a realistic and a fruitful theoretical framework for asking important questions about the uses to which the media are put. Of particular importance is the question of whether the media serve privileged interests or exist for the good of all. That crucial deliberation has probably influenced more media research agendas than any other in the entire field of media studies.
+ Marxists convincingly remind us that economic power and ideological control are unevenly divided in society. People with money – lots of money – carry considerably more ideological clout (hegemony) *vis-à-vis* the media than middle and low income groups. Marx himself accurately highlighted the links between money and press influence in nineteenth-century England. Even though these links were more transparent then than today, modern marxists are still adept at flushing out the connections between financial and media power blocs.
+ One of the leading media research groups in the world (the Glasgow University Media Group) adopts a marxist-oriented approach. In their capacity as empirical researchers, the members of this group practise the best kind of marxism: the kind which supports its contention that media selection and representations favour some groups over others with hard evidence.

AGAINST

− Marxists sometimes over-estimate the extent to which media moguls and other power-brokers work hand-in-hand. The commercial media compete with each other, and pursue their interests even when that entails taking on the government or fighting the restraints placed upon them by the courts, the military and other establishment institutions.
− Marxists claim that media production is ideologically saturated with the values of the ruling class. They overlook, however, that marxism itself is inherently ideological because it proposes a radical and a different set of values. Orthodox marxists retort that marxism is scientific and non-ideological. However, while marxists are excellent social scientists when they want to be, they also have a tendency to let political sentiments cloud their judgement.
− Contrary to what marxists claim, lots of different voices find expression through the media. Moreover, anti-establishment voices often carry a great deal of influence. Greenpeace, for example, successfully uses the media to effectively mobilise popular opinion against big corporations who put profit before the environmental health of the planet.

'Collor, the telegenic young politician who won office in 1989 partly by promising to end the corruption plaguing Brazilian politics throughout history, had been unmasked by the very media that helped elect him.'

(Lull 1995: 128)

Given that Brazilian media have been traditionally regarded as a propaganda instrument of the ruling class, the fact that TV Globo brought down the president was proof that the media weren't in the pocket of the rich and powerful. Collor was accused by a former presidential motorpool driver of continuing the corruption that many Brazilians thought his presidency would put an end to. The testimony of the driver, a poor man, was delivered to a congressional committee which had recently begun investigating possible abuses of power by President Collor. The hearing was televised, and an enormous national audience had tuned in. At that moment, says James Lull:

'Television had asserted a moral authority that resonated with popular sensibilities and stood in direct conflict with the vested interests of the powerful.'

(Lull 1995: 133)

Given that TV Globo's owner, Roberto Marinho, had some years earlier said, 'So long as the politicians remain stronger (than audience opinion) we will continue to support them' (cited by Lull 1995: 130), this represented a dramatic about-turn. The once 'in the pocket of the rich and powerful' television company had played a sharply critical, investigative role in the process leading up to the impeachment of a president.

The marxist retort to the view that TV Globo suddenly became the voice of the people is that the media are opportunistic and fickle. Their natural role is to support powerful interests, but they will go with the flow when social change is imminent and unstoppable – they have no other option if they want to survive. Other sociologists aren't convinced that one particular group in society ever holds sway over what the media produce. These sociologists argue that everyone's voice is in some way represented in what comes out of the media. They're called pluralists.

Pluralist theory

Proponents of pluralist theory argue that the media don't privilege particular viewpoints over others. This doesn't mean that newspapers, radio and television put lots of different viewpoints into a melting pot and pull out a consensus view of things. Instead, the media operate as a sort of multi-cultural kaleidoscope, giving the competing ideologies of all kinds of different groups balanced and equitable coverage. Pluralist theory thereby rejects the notion that one ideology gets special favours. Instead, it contends that the diversity of individuals and groups in society ensures that adequate access to the media exists both for 'official' voices and for critical, alternative opinions. That said, pluralist social scientists do tend to adopt a rather consensual position, because they usually assume that divergent views are articulated within an overarching framework of common agreement. Thus, for example, the media will run stories that offer contradictory views on the National Health Service, while simultaneously assuming that their audiences generally support the principle of free health care.

Just to re-emphasise what this book has been saying all along, pluralism and marxism, like any other perspectives, shouldn't be regarded as exclusively either/or options. There are overlaps. Witness, for example, the marxist-oriented Greg Philo – of the Glasgow Group – noting that:

'Newspapers exist within a highly competitive market. If the disjunction between their preferred policy and the views of their readership becomes so great that it could affect sales, then editors may have to think again. This is the continual problem facing a paper such as Rupert Murdoch's *Sun* which advocates Conservative politics to a readership which very substantially votes for the Labour Party. At times, the *Sun* has employed individual columnists to broaden its appeal. In 1991 it featured a regular column from none other than Ken Livingstone under the banner "A View from Labour".'

(Philo 1995: 220)

Philo's point is that a pluralistic reporting style might be invoked even by a tabloid that usually takes a partisan political line, especially if it senses that the various subgroups that make up its client base want a newspaper which offers more than just one viewpoint. The press are also adept at presenting a kind of 'pluralistic consensus' which emerges when journalists sense they've tapped into an opinion that echoes the sentiments of the majority. Illustrative of this point is the press coverage of the run-up to the US presidential election in October 1992. As Jeffrey L. Katz notes:

'The aftermath of the second presidential debate in mid-October seemed to produce a coast-to-coast journalistic consensus. A full two weeks before Americans voted, the news media declared Bill Clinton the winner . . . Most journalists insist they were simply reflecting public sentiment . . . '

(Katz 1993: 277)

But was pluralism really at work here? 'No', claim the conservative (with a small 'c') Center for Media and Public Affairs. Based on its analysis of network evening newscasts during the autumn campaign, the Center characterised 71 per cent of the comments about President Bush as negative. Another Clinton opponent, Perot, received 55 per cent negative comments. Yet Clinton, the eventual winner, only had 48 per cent negative comments. However, even if a majority of journalists were rooting for Clinton, newspapers and television channels are too competitive with each other to take sides that simplistically. In that respect, it's fair to note that Clinton took a severe pounding from the media over his alleged affair with Gennifer Flowers, dodging the draft (a lottery-style form of military conscription), and being shifty in his replies about smoking marijuana.

Having carefully considered the available evidence, Jeffrey L. Katz concludes that:

'A plurality of voters in 1992 felt that the Democratic candidate best embodied their hopes for the future and was best prepared to improve the economy. The campaign coverage reflected that. Ignoring this critical element would have been a distortion indeed.'

(Katz 1993: 284)

So in the context of the 1992 US Presidential election campaign, it's argued that the media faithfully reflected the views of the electorate. That doesn't stop supporters of the losers suggesting that their candidate didn't get a fair hearing. But such supporters are more likely to make allegations because of political sentiments than on the basis of hard, social scientific evidence. Even in 1980s UK, when Margaret Thatcher's New Right agenda was actively promoted in the tabloid press, the Conservative government was complaining that news and current affairs on television were biased in favour of left-wing politics. This allegation, however fervently it's made, doesn't really square with the facts. From the mid-1980s, the media were generally quite well-disposed to the Conservative government's claim that it had revitalised the British economy. As Philo notes, 'The routine deference to City "experts" for opinions on economic news, for example, was a product of this time' (1995: 217). What these so-called experts had to say was, of course, generally in line with the government's monetarist policies.

Nevertheless, it would be wrong to assume that the media were simply at the beck and call of the then establishment. To be sure, there were nods and winks in the government's direction, but partisanship (supporting just one side) wasn't so blatant as to constitute a one-way flow of 'information' from government, via media, to public. Points of view, even when they emanated from the lofty heights of the City, were contested. Pluralism was apparent. The Labour-controlled, fiercely anti-City, Greater London Council, for example, wasn't only supported by a majority of Londoners (66 per cent in 1985), but also by 'quality' newspapers, like the *Guardian* and the *Observer*. The City experts didn't have everything their way. Things really took a turn against the government and its City spokespersons towards the end

PLURALIST THEORY

FOR

+ Pluralists correctly recognise that society contains a plurality of groups (admittedly, not equally as powerful as each other) who are engaged in an ideological contest for media ascendancy. For example, 'grassmoors gentry' types who subscribe to hunting and fishing magazines confront 'new age' people who read about alternative views in Greenpeace publications.
+ Subsequent to the preceding point, there exists a plurality of media production that, mirror-like, reflects the ideological struggle between these competing groups. Evidence shows that this is so because there are numerous examples of media messages that directly confront each other (for example, the *Daily Mirror* versus *The Times* on politics; BBC's *Watchdog* versus the public relations departments of allegedly corrupt corporations, etc.).
+ Ultimately, no single group and no unitary media viewpoint gains the upper hand. The media simply act as the means through which the contest is conducted, and, ultimately, the public are left to decide which group or which ideology they support. Thus, for example, members of the public exercise choice as consumers (for example, shall I subscribe to *The Economist* or *The New Internationalist*?) and as advocates (for example, exercising the right of reply in newspaper letter columns).

AGAINST

– Pluralists underestimate the extent to which some groups in society are both allied to each other and exercise considerably more leverage over media production than ordinary citizens. For example, some media moguls are on very cosy terms with high-ranking politicians, and both 'conspire' to produce news that supports their respective (and often common) ideologies.
– It's true that the media represent ideological diversity, but there isn't parity of status here. Some issues receive much more prominent coverage than others. Moreover, certain viewpoints obtain more column inches and more sound bites than others.
– Content analysis reveals that there are clear winners and losers in the ideological 'wars' that find expression in the media. You or I might have a right of reply to a programme whose content offends us. However, that programme's message might be halfway round the world before our view has time to tie its laces.

of the 1980s. The issue was the very unpopular poll tax. Media coverage was consistently opposed to the tax.

Even the Tory tabloids sensed and reflected, in a pluralistic way, the public mood towards the poll tax. One of the great strengths of the Glasgow Group is that, despite its marxist orientation, it doesn't let political sentiments get in the way of critical analysis. One of its leading lights, Greg Philo, demonstrates this readiness to go with the evidence rather than other considerations when he writes:

'The Conservative press obviously wish to promote Conservative views but they tread a fine line between how they invite their readers to understand the world and the actual material conditions and experience of those who buy their papers. It is the fine line that all political communicators tread. This does not mean that there is an immediate and necessary relationship between a change in "reality" and the public perception of this change. But it does seem clear that some major changes in material circumstances such as the increase in unemployment in the 1980s or the radical drop in house prices pose very great difficulties for "good" public relations and effective media management. The credibility gap can indeed yawn wide but where and when it exactly does so forms the site of a constant struggle between contending forces. It is a struggle in which the structural position of the state and its information managers is one of privilege and potential dominance. But it is a dominance which is contested by oppositional groups and through the interplay of the different organizational and commercial priorities of the media.'

(Philo 1995: 222)

Putting this rather complicated-sounding argument into more simple language, Philo is saying that:

- Tory newspapers want to support Tory ideologies.
- It's commercially risky to support Tory policies that create economic hardships for the readers of Tory newspapers.
- Editors of Tory newspapers, even though they tend to play the Tory card, must run stories that take account of the opinions of their readers, even when these opinions run counter to received wisdom in Tory circles.

More to the point, Philo is actually constructing a bridge between the marxist and the pluralist perspectives on the role of the media. Essentially, he's arguing that while journalists work with routine assumptions about who knows best (for example, politicians), they're also obliged to consider the fact that the agendas for economic and political debate are sometimes set by people who contest the existing power elite. Philo lets his marxist tilt slip though when he acknowledges that much of what passes as independent media comment is influenced by government and City opinion. But, at the same time, he acknowledges that the possibility of a free and critical press exists within the pluralistic society we occupy.

In that context, it's apposite to note that during the 1984–5 Miners' Strike, *Channel 4 News* supplied the two main protagonists, National Union of Mineworkers President, Arthur Scargill, and National Coal Board Chairperson, Ian MacGregor, with a television crew and the chance to provide their own reports on pit closures. Both men accepted the offer and prepared their respective filmed reports, thereby allowing British television viewers the opportunity to see two sides of the story.

So, in the spirit of trying to unite the different perspectives that make up the discipline we call sociology, we're mindful that marxists and pluralists both have important contributions to make to media research. Marxists rightly note that people in high places often have the ear of editors and journalists. But pluralists remind us that the commercial viability of media enterprise exists on the sufferance of the people who buy newspapers or tune into television stations. The upshot is that the information we receive of the world which exists beyond our immediately lived experiences is unduly influenced by the ideologies of the rich and powerful, but doesn't always exclude the opinions of 'ordinary' people.

Taking account of the fact that the distinction between pluralist and marxist interpretations of the media is *ideal-typical* (that is, each model's arguments are accentuated for the sake of conceptual clarity), the table below will help you to grasp the most important differences. McQuail's 'Dominance Model' is an orthodox marxist one.

Alternative models of media power

	Dominance	**Pluralism**
Societal source	Ruling class or dominant elite	Competing political, social, cultural interests and groups
Media	Under concentrated ownership and of uniform type	Many and independent of each other
Production	Standardised, routinised, controlled	Creative, free, original
Content and world view	Selective and coherent; decided from 'above'	Diverse and competing views; responsive to audience demand
Audience	Dependent, passive, organised on large scale	Fragmented, selective, reactive and active
Effects	Strong and confirmative of established social order	Numerous, without consistency or predictability of direction, but often 'no effect'

(McQuail 1987: 86)

EXAM TIP

Don't adopt a 'conspiracy theory' view that the media are entirely in the pockets of powerful elites who use them to 'brainwash' the public. Even marxists – who do contend that powerful interests exert leverage on media influence – reject the exaggerated claims of the conspiratorial argument.

It's now time to consider another issue that connects with ideology: the selection and presentation of media content.

Selection and presentation of mass media content

This section focuses on how what the media transmit are both *selected* (for example, a television news broadcast on the Gulf War might predominantly select material from US military sources) and *presented* (for example, the same broadcast might use reporting language that presents the US military as a 'humanitarian' force). Do the media transmit balanced and truthful representations of the world that lies beyond your personal knowledge, one-sided and distorted (i.e. ideological) representations, or a mixture of both? We think a mixture of both, but with a preponderance of the one-sided, distorted stuff!

Each day, journalists decide which news to report, what to ignore, and how to present what they select. For a typical daily newspaper, over 75 per cent of potential news is discarded (McCombs 1994). The selection of what constitutes 'newsworthiness' is called *agenda-setting*. Moreover, selection and presentation go hand-in-hand. Not only do the news media largely influence what we see of the world at large, they also shape our perception of that world. Research (for example, Brosius and Kepplinger 1990, cited by McCombs 1994) suggests that media agenda-setting also affects public agenda-setting. In other words, audiences quite often attach importance to the same issues that the media emphasise in television news coverage. It's therefore very important to consider who are the agenda-setters and presenters, as well as what these people select and how they represent the social world.

We don't adopt the very orthodox (and now outmoded) marxist view that the media are the willing mouthpieces of ruling class ideology. Things are more complex than that. We support Stuart Hall's contention that the 'criticism is not of the wilful, intentional bias of editors and newscasters, but of the institutionalized ethos of the news media as a whole' (Hall 1976: 89). Moreover, we don't accept that it's only the ruling class who are ideological in the way they present their views. Instead, we use the term 'ideological' to refer to beliefs that reflect the distinctive outlooks of a wide range of social groups. At the same time, we recognise that some of those groups are more successful than others in ensuring that the media select and present their viewpoints. Mass media in America and the UK are produced mainly by white, middle- and upper-class males, and media selection and content largely reflect their ideological agendas.

Take Chicago, for example. The population there is 36.5 per cent white, 41.1 per cent black, 17.9 per cent Latino, and 4.5 per cent other minorities. In the late 1980s, the *Chicago Tribune* had 594 newsroom employees, of whom only 10 per cent were recruited from minority groups. At the *Chicago Sun-Times*, only one of 37 editorial employees occupying management positions was black, and only two of the newspaper's 52 copy-desk employees were black (Jackson 1987, cited by Hiebert 1995).

The press and broadcasting are male dominated. The higher up the hierarchies, or the more prestigious a particular medium, the fewer women there are. As for working-class people, they probably have even less influence than middle-class women and middle-class ethnic minority employees in the media industries. Ten years ago, the more prosperous of their number were skilled metal block printers. Now, however, in the age of the word-processor, they answer telephones, make the tea and clean the premises.

Media personnel who come from different classes and ethnic and gender groups are likely to have different perspectives on how the world is and how it should be. Yet, says Hiebert, 'One problem with mainstream gatekeepers of mass media is that they often think they have a franchise on objective observation and the presentation of truth' (1995: 363). But, just like the sub-groups of the population, notably women and ethnic minorities, whose presence they symbolically annihilate, these predominantly white male, middle- and upper-class gatekeepers are also influenced by their backgrounds and prior experiences. They really don't have a monopoly on what constitutes truth, even if they think they do.

Even though much remains to be done, some progress has been made by women in the media industry. In the UK, the US and the Netherlands, for example, more women are entering schools of journalism. Advertising and public relations media are also increasingly opening their doors to (white) women. That said, advertising isn't taken very seriously by some media professionals, who regard it just as a way of financing what is regarded as the 'real' media: newspapers and television. When they do work in more prestigious media fields, women still tend to predominate in areas that are an extension of their 'domestic responsibilities': in human interest and feature sections of newspapers and in children's and educational television. This gendered selection of media personnel reinforces the stereotyped treatment of women in entertainment and news programmes.

The fact that women, black people, working-class people and the very young and very old have little influence in what the media produce means that white, middle-aged, middle- and upper-class males make most of the decisions about the inclusion/exclusion and 'representation' of age, class, ethnicity and gender. It's now time to look at each of these groupings in turn – not forgetting, of course, that they interact with each other.

Age

Consider, for a moment, the kinds of age stereotype that pervade television sitcoms and soaps: irritable old men, 'nagging' mother-in-laws, successful young and middle-aged adults (especially white males), angst-ridden teenagers, some of whom (especially boys) get into trouble with the law. If we look at media selections and representations of age groups, here are some recurrent themes:

- *Babies* generally receive sympathetic treatment, but white babies tend more often to be portrayed as healthy and happy, compared to black babies who, when they appear at all, are sometimes represented as the unwitting 'crack addicts' of one-parent, drug-taking mothers or as the disease-ridden, starving poor of sub-Saharan Africa.
- *Children* (aged about 2–14) are typically depicted as 'nice but naive', and in need of adult protection and supervision. Advertisers also, for obvious commercial reasons, envisage children as having insatiable appetites for 'toys', and they are very receptive to (and positively encourage) children's 'gendered' preferences for these products. Black children are more often featured in the media than previously, and are generally represented in positive ways. This is particularly the case in television advertising in the UK and the US. Not all advertising, however, portrays black children in a positive way. For example, Benetton's advert (above) with a black child as the devil and a white child as an angel caused much concern.
- *Youths* (aged about 15–20) tend to get a rather 'bad press', especially if they're black, male and working-class, and live on low-income council estates in the UK or so-called 'projects' in big American cities. Like children, all youths are assumed by advertisers to want lots of consumer products. Cosmetics, athletic footwear, clothes, computers (including games and other software) and music CDs are especially promoted. Media representations of young people tend to be gendered in ways that advantage boys and disadvantage girls. Girls' magazines sometimes foster what Marjorie Ferguson (1983) has termed a 'cult of femininity' (for example, girls should be 'pretty' and therefore very concerned with beauty products)
- *Young adults* (aged about 21–40) usually receive very favourable media representations, especially if they're white, male and middle-class. Those three factors add up to success. These are the 'Gillette men': racket ball players; stockbrokers; airline pilots; and 'new man' dads. Women and ethnic minorities of both sexes in this age group are faring quite well in American television series (witness, for instance, the female African–American chief surgeon in the hospital drama, *ER*). However, they're still under-represented and over-stereotyped on British television
- *'Middle-aged' adults* (aged about 41–early sixties) often do as well, sometimes better, in the media than young adults. Again, being white, male and middle-class works wonders for one's media image, greying temples providing just the right amount of senatorial gravitas. Yet successful female role models in this age group are few and far between in advertisements, younger 'career women' tending to feature more often. Once again though, American television series are ahead of their British counterparts. In the US, middle-aged women (including African–Americans) are often cast as judges, district attorneys and doctors
- *'Elderly' adults* (aged about 65 and upwards), unless they're 'young at heart', insufferably rich and very famous, don't do too well in media representations. Negative stereotypes abound, especially in television sitcoms, where grouchiness and senility are all too common themes. Another common theme in newspapers and on television is the old woman as victim of violent assault in her home.

OVER TO YOU

Taking each of the above age groups in turn, write down:

a a stereotype of each

b a counter-stereotype (i.e. an opposite) of each stereotype you selected.

One of the largest content analyses of age is reported by N. Signorielli (1984, cited by Guy Cumberbatch 1989). It's based on 14,037 characters on American television. She concludes that the old and the very young were under-selected in prime-time dramatic fiction. Older characters were less likely to be represented as 'good', but were also less likely to be involved in violence than younger characters. Older men were more likely than younger men to appear in a comic role, and old women tended to be portrayed as unsuccessful and as victims. About 70 per cent of old men and 80 per cent of old women were judged to be held in low esteem and treated discourteously.

Some studies, however, have found more positive representations of old people. Ansello (1978, cited by Cumberbatch 1989) found that old women in soap operas were generally portrayed in a positive way. Moreover, British research (Lambert, Laslett and Clay 1984, cited by Cumberbatch 1989) has also found, despite under-selection of the old on television, that the roles they portrayed and the treatment they received were mainly positive. Significantly, a 1990s advertising campaign for Levi's red tab denims uses older weather-beaten faces instead of softer youthful ones. These older models reflect the fact that people of their generation wore these clothes not long after the death of Levi Strauss in 1902. Two of the models are shown below.

QUESTION

What images of old age are portrayed in the two photos below?

Things might be changing, but the many negative media stereotypes of old people that still abound continue to promote and reinforce ageism. Here are some examples of ageist stereotypes about older Americans provided, and – importantly – rebutted on the basis of empirical evidence, by Alex Thio:

'1 Old people are usually senile.
2 Older workers are not as productive as younger ones.
3 Most old people live in poverty.
4 Most old people are lonely.
5 Most old people end up in nursing homes and other institutions.
6 Most old people have no interest in or capacity for sexual relations.
7 Most old people are set in their ways and unable to change.
8 Most old people feel miserable.'

(Thio 1989: 300)

OVER TO YOU

How many of the eight stereotypes listed above can you find in any of the media that you are familiar with? Discuss your findings.

Here are some examples of stereotypes that we (me and my A-level Sociology students) found:

- The *Daily Star* (22 February 1996) reported that 'Randy wrinklies are having afternoons of steamy sex and free love in an OAPs' wife-swapping club'. This tabloid stereotype insults old people by referring to them as 'wrinklies'. By subtle implication, it also suggests that

'Josephine, 79, a teacher soon to receive her black belt in karate, wears Levi's Women's Fit 534 jeans.'

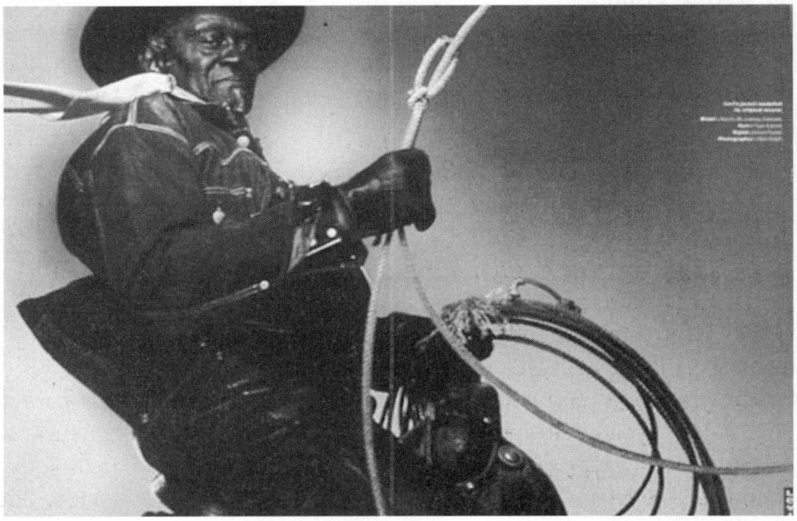

'Alonzo, 86, is the oldest surviving black cowboy in Colorado and still rides in the Rodeo. He wears Levi's Type II jacket.'

(Both photos appeared with these captions in *Observer Life*, 12 May 1996) there's something unusual about old people having sex.

- *Scotland on Sunday* (5 September 1993) quoted the historical novelist, Nigel Tranter, as saying: 'I'd have my doubts about living to 115. I wouldn't want to be a decrepit old nuisance.' The same newspaper also cites biology student, Peter Roan Edwards: 'I'm going to keep rolling till I'm about 40; then they can put me down like a dog.' Here we have two stereotypes about old age – and even middle age – being identified with ill-health.
- The Conservative politician, John Redwood, writing about council-managed 'old people's homes' in the *Mail on Sunday* (25 February 1996) observed that, 'It makes my blood boil when there never seems to be enough to look after granny.' No doubt, his sentiments are genuine, but the 'looking after granny' image conveys a sense of female, old-age senility.
- *The Times* (9 October 1992), referring to the US, wrote, 'The new big spenders, the darlings of marketing and advertising departments throughout the country, are the grumpies, grown-up urban mature professionals.' Big spenders they might be, but calling them 'grumpies' emphasises their alleged tendency of being miserable.

Fighting fire with fire, Age Concern launched an ingenious anti-ageist campaign in 1993. Using a poster that featured a 70-year-old man referred to as an 'old codger' and a woman labelled a 'silly old moo', the punchline was a very pointed question and a call to action: 'How long before people call you names? Fight ageism now.' In its lobbying actions for legislation against age discrimination similar to that for racism and sexism, Age Concern said that the stereotype of an old person was someone in poor health, who lived in poverty, and had lost interest in sex. In reality, however, only 3 per cent of people over 65 lived in institutions, and only 22 per cent of people over 55 said their health was bad. Newspaper articles about hang-gliding grandmothers and old people being attacked or conned, added Age Concern, were patronising, and reinforced stereotypes.

While media stereotypes of old people are often very up-front, newspaper and television portrayals of middle-age success tend to be under-stated. When we see a courtroom lawyer on a television series, an anchorwoman on a news programme, a politician in a newspaper, it's almost taken for granted that these people will, in most cases, be middle-aged. Pluralists might argue that this has less to do with stereotyping and more to do with how the world is: the media simply reflect the fact that the most successful people, careerwise, are generally middle-aged. On the other hand, it would certainly be possible for the media to select other examples of career success. And we don't mean just professional sportspeople and grunge musicians, who are usually younger people. There are young and old high-flyers in all walks of life: young legal eagles, old surgeons, young and old human rights workers.

Before looking at ethnicity in the media, it's apposite to note these points:

- There's a definite need for more social scientific research into the selection and representation of age groups in the media. This is especially so with regard to middle-aged people.
- Existing research into media and age tends to focus on age in relation to other issues – for example, young, black LA 'rioters', old 'victims' of crime, etc. It's time to look more at age groups in their own right rather than as categories that simply connect with other research issues. It's still important, however, to regard people as belonging to more than one social group – middle-aged women, black children, etc.

Ethnicity

The UK has a long history of ethnic diversity. Black troops of the Roman army were garrisoned here some 1,600 years ago; the 'Anglo–Saxon English' from Germany invaded and settled shortly thereafter; as did Scandinavians in the late eighth century and the French in 1066. The past 1,000 years have also witnessed the, generally more peaceful, immigration of other ethnic groups: Belgians, Irish, Indians and African–Caribbeans, to name just some. This section focuses on very recent (post-Second World War) ethnic issues, including the lives of immigrants, the experiences of British-born people whose parents or grandparents migrated here in the past, and 'foreign enemies'.

Since 1948, when the first post-war West Indian immigrants arrived in the UK, the number of black people living in the country has risen to more than a million. Although many white people have migrated to the UK during this period, the term 'immigrant' tends to be associated with black people (Braham 1992: 268). This misnomer overlooks the large number of British-born black people, as well as a large number of white immigrants, notably, the Irish. It's an ill-informed assumption based on an out-dated colonial view of black people as 'outsiders'. If that weren't enough of a stigma for black people to suffer, tabloid newspapers have created in some white people's minds an association between being black and being a 'mugger' or a welfare recipient.

Nor have the advertising media done much to counter negative stereotypes of people from ethnic minorities. Says Peter Popham, 'Britain might be a multicultural society, but its advertising industry has been slow to catch on' (1996: 14). Some adverts even fuel the problem of racial division. Referring to Britain, Popham puts the position powerfully in a telling juxtaposition:

'On the one hand are the basket cases and low-lifes: the actors in ads for HIV awareness, drug warnings, income support, campaigns against domestic violence, recruiting campaigns for the police. Often shot in grainy monochrome, these feature blacks in almost over-generous measure. But then in a flash we are transported to another world of whiter-than-white underclothes, of perfect dinners, charming interiors, exciting car rides, brilliant sunshine; a world almost entirely – *pace* the latest Persil ad – populated by whites.'

(Popham 1996: 14)

Television has played an important stigmatising role in its portrayal of black people. A study by Preethi Manuel (1985, cited by van Zoonen 1994) of people of African, Indian, Pakistani and West Indian origin in British television drama found they were mainly cast as law-breakers, low-paid workers, and students, or as background figures. This is a very one-sided selection of the roles black people occupy in society. In a different context, William Raspberry of the *Washington Post* tells the story of an 11-year-old-boy who asked his father, 'Daddy, do white people take drugs?' 'Of course', replied his father. 'Well', said the boy, 'I never heard anything about it' (Raspberry 1990, cited by Hiebert 1995: 351). That brief discourse, notes Raspberry, is an indictment of journalism. He points out that 70 to 80 per cent of the consumption of illicit drugs happens outside of black ghettos. 'But that knowledge rarely informs our stories and commentaries', writes Raspberry.

R. M. Entman (1992, cited by Greenberg and Brand 1994) analysed local television coverage of four Chicago stations for 55 days from December 1989 to May 1990. Their aim was to gauge whether crime and political reporting depicted black people as more physically threatening and demanding than white people. Among a variety of findings about the selection and portrayal of black people on television news, Entman discovered that, compared to white people, they:

- were less often named
- less likely to be shown in motion
- more likely to be filmed in custody
- less likely to be defended in the story text
- more often talked about by black and white police officials.

As for political news coverage, Entman found that black leaders were more often depicted defending black community interests, whereas white leaders more often seemed to represent all constituents. He therefore concluded that television news conveyed the impression that black politicians advanced special interests rather than the public interest.

Even media representations of black success tend to be stereotypical, typically focusing on sporting prowess rather than intellectual acumen. Not that one or other of these attributes are more or less worthy. The point is that different types of ability get undue prominence. Moreover, media selections and representations of black athletes over-emphasise the 'bad boy with attitude' persona. Nike Inc. candidly owned up to pursuing actively attention-getting, 'bad boy' athletes to represent their products (Lull 1995).

Latino–Americans also suffer negative stereotyping at the hands of the media. To discover how some of the most influential papers in the United States covered Latino (also called Hispanic) communities in their respective cities, a magazine called *Hispanic* conducted an analysis of the *Chicago Tribune*, *Los Angeles Times*, *New York Times*, *San Antonio Light*, and *Washington Post* during the week of 24–30 August 1992. The study counted the number of stories about Hispanics, and classified them into five categories: crime, culture, business, people and issues. The stories were also graded as either positive or negative. From a selection angle, it was noteworthy that Hispanic culture had a very limited coverage. When a story about an Hispanic was stumbled across, she or he was likely to appear in a crime story – as the perpetrator, victim, cop, or all three. Here are some examples of what appeared during that week.

The *Chicago Tribune* managed to hit two stereotypes in just one paragraph about an Hispanic named Noe Martinez. He was:

'interviewed as he picked fruit for [greenhouse manager Carl] Ford last week. Martinez, an immigrant from Chihuahua, Mexico, estimated his pay at $200 a week and noted that most places to rent cost more than $300 a month.'

Have you detected the stereotypes? They are: Hispanics are manual workers, and they don't earn enough money to make ends meet. But a few paragraphs later, Joe Medina, 'a local businessman and former Chamber of Commerce president', voices his opinion on an important community issue at a city council meeting. Here we learn that Hispanics also exist in the business world and that they have a say in local politics. However, although the *Chicago Tribune* achieves some balance, it simply doesn't give Hispanic issues much coverage.

Hispanics were also quite hard to find in the *New York Times*. Moreover, of the week's 19 stories on Hispanics, only eight presented them in a positive way. Hispanics in New York – where one in four residents is Hispanic – were very often portrayed as murderers, sex maniacs, swindlers and residents of crime-ridden neighbourhoods. In the *Los Angeles Times*, stories about Hispanics are much more abundant. The problem is that they also promote negative stereotypes. Of the 56 Hispanic stories counted in the one week study, 25 were negative. While giving due prominence to issues that engaged the interests of the Hispanic business community, there were plenty of stories linking Hispanics to gangs and the after-effects of the LA riots. Even ostensibly complimentary reports about Hispanic community workers were hedged with comments that portrayed them as the odd ones out in an otherwise violent subculture.

Turning to the *Washington Post*, only 15 of the hundreds of the stories run by this prestigious newspaper in the week were about Hispanics or Hispanic issues. That said, ten of the 15 stories showed insight and receptiveness to matters affecting the Hispanic community, both in Washington and further afield. But alongside positive coverage, the *Post* sneaked in a story portraying Hispanics as new immigrants, non-English speaking, unemployed, poor and ignorant of American law.

The smaller *San Antonio Light* has what its more worldly cousins lack: fair and balanced coverage of its population, 56 per cent of whom are Hispanic. With only half the pages of the *LA Times*, *NY Times* and *Washington Post*, the *Light* nevertheless ran 49 Hispanic stories in its daily editions. Of these, 37 were positive. In short, the *Light* knows that the selection and representation of Hispanic news don't have to contain a preponderance of stereotypical images. Certainly, there are stories of Hispanic crime in San Antonio, but there's much more too. For example, a front-page profile on an Hispanic nurse, Paul Rivera, described him as intelligent, professional and active in the community. His name apart, the fact that Paul is Hispanic isn't made an issue in the story, thereby allowing his accomplishments rather than his ethnicity to take the centre stage they deserve.

On this more positive front and on this side of the Atlantic, there have been some encouraging attempts by the London Metropolitan Police to challenge racist stereotypes through an ingenious poster campaign. The text of the poster (see below) explains that, contrary to anticipated impressions, the black man is a plain-clothes police officer leading a chase after an unseen criminal.

Critics, of course, might argue that this is simply a clever propaganda campaign by the police designed to turn the tables on those who accuse them of being racist. What do you think? Is the message genuine? Should all intending police officers take compulsory courses in sociology, especially, labelling theory?

Whether or not the police are genuinely committed to challenging negative media selections and representations of minority ethnic groups, black people and also 'foreigners' don't often receive sympathetic treatment in newspapers and on television. In times of war, for example, the sufferings of a 'foreign enemy' are sometimes construed as less painful than the trials and tribulations of 'our boys'. The Glasgow Group (1985) illuminated this point in an important content analysis of British television news coverage of the sinking of the Argentine cruiser *Belgrano* and the later sinking of the British destroyer HMS *Sheffield* during the Falklands/Malvinos War of 1982.

CRIT THINK CRIT THINK CRIT THINK CRIT THINK CRIT THINK CRIT THINK

TACKLING STEREOTYPES BY USING POSITIVE IMAGES

Imagine that you're part of a team of sociologists who've been asked by a Department of Health committee to design a full-page advertisement in a national newspaper to encourage more students from minority ethnic groups to study medicine.

This exercise can be done as a group activity, with each group making a presentation to the rest of the class, who act as the committee. The committee can ask the sociologists questions about their advertisement.

If you do the exercise as a piece of written work, you will need to justify your ideas and design (i.e. anticipate the sorts of question the committee might ask).

1. *Take some time to think of ideas and plan your advertisement, using pictures and text. Discuss your ideas and plans using sociological concepts and reasoning.*
2. *Design and produce your advertisement.*
3. *Prepare and, if possible, make a presentation to promote the advertisement to the committee.*

CRIT THINK CRIT THINK CRIT THINK CRIT THINK CRIT THINK CRIT THINK CRIT

The Glasgow Group noted a reticence by the BBC and ITN to use 'hard' terms when referring to the fate of the crew of the *Belgrano*. The term 'killed', for example, wasn't employed. The phrase 'drowning Argentineans' was used, but was related to a story about the rescue of Argentinean sailors. In stark contrast, the reporting of the sinking of HMS *Sheffield* emphasised the casualties and the human tragedy involved. 'Harder' terms were deployed in describing those who lost their lives aboard the *Sheffield*. Moreover, 'emotive' links were made by reporting about personal grief and the loss of the ship on a community level.

In reality, of course, military personnel from both sides suffered appalling death agonies, and they left mums and dads, daughters and sons, and brothers and sisters to grieve this tragic loss of young lives. The tears of an Argentinean mum are just as real as those of a British mum. Yet somehow, the British television media don't convey this parity of suffering in the material they select and broadcast. What do you think? Do the media have a right, in times of war, to place patriotism before balanced judgement? Are sociologists who favour honest, up-front reporting in such times good social scientists or 'traitors to the cause' – or both? Get your teacher to organise a class debate on these important questions.

A more recent 'foreign enemy' has been Iraq. When the 'Gulf crisis' began in August 1990, most Britons had little knowledge of Middle East affairs, and there was no public desire to wage war on Iraq. Despite this, in a short time, a highly successful campaign by politicians, the media and pro-war groups persuaded a majority of the population that a war was morally justifiable and necessary. Much of the success of the campaign was the media's ability to represent the Iraqi leader, Saddam Hussein, as a latter-day Hitler figure. Little, however, was said in the media about ordinary Iraqi citizens, even though most Iraqis were Shi'a Muslims and Kurds who were themselves oppressed within Iraq. Moreover, the ensuing destruction would be mostly suffered by the civilian populations of cities and a conscript army which occupied neighbouring Kuwait.

In the national press, only the *Guardian* argued against the military option, pointing out that economic sanctions had already halted 97 per cent of Iraqi exports. BBC News also ran a brief story two days prior to the outbreak of hostilities that highlighted the success of sanctions. However, the general flow of media messages were characterised by a war-mongering spirit, the suggestion being that war was inevitable if 'negotiations' failed. This mood is epitomised in a *Sun* front-page declaration: 'It looks like war – Battle stations as Gulf talks collapse. War in the Gulf looked inevitable last night after last ditch peace talks failed' (10 January 1991).

Once the war had started, however, some discontent was expressed by British journalists about manipulation of the media by politicians and military people. True to form, though, the tabloid press had a jingoistic (exaggeratedly patriotic) field day, the *Sun* baying for vengeance after British casualties were reported and captured pilots were shown on Iraqi television. Even the BBC was attacked in the popular press for referring to 'the British troops' instead of saying 'our troops' or 'our boys'. Another theme that the tabloid press promoted was the patently absurd notion that the war could be fought with virtually no casualties. 'Western' commanders perpetuated this nonsensical propaganda by using phrases like 'precision', 'smart' and 'surgical' when describing their bombing raids. After the war, it was revealed that only 7 per cent of the bombs dropped were 'precision' or laser-guided weapons.

Some newspapers, such as the *Sun*, openly revelled in the destructive power of the allied forces. On 24 January 1991, the *Sun* ran a full-page feature on the weaponry of the B-52 bomber, leading with the headline: 'Death cargo of the jolly green giant'. The report concluded with a quote from former defence chief Alexander Haig: 'I ordered B-52 carpet bombing raids in Vietnam and I have seen them reduce men and material to jelly. They will turn Iraq into a talcum powder bowl.' In the *Daily Mirror*, the 19 January 1991 edition gave a complete front page to its headline: 'We'll bomb them till they're not there any more.'

Given the media's efforts to sanitise – and in some cases to exclude – the casualties suffered by the Iraqis, pictures of casualties from Iraqi sources that did get out were hedged by warnings that they could be fabrications. Both the BBC and the ITN were afraid that they might be accused by British politicians of distributing Iraqi propaganda. As Greg Philo and Greg McLaughlin correctly write, 'it was only after the war had ended that its full human costs were made more apparent' (1995: 153). Such was the power of the establishment to shape the majority view on the 'ethics' of the Gulf War, that only when patriotic fervour had waned some time after the ensuing victory was it possible for some sections of the media to report the facts without pulling punches.

While it's still possible for the media to get away with running down a 'foreign enemy' in a fairly propagandist sort of way, such isn't any longer the case in the way media personnel represent social classes. Here, things are usually more subtle.

Social class

In the 1970s, a British 'alternative comedy' show, *Monty Python*, regularly made fun of the British class system. Using three males of different heights and accents and in different attire, the upper class was represented by a tall, 'grassmoors-gentry' type who spoke the Queen's English; the middle class as an average height, pin-striped, bowler-hatted city gent with a rather studied BBC accent; and the working class as a short, cloth-capped cockney. Things have changed somewhat since then. While classes still exist as real economic entities, the media stereotypes are less sharp than previously. Indeed, a *Monty Python* sketch re-run would be precisely that: a re-run of something that belongs to another era. Even the 'loads of money' Essex Man stereotype, both as comic figure and stockbroker type, seems rather dated these days.

Stark images of 'working classness' are more likely to focus on alleged 'underclass undesirables' – lone-parent women on welfare who can't control their unruly, thuggish sons – rather than on gritty, but respectable, heavy industry communities where everybody pulls together. Working-class toughness gets limited exposure on blue jeans commercials where jean-clad, gym-conditioned actors carry truck tyres and steel wrenches. But here it's packaged as 'blue-collar, hard masculinity' in a quite overtly sexual manner. Cultural connotations don't feature in the imagery.

Negative media representations of working-class people go much further back than the *Monty Python* stereotypes (which incidentally, poked as much fun at middle- and upper-class types as it did at the working class) of the 1970s. The historian E. P. Thompson (1976) notes how, in the nineteenth century, *The Times* letters page allowed middle- and upper-class readers to express their opposition to working-class unrest. Thus, for example, after the 'Trafalgar Square Riots' of February 1886, when unemployed demonstrators threw bricks at select London clubs, an irate gentleman whose carriage windows had been smashed wrote:

'Sir,
I am a subscriber to various charities and hospitals, which I shall discontinue. I have always advocated the cause of the people. I shall do so no more.'

(cited by E. P. Thompson 1976: 262)

Another correspondent enquired in the same year:

'Sir,
What is the use of having a highly-paid Commissioner of Police, with proportionately highly-paid deputies, if they are afraid of the responsibility attaching to their posts? . . When there is a kennel riot in any kennel of hounds, the huntsman and whips do not wait to get the special orders of the master, but proceed to restore order at once.'

(cited by E. P. Thompson 1976: 263)

Some nineteenth-century 'gentlemen', it seems, used the 'respectable' press to vent their own self-righteousness, and to encourage the forces of law and order to return working people to their 'kennels'. It's funny how people at the top always seem to be experts on the 'there ought to be a law against . . .' theme. Today, they still get plenty of opportunities to uphold the national conscience and admonish the delinquent and the depraved. Strikers are fair game, as are subcultural deviants, especially ones from low-income council estates. Admittedly, *The Times* isn't as strident as it was a hundred years ago, but its close cousin, the *Sun* (which comes from the same Rupert Murdoch media stable) readily adopts a bare-knuckle reporting style when laying in to the urban 'underclass'.

However, it's usually in more subtle ways that working-class people get a raw deal. Typically, their voices are either excluded or find limited and rather stereotypical expression in the media. The 'experts' on news programmes whose views are solicited by middle-class presenters are, for the most part, white, middle- and upper-class men: treasury officials, lawyers, city economists, politicians, and the like. When working-class people are in the frame, it's quite often in the context of industrial disputes. And, as the Glasgow Group have discovered, the coverage is typically negative. When Philo (1995) asked people about their memories of the 1984–5 miners' strike, nearly all of them thought that most picketing shown on television news portrayed violent episodes. Yet among those respondents who had actually been to a picket line, none believed that the picketing was mainly violent. One respondent, a police officer, commented: 'A lot of it was good-natured banter' and 'Come on, lads, it's time for a good heave' (cited by Philo 1995: 38).

Yet the pervasive newsreel images of the miners' strike is one of embittered strikers on the rampage in muddy fields doing battle with serried ranks of police who banged truncheons on riot shields. When the miners' leaders were interviewed, it was often in the midst of all this turmoil. Indeed, one camera crew tried to interview Arthur Scargill, President of the National Union of Mineworkers, while he was being unceremoniously arrested and dragged off by police. Yet when the managers and bosses of the then National Coal Board were interviewed by television journalists, the setting was altogether different. No hustle and bustle, no blood, sweat and tears here – just men in suits talking to other men in suits in smart surroundings.

Remembering that social class interacts with other social indicators, it's especially apposite to say something about young working-class males. The media aren't known to be kind in what they say about these people. Rather than rehearsing in any detail arguments that have been stated in an earlier chapter, we'll very briefly summarise what's already been said:

Young working-class males who belong to distinctive subcultures (for example, mods and rockers) often get a very bad press. Sociologists (for example, Stanley Cohen) have noted how the media exaggerate the alleged criminal behaviours of people who belong to these subcultures, and even trigger off pro-active policing strategies against these people. Add black skin colour to the 'young working-class male subcultural deviant' configuration, and the stereotype become even more demonised.

In an interesting contrast, a very popular – and equally controversial – American television cartoon series, *Beavis and Butt-Head*, 'presents the revenge of youth and those who are terminally downwardly mobile against more privileged classes and individuals' (Douglas Kellner 1995: 148). Beavis and Butt-Head sit in a shabby house most of the day, watching television – especially music videos. Anything that contains sex and violence is usually judged as 'cool'. Everything else 'sucks'. They hate school and the fast-food restaurant where they sometimes work. They're particularly disdainful of adult figures whom they encounter, most of whom are white conservative males and liberal yuppies. Says Kellner, the series thereby enacts class and youth revenge against older, middle-class authority figures.

Beavis and Butt-Head's neighbour, Tom Anderson – a conservative World War Two veteran – is the hapless victim of many of their escapades. They cut down his trees, one of which falls on his house; they put his dog in a washing machine; they throw mud baseballs into his yard; and torment him in other ways. They also blow up an army recruiting office as the officer attempts to get them to join up; and they put rats and worms into the food they serve to 'obnoxious' customers at a fast food outlet. Another favourite victim is their 'friend', Stewart – lavishly pampered by his yuppie parents – whose house they love to trash. Nor have they any time for their liberal hippie teacher, Mr Van Driessen, who tries, in vain, to make Beavis and Butt-Head politically correct. They continue to regard naked women, fire and violence as 'cool', and when their teacher lets them clean his house to learn the value of work and money, they destroy his irreplaceable eight-track music collection.

Beavis and Butt-Head hit back at authoritarian people, whatever their liberal guises, but they don't offer politically-correct alternatives. Instead they represent a caricaturised mirror image of what Kellner describes as a 'large teenage underclass' who have nothing to look forward to other than three bucks an hour at a '7–11' store and a bullet in the mouth before they reach 20. In that sense, they provide an indictment of both their own 'lower' social class, and the more privileged sections of society whom they constantly bemoan. Importantly, however, by challenging affluence and respectability, they provide a radical departure from conventional media representations of the American middle class. Beavis and Butt-Head are contemptuous of the middle class, and their secure and predictable lives.

But even though they have a big following, the people who watch Beavis and Butt-Head (mainly young MTV viewers) are in a minority, compared to people who watch more mainstream programmes. Our point is that the middle and upper classes can quite easily suffer a bit of bashing and retain their 'superior' image, provided most of what goes out on the air is generally complimentary. In that wider context, the working class still fares badly in media selection and representation. There are few working-class people in positions of prominence in the media as a whole (both in relation to content and personnel), and images of 'working classness' are too often presented through negative stereotypes.

Gender

Important pioneering work in the field of gendered media stereotypes was conducted by G. Tuchman in the 1970s. Drawing from different research data, she argued that, in America, television symbolically 'annihilates' women by showing an overwhelming majority of men in all kinds of television programme. A notable exception to male domination was in soaps, where women were the majority. Television stresses that women have important roles to play as mothers and 'housewives'. But, says Tuchman, 'Girls exposed to "television women" may hope to be homemakers when they are adults, but not workers outside the home' (Tuchman 1978, cited by van Zoonen 1994: 17).

OVER TO YOU

1. ***Consider and discuss the importance of content analysis in media research.***
2. ***What kind of 'television women' does British television select and present in the 1990s? Discuss your impressions. Then set up and conduct a content analysis study in order to test your hypotheses.***

Extensive research of the Tuchman type has since been carried out worldwide, much of it based on content analysis. Liesbet van Zoonen (1994) reports that this research reveals 'depressing similarities'. Women who do appear in the media, while under-represented in production and content are, contentwise:

- usually young and conventionally 'pretty'
- represented in relation to their husband, father, son, boss or another man
- portrayed as dependent, indecisive, passive and submissive.

When we introduce the issue of ethnicity to the debate about gender stereotypes, we find in the UK that black women hardly appear at all in television drama, and rarely as part of a family. As for the portrayal of black family life on American television, widespread stereotypes abound (Melbourne Cummings 1988, cited by van Zoonen 1994), notably:

- the loud, loveable 'mammy to massa's three little children'
- the overpowering black woman
- the sexually insatiable black woman.

The last stereotype is very prevalent in European colonial racist and sexist myths about uninhibited, black female sexual appetites. It is a perennial theme in the works of British and French painters and writers. With regard to media representations of women in general as 'sexual objects', it's pertinent to note that much of this has been designed by men for men. Although media sex on network television contains plenty of variations on heterosexual intercourse, there's very little emphasis on tenderness. To quote Richard Jackson Harris, 'Women are seen eagerly desiring and participating in sex, often with hysterical euphoria' (Harris 1994: 250). Observes Harris, there's minimal concern with the consequences of sex or the relationships within which most adults find it. Harris notes, however, that things are changing here, with more emphasis on relationships and women's points of view – but only slightly.

The theme of sexual aggression against women is very prevalent in cinema and television media. Moreover, this theme isn't limited to pornographic and horror movie material. It pervades the mainstream too. For example, in their content analysis research, D. T. Lowry, G. Love, and M. Kirby (1981, cited by Harris 1994) found that, apart from erotic touching among unmarried people, aggressive sexuality was the most common type of sexual interaction in daytime soaps. In its most savage form – pornography – masculine power over and violence towards women is starkly represented. Unlike 'erotica', which typically represents sexual behaviour between consenting, equal, heterosexual partners, pornographic media more commonly show sexuality as male-dominated and cruel. Some feminists claim that pornography is the 'theory' and rape the 'practice'. But the extent to which pornography adversely affects male behaviour towards women is contested – more about that debate in the section on media effects.

Whether as a victim of violence or as an object of sexual desire, the display of women as a spectacle to be looked at by men underpins media representations. The 'objectification' of women's bodies is commonplace in commercials, television game shows and tabloid 'page 3 girls'. It's very likely that this process has damaged women's sense of well-being, probably accounting, in part, for the eating disorders that occur when the pressure to be 'slim and beautiful' gets out of hand. While things are starting to change, it's still much less common to see media representations of the male body in ways similar to the display of women's bodies. When men are seen partly clothed, it's more commonly associated with sport or blue-collar work than with sex: the high board diver; the surfer; the construction worker; the truck mechanic. Contrast this with the more sexually-explicit poses of the semi-clad or naked woman. Even male 'pin-ups' are different to their female equivalents: a man stares; a woman 'pouts'; a man threatens; a woman invites.

In an analysis of the women's magazine, *Playgirl*, Ien Ang (1983, cited by van Zoonen 1994) found that male pin-ups display very active masculine features: taut muscles, physical endeavour; the suggestion of manual labour. The difference between gender representations in *Playgirl* and *Playboy* (a men's magazine) is that the *Playgirl* man is portrayed as a romantic rather than a sexual object. According to Ang, this is accomplished in a number of ways:

- Unlike other male pin-ups, *Playgirl* men look at their women readers as if both parties know each other.
- They're smiling, friendly and reassuring, conveying the idea that women are looking at a friend, not a body.
- The stark sexuality associated with pornography is suppressed by aesthetic compositions and lighting.
- The text that accompanies the male pin-up emphasises the identity, personality and human qualities of the man.

Developing the last point, it's noteworthy that male pin-ups are typically introduced by their first and last names, which emphasises their 'human' as opposed to 'body' aspects. Thus, for example, *Playgirl* Man of the Month for March 1992 was introduced as:

'Handsome prince personified. Looking as though he'd been plucked from the pages of a fairy tale, Robert Johnston undoubtedly qualifies for the role of Prince Charming . . . Bobby is a marine biologist whose fascination with ocean depths often send him into the far reaches of the deep blue sea [*sic*!] . . . Single, but always looking, Bob says he never enters a relationship with any "expectations about how it's going to be. Each experience is always new and rewarding." Indeed, this taut 26-year-old proves wise beyond his years. "I am a big believer in the notion that love can cure society's travails", he declares.'

(cited by van Zoonen 1994: 101)

In the same issue, the picture series of that month's 'Mr Big' – 'proportions like these get noticed' – gave the body a personality. 'Mr Big', Tom Marinelli, has a body etched by rigorous workouts, and the presence of his motorbike in the picture tells us this guy is on the move. The accompanying text read:

'At 23, Tom Marinelli has the confidence it takes most people several decades to acquire. But then, this is no ordinary guy. You're looking at someone who actually wakes up every morning feeling good – in fact rarin' to go! . . . Tom the Triumphant credits his parents with instilling in him such old-fashioned values as the work ethic. "Besides building my pride, doing a good job helps to get the bills paid", he notes pragmatically. Those close family ties may also account for the way he guards his private life – fiercely. Not one to blather about his special lady, Tom just smiles when *Playgirl* scribes attempt to pry.'

(cited by van Zoonen 1994: 102)

Ang asserts that the *Playgirl* male pin-up encourages a fantasy of heterosexual romance rather than of female heterosexual desire. Even the sex appeal of the *Playgirl* man is based more on his character than on his body. The situation is typically reversed in *Playboy* and other heterosexual men's sex magazines. The dominant portrayal is one where men look at women as sex objects and women look at men as more rounded human beings. In television commercials, however, things seem to be changing. Women are starting to look at male bodies without the romantic asides. The Levi-Strauss, blue jean man bathing in a clearwater creek while two young women look on, and the 11.30 man-watching break, as female office workers gaze at a construction worker taking off his shirt before drinking a Diet Coke, exemplify this new trend.

It's also important to recognise that, even in earlier decades, there have been media representations that proclaim a strong womanhood, even though such representations have been few and far between. In another study by Ien Ang (1991), this point is made with reference to female heroes in popular television fiction shows from the 1970s and 1980s, like Maddie Hayes (*Moonlighting*) and Christine Cagney (*Cagney & Lacey*). Notes Ang, these figures:

'do not fit into the traditional ways in which female characters have generally been represented in prime-time television fiction: passive and powerless on the one hand, and sexual objects for men on the other.'

(Ang 1991: 75)

Cagney, a feisty detective, forcefully takes on the male hierarchy of the police department, and often 'wins' the ensuing battles. Hayes, an energetic businesswomen, challenges the machismo of her business partner, David Addison, and gains respect in the process.

In concluding this section, we turn to a review of key research findings into the selection and presentation of media images, compiled by Denis McQuail (1987).

From extensive studies of *news*, these kinds of biases have been identified:

- There's consistent over-selection of powerful people (for example, politicians) as sources of news and under-selection of 'ordinary people'. Women figure less often than men in news, and in less varied roles.
- Powerful people are more likely than other people to be reported about.
- Large-scale, dramatic, sudden or violent events are more likely to figure in the news than more routine, more typical and more common occurrences. Crime reporting tends to very much exaggerate the extent of violent crimes.
- Reporting styles tend to show a bias towards dominant social and community values.
- Reporting of international issues are often biased by nationalistic orientations.

- Minorities who aren't considered troublesome (by the media) are commonly ignored in the news. Minorities who allegedly have 'attitude' (a label commonly applied to black people in predominantly white societies) and other alleged 'deviants' are usually portrayed in negative ways, which can involve exaggeration or misrepresentation of facts.
- Even when some members of minorities (for example, victims of racism) receive 'sympathetic' treatment from the media, they're often represented as people with social problems. Being represented as an aggressor or as a victim isn't positive.

As for media selections and representations of fiction, these are some typical findings:

- Generally, there's an over-selection of characters in high-status occupations (notably, legal, medical, law-enforcement, military and show business – at their higher levels).
- Ethnic minorities are frequently represented in low-status or 'dubious' roles, even though there has been some improvement in that respect since the 1940s.
- Women, when not 'invisible', tend to appear in stereotyped occupational and domestic roles.
- The incidence of violence is exaggerated, and this has an effect on some viewers. For example, television viewers in the US who gave 'TV version' rather than real version (i.e. statistically accurate) replies to the question, 'What are your chances of being involved in some kind of violence in any week?' said 10 per cent, whereas the 'right answer' (based on crime statistics) was 1 per cent (Gerbner and Gross 1976, cited by McQuail 1987).
- Media fiction continues to perpetuate myths about human behaviour, history and present-day society and its institutions, especially in relation to the 'nation', sexuality, war and crime.
- Media fiction designed for very big (including international) audiences is likely to echo dominant, 'official' or non-controversial viewpoints.

Despite some past precedents and some recent developments, the media are still peppered with negative representations of females and positive ones of males. If, as the next section argues, the media influence people's attitudes and behaviour, this should be cause for serious concern.

QUESTIONS

1 Identify the factors that influence the *selection* and *presentation* of media content.
2 Outline the different ways in which the media *represent*: age groups, ethnic groups, social classes, and gender groups.

EXAM TIP

A common error in exams is for cand dates not to distinguish between media *selection* and media *representation*.

- Selection is about what's included and what's left out.
- Representation is about how what's included is portrayed.

Influence of the mass media

Most sociologists accept that the media influence how we think and behave. Most of them also believe that this influence is pervasive, varying from shaping political beliefs and voting patterns, to fanning the responses of law enforcers to reported levels of crime, to producing a generation of young women who suffer from eating disorders like anorexia nervosa and bulimia. However, despite the huge amount of media research conducted over the past 50 years, claims made about media effects are still equivocal.

The best we can say is that some media affect some people some of the time in some ways.

Consider these situations:

1 You're watching a film on TV. During a commercial break, there's a commercial about an ice cream product that you happen to have in your freezer. The commercial jogs your memory about this, and you decide that you want to eat the ice cream now. You fetch the product, and eat it.
2 You're watching a film on TV. Dur ng a commercial break, there's a commercial about a yoghurt that your mum likes, but which you don't. The product is in your fridge. You don't fetch it and you don't eat it.
3 You've decided to go off-road mountain biking tomorrow if the early morning radio weather forecast predicts a dry day. Tomorrow arrives, you listen to the weather forecast. Sunshine is expected, so you set off on your mountain bike.
4 You have no interest whatsoever in sailing. While listening to the radio, you happen to hear that gale force winds are expected off the west coast of Scotland tomorrow morning. You won't be in that area and you wouldn't be going sailing, whatever the weather forecast. The information changes neither your plans for tomorrow, nor your activities on that day.

In situations 1 and 3, there's quite a direct media effect on both your thoughts and your behaviour. In situations 2 and 4, the media messages might prompt some fleeting thoughts, but there's no obvious effect on your behaviour.

In social scientific language, the first pair of outcomes might be explained in terms of:

- the *hypodermic syringe model*: in goes the media message, just like an injection, out comes a fairly immediate behavioural change (with a jab, a painful grimace; with an ice cream commercial, the initiation of eating)
- the *uses and gratifications model*: the media message is used by the viewer to gratify a prompted want.

The second pair of outcomes can't be explained by the hypodermic syringe model because even if the viewer registers the message, there's no behavioural change. However, the uses and gratifications model could be used to explain how the viewer hasn't been persuaded to change her or his behaviour: there's no need to use something that doesn't gratify.

We hope you've noticed two important things:

- These models don't always have to be viewed as either/or explanations. Sometimes both models are helpful.
- The hypodermic syringe model is more positivistic (and thereby more deterministic) than the uses and gratifications model. The first model regards the mass media as having a fairly direct causal effect on audience behaviour. The second model puts the audience in the driving seat as a user, not simply a pawn, of the mass media. In that respect, it adopts a rather interpretivistic approach.

The hypodermic syringe theory and the uses and gratifications theory are at two ends of a continuum. The one gives overwhelming power to the media; the other turns the individual into an independent decision-maker. In between these two extremes are other explanations, notably, *two-step-flow theory* and *cultural effects theory*. The first of these proposes that media influences aren't always as direct as hypodermic syringe theory suggests. The idea here is that media influences often reach people in a step-by-step process. Some individuals are exposed to the media firsthand and, subsequently, pass on their interpretations of what they see, hear and read to other people. Cultural effects theory takes this concept even further by suggesting that media influences cascade upon people in lots of different ways. We'll now consider each of the four main theories in turn.

Hypodermic syringe theory

This theory is referred to as a *direct effects model*. It goes by a number of other names, among them, the *magic bullet theory* and the *transmission belt theory*. The essential idea behind these terms is that media messages are received in uniform ways by audiences, and that fairly immediate and direct responses are triggered. For example, you watch a violent film and you go out and beat someone up. This stimulus-response model of media effects was popular in the early nineteenth century, and it derived from the belief that all human behaviour was pretty much the same. People inherit, so the theory argued, the same set of fixed responses to given stimuli. It therefore followed that media stimuli tapped pre-programmed behaviours that were wired into all human brains. These beliefs led to the exaggerated claim that the media were able to brainwash the masses.

Many social scientists in the 1920s and 1930s (for example, H. W. Lasswell, W. Lippmann, L. Doob) subscribed to hypodermic syringe theory. Around that time, some very dramatic events (for example, the mass panic when people feared a Martian invasion after listening to Orson Welles', *War of the Worlds* broadcast on the radio; and the adulatory crowd responses of people at packed nazi conventions) suggested that ordinary citizens were easily swayed by the impact of mass communications.

In a more up-to-date context, proponents of hypodermic syringe theory argue that the portrayal of violence by the media can trigger violent audience responses. If, for example, you watch Mike Tyson in the boxing ring, you might, so the argument goes, be stimulated to behave in an aggressive manner. Here we have a classic stimulus-response explanation: you watch a televised boxing match (the stimulus) and you start laying into the guy next door (the response). It's a very simplistic and – dare we say – not a very convincing explanation of the relationship between the media and the audience. Think about it! If the theory were accurate, it would be dangerous to leave your home after watching a boxing match on television because the streets would be full of Mike Tyson 'wannabes' ready to take on all-comers. In reality, of course, not all members of an audience respond in the same way to what they see on television. To be sure, there might be some individuals who decide to brush up on their boxing after watching a televised fight. But experience tells us that most of us won't respond in this way.

Nevertheless, hypodermic syringe theorists do believe that audiences are sometimes overwhelmed by media messages. The most quoted instance is the Orson Welles' radio broadcast, referred to above. Listeners allegedly took the message literally, and mass panic ensued because many people believed that Martians had invaded Earth. Well, so the story goes. In fact, there remains considerable uncertainty about the actual scale of the alleged *War of the Worlds* 'panic'. Perhaps a number of listeners did take the 'bulletin' seriously, but one suspects that many took it for what it was – fiction. Martians aside, there are commentators who still claim that large-scale persuasion of entire populations can be achieved through using the media in propagandist ways. That's why totalitarian regimes are very anxious to control the media and to ensure that those who might incite civil disobedience – pro-democracy activists and the like – don't get access to radio and television stations.

It's fashionable these days to dismiss hypodermic syringe theory as out-dated and too deterministic. But hold on a moment! While human behaviour is certainly the product of multiple influences operating in concert, sometimes one or more of those influences do carry more weight than others. You might be influenced fairly directly by a movie. Perhaps it contains a central character who is an expert skydiver. You've been thinking about doing a charity parachute jump, and the movie star gives you the media-generated nudge (excuse the pun!) to actually do it.

On an empirical level, the question of whether or not the media can produce fairly direct effects is probably not resolved. Take pornography, for example. Some feminists have coined the expression: 'Pornography is the theory and rape the practice'. Two US presidential committees that extensively studied the effects of pornography produced contradictory results. In 1970, the Lockhart Commission on Obscenity and Pornography found no evidence that pornography use played a role in criminal behaviour among youths or adults. More than a decade on, the Meese Commission concluded that violent pornography did have an effect on aggressive male behaviour.

Liesbet van Zoonen identifies an integrated model of media effects in feminist theory (see opposite), the pornographic strand of which represents a direct type.

HYPODERMIC SYRINGE THEORY

FOR

+ At the turn of the nineteenth century, the media, where they were well-developed, probably did exert more transparent influence on people who were exposed to them. For one thing, there weren't many media studies experts around to warn audiences of bias in the media. Moreover, people were less well-travelled, and were probably more inclined to trust media accounts of incidents and issues that personal experiences might otherwise disconfirm.
+ The first half of the twentieth century witnessed the effective (and immoral) use of the media by dictatorial regimes. Nazi Germany and 'communist' Russia are two examples of this.
+ The sometimes unscientific assumptions that the media could be immensely powerful, encouraged social scientists to put these assumptions to the test. In that respect, hypodermic syringe theory pioneered a resolve to go beyond speculation and conduct systematic research.
+ Notwithstanding the over-simplified explanation of media effects associated with hypodermic syringe theory, there are clearly times when some such effects are pretty immediate: going to see a film advertised in a newspaper, reacting to a newsflash, etc.
+ Hypodermic syringe theory echoes the persuasive sociological contention that social forces (in this case, the media) are far more powerful than individuals tend to reckon with.

AGAINST

– Being exposed to media and being aware of media messages often occurs without related attitude and behavioural change. For example, if you can't stand soap operas, it doesn't much matter how often they're advertised, you're unlikely to change your opinion of them and even less likely to watch them.

– With the excessive emphasis placed by hypodermic syringe theorists on quantitative, cause and effect measurements, there's the risk that the complexities of human social behaviour become reduced to statistical data.

– The hypodermic syringe model is too much wedded to rather out-dated aspects of positivist methodology. In that respect, there's the risk that social phenomena are treated like natural phenomena because both are explained by cause and effect (for example, watering a plant *causes* it to grow faster; watching a commercial *causes* an individual to buy a product).

– Some proponents of hypodermic syringe theory might overstate media effects because their livelihoods depend on predicting and plotting such effects. Consider in that context the social scientist employed by an advertising firm whose income is linked to the claim that her or his marketing strategy is going to persuade lots of people to buy a particular product. When one's salary is justified by claiming strong effects, there's an increased danger that wanting something to happen takes precedence over objective judgement.

– Hypodermic syringe theory regards mass audiences as captive and gullible. The major assumption is that exposure to media has a direct and measurable effect on audience behaviour, with little or no voluntary control exercised by the individual.

	Sender	Process	Message	Process	Effect
Stereotypes	men	distortion	stereotype	socialisation	sexism
Pornography	patriarchy	distortion	pornography	imitation	oppression
Ideology	capitalism	distortion	hegemony	familiarisation	commonsense

(van Zoonen 1994: 29)

Looking at the words in van Zoonen's diagram that need explanation:

- *distortion* refers to the under- and mis-representation of women
- *hegemony* refers to the self-proclaimed, 'we know best' projections of the rich and powerful
- *patriarchy* refers to a male-dominated power structure.

The relationship between pornography use and imitation is the direct link. Use is accompanied by imitative behaviour. That's one theory, but we still have to decide if there's compelling evidence to say that what's predicted actually happens. It seems the jury is still out on this complex issue. What do you think?

To some extent, orthodox marxism aligns itself with hypodermic syringe theory. Early marxists proposed that the media were agents of a ruling class whose task was to 'inject' a 'reassuring false consciousness' – that is, a feeling among working-class people that their interests were best looked after by 'social superiors'. More recent marxist theory has shifted the emphasis away from a dominant elite calling the shots, in favour of a more subtle process of hegemony, whereby the media act as guardians of prevailing othodoxies without being directly propagandist. This theme is very much associated with what is called *cultural effects theory*, which posits that the outlook of the rich and powerful, of white people and males, disseminates – via the media – the everyday, taken-for-granted social world that the rest of us inhabit. The onus here is less on a direct injection effect, and more on a slow, drip, drip, saturation.

Two-step-flow theory

Here we have a *chain reaction theory*, in which the effects of the media move from one individual to the next. Your best friend watches a television commercial about blue jeans, buys a pair the next day, as do you the day after, following her example. There are two steps here:

1. Media effect upon first individual
2. Media effect, via first individual, upon second individual.

Of course, there could be more than two steps. You might, for example, influence the consumer behaviour of your older sister, who, in turn, might have an effect on someone else. So perhaps it would be better to call this model the 'multi-step-flow-theory'!

Two-step-flow theory gained prominence in the 1950s through the work of Elihu Katz and Paul F. Lazarsfeld. In reviewing the early twentieth-century work on media effects, these two social scientists noted that people who regarded the media as the enemies of democracy, feared the newspaper and the radio 'as powerful weapons able to rubber-stamp ideas upon the minds of defenseless readers and listeners' (Katz and Lazarsfeld 1965: 16). Yet, they argued, this kind of direct brainwashing effects model didn't take full account of the fact that individuals' predispositions could modify or distort the meanings of a particular message. For example, 'a prejudiced person . . . may actively resist a message of tolerance' (1965: 23). Similarly, if you're a supporter of the Conservative Party, you might refuse to believe the claims of a Labour Party political broadcast. What Katz and Lazarsfeld were able to offer social science was a less deterministic view of media effects. People aren't robots. They have feelings and ideas, and they either accept, modify or reject what they receive from the media.

Nor, argued Katz and Lazarsfeld, do all people have the same amount of direct exposure to media messages. Contrast, for example, the once-a-week cinema-goer with the once-a-year movie watcher, the person who reads three national daily newspapers with the person who reads one Sunday newspaper, the 'couch potato' who watches eight hours of commercial television every day with the one who just tunes into BBC *Nine O'Clock News* on weekdays. People who are regular users of the media do, of course, associate with those of us who use it less often. It's in that interaction between these two groups that media messages sometimes continue to flow. Thus, for example, the 'three-newspapers-a-day' reader is asked by the 'once-a-week' reader for advice on whether to vote for a common European currency in a forthcoming referendum. The regular reader has acquired lots of information on this subject from newspapers and offers an 'informed' opinion. At that point, she or he becomes what Katz and Lazarsfeld term an 'opinion leader'.

It's these opinion leaders who pick up new ideas and behaviours from the media (one step) and pass them onto their peers (two steps), who in turn influence other peers (three or more steps) – and so the process continues. In the words of Katz and Lazarsfeld: 'ideas, often, seem to flow from radio and print to opinion leaders and from them to the less active sections of the population' (1965: 32).

The original evidence for this theory was presented in a study by Katz and Lazarsfeld (1965) of the 1940 US presidential election campaign. The supposition is that individuals are, to some extent, shielded from direct media exposure by the strength of their personal ties to families, peers and other social groups in society. It's within the context of this group structure that they receive media messages and ultimately form judgements. Especially important within the group are the 'opinion leaders'. These are the people who receive media messages firsthand and pass this information (sometimes selectively) to other people with whom they associate.

In practice, of course, all of us receive first-hand exposure to the media. We all watch television, most of us read newspapers, etc. What the two-step-flow theorists seem to be suggesting is that:

- some (generally, 'well-informed') people have lots of exposure to the media. They might include teachers who read more than one newspaper daily, politicians who watch hours of television news programmes, school students who never miss an episode of *Neighbours*, etc. These people are 'opinion leaders'
- other (generally, less 'well-informed') people have more limited exposure to the media. They might include people who don't watch much television or who don't read a daily newspaper. These people are sometimes influenced by those of their acquaintances who are 'opinion leaders'.

The opinion leader doesn't just pass on uncontested information (for example, football results), but also interpretations of media messages (for example, how a preview has persuaded her or him to watch a particular film). Media messages thereby do a 'two-step'. Firstly, the opinion leader is influenced through direct exposure. Secondly, people who respect and heed the views of the opinion leader are influenced. In general, it's been found

TWO-STEP-FLOW THEORY

FOR

+ It represents a theoretical and an empirical shift from the somewhat crude belief that the media have unshakeable, direct effects upon gullible individuals. Two-step-flow theory also represents an intellectual step forward in communications studies, because it correctly recognises that human social behaviour is shaped by multiple effects, among which the media play a greater or lesser role.
+ It astutely notes that personal relationships and conversation with respected peers and other significant contacts accompany and sometimes modify media influence. Maybe, for example, your initial decision to buy a particular type of CD-player after watching a television commercial might be changed when you listen to music on your 'techo' friend's superior music system.
+ Its assertions, as McQuail (1987) observes, have been taken very seriously by sophisticated political campaign managers, who have incorporated the factor of 'personal influence' into their electioneering strategies. These people don't invest time and money in projects unless they're convinced that there are likely to be favourable outcomes.
+ In some 'communities' (for example, gang neighbourhoods), when new ideas come from the media (for example, the latest, most 'cool' baseball caps), the responses of key figures (for example, gang leaders) can influence whether the message is adopted on a wider scale.

AGAINST

− Some audiences have a single-link relationship with media sources. For example, socially isolated individuals sometimes use television to reduce loneliness. There are no second-link opinion leaders here, just the television screen and the viewer.
− While it emphasises 'mediated media' effects (i.e. opinion leaders mediate from the media to their associates), the onus is still on fairly direct influences. The opinion leader gets 'zapped' by a media message, which is then transferred to other people. The process is one-directional, and the audiences are theorised as being more uniform and passive than they actually are.
− There are times when the influence of opinion leaders is secondary to the direct effect of a particular media stimulus on a respondent's 'fast-forward' attitudinal and behavioural changes. For example, a person might immediately renounce any desire to wear seal fur garments, and decide to join a citizens' lobby group after watching an anti-fur trade Greenpeace programme on television. Even if this person's friends exert strong counteractive pressures, she or he might resolve to remain firm.
− It's often said that two-step-flow theory stops short of three, four or more steps. We think this criticism is a bit pernickety, because two-step-flow theorists probably envisaged that the cascading process might keep going. On the other hand, it's a criticism that reminds us that two or just a few steps don't tell the whole story. How people are influenced by the media is potentially much more complex than that.

that influential opinion leaders are, in certain respects, very much like the people they influence. As Melvin L. De Fleur and Sandra Ball-Rokeach note: 'Opinion leadership does not seem to travel down the social structure, but is more likely to be horizontal' (De Fleur and Ball-Rokeach 1982: 194). In other words, opinion leaders and their acquaintances usually have similar social backgrounds. Katz and Lazarsfeld (cited by De Fleur and Ball-Rokeach 1982) discovered that social position was a key factor in determining who would influence whom in areas like fashion and public issues. For example, young working women who regularly read fashion magazines were consulted by the less informed for advice on clothing, hairstyle, and such like. Married women with large families, who – via the media – knew a lot about household products, were sought as consultants on trying out new products, and so on.

Two-step-flow theory represents an important departure from the more direct effects model of hypodermic syringe theory. Nevertheless, in both models, the flow of influence starts from the media and – more or less speedily – reaches the audience. The next model for consideration, uses and gratifications theory, challenges the notion that audiences are always on the receiving end of media messages. Sometimes the media are on the receiving end of the uses that audiences choose to put them.

Uses and gratifications theory

As its name implies, this model proposes that people use the media in order to obtain gratification. For example, you tune your satellite receiver to MTV (a *use* of media) because you enjoy watching and listening to the music on that channel (a *gratification*). It's not a case of the media manipulating you; it's you deciding what to do with the media. The question to ask, says Elihu Katz (1977, cited by Lull 1995: 90) is: 'what do people do with the media?'

Taken to its logical conclusion, uses and gratifications theory almost ceases to be an explanation of media effects, because the audience rather than the media are in the driving seat. Indeed, K. E. Rosengren and S. Windahl (1972) propose that the two concepts of 'media effects' and 'media uses' should merge, and that it's possible 'to ask what effect a given use made of the mass media, or a given gratification obtained from them, may have' (cited by Rubin 1994: 422). In other words, social scientists must consider how you, a user of media, affects them, and how they, as providers of your needs, affect you. It's conceded, of course, by exponents of uses and gratifications theory that people make choices which are, to some extent, 'shaped' by social influences – including media exposure. At the same time, people bounce back at the media with their uses and their needs.

And those needs, say uses and gratifications theorists, aren't merely social. They involve biological and psychological dimensions. As the Swedish sociologist and uses and gratifications theorist Karl Erik Rosengren (1974) contends, *need* is 'the biological and psychological infrastructure that forms the basis of all human social behavior' (cited by Lull 1995: 98). What he's saying here is that our biologies and psychologies motivate us to seek social interaction (this includes the interaction between the individual and the media) in order to satisfy our goals. For example, my biological need to get fit and my psychological wish to feel good might prompt me to 'work out' while watching aerobic exercise demonstrations on 'breakfast TV'.

While uses and gratifications theorists generally accept that the media are potential sources of influence, they also emphasise that audience behaviour and motivation reduce or heighten such effects. According to Alan M. Rubin (1994: 420), uses and gratifications theory is based on these assumptions:

- ◆ People select and use the media in a goal-directed, purposive manner to satisfy felt needs.
- ◆ People's interaction with the media is based on their particular psychological and social profiles.
- ◆ Media compete with other forms of communication (for example, telephones) for people's attention, selection and use.
- ◆ People are typically – but not always – more influential in the relationship between them and the media (i.e. they're more likely to decide what they want to do with the media than what the media want to do with them).

Uses and gratifications research focuses on audience motivation and consumption. With those considerations in mind, D. McQuail, J. G. Blumler and J. R. Brown (1972, cited by Rubin 1994), have developed a model of media–person interactions, noting that people are motivated to use television for:

- ◆ diversion (for example, escape)
- ◆ personal relationships (for example, companionship)
- ◆ personal identity (for example, value reinforcement)
- ◆ surveillance (for example, getting information and news).

This multi-dimensional appeal of television to viewers suggests that what audiences seek to obtain from the media can't be pinned down to one or two simple needs. To quote D. McQuail *et al.* (1972), 'the relationship between content categories and audience needs is far less tidy and more complex than most commentators have appreciated' (cited by Rubin 1994: 422). This recognition of complexity is a welcome departure from the simpler, 'knee-jerk' effect model of the hypodermic syringe theorists, because it rightly emphasises that audiences aren't the passive dupes they were once thought to be. Audiences are made up of people who have different needs and their own, sometimes very personal, ways of satisfying those needs. I might watch the film *Braveheart* to learn something about medieval military tactics. The person in the seat next to me might watch it because she wants to 'connect', in a very vital way, with her Scottish heritage. The person sitting next to her might be watching it because he accidentally entered the wrong door in a multi-screen cinema!

Adding to – and, to some extent, complementing – the list of uses to which viewers put their televisions noted by McQuail *et al.* above, James Lull (1995) has documented these various ways in which people engage the media for personal and social reasons:

- Radio listeners have used quiz programmes and soap operas to obtain advice about personal problems, and for learning social skills. They've also listened to the radio for companionship and entertainment.
- Adults have read newspapers to help them to participate effectively in public life.
- Families have used television to provide group entertainment, as a fantasy stimulant, and as a conversational resource. An ethnographic study of Boston's East End Italian population of the 1950s by H. Gans (1962, cited by Lull 1995) found that family discussions about television programmes 'helped' people to define and reinforce gender roles, solve everyday problems, and criticise social institutions.

This emphasis on how people use the media is important and helpful. However, it's also crucial to recognise that 'needs' are sometimes manufactured in the first instance by the media. This is especially so in the context of effective advertising. If an advertisement persuades you that you 'need' a particular product even when you probably don't (we can probably all think of examples from personal experience here), then the 'need' has become a 'media effect'. In that respect, you aren't defining your needs on the basis of personal autonomy; rather, the media are defining your needs for you.

Nevertheless, it's right to acknowledge our debt to the work of social scientists who work within the uses and gratifications paradigm (model). They keep reminding us that there's much more to the understanding of human social behaviour than just looking for effects that move in one direction from television screens and newspaper print to viewers and readers.

It's now time to look at a theory of media effects that adopts more of a 'flow from media to audience' approach: the cultural effects model.

Cultural effects model

Whereas the hypodermic syringe model envisages a media 'quick shot in the arm' followed by a fairly direct, often immediate effect on the audience, the cultural effects model suggests a 'slow, drip, drip' process, accompanied by a less direct, longer term influence. It

USES AND GRATIFICATIONS THEORY

FOR

+ It demonstrates that people use media for their personal and social interests. They choose to do this because they are wilful beings. In short, uses and gratifications research shows us that human social behaviour can't just be reduced to a stimulus-response model.
+ Its argument that audiences are active selectors and interpreters of media messages is widely supported by extensive empirical research, as documented for example by James Lull (1995).
+ With its emphasis on the felt needs of the individual, it combines the insights of biological, psychological and sociological sciences. Put another way, it properly takes account of the fact that people's needs are explained on more than one level. We have bodies, minds and sociabilities.

AGAINST

– It invests the viewer with too much autonomy, thereby underestimating the extent to which people in society are socialised (by, among other things, the media) into some of the apparent 'choices' they make. In that respect, a 'need' is sometimes manufactured by the media (for example, through advertising) rather than emanating from the individual.
– It's a very individualistic theory, and doesn't give sufficient attention to the social dimensions of media organisation and production. That part of the story is almost 'forgotten'. The individual versus the media is a very unequal contest in which, arguably, the media often have the upper hand.
– Linked to the last point, the individualistic orientation employed in uses and gratifications research makes it difficult to generalise beyond individual cases. Put simply, if we argue that lots of different individuals use the media for lots of different reasons, it becomes difficult to identify more general trends.

envisages media effects as shaping, over time, people's taken-for-granted assumptions. Who, for example, among the many tabloid newspaper readers in the UK would question the taken-for-granted view that our nation needs a strong army, that 'panhandlers' aren't prepared to earn a living like the rest of us, that young offenders need boot camps rather than therapy-based 'holidays'? Perhaps sociologists would question these tabloid-manufactured stereotypes. But tabloids, and the culture they spin, have never had much time for sociologists. When they do write about us, it's usually to tell their readers how misguided and out of touch with reality sociologists are. And there's another stereotype!

Among the taken-for-granted cultural assumptions that are fuelled by some tabloid media in the UK are:

- Women should look beautiful and slender.
- Young black males are potential muggers.
- One-parent families headed by single mothers are welfare scroungers.
- 'Immigrants' come here to get free housing.

OVER TO YOU

Add to the above list, and identify the kinds of source from which your examples come.

Cultural effects theory has informed media effects research from at least as far back as the 1960s. Particularly important in that decade was the US-based Cultural Indicators Project. Launched in 1967, the Project began with a study for the National Commission on the Causes and Prevention of Violence. Since that year, annual week-long samples of US network television drama have been content-analysed in order to identify selected features and trends in the 'world' that television presents to viewers. The next step is to ask viewers questions about their perceptions of social issues (for example, 'Is crime a big problem in society today?'). The object is to see if frequent viewers are more likely than infrequent viewers (both groups sharing similar demographic profiles, for example, same social classes, same age groups, etc.) to give 'television answers' to the questions.

Cultural effects research of this kind, based on longitudinal studies of adolescent viewing (for example, Morgan, Alexander *et al.*, 1990, cited by Bryant and Zillmann 1994), shows that television can exert an independent influence on attitudes and behaviours over time, but that the beliefs of young viewers can also influence subsequent viewing. The point here is that cultural effects aren't seen as simple one-directional, *from* television *to* viewer influences. For example, children who are strongly integrated into cohesive peer or family groups are more resistant to adopting a television view of the world. Even allowing for such variations, however, cultural effects research still identifies in many viewers a gradual entrenchment over time of television-orchestrated, mainstream outlooks.

In cultural effects theory, it's accepted that people are born into a symbolic environment (i.e. a social world where assumptions and attitudes have been and are being shaped) in which the media, especially television, is a key shaper. In that sense, as George Gerbner, Larry Cross, Michael Morgan and Nancy Signorielli note:

> 'Television viewing both shapes and is a stable part of lifestyles and outlooks. It links the individual to a larger if synthetic world, a world of television's own making.'
> (Gerbner *et al.* 1994: 23–4)

This isn't to suggest that television – and, indeed, other media – effects can be measured by straightforward 'before and after' experiments. For how, in a world where even the newborn are exposed to television, is it possible to talk of people who have certain attitudes before and different attitudes after watching it? You might reply that it's possible to study the effects of long-term exposure to television violence on people before and after the viewing started. But even here, there might have been much earlier, perhaps even forgotten, exposure to television programmes featuring violence. Won't this also have to become part of the equation, even though it doesn't fit into the experimenter's time-frame? If such is the case, how is it possible to disentangle one set of effects from another?

These are difficult questions, and the best that social scientists can do is to ensure, as far as possible, that their 'control' and 'experimental' samples contain people with broadly similar characteristics. Otherwise, it's very likely that the viewer samples will respond in different ways to the content of the programmes they watch. A viewer's age, ethnicity, sex, social class, etc., can and often do affect how a particular content is interpreted. These distinct identities of different kinds of viewer caution against the early hypodermic syringe model notion that mass media messages were uncritically imbibed by undifferentiated mass audiences. People sometimes see different things. Take, for example, early television depictions of the incorrectly termed 'American Indian'. In the 1940s and 1950s, some white Americans who watched Native American people attacking white settlers were probably repelled by the 'brutish savagery' of the 'redskins'. Yet when young Aboriginal Australians watch old 'westerns', some of them identify with the 'Indians', and 'cheer them on as they attack the wagon train or homestead' (Fiske, cited by Lull 1995: 73).

A key assumption of cultural effects theory is that audiences aren't blank cheques to be filled in by scripts created by the media. People encounter the media with lots of cultural and experiential baggage already on board. The Glasgow Group found this when they interviewed people who watched news footage about the 1984–5 miners' strike in the UK. As mentioned earlier, these people responded to the media not in some robotic, knee-jerk fashion, but in a considered way, based on their prior knowledge – sometimes first-hand – of the events that were portrayed. The in-depth interview is a very important tool in cultural effects research – it enables social scientists to prize out the different ways in which audiences interpret, make sense of and sometimes resist the messages they receive from the media.

But, as its description implies, cultural *effects* theory is also concerned with effects. Nevertheless, even though many of them are marxists, cultural effects theorists reject the simplistic notion that the media are a brainwashing tool of the ruling class. Instead, they adopt the more realistic view that some media help powerful groups in society to obtain the 'active consent' of people whose real interests run counter to giving that consent. What we have in mind here are the taken-for-granted assumptions that arise, for example, when people on low incomes start believing – because of heavy exposure to tabloid media – that they have no moral right to accept welfare payments. If the *Sun* hammers home the message that welfare recipients are 'scroungers', and this persuades some of its poorer readers not to claim what's legally (and morally) theirs, needy people are 'colluding' with a system that oppresses them.

Cultural effects theory recognises that people make their own sense of media messages (you and I might read different things into a television advertisement, for example), but only within determinate limits. In that respect, it neither conflates the 'audience's uses' nor the 'media effects' side of things. Both play a part. It's reasonable to expect that individuals don't simply fall into line with what media producers seek to convey. Simultaneously, it's sensible to conclude that the long-term exposure of individuals to media does have some 'effect' on how they think and behave in general terms, and, to some extent, on how they 'make sense' of what the media produce. For example, if, over the past ten years, I've largely relied on the *Daily Mirror* for knowledge of national news, then it's very likely that what I've read will influence my thoughts (for example, thinking that 'New' Labour has got it right), behaviour (for example, voting Labour at the last general election), and my level of trust in the newspaper (for example, regarding it as reliable). To be sure, some of what's going on will be a process of reinforcement (i.e. confirming what I already believe), but the *Daily Mirror* will, no doubt, influence me too.

Of the four models of media effects considered above, three – hypodermic syringe, two-step-flow and cultural effects – tend to see the media, to a greater or lesser extent and more or less directly, as influencing the way people think and behave. At the heart of these models is the assumption that the media can implant ideas in people, either through direct exposure or through the 'copycatting' of those who have been exposed. Social scientists who adopt these models adopt a research outlook characterised by the attempt to measure the effect of media input on those exposed to the input and those not so exposed. One of the models – uses

CULTURAL EFFECTS THEORY

FOR

+ It studies media effects as they operate within a social structure of pre-existing power relationships and a cultural context of prior assumptions. In those respects, account is taken of who pulls the strings, as well as the beliefs people already have.
+ It focuses on the relationship between media exposure and long-term effects, rather than on immediate 'knee-jerk' reactions to the media. With few exceptions, being influenced by the media takes time.
+ It correctly notes that the modern media (especially television) dominate people's 'symbolic environment', substituting communications messages for personal experiences. Persistent exposure to these messages clearly has a shaping effect on how people think and behave.

AGAINST

– Its assertions are, by its own admission, guarded and circumspect. Unlike theories that offer more direct explanations, cultural effects theory is much more tentative and inexact about what it attempts to predict. In that sense, it lacks the bold scientific edge of 'cause and effect' explanations.
– It claims to tease out biases and distortions in the media, but its proponents tend to question the reliability of any media accounts of reality that don't square with their own interpretations. This is especially so with the more marxist-oriented advocates of cultural effects theory.
– Cultural effects theorists often assume that the media privilege the views of the rich and powerful over other groups. This under-estimates the extent to which media personnel exercise a strong claim to professional autonomy. The duty of the journalist, for example, is to the public's 'right to know', not to present the personal views of media bosses.

and gratifications – turns things around by suggesting that people, through consumer choice, decide what to do with the media.

Research into media effects often combines more than one theory in order to obtain a better purchase on complex phenomena. For example, the better parts of hypodermic syringe and cultural effects theories fuse to form another one – *amplification theory* (see Chapter 16, Deviance, page 507). Amplification theory argues that certain behaviours can be *amplified* (i.e. escalated) because of the way the media present them. This can occur in actual and in socially constructed ways. For example, if a television bulletin reports that an LA gang is expected to carry out a series of drive-by shootings over the weekend, this might – in hypodermic syringe manner – prompt some gang members to fulfil the expectation. Here we have a self-fulfilling prophesy that leads to an actual increase in violence. On a socially constructed level, a newspaper campaign which claims that Leeds is the 'car-theft capital' of the UK might – through cultural effects saturation – create a law enforcement moral panic, thereby leading to more arrests of car thieves. In this instance, car theft crime statistics increase even if there's no actual rise in the number of stolen cars.

Violence and the media

Amplification theory – a composite of hypodermic and cultural effects theories – has an interesting application in the study of terrorism. Some terrorist violence is given advance notice, via the media, by terrorists who want maximum publicity for political reasons. In a study of this phenomenon, A. P. Schmid and J. de Graf (1982, cited by McQuail 1987) contend that violence is often a means of access to mass media, and can be a message in itself. The media play a role here because they attach huge weight to reporting violence. Schmid and de Graf also refer to the strong beliefs of police – and also a moderate belief by media personnel – that live coverage of terrorist actions does encourage terrorism. Copycat behaviours and the belief that one's cause is 'celebrated' worldwide might both feature here.

The argument that violence on the media – especially the kind that sensationalises assaults, rapes and murders – actually causes some people to commit violent acts is supported by some social scientists, but is treated with scepticism by others. Certainly, politicians are coming round to the idea that TV violence begets real violence. President Clinton, for example, has decided that all new television sets in the US will be fitted with so-called V-chips (short for violence chips) from 1998. The European Parliament has also proposed the introduction of these devices. The V-chip (promoted as a barrier to the ill-effects of television, and which only costs 60p) scrambles any programmes that parents decide are too violent or

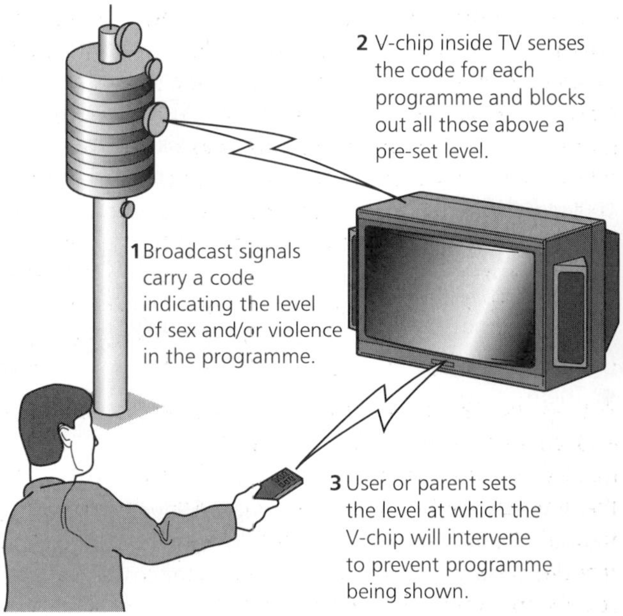

2 V-chip inside TV senses the code for each programme and blocks out all those above a pre-set level.
1 Broadcast signals carry a code indicating the level of sex and/or violence in the programme.
3 User or parent sets the level at which the V-chip will intervene to prevent programme being shown.

(*The Times*, 19 March 1996, page 6)
How the V-chip can scramble violent programmes

in other ways unsuitable for their children. The diagram above shows how the new technology works.

Clearly, the logic behind the V-chip is that violent programmes are a bad influence on young viewers. But is it a logic supported by the findings of social scientific research? According to Tim Newburn and Ann Hagell, public debate about the 'effect of violence in television and film . . . remains dominated by anecdotal evidence' (Newburn and Hagell 1995: 7). So what does social science have to say about the matter?

Some of the earliest social scientific research into the impact of media violence was conducted in the 1920s in the US. During that decade, the film industry became a major source of mass entertainment. Yet, notes Barrie Gunter (1994), no equivocal evidence emerged to support the widely held fear that films had damaging effects on their audiences. In the 1950s, media researchers became very interested in another popular entertainment medium – comics. One very scathing attack on the alleged bad influence of comics came from F. Werthman (1954, cited by Gunter 1994) in his book, *The Seduction of the Innocent*. As the title of the book implies, Gunter argued that children imitated violent acts they found in crime comics. Werthman actually claimed that there was a significant correlation between reading crime comics and very serious forms of juvenile delinquency. His 'evidence' was largely based on interviews of children in clinical settings, which, from an interpretivist standpoint, compromise validity by their artificiality. Gunter contends, moreover, that there were inconsistencies in Werthman's analysis. Nevertheless, the publication of *The Seduction of the Innocent* seriously undermined the comic industry at that time.

Moving forward to the next decade, President Johnson's National Commission on the Causes and Prevention of Violence (1968) didn't find that television was a major cause of social violence. However, the Surgeon General's Scientific Advisory Committee on Television and Social Behaviour – set up in 1969 and reporting in 1972 – concluded that:

- Television content is very substantially laden with violence.
- Adults and children spend increasingly more time watching this violence.
- There is some evidence that, on balance, watching violent entertainment on television increases the prospect of aggressive behaviour among viewers.

A ten-year follow-up to the Surgeon General's Report by the US National Institute of Mental Health concluded that the short-term and long-term consequences of violence on television were to help stir up aggressive behaviour. In very unequivocal terms, the National Institute of Mental Health (1982) reported:

'The consensus among most of the research community is that violence on television does lead to aggressive behavior by children and teenagers who watch the programs.'

(cited by Barry 1993: 237)

A 1985 task force for the American Psychological Association Commission on Youth and Violence arrived at the same conclusion. In 1992, a study by the same body noted that the National Institute for Mental Health, the American Psychological Association and the Center for Disease Control agreed that research confirmed the following finding: *childhood viewing of television violence is directly related to criminally violent behaviour later on*. Moreover, a study by Dr Brandon Centerwall (1992, cited by Barry 1993), of the University of Washington Department of Epidemiology and Psychiatry, into the statistical relationship between the change in violent crime rates following the introduction of television in the US, found that:

- Murder rates in Canada and the US increased nearly 100 per cent (92 per cent in Canada, 93 per cent in the US, corrected for population increase) between 1945 and 1970.
- In both countries, television ownership increased in almost the same proportion as the murder rate.
- White murder rates in Canada, the USA – and also in South Africa – were stable or declining until the introduction of television. Thereafter, in the course of a generation, the murder rates doubled.

Taken as a whole, the general finding of the various positivistic studies referred to above is that violence in the media, particularly on television, tends to incite violent behaviour among certain members of society, younger people being particularly susceptible. It's a finding, however, whose validity is questioned by social scientists who adopt a more interpretivistic approach to media research. They regard the positivistic assertion that exposure to violence in the media heightens the incidence of violence in society as tentative at best and speculative at worst. For example, Philip Schlesinger *et al.* write:

'Mass-mediated violence has been studied by using a wide range of models and theories, but there is no undisputed evidence of what the effects of such highly varied representations may be.'

(Schlesinger *et al.* 1992: 2)

Working within an interpretivist framework, Shlesinger *et al.* (1992) are less interested in cause–effect analysis than in how people, particularly women, make sense of the violence they see in the media. This focus on how people interpret media messages asks different questions to the ones posed by social scientists who are more concerned with how the media might harmfully influence vulnerable viewers. Foremost in this context is the endeavour to find out how people's backgrounds and experiences interact with what the media produce. nstead of asking, 'Will these violent films make more people violent?' interpretivists ask, 'How do different individuals *interpret* and, thereafter, respond to the films?' This last question suggests that simple cause–effect models of media effects don't take sufficient account of audience variety. Individual A might look at a 'bad guy' shooting a police officer on the streets of Los Angeles in the film *Reservoir Dogs*, and think, 'That's how I'm gonna take care of any cop who gets in my way', and actually go out and shoot a police officer. Individual B, on the other hand, might merely find the scene 'entertaining', and won't, under any circumstances, carry out a real-life shooting.

Put simply, the results of research into the relationship between media violence and violence in society remain stubbornly inconclusive – which brings us back to our original assertion, and it's one that we stand by:

Some media affect some people some of the time in some ways.

Taking stock of media effects, we can make these observations:

- The study of mass media is largely based on the assumption that the media affect us. But how and to what extent this happens is still uncertain.
- Despite the above uncertainty, the assumption is very sensible. All of us know, from personal experience, of times when the media has had an affect on how we behave: wearing a raincoat when the weather forecast predicts rain, running out to the corner shop to buy an ice cream when a television commercial reminds us we want our favourite product – right now!

Watching this film might have the effect of making some people engage in copy-cat violence. Other people who watch the same film won't experience the same ill-effects.

- When we consider more complex issues – such as, why people vote the way they do, why some people are violent, why some people challenge the opinions of newspaper editors, etc. – media effects theory offers lots of (and sometimes 'competing') explanations.
- Most sociologists accept that the way people behave and think is rarely, if ever, only explained by exposure to media. In that sense, the problem becomes one of measuring the influence of the media, compared to the influence of other factors.

Owning up to the inevitable inconclusiveness of media effects research isn't an admission of defeat. Far from it. It represents both intellectual honesty and the resolve to keep on looking for better answers.

QUESTIONS

1. Outline and evaluate the four main models of media effects: hypodermic syringe; two-step-flow; uses and gratifications; cultural effects.
2. Explain the links between positivism and the hypodermic syringe model, and between interpretivism and the uses and gratifications model.
3. Why is the study of deviancy amplification an essential part of media effects research?
4. Assess the argument that media violence causes actual violence.

Ownership and control of the mass media

Karl Marx wasn't just a social scientist; he was a journalist too. In one of his articles, 'The opinion of the press and the opinion of the people' (1861, cited by Murdock 1995), he pondered the various links between newspaper owners, editors and ruling class politicians. The American Civil War was raging at the time, and Marx sought to explain why prominent London newspapers were campaigning for intervention on the side of the pro-slavery South. He argued that the proposed intervention served the interests of an important section of the English ruling class led by the Prime Minister, Lord Palmerston. Moreover, Marx claimed that these powerful people were able to influence press coverage because they owned leading newspapers and had political and social connections with key editors. Identifying this constellation of ownership, control and influence, Marx wrote:

'Consider the London press. At its head stands The Times, whose chief editor, Bob Lowe, is a subordinate member of the cabinet and a mere creature of Palmerston. The Principal Editor of Punch was accommodated by Palmerston with a seat on the Board of Health and an annual salary of a thousand pounds sterling. The Morning Post is in part Palmerston's private property . . . The Morning Advertiser is the joint property of the licenced victuallers . . . The editor, Mr Grant, has had the honour to get invited to Palmerston's private soirees . . . It must be added that the pious patrons of this liquor-journal stand under the ruling rod of the Earl of Shaftsbury and that Shaftsbury is Palmerston's son-in-law.'

(Marx 1861, cited by Murdock 1995: 126)

Marx believed that editors, while nominally in control of day-to-day operations, ultimately complied with the ideological interests of the owners. His personal experience as one of the *New York Daily Tribune*'s European correspondents, reinforced this opinion. He was initially regarded as one of the best reporters on the 'foreign' staff. However, his views increasingly began to alarm the proprietor of the paper, Horace Greely. So concerned was

Greely, that he asked the editor, Charles Dana, to fire Marx. Bravely, Dana refused, but publication of Marx's articles was temporarily suspended, and soon afterwards he was taken off the payroll – allegedly because more space was needed for coverage of the American Civil War.

Unlike Marx and his theoretical advocates, pluralist sociologists rebut the argument that the mass media serve the ideological interests of the ruling class. Rather, claim the pluralists, the professional managers of communications corporations have agendas that support widely ranging ideologies. Take the British press in the mid-1990s, for example. The *Daily Mirror* supported the Labour Party, the *Sun* favoured Thatcher-style Conservatism and gave the Conservative Prime Minister, John Major, a hard time, the *Financial Times* offered a plurality of political opinions, but its leader articles were very pro-Tony Blair, the Labour Party leader.

Ultimately, argue the pluralists, 'Consumer sovereignty rules, OK!' In short, the owners and managers of the mass media aren't free to follow the personal preferences and whims of a ruling class because proprietorial and managerial influence must defer to the demands of mass consumers. In that sense, contends Martin Seiden:

'It is with the audience and not with the media that the power resides . . . Because the audience's attention is so essential to the success of the system, its influence over the media is exercised in its day-to-day operation rather than as some vague, intangible desire on the part of those who own the media.'

(Seiden 1974, cited by Murdock 1995: 129)

The pluralists have quite a strong case. Indeed, sometimes the press are among the staunchest critics of government. In its Commentary, 'Lies, damned lies and logistics', on 18 February 1996, the *Observer* noted of the UK arms to Iraq scandal that:

'All the vices the Scott inquiry should have put a stop to were on display last week. Parliament was misled, civil servants were misused, and Ministers covered up all over again. The Whitehall lie machine went into overdrive the moment Sir Richard Scott's report landed on Ministers' desks. The Government press pack, prepared by civil servants, was a master of disinformation. Conservative politicians repeated the party line, parrot-fashion, in Parliament and outside. Nothing had gone wrong; and nobody was to blame. We are ruled, we are told, by honourable men. But men of honour do not treat the public with such blatant contempt . . .

The lie machine began operating according to its own twisted rules long ago. In the Thatcher years, Britain became an arms bazaar, pushing weapons to some of the world's most despicable regimes. With muck, came brass, but it was not honourably gained. Britain knew that Saddam Hussein had used poison gas against the Kurdish people. Photographs were published of their torment and extermination. But secretly, unofficially, Saddam's Iraq remained a friend. Parliament was kept in the dark, not for reasons of nationa security as the Government pretended, but because of the fear of strong public opposition to such a murky, lucrative trade.'

(*Observer Review*, 18 February 1996, page 3)

Harsh words indeed from one of the nation's most respected broadsheet newspapers. They indict political leaders for their wrongdoing, and they cite, as evidence, a report prepared by a fox-hunting, titled judge: Sir Richard Scott.

Not only do newspaper staff sometimes take a swipe at the rich and powerful, they also occasionally let 'ordinary' citizens have a voice in the media. During the 1984–5 miners' strike, for example, Bill Keys, General Secretary of the Society of Graphical and Allied Trades, demanded a right of reply on behalf of Arthur Scargill, President of the National Union of Mineworkers, the day after a scathing attack appeared in the *Daily Express* (9 May 1984). Keys, who represented some of the *Daily Express* printworkers, said he had never come across a more politically biased article in his 47 years as a trade union official. Lord Matthews, Chairperson of the *Daily Express*, agreed to print a reply. However, when Keys insisted it should appear on the front page, the newspaper's editor, Sir Larry Lamb, believed his position had become compromised and offered to resign. When Scargill's letter arrived, Lord Matthews refused to print all of it on the alleged grounds that it contained 'rhetorical abuse'. Keys responded by threatening to halt production of the newspaper through withdrawing the printworkers, which, in turn, set the journalists against Keys. The upshot was that the *Daily Express* lost all editions that should have been printed in London that night. The next day, an agreement was reached with the unions over the content of Scargill's reply, and Sir Larry Lamb withdrew his resignation.

Three days later, an article by Scargill appeared in the *Daily Express*, but on the front page was a picture of the miners' leader showing him with his arm outstretched. The same picture, headlined 'Mine Fuhrer', was prepared for publication on the front page of the *Sun*, accompanied by a story which reported that Scargill had given his supporters a Hitler-style salute. When *Sun* printworkers saw the front page, they refused to let production continue, and the *Sun* appeared without the picture or the headline. The retaliatory action by the printworkers shows that the managers and the owners of newspapers aren't the only people who exercise control over what the media produce. On several other occasions, the printworkers successfully challenged the editors and proprietors. In February 1984, for example, members of the National Graphical Association at the *Sunday Times* obtained equal space for Scargill to reply to an article by the head of the coal industry, Ian MacGregor.

But the pluralist argument sounds less convincing in relation to captive audiences. During a bit of 'world wide web surfing' at a cyberspace cafe in York, I came across an American lobby group called Campaign for a Non-Commercial Classroom. On downloading their file, I discovered that the members of this group have launched a campaign to keep Channel 1 outside of American classrooms. Channel 1 is a satellite-based television feed system that transmits so-called educational programmes. Owned by K-111, a big media company whose publications include *Hand Gunning*, *Daily Racing Form* and *Soap Opera Weekly*, Channel 1's best known offering is a 'current events' programme which also contains commercials for junk food, cosmetics and athletics clothing – all specifically packaged for teenagers. Companies that advertise on this channel (among them, Pepsi, McDonald's, Reebok, Nintendo, Wrigley and Disney) pay $200,000 per half minute spot.

They pay because their audience is truly captive (the students in 12,000 US public schools who watch TV in classrooms every day). Moreover, what these companies sell is targeted to an age group who buy their products. Almost all the materials K-111 produces for the classroom carry some kind of advertising. Says the Campaign for a Non-Commercial Classroom: 'It thrives on the support of advertisers who target specific audiences that they can reach through classroom materials.'

The influence of powerful American corporations over media production isn't, of course, confined to its own domestic markets. Just outside Tokyo, 300,000 people visit Japan's Disneyland. In Brazil, 70 per cent of songs played each night on the radio are in English. American authors line up prominently in Italian best-seller lists, and American films (mostly action-adventure epics like *Jurassic Park* and *Heat*) get some 70 per cent of the European gate. Says Carl Bernstein: 'America is saturating the world with its myths, its fantasies, its tunes and dreams' (Bernstein 1990: 10). It's doing this through the ownership and control of global entertainment empires by the likes of Dreamworks' Steven Spielberg, Fox's Rupert Murdoch, and Microsoft's Bill Gates.

Consider, for a moment, the global communications empire of media mogul Rupert Murdoch. As at July 1995:

- in the USA, he owned the Fox Television Network, the film studio Twentieth Century Fox, the FX cable channel, a clutch of local television stations, *TV Guide*, the *New York Daily Post* and the book publishers, Harper Collins
- in Asia, he held a 63.6 per cent stake in Star TV, whose satellite television was capable of reaching two-thirds of the world's population
- in Australia, he had a 15 per cent share of Channel 7, the national newspaper, *The Australian*, as well as numerous regional newspapers and magazines

Media moguls like Bill Gates, boss of Microsoft, own and control much of global mass media.

- in the UK, his press empire owned the *Sunday Times*, *The Times*, the *Sun*, *News of the World* and *Today*. He also had a 40 per cent holding in the television satellite company BSkyB

. . . and the list goes on! (See the map on page 482.)

Of course, it's very hard to prove that people like Rupert Murdoch exert 'editorial control' over the media companies they own. But it seems likely that they do exercise some leverage. Murdoch, for example, was a favoured dinner guest at Prime Minister Thatcher's table, and the *Sun* was an ardent fan of the 'Iron Lady'. The late Robert Maxwell sometimes used his media for purposes of self-publicity, and Tiny Rowlands, who was once a newspaper proprietor, is known to have influenced an *Observer* piece. Moreover, the owners of the media have an important say in who works for them, especially at the higher levels of the operation. So it's reasonable to assume that top managers share some affinity of opinion with their bosses. Unless, of course, one believes Lord Thompson, who said he didn't care what his newspapers printed, as long as they made a profit. One of the authors recently (March 1996) asked the editor of the *Financial Times* if he were ever leaned upon by the Pearson family (who own the newspaper) to take a particular editorial line. He replied that, in the five years he had been editor, he had never met any member of the Pearson family, and that they were happy for him to take full editorial responsibility, provided the paper made a profit. We believe him.

Profit does, of course, play an important role in what the commercial media are prepared to run with. For example, MTV's hugely popular Beavis and Butt-Head

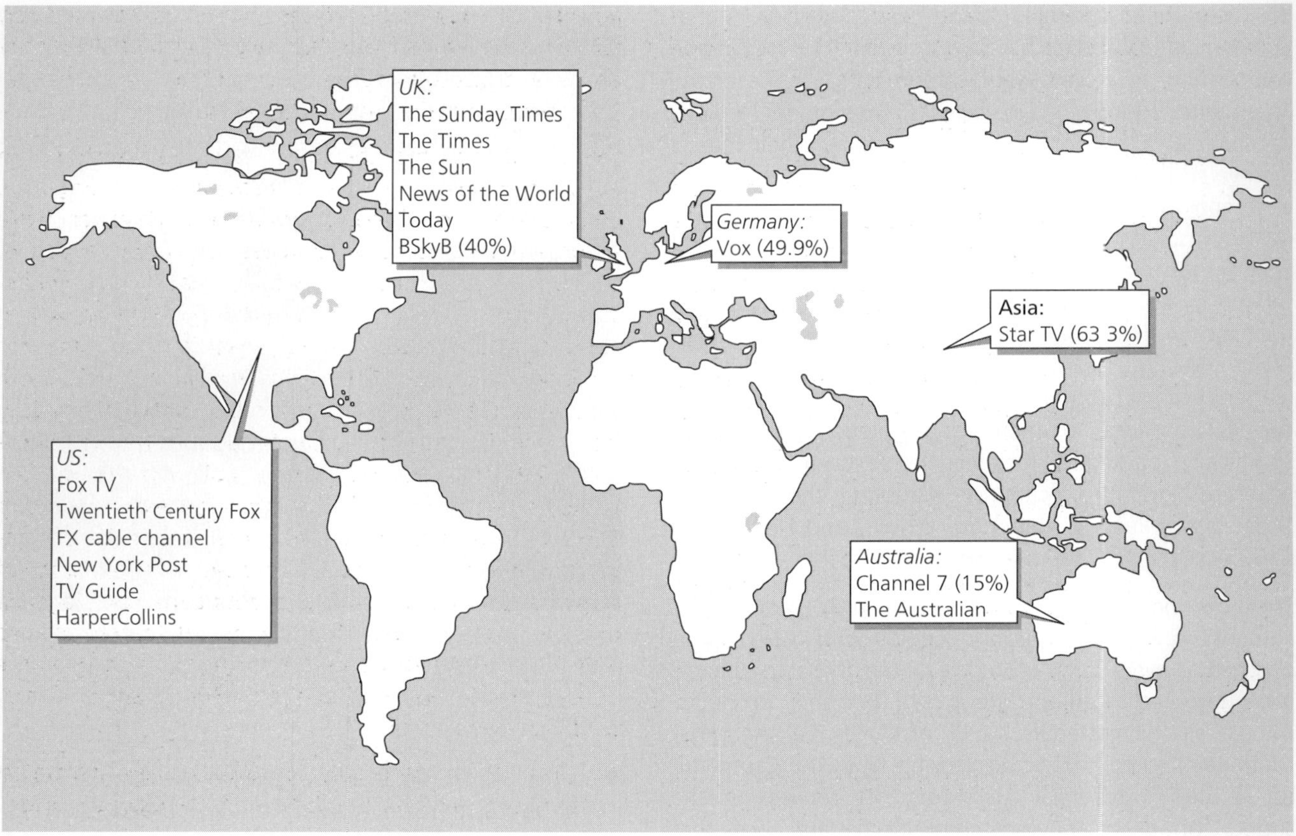

(The *European*, 7–13 July 1995)

The Murdoch empire (in 1995)

series in the USA makes huge profits for a capitalist corporation whose values and concerns are precisely those that Beavis and Butt-Head despise and attack. That part of the equation didn't seem to worry the corporation, so long as the big bucks came rolling in. However, intense criticism of the show's violence, coupled with Congressional threats to regulate television violence in the US, persuaded MTV to screen it later in the evening. There was also a promise not to replay the more violent episodes and not to show Beavis and Butt-Head starting fires, or Beavis shouting 'Fire, Fire!' MTV decided to walk a line between continuing to screen its most popular and profitable product, and avoiding lots of criticism. The upshot was to soften the edge of the series, while still preserving its huge – and profitable – popularity.

Whatever the extent of media moguls' influence on what papers print and televisions broadcast, to suggest, as pluralists do, that the media act as honest brokers between would-be advocates in society who have something to say and a public that wants to hear both sides of the story isn't supported by empirical evidence. The reality is that some advocates exert much more leverage on editors and journalists than other groups. The outcome is, to be sure, more complex than a straight ruling-class conspiracy theory would have. Nevertheless, media managers are leaned upon by powerful groups in society: 'City experts', clients (notably, advertisers), captains of industry and commerce, media bosses, competitors (notably, rival media), politicians, warlords and lawyers. The audience is powerful too but, as a 'mass', it's an aggregate that hasn't got the capacity to flex individual muscles. This isn't so when we consider the other powerful groups. They often call the shots in a manner that's very disproportionate to their number. Consider, for example, how media bosses hire and fire editors, how politicians use the courts to block controversial broadcasting, and how army officers prevent the untrammelled reporting of war stories.

Illustrative of the potential power exercised by advertisers over the media, one has only to look at the historically cosy relationship between the car industry and the communications industry. In what has become a classic indictment of this symbiotic love affair, Ralph Nader, in his book *Unsafe at any Speed*, contended that the car industry:

'by dominating the channels of communications through which the customer receives his [*sic*] information about automobiles, has obscured the relation of vehicle design to life and limb and has kept quiet its technical capability of building crash-worthy vehicles.'

(Nader 1965, cited by Cirino 1976: 48)

Observing that pressure can be applied by advertising money and other subtle forms of leverage, Nader added:

'It is more than coincidental that radio, television, newspapers and magazines have so long ignored the role of vehicle design in producing . . . collisions.'

Illustrative of this powerful argument, not one out of over 700 newspapers accepted an offer by Nader to run his book as a serialisation. Research by Robert Cirino (1976) strongly supports Nader's assertion that the media are to blame for failing to inform people about flawed car design. It's not as if the matter suddenly became an issue in the 1960s. As far back as 1937, Dr Clair Straith (cited by Cirino 1976), an acclaimed facial injury plastic surgeon, pointed out that the majority of severe, crushing, facial injuries were suffered by young women sitting in the seat next to the driver. In seeking to do something practical about this serious problem, Dr Straith made some suggestions to car manufacturers:

'projecting objects on the instrument panels (handles, knobs and cranks) add to the hazard. Elimination of such objects from the passenger's side of the instrument panel should be attempted by motor car engineers. The use of "crash padding" might do much to minimize the seriousness and extent of these injuries.'

(cited by Cirino 1976: 49)

The Associated Press dispatched a short news release on Dr Straith's article, but the release contained nothing about the good doctor's view that many cases of disfigurement could be prevented by a better designed car. Moreover, the press didn't pursue the lead, and so the public were kept largely unaware of the matter. Dr Straith, however, wouldn't be silenced, and later in the same year, he wrote another article, which included harrowing details of car accidents he knew about from first-hand experience. To emphasise his point, he even included a photograph of the interior of his own car, which contained padding that he had installed. Both the article and the photograph were ignored by the *New York Times* and the rest of the media.

One might think that things are much different today in a world where driver and passenger air bags are commonplace in television commercials. However, while a concern with some safety measures is now a part of car culture, there are still hazards that remain understated (even unspoken) in advertising. Notable in that context is the reluctance of advertisers to take the carcinogenic and other disease-producing effects of exhaust emissions seriously. Nor has much, if anything been said by advertising media about the well-documented hazards associated with bull bars. To be fair, however, the news media are more honest in reporting concerns over both issues. And here we make a noteworthy point: the media comprise lots of different organisations, not all of whom adopt the same agenda and the same motives. Whether or not the relationship between news media and advertising is as co-operative as it evidently was during the 1930s is an issue that deserves serious research.

McQuail clarifies matters by defining the main contenders for media 'control' and influence in the diagram below.

> ***OVER TO YOU***
>
> ***Match McQuail's diagram, or part of it, to a real example of how media select and present 'news' (for example, a newspaper, a television channel, etc.).***

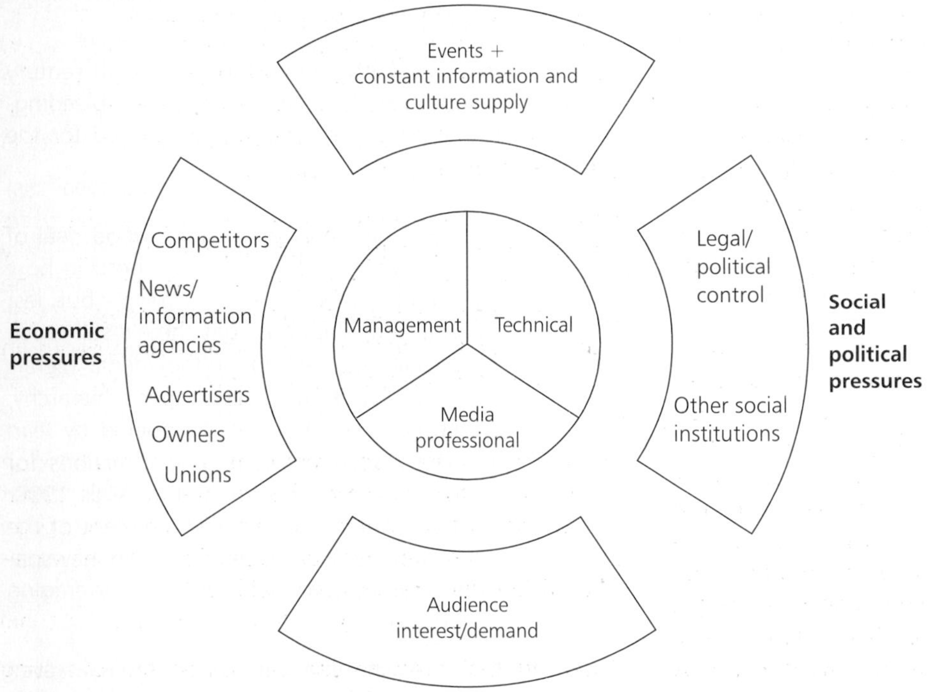

Media organisation in a field of social force

(McQuail 1987: 142)

The clamouring of different voices for access to news media eventually succumbs, concludes J. H. Altschull (1984, cited by McQuail 1987), to 'seven laws of journalism':

1. In all press systems, the news media are the agents of people who exercise economic and political power.
2. The content of the news media reflects the interests of people who finance the press.
3. Press systems are based on the belief in freedom of expression; but freedom of expression is defined in different ways.
4. Press systems claim they serve the public interest, and state their willingness to provide access to the public.
5. Press systems claim that their rivals are deviants.
6. Schools of journalism transmit the ideologies of the societies in which they exist, and help people in power to maintain their control over the news media.
7. Press practices always differ from theory.

According to McQuail, 'These "laws" are not prescriptions about what ought to happen, but summary observations about what does happen in practice' (1987: 124).

OVER TO YOU

How might pluralist theorists dispute Altschull's seven laws?

If McQuail is right, the 'piper's paymaster' calls the tune in private sector media. That said, there are many different kinds of arrangement to be made between the 'paymaster' and the 'piper'. This is partly facilitated by the tendency for private media to have multiple sources of financing: from investors, advertisers, consumers, etc. In these contexts, it's sometimes possible for media managers to play one 'paymaster' off against another, and perhaps even to discard one source of finance if support is found in other quarters. There's also, of course, the consideration that editors and journalists are well-educated, professional people who don't like being told what to do by financiers and money-lenders.

One of the authors has a brother who is a senior editor in a UK broadsheet newspaper, and he tells us that Arthur Scargill trusted his journalist colleagues to run Mr Scargill's 'version of events' during the 1984–5 miners' strike – despite the fact that rich and powerful people own the paper. Anecdotal this is, but it makes an important point. Some journalists regard themselves as free-standing professionals who aren't afraid to take on political and economic elites, holding them to account, whether or not such elites own and control media and other enterprises. Inherent in this belief is the notion that media professionals constitute a 'Fourth Estate': critic of the government and champion of the ordinary citizen.

It sounds romantic, but what does the evidence show? Says McQuail:

> 'The weight of evidence is that the neutral, informative role is most preferred by journalists and it goes with the importance of objectivity as a core value and an element in the new professionalism.'
>
> (McQuail 1987: 146)

To some extent, though, the particular society in which media professionals work probably has a bearing on their readiness to adopt a neutral or an adversarial role. In the US, for example, there exists a ong tradition of scrutinising claims and statements made by federal government. And, in true American style, when federal government is found wanting, journalists don't pull any punches. The *Washington Post* demolished a former US President (Richard Nixon), and the press and television media have had a field day over allegations that President Clinton's wife might have acted improperly in a company where she once worked as a lawyer. A survey of American journalists by D. Weaver and C. G. Wilhoit (1986, cited by McQuail 1987) showed that, although there was some decline in the critical journalism of the 1970s (when, incidentally, Nixon fell), there was still a reformist spirit among journalists who, on balance, were more 'left'-inclined than 'right', politically.

While it's true that an independent zeal characterises the professional work of some journalists, independently of who owns the 'show', what kind of people are journalists? In America, especially at the editorial decision-making level, most of them are white men. 'Second-class citizenship' is commonplace for women in newsrooms. Moreover, as Kay Mills points out:

> 'most women in the 19th and well into the 20th century were either "sob sisters", covering trials and bleeding-heart human interest stories, or they were hired for the women's pages.'
>
> (Mills 1990: 385)

Kay Mills argues that women have made a good deal of progress in media over the past 30 years – both in how they're portrayed and in their gatekeeper roles – but, lest we become complacent, she adds that there's still much to be done, especially at the top of the media hierarchies. The higher you look in a newspaper's hierarchy, the fewer women you see. A survey conducted by Jean Gaddy Wilson, executive director of New Directions for News at the University of Missouri (cited by Mills 1990: 387), revealed that women have only 14 per cent of the top decision-making editor posts in American newspapers. As publishers, they fare even less well, averaging 6 per cent of the total.

Black, Latina and Asian–American women remain even more under-represented at the top, and the white women who make it to the top often don't include the concerns of these women on their media agendas. There are, of course, individual success stories, such as Pam Johnson, a black woman who is publisher of *The Ithaca Journal* in New York State. The number of black women editors is also growing. But as one of them (anonymously cited by Mills 1990) astutely observes, an editorial writer affects only one editorial on any one day, while a black woman who attends the page-one conference or produces a news staff budget can exercise much more control over the operation of an entire newspaper.

Having looked at the private media in some detail, we'll conclude this section by considering media that aren't in private hands: government information agencies and the BBC. Both of these media are in the public domain, and – in theory, at least – they're 'owned' by voters and viewers.

The job of government information agencies is to provide press releases to journalists on policy initiatives and other state matters. Thus, for example, the Department for Education and Employment issues press releases on the latest developments in the National Curriculum, the reform of post-sixteen education, etc. These are the leads from which some reporters pick up a 'story' and take it further. It must be said, however, that the government and its information agencies enjoy a 'cosy' relationship. In that sense, the agencies function as the 'noticeboard' of the establishment, being largely under the control of their political 'masters'.

So can they be trusted to disseminate objective information or are they in the business of producing propaganda?

A bit of both, we suspect, is the best answer to this question. When dealing with straightforwardly factual information (for example, the number of students in England and Wales passing A-levels), it's likely that the agencies tell the truth. On the other hand, when controversial issues are in the frame (for example, the government's handling of the 'mad cow disease' scare in 1996), it's probably right that the public exercises a degree of scepticism. This is because the government might sometimes choose to withhold important information, or to produce information that accords with what it wants to hear. In relation to the 'mad cow disease' (the disease is also called BSE) affair, the *Independent on Sunday*'s Comment column on 24 March 1996 was scathing of the then government's role in providing – or not, as the case might be – the British public with the information citizens had a right to know:

'They [the government] have become so enamoured of the sound-bite, so convinced that "presentation" is all, so accustomed to dealing in evasions and half-truths that they have lost the art of conveying plain, simple, unvarnished information . . . Farming and food . . . are enfolded into government and so become part of the never-never land of Whitehall-speak, in which everything is packaged to minimise ministerial embarrassment and calm public criticism or concern.'

(The *Independent on Sunday*, 24 March 1996, page 20)

The hard-hitting editorial was accompanied by the cartoon depiction below of how little trust the British public had in government statements and press releases on BSE.

The then government's handling of the BSE affair is just one more example of a long series of denials of danger: from asbestos, to lead in petrol, to radiation, to acid rain, to pesticides, to the ozone layer. Once again, the government has only conceded that risks exist when

NO NEED TO PANIC... IT'S QUITE SAFE.!!

(The *Independent on Sunday*, 24 March 1996, page 20)

confronted with personal tragedies, in this case, ten human fatalities with possible links to BSE. It seems the British public, on this occasion, decided to place its trust in media sources other than the government. Shoppers delivered their own verdict on the government's assurances about beef safety by keeping beef off the menu.

Government sources of information, whether issuing from Labour or Conservative administrations, are likely to remain suspect for quite some time, in the wake of the BSE crisis. For as long as politicians pick their own 'experts' to make pronouncements on matters of public safety while rubbishing 'experts' who say things the government doesn't want to hear, people won't trust ministerial press releases. Clearly, the government has a vested interest in controlling information dissemination from departments of state that it doesn't own, but does preside over.

But what about that other non-commercially-owned medium, the BBC? Can it be trusted to report the facts openly and honestly or, like government information agencies, is it a largely self-serving instrument of 'propaganda'? In an article called 'You call the tune by paying for the BBC' (*Sunday Express*, 9 January 1994), the then Director-General of the BBC, John Birt, claimed that 'the BBC belongs, body and soul, to the public who pay for it. We have to listen to what our licence payers tell us, tune in to their concerns . . . ' Birt added that the BBC 'news machine is unrivalled in the world in its breadth and depth, and reputation for fairness and decency.' We hear you saying, 'He would say that wouldn't he?' So let's look at the evidence. Who controls what the BBC broadcast, and do the controllers provide the British public and the world with fair and balanced coverage?

The BBC had a monopoly on television in the UK until 1954, and on radio until 1972. Although it is ultimately responsible to Parliament, the BBC is relatively independent in its broadcasting activities. Day-to-day operations are controlled by a board of governors, appointed by the Queen. The BBC is financed by annual licence fees paid by the owners of televisions and radios. So, in that respect, Birt is right: we, the public, own the corporation. Under the terms of its charter, the BBC isn't permitted to advertise or broadcast sponsored programmes. This means that it isn't under the sway of advertising corporations who do exercise some control over private sector broadcasting – even if that control only means 'plugging' a commercial product. Weather forecasts on Sky TV, for example, are sponsored by Tulip Computers, who advertise this fact to cable and satellite TV viewers just before the forecasts are made.

Nevertheless, it would be a mistake to assume that the BBC is a neutral disseminator of information and entertainment. Its current charter defines a statutory role for BBC governors, part of which involves them overseeing the 'taste and decency' of the corporation's media output. But who are these people, these governors, these arbiters of 'good taste'? In 1996, they included a girls' public school headmistress, a member of a former Labour Government, a senior clergyman from one of the Scottish churches, an erstwhile permanent secretary, a powerful captain of industry and a right-wing trade unionist. Far from being a representative cross-section of the British public, these governors have been recruited from a rather select wedge of the British establishment.

The BBC's licence requires it not to editorialise its news programmes, and the Independent Broadcasting Act of 1973 held that impartiality must be maintained by programme providers on matters of industrial and political controversy, and current public policy. In that respect, public television and radio journalism is – at least, in theory – different from print journalism, where editorial viewpoints abound. In practice, however, more often than not it's television broadcasters who seem to bear the brunt of criticisms from politicians of being politically biased. This, in itself, cautions us to be wary of over-simplistic notions that media personnel are simply in the pockets of powerful people. What the media report and how they present it, argue pluralist sociologists, is constantly being contested and influenced by all manner of different groups in society: animal rights activists, the pro-hunting lobby, trade unionists, managerial associations, etc. Against this position, marxist sociologists claim that the media consistently select and present the news in ways that support vested interests, rather than in a balanced manner which reflects widespread opinion.

OVER TO YOU

Based on your own experiences of media news-reporting, which of the above views, pluralist or marxist, seem more convincing? Discuss whether you would consider your personal exposure to the media as a source of reliable and valid social scientific evidence.

But let's not think that pluralists and marxists are always easily discernible groups. There are cross-overs between the two camps. Notable in that context is the marxist-oriented sociologist, Charles Wright Mills, one of the leading social scientists America has produced. Mills wrote an essay on the mass media after the 1948 presidential election of Truman, who, against the predictions of opinion pollsters, defeated his Republican opponent, Governor Dewey. Given that Dewey had also received strong support from the media, Mills discovered it was unrealistic to assume that public opinion is entirely controlled and manipulated by one-sided media accounts. Despite his inherent leanings towards marxism,

Mills was also a sociologist who heeded the evidence. He recognised that the media provided opportunities for different and contesting voices to be heard. In short, he accepted that the media were receptive to pluralistic forces, rather than under the sway of a dominant minority.

At the same time, Mills accepted that in societies where democratic processes are being eroded, there evolves a definite centralisation of the media. Consider the fictional society in George Orwell's *Nineteen Eighty-Four* as an extreme illustration of the kind of centralisation Mills has in mind: where people lack individuality, becoming a 'mass' who are easily controlled and manipulated by a propagandist ruling class who run and shape media production. But *Nineteen Eighty-Four* is, as said, a piece of fiction. In reality, the notion that a ruling class exercises direct ownership and control over media production isn't supported by the evidence. That said, it would be fair to argue that white middle- and upper-class males, either in their role as media moguls, 'City experts' or government ministers, do have some serious leverage over media managers. Nevertheless, it's more accurate to say such people 'influence' rather than 'control' what we read in newspapers and see on television. Moreover, sociologists also know that other influences play an important role in the mediation process. Among the more notable are:

- the contacts journalists have with a wide range of individuals and organisations (ranging from the parliamentary lobby to citizen action groups like Greenpeace)
- investigative journalism based on research, interviews and direct observation
- use of formal information providers, sometimes involving other media sources (for example, news agencies like Reuters, the worldwide web, etc.).

To be sure, there are instances of obvious collusion between media producers and political and economic elites, as when, for example, political leaders get opportunities to address large publics. But there are also cases when media personnel eschew elitist versions of reality and use their own professional skills, as well as non-elite considerations and sources, in the manufacture of news and entertainment. Sometimes, for some journalists, the only responsibility of the media is to tell the truth rather than to play the piper's tune.

EXAM TIP

Be sure to distinguish between private media and public media. Some exam candidates assume that *all* media in the UK are privately owned. That's not the case.

Concluding remarks

The appearance of the mass press in the sixteenth century heralded a new epoch in world history. It meant that people would communicate with each other on a scale beyond the wildest flights of imagination of earlier generations. When the press was accompanied by motion pictures in the early nineteenth century, this was the dawn of a new and powerful technology – electronic media. Today, television touches the lives of virtually everyone on the planet, and it exerts an influence more powerful than any other medium.

Powerful though their influence is, the media exist alongside other socialising agencies – families, peers, schools, etc. Moreover, the media influence some people more than others. For example, frequent viewers of television news bulletins are probably more likely than infrequent viewers to have 'television opinions' about national and international issues. By the same token, people's individual and social circumstances affect why and how they use the media. Lonely people, for example, might watch more television soaps for 'company' than people who have active social lives.

While it's true that the media do flow from their technological sources (often owned and controlled by powerful groups) to the 'masses' beyond, people also exercise choices. The degree to which those 'choices' are relatively autonomous or affected by media (for example, advertising) is difficult to gauge. Children are more likely than (some!) adults to succumb to the pressures of aggressive consumer advertising. Women might be more at risk than men of suffering media-induced eating disorders. Undecided voters who read the *Sun* may, in the past, have become more inclined to vote Conservative than if they read the *Daily Mirror*.

How far it makes good social scientific sense to trust media selections and presentations as balanced and reliable is fiercely contested. Pluralists claim that the media are honest brokers, marxists that they're in the hands of the rich and powerful. The truth is probably somewhere in-between. That said, empirical evidence does show that the media are largely owned and controlled by white, middle- and upper-class males. Even the BBC is mainly governed by establishment figures, despite being 'owned' by the public. It's also the case that the media consistently under-select and exaggeratedly stereotype some people more than others. Black people, old people, girls and women, gay people, working-class people and people who are disabled incur a great deal of biased treatment in these respects. Their 'opposite numbers', by contrast, receive undue prominence and generally very favourable portrayals.

The debate will continue about the extent to which the media influence the way people think and behave. One thing is clear, though – the directors of corporations like

Pepsico wouldn't spend £200 million on changing Pepsi cans to 'electronic blue' if they didn't expect a return on their investment. They know, as we do, that the media have very powerful effects.

Glossary of key terms

Agenda setting Deciding what to include and what to omit in the transmission of news, entertainment and other media outputs. Sometimes also known as *selection*

Cultural effects theory This theory argues that the media influence people by playing a prominent role in constructing the culture they inhabit and experience. It draws upon marxist theory by emphasising the major part played by powerful people in media production, and upon social constructionist theory by identifying the role of stereotyping in media imagery

Culture The way people live, their lifestyles. Do they like surfing more than football, cinema, as well as theatre, television more than radio, the *Guardian*, as well as the *Independent*?

Deviancy amplification A process, often media orchestrated, whereby the social perception of the actual incidence of deviance becomes exaggerated. This, in turn, leads to reactions to the perceived threat (for example, tough, pro-active policing) that are 'over the top'. Sometimes deviancy amplification refers to an actual – typically, media fanned – increase in crime. For example, if a news bulletin forecasts a likely confrontation between two rival gangs, that might become a self-fulfilling prophecy

Hegemony The power that one group holds over another by persuasion and/or manipulation rather than brute force. In a crude sense, this can be regarded as the process of brainwashing. In a more subtle sense, it's a form of gentle coaxing

Hypodermic syringe theory A direct media effects model based on stimulus-response explanations. People are regarded as rather gullible mass audiences who respond in predictable and uniform ways to media stimuli

Ideology A set of beliefs and ideas that are held by a group (for example, the ideology of Conservative voters, the ideology of Greenpeace, the ideology of the ruling class)

Marxist perspective of media The media serve the economic and political interests of the rich and powerful. They are the disseminators of ruling-class ideology. Orthodox marxists argue that the ruling class own and control the private media, and also use public media to actively promote their own ends. Neo-marxists generally accept this argument, but they don't push the conspiracy angle to the same extent as their orthodox cousins

Mass media Communication organisations (private and public) that principally comprise newspapers, magazines, radio, television, cinema and – increasingly – parts of the Internet. 'Mass' refers to the many people (also called audiences) who are reached by the media. Note that media *are* plural

Pluralist perspective of media The media are honest brokers. They act as a mirror that reflects back to society the wide diversity of its citizens' outlooks, needs and demands

Representation How things are portrayed (for example, how the mass media portray people who are disabled)

Stereotype An exaggerated and, most usually, a degrading representation (for example, the portrayal of people who are disabled as 'helpless')

Two-step-flow theory A model of media effects that identifies two steps in the flow from the media source to the audience. The first step is the passage of the media message to a front-line audience (for example, readers of a daily newspaper). The second step is the passage of the message from influential members of the front-line audience to their less influential peers

Uses and gratifications theory According to this theory, people *use* the media to obtain *gratifications*. The emphasis here is on active audiences who decide what to do with the media rather than being directly influenced by the media

References

Ang, Ien (1991) Melodramatic identifications: Television fiction and women's fantasy, pp 75–88, in Brown, Mary Ellen (ed.) (1991) *Television and Women's Culture*. London: Sage Publications

Barry, David S. (1993) Growing up violent, pp 235–9, in Hiebert, Ray Eldon (ed.) (1995) op. cit.

Bennett, Tony (1995) Theories of the media, theories of society, pp 30–55, in Gurevitch, Michael *et al.* (eds) (1995) op. cit.

Braham, Peter (1995) How the media report race, pp 268–86, in Gurevitch, Michael *et al.* (eds) (1995) op. cit

Bernstein, Carl (1990) Global mass media empires, pp 9–16, in Hiebert, Ray Eldon (ed.) (1995) op. cit.

Bryant, Jennings and Zillmann, Dolf (eds) (1994) *Media Effects*. New Jersey: Lawrence Erlbaum Associates

Cirino, Robert (1971) Bias through selection and omission: Automobile safety, smoking, pp 40–61, in Cohen, Stanley and Young, Jock (eds) (1973) *The Manufacture of News*. London: Constable

Conroy, Sarah Booth (1989) Culture in the hands of corporate sponsors, pp 425–7, in Hiebert, Ray Eldon (ed.) (1995) op. cit.

Cumberbatch, Guy (1989) Overview of the effects of the mass media, pp 1–29, in Cumberbatch, Guy and Howitt, Dennis (1989) *A Measure of Uncertainty: The Effects of the Mass Media*. London: John Libbey

Dayan, Daniel and Katz, Elihu (1992) *Media Events*. Cambridge, Massachusetts: Harvard University Press

De Fleur, Melvin L. and Ball-Rokeach, Sandra (1982) *Theories of Mass Communication*, Fourth Edition. New York: Longman

Ferguson, Marjorie (1983) *Forever Feminine*. London: Heinemann

Gerbner, George, Cross, Larry, Morgan, Michael and Signorielli, Nancy (1994) Growing up with television: The cultivation perspective, pp 17–41, in Bryant, Jennings and Zillmann, Dolf (eds) (1994) op. cit.

Glasgow University Media Group (1985) *War and Peace News*. Milton Keynes: Open University Press

Greenberg, Bradley S. and Brand, Jeffrey E. (1994) Minorities and the mass media: 1970s to 1990s, pp 273–314, in Bryant, Jennings and Zillmann, Dolf (eds) (1994) op. cit.

Gunter, Barrie (1994) The question of media violence, pp 163–211, in Bryant, Jennings and Zillmann, Dolf (eds) (1994) op. cit.

Gurevitch, Michael, Bennett, Tony, Curran, James and Woollacott, Janet (eds) (1995) *Culture, Society and the Media*. London: Routledge

Hall, Stuart (1976) A world at one with itself, pp 85–94, in Cohen, Stanley and Young, Jock (eds) (1976) op. cit.

Hall, Stuart (1992) The rediscovery of 'ideology': Return of the repressed in media studies, pp 56–90, in Gurevitch *et al.* (eds) (1995) op. cit.

Harris, Richard Jackson (1994) The impact of sexually explicit media, pp 247–72, in Bryant, Jennings and Zillmann, Dolf (eds) (1994) op. cit.

Hiebert, Ray Eldon (ed.) (1995) *Impact of Mass Media*, Third Edition. White Plains, New York: Longman

Katz, Elihu and Lazarsfeld, Paul F. (1965) *Personal Influence*. New York: The Free Press

Katz, Jeffrey L. (1993) No, the press was not biased in 1992, pp 277–84, in Hiebert, Ray Eldon (ed.) (1995) op. cit.

Kellner, Douglas (1995) *Media Culture*. London: Routledge

Lull, James (1995) *Media, Communication, Culture*. Cambridge: Polity Press

Marx, Karl and Engels, Frederick (1965) *The German Ideology*. London: Lawrence & Wishart

McCombs, Maxwell (1994) News influence on our pictures of the world, pp 1–16, in Bryant, Jennings and Zillman, Dolf (eds) (1994) op. cit.

McQuail, Denis (1987) *Mass Communication Theory*, Second Edition. London: Sage Publications

Mills, Kay (1990) We've come a long way, maybe, pp 383–9, in Hiebert, Ray Eldon (ed.) (1995) op. cit.

Murdock, Graham (1995) Large corporations and the control of the communications industries, pp 118–50, in Gurevitch *et al.* (eds) (1995) op. cit.

Newburn, Tim and Hagell, Ann (1995) Violence on screen, pp 7–10, *Sociology Review*, February

Philo, Greg (1995) Television, politics and the rise of the New Right, pp 198–233, in Philo, Greg (ed.) (1995) *Glasgow Media Group Reader*, Volume 2. London: Routledge

Philo, Greg and McLaughlin, Greg (1995) The British media and the Gulf War, pp 146–56, in Philo, Greg (ed.) (1995) op. cit.

Popham, Peter (1996) The *Independent*, 27 February, Section 2, p. 14

Rubin, Alan M. (1994) Media uses and effects: A uses-and-gratifications perspective, pp 417–36, in Bryant, Jennings and Zillmann, Dolf (eds) (1994) op. cit.

Thio, Alex (1989) *Sociology: An Introduction*, Second Edition. New York: Harper & Row

Thompson, E. P. (1970) Sir, Writing by candlelight . . ., pp 262–9, in Cohen, Stanley and Young, Jock (eds) (1973) op. cit.

van Zoonen, Liesbet (1994) *Feminist Media Studies*. London: Sage Publications

---

Exam practice: Mass media

Essay questions

1 Examine sociological contributions to an understanding of the production and presentation of news by the mass media. *(25 marks)*

2 Assess the view that the mass media both reflect and promote a bias against ethnic minorities in Britain. *(25 marks)*

(Summer 1997 AEB AS-level Sociology, Paper 2, © 1997 AEB)

3 Assess the view that the output of the media is always ideological. *(25 marks)*

(Summer 1997 AEB A-level Sociology, Paper 2, © 1997 AEB)

4 'Newspapers may appear to be run by professional managers and journalists but, in reality, it is the owners who wield ultimate power.'
Discuss this statement with reference to sociological evidence and arguments. *(25 marks)*

(Summer 1993 AEB A-level Sociology, Paper 2, © 1993 AEB)

16 Deviance

Topics covered in this chapter
- *Defining deviance*
- *Theories and studies of crime*
- *Crime statistics*
- *Cops, courts and chain gangs*
- *Suicide*

Deviance is a crowd-puller. It generates curiosity and interest. Perhaps this has something to do with the fact that deviance, as Durkheim reminds us, is exciting and innovative. For without deviance, societies would get stale and static. Would South Africa have become a democracy without the 'deviant' rebelliousness of its president, Nelson Mandela? Would African–Americans be allowed to drink water from all public drinking fountains if Dr Martin Luther King hadn't broken unjust laws during the civil rights movement of the 1960s?

But not all deviance is 'noble'. The subway poison gassings that killed passengers in Japan in March 1995, the so-called 'ethnic cleansings' that led to the deaths of civilians in Bosnia and Rwanda, the April 1995 Oklahoma City bombing that resulted in the slaying of adults and children (the baby in the picture on page 492 was one of the victims) were truly 'horrific' forms of deviance. They were so, not only for their fateful consequences, but also because they shocked and offended world opinion.

Things aren't always so 'cut and dry'. The director of the film *Natural Born Killers* might be seen as a harmless entertainer by some film-goers but as a menacing deviant by others.

Nelson Mandela, President of the now democratic South Africa, was considered a criminal terrorist by former white rulers, and locked up in prison for over 25 years. Now he's widely regarded as a dignified, respectable leader whose earlier exploits were justified in the context of the oppressive apartheid regime he sought to overthrow.

Aftermath of the 1995 Oklahoma bombing

Defining deviance

Not so easy as it might appear! What is deviant in one society might be acceptable in another. As David Matza (1969: 348) notes: 'one man's [*sic*] deviation may be another's custom'. What he means is that people's perceptions of what and who are deviant vary from society to society, and even between individuals in the same society. For example, the consumption of alcohol by adults in some Islamic countries is considered seriously deviant, but the same practice – in moderation and not mixed with driving – is regarded as entirely normal in most European countries.

So how do we resolve the dilemma of defining what deviance actually is?

At the two extremes are these arguments:

- Defining deviance is like trying to nail a jelly to the wall: it's so elusive and slippery that it's impossible to define. This view is very *social constructionist* and *qualitative*: deviance is socially constructed and must be interpreted.
- Defining deviance is straightforward: actions that offend conventional norms are deviant. This view is very *structural* and *quantitative*: deviance is socially caused and measurable.

Both definitions are insightful, but each, on its own, is limiting. However, if we distil from each their combined 'wisdoms', we arrive at a better definition:

Deviance is action that offends the norms of a particular society or of a particular group.

For example, to say 'Hi, I'm Veena. What's your name?' to a party guest in Leeds would be considered acceptable behaviour. Yet for a tourist to ask a Native American her name at a social function on an Arizona reservation might be regarded as deviant: such questions are sometimes considered discourteous in Native American culture.

> ***EXAM TIP***
>
> Whatever exam you take, the examiners will expect you to realise that any attempt to define deviance is 'problematic'; that is, no one definition will satisfy all sociologists. Nevertheless, some definitions – as suggested above – are better than others. We hope you think that our 'distilled' definition is a good one. But we would expect you, as 'critical' (that is, evaluative) social scientists, not to take our word for it.

QUESTIONS

1. Why is it difficult to pin down a definition of deviance that everyone agrees on?
2. What factors might explain the different perceptions of a US cavalry soldier and a Blackfoot warrior towards showing mercy to an enemy in the heat of battle?

Conformity

Not so easy to define either! Saying it's the opposite of deviance, is a good start though:

Conformity is action that accords with the norms of a particular society or of a particular group.

But hold on. Didn't Matza say that one person's deviance might be another's conformity? Yes, he did! So Veena's conforming inquisitiveness at a Leeds party becomes a tourist's deviant intrusiveness on an Arizona reservation. Conformity, like deviance, is contextually defined. In different contexts, each can be the other. Even committing an assault might be regarded by some individuals as conforming behaviour. Gang members in Little Rock, Arkansas, for example, sometimes have initiation rites that involve assaulting the initiates. Not taking one's punishment would be seen as deviant in the eyes of the gang.

That's a group context, however, and a fairly untypical one too! If we want to avoid the interminable debates which arise from arguing that anything goes, provided it's acceptable to two or more people, we need to define conformity on a whole society level. Then conformity becomes what is generally regarded as acceptable behaviour.

OVER TO YOU

List three examples of behaviour that are considered deviant by some individuals, but conforming by other individuals.

Crime

In a strictly legalistic sense:

Crime is action whose commission – or, in some cases, whose omission – results in the breaking of criminal law.

But people sometimes speak of crime to denote a serious breach of ethical conduct, even if such action doesn't necessarily break the criminal law. For example, because the UK, unlike all other EU countries, hadn't, until the late 1990s, implemented a minimum legal wage, some UK employers paid employees less than £1 per hour. There was no breach of criminal law here, but some people might regard the conduct of such employers as 'criminal' in a moral sense. Nor do some arms dealers break criminal laws, even though some of people who buy their bombs and guns use them in violation of the human rights of others. Would these dealers be considered 'criminal' in a moral sense, or are they just good business people?

Instead then of taking a purely legalistic view of crime, it's important to heed what Edwin H. Sutherland (1974) said:

'Obviously, legal definitions should not confine the work of the criminologist; he [*sic*] should be completely free to push across the barriers of legal definitions whenever he sees noncriminal behaviour which resembles criminal behaviour.'

(cited by Vold and Bernard 1986: 12, footnote 23)

Conversely, don't make the mistake of assuming that all legally defined crimes are deviant. If that were so, brave people like Oskar Schindler (played by the screen actor Liam Neeson in the acclaimed film, *Schindler's List*) who broke nazi criminal law by saving Jews from the Holocaust, were deviant. Clearly, they weren't, by any humane, moral, reasonable standards. Other crimes are so common as to be almost 'normal', for example, using paper clips from work for personal use.

The more obviously serious crimes – murder, rape, robbery, etc. – are generally considered by most people (including sociologists) to be deviant also. However, while the majority of sociologists are as equally dismayed as anyone else about destructive deviance, their first concern, as social scientists, is to explain rather than condemn such conduct. Here we encounter that important debate about whether or not personal values should intrude into the conducting of sociological research. We think that, as far as is possible, they shouldn't. If we may here draw a parallel: imagine an 'emergency room' surgeon who is called upon to treat a gunshot victim. She knows he's a drug dealer and that he carries a handgun when he's dealing, and she disapproves of his lifestyle. She also knows that it's her job, as a doctor, to do what she can to save his life. In that sense, she's obliged to put her feelings of personal disgust on the back-burner, and to get on with being a surgeon.

People like Oskar Schindler, who broke unjust laws to prevent Jews ending up in death camps, are today considered heroes rather than criminals.

In order to remain as objective as possible, sociologists must do the same. Their task, as social scientists is to conduct studies and formulate theories. This doesn't mean that sociologists cease to regard crime as a social problem. Who doesn't regard corporate laundering of drugs money, racist assaults and burglaries as problems? Perhaps not the perpetrators, but certainly the victims and most members of the public. That's why criminal deviance is more likely to figure on the research agendas of sociologists than eccentric, but harmless, forms of deviance, such as speaking to oneself in a busy shopping centre. This chapter is therefore mainly, but not exclusively, concerned with deviance that is defined as criminal.

Theories and studies of crime

This section deals with sociological explanations of crime, notably, those explanations that address:

- power, social control and social order
- criminal youth subcultures and criminal neighbourhoods
- the social construction of crime (including the role of media and law enforcers).

Although a simplification, it helps to think of theories of crime under these two headings:

- Theories of distinct criminal and conforming populations
- Theories of widespread crime and selective law enforcement.

Deviant and conforming population theories suggest that the differing biologies, psychologies and sociologies of individuals, either independently but more usually in combination, account for criminal behaviour in some people – a criminal population – and conforming behaviour among other people – a conforming population. For example, some criminologists believe that serial killers are formed through a fusion of biological factors (for example, brain trauma), psychological factors (for example, sadistic sexual fantasies) and sociological factors (for example, inability to relate to peers). Here we have a 'poker flush' type of analysis. It takes a number of factors, in a particular configuration, to create a human being who kills and kills again.

EXAM TIP

While biologists and psychologists make important contributions to the study of crime, make sure that you concentrate on *sociological theories* in the exam.

Sociologists who adopt 'deviant and conforming population' theories are usually structural social scientists. That said, because they usually claim a causal link between 'working classness' and criminal behaviour, they don't count many marxists among their number. Quantitative research methods are generally favoured by the exponents of 'deviant and conforming population' theories.

Widespread crime and selective law enforcement theories propose that most people commit crimes, but the law is enforced selectively by the police and courts. Working-class, minority ethnic 'criminals' go to jail; middle- and upper-class ethnic majority 'criminals' get de-selected from the board of directors! The emphasis here is less on the criminal act and more on how the act is reacted to by law enforcers. The commission of a criminal act – *primary deviance* – might originate from a configuration of biological, psychological and sociological factors in a person's life, but what counts is whether the act, if it's detected, is responded to by law enforcers as though it really were a criminal deed – *secondary deviance*. For example, a Beverly Hills film star, who uses illegal violence with a handgun against an intruder in a society that tolerates certain types of gun culture, might be excused by some police officers if they think she's 'only protecting her property'. On the other hand, the courts would probably take a dim view of a young Latino male from east LA striking a police officer who is using unreasonable force on a local resident.

Widespread crime and selective law enforcement theories are most often advocated by social constructionist and marxist sociologists. They frequently use qualitative research methods when studying crime. Marxists also often supplement this with quantitative approaches.

Now it's time to examine in more detail the various theories and studies that are associated with each of the two broad theoretical headings.

Major deviant and conforming population theories and studies

14:41

There are lots of these, ranging from the ridiculous – thieves tend to have flattened noses; honest types don't – to the sensible – being long-term unemployed increases the likelihood that people will commit property crimes, compared to those who have secure jobs. This is a book about sociology, so we'll concentrate on the main *sociological* theories and studies.

Ecological theory and studies

16:30

If the flattened nose theory is right, gangsters must spend a lot of money on cosmetic surgery to hide their outwardly criminal appearances! We'll dispense with that theory without further ado and have a look at ecological theory.

Ecological theory emerged from the Chicago of Al Capone in the 1920s. The Department of Sociology at the University of Chicago set itself the task of identifying the environmental factors associated with crime. This involved correlating the social characteristics and the crime rates of different neighbourhoods. Since the research was based on a conception of human communities borrowed from plant ecology, the perspective supported by this research became known as the Chicago School of Human Ecology.

The basic idea behind this is the notion that human communities, like plant communities, tend to have common characteristics. No, we're not suggesting that the residents of Bethnal Green in East London exhibit the same properties as a row of King Edward potatoes in the local allotment! The comparison is metaphorical: just as potatoes which grow in the same soil conditions tend to be of similar texture and size, so the residents of a particular neighbourhood are inclined to develop similar lifestyles. In this way, just as a potato patch has an organic unity, so does a neighbourhood have a character of its own. But these characteristics, the vegetable and the human variety, can be upset by outside influences: potato patches can be taken over by weeds; Native American communities by white Americans. This process is referred to by ecologists as one of 'invasion, dominance and succession', a theme which was taken up, in the context of urban environments, by two Chicago School sociologists, Robert Park and Ernest Burgess.

Park and Burgess used 1920s Chicago as the urban environment of their study. They noticed that, like many cities, Chicago had a tendency to expand from its centre in a series of concentric circles, like ripples moving out from the point where a stone strikes water.

This pattern is illustrated in the map below. Zone I, the central business zone, gradually 'invades' Zone II, the area of transition and high crime rates. This area already has a derelict feel about it because buildings have been torn down to make way for the expanding business complexes. It's also the first port of call for new arrivals to the city, many of whom are poor and unemployed. Their first address is likely to be a cheap 'flop house'.

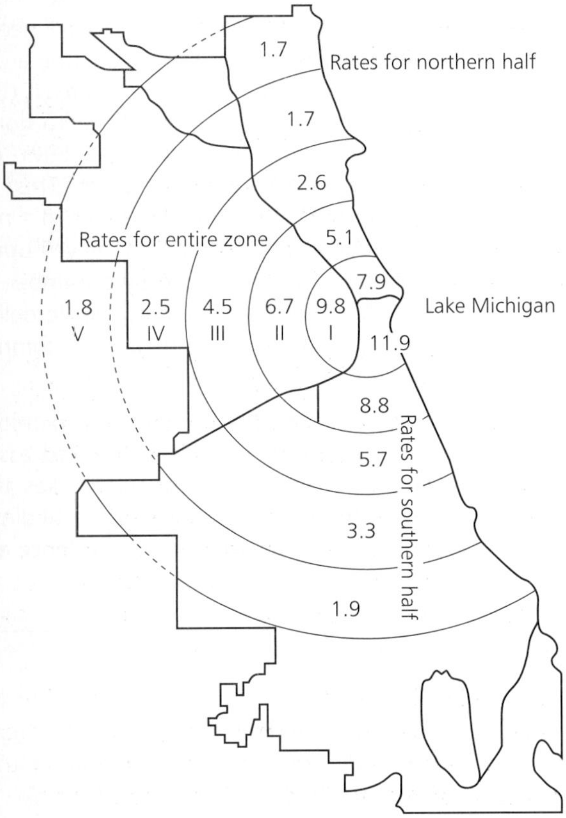

(Shaw and McKay 1942: 74, in Vold and Thomas 1986)
Map of Chicago showing zone rates of male juvenile delinquents from 1927 to 1933

But if they find a job, after a few years' hard toil, they might be able to save up enough money to move to a 'better', more settled neighbourhood. However, during the interim period, they and their children are living in a social environment that, with all the migrations into and out of the area, doesn't engender a sense of belonging to a common culture. In such a setting, normlessness – or 'anomie', to use its sociological description – is prevalent. An 'anything goes' outlook develops, especially among young males, who increasingly turn to crime in search of excitement and material gain. There are few informal surveillance controls – the defining feature of more permanent communities – to keep delinquency at bay.

Within this framework and against the backdrop of a rising crime wave generated in part by widespread resistance to Prohibition, Park and his colleagues studied the particular problems faced by the city of Chicago. One of those colleagues, Clifford R. Shaw, worked as a probation and parole officer. He became convinced that juvenile delinquency was associated with young people's detachment from conventional culture, and set about analysing the social characteristics of neighbourhoods that, based on court and police records, had the most delinquents. Perhaps to his surprise, Shaw discovered that only about 20 per cent of youths in such neighbourhoods had run-ins with the courts. So he began compiling detailed life histories of individual delinquents in an attempt to find out how they interacted with their environment.

Shaw published his study in 1929 in a volume called *Delinquency Areas*. Subsequently, with Henry D. McKay, he wrote *Social Factors in Juvenile Delinquency* (1931), and *Juvenile Delinquency and Urban Areas* (1942) (all cited by Vold and Thomas 1986). In these investigations, Shaw and McKay pinpointed the residences of juveniles who had run foul of the criminal justice system. Other 'spot maps' were constructed depicting, for example, the homes of truants, the location of demolished buildings, and the rate of tuberculosis. (Incidentally, this disease, which strongly correlates with poverty and bad housing, has returned to the UK and the US in the 1990s.) Rate maps representing the percentage of the juvenile population who were 'in trouble' with law enforcement agencies were also produced. Finally, zone maps were created to show that there was a general tendency for community problems to be concentrated near the centre of Chicago.

With this information available to them, Shaw and McKay arrived at these conclusions:

- *Physical conditions* The highest delinquency rates correlated with neighbourhoods in or right next to areas of commerce or heavy industry, and in districts with the highest number of condemned buildings and of decreasing population.

- *Economic conditions* The highest delinquency rates were in areas where poverty was at its worse. Nevertheless, Shaw and McKay concluded that economic conditions didn't, in themselves, cause crime.
- *Population composition* Areas of highest delinquency were consistently associated with higher concentrations of black and of 'foreign-born' heads of families. Importantly, however, Shaw and McKay found that within *similar* neighbourhoods, whether the residents were foreign-born or native-born, recent or more established immigrants, black or white, the delinquency rate of these different groups was about the same. In other words, factors like ethnicity didn't 'cause' a particular level of delinquency.

This last point deserves special emphasis. It was the social ecology of a neighbourhood, concluded Shaw and McKay, that determined its rate of delinquency and other social problems, not whether the people who lived in a neighbourhood were black or white. Some 35 years on – in the 1960s – the same point was forcefully and persuasively made by another sociologist: Martin Luther King. Responding to the flawed 'sociological' argument that black neighbourhoods generate high crime rates, Dr King pointed out that the proponents of this view:

> 'never stop to realize that criminal responses are environmental, not racial. To hem a people up in the prison walls of overcrowded ghettos and to confine them in rat-infested slums is to breed crime, whatever the racial group may be.'
>
> (King 1969: 117)

Returning to Shaw and McKay's study, in areas where people didn't settle – so-called 'zones of transition' – there existed a marked lack of 'neighbourliness' and an attendant inability of parents to control their wayward young. The situation was reversed in established Zone III neighbourhoods. When immigrants saved enough money and moved into Zone III, social problems generally diminished. Although Shaw and McKay identified an association between residency and crime, they didn't push a straightforward cause and effect model. As good social scientists, they knew that associations between variables can't, in purely statistical terms, be treated as causes, even though 'causality' can sometimes reasonably be inferred. Moreover, they also recognised that over-rigorous policing of some neighbourhoods could push up the crime figures, because more people are arrested when law-enforcement is pro-active.

As originally formulated, ecological theory explained high rates of delinquency by the absence of community norms and values. When young people don't feel attached to the social structure in which they grow up, they don't experience a sense of being controlled, and their behaviour 'runs wild'. However, ecological theory also identified the formation of enduring delinquent subcultures among disaffected young people who, finding no sense of community in society at large, discovered a compensatory community of their peers in criminal gangs. In that sense, social disorganisation leads to lawlessness, but lawless individuals develop alternative cultures which are subsequently supported over time by later generations. It's at this point that ecological theory merges with – or even foreshadows – another criminological perspective: *subcultural theory* (the topic of the next section).

Ecological theory is still important in modern criminological thinking. Per-Olof Wikstrom (1991, cited by Bottoms 1995: 585–656), for example, has conducted a comprehensive ecological study of recorded offences in Sweden's capital city, Stockholm. He found that vandalism and violence in public, and theft of and from cars were very much clustered in the downtown area (i.e. the city centre). However, the highest rates of family violence were found in certain outer-city areas which were characterised by comparatively high levels of:

- residents on social welfare
- immigrant residents
- working-class residents
- children with single, working parents
- non-profit housing (similar to council housing in the UK).

Wikstrom discovered that residential burglaries tended to occur in prosperous neighbourhoods, especially when such neighbourhoods were in close proximity to 'high offender rate areas'. An important distinction here needs to be made between 'high offender rate areas' (the areas where offenders live) and 'high offence rate areas' (the areas where offences are committed). For the two don't always go hand-in-hand. Sometimes the 'bad guys' do their offending in areas where they don't live. This, of course, occurred in Wikstrom's study. However, it's not always like that. Sometimes poor people are preyed upon by their poor neighbours, a point made by a number of marxist sociologists. It's also the case that juvenile delinquents are more likely than adult offenders to commit crimes in the neighbourhoods where they live.

Even so, in keeping with the ecological tradition, Wikstrom's research reveals that there are marked associations between areas and crimes. He also makes the important point, which, in a sense, adds to the findings of the Chicago School, that different types of offence are linked to different types of environment.

EXAM TIP

There's a tendency for candidates to remain stuck in the 1920s and 1930s when they write about ecological theory. The pioneering work in those decades is important and relevant, but do bring in more recent research as well.

ECOLOGICAL THEORY OF DEVIANCE

FOR

+ It demonstrates that neighbourhood factors, notably, poverty, poor housing, disease and high residency turnover, as opposed to individual personality traits, ethnicity and being native or overseas born, are the 'determinants' of differing delinquency rates.
+ It's a very scientific approach, based on the careful computation of statistical associations between types of neighbourhood and levels of delinquency. At the same time, it doesn't fall into the trap of implying that associations, in themselves, represent 'hard and fast' causal relationships.
+ It's suggestive of neighbourhood improvement schemes whose aim is to 'design out' crime. This approach is currently advocated by Jock Young in his advocacy of, for example, better street lighting aimed at reducing the risk of street crimes.

AGAINST

– People aren't plants. The plant ecology model that underpins the early models of ecological theory is misplaced. Social life requires its own sociological explanations, and should dispense with concepts borrowed from the biological sciences.
– Self-report studies, like the British Crime Survey (where sociologists ask delinquents and alleged non-delinquents to own up, in confidence, to crimes they've committed), reveal that delinquency is fairly widespread throughout society rather than concentrated among 'lower-class, wrong side of town' residents. That said, some self-report studies reveal that court and police records quite accurately record the distribution of those kinds of crime that are likely to get any young people into trouble with law enforcers.
– Shaw and McKays' suggestion that ethnicity isn't a good predictor of delinquency rates was challenged by Norman S. Hayner (1933, cited by Vold and Bernard 1986: 175). He found that Japanese people living in 'slum' areas had very low rates of delinquency.

OVER TO YOU

Using statistics on local crime rates (where do you think you might obtain these?), construct a local zone map.

Subcultural theory and studies

Very much linked to ecological theory, subcultural theory is in the 'deviant and conforming population' tradition. It proposes that some people are socialised into criminal subcultures – that is, lifestyles where law-breaking is accepted and even encouraged. The emphasis here is on criminal ways being learned and internalised (for example, through being a Chicago gang homeboy or girl) in much the same way that conforming behaviour is acquired in mainstream culture or in 'acceptable' subcultures (for example, kibbutz communities in Israel). This perspective is very well exemplified by Edwin H. Sutherland's *differential association theory*:

'Criminal behaviour is learned . . . A person becomes delinquent because of an excess of definitions favorable to violation of law over definitions unfavorable to violation of law . . . The process of learning criminal behaviour by association with criminal and anticriminal patterns involves all the mechanisms that are involved in any other learning . . .'

(Sutherland 1947, cited by Vold and Bernard 1986: 210)

OVER TO YOU

Put the preceding 'cut and pasted' statements from Sutherland into 'plain English'.

Some sociologists make a distinction between 'cultural' and 'structural' causes of crime. Cultural factors are said to do with the learning of criminal habits; structural factors are considered as propelling social forces (for example, desperate poverty) that push people into crime. We don't think such a clearcut distinction should be made. Culture is a product of structure and structure is a product of culture: both bounce off, and affect, each other. For example, structural isolation in a crime-ridden neighbourhood like Seacroft in Leeds might make it more likely that children who are largely socialised outside of mainstream culture will engage in crime than children reared in leafy, middle-class suburbs. At the same time, the criminal subculture that some (remember, not all) the Seacroft children learn and acquire, makes it more likely that they'll remain in the neighbourhood where deviant 'innovation' (for example, selling crack) yields a sizeable income.

Popular tabloids often describe the behaviour of these young people as thugs who belong to a criminal 'underclass'. Yet their behaviour, on closer sociological inspection, isn't so strange. Middle- and upper-class

Guns are the ultimate symbols of criminal subcultural machismo. 'You fire a gun and you just hear the power,' says Doug (pseudonym), a 16-year-old from a white, working-class neighbourhood in Benson, USA. 'It's like yeah!' In downtown Omaha, a teenager carries a sawn-off shotgun.

youths get their kudos and status by going to university, buying expensive cars, and living in fashionable neighbourhoods. Working-class youths who live on run-down estates in 'wrong side of town' neighbourhoods derive peer status by craving excitement and danger: a daring car theft, packing a handgun, and dealing narcotics.

The theoretical underpinning behind this argument can be found in the work of Walter B. Miller (1958, cited by Vold and Bernard 1986). Considering the reason for gang delinquency in 1950s USA, Miller argued that 'lower'-class culture has long been distinct from middle-class culture. Where middle-class people emphasise 'conventional' forms of achievement, 'lower'-class people (read lower-class males; so what's happened to the females?) have different 'focal concerns', notably:

- trouble (both getting into and staying out of it)
- toughness (macho ruggedness is prized)
- smartness (the streetwise variety rather than high IQ)
- excitement (a relentless search for thrills)
- fate (the feeling that what will be will be: so just do it!)
- autonomy (an antipathy towards conventional authority and rules).

Miller sees these 'lower'-class preoccupations as a 'generating milieu' for gang delinquency. It's not that the boys are challenging middle-class norms head-on. Rather, they're acting out, in an intensified fashion, the culture of their own working-class communities. Miller noted too that 'lower'-class male delinquents often lived in lone-parent families headed by mothers. The absence of a male role model, in the person of a wage-earning father, meant that these boys copied the masculinities of their male peers, out on the streets in gangs. Miller's lone female parent explanation is much in vogue these days, particularly – but not exclusively – among some right-wing commentators.

It's perhaps more speculative though than accurate. The quality of parenting rather than the presence or otherwise of a female and a male parent is a better predictor of how children 'turn out'. In Sweden, for example, where families headed by females are quite common, the tendency for males to enter gangland subcultures is much lower than for males growing up in South Central Los Angeles. That said, the absence of a father, in combination with other social factors, might encourage some young males to develop an exaggerated and delinquent sense of masculinity through the peer influence of male gang members. Such 'tough guy' machismo often finds expression in the carrying and the use of guns.

What's needed is more research in this area. Female rebelliousness also needs more attention. For girl and women deviants have their own subcultural forms of 'tough femininity'. In San Antonio, USA, for example, one gang allegedly requires female initiates to have unprotected sex with a known AIDS-carrier. The would-be gang member subsequently has an AIDS test. If its negative, she's accepted. Females (and males) who want to join the Playboy Gang, a Latino Los Angeles gang, have to get 'jumped in': set upon by three gang members with only limited means to defend themselves. On the other side of the coin, women researchers who, as part of a team, investigated young adults in north-east England (Frank Coffield, Carol Borrill and Sarah Marshall, cited by Jeremy Seabrook 1986), found that male working-class culture isn't all hard masculinity: deep down there was genuine tenderness.

Another early and influential exponent of subcultural theory was Albert K. Cohen (not Stanley: we'll come to him later). Albert Cohen, like Miller, was a sociologist interested in the America of the 1950s, with its soda fountain drugstores, Levi Strauss 501s, rock and roll, rhythm and blues, and a vibrant new youth culture centred on 'hanging out', fashion, dancing and 'knocking' the traditional establishment. So why were some guys turning to delinquent ways?, mused Albert in his professional work with juveniles. He found the answer in subcultural theory.

Albert Cohen (1955, cited by Vold and Bernard 1986: 194) noted that most delinquent behaviour occurred in gangs, and that it was generally 'non-utilitarian, malicious, and negativistic'. Unlike Merton's utilitarian innovators (see the next section), who stole for money, Cohen's delinquent boys belonged to a youth culture that prized stealing for kicks. These boys went to schools whose middle-class culture exerted a destruction of their 'lower-class' self-worth so great that they searched for kudos outside the values endorsed by teachers. Some of their working-class peers, of course, surrendered to the system, but those who didn't rebelled against middle-class values by exaggeratedly embracing gang-validated symbols of success: unleashing physical aggression instead of controlling it; destroying property rather than respecting it; living for the day against preparing for tomorrow. As Cohen says:

'They not only reject the dominant value system, but do so with a vengeance. They "stand it on its head"; they exalt its opposition.'

(Cohen 1966: 66)

There are parallels here with Paul Willis' West Midlands 'lads' in a 1970s boys' secondary school:

'Settled in class, as near a group as they can manage, there is a continuous scraping of chairs . . . and a continuous fidgeting about which explores every permutation of sitting or lying on a chair . . . There is an aimless air of insubordination ready with spurious justification and impossible to nail down.'

(Willis 1978: 13)

Subcultural theory is still an important perspective in 1990s sociology. Gerry P. T. Finn, for example, uses subcultural theory in his study of football violence:

'The socialization of the football fan leads individuals to adopt a cultural framework that stresses different values from those normally proclaimed appropriate for everyday social life. Both players and supporters are socialized into a culture of quasi-violence: a culture that accepts aggression and violence as central to the game.'

(Finn 1994: 102–3)

The hard masculinity imbued in the culture of professional football sometimes spills over into off-field violence between rival fans. This is hardly surprising, given the aura of aggression that is so pervasive in the subculture of the 'hard fan'. Don't imagine that this type of deviant youth subculture is a new phenomenon. It has a very long history indeed, even if the lino-cutter knives of today have replaced the broken bottles of football terraces and the streets around the stadium during the 1930s.

SUBCULTURAL THEORY OF DEVIANCE

FOR

+ It has had a huge influence on criminology. In that context, it successfully challenged the view that the causes of criminal behaviour were mainly linked to biological and psychological 'abnormalities'. As an alternative explanation, it convincingly argued that some biologically and psychologically 'normal' individuals might commit crimes simply by being socialised into a criminal subculture.
+ It demystifies criminal subcultures by revealing that people, especially young people, who live outside of mainstream conventional culture sometimes learn to be criminal in much the same way that other people learn to conform. In that respect, it dispenses with common-sense 'they're just bad kids' theories – or should one say, half-truth hearsay assumptions!?
+ It's an enduring perspective whose insights have promoted (and still do promote) the application of social scientific theories to the solution of social problems. For example, Robert Kennedy, brother of JFK and US Attorney-General in the 1960s, asked Lloyd Ohlin, a subcultural/strain theorist, to help develop a new federal policy on juvenile delinquency. This led to the Juvenile Delinquency Prevention and Control Act (1961). The ensuing programme – which included school improvement and job creation schemes – was later expanded in Lyndon Johnston's War on Poverty.

AGAINST

– The unintended sexism aside (early subcultural theorists were products of their own time and culture rather than wilful sexists), subcultural theory is way too male-oriented. Things are changing though: mixed and girl-only gangs are known to exist in 1990s USA. According to a report by the University of Southern California's Center for Research on Crime and Social Control, mixed gangs with up to 25,000 members are believed to be active in 177 of 189 major American cities. Subcultural theory is having to get right up-to-date in order to address this phenomenon, and 'male culture only' explanations just won't do.

– There's too much of an 'us' and 'them' emphasis in subcultural theory. Conforming people also live in so-called 'wrong-side-of-town' neighbourhoods, as do gangsters in 'leafy suburbs'. That said, most subcultural theorists recognise that labelling plays an important role in the stigmatisation by law enforcers of certain neighbourhoods and of the people who live there.

– Subcultural theory seems preoccupied with 'lower'-class criminality. This can be responded to in a number of ways. Critics would say that it largely overlooks middle- and upper-class crime. Advocates would argue that it doesn't pretend to be a general theory of crime: its main concern is with working-class crime, but it doesn't ignore the criminality of more affluent youths.

CRIT THINK CRIT THINK CRIT THINK CRIT THINK CRIT THINK CRIT THINK

WHY JOIN A GANG?

While it's fair to say that subcultural theory – and, for that matter, ecological theory – largely focuses on working-class criminality in 'downtown' neighbourhoods, it would be a mistake to assume that middle-class youths from suburban areas don't commit crimes. In his book, *Suburban Gangs: The Affluent Rebels*, Dan Korem claims that:

'For the first time in American history, youth gangs are forming in persistent numbers in suburban middle- and upper-middle class communities. This new and dangerous trend is also growing in Europe. There have been isolated cases of affluent gangs in the past, but the current trend is unprecedented. The emergence of these gangs must be acknowledged, respected, understood, and successfully addressed.' (Korem 1994: 5)

Based on his research over seven years in the US and other countries – the UK included – Korem (1994) noted that affluent and non-affluent youths who are likely to join gangs have a typical profile. When these youths are faced with problems and don't have family members to call upon for support, their anxiety increases and they tend to seek solutions elsewhere. Joining a gang – a new kind of family – is one such solution. It's not only working-class young people from 'broken homes' who adopt this behaviour, so too do some middle-class youths when faced with family problems and an acute sense of social isolation. There are echoes here of Emile Durkheim's research (1968, first published in 1897) into the link between feeling cut off from a social group and an increased risk of taking one's life.

Suicide isn't, however, the only response to family crisis. For most youths, middle-class or working-class, joining a gang or committing suicide are probably relatively uncommon outcomes if the family doesn't provide what Korem calls a 'protective factor' when personal problems loom. It's likely that the majority of young people get through these crises without doing anything drastic. Nevertheless, sociology is interested in heightened risks associated with particular social factors, and, in that context, problems at home seem more likely than economic factors to propel some youths into gangs for the solace that they don't find in their families.

This finding has important implications for policy-makers. Whether coming from poor or affluent backgrounds, Korem found that family problems are a better predictor than low income of young people turning to gangs. It might therefore make sense to develop strategies designed to help young people from 'difficult' home circumstances either to cope better with their problems or to find alternative routes from the problems than joining gangs. Just concentrating on doing something about low incomes isn't enough, as evidenced by the fact that young people from high-income families are still more prone to join gangs when they encounter severe family problems than are their peers – poor or otherwise – from stable family backgrounds. The big question is: what kind of intervention is likely to reduce the risk that young people from 'broken homes' will join street gangs?

Taking the above into account, and other relevant sociological considerations (for example, theories about crime), imagine that you're part of a sociological task team whose brief is to

- *research the causes of growing involvement of youths in gangs in your area*
- *come up with sociological strategies to prevent this from happening.*

1. *Prepare and present a report on the reasons why young people are joining gangs (imagination is allowed here, but make sure it's a sociological imagination!).*
2. *Based on your assessment of the causes, produce an action plan with the aim of dissuading young people from joining gangs.*
3. *Discuss how an over-concentration on the link between family problems and gang membership might provide politicians with an excuse to play down the impact of poverty and unemployment on youth crime. In that context, you might wish to reflect on the possible relationship between low income and family problems.*

CRIT THINK CRIT THINK CRIT THINK CRIT THINK CRIT THINK CRIT THINK CRIT

Strain theory and studies

Strain theory claims that there exists in society a *strain* (or, to put it another way, a tension) between what people are reasonably expected to achieve in life – a decent wage, good health, etc. – and what they are actually able to achieve. The emphasis here is on frustrated legitimate aspirations. The frustration is most likely to occur among people at the bottom of the social hierarchy – low-paid and unemployed people, members of oppressed ethnic minorities, people who are disabled. Most of these individuals don't turn to crime in order to acquire what they can't easily achieve through conventional ways – reasonably paid employment, a good pension, etc. However, some individuals, faced with the bleak prospect of not obtaining society's prizes by legal means, resort to crime, especially theft.

This theme has received much attention in the important work of the American functionalist, Robert K. Merton, whose strain theory is one of the most frequently quoted concepts in the sociology of deviance and in criminology generally. Merton, in the manner of the classical sociologists, was a bit of a grand theorist. Although a functionalist, he recognised that 'full or overwhelming consensus in a complex, differentiated society exists for only a limited number of values, interests, and derived standards for conduct' (Merton, 1971: 804). In other words, people live in societies where some behaviours are generally accepted by most of them, while other behaviours are accepted by some and not by others. For example, in the UK, most people form a queue at a bus stop, but many people decorate their homes in a variety of styles.

Merton was fully aware of the importance of social constructionist and marxist explanations of crime. In that context, he wrote:

'Those occupying strategic positions of authority and power of course carry more weight than others in . . . identifying for the rest what are to be taken as significant departures from social standards.'

(Merton 1971: 803)

At heart though, Merton was, in the structural tradition, a broad canvas thinker. He was also more inclined perhaps to put forward ingenious hunches than to conduct empirical studies. He did, however, draw upon a number of examples of 'exhortational literature', which 'preached' that anyone can make it to the top in the US, provided they have lofty goals, and a steely determination to be a winner.

There are clear echoes of Merton's argument in Jeremy Seabrook's account of property crime in the UK in the 1990s:

'the upsurge in crime is the only logical response by certain sections of the poor to the exacerbation of their condition . . . They are not only relatively poorer, but they also see the good life, which requires ever more money, receding from them at an accelerating pace . . . Their only hope is to determine their own fate, even if this means rectifying, by private acts of plunder, their disadvantage and rejection.'

(Seabrook 1990: 18)

Other sociologists, many of them subcultural theorists, have conducted empirical studies, some of which support Merton's argument. While Merton probably preferred theorising to carrying out practical investigations, his work was premised on his study of an existing sociological theory: Emile Durkheim's concept of *anomie*.

Durkheim defined anomie as a 'pathological' breakdown in society's capacity to restrain untrammelled and potentially criminal drives among its members. Merton developed and refined this idea to produce a theory of a tension between driving and restraining social forces. The driving forces are the culturally-generated pressures to advance oneself in the true American way: by getting a good job, a fine home and an expensive car. The restraining forces are the internalised norms – products of socialisation – that keep in check any possible inclination to obtain these material goals through crime. Put simply, we're encouraged to want lots of material things, but some of us find we can't earn enough money or even get a job to enable us to obtain those things.

When the restraining forces are overwhelmed by the driving forces, crime sometimes results. Consider a Liverpool 8 resident who constantly encounters postcode discrimination from employers who don't like the sound of her neighbourhood, and won't even consider her job applications – it happens! Like you and me, this individual is relentlessly bombarded by media messages to measure her status on the basis of material success. But this 'legitimate aspiration', this commonplace value of ordinary Britons, is thwarted by the structural arrangements of the society in which she lives: in this case, 'wrong side of town' discrimination. In such circumstances, according to Merton's strain theory, there exists a heightened risk that the woman might *innovate* (to use Merton's term) in order to obtain what she can't reasonably achieve through legitimate channels. In this sense, to innovate means to come upon a new, deviant, way of attaining a desired goal: theft is the most common outcome.

Take some of the people who live in Manchester's Hulme district, where poverty is rampant and poor housing widespread. Unemployment among some young black people there is 75 per cent. Moreover, postcode discrimination against job applications from residents living in Manchester 14, 15 and 16 districts adds to the understandable feelings of frustration. In Manchester Moss Side, next door to Hulme, a youth worker speaks to a young man dealing drugs in a dimly lit shopping centre.

In a reply that perfectly echoes the insights of strain theory, the dealer says:

'"Look, I have never had a job. I tried for a long time and ended up on the dole. Two years ago, I started selling drugs. Since then I've stayed in the best hotels, I've eaten at the finest restaurants and I wear the most expensive clothes. I might end up in prison, but that can't be worse than being on the dole in Moss Side."'

(reported by Steve Boggan in the *Independent*, 6 July 1991, page 8)

However, while innovators might be more likely to be found among those members of society who have least access to conventional means of making a living, Merton's theory doesn't preclude middle- and upper-class criminals: the rich lawyer who gets even richer by dealing cocaine obtained as 'fees' from drug trafficking clients; the corrupt politician who accepts illicit payments from arms dealers who want their interests promoted by the government. In these cases, even reasonable access to the high life – a lucrative occupation or directorship – isn't always enough for some individuals in their pursuit of material trappings. They want more, and so they supplement legally obtained incomes with a bit (or a lot!) of criminal innovation on the side.

Although Merton places a great deal of emphasis on *innovation* as a deviant response to frustrated ambition, he also recognises that, faced with the same objective circumstances, most people simply conform, and some adopt different deviant responses. Even if, for example, I live in a crime-ridden neighbourhood, and there's more likelihood that I'll turn to crime than other people, chances are I'll still conform. If I do conform, this can happen in two main ways:

- Straight-down-the-line *conformity*: I accept that getting on in a material sense is a goal worth striving for, and I do my best to obtain this goal by getting a job and working hard.
- *Ritualism*: I'm a conformist in the sense of not breaking the law, but I don't aspire to the 'American Dream' of becoming wealthy. There's a ritualistic (i.e. habitual, almost over-scrupulous) adherence to the rules here, but a 'play it safe' lack of material ambition.

There are also different ways of being deviant than stealing cars. Merton identified two other variants:

- *Retreatism*: I opt out of the conventional value system and I adopt unconventional behaviours. This can vary from becoming a non-drug-taking New Age person, a nun in a closed community, to a solvent-using drifter. Some retreatist 'deviants' are deviant by dint of leading very untypical lives while not breaking the law, while others break laws.
- *Rebellion*: I challenge the existing value system and seek to replace conventional values with alternative ones. I might become a Greenpeace activist or a Buddhist monk. Merton has a 'soft spot' for rebels.

STRAIN THEORY OF DEVIANCE

FOR

+ Crime isn't simplistically seen as simply a product of human weakness and low morals. Strain theory points to underlying structural pressures that push some people to commit crimes when they perceive that they can't get what they 'reasonably' want through ordinary legal means.
+ Strain theory helps policy-makers tackle some of the underlying causes of crime rather than merely blaming the perpetrator. The British Prime Minister, Tony Blair, for example, argues that social policies designed to reduce crime should root out structural incentives to commit crime – unemployment, low pay, etc. – as well as dealing, through the deployment of law enforcers, with the symptoms of these deviant incentives.
+ Crime statistics demonstrate that there's a positive correlation between increased levels of unemployment and increased levels of property crimes. This is consistent with the prediction of strain theorists that economic adversity heightens the pressure on people to steal.

AGAINST

– Strain theory seems a plausible explanation of certain types of property crime, but it's based more on clever hunches rather than on evidence. In reviewing empirical research into the aspirations and expectations of delinquents, Ruth Kornhauser (1978, cited by Vold and Bernard 1986) claimed that the research revealed low aspirations and low expectations associated with delinquency. In short, delinquents don't aspire to much, nor do they expect to get much, so how can one talk of strain?

– Linked to the criticism above, strain theory doesn't seem to offer convincing explanations of crimes that have no materialistic motives. How, for example, might strain theory explain why a young male in Birmingham walks into a museum and paint sprays graffiti on the exhibits? Once again, it's apposite to ask, 'Where's the strain?'

– Strain theory places too much emphasis on blue-collar crime and doesn't give sufficient attention to white-collar/corporate crime. Merton, of course, wasn't seeking to offer a general theory of crime, so he could argue that this criticism is misplaced.

Merton's five adaptations – conformity, innovation, ritualism, retreatism, rebellion – don't describe personality types, but rather individuals' choice of behaviours in response to strain. Some individuals might consistently opt for one adaptation, but other people use several – either one at a time or simultaneously. For example, a young burglar (an innovator) might become a law-abiding citizen (a conformist). On the other hand, a career burglar (an innovator) might also use narcotics (retreatism).

OVER TO YOU

Imagine you've been given £100,000 to lead an investigation over one year into the causes of car theft in an area of high unemployment. How might the insights of strain theory help you in this research project?

EXAM TIP

Merton's functionalist-strain theory is the single most influential theory in modern criminology. Despite its functionalist pedigree, it's very radical, so don't fall into the trap of dismissing it as just another 'conservative functionalist theory'. Merton respected 'deviant rebels' who confronted what they regarded as unjust values in the pursuit of a 'better society'.

Marxist theory and studies

While he didn't write at length about crime, Marx argued that laws were generally the codified means by which one class, the rulers, kept another class, the rest of us, in check. He was particularly scathing about the legislation imposed by the English landed ruling class that enabled them to 'enclose' common land. Marx called this the systematic robbery of the people. There's something very 'Robin Hoodish' here: the notion that wherever deer roam, they belong to the king alone, and that the poacher who takes one for her hungry family is a common criminal.

The idea that the poor are driven to commit crime strongly underpins the theories of those criminologists who have taken Marx's ideas further. An early marxist criminologist, Willem Bonger (1916, cited by Vold and Bernard 1986), argued that the capitalist system encourages people to pursue self-interest without regard to the well-being of others. However, said Bonger, this manifest greed is criminalised among the poor, yet tolerated among the rich. Put another way, when greedy working-class people commit crimes, they go to the 'slammer', but when greedy upper-class people break the law, the 'justice' system 'tolerates' their transgressions.

This line of argument actually forms the basis of a theory of widespread crime and selective law enforcement: crime occurs throughout society, but poor criminals receive harsher treatment than rich criminals. As will be seen later, marxist theories of crime contain aspects of both deviant-and-conforming and widespread-crime-and-selective-law-enforcement insights. However, unlike other structural sociologists, marxists tend to emphasise 'white-collar, corporate crime' and pay less attention to 'blue-collar' variants. In that respect, the

Just as the English poor had common land expropriated from them in the past by the landed aristocracy, so did the New Zealand Maoris have their rights to traditional land rights removed by white European 'robber barons'.

'deviants' are more likely to be identified among the rich and powerful than among the poor and oppressed. In a positivistic way (marxists are some of the most sophisticated positivists around), marxist criminologists note that:

- The crimes of the upper class exert a greater economic toll on society than the crimes of 'ordinary' people. Thio (1989) notes that the economic cost of corporate crime in America is about 27 to 42 times greater than losses accounted for by 'traditional property crimes', like burglary and robbery.
- Violence against members of the American public by corporate 'gangsters' in pursuit of profit far exceeds violence by 'lower-class street criminals' (Thio 1989). Of the four million workers exposed to asbestos in America, about 1.6 million are expected to die from lung cancer (Balkan, Berger and Schmidt 1980, cited by Thio 1989)
- Law enforcers are, in an important sense, the servants of the middle and upper classes: they police blue-collar crime more aggressively and vigorously than white-collar crime. Given that middle- and upper-class people have far more to lose, potentially, from property crime than the poor, the prosperous seem to need more protection. Yet, perversely, it's often those on low incomes who are more likely to be burgled than rich people.
- Although some working-class criminals engender the romanticism of the Robin Hood legend, this argument mustn't be pushed too far. Those burglary victims referred to above are likely to have been the victims of working-class criminals. This approach is adopted by so-called 'new left realists', like Trevor Jones and Jock Young.

Taking the theme of *new left realism* a little further, here we have quite a curious stand-off between two types of marxist: the classical and the new. Not forgetting that classical knowledge confers past wisdoms even to the modern age, we mustn't assume that the classical version is out-of-date. But what are the essential differences between the two types?

In its most moderate form, the new marxism is looking for a different name. Like Clause Four of the pre-1995 British Labour Party, the very mention of marxism sends shudders down the spines of those in the Party who are eager, like their leader, Tony Blair, to create a market economy-friendly version of socialism.

So, to illuminate matters, the latest version of *new left realism* runs like this:

- Long term unemployment and relentless poverty are important causes of working-class property crime.
- At the other end of the spectrum, the increasing prosperity of the rich is sometimes premised on their engaging in 'social crimes' (for example, ruthlessly laying off workers and giving themselves huge pay rises) and 'legal crimes' (for example, encouraging MPs to promote their business interests).
- The real victims are poor people: people who are disabled, homeless, low paid, old, female heads of lone-parent families, and long-term unemployed. Not only are they on very low incomes, they also tend to live in areas where they're exploited by predatory members of their own social class: working-class burglars, muggers and the like.
- These victims need better pay, better police protection and access to improved crime prevention measures (for example, security locks provided by the city council in the event of becoming 'serial burglary' victims). It's this 'let's get *real* about the working class victim' approach that gives 'new left *realism*' its name.

Classical marxists go along with much of the above, but they:

- emphasise the crimes of the rich and powerful much more than the 'anti-social lumpen-proletarian' criminal habits of those members of the working class who prey on their own kind
- don't have much confidence in the police, nor in crime prevention strategies. They claim that social justice and equality are the best ways of getting rid of property crime altogether.

It's appropriate to conclude this section with a reference to Ian Taylor, who was a pioneer of what, in the early 1970s, became known as the 'new criminology'. It's hardly new now though, some 30 years on. So perhaps this school of thought needs a new name! The new criminology is more or less synonymous with new left realism: it's very much into pro-active radicalism, of identifying a problem and tackling it in a practical way. But Taylor, despite his new criminology leanings, still emphasises that some of the really 'big villains' are higher up the social class ladder than the working-class mugger. In that context, he notes that the laundering of money obtained through the marketing of cocaine and other illicit drugs is widely reported to have escalated. Moreover:

'any adequate account of the phenomenon of money-laundering itself must suspend a purely criminological framework focusing on crooked and socially-marginal corrupters and pay attention to the involvement of very familiar, respectable "High Street banks" and other financial institutions.'

(Taylor 1991a: 124)

OVER TO YOU

Using up-to-date evidence from a wide range of secondary sources, find out what you can about present-day corporate crime. Write up your findings in a short report.

MARXIST THEORY OF DEVIANCE

FOR

+ It scores top marks for corroborating its claims about corporate 'gangsterism' with impressive empirical evidence.
+ It goes beyond simple criminal population theory explanations by demonstrating that crime is endemic among all social groups. That said, you'd be forgiven for thinking that some of the more orthodox marxists have developed their own version of criminal population theory: the claim that all the 'bad guys' are middle and upper class!
+ It urges real macro, structural changes in society in order to get rid of crime. High on the agenda are anti-poverty and full employment measures. Remember too that the more moderate marxists (new left realists) advocate more hard target measures, like community policing in poor neighbourhoods where burglary rates are high.
+ It draws on social constructionist theories and studies of crime, and, in the best sociological tradition, shows that people make the social structures that turn back on them. For example, politicians make laws that decree what behaviours are allowable and what are criminal. This has consequences: an upper-class interpretation of law presides over 'lower'-class conceptions, to the benefit of the former and the detriment of the latter.

AGAINST

− It's very ideological because it makes no bones at all about its antipathy towards the middle and upper classes and its sympathy with the working class. Of course, orthodox marxists would never accept the charge of being ideological: they believe that marxism is objective, and all other thought forms are ideological. One might accuse them of being imperious, to say the least.

− Its theoretical approach isn't renowned for being particularly flexible. There's an in-built assumption that laws are installed by a corrupt, self-serving upper class, who are aided and abetted by a loyal – but, from a working-class view, treacherous – criminal 'justice' system. Credit where it's due though. Marx himself spoke highly of the nineteenth-century factory inspectors, a body of men whom he regarded as fiercely independent and ready to expose breaches of health and safety regulations by corrupt factory owners.

− With the exception of the new left realists, marxists aren't generally favourable towards gradual, piecemeal reform; they prefer things to be much more radical. Given though that not a few professors make a rather good living out of lecture hall marxism, perhaps it's not such a bad thing after all to endorse some reform, especially if it makes impoverished lives a little better.

− It doesn't pay sufficient attention to oppressed social groups other than the working class, notably babies (more likely than any other individuals to be victims of homicide), ethnic minorities, people who are disabled, old and young people, girls and women.

All theories of distinct criminal and conforming populations derive from the structural view that human social behaviour is shaped by social forces. *Functionalist-strain theorists* describe these forces in terms of the difficulties encountered by some (usually 'lower'-class) people to obtain socially valued material goals without breaking the law. *Subcultural theorists* and *ecological theorists* explain how 'lower-class' values and run-down neighbourhoods combine to socialise certain individuals into criminal habits. *Marxist theory* is the joker in the pack because it readily combines structural with interpretive insights. Its exponents show how the different life chances generated by the social class position of individuals create different pressures and opportunities for the commission of crime. At the same time, the socially constructed perceptions of the police and courts towards different types of criminal lead to selective law enforcement: blue-collar crimes are more vigorously prosecuted than white-collar ones.

The strength of structural theories lies in their ability to account for crime on the basis of sociological explanations rather than 'common-sense' notions of individual weakness. If you grew up in a neighbourhood where employment prospects were scarce and drug-dealing offered lucrative pickings, as well as high peer status, isn't it more likely that you might turn to crime than if you grew up in a prosperous tree-lined suburb, where most young people entered university, and, thereafter, well-paid career ladder occupations? That isn't to say that you'd automatically become a crack-dealer if you were raised in Moss Side, Manchester, or a barrister if you were brought up in Hampstead, London.

What structural theorists assert, an assertion supported by numerous empirical studies, is that social factors play a very significant role in what we become. In statistical terms, this means that there are strong associations between different sets of social circumstances that individuals encounter and the likelihood of them generally committing crimes or generally conforming. The 'generally' qualification is important because most people (especially most males) commit some – usually, not very serious – crimes. However, for most people, this isn't usually a life-time habit.

Arguably, a major shortcoming of all structural theories is the tendency to focus on male crime and to under-investigate female crime. This sexist research orientation is increasingly being challenged both on ethical and methodological grounds. It's offensive to assume that only male lifestyles are worthy of study; moreover, to ignore what females do is simply bad social science. Even if one accepts the plausible argument that males generally commit more crimes than females, it's still important to research female criminality. Structural theories also have a tendency to underestimate the influence of labelling processes on what comes to be defined as criminal behaviour. In that sense, too much attention is placed on criminal behaviour as an easily identifiable phenomenon with 'causes' that can be unproblematically plotted. As you'll discover when you read the next section, sociologists of a more interpretive disposition adopt a different view: crime isn't a clear-cut, 'cause and effect' issue – it's socially constructed.

Major widespread crime and selective law enforcement theories

Labelling theory and studies

David Matza writes: 'Straying from a path need be regarded as no less comprehensible nor more bewildering than walking it' (1969: 350). He's a labelling theorist. He believes that becoming deviant has more to do with how some people *become* deviant by being so labelled than with how people are *made* deviant by social forces. Out goes structural preoccupations with the social backgrounds of offenders. The emphasis is on how easy it is for certain people to drift away from the usual controlling constraints (for example, families, schools, etc.) and to stray into the path of the label-makers: police, probation officers, social workers, teachers. This emphasis on the lifting of those aspects of socialisation that control our behaviour has led to Matza sometimes being referred to as a 'control theorist'.

While most people commit crimes (there's a bit of drift and stray in all of us), only some are regarded as real criminals. Take a street party as an example. One occurs on a run-down Newcastle estate: an argument breaks out; punches are thrown; the police arrive and charge two working-class men with drunk and disorderly conduct. Picture another street party. It takes place in a plush, tree-lined Oxford suburb: an argument breaks out; punches are thrown; the police arrive and . . .

OVER TO YOU

You fill in the ensuing details! Explain your ending, sociologically.

We hope you've concluded, like us, that the second street party is more likely than the first not to end with charges. Middle- and upper-class criminality, in contrast with the blue-collar variety, more often results in an informal warning than with further proceedings. Yet the criminal acts are the same: what's different is the reaction by law enforcers to the acts. All of the individuals, irrespective of their social class, commit what Edwin Lemert (1967, cited by Schull 1988) refers to as *primary deviance*, in this case, actual crimes. For some individuals things don't go beyond a non-recorded verbal caution. For others, there are different outcomes: they're charged and 'confirmed' in their criminality, thereby experiencing what Lemert describes as *secondary deviance*.

Lemert's distinction between the two phases of deviance, the second of which may or may not occur, rescues labelling theory from the charge that it forgets 'causes' and just looks at 'effects'. His ingenious theory demonstrates that primary deviance has an 'original cause' which remains unimportant so long as its perpetrator is considered to be acting within the bounds of acceptable behaviour. Secondary deviance, however, is the 'definitive cause' because it confirms society's serious disapproval of both the act and the actor.

EXAM TIP

In evaluating labelling theory, be sure to note that the concepts of primary and secondary deviation together take account of *causes* (why someone becomes deviant in the first place) and *reactions* (how a negative reaction to an initial deviant act triggers more deviance).

Why is it that working-class violence is often interpreted as heavy duty crime, while violence by higher social classes is frequently perceived as high-spirited or out-of-character behaviour? Labelling theorists reply that rule-makers – judges, politicians and the like – are middle- and upper-class. They tend to treat the infractions of their own kind more leniently than the deviance of working-class people. This assertion echoes the marxist argument that:

- the definitions of deviance put forward by the rich and powerful carry more clout, being more energetically acted upon than the views of those who occupy positions lower in the social hierarchy

- crimes occur among all social groups, but the law is enforced selectively: those at the top and middle are given greater levity and granted more lenience than those at the bottom.

It's not only poor people who are more likely than other groups to be labelled as criminal, ethnic minorities encounter a great deal of negative stigmatisation too. In a famous study of two Californian cities, the ethnomethodologist, Aaron Cicourel (1976), drew attention to this phenomenon. Although both cities were of similar size, they had different rates of juvenile delinquency. City A had higher general delinquency rates, but City B had higher rates of African–American and Mexican–American delinquency. Cicourel attributed this to the fact that the police department in City B was strongly disposed to view ethnic minorities as 'trouble-makers'. Thus these groups were more aggressively monitored and policed, and their actual delinquency was thereby probably exaggerated (or *amplified*, to use a sociological term). We'll elaborate on amplification, particularly with regard to the mass media, because it's an important issue in itself, and because it's a popular topic in A-level sociology exams.

The mass media and deviancy amplification

Let's consider a Saturday night disturbance in a pub during which two young males get into a fight and both end up with minor injuries. You weren't at the pub at the time, but you read about the incident in a newspaper. Unknown to you, however, the reporter who works for the newspaper has a vivid imagination and a marked tendency to exaggerate. Minor injuries are 'amplified' into serious ones and an untypical episode into a long legacy of violent behaviour.

Here we have the beginnings of a media-generated *moral panic*. The local chief constable over-reacts to bad publicity. The impression conveyed by the sensationalist reporter, that violence is commonplace in the pub, prompts the chief constable to engage in some pro-active law enforcement. Undercover officers are placed in the pub and in neighbouring clubs and bars over the next few weeks, and they're ordered to make arrests if even the smallest disturbances arise. The upshot is that:

- quite a lot of young men are arrested for minor squabbles that would otherwise have run out of steam without police intervention
- the arrests lead to some convictions, and, for a while, these convictions make it appear as if the crime rate is going up. It's not of course: more undercover officers means more convictions, even if the number of offences doesn't actually increase
- the excitable reporter, either through lack of understanding or through sheer misrepresentation, runs another story alleging that violent crime rates in the area are up
- this puts even more pressure on the chief constable to sort out the perceived problem, and more police are sent in, and, hey presto!, more arrests occur
- the pub begins to acquire a 'hard man' reputation – media fanned and, unwittingly, police behaviour-related – among 'wannabe tough guys' who've heard it's the place to go for a punch-up on a Friday night
- the self-fulfilling prophecy really takes off when 'out for trouble lads' go to the pub on weekends and get into fights
- yet more arrests are made, the crime figures increase, the reporter keeps spinning his tale (this time with some semblance of truth), the chief constable keeps up the pro-active policing, and so the cycle continues.

The hypothetical process charted above is defined by sociologists as *deviancy amplification*. We hope you've noticed that it's actually an example of a self-fulfilling prophecy: what's prophesied happens in earnest! In that respect, minor deviance is reported in an exaggerated fashion which sets in motion a train of events that eventually lead to more serious versions. The relationship between the media and deviancy amplification, although not simply one-directional, also highlights an area of media effects.

It's very important to note that the deviancy amplification model contains both the recognition that:

- the initial commission of fairly minor acts of deviance can be exaggerated out of all proportion
- serious acts of deviance can result from exaggerated societal reactions, because the reactions become a form of 'advanced billing' for worse things to come.

A path-breaking British sociological study of the deviancy amplification effect of mass media was conducted in the 1960s by Stanley Cohen (1973). Dated it might be, but a classic that still informs current research it remains. The study investigated encounters between mods and rockers in south and east England seaside towns. Adopting an interactionist approach, Cohen examined the processes whereby society labels rule-breakers as deviant and how, once type-cast, their actions become interpreted in relation to the deviant status they're assigned.

Substantially agreeing that subcultural theory provides 'the structural setting for explaining the Mods and Rockers phenomenon as a form of adolescent deviance among working-class youth in Britain' (Cohen 1973: 19), Cohen proceeds to focus attention on the hyped rhetoric of 'moral panics' fostered by the press. In that context, the message that 'We won't allow our seasides to be taken over by hooligans' became firmly established. The media, with editorials coining labels of 'ill-conditioned odious louts' (*Daily Express*), 'retarded vain young hot-blooded paycocks' (*Daily Sketch*) and 'grubby hordes of louts and sluts' (*Daily Telegraph*), fanned a panic of 'clear and present danger'. This, in turn, encouraged law enforcers to escalate the measures they took in dealing with the perceived threat to 'law and order'.

In responding to the amplification process, the police resorted to the 'show of force' principle by increasing the number of officers on duty. In August 1964, the Chief Constable of Hastings called on the Metropolitan Police 'Sky Squad' and neighbouring forces, thereby trebling the police presence. Reinforcements were accompanied by wider use of truncheons, police dogs and horses. Brighton even converted civil defence vehicles into police vans. While each local force had their own specific strategies, most used similar control tactics. These included:

- keeping 'suspicious-looking' youths in one area, usually on the beach
- keeping previously designated 'trouble spots' clear of likely looking mods and rockers
- pre-emptive strikes on putative troublemakers, for example, stopping scooter riders to produce their driving licences and confiscating studded belts.

Clothing styles and distinct hairstyles were considered suitable grounds for regarding certain persons legitimate targets for police control, and in 'certain cases, purely on the basis of symbolization, young people were in fact forced out of town' (Cohen 1973: 94). Cohen argued that the actual extent of the criminality of mods and rockers was amplified by the mass media way beyond its real incidence. In that sense, he claims, the mass media create moral panics and 'folk devils'. Here's how this happens:

1 An initial act of deviance, say, a seaside punch-up between several mods and rockers, leads to arrests and legal sanctions.
2 This event catches the headlines, is blown out of proportion, and sensationalised, leading to a 'moral panic'.
3 Other mods and rockers are treated by the media and by 'law-abiding folk' and law enforcers as 'folk devils', and are pro-actively policed to the point of harassment.
4 Mods and rockers in general become aware of this negative labelling, come to perceive themselves as deviant, gang up with other members of the same youth culture and 'live up' to their media reputation by going on the rampage.
5 More arrests and punitive measures occur, and a 'vicious circle' ensues.

More recently, the theme of deviancy amplification has been taken up by Ian Taylor. He's a professor of sociology at Salford University, Manchester, and he's particularly interested in the way this city has become 'demonised' by the press:

'Manchester . . . is now well and truly launched into a powerful new moral panic, focusing on a widely reported increase in the carrying of arms and the use of violence . . . By May, The Observer (5 May 1991), was running Manchester crime stories using headlines such as Drugs Gangs Wage War for Control of Moss Side. The ratchet of panic in the public mind was turned even tighter.'

(Taylor 1991b: 28)

Yet, as Taylor notes, this kind of publicity doesn't give a balanced account of the Manchester crime scene. The number of murders known to the Greater Manchester police force in 1990, in a population of 2.6 million, was 23, ten down on 1989: a rate of slightly less than one per 100,000. Compare this to the US, where the overall homicide rate for all areas stood at nine per 100,000 in 1989. Given that murders have a very high police clear-up rate, these figures are likely to be fairly accurate.

Despite the statistics, the rhetoric of moral panic, fuelled by media amplification, is alive and kicking in Manchester. The sensationalisation of crack and gun culture is likely to provide new recruits – lured by the imagery of masculine toughness – to the criminal scene. It's a problem not as big as the media would have us imagine. But try telling that to the young people whose lives it damages and sometimes destroys in areas like Hulme and Moss Side.

Moral panics are also at work in media predictions of football fan violence. Colin Ward, for example, suggested that such forewarnings during the 1990 World Cup might become a self-fulfilling prophecy: 'The problem is that the media have created a forest fire that needs ever more combustible material to satisfy demand' (Ward 1990: 24).

One of the more recent moral panics whipped up by the press is the theme of young Britons behaving as 'badly or worse' than their American counterparts. America is seen as a dangerous, powerful, global agenda-setter whose media images of deviant identities are readily sold as commodities via satellite and fibre optics into the heart of British youth subcultures.

Consider these press reports:

- 'Bronx violence, Sheffield accent' (*Independent*, 28 November 1994)
- 'Sub-machine guns in big arms seizure by Liverpool police . . . were probably intended for criminals . . . ' (*Guardian*, 8 February 1994)
- 'Menace of the all-girl gangs: Liz Hurley mob copy US thugs' (*Sun*, 26 November 1994).

As usual, Manchester is getting a lot of stick, being described, for example, by the *Manchester Guardian* on 11 February 1994, as 'worse than New York'. But well done, Ian Taylor for reminding the readers of the *Guardian* on 12 February 1994 that New York is 'a city where there are as many murders every two days as there is in Greater Manchester in a year . . .'

Other perplexing side effects of moral panics have been highlighted by Chris Grover and Keith Soothill (1995) in their study of the social construction of sex offenders. The media tend to portray a selective image of sex crime that obscures an understanding of its real nature and extent. By focusing on the unusual and sensational, the press construct an image which suggests that women only need be wary of strangers, and that only a minority of men are capable of sex offending. This denies, argue Grover and Soothill, the generalised nature of sex offences against both women and children. Moreover, male sex offenders are labelled as 'monsters' who are often led astray by booze or drugs into attacking women: 'The image thus created is that men do not have any responsibility for their actions' (Grover and Soothill 1995: 33). But this overlooks the importance of understanding how males in general are socialised into becoming potential or actual sex attackers. It's a stereotype that also underplays the need to consider the routine – as opposed to the sensational – nature of sexual violence that's embedded in society. Sex attackers aren't just folk devils; sometimes they're the guys 'next door'.

Marxist theories and studies (what, again?)

Yes, again. We'll re-visit the marxists, but this time looking at the social constructionist insights they employ. If you've studied the sociology of education, you'll have come across the marxist-cum-social constructionist Paul Willis. He suggests that working-class school students 'suffer' the double blows of negative labelling from teachers, and the drudgery of low-paid, tedious manual work in the social structure of the world beyond the school when they enter employment. Similarly, marxists with social constructionist leanings note that working-class behaviour is often stereotyped by law enforcers as

LABELLING THEORY OF DEVIANCE

FOR

+ It doesn't fall into the simplistic trap of dividing 'mobsters' and 'ordinary folk' into 'bad guy' and 'good guy' categories: crime is recognised to be fairly widespread among all social groups.
+ It correctly draws attention to the fact that reactions are as important as (sometimes more important than) actions. Throwing a plate on the ground in a restaurant would usually be considered a criminal action; but not in a 'plate-smashing' Greek restaurant.
+ It cautions against taking official crime statistics at face value. The compiling of these statistics are influenced by negative and positive labelling. For example, the police tend to 'label' young streetcorner males who don't show them respect as 'bad boys', but are more likely to define college boys who are out on the town as just high-spirited.

AGAINST

– While crime is committed by most people, it's necessary to distinguish between minor, short-term criminal behaviour (most young offenders grow out of crime) and serious, career crime. Labelling theory doesn't perhaps make this distinction as explicit as it might.
– Isn't there just a bit of a 'stand by the underdog' tendency among labelling theorists? But hey, so what!? As Howard Becker (1967: 5) remarks, 'unconventional sentimentality . . . is the lesser evil.'
– There's a tendency to underestimate the importance of structural 'causes' of crime, for example, the relationship between property crime and unemployment. That said, few, if any labelling theorists, would go so far as to say that labels creep up by stealth and fasten themselves to the backs of innocents. Yet this criticism is sometimes levelled at labelling theory.

criminal, while similar behaviour is 'permitted' when carried out by members of 'higher' social classes. At the same time, the structural position of working-class criminals – low income, poor quality housing, etc. – places great pressures (echoes here of strain theory) on them to turn to crime for economic reasons.

The tendency for marxist criminologists to use labelling theory in their research is readily illustrated by the comments of the marxist William Chambliss:

'Instead of asking "why do some people commit crimes and others not" we ask "why are some acts defined as criminal while others are not." Instead of asking "why is crime more often committed in this part of a city than in that" we ask why the law enforcement agencies make more arrests "here" than "there".'

(Chambliss 1975: Preface)

In their now classic 1960s study of an American metropolitan police department in an industrial city of 450,000 inhabitants, sociologists Irving Piliavin and Scott Briar (1964) addressed these important questions. During nine months' observation of all juvenile police officers in the department, supplemented by interviews with officers, they found 'officially frowned-upon practices' were openly apparent, even when the officers knew they were being watched by the sociologists.

Police dispositions towards potential suspects played a crucial role in deciding whether or not young males were labelled as 'would-be tough guys' or good boys temporarily gone astray. Other than prior record, the most important cue to a youth's character from a juvenile patrolman's point of view, was the young person's demeanour. Boys who were contrite about their infractions and respectful to police officers were seen as misguided but salvageable. Informal or formal reprimands were considered sufficient to bring them back in line. By contrast, youths who were fractious and 'laid-back' in their dealings with patrolmen were likely to be regarded as 'punks' (yes, the word is much older than the Sex Pistols!) who deserved to be arrested.

However, from a law enforcer's point of view, demeanour was often associated with ethnicity. Of 27 officers interviewed by Piliavin and Briar, 18 openly admitted a dislike for African–Americans, who, said the patrolmen, were more likely to 'give us a hard time', to be uncooperative and to show no remorse for their infractions. Such prejudicial attitudes, noted Piliavin and Briar, led to closer surveillance of black neighbourhoods and more frequent encounters with young African–Americans. Moreover:

'the consequences of this chain of events are reflected in police statistics showing a disproportionately high percentage of Negroes [*sic*] among juvenile offenders, thereby providing "objective" justification for concentrating police attention on Negro youths.'

(Piliavin and Briar 1964: 219–20)

The stereotyping of disadvantaged social groups by law enforcers is well expressed by Chambliss when he writes:

'Selective perception and labeling – finding, processing and punishing some kinds of criminality and not others – means that visible, poor, nonmobile, outspoken, undiplomatic "tough" kids will be noticed, whether their actions are seriously delinquent or not.'

(Chambliss 1973: 160)

Conversely, less visible, rich, jet-setting, 'well-spoken', diplomatic 'decent' kids are less likely to be noticed, even when they're 'up to no good'.

More recently, Chambliss (1994) conducted an observational study of the Rapid Deployment Unit (RDU) of the Washington DC Metropolitan Police, whose members are described by other police officers 'as the "Dirty Harrys" and "very serious bad-ass individuals"'. The RDU is deployed in teams of three patrol cars with two officers per car. They patrol what has been termed the 'urban ghetto', namely, the area of the city where 40 per cent of the black population lives below the poverty line.

Chambliss and some of his students spent more than 100 hours riding with the RDU and other police officers. On the basis of extensive observation and discussions with the officers, he discovered selective law enforcement. For example, he noted that when the RDU patrols the ghetto, they're constantly on the lookout for cars driven by young black men. They're especially attentive to newer-model cars – BMWs, Honda Accords, Isuzu four-wheel-drive vehicles – on the assumption that such cars are favoured by drug dealers. Interestingly, during his observations, Chambliss found that RDU officers had concluded that drug dealers were leaving their 'flashy' cars at home to avoid being stopped. 'It thus became commonplace for RDU officers to stop any car with young black men in it' (Chambliss 1994: 179). Once a car is stopped, the officers radio for backup. Nor are they averse to breaking the law themselves if they want to justify a vehicular stop. They're supposed to stop a car only when a violation has occurred, so sometimes they will break a tail light as they approach the stationary vehicle. In the words of one of the officers:

'This is the jungle . . . we rewrite the constitution every day down here . . . If we pull everyone over they will eventually learn that we aren't playing games any more. We are real serious about getting the crap off the streets.'

(Chambliss 1994: 179)

Racist behaviour by the police also extends to the way they handle suspects. Thus, for example, during a 'rip' (when undercover agents pose as crack buyers), a young black male is arrested. With guns drawn, the police enter an apartment he's entered. Small children begin to cry and scream, adults are thrown to the floor, the police are shouting too, as are three women in the apartment. While the suspect is being questioned, one officer says:

'"I should kick your little black ass right here for dealing that shit. You are a worthless little scumbag, do you realise that?"

[Another officer asks:]

"What is your mother's name, son? My mistake . . . she is probably a whore and you are just a ghetto bastard. Am I right?"'

(Chambliss 1994: 178)

The RDU doesn't patrol the mainly white neighbourhoods of Washington DC. Policing in these areas is very different. There are no 'rips' and no vehicular stops unless there has been a clear violation. Officers aren't looking for cars driven by black people. If a car is stopped, unlike in black parts of the city, backup isn't summoned. Moreover, when white suspects are arrested, the police are significantly less aggressive in their demeanour towards the suspects and the bystanders. Selective law enforcement is certainly alive and kicking in Washington DC!

The for and against critique of those aspects of marxist thought that are linked to widespread crime and selective enforcement theories are essentially the same as those for labelling theory and don't need to be repeated.

Theories of widespread crime and selective enforcement remind us that a cause–effect model of crime is only part of the story. If we place criminals and law-abiding citizens into 'bad guy/good guy' groups, and seek to identify what social factors 'cause' people to end up in one or other of these categories, we overlook the important process of labelling in the social construction of crime and conformity. Put simply, how can a simple cause–effect model be helpful when we know that people from all kinds of social background and group commit crimes? Shouldn't we instead concentrate on how it is that similar behaviours can be labelled by law enforcers as criminal or otherwise, depending on how the perpetrators are perceived? Taking different readings of the same kind of behaviour, for example being drunk and disorderly in public – 'People from that council estate are always drunk'/'They're just a few high-spirited medical students having fun after the graduation party' – suggests that the reaction to a behaviour might be a more important explanation of crime than the reason for the behaviour.

The strength of theories of widespread crime and selective law enforcement lies in their readiness to study crime in its entire social context. It's only then that sociologists can take account of crime as a phenomenon which is defined in terms of behaviour so labelled. By focusing on the process of criminal labelling, these theories make us question the seemingly obvious validity of official crime statistics. Such data are at best a rough approximation of actual criminal acts. However, they tell us much about the interactions that occur between law enforcers and potential offenders. For it's the nature of this interaction that largely determines whether or not a behaviour is considered and recorded as a crime, and whether or not it comes to be recorded as a crime statistic. In that context, a social constructionist approach to the study of crime correctly draws attention to the victimisation experienced by 'low status' social groups in society because of the prejudiced assumptions of law-makers and law enforcers.

Yet although theories of widespread crime and selective law enforcement usefully highlight the importance of the labelling process in relation to what's defined as criminal behaviour, they sometimes push this argument too far. After all, not all police officers and court officials are out to give working-class people and ethnic minorities a hard time. Moreover, as Ronald L. Akers astutely comments:

'One sometimes gets the impression . . . that people go about minding their own business, and then – "wham" – bad society comes along and slaps them with a stigmatized label. Forced into the role of deviant the individual has little choice but to be deviant.'

(Akers 1967, cited by Vold and Bernard 1986: 256)

Akers here makes a charge against social constructionists that is more usually levelled against structural theorists, namely, the adoption of an over-deterministic approach. It's as if the person labelled as a deviant is somehow locked into a perpetual criminal career, and any resistance to the label is pointless. There are parallels here with the structural view that once individuals are drawn into a criminal subculture they get sucked into a hard-to-get-out-of, 'subterranean low-life existence'. Lemert's concepts of primary and secondary deviation provide an insightful bridge between the two theoretical camps. For he recognises that any number of factors – sociological, psychological, even biological – might lead people to commit crimes. This primary deviance can be 'caused' by structural factors, but it only 'graduates' to secondary deviance when individuals are labelled as criminals.

QUESTIONS

1 How might R. K. Merton's functionalist-strain theory help sociologists to understand why some unemployed young people commit burglary and car theft?
2 What reasons did the Chicago urban ecology sociologists give for higher rates of crime in some neighbourhoods than in others?
3 What do subcultural explanations of crime contribute to our understanding of gang behaviour?
4 How do some marxist sociologists combine structural and social constructionist insights when they research crime?
5 Why do some social constructionist sociologists argue that structural explanations of crime don't provide a complete picture?
6 To what extent, if at all, is it fair to claim that labelling theory is too deterministic?

Crime statistics

Consider the following statistics.

In England and Wales:

- Only a half of all crimes are reported, three in ten are recorded, and fewer than one in ten is cleared up (*Social Trends 23*).
- One third of all men born in the early 1950s had a conviction by the time they were 31; one in 14 were convicted for violent crime (*Social Trends 23*).
- Car theft was the most common crime recorded by the police in 1991 (*Social Trends 23*).
- The probability of being a victim tends to be higher among ethnic minority people (*Social Trends 23*).
- Homicide victims often knew their killer: almost two-thirds of male victims and four-fifths of female victims knew, or were related to, their killer (*Social Trends 23*).

In America:

- Crime and imprisonment rates are the highest in the industrial world (Henwood 1994).
- The FBI (1988, cited by Thio 1989) estimate that one American is murdered every 26 minutes.
- The risk of being murdered is 1 out of 157 for all Americans, but 1 out of 29 for black males (Thio 1989).
- 92.7 per cent of victims of black murderers are black; 84.7 per cent of victims of white murderers are white (Henwood 1994).
- One quarter of all black men in their twenties are either in jail or on parole or probation. This is four times the rate of white men (Henwood 1994).
- Homicide is most frequent on weekend evenings, especially Saturday nights. This is largely so when working-class murderers slay. However, middle- and upper-class offenders kill on any day of the week (Thio 1989).
- Higher-class murders are more likely to be premeditated than lower-class homicides – thus less likely to be prompted by weekend drinking (Green and Wakefield 1979, cited by Thio 1989).

How far can we rely on such figures? Crime statistics generally come from these sources:

- *Crimes known to the police* These are the crimes they come across, usually through incidents that are reported by members of the public
- *Crimes reported by victims in probability surveys* (notably, the British Crime Surveys)
- *Crimes owned up to in social scientific studies* These are self-reported, usually in local research projects.

Taken together, these and other sources still probably underestimate the actual extent of crime (mainly due to under-reporting by victims). They also don't provide a complete picture of how crime is committed by different sections of society (because, for example, of selective law enforcement).

This section considers the question further in the context of the statistical distribution of different social groups in reported crime rates. The main focus is on age, class, ethnicity, sex and region. The relationship between these groups and crime figures shouldn't just be considered though in 'splendid isolation'. For example, although black and Asian people in England and Wales are more likely than white people to be the victims of many types of crime, this has much to do with the neighbourhoods where they live.

Since the Conservatives came to power in 1979, the official crime figures have doubled. In 1994, 5,251,100 crimes were reported to the police. Social scientists know this figure is open to a number of interpretations. That said, whichever way they look at it, crime has almost certainly increased. According to the Home Office's British Crime Survey of 14,500 households, the 'real' number of crimes is 15 million a year, three times higher than the police figures reveal.

Nevertheless, it would be arrogant and irresponsible for social scientists to suggest that crime statistics can be calibrated with the fine-tuned accuracy of an oil pressure gauge. Social statistics, especially those dealing with crime, must be treated with great circumspection and caution. To cite an illustrative example, in one year, the store detectives of a Chicago department store arrested two-thirds as many women for shoplifting as were formally charged with all forms of petty larceny (shoplifting included) by police in the entire city of Chicago. Yet only about 25 per cent of apprehended alleged shoplifters were handed over by store detectives to the police (Sutherland and Cressey 1978). Put simply, there was a discrepancy between the number of alleged offences committed and the number of alleged shoplifters charged.

This is but one example of the many different ways in which crimes can be 'lost' between an initial arrest and an actual prosecution. The so-called 'chivalry factor', for example, can lead to male police officers acting more 'leniently' towards female suspects by issuing a warning rather than pressing a charge. This social constructionist (that is, labelling) concept shouldn't, however, be pushed too far. In certain cases, female suspects might be treated more harshly than males by law enforcers. Soliciting client sex is an example here.

Sex and crime rates

On a purely positivistic level, Albert K. Cohen and James F. Short Jr write:

'If an investigator were asked to use a single trait to predict which persons in any given town would become criminals, he [*sic*] would make the fewest mistakes if he simply chose sex status and predicted criminality for the males and noncriminality for the females.'

(Cohen and Short 1971: 107)

This view receives support today from Pamela Abbott and Claire Wallace, who assert that:

'One of the reasons that "women and crime" has been a neglected area in sociology is that women appear to be remarkably non-criminal.'

(Abbott and Wallace 1993: 153)

As for male crime, note Abbott and Wallace:

'Much male deviance is associated with what it means to be "a man" – theft using force, fighting in gangs, football violence, and so on.'

(Abbott and Wallace 1993: 153)

While official statistics (*Social Trends 25*) certainly support the view that in 1990s England and Wales, males are more likely than females to be convicted of – or cautioned for – crime, do these figures reflect real differences or harsher treatment by law enforcers towards males? Probably, more of the first factor and a bit of the last factor is as close as we'll get to the truth. This means that, even if we make allowances for some discriminatory behaviour on the part of law enforcers towards men, there are still likely to be real differences between rates of male and female crime. In other words, the differences recorded in official statistics are too big to be explained largely on the basis of gendered discrimination.

So what do the official figures show?

In the UK, the rate of females aged 21 and above serving prison sentences in 1991 was five per 100,000 females aged 21 and above in the female population as a whole. For males, the comparable rate was 163 per 100,000. These rates remained relatively stable during the period 1986–91 (*Social Trends 23*). In short, males are about 33 times more likely to end up in prison than women. The very small number of women in prison might explain why those who are, especially women convicted of violence, seem to get harsher condemnation than men in the media. In the patriarchal society of the UK, women are 'supposed' to be 'biologically determined mums and wives', and criminal behaviour represents a very serious departure from this norm.

Let's now look at the official statistics for offenders aged under 21 found guilty of, or cautioned for, indictable (fairly to very serious) offences, in the line graph above.

QUESTION

Interpret the line graph above by translating the main statistical trends into accurate and concise language.

We hope you've noticed that throughout the 28-year time span of the graph, the rate of young female offenders

Offenders aged under 21 found guilty of, or cautioned for, indictable offences: by sex and age, England and Wales

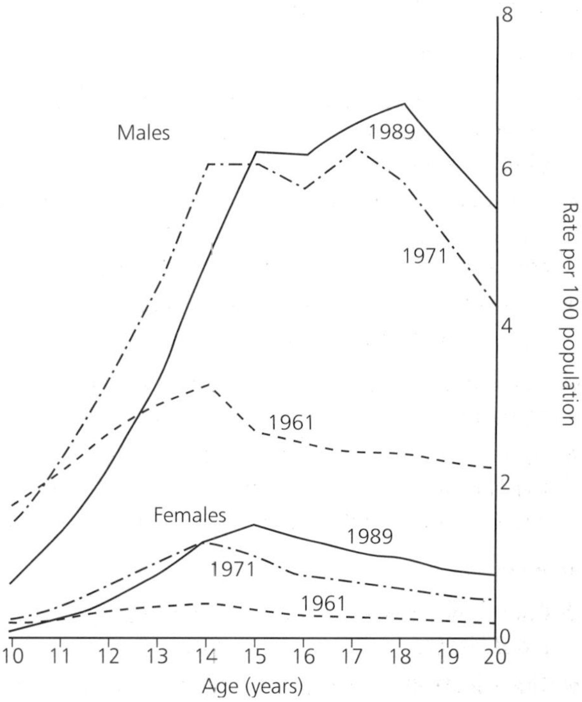

(*Social Trends 22*: 212, based on Home Office statistics)

was consistently, and generally, very substantially below the rate of young male offenders. In 1989, for example, the rate of offenders per 100 young persons aged 18 in the general population was about one per 100 females and about seven per 100 males.

Frances Heidensohn provides a useful summary of trends in female criminality when she writes:

'1. Women commit a small share of all crimes.
2. Women's crimes are fewer, less serious, and more rarely professional than men's.
3. In consequence, women are represented in very small numbers in penal establishments.'

(Heidensohn 1995: 998)

Heidensohn also found that crime is overwhelmingly dominated by men in all European countries. She notes too, with some caution, that some commentators consider women to be only 10 per cent of 'the trouble'. However, when one considers different types of offence, Heidensohn rightly points out that a more complicated picture emerges. Who commits what crimes is quite strikingly gendered. In 1990, for example, about 21 per cent of the women's sentenced population in this country were convicted for robbery, the figure for men being 43 per cent. Women are more likely than men to be found guilty of theft, handling stolen goods, fraud and forgery (20 per cent, against 11 per cent for men), and for drug offences (25 per cent, against 8 per cent for men). Theft and handling offences committed by women are most typically associated with shoplifting. Female crime involving fraud and forgery is usually linked to welfare scams.

While men are more likely than women to murder, some women are killers. But women tend to murder husbands and lovers, while men are more inclined to murder friends and strangers. Women usually employ less violence than men, and they tend to murder in their homes, using kitchen implements. It's also the case that women who kill quite often do so in anger or self-defence, the victim frequently being the original aggressor. Moreover, most women attack men who are drunk or asleep.

Allowing for the fact that negative labelling probably works more against male than female offenders in most criminal proceedings, the positivistic claim that the official statistics demonstrate a real and significant excess of male over female criminality seems very convincing. That's why it might be more helpful, from a social policy angle, to direct more interventionist strategies at male socialisation patterns, especially in the early years of schooling when 'mini-macho man' starts to hatch and develop.

But what about moral panics? Don't they inflate the probability that young male 'folk devils' are more likely than women in general and older people to end up being more harshly dealt with because of negative labelling? Yes, they probably do. D. Steffensmeir (1980, cited by Leonard 1995), for example, asserts that women tend to receive more lenient treatment from the courts, thereby ending up less often in the statistics. But this alleged leniency is rarely extended to adolescent girls, who, notes Leonard (1995), are more likely than boys to be put into care or receive custodial sentences. In that context, girls are often referred to courts for being in need of care and of protection from their own promiscuity. Contrast this with boys, who in our society, are more likely to have their sexual escapades tolerated compared to their female peers.

One must conclude that young males do commit more crimes than other people.

Gender is only one of a number of factors that can influence police–suspect interactions. As R. Harris observes, 'To be older, apologetic and "respectable" is as advantageous for men as for women' (Harris 1992, cited by Heidensohn: 1007). Even accounting for a degree of leniency by some male police officers towards female offenders, the very big difference in the crime rates of young males and all other groups can't adequately be accounted for just in terms of discriminatory labelling. Males probably do commit more crimes than women.

Ethnicity and crime rates

Numerous studies (for example, Sutherland and Cressey 1978) reveal that black Americans are more likely than white Americans who have committed the same crimes to be:

- arrested
- indicted, that is, charged in a criminal court
- committed to an institution.

Sutherland and Cressey (1978) also note that black Americans have a poorer chance than white Americans of receiving:

- probation
- a suspended sentence
- parole
- commutation of a death sentence or a pardon.

Moreover, a 1991 US survey (cited by Jonathan Sale in the *Independent on Sunday*, 11 February 1996, pages 26–7) showed that on a typical day, 42 per cent of all black males aged 18–35 in Washington DC would be under the jurisdiction of the criminal justice system. Fifteen per cent would be in jail, 21 per cent on probation or parole, and 6 per cent waiting for, or avoiding, trial.

It seems very likely indeed that official US crime statistics exaggerate the actual rate of crimes committed by black Americans as compared to white Americans.

In the UK, Errol Lawrence (1982, cited by Aggleton 1991: 102) has highlighted the stereotyping destructiveness of 'common-sense' racist ideologies that influence white perceptions of black culture. In this way, through what Lawrence calls the 'pathologization of black culture', black people are portrayed as 'deviant', 'irrational' and 'sick'. Given that some law enforcers probably apply such negative labels, black suspects are at risk of being handled differently to white suspects. It's also apposite to note that in America, drug offences involving crack typically carry a five-year prison sentence, while probation is more common for crimes related to powdered cocaine (BBC *Panorama*, 27 November 1995). What's significant here is that black drug users tend to go for crack, and their white counterparts are more likely to use powder.

Certainly, the statistical profile of the British prison population reflects differential and unfair handling of offenders by law enforcers. Among adult males, the rate of imprisonment is roughly the same for persons of south Asian origin (Bangladesh, India and Pakistan) as for persons of white British origin. However, the rate is almost seven times higher among persons of African–Caribbean origin. Among young males, the rate of imprisonment is significantly lower for south Asians than for whites, but about five and a half times as high for blacks as for whites.

While black people are much more likely to be imprisoned than white people for all offences, about 27 times as many black as white adult males per head of population are in prison for drug offences, and eight to nine times as many for rape and for robbery. Among south Asian adult males, the rate of imprisonment for drug crimes is also very high, being about four times as high as for white men. However, a much smaller proportion of south Asian men are in prison for burglary: only about one fifth the rate for white men. Ethnic variations in imprisonment rates are broadly the same for young offenders.

The above figures don't necessarily imply that black people are more likely than white people to commit crimes. Rather, in the context of young black men, there's a concern about racial discrimination in the form of police targeting of black communities, 'which increases the likelihood of criminalisation of young blacks' (Blackstone 1990: 26). Certainly, among juvenile suspects, there is clear evidence, reports David J. Smith (1995), that a higher proportion of African–Caribbean than white youths are prosecuted, mainly because of direct discrimination. It has also been argued by L. Blom-Cooper and R. Drabble (1982, cited by Smith 1995) that black people tend to be charged with robbery in circumstances where a white person would be charged with the lesser offence of theft.

Summarising and adding to the above details, David J. Smith (1995) provides this tentative picture of the British experience:

- There's evidence of bias against black people in: the targeting of pro-active law enforcement (i.e. 'go in and find 'em' policing) as opposed to the reactive variety, (i.e. responding to emergency calls, etc.); in decisions to prosecute juveniles; and in Crown Court sentencing.
- Most of the above biases are the result of direct discrimination.
- The magnitude of these biases is small compared with the stark contrast in rates of arrest and imprisonment between black and white people. What seems to be implied here is that, allowing for some degree of selective law enforcement which discriminates against black people, they might actually be more likely than white people to commit crimes.
- South Asians are not over-represented among offenders described by victims, persons arrested, or the prison population. To some extent, they appear to be favoured compared to black or white people.

Returning to the American scene, consider these facts. The prison population in the US increased by 167 per cent between 1980 and 1992, the greatest percentage increase being in drug law violations. The US locks up a higher percentage of its population than any country in the world, and young African–Americans and Latinos are disproportionately arrested, convicted and sentenced to prison terms. In 1991, African–American males between the ages of 15 and 34 comprised 14 per cent of the general population but more than 40 per cent of the prison population. White males make up 82 per cent of this age group, but less than 60 per cent of the prison population. In Washington DC and Baltimore, 40 to 50 per cent of all black males between the ages of 18 and 35 are either in prison, jail, on probation or parole, or there's a warrant out for their arrest. In the country as a whole, African–Americans accounted for more than 40 per cent of all drug arrests, despite the fact that self-report surveys (when people 'own up' to crimes) show that, except for crack cocaine, white people are three to five times more likely to use drugs as black people. Thus more white people than black people use illegal drugs and more than 80 per cent of the general population is white. However, 66 per cent of the inmates of state prisons who are convicted of drug offences are black, and only 33 per cent are white.

Social class and crime rates

Social class affects the ways in which crimes come to be reported. In his now classic study of corporate gangsterism in Seattle, William J. Chambliss writes:

'In Seattle . . . one can find any type of vice that suits the palate . . . Gambling, prostitution, pornography, and usury (high-interest loans) exist with the compliance, encouragement, and cooperation of the major political and law enforcement officials in the city . . . There were innumerable instances of payoffs to politicians and government officials for real estate deals, businesses, and stock transactions. In each case the participants were a combination of local businessmen, racketeers, local politicians, and government officials . . . all of this corruption, bribery, and blatant violation of the law was taking place while arrests were being made and people sent to jail or prison for other offenses. In Seattle over 70 per cent of all arrests during the time of the study were for public drunkeness. The police were actually arresting drunks on one side of a building while on the other side a vast array of other offenses was being committed.'

(Chambliss 1976: 20–3)

Chambliss concludes that 'Everyone commits crime . . . but the label "criminal" is a matter of whom can pin the label on whom' (1976: 23). If Chambliss is right, this means that working-class crimes (notably, public drunkeness) will figure more prominently in crime statistics than middle- and upper-class crimes (notably, bribery). Some words of caution though. Chambliss' study is:

- a case study (case stud*ies* would be fairer because he conducted a comparative study of Seattle, USA, and Ibadan, Nigeria). Therefore generalisations beyond those two cities aren't necessarily valid. That said, his findings are suggestive and merit more extensive research
- mainly based on participant observation, supplemented by extensive interviewing of a 'convenience' sample of informants from a wide range of people: racketeers, prostitutes, police officers, government officials, businessmen, professional thieves, etc. In short, because non-representative samples were used (for very good reasons: can you imagine sending a random sample questionnaire to every tenth Seattle resident asking them to report how many liquor stores they robbed last year!?), as well as participant observation, statistical reliability is compromised
- dated: the Seattle study was conducted between 1962 and 1972. Chambliss' findings are now 'history', unless – as is possible, but needs to be studied – things haven't changed much over the past 30 years or so.

In the UK, the official crime statistics don't refer to the social class of convicted people. Criminological studies generally show, however, that more working-class than middle- and upper-class people are convicted. While selective law enforcement plays a role here, working-class Britons probably commit more street crimes, burglaries and robberies than their 'higher'-class counterparts. Very serious but less aggressively policed crimes, like corporate manslaughter (for example, criminal negligence by a shipping company, resulting in the deaths of passengers), are almost certainly the province of the middle and upper classes. Corporate and white-collar crimes are also unlikely to turn up in victim surveys. People know they're a victim if they're assaulted in a working-class bar. But how many people who work on dangerous construction sites and in hazardous private coal mines know that they're victims of the crimes of the rich and powerful?

While it's very difficult to come up with reliable statistics on the relationship between social class and crime rates, one of the most thorough reviews of the evidence has been provided by J. Braithwaite (1979, cited by Maguire 1995). He analysed 41 self-report studies, as well as over 250 other studies on social class and crime. He concluded that, although the evidence was often contradictory and confusing, police bias probably exaggerated the relative amount of working-class delinquency, and self-report studies tended to overstate the relative extent of middle-class delinquency, the following statements could be fairly confidently made:

- Working-class adults commit those types of crime that are handled by the police at a higher rate than middle-class adults.
- Adults living in working-class areas commit those types of crime that are handled by the police at a higher rate than adults who live in middle-class areas.
- Working-class juveniles commit crime at a higher rate than middle-class juveniles.
- Juveniles who live in working-class areas commit crime at a higher rate than juveniles who live in middle-class areas.

Age and crime statistics

Being young is a good predictor of ending up in crime statistics. In America, for example, most arrests are of people under the age of 20. Young people are twice as likely to be arrested there for 'index offences' (serious crimes) than their proportion in the population would suggest (US Department of Justice 1987). Even accounting for the fact that law enforcers tend to police young people more vigorously than other people, the young are more likely to commit crimes than their elders. In England, Wales and Scotland, the peak offending age for males is 18. The peak offending age for females in England and Wales is 15. A 15-year-old female is more likely to commit an offence than a man aged 31 or over (*Social Trends 25*). It's important, however, to recognise that the extent to which youthful crime is greater than the crime rate among other age groups varies by type of offence and other social groupings.

Take threats and assaults in America. As Sally S. Simpson and Lori Elis note, 'female juveniles in higher class fractions tend to be less frequently involved in these acts than those in lower fractions' (Simpson and Elis 1994: 466). In Scotland, a crime survey (questionnaires that asked about offending behaviour and victimisation experiences were used) in 1990 of 11–15-year-old teenagers in an inner-city Glasgow school revealed that: 'Some 68 per cent of respondents had been involved in a fighting offence, evenly distributed by age but predominantly male (66 per cent)' (Hartless, Ditton, Nair and Phillips 1995: 126–7). Yet, of the 23 per cent of teenagers who had been involved in drug offences, there was no sharp differentiation between the sexes (Hartless *et al.* 1995). Like the sentenced and cautioned population, the prison population in England and Wales is predominantly young. Excluding juveniles in both cases, in 1991, 62 per cent of inmates were aged under 30, compared with 25 per cent of the general population.

Allowing for the likelihood that young people (especially, young, black males) are more likely to be victims of selective law enforcement than other age groups, it's very likely that young people do commit more crimes than other people. The statistics, although partly socially constructed by moral panics and deviancy amplification, must also be interpreted as revealing real differences between the criminality of the young and that of their elders.

> ***EXAM TIP***
>
> By re-reading and learning the earlier section on deviancy amplification (pages 507–9), you'll glean important insights into the social construction of young offender crime statistics.

Region and crime rates

04:59

Crime rates are characterised by important regional differences. In England and Wales, Metropolitan London has a robbery rate over twice that of any other police district. Generally, crime is concentrated in inner cities and in poor neighbourhoods. In agricultural areas, the risk of burglary is about one per year per every 100 houses; it's as high as one in ten houses per year in some inner-city areas. Even this figure isn't evenly distributed across the whole of a particular city. Pockets of the inner city, especially the most impoverished areas, have higher crime rates than others. Thus, for example, the one in ten rate for the inner city rises to one in five or more on some housing estates.

There have been a number of local victimisation surveys, both in the UK and abroad. The findings from these surveys show that area and crime are linked. The Second Islington Crime Survey, for example, reported a burglary rate twice the national average. Ironically, such research often shows that the risk and impact of criminal victimisation are greatest in neighbourhoods where people are often poor. From a 'new left realism' perspective, this implies that the working-class poor are preyed upon by members of their own social class. We're not talking Robin Hood romanticism here; rather, 'lumpen-proletarian' duplicity. The 'lumpen-proletariat' were described by Marx as those members of the working class who take advantage of their own kind. It's a very loaded, value-judgmental term, but in the context just described, it's a useful metaphor.

Justifiable fear of crime in certain neighbourhoods empties the streets of people, and reduces the effectiveness of informal surveillance. This problem has been addressed by the Home Office in a policy-oriented perspective introduced by its criminologists called *situational theory*. This approach, which is essentially a revised form of ecological theory, focuses on the immediate situational features of the environment in which offences are committed. 'Hard-to-let' council estates, for example, have high burglary rates because the commission of crime is easy: poor people can't afford strong security locks, entry phone devices, etc.

Recognising this, situational theorists (note here the close affinity too with new left realism) advocate target hardening strategies: improved locks, video camera surveillance, etc. *Designing Out Crime*, the title of a book edited by situational theorists R. V. Clarke and P. M. Mayhew (1980), lies at the heart of this very preventative approach to dealing with crime. Sadly, however, target hardening on its own doesn't get to the root causes of the crimes that hurt the poor and the powerless: the breakdown of community life, low pay and unemployment.

> ***OVER TO YOU***
>
> ***Re-read and learn the section on ecology theory and studies (pages 494–7), and indicate how its findings are appropriate to the issue of regions and crime rates.***

QUESTIONS

1 Why is it unwise to take crime statistics at face value?
2 What are the arguments for and against the view that males commit more crimes than females?
3 What does sociological evidence reveal about the selective law enforcement of black people and white people?
4 What is the relationship between social class and crime rates, and age and crime rates?
5 What do situational theorists and new left realists share in common in their approach to crime?

> ***EXAM TIP***
>
> In general, questions on crime rates require a consideration of both positivist (treating the actual figures as helpful in their own right) and interpretivist (treating the actual figures as saying a great deal about selective law enforcement) insights.

Cops, courts and chain gangs

10:35

It's official: the State of Alabama, USA, re-introduced chain gangs in 1995. It doesn't surprise us. Most Americans take a tough line on law enforcement, whether it's the use of deadly force by police officers, electric chair sentences from the courts, and chaining prisoners on work details in the states of the Deep South. Public support for the death penalty in America for persons convicted of murder has actually increased from 51 per cent in 1969 to 78 per cent in 1991 (*The Gallup Report* 1991, cited by Aguirre and Baker 1993). Closer to home, in the UK, tougher sentences for violent crimes have been proposed, and prosecution lawyers have been given powers to appeal against allegedly lenient sentences. The 'get tough on crime' philosophy is bigger in the UK and the US than in most other post-industrial countries. But where does this philosophy – 'new right realism' – come from, and do the policies contingent upon it actually reduce crime?

The simple answers are: from right wing quarters; and, No!, they don't. Yet Michael Howard (the last Home Secretary) persistently argued that the solution to crime is prison. His researchers, and even the police and the courts, urged him to think again. But he wouldn't. More people are imprisoned and, generally, the recorded crime rate keeps rising. The 1994 Criminal Justice and Public Order Act further emphasised the retributive approach of new right politicians. Among its provisions, for example, are restrictions on peaceful protest.

There's something very Durkheimian at work here. Durkheim argued that the ritual of punishing criminals, particularly as a form of public spectacle, functioned to reinforce the sense of self-righteousness of the allegedly law-abiding public. Think about it. When people get together and talk about giving someone else a hard time because that person has acted selfishly, the thought that she or he 'deserves' punishing, heightens the feeling of being on the right side among the would-be punishers. New right realism endorses this 'cause' with a vengeance. No matter that retributive measures do little or nothing to keep crime at bay – when pick-pockets were hanged in eighteenth-century England, their accomplices picked pockets from the crowd – so long as the public's appetite for reprisal is satisfied.

Research in America (Henwood 1994) confirms that, even though no credible evidence shows that the death penalty deters crime, it still remains popular with the public. Perhaps this suggests that a desire for retribution – some would call it revenge – is a more powerful consideration than the findings of rational social scientific research.

Yet the UK government, pandering more to its perception of public opinion than to actual research, also favours the 'tough on crime' approach. Police officers, already equipped with American-style, side-handled batons, might soon be routinely issued with CS canisters. Military scientists are also looking at non-lethal weaponry. Take the 'toffee gun', for example. It fires a jet of foam that envelops aggressive suspected felons and sticks them to the ground. Comic-book stuff, vaguely humorous, you might think. But, in reality, it signals a 'new right' agenda that violently attacks the manifestations of crime without sensibly tackling the underlying causes.

Preceding sections (notably those about labelling theory and studies, and crime statistics) have highlighted the differential treatment meted out by law enforcers to different social groups. By way of summary and augmentation, we can say that:

Along a highway close to the Alabama–Tennessee border, 320 convicts from the Limestone Correctional Facility are shackled in a chain gang. It's 1995, and the Alabama Governor, Fob James, has revived an old and harsh punishment.

- police officers tend to be harsher in their enforcement of the law when dealing with black people, working-class people and young males
- courts hand out tougher sentences to black people than to white people for similar offences. It's apposite to note that recent research suggests that in America white people who discriminate against black people are more likely to support the death penalty (Aguirre and Baker 1993)
- poor people and people without 'influence' accused of minor crimes are rushed through the courts (so-called 'cash-register justice'). One Philadelphia judge disposed of 55 cases of drunkeness, disorderly behaviour and vagrancy in 15 minutes (Sutherland and Cressey 1978). In the UK, Michael Levi (1990, cited by Stern 1990) shows how poor offenders pay relatively more than better-off offenders in fines and in diminished life chances after prison sentences. He notes too that poor offenders are more likely to get caught and prosecuted
- racist attitudes are rife among British prison guards: out of 100 prison officers who were interviewed, only six didn't report negative stereotypes of black prisoners: belligerent, noisy ('They remind me of a monkey colony', said one prison officer), demanding, lazy, and unintelligent (Gender and Player 1989, cited by Blackstone 1990: 28)
- gendered discrimination probably operates against males in the majority of arrests and charges. But this needs to be qualified: males almost certainly commit more crimes than females, and females are probably treated either equally or more harshly than males when they're charged and convicted of soliciting and, in some cases, of violence (consider the case of Myra Hindley).

QUESTION

What, according to Durkheim, is the function of punishment?

Suicide

In a purely statistical sense – insofar as suicide statistics are accurate – suicide is 'deviant' because of its rarity. Even so, in some circumstances, suicide might be construed as a conforming act. Consider, for example, a brave woman who offers to die in the place of a hostage. Such a woman would be called a hero rather than a deviant.

It's also important to take into account cross-cultural interpretations of suicide. In Sweden, for example, there's probably less stigma attached to the act of suicide than in Italy. Sweden is a more secular society than Italy. Suicide might therefore be recorded accurately in Stockholm. In Naples, however, religious condemnation of suicides might put pressure on officials to attribute some of these deaths to misadventure. Such factors must be taken into account when we consider the accuracy of suicide statistics. Commenting on the presence or absence of suicide notes, J. Maxwell Atkinson remarks: 'according to a police officer who had encountered many suicides, many notes end up on fires long before the law arrives on the scene' (Atkinson 1973: 175). The implication is that such notes are destroyed by friends or relatives of the deceased, so that the act of suicide is concealed and no social stigma arises.

Conventional textbook coverage of suicide sometimes considers the issue in terms of positivist versus interpretivist accounts. On the one side are the positivists, who argue that suicide is a real and scientifically measurable social fact. Against them stand the interpretivists, the advocates of qualitative insights rather than 'pin-it-down measuring rods'.

In their 'ideal type' (i.e. caricatured) forms:

- *positivists* argue that suicides are 'caused' by an interplay of biological, psychological and sociological factors (for example, depression, coupled with a sense of worthlessness and social isolation), and that their incidence can reasonably be measured by coroners (professionally-trained experts who determine cause of deaths not attributable to usual circumstances)
- *interpretivists* claim that suicides are 'socially constructed' by people who are involved in interpreting how other people have died. For example, some coroners interpret the signs that 'add up to suicide' in different ways. Also, people like doctors and relatives might, in certain circumstances, feel pressured to masquerade an apparent suicide as something different. Ultimately, then suicides are deaths so defined, whether or not the definitions are factually accurate.

We think that pitting positivism against interpretivism is unhelpful. Take that so-called arch-defender of positivism, Emile Durkheim. Although it's fashionable to suggest that this notable scholar of the causes of suicide ignored the role of officials in the social construction of suicide statistics, he didn't. In his celebrated work, *Suicide*, Durkheim wrote:

> 'But as Wagner long ago remarked, what are called statistics of the motives of suicides are actually statistics of the opinions concerning such motives of officials, often of lower officials, in charge of this information service. Unfortunately, official establishments of fact are known to be often defective even when applied to obvious material facts comprehensible to any conscientious observer and leaving no room for evaluation. How suspect must they be considered when applied not simply to recording an accomplished fact but to its interpretation and explanation!'
>
> (Durkeim 1968: 148)

What Durkheim is saying here is what phenomenologists (they're very social constructionist in outlook) seem to accuse him of not saying, namely, that certain aspects of suicide statistics – notably, assumed motives of people who commit suicide – are shaped by the interpretations of the compilers of those statistics. Here, Durkheim is recognising the important fact that the motives that one official attributes (for example, relentless physical pain) to a particular suicide might be different to the motives attributed by a different official (for example, marital problems). Unlike phenomenologists, however, Durkheim regards suicides as real events (which of course they are) that have real causes. He recognises that individuals might have psychologies that dispose them to take their lives, but he also emphasises that suicides are associated with social forces. In this manner, Durkheim identifies four main types of suicide:

- *Anomic suicide* Think of an old man who showed respect to his elders when he was a child, but who has grown old in a society where children are less respectful towards their elders. His world has been turned upside down. The norms and values that structured his earlier experiences have been shattered. Old certainties and comfortable habits have gone. He's left confused and unable to adapt to the new ways. This is anomie; it might drive him to take his life.

  In her study of Native Americans in Alaska, Lydia Conway captures the essence of anomic suicide when she writes:

  'With the loss of their cultural anchor, many natives have chosen to opt out. Suicide is quick with a bullet, slow from a whisky bottle. The slowest of all is the lingering misery of a disconnected life on the edge of existence. Drinking fills the day.'

  (Conway 1988: 20)

- *Fatalistic suicide* Consider a prisoner whose every move, 24 hours a day, seven days a week, year after year, is controlled and organised by guards. She's no longer the arbiter of her own fortune. Her sense of self-dignity has eroded; she's merely a cog in a system wheel that's much bigger and more powerful than her. The sense of hopelessness engendered by this condition might push her over the edge, might lead her to fatalistic suicide.
- *Egoistic suicide* Think of a woman who tragically loses her partner, daughter and son in a car crash. She's isolated and lonely, no longer integrated into the family that once was. Her bereavement is likely to cause deep depression, but she has no family to support her in her grief. In such circumstances, the pressure on her to commit egoistic suicide is increased. Such suicides are very common among farmers and other rural inhabitants in the UK (Peter Jones, *The Guardian*, 22 March 1994). Catriona Marchant (1994) has also identified worrying rates of suicide among young Asian women in Wolverhampton, where, contrary to popular belief, young relatives who are mentally ill aren't well integrated into family networks.
- *Altruistic suicide* Contemplate an officer whose infantry platoon has been wiped out in front line action because he mistakenly sent them headlong into heavy machine gun fire. He's the sole survivor. He can choose to surrender to the enemy. However, the sense of loss caused through his error and the knowledge that he escaped the fate that his men suffered might urge him to take the 'honourable way out' by shooting himself.

Anomic suicide is a big problem today and it doesn't only affect the native communities of Alaska. Simon Armson, chief executive of the Samaritans (as referred to in *The Observer*, 14 November 1993, page 27), regards the normative confusion of British men as an important explanation of the recorded 80 per cent increase in male suicides from 1983–93. Caught in the flux of new and receding forms of masculine identity, men are half-way down the road to cultural change. The resultant pressure can, and does, lead to anomic suicide.

While official suicide statistics help sociologists to identify causal patterns behind suicides (for example, depression and unemployment are statistically linked to suicide), the same statistics are the products of complex social processes. This is where the social constructionists come into their own. Their work into how some deaths come to be categorised as suicides cautions us against taking official suicide statistics over-literally. In that context, social constructionists (for example, Jack D. Douglas 1967; J. Maxwell Atkinson 1973) argue that coroners play an important interpretive role in the compiling of suicide statistics.

Douglas goes so far as to suggest that it's invalid to treat coroners' records as sources of 'real' suicide rates because they merely reflect what coroners perceive as suicides. An extreme view you might think (we do!), given that coroners are highly trained experts in determining causes of death. Atkinson (like Douglas, a social constructionist) takes a rather more 'objective' position, noting that an argument such as Douglas' taken 'to its logical conclusion . . . suggests that there are no valid sources of data on suicide and hence that no further research is possible' (Atkinson 1973: 168). Atkinson applauds Douglas for making us aware of the dangers of taking official suicide statistics at face value without consideration for how those statistics are compiled. At the same time, he thinks that Douglas pushes his case too far down the social constructionist continuum. Put another way, Atkinson isn't so 'extreme' an interpretivist as Douglas.

The social constructionists ('extreme' or 'moderate') do, however, alert us to the fact that the accuracy of official suicide statistics is crucially linked to the work that coroners do. Consider, for example, when a coroner decides that an autopsy should be conducted to determine whether the deaths of two people are the result of murder or suicide, she'll pay close attention to the report of the forensic pathologist who carries out the autopsy. Has the pathologist indicated that the cut throat of the first subject looks like a self-inflicted wound? – tentative and experimental cuts before the final slash. And does the gunshot wound to the second subject suggest, by its star-shaped feature, that this was a suicide? Forensic pathologists and coroners concern themselves with such details. If they get it right – probably most of the time – the statistic is accurately recorded as a murder or a suicide. But when they get it wrong, what appears as an official murder or an official suicide statistic is a socially constructed mistake.

But the problem is even more complicated. Their usually very private nature makes it rare for suicides to be observed, or for prior interviews to be conducted. Instead, the 'experts', the people whose decisions shape the final statistics, have to consider what evidence they can get hold of: suicide notes, modes of death, location and circumstances of death, life and medical histories, etc. This isn't an exact science. So we must treat the official statistics cautiously and with circumspection.

It would be folly though to imagine that there are no valid sources on suicide. All the above forms of evidence, in professionally trained and honed hands, give social scientists a reasonable approximation of the extent of suicide. To adopt an extreme ethnomethodological view that it's impossible to adjudicate between different claims to truth – the considered judgement of a coroner versus the hearsay opinion of a tabloid journalist – is unhelpful. Ultimately, some opinions are more likely to be more truthful than others. If we don't accept this, then sociology itself becomes no more or less convincing than the musings of anecdotal hunches.

One of the world's leading authorities on suicide, the Norwegian psychiatrist Professor Nils Retterstol, stands firmly in the scientific tradition by acknowledging the:

'commonly held view on the basis of international surveys that the "correct" number of suicides in a population is 25% higher than that officially registered.'

(Retterstol 1993: 2)

Like Durkheim, Retterstol is a quantifier of suicide rates. He even sounds like Durkheim when he writes: 'Today, social integration or lack of social integration is regarded as a key factor in the problem of suicide' (1993: 81). So what about the overworked argument that the study of suicide is the study of positivism versus interpretivism? The combined insights of both approaches give a more accurate picture of the issue under scrutiny. This view is adopted by Retterstol, even though he errs on the positivistic side.

Of course, how coroners and other officials interpret the complex pieces of evidence surrounding suicide does affect the compilation of statistics. But suicides are real events, not socially constructed imaginings. So let's get the balance right. The official statistics are imperfect estimates, but they do help us to gauge the relationship between social conditions and individual psychologies. We owe much to Durkheim for making this point so forcibly.

EXAM TIP

Don't make the common, but mistaken, assumption that Durkheim's theory of suicide is *passé*. It's bang up-to-date in the insights it offers.

QUESTIONS

1 How might Durkheim's turn-of-the-nineteenth-century research into European suicide help sociologists to understand the causes of suicide today?
2 Why is the 'positivism versus interpretivism' debate potentially damaging to a sociological understanding of suicide?

Concluding remarks

Social scientists haven't yet formulated a definitive and final explanation of crime and other forms of deviance. Yet the combined perspectives of 'causal' and 'labelling' models have brought us much closer to a social scientific understanding of these phenomena than speculative, 'common-sense' assumptions. In that context, Edwin Lemert's distinction between primary deviation (which can arise from a number of different causes) and secondary deviation (which determines whether the *caused* deviance becomes *labelled* as deviance) is a brilliant example of social scientific insight. Take a bow Edwin for making us understand that shadow-boxing between structural and social constructionist theorists of crime is much less helpful than an emphasis on both 'causes' and 'reactions'.

Good criminologists make assertions that are supported by evidence. This holds true even when they have strong personal beliefs and convictions about crime and criminals. Whether or not you think that executing murderers is morally justifiable, you need to know that social scientific evidence rebuts the view that capital punishment reduces the homicide rate. As a private citizen, you have a right to a personal opinion on a moral issue. However, as a social scientist, you must report the facts as you find them.

Sociological theories of crime fall into two broad categories:

- *Distinct criminal and conforming populations* These argue that behaviour is 'caused' by factors largely beyond the individual's control. The approach is distinctly positivistic: it's premised on the belief that social factors are the determinants of crime and conformity. Within this frame of reference, the most notable theories are:
  - *Functionalist-strain theory* – frustrated ambition causes crime; achievable ambition encourages conformity
  - *Ecological theory* – poor neighbourhoods are associated with high crime rates; prosperous ones with low rates
  - *Subcultural theory* – criminal populations pass on criminal norms; conformists are socialised within conforming populations
  - *Marxist theory* – capitalism pushes the poor into committing crimes for survival, and the criminal justice system enforces the will of the ruling class. The 'new left' variant emphasises that some working-class criminals prey on poor people, and that community policing can 'cause' a reduction of this problem.
- *Widespread crime and selective law enforcement* These claim that human social behaviour is 'defined' rather than 'caused' by particular contexts. This model is clearly interpretivistic. What passes as crime in one society is accepted as conforming behaviour in another – so how can one talk of mere 'causes'? The main theories associated with this approach are:
  - *Labelling theory* (essentially, an umbrella term for the social constructionist perspective) – crime and conformity are behaviours so labelled
  - *Aspects of Marxist theory* – crimes occur among all social groups, but the law is enforced more severely against black, working-class, young males than against white, middle- and upper-class, middle-aged and older females and males. Conformity and crime are defined and constructed by powerful interest groups.

We hope you won't feel that any one of these theories (and the various studies that support each of them) is somehow more 'correct' than the others. The best sociology adopts a variety of perspectives. Sometimes this involves selecting the most suitable approach for a particular study (for example, a subcultural explanation account of gang life). On other occasions, a number of perspectives and research methods are used in combination in order to obtain a fuller picture (for example, a 'mixed toolbag' blend of labelling and urban ecology interpretations of neighbourhood crime).

Whatever orientation is adopted, an unswerving resolve to obtain reliable and valid results is the goal of all sociologists of deviance.

Glossary of key terms

Conformity Behaviour that is considered 'normal' by a group or by a society

Crime The commission or, in some cases, omission, of an act that results in the breaking of criminal law

Deviance Behaviour that is considered offensive by a group or by a society

Ecological theories Structural explanations of crime that link its commission to geographical areas. These theories are associated with the Chicago School of Human Ecology

Folk devils The people whose alleged or actual deviance are the targets of moral panics

Functionalist-strain theories Structural explanations of crime that account for its commission on the basis of frustrated but legitimate ambitions

Labelling theory Essentially an umbrella term for social constructionist theories, this perspective claims that law enforcers interpret similar actions differently on the basis of who carries them out: 'rowdy' behaviour by white, middle class women might be tolerated, but the same behaviour, if committed by black working class women might be 'labelled' as criminal

Marxist theories Structural explanations of crime that often contain social constructionist insights. Crimes of the powerful occur because the upper class make (or influence the making of) laws that tolerate their indiscretions but which come down hard on working-class 'criminals'

Moral panic An exaggerated response (typically from law enforcers) to either the misconceived perception that deviance is occurring when it isn't, or to a small amount of deviance. The response is usually fuelled by sensationalist media reporting

New left realism Linked to marxist theory, with a self-proclaimed 'let's get real' message: crime hurts victims and most victims are poor

New right realism Linked to 'Thatcherism', with a self-proclaimed 'let's get real' message: the best way to tackle crime is by removing criminals from circulation by locking them up

Social constructionist theories of crime Explanations of crime that are based on the argument that crimes are actions so labelled

Structural theories of crime Explanations of crime that are based on causes in the structure of society, for example, growing up in a gang neighbourhood

Subcultural theories Structural explanations of crime that are linked to 'differential association'. The argument is that associations with criminal or conforming ways of life lead, respectively, to greater likelihoods of criminal or of conforming behaviour

References

Abbott, Pamela and Wallace, Claire (1993) *An Introduction to Sociology: Feminist Perspectives*. London: Routledge

Aggleton, Peter (1991) *Deviance*. London: Routledge

Aguirre, Adalberto and Baker, David V. (1993) Racial prejudice and the death penalty: A research note, pp 150–5, *Social Justice*, Vol. 20, Nos 1–2, Issues 51–52, Spring-Summer

Atkinson, J. Maxwell (1973) Societal reactions to suicide: The role of coroners' definitions, pp 165–91, in Cohen, Stanley (ed.) (1973) *Images of Deviance*. Harmondsworth: Penguin

Becker, Howard S. (ed.) (1967) *The Other Side*. New York: The Free Press.

Blackstone, Tessa (1990) *Prisons and Penal Reform*. London: Chatto & Windus

Bottoms, Anthony E. (1995) Environmental criminology, pp 585–656, in Maguire, Mike, *et al.* (eds) (1995) op. cit.

Chambliss, William J. (1973) The saints and the roughnecks, pp 148–61, in Chambliss, William J. and Mankoff, Milton (eds) (1976) *Whose Law, What Order?* New York: John Wiley & Sons, Inc

Chambliss, William J. (ed.) (1975) *Criminal Law in Action*. Santa Barbara: Hamilton Publishing Company

Chambliss, William J. (1976a) Functional and conflict theories of crime: The heritage of Emile Durkheim and Karl Marx, pp 1–28, in Chambliss, William J. and Mankoff, Milton (eds) (1976) op. cit.

Chambliss, William J. (1976b) The state and criminal law, pp 66–106, in Chambliss, William J. and Mankoff, Milton (eds) (1976) op. cit.

Chambliss, William J. (1994) Policing the ghetto underclass: The politics of law and law enforcement, pp 177–94, *Social Problems*, Vol. 41, No. 2, May

Cicourel, Aaron V. (1976) *The Social Organization of Juvenile Justice*. London: Heinemann

Clarke, R. V. and Mayhew, P. M. (eds) (1980) *Designing Out Crime*. London: HMSO

Cohen, Albert K. (1966) *Deviance and Control*. Englewood Cliffs, New Jersey: Prentice-Hall

Cohen, Albert K. and Short Jr, James F. (1971) Crime and juvenile delinquency, pp 89–146, in Merton, Robert K. and Nisbet, Robert (eds) (1971) *Contemporary Social Problems*, Third Edition. New York: Harcourt Brace Jovanovich

Cohen, Stanley (1973) *Folk Devils and Moral Panics*. St Albans: Paladin

Conway, Lydia (1988) The lost people, pp 18–20, *New Society*, Vol. 84, No. 1322, 29 April

Douglas, Jack D. (1967) *The Social Meanings of Suicide*. Princeton, New Jersey: Princeton University Press

Durkheim, Emile (1968; first published 1897) *Suicide*. London: Routledge & Kegan Paul

Finn, Gerry P. T. (1994) Football violence: A societal psychological perspective, pp 90–127, in Giulianotti, Richard, Bonney, Norman, and Hepworth, Mike (eds) (1994) *Football, Violence and Social Identity*. London: Routledge

Grover, Chris and Soothill, Keith (1995) The social construction of sex offenders, pp 29–33, *Sociology Review*, Vol. 4, No. 3, February

Hartless, Julie M., Ditton, Jason, Nair, Gwyneth and Phillips, Samuel (1995) More sinned against than sinning: A study of young teenagers' experience of crime, pp 114–33, *British Journal of Criminology*, Vol. 35, No. 1, Winter

Heidensohn, Frances (1995) Gender and crime, pp 997–1039, in Maguire, Mike, *et al.* (eds) (1995) op. cit.

Henwood, Doug (1994) *The State of the USA Atlas*. Harmondsworth: Penguin

Korem, Dan (1994) *Suburban Gangs: The Affluent Rebels*. Richardson, Texas: International Focus Press

King, Martin Luther (1969) *Chaos or Community?* Harmondsworth: Penguin

Leonard, Madeleine (1995) Masculinity, femininity and crime, pp 2–7, *Sociology Review*, September

Maguire, Mike (1995) Crime statistics, patterns and trends: Changing perceptions and their implications, pp 233–91, in Maguire, Mike, *et al.* (eds) (1995) op. cit.

Maguire, Mike, Morgan, Rod and Reiner, Robert (eds) (1995) *The Oxford Handbook of Criminology*. Oxford: Clarendon Press

Marchant, Catriona (1994) Heart to heart, p. 18, *Community Care*, 24 February

Matza, D. (1969) Becoming deviant, pp 347–50, in Worsley, Peter (ed.) (1972) *Problems of Modern Society*. Harmondsworth: Penguin

Piliavin, Irving and Briar, Scott (1964) Police encounters with juveniles, pp 214–21, in Chambliss, William J. (ed.) (1975) op. cit.

Retterstol, Nils (1993) *Suicide: A European Perspective*. Cambridge: Cambridge University Press

Scull, Andrew T. (1988) Deviance and social control, pp 667–93, in Smelser, Neil J. (ed.) (1988) *Handbook of Sociology*. Newbury Park, California: Sage Publications

Seabrook, Jeremy (1986) A generation in exile, pp 24–5, *New Society*, 13 June

Seabrook, Jeremy (1990) Law and disorder, p. 18, *New Statesman & Society*, 5 October

Simpson, Sally S. and Elis, Lori (1994) Is gender subordinate to class? An empirical assessment of Colvin and Pauly's structural marxist theory of delinquency, pp 453–80, *Journal of Criminal Law and Criminology*, Vol. 85, No. 2, Fall

Social Trends 22 (1992). London: HMSO

Social Trends 23 (1993). London: HMSO

Social Trends 25 (1995). London: HMSO

Smith, David J. (1995) Race, crime, and criminal justice, pp 1041–117, in Maguire, Mike, *et al.* (eds) (1995) op. cit.

Stern, Vivien (1990) Lock-up, p. 36, *New Statesman & Society*, Vol. 3, No. 85, 26 January

Sutherland, Edwin H. and Cressey, Donald R. (1978) *Criminology*, Tenth Edition. Philadelphia: J. B. Lippincott Co.

Taylor, Ian (1991a) Big crime: The international drug trade, pp 121–4, *Social Studies Review*, Vol. 6, No. 3, January

Taylor, Ian (1991b) Moral panics, crime and urban policy in Manchester, pp 28–30, *Sociology Review*, Vol. 1, No. 1, September

Thom, Laine (1992) *Becoming Brave*. Del Mar, California: McQuiston & Partners

Vold, George B. and Thomas, J. Bernard (1986) *Theoretical Criminology*, Third Edition. New York: Oxford University Press

Ward, Colin (1990) Fighting talk, pp 24–5, *New Statesman & Society*, Vol. 3, No. 103, 1 June

Willis, Paul (1978) *Learning to Labour: How Working-Class Kids Get Working-Class Jobs*. Farnborough, Hants: Saxon House

Exam practice: Deviance

Essay questions

1 'The usefullness of crime statistics in sociological research depends on the theoretical approach adopted by the sociologist.'
Critically explain this view. *(25 marks)*
(Summer 1996 AEB A-level Sociology, Paper 2, © 1996 AEB)

2 Some explanations of crime focus on the background of offenders, whilst others focus on the practices of the police and courts.
Assess the usefulness of these two approaches in explaining the social characteristics of convicted criminals. *(25 marks)*
(Summer 1997 AEB A-level Sociology, Paper 2, © 1997 AEB)

3 Critically examine the contribution of studies of suicide to a sociological understanding of deviance in society. *(25 marks)*
(From Summer 1994 AEB A-Level Sociology, Paper 2, © 1994 AEB)

4 Critically discuss Becker's argument that a value-free sociology of deviance is not possible because sociologists have personal and political sympathies. *(25 marks)*
(From June 1993 AEB A-Level Sociology, Paper 2, © 1993 AEB)

17 Sociology of locality

Topics covered in this chapter

- *Social stability and social change*
- *Urbanisation, industrialisation and community*
- *Loss of community?*
- *Environmental sociology*
- *Power, policy and conflict in the city*

Recently, I found myself on the wrong side of town at night in Lafayette, Louisiana – one of the most dangerous states in the US. As I was walking along the pavement, a car cruised menacingly towards me, headlights full on. I feared the people in the vehicle might be gang members.

Here I was, a lone sociologist, an outsider, the only person in sight, on somebody else's patch. I was carrying a small reporter's Dictaphone which lit up red when the record button was pressed. I hit the button and talked into the machine, tried to look confident, and hoped the men in the car would take me for a detective or an FBI agent calling for back-up. The ruse worked. The car glided by without incident.

Localities are places where people follow local norms and values. In the UK, this might mean having a beer with friends and family in the local pub, going to the gym with work colleagues, or having a street party with the neighbours. It might also, in some localities, involve hanging out with the 'kids on the block', robbing a petrol station with a few pals, or dealing crack with gang members.

At the dawn of the twenty-first century, localities are becoming increasingly urban – not just in rich countries like the UK, but also in the poor nations of the majority world. Some commentators contend that urbanisation lies at the root of today's ills. With the demise of village life, so we're told, people 'go mad' in the city. This 'loss of community' thesis is important, but it's also contested. Was country life ever that cosy? And is the big city really a place of crime, homelessness, unrest and instability? These are questions we'll return to.

We'll also look at the sociology of the environment. While great sociologists like Marx, Durkheim and Weber didn't ignore the human and physical environment which people inhabit, environmental sociology didn't gain real momentum until the 1970s. In that sense, it's a relatively new sub-discipline within sociology. That doesn't diminish its importance. We interact with human and physical environments on a daily basis, and we invest part of our own humanity in that encounter. Some sociologists even reckon that we and the environment are one. We'll see.

Social stability and social change

What causes social stability and what causes social change? These questions lie at the heart of sociology. *Stability* suggests that things stay as they are or, to put it another way, that society is characterised by social order. *Change* implies the opposite: instability or disorder. In the UK, enjoying a pint in the pub is a longstanding tradition. It's an example of stability. Lots of young Britons have very different musical tastes to those of their grandparents. That's an example of change.

Stability and change aren't, however, simple either/or things. They occur simultaneously. Emile Durkheim (1964, originally published 1893), for example, noted that while England was undergoing an industrial revolution, traditional lifestyles still endured in some parts of the country. More recently, Talcott Parsons wrote:

'Thus, in a broad sense, the American Constitution has remained a stable reference point over a period of more than a century and a half. During this time, of course, the structure of American society has changed very greatly in certain respects.'
(Parsons 1961, in Demerath and Peterson 1967: 190)

While stability and change co-exist, there's usually one or more of the other. Consider, for example, a rural Irish town like Kiltimagh, where custom and tradition ensure that change is kept at bay for as long as possible. In such a community, you might experience the same kind of values today as those that prevailed in the time of the present inhabitants' grandparents. Certainly, there will be some change – no society is completely static – but change is often resisted and occurs at a snail's pace. Contrast this setting with a big urban city like Newcastle. Dubbed the 'party town' of Europe, the people of Newcastle eagerly embrace change, and experience a fast pace of life. The city pulses with energy. Within the last decade, Newcastle has bought the then most expensive football player in the world, revitalised its city centre, cleaned up historic buildings, and opened one of the most famous shopping and entertainment centres in the world.

Another way of looking at stability and change is to use the analogy of structure and function. In that context, Auguste Comte (1798–1857) applies two important concepts:

- *social statics* – the frozen-in-its tracks study of the structure of society or, to use a biological analogy, the 'anatomy' of society
- *social dynamics* – the process study of the functions of society or, to use a biological analogy, the 'physiology' of society.

The first concept envisages a stable state, the second, a state of motion. Put the two together, and we get a model of society as a social structure which is neither completely still nor totally in motion. It's a useful model, but it tends to describe a society whose static and dynamic parts work together to produce an overall state of harmony. In reality, though, some societies are remarkably stable and others are prone to rapid change.

Before reading any further, re-acquaint yourself with the theories of Durkheim, Marx and Weber by consulting Chapter 4. These 'founding fathers' have important things to say about stability and change. This, in summary, is what they said:

Durkheim argues that most people are socialised into accepting the culture of their societies. In this way, *consensus* ensures *social stability*. As societies get bigger, however, people have to move into bigger localities called towns and cities. Here they escape the surveillance of village life, and more levity is permitted to individuals who want to be different. Therein lies the motor of *social change* – the social possibility to challenge convention and build an alternative future. Durkheim refers to the transition from traditional to modern society as a move from *mechanical solidarity* to *organic solidarity*. By this, he means that an increasing division of labour (whereby lots of different people divide various job roles between them) leads to the breakdown of 'sameness' and the celebration of 'difference'. The differences still bind people though because different work roles are directed towards a common goal – just like on the TV series, *ER*.

Marx contends that socialisation in industrial capitalist society is actually a form of indoctrination. If working-class people – the majority of most populations – contest their socialisation into submissive roles, *social stability* is fractured by *social change*. The impetus of such change, argues Marx, is *conflict* between the greed of the rich and powerful and the rights of the poor and oppressed. At the heart of this conflict lies unequal access to economic resources. Society changes when brave individuals – revolutionaries – wrest power from the ruling class when dominant but outworn institutions are about to topple. Industrialisation and urbanisation pits workers against capitalists, and when the time is ripe, claims Marx, the working class – through peaceful or violent means – will take over the economy and create an equal society based on socialism and, later, communism.

Weber developed a theory of change based on individual human endeavour. He applied the theory to the emergence of capitalism, which moved society beyond the stability of pre-industrial forms. Like Marx, Weber accepts that economic factors can cause social change. Unlike Marx, however, he doesn't assume that individuals have to wait for critical economic turning points before they can become active agents in changing society. For Weber, society remains stable or changes largely as a result of the force of ideas. In his famous work, *The Protestant Ethic and the Spirit of Capitalism* (1974, originally published 1904–5), Weber develops the thesis that strong religious beliefs can galvanise human wilfulness in such a way that new economic systems are created. Thus, the Protestant creed of Calvinism became the main driving force behind the rise of modern capitalism because it encouraged its followers to pursue profit not out of greed, but from conviction. Here we have an historical example of a macro-domain change in society that was initiated, claims Weber, from within the micro-domain of human beliefs.

Consult pages 575–9 of Chapter 18, which examines evolutionary and revolutionary theories of change in the context of poor and rich countries. Before considering change in this chapter, however, we'll first examine its opposite number: stability.

Social stability

In the 1960s and 1970s, the first thing undergraduate students of sociology studied was the 'problem of order'. I always wondered why order was described as a 'problem' until I read a book called *The Crisis of Western Sociology*. The author, Alvin W. Gouldner (1972), argues that the 'problem of order' is actually a fear of disorder by the conservative middle class. The problem of order only becomes a *problem* if social order – or to give it another name, *social stability* – is threatened. The notion of a problem is an ideological rather than an academic concern.

Talcott Parsons (1963, in Parsons 1967a) thinks the best guarantor of compliance is when compliance is optional rather than enforced. He's right. The most socially stable societies are those where people 'choose' to follow the rules. Whether Parsons personally approved of social order is, I think, difficult to gauge. I suspect, like most of us, he favours order generally, but not at all costs.

Percy S. Cohen (1970) reckons there are five key meanings in sociology to the concept of social order:

- *restraint* – the inhibition of impulse (including violence)
- *reciprocity* (or mutuality) – human social behaviour isn't random; it takes account of and complements the conduct of others
- *predictability* – social life is possible only when individuals know what to expect of one another
- *consistency* – the above expectations have to be fairly compatible with each other
- *persistence* – predictable and consistent social behaviours are only feasible if they endure.

OVER TO YOU

Find some real-life examples of each of Percy Cohen's five points.

If possible, divide into five groups for this activity, each group addressing one of the points. Report your deliberations in sociological language to the rest of the class.

EXAM TIP

There are lots of sociologists called Cohen. The three main ones, for your purposes, are Albert, Stanley and Percy. Albert and Stanley are criminologists – the first a subcultural theorist, the second a labelling theorist. Percy is a scholar of general sociological theory.

Percy Cohen's list of five contains guarantors of social order that are all linked to each other. Thus, for example, individuals exercise restraint because they anticipate others will do the same. A good example of this is when two individuals who don't like each other adopt professional courtesies at work. Cohen also notes how the unintended consequences of social behaviour can preserve order. Each person separately pursues her or his interests. In so doing, they unwittingly come into contact with other people. These encounters require the individual to adjust to and take account of other people's ways. Invariably, there will be some clashes. However, over time, each person will find that her or his interests are best served by avoiding confrontations and being co-operative. This leads to the institutionalisation (i.e. laying down in structured form) of mutual expectations of conduct, and their gradual fine-tuning to a point where a balance is reached. Cohen refers to the above unintended consequences model as an *interest theory* of social order.

Whilst, as Cohen recognises, interest theory doesn't explain where interests derive from, most people discover that order is helpful, and therefore support it. Without order (hereafter, in keeping with the title of this subsection, generally referred to as stability), there would be no codes of acceptable conduct, no laws, no rules, no conventions – no society. Imagine, for example, if there were no Highway Code. Some motorists would give way at T-junctions; others would drive on; some would overtake when it was safe to do so; others would risk head-on collisions. Chaos would prevail on our roads. That's why (most) motorists agree to follow a Highway Code. Put simply, they agree to conform to a consensus. The existence of consensus makes society possible. It's the common denominator of stability.

To be sure, there's no such thing as a totally stable society. A society is a continuous process rather than a fixed entity. Bits of yesterday slide into today, and today itself is influenced by the anticipation of tomorrow. That's why the concept of stability is a relative, not an absolute one. Put simply, some societies are more stable than others, and even fast-changing societies have their stable moments.

By now, we hope you've realised that the sociological study of stability has its roots in functionalism. Functionalism is a theory that sets out to understand why individuals agree to follow common norms. In this respect, it rejects the notion of a non-social individual. Societies exist and continue to exist because individuals allow this to happen. Why do they allow this to happen? Because they're socialised into conformity. What about criminals?, you might ask. Even they conform in certain important respects. They might break into bank vaults by night, but during the day they wear conventional clothes, stand in line in stores, and pay for their meals in restaurants.

OVER TO YOU

Keep a diary of all the routine things you do in one day that you think your friends also probably do. Then compare notes. In what ways do the behaviours you and your friends have in common help to ensure stability in your lives?

Through being socialised into norms and values, individuals learn to comply. Allowing for some necessary challenges to conventions, societies are generally fairly stable. That's why social change is usually a gentle easing in of new ideas rather than a radical departure from prevailing ways. The emphasis is on evolution, not revolution. Things change, but at a controlled pace. Even conflict theorists accept that societies exhibit social stability. Unlike functionalists, however, they begin from the premise that order is possible because powerful people keep other people in check. As long as the powerful are able to do this – through persuasion and/or force – society remains relatively stable.

According to conflict theorists, stability is precarious because it's engineered rather than willingly agreed to. Conflict is likely to erupt at critical moments and, in extreme cases, it can topple the existing social order. This doesn't happen too often because differences of opinion are usually resolved through conflict resolution. For example, when trade unionists and corporation bosses argue over pay, both parties usually reach a compromise. This is an example of what sociologists call the *institutionalisation of conflict*.

That rather complex sounding concept means that people respect each other's right to disagree. Out of mutual tolerance, it's hoped that a rapprochement will be reached. The use of the term *institutionalisation* suggests that accepted procedures endure over time. For that is what an institution is – a durable set of norms. Norms endure – not just in relation to settling disputes, but also in openly consensual behaviour – because of socialisation.

How is it though that children aren't social mirror images of parents? Nobody is suggesting that you and your parents are identical. If it were so, society would never change. What sociologists argue is that socialisation generally results in safeguarding certain essential norms and values in society (thereby preserving relative stability), while simultaneously offering the next generation enough levity to reshape aspects of the existing arrangements. Socialisation transmits the cultural heritage of our parents which we learn, adopt, adapt and contest in different degrees.

Social control is triggered if our protestations become too bellicose. There are soft and hard forms of social control, both of which help to ensure a minimum degree of stable continuity from one generation to the next, in spite of some inevitable breaches. Soft forms operate, for example, through etiquette, as in a stern glance from significant adults when children speak with their mouths full. The hard variety uses the threat or use of punishment (including force). Detentions, smacking and confinement are examples.

The impact of socialisation varies between individuals, societies and periods. In the late, or postmodern, era of the 1990s, the capacity for individuals in 'western' societies to break loose from convention is greater than in the past. Revolutionaries have long held a monopoly on that prerogative, tipping the scales when society was on the brink of a new era. Now many more people have the opportunity to be rebels. Consider, for example, the things you might 'get away with' at school, compared to your grandparents when they were students.

The 'hardest' forms of social control in society are used by the police and the military.

While Durkheim was a modernist, he acknowledged that people who lived in industrial, urban societies don't all agree with each other. Consensus has to make do with minimal agreement on certain core values rather than with detailed moral rules. This position suggests that some degree of common agreement is a necessary condition for social stability. Even Marx anticipated that a future communist society could only become a reality if people accepted the basic moral belief that all human beings are inherently equal. In short, the most famous of the conflict theorists advocated 'politically correct' consensus.

Cyclical theorists like, for example, Pitirim A. Sorokin (1889–1968) adopt, as the term 'cyclical' implies, an approach to stability which sees it as part of a cycle. There are similarities with functionalism here – equilibrium is followed by disequilibrium, is followed by equilibrium, *ad infinitum*. The main difference between functionalist and cyclical theories is that the first see this process in terms of a directional sequence, whereas the second envisages the repetition of similar social forms. Put simply, for the functionalist, there's a sequence whereby stability 1 is followed by instability 1 which is followed by stability 2. In cyclical theory stability 1 is succeeded by instability 1, is succeeded by stability 1 (i.e. again, albeit in modified form).

Social constructionist theorists regard stability as a transitional phase. If people define a situation as stable, to all intents and purpose it is, because by acting on this belief they make it so. When the Mexican revolutionary general, Emiliano Zapata, told his army that it was better to die on one's feet than to live on one's knees, he de-constructed the image of the patrician order he so despised. The people who heeded his memorable war cry replaced the icon of lord and master with the image of enemy and oppressor. That new social construction galvanised the resolve of the revolutionary army to fight for what they defined as social justice. Their struggle was successful, and the old rulers were toppled.

Weber, whose work had a profound influence on social constructionist thought, shows how stability endures only until one set of established beliefs is knocked off its pedestal. Illustrative of this point, he (1974) noted how the medieval notion of dutifully accepting one's ascribed station in life was powerfully challenged by the Protestant conviction that hard work determined the measure of a human being. This isn't to say that the old ways were relinquished by everyone. Some people clung to them, others set up a new marker. It just so happened that this marker, says Weber, took off in big way, lighting the fuse that led to modern capitalism.

Before examining the opposite condition of social stability – social change – (recognising, of course, that the two typically co-exist), it must be acknowledged that there's a bit of a 'chicken and egg' dilemma in the sociological study of order. Which comes first – consensus or the perpetuation of consensus? Confused? Don't worry if you are. This is a puzzling issue. Sociologists might argue that people are born into a society where consensus prevails, and that socialisation helps to preserve important core values. However, what they don't seem to have solved yet is where the consensus comes from in the first place. In other words, we know many of the reasons why stability endures, but we don't yet fully understand the origins of stability. Now there's a worthy Ph.D. topic if you want to take your study of sociology to lofty heights!

Social change

All societies change. Look at some old black and white newsreel from the 1930s. The way people lived then compared to now is apparent. A comparison of media images of royalty in the 1950s and 1990s, for example, strongly suggests that the Royal Family were held in higher esteem in the earlier decade. Change is a complex issue in sociology because nobody knows for certain what sets it in motion. Some sociologists argue that economic factors are the prime movers of change. Thus, for example, the discovery of gold in 1840s San Francisco led to a goldrush that changed the lives of Bay Area residents. Other sociologists contend that pivotal ideas are what bring about change. Illustrative of this, Newton's laws of motion laid the foundation for new kinds of technology. One might add that Newton was a scientist whose *individual* genius was as a mover of social change. However, Newton drew his inspiration by standing on the shoulders of other great thinkers.

Individuals as agents of change?

One sometimes gets the impression that history is shaped by powerful individuals. History books sometimes convey the idea that change is brought about by 'great men' – kings, generals, popes and prime ministers. These individuals have immense but not limitless power. An English king who tried to exercise too much royal prerogative lost his head in the seventeenth century. People, not individuals, are the agents of social change. People are, of course, individuals, but they act in concert (and sometimes in conflict) rather than alone. Don't think we're denigrating the power of ordinary people. Individually minuscule they might be but, as Piotr Sztompka perceptively remarks, they are 'in their aggregation decisive for the course of change' (1994: 261).

To be sure, some individuals are exceptional – Julius Caesar, Shakespeare, Galileo and Martin Luther King come to mind. Their exceptional qualities aside, such individuals act as the representatives of other people. Moreover, Sztompka reminds us that 'Objective consequences and subjective intentions do not necessarily coincide' (1994: 261). Thus, for example, the famous physicist, Niels Bohr, didn't intend or anticipate that his atomic particle research would promote the development and production of nuclear warheads.

Social movements (for example, civil rights lobbies) are often given added momentum by the sheer mass of like-minded people in urban areas. Marx recognised the importance of the 'political density' of a population when he urged all factory workers to unite in common cause. In the context of the American civil rights movement, black people were densely segregated in both urban and rural neighbourhoods, which maximised their opportunity to develop common points of view and recruit supporters. Add some precipitating individual acts of heroism to this heady social mix, and what might otherwise have been seen as trivial events become catalysts for change.

To count as an exceptional individual, one's actions must be public, not private, social, not personal. Moreover, appropriate social conditions generate opportunities for individual greatness. This point was persuasively made by R. K. Merton (1973, cited by Sztompka 1994) who reports that multiple independent scientific discoveries appear in clusters when scientific communities are ready for breakthroughs. Social contexts (for example, the Renaissance) are conducive to the nurturing of genius. But genius is typically socially defined as a white, masculine attribute. Given that there aren't any inborn intellectual differences between 'racial' groups or between women and men, we must conclude that genius is, at least in part, socially constructed. To quote Sztompka:

'Here negative social selection is clearly at work, denying to members of certain gender categories, racial and ethnic groups the equitable recognition of their achievements and preventing them from entering the pantheon of heroes.'

(Sztompka 1994: 268)

The opportunity to be a hero who can alter the course of history occurs within the limits of the sociologically possible. This might happen in a marxist and a weberian sense when a charismatic individual grasps the moment and tips the scales. Ghandi was such a hero. Notwithstanding their individual greatness, heroes are nurtured by critical opportunities. Moreover, they have a huge following. Notwithstanding the important role of great individuals, sociology places more emphasis on the collective nature of social change. In this context, it adopts three main structural approaches:

- evolutionary theory
- revolutionary theory
- cyclical theory

and one main interpretive approach:

- social constructionist theory.

The evolutionary theory of social change

This theory envisages an 'orderly' process of social change – partial shift rather than radical transformation. This isn't to suggest that sometimes things can't be more radical. Parsons, for example, a functionalist evolutionary theorist, adopts a pacey tone when he refers to 'the process of "breaking out" of what may be called the "primitive" stage of societal evolution' into 'the development of a well-marked system of social stratification' (1964, in Parsons 1967a: 496). His use of the term 'development', though, puts a break on things. Lots of little shifts can, of course, upset the overall equilibrium, and, if they move in the same direction, small steps can lead to significant change. Here we have an *evolutionary* theory of change.

The founder of sociology, Auguste Comte (1798–1857), was an evolutionary theorist. He developed the 'law of three stages' to describe the process of social change (see page 575 in Chapter 18). In the first stage, people invoke gods and, finally, one omnipotent God to understand earthly events. The second – metaphysical stage – arrives when God is 'replaced' (or, at least, complemented) with reason. Finally, the third – positive stage – occurs when people, especially sociologists, discover laws based on empirical evidence. Herbert Spencer (1820–1903), a nineteenth-century English sociologist, also adopted an evolutionary theory of social change. He argued that evolution is the driving force of all natural and social things. According to Spencer, societies evolve from simple and uniform to complex and specialised forms. The impetus to change lies in the inherent instability of simple, uniform societies. As people begin to recognise they're unequal, they cannot remain as one homogenous mass. They begin to magnify initial differences into distinct social groups, notably social classes.

Social evolutionists, like Comte and Spencer, believe there's an innate impulse towards change in society derived from a human need for self-realisation and self-transformation. Evolutionary change is thus a gradual unfolding of in-built potentialities from simple to mature – and to better – forms. Evolutionary theory also proposes that change is gradual, incremental and cumulative. It can weather one-off eruptions and occasional discontinuities because, ultimately, this kind of change, like the Mississippi River, keeps rolling.

Conflict theorists contest this assumption, arguing that some changes in human history are so sudden and cataclysmic, that they can't be explained by gradualism. Some events are too sudden and dramatic to be accounted for on the basis of social evolution. That said, recent versions of evolutionary theory, notably the work of Parsons, are more sophisticated than their over-deterministic predecessors. These newer theories are circumspect about clearly charted trajectories towards progress and development. Outcomes are seen as

EVOLUTIONARY THEORY OF SOCIAL CHANGE

FOR

+ History demonstrates that societies do grow and develop, and that this is generally a gradual process, as evolutionary theory posits, from simple, uniform forms to more complex, differentiated types. Consider the history of the UK, for example. Its pre-industrial past was less complex in technological and social terms than today's society. The division of labour has also resulted in extensive differentiation between occupations.
+ All societies have universal material needs, which can only be met through technological innovations. Thus, for example, the need for healthy living provided a stimulus for the invention and development of safe sanitation methods. Once new technology arrives, it changes the entire character of social life. True, as the marxists remind us, the pace of change can get very fast, but quick steps are typically preceded by a gradual evolutionary build-up – another point that Marx himself acknowledged.
+ Evolutionary theory recognises that human beings have a need for self-realisation and self-transformation. The unfolding of this human potentiality is the creative energy which fuels social change. Most of us have ambitions. We want to get on – some people in material terms, some in intellectual terms, others in moral terms, and indeed, for many a combination of all these. We learn through socialisation that such aspirations are not usually realised overnight, and we know that a readiness to grow and develop are pre-requisites for success. In short, our micro-lives are mirrored in macro-evolutionary trends.

AGAINST

− Social change isn't always orderly and predictable. History is full of backlashes, false starts, breakdowns, and even reversals. Yet these important events don't figure prominently in evolutionary thought. In its over-generalised assumption of sequential (step-by-step) development, evolutionary theory underestimates the variety of forms that social processes take. Just because some countries have histories that fit the expectations of evolutionary theory doesn't mean that the pattern is universal.

− Although Parsons recognises the importance of exogenous (outside) causes of social change, evolutionary theory has under-estimated the impact of these factors. Natural disasters, environmental changes (for good and bad), invasions, conquests, etc. have all played pivotal roles in the process of social change. There's no human design or planning behind an earthquake or a volcanic eruptions. Yet these natural events can raze villages and towns, and wipe out whole communities.

− Chronological ageing isn't always matched by chronological progress. Consider, for example, the collapse of Ancient Greek civilisation, a nation so civilised it asked its conqueror, Rome, not to stage gladiatorial blood-letting, and whose dramatist, Euripides, spoke out against slavery. On the other side of the coin, think of the rise of nazi Germany in the 1930s, and the subsequent murder of six million Jews. This represents a reversal of progress.

open-ended, and individual wilfulness is considered important, even though it usually succumbs to prevailing social trends. Parsons, for example, notes that some artistic people take a stand against social convention.

Rather than seeing the triggers of social change in either/or categories, Parsons (1961, in Demerath and Peterson 1967) also suggests that these initiators typically occur in combination. He proceeds to identify two potential sources of structural change:

- *exogenous sources*, which are 'outside' factors (for example, environmental change)
- *endogenous sources*, which are 'inside' factors (for example, strains within institutions).

A key contribution of evolutionary theory has been its ability to plot the relationship between population growth and change. As a population gets bigger, the migration from rural villages to towns and cities (*urbanisation*) gathers pace. This, in turn, leads to changes in the way people live. Thus, for example, one of the knock-on effects of urbanisation is the development of improved sanitation. The basic technology of rural plumbing eventually yields to more advanced techniques. There are social changes too. Mass populations enjoy mass entertainment. City life led to a huge expansion in dance halls, football grounds, cinemas, pubs, greyhound stadiums, and lots more. In this and other ways, societies evolve from simple into more complex structures. That word *evolve* is important. The emphasis is on gradualism rather than rapid motion.

The revolutionary theory of social change

Interestingly, revolutionary theorists of social change generally accept that societies have an evolutionary momentum. They significantly add, however, that no-turning-back points are finally reached. Thenceforth, things move quickly, and change becomes *revolutionary*. There are, to be sure, differences in the speed, intensity and rhythm of revolutions. Some are quite speedy – but nevertheless gradual – processes towards different futures. Others are very sudden indeed, marking a rapid, cataclysmic break with the past. The English Industrial Revolution of the eighteenth and nineteenth centuries is of the first type. The French Revolution of 1789 is of the second.

More than those of any other social scientist, the writings of Karl Marx (1818–83), the 'founder' of conflict theory, exemplifies the *revolutionary theory of social change*. Importantly, though, his theory also contains an evolutionary theme. Marx charted an evolutionary build-up phase of accumulated tensions, followed by a revolutionary eruption when pent-up discontents pass a critical threshold. The theory places emphasis on structural conflict, but the final push is the result of human wilfulness hitting a ripe moment. The successful revolutionary isn't the one who acts in a precipitate way, but rather the one who strikes when the iron is hot.

Take, for example, the 1997 revolution in the African country of Zaire (now the Democratic Republic of Congo). The deposed dictator, Mobuto Sese Seko, was only ousted by revolutionary leader, Laurent Kabila, because the regime of the dictator had run out of steam. Although they initially received help from other governments – primarily of Rwanda and Uganda – Kabila and his revolutionary troops were sustained by extensive home-spun discontent. The revolution took on a momentum of its own, because the people (or lots of them) were behind it.

The course of revolutions contain fairly typical sequences, what Sztompka (1994) says are commonly taken to consist of ten stages:

1. All revolutions are preceded by the intensification of discontent and conflict due to economic crises. These are experienced most sensitively by social classes 'on the make' rather than people who are at the bottom of the pile.
2. At the second stage, there is a transfer of allegiance of the intellectuals in society in favour of revolution. The intellectual roll call during the French Revolution, for example, included Condorcet, Diderot, Rousseau and Voltaire, all of whom embraced and fanned a revolutionary spirit.
3. Next comes the attempt by the existing regime to appease the growing rebels by limited reform. This occurred, for example, in South Africa prior to the release of Nelson Mandela from Robben Island Prison. These attempts are, however, read as belated, too little too late signs of weakness, and bolster the revolutionary spirit even more.
4. The state eventually seizes up, its legitimacy or naked coercive power shattered. This is the critical moment when rebels become revolutionaries, seizing power by peaceful or violent means.
5. The old order collapses, and a 'revolutionary honeymoon' ensues, rather like the period of euphoria and expectation after Tony Blair's victory in the 1997 General Election.
6. Internal divisions start to fracture the internal cohesiveness of the revolutionary leadership. Radicals seek to take the revolution further; moderates want to slow things down; conservatives try to minimise change.
7. Moderate reformers gradually take over, and certain aspects of the 'comfortable old ways' start to reappear. This blunts the revolutionary aspirations of the masses, and creates a period of post-revolutionary malaise.
8. Mindful of widespread dissatisfaction, radicals mobilise the people and replace the moderates. Such in-fighting isn't always successful though. In the post-English Civil War period, for example, disillusioned soldiers put their case to the Cromwellian leadership at the so-called Putney Conference. Cromwell responded by hunting down dissidents who claimed he hadn't delivered on his promises.
9. A period of 'terror' ensues as radicals seek to usurp the moderates and eradicate all traces of the old regime. This often provides an opportunity for a dictator to size power through a military *putsch*.
10. Finally, a balance is arrived at, when the excesses of radicalism are condemned, and a framework of stable institutions is installed.

The above sequence isn't faithfully followed in all revolutions. However, allowing for the historically 'unique' backgrounds of such revolutions as the English (1640), American (1776), French (1789), Russian (1917), Chinese (1949), Cuban (1959), Philippine (1985) and central and eastern European (1989), they plot stages that are generally recognisable. In that sense, they represent an idealised (or ideal typical) revolutionary sequence. One might add, however, that dissatisfaction isn't just experienced by the intellectuals who form the vanguard of many revolutionary movements. Injustice is acutely felt by the poorest members of society, and collective misery often motivates a collective struggle for a just society.

Jack A. Goldstone (1982, cited by Sztompka 1994) likens the study of revolutions to the study of earthquakes. When a revolution or an earthquake happens, social scientists and geologists try to make sense of the data that arises, and build predictive theories to account for and time the next ones. Yet when the next ones occur, we're still surprised by them, because elements of unpredictability still remain.

EXAM TIP

Be aware of the complementary roles that evolutionary and revolutionary processes have in social change. Guard against treating them as either/or concepts.

REVOLUTIONARY THEORY OF SOCIAL CHANGE

FOR

+ Revolutionary theory is mindful of both structural contraint and individual potentiality. Successful revolutions only occur when the alignment of these two forces coincide at critical moments in the historical process. Empirical evidence supports this assertion. The Russian Revolution, for example, only became possible when the mass of the Russian people were persuaded by a handful of communist intellectuals that a threshold of unbearable economic frustrations could be ended if apathy were replaced by a collective and resolute will to fight.
+ History tells us that social change is a very variable phenomenon. Sometimes it's slow; other times it's fast. It's with regard to the last category that revolutionary theory comes into its own. The events that swept through eastern and central Europe following the citizen demolition in 1989 of the Berlin Wall happened so rapidly that they require an explanation which addresses the social dynamics of radical breakthroughs. With its emphasis on the kind of change that's characterised by sudden leaps to dramatically different futures, revolutionary theory provides just such an explanation.
+ Revolutionary theory demonstrates that slavish devotion to convention can be overcome by a wilful human spirit, provided the wilfulness strikes while the iron is hot. The emanicipation from customs that oppress the people is a noble project. It has encouraged heroes to wage war – sometimes literally, sometimes figuratively – on oppressive regimes. It has given them the intellectual insight to understand that rapid and radical change is possible provided the collective will of the people can be harnessed in common cause. The promise of revolutionary theory has sometimes led to the creation of better, more just societies, as, for example, in South Africa.

AGAINST

– No sociologist can say what precisely creates the unique explosive mix that leads to particular revolutions. The best sociologists can do is to provide general pointers which may or may not precipitate a revolution. This is all too general. Each and every revolution is a special case, and therefore requires fine grain rather than broad spectrum analysis. It might therefore be the case that ideographic historians rather than generalist sociologists are better informed on revolutions.
– While it's true that the most famous revolutionary theorist of them all, Karl Marx, did recognise the importance of social evolution, revolutionary theory gives undue and exaggerated prominence to sudden cataclysmic events. Moreover, it's wrong to assume, as Marx seems to do, that evolution is merely a prelude to a big social bang. Evolutionary trends sometimes lead to revolutions, but there's nothing inevitable about this. Whether such trends do or don't culminate in revolution is a matter for empirical investigation, not theoretical or ideological speculation.
– While revolutionary theory provides would-be revolutionaries with blueprints and inspiration for their own actions, it would be naive to imagine that all revolutions are just. Some lead to little more than a recycling of dominant elites. One oppressor becomes replaced with another. Trotsky protested that this had happened in post-revolution Russia, and ended up being murdered. Moreover, violent revolutions often involve a great deal of blood-letting, and are opposed by proponents of non-violent social movements (for example, the civil rights campaign of Martin Luther King, and the 'peaceful revolution' of Polish Solidarity).

Cyclical theory of social change

Unlike evolutionism, revolutionism and (in the case of Weber) social constructionism, theories of historical cycles don't envisage a 'march of history' approach. The emphasis is on recurrence: what goes around, comes around! On the big canvas, no matter how many times our ancestors have experienced the tragedy of war, it keeps recurring. Instead of going forwards, we go round in a circle. In the other three theories, what happened yesterday won't be repeated, and what happens tomorrow will be unique. In cyclical theory, change brings – sooner or later – a return to the semblance of an earlier state.

A big name in cyclical theory is Pitirim A. Sorokin, a Russian-born American sociologist. Sorokin says that change occurs because a dominant culture eventually confronts a contending culture. One is a spent force, the other a rising giant. Sorokin uses rather complex language to describe the two main types of culture that square up to each other: the *sensate* and the *ideational*. The first attempts to conquer the material world; the second seeks to understand the inner human. The one is 'materialistic' (pertaining to the senses) – sometimes decent (for example, conquering disease), sometimes greedy (for example, mining for gold). The other is 'spiritual' (concerning the mind and the sacred) – sometimes honourable (for example, rejecting wealth), sometimes irresponsible (for example, neglecting the impact of famine).

Sorokin also adds a third type of culture: the *idealistic*. This culture is a tentative, fragile combination of the other two, tending to be more short-lived. Sorokin thinks twentieth-century Europe is a sensate culture, but he eagerly anticipated a return to an ideational type. This *might* suggest that Sorokin is, after all, a directional theorist, like, for example, evolutionary or revolutionary theorists. However, even though he addresses the issue of directional change, his arguments are generally based on cyclical assumptions.

Sorokin doesn't predict any fixed sequence, but he does, by reading the mood of a particular age, have an inkling of where the future might be (temporarily) heading. Being prudent, he also distinguishes between 'completely cyclical' and 'relatively cyclical' recurrences:

'In the *completely cyclical* process the last phase of a given recurrence returns to its first phase . . . [However] in the *relatively cyclical* process . . . the direction of the recurring process does not coincide completely with that of the series of previous recurrences. There is some deviation from cycle to cycle.'

(Sorokin 1957: 62)

Incidentally, Sorokin doesn't especially favour the ideational over the sensate, but he does think it's time for a change. His argument that all forms of 'truth' are subject to a *dialectical destiny* (a tough concept this; it means destined to change) sounds rather postmodernist, but he certainly wouldn't have described himself as such.

Another notable exponent of cyclical theory is the Italian sociologist, Vilfredo Pareto (1848–1923) (see pages 365–6). A systems theorist at heart, Pareto viewed society as a structure of interdependent elements with a tendency to equilibrium. He added, however, that extraordinary modifications do occur, thereby destabilising the equilibrium. Disequilibrium ensues, but eventually a new equilibrium is installed. The social system, says Pareto, consists of three essential components:

CYCLICAL THEORY OF SOCIAL CHANGE

FOR

+ Cyclical theory isn't over-deterministic. Sorokin, for example, regarded nothing as 'necessary' or 'inevitable' in the cyclical course of history that he expounded. This allows for a more empirical judgement of social change. The facts don't have to fit into a fixed, directional sequence. Instead, the facts let sociologists use theory to gain a better understanding of change.
+ History demonstrates that human social behaviour keeps repeating itself. For example, the classical culture of ancient Greece was rediscovered and emulated during the European Renaissance in the sixteenth and seventeenth centuries, bringing an end to the so-called 'dark ages'. This reawakened version of the Greek classical spirit was, of course, different to the original. Cyclical theory doesn't say that earlier epochs return in identikit form. What does re-occur is a *Zeitgeist* – a spirit of the time.
+ Pareto's theory of the circulation of elites is supported by empirical evidence. Take, for example, the expansion of the Roman Empire. Its military might eventually became codified into laws and regulations. Thus, the *Pax Romana* (Roman Peace) was guaranteed by lawyers and administrators ('foxes') to countries which generals ('lions') had earlier taken by storm.

AGAINST

– Pareto's calculation of the distribution of residues is hypothetical. History often reveals different distributions and, of course, obvious mixtures. British imperialists, for example, relied on fox and lion-like qualities to conquer different parts of the world. If diplomacy didn't work, they sent in the redcoats! To be fair to Pareto though, he did envisage the co-existence of mixed residues, but perhaps he under-estimated the extent to which they prevail. Similarly, as Sorokin himself admitted, societies often simultaneously contain sensate, ideational and idealistic cultural tendencies.

– Cyclical theory exaggerates the extent to which earlier cultures re-assert themselves. Sure, there are certain enduring human qualities – generosity, cruelty and inquisitiveness among them. However, social systems reforge primary ingredients into new and radically different forms. The Italy of today, which sends many of its best football players to English clubs, is a very different place to the land that brought Ancient British hostages in chains to the thrones of emperors.

– Cyclical theory doesn't pay sufficient attention to environmental and 'great leader' triggers of social change. What happens if a natural disaster hits, or a charismatic revolutionary shakes things up? Sorokin's theory, in particular, envisages change as an inevitable, in-built force. The assumption here is that social systems are bound to change because they're 'predestined' to run out. If such is the case, Sorokin needs to say where this inner 'clock' comes from and who or what winds it up.

- *residues* – manifestations of sentiments, or even sentiments themselves
- *interests* – things that serve human needs
- *derivations* – justifications that people use to defend their residues and interests.

Residues are the driving forces of human social life. Indeed, Pareto even refers to them as corresponding 'to certain instincts in human beings' (1935: 509), and, in this context, he identifies the 'sex residue' (1935: 519). Sounding very positivist, he also writes that:

'The residues are the manifestations of sentiments and instincts just as the rising of the mercury in a thermometer is a manifestation of the rise in temperature.'

(Pareto 1935: 511)

Two alternative general types of residue are especially noteworthy, representing the different strategies people use to attain their interests. These are:

- *combination (so-called class I) residues*, which include such personality traits as innovativeness, risk-taking, activeness, entrepreneurial spirit and originality
- *persistence (so-called class II) residues*, which include prudence, caution, traditionalism, patriotism and legalism.

Society is typically headed by elites. These are people who excel in their particular field (for example, in politics, business, academia). Elites tend to have a preponderance of either class I or class II residues. In a political cycle, the main players are strong rulers (the 'lions') and cunning administrators (the 'foxes'). Lions espouse military values and take power through force. Once established, they display patriotism and traditionalism (class II residues). But in peacetime, these values are contested by innovativeness and entrepreneurialism (class I residues). Foxes adopt these latter values, and they slowly penetrate the militaristic lions.

This takeover by stealth enables the foxes to outwit the lions, and the foxes take power. In turn, they have their 'come-uppance'. There's gradually a conservative backlash, and the lions overthrow the foxes using their favourite weapon – force. Then the cycle begins anew. In this manner, as Pareto aptly puts it, 'aristocracies do not last but are constantly renewed. This phenomenon may be called the *circulation of elites*' (selections from 1896–1921: 155). In the business cycle, the elites who confront each other might be landlords versus industrialists, in the academic cycle modernists versus postmodernists – and so it goes on.

Social constructionist theory of social change

Social constructionists, following Weber, place even more emphasis than marxists on the continuous role of human agency in the process of social change. People construct social structures, and they also deconstruct and reconstruct them continuously. They don't always have to wait, as the marxists tend to imply, for critical moments. Once created, though, 'structures' influence people, a point conceded by most social constructionists. However, the influence is seldom so strong as to stop individuals from contesting, side-stepping, or even demolishing the 'rules'.

In his famous critique of one of the most important examples of social change in modern society, the rise of capitalism, Weber emphasised the crucial role of Protestant ideas and values in the process of change. While he accepted that the strong work ethic of Protestantism didn't provide a full explanation for the change to modern capitalism, he recognised that the human wilfulness of religious conviction was a potent force for change. By insisting that hard work was an earthly sign of God's grace, Protestantism fostered outlooks that were conducive to capitalistic behaviour.

Realising that capitalism was the product of human action, Weber postulated that the crucial agents behind the transition from traditional to capitalist society were Protestants. He found the preponderance of Protestants in entrepreneurial activity was striking, irrespective of the kind of society they inhabited. Weber consequently concluded that the development of capitalism was causally linked to 'the permanent intrinsic character of their [Protestants'] religious beliefs, and not only in their temporary external historico-political situations' (1974: 40). Importantly, Weber argued, as Parsons puts it:

'that the "spirit" [of Protestantism] forms a fundamental causal factor in the genesis of the concrete capitalistic order and is not merely a "reflection" of its "material" elements.'

(Parsons 1967b: 517)

This is complex stuff! What Parsons means is that Weber had discovered that ideas, not just material things (for example, population increase), can change society. On the face of it, this looks anti-marxist. Sensibly, however, Weber played safe by indicating that some forms of social change might be caused by material factors. He also noted that Protestantism was located within social contexts. In that respect, it wasn't an entirely free-floating spiritual energy. Later in his life, Weber actually toned down the causal side of his original thesis, and suggested that Protestantism *contributed* to the rise of capitalism. This point has perhaps been overlooked by Parsons.

Weber's belief that the origins of social change might be found in the personal behaviours of individual social actors lies at the heart of social constructionist theory. For interactionists and phenomenologists contend that the way people interpret their social worlds can and does exercise powerful influences on social change. Imagine, for example, that you live on an island where a male ruler calls himself the lord and provider of you and all the other islanders. This guy also happens to live in the best house, eats the nicest food, and drinks the finest fruit juice on the island.

You and your peers, however, live in ramshackle homes, eat unpleasant food and drink polluted water. How long do you think it's going to be before you and other 'subordinates' start redefining your leader, calling him a tyrant rather than a provider? Thereafter, if the new adage sticks, collective grievances might become galvanised into a resolve to make him stand down. In that way, the inter-subjective (i.e. agreed between individuals) deconstruction of the first label and the construction of a new one have real consequences. Out goes the newly defined tyrant, and in comes a more just society.

Weber's work has strongly influenced social constructionist thought. It was he who conspicuously placed human beings and their actions at the forefront of sociological debates on social change. It would be remiss, however, to imagine that Weber didn't attach importance to the shaping power of social structure. He did. In a strikingly modest and sincere gesture, Weber declared that his wish wasn't:

SOCIAL CONSTRUCTIONIST THEORY OF SOCIAL CHANGE

FOR

+ It forces us, and rightly so, not to forget that behind the macro forces of social change there are underlying human aspirations, motivations and sheer wilfulness. There's nothing in human history that isn't influenced, intentionally or otherwise, by the actions of women, men and children. People are literally the stuff of social change. Moreover, within the collectivity we refer to as people, there are exceptional individuals whose actions exercise intended and real effects on the course of history. When people attach meanings to social processes and act upon them, if the meanings stick, subjective interpretations can become objective realities. This is the principle of the self-fulfilling prophecy.
+ Even the ravages of natural disasters are responded to in a socially constructed manner. Society's readiness to develop risk technologies in response to such events rests largely upon the perceptions and proposals of key decision-makers. In that respect, the social construction of what constitute environmental risks and how to deal with them is an eminently human activity. The consequent 'understanding' of what constitutes environmental problems can and does trigger societal reposes. Thus, for example, the perception that ozone layer depletion is damaging the planet and causing more skin cancer has led to new kinds of aerosol and weather forecast tips on minimising sun exposure.
+ The assertion that human agency lies at the heart of social change is amply and impressively supported by Weber's comparative analysis of the 'causal' relationship between the rise of Protestantism and the development of capitalism. Although he took account of the argument that ideas don't operate in a social vacuum, Weber demonstrated that religious ideas and behaviours can and do exercise a pivotal force in the transition to modern capitalism.

AGAINST

− While it's true that people make history, as Marx persuasively reminds us, our capacity to do this is either constrained or accelerated by social conditions. In short, opportunities for individual agency in the process of social change have to be seized at the right moment. However compelling the arguments of a revolutionary leader might be, she or he won't be able to effect a change in society unless the will of the mass of the people is fully mobilised. It's only when they're within striking distance of pushing the march of history forward that individuals can ever hope to be agents of change.

− Linked to the preceding point, the social constructionist theory of social change is sometimes unhistorical and unsociological. It under-estimates the powerful effect of economic and political forces in society, and has very little to say about the impact of physical factors, like earthquakes and twisters. It won't do simply to wish these forces away on the grounds that they're mere social constructions that can be replaced by other interpretations. For an earthquake-prone society not to incorporate safeguards in building designs is both unwise and irresponsible. Individuals have to acknowledge the fact that, on their own, they're less powerful as agents of change than they might think.

− Social construction, by itself, can't conjure up change from 'thin air'. Here we need to distinguish between wanting something to happen and realistically judging what is likely to occur. In the 1997 General Election, Conservative voters wanted John Major to continue as prime minister, but that didn't stop the 'inevitable' from happening: a landslide victory for Labour and Tony Blair – which, incidentally, had been predicted by social scientists. This isn't, of course, to suggest that wilful, self-fulfilling prophecies don't have an effect on social outcomes. They do. However, if they work against the grain of powerful social forces, they're unlikely to have much impact.

'to substitute for a one-sided materialistic an equally one-sided spiritualistic causal interpretation of culture and of history. Each is equally possible, but each, if it does not serve as the preparation, but as the conclusion of an investigation, accomplishes equally little in the interest of historical truth.'

(Weber 1974: 183)

Put simply, Weber recognises that ideas and structures can both be causes of social change. He also notes that it's necessary to investigate how Protestantism was 'influenced in its development and its character by the totality of social conditions, especially economic' (1974: 183). True to his word, in his later work Weber emphasised that religion may have different – even opposite – influences on social life, depending on local, historical conditions.

> **EXAM TIP**
>
> Remind the examiner that Weber's analysis of social change, while at times placing human agency centre stage, also recognises the influence of social structure.

Weber's readiness to consider individual capacities and social structures in the analysis of social change has left a sensible legacy to social constructionists. Only the really 'hard' theorists in this camp – certain ethnomethodologists perhaps – would seriously suggest that change can be understood simply on the basis of the meanings people attach to social processes. If, for example, I incorrectly attach a radical meaning to a policy which turns out to have conservative influences, I have interpreted the situation wrongly – simple as that! No amount of wishful thinking on my part is going to undo this, unless, of course, I learn from my mistake and try another strategy.

Arguably, the most significant changes over the past 200 years are the movement of people from rural villages to industrial towns, and the replacement of manual with machine technology. Intertwined with these developments is the changing – some would say, declining – influence of community life. This important configuration of social processes will be examined in the next section.

QUESTIONS

1. Briefly define these terms: social stability; social change; social statics; social dynamics.
2. Illustrate the concepts of stability and change with real-life events.
3. Briefly, what do the exponents of the functionalist, marxist, cyclical and social constructionist theories have to say about social order?
4. What are the main features of the functionalist, marxist, cyclical and social constructionist approaches to social change?

Urbanisation, industrialisation and community

There are terms to define first:

- *industrialisation* – the development of mass production in factories
- *urbanisation* – the migration of people from villages into cities and sizeable towns
- *community* – a sense of common purpose among people who typically live in the same locality.

The nineteenth-century social scientist, Ferdinand Tonnies (1855–1936), bemoaned what he described as the loss of community which ushered in urbanisation and industrialisation. When tradition and loyalty confront rationality and self-interest, something has to give. In the nineteenth century, the former sentiments surrendered to the latter ones, as evidenced by the replacement of personal with impersonal forms of association. Thus, for example, the personal handshake which assures a deal on a face-to-face level yields to the impersonal contract between two lawyers whose clients might never see each other.

Tonnies argued that the breakdown of community spirit led to urbanisation and industrialisation rather than the other way round. Sure, there was a bit of influence from both directions, but essentially, says Tonnies, the decline of rural solidarity made the growth of towns and factories more likely. When people start moving from villages to towns and swap the horse and plough for the factory machine, the retreat of community life gains added momentum.

Tonnies coined the German terms:

- *Gemeinschaft* to distinguish the 'community-type' society of the pre-industrial world
- *Gesellschaft* to distinguish the 'organisation-type' society of its industrial heir.

While he said that rural areas tended strongly towards Gemeinschaft and urban ones towards Gesellschaft, he recognised that Gemeinschaft and Gesellschaft relationships could exist in both rural and urban settings.

> **EXAM TIP**
>
> Saying 'My community is mine' will help you to remember that Ge*mein*schaft is Tonnies' community model.

Here are the main characteristics of each of the society types envisaged by Tonnies. It's important to realise that these are models – *ideal types*, to use Max Weber's term. So don't expect to find perfect replications in the real world. Tendencies will suffice.

Gemeinschaft

- Social relationships are face-to-face, enduring, and based on *who* a person is, rather than on what she or he has achieved.
- Linked to the previous point, an individual's status in society is *ascribed* (endowed by birth), rather than *achieved* (obtained through merit).
- People in Gemeinschaft localities are relatively geographically and socially immobile: they don't venture forth into the big wide world, and they don't ascend or descend the social ladder.
- Gemeinschaft culture is based on consensus because norms and values are transmitted, enforced and overseen by accepted moral custodians – notably, the family and the church.
- Locality and kinship are highly prized. Sharing the same earth and the same blood mean a great deal in Gemeinschaft culture.

Gesellschaft

- Social relationships are impersonal, and sometimes mediated through lawyers and other middle parties.
- Related to the previous point, contractual relationships are common. Handshakes are replaced with legal documents.
- Behaviours are individualised rather than reflecting the norms of the group.
- Gesellschaft society creates tensions between competing individuals. Conflict rather than consensus is the norm.
- People relate to each other in a rational rather than an emotional way. In that sense, relationships are often calculative.

> **EXAM TIP**
>
> The first letter of a German noun is a capital. So always write Gemeinschaft and Gesellschaft.

Like Tonnies, Durkheim was also interested in different types of social environment. In his path-breaking analysis of the transition from traditional to industrial society, Durkheim identified two types of social relationship:

- *mechanical solidarity*, which denotes the social relationships that prevail in traditional society, and which approximates to Tonnies' community-type Gemeinschaft
- *organic solidarity*, which denotes the social relationships that prevail in modern society, and which resembles Tonnies' organisation-type Gesellschaft.

These are tricky concepts, and require a bit of unpacking.

Characteristics of mechanical solidarity

- Individuals are strongly bound to the *same* large social group to which they belong. Solidarity is guaranteed by likeness, and team spirit is valued above individual ambition.
- Following on from the previous point, departures from group values, from what Durkheim called the *collective conscience*, are severely sanctioned. Criminal law is therefore very punitive because, to quote Durkheim, 'What we avenge, what the criminal expiates, is the outrage to morality' (1964: 89, first published in 1893).
- There's limited *division of labour* (i.e. job specialisation). Adults are farmers, carers and warriors, rather than one or the other.
- Owing to the similar roles and skills which its members have, the larger group can carry on even if numbers are depleted (for example, because of war and natural disasters). This gives a *segmental* character to society (cut one piece off and the rest makes good, just like a worm).

Characteristics of organic solidarity

- Individuals are dependent on those parts of society which, although *different*, complement each other – hence the biological analogy of organic. Bodily organs are different but they work in harmony. Social institutions like the family and school also tend to support each other, thereby promoting solidarity.
- People who are deviant are responded to in a restitutive rather than a retributive manner. As Durkheim puts it, 'the judge . . . speaks of law; he [*sic*] says nothing of punishment' (1964: 111).
- There's a pronounced division of labour. People specialise in different occupations rather than doing lots of different tasks.
- The different groups which make up society are highly interdependent and can't easily survive as separate units. A large company, for example, can't survive if it loses all its information technology specialists.

Durkheim recognised that, although organic solidarity engenders a different kind of social bonding than mechanical solidarity, sometimes the division of labour literally produces social divisions. Sounding remarkably like Marx, Durkheim illustrates this point when he writes:

'The conflict between capital and labor is another example, more striking, of the same phenomenon. In so far as industrial functions become more specialized, the conflict becomes more lively, instead of solidarity increasing.'

(Durkheim 1964: 354)

Despite the clarity that both Tonnies' and Durkheim's analyses bring to the debate on social change, both models over-simplify things. Thus, for example, conflict also exists in pre-industrial societies, and consensus is found in modern societies too. Similarly, attachments to blood and soil still endure in present-day settings, and interdependence has characterised important aspects of past social life. Durkheim didn't generally lament the emergence of organic solidarity, but he accepted that the demise of strong community bonds created social vulnerabilities. For example, he noted that the loosening of social cohesion could make some people desperately lonely and more likely to commit suicide.

Tonnies, however, was quite openly concerned about urbanisation and industrialisation. He feared the breakdown of Gemeinschaft order and community and its replacement with Gesellschaft instability and fragmentation. These fears were shared by his German contemporary, the sociologist, Georg Simmel. Like Tonnies, Simmel believed that *urbanism* (city living) was rational. In that sense, the city becomes a place where people relate to each other in a matter-of-fact sort of way instead of on the basis of filiality, producing what Simmel describes as a blasé outlook. The city is also, he argues, the centre of the capitalist economy in which money counts, not people.

On perhaps a more positive note, Simmel envisages the metropolis as a locality in which reason and intellect prevail, as against the emotional relationships that characterise small towns and rural settings. Even here though, his position is guarded. He regards the intellectual culture of the city as an attempt by the individuals who live there to protect themselves against the 'domination of the metropolis' (Simmel 1948: 326, first published in 1903). While he clearly doesn't like the loss of community engendered by the rise of the modern city and its 'unrelenting hardness' (Simmel 1948: 326), as a sociologist, Simmel contends that the commentator shouldn't pass judgement on social processes: 'it is our task not to complain or to condone but only to understand' (Simmel 1948: 339).

This is often difficult to accomplish, but Simmel is right to remind us that the primary goal of sociology is to understand social phenomena. Once it has assembled its data, sociology is in a better position to apply values. For example, if we find that the axing of local bus services diminishes a sense of community spirit in an area, we might advocate a reversal of the policy in order to revitalise and repopulate the area. Here empirical investigation sensibly informs a plan of action.

Industrialisation, urbanisation and urbanism

You might find it useful to read pages 597–601, Chapter 18, where industrialisation and urbanisation are discussed in relation to poor countries. The chapter also refers to industrialisation and urbanisation in rich countries, but not in great detail. In this section, we'll look at the European experience, in particular the UK.

First, though, we'll recap on two definitions and add a third:

- *Industrialisation* is the development of mass production in large factories.
- *Urbanisation* is the migration of people into densely populated areas which become (or already are) towns and cities.
- *Urbanism* is the way of life of people who live in towns and cities.

What kind of locality do you live in? Chances are it's urban – a town, a city or the outer limits of either, in which case *urbanism* is your way of life. If you live in the country – a *rural* environment – you're in a minority: some might add, the fortunate minority, and *ruralism* is your lifestyle. If you're a Londoner, the city is the best place. But if you've been raised in the Yorkshire Dales, nothing can beat that. We respond to locality on the basis of prior experience. That's not to say we don't sometimes want a change. Most people, from time to time, tire of their immediate environment, and yearn for something different. Temporary escapades to other localities for holidays make for an interesting life.

In the nineteenth century, when industrialisation was in full swing in Britain, holidays were the prerogative of the rich who sent their sons on Grand Tours of Europe. The Europe these young men saw, as part of their finishing 'education', was predominantly rural in character, even though it boasted great cities like Paris and Rome. But this was not to last. The processes of industrialisation and urbanisation that began in Britain in around the 1760s were soon to take over the rest of Europe. The upshot of these combined forces was *urban industrialism*. They were forces which had a profound impact on patterns of migration.

Britain became the most urbanised country in the world, and had the fastest growing population. Industrial towns and mining villages grew rapidly, and, by 1850, half the population lived in cities of more than 10,000 people – way ahead of other European countries. Urbanisation went hand in hand in the shift from an agricultural to an industrial workforce. However, house building in towns struggled to keep pace with rapid urban growth. Between 1821 and 1831, for example, Bradford's population increased by 78 per cent. Urban rents were lucrative, taking 10–20 per cent of wages, in contrast to 5 per cent or so in the countryside.

Back-to-back terraced houses with a front door on each side and a transverse party wall were particularly cramped, and had no back yard or through ventilation. Later versions of these houses still exist in Leeds and other northern cities. Some easing of overcrowded conditions occurred towards the end of the nineteenth century because better wages and a falling birth rate enabled workers to rent more spacious and better accommodation. In fact, by that time, nearly all houses had their own outside toilet, and some had an inside bathroom. Some of the more prosperous workers – 'foremen' and the like – moved to better houses on the outskirts of urban centres. In that way, *suburbanisation* became an important vehicle of population redistribution. Business people, in particular, often preferred to commute into town from outlying, high-status suburbs.

Much more recently – from about 1951 to 1971 – Britain urbanised through an outward expansion of commuter hinterlands, the populations of urban cores falling from 53.7 per cent of the national total to 47.9 per cent. By the 1960s, however, the London ring's increase had settled (and even fallen), and was unable to compensate depletion from the central core. Similar patterns were evident in Manchester, Newcastle and Glasgow. Elsewhere, for example, in Birmingham, Leeds, Nottingham and Sheffield, decentralisation gathered momentum in the 1960s. Today, despite decentralisation, the British population is still quite highly concentrated in urban cores. In America, however, metropolitan rings have turned into massive urban sprawls such that some cities almost merge into each other. Consider, for example, eastern cities like Washington DC and Baltimore.

During the nineteenth century, Britain became the world's first modern urbanised nation. At the beginning of that century only about one third of the population lived in towns. By 1914, about three-quarters did – which is close to the proportion today. In the hundred years before the mid-nineteenth century, the rural population only grew by about 0.5 per cent per year. In the same period, the growth rate for towns was almost 2 per cent. The number of people living in rural areas actually fell by about half a million between 1831 and 1911, losses reaching a peak during the 1880s. Migration to towns and emigration abroad (which was also high, especially in Ireland) largely accounted for this. In 1851, half of the migrants to Liverpool came from Lancashire and most of the rest were from Ireland.

Internal migration tended to be within limited geographical areas. Farm labourers in the south-east, for example, didn't often leave their horse and hoe in Kentish fields to work in Yorkshire coal mines. Instead, they typically migrated to London. The pit villages of the north were also largely populated by people who used to live in nearby agricultural districts. While town and city populations generally increased, and rural village populations typically dwindled, there were some exceptions. Thus, for example, a few areas of early industrialisation in north-east Lancashire and west Yorkshire incurred population losses because their water power technology was replaced by steam and coal in other parts of the counties.

The last 50 years have witnessed a number of important trends in the changing distribution of the UK population. Among the more notable are:

- a drift from the north to the south
- rural decline and later revitalisation (for example, the growth of 'heritage' villages)
- decentralisation from cities (especially from about 1960), and planned urban overspill into 'commuter-land'
- small town growth and, more recently, perhaps, a halt to a decline in big city growth.

Today, the UK is one of the most densely populated countries in the world. Its average density in 1981 was 242 people per square kilometre. Of course, there are some wide variations in population density. London is very crowded, while the North Yorkshire Dales are very sparsely inhabited. The high overall density reflects the fact that more than 90 per cent of the population now effectively live in an urban environment. Urbanism is definitely the norm.

So where are we today in relation to population distribution?

- The south-east has expanded in both absolute numbers and share of the national population.
- The older industrial regions of the north have fallen back in population terms.
- The more rural areas of East Anglia the south-west, and to a lesser extent, the East Midlands have experienced a population upturn.
- The population of Wales has been relatively stable, as has the population of Northern Ireland.
- Scotland's population has steadily declined.

There have long been immigrant populations in Britain, mainly in large towns. From the nineteenth century, the Irish were the largest group of immigrants. Many Irish people still move to Britain, and an Irish presence in cities like London, Leeds and Liverpool is apparent. The arrival after the 1940s of large numbers of immigrants from poor countries is also significant. Their entry into Britain coincided with the collapse of the British 'Empire', and the ensuing migration of citizens from former Commonwealth countries who retained a right of entry into the UK. Many black immigrants obtained jobs in manufacturing and other manual jobs. This made them susceptible to a greater risk of unemployment in later decades when heavy industry began its steep decline. The fact that these immigrants often lived close to city centre factories meant that they and their children and grandchildren bore the brunt of industry's exodus from the inner city.

Initially, before they were eligible for council homes, many immigrants lived in private rented accommodation in the older properties of inner cities. A large number of Asian people, however, became owner-occupiers. Today, a higher proportion of South Asians – who have tended to be more economically successful than other minorities – own their own homes than white people. Bangladeshi people, however, among the most recent and the poorest immigrants, generally live in council homes. They have high levels of segregation in Britain. Black people are also heavily concentrated on council estates, but are generally less segregated. Irish-born people in Britain are more widely dispersed than black and Asian groups, but are nevertheless concentrated in urban areas.

We now live in a multi-ethnic society, where the vast majority of young black people and young persons of Irish descent are native-born Britons. However, minority ethnic groups are markedly concentrated in geographical terms. Historically, this was linked to the availability of work (often close to ports of entry) when the grandparents – and in the case of middle-aged people, the parents – of young people from minority ethnic groups first emigrated to Britain. Irish immigrants and their families are concentrated in the north-west (especially Manchester), the West Midlands, London and other parts of the south-east. People from black and Asian minority ethnic groups, typically in households headed by Commonwealth immigrants, usually live in big cities. In the mid-1980s, 64 per cent of British residents of African origin, 57 per cent of West Indian origin, 54 per cent of Bangladeshi origin, and 14 per cent of Pakistani origin lived in London.

Today, four out of every five Britons live in towns and cities. It's important to grasp this even though, over the past 25 years, Britons have moved away from major cities. This trend is a new kind of urbanisation rather than a return to country living. Every year, an area of countryside the size of Bristol is built over to provide homes, offices, shops and roads for these new migrants. If this trend continues, soon our countryside will contain large tracts of housing which will form urban corridors between towns and cities. This has already happened, for example, between Bradford and Leeds.

Much of the preceding data on patterns of urban migration is based on the work of David Coleman and John Salt, published in *The British Population* (1996). Their book is an authoritative and a relatively easy-to-read reference source. Do consult it for more facts about British population trends. Having considered migration patterns in Britain, it's now time to look at what happens at the end of the journey – the homes people go to.

Access to housing

On the face of things, housing need in the UK is largely satisfied. After the Second World War, there was a big growth in owner-occupation and council housing, and a fall in private rented accommodation. By the early 1970s, a surplus of dwellings over households occurred, which, with dips and peaks, continued into the 1990s. The surplus, however, doesn't give a true picture of the real relationship between supply and need. Of the 23.6 million dwellings in 1991, substantially over a million were unfit for occupation or were otherwise vacant. These included homes without basic amenities, properties undergoing extensive conversion or improvement, and second homes. Added to this, were about half a million of what are called 'concealed households' (for example, couples living with parents and in-laws). Taking these concealments into the reckoning, there was a real shortage of housing – approaching three million. There was also a surplus of expensive houses in the countryside and in outer urban suburbs, and a shortage of affordable housing in urban centres.

In 1967, 447,100 dwellings were started in Britain, of which 213,900 were council homes. By 1992, the number of starts had fallen to 156,000, with only 36,400 in the council sector. Housing shortages have precipitated a high level of homelessness in the UK. The official number (an under-estimate) of homeless households in England was 145,800 in 1991. Many of the people not counted in the statistics were deemed 'intentionally homeless'. Given that not being able to keep up with mortgage payments accounted for much of this, one wonders how the term 'intentionally' can be justified. Additionally, the number of homeless single people increased to about 80,000 by 1991. At precisely the same time that council waiting lists and the number of homeless people reached record high levels in the early 1990s, nearly half a million construction workers had been made redundant by a huge slump in the building industry.

Access to housing for households who can't or prefer not to buy will only improve if more council accommodation is made available at affordable rents. Yet council home waiting lists have grown. Importantly, because of the right-to-buy policies of successive Conservative governments, the sale of council homes has exacerbated the problem. Says Balchin:

> 'From 1979 into the 1990s, Conservative governments presided over the greatest onslaught on the direct provision of local authority housing since its inception.'
>
> (Balchin 1996: 11)

So great was this onslaught that, by the end of the 1980s, the British state housing sector was thrown into sharp collapse for the first time in 60 years. Adopting an openly value-judgmental tone, Balchin concludes that Conservative housing policy has exhibited a 'biased, profligate and irresponsible support for the owner-occupier and neglect of the tenant or homeless' (1996: 13).

Despite the growth in owner-occupation (accounting for 66 per cent of British housing stock in 1991), it's often difficult for prospective first-time buyers to acquire a property. Average house prices are in excess of £60,000, which requires an income of at least £22,000. This poses special problems for women, black people and old people, all of whom are disadvantaged in relative income terms. Added to the economic disadvantages they encounter, black people also suffer racial discrimination in relation to their housing needs and aspirations.

Women

Housing policies in Britain, claims Balchin (1996), have been based around the family. About 66 per cent of the British housing stock is owner-occupied. Women, however, fare less well than men because building societies give preferential treatment to male applicants. Men are seen to be less of a financial risk because it's assumed they will have relatively uninterrupted employment. Moreover, mortgage loans are calculated on the basis of about three times the average male salary, which again discriminates against women. Female income is only about two-thirds that of male income. Women are over-represented in low-paid jobs, and often occupy relatively junior positions. Moreover, the domestic and caring work undertaken by women means that they're more often than men found in part-time employment.

In terms of poverty, women outnumber men by about 1.2 million, making up approximately 56 per cent of poor adults. Stephen Webb (1993, cited by Oppenheim and Harker 1996) found in 1991 that around two-thirds of adults in the poorest households were women. He discovered too that women in these households had about half as much independent income as men. Unsurprisingly, access to an independent income from paid employment was associated with not having dependent children.

Relationship breakdowns make women especially vulnerable in housing terms. Only 38 per cent of women are owner-occupiers following these breakdowns, in contrast to 50 per cent of men. These figures, notes Balchin (1996), counter the common assumption that women retain the home when a relationship ends in separation or divorce. It's pertinent to add that about one in five property transactions probably stem from a broken relationship. The economic disadvantages that women suffer relative to men, both in terms of post-relationship settlements and also of pay, forces many of them into the public rented sector. Balchin adds that 'it is probable that many more women than men have to leave the marital home due to domestic violence, abuse or harassment' (1996: 243). This increases the risk that women will face the prospect of homelessness. In fact, relationship breakdown is the second most common reason given by homeless people for becoming homeless.

Black women, in particular, face grim prospects. Balchin (1996) has documented this, noting that they:

- are twice as likely as white women to suffer long periods of homelessness
- tend to be allocated the worst council properties in less popular locations
- often have to wait longer than other people to obtain the council property
- are likely to have to share amenities and have lack of security of tenure.

Minority ethnic groups

People from minority ethnic groups are often concentrated in inner-city areas in cheap, poor quality housing. Despite legislation (notably, the Race Relations Act 1976) which prohibits discrimination, black people still encounter unequal treatment from private landlords. Nor do they always fare better in the council sector. Ginsburg (1992, cited by Balchin 1996) has highlighted three kinds of discrimination here:

- relative inadequacy in the physical standards of homes in relation to the needs of black applicants. This is particularly so with regard to the number of bedrooms that are offered
- local policies, such as residency requirements and the exclusion from housing lists of co-habitees, joint families and single people, discriminate against black applicants
- 'managerial landlordism' involving racist assessment of the deserving status and respectability of applicants, erroneous assumptions about the preferred areas of residence for different ethnic groups, and about the threat of racist harassment by white people.

These and other forms of racism in the public sector pose special problems at a time when large numbers of black households have to rely on council housing because they're poor and also because they face discrimination in other housing tenures. Faced with this, many black households seek owner-occupation rather than run the risk of homelessness.

Balchin adds that within the context of housing, black people have long been victims of racist attacks. Yet racial harassment against black residents on council estates wasn't officially recognised as a problem until the 1980s. Moreover, Balchin reports that when racial harassment is investigated by local authorities, the typical solution is to transfer the black household which has suffered the problem rather than take legal action against the perpetrator. In this and other ways, it's evident that housing policy in the UK is based on the assumption that minority ethnic groups need to adapt to the existing structures that have been developed by and for white people.

Old people

In 1991, there were about ten million pensioners in Britain out of a total population of around 56 million. The number of old people living alone has increased: up from 14.2 per cent in 1981 to 15.1 per cent in 1991. Since 1945, there's been an increasing trend for older people to live either with a spouse or alone, and not with other relatives or friends. Significantly more older women than older men have been affected by this. However, there's a trend towards more and more men living alone. Many already do so, and more are likely to. There's an important planning implication here – more single homes need to be built.

In 1987, 61 per cent of households headed by old people were owner-occupied, and 80.5 per cent of these individuals lived in houses as opposed to apartments. Although women generally live longer than men, the morbidity (illness) rate among older women is typically higher than among older men. The prospect of becoming disabled increases with age. There are design messages here. The construction industry in both the private and public sectors must be mindful that some old people have functional problems, such as the inability to wash, dress, move around, go up and down stairs, and cook. Bearing in mind that most pensioners are income-poor, even if some are asset-'rich', the cost of constructing specially equipped homes or adapting existing properties must largely be borne by the community.

Actually, from the 1970s, some homes have been specifically designed for old people. Examples of initiatives include low-dependency housing (for example, well-maintained heated apartments and bungalows near shops and services), and medium-dependency housing (for example, sheltered homes). Further up the needs scale are the high-dependency homes, mainly in the form of very sheltered or extra care provision, as well as residential and nursing care. For many older people who aren't as independent as they once were, access to some form of sheltered housing is an attractive option. This is the kind of provision that typically contains a resident warden, alarm system and communal facilities, like a residents' lounge, guest rooms and laundry services.

The standard of sheltered accommodation – especially in the private sector – is generally high. However, private homes are beyond the means of old people who are poor, as are the high service charges levied in these properties. They haven't been helped by severe cuts in the supply of public sheltered housing in the 1980s and early 1990s. For the most frail and least independent old people, the only realistic option, other than a geriatric hospital bed, is to move to a residential home or a nursing home. Perhaps up to 5 per cent of people aged over 65 live in communal establishments that offer personal or nursing care. From the age of 85, however, the percentage reaches about 20 per cent.

Residential and nursing care is costly, especially in the private sector. Yet it's in the public sector that one is more likely to find special provision (for example, level or ramped access, wide doorways) for the needs of old people with disabilities. Moreover, old people are understandably concerned that they sometimes have to sell their own homes to meet the costs of care. This means they can't pass their homes on after they die to their children. In practice, though, most old people stay put, continuing to live in their own homes. This is sometimes made possible by the use of public 'staying put' schemes, which allow conversion of homes into low-dependency accommodation.

Facilities offered include the use of mobile council wardens and the distribution of dispersed alarm systems. In fact, I have an elderly neighbour who carries a personal alarm that gives him quick access to emergency services if he falls or becomes seriously ill. The 'staying put' deal is, arguably, a cheaper option for the government, and – for that reason – it might not always be in the best interests of old people.

Many old Britons are poor, and many live in homes that aren't fit for habitation. In the mid-1980s, households aged 75 and above were more likely than other groups to inhabit unfit dwellings or homes that lacked amenities. The same is almost certainly true today. The figures for 1986, reports Balchin (1996), revealed that although comprising only 10 per cent of all households, this age group occupied as much as 33 per cent of properties which lacked amenities, and 16 per cent of those that were unfit.

Housing access is linked to sex, ethnicity and age, as the above paragraphs have demonstrated. If we had more space in this book, we could extend the discussion to other important groups, notably, working-class people and people with disabilties. In both those groups, we would find significantly reduced life chances in relation to housing need and housing provision. It's also the case that the most severe form of housing need – homelessness – contains disproportionately high numbers of people from all these relatively disadvantaged groups.

Homelessness

Alongside the decline in council house construction programmes, there's been a steep rise in the number of homeless people. This problem has affected people from all ethnic groups, but black people often fare worse than

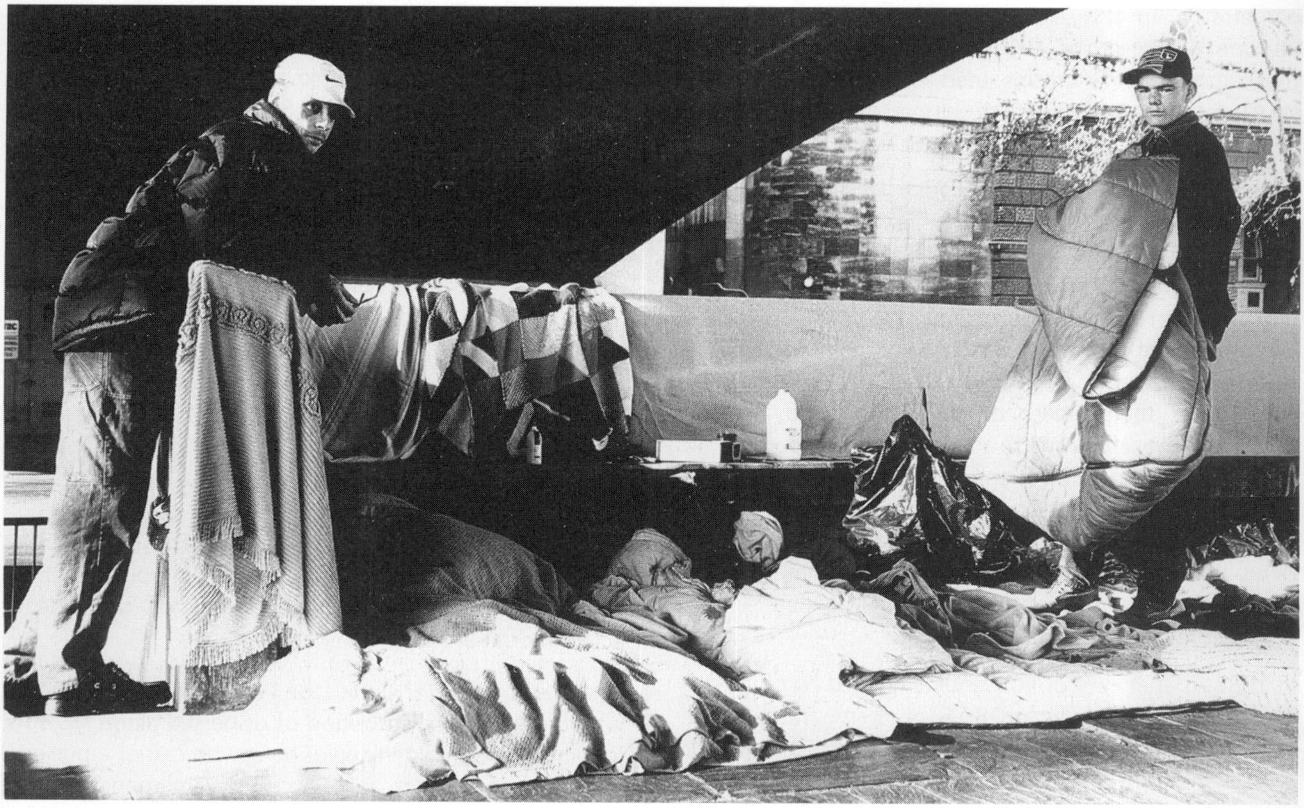

Behind the figures, disturbing in their own right, is the even starker human face of homelessness.

white people. In 1979 there were 56,750 statutory homeless households in England. The number rose to 134,190 in 1993 (equivalent to about 400,000 people). Regional disparities are evident, with a concentration of homeless households and households in temporary accommodation in Greater London. Homelessness is particularly severe in the larger cities.

Official statistics have been confined to households who are 'accepted' as homeless by councils under the terms of the Housing Act of 1985 and Housing (Scotland) Act of 1987. The statutory figures only include people who haven't 'intentionally' made themselves homeless. This definition automatically excludes anyone who has 'voluntarily' made a decision to leave home. Consequently, large numbers of homeless people (for example, over 80,000 single people in England and Wales, of whom possibly up to 20,000 are 'rough sleepers') escape official notice, and, no doubt, often official concern.

Between 1979 and 1997 the Conservative government introduced the right-to-buy programme, and forbade councils to use more than 25 per cent of the receipts thereof. They also criticised councils for retaining a number of empty dwellings. Ironically, if the councils could have spent more than the permitted 25 per cent, they might have been able to have returned these dwellings into a fit state for habitation.

The number of empty dwellings in private sector housing has been more than ten times greater than the number of void council units. A large proportion of empty private accommodation is deliberately kept off the market by owners who are anticipating upturns in the housing market. Another reason for the high void rate in this sector, especially among former rented properties, is disrepair and the difficulty of obtaining an improvement grant.

In 1989, the National Audit Office reported that it cost an estimated average of £15,500 a year to maintain a homeless family in bed and breakfast, as against only £8,200 to supply a new council home. In 1992, Shelter found that, whereas the then total cost of bed and breakfast accommodation came to £146 million each year, the first year cost of providing new council housing was just £78 million.

Perhaps you might have wondered why there seem to be a lot of homeless beggars on the streets in the 1990s. One of the reasons for this is that the provision of welfare benefits to homeless single people has been severely curtailed. Moreover, many people who sleep rough by night and beg by day have mental disorders, and have been adversely affected by the closure of psychiatric wards. Just in case you might think that the rough sleepers who sit in doorways with a dog as a companion (and as a 'hot water bottle' for cold nights) choose this way of life, the average life expectancy of a rough sleeper in Britain is around the mid-forties! The decision to take to the streets is often a desperate last resort or not a choice at all.

Homeless people can suffer from harrassment, as happened to Brian, a homeless man who, in 1996, was 'run out of town' in York. Passers-by threw broken glass and rubbish at him. Brian isn't the only street seller of the *Big Issue* – a weekly magazine sold by the homeless – to be abused and attacked. Many have been so harassed, they've found it difficult to sell their papers, leaving them virtually penniless. Sometimes they are the victims of media-generated moral panics whipped up by newspapers like the *Sun*. The *Sun* report, reproduced on page 546, had a big effect on sales. Normally, about 350,000 copies of the *Big Issue* are sold weekly by homeless and ex-homeless people who retain 45 pence of the 80 pence cover price. The profits go to the Big Issue Foundation, a charity that funds drug rehabilitation, housing advice, training and other services for homeless people. Around the time that the *Sun* report appeared, sales of the magazine dipped by at least 4,000 on the previous week.

> **OVER TO YOU**
>
> **Read pages 507–9 in Chapter 16. Then analyse the articles from the Sun on page 546. How might some of the reporting lead to the stigmatisation of Big Issue vendors as 'folk devils' and to the ignition of 'moral panics'?**

The main reference source for the data on housing referred to above is *Housing Policy*, by the urban economist, Paul Balchin (1996). This is a well-written, very accessible book, and I recommend that you consult it.

The effects of urbanism

The predominantly urban environment that most Britons (black and white) inhabit profoundly affects how they live. Their urban locality isn't just a collection of buildings, but a way of life. Urban residents don't necessarily have fewer acquaintances than their rural counterparts, but cities and towns tend to engender more superficial relationships. Individuals might know as many people as a village dweller, but urban interactions lack the warmth and intimacy of rural association. Put simply, there's less 'community' in the city than in the countryside. Brief encounters and a sense of loneliness in the midst of a crowd are often features of city life. This isn't to say that village life is a folksy idyllic existence. On the contrary, as David Lee and Howard Newby note, 'While the city emancipates the individual from the crushing conformities of Gemeinschaft, it also leaves the individual rootless and unintegrated' (1986: 48).

The city also sets in high relief the gulf between the rich and poor. Cities with social faultlines suggest an absence of community and an excess of division. The debate about this is, however, a difficult one. For cities are too complex to be defined in simple either/or terms. It's important to understand this when we investigate the claim that urbanisation and urbanism have heralded the loss of community.

QUESTIONS

1. Define these terms: industrialisation; urbanisation; urbanism; Gemeinschaft; Gesellschaft
2. Why do some sociologists seem to be anti-urban in outlook?
3. Briefly describe the main changes in the distribution of the UK population over the past 50 years.
4. What kinds of problems do women, members of minority ethnic groups and old people encounter in relation to housing access?

Loss of community?

'The community is a place to share feelings and expose one's tender inner core', says the sociologist, G. D. Suttles (1972, in Thompson 1996: 25). It's an eloquent way of putting things, and it emphasises the link between place (or locality) and meaningful identification with other individuals.

The sociologists who featured in the preceding section tend to regard industrialisation and urbanisation as damaging to community because these processes loosen social bonds. Whether they used terms like *Gemeinschaft* and *Gesellschaft* (Tonnies), or *mechanical solidarity* and *organic solidarity* (Durkheim), the community idyll was envisaged as a product of country living, and its demise was associated with the teeming city.

The notion that the peasant cultures of grandparents would be lost in an urban–industrial maelstrom was frequently asserted in early and mid-twentieth century sociological circles. But it was rarely tested empirically. Much more recently, Ulrich Beck (1994) has likened the individualising process of industrialisation to 'risky freedoms'. In his analysis of what he calls the risk society, Beck notes that industrial society produces risks which it can't control. Put another way, when society innovates, opting for an industrial as opposed to an agricultural path, it takes economic, ecological, political and social risks. For example, mass production increases the risk of pollution-related lung disorders because factories belch smoke into what was once cleaner village air.

The Big Earner

I take home pocketfuls of money every night

By Jamie Pyatt

Greedy Big Issue seller Mark Harris boasted of taking home 'pocketfuls of money every night' when an undercover Sun reporter asked him about the magazine.

Harris, who sells around 200 copies a day and also gets handouts from kind-hearted shoppers added: 'Yeah it really pays'.

Our reporter, posing as a homeless man, approached Harris, 38, after watching him work his patch in Kingston, South-West London.

The conversation between the two went like this:

Sun: I'm looking for a bit of work – does it pay to sell those?

Harris: Yeah. I do alright on it.

Sun: How do you get into it?

Harris: There's offices up town near Blackfriars, just go in there about 10 o'clock, say you're squatting or whatever, sleeping rough, and they'll give you a badge like. *(Proof you are an authorised seller)*

Sun: I'm on the dole as well. Do you have to tell them?

Harris: You're not supposed to sign on – you just give a dodgy name though, don't ya? I don't sign on because I do well enough – it ain't worth my while.

Sun: Is it worthwhile then?

Harris: I do well but I've been here four years. I've got a lot of mates up here and a lot of regulars. If you're not earning £50 a day you're doing something wrong. I sell about 200 a day.

Sun: Do you get a lot of hastle doing this?

Harris: No, the Old Bill leave you alone. If they do say something it's in one ear, out the other, just bring home a pocketful of money every night.

Just give them a name. There's nothing they can find out and even if they did, just say you've earned £20 a week. There's no way they can prove otherwise.

Sun: Do you do it every day?

Harris: Yeah, I do six days.

Sun: Apart from the rain, yeah?

Harris: Yeah, but it pays to stand out in the rain. Sometimes people see you here and they think at least you're doing something, you know what I mean?

Sun: How much are they?

Harris: We pay £35 for 100 – 35p each. We sell them for 80p and most people give you a nugget, so it's £1 a paper. I make about £110 from 100 papers, maybe £120. Some days you get a £20 drop. I do 10 a.m. to 5 p.m.

Sun: It's definitely worth it then . . .

Harris: Sure enough, it's better than being on the dole.

Bearded Harris is a well-known figure in Kingston's busy shopping precinct.

Always standing outside the mall's popular Marks & Spencer store, he woos shoppers by crying: 'Big Issue, sir? Big Issue, madam?' in a booming but polite voice.

Chat

Well-healed women often chat to him, hand over £1 for the magazine – then bin it further down the street.

We revealed our investigation to Harris on Saturday afternoon, challenging him at the bureau de change, tucking away a pile of notes. He let fly a stream of four-letter abuse and – changed his story by claiming that he made £500 a week (at the most).

Even that is £25,000 a year, tax-free.

Harris said: 'I haven't got a fancy car – I come to work by train. I do have my own flat and I pay rent and I don't ponse off the f***ing dole.

'I work hard for what I get. It's f***ing hard graft. I'd like to see you stand there for eight hours every day shouting your ass off.

'There are plenty of sellers doing better than me.'

But he stayed silent when asked if he thought shoppers bought The Big Issue from him because they believed he needed help.

I only shift 30 . . . but it's better than just begging

By Chris Pharo

Most Big Issue sellers struggle desperately to make a living – and are often lucky to make more than £20 from a days work.

Homeless Dave Jones sells around 30 copies on an average day. Dave, 32, who lives in a car park under Bristol's ice rink, said yesterday: 'I would never try and con anyone.'

We recently counted 33 people buying the magazine from him in the city centre – and Dave happily admitted it had been a good eight hours.

At the last count in 1994, there were 3,000 Big Issue vendors. They sold an average of 115 copies a week each, earning £50.

Dave, wearing ripped jeans and a torn green jacket, said: 'It's better than begging.'

'I can't understand why people would lie about how many they sell – you are going to get caught in the end.'

Dawn Smythe, 16, sold 140 copies in the two days we watched her in Bristol.

She did not try to hide the total, saying: 'I sell about 70 a day.'

'Sometimes people give me £1, which means I keep more money.'

In Birmingham, Paul Fellon, told how every morning he buys 40 magazines to sell, then uses the profit to buy 40 more.

Paul, 30, who has been homeless since the age of 15, said: 'In an average week I get about £120, but on a really good week, £140 plus.

'But there are days when you make nothing and it's straight down the soup kitchen.'

Elsewhere in the city, another vendor Gary, who likes to serenade prospective purchasers, struggles to sell just three copies.

He said: 'My singing puts some people off.'

We'll root out mickey takers

By Ian Hepburn

The Big Issue last night promised to investigate our findings on Mark Harris – and said: 'We are keen to find those who are taking the mickey.'

Spokeswoman Sally Stainton admitted she was 'astounded' by the huge sum being made by Harris.

And she added: 'We will look at this case and go back over our files. But it's difficult to keep track as our system is open.'

Sally insisted that Harris was far from being a typical Big Issue seller.

She said: 'In contrast, we have people who are incapable of selling more than five copies a day.

'They rely on us. A lot are homeless or have alcohol or drug problems. Some are Care in the Community cases. We just hope your story doesn't stop people helping those who really do need help.'

Sally said The Big Issue enabled struggling people to regain their self-respect and stability by 'making money for themselves'.

And she added: 'In a way I suppose this man is a success story.'

But successful sellers were 'expected to move on'. Sally said: 'We want people to get back on their feet, not make fortunes out of it.'

(All three articles: The *Sun*, 28 October 1995)

On a social level, the risks are many. Crime rates are generally higher in urban than in rural areas; the self – disembedded from the local support structures of the village – is prone to heightened feelings of insecurity; and individuals confront their fear of freedom. Cutting loose is risky. A community engenders a sense of security because the individual has a group to turn to in times of crisis. Communities also offer routine everyday support. But rural communities aren't the only ones. Tight-knit social bonds exist in lots of different settings, including urban enclaves. Common conviction can also create communities, as evidenced, for example, by eco-warrior settlements. Perhaps sociologists should be saying that rural environments create different rather than stronger communities.

Eco-warriors like Swampy inhabit communities of like-minded individuals who look to each other's needs and are united in common cause against environmental destruction.

OVER TO YOU

What do you think of Swampy and his eco-warrior soul-mates?

Louis Wirth makes the significant point that urban influences:

'are greater than the ratio of the urban population would indicate; for the city . . . is the controlling center of economic, political and cultural life that has drawn the most remote communities of the world into its orbit and woven diverse areas, peoples, and activities into a cosmos.'

(Wirth 1964: 60–1, first published in 1938)

As indicated, Wirth originally wrote these words in the 1930s. Think about that when grandparents and older people tell you that community life was an integral feature of the 'good old days'. Even certain sociologists have a rose-tinted sentimentality about community life in bygone times. Thus, for example, in his polemical book, *Spirit of Community*, Amitai Etzioni laments the passing of American communities, and eagerly embraces the goal of building the 'supracommunity, a community of communities – *the* American society' (1993: 160). Through what he terms *communitarianism* – the active promotion, especially through schooling, of playing down our selfish 'I' and developing our collective 'we' – Etzioni wants the celebration of self to yield to the avowal of communal responsibility.

Here comes the polemical part though. Etzioni, a distinguished sociologist with an international reputation, advocates the introduction of national service in the US as 'a major way to build up the moral tenor and sense of social responsibility among the young' (1993: 113). Granted he acknowledges that this might take place in the armed forces, the Peace Corps or other organisations. But isn't this a conservative value-judgemental position, or what!?

It's also pertinent to add that some earlier versions of community life were brutal and ugly. The clan-ridden white communities of Mississippi in the 1950s and 1960s may have forged common purpose among racist whites, but what kind of purpose?, is the obvious question. It took heroes like Dr Martin Luther King and other civil rights protesters (black and white) to make white America understand that community life is pretty difficult when people are bombing your home, threatening your children, and when congressmen spend their time trying to defeat civil rights.

In case we think that community life has been swept away with the growth of a 'new' phenomenon – urbanism – it's important to emphasise that the only thing 'new' here is the present variety of urban forms. For great cities existed in pre-industrial times. It's interesting to note Simmel's (1948) point that the ancient *polis* (Greek for city) seems to have had a small town character in terms of the cohesion of its inhabitants. Simmel adds that this cohesion could be enforced by political and military authorities.

'It is pretty difficult to like some people. Like is sentimental and it is pretty difficult to like someone bombing your home; it is pretty difficult to like somebody threatening your children; it is difficult to like congressmen who spend all of their time trying to defeat civil rights. But Jesus says love them, and love is greater than like.'

(Martin Luther King, in King 1985: 37)

OVER TO YOU

Select a pre-industrial city (for example, ancient Rome or Athens), research its essential characteristics, and compare and contrast these with an industrial city (for example, nineteenth-century Manchester or Leeds).

Besides its neglect of alternative community styles and pre-industrial urbanism, the 'standard' portrayal of the loss of community thesis fails to take due account of the human capacity to build decent communities in all kinds of physical locality. While the bulldozing of working-class terraced houses in the 1950s and their replacement with dreary high-rise flats might have driven certain types of community off the geographical and social map, we mustn't assume that other forms of meaningful association haven't emerged. Much more research is needed here. That's why I applaud the pioneering work of the photo-journalist and sociologist, Camilo Vergara, who has engaged 'an uninterrupted dialogue with poor *communities*, their residents, and the scholars who study them' (1997: xii, my italics).

In the midst of the stark devastation of American inner cities over the last 30 years, Vergara encountered a young maintenance man in Chicago's Lawndale who asked him not to use his photos of the neighbourhood 'against his "people"' (1997: 8). In New York, he was criticised for taking photos of all the dirty spots, and in Detroit he was repeatedly asked not to make the city look ugly. One of his most moving meetings was with a group of older women, members of the local residents' council, in Altgeld Gardens – a Chicago housing project (the equivalent of council homes) in the city's poorest neighbourhood. They told Vergara to tell about the good things in their community. These women had a sense of common pride that looked beyond the drab barrack-like buildings, boarded up flats, and broken playgrounds of their physical surroundings.

Similarly, the sociologist, Seán Damer (1990), found a masculine community spirit – some of it oppressive, some of it just – at the beginning of the nineteenth century in the tenement slums of Glasgow. Says Damer:

'The dominant version of this culture was definitely *macho*, brutally hard-drinking, aggressive with undertones of real violence, massively exploitative of women and children, unhealthy to a degree, disgustingly sectarian, introverted – and yet at the same time astonishingly democratic, friendly, witty, well-read, internationally aware and politically conscious.'

(Damer 1990: 102)

Less visible, Damer also highlights the world of Glasgow women. Against terrible odds, they worked hard in both waged and household labour, creating the circumstances at home and in the community that allowed their men to go to football matches and discuss politics over pints of strong beer in the pub.

In a powerful critique of Wirth's representation of the city as a prototype of American mass society, Herbert J. Gans argues that 'the conclusions derived from a study of the inner city cannot be generalized to the entire urban area' (1991; in Kasinitz 1995: 173). Gans also contends that even if the dire consequences of urbanism lamented by Wirth do occur – and there's no conclusive proof that they do or don't – many urban inhabitants are protected from such problems by cultural patterns they either brought to the city or developed by living there.

A good example of this, in a British context, is the vibrant community life of Bangladeshi people in the Brick Lane area of London's East End. The strong family and neighbourhood ties that prevail here reflect the customs of Bangladesh and the solidarity that's engendered by having to confront poverty and racism on a daily basis.

It's very easy to slip into the bad habit of treating poor urban neighbourhoods as suffering from an absence of community and a prevalence of social dislocation. There's a marked tendency here to view any departure from the high-water mark of assumed normality as deviant and disturbing. Yet, seen from the inside, poor people are often adept at defining and building their own forms of community life. Thus, for example, in his famous study of the Addams area – one of the oldest Chicago slums – in the 1960s, Gerald D. Suttles commented that for someone first entering the area, the most striking thing was its street life:

'On the streets, age, sex, ethnic, and territorial groups share boundaries that open them to mutual inspection, thus giving the occasion for transient interaction between groups, for gossip, and for interpretive observation . . . Street life is especially active in the afternoon after school or work. The front steps are crowded with old people chatting back and forth between households while some occasionally bring out chairs when sitting space gets scarce.'

(Suttles 1968: 73–4)

Of course, we're not suggesting that all low-income localities exhibit a thriving community spirit. When poor people physically distance themselves from criminal environments by living behind reinforced doors, bars and high fences, they lead isolated lives. In these localities, burglaries, drug-dealing and other crimes keep them indoors, or force them to spend their low incomes on taxis in order to minimise the risk of being mugged when they do leave their homes. It's also the case that some building designs, like the concrete tower blocks of the 1960s, make it physically difficult for residents to engage in community activities.

Physical and social dimensions are both important when one considers the absence or presence of community. However, in the final analysis, we give more weight to human factors. Consider, for example, two physically similar environments: bleak high-rise buildings, crumbling plaster in the entrance hall, broken lifts, damp flats, and not a police officer in sight. On the one estate, drug dealers have moved in, and among those residents who can 'afford' to buy crack, many do. On the other estate, a residents' lobby group have run the drug dealers out, have persuaded the local police to provide high visibility law enforcement, and have set up a building improvement scheme which pools the skills of the tenants.

It would be a mistake to imagine that urbanism is synonymous with the loss of community. Towns and cities vary considerably, not only between each other but also within different parts of the same urban area. Some cityscapes are full of defences against an imagined or a real intruder. Metal wired windows, entrance phones and other signs of physical hardening proclaim a stark message: keep out. Yet I live in a city neighbourhood where front doors aren't always locked, where people brew tea on a communal green, and neighbours regularly check on the well-being of the sick and old. Here we have a micro-environment which is conducive to community life even though other parts of the city might not be. And this is 1998, not some rosy-tinted bygone age.

A short car ride, however, takes me to a 'postcard-pretty' Dales village where behind the polished red letterboxes, and brightly painted tourist shops, many old people live in poverty – neglected by some of their better-off neighbours. There's a danger in imagining that rural England is the setting of warm beer and cricket on the village green. This cosmetic image of 'merrie England' is just that, a fabrication. It hides the problems that rural inhabitants face, not just the poverty of many of the old, but the dashed hopes of young people who can't find a job, and the desperate loneliness that drives so many farmers to suicide.

So don't put the loss of community debate into a rural–urban continuum, where its presence or absence becomes grounded in rural or urban localities. The issue is more complex. A community is more than a physical environment. It's essentially a human thing. This cautions us against adopting an over-deterministic ecological view of things. Our ecology (habitat) is important, but architects who imagine they can create human communities just by making the built environment a collection of 'garden cities' and 'urban villages' are mistaken. People make communities, not bricks and mortar. It helps if the building design facilitates meaningful interaction between neighbours, but you can't bring a horse to water if it doesn't want to drink.

OVER TO YOU

Design a brand new council estate whose architecture <u>might</u> encourage community relations between the residents. Use sociological evidence and arguments to justify your proposals. Why do you think we've underlined might?

The 'recovery' of a community that was allegedly corrupted by the ravages of urbanism is a thankless quest.

Even if 'merrie old England' really did exist, how would it be possible to restore such a setting in the twenty-first century? Communities come and go, take many different forms, and exist because some people collectively embrace core values. That they *choose* to do so is the key to community spirit, not because communitarian sociologists like Etzioni (1993) say that schools *ought* to instil community values. Etzioni is a classic 'loss of community' theorist who believes that, 'If the moral infrastructure of our communities is to be *restored* [my italics], schools will have to step in where the family, neighbourhoods and religious institutions have been failing' (1993: 89). His emphasis, however, on restoring an assumed better past is in our opinion rather fanciful and, frankly, quite conservative.

This isn't to say that we shouldn't be trying to build a community spirit in our towns and cities. The sociologist, Michael Young, is all in favour of new owner-occupiers on a hillside of inner-city Bradford signing a 'mutual aid clause' which would oblige them to offer their services to a housing association 'for the benefit of other local residents and, more particularly, for the support of elderly, disabled and sick people and young children' (The *Guardian*, 18 September 1996, page 6). Young applauds the fact that tenants for new housing in the area have been chosen on the basis of need, but laments the fact that families on housing waiting lists have in most instances been rehoused on their own, instead of with their kin and friends. Nevertheless, the scheme is intended to encourage the residents to lend a helping hand to the rest of the *community*. For therein lies the heart of community life – a 'one for all and all for one' spirit.

QUESTIONS

1 In what ways might urbanism make it difficult for communities to flourish?
2 How might a community thrive in an urban environment?
3 Has the dawn of the new millennium witnessed the loss of community?

LOSS OF COMMUNITY THESIS

FOR

+ Urbanism has replaced the close emotional ties of village life with the impersonal calculating relations that prevail in cities. Georg Simmel's argument that this has led to a loss of community is convincing. City life lacks the local intimacy of the rural community because nobody can possibly get to know all the inhabitants of a metropolis.
+ The unsettled nature of inner city areas, with the constant coming and going of new waves of migrants, make it hard for community life to flourish. This point was made by the Chicago School theorists who highlighted the instability of the city of Chicago in the first half of the twentieth century (see pages 494–7 in Chapter 16, and pages 555–6 of this chapter).
+ Urban decay, spiralling crime, and inner-city fortification make it hard for community life to take root, let alone flourish. Consider, for example, an environment where the few remaining shops have bullet-proof glass between proprietor and customer, vacant car parks are overgrown with weeds and shrubs, old steelworks are boarded up, and wild dogs roam the streets. This kind of setting doesn't make for community.

AGAINST

– The 'rural–community'/'urban–loss of community' dichotomy is over-simplistic. Communities flourish in a wide range of settings which span the rural–urban continuum. Not all country villages exhibit strong community ties. If that were so, the rick-burning rebellion of English agricultural workers in the eighteenth century wouldn't have happened. Nor, for that matter, would television series like *EastEnders*, which dramatise urban community life, have any resonance with viewers.

– Communities are very diverse. They don't therefore easily fit into predefined lists of what a community is supposed to be like. It's important, in that context, not to suppose that rose-tinted memories of folksy, apple-pie, rural communities – if they ever existed – are the only form that communities take. Some communities are traditional, like that of the Hasidic orthodox Jews in North London. Other communities are radical. Consider, for example, the tree-dwelling new age communities in various parts of the UK.

– In the most extreme conditions of urban poverty, there are examples of community life. People don't always react to environments in predictable ways. Faced with the same objective conditions of inner-city squalor, some people barricade themselves from drug-dealers into private, isolated existences, while others build strong community links and reclaim their neighbourhoods from those who would control them. It's important to recognise that urban environments are social mosaics, not homogenous slabs. Variety, not sameness, is the name of the game.

> ***EXAM TIP***
>
> Don't confuse a critique of the loss of community thesis with a value-judgement about whether community life is desirable or not. The issue isn't about what's good or bad. It's to do with whether or not communities are diminishing.

Environmental sociology

Our environment consists of the surroundings we inhabit. One way of looking at the environment is to view it as a determining factor. An earthquake region, for example, determines the design and construction of buildings. Paper houses in earthquake-prone Japan make good sense when the earth starts to shake and you're indoors! In Ancient Greece, the mountainous terrain and sun-scorched grass didn't make for good pasture land, so Greeks got their milk from mountain goats, not cows, and their soldiers generally fought battles on foot rather than horseback. Among the Apache people of the nineteenth century, the rugged lands they roamed made co-operation among households essential for protection and obtaining food. Says Donald E. Worcester, 'It became customary, therefore, to share labors and their fruits with neighbors and related households, so that all fared equally' (1992: xiv).

The notion that geography shapes human lives is compelling. But let's not forget that people also influence their environment. The built environment of museums, concert halls, places of worship, schools and hospitals isn't just a response to earth tremors. The Sistine Chapel, whose ceiling was painted by the Renaissance genius, Michelangelo, is a work of art as well as a building whose structure conforms to the contours of the land. It has the imprint of human genius on its plaster. There's also a social environment of institutions which form the behavioural network within which we live our lives and relate to other people. Much of this environment isn't visible in the way a mountain or a building is. Instead, it's a symbolic setting of language, gestures and other signs. Thus, for example, a disapproving gesture by a teacher which is read and interpreted by the students forms part of the social environment of a classroom.

Although there are different types of environment, it's true to say that environmental sociology tends to focus on the relationship between people and nature. Keeping with that convention, this section mainly addresses the interplay between us and the physical world. However, one of the sub-sections – ecology – returns the discussion to the built and social environments.

Sociology regards the natural environment as both a determining and a determined thing. It shapes people's lives and people shape it. Marx made this point when he wrote:

> 'the nature that preceded human history, is not by any means the nature in which Feuerbach [a nineteenth century philosopher] lives, it is nature which today no longer exists anywhere (except perhaps on a few Australian coral islands of recent origin) and which, therefore, does not exist for Feuerbach either.'
>
> (cited by Maguire 1996, in Lash *et al.* 1996: 185)

However, were Marx alive today he might find it hard to find an 'unspoilt by human hand' Australian coral island, given the extensive environmental degradation which besets our planet.

> ***EXAM TIP***
>
> Convey to the examiner an understanding of both the *shaping* and *human shaped* aspects of the environment. You might add that the relative degree of this varies. For example, a volcano shapes a bay without much human intervention, whereas you choose a wallpaper design without consulting a vulcanologist.

Marx adopted what is known as a *modernist* approach to the environment. Modernism is the dominant outlook that characterised European intellectual thought during the period known as the Enlightenment. Also called the Age of Reason, this period roughly stretches from 1650 to 1800. Modernism embraces reason and rejects superstition. It elevates science above magic, believing in material things rather than ghosts. Consult pages 118–20 in Chapter 6, for more about modernism.

The modernist view of nature

Much of the academic discourse about our natural surroundings is couched in the language of science. This has led to a view of environment as a material thing. The materialist presentation is very much in line with the *modernist* thinking that sprung from the age of the Enlightenment. No longer would natural catastrophes be attributed to gods, demons and magic, but would be transformed into calculable risks that science would wrestle with and eventually overcome. Society and nature are thus pitted against each other in a battle for supremacy. The confrontation presumes that humankind will eventually win if it lets scientists and their political 'masters' (most are male) use expert knowledge to overcome nature. 'Ordinary' people aren't invited to participate in the discourse, but are expected to place their trust in the 'experts.'

The main distinction between pre-modern and modern perspectives on the environment is helpfully presented in diagrammatic form (below) by Peter Dickens.

The modernists see nature 'out there' – a powerful physical force to be reckoned with and somehow tamed. Marx believed that nature, harnessed to the needs of humankind, would lead to freedom. While acknowledging that people and nature interact with each other, he tended to see the two as fairly distinct. Marx may have referred to nature as 'man's [*sic*] inorganic body' (cited by Dickens 1996: 204), but he also wanted 'man' to conquer nature. However, nature as the servant of capitalism compromised human dignity. Capitalist-owned coal mines and factories created appalling employment conditions, and produced fuels that belched poisonous smoke into the atmosphere. By damaging the environment from which they extracted coal and other natural products, the capitalists were, to coin a marxist phrase (and here a literal one), digging their own graves. Commenting on the destructive impact of capitalistic modes of land use, Marx wrote:

'All progress in capitalistic agriculture is a progress in the art, not only of robbing the labourer, but of robbing the soil; all progress in increasing the fertility of the soil for a given time, is a progress towards ruining the lasting sources of that fertility.'

(Marx, quoted by Dickens 1996: 30)

Against Marx's argument, one might substitute 'industrialisation' for 'capitalism'. For industrialisation, whether it occurs in capitalist or communist countries, has accelerated the build-up of greenhouse gases on earth. These gases, especially carbon dioxide, reflect infra-radiation from the planet that would otherwise pass beyond the atmosphere back to earth, thereby causing global warming. It's the people from the industrialised nations, particularly, the former Soviet Union and the present US, who bear much of the responsibility for global warming. Both of these countries operated a massive military–industrial complex which has maximised output and minimised preservation of the environment. Outrage over irreparable environmental damage was one of the main catalysts of the political upheaval in the late 1980s that finally led to the break-up of the old Soviet empire.

As the functionalist sociologist, Neil J. Smelser – who worked with Parsons – observes, the destruction of the natural world is a universal threat:

'because it involves the fate of the entire human species in relation to the sustaining environment – no respecter of nation, class, or group in its ultimate consequences.'

(Smelser 1997: 81)

Smelser also notes that:

'The ravaging of the earth, its oceans, and its atmosphere is not new, but all signs point to the fact that it is increasingly massive and in the end constitutes the most important threat to humanity.'

(Smelser 1997: 80)

Pre-modern societies

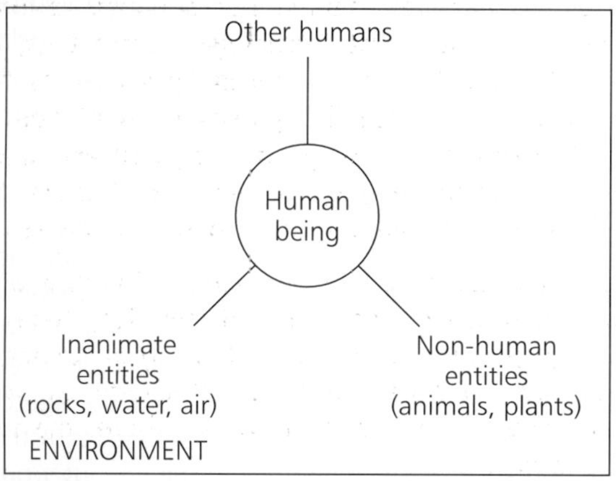

Human beings in pre-modern societies do not usually distinguish between 'society' and 'nature'. For them there is only one world, containing humans, inanimate entities and non-human entities. Knowledge of that world is gained through dwelling in it and interacting with it.

Modern societies

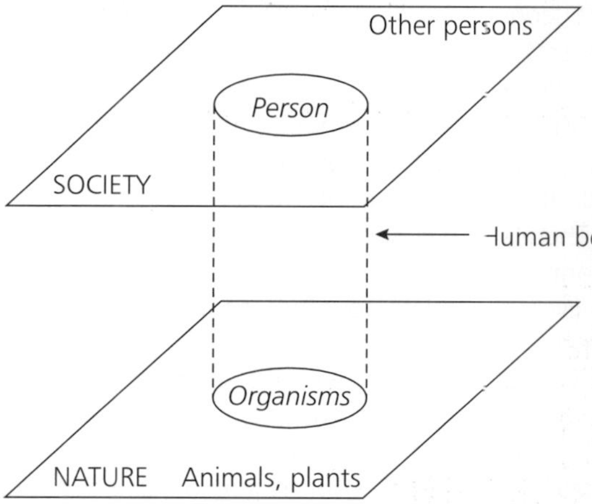

Human beings in modern societies typically distinguish between *two* worlds: human society on the one hand and 'nature' on the other. Yet in practice people are, as *human organisms*, part of both these worlds. In modern societies humans depend less on knowledge gained through direct interaction with the environment and much more on abstract knowledge gained through stepping out of the environment.

(Dickens 1996: 6)

Concepts of people and environment (after Ingold 1990)

Far from being the stereotypical 'stick-in-the-mud' that functionalists, according to their critics, are supposed to be, Smelser speaks approvingly of 'the ennoblement of human control of human affairs', noting that 'only human beings can set right the balance between humanity and nature, just as human beings have been the agents who have threatened to ruin it' (1997: 81).

Protestations against environmental degradation are typically expressed in the scientific discourse of modernism, where tonnage and cubic centimetres prevail. This is especially so in relation to what Joni Seager describes as 'The largest single output of all manufacturing industry [which] is pollution' (1995: 116). This has the advantage of cutting across political debates to provide objective measurements. The millions of tons of industrial waste – much of it toxic – that is blighting our planet doesn't cause less damage if it happens to issue from a communist or a capitalist factory. The evidence for this assertion is clearly revealed in the chart below. However, it's the people from the so-called 'Third World' nations who are most immediately affected by that destructive process.

The response of the business community to these problems is that nature is largely a manageable system which can be manipulated by rational human intervention. The assumption here is that human beings can convert nature into things they want. Moreover, business people and the scientific advisers whom they employ, point to the fact that heavy industry is in decline and that the growth of the service sector and new technologies signal a less polluted future. But things aren't so simple and clear-cut. Car ownership rates, for example, have significantly increased, and it doesn't much matter if noxious gases spout out of a factory chimney or a car exhaust.

Current annual carbon dioxide release per person

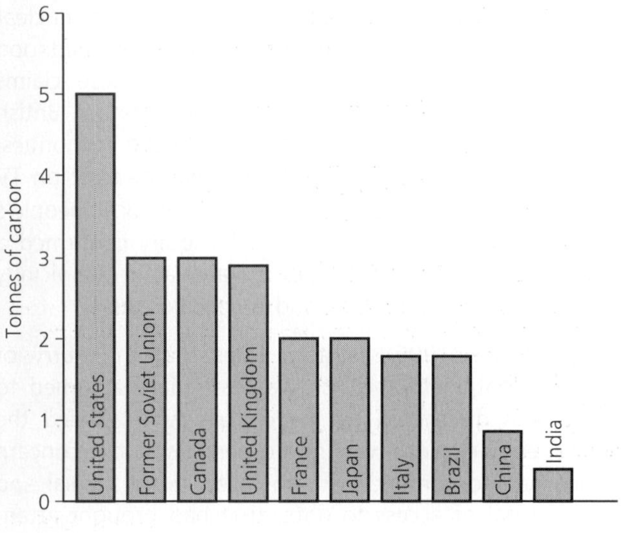

(Watkins 1995: 156, using figures from Friends of the Earth)

Today, 19 million Britons breathe air more polluted than World Health Organisation standards permit – mainly caused by gases from car exhausts. One exhaust pollutant – particulates – alone kills 10,000 people in the UK each year. If the government is serious about its intention to reduce dependence on the private car, it needs to invest heavily in public transport, reduce bus and train fares, and cut the need to use cars for short trips (by, for example, curbing the growth of out-of-town shopping centres).

While it's important and necessary to work towards a cleaner future, we must be mindful of the fact that industry has left a grim legacy. As Vergara (1997) observes, when factories are razed, they leave a treacherous labyrinth of subterranean tunnels under railway tracks, parking docks, and roads and other paved surfaces. Polluted fluids – toxic cocktails of oil, rainwater, solvents and other chemicals used during their many years of industrial operation – collect in open sewer holes. These noxious substances don't disappear overnight. Nor do the 300 million metric tons of hazardous waste produced each year by the world's more prosperous nations. If the waste is dumped in landfills and storage pits, poisons leak into drinking water and residential areas. If it's burned, a toxic residue remains. If it's dumped at sea (now banned by most countries), it harms marine mammal and fish life. Industry has unleashed a monster whose death cries are still being felt.

In capitalist and communist (former and current) countries, there are obvious pressures on government scientists not to produce evidence which might implicate their political 'masters' in relation to environmental problems. Even the scientists who do tell the truth as best they can don't always deliver. This argument is forcibly presented by the German sociologist, Ulrich Beck, who claims that the hazards produced by society can't be contained within scientific systems of prediction and control. Faced with a range of biological and nuclear dangers, a self-endangering 'modern' world, it won't do, says Beck, to leave things to the 'experts'. Continues Beck:

> 'In the nineteenth century, privileges of rank and religious world views were being demystified; today the same is happening to the understanding of science and technology in the classical industrial society, as well as to the modes of existence in work, leisure, the family and sexuality.'
>
> (Beck 1994: 10)

Beck's work displays a pull towards 'sensible' modernist thinking, as well as a taste for 'moderate' forms of what is known as *postmodernist* thought. Postmodernism is a critique more than an outlook. It debunks the claims of the Enlightenment and argues that science is just another ideology. What does it offer instead? That's a tough one. I think its offering is similar to the argument put forward by a famous marxist, Antonio Gramsci, who said that everyone is an intellectual. Put as simply as I can, postmodernism says that no single body of knowledge is privileged. Everything is open to challenge. There's no single truth, but there are claims to truth. The roots of postmodernism go back to the 1800s, but it's especially associated with the late twentieth century. Consult pages 120–3 in Chapter 6 for a simplified critique of postmodernism.

Beck, himself, has no truck with either the sociologists 'who now cling more tightly than ever to the Enlightenment', nor with the sociologists 'who would wash the whole project of modernity . . . down the river' (1994: 10). In other words, Beck is warning us to be wary of extremists in either camp. Instead of looking for a 'post', a beyond, that eludes description, Beck believes that a new form of modernity is taking shape: 'we are witnessing not the end but the beginning of modernity – that is, of a modernity beyond its classical industrial design' (1994: 10).

Even so, Beck's natural scepticism does seem to echo a 'postmodernist' antipathy towards scientific claims.

The postmodernist view of nature

Postmodernists, as the name implies, look beyond the modern outlook. They're mistrusting of the modernist claim that human progress depends on the rational, scientific control of nature. Instead, they argue that nature is what people define it to be, which is, of course, a very social constructionist outlook. While, for example, a meteorologist can describe low and high pressure air in technical terms, for you and me that translates into rainy and sunny weather. We have our own interpretations of this. If I'm a farmer, low pressure might mean good crop yields this year. If you're a tourist, high pressure might mean sipping a coffee and munching a croissant under the parasol of a Parisian pavement cafe. Both experiences are joyful for us in different ways.

According to postmodernists, there's no nature as such, only natures. These natures are socially constructed. When, for example, scientists refer to holes in the ozone layer, they're referring to socially perceived crises. There is no objective definition of global crisis. It amounts to what people say this is. Green organisations like Greenpeace say there is a crisis, scientific journals disagree about this, and capitalist company bosses who dump waste in rivers don't mind as long as the problem isn't in their back yard. Some politicians in poor countries even regard industry – for all its problems – as a way out of poverty. So how do postmodernists respond to different claims?

They urge us not to privilege the ideas of experts who think they know better than us. After all, experts don't always live up to their claims of managing and controlling nature. In fact, some scientists are responsible for the physical dangers and economic problems that emanate from technology itself. The technology that produces the greenhouse effect, for example, leads, in turn, to a heightened tornado risk. At least nine insurance companies have gone bankrupt because of hurricane damage claims in Florida and Hawaii. Indeed, new house owners in Hawaii can no longer obtain insurance cover. We're talking serious environmental hazards here, not minor side-effects!

Scientific expertise is increasingly contested by the public. Consider, for example, the scientific advice provided by the previous Conservative government on the risks of contracting BSE from meat products. Some parents didn't trust the government's attempt to downplay the risks. The public furore over the former Conservative government's handling of the BSE crisis was a factor in their downfall in the General Election of 1997. Sounding very marxist in tone, Beck writes: 'Politics is becoming a publicly financed advertising agency for the sunny sides of a development it does not know' (1994: 224). In other words, 'Don't trust politicians. They make even the bad things seem good. They're purveyors of ideology, not truth.'

OVER TO YOU

Can politicians be trusted? How might one give a sociological as opposed to a 'common-sense' answer to this question?

Public mistrust of politicians and their scientific servants isn't, of course, a new phenomenon. In the 1970s, for example, people who lived near the Sellafield nuclear reprocessing complex claimed that excessive childhood leukaemias were occurring in the area. These claims endured, despite official denials by the operators, British Nuclear Fuels, and even by the public health authorities. Eventually a national documentary was broadcast on TV in 1983 which essentially supported the local people's observations. A subsequent official enquiry confirmed a persistent cluster of childhood leukaemias in the vicinity of the plant, but failed to find a specific cause.

Brian Wynne (1996) astutely notes that the flurry of expert attention to this risk was essentially assumed to have been discovered by the experts who advised the official enquiry. Yet it was non-expert, lay public concern which had to contend with so-called expert denial and even refusal of access to data, that had brought attention to the issue in the first instance. In this way, as

Wynne writes, 'It is easy to see how non-institutional forms of experience and knowledge come to be systematically deleted from recognition' (1996: 49). Wynne strongly rebuts the 'cultural dupe' notion of the place of ordinary folk in relation to expert claims. There are, he suggests, deep public concerns about the trustworthiness of the 'I know best' expert. Alternative knowledge, especially the kind possessed by people who work with nature rather than study it from afar, is sometimes more reliable.

There are strong echoes here of the postmodernist distrust of claims to certainty, especially when such avowals come from science and industry. In that context, John A. Hannigan has noted how organisations like Greenpeace have 'depicted whalers, nuclear operators, forestry companies and others as evil personified' (1997: 180). The upshot, says Hannigan, is a weakening of confidence in the scientific community, a sense that scientists aren't telling it like it is to the public-at-large. This unmasking of the experts isn't just about differences of opinion or politics. On numerous occasions the scientists have been floored by their own evidence. Nuclear power, toxic waste incinerators, herbicides and plastics – all products of scientific technology – have been demonstrated to have damaging effects on the planet. Now the film producers are clamouring to make this point, as, for example, *Outbreak* demonstrates.

Although postmodernists are sometimes portrayed by their critics as opting out of real environmental issues, this stereotype misjudges (or pre-judges) the postmodernist position. Yes, there are some postmodernists who push the hyper-real too far, just as there are modernists who exaggerate the explanatory powers of science. But even certain postmodernists make a distinction between rocks and people! Thus, for example, the postmodernist sociologist, Jean Baudrillard, is in no doubt that geological events carried their own momentum long before humans walked the planet:

'The very idea of the millions and hundreds of millions of years that were needed peacefully to ravage the surface of the earth here is a perverse one, since it brings with it an awareness of signs originating, long before man [*sic*] appeared, in a sort of pact of wear and erosion struck between the elements.'

(Baudrillard 1993: 3)

Baudrillard shows his postmodernist hand though when he adds that magnificent geological formations like Monument Valley in Arizona cease to be natural when they 'become, like all that is cultivated – like all culture – natural parks' (1993: 4). In this way, we see that Baudrillard, the postmodernist, recognises that nature has its physical, scientific and its social, cultural side. Setting the one against the other is disingenuous. Baudrillard also engages the issue of the built environment wherein people use natural materials to create cultural objects: motorways; cinemas; soaring skyscrapers. Baudrillard is comfortable in both natural and people-made environments: 'My hunting grounds are the deserts, the mountains, Los Angeles, the freeways, the Safeways, the ghost towns, or the downtowns' (1993: 63).

The sociology of the environment, then, goes beyond the interaction between people and geology. It's also about the impact of the built environment on human social behaviour. A key concept here is that of *ecology*.

Ecology

The urban ecologists of the Chicago School of Sociology (their most notable exponent being Robert Park) borrowed heavily from plant biology. Just as plants are affected by their natural environment, so are people affected by the built environment in which they live. Turning the city in which they studied into a giant sociological 'laboratory', the Chicago sociologists noted that it formed a pattern of concentric semi-circles (see page 495 in Chapter 16), each of which had its distinctive lifestyles. Incidentally, you geographers might have guessed that Chicago's areas could never form literal concentric circles, because part of it borders on massive Lake Michigan.

While social constructionists claim that their heritage springs from the University of Chicago, the early Chicago sociologists also used quantitative methods. Robert Park, for example, while recognising the crucial significance of the meanings of social action, also took account of quantitative factors like land values, street car transfers (people hopping on and off trams), and the volume of traffic at intersections. That said, Park was outspoken about number-crunching for the sake of it. He strongly objected to sociologists starting on a research problem with a 'let's collect loads of statistical data' approach.

His colleague, Ernest Burgess, though, had a keen interest in the statistical relationship between city environments and social behaviours. One of the first courses Burgess taught at the University of Chicago was social pathology. His students were required to prepare maps that pinpointed the geographical distribution of social problems throughout Chicago. Burgess's ecological approach eventually led (in 1925) to the famous theory of concentric zones referred to above. Said Burgess:

'In every course I gave I am sure there were one or two students who made maps. I think the maps of juvenile delinquency were the first ones undertaken. They were followed by maps showing the distribution of motion picture houses. Then came maps showing the distribution of patrons of the public dance halls ... We were very impressed with the great differences between the various neighbourhoods in the city, and one of the earliest goals was to try to find a pattern to this patchwork of differences, and to "make sense of it". Mapping was the method which seemed most appropriate for such a problem.'

(Burgess 1964, cited by Bulmer 1986: 154–5)

The spot maps of urban ecologists like Burgess identified zones and associated human social behaviours. The downtown area was full of stores, theatres, hotels, banks and skyscraper corporations. People went there to shop, to have fun, and to work in white-collar settings. The next layer of the onion was characterised by slums, 'flophouses' (cheap lodging houses), pawnbrokers, cheap truckstop cafes and heavy industry. The people in this part of town lived in an environment of urban decay and acute material deprivation. Outside this was a ring of middle-class suburbs – the residential area of the people who worked in the downtown area but who lived in spacious, comfortable houses.

Much of the work of the early urban ecologists focuses on the relationship between 'dodgy' areas and social 'pathology'. Starting with seven foot long blank maps of Chicago, the sociologists plotted clusters of particular behaviours, for example, areas with high levels of alcoholism and divorce. Personal 'pathologies' were subsequently linked to different degrees of urban disorganisation. So committed were the urban ecologists to the spot map, it was apparently difficult for a Chicago sociologist in the 1920s to obtain a Ph.D. without doing one.

The measurement of ecological effects was integral to the Chicago School. Thus, male juvenile delinquency rates were calculated within zones radiating from the Loop – Chicago's central train route. As one moved from the centre outwards, a declining crime rate became apparent. The Chicago sociologists had discovered a phenomenon that holds true today in many cities. Young males from the slum neighbourhood are more likely than their counterparts in the outlying district to have run-ins with the police. By contrast, residents of prosperous suburbs are often involved in the kind of activities that keep crime at bay – forming neighbourhood watch groups, sending their children to pre-school groups, and earning a living from well-paid jobs rather than committing crimes.

The argument here is a compelling one: deviant and conforming behaviours are importantly linked to the degree of exposure people have to deviant and conforming cultures – to *differential association*. This isn't to say that people who live on the 'wrong side of town' are bound to become criminals and that those who don't will definitely become upright citizens. The position of the urban ecology theorists is a qualified one. Likelihoods and tendencies, rather than certainties and dispositions, are all that can be ventured.

> **EXAM TIP**
>
> Beginning students of sociology have a tendency to over-state sociological claims. The best that sociology can do is to make statements of *probability*. Thus, for example, the chances of you joining a gang are greater if you live in South Central LA than if you live in Beverley Hills.

It's also significant that the Chicago sociologists complemented spot maps with qualitative methods. This made it possible to check statistical patterns against observation and the content analysis of documents.

The Chicago School sociologists weren't just interested in the study of social 'problems', they also wanted to help solve them. From their work emerged the Chicago Area Project, in which sociologists worked with community volunteers to tackle delinquency. Park and Burgess regarded the community, with its strong primary group relations – blood, kin and kin-like friendship – as the main defence against the assumed social crises of urbanism. But they didn't regard the community as some defrosted version of the past. On the contrary, Park and Burgess envisaged communities as processes – as social networks that grow and adapt, but still retain an affinity to collective loyalties. They took sociology out of its ivory tower and placed it right at the centre of the community. In that manner, they turned the city of Chicago into an extension of the lecture hall.

Even today, we can see the legacy of Chicago School thinking behind inner-city youth programmes that offer tantalising alternatives to the excitement of crime. A recent example of this is a homelessness programme led by the African–American, Ted Hayes, in Compton, South-Central Los Angeles. In 1997, Hayes brought some Compton youths to Lord's Cricket Ground in London. Says Hayes of cricket:

'It's the discipline the game demands. It's about good manners and gentlemanship in an intense environment – and young people in our inner cities are in very intense environments.'

(cited in the *Guardian*, 17 May 1997, page 4)

Hayes believes these are skills that might save his Compton boys (who play cricket in LA) from death on the mean streets back home.

While not wanting to knock the good intentions, and – in some cases – the good effects, of programmes like

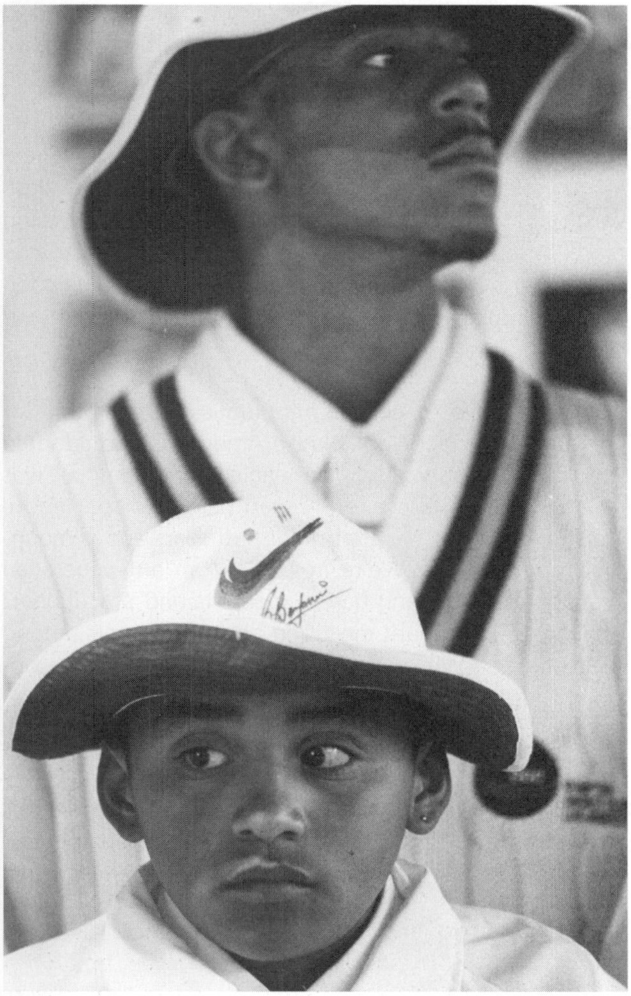

Compton boys at Lord's Cricket Ground

this, it makes good social scientific sense to supplement them with training and employment initiatives. Cricket and other sports, together with the prospect of a decent job, offer disaffected young people hope. Scott H. Decker and Barrik Van Winkle recently conducted a three-year study of 99 active gang members (most of whom were male African–Americans) in St Louis.

Decker and Van Winkle's study is up-to-date and illuminating. The study also provides implicit support for Robert K. Merton's argument that material ambition plus no job make for an explosive mix (see the section on *Power, policy and conflict in the city* on page 559). Decker and Van Winkle found that the decline of the St Louis industrial base and the resultant unemployment hit some neighbourhoods badly. The loss of steady, well-paid work in this rust-belt, mid-western city had an ecological impact. It led to social dislocation from the mainstream, and created conditions that led to the growth of gangs. When people, especially young males, don't have a job or one to look forward to, they're more inclined to hang out, sell drugs, and use violence in the company of their peers.

In such settings, the deviant culture of the neighbourhood exerts a powerful effect on young people. Most young people in a neighbourhood with an active gang, note Decker and Van Winkle:

'could expect to be "tested" to determine if they were interested in or worthy of joining the gang. Many would decide that joining the gang was their most prudent choice, especially in those neighborhoods plagued by the highest levels of violence.'

(Decker and Van Winkle 1997: 106)

Once in the gang, members who left the (neighbour)-hood were still expected to 'hang' with their 'homies'. Said 16-year-old Crenshaw, a male member of the St Louis Mob Gangster Blood: 'You don't necessarily have to stay in the hood as long as you be over there hangin' with the boys' (Decker and Van Winkle 1997: 108).

Urban ecology theory, with its origins in the criminological interests of the Chicago School sociologists, has largely focused on the relationship between 'bad' neighbourhoods and deviant norms. However, in a more general sense, to cite Barry Commoner (from Bronislaw Szerszynski, in Lash *et al.* 1996: 112), ecology is based on four 'laws':

- 'Everything is connected to everything else.'
- 'Everything must go somewhere.'
- 'Nature knows best.'
- 'There is no such thing as a free lunch.'

OVER TO YOU

What do Commoner's four laws mean? Use your own language to discuss this. Do you agree with Commoner?

As indicated earlier, the Chicago School urban ecologists weren't just interested in statistics. They also used observation and other qualitative techniques to get at the people behind the figures. That said, there was a tendency to err on the side of seeing the environment as a determining force. On the other side of the continuum is the view that ecology is a people product. This position is enjoined by many social constructionists, and also strikes a chord with postmodernist thinking. In these contexts, it's contended that people give meaning to a natural (and social) world that has no meanings of its own.

Rocks can't talk, but people can carve them into sculptures, and give that art form a name. From this perspective, nature doesn't know best because nature doesn't know anything – it just is. People give nature meaning when they describe it, mould it, and even when they're constrained by it. Giving a name to a spiralling wind by calling it a twister invests it with a human dimension. We might not be able to tame a twister but we know what to call it. Similarly, people define their social worlds in terms that invoke distinctively human qualities – class-ridden, egalitarian, democratic, racist, communal, and so forth.

One way of getting beyond the idea of environment as, on the one hand, an 'out there' thing that confronts us, and, on the other, a socially defined construct, is to adopt a perspective known as 'deep ecology' – deep because it requires deep thought and reflection. First outlined in a 1972 lecture by the Norwegian philosopher, Arne Naess, deep ecology is premised on two fundamental beliefs:

- the recognition that people are part of nature
- a respect for all human and non-human life forms.

Naess made this outlook explicit, but it has been around for some time. In Native American culture, for example, the killing of deer for food was accompanied by asking forgiveness from the animal – *post mortem* or as its life blood ebbed – for slaying it. Kind words were also said about the gift its body bequeathed. Laine Thom, a Native American from Utah, reawakens those sentiments when he writes:

'O vanished buffalo, you were truly a gift from the Great Spirit; you sacrificed your life that we may live. Your flesh was our food, your skin our clothing and our dwelling place. After you were gone your spirit came back as a messenger from the Great Spirit to grant our people good health, happiness, and long life. Once again we use your skull in our Sacred Sun Dance.'
(Thom 1992: 29)

Killing in Native American communities wasn't done for pleasure, but for survival. Native Americans also adopted the 'spirit' of animals. The eagle, for example, was revered because it inspired human beings to soar above life's problems, just as that great bird soars above mountains and canyons. We're not taking an anti-vegetarian or an anti-vegan stand here. Exponents and practitioners of deep ecology count meat and non-meat eaters among their number. While the non-meat eaters might reasonably argue that their respect for non-humans is greater than people who eat bacon and eggs for breakfast, this is a moral rather than a sociological debate.

According to deep ecologists, the modern world has created an artificial dualism – a two-sided separation – which places people against nature and nature against

CRIT THINK CRIT THINK CRIT THINK CRIT THINK CRIT THINK CRIT THINK

PEOPLE AND THE BUILT ENVIRONMENT

Read the following passage.

'In their earnest pleas for the abolition of tenements and the construction of philanthropic housing and playgrounds, social reformers of the late nineteenth century expressed a belief in the power of urban environments to shape lives. Two generations later, architects and planners proclaimed their ability to design healthier and happier surroundings where human needs could be satisfied. Ironically, their rational designs, in the form of "towers in the park", now characterize troubled housing developments in cities throughout the nation [USA]. But today, when overcrowding and the deterioration of the urban fabric have re-created conditions prevalent in slums a century ago, the call to rebuild our cities lacks public resonance. Although the physical environment of the ghetto is becoming more fragmented, isolated, and hostile, we continue to neglect its influence on the people living there, and on ourselves.'
(Vergara 1997: 2–3)

1 *What do you think are the best methods to use when studying the relationship between a neighbourhood and the lives of the people in it?*

2 *Do you think Vergara's contention, that some architects and planners have failed in their attempt to 'design in' happiness, suggests that social science hasn't got much to offer city planners?*

3 *How might a 'fragmented, isolated, and hostile' environment influence the lives of people who live:*
a *in a ghetto?*
b *outside a ghetto?*

CRIT THINK CRIT THINK CRIT THINK CRIT THINK CRIT THINK CRIT THINK CRIT

people. This 'us' and 'it' dichotomy is, argue deep ecologists, unhelpful. What's needed, they propose, is a participatory experience of nature. In this respect, people need to reconnect with their environment in a holistic way, thereby developing a cosmic consciousness. This gives rise to a sense of being at one with the world, of being a child of the universe, not its enemy nor its victim.

In its social context, the notion of people participation has important implications for life in the city. For, in the urban centres of the late twentieth century, the poor are less likely to participate in their environment than to be oppressed by it.

Power, policy and conflict in the city

In a hard-hitting article entitled 'One motorway: Two Britains', Ros Wynne-Jones reports that in West London two communities (poor West 12 and prosperous West 11) are divided by a wide road:

'On one side, in the poverty of the White City estate, a nine-year-old girl was allegedly raped last week by five nine- and ten-year-old boys. On the other is Notting Hill and Holland Park, the new seat of media and business power. These opinion-formers never cross the road, turning a blind eye to the underclass within yards of their luxury homes.'

(The *Independent on Sunday*, 11 May 1997)

Geographical and social divisions in the city

The White City estate, Hammersmith and Fulham's poorest area – and reputedly a centre for crack dealing – accommodates about 8,000 people. They don't think much of the media moguls who occupy the BBC Television Centre, which is located close to the stubby council blocks. Says Courttia Newland, one of the few (if not the only) novelists who comes from the area:

'And you live with the BBC richies all the time. There's a lot of money around, but none of it's coming our way. West London is supposed to be the richest side of the capital – for people not in that bracket who live there, that's hard.'

(The *Independent on Sunday*, 11 May 1997)

The American social commentator, Jonathan Kozol (1992), highlights an even starker geographical and social division on the other side of the Atlantic. Here, the dividing line is between the mainly black residents who live in the Bottoms floodplain of the Mississippi River opposite St Louis and the predominantly white inhabitants who live on the Illinois Bluffs, which surround the floodplain in a semi-circle. The two tiers – 'Bluffs' and 'Bottoms' – inhabit different worlds, and the Bluffs residents overwhelmingly want this to continue. In the Bottoms, the city of East St Louis doesn't have the funds to cope with flooding problems on its own, or to reconstruct its sewer system. The problem is made worse because chemical plants have been releasing toxic substances into the sewer. Towns on the Bluffs don't pay taxes to deal with flood problems in the Bottoms – even though much of the problem is caused by water draining from the Bluffs.

Says Kozol (1992), the practice of concentrating black people in flood-risk lowland areas isn't uncommon in the United States. Farther down the river, for example, in the delta town of Tunica, Mississippi, the residents of the predominantly black community of Sugar Ditch live in shacks by open sewers. These conditions, adds Kozol, are commonly held to be the cause of the high incidence of liver tumours and abscesses among the children there. People who live in localities like this have little power. Their lives and their chances of reaching old age are largely determined by the power and the policy decisions of white middle- and upper-class people.

The decision-makers have good well-paid jobs, and live in plush neighbourhoods. They make it hard for the poor to enter their social and geographical space. In 1993, for example, a survey of the Metro North evening trains which take corporate executives to their suburban homes in places like Rye, New York, and Greenwich, Connecticut, found that virtually no black passengers were on board (Vergara 1997). While America has its share of black middle-class neighbourhoods, the typical 'black part of town' is notably poorer than its white counterpart. Residential segregation is widespread. Even in the rural areas, some black sections have dirt roads and houses on the verge of collapse. More worryingly, parts of the South, as I discovered still celebrate the confederacy. In downtown Baton Rouge, for example, I came across a statue of a Confederate soldier with an inscription that paid tribute to the soldiers of the south who fought to uphold black slavery.

In some parts of the south, the 'rebel yell' isn't just the brand name of a bourbon whiskey. On the other hand, in the Alabama city of Mobile, a man whom I took to be a redneck (he boasted of shooting lots of rabbits and deer, sported a pot belly, etc.) addressed a poor African–American as 'sir'. The salutation was genuine and polite. The south is different today. Stubborn pockets of white supremacist bigotry still endure, but there are also decent white folk who repent of the racism that haunted the past.

Even President Clinton lamented the sins of his 'fathers' when, in 1997, he begged forgiveness for one of the most shameful episodes in American history: the use of poor black syphilis victims for a 30-year medical research programme without their knowledge or consent.

President Clinton hugs Herman Shaw, from Tuskeegee, Alabama, a survivor of the syphilis medical experiments which were carried out by the US government.

Despite the progress that has been made to improve the economic and social position of black Americans, the south is still a place of mixed values, practices and beliefs. Peter Applebome, of the *New York Times*, captures this mood when he writes of 'the insane jumble of progress and stagnation that is the South three decades after the civil rights revolution petered out' (1996: 17). More recently, a young black Briton, Gary Younge, has added to this picture. In optimistic vein, he says:

'A young black man with a credit card, a hire car and an English accent can go almost anywhere he chooses in the Deep South. As recently as 20 years ago, this would have been little short of amazing.'

(The *Guardian Weekend*, 3 May 1997, page 52)

In more pensive mood, however, Younge adds that all isn't what it seems. He found Confederate flags flying on government buildings and reported that black churches are still being burned.

The fault lines between the haves and the have-nots in today's cities are easily discernible. The rich live in fortified residences, and the poor 'survive' and sometimes die in low-income housing and on the streets. The rich are powerful in economic and political terms. The poor lack economic muscle, but some poor people do contest the political decisions that oppress them. This challenge takes a number of forms. When Vergara conducted research for his book, *The New American Ghetto* (1997), he listened to the voices of the poor: the anonymous writing on bulletin boards, sketchings on walls, and the overheard conversations on buses and subway trains that give meaning to the daily lives of ordinary people. In ghettos, observes Vergara:

'the walls have become surfaces on which to vent anger, to display models worthy of emulation, to represent African American and Latino culture, and to remember the dead.'

(Vergara 1997: 2)

As in the US, so in the UK, inner-city areas have become increasingly depopulated. The main reason for this is the decline of heavy manufacturing, much of which was once located in inner-city areas. Coupled with this is the tendency for light manufacturing and service enterprises to be sited in locations on city outskirts – often in so-called industrial parks. The resultant emptying out of the central urban district leaves people there who can't afford to move to the leafy suburbs. They're often without jobs too. Eloquently chronicling a tragic situation, Philip Kasinitz describes the American experience of this phenomenon as one where:

'Once characterized by the exploitation of industrial labor, urban poverty is now marked by the lack of it. As many of the poor have been "deprolitarianized", large parts of American central cities have been reduced to virtual reservations for redundant populations excluded from the new, information-oriented economy.'

(Kasinitz 1995: 392)

Poverty in Britain's cities is pervasive, especially in London, which contains 15 of the 20 most materially-deprived districts in the country (Goodwin 1995, in Philo 1995). The worst instances of urban deprivation typically occur in inner-city areas, and outer council estates. Rented bedsits, bed and breakfast 'flop houses' (cheap lodgings), and high-rise flats make life hard – sometimes unbearable – for millions of Britons. Homelessness is even worse, and it's a huge problem. According to the 1991 Census, 2,674 people were sleeping rough. This is almost certainly a very substantial under-estimate. Official figures often don't get at the people who sleep in doorways, barns and sheds. We see them, but they remain invisible to the enumerators. If these 'rough' sleepers are officially accepted as homeless by local councils, they will appear in the statistics. However, if they fall outside the category of 'priority need' – which, of course, they do even if officials say otherwise – the 'unofficial homeless' don't always get recorded.

The poor in the city, as Goodwin points out, 'face constant reminders of those who are wealthier and more fortunate' (1995, in Philo 1995: 75). Not surprisingly, when they see opulence and grandeur on the other side of town, the poor are particularly prone to feelings of low self-esteem. This isn't about envy. It's about huge differences in income, wealth and power, and the inevitable social polarisation between people who live in the same city. So substantially different are the economic life chances of people in England's capital, that on some measures Greater London is one of the richest regions in the country, while Greater London boroughs like Hackney and Tower Hamlets contain some of the poorest people in the nation.

Gangs in the city

We have to turn to the US if we really want to explore the sociology of gangs. For there they exist in plenty, and they're big – very big. Los Angeles has a reputation for some of the most prominent gangs. The biggest and perhaps the most violent gang there is called 18th Street. It numbers around 20,000 members in southern California alone, bigger than the infamous Bloods and Crips. Although primarily Latino in composition, 18th Street recruits members from all ethnic groups in working-class neighbourhoods. The power of the gang comes from the barrel of a gun. 18th Street has allegedly committed more than 100 murders in the city of Los Angeles since 1990 – three times more than many of the city's most active gangs.

As in all American gangs, the emphasis is on unity, and many members say they're in *por vida* – for life. Socialisation starts early. The *Observer* (24 November 1996) reports that a 'little homey', a four-year-old called Baby Midget, is already learning to flash the gang's 'E' sign. When asked where he's from, Baby Midget says 'Southside 18th Street'. Young homeboys teach him the norms and values of the gang. When asked if he likes school and the police – symbols of, respectively, middle-class respectability and middle-class protection – he shakes his head and says no. Baby Midget is beginning to learn that the way to power is to hang out and act tough with the other 'homies'. Soon he'll find that the way to protect his turf is to learn how to use a gun.

In Decker and Van Winkle's (1997) study of gang life in St Louis, 81 per cent of gang members who were interviewed in the investigation attached symbolic importance to their turf – either because the gang started there, they lived there or, most significantly, it was theirs and defending it was a matter of honour. A much smaller proportion reported more 'practical' reasons for defending turf. Selling drugs, in particular, required a secure turf. Nearly 90 per cent of gang members said they had defended their turf against members of rival gangs over the past year. Typically, this involved fighting, and guns were used in over 95 per cent of the skirmishes. Most gang members accept that incursions on their turf will be violently repelled. When asked by one of the interviewers if someone from another turf entered his part of town, what his gang (the Crips) would do, Anthony, a 22-year-old said:

> '"First try to tell him to leave."
> [Interviewer]: "If he don't leave?"
> [Gang member]: "He'll leave one way or the other, carry him out in a Hefty bag."'
>
> (Decker and Van Winkle 1997: 113)

When resources are scarce, as they are in the inner city, poor people sometimes wage war against each other. Among gangs, for example, there's money to be made in dealing drugs on a particular patch. Families are also put under enormous pressure in desperate bids for scare resources. In his study of a poor British inner-city area, the London Borough of Hackney, journalist and sociologist, Paul Harrison notes:

An 18th Street youth plays with a gun as fellow gang members make shadows in the shape of XVIII.

'Where better-off families can usually accommodate multiple demands out of more ample funds, poor families often find themselves in a situation where one person's need for shoes can be met only at the expense of another's need for a winter coat, or a man's desire for a drink and a gamble can only be satisfied at the expense of his family's food or fuel.'

(Harrison 1985: 301)

Although gangs, in their large-scale American sense, don't exist in the UK, poor neighbourhoods do encounter high rates of crime. This typically takes a predatory form, with the poor preying on the poor. For the victim, an impoverished life becomes even more unbearable. When, for example, a television is stolen, a piece of technology that makes a bleak life a little more tolerable can't be replaced. The devastating effects of crime on victims and their families aside, the fear of crime in some inner-city areas creates a tense atmosphere. Some poor people stay indoors through fear of being mugged.

Policing the city

The response to breakdown of order in the inner city is often heavy policing. From their central headquarters, the police venture forth, more heavily armed than usual, into 'enemy territory'. The use of zero-tolerance tactics – whereby minor infractions are severely dealt with to prevent escalation – pushes certain members of poor neighbourhoods (notably, young males, and 'rough' sleepers) into open confrontation with the police. Illustrative of this new aggressive policing style, David and his 'drinking buddies', who normally wouldn't attract official attention as they sit huddled in the cold in King's Cross, London, are now told by police officers to move on. Says David:

'They told us to find a park and go and drink there. But I can't earn any money in the parks, especially in this weather. I stand near the station because I can beg for money here.'

(cited by Vivek Chaudhary and Martin Walker in the *Guardian*, 21 November 1996, page 2)

This isn't a one-off experience. David and his pals were experiencing a police initiative launched in the King's Cross area in November 1996 called Operation Zero Tolerance. It involved 25 police officers over a six-week trial period who were instructed to clamp down on all crime in the area – irrespective of how trivial or irrelevant it might seem. Homeless beggars are, of course, prime targets in the new 'get tough' approach. To find the thinking behind this British version of an American law enforcement strategy, you need to visit the Big Apple and talk to Mayor Rusi Giuliani. The New York City Mayor claims that his town has become just about the safest big city in the US. At face value, the claim seems supported by the figures. Murders have halved and robberies have dropped by a third in New York City since zero tolerance policing methods were introduced in the summer of 1994.

Origins of 'zero tolerance' policing

In 1994 in North Brooklyn, one of the poorest areas of the city, there were 126 homicides in the 75th precinct of New York City Police Department. In 1995, there were 44. The story of this apparent turn-around, from a city supposedly sinking under the weight of rocketing crime rates into one where the police are back in charge, began in 1990 on the New York subway. The man in charge of the subway police, William J. Bratton, decided in that year of unprecedented violence that enough was enough. He was influenced by the famous 'broken window' experiment of Stanford University social psychologist, Philip Zimbardo. In 1969, Zimbardo parked a car on a local street in California's Palo Alto for a week, where it remained untouched. Then he placed another car on a similar street in a similar neighbourhood in the Bronx district of New York, with its licence plates removed and the hood left often. Within a day, it was stripped of batteries, seats and tyres, and then wrecked.

Next, Zimbardo broke one of the windows of the car in Palo Alto. Within 24 hours it was stripped and vandalised. He concluded that one broken window was perceived as a licence to break the rest of the rules. In other words, one crime begot more crime. Impressed by this social scientific evidence, Chief Bratton cleaned graffiti from all the subway cars in the New York City transit system. Then he got tough with fare-dodging turnstile hoppers, figuring that waging war on those who vault over the token-operated turnstiles would diminish an atmosphere of lawlessness. Appointed Police Commissioner for the whole of New York in 1994, Bratton applied the broken window theory city-wide, telling police officers to clamp down on beggars, people who ride bikes on pavements, petty drug dealers, street 'prostitutes', and people who urinate in public.

On a 'softer' level, he also introduced community leaders not just to station chiefs, but to patrol officers, many of whom get out of their cars and walk the streets. Bringing statistical data into play, Bratton maps crimes daily and police deployments weekly. Responding to the obvious (and, arguably, valid) criticism that zero tolerance policing just moves the crime problem to other districts, David Walden, Chief of Staff to the Mayor of Houston – where similar techniques are claimed to have dropped the murder rate to its lowest since 1976 – says:

'You have to keep the heat on, permanently, shifting resources every week, watching the crime map, getting the community to trust the cops because they see this is serious and sustained.'

(cited by Vivek Chaudhary and Martin Walker in the *Guardian*, 21 November 1996, page 2)

How effective is zero tolerance?

Closer to home, local residents in the King's Cross area are reported to have welcomed the London initiative, regarding it as an opportunity to clean up the area – both literally and in terms of reputation. But is it going to work in the UK? That's a tough one to answer. Sociologists could argue, for example, that zero-tolerance policing is tough on crime, but not on the causes of crime. Some 26 per cent of all known offenders in Britain are aged 10 to 17, and successive government responses to them have been misguided and confused. There's a real and urgent need to respond to this problem by shifting from punitive to preventive measures. This view is backed by the findings and recommendations of the National Audit Commission, which reported in late 1996. This is an official government body which is responsible for overseeing and identifying best practice and efficiency in the National Health Service and other public agencies, including the police.

Moreover, there's the danger that pro-active law enforcement styles can criminalise certain groups – notably, young, working-class, black males. In America, for example, on current trends, nearly 75 per cent of African–Americans and millions of Latino–Americans will have been arrested and charged by the time they reach 35. There are cities in America where one black male in three is either in prison, on probation or awaiting trial. Then there are demographic trends to consider. As young people turn into more mellow adults, provided they persuade their children to be law-abiding, crime rates might drop.

Even schemes like Tony Blair's £3 billion programme to get the long-term jobless and the young into work might encourage more young people to turn from crime. Here we have the chance to test Robert K. Merton's theory that a major cause of crime is the tantalisation of acquiring material trappings when lawful means of doing so (for example, getting a job) aren't easily available. The magic bullet appeal of zero tolerance must be tempered, however, with prudent sociological reasoning. In that context, we need to be mindful of the evidence – which, at this stage, isn't conclusive. Take Washington DC, for example. Despite the use of zero tolerance there, little has changed in relation to crime rates.

It might be a tool for decreasing crime, but zero tolerance isn't a panacea. Moreover, as indicated, it has drawbacks, not least of which is the risk of criminalising and, frankly, intimidating, the inhabitants of entire neighbourhoods – the innocent and the guilty. Fear and even hatred of the police among some young people is deep. It's not just a matter of perception. If, for whatever reason, a young person is unjustly harassed and intimidated by police officers, she or he is unlikely to be favourably disposed towards them. Recently, while travelling from Miami to Los Angeles, I spoke to a young African–American professional – a teacher, in fact – who told me that a police officer had once held a gun to his head. If you or I experienced such a frightening encounter, I suspect we too might adopt negative attitudes to police in general.

Of course, we are not suggesting that all white police officers are racist and that all black people are innocent law-abiding citizens. There are 'good' and 'bad' in both camps. The problem, as Harrison puts it, is that:

'There is a tendency among police officers – based on previous experience – to expect trouble when arresting or questioning Afro-Caribbeans, and to be prepared for it, just as Afro-Caribbeans, again from experience, expect trouble from the police. These mutual expectations create tense situations in which gestures are easily misinterpreted and rapid escalation to high levels of violence is facilitated.'

(Harrison 1985: 362)

OVER TO YOU

In what ways does the preceding quote from Paul Harrison's book,* Inside the Inner City *(1985), draw upon labelling theory (in particular, the self-fulfilling prophecy)?

Whilst zero tolerance policing has been getting a lot of public attention, it is, of course, important to point out that less aggressive policing methods are also employed by law enforcement. In Britain, for example, community-style policing is apparent in 'back to the beat' initiatives, visits to schools, liaison with minority ethnic group community leaders, and so forth. It's also apposite to note, as New Left realists argue (see the section on region and crime rates in Chapter 16, Deviance), that poor communities need police protection from those who would prey upon them.

People who are menaced by burglary, robbery, intimidation, violence, and indeed, by the psychological fear of crime, are probably reassured by high profile community policing. Ironically, though, trends towards the privatisation of law enforcement (security guard car patrols, etc) might be bad news for potential victims in poor neighbourhoods. For, as Nils Christie (1994: 110) remarks:

'A private police, caring for those able and willing to pay, might reduce the interest among the upper classes in having a good, public police, and thus leave the other classes and the inner cities in an even worse situation'.

A public police which gets out of its squad cars and onto the beat, talking to people, and taking an interest in their general well-being, offers a better service to the poor of the inner city. Dixon of Dock Green – a caricature, to be sure, – is, in that sense, the sociological *ideal type* of a community beat officer. Dixon, however, frequented not only a television world, but also a different era – the London of the 1950s. Today, the police do their work in a high-tech environment, often unavoidably distanced from the public they serve.

Many senior police officers attend courses in criminology and sociology these days. They are therefore aware that crimes do have 'causes', and that pro-active, zero tolerance law enforcement can offend and provoke the law-abiding members of groups in society whom aggressive policing often targets. These police officers support Tony Blair's resolve to focus as much on preventative strategies (ie tackling the causes of crime) as on symptom-oriented strategies such as zero tolerance.

At various junctures in this chapter, we've made the point that not all is bad in the inner city. Some poor people, faced with urban blight and widespread conflict, develop community action projects and neighbourhood self-help schemes. Some of them take to the streets in peaceful protest against social injustice and for a better deal. There's no doubt that these initiative can lead to improvement. That said, the more people in poor neighbourhoods have a right to a better future, the less likely are they to have the political muscle to bring about change.

QUESTIONS

1 Outline some of the important divisions between the 'haves' and the 'have nots' in the city.
2 What did Scott H. Decker and Barrik Van Winkle (1997) find out about gang life in St Louis, USA?
3 To what extent, if at all, would it be accurate to describe zero tolerance policing as wishful thinking?

Concluding remarks

We've covered a lot of ground in this chapter: how societies endure and change; how this relates to urbanisation and industrialisation and the important debate on community; what and how the environment is and is becoming, and how it affects us and we affect it; and the trials and tribulations of the city.

What have you learnt from all this? In general terms, perhaps you've come to understand that:

- stability and change are *ideal types*. Society is a process which contains static and dynamic elements. An excess of static tendencies leads to order and gradual change (evolution); a lot of dynamism results in explosive, rapid change (revolution). If things repeat themselves over time, we have cyclical change. How people socially construct things and act upon these their perceptions also affects change
- urbanisation and industrialisation are prime movers of change and have profound effects on people's lives. These effects are typically differentiated in ways that benefit certain groups (for example, company bosses) and oppress other groups (for example, low-paid black employees)
- community forms, like other things in society, are subject to change. However, different types of community can and do develop. The loss of community, in an empirical sense, can only refer to the loss of a particular kind of community rather than community spirit
- the natural and social environments bounce of and affect each other. The relative weight and direction of these mutual influences must be determined empirically. An earthquake has the upper hand on an unprepared community. A fishing community directly affects marine biology. The built environment influences human social behaviour
- life in the city is often characterised by stark divisions of power, and is punctuated by conflict. So-called legitimate power (for example, that of politicians and the police) is frequently contested by people who don't have a stake in the town hall.

Locality isn't so fixed as it was in the past – unless you were always on the move like Hannibal or Captain Cook! Even if you are a bit of a 'stick in the mud', chances are you'll have a wider-lens view – courtesy of the electronic media – than your predecessors.

Glossary of key terms

Community A social group whose members are closely knit, share similar values, help each other and typically live in the same locality

Derivations Justifications that people use to defend their *residues* and *interests* (*see below*)

Ecology The study of the relationship between inhabitants and their environment

Elites People who excel in their particular field (for example, in politics, business, academia)

Gemeinschaft The 'community-type' society of the pre-industrial world

Gesellschaft The 'organisation-type' society of the industrial world

Ideational culture A culture characterised by other-worldly, sacred values

Institutionalisation of conflict The settling of disputes through established procedures

Industrialisation The development of mass forms of factory production

Interests (as used by Vilfredo Pareto) Things that serve human needs

Mechanical solidarity The social relationships that prevail in traditional society, and which approximate to Tonnies' community-type Gemeinschaft

Organic solidarity The social relationships that prevail in modern society, and which resemble Tonnies' organisation-type Gesellschaft

Residues Manifestations of sentiments, or even sentiments themselves

Risk society A societal condition where natural and social hazards are created – but not contained – by industrialisation. *Risk Society* is the title of a very important book by Ulrich Beck, who is a professor of sociology at the University of Munich

Ruralism The way of life of people who live in the countryside

Sensate culture A culture characterised by material, sense-recognised values

Social change Instability or disorder, leading – for 'good' or 'bad' – to social alteration and social shift

Social dynamics The process study of the functions of society or, to use a biological analogy, the 'physiology' of society

Social stability Things staying as they are, or, to put it another way, social order

Social statics The study of the structure of society or, to use a biological analogy, the 'anatomy' of society

Urbanisation The migration of people into towns and cities

Urbanism The way of life of people who live in towns and cities

References

Applebome, Peter (1996) *Dixie Rising*. New York: Times Books

Balchin, Paul (1996) *Housing Policy*, Third Edition. London: Routledge

Baudrillard, Jean (1993) *America*. London: Verso

Beck, Ulrich (1994) *Risk Society: Towards a New Modernity*. London: Sage Publications

Bulmer, Martin (1986) *The Chicago School of Sociology*. Chicago: University of Chicago Press

Christie, Nils (1994) *Crime Control as Industry*. Second enlarged edition. London: Routledge

Cohen, Percy S. (1970) *Modern Social Theory*. London: Heinemann

Coleman, David and Salt, John (1996) *The British Population*. Oxford: Oxford University Press

Damer, Seán (1990) *Glasgow: Going for a Song*. London: Lawrence & Wishart

Decker, Scott H. and Van Winkle, Barrik (1997) *Life in the Gang*. Cambridge: Cambridge University Press

Demerath III, N. J. and Peterson, Richard A. (eds) (1967) *System, Change and Conflict*. New York: The Free Press

Dickens, Peter (1996) *Reconstructing Nature*. London: Routledge

Durkheim, Emile (1964) *The Division of Labor in Society*. New York: The Free Press

Etzioni, Amitai (1993) *Spirit of Community*. London: Fontana

Gans, Herbert J. (1991) Urbanism and suburbanism as ways of life: A reevaluation of definitions, pp 170–95, in Kasinitz, Philip (ed.) (1995) op. cit.

Goodwin, Mark (1995) Poverty in the city: 'You can raise your voice, but who is listening?', pp 65–82, in Philo, Chris (ed.) (1995) op. cit.

Gouldner, Alvin W. (1972) *The Coming Crisis of Western Sociology*. London: Heinemann

Hannigan, John A. (1997) *Environmental Sociology*. London: Routledge

Harrison, Paul (1985) *Inside the Inner City*. Harmondsworth: Penguin

Kasinitz, Philip (ed.) (1995) *Metropolis*. Basingstoke: Macmillan

King, Coretta Scott (ed.) (1985) *The Words of Martin Luther King*. London: Fount

Kozol, Jonathan (1992) *Savage Inequalities*. New York: Harper Perennial

Lash, Scott, Szerszynski, Bronislaw and Wynne, Brian (eds) (1996) *Risk, Environment and Modernity*. London: Sage Publications

Lee, David and Newby, Howard (1986) *The Problem of Sociology*. London: Hutchinson

Maguire, John (1996) The tears inside the stone: Reflections on the ecology of fear, pp 169–88, in Lash *et al.* (eds) (1996) op. cit.

Oppenheim, Carey and Harker, Lisa (1996) *Poverty: The Facts*, Third Edition. London: CPAG

Pareto, Vilfredo (selections from 1896–1921) *Sociological Writings*, selected and introduced by Finer, S. E. (1976) Oxford: Blackwell

Pareto, Vilfredo (1935) *The Mind and Society*, Volume Two. New York: Harcourt, Brace and Company

Parsons, Talcott (1961) A paradigm for the analysis of social systems and change, pp 189–212, in Demerath III, N. J. and Peterson, Richard A. (eds) (1967) op. cit.

Parsons, Talcott (1967a) *Sociological Theory and Modern Society*. New York: The Free Press

Parsons, Talcott (1967b) *The Structure of Social Action*. New York: The Free Press

Philo, Chris (ed.) (1995) *Off the Map: The Social Geography of Poverty in the UK*. London: CPAG

Philo, Chris, McCormick and Child Poverty Action Group (1995) 'Poor places' and beyond: Summary findings and policy implications, pp 175–88, in Philo, Chris (ed.) (1995) op. cit.

Seager, Joni (1995) *The State of the Environment Atlas*. London: Penguin Books

Simmel, Georg (1948) The metropolis and mental life, pp 324–39, in Levine, Donald N. (ed.) (1971) *On Individuality and Social Forms*. Chicago: University of Chicago Press

Smelser, Neil J. (1997) *Problematics of Sociology: The Georg Simmel Lectures, 1995*. Berkeley University of California Press

Sorokin, Pitirim A. (1957) *Social and Cultural Dynamics*. Boston: Porter Sargent Publisher

Suttles, Gerald D. (1968) *The Social Order of the Slum*. Chicago: University of Chicago Press

Szerszynski, Bronislaw (1996) On knowing what to do: Environmentalism and the modern problematic, pp 104–37, in Lash *et al.* (eds) (1996) op. cit.

Sztompka, Piotr (1994) *The Sociology of Social Change*. Oxford: Blackwell

Thom, Laine (1992) *Becoming Brave*. San Francisco: Chronicle Books

Thompson, Kenneth (1996) *Key Quotations in Sociology*. London: Routledge

Vergara, Camilo Jose (1997) *The New American Ghetto*. New Brunswick, New Jersey: Rutgers University Press

Watkins, Kevin (1995) *The Oxfam Poverty Report*. Oxford: Oxfam (UK and Ireland)

Wirth, Louis (1964) *On Cities and Social Life*. Chicago: University of Chicago Press

Weber, Max (1974) *The Protestant Ethic and the Spirit of Capitalism*. London: Unwin University Books

Worcester, Donald E. (1992) *The Apaches: Eagles of the Southwest*. Norman: University of Oklahoma Press

Wynne, Brian (1996) May the sheep safely graze? A reflexive view of the expert-lay knowledge divide, pp 44–83, in Lash, Scott *et al.* (eds) (1996) op. cit.

Exam practice: Sociology of locality

Essay questions

1 Examine sociological contributions to an understanding of urban unrest in Britain. *(25 marks)*

2 Compare and contrast Weberian and Marxist approaches to urban sociology. *(25 marks)*

(November 1993 AEB A-level Sociology, Paper 2, © 1993 AEB)

3 Critically examine sociological contributions to an understanding of the factors which influence access to housing. *(25 marks)*

(Summer 1991 AEB A-level Sociology, Paper 2, © 1991 AEB)

4 Critically examine the view that de-urbanisation has blurred the distinctions between rural and urban life. *(25 marks)*

(Summer 1996 AEB A-level Sociology, Paper 2, © 1996 AEB)

18 World sociology

Topics covered in this chapter
- *World sociology theories*
- *Measuring development*
- *Colonialism and its legacies*
- *Causes and consequences of demographic trends*
- *Alternative development strategies*
- *Industrialisation, employment and urbanisation*
- *Education and health*
- *Gender inequalities and equal opportunity initiatives*
- *One planet, one world: The global environment*

When a floating pollen seed touches a spider's web, it sends a tremor that moves through the entire structure. When you buy a packet of fairly traded coffee, your purchase sends a tremor that touches the lives of poor people on the other side of the world.

World sociology considers such matters. In its emancipatory form, world sociology also seeks to promote a global civic ethic. This is a compelling and a tantalising vision. It harkens back – while simultaneously looking forward – to the authentic implementation of the original Charter of the United Nations:

'And for these ends . . .
to practice tolerance and live together in peace with one another as good neighbours'

The message is clear: we're already global neighbours. Now let's be part of a global humanity.

'The Spaniards are troubled with a disease of the heart for which gold is the specific remedy.' These words are from Cortes, the sixteenth-century Spanish invader and, some would say, plunderer of Native (later so-called Latin) America. According to marxist social scientists, what Cortes and others like him did, in the Americas of their time, was to turn the clock back for the people whose livelihoods they destroyed. This is why, contends Andre Gunder Frank:

'The Indian [*sic*] settlements of later times . . . are not then survivals of pre-conquest times. They are, on the contrary, the underdeveloped product of capitalist development.'

(Frank 1969a: 128)

What marxists like Frank are saying is that sixteenth-century, gold-prospecting Europeans removed the land-use rights of Native Americans, thereby *holding back* and *pushing back* the cultural and economic development of civilisations which were at least as advanced as their European counterparts. This is the catastrophic flaw of ethno-centricity (judging other societies by the standards of our own): it equates 'different' with 'inferior', and 'traditional' with 'primitive'.

EXAM TIP

Frank's interpretations of world sociology issues are openly value-judgmental. This point needs to be emphasised when evaluating Frank's and other marxist critiques.

The above perspective is a variant of the crude, racist, colonial mentality which believes – incorrectly – that white Englishmen went out to Africa, India and other 'uncivilised' lands, and 'civilised' the natives. In its American context, this ideology has been promoted on the silver screen by 'cowboy and indian' films that presented a picture of 'white frontier heroism'

ATTRACTIVE, DETACHED RESIDENCE
Believed to be unique, this magnificent dwelling has been sadly neglected in recent years. Some outstanding features have been lost. However it still offers an exceptional home to those prepared to maintain it with care.

We're all global neighbours.

confronting 'redskin debauchery and savagery'. In more recent years, that outlook has been convincingly challenged in films like *Dances with Wolves* (1990), and documentaries like Channel 4's *The American West* (1995). In the first production, Lieutenant Dunbar (played by Kevin Costner) finds the customs and practices of the Sioux much more refined than the genocidal behaviour of US cavalry soldiers. The Channel 4 documentary describes the confrontation between a Native American culture that regards the earth as something to be nurtured and shared, and an invading European culture which sees it as property to be exploited and divided.

Some social scientists reckon that, whatever happened in the past, things have changed today, and that rich nations are now better placed to help their poorer neighbours. Others argue that poor countries are still exploited by rich countries, but not in so vividly a brutal manner as previously. Yet other social scientists adopt a midway position, arguing that the rich world both oppresses and liberates the poor world in different contexts. When, for example, American and British companies buy cocoa from West Africa at market rather than fair prices, the cocoa pickers receive low wages. That's oppression. However, when American and British health workers provide mass vaccination programmes that significantly reduce infant mortality rates in poor countries, that's liberation.

We'll begin this chapter by putting what's been briefly commented upon in the preceding paragraph into more explicit theoretical frameworks, starting with a consideration of the view that nowadays rich countries help poor countries to develop.

EXAM TIP

Demonstrating an awareness of the problematic nature of world sociology terminology is an important evaluative skill, and will earn you marks in an exam.

A note on terminology

There are a number of ways to describe the different nations that make up our world. A rather old-fashioned (and elitist) model divides the world into three blocs:

- the First World (USA and other rich countries)
- the Second World (China and other communist societies)
- the Third World (most African and other poor countries).

Some commentators describe countries as:

- 'developed' (mainly First World, but some Second World)
- 'newly industrialising' (some Second World and the 'up-and-coming' Third World countries)
- 'underdeveloped' (most Third World countries).

There are other variants, for example, rich 'North' or 'Western' countries and poor 'South' countries. This book generally uses two broad, but accurate, categories:

- *the majority world* (also referred to as poor countries)
- *the rich world* (sometimes also referred to as 'western' countries).

World sociology theories

This section examines the *main* world sociology theories:

- modernisation theory
- dependency theory (sometimes, in its more recent form, called world systems theory)
- convergence theory.

Two other theories are also considered:

- evolutionary theory
- revolutionary theory.

As will be seen, evolutionary theory is the guiding paradigm (model) of modernisation and convergence theorists, and revolutionary theory strongly influences dependency theorists.

Modernisation theory

There's still an assumption among some people in 'western' countries today that 'what's good for the west, is good for the rest'. This outlook has its academic as well as its popular followers. The academics are called 'modernisation theorists' (and 'doers', because they're into getting things done, as well as theorising). Their most notable exponent is Walt Whitman Rostow (1965), an American professor of political economy. Rostow claims that there are five stages of economic growth through which all societies who would be modern must pass. These are:

1. *Traditional society* – pre-industrial, agricultural societies with old technology, and paternalistic power structures. In very 'modernist language', Rostow says that a traditional society is 'based on pre-Newtonian science and technology, and on pre-Newtonian attitudes towards the physical world' (1965: 4)
2. *Preconditions for take-off* – growth of trade and of infant industries are set in motion, triggered perhaps by newly discovered technologies, and a new kind of 'leader': the entrepreneur
3. *The take-off* – a period of about 20 years when industry starts to replace agriculture, towns become magnets to rural populations, and entrepreneurs come knocking hard on the doors of a ruling class in decline: the old paternalistic landowners. Britain was the 'first' country to take off, which it did, says Rostow (1965) approximately in the two decades after 1783. France and the US 'took off' during the several decades preceding 1860
4. *The drive to maturity* – a period of about 40 years, during which a country consolidates what's been gained in the take-off period, and builds on that progress, especially in international markets
5. *The age of high mass consumption* – the upshot of the drive to maturity race, when increased industrialisation, followed by the expansion of a service sector (leisure, welfare, education, health, etc.) leads to mass consumption, and better living standards.

Rostow's model of modernisation is evolutionary. It doesn't assume any leap-frogging over the different stages, but a successive progression through each of them in turn. He does, however, accept that economic strategies might have to be different for the development of rich and poor countries. In that respect, he believes, for example, that poor countries might need to be 'kick-started' into modernisation by receiving economic aid and political (anti-communist) guidance from their richer neighbours.

EXAM TIP

Like Frank, but on the opposite side of the political fence (i.e. right-wing rather than left-wing), Rostow is morally committed to his argument. This needs to be emphasised when evaluating modernisation theory.

Rostow and modernisation theorists in general are of the opinion that what poor countries require is a 'good dose' of 'western-style culture and know-how' to set them right and get them on the path to a more prosperous future. Much of what they advocate seems to make good sense:

- Rich countries have become even richer by debunking tradition and superstition, and replacing these with modern and rational thought. If poor countries do the same, they'll reap the same benefits.
- Rich countries have the economic expertise and the economic resources to set themselves up as the financial advisers, the bankers and the providers of 'aid' (usually with 'payback' plus interest, of course) to poor countries.
- Rich countries need to expand their free market business by setting up shop in poor countries. The pay-off to the poor of this expansion is that 'western' transnational corporations (TNCs) provide them with training, employment and the prospect of a better future.
- Rich countries have generally prospered by making it the norm for families to have fewer children than in the past. They're ready and willing to share this knowledge with people in poor countries, so that they too will become committed family planners.

The practical implications of modernisation theory were advocated by leaders from the rich world in 1944, at a conference held at Bretton Woods – a fashionable old hotel located in the hill country of New Hampshire, USA. At the meeting, those gathered set a global agenda that aimed to get rid of 1930s-style protectionism and open up national borders worldwide to free trade. To implement this plan, they established two new financial institutions: the International Monetary Fund (IMF) and the World Bank. Shortly thereafter, another institution was set up, the General Agreement on Trades and Tariffs (GATT) which laid down the 'rules' for open economies and free trade. This has since been replaced in 1995 by the World Trade Organization (WTO).

Taken together, and with the inclusion of the regional development banks, these bodies are collectively called the international financial institutions (IFIs). They support global competition and corporate enterprise. But, say their critics, they haven't got a good track-record. IFI opponents – often left-wing in disposition – claim that the outcomes of IFI policies up to the present are these:

- There are budget and trade deficits worldwide – in rich and poor countries.
- Majority world debt has crushed the ability of poor countries to fund education, health and welfare from tax revenues.
- TNCs have become 'global plunderers', plying their trade by bidding down the wages of employees, circumventing environmental regulations and pillaging natural resources.

Yet, despite this abysmal showing, say the IFI critics, the Bretton Woods Conference still shapes poor world–rich world relations, especially with regard to 'the high-handed fashion in which the World Bank and the IMF have tried to impose their economic blueprint' (Swift 1994: 1).

A little harsh, you might say, towards modernisation theory? Perhaps the theory has been applied too literally, in which case there might be an argument for it to be adopted in a more flexible manner. If such is so, we can't think of a better advocate than Mahbub ul-Haq – former Finance Minister in Pakistan, and visionary initiator of the United Nations Human Development Reports – who argues that 'The dialogue of the future is about more access to global opportunities for trade and investment and migration and the free movement of the market' (1994: 21). He also believes that a 'fair market' is a more effective way than aid to get poor nations economically healthy. But what's a 'fair' market? ul-Haq has this in mind:

- It's a market where the majority world is an attractive economic proposition because it offers cheaper (and increasingly skilled) labour than the rich world. By out-competing the 'west' here, it attracts capital like a magnet, as has happened in Pacific Rim countries like Malaysia and Singapore.
- It's a market in which any countries who violate market principles by erecting trade and migration barriers, and who pollute the environment should pay compensation. This could lead to poor countries receiving about a 5–10 per cent transfer of resources as recompense, calculates ul-Haq. He notes too that poor countries 'have been fighting for 0.7 per cent of aid for so long as a charity principle – they should chance the market principle' (1994: 22).
- Unlike certain hard-line modernisation theorists, ul-Haq recognises that the 'free market', as it operates in the world today, isn't free at all. His version of a free market is one where the tariffs that prevent poor countries from exporting processed (as opposed to raw) goods to rich countries must be brought tumbling down. No doubt, as an authentic free marketeer, he would also like to see the removal of subsidies that are given to rich world farmers (billions of dollars each year) to produce too much food. Such subsidies lead to those EU milk lakes, and butter and beef mountains that we keep hearing about.

You might recall that Band Aid founder, Bob Geldoff, urged the EU to send these excess food supplies to Ethiopia during the famines there in the 1980s. He took the intellectuals and the bureaucrats to task, telling them

MODERNISATION THEORY

FOR

- **+** Rationality does appear to be a feature of all 'modern' societies.
- **+** Modernisation theory is in touch with the economics of the real world. A market economy is the way rich nations conduct their business. If the majority world wants to 'join the banquet', it will need to learn and apply the same business habits.
- **+** While it's true that the comparative pay and conditions and the environmental codes of practice provided by TNCs in the majority world aren't up to the standards in the rich world, there's still the 'better than otherwise' argument to consider. Put simply, poor people who have jobs and a pay packet are better off than when they're unemployed and unwaged.
- **+** Whatever the particular concerns of individual families might be in terms of trying to secure more prosperity by having lots of children, when too many people outstrip available resources, poverty and starvation are certain. The 'west' has the 'know-how' in birth control practices, and it's ready to share that expertise with poor countries.

AGAINST

- **–** Rostow's model of modernisation ignores the wide diversity that exists among pre-industrial countries, theorises, without empirical evidence, that such countries can't leap-frog over his five stages or find different routes to modernisation, under-estimates the economic successes of communist countries, and provides an ideological justification for American imperialism.
- **–** The rich world might be relatively prosperous, but its own development is very uneven and unequal: some American and British inner-city neighbourhoods, for example, are strewn with the homeless poor, many of whom are mentally ill. Is this 'development'? Are we really talking 'development' too when one in three Americans, through over-eating and under-exercising, is obese?
- **–** Market economies are profit- rather than people-oriented. TNCs which produce chocolate beverages and confectionery, for example, are usually more concerned with buying cocoa at the lowest possible price than with paying cocoa farmers a fair price for their produce. Linked to modernisation theory's endorsement of the 'free market' is an underlying commitment to right-wing politics. This compromises social scientific objectivity.

to stop talking and do something – fast. In moral terms, we think he was right. While sending food aid to poor countries might put local farmers out of work (they can't sell produce if it has already arrived in food parcels), when your family is starving to death, what you don't need is a lecture on economic theory. You need food in your belly. Longer term, you might listen to the argument that sustainable self-sufficiency is the goal to aim for. Short-term, however, food aid is life to people who are starving.

More about aid in the section on *Alternative development strategies* (page 592).

Dependency theory

The strongest critics of modernisation theory are dependency theorists (who are also doers). They're called dependency theorists because they claim that poor countries are forced to *depend* on 'western' economic policies. Their staunchest advocate is Andre Gunder Frank. A Berlin-born, US-educated social scientist, he argues that the majority world has 'under-developed' (i.e. gone backwards) because 'western' powers have invaded poor countries, and exploited their human and material resources through colonialism. There thus emerged, argues Frank, a world system of dependency of *peripheral* countries like Ethiopia and Pakistan on *core* countries like the US and the UK. The key link in this dependency chain has been and still is the city. Core nations use cities in poor countries as a conduit through which they drain labour power and commodities. Moreover, rich colonists have cut lucrative deals with local city-dwelling elites who, though born and raised in the majority world, have been encouraged to adopt 'western' mannerisms, and to collaborate with the colonists.

Today, argues Frank, the chain is still intact, although it's more likely to manifest itself in economic rather than military invasion terms. For example, rich countries set the price of coffee on the world commodities markets in London, New York and Tokyo, and poor countries have to sell their produce at that price – even when, as it usually is, an 'unfair' price. When one considers the plight of the poorest of the poor in the majority world – subsistence farmers, landless labourers and those who scratch a living in the informal economy (street-vending, shoe-shining, etc.) of the cities – they are, to quote Tony Killick, 'generally left behind by economic expansion' (1995: 309). These are the people who don't show up on the stock market computer screens.

Dependency-oriented social scientists argue that:

- traditional ways aren't necessarily 'backward'. For example, farmers in the majority world often use agricultural methods that don't belch toxic fumes from petrol-driven vehicles into the environment. They have a stake in preserving the resources they use
- the argument that 'western' bankers know what's best for the majority world is ideological cant rather than evidence-based fact. In 1993, for every dollar 'given' as aid to poor countries, rich countries took back three as debt repayments
- the terms of 'free market' international trade favour rich countries, and they generally 'call the shots'. For example, they 'force' poor countries to sell them cash crops (such as oranges) rather than manufactured goods (such as clothing). They do this by imposing heavy trade tariffs (payable by poor countries) on the manufactured goods they import from the majority world. Subsequently, very little financial benefit, barely a trickle, flows from rich to poor countries
- from the point of view of poor people in the majority world, it makes good sense to have lots of children: the extra hands provide more help and more income, especially if some of the children enter relatively well-paid employment in adult life
- poor people are most successful when they set their own development agendas, rather than being told what to do by self-styled experts from the rich world. The poor must participate in their own liberation, even if this means forcibly removing from office those leaders of their own nations who are in the pockets of 'western' economic, political, and military elites.

Many of the basic principles of dependency theory have been reformulated in less overtly 'left-wing' terms by the advocates of a fairly recent model called *World Systems Theory* (WST). The main thinker behind this theory is Immanuel Wallerstein who, when he writes, 'Incorporation into the capitalist world-economy was never at the initiative of those being incorporated' (1989: 129), expresses views not dissimilar to those of Frank.

David Kowalewski and Dean Hoover (1994), who subscribe to WST, summarise the theory's main arguments in a series of propositions:

According to dependency theorists, 'Trickle-down Theory' (the assumption that economic growth in the rich world benefits the majority world because benefits trickle down) is a sham: the rich get richer and the poor stay poor.

- Since the beginning of 'modernity' (at least 500 years ago), the growth of capitalism and the trends which it triggered (notably, 'western' colonialism) have led to development in the *core world* (another name for the rich world) and underdevelopment in the *periphery world* (another name for the majority world).
- This 'core–periphery' structure has persisted and still endures.
- The core's economies are diversified and don't depend on single foreign markets.
- The periphery's economies are less diversified and highly dependent on single core markets.
- The social class structures of core and periphery nations are very different: the core's structure is more equal than the periphery's. Consequently, the periphery has more poverty, social and cultural divisions, instability, and authoritarianism than the core.

Put simply, WST maintains that capitalism has turned the rich world into an exploiter of the majority world's resources, and that, while there are social class divisions in rich countries, they aren't as pronounced as in poor countries.

DEPENDENCY/WS THEORY

FOR

+ There's nothing wrong with traditional ideas, provided they work. Dependency/WS theorists aren't anti-modern, but they don't advocate replacing perfectly good traditional systems with modern ways just for the sake of it.
+ While recognising that the rich world sets the economic stage on the broader canvas, dependency/WS theorists are aware that countries of the majority world can forge mutually beneficial economic alliances between each other. Such arrangements can create alternative trading links. For example, a banana-producing country might swap fruit for the tea of another country.
+ Dependency/WS theories emphasise the importance of developing polutions to poverty *with* not *for* poor people.

AGAINST

– Urging poor people to overthrow their rich world rulers might sound 'Che Guevara-romantic', but is it practical, and who is likely to suffer most as a result of such actions? Comprador s – those majority world rulers who've adopted 'western' ways – wield huge economic, military and political power. They often control the army and the police, which makes it easy for them to put down any opposition.
– Are the advocates of alternative trade coming to terms with hard economic facts? Perhaps some of their ideas might work on a small-scale level (for example, selling coffee at a just – not a stock market – price through fair trade 'western' organisations like Traidcraft). But these ventures are too small to make a big dent.
– It's unrealistic, in a global market economy, to expect employees in the majority world to earn the same wages as workers in the 'west'. But that's free market economics for you. Moreover, regional pay differences occur in rich countries. For example, people in south-east England are paid higher wages than people in north-east England. But buying a house in the north-east is cheaper than in the south-east. TNCs have to work with market forces. However, that doesn't mean they're not keen to train local workforces (including their managers), provide clean, safe work environments and fair local wages.
– Evidence suggests that widespread use of birth control in majority world countries is a powerful predictor of fewer children per family. The dependency/WST view that poor people will be keener to have fewer children voluntarily when they become prosperous sounds a reasonable argument. However, with population increasing at a rate of 90 million more people each year, it may be dangerous to wait for the spur of prosperity.

Convergence theory

An important perspective in world sociology, convergence theory is, in many respects, an extension of modernisation theory. For it sees 'modernity' as the destination towards which the 'first, second and third worlds' are converging. So whose kind of 'modernity' are we talking about? You've guessed it, the 'modernity' (or is it 'post-modernity' these days?) of rich world globalisation. In that sense, the rich world isn't really converging. It's staying on a straight track, moving happily along into some so-called postmodern state, while the rest of the world is converging towards its alluring beacon.

But there are other ways forward. As Erhard Berner and Rudiger Korff point out:

'globalization should not be misunderstood as homogenization . . . Globalization is not the global extension of one particular culture or society, which then is as closely integrated as a national culture, but the selective transnationalization of diverse parts of cultures . . . Through globalization, the limits of national cultures and societies are ultimately transcended.'

(Berner and Korff 1995: 208)

These social scientists have a good point, but they use complex language. What they're saying is this: a future world society doesn't have to be based on one type of existing society. It can be based on a mosaic-style mixture of lots of different national cultures.

CONVERGENCE THEORY

In lots of ways, the earlier evaluation of modernisation theory is also an evaluation of convergence theory. The two theories have so much in common. That said, here are some additional points which more specifically deal with convergence theory.

FOR

+ Events in Eastern Europe – namely, the imploding of the Soviet empire and the development of democracies and market economies in former Eastern Bloc countries – suggest that the predictions of convergence theory are happening. That's as may be, but the so-called 'second world communist' countries haven't all disappeared. China, North Korea and Cuba, for example, are still 'communist'. Maybe though it's just a matter of time before they become 'westernised'.
+ There's no doubt that global technologies do shape social conditions. It's also pertinent to note that many of these technologies are developed and marketed by 'western' corporations. Take communications, for example. Bill Gates, the American founder and chairperson of Microsoft, dominates a communications technology so powerful that it touches nearly every desktop, office and school in the US. And it's getting bigger: eight out of ten of the world's personal computers can't boot up (start) without the use of Microsoft operating-system software, like MS-DOS, Windows and Windows NT. Now that Microsoft is into interactive TV, TV movies, E-mail, banking services, electronic shopping and multimedia games, its transmissions are bound to exercise an important influence on global culture.
+ Convergence theorists have an inspired vision of a world where damaging differences – class and ethnic divisions, poor and rich nations, communists and capitalists – are eventually replaced by a global society which is united on the basis of common economic, political and social goals. Clearly, in such a utopian future, the idea that nations will want to wage wars against each other is unthinkable. Already, the collapse of the East–West 'iron curtain' is creating a 'peace dividend', namely, the use of funds previously earmarked for military spending for health, welfare and other socially useful programmes.

AGAINST

– Nobody knows yet where the new Europe, following the demise of the Soviet Union, is heading. It's far too early and much too simplistic to predict that this former part of the 'second world' is going down a 'western' road. Wars and battles are still being fought, as in the former Yugoslavia, and final outcomes aren't known. Some commentators envisage a move towards authentic socialism, others towards 'western-style' capitalism, and yet others a return to totalitarian communism. As things stand, however, the 'western' way is very much in the frame.

– Although technology is becoming much more standardised, local knowledge and local technologies in majority world countries are still – and will continue to be – very important. Moreover, there's no one single path towards the future. Take the experience of industrialisation, for instance. Both South Korea and Taiwan have undergone rapid industrialisation. Yet that process in South Korea is of a capital-intensive (technology replaces manual labour), large urban conglomerate type. By contrast, in Taiwan, industrialisation has been labour-intensive (manual work hasn't been taken over by machines), accompanied by dispersed living patterns of industrial workers.

– It's right to be idealistic and optimistic, but do current trends in the world really suggest that we're en route to a more stable, peaceful, egalitarian global society based on a 'western', free market model? There have been some important narrowings of the gaps between rich and poor, but this has less to do with the 'free market' and more to do with fiscal (tax-based) policies, especially those of a social democratic kind.

'No way!', says Clark Kerr, perhaps the most well-known exponent of convergence theory. He's an American professor of industrial relations and was born in 1911. In his book *Industrialism and Industrial Man* (1960), which he co-authored with other social scientists, Kerr argues that industrialisation has become the dominant feature of societies worldwide. He acknowledges that the economic, political and social systems differ between societies, but predicts that these differences will ultimately be swept away as the 'first, second and third worlds' converge into one single, mass industrial society, '*à la* USA'. When this happens, suggest convergence theorists, the world will become a peaceful, unified planet of plenty and stability.

According to Kerr, technology is the driving force behind the impending convergence of the three world systems. For it makes no difference if you're affixing labels to beer bottles in Athens, Greece or Athens, Georgia, USA, your production plants will be using the same or similar technology. While not himself a marxist, Kerr applied a similar idea to Marx in his analysis of social change, namely, that technology is the driving force that brings other aspects of society under its sway. During Britain's Industrial Revolution, for example, the notion that working-class children could learn all that they needed to know out in the fields with the hoe and plough was gradually replaced with the recognition that schooling was necessary to instil the requisite habits of factory discipline (Stephens 1987). Similarly, Kerr believes that a new consensus on norms and values will evolve (convergence theory is premised on *social evolution*) as all industrial societies submit to mass education, mass media and the rational orientation of science and technology.

But who will the rest of the world be becoming more like? Convergence theorists, like their modernisation cousins, are confident that the 'west' is the prototype towards which other societies aspire and evolve. So, as indicated earlier, we're not talking about 'real' convergence: the 'west' keeps going forward in a straight line and the *rest* gravitate (converge) towards that line. Genuine convergence, of course, would be a meeting of the three worlds in a manner that shared equal parts of each's heritage.

EXAM TIP

When answering questions on convergence theory, be sure to emphasise its close links with modernisation theory. It's an important point to make and it extends your essay.

Evolutionary theory

Evolutionary theory, in its social scientific usage, was formulated by the French sociologist, Auguste Comte. He was the man, you'll recall, who, in the nineteenth century first coined the word 'sociology' – a 'founding father', so to speak. As an evolutionary theorist, Comte believed that societies evolve (develop) from less to more complex forms in a one-directional way. The underlying assumption here is that societies become increasingly 'civilised'. Being a grand theorist, Comte plotted this 'progress' in terms of a sequential (i.e. one follows the other) Law of Three Stages:

1 the *Theological Stage*, during which people explained their existence on the basis of supernatural forces and gods, leading eventually to a belief in one almighty God

2 the *Metaphysical Stage*, during which supernatural forces were still prominent explanations for existence, but were more consistent and predictable than the more arbitrary gods of bygone ages

3 the *Positivist Stage*, during which science is the only explanation of existence, and when real evidence, rather than faith or speculation, becomes the principle arbiter of truth – and that's the end of the line!

According to Comte, each stage of human society has been predominantly associated with each of these three phases, starting with the theological, evolving to the metaphysical, and then to the positivist. To be sure, this is a caricatured version of events (what sociologists call an *ideal type model*), but it does focus attention on the bold outlines. Comte recognised that there are transitional stages, when an existing stage tries to fend off a rising usurper. This happened, for example, when the theological stage refuted Galileo's scientific argument that the earth is spherical. Eventually, science won the day here, but theologians came to realise too that his argument wasn't inconsistent with the existence of God. Essentially, this compromise position approximates to the metaphysical stage.

This will get the biologists, chemists and physicists mad, but Comte also claimed that, of all the sciences, sociology was the 'top dog'. It was the great intellectual and practical achievement of the positivist stage. For, believed Comte, it was a science whose insights could provide social policymakers with the knowledge to make society a better place in which to live. He even envisaged a 'sociocracy', a society led by sociologists. That's not such a bad idea perhaps, especially if the 'sociologist-rulers' are social scientists who apply their science justly and wisely, using its insights as a humanising force. But isn't it just a bit far-fetched to imagine such a society will arise? At least, that's what some of Comte's critics wonder.

Comte wasn't the only visionary of his time. Marx also anticipated a more just future towards which society would 'evolve', helped on its way, if necessary, by revolution. Yes, Marx was an evolutionary theorist too! He argued that societies evolved through sequential stages, from slavery to feudalism, from feudalism to capitalism, and from capitalism to socialism/communism. Like Comte, he asserted that the transition from one stage to the next is accompanied by conflict, as one social system wrestles with its successor – sometimes through 'democratic' means, but often through revolution. For Marx, the effective revolutionary is the one who recognises the unstoppable march of history and makes it happen just that bit faster – a sort of 'fast-forward evolutionist', if you like! But more about Marx in the next section.

Another prominent evolutionary theorist of the nineteenth century was the British sociologist, Herbert

EVOLUTIONARY THEORY

FOR

+ The model does seem to be supported by the evidence. While societies might temporarily go backwards – *underdevelop,* as dependency theorists put it – the forward march of history from simple to complex always seems to win the day. If that weren't the case, we wouldn't be playing with and learning from interactive software, or curing cancer patients through new medical techniques. Remember this, when people make anecdotal and unsupported assertions like, 'School students were better educated when I was a child'. No, they weren't.
+ In its Comtean version (but less so from the Spencerian perspective), evolutionary theory helpfully advocates using applied sociology to develop more just societies. While it's conceded that evolutionary forces have their own momentum, there's also a recognition that social scientific knowledge can sometimes prod social change in desirable directions. The idea that social science can be harnessed in the service of humanity is succinctly captured in Ian Lister's view that 'social prosperity, and the alleviation of suffering, are possible through the application of reason' (1984: 3) .
+ As an endeavour to understand society and social change, evolutionary theory was a very important intellectual force of its time. By identifying predictable social patterns, it laid the foundations for the *scientific study of society* – sociology – and greatly influenced the ideas of famous sociologists, like Emile Durkheim and Talcott Parsons. These sociologists keep reminding us that human social behaviour isn't some random event; it's explained on the basis of accumulated social experiences.
+ Continuing on from the above point, evolutionary theory forms the basis for the single most influential school of thought in twentieth-century (at least up to the late 1960s) sociology: *functionalism*. While it has recently fallen into some disrepute, functionalism is still a very important and insightful perspective, especially in its contributions to the study of crime and social order. Merton, for example, a student of Talcott Parsons and a functionalist, is one of the most cited criminologists in the world today. Such is the respect for his immense scholarship.

AGAINST

– Are we really moving forward? In the space of a couple of centuries, so-called progress, fuelled by the industrial revolution, has created a planet in the midst of the largest epoch of animal and plant extinction in 65 million years. Every year there are more people in the world who go hungry. Is this progress? Isn't it time to adopt the ecological sensitivity and community spirit of our New Age sisters and brothers, reversing the complex and destructive and returning to the simple and productive?

– Despite Comte, evolutionary theory has its 'what will be, will be' advocates. Spencer was a bit that way. Indeed, these days his work tends to be regarded as very supportive of 'don't rock the boat' philosophies. Such outlooks underpin conservative social thought, and sometimes justify the 'survival of the fittest' ethos as both natural and right.

– The evolutionary/functionalist way of investigating society is very 'biological'. Sociology is arguably scientific, but it needs its own theoretical orientation and distinctive methods. Trying to figure out why I like films and you like chat shows, requires interpretivistic as well as positivistic reasoning.

– Evolutionary theory might have laid the intellectual basis for functionalist theory, but both these theories have been largely surpassed by radical marxist and social constructionist perspectives, both of which often join up to provide an even more formidable alternative.

Spencer. Because he argued that, like nature, societies have evolved according to laws of selection, survival and adaptation, Spencer has been described as an exponent of 'Social Darwinism'. Darwin, of course, was the pioneer of biological evolution. Like biological organisms, said Spencer, societies have:

- evolved from *simple* to *complex* forms (echoes of Comte here) through a process of natural selection: the strong society has endured; the weak society has succumbed. It was Spencer, not Darwin, who coined the term 'survival of the fittest'
- adapted to their environment through a process of *differentiation* (modern people have specialised functions – one might be a teacher, another a mechanic, etc. – compared to the more uniformly similar functions of their ancestors) and *integration* (feeling and acting as though one is a part of society, as opposed to anarchy)
- progressed from the *homogenous* (not the milk variety!; the type where 'sameness rules' – everyone is a cave-dwelling hunter gatherer, for instance) to the *heterogeneous* (where, as indicated in the preceding point, people become specialised in their activities).

But how do societies make the jump from one stage to the next? Something upsets the equilibrium, is the simple answer. Imagine you're living in a peaceful society that's suddenly attacked by an aggressive invader, as happened, for example, when Native Americans found their world turned upside down by marauding white invader-settlers. This important event challenges the existing equilibrium – that is, the stable, enduring aspects – of Native American culture. Surrender, mass suicide or war are the main choices. But whatever option is selected (often more than one is chosen, for example, war followed by surrender), when the dust settles, a different society emerges. Stronger has triumphed over weaker, and the fittest contender constructs the new society. Invasion is, of course, only one possible trigger of social change. Natural disasters, path-breaking discoveries or new technology can all set things in motion.

Perhaps you've figured it out already, but evolutionary theory largely underpins modernisation theory. Both perspectives envisage societies evolving from old to new forms. In many ways, modernisation theory – and its close cousin, convergence theory – represent a fusion of evolutionary theory and functionalism. What a complex recipe this sounds. Let's simplify things by unpacking the connections. Modernisation and convergence theories:

- are gradualist models of social change that emphasise evolution rather than revolution. While exponents of these theories sensibly recognise that sharp shocks to a social system (for example, sudden widespread disease) can precipitate fairly swift social transformations (for example, rapid medical advances), they emphasise that social change is more commonly a gradual process
- are macro perspectives that chart functional relationships between different stages of development and different types of thought. For example, modern, industrial society fosters rational scientific thinking.

Revolutionary theory

Revolutions are speedy affairs. They also change societies profoundly. Consider the English Revolution of the seventeenth century: within a few years, out went the monarchy and the House of Lords. More importantly, real political power thenceforth resided with Members of Parliament, not with monarchs or peers of the realm – despite their restoration to office not long after the Civil War. The late eighteenth-century French and American and the early nineteenth-century Russian Revolutions also changed old ways fast and decisively. All of these revolutions were violent, which tends to be the case with the most rapid forms of social change. But there are non-violent revolutions (sometimes called economic and cultural revolutions) during which societies change quite quickly (a century isn't uncommon) without the catalyst of sabres, muskets and rocket launchers. The British Industrial Revolution was of this type.

That said, most revolutions contain some violence and some economic and cultural shift. When contemporary revolutionaries engage in armed struggle, among their primary targets are radio and TV broadcasting centres. Whoever has power over the media has potential power over the hearts and minds of the people. Not that instant conversion is on the agenda. The violence that topples an existing regime has usually been preceded by deep-seated ideological confrontation between contending groups – radicals and conservatives – for a considerable period. The call to arms by those who seek to remove the *status quo* by force is usually a 'no turning back' revolutionary flourish to a long-standing war of words between those who cling to tradition and those who urge decisive change.

This forces us to re-iterate what we said earlier: revolutionary theory isn't unrelated to evolutionary theory. This is because revolutions are typically the 'fast-forward' phase of fairly long-standing evolution towards a new kind of society. But what triggers this last quick-paced stage we call revolution? Marx and marxists say it's prompted by the realisation among those who would change society swiftly and dramatically that their moment has come. Now is the time for action.

Let's put this into something a bit more familiar. Imagine you're seeking to change a particular school policy, for example, to end the requirement that students have to wear uniform. A debate about this has endured (evolution!) in your school for some years, but the headteacher and the chair of governors are determined that uniform must remain. But over the years, a majority of teachers and quite a few governors have begun to favour a change. You sense that the mood is right to tip the scales even further, and so you call a meeting of the school student council. They unanimously vote to abolish school uniform. The headteacher and the chair of governors now realise that they're fighting a rearguard action, and they throw in the towel. There's your revolution! And what got things finally decided was you mobilising opinion among the student council, who then seized the moment.

So it is with larger scale revolutions. A collective resolve to radically change the system must be forged. Marxists refer to this as a *revolutionary consciousness*. As Frank remarks, 'For revolutionaries . . . the battlefield includes the field of ideology' (1969b: 402). He controversially (Frank is nearly always polemical!) adds, 'For revolutionary social scientists, the ideological battle extends to the field of social science' (1969b: 402). So what's Frank driving at? He's saying that military revolutionaries and revolutionary social scientists must seek to persuade the majority of the people that revolution is achievable and just. Like most marxists, Frank believes that social science should be an emancipatory discipline rather than mere theoretical discourse. Don't forget, however, that many functionalists adopt this view, even, if sometimes their view of what constitutes 'emancipatory' is different. Let's put the essentials of revolutionary theory into sequential order:

1 Social conditions in society create tensions between existing practices and new ideas. For example, pressing

REVOLUTIONARY THEORY

FOR

+ It's a theory that accurately describes and explains real historical and contemporary events. Witness, for example, rapid social transformations like the late eighteenth-century American Revolution and the late nineteenth-century Eastern European Revolution (which is still going on in former Yugoslavia). Consider too the revolution in South Africa (a mixture of violent and cultural change) that abolished apartheid and introduced democracy. On the cultural revolutionary front, Martin Luther King and the American Civil Rights Movement of the 1960s, radically overhauled legislation that previously permitted racist practices.
+ It provides a moving picture, as opposed to a snapshot view of development. This is the most accurate way to visualise rapid social change: the theory is in harmony with the process it describes. How else could one account for the events referred to in the preceding point without a theory that pays particular attention to moving target rather than static affairs?
+ It combines a sense of structure (i.e. powerful social forces) with an awareness of human agency (i.e. the capacity of people to change society). This it does by highlighting the capacity of successful revolutionaries to 'strike while the iron is hot', of being both shaped by and participating in the historical process. In that respect, it addresses one of the most profound questions in social science: are human beings free? The reply, to paraphrase a famous observation of Karl Marx, is 'Yes, but not in circumstances entirely of their own choosing'.
+ It makes social science a liberating discipline whose purpose is to help set people free. By studying society and knowing its ways, exponents of revolutionary theory are able to provide the poor and oppressed with a vision of a better future worth fighting for.

AGAINST

– How does revolutionary theory account for social stability? There's also that slow, gradual change we call social evolution. Surely evolution is more common than revolution. So if evolution is the 'norm', isn't evolutionary theory a more useful explanation of social change. On the other hand, it's arguably better to let revolutionary theorists explain revolution, and to let evolutionary theorists handle evolution. Better still, integrate them by recognising that evolution precedes revolution – well, most of the time!
– It's a very polemical theory. Revolutionary theorists are generally left-wing, and their political leanings can interfere with their social scientific judgement. In that context, it's important to distinguish between what their hearts want and what their minds know is possible. Marx experienced this dilemma. Sometimes he urged workers to unite in revolutionary purpose; on other occasions, he emphasised that history would run its own course.
– Most revolutionary theorists envisage an egalitarian, utopian future where the oppressed are liberated from capitalistic exploitation, and capitalists are liberated from their own inhumanity. This utopia is invariably a socialist one. Critics aren't convinced, however, that global socialism offers a better future than global capitalism. They doubt whether such a political system will be any more equitable than the socialist countries of today, where income and wealth are unevenly divided.
– Revolutionary theory and its marxist thought forms are increasingly out of touch with present-day social scientific research. Such research is often funded by organisations whose agendas don't support revolutionary action.

poverty – perhaps, aggravated by a food shortage – causes the impoverished to define their circumstances differently. Yesterday, they doffed their caps to the local rulers whom – when the harvest was abundant – ensured that the local populace was well fed. Today, when most of the crop fails, the same rulers don't share what food remains.

2 A generalised belief develops among the poor, fanned by 'intellectuals' (notably, 'educated' people of working-class origin), that yesterday's benefactor is today's oppressor.

3 Typically, a precipitating factor 'pulls the trigger'. For example, a 'riot of the belly' is harshly put down by the army or police, who are protecting the property of the rich and powerful. This event sets in motion widespread protests and mass riots.

4 A revolution erupts. There are three possible outcomes now: the revolutionaries topple the ruling class and shape a new society; the rulers' armed response is too powerful for the insurgents and the beginning revolution is held in check; the struggle is evenly balanced, and a deal is struck leading to 'negotiated reforms'.

The above model focuses on the potential for violent revolutionary change. Economic and cultural revolutions are characterised by similar tensions, but more peaceful – sometimes democratic – processes lead to change. Such change, however, is sometimes underpinned by the threat of violence if a new order isn't forthcoming or is too slow to emerge. Moreover, economic and cultural revolutions quite commonly follow violent ones, as happened in China after the Second World War. Once the ruling class had been overthrown, the Chinese revolutionary leader, Mao Tse Tung, consolidated his victory through educational and training programmes designed to persuade (some would say indoctrinate) the people in the ways of Mao's version of 'communism'.

While revolutionary theory is most obviously linked to marxism, certain functionalists (notably, Emile Durkheim, Neil Smelser and Robert K. Merton) – contrary to the impression conveyed in some textbooks – also envisaged revolution as a possible mover of rapid social change. Merton, for example, spoke (one senses, with some admiration for them) of 'rebels' who 'waged war' on existing institutional arrangements.

All the perspectives discussed above have in common the fact that they're macro (i.e. big frame), structural (i.e. explaining causes and finding remedies on the basis of whole society(ies) analyses) theories. Moreover, in their 'different' ways, they all see development of the majority world as something good. In that sense, modernisation, dependency/WS, convergence, evolutionary and revolutionary theorists want to see an end to world poverty and hunger, even though they sometimes adopt different stances towards the causes of those problems and their remedies.

These days, world sociologists are less inclined than in previous decades to declare their theoretical allegiances explicitly. But they quite commonly adopt one or other of two approaches identified by Paul Streeten (1995):

- *Human resource development* Advocates of this standpoint emphasise the economic productivity aspect of development, and rest their case on applied and theoretical economics derived from 'mainstream' (read 'city-style') economists, bankers (including personnel of the World Bank), and technocrats. While accepting that *per capita Gross National Product (GNP)*[1] measures of development don't provide the whole picture, they point out that these measures give economists a good idea of how societies are more or less developed compared to each other.
- *Humanitarianism* Proponents of this outlook, while taking account of production issues, also stress the 'share of the cake' aspect of development, something that stock market indicators tend to gloss over. Social scientists who adopt the humanitarian approach consider the so-called 'unproductive' members of society – people who are chronically ill or disabled, etc. – too. In that context, humanitarians note that if parents in the majority world know that the community will look after them if they become infirm, an important reason for large families (i.e. as carers of the old) disappears.

No doubt, you'll have seen aspects of modernisation and convergence theories in the first of these models, and of dependency/WS theories in the second. But remember that all theories simply help us to sharpen our outlook(s). They must be modified and adjusted in the light of new evidence and more convincing arguments. So don't be too rigid in adhering to just one perspective, even if your intellectual and ethical commitment might align itself more with one view than with another.

QUESTION

How do each of the theories below characterise the relationship between poor and rich countries?

a modernisation theory
b dependency/WS theory
c convergence theory
d evolutionary theory
e revolutionary theory

[1] GNP refers to the value of all the goods and services produced by a country, plus the value of its net revenue from overseas investment. Per capita GNP refers to the average (mean) value of GNP received by each individual in a country.

Measuring development

Now that we've considered the main theories in world sociology, we're better placed to examine how development can be measured. None of the perspectives adopt a social constructionist 'people are as developed as they feel' approach. That would make a nonsense of the very real inequalities that exist between the majority and rich worlds. What would we make, for example, of a poor Indian woman who says she lives in a developed country when she and many of her citizens don't have access to clean mains water? Conversely, how would we respond to a rich British woman who hires three Filipino maids to attend to household chores and who claims her country is undeveloped?

While, as social scientists, we need to take account of how people feel, development is one of those areas where it's usually more helpful to quantify things. How many people can read? How many children live to adulthood? Is anyone in prison because their views don't accord with those of the government? Ideally, all of these and other important indicators of development could be fed into a computer, and out would come a single number measurement of how developed a society is. Efforts have been made to measure human rights in different countries, to include civil and political and social and economic rights (Fraser: 1994). But this quest, though noble, is far from simple.

When, for example, do we stop adding indicators to the list? Furthermore, what about the high murder rates in a country like the US – does that mean it's not really developed after all? Also, whose definitions do we use when we talk of human rights? Some issues are self-evident, for example, the right not to be subjected to cruel and unusual punishments. But what do we make of 'western'-style indicators of human rights that include the constitutional right to own one's home (Fraser 1994)? Some socialists regard this as an unethical encroachment on the rights of homeless people, and favour community housing projects to home-owner schemes. These are very debatable issues, and the 'experts' haven't stopped pondering them. Nor have they come up with answers that satisfy everyone.

So how then can we begin to 'measure' development?

Economic growth (i.e. an increase in per capita GNP) is a starting point, but not a sufficient condition for development. For, 'Depending on the assessment criteria used, the same process of economic growth may be welcomed as . . . a trend favourable for some and unfavourable for others' (Sachs 1995: 1).

To illustrate this important point, consider an imaginary island inhabited by 100 people. Five of them are ruling class, and the other 95 belong to the working class. Every day, a gigantic apple pie weighing 100 kilos is baked by the workers. If this were shared equally, each individual would get 1 kilo of pie. However, half of the pie is consumed by the rulers, and the other half by the 95 workers. This means that each ruler scoffs 10 kilos of pie a day (yes, they're overweight!), and each worker chomps through just over a half kilo a day (that's quite a lot too). Nevertheless, the per capita GNP (roughly, the 'mean average' product consumed per person) is 1 kilo of pie. Next year, the fruit pies get bigger, increasing to 150 kilos in weight (i.e. an increased per capita GNP of 1.5 kilos of pie). But the five rulers consume much more of the pie, now eating 100 kilos per day, namely, 20 kilos each. This leaves 50 kilos to be shared between the 95 workers, who are no better off than before, even though per capita GNP is up from one to 1.5 kilos. So you see, while per capita GNP is up, the trend is more favourable for the ruling group and less favourable for the worker group (discounting, of course, the increasing weight-related disorders experienced by the rulers!).

Supporting this point further with concrete examples, consider the figures opposite. What they show is that many countries have a relatively high GNP per capita, but low human development indicators (so-called HDIs, as measured on the basis of life expectancy, adult literacy and infant deaths) – and vice versa.

QUESTION

Summarise, in concise social scientific language, the *main* points that are highlighted by the table and chart opposite.

Clearly, we must move away from the view that what counts, so far as measurable development is concerned, is growth in per capita GNP. Such a measurement might satisfy Wall Street stockbrokers, but it doesn't give a full picture of how the 'apple pie' is really divided. Nor does it say anything about how citizens are treated in terms of 'social development': their participation in democratic decision-making, whether they're denied fundamental human rights, the quality of their physical and social environment, etc.

In seeking to arrive at a wider-reaching measurement of what would constitute 'social development' in terms of future-oriented 'action targets' in the majority world, the Director General of UNESCO (1995) identified these factors:

- expansion of education and training, especially in rural areas, and the harnessing of science and technology
- combating poverty by ensuring that poor people are involved in the design and implementation of social programmes
- paying proper regard to the cultural, historical and social contexts of poor countries, namely, avoiding policy initiatives that ride roughshod over people's customs

Similar income, different HDI, 1991–2

Country	GNP per capita (US$)	HDI value	HDI rank	Life expectancy (years)	Adult literacy (%)	Infant mortality (per 1,000 live births)
GNP per capita around $400 to $500						
Sri Lanka	500	0.665	90	71.2	89	24
Nicaragua	400	0.583	106	65.4	78	53
Pakistan	400	0.393	132	58.3	36	99
Guinea	500	0.191	173	43.9	27	135
GNP per capita around $1,000 to $1,100						
Ecuador	1,010	0.718	74	66.2	87	58
Jordan	1,060	0.628	98	67.3	82	37
El Salvador	1,090	0.543	112	65.2	75	46
Congo	1,040	0.461	123	51.7	59	83
GNP per capita around $2,300 to $2,600						
Chile	2,360	0.848	38	71.9	94	17
Malaysia	2,520	0.794	57	70.4	80	14
South Africa	2,540	0.650	93	62.2	80	53
Iraq	2,550	0.614	100	65.7	63	59

(United Nations Development Programme 1994: 15)

Similar incomes – different human development (GNP per capita around $400 – $500)

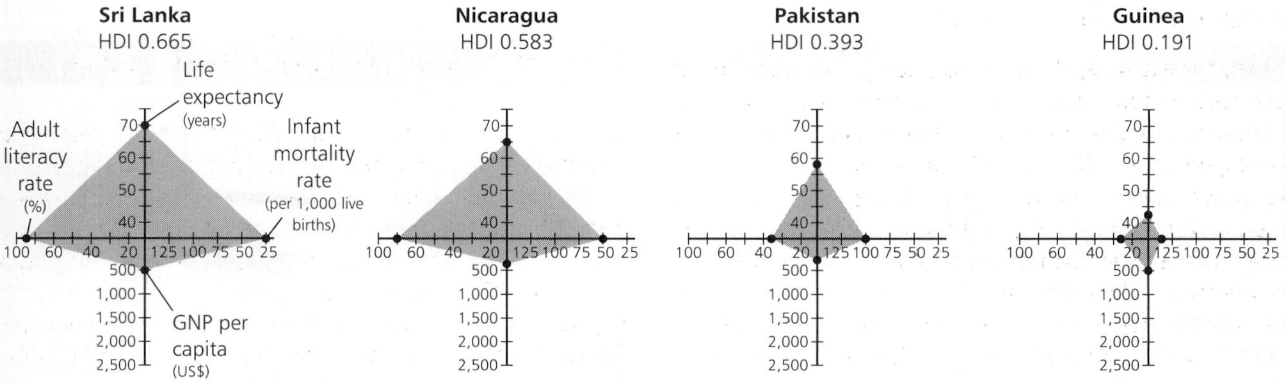

(United Nations Development Programme 1994: 16)

- promoting a vision of employment and work that celebrates the notion of an 'active life', that is, a life which embraces leisure as well as production
- enhancing the life quality of the rural poor by promoting employment in cultural and eco-tourism, shelter-building using local materials, developing local health and social service provisions, and creating community media
- advancing people's awareness of the environment and their participation in equitable and sensible use of resources for 'sustainable development' (i.e. ensuring that one generation's development doesn't hinder the development of future generations)
- strengthening social policy skills and devising an 'early warning system' that enables governments to check that social policies actually promote the life quality of the poor.

These 'action targets' clarify what the Director General of UNESCO believes would constitute aspects of social development that aren't merely confined to computer print-outs of GNP trends from a rich world city bank.

A more shorthand and a rather ingenious way of defining human development (which is a precursor of trying to measure it) is provided by Paul Streeten in his variation on Abraham Lincoln's definition of government:

'It is development *of* the people, *for* the people, *by* the people. *Of* the people implies adequate income generation through jobs and the generation of primary incomes; *for* the people implies social services for those who need help and the generation of secondary incomes; and *by* the people means participation. It could also be interpreted as the economic, social and political dimensions of development.'

(Streeten 1995: 28)

Still a bit vague for you positivists out there, perhaps!? In that case, let's consider a very quantitative form of measurement: the UNDP Human Development Index. Although this index can't hope to capture the entire concept of development in a single number, it's certainly an improvement on the per capita GNP index. The HDI below (similar to the previous one, but, surprisingly, not separating out infant mortality) comprises:

- the calculation of average real purchasing power in relation up to an international poverty line
- the literacy rate and the mean (average) years of schooling
- the life expectancy at birth.

These three components are calculated to a common denominator by counting the distance between the best and worst performances. This provides a ranking of countries. The HDI has been adjusted for sex disparities to measure the extent of sexual equality between the three components. Thus a country, which came out well before this adjustment, would come out badly if it were found that income and wealth were largely in the hands of men. Top of the scale, incidentally, is Sweden.

Looking at development in its human manifestations, provides a more optimistic picture than in income terms alone. Since 1960, average life expectancy has gone up by 16 years, adult literacy by 40 per cent, nutritional levels by more than 40 per cent, and child mortality rates have been halved. In these important respects, the international divide, unlike that regarding income per head, has closed significantly. Thus, while the average income per head in the majority world is 6 per cent of that in the rich world, life expectancy is now 80 per cent, literacy 66 per cent, and nutrition 85 per cent (Streeten 1995).

If you want to consult a simply presented, but very informative, way of measuring how far countries have developed, look at the regular snapshot feature called, 'Country Profile', in *New Internationalist* magazine. Reproduced below is the feature for Uganda which, while

UGANDA: AT A GLANCE

Leader President Yoweri Kaguta Museveni

Economy GNP per capita: $170 – the seventh lowest in the world (US$23,240)
Monetary unit: Ugandan Shilling
Main exports: Coffee (70% of total), cotton.
New exports – hides, maize, sesame and fish
Main imports: Capital goods, manufactured goods, foodstuffs, fuels
External debt: $3 billion

People 19.3 million

Health Infant mortality 114 per 1,000 live births (Australia 7 per 1,000). An estimated one in five (nine per cent of the general population) of the sexually active population is infected with HIV. Encouragingly, though, rates of infection among women attending antenatal clinics have been falling since 1992.

Culture Most Ugandans come from the integration of various ethnic groups, mainly the Baganda, Bunyoro and Batoro.
Religion: Christian (Catholic and various Protestant sects) 50%; traditional (mostly animist) 40%; Muslim 10%.
Languages: English is the official language but Nilotic languages are spoken in the north and Bantu in the south. The most common are Kiswahili, Luganda and Luo.

Sources: *New Africa Year Book 1995–96, Africa Review 1995; The Statesman Year Book 94–95; The State of the World's Children 1995; Amnesty International; Oxfam; AIDS Analysis Africa*

Previously profiled October 1983

NI star rating

Excellent ★★★★★
Good ★★★★
Fair ★★★
Poor ★★
Appalling ★

STAR RATINGS

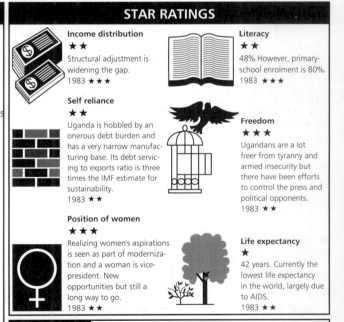

Income distribution
★★
Structural adjustment is widening the gap.
1983 ★★★

Literacy
★★
48% However, primary-school enrolment is 80%.
1983 ★★★

Self reliance
★★
Uganda is hobbled by an onerous debt burden and has a very narrow manufacturing base. Its debt servicing to exports ratio is three times the IMF estimate for sustainability.
1983 ★★

Freedom
★★★
Ugandans are a lot freer from tyranny and armed insecurity but there have been efforts to control the press and political opponents.
1983 ★★

Position of women
★★★
Realizing women's aspirations is seen as part of modernization and a woman is vice-president. New opportunities but still a long way to go.
1983 ★★

Life expectancy
★
42 years. Currently the lowest life expectancy in the world, largely due to AIDS.
1983 ★★

POLITICS

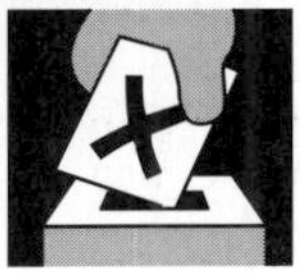

NI Assessment ★★★★★
The NRM Government deserves credit for pulling Uganda out of the horror of the Amin and Obote years – and for its moves against sectarianism and towards local democracy. But its economic policies may work against its claim to be acting in the interests of all Ugandans at a time when it is resisting pressure for multi-party democracy.

(Adapted from *New Internationalist*, October 1995, page 36)

the 'darling' of the International Monetary Fund (having followed its recommendations and achieved an annual growth rate of nearly 6 per cent over the past nine years), still remains a very poor African country. The sense of progress certainly isn't felt by all the people, especially the residents of north Uganda.

OVER TO YOU

What factors would you include in an international table measuring the extent to which countries are developed? Give reasons for your decision.

Colonialism and its legacies

One important factor that, according to many social scientists – especially, dependency/WS theorists – has had an oppressive rather than a liberating influence on the development of poor countries is *colonialism*. Colonialists have an outlook like that described by Paulo Freire:

'The oppressor consciousness tends to transform everything surrounding it into an object of its domination. The earth, property, production, the creations of men [*sic*], men themselves, time – everything is reduced to the status of objects at its disposal.'

(Freire 1972: 34)

A colony is an outpost of a 'parent' nation. Some social scientists, notably, dependency theorists, would change that to 'of an "exploiter" nation'. They have a strong case. Colonialism has oftentimes brutalised the cultural heritage and the economic practices of traditional societies and communities. Consider these facts:

- Writing to the King and Queen of Spain of the Indios (as he called them) on the island that was named San Salvador, Christopher Columbus remarked: 'So tractable, so peaceable, are these people, that I swear to your Majesties there is not in the world a better nation' (cited by Brown 1991: 1). Columbus added that the people should be 'made to work, sow and do all that is necessary and to adopt our ways' (ibid.). Over the next 400 years (1492–1890), millions of Europeans and their descendants enforced their ways upon the people of the so-called 'New World'.
- The 'slash and burn logging' of rich world corporations in their majority world outposts has long been – and still is – a threat to the tribal inhabitants of tropical forests. These traditional groups:

'possess sophisticated ecological knowledge about the forest . . . As fewer tribal people engage in traditional practices, valuable knowledge gained over hundreds of years in tropical forests is being lost.'

(Gradwohl and Greenberg 1988: 47–8)

European colonialism and expansion over the last 400 years has led to a few countries, mainly European and North American, consuming a disproportionately large share of world timber, and to the displacement of poor people from the land.

- In seventeenth-century Virginia, a white colonialist master could kill his black slave and yet not be charged with murder. Eugene D. Genovese writes disapprovingly:

'Would a man willingly destroy his own property? Certainly not. Therefore, no such crime as the murder of one's own slave could present itself to a court of reasonable men.'

(Genovese 1975: 37)

Having colonised eastern America, white Europeans shipped human cargo in chains from Africa, enslaved these black Africans on Deep South plantations, raised their children in bondage, and treated all of them as property, thereby denying their inherent humanity.

- 'Western' colonists imposed homogenous (lacking in variety) food systems on the heterogeneous (rich in variety) food systems of the majority world. Traditional cultivation practices adopted multi-crop principles, so if one crop failed, there would be a reserve crop in the form of other vegetables. Over-reliance on one or a few crops is potentially disastrous: Irish potato famines and US corn blights demonstrate this. There's no suggestion that the majority world should re-enact ancient ways. However, aspects of modern systems can usefully be incorporated into traditional farming methods, provided the farmers are in control of the incorporation.
- Edward Sjöblom, a missionary, arrived in the Congo in July 1892. Travelling by steamer up the Congo, he witnessed a flogging with a hippo-hide whip. All the white men on board were of the opinion that only the whip can civilise 'the black'. Sjöblom noted:

'The captain often showed the boy the *chicotte* [a whip of raw hippopotamus hide], but made him wait all day before letting him taste it. However, the moment of suffering came. I tried to count the lashes and think they were about sixty, apart from the kicks to his head and back. The captain smiled with satisfaction when he saw the boy's thin garb soaked with blood. The boy lay there on deck in his torment, wriggling like a worm, and every time the captain or one of the trading agents passed him by, he was given a kick or several.'

(cited by Lingqvist 1997: 20)

- After the English landed in Plymouth, America, in 1620, they were saved from probable starvation by Native Americans, one of whom was a Pemaquid called

Samoset. He and other Native Americans gave the English corn and showed them how to cultivate it. In 1625, the English colonists asked Samoset to 'give' them 12,000 additional acres of Pemaquid land. Samoset, like other Native Americans, didn't believe that land could be owned but, to humour the white settlers, he signed a land transfer document. This was the first deed of Native American land to English colonists. It signalled the gradual erosion of a native land-use culture by a colonising culture that fenced in and turned common land into private property.

These are but a few examples of the many different ways in which majority world cultures and economies were 'colonised' by rich European nations. Far from promoting the development of poor countries, they often led to what Frank calls the 'development of underdevelopment'. In that sense, they and other exploitative forms of colonialism left a legacy of cultural decimation and economic hardship. Such deprivations were, however, unevenly felt. Some leaders in the majority world cut a deal with white rulers, whereby they retained certain privileges in return for 'betraying' their people by encouraging – sometimes forcing – their submission. Such leaders, 'compradors', as they're called, are still doing 'very nicely, thank you' today, amidst widespread poverty in their nations.

Incidentally, 'neo-colonial' means 'new-colonial': it refers to modern-style colonialism which tends to enforce dependency of the majority world on the rich world through trade rather than 'old-style' military might. To be sure, there has always been a bit of economic coercion and military muscle in the old and the new varieties of colonial domination. However, the former type was often a warlike, setting-up, 'we're in charge' venture. The new type is an 'after the conquest' consolidation of what's often been obtained through military means. It's largely based on 'persuading' the now 'independent' colonies that they need to sell their commodities to the rich world countries.

On the cultural front, colonists have often 'demonised' the norms and values of the colonised. White European culture, however, with a possessive consciousness that turned all it saw into private property, was revered as civilised. Subject culture was presented as barbaric, primitive and savage. Some pseudo-scientists even claimed that the skulls of white people housed larger brains than those of black people. To 'prove' this point, 'white' skulls were filled with gunshot which was then tipped into measuring jugs to calculate the volume of the brain cavity. Similar procedures were carried out with 'black' skulls, but the gun shot was not so firmly packed as with the 'white' skulls. The falsified conclusion was that white people had bigger brains than black people, and were therefore more 'intelligent' and 'civilised'.

Let the scientific record show that brain size doesn't correlate with 'intelligence' or 'civilisation', and that, anyway, the skulls which house the largest human brains in the world are of the black Masai tribe of Kenya. Reliable scientific knowledge is, of course, incompatible with ill-informed racist prejudice. That's why the eminent anthropologist, Louis Leakey, balked at the absurd notion that Africa wasn't a fit place for the origin of the human species and, to quote his also very famous son, Richard Leakey, 'went on to establish East Africa as a vital region in the history of our early evolution' (1994: 2–3).

Having de-humanised colonised people as uncivilised, white Europeans had found an easy excuse to behave badly. The sixteenth-century Catholic priest, Batolome de Las Casas, provides a powerful account of the depredations of the Spanish, who flung themselves upon the native people 'like wolves after days of starvation'. He continued:

'For 40 years they have done nothing but torture, murder, harass, afflict torment and destroy them with extraordinary, incredible, innovative and previously unheard of cruelty.'

(cited by Ellwood 1991: 6)

Las Cas estimated that 50 million native people perished in Latin America and the Caribbean within 50 years of Columbus' landing in the 'New World'. It's now reckoned that 90 per cent of the indigenous (native-born) population of the Americas was wiped out in a century and a half: 'the greatest demographic collapse in the history of the planet', writes Wayne Ellwood (1991: 6).

While murder played its part, it has to be said that much of this mayhem was inadvertently caused by diseases brought from Europe by the colonists. There's a perverse irony here: the self-proclaimed 'tamers of savages' brought diseases to people whose bodies were healthy but, sadly, unused and barely resistant to Old World illnesses like influenza, measles and smallpox.

Today, the old-style colonialism of the conquistadors has been replaced with the neo-colonialism of international corporations. It's they, not the US cavalry, who now occupy the lands of the Apache and the Commanche. Today, says Adrian Esquina Lisco (Spiritual Chief of the National Association of Indigenous Peoples of El Salvador), 'the white world wants to celebrate its 500th anniversary of invasion and genocide and call it "the discovery" or the "encounter"' (Lisco 1991:17).

It's this, essentially racist, legacy that colonialism has left. In that context, consider present-day Brazil. Portuguese colonists brought the first African slaves to that country in 1549. Before slavery was abolished in 1888, nearly eight million slaves had been shipped to Brazil. Today, racism is banned by the constitution. Yet racist attacks are an everyday occurrence. Other more subtle forms of racism also exist: school books are commonly written by white authors, and there's little reference to the ancestors of black children; job advertisements often require a 'good appearance' – a shorthand for 'don't apply if you're black'. As the African–Brazilian sociologist, Lourdes Teodoro, comments:

'the only Afro-Brazilians you see in Brasilia's government buildings are serving coffee, mopping floors or chauffeuring around white Brazilian bureaucrats.'

(Teodoro 1991: 26)

Teodoro also reports that, in 1988, an adviser to the then Sao Paulo governor proposed a national birth control campaign targeting black people, people of 'mixed race' and 'Indians'. The idea was to prevent these ethnic groups becoming a majority.

The impact of colonial values is also felt among those elites in the majority world who hanker after rich world lifestyles. These 'westernised rulers' – politicians, generals, businessmen (there are few women) and the like – have surrendered their own ethnic identities to become the carriers of 'colonial culture'. They promote this – often Anglicised – culture in educational institutions that were originally established by former white colonists. In this manner, as Raymond L. M. Lee writes:

'colonial education [has] violated the natives' sense of self by derogating indigenous knowledge for the impression of Western knowledge as infallible, absolute and uncompromising.'

(Lee 1994: 44–5)

In other words, the colonists, through the schools they set up in days gone by, have left a cultural imprint that says, 'what's good for the white west is good for the rest'. This cultural hegemony (ideological domination) is strongly buttressed by media representations (usually of 'successful' white people) of the 'good life' in the 'west'. The main message here is that it's desirable for poor people to buy goods and services that are eagerly supplied by TNCs: expensive soda, cigarettes, jeans, etc. To quote Lee again:

'The reshaping of cultures around the world under the juggernaut of the culture industry appears inevitable, given the quest for modernity in many non-Western societies . . . The penetration of multinational capitalism into non-Western societies brings with it popular TV serials, fast-food chains, shopping malls, freeways, theme parks and sports entertainment. These cultural forms signify instances of the good life desired by non-Western consumers.'

(Lee 1994: 29)

But the adoption by majority world people of 'western' lifestyles doesn't always go unchallenged. Cultural resistance is quite widespread, and sometimes comes from unexpected quarters. Take Malaysia, for instance. It's part of the majority world, but it's a rapidly developing nation, a so-called 'newly industrialising country' (NIC) or 'semi-peripheral country'. And it's caught between two lifestyles. The tension is highlighted by the position of the so-called 'liberated', TNC-employed, Malay female. No longer living in rural villages, this 'new woman' is now working on the electronic assembly lines of the big city. Much to the consternation of the Malay establishment, which still cherishes strict female dress codes and 'feminine coyness', the rebound effect of exposure to TNC culture has been the rise of a jeans-clad, cosmetics-adorned, 'westernised', Malay female employee. This is just one example of the unease created in majority world countries when the option of acquiring 'western-style' technological success has to be weighed against the 'liberalising' effects of rich world culture.

Sometimes, of course, majority world countries don't see a contradiction between retaining traditional values and moving forward in developmental terms. Thus, for example, NICs like Hong Kong, Singapore, South Korea and Taiwan have engineered their own 'eastern' versions of modernity without becoming totally immersed in 'western' ways. These countries still cherish a Confucian philosophy (from the ancient Chinese sage, Confucius) that emphasises frugality, hard work, moral integrity, and self-control. Such values – contrary to what some modernisation theorists might expect – are firmly anchored to a business ethos that has led to very rapid economic growth over recent decades.

So there's really no need, it seems, for poor countries to adopt those 'modern man' values (read 'American man' values) so fervently propagated in the 1950s and 1960s by modernisation theorists like Daniel Lerner. These social scientists argued that majority world culture needed a 'good dose' of rich world know-how if poor people were to replace fatalism with rationality and superstition with science. This is an imperious view. It suggests that 'west knows best', whatever the circumstances. At the other extreme would be the opinion that only majority world knowledge is worthwhile. This is inverted snobbery and is clearly untenable. What we really need is for people to listen to each other. The poor have important things to say; so have the more prosperous. Both might learn from each other, as indeed happens when traditional healers and 'western' doctors share their valuable knowledge and work towards the common goal of helping their patients.

In that context, it's important to recognise that a culture's inherent value mustn't be measured against a yardstick

WORK
Racial prejudice affects access to jobs.

Canada – Indigenous people are twice as likely to be jobless as the rest of the population.

US – Blacks are twice as likely to be jobless as whites.

UK – Ethnic minorities are twice as likely to be jobless. Ethnic minority women are three times as likely to be jobless as other women.

Australia – Aboriginal people are more than three times as likely to be jobless as the general population.

But in **India** 10% of higher level jobs in the public sector now go to people from the Scheduled Castes (more than 16% of the total population) compared with only 3.5% in 1972.

HEALTH, WEALTH AND HOUSING
How we live and how long we live may often be determined by 'race'.

In the **US**:

- Nearly 50% of the black population live in polluted areas, compared to 30% of the white population.
- 40% of Native Americans live below the poverty line. 37% die before the age of 45. They are 10 times as likely to die of alcohol abuse.

In **Australia**:

- Aboriginal people's life expectancy is 15 years lower than the rest of the population. Infant mortality is three times higher.
- The suicide rate is six times higher.
- Aboriginal family income is about half the Australian average.

In **South Africa**:

- The white 14% of the population owns almost 90% of the land.
- Life expectancy for whites is 73 years, for blacks 57. Infant mortality among whites is 13 per 1,000; among blacks, 57 per 1,000.

In the **UK**:

- People from ethnic minorities are four times more likely to be homeless in London than whites.

(Adapted from *New Internationalist*, October 1994, page 18)

which has been constructed by rich world nations. Can we really say, for example, that the higher the rate of urban dwelling, the higher the level of 'civilisation'? In 1995, 89.5 per cent of UK inhabitants were urban dwellers. But does that mean they're more culturally sophisticated than nomadic Arabs? We don't think so. Traveller 'New Age' Britons and nomadic Arabs define the 'good life' in terms of service to each other, generosity, austerity, lack of residential confinement and access to clean, fresh air. Not for them, the notion that urban dwelling is a superior lifestyle. And is it right to suggest that the rich world offers a more 'civilised' lifestyle when it discriminates against those of its citizens who have black or brown skins? (Look at the examples on the left.) Again, we don't believe so.

While, 'At the level of postcolonial governments, emulating successful foreign economic models was and still is a conscious policy' (Bamyeh 1993: 45), this needn't be the model for the majority world's poor. For there are different types of dignified futures, none of which have to be based on the economic and social systems of the neo-colonial powers. It's achieving alternative futures that's the hard part, a goal considered in a later section, *Alternative development strategies*, page 592.

In what some social scientists have called our 'post-modern world' – a world where it's no longer assumed that the most powerful people and the most powerful nations know more than everyone else – white colonial representations of majority world people as members of inferior ethnic and 'racial' groups have become increasingly absurd, not to say downright offensive. Most, if not all, global sociologists are now of the opinion that the self-proclaimed superiority of colonial culture, in both its old and 'neo' forms, must be taken down from its pedestal. That's a lesson that particularly needs to be applied in the context of the next issue for consideration: what to do about population growth.

Causes and consequences of demographic trends

In about 26 years from now – a generation time-frame – eight billion human beings will be living on this earth. On present trends, three billion people will be poor; over two and a half billion people will be homeless; and two billion people will be without mains water. In these anticipated circumstances, notes Riccardo Petrella:

'satisfaction of the basic needs and expectations of eight billion people is the only true and compelling objective for economic and social development . . . It is therefore time to recognize the right of every individual to enjoy access to an income making it possible to live in society and providing for housing, food, medical care, education and clothing.'

(Petrella 1995: 20)

Demography is the study of population trends. *Demographers* examine the causes and consequences of predicted trends, like those referred to. They also, in an applied context, propose interventionist strategies that aim to influence and/or deal with the trends. For example, demographers who adopt a modernisation stance tend to advocate the promotion of birth control programmes in the majority world to stem population growth. Demographers of a dependency persuasion are generally in favour of population reduction policies too. However, they advocate poverty elimination programmes as the most effective – and, importantly, the most just – way to reduce human reproductivity: poverty leads to large families, prosperity to small families.

Causes of population increase and decrease

Here we find very complex and hotly debated arguments and explanations, much of them located in a modernisation versus dependency framework. There is, however, broad agreement that population trends are mainly dependent on three factors:

- *birth rates* (total births per year, per 1,000 of the population)
- *death rates* (total deaths per year, per 1,000 of the population)
- *migration*.

The first two factors affect total world population. Migration, however, while one of the determinants of local population size, has no effect on the total global scene. Space travel might change that one day!

In the crudest sense, population increase or decrease depends on the difference between births and deaths. For example, if the difference between birth rates and death rates is 0.1 per cent (that is, each year, 0.1 per cent more people are born than die, as is the current European experience), it takes more than 1,000 years for the population to double. However, if the annual rate of natural increase is 2.9 per cent – as in Africa – the population doubles in only 24 years.

One of the most influential models of demographic change used by social scientists is called *demographic transition theory*, the 'demographic transition' referring to how societies move from one set of population circumstances to another. Illustrative of this point, deaths rates fell in the Europe of the 1800s, as a result of improved living conditions and better medical science. This led to a rapid increase in population, spurring overseas migration. By the 1900s, however, birth rates fell, slowing population growth.

These events accord with the predictions of demographic transition theory, which proposes that:

1. Societies have initially high birth and high death rates. The population doesn't grow.
2. The above phase is followed by an intermediate stage in which modernisation begins, and mortality declines but fertility remains high. The upshot is rapid population growth.
3. The 'last era' is one of relatively stable population growth, caused by low birth and low death rates. This describes the present state of most of the rich world.

According to convergence, evolutionary and modernisation theories, one would expect the same 'last era' pattern to be gradually occurring in the majority world. But, claim Bryant Robey, Shea O. Rutstein and Leo Morris (1993), different rates of change are apparent. Majority world fertility rates have fallen much more rapidly than they did during the 'last era' demographic transition in Europe. Moreover, Robey *et al.* note that birth rates in the majority world have fallen, even in the absence of better living conditions. Their observation perhaps challenges the dependency theory claim that poor people will have fewer babies if they become more prosperous. Robey *et al.* assert that:

> 'Developing countries appear to have benefited from the growing influence and scope of family-planning programs, from new contraceptive technologies and from the educational power of mass media.'
>
> (Robey *et al.* 1993: 30)

Employing positivistic analyses of recent data about fertility in the majority world drawn from 44 representative, comparable surveys of more than 300,000 women conducted from 1985–93, Robey *et al.* found that the *fertility rate* (number of births per year, per 1,000 females of child-bearing age) had declined very significantly since the 1970s. In Thailand, for example, fertility rates have fallen 50 per cent in 12 years, from 4.6 children per woman in 1975, to 2.3 children in 1987. In Columbia, the fertility rate went down from an average of 4.7 children per woman in 1976, to 2.8 children in 1990. In eight Latin American and Caribbean countries, women in the 1990s are having an average of one less child than did women 20 or so years ago.

A number of factors, notably, the use of contraception, the age at which women first marry, the length of time after childbirth when a woman can't conceive (due to breast-feeding or sexual abstinence), and the use of abortion are all directly implicated. More indirect factors affecting birth rates are education, location, occupation, religious belief, social status and wealth.

Of the direct influences, the most significant is family planning, argue Robey *et al.* (1993). According to them, the data reveal that differences in contraceptive prevalence explain about 90 per cent of the variation in fertility rates. Excluding China, 38 per cent of women in their childbearing years in majority world countries practise family planning in the 1990s: a total of some 375 million women. When China is included as a majority world country, the figure rises to 51 per cent. While quite high, this rate is still significantly below the more than 70 per cent of women in most rich world countries who use contraception. In Japan and some European countries, the total fertility rate is actually approaching, or is below, the *replacement level* of 2.1 children per couple. The *replacement level* refers to the rate at which the population eventually stops growing.

Contraceptive use is regarded as a direct 'cause' of a reduced fertility rate, as 'demonstrated' in the graph below. The bar chart illustrates the relationship between women's education and fertility rates in three countries. It's a relationship that's regarded as an indirect 'cause', that is, more education 'causes' more women to know about, think about and actually use contraceptives, assuming, of course, that contraceptives are available.

The education of girls is an important determinant of family size, even if it's regarded as an indirect cause. Educated women usually have more awareness of family planning and more power to shape their own lives. They're also likely to marry later, to postpone their first pregnancy, to leave more time between births, and to have fewer children. As the chart below indicates, the impact of secondary education is particularly marked.

QUESTION

What do the three charts reveal about the relationship between:

a contraceptive use and fertility rates in poor countries?

b schooling and fertility rates in poor countries?

Although the use of birth control and the development of female education programmes in poor countries are good predictors of smaller families, the world's population will continue to grow, pushed upwards by the sheer momentum of present numbers. It's true that fertility rates have been falling for many years everywhere in the world except Africa – where now the first signs of decline are also evident in countries such as Botswana, Kenya and Zimbabwe. Yet, according to World Bank projections, more than half the countries of sub-Saharan Africa will see their present populations increase five-fold before stabilising. Even when stabilisation occurs (probably not until well into the twenty-first century), there's likely to be more than double today's global population.

Relation between contraceptive use and fertility rates, 1984–92

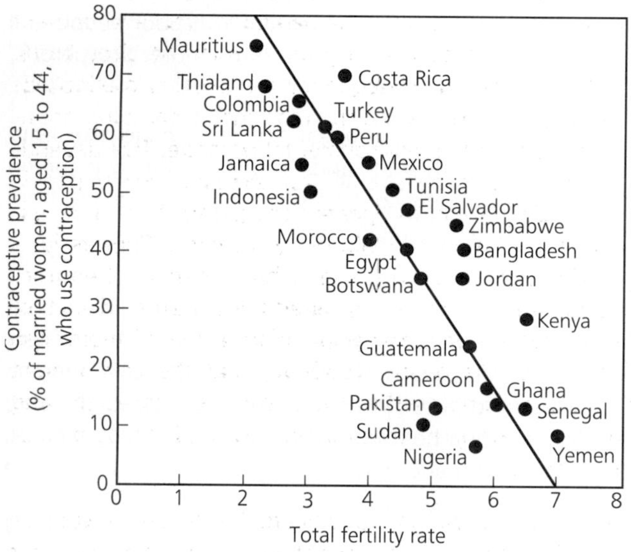

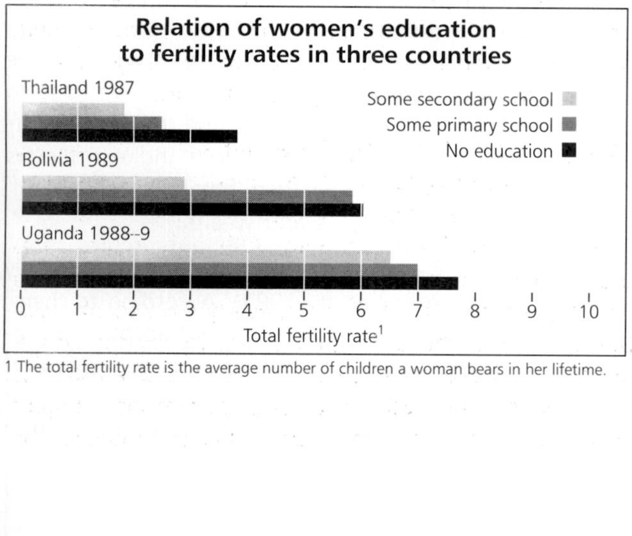

1 The total fertility rate is the average number of children a woman bears in her lifetime.

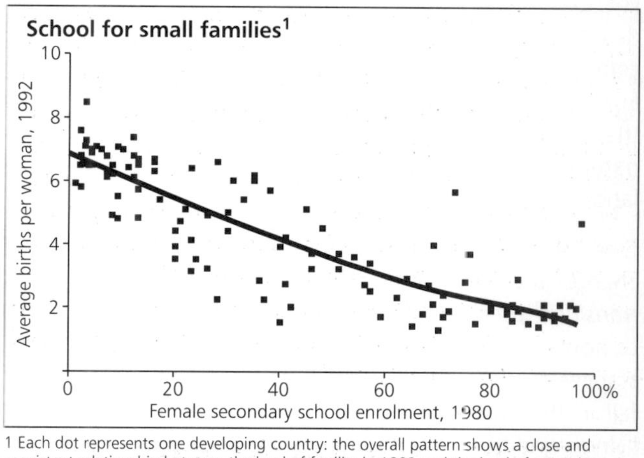

1 Each dot represents one developing country: the overall pattern shows a close and consistent relationship between the level of fertility in 1992 and the level of secondary education for girls a decade earlier.

(UNICEF 1994: 27, figures for total fertility rate from United Nations Population Division [1993] *World Population Prospects: The 1992 Revision*, and education figures from UNESCO [1993] *Statistical Yearbooks* and earlier years)

Nevertheless, it needs to be recognised that in much of the world, desired (or is it 'socially pressured'?) family size is still much higher than the replacement level. In these circumstances, argues the then President of the Population Council, Margaret Catley-Carlson (1994), it's necessary to seek to create the conditions that will increase the desire for smaller families. These conditions include, says Catley-Carlson:

- rising incomes
- falling child death rates
- increasing levels of female education
- greater gender equality
- widespread access to the kind of family planning services in which people can have confidence.

There are echoes here of the conclusions reached at the 1994 International Conference on Population and Development in Cairo (UNICEF 1995). Drawing on the previous 20 years of study and experience, the Cairo Conference showed that the main forces behind falling fertility are:

- rising levels of education, especially for girls
- lower child death rates, enabling parents to be confident that their children will survive
- increasing economic security
- progress towards gender equality, helping to reduce a preference for sons, and offering women choices beyond unbroken child-bearing years
- widespread availability of family planning information and services.

However, while women might choose to have fewer children, more women in the population means more children will be born overall, even if family sizes are reduced. It's this momentum that's a continuing cause of increased birth rates. So will things eventually slow down? Not, it seems, in the foreseeable future. Despite the preceding arguments about the efficacy of birth control, the world's population continues to grow by about 90 million people a year. In a world of such massive inequalities between nations, where more than a billion people don't have access to safe drinking water, where every day at least 25,000 people die from illnesses caused by unsafe water, where each year there are more people who don't get enough to eat, women have to bear higher numbers of children to satisfy *perceived* population replacement levels.

Consequences of population increase and decrease

These consequences must be seen in particular contexts. Population increase in a densely populated 'western' city might cause more homelessness. Population decrease, perhaps occasioned by migration to other cities, could ease this problem. On the other hand, many 'western' countries are having 'too few' babies. The consequences of this might be unemployed school teachers when fewer babies than usual reach school age. If more babies are born, when they reach school age, job prospects will be better for school teachers. Similar consequences might occur in some majority world countries. It's important to recognise this because there's a tendency in the 'west' to assume that people in majority world countries are hungry simply because their large populations outstrip scarce resources. Yet, as Dinyar Godrej observes, 'Hunger is not due to scarcity; it is created by wealth' (1995: 9). The richest fifth of the population – who mainly live in the west – receive 85 per cent of the world's income. The poorest fifth, most of whom inhabit the majority world, get just 1.4 per cent.

This richest fifth also cause 80 per cent of global pollution and resource depletion. It's therefore salutary to remember 'that the birth of one potentially rich new consumer may be more damaging to the environment than 50 babies born in a poor country' (Buckley 1994: 7). Now there's a consequence that's often overlooked! That said, it's not always the case that a declining population leads to less environmental damage. This depends on how people behave. If, for example, fewer people in a society leads to greater prosperity, but more use of cars, pollution can obviously increase. Conversely, a growing population sometimes has a beneficial environmental impact. In the semi-arid Machakos District of Kenya, for example, the population increased more than five-fold in the period 1930–90, and the environment has greatly improved. People can be respecters and cultivators of global resources, as well as agents of destruction.

The preceding two paragraphs aren't intended to confuse you. They make an important point: the consequences of population change must be considered in the contexts of the countries and the circumstances it occurs. For all that, some commentators warn of global chaos and environmental catastrophe if the world population keeps growing. Even though every child born in the rich world consumes much more of the planet's resources (20–30 times as much) than a child born in the majority world, this doesn't mean we can ignore the consequences of rapid population growth in poor countries.

That growth is degrading the environment and making the economic prospects of many hundreds of millions of people very bleak indeed. Moreover, there's a definite momentum for further growth. Although fertility rates are declining in most countries, the high proportion of young people in the 1990s (especially women of child-bearing age) is the underlying cause. As for the consequences, opinions are divided. The chaos/catastrophe theorists envisage, well, chaos and catastrophe if urgent action isn't taken by the international community. The action is typically framed in the language of modernisation theory: 'contraception is the best contraception'; not poverty reduction, accompanied by voluntary use of contraceptives as people become more prosperous.

However much more rich world citizens damage the environment than their majority world neighbours, modernisation theorists nevertheless point out that the growing world population burdens natural ecosystems. This is because there's an imbalance between what people consume and what the planet can provide. In short, available resources get used at an unsustainable (unreplaceable) rate. When the imbalance is one where the need for food isn't met, hunger is the outcome. This manifests itself in terms of *malnutrition* (not having a properly balanced diet: which occurs in the low-income, high-rise council estates of present-day Glasgow, as well as in the majority world) and *starvation* (not having enough food to sustain life).

It's essential to understand that hunger isn't caused by too many people. There's more than enough food in the world to feed the entire population. The simple truth is that the rich world eats too much and the majority world too little, as the data opposite clearly illustrate.

Nevertheless, when there isn't enough food to go around and poor people still have large families, then there *is* a contextual link (a relation caused by particular circumstances) between population growth and hunger. On a global level, food production is rising. Such is the case also in Africa. Yet almost two-thirds of the majority world – Africa included – face stagnant or declining levels of per capita (i.e. per person) food production in the 1990s. Why is this? One reason is that many countries where hunger is common are still exporting food. Another reason is that poor people simply don't get to share in the national cake because majority world elites, like their 'western' counterparts, take too much. The upshot is that too little food gets to the poor, and the problem gets worse when the poor have lots of children.

Another consequence of population increase is that more people migrate to cities and to more prosperous countries. Urbanisation in poor countries is currently occurring at breakneck speed. This massive rural to urban shift is having harmful consequences. Under the strain of urban sprawl, natural habitats are ruined, wetlands are drained, pollutants become concentrated in cities, and increased crime further adds to the problems of beleaguered city-dwellers. Nor are those who move to cities necessarily guaranteed a better life. Many end up in sweat shops and other 'informal economy' employment: street vending, shoe-shining, begging and soliciting for sex.

As far as international migration is concerned, population growth and poverty are important causes of this phenomenon. At least 35 million people from the majority world have taken up residence in the rich world over the past three decades. About one million join them each year. Another million or so are working abroad on fixed period contracts. It's estimated that the number of illegal international migrants is around 15–30 million. Exodus pressures are likely to increase as populations continue to grow. But the rich nations are closing their doors. There's a bitter irony here. The rich world creates unemployment in poor countries when it raises trade and tariff barriers, because when the majority world can't afford to export its products, workers get laid off. The result is that when jobs don't move towards people in their own countries, people are more likely to move towards jobs in other countries.

Turning now to the consequences of population decrease in the majority world, it's necessary to consider what *might* be, rather than what is. For in poor countries, unlike in the rich world, populations are increasing. So let's consider, as does Catley-Carlson (1994), 'what might be?' were a major effort made to get family planning services universally available by the year 2000.

This goal – agreed upon by almost every nation at the 1990 World Summit for Children – is achievable. A great deal of low-cost technology is available, and more is on the way. We also know more than before about 'how family planning can be made available in human and respectful ways' (Catley-Carlson 1994: 25). It's no good having the means available to reduce fertility rates if people object to particular methods. In short, one has to offer family planning options that don't offend the beliefs and convictions of the people who might use them: Jews, Muslims, Roman Catholics or whoever.

Here, suggests Catley-Carlson (1994), are five beneficial consequences, were the above Year 2000 goal of universal family planning services to be achieved:

- a 50 per cent decline in maternal deaths in the majority world if women who didn't want children had access to reliable family planning methods. Half a million young women die each year from causes linked to pregnancy and birth
- a radical decline in the number of abortions – estimated at 25 million per year in the majority world and as many again or more in the rich world
- a 30 per cent reduction in child deaths. Most deaths under the age of five are of children born within two years of a previous birth, or to mothers under 18 or over 35. Delaying births until mothers want to become pregnant would decrease under-five deaths by 24–30 per cent, and by even more where the present interval between births is under two years
- a better future for young girls – mothers under the age of 18 run three times the risk of death of mothers aged 20–29. Moreover, very few of them are able to remain at school, or develop their potential

Shares of the crop

The rich world's proportion of grain production is significantly higher than its share of the world population.

	% of world grain production	% of world population
Africa	5.5	12.4
North America (USA and Canada)	18.2	5.2
Central and South America	6.7	8.4
Asia	52.7	59.0
Europe	15.2	14.5
Oceania	1.7	0.5

Feast and famine

The rich world has a glut – of food and obese citizens: in the US about a third of the population is overweight – $33 billion is spent each year in attempts to lose weight. In the poor world millions subsist on an amount of food that is simply inadequate for good health. An estimated 190 million children under the age of five are chronically malnourished.

The feast

Countries with highest daily supply of calories per head as % of requirements[1] 1988–90

Ireland	157
Greece	151
Belgium	149
Bulgaria	148
France	143
Spain	141
Italy	139
US	138
Hungary	137
Singapore	136
Aotearoa/NZ	130
UK	130
South Africa	128
Australia	124

The famine

Countries with lowest daily supply of calories per head as % of requirements[1] 1988–90

72	Afghanistan
73	Chad
73	Ethiopia
77	Mozambique
80	Angola
81	Somalia
82	Central African Republic
82	Rwanda
83	Sierra Leone
84	Burundi
84	Bolivia

[1] An adequate adult calorie intake is between 2,350 and 2,600 calories per day, depending on climate and kinds of work performed.

Shocking as they may be, these figures are only averages. There are hungry people in rich countries and those who can afford more than they need in poorer ones, which makes the contrast between greed and need even more dramatic.

Grain for meat

Farm animals consume nearly half the world's cereal produce. Growing grain to feed animals to turn them into meat is an inefficient business – an acre of cereals can produce five times more protein than an acre devoted to meat production.

World cereal use

In millions of tonnes, 1988–90

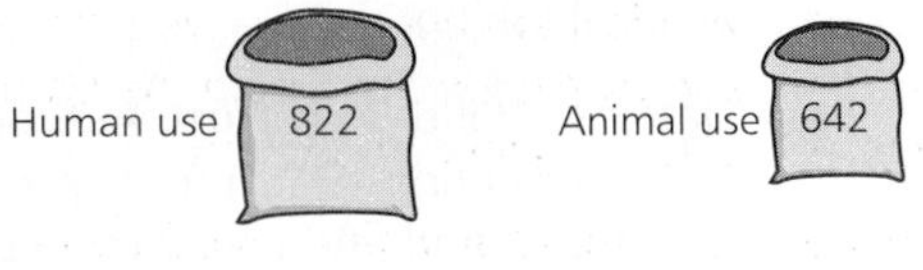

As a % of total cereal available, selected regions, 1990

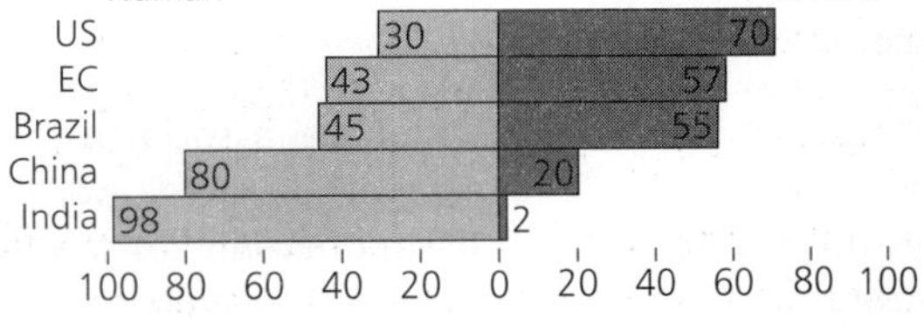

(Adapted from *New Internationalist*, May 1995, page 19)

- a very different pattern of planned parenthood. Outside of Africa, at least half of all married women don't want any more children; within Africa, half would like to postpone the next birth or don't want any more children. When women and families are able to devote their energies and resources to their existing children and to themselves, child care and family nutrition improve, and women have a better chance of enhancing their own life chances.

The 1990s is a decisive decade. It will largely determine whether eventual global population stabilises closer to 10 billion (the most optimistic forecast), or at 20 billion (the top-end prediction). According to Catley-Carlson:

'The difference between these two figures might well be the difference between success and failure in managing the transition to sustainable development.'

(Catley-Carlson 1994: 25).

While world population is now growing by about 90 million people a year, Europe's population is expected to grow by less than 4 million by 2025. During the same period, population in North Africa is predicted to grow by 123 million, and in Western Asia by 169 million. The pressure to migrate to Europe will be considerable. Similar pressures will be felt in other parts of the rich world. Some Northern European countries have admitted workers from other countries for limited stays by issuing temporary work permits. This practice has supplied labour to rich world countries and has provided work (usually menial) to people from more populous countries. However, in periods of economic recession, these workers are often laid off and sent home, which places the burden of unemployment on them and their countries of origin.

Migration from poor to rich countries won't be the only consequence of predicted demographic trends. While populations might stop growing in the rich worlds over the next 30 years, it's likely that in countries like the US, the proportion of old people will increase – unless an unexpected 'baby boom' occurs or immigration surges. In 1970, there were 17 old Americans per 100 working-age Americans. By 2040, it's expected that there will be 40 old Americans per 100 working-age Americans. Since social security payments are financed out of the payments of current workers, this means more people will be on benefits and fewer people will be supporting the benefits system. That said, the situation might be eased if women continue to become a growing proportion of the workforce.

Given the obvious problems that are associated with rapid population growth in a world where available resources might be enough but are unevenly distributed, social scientists must find ways for sustainable development. They must examine and consider alternative development strategies, and advise governments and non-governmental organisations (NGOs, such as Oxfam) on the most realistic and the most beneficial ways forward for the people on this planet who still live in poverty.

QUESTIONS

1. What are the main causes of population growth in the world today?
2. What is the relationship between the education of girls and women and fertility rates in the majority world?
3. Explain what is meant by the argument that the consequences of population increase and decrease must be seen in context.

Alternative development strategies

What are the alternative strategies available for bringing the majority world into a better future – a future where all their people have enough to eat, a decent home to live in, a good education, a well-paid job or a reasonable fixed income (for example, a pension), high quality medical care (especially, of the preventive kind), clean air to breathe and pure water to drink, a world without war, a world in which human rights are respected?

Don't think of such contemplations as lofty but unrealistic dreams. Providing for the educational, health and nutritional needs of the world's poor is a feasible and an affordable goal whose realisation will weaken the grip of environmental destruction, population growth and the very worst aspects of poverty. We can get there, or if not quite there, then fairly close. Better to get closer to an ideal than to be far from it.

Let's first consider a development strategy put forward by Riccardo Petrella (1995). He proposes the setting up of a *world social contract* designed to:

- adopt new worldwide economic 'rules of the game' that are codified in a globalised, legal and political framework. Such rules might include, for example, a legally enforceable global minimum wage
- enact a series of instruments and measures to ensure the effective check, through an international inspectorate, that a global minimum wage is actually applied, and to 'persuade' any countries who don't abide by the rules to change their ways.

In part, suggests Petrella, the world social contract could be achieved by establishing:

- a United Nations World Anti-Trust Authority, to be responsible for preventing the formation of powerful rich world financial and industrial oligarchies (economic power elites who seize and control particular markets) who are able to unduly influence world economic trends

- a World Economic Tribunal to secure adherence by nations to ethical principles in world economic affairs, and to audit the use of world public financing for co-operation and development.

Petrella lets slip his 'dependency theory' orientation when he writes:

'The twenty-first century will bring us into the third millenium AD . . . conquerors need not apply . . . But you builders of new boroughs and agoras [the Greek word for markets] and of new cities of the planet, please step right in.'

(Petrella 1995: 23)

But what kind of development strategy might proponents of a more modernisation theory approach come up with? What do you think?

OVER TO YOU

Draw up a development strategy based on the principles of modernisation theory.

Did your model include any of the following features? They're all based on modernisation theory:

- linking aid (whether repayable with/without interest or non-repayable) from rich world 'donors' to majority world 'recipients' to economic plans mapped out by the donor countries. For example, in exchange for the setting up of hospitals, poor countries might have to agree to have their doctors educated (at a fee) in rich countries. Other aid conditions could include *structural re-adjustment plans*, whereby recipient nations might be required, for instance, to raise interest rates on consumer borrowing
- setting up strong trade links between rich and poor countries, particularly involving TNCs, and recruitment and training by these companies of local labour in poor countries – including 'western-style' management training schemes for aspiring majority world managers. The emphasis in these training schemes is likely to be on accepting the 'realities' of 'free trade' economics, and using those 'realities' to build stronger majority world economies. There's also the presumption that the General Agreement on Tariffs and Trade (GATT; since replaced in 1995 by the World Trade Organisation) and the North American Free Trade Agreement (NAFTA), which form the cornerstone of rich world economic theories and practices, should set the economic agendas for rich and poor nations alike
- persuading the majority world to adopt rich world birth control methods in order to reduce population growth in poor countries, thereby enabling the smaller populations to become more prosperous by having larger shares of the economic cake. Education will play a key role here, especially the education of women because 'educated' women tend to have smaller families. The majority world needs to be persuaded that family planning in itself – rather than waiting for more prosperity, to be followed by family planning – is the most powerful means of keeping population growth at bay
- promoting the democratisation of majority world countries whose regimes are undemocratic, both extreme left and extreme right wing versions. The US, for example, imposed economic sanctions against apartheid South Africa (arguably a majority world country because of the massive poverty among the largely black population) because it hadn't, prior to the election of President Mandela, allowed black citizens equal voting rights with white citizens.

Dependency/WS theorists aren't convinced that modernisation theory offers the best development strategies for the majority world. Very orthodox marxists argue that poor countries need to 'go it alone' in a union of satellite countries who break free from the rich core. But such an idea, however noble it might be, isn't really practical. Like it or not, poor countries are inextricably linked to the economies of the rich world. So perhaps a more realistic development strategy is to 'civilise' the oppressor by turning the neo-colonial 'west' into a fair trading partner. Easier said than done. But this approach is being increasingly adopted by NGOs, many of whom are sympathetic to a dependency/WS approach – provided it's achievable rather than theoretical.

NGOs are groups that harness the efforts and the financial donations of citizens worldwide for the purpose of promoting the development of the majority world. One of the best known NGOs is Oxfam. Founded in 1942 to relieve famine and sickness in nazi-occupied Greece and Belgium, Oxfam mainly funds projects of other groups and organisations in the majority world. It takes a special interest in agriculture, education, emergency relief and production. Oxfam also promotes public awareness in the rich world of the causes of poverty. This NGO has around 1,000 shops in the UK, and it also runs Oxfam Trading, which sells produce made by poor people in the majority world, returning the profits to them.

Don't think of Oxfam and other NGOs as 'drop in the ocean' ventures. While their activities don't touch the lives of all poor people, any improvement to the lives of other human beings, however small the number, is consequential. Moreover, growing awareness of the need for more directly targeted, grassroots developmental action, coupled with a disenchantment of banks and governments, has given momentum to the growth of NGOs. For their part, civil servants in inter-governmental organisations haven't always been especially well-disposed to NGOs. The good news, however, is that the relationship between the United Nations and NGOs is now good, and getting better. A significant high point was met in Rio at the 1992 UN Conference on Environment and Development. Upwards of 1,400 NGOs were accredited to the official conference, and thousands more attended the parallel Global Forum. NGO influences have also been felt at UN conferences: on human rights in Vienna in 1993, on small island states in Barbados in 1994, and – also in 1994 – on population and development in Cairo.

NGOs play a crucial role as ethical pressure groups, challenging the 'western-style' economic policies of international organisations like the International Monetary Fund and the World Bank, which – incidentally and importantly – are *largely* run by white middle- and upper-class 'western' males.

In that context, Christian Aid, for example, has strongly attacked World Bank and IMF Structural Adjustment Programmes (SAPs). These programmes, which are largely premised on modernisation theory, encourage (some would say, force) poor countries to 'develop' by making exports a priority, devaluing their currencies, and cutting their own government expenditure. This often leads to drastic reductions in health and education provision, while the price of imported food and medicine rises because of a weaker currency. In his support of Christian Aid's campaign, Archbishop Desmond Tutu, of South Africa, has urged those who run the IMF and the World Bank to start reflecting the aspirations and views of the victims of an unjust world economic order. His and Christian Aid's view echo the WST/dependency argument that poor people have the right to participate in and contribute to the development of economic justice.

NGOs do make a difference in development strategies. Using Oxfam again as an example, in the early 1990s *New Internationalist* magazine (February 1992) sent local journalists from Bangladesh, Brazil and Zambia to visit an Oxfam project of their choice. The purpose was to get these journalists to talk to people in the communities the organisation aims to help, without being guided by the views of Oxfam workers.

Let's start with Faruq Faisal's report on an organisation in Bangladesh called Dwip Unnayon Sangstah (DUS). It works for landless people, and it's funded by Oxfam UK. DUS began organising landless people into groups in 1985, and later started implementing the Bangladeshi government's land-reform programme, whereby each landless family was guaranteed two acres of land. The organisation has also provided villages with tubewells for drinking water, taken charge of schooling, and launched a mother-and-child health programme. The verdict is that DUS (and, by implication its funder, Oxfam) has done a fine job.

Now we'll consider an article by Tarciana Portella about a town called Nova Petrolandia in Brazil. In 1986, the original town disappeared beneath the Sao Francisco River, which had been diverted and dammed to build the hydroelectric plant of Itaparica. Local people said that the Hydroelectric Company of Sao Francisco made life miserable for them by not meeting their main claim to land, and by paying workers less than was previously agreed. Against this backdrop, Oxfam UK helped set up and supported a Human Rights Centre. Vicente da Costa Coelhoe, the Centre's Director, reported that Oxfam provided the cost of three advisers – an agronomist, a social worker and a lawyer. It also supplied two vehicles (plus fuel and running costs), which are essential for maintaining contact between isolated agricultural settlements. Moreover, Oxfam denounced – at both national and international levels – those who oppress rural workers, as well as putting pressure on the World Bank to suspend funds destined for the Hydroelectric Company. The judgement is that Oxfam has played an important and a valuable role.

Finally, Mary Namakando documents Oxfam's work in the rural town of Mumbwa, Zambia. In this area, where

The Executive Board of the World Bank, 1995, with few women in sight

malnutrition and poverty are prevalent, Oxfam has been operating as a 'mini bank', offering local farmers loans to buy fertiliser and maize seed. Unlike conventional banks, no collateral is required when poor people take out loans. Collateral is security against a loan (for example, personal possessions) that can be seized by the lender if the borrower can't pay back the money. While the farmers appreciate and gain from the loans, there's a local view that they aren't big enough to expand the maize fields. The conclusion here about Oxfam seems to be: 'doing well, but could do better'.

Overall then, a very encouraging report emerges on Oxfam's work in these local examples. It's an NGO that does make a difference – for the good – to the lives of poor people, even though the ventures considered are relatively small-scale. Just remember that any improvement to the lives of those who are oppressed, whatever their number, is important and valuable. Moreover, unlike certain 'grand plan' proposals for majority world development, what Oxfam does is on a practical level – not a theoretical one. Perhaps that's why, as Aidan Foster-Carter (1991: 10) notes, Oxfam and other NGOs launched a new journal in 1991 called *Development in Practice*. Says Foster-Carter: 'Evidently, "Rostow versus Gunder Frank" is of even less use to people *doing* development, in the field and at the grass roots' (1991: 10).

Another – at this stage, rather modest but expanding – 'hands-on' development strategy is 'alternative trading'. This often involves NGOs known as Alternative Trading Organisations (ATOs). These organisations operate on the basis of principled rather than exploitative trade, paying for goods made by poor people at a fair price, even if it's above the market price. They also recognise the important fact that fair trade is more important for the development of poor countries than 'aid'. Trade already yields 80 per cent of the majority world's income (fair trade would make much more); aid makes only 5 per cent.

ATOs depend, in large part, for their success on *you*, the rich world consumer. Many of the commodities the UK imports from the majority world are grown on plantations that are owned by corporations and local elites. Yet the productivity of small farms is often higher than big plantations – mainly, because poor farmers' livelihoods are based on the success of the crop yield. Such smallholdings can benefit when 'western' consumers wield their purchase power to persuade companies to buy goods from ATOs. Given that the average 16-year-old in the UK and Ireland will spend £1 million in her or his lifetime, how this money is spent can make a difference to the lives of poor producers. Supermarkets are already listening to consumer power when it comes to environment-friendly goods. They're also beginning to apply similar business ethics in the context of people-friendly products.

Consider these facts:

- Traidcraft is a company that specialises in fairly traded goods from the majority world. Its filter coffee, Cafedirect, sells for around £1.55 (1995 price), of which 43p goes to the farmers and pickers who produced it – over twice as much as from average coffee.
- With money from Christian Aid, the villagers from the Wend Yam Federation in Burkina Faso, Africa, have started to grow green beans to sell to Europe, mainly to France. They sell the beans to a company called Flexfaso, which pays the farmers a fair price for the product. The revenue means more food, medicine and schooling, and a better future for local people.
- In 1985, the year of Live Aid when millions of people starved in the Ethiopian famine, more than US$3 billion of emergency help was sent to Africa. Yet in the same year, with a dramatic fall in the price of African goods and rising costs of what Africa bought from the rest of the world, unfair trade left the continent US $19 billion worse off.

Alternative trade might be small-scale, but it has outcomes that could help poor people like Lova Constance, a sugar cane cutter in the Dominican Republic. His impoverished life is graphically described in Christian Aid's *Trade for Change Youth Campaign Action Pack*.

Hard labour: Bitter sweet

Lova Constance is a sugar cane cutter working in Dominican Republic. He is 81 and, using his bare hands, still harvests over two tonnes of sugar cane a day.

He lives in a bamboo hut with a banana leaf roof and shares one water tap with 800 people.

The cane Lova cuts in a day is enough to make 280 bags of sugar – worth about £182 in your local supermarket. He gets paid £1.80, hardly enough to feed his family.

(*Trade for Change Youth Campaign Action Pack*, Christian Aid)

ATOs look forward to a future when the concept of 'alternative trade' is replaced with 'universal fair trade'. As part of their campaign to secure this goal, they're urging 'western' consumers not only to buy fairly traded goods and services, but also to petition corporations to pay majority world farmers more money, and to request food stores and other retailers to offer people-friendly products. On page 596 is an example of a Christian Aid initiative, a voucher that customers are asked to give to the checkout operators at supermarkets, with a request for it to be passed to the manager.

TRADE FOR CHANGE

Dear store manager

As a customer at your store I would like to see you stocking goods from the Third World which give poor people a fair return for their labour.

Yours faithfully

Signed.................................... Name..

Address..

....

Another venture is the Fairtrade Mark, launched in 1994 by the Fairtrade Foundation. Goods that bear this mark guarantee a fair deal for the person who grew or made them. Specifically, the Fairtrade Mark guarantees that the price paid by a UK company should cover:

- the cost of production
- the cost of living (education and health care included)
- some additional money for investment.

Set out in the Fairtrade criteria is a guarantee of long-term trading: the security that when a crop is ripe, producers can sell. One of the products in the UK that carries the Fairtrade Mark is the Maya Gold chocolate bar, which sells in most supermarkets, as well as through Oxfam and wholefood outlets. To emphasise that fair trade does make a difference, Green & Black's (the UK company that manufactures Maya Gold) have turned a potential financial disaster for central American cocoa farmers into a bright future. During 1992 and 1993, many farmers in that part of the majority world abandoned their cocoa crop after the price dropped so low it wasn't cost-effective to harvest. Fairtrading Green & Black's stepped in, and offered nearly double the price, as well as a commitment to buy all the cocoa the farmers could harvest for at least the next three years. Incidentally, when you buy a £1 bar of chocolate in the UK that isn't fairly traded, the British Treasury earns more in VAT than the cocoa farmer.

A £1 bar of chocolate – where the money goes

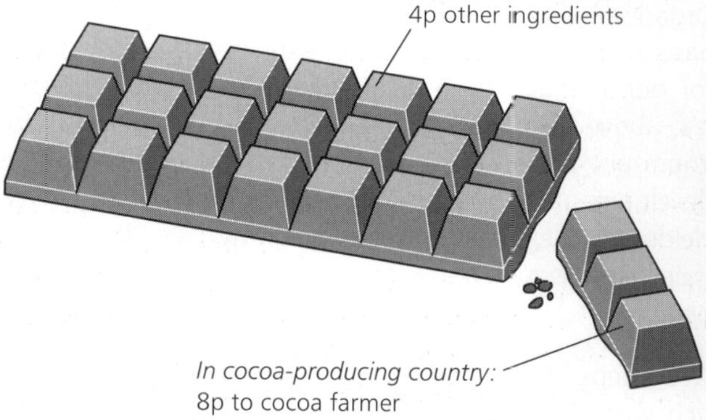

(From a World Development Movement pamphlet, *Trade*)

Fairly-traded bananas are also in the frame. Fifteen European banana trade groups have joined in urging the EU to support fair trade in this important crop. Small producers in the Caribbean and plantation workers in Latin America have asked for a reform of European banana import regulations to support the adoption of fair trade bananas to the EU. Bananas from Latin American plantations are cheaper than their Caribbean counterparts. However, this is accomplished through cheap labour and very high level use of agrochemicals. 'Cheaper' bananas thereby threaten the livelihoods of less environmentally destructive Caribbean farmers. Fairly-traded bananas meet agreed ecological and social standards. They're produced with more respect for the environment and for the rights of workers.

CRIT THINK CRIT THINK CRIT THINK CRIT THINK CRIT THINK CRIT THINK

TRADE AND SOCIAL JUSTICE

1 Select one non-governmental organisation (NGO) which is also an alternative trading organisation (ATO). Contact the organisation, and ask them to send you materials that promote their fair trade activities.

2 Prepare a critique (i.e. consider good features and where improvements might be made) of the supplied materials.

3 Using the supplied materials and/or other resources, prepare an action plan that contributes, in a practical way, to global fair trade. If, for example, you have a school or college shop, consider ordering some Fairtrade Mark drinks, snacks, handicrafts and other products.

4 If possible, implement your action plan. Then, at appropriate intervals, review the progress and outcomes of your action plan, and report on them.

This exercise can be done as a group activity, with each group choosing a different NGO/ATO, and presenting the critique of the materials to the rest of the class.

CRIT THINK CRIT THINK CRIT THINK CRIT THINK CRIT THINK CRIT THINK CRIT

EXAM TIP

The Crit Think venture above could (with appropriate developments) become a coursework submission. It has an obvious link, for example, with the important debate about using social scientific knowledge to promote social justice. Discuss the potential of this with your teacher.

You've probably noticed that it's inappropriate to cast dependency theorists and modernisation theorists in the roles of more or less righteous groups. Both camps can be very sincere in their convictions, and there's quite a lot of overlap between their aims, if not always between their preferred means. For example, dependency theorist, Frank, dedicated his book, *Latin America: Underdevelopment or Revolution* (1969), to: 'Marta and all other Latin American comrades whose own dedication is to the Revolution'. By contrast, the book by modernisation theorist, Rostow, *The Stages of Economic Growth: A Non-Communist Manifesto* (1965), is an avowal of how rich world aid, especially American, should be mobilised to fight off the threat of communism. Despite these very obviously different missions, both social scientists want to see a majority world in which hunger and poverty no longer exist, and in which human rights are not trampled upon by corrupt dictatorial regimes – whether of the left or right.

The message of ATOs to the United Nations is the poor want action, not words. Eloquently turned phrases and expressions of intent from the leaders of rich nations at world summits, on what to do about majority world poverty, won't touch people's lives unless the sentiments are galvanised into action programmes. If these summits led to big changes – a world employment programme, an international shift of investment from defence to education and health, the dismantling of tariff and non-tariff barriers to majority world trade, the stabilisation of falling commodity prices (so that for example, poor farmers find it worthwhile to produce coffee beans), a global tax, and cancelling the poorest countries' debts – they would then have real teeth and effective outcomes.

The question is, has social science produced a feasible strategy for real development? Are 'revolution and socialism' or 'the ballot box and capitalism' the best way forward? Marx himself advocated revolution only as a last resort against what he regarded as oppressive regimes whose leaders couldn't be removed through democratic means. Indeed, in his private life, he may accurately be described as an 'extreme democrat'. True, his writings have often been corrupted by socialists and communists in name only (like Stalin, for example). But Marx can hardly be blamed for that. Moreover, it's not only dependency theorists (or some of them) who advocate 'justifiable violence' in the quest for a better world. Modernisation theorist, Rostow, was special adviser to American Presidents Kennedy and Johnson, who regarded United States GIs as 'freedom fighters' in the war against communism in a country called Vietnam!

Industrialisation, employment and urbanisation

These three processes go together, often in the majority world, like this:

- Transnational corporations (TNCs) set up shop in majority world countries. The economic gains are very lucrative. Industrial corporations (for example, jeans manufacturers) can buy local labour in low-wage markets and sell their products in the high-wage markets of the rich world (check where your jeans are made). Such corporations are often the trigger of *industrialisation*, namely, the development of mass production in large factories.
- Industry encourages the rural poor to seek jobs in cities. In this manner, it exerts, like a magnet, what's called a 'pull factor'. The process whereby people move from the dispersed settlements and livelihoods of the 'countryside' to the more concentrated residences and workplaces of the cities is called *urbanisation*.
- These new urban, industrial workers get a job, a pay packet and the chance of a better living. 'Chance' is the operative word here because there are hazards: like working without the protection of key health and safety provisions that are generally taken for granted in the 'west', and living in squatter settlements in shanty housing of corrugated iron on vacant land in derelict areas. But, on the plus side, *employment* in a city is likely to pay more than what can be earned in a rural village.

Industrialisation

The largest single product of all manufacturing industry is pollution. About 350 million metric tons of hazardous industrial wastes are generated worldwide each year, of which some 90 per cent comes from the rich world. There are upwards of 35,000 TNCs in the world, with around 150,000 overseas affiliates. The leading players are concentrated in these industries: motor vehicles/parts; petroleum refining; computers/office equipment; and electronics. TNCs are at the forefront of a 'Second Industrial Revolution', one which is happening in the majority world. Industrialisation is creating a relocation of factories from rich to poor countries, and a 24-hour-a-day, worldwide, financial trading system. Most corporate investment ends up in the hands of the 'west'. Of the $150 billion of overseas direct investment in 1991, more than two-thirds went to the rich world.

From a modernisation perspective, industrialisation is applauded as a desirable forerunner of economic growth and employment (especially in a TNC), as a way out of rural poverty, and a way into urbanisation. The TNC-led Industrial Revolution in the majority world is regarded as:

- the means whereby poor countries gain more access to global opportunities for trade and investment. Given that 'free trade' is here to stay – 'western' capitalism is far too powerful for things to be otherwise – poor countries must work and be successful within that system. If 'free marketeers' have their way, not only will trade and investment flow unimpeded worldwide, so too will labour. A truly free labour market, allowing people to work anywhere in the world, would give the majority world between $300–500 billion a year in transfers (that is, money sent home by employees to their families), compared to the $60 billion they receive in aid. 'Real free trade, not aid' is what poor countries need
- an opportunity for people in poor countries to leave the ox and the hoe and to become acquainted with the technologies of the future. Given that new technology is the motor of social change the sooner the majority world adopts and acquires technical skills from working in large industrial plants, the quicker its people will reap the material rewards of mass production and mass consumption. Moreover, manufactured exports, once the preserve of the rich world, don't risk the potentially disastrous price fluctuations of commodities like coffee and sugar. Gone is the commodity export ghetto which the majority world traditionally inhabits. By manufacturing jacuzzis, car parts and VCRs, poor people are guaranteed a better pay packet. Given time, they'll become affluent, and – like their 'western' counterparts – they'll have leisure on their hands and the money to enjoy it
- a meeting point, to the benefit of both parties, of re-located 'western' capital and an abundant supply of competitively priced majority world labour. In Mexico, for example, the comparatively low labour costs make workers there far more competitive from a company perspective than their higher paid cousins in the US and Canada. Capital is therefore given added incentive to move south, creating more jobs and more prosperity for Mexicans

Social scientists of a more dependency-oriented outlook aren't convinced. They argue that:

- the wider the free trade areas available to TNCs, the less accountable powerful and footloose corporations become to the local communities in which they conduct their operations. For 'free traders' who extend their operations to the majority world want to maximise profits, without regard for social and environmental considerations. They pay low wages, exploit women (a worldwide scandal), take advantage of lax or non-existent health and safety regulations, and don't fit costly anti-pollution devices. These costs are, to use the terminology of economics, 'externalised'. This means that the rich world TNCs don't clear up after the damage – social and environmental – they do in the majority world. By being 'externalised', the costs are 'paid for' by people who live and work in poor countries – as when, for example, they suffer the stench and the bad air of smoke-belching industrial plants

- TNCs set up 'export only' industrial plants in the majority world. This goes back to the colonial tradition of coercing poor countries to produce cash crops for export to the 'west': the 'breadbasket of the world syndrome'. It's a practice that continues – a perverse state of affairs, given that many countries where hunger is prevalent are exporters of food. In Mexico, it's more a case of 'maquila sunrise' than the tequila version. The so-called 'maquila plants' there import raw materials and parts without restriction, for processing in Mexico and export to the US. It's rather like using another country as a laundry delivery service. NAFTA, however, is likely to reduce the economic advantages enjoyed by maquila plants because it's making trade between Mexico, the US and Canada enticing for other companies, not just the maquila variety. That said, NAFTA will help more North American companies to tap into the very low labour costs available by employing Mexican workers
- TNCs export a corporate culture that's based on competition and hierarchy. When they move their industrial plants to the majority world, co-operation and sharing are off the agenda. Climbing the corporate ladder is the defined goal of those who want to be managers – locally recruited or brought in from the 'west'. Orders flow from the top to the bottom, and the opinions of the poor, who carry out the most menial of tasks, are seldom, if ever, solicited. The scene is aptly illustrated in the film *On Deadly Ground* (1994), when rich oil barons place corporate greed above the ecological values of Native Americans. The sites of traditional communities are so many cubic metres of oil.

It's for you to make an informed judgement about which of these two versions are more or less accurate. Perhaps you would prefer a more 'balanced' appraisal of the situation. That said, 'extreme' views aren't necessarily inaccurate. Like any standpoints, they must be weighed against the evidence. Ultimately, one has to come to a conclusion based on a consideration of the disadvantages and the advantages. Take the experience of industrialisation in Hong Kong and South Korea, for example:

- In Hong Kong, the most densely populated city in the world, the squatter population is in excess of 250,000, and Hong Kong harbour and surrounding waters are badly polluted. South Korea has one of the worst records for industrial disputes over pay and conditions. Pay is low, and an average of five workers are killed at work every day; 390 more are injured. This represents one of the highest occupational accident rates in the world. Moreover, women workers earn less than 60 per cent of male wages.
- The rate of economic growth – prompted in no small measure by industrialisation – has led to decreases in infant mortality and higher enrolments of women in secondary education. In these two countries, for instance, infant mortality rates are down: in Hong Kong from 15 per 1,000 live births in 1970–5 to 7 per 1,000 in 1991; in South Korea from 40 per 1,000 live births in 1970–5 to 17 per 1,000 in 1991.

So, are these two countries going forward, as modernisation theorists would have it, or backward, as dependency/WS theorists would claim? Perhaps the most accurate answer is that they're experiencing *uneven development*: some forward movement, some backward movement.

Employment

For most people, economic security requires a guaranteed income – usually from paid employment, or from publicly financed sources (notably, social welfare and state pensions). Yet only about one quarter of the world's population may enjoy this kind of income provision. In the past two decades, the number of jobs in rich countries has failed to keep pace with the growth in the labour force. Young people are especially at risk of unemployment, with young ethnic minorities being hit hardest.

The problem is worse in the majority world, where official unemployment is often above 10 per cent, and actual unemployment probably much higher. As in the 'west', the problem is particularly acute for youths. Moreover, official figures on unemployment tend to understate the extent of the crisis because many working people are seriously underemployed. Without an assured social welfare net, the poorest people can't survive even a short period without an income. In that context, it's important to realise that when food is available and poor people can't afford to buy it, they go hungry.

Some poor people get work in TNCs which, while offering 'formal sector' employment and a modicum of job security, tend to underpay and overwork majority world employees. The pros and cons of this kind of employment have already been discussed in the section on *Industrialisation*. The most insecure employment conditions are commonly in the 'informal sector' of street vending, pavement distribution of flyers, and the like. Paradoxically, this type of sector accounts for a great deal of available work in poor countries. In 1991, it provided 30 per cent of all jobs in Latin America, and 60 per cent of jobs in Africa. The global shift towards less secure employment is affecting poor and rich countries. It's largely accounted for by the worldwide contraction in manufacturing, and the expansion of service sector work – where jobs are often part-time or temporary and less protected by trade unions.

In the majority world, when jobs are hard to come by, self-employment is often the only option. It tends to offer less security than waged work, and the poorest among the self-employed find it hard to make ends meet. In rural areas, for example, the poorest farmers have very little access to land, whose distribution can be measured by the so-called Gini coefficient – a calibration of inequality that ranges from 0 (perfect equality) to 1 (absolute inequality). In Kenya, the land Gini coefficient is 0.77, in Saudi Arabia 0.83 and in Brazil 0.86 – far from equitable. Yet even small landholders often find it difficult to farm because they have limited credit – a sad state of affairs indeed, given the mounting evidence that the poor are creditworthy.

Precarious employment is invariably accompanied by poor wages, which tend to remain stagnant or, if they rise slightly, are eroded by inflation. The upshot is that real wages in many parts of the majority world have fallen. Worst hit are women, who typically earn 30–40 per cent less than men for doing the same jobs: more about this in the section on *Gender inequalities and equal opportunity initiatives*. Gender discrimination against women is also common in the rich world. In Japan, for example, women who work in manufacturing earn only about half as much as men.

Minority ethnic groups and disabled people encounter employment discrimination too. For example, in 1994 about 65 million disabled people required training and job placements in order to obtain economic security in their lives. However, only about 1 per cent will have received the needed support. Generally speaking, disabled people are found among the poorest quarter of the population. In Mauritius, their unemployment rate is 84 per cent, and in China, 46 per cent.

There's little if any recourse to social welfare for those in the majority world who can't find a job. Nor are things looking very hopeful in that context in the rich world. In the US, between 1987 and 1990, real benefits per pensioner decreased by 40 per cent, and in Austria by 50 per cent. Today, in both the US and the EU, nearly 15 per cent of people live below the poverty line. In the majority world, more than a third of people live below the poverty line, and over one billion people receive a daily income of less than $1.

According to the *Human Development Report* (United Nations Development Programme 1994), creating enough opportunities for productive employment and sustainable livelihoods, needs these strategies:

- education and skills training
- fair and stable macro-economic policies, an equitable legal system, sufficient physical infrastructure (roads, bridges, etc.), and incentives for private investment (hint of a modernisation perspective here!)
- a more equitable distribution of land and better access to credit
- labour-intensive technologies (i.e. human workers, rather than automated machines) that take advantage of the abundant supply of labour in poor countries
- public works programmes (i.e. state-provided employment) when private markets don't offer enough jobs
- targetted interventions or programmes of affirmative action (i.e. giving priority to disadvantaged people) when private market employment discriminates against particular groups, for example, ethnic minorities and women
- job-sharing.

Urbanisation

The majority world already contains 78 per cent of the global population. Moreover, 94 per cent of current population increase occurs in poor countries. Majority world cities will consequently face more strain as rural-dwellers become urban dwellers in search of jobs and better living conditions. The pace of urbanisation is much faster in the majority world than that experienced in the past by rich countries. During the first half of the twentieth century, the world's major cities were in Europe and North America. By 2000, eight of the world's 15 biggest cities will be in Asia.

Modernisation theory commonly associates urbanisation with development. Yet, in reality, majority world countries are urbanising faster than they're industrialising. People are drawn to cities ahead of the economic capacity to provide jobs, homes, sanitation, water and other essential services. The upshot is urban squalor rather than development.

On a somewhat different note, it seems that modernisation theory needs a history lesson. For if the advocates of that theory envisage urbanisation as a feature of modernisation, they should be reminded that people lived in big cities in ancient times. Asia has an urban tradition at least 5,000 years old. Batavia (now Jakarta, Indonesia), for example, was a vibrant port city long before Manchester became an industrial city.

Notwithstanding its ancient heritage, recent urbanisation has forged a different type of city, characterised most obviously by its sheer size. Cities of one million and above are a twentieth-century phenomenon. It's also important to note that, compared with rich world cities, a disproportionate number of people live in the larger cities of the majority world, with relatively few people in medium-size towns. This tendency for urbanisation in poor countries to become dominated by very large (so-called primate) cities is prompted by:

- the inclination of rich nation investors to locate their industries in a single city, thereby taking advantage of infrastructure (airports, harbours, transit systems, etc.) and central government trade bureaus
- the concentration of education and other public services in large cities

- the weak development of internal markets, leading to the development of export-oriented production centres.

From a modernisation perspective, these big cities offer an economic and cultural window onto the rich world. When, for example, a US jeans manufacturer sets up shop in such a place, those who would move from farming communities into an urban-industrial setting to make an 'all-American' product are provided with new and exciting job prospects. This exposure to rich world ways of doing things allegedly rescues the more ambitious and forward-looking of village dwellers from the rural impoverishment that would otherwise be their plight. True, many of them probably won't be able to afford the urban lifestyle that they might aspire to. But they'll be better off in the big city than in a rural 'backwater'.

The minimum daily wage at an electronics factory in Manila, in the Philippines, for instance, is usually more than twice what a worker would get from working in the fields. People who move to cities also become more acquainted with 'western' lifestyles, especially if they secure employment in the burgeoning tourism sector of the majority world. By rubbing shoulders with people from the rich world, even though on unequal terms, urban workers are encouraged to replace the fatalism and traditionalism of rural life with a 'can-do', modern outlook and a resolve to 'get on'. Given that economic growth is largely urban-based, what better way than for the rural poor to move to the cities in pursuit of a more prosperous future?

Social scientists of a dependency/WST orientation are wary of the 'bright city lights' optimism of modernisation theorists. In their rebuttal of this rosy picture, they point out that urbanisation in the majority world is often markedly different to urbanisation in the rich world. For one thing, it's more likely to be rapid and unplanned. This means that when poor people flock to cities from villages, they often don't have access to the kind of facilities more commonly associated with 'western' cities: education and welfare services, health care, etc. Frequently, they end up in the improvised, 'make-do' circumstances of urban squatter settlements: the *bustees* of India, the *barangays* of the Philippines, the *barrios* of Latin America.

These settlements rapidly spring up to house rural migrants who can't afford anything better. Generally, they consist of shanty dwellings made of corrugated iron, plywood and any bits of material people can get their hands on. They sometimes accommodate hundreds of thousands of people in grim, shabby environments: along railway tracks, under motorways, and by ports. Hardly a case of improved living conditions!

What needs to be remembered is that the experience of urbanisation in the majority world is often different to what happens in the rich world. While some of us in the UK might regard city life as more enticing and more modern than a village environment, we must guard against assuming that our experience is replicated in a poor country. Imagine what you would feel if you lived in a squatter settlement *barrio* in São Paulo, Brazil. You might be in close proximity to wealthy business and tourist districts, but you'd be an observer rather than a beneficiary of prosperity.

At the same time, it's important not to over-romanticise urbanisation in the rich world. Consider, for example, those big pockets of urban poverty and squalor in British cities like Leeds, Liverpool and London. Is it really progress to live on a run-down council estate in Seacroft, Toxteth or Hackney, without a job, no regular access to a GP, just a welfare cheque away from grinding poverty? It's also relevant to note that growing numbers of Britons are recognising that there's 'civilisation' outside of urban centres. Recent developments in telecommunications mean that the countryside can keep in touch with the city, as well as providing cleaner air, more pleasant surroundings and a less stressful lifestyle.

OVER TO YOU

How do the preceding two paragraphs challenge some of the assumptions of convergence theory?

Education and health

If the relationships between employment, industrialisation and urbanisation, and development aren't as clearcut as some commentators might have us believe, what can education and health programmes do to promote development?

Education

The education of a nation is one of its most cherished assets. Education is fundamental for development in any country, rich or poor. About a third of majority world children aren't completing even four years of education – either because they simply don't enter school or because they discontinue after they've started. But it's not all gloomy. Most nations in the majority world have accepted the goal of providing a primary school education for at least 80 per cent of their children by the year 2000. Of the most populous poor countries, China, Egypt, Indonesia and Mexico are on target. Brazil and India could achieve the goal with an accelerated effort. Moreover, the 1990s have witnessed a real breakthrough in pre-school education. In five years, the number of children in early years education has increased by over 40 per cent from about 45 million to about 65 million worldwide.

But the 'western' approach, based on teacher education programmes and custom-built schools, mightn't be the best model for educational development in poor countries. During the time it takes to implement such programmes and to set in motion a school building project, two or three generations of young people would grow up without an education. The then Chief of Education for UNICEF, Fay Chung (1994), recognised these problems when she was serving as first head of the Zimbabwe Integrated Teacher Education Course, soon after Zimbabwe became independent in 1980. Faced with the challenge of Zimbabwe's post-Independence drive to achieve education for all within five years, she turned to non-conventional, but highly successful strategies. These were:

- the recruitment of 900 student teachers for a four-month course based on once weekly meetings with tutors, supplemented by distance education and on-the-job training. The programme contained a core curriculum, focusing on reading, writing, maths and practical skills linked to community development and farm productivity
- telling communities who wanted schools to build them. Nearly all the new schools – many thousands of them shacks with thatched roofs – were built by school students' own parents and other community members.

Added to these strategies was a pent-up, post-colonial thirst for universal education, as well as international support (especially from Sweden) to carry the plans into the poorest parts of the country. Within 18 months, the number of schools had risen from 1,700 to 4,500, and the number of primary school students had surged from 800,000 to 2.3 million. Secondary schools also witnessed a huge expansion – from 66,000 students in 173 schools in 1980 to 700,000 students in 1,500 schools by 1985.

According to Chung (1994) – who also served as Zimbabwe's Minister of Education from 1988 to 1993 – these are the common elements in widening educational opportunities in the majority world:

- the effective deployment of large numbers of high calibre, 'para-professional' (quickly trained) teachers
- parental and community involvement, and high expectations of teachers
- school fees – although the ideal is for free universal education, at least up to primary level, in most countries school fees need to be part of the strategy. Such fees should be under community control
- government funding concentrating on the education of the poorest people so that they don't fall by the wayside
- sustained and stable government commitment, based on high quality personnel who stay in the job long enough to see it through, rather than on short-term contract expatriates (i.e. non-nationals: often 'westerners')
- re-allocation of aid (over 80 per cent currently goes to secondary and higher education) to particularly target a basic education for all children.

Chung's insistence that education must relate to local needs is especially apposite when we consider what goes on in majority world 'classrooms'. Take, for example, teaching children about the geography of world maps. Latin American educators have long proposed that these maps should be inverted, with the south at the top and the north at the bottom. For the world seen from the south challenges the idea that the rich north is 'above' the south. Such a map doesn't pretend to be 'unbiased', but it does force a reconsideration of the view that everything starts in Greenwich, London!

There's been a tendency among modernisation theorists to suggest that 'western-style' education 'works for us, so why not for them?' This view is ethno-centric and unhelpful. Turning the map upside down is a symbolic recognition of these facts. Why should we imagine that Somali children reared on a history of English queens and kings are going to obtain an education that they can use to make their society more prosperous? Isn't it more important to consider the local needs of Somali children – knowledge about farming and water purification, perhaps – and fit the curriculum to these needs? Yet 'western' models of schooling are sometimes represented – even by majority world elites – as superior forms of knowledge than traditional culture. As Yumi Lee and Peter Ninnes note:

> 'In many cases, the effort to duplicate classrooms developed in the North has been so great that many aspects of schools found in La Paz, Bolivia, are not much different from those found in Los Angeles, California.'
>
> (Lee and Ninnes 1995: 175)

Such dissonance between a 'western' import education and the home culture of school students can have very damaging effects. In the Solomon Islands, for example, traditional culture endorses equality and group loyalty. Yet the 'western-style' certificated schooling that has taken root there celebrates a 'go for it, gung-ho', individualistic ethos. The upshot is the erosion of traditional values and, for those school students who don't make the grade, a 'lack of status they would have achieved through the mastery of village tasks' (Lee and Ninnes 1995: 176), if they hadn't spent so much time away from village life.

The cultural dimension of education has also been taken up by Orlando Albonoz (1993) in the context of Latin

America. While Albonoz recognises that universities have a crucial role to play in promoting economic and social progress, he laments the fact that Latin American universities too often act as vehicles for the self-recruitment of majority world elites. Even in Venezuela – where educational reforms (on paper!) have been concerned with more equal access – the reality has been otherwise: increasing private sector encroachment, mainly focused on educating the elites.

Paulo Freire's (1972) heroic vision of popular education in Latin America, specifically Brazil, hasn't yet been realised. But his message still has a persuasive resonance. Speaking from and for the majority world, Freire urged illiterate poor people to become free subjects by learning to read and write, and using that knowledge to forge a more dignified and a more just future. Time and time again, poor people, after just a few hours of class, began to discover a new and important worth:

'"I now realize I am a man, an educated man." "We were blind, now our eyes have been opened." "Before this, words meant nothing to me; now they speak to me and I can make them speak." "Now we will no longer be a dead weight on the cooperative farm."'

(Freire 1972: 12–13)

Freire dedicated his book, *Pedagogy of the Oppressed* (1972), 'To the oppressed and to those who suffer with them and fight at their side'. No stranger to oppression himself, his adult literacy campaign was considered such a threat to the old order of Brazil, that he was jailed immediately after a military coup in 1964. Following his release, he was 'encouraged' to leave the country, and he became a political exile.

For education to be of real value to the people of the majority world, it's vital to design policy frameworks that are nation-specific. The stake-holders must also be fully involved in the policy-making. Standard recipe knowledge imported from the rich world and implemented by visiting 'western' professors won't do. At last the World Bank is beginning to realise this important lesson, and is actively promoting:

- matching educational policy to real local contexts and needs
- encouraging central state strategic planning, instead of relying on private sector involvement.

There are also encouraging signs in 'western' countries of movements towards a more global, less 'westo-centric' curriculum. Not all 'western' teachers are exponents of the 'English queens and kings' outlook. For example, British high school teachers, Paul Stephens and Tim Crawley (1994), practise – and promote in their writing – a global approach to teaching. Theirs is a global classroom where the histories of marginalised peoples are right in the frame. They would like to create a cyberspace resource to enable internet communication between children in different countries. The aim is to challenge ethno-centricity and to foster global awareness. Similarly, in Japan, the sociologist, Kazuko Ohtsu (1992), has written a book for use in social studies classes that enables school students to track the passage of bananas from poor to rich nations. Through the journey, they are able to find out about the lives of banana workers: the harsh employment conditions, and the low pay and 'back-breaking' pain they suffer. If rich world schooling embraces global rather than 'national curriculums', then maybe 'western' educators will have something to offer their poorer neighbours. This applies as much to science as it does to humanities education. For science itself develops out of social contexts. The majority world will gain and give much more if scientists from rich countries work with them on food science than on rocket fuel production!

OVER TO YOU

Trace the journey of the coffee bean from the majority world crop to the rich world coffee pot, commenting upon what you discover.

Coffee: Instant profit

Coffee is the world's favourite stimulant – and second most heavily-traded commodity. Yet the 20 million people who produce it live in extreme poverty.

Most of the price you pay for your instant coffee goes to the powerful companies who ship, roast and retail the product. Only a fraction reaches the people whose lives are spent growing and harvesting it.

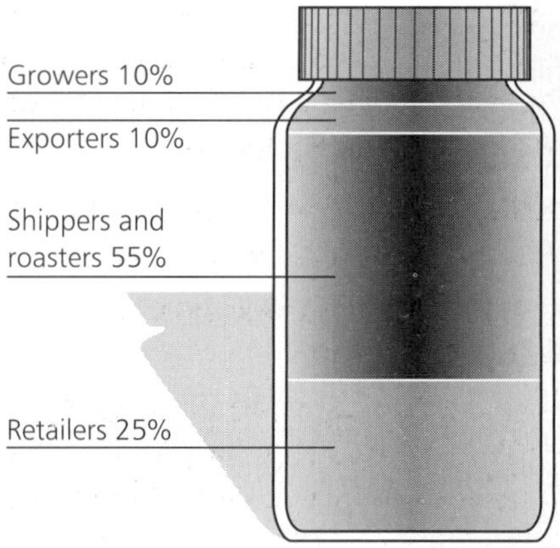

(Adapted from *New Internationalist*, July 1995, pages 18–19)

Replacing ethno-centric approaches towards majority world education with a global curriculum must also be complemented with a willingness on the part of rich donor countries to confront the damaging impact of the global (read 'western-orchestrated') economy on schools in poor countries. Faced with the daunting challenge of operating within an unequal global trading system – to which is added the weight of debt repayments to the International Monetary fund and the World Bank – the majority world has to increase its export revenues by selling goods to rich countries, often at an absurdly low price. The revenues received have to be spent in paying off debt (plus interest) rather than on education and health programmes. In such circumstances, education and medical care usually go to the wall.

On the subject of health, the next section examines the important relationship between health and development.

Health

The three greatest threats to the health of children in the majority world are diarrhoea, measles and pneumonia. Abetted by poor nutrition, these diseases kill about seven million children each year. Low-cost methods of preventing or treating all three – oral rehydration therapy (ORT) for diarrhoea, vaccine for measles and antibiotics for pneumonia – are available.

Fifteen years ago, the benefits of immunisation reached no more than 15 per cent of the majority world population. Today, they reach close to 80 per cent, and prevent about three million child deaths and half a million cases of polio every year. Moreover, ORT is used by almost 40 per cent of all families in the majority world, saving around a million lives annually. This all adds up to a remarkable success story that should make us question the view that the problems of the majority world are too big to handle. That said, lest we become complacent, two million children still die of vaccination-preventable disease. Another three million succumb to diarrhoeal disease. Moreover, pneumonia remains the biggest single cause of child deaths in the world, killing an estimated 3.6 million under-fives each year. That's why immunisation and ORT, as well as the ready availability of antibiotics, are among the most important public health challenges of the 1990s.

Incidentally, talking of ORT, it's ironic that few parents in rich world countries know about this treatment, and most doctors prescribe antidiarrhoeal drugs. Yet a World Health Organisation report concluded that 'antidiarrhoeal drugs should never be used. None has any proven value and some are dangerous' (cited by UNICEF 1994: 15). The cost of inappropriate treatment in the US is more than $1 billion a year. Only about 20 per cent of American families know about ORT: half the rate in the majority world. Given that most health services and medical schools recommend ORT as the first treatment of choice for diarrhoea, perhaps rich world parents have a lesson to learn from their majority world counterparts. This reminds us to avoid the dangers of ethnocentricity. Not only is it unethical, there are also times when the 'west' doesn't seem to know best.

The effectiveness of ORT and immunisation is given added impetus by education programmes, especially those directed towards women. In India, for example, safe motherhood programmes are linked to monthly immunisation sessions, where pregnant women obtain appropriate medical care, are taught about potential danger signs, and are told where they can receive emergency obstetric care if complications arise.

While curative treatment (i.e. tackling a medical condition that has already arisen) plays a role in all health-care programmes, prevention is, of course, better than cure. Getting to the root causes of diseases before they take a grip makes good medical and economic sense. Immunising a child and providing her with proper nutrition and access to clean water keep her healthy, and are less costly methods than providing lengthy treatment for a preventable disease. Even dependency theorists and modernisation theorists agree on this. But what's the most effective preventive of all? The elimination of poverty – that's what! It's a sad fact, but when we in the UK watch starving African children on TV, little do some of us realise that often they could get enough to eat if only their parents could afford to buy food. Even the past teaches us that important lesson. When, for example, more than a million people starved to death during the Irish famines of the 1840s, there was food available to feed them if they had enough money to buy it.

The hard truth is that all manner of diseases in the majority world have always been most common among the least well nourished, as well as among people who have minimum access to health care. Every year, two million children die from vaccine-preventable disease. Moreover, rich world citizens are also dying needlessly because their eating and other lifestyle habits are causing rather than preventing the onset of diseases like clogged arteries, cirrhosis of the liver, and lung and bowel cancer. As far as bowel cancer (a major killer in the UK) is concerned, we 'westerners' could gain much by adopting the high fibre, more vegetarian eating habits of many majority world people. This point is raised by Parveen J. Kumar MD and Michael L. Clark MD in a standard medical text, *Clinical Medicine*:

'Adenocarcinoma [a cancer] of the large bowel is the second commonest tumour in the UK . . . The disease is rare in Africa and Asia and this difference is thought to be largely environmental rather than racial. There is a correlation between the consumption of meat and animal fat and colonic (large intestine) cancer. Western diets are low in fibre and the resulting intestinal stasis [lack of "exercise" of the intestine] increases the time for which any potential carcinogen [cancer causing agent] is in contact with the bowel wall.'

(Kumar and Clark 1991: 234–5)

While an emphasis on 'preventive medicine' is wholly appropriate, it would be harsh indeed to suggest that 'curative medicine' shouldn't feature in majority world health programmes. Yet there's a lack of resolve among donors to African AIDS programmes to 'waste' money on AIDS patients. Even the World Bank has expressed the view that treatment isn't cost-effective, and that prevention is the real solution. But is denying care to an African AIDS patient a moral option? Would such care be refused to a European AIDS patient? Is an African's suffering any less painful than the suffering of a European? These are truly important questions. For they force us to confront the sad reality that the 'west' sometimes puts a higher value on the health of people in the rich world than on the same well-being of people in poor countries.

While it's absolutely essential to develop preventive strategies, it's folly and immoral to do nothing when people are ill: whether the patients are in the UK or Rwanda. In combination, preventive and curative health-care programmes are essential for the development of all our world. Of course, whether we're treating AIDS patients in Africa or TB patients in the USA, simultaneously, we must be devising ways of preventing these and other diseases arising in the first place. So don't regard rich world and majority world health challenges as altogether different. Preventive medicine is always the best medicine, but nobody wants to see people who need curative treatment going to the wall. The best way forward is to remove the causes of ill-health, but to retain curative options as and when necessary.

A woman's lot

Women:

- contribute 66 per cent of the hours worked in the world
- earn about 10 per cent of the world's income
- own only 1 per cent of the world's property.

Kenya

- 58 per cent of rural Kenyan women work in four or more activities, compared with only 13 per cent of men.
- 41.5 per cent of women are illiterate, compared with a national average of 31 per cent.

Ghana

- Women make up 40 per cent of the labour force (i.e. people bringing in an income). 47 per cent of women are farm workers, 56 per cent are self-employed and 67 per cent are unpaid family workers.
- 49 per cent of women are illiterate, compared with a national average of 39.7 per cent.

UK

Women comprise:

- less than 4 per cent of the total number of people on the boards of major UK companies
- 2 per cent of science professors
- 9 per cent of MPs (in the mid-1990s), even though women won the right to vote 77 years ago
- 2.8 per cent of managers
- 90 per cent of part-timers.

(Adapted from *Guardian Education*, 30 May 1995, page 15, based on data from *Intermediate Technology*)

Gender inequalities and equal opportunity initiatives

Look at the extract entitled 'A woman's lot'. It contains some important facts about the situation of women in the majority and the rich worlds.

In most rich nations, women, compared with men, are under-represented in the higher professions and in politics, underpaid in the workplace, and overworked by their assumed and combined responsibilities as 'homemakers' and income earners. In the majority world, women are even worse off. They're poorer than men, they do most of the arduous tasks of fetching, carrying and pounding, and they face lifelong discrimination in health care and nutrition. It's also the case, as Ben Jackson (1990) points out, that the role of women in development projects is often overlooked. For example, while most African farmers are women, only a few projects are targeted towards helping them grow more food. Moreover, women frequently find it hard to get credit and seeds. Lip service rhetoric on the part of development agencies to the role of women in producing better futures, won't do, warns Jackson. What's needed is more women-focused aid.

There's also the need, through education, media and other forms of persuasion, to change traditionally *patriarchal* (i.e. 'males rule, OK') attitudes of men towards women. In Africa, a woman who has three boys will often receive more admiration from friends and neighbours than a woman who has three daughters. In those parts of Asia where the parents of a bride are obliged to provide the family of the groom with a substantial payment (a dowry), financial ruin might be the plight of a family with three daughters. Says Gertrude Mongella:

'The challenge we face is the challenge of moving to the point at which these all-important differences are of no importance' (1994: 31). She's right. How can we possibly talk of progress, of development in the majority world when half of its population – girls and women – encounter exploitation, inequality and oppression? How can we take constructive steps to remove the obstacles to equality of opportunity that women encounter world-wide in educational systems, governments and the professions?

A good start would be to recognise, as Frene Grinwala (1995), Speaker of the South African National Assembly, points out, that the kind of development which fosters a better future for women requires:

- changing male-dominated institutions in society rather than merely letting women gain admittance. Don't just open doors; think about what needs to change once the doors are open
- providing real equality that enables women to claim and exercise their rights by enshrining women's charters in, for example, Bills of Rights.

What Grinwala has in mind is development that transforms society, rather than just the position of women within society. Her vision is one 'of bringing the experience and perceptions of women to bear on the reshaping of society', thereby forging 'a different and a better democracy' (1995: 39).

Achieving equality of opportunity and, even more importantly, equality of condition between the sexes is a necessary step towards a better and a more just world. But if girls and women are to aspire to these goals, they must acquire an education. An educated woman, notes Mongella (1994):

- usually has more status in the eyes of her family and her community
- is likely to have more opportunities and more self-confidence
- is often inclined to share in family decisions, including: how many children to have, how to spend family income, and how to care for her own and her family's health.

These factors enhance a woman's status, 'and make it more likely that the gender conditioning of the next generation will be less severely discriminatory' (Mongella 1994).

OVER TO YOU

Using the insights of labelling theory, explain the thinking behind Mongella's last assertion.

Another very important factor in the transformation of women's lives is the development of family planning services. The number of children a woman has affects her health, her opportunities to start a career, and the health and future prospects of her children. A girl growing up in Africa, for example, encounters a one in 20 risk of dying during pregnancy or childbirth. UNICEF has long regarded responsible family planning, especially birth spacing, as a crucial part of maternal and child health services. In 1994, the Cairo International Conference on Population and Development emphasised that family planning programmes must be integral aspects of a wider endeavour for improved child survival, safe motherhood and reproductive health. However, as a matter of policy, approved by its Executive Board, UNICEF doesn't promote any particular method of family planning. Instead, it adopts the rather dependency theory-oriented view that this is a matter best decided by people themselves, based on their needs, preferences and values. This contrasts with that, by now, rather dated modernisation theory view that poor people need to have their decisions made for them by 'we know best' experts in the 'west'.

Women's health is also affected by patriarchal attitudes that put pressure on them to:

- eat last and least – males get the first and the biggest shares
- put up with health problems that wouldn't be tolerated by males
- bear pain and suffering with acceptance and fortitude.

This relative neglect of their health makes it difficult for women to get on in life, not least in terms of advancing their economic and political influence. For some women, poor health and inadequate nutrition during childhood and puberty cause problems in childbearing years, and are a major cause of low-birth-weight syndrome, which, itself, propels the problem of ill-health onto future generations. Yet again, here is where education can come to the rescue of women's futures. For without it, they'll find it difficult to acquire the knowledge and the change in attitude that are needed to give them a stronger voice. As far as changing attitudes are concerned, in Jamaica, for example, UNICEF has supported video productions that seek to reduce stereotyping among girls and boys in secondary and higher education.

Another step in the right direction for women is the introduction of technology that reduces their burdensome work. This technology is available and it's cheap. Standpipes and handpumps, small tools to help with ploughing and weeding, powered grain-grinding mills, and cooking stoves that reduce the amount of firewood to be collected – these are the tools that can change women's lives for the better, improving their health, and releasing time and energy for them to pursue other ambitions.

But what about boys and men? you might reasonably ask. Aren't males in the majority world also poor? Don't they deserve the right to get on? Yes, they're poor and, of course, they're entitled to a brighter tomorrow. But not at the expense and suffering of girls and women. Entitlement to food and access to school must be based on the needs of people, not the prerogatives of males. How difficult it's going to be to persuade the majority of males that this is what real development and real justice demand. We in the rich world know all too well that our own women generally encounter diminished life chances relative to men. So we mustn't set ourselves up as role models for our poorer sisters and brothers, not unless we really have something worthwhile for them to learn from. Perhaps the most effective way the 'west' can change male sexist attitudes in poor countries is to target more aid to women's economic needs. That will enhance their opportunity to obtain more material equality with men, and, hopefully, will encourage them (and men!) to challenge stereotypes of female inferiority.

QUESTIONS

1 In what ways are the processes of industrialisation, employment and urbanisation in the majority world interrelated?
2 What kinds of educational and health development are most likely to make better futures for the poor of the majority world? Explain your answer.
3 What are the problems faced by females in poor countries, and how might those problems be tackled effectively?

One planet, one world: The global environment

We're all affected by our global environment: the 80 per cent of us who live in the majority world and the 20 per cent of us who live in the rich world. It's an environment that's directly influenced by the inequalities that divide us.

Poverty pushes people (and nations) to desperate measures. This is especially apparent in the exploitation of available resources. The overuse of fuelwood, which adds to the problem of deforestation, is illustrative of this point. Many people in majority world countries rely on traditional fuels – wood, dung and charcoal – for cooking, energy and warmth. About 70–95 per cent of such fuels are used at home, and the remainder in cottage industries and small-scale enterprises. As fuel shortages, especially of fuelwood, become even more scarce, the effort and time expended on finding and collecting wood is becoming increasingly acute. Many women in rural areas of poor countries report that because they spend so much time collecting firewood, they have little time over for growing and cooking food. With less time available for food preparation, less nutritious diets are adopted. For example, in the Sahel, many women now cook rice instead of millet: poor nutrition is the outcome.

Industrialisation is seen by some commentators, especially those of a modernisation theory disposition, to be a better way forward for these rural inhabitants. But let's not forget that the urbanisation which accompanies industrialisation is itself implicated in the destruction of forests. In the late 1980s, for example, it's estimated that 6 hectares of forest a day had to be felled to meet the firewood demand for the industrial city of Delhi, India. Every year, vast tracts of Brazil's land are left bereft of trees as the poor push deeper into the Amazon rainforest, clearing patches of earth by torching the trees. Tragically, it's a largely self-defeating exercise, because forest soil isn't much good for farming. Yet 1995 witnessed one of the most intensive torching seasons to date.

Don't imagine, however, that it's only the majority world who are 'behaving badly'. Rich nations have a great deal to answer for. The industrialisation that heralded their burgeoning economic prosperity has produced a nasty by-product called acid rain. It's caused by sulphur and nitrogen emissions from the burning of fossil fuels, notably, coal in power stations and oil in motor vehicles. Acid rain crosses national boundaries, eroding railway tracks, corroding masonry, destroying fish in lakes, killing off forests and damaging crops. The rich world, especially Canada and north Europe, is taking much of the brunt of the consequences of acid rain. But it's also a growing problem in newly industrialising countries of the majority world – both for them and, when it drifts, for their richer neighbours. That's why we in the 'west' need to ask ourselves, 'Is industrialisation really the best way forward for our poorer neighbours?'

While the rich world has now, say some commentators, entered a post-industrial age, its industrial remnants pack a hefty punch. 'Western' car plants still turn out growing numbers of gas-guzzling cars. The costs of this are high. Not only do cars clog the streets of urban centres, their emissions are the largest single source of air pollutants. Increasing car ownership also tends to reduce government investment in public transport systems. This has the effect of further marginalising people who occupy the economic and social fringes of society – the old, the poor and women. As car production increases, majority world markets beckon. Car culture has a firm grip on the large cities of Brazil, India and Mexico, and is moving steadily into other poor countries.

Surely if, as modernisation theorists believe, the majority world are to move into a more prosperous future by adopting rich world habits, then it's vital that those habits are worthy of imitation. Development measures that are based on macro-indicators like GNP aren't the only, nor even the best ways of gauging the progress of a nation. What do we make, for example, of the argument that more car plants in Brazil equates with a higher GNP if only relatively well-paid people can afford to buy cars, and if the resultant environmental degradation caused by noxious emissions makes the lives of the very poor even more unbearable?

When poor people's existing living arrangements and the land they occupy worsen because of pollution, is it really surprising that they seek other habitats that offer better shelter and more arable land? We don't think so. Not for these people the theoretical luxury of pondering the environmental outcomes of the desperate measures – tree felling, over-farming, etc. – they're forced, in the short-term, to adopt. They've got children to keep warm and mouths to feed. Sure, they're going to make inroads into neighbourhoods or land tracts that they think might make things better for their families. But where are they going to go if we're running out of land? According to Washington's Worldwatch Institute, the average amount of grainland per person has decreased in 30 years from more than 0.2 hectares to not much above 0.1 hectare. Arable land is straining under the multiple destructiveness of chemical pollution, desertification, overuse of water and urbanisation. Land depletion is leading to the displacement of what are called 'environmental migrants'. These nomadic poor are forced to move from one shoddy environment to the (perhaps not quite so shoddy) next. Once that's been exploited to the full, it's time to move on again, and so the cycle continues.

Although things look rather bleak, it's important and necessary to recognise that not all is doom and gloom. The architects of a Green Revolution are rising to the challenges facing the planet's environmental degradation. In 1994, for example, the Philippines' International Rice Research Institute developed a new strain of 'super-rice', which is expected to increase the annual global rice harvest by 100 million tons, or 30 per cent. In 1995, Greenpeace used solar energy to power two Internet cafes in Edinburgh and London to launch its solar information page on the World Wide Web. For those of you out there who like to 'surf the Internet', it's at http://www.greenpeace.org/.

Solar power transforms sunlight into electricity. It's up and running in several countries, and it works. Unlike conventional energy sources, it produces no CO_2 and no radioactive waste. It's an outstanding solution to the problems of global warming and nuclear hazards – two of the greatest threats to the global environment. Even on the forestry front, things needn't be so bleak. Greenpeace's campaign for better forestry practices has been so successful that new forests are now being logged according to its guidelines in Austria, British Columbia (Canada) and Germany. In these operations, clearcutting – the stripping of every bit of standing vegetation in a forest – is prohibited. Enough old and dead trees are left in the forest to provide habitats for birds and insects, and to nourish new growth. These sustainable principles also preclude the use of chemicals, so minimal damage is done to soil. Moreover, a strong European resolve to reduce sulphur dioxide emissions is gradually paying off. The emissions are coming down, and the EU has mandated that large fossil fuel plants will have to cut emissions of sulphur dioxide by 60 per cent by 2003.

Perhaps the most important thing to remember, when we look at the relationship between development and the environment, is that increased GNPs that lead, through the pursuit of 'quick-bucks' profit and planet-destroying technologies, don't measure real development at all. For real development is much more than crude macro-economic indicators. It's about confronting environmental problems with practical sustainable solutions, and in challenging industrialists, politicians and trade unions to adopt them – for all our sakes.

Concluding remarks

Recent years have witnessed very significant steps towards improving the lives of people in poor countries. Moreover, existing resources and knowledge can drastically reduce disease, illiteracy and malnutrition by the year 2000. Social scientists differ about the paths they advocate to reach this goal. However, there's general agreement among most dependency/WS and modernisation theorists that rich nations could improve things greatly by providing aid for: adequate nutrition, basic education, primary health care (including safe water supplies) and family planning. Investment in these important areas not only improves human well-being worldwide, it also helps to reduce population growth and mitigates against environmental destruction. These are investments rich countries can and need to afford. The beneficial effects would be many times greater than the sum of their individual outcomes. Providing basic education, for example, leads to an upward spiral of improvement across many different fronts: more awareness about hygiene, a better educated workforce, etc. In that sense, it's appropriate to talk of a multiplier effect, whereby one set of improved circumstances triggers off improvement elsewhere. The diagram opposite highlights these spiralling outcomes.

Countries and regions that prioritised such investments in poor people's futures in the 1950s and 1960s have controlled population growth, and will eventually stabilise their populations at considerably lower levels than would otherwise have been the case. Placing the financial wherewithal to forge a better future at the disposal of the majority world poses a worthy challenge to the 'west'. But that's only part of the story. We, in the rich world, must also recognise that our poorer neighbours

The upward spiral

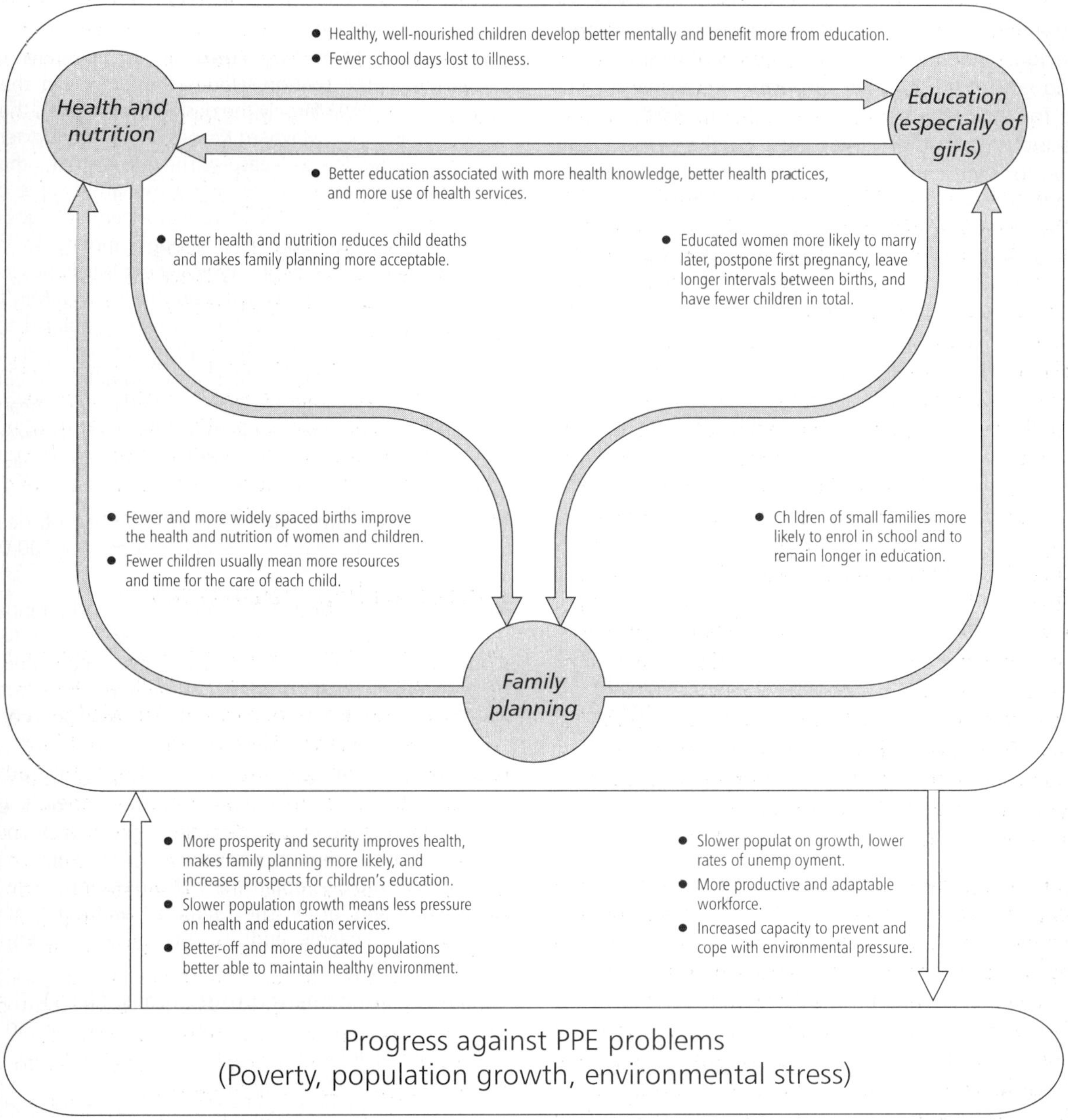

(UNICEF 1994: 49)

need to participate in the planning, the implementation and the consequences of effective development strategies. Our task isn't to work for the poor, but with them. For the poor have a right to shape their own futures. However, that isn't going to happen if they simply 'opt out' of the admittedly unjust system of the global market. In theory, going it 'alone' in a majority world trading bloc sounds like a good idea. But in a world where the rich world is rich because it owns and controls most of the world's resources, poor countries must 'co-operate' with their more prosperous neighbours.

This doesn't mean treading a 'western' path. But it does mean persuading the rich world, through the advocacy channels offered by NGOs and sympathetic media, to drastically write down majority world debt. Three-quarters of Africa's total debt, for example, is to the governments of rich world nations. Think what debt relief could do for that great continent, the cradle of humankind, the place where our first human ancestors walked the earth. It would release expenditures for education, health, nutrition and family planning, especially if a condition of the relief were that it shouldn't be used on military purchases. Debt relief in Africa and other parts of the majority world would truly create a much more hopeful framework for genuine basic needs human development, and would constitute an important step towards the future described below:

'The day will come when the progress of nations will be judged not by their military or economic strength, nor by the splendour of their public buildings, but by the well-being of their peoples: by their levels of health, nutrition and education; by their opportunities to earn a fair reward for their labours; by their ability to participate in the decisions that affect their lives; by the respect that is shown for their civil and political liberties; by the provision that is made for those who are vulnerable and disadvantaged; and by the protection that is afforded to the growing minds and bodies of their children.'

(UNICEF 1995)

Glossary of key terms

Adult literacy rate Percentage of people aged 15 and over who can read and write

Colonialism The enforced take-over by powerful nations of weaker nations, often through military means, but, in its *neo* (new) form, by locking poor countries into an economic market that benefits the 'west' and exploits the 'rest'

Convergence theory Strongly associated with Clerk Kerr, this perspective proposes that majority and rich countries alike will prosper when all nations converge along the path of modern technological liberation. It's a close cousin of modernisation theory, but perhaps it could also be interpreted as a 'left-wing' model in the context of a convergence that has democratic socialism as a guiding light

Crude birth rate Annual number of births per 1,000 population

Crude death rate Annual number of deaths per 1,000 population

Dependency theory The 'arch-rival' of modernisation theory and advocated by the marxist, Andre Gunder Frank, this perspective claims that 'what's good for the "west" is bad for the rest'. It's both an evolutionary and a revolutionary theory, and it proposes that poor countries will enter better futures if they uncouple, as far as is practical, their ties to the 'west' and join with like-minded poor countries to form an international socialist trading bloc

Evolutionary theory Pioneered by August Comte and Herbert Spencer and, later, by modernisation theorists, this perspective asserts that nations experience gradual social change through a step-by-step progression from tradition to modernity

Gross national product (GNP) The value, expressed in current US$, of everything that a country produces and sells in the course of a year. It includes private and public sector goods and services. Per capita GNP is the mean average of GNP per head of the population of a country, again over the course of a year. On an imaginary island of 100 inhabitants with a GNP of $100,000 dollars, the per capita GNP would be 100,000 divided by 100, which equals $1,000 each. Of course, that doesn't imply that each person would receive $1,000. This would only be so if the GNP were *equally* divided

Infant mortality rate The probability of dying between birth and exactly one year of age, expressed per 1,000 live births

International Monetary Fund Set up by leaders of rich nations at the Bretton Woods Conference in the US in July 1944. It was largely the design of two men, the British economist, John Maynard Keynes, and Harry Dexter White of the United States Treasury. The IMF is a bank that lends to countries who, at the going exchange value of their currencies, find it difficult to export enough goods and services so they can earn enough money to pay for imports and settle debts. Typically the IMF issues loans on condition that the recipient country follows IMF 'advice'. This usually means that the borrower is obliged to introduce a 'structural adjustment programme' (SAP). In practice, this often requires the borrowing nation to cut down on public expenditure (notably, education, health and social welfare). Understandably, the IMF is viewed with suspicion by many poor countries, who regard it as a 'take your medicine' bank of the rich world

Maternal mortality rate Annual number of deaths of women from pregnancy-related causes, per 100,000 live births

Modernisation theory The perspective, championed by Walt Rostow, that says 'what's good for the "west" is good for the rest'. It's an evolutionary theory, and it proposes that poor countries will enter better futures if they imitate the cultural, economic and political habits of their richer neighbours

Revolutionary theory Vigorously enjoined by Karl Marx and, later, by dependency theorists, this perspective claims that nations *evolve* to critical 'no-turning back points', at which time, revolutionaries recognise and seize the moment, rapidly topple the old order, and forge a radically different future. The 'ultimate best future', when history will allegedly end, is, say marxists, international communism

Structural adjustment programmes (SAPs) These are typically required of poor countries if they want to receive loans from international financial organisations like the IMF and the World Bank. In practice, such bodies tell borrower nations to deflate their economies and to cut back on public expenditure, even if this means, as it usually does, withdrawing the compassionate support of the basic health and welfare needs of the most vulnerable members of society. Some poor people actively resist SAPs by taking to the streets in protest. Nevertheless, this 'hard medicine' for ailing economies is widespread throughout Africa, where SAPs have been implemented by virtually every country

Total fertility rate The number of children who would be born per woman if she were to live to the end of her child-bearing years, and bear children at the fertility rate prevailing in her society

World Bank Like its cousin, the IMF, this was also established at the 1944 Bretton Woods Conference. Its function is to borrow money from rich countries and invest it in the development of poor countries. Like the IMF, it imposes structural adjustment programmes on borrowers as a condition of the loan

World systems theory A less politically strident, 'modified version' of dependency theory, this perspective challenges more orthodox marxists to 'get real', by proposing that poor countries will only prosper when rich countries resolve to treat them justly and to trade with them fairly. Telling the majority world to go it alone, say world systems theorists, might appeal to herringbone-jacketed marxist professors, but poor people will suffer if that happens

References

Albonoz, Orlando (1993) *Education and Society in Latin America*. Basingstoke: Macmillan

Bamyeh, Mohammed A. (1993) Transnationalism, pp 1–101, *Current Sociology*, Vol. 41, No. 3, Winter

Berner, Erhard and Korff, Rudiger (1995) Globalization and local resistance: The creation of localities in Manila and Bangkok, pp 208–22, *International Journal of Urban and Regional Research*, Vol. 19, No. 2, March

Brown, Dee (1991) *Bury My Heart at Wounded Knee*. London: Vintage

Buckley, Richard (ed.) (1994) *World Population: The Biggest Problem of All?* Cheltenham: European Schoolbooks

Catley-Carlson, Margaret (1994) The decision decade, p. 25, in UNICEF (1994) op. cit.

Chung, Fay (1994) Education for all can still be achieved, p. 19, in UNICEF (1994) op. cit.

Ellwood, Wayne (1991) Hidden history: Columbus and the colonial legacy, pp 4–7, *New Internationalist*, December

Foster-Carter, Aidan (1991) Development sociology: Whither now?, pp 10–14, *Sociology Review*, November

Frank, Andre Gunder (1969a) *Capitalism and Underdevelopment in Latin America*. New York: Monthly Review Press

Frank, Andre Gunder (1969b) *Latin America: Underdevelopment or Revolution*. New York: Monthly Review Press

Fraser, Elvis E. (1994) Reconciling conceptual and measurement problems in the comparative study of human rights, pp 1–18, *International Journal of Comparative Sociology*, Vol. XXXV, Nos 1–2, January–April

Freire, Paolo (1972) *Pedagogy of the Oppressed*. Harmondsworth: Penguin

Genovese, Eugene D. (1975) *Roll, Jordan, Roll*. London: Andre Deutsch

Godrej, Dinyar (1995) Hunger in a world of plenty, pp 7–10, *New Internationalist*, May

Gradwohl, Judith and Greenberg, Russell (1988) *Saving the Tropical Forests*. London: Earthscan Publications

Grinwala, Frene (1995) Discrimination not the problem, pp 37–9, in UNICEF (1994) op. cit.

Jackson, Ben (1990) *Poverty and the Planet*. London: Penguin

Kerr, C., Dunlop, J. T., Harbin, F. H. and Myers, C. (1960) *Industrialism and Industrial Man*. London: Heinemann

Killick, Tony (1995) Structural adjustment and poverty alleviation: An interpretative survey, pp 305–31, *Development & Change*, Vol. 26, No. 2, April

Kowalewski, David and Hoover, Dean (1994) Dissent and repression in the world system: A model of future dynamics, pp 161–87, *International Journal of Comparative Sociology*, Vol. XXXV, Nos 3–4, Sept–Dec

Kumar, Parveen J. and Clark, Michael L. (1991) *Clinical Medicine*, Second Edition. London: Baillière Tindall

Leakey, Richard (1994) *The Origin of Humankind*. London: Weidenfeld & Nicolson

Lee, Raymond L. M. (1994) Modernization, postmodernism and the Third World, pp 1–66, *Current Sociology*, Vol. 42, No. 2, Summer

Lee, Yumi and Ninnes, Peter (1995) A multilevel global and cultural critique of the 'Diploma Disease', pp 169–77, *Comparative Education Review*, Vol. 39, No. 2, May

Lindqvist, Sven (1997) *'Exterminate All the Brutes'*. London: Granta Books

Lisco, Adrian Esquina (1991) The pain of Mother Earth, pp 16–17, *New Internationalist*, December

Lister, Ian (1984) *Teaching and Learning about Human Rights*. Strasbourg: School Education Division, Council of Europe

Mongella, Gertrude (1994) Change for the last and the least, p. 31, in UNICEF (1994) op. cit.

Petrella, Riccardo (1995) Europe between competitive innovation and a new social contract, pp 11–23, *International Social Science Journal*, Vol. XLVII, No. 1, March

Robey, Bryant, Rutstein, Shea O. and Morris, Leo (1993) The fertility decline in developing countries, *Scientific American*, December

Rostow, Walt Whitman (1965) *The Stages of Economic Growth: A Non-Communist Manifesto*. London: The Syndics of the Cambridge University Press

Sachs, Ignacy (1995) The quantitative and qualitative measurement of development: Its implications and limitations, pp 1–10, *International Social Science Journal*, Vol. XLVII, No. 1, March

Stephens, Paul (1987) 'The landed interest and the education of the English working class 1807–1833: A sociological study of aristocratic debate and policy'. Ph.D. thesis, University of London

Streeten, Paul (1995) Human development: The debate about the index, pp 25–37, *International Social Science Journal*, Vol. XLVII, No. 1, March

Swift, Richard (1994) Bretton Woods, p. 1, *New Internationalist*, July

Teodoro, Lourdes (1991) Black Brazil, pp 26–7, *New Internationalist*, December

ul-Haq, Mahbub (1994) The new deal, pp 20–3, *New Internationalist*, December

UNICEF (1994) *The Progress of Nations 1994*. New York: Unicef House

UNICEF (1995) *The State of the World's Children 1995*. Oxford: UNICEF/Oxford University Press

United Nations Development Programme (1994) *Human Development Report*. Oxford: UNDP/Oxford University Press

Wallerstein, Immanuel (1989) *The Modern World – System III*. San Diego: Academic Press

Exam practice: World sociology

Essay questions

1 Assess the claim that gender issues have been ignored in studies of Third World development. *(25 marks)*

2 Evaluate the usefullness of the concepts of development and underdevelopment in the analysis of the relationships between First and Third World countries. *(25 marks)*

(November 1993 AEB A-level Sociology, Paper 2, © 1993 AEB)

3 'Definitions and explanations of development reflect different ideological perspectives'.
Assess this view. *(25 marks)*

4 'Modernisation, mainly through education, is the most important influence on economic development.'
Assess sociological arguments and evidence which support this view. *(25 marks)*

(Summer 1997 AEB A-level Sociology, Paper 2, © 1997 AEB)

Author index

Page references in **bold** indicate entry in bibliographies, those in *italics* indicate tables, diagrams etc. Multiple (i.e. more than two) authors are entered under first named author only.

General Index

Page reference in **bold** indicate glossary entry, those in *italic* indicate diagrams, tables etc.